TAXATION:
LAW, PLANNING, AND POLICY
Second Edition
Second Edition

TAXATION: LAW, PLANNING, AND POLICY

Second Edition

MICHAEL A. LIVINGSTON
Professor of Law
Rutgers School of Law–Camden

DAVID S. GAMAGE
Assistant Professor of Law
UC Berkeley School of Law

Library of Congress Cataloging-in-Publication Data

Livingston, Michael A.
    Taxation : law, planning, and policy / Michael A. Livingston, David S. Gamage. -- 2nd ed.
        p. cm.
    Includes index.
    ISBN: 978-1-4224-7680-2 (hardbound)
    1. Income tax--Law and legislation--United States--Cases. 2. Taxation--Law and legislation--United States--Cases. I. Gamage, David S. II. Title.
    KF6368.L58 2010
    343.7304--dc22

                                                                        2010008101

NOTE TO USERS

To ensure that you are using the latest materials available in this area, please be sure to periodically check the LexisNexis Law School web site for downloadable updates and supplements at www.lexisnexis.com/lawschool.

Editorial Offices
121 Chanlon Rd., New Providence, NJ 07974 (908) 464-6800
201 Mission St., San Francisco, CA 94105-1831 (415) 908-3200
www.lexisnexis.com

MATTHEW◆BENDER

                                                                (2010–Pub.3615)

DEDICATIONS

There is not enough room to thank everyone who has helped me, directly or indirectly, on this project, but special mention must surely be made of my law school Dean, Rayman Solomon; my research assistants, Travis Weitzel, Becky Lawnicki, Ann McDonough, and Jana Taylor on the first edition and Erica DiMarco, Shefali Jaiswal, Marissa Sharples, and Zoha Barkeshli on the second edition; my secretary, Kaeko Jackson on the first edition and Debbie Carr on the second edition; and all the others at Rutgers who have supported me throughout. My editors, Keith Moore at Anderson and Cristina Gegenschatz at Lexis, deserve special praise for their unfailing patience and understanding, as does Prof. Nancy Staudt who — although not claiming credit as a co-author — read several drafts and was instrumental in the conception and execution of the first edition. My wife, Anne Weiss, and my children, Benjamin and Daniel, are to be thanked for their constant encouragement and for providing the meaning in life that makes me want to learn new subjects and explore new territories. Finally, I wish to thank the Source of Life for creating and sustaining me and enabling me to reach this happy occasion. Without all of them nothing would matter.

— Michael A. Livingston

I began using the first edition of this casebook because I felt it superior in many important respects — most significantly, in its offering a reasonable introduction to the areas of business and international taxation. I felt honored when Michael Livingston asked me to join him as a co-author for the second edition, and I hope that my efforts to improve the text have been worthy of his trust. I owe special thanks to my research assistants, Amanda Cleaver, Ora Sraboyants, Ketki Buddhisagar, and Kelly Stevens. I additionally owe thanks to my assistant, Chris Swain; to my Dean, Christopher Edley; to my editor, Cristina Gegenschatz; and to my colleagues at Berkeley who have been unwaveringly supportive. I am always thankful for the support of my wife, Amy Coren, who brings joy to my life. Finally, I would like to thank my students, who endure first-hand my efforts to improve my teaching.

— David S. Gamage

INTRODUCTION

Taxation may well be the least popular subject in the law school curriculum. Tax concepts are difficult to master, the course involves lots of numbers, and most of you probably don't want to be tax lawyers, anyway. So why are you (more or less) expected to take it, and what are you supposed to get out of it?

The best reason for studying taxation has always been its inherent importance as an area of law. Taxes — most notably, the Federal income tax — are the lifeblood of democratic government. They affect virtually all business transactions and an astonishing variety of personal decisions, from buying a home to planning for one's retirement or estate needs. Even nontax practitioners are expected to know, if not the answers, then at least the questions posed by tax law in these areas, so that their clients will not be unpleasantly surprised or (even worse) tempted to consult another law firm for these matters. Tax policy is likewise a matter of broad public concern, raising basic questions of fairness, efficiency, and ultimately of the very nature of government and its role in our everyday lives. No legal education is complete without considering these subjects.

A second reason is less parochial in nature. A good tax course provides an incomparable introduction to statutory reasoning and interpretation and, more generally, to the nature and function of statutory law. Most of your courses to date have been in common law subjects, that is, subjects (e.g., torts, contracts, property) in which the law originally developed in judicial decisions and was only later, if ever, codified in statutes or scholarly treatises. By contrast tax law is statutory in origin and application. The principal tax statute, the Internal Revenue Code, did not even exist until 1913, and many of its important provisions are much more recent in origin, enacted in response to demands for additional revenue or other social and political goals. Although there is by now a large body of tax judicial decisions, all of these decisions eventually lead back to the statutory language itself, and to the large body of legislative and administrative materials that explain and expand on that language.

Learning to deal with these materials — statutes, regulations, committee reports and other legislative documents — is a large part of learning to be a tax lawyer. Tax students learn quickly that the statute is sometimes dispositive, but other times contradictory or unclear, requiring one to look at the underlying intent or policy of the provision in question in order to provide an answer to a client's problem. The skills acquired in a tax course are thus useful in all the areas of law — antitrust, environmental law, employment law, civil rights and anti-discrimination law, and so forth — that are statutory in origin and raise many of the same theoretical and practical issues. Since the great majority of new law (and especially Federal law) is statutory in nature, these lessons are vital indeed.

Finally, tax law is exciting because it emphasizes practical as well as legal concerns. A good tax lawyer tries to reduce her client's taxes, but must do so in a way that achieves the client's business or personal goals, too. (Imagine the fate of a lawyer who counseled his clients to reduce taxes by refusing to make any money.) To accomplish these goals, the tax lawyer must be a planner as well as a litigator, striving to arrange her client's affairs so that the client will reduce taxes without ever seeing the inside of a courtroom or IRS office. Of course, this planning element is important in all areas of law, but law

INTRODUCTION

school tends to obscure it, emphasizing judicial decisions that are based upon fixed factual circumstances and that typically pay little attention to business or other practical concerns. The tax course hopes to be an antidote to this problem, emphasizing planning and practical considerations and beginning the students' transition from passive observers to active participants in legal practice.

To accomplish the goals above, this casebook does things a little bit differently than previous models. First, the book emphasizes the acquisition of skills as much as or more than information. The first of these skills involves the understanding and application of tax and (by extension) other forms of statutory law. Right from the start students are challenged to read the statute and regulations, often without additional explanatory material, determining which questions are answered by the statutory language and, when it is necessary to look beyond the "four corners" of the statute, where that search should begin. When posing questions ("Using the Sources"), the book challenges students to identify the authority for their answers, whether it be the Code, Regulations, or case law, avoiding the usual law school notion that it is possible to argue almost any position if one does so with a straight face. (It isn't, or at any rate, not in tax practice.) The skills acquired in these exercises — weighing the "plain meaning" of the statute against the legislative history, administrative decisions, and other interpretive sources — are relevant even for the student who will never take another tax course.

Together with questions on law and legal sources, the book includes numerous questions on tax planning and policy. Along with the usual judicial perspective, these questions aim to familiarize the students with the perspective of the real-world tax practitioner, who must balance tax and nontax concerns in planning business transactions, and of the tax policy-maker, who may be influenced by political and practical as well as more purely technical issues. In addition to "livening up" the classroom discussion — even tax lawyers don't want to parse Code sections twenty-four hours a day — these materials combat the isolation of most tax courses by enabling students to see the relationships between taxation and the other subjects they have studied or will study in law school. To prevent confusion, the questions are labeled "Law and Planning" or "Politics and Policy," as appropriate; it should be clear at the outset which questions have a "right" or "wrong" answer and which involve the exercise of professional judgment at a more sophisticated level.

To educate the student in the proactive as well as the reactive aspect of tax practice, each of the twelve chapters concludes with a detailed planning or policy problem, designed to emphasize the interplay of tax and business goals or (for the policy problems) the balance between legal theory and hard political reality. Unlike the questions in many casebooks, these problems are designed not as technical brain-teasers, but as realistic situations intended to provoke creative thought at a level beyond that possible in regular classes. For example, one of the first problems requires students to consider the relative advantages provided by various tax-free fringe benefits, while later problems ask them to prepare a client memo, an incentive compensation strategy, and a legislative drafting proposal. It is anticipated that, in many courses, at least some of these problems will serve as the basis for take-home writing assignments. In other courses, the problems may serve primarily as a basis for organizing in-class discussion. In either case, the problem approach aims to restore the "lawyering" aspect to a course in tax law, sacrificing some breadth of coverage for a deeper, more fundamental understanding of what it is that practicing tax (and other) lawyers really do. The problems and associated feedback may

INTRODUCTION

also provide for a less confrontational classroom and lessen the terror associated with a single, all-or-nothing final exam.

Finally, in contrast to other introductory tax casebooks, the book includes significant materials (primarily Chapters 11 and 12) on business and international taxation, subjects traditionally relegated exclusively to advanced tax courses. The inclusion of these materials is, in our judgment, simply a recognition of reality. The vast majority of students in a basic income tax classroom will never take a second tax course. To ask them to devote hours to the fine points of installment sales or tax-exempt securities, without teaching them anything about business or international tax issues, seems to us irrational and unfair, especially since the latter areas are among those that a modern, interdisciplinary practitioner is most likely to need in her general practice. The exclusion of international materials seems further short-sighted in an increasingly globalized, borderless world. There is little danger that the inclusion of such materials will discourage serious tax students from taking further J.D. or LL.M. courses; to the contrary, a taste of such materials may result in increased enrollments, much as students register for commercial law to pursue topics originally encountered in their basic contracts class, or criminal procedure to supplement a first-year criminal law course. The inclusion of new materials also heightens the planning orientation of the casebook and dramatizes the tension between tax and nontax goals that is a central theme of the course.

The paragraphs above may make the course seem more serious and heavy-handed than it actually is. In fact, tax is an enjoyable subject, and with a little bit of effort should be one of the most entertaining courses in the legal academy. Everything is here: logic and illogic; high-minded ideals and cynical manipulation; sublime concepts and ridiculous or near-ridiculous exceptions to those concepts. Unlike many areas of law, which sometimes strike students as no more than judicial politics, tax involves a systematic, logical framework, the deviations from which only heighten the excitement of uncovering the framework and (just as quickly) discovering its many limitations. Learning to comprehend that framework, and to appreciate those limitations, is one of the premier experiences of law school. By adopting a practice-oriented perspective, and emphasizing those materials most likely to be useful to a general practitioner, this book aims to make the experience all the more pleasant.

One additional note, especially for students who suffer from "numbers anxiety" and similar phobias: Tax is an unavoidably quantitative subject. One cannot understand progressive tax rates without doing a little bit of multiplication, or recognize the significance of tax avoidance without knowing how much tax one would otherwise pay. But the numerical aspect of tax law is often exaggerated. Accountants, not lawyers, fill out tax returns; even for them, most computations are relatively simple, and the most important work is qualitative rather than quantitative in nature. The day-to-day fare of tax lawyers involves planning, litigation, and the evaluation of difficult legal issues in a manner not terribly different from other practitioners. In thirty-some years of combined tax teaching and practice, we cannot recall seeing a tax lawyer use a calculator or, with one exception, keep a pencil behind his or her ear. (The exception may have also had an accounting degree.) A fear of numbers may deter some people from pursuing tax law, but the reality of the subject need not, and an English major is no less likely to succeed in this course than her colleague who has a computer in every room of the house.[1]

One final note about studying for a tax course: Students often ask which aspects of the course — statutes, cases, problems — are most important, and whether they will benefit from participating in a student-run study group. The answers to these questions are, essentially, "yes, yes, and yes." All course materials are important; the best indication of what you should emphasize is what your professor emphasizes in class, or has chosen to test on in previous courses. (It is (s)he, after all, who will be writing your final exam.) Study groups are frequently quite valuable, although they are obviously not a substitute for individual preparation, attentiveness to class discussions, and so forth. The best study method, although not necessarily the most pleasant, is probably to review one's class notes, together with statutes, cases, etc., at the end of each week, trying to "digest" that week's materials and figure out where they fit in with the rest of the course. A good review book is sometimes, although not always, helpful in this process.[2] In these dynamics, as in others, tax is not especially different from other courses; only more challenging, and more enjoyable.

Enough background material. Good luck, and as the Italians say, "Buon divertimenti." Don't forget to have fun.

The Second Edition follows the same general approach as the first, with three major changes. First, Professor David Gamage of the UC Berkeley School of Law has become a co-author. Second, largely as a result of Prof. Gamage's efforts, the book has been streamlined so as to reduce the number of chapters from fourteen to twelve and eliminate a certain amount of well-intentioned but ultimately excessive or duplicative material. In particular, the materials on the estate tax (former Chapter 11) have been largely eliminated, with remaining material from that chapter included in the new Chapter 10, and Chapter 14 (readings in tax policy) has been radically shortened and combined with the original Background section. Finally, a number of typographical errors have been corrected and the book has been updated for new developments, although — given the skills approach of the volume — these changes have been somewhat less extensive than is typically the case. We believe that old users will find these changes easy to adjust to, and that new ones will find the book that much more attractive.

---

[1] To make sure of this point, the next section includes a brief introduction to business and economic terms.

[2] Among the better available review books are Marvin A. Chirelstein, FEDERAL INCOME TAXATION: A LAW STUDENT'S GUIDE TO THE LEADING CASES AND CONCEPTS (11th ed. 2009) and Joseph Bankman, Thomas D. Griffith & Katherine Pratt, FEDERAL INCOME TAX: EXAMPLES AND EXPLANATIONS (5th ed. 2008). The former is generally most useful as an overall review, and the latter as a chapter-by-chapter companion. Anything that purports to explain the entire tax law on one index card is best avoided.

TABLE OF CONTENTS

TABLE OF CONTENTS

TABLE OF CONTENTS

TABLE OF CONTENTS

TABLE OF CONTENTS

TABLE OF CONTENTS

TABLE OF CONTENTS

TABLE OF CONTENTS

TABLE OF CONTENTS

TABLE OF CONTENTS

TABLE OF CONTENTS

BACKGROUND AND BASIC THEMES

It is customary, at the beginning of a tax course, to provide students with background information regarding the structure of the tax system and the underlying themes of tax policy. Because much of this information has been integrated into the regular course materials, this introduction will be shorter than many students (and some teachers) are used to. Nevertheless, it seems useful to set forth a few basic concepts at the outset, to ensure that everyone is on the same "wavelength" and avoid possible confusion later on. The materials that follow are divided into three principal sections: (a) the sources of federal tax law; (b) the basic principles of tax policy, including the choice of an overall tax base (income tax, consumption tax, value added tax, etc.) and the goals of a good income (or other) tax once that original choice has been made; and (c) a brief introduction to economic and business vocabulary, which is important for understanding many tax provisions but with which some students may be unfamiliar. Read the materials now, even if they appear theoretical or abstract in nature: you will have ample opportunity to apply these ideas to specific cases as the course progresses. The materials conclude with a brief exercise in completing a standard income tax return (Form 1040), which will refocus our attention on "black-letter" law and serve as a sort of informal overview of the rest of the course.

I. SOURCES OF FEDERAL TAX LAW

The first point concerns the sources of federal tax law.[1] Like any statutory law, tax law has three principal sources: legislative sources (i.e., the statute itself and its accompanying legislative history); administrative sources (i.e., Treasury Regulations and IRS rulings); and judicial sources (i.e., the holdings, rationales, and outcomes of previously decided tax cases). In addition, numerous secondary sources, including scholarly books, treatises, articles, and other computerized and hard-copy materials, are often consulted as sources of tax law, especially in close or difficult cases. This differs from common law subjects, where judicial sources are paramount and other materials (restatements, treatises, etc.) largely derive from these judicial decisions.

Begin with legislative sources. The most important of these is the statute itself, which for (United States) federal taxes is the Internal Revenue Code of 1986 (the "Code"), as amended by subsequent tax bills. All major federal taxes, including the income, estate and gift, excise and employment (i.e., social security and Medicare) taxes, are contained in the Code, with the largest single part being devoted to the

---

[1] Because most of the course is devoted to (United States) federal taxes, and especially the federal income tax, this introduction emphasizes the sources of federal tax law. State and foreign taxes have essentially equivalent sources (statutes, administrative regulations, and so on), although foreign sources may differ because of the differing allocation of authority in different legal systems. For example, as compared to common law jurisdictions, France and other civil law countries tend to rely more heavily on administrative than judicial decision-making, so more of their tax (and other) law is likely to be found in administrative sources. Yes, and it is also written in French.

income tax. The Code is, of course, the law, and when it addresses an issue squarely that's the end of it; but like many statutes it has an annoying habit of leaving important questions unanswered, while rambling on for pages on matters of interest to only a handful of taxpayers. For example, the definition of income, in section 61 of the Code, is less than one page long, and provides virtually no guidance on any important issue. By contrast, the so-called "at risk" rules (section 465), limitations on tax shelters that were never particularly effective and have largely been superseded by other provisions, occupy numerous pages; credits for various unprofitable energy sources (solar, wind, geothermal) fill up several more; and an entire Code section was once drafted to allow Alaska residents to share in that state's oil revenues without sharing them with more recent arrivals. This random quality means that, for all its impressive length, the Code leaves many key questions unanswered; in a difficult tax case, the question is likely to be not whether to look outside the statute, but which outside source (judicial decisions, legislative history, scholarly treatises, etc.) proves most convincing or persuasive. Yet even in these cases, the Code sets the parameters for the debate, and is the starting point for the discussion of any tax issue.

A second, more controversial source is legislative history, which usually means committee reports and similar documents written by congressional staff in connection with tax legislation. Legislative history is important for any statute, but tends to be especially so in taxation, given that the statute leaves so many questions unanswered and it often takes years for regulations or other administrative guidance to be issued. As a general rule, it tends to be most important for new provisions and becomes less so, although still retaining some importance, as the statute becomes older and alternate forms of guidance (regulations, rulings, and so forth) become available. In recent years, there has been an assault on legislative history led by Justice Scalia and his allies, who ask — not altogether unreasonably — why judges should be bound by documents written by young congressional staffers and rarely read, much less written, by any elected official. The Scalia-led assault has reduced, but by no means eliminated, reliance on legislative history, and especially for new statutes it is likely to remain important for some years to come.

Administrative sources include regulations and rulings authored by the Treasury Department and its tax administrative arm, the Internal Revenue Service (IRS).[2] Of these the most important are Treasury Regulations, which are carefully drafted and subject to an extensive Notice and Comment procedure although often available in Proposed or Temporary form prior to the completion of that process. The regulations, which are organized according to Code section,[3] serve three principal functions: they restate the Code language in a somewhat more readable form; provide additional detail regarding the meaning and application of the relevant Code provision; and, in some cases, include examples that demonstrate the effect of the rule in a series of hypothetical situations. The regulations (other than examples) are usually written in a textual form, not wholly unlike that of the statute, although some use a question and answer ("Q & A") format in place of the traditional model.

---

[2] The IRS remains is attached to the Treasury Department although it has its own Commissioner and a high degree of autonomy.

[3] For example, Regulation 1.61-1 is the first regulation under section 61 of the Code.

Although much ink has been spilled regarding the interpretive authority of Treasury Regulations, in practice it is extremely difficult to overcome them, especially for final regulations that have been in effect for several years without successfully being challenged in court. For regulations that adopt a pro-taxpayer position — for example, permitting a transaction that the statute might otherwise seem to prohibit — it is unlikely that the challenge will even be made. So, especially for older provisions, the Regulations have the status of near-law: not quite the statute, but close to it, and subject to challenge only if they are manifestly inconsistent with the underlying Code section.

In addition to regulations, the IRS issues several subsidiary forms of taxpayer guidance. Revenue Rulings and Revenue Procedures provide published guidance regarding the application of the law to specific situations, frequently new or emerging kinds of transactions that are not yet covered by existing regulations. Revenue Rulings adopt a format similar to a judicial opinion, setting forth a hypothetical fact pattern, a question to be resolved, and the answer to that question, usually without very extensive discussion. Revenue Procedures set forth rules applicable to a broader range of factual situations. Revenue Rulings and Procedures are subject to less review than regulations, and they have relatively low precedential value, although an old and time-tested ruling may begin to assume a status approaching that of law, especially if no other guidance is available on the issue. In addition to these public materials the IRS issues particularized guidance ("private letter rulings") in response to requests from individual taxpayers; these have in theory no precedential value whatsoever, but have been collected and published by private companies following a Freedom of Information Act suit and are inevitably consulted by taxpayers when no reliable alternate source is available.

Judicial sources include decisions in previous tax cases, the persuasiveness of which is (as in any area of law) dependent on the status of the court in question and the specificity with which it addresses the relevant issue. Two special points about tax cases are worth mentioning here. First, the unusual structure of the tax judiciary means that there will often be conflicting or at least alternate precedents on the same issue.[4] Second, as noted above, all tax decisions are, in theory at least, interpretations of one or more Code provisions, so it will be relatively rare for a case to be the sole authority on an issue. More likely, judicial, administrative, and legislative sources will each be relevant, the precise mix of importance depending upon the issue in question.

In addition to the materials described above, so-called secondary sources — books, treatises, articles, etc. — function as additional sources of tax law, especially in close or difficult cases. For example, the opinions in a number of cases have suggested that so-called "tax theory" or "tax logic" can be controlling even in the absence of a specific Code provision — because to permit otherwise would

---

[4] Taxpayers challenging an IRS assessment have the choice of bringing suit in their local United States District Court; the United States Claims Court; or the United States Tax Court, the third alternative permitting them to delay payment of the disputed tax (plus interest) until the case is resolved. Tax Court, together with District Court, decisions are appealable to the regional Courts of Appeals, and Claims Court decisions to the Court of Appeals for the Federal Circuit, with all these decisions ultimately appealable to the Supreme Court. Proposals for a National Tax Court of Appeals, which would relieve the general courts of tax matters, surface from time to time, but none has yet been enacted.

undermine the logical structure of the income tax as a whole.[5] Other cases have given rise to more modest interpretive doctrines, including the prevention of tax avoidance; the need to identify the substance rather than the form of a transaction; and other similar ideas.[6] Here again, the statute is the starting — but by no means the end — point of tax law, and the capable practitioner must be aware of all sources relevant to the problem at hand.

What all this means is that a court (or student) faced with a tax question always begins with the Code but may have many possible places to turn to if the Code is ambiguous or incomplete. Depending upon the issue in question, the answer may lie in legislative history, regulations and rulings, judicial decisions, or the unwritten structure and policy of tax law; or (most likely) in a combination of each of these elements, the precise weight of each items depending upon the provision in question and the facts of the particular case. This does not mean, as is sometimes suspected, that one can argue any position in any tax case, or that lawyers can take whatever positions their clients wish and hope that they will avoid being audited. Much of the time, there will be a relatively clear answer, and the different forms of evidence will point largely in the same direction. But hard cases are, almost by definition, those in which the evidence conflicts; and law school, as we all know, is largely about the hard cases.

Rather than worrying too much about which source is most important — an unanswerable question, in any event — it may be useful for the student simply to list the sources at issue in each case and think how the court or other relevant party applies them. What Code section, or sections, are at issue? Are any regulations or rulings relevant, and what have prior courts held on the matter? What, if anything, does tax theory or logic have to say about the facts in the case? Finally, having taken the inventory above, which source(s) is (are) most convincing on these particular facts, and has the court applied them in a convincing manner? Asking these questions can be a frustrating enterprise, since courts themselves are sometimes unclear as to exactly which source they rely on. For some (especially older) cases, there may be few sources at all. But the habit of asking these questions is a good one, and will provide the student with a skill that is useful well beyond the tax field.

II. TAX POLICY AND TAX REFORM

Together with law, a tax course inevitably involves a healthy dose of tax policy. Questions of policy arise with regard both to the choice of tax base (income tax, consumption tax, and so forth) and how a particular tax base should be implemented once it is chosen. Indeed, these are by and large the same question, since a key criterion in choosing a new tax base is whether it will advance existing policy goals,

---

[5] *See, e.g.*, Comm'r v. Tufts, 461 U.S. 300 (1983).

[6] One of us (Livingston) having spent a fair amount of time refuting the idea of a unified theory of taxation, we are perhaps ill-suited to present it here; but it is certainly true that there is a large body of accumulated tax wisdom and that this wisdom, together with the Code and other primary sources, must be consulted in applying tax rules. *See* Michael A. Livingston, *Practical Reason, "Purposivism," and the Interpretation of Tax Statutes*, 51 TAX L. REV. 677 (1996). For differing views, see Deborah A. Geier, *Interpreting Tax Legislation: The Role of Purpose*, 2 FLA. TAX REV. 492 (1995); Lawrence Zelenak, *Thinking About Nonliteral Interpretations of the Internal Revenue Code*, 64 N.C. L. REV. 623 (1986).

such as fairness, simplicity, and economic efficiency, better than the other available alternatives. Students often wince at policy discussions, but in a field like taxation they are inseparable from legal analysis, and provide an important tool for understanding and critiquing even the most simple practical outcomes.

A.   Alternative Tax Bases and "Big Picture" Tax Reform

The first choice in designing a tax system is determining what the tax base (or tax bases) will be. Historically this was a more constricted choice than it is today. Since traditional societies lacked the capacity to measure items like "income" or "consumption," a property tax was especially common in this era. A property tax requires the owner of property (land, money, materials) either to turn over a portion of their property to the sovereign, or to pay an amount based on the estimated value of that property, on an annual or some other basis. For example, the Biblical tithe required individuals to turn over one tenth of their property or produce to the sovereign for the relief of poor people and other worthy purposes. A more modern version might provide a formula for valuing various types of property and require some (presumably low) percentage of the assessed value to be paid to the Government in each year. Property taxes are a useful if not especially popular source of revenue, but they are subject to two principal difficulties: they rely on arbitrary assessments of value and, if applied repeatedly to the same property, may effectively confiscate that property from its private owners in favor of governmental authorities. Property taxes survive today in many countries and in some places, including both European and Third World nations, are a significant part of the revenue mix. In the United States, property (especially real property) taxes are a principal source of revenues for financing schools and other projects at the local level, while the federal estate tax, a sort of once-in-a-lifetime property tax, accounts for a significant but not very large part of national revenues.[7] But there is no annual wealth or property tax at the federal level, and for political reasons there is unlikely to be one in the foreseeable future.

As societies developed, and trade became more important, governments naturally wished to capitalize on this trade as a revenue source. They accomplished this by imposing excise taxes, that is, taxes on various forms of transactions, typically the sale or purchase of commodities rendered taxable by appropriate royal or parliamentary action. In particular, many nations imposed taxes on alcohol, tobacco, salt, and other commodities considered luxuries by the standards of those times. The Stamp Tax, famous for its role in provoking the American Revolution, was essentially an excise tax on legal documents (wills, conveyances, etc.), which were considered invalid without attaching the proper tax stamp. Excise taxes have many advantages: they are relatively easy to collect, especially in industries with a relatively small number of wholesale dealers, and provide a large volume of revenue without the confiscatory features of a property tax. Until this century, they were the primary source of revenues for the federal government, together with import duties which are in essence another form of excise tax. But

---

[7] The estate tax and its cousin, the gift tax, may also be conceived as an indirect form of inheritance tax, that is, a tax on the act of passing one's wealth to one's heirs or successors, rather than on the underlying wealth itself. Many states, as well as the federal government, impose an inheritance tax.

excise taxes are highly regressive, that is, they tend to fall more heavily on poor than on wealthy people,[8] and they distort the economy by discouraging production of the product subject to tax. In the past thirty years, excise taxes have declined sharply as a percentage of aggregate federal revenues, being now limited largely to "sin" taxes on disfavored activities (smoking, drinking, and so forth) and public trust fund taxes which are used for related spending purposes (e.g., gasoline taxes which are deposited in the Highway Trust Fund). More broad-based excise taxes survive in the form of State and local sales taxes — essentially, an excise tax on all retail sales — and in proposals for a federal sales or value added tax (VAT) to replace or supplement the existing income tax.[9] Many State taxes deal with the regressivity issue, albeit clumsily, by exempting food and other necessities from the list of taxable items.

Sometime in the late 1800s it became apparent that excise and property taxes could not meet governments' growing demand for revenue for social and (some would say) less beneficent military and other purposes. At the same time it was apparent that many emerging forms of wealth — especially those arising from new industrial and commercial enterprises — were exempt from tax or else being taxed at very low rates. (A similar concern for unchecked accumulations of wealth helped give rise to the antitrust laws.) Meanwhile modern accounting methods, and the rise of a cash-based, wage-paying economy, removed many of the previous objections to income taxation.

This combination of hunger for new revenue, an incipient demand for social justice, and an attractive new revenue source led most industrial nations eventually to impose some form of wage or income tax. The United States enacted its first peacetime income tax in 1894, but the Supreme Court held the tax unconstitutional; the Sixteenth Amendment was subsequently amended and the predecessor of today's income tax enacted in 1913. For its first thirty years the income tax remained largely a "soak the rich" affair, a situation which is reflected in early judicial opinions, in which conservative judges displaying a thinly veiled hostility to the tax and sought to restrict it by narrow interpretations whenever possible. Only during World War II was the tax extended to middle-income Americans; at this point the IRS began to withhold the income tax from individual paychecks and the tax became the mass-based levy that it is today.

---

[8] For example, an excise tax on tobacco is imposed equally on a wealthy or poor individual, but is likely to take up a larger percentage of the poor person's income.

[9] A value added tax differs from a sales tax because it is imposed at all levels of production and not merely at the final, retail stage. For example, assume that A chops down a tree, paying $100 for an ax and other supplies, and sells the lumber to B for $1,000; B processes the lumber into wood which he sells to C for $10,000; and C uses the wood to make furniture which she sells, at retail, for a total of $100,000. A, B, and C would pay VAT at the applicable rate on $900, $9,000, and $90,000 respectively, or the amount of value that he or she added at each phase of the production process. The aggregate amount taxed ($99,900) would be similar to that under a sales tax, but the tax would be imposed in three stages instead of exclusively at the retail level. VATs are especially popular in European countries, in part because they are relatively easy to impose on imports, although the increasing unification of Europe makes this a somewhat less important factor. *See infra.*

Today the income tax is the single largest source of federal revenues, having left the estate, excise, and other miscellaneous taxes far behind.[10] Income taxes are also imposed by most states and many foreign countries, in most cases constituting a major or even dominant portion of the overall revenue mix. The tax has become so well established as to be part of our popular culture: phrases like "tax shelter" or "it's deductible" are part of our daily vocabulary, and April 15 is a universal synonym for something simultaneously unavoidable and dreaded.

When a rule has existed for a long time, there is a tendency to see it as inevitable, and to invent rationalizations that may have little to do with its original causes. Thus it is sometimes suggested that the income tax is superior to other taxes because it is based on the taxpayer's "ability to pay" and thereby avoids the problems of a large-scale excise or property levy. But this is circular logic: an income tax measures ability to pay only if one believes that ability to pay is measured by income, rather than by wealth, property, or some mixture of wealth- or income-based factors. For example, it is hardly intuitive that A, with a $50,000 salary and no wealth to speak of, has more taxpaying capacity than B, with a $40,000 salary and vast inherited property, although the income tax makes precisely this judgment. Other theories, purporting to derive a scientific or mathematical basis for income taxation, are similarly unconvincing.[11] It is probably more honest to say that the income tax arose for a mix of historical and policy reasons, including its own appeal and the limitations of other taxes, and that once stuck with it Governments and policy-makers have done their best to make the tax as fair, efficient, and administrable as possible. That is reason enough for professors to study the income tax, and for students to spend most (although not all) of a basic course on it. But there is no guarantee that the income tax will remain dominant for another hundred or even twenty-five years, or that what we call an income tax may not change beyond recognition within that or a still shorter period.

In the past two decades there has been increasing dissatisfaction with the income tax, in part resulting from political opportunism but in part an honest response to the limitations of the tax. In particular, critics have suggested that the income tax is unnecessarily complex; that high tax rates discourage hard work and innovation; and that the taxation of interest, dividends, and other investment

---

[10] The most important competitor of the income tax is no longer the excise, estate, or other traditional taxes but the employment taxes used to fund the social security and similar retirement programs. Although frequently thought of as investments rather than taxes, these payments have most of the features of taxes and occupy an increasing percentage of the federal budget. Social security taxes are increasingly controversial because of their regressive tax base, which includes wages but not interest, dividends, or other income, and because they tend to redistribute income from younger to older taxpayers. *See infra.*

[11] Perhaps the most famous effort to define a systematic approach to income taxation was that of the economist Henry Simons, who argued that all economic income should be taxed at the same rate while noting that the existing income tax contained numerous exceptions to this rule. HENRY C. SIMONS, PERSONAL INCOME TAXATION: THE DEFINITION OF INCOME AS A PROBLEM OF FISCAL POLICY (1938). The problem, of course, is that it turns out not to be so easy to define what economic income consists of. Thus, while Simons and his predecessor R.M. Haig remain justly famous — and reformers frequently state as their goal the taxation of "Haig-Simons income" — in practice it remains an aspirational rather than a scientific standard.

income discourages savings and encourages excessive consumption activity. Some of these critics have been content to propose changes in the existing income tax while retaining its underlying structure. For example, several prominent Republicans have proposed a so-called "flat tax," i.e., an income tax with one basic tax rate, in place of the current progressive income tax which imposes higher rates on higher levels of income. More creative opponents have proposed replacing the income tax with a consumption tax — essentially, an income tax with a deduction for all savings or investment by the taxpayer — or with a hybrid combining some aspects of an income, consumption, or other taxes. Still others have proposed a national sales or value added tax, of a type now used by various states or foreign countries, either as a replacement or supplement for the existing tax system. These proposals are frequently accompanied by colorful language, such as promises to "tear the income tax out by its roots," and impossibly optimistic revenue projections, which suggest that everyone can pay less tax in the new system while somehow raising the same sum of money. Many of the proposals may never make it past the discussion stage. But there is a strong undercurrent of dissatisfaction with the income tax, and it seems likely that, if not replaced, the tax is likely to be overhauled substantially in the next decade. While emphasizing current law, this book will also consider the most important of the emerging alternatives, together with existing nonincome taxes that will remain important even assuming the income tax (for all its faults) is retained.

B.   The Goals of a Good Income (or Nonincome) Tax

Once an overall tax base has been selected, attention turns to application. Traditionally, scholars have identified three principal criteria for evaluating a tax system: fairness, efficiency, and simplicity, the third sometimes being demoted to "administrative feasibility" or some weaker term. These terms are most commonly applied to the income tax, but are equally relevant for other taxes, and indeed for any kind of law that deals with economic or financial issues. The criteria can be applied to broad features of a tax system or to highly specific provisions. For example, it is frequently argued that tax breaks for particular industries are unfair because they treat these industries better than other endeavors, or inefficient because they cause excessive amounts of money to be invested in favored activities.

Fairness is traditionally divided into two components, horizontal equity and vertical equity. Horizontal equity means fairness in the sense of treating like cases alike, or in the words of the famous tax tongue-twister, "similarly situated taxpayers ought to be treated similarly." For example, if two families each have $50,000 of economic income, horizontal equity suggests that they ought to pay the same amount of tax. Getting just a little bit more daring, if company A makes $1 million in the oil business, and company B makes $1 million selling cars, these businesses likewise should pay a similar tax. Of course, we might choose to make differentiations in either of these cases, favoring one family over the other because (say) part of its income came from tax-free municipal bonds, or one company over another because we believed that subsidies for the oil and gas industry were in our national interest. But these deviations would be violations of the horizontal equity concept, and would have to be justified by an overriding, external concern.

Horizontal equity comes naturally for Americans, who are used to concepts like equal protection and equal rights, and in my experience few students have much trouble with it. The problem is that it tells you little about difficult cases. Take the case of the two families described above. Suppose now that one couple earns $50,000 of income, but has $10,000 of child-care expenses, so that its remaining income is only $40,000, while the second couple has a stay-at-home parent and gets to keep all $50,000. Should these couples still pay the same tax? Well, yes, if you think that income should be measured without regard to child care expenses (in which case both families still have $50,000 of income), but no, if you think that child-care is a legitimate business deduction (in which case the couples no longer have equivalent incomes). What if an oil company argues that it has not really made $1 million, because it has taken economic risks (dry holes, changes in oil prices, etc.) not faced by an automobile manufacturer, and that ought to be reflected in its accounting method and hence its tax bill? In cases like these horizontal equity tends to degenerate into a morass of political and technical arguments, not terribly different than those which would have been made if the concept had never existed. To paraphrase our original formula, we cannot say what it means to treat similar cases in a similar fashion because we cannot agree on which cases are similar.

The frequency of such cases has led some scholars to believe that horizontal equity is meaningless, a vague goal that has no impact on real-world cases. That's probably an exaggeration, and horizontal equity remains an important analytic tool, enabling us to identify obvious inequalities and providing at least some language for approaching more difficult cases. But it's probably better to think of horizontal equity as an argumentative structure rather than a magic formula: only rarely will it provide a clear solution to a tax problem.

The second category of fairness, vertical equity, is more potent but more controversial. While horizontal equity concerns the treatment of similar (or at least equivalent) taxpayers, vertical equity considers the impact of the tax system on broad economic or social classes. It asks whether the tax structure imposes an unfair burden on poorer individuals, or (more radically) whether it ought actively to redistribute income from wealthier to poorer taxpayers. In large part this is a matter of tax rates, and vertical equity is often taken to support the imposition of progressive tax rates, that is, higher tax rates on higher levels of income.[12] But

---

[12] Progressive taxation refers to the imposition of higher marginal rates of taxation on higher levels of income. Assume, for example, that there were two tax brackets, with all income up to $40,000 being taxed at a 15 percent rate and all income above $40,000 being taxed at 30 percent. A taxpayer with $50,000 of income would play $9,000 of tax (15 percent × $40,000 $6,000 tax on the first $40,000 of income and 30 percent × $10,000 $3,000 tax on the last $10,000 of income). The "marginal tax rate" for this taxpayer would be said to be 30 percent (alternatively, she would be said to be in the "30 percent tax bracket") although her average rate is somewhat lower, reflecting the lower rate on her first $40,000 of income. Marginal rate is usually considered more important for tax purposes, since people tend to make decisions at the margins. For example, if our hypothetical taxpayers earns an additional dollar, it will be taxed at a 30 percent rate, while an additional dollar of deduction will save her 30 cents in taxes.

Progressive taxation has been justified on various grounds, including diminishing marginal utility (roughly speaking, the idea that rich people need their last dollar less than poor ones), the benefit theory (the rich derive more from Government and should accordingly pay more taxes), and a simple desire to redistribute income and thereby improve social justice. The arguments against progressivity include the alleged disincentive of high taxes (people will supposedly work less if they have to share income with the

vertical equity may also be used to argue for or against specific provisions. For example, allowing businesspersons to deduct a "three martini lunch," while their employees received no similar benefit, is arguably inconsistent with vertical equity, while an exclusion for welfare or unemployment payments might be supported on vertical equity grounds.[13]

Arguments grounded in vertical equity tend to be more emotional than the horizontal variety, and are often supported by impressive statistical data, such as tables showing the impact of proposed tax changes on different economic and social classes. But they are also more politically controversial. How the tax system should treat richer and poorer taxpayers is a highly political issue, part of the broader question regarding the role of government in a modern, post-industrial society. An increasingly vociferous minority rejects the very concept of redistributive taxation, preferring a "flat" tax that ignores differences in income level. Even for political liberals, the goal of vertical equity may conflict with other objectives, such as promoting economic efficiency or providing incentives to wealthy taxpayers to invest money in favored ways. Vertical equity is thus an important part of tax policy analysis, but a highly subjective one, and difficult or impossible to separate from one's broader political views.

Along with fairness, the most widely cited goal for tax law is economic efficiency. Where fairness emphasizes the distribution of the tax (or broader economic) pie, efficiency concerns how to make the pie bigger. Efficiency analysis expresses itself at two distinct levels. First, as a general principle, the imposition of tax reduces the marginal incentive to earn extra income, since a taxpayer will keep less than a full hundred cents on each additional dollar she earns. Many (and especially conservative) tax analysts believe that it is important to reduce tax rates in order to increase this incentive. Second, taxes cause distortion in favor of specific activities or industries that benefit from lower taxation and against their higher-taxed competitors. For example, a tax break for the health or housing industries will cause somewhat more money to flow into these activities, but proportionately less to be available for other sectors, so that the allocation of resources will be different than that which would be provided by the pre-tax market. A portion of economic activity will thus be determined not by the market, but by the Government, which has distorted the market in favor of the chosen activities. Since economists generally assume that the free market distributes goods and services in the most efficient manner, reducing this sort of distortion is usually thought to promote economic efficiency.

Efficiency is much in vogue in contemporary tax policy, reflecting both the influence of economists and the increasing prominence of political conservatives,

---

Government), the right of individuals to keep their own income, and other arguments. *See* Walter J. Blum & Harry Kalven, Jr., *The Uneasy Case for Progressive Taxation*, 19 U. Chi. L. Rev. 417 (1952). Tax rates have changed several times in recent years, and are likely to do so again, although the general trend has been toward somewhat lower and flatter tax rates in the U.S. and other countries. Year 2009 U.S. individual tax rates range from 10 to 35 percent.

[13] To constitute a vertical equity issue, the differences in income and class level should be significant in degree. For example, a comparison between two equivalent wage-earners, one of whom has free commuting or child care and the other of whom must pay for these services, would normally be considered a horizontal rather than a vertical equity issue.

who tend to prefer efficiency to fairness rhetoric.[14] But efficiency, like fairness, also has limitations. At its broadest level efficiency is tied to behavioral assumptions that are difficult or impossible to prove, and tends to obscure political tradeoffs behind a superficially apolitical analysis. Thus, while an 80 percent tax rate would surely discourage some people from working, it is by no means clear that a 30 or 40 percent tax rate will do so; even if it did, the cost might be acceptable if it contributed to vertical equity or other objectives. At a more detailed level, efficiency analysis tends to overstate the efficiency of the free market and (perhaps) to exaggerate the costs of Government interference in the economy. For example, tax breaks for housing may help prospective home buyers overcome "barriers to entry" in the retail housing market, while research and development (R & D) incentives arguably correct for inefficiencies in the pretax economy. Further incentives, like those for health care or retirement security, may indeed distort the economy, but in ways that the Government (and a majority of citizens) believe to be necessary or proper. In still other cases, a certain amount of distortion may be acceptable to achieve fairness or other goals. These limitations by no means suggest that efficiency is irrelevant or unimportant, but its limitations should be understood.

The third goal of a good tax system, simplicity or (at least) administrability, is historically the weakest of the three elements. One look at the tax code suggests that it is anything but simple. This complexity results, in large part, from the need to meet the conflicting goals of horizontal and vertical equity and economic efficiency in a variety of personal and business settings. For example, a flat wage tax, with only one tax rate and ignoring interests, dividends, and other nonwage income, would be simple and perhaps even efficient, but would be unfair to wage earners and provide an arguably unmerited advantage to wealthier taxpayers. By contrast an individualized tax system, in which each person negotiated their tax payment based on their own personal facts and circumstances, would be extremely fair but also quite inefficient, and make it difficult for taxpayers to rely on tax law in planning business transactions. Trying to bridge this gap — to write general rules and yet take into account a broad range of personal and business circumstances — inevitably leads to complexity. Yet the tax laws, to be enforced, must first be comprehensible, and the authors of the tax code must devote at least some attention to fostering simplicity while trying to achieve other goals.[15]

What do fairness, efficiency, and simplicity mean to a student in a tax course? Like the principles of statutory interpretation, they constitute a sort of persistent

---

[14] Rhetoric is probably the right word: one observer has noted that both equity (*i.e.*, fairness) and efficiency arguments can be made in virtually any circumstances, since a higher tax would always redistribute income to at least some degree and a lower tax would always reduce distortion by at least some minimal amount. LOUIS EISTENSTEIN, THE IDEOLOGIES OF TAXATION 3-16 (1961).

[15] Part of the ambivalence regarding "simplification" of the tax code stems from the different meanings ascribed to the term. For example, the sort of simplicity sought by professors, who tend to prefer grand, ideological schemes, may be worth relatively little to individual taxpayers, who are largely interested in how long it takes to complete their returns. *See* Deborah L. Paul, *The Sources of Tax Complexity: How Much Simplicity Can Fundamental Tax Reform Achieve?*, 76 N.C. L. REV. 151 (1997) (dividing complexity into complication, intractability, and [logical] incoherence and suggesting that each may have different cures).

background music, a series of themes that rise and recede but are never very far from the action. A good habit is to ask, after reading each case or code section, what each of these concepts would have to say about the particular issue in question. For example, in a case involving taxation of employee fringe benefits, horizontal equity would likely argue in favor of taxation, since an exemption would discriminate against taxpayers who receive equivalent cash income, while simplicity or administrability might argue against taxation, since enforcing the tax is difficult in such cases and would require substantial administrative resources. Both horizontal and vertical equity would likely argue against most business tax incentives, although the recipients of these benefits sometimes argue that they improve economic efficiency, by encouraging investment or other positive economic activity. In other cases, these two concepts would clash, as in the case of (say) a proposed deduction for commuting or childcare expenditures, which might seem justified on grounds of horizontal equity but would arguably give a larger benefit to wealthier taxpayers.

The role of policy arguments varies in different contexts. In judicial decisions, they are determinative only if there is no clear case or statute on point, while in a legislative context they may be the starting point for your analysis. Sometimes all three criteria are overwhelmed by sheer political convenience. But understanding the policy implications is helpful in all of these contexts, enabling one to see tax law as a web of related choices rather than a series of disjointed parts.

In addition to specific tax provisions, the goals of fairness, efficiency, and simplicity are frequently invoked in arguments for comprehensive tax reform. For example, consumption tax supporters argue that a consumption tax would improve economic efficiency by encouraging investment and savings, while opponents argue that it would reduce vertical equity, since the poor typically consume a larger portion of their income than the rich. The same criteria are also used to evaluate sales, value added, and other kinds of nonincome taxes. During the course, you will have occasion to evaluate these broader issues, considering how tax policy is used not just to resolve individual issues, but to determine the overall direction and character of the tax system.[16]

III.   PRACTICAL CONSIDERATIONS: THE REAL WORLD CONTEXT FOR TAX LAW

Taxation is often the first law school subject to involve a large number of business transactions and terminology. As such, its language and mindset can be intimidating to beginning students. It is hard to appreciate the significance of tax decisions

---

[16] A particular application of tax policy is the concept of "tax expenditures," pioneered by the late Stanley Surrey and now a regular part of tax analysis. The basic idea is to see tax breaks for different activities as not really tax provisions at all, but a form of disguised spending, forcing other taxpayers to pay higher taxes in order to raise the same amount of net revenue. For example, the deductibility of home mortgage interest might be seen as a form of disguised spending for residential housing, while tax breaks for oil drilling would constitute a form of hidden assistance to the oil and gas industry. The implicit suggestion is that these programs would not survive scrutiny as direct spending and that many or most of them should be either reduced or eliminated.

without understanding their economic or business context; sometimes, it is hard even to state the facts of a case.

The ensuing materials provide an introduction to three topics that appear throughout the course: the structure of business enterprise, the time value of money, and the significance of accounting methods. While hardly a substitute for a course in corporations or business entities, these materials aim to provide at least a minimal economic and business vocabulary, ensuring that all students are on a "level playing field" in approaching the course materials. A subsequent section considers the values of the tax lawyer and the ethical standards applicable to tax practice.

A.   The Capitalist Economy and the Structure of Business Enterprise

We begin with the basic forms of business entity and investment. As you have probably noticed, the United States is a capitalist society in which the majority of business activity is controlled by private actors. Businesses in this country are usually conducted in one of three forms: a sole proprietorship, that is, a business wholly owned and operated by one person; a partnership, that is, a business jointly owned and operated by two or more persons, but treated for most purposes as an aggregate of its individual members rather than as a separate legal entity; and a corporation, which is treated as a separate legal entity and is (in most cases) managed by a Board of Directors distinct from its individual owners. Corporations are separate from their owners for income tax purposes, the so-called corporate income tax,[17] while partnership and sole proprietorship income "flows through" to the returns of the individual owners. (These issues, and the special cases of subchapter S corporations and limited liability companies, are discussed further in Chapter 11.)

The owners of a business, who are called stockholders or shareholders in a corporation and partners in a partnership, make money in two principal ways. First, the business may distribute money to its owners at any time, especially if it has been a profitable year and the business has extra cash that it does not need for its day-to-day operations. These distributions, which are called dividends in corporations and go by various names in a partnership, are usually taxable to the owners when received, in the same manner as salaries, interest, or other receipts. Both large and small corporations may pay dividends, but they tend to be more reliable in larger companies, so that people who depend on dividend income (e.g., older or retired persons) are more likely to invest in larger, more established businesses.

Second, the owner may hope to make money by an increase in value of his her ownership interest ("capital appreciation"), as when a stock increases in price because the company has performed well or because the economy in general has been strong. In this latter case, the owner pays income tax only when and if he sells

---

[17] The corporate income tax is, really, the same as the individual income tax, but with special rates for corporations (sec. 11) and subject to various special provisions that are only applicable to them (sec. 301 *et seq.*).

the relevant asset, the gain (or loss) being measured by the difference between the price that he paid for the stock or partnership interest and the price for which he sold it. This delay in tax, until an appreciated asset is sold or otherwise disposed of, is known as the "realization" requirement and is an important theme in the taxation of investment income. The tax upon sale of a stock or similar investment is also frequently imposed at the lower tax rate applicable to capital gains. (Investment for capital appreciation is often associated with younger, more aggressive investors, who can afford to forego current income in the hope of a more significant gain later on.)[18]

Instead of buying ownership interests, investors sometimes lend money to businesses, by buying bonds, notes, or other forms of debt instruments which the business repays, with interest, over the course of one or many years. In this case, the investor plays the role usually taken by a bank, seeking a return on her money (i.e., interest) that is likely to be lower than that available in the stock market, but also somewhat less risky. Individuals may be borrowers as well as lenders, as when a family takes out a mortgage loan on its residence or a loan to finance college tuition, a car, or other large expenses. Here it is the individual who must pay interest and the bank or other lending institution that receives it; the bank makes money by charging higher interest rates on such loans than it pays out to its own depositors. The tax treatment of these transactions is discussed in Chapter Five.

Finally, some individuals hedge their financial bets by investing in tangible assets, like real estate, cattle, or oil and gas wells, as well in stocks and other intangibles. The income tax treatment of these assets is generally similar to the rules above: income distributed by these activities (rents, royalties, and so forth) is taxable in the year received, while appreciation in value of the underlying asset is taxable only when the asset is sold, and frequently at reduced capital gain rates. Many of these areas, notably real estate investment, benefit from special deductions and credits that provide a significant tax incentive for the favored type of investment. Others, notably tax shelter investments, are subject to limitations designed to prevent excessive tax benefits accruing to the relevant investors.

You may have noticed that there is a certain "rich get richer" feeling to the rules above. Thus, the average person, who receives salary and (perhaps) a few interest and dividend payments, must pay tax on all of her income when received, while the wealthy, who hold stock and other appreciated property, can delay tax until they sell the relevant assets, and even then benefit from lower capital gain tax rates. The interest rules likewise seem to favor those who can afford large home mortgages or other deductible interest payments. Your instincts are correct: the realization requirement has long been a controversial feature of the tax system, while both the capital gain and interest deduction rules have been widely criticized for their potentially inequitable effect. In general, the income tax does a better job of taxing income from labor than income from property or capital, a situation which numerous reforms have tackled but none has completely corrected. We will discuss each of these issues in greater detail as the course progresses.

---

[18] In addition to distributions and capital appreciation, the owners of many small businesses may double as executives or other employees of the business and receive salaries for performing these functions. These salaries are taxed to the recipients in the same manner as any other wage-earner.

B.   Interest, Deferral and the "Time Value of Money"

A particularly important concept in the tax world is the time value of money. Although volumes have been written on time value, in essence it comes down to a simple observation: $1 today is worth more than $1 a year from today, which is worth more than $1 two years from today, and so on, until $1 (say) thirty or forty years from now has virtually no present value, at all. There are at least two reasons why this is true. In a subjective sense, it is simply more fun to have money now than later; you can always choose to save the money if you wish, but you have the further option of spending it if you desire. In a more objective sense, money is worth more now than in future years because of the existence of interest.

Assume that the interest rate for a given society is 10 percent (for simplicity we will assume that the same rate applies to all borrowing). At this interest rate, $1 invested today will increase to $1.10 a year from today; $1.21, with compound interest, two years hence; and about $17.50 thirty years from today, or more than 17 times the initial investment. Looking at the same transaction in reverse, in order to have $1 a year from today, I need invest approximately 91 cents today; to have $1 two years from today, about 81 cents; and to have $1 thirty years from today, I need set aside only bout 6 cents this afternoon. In economist's terms, the present value of $1, thirty years from now, at 10 percent interest, is said to be 6 cents.[19]

Since taxes are, essentially, debts of the taxpayer to the federal (or state) government, the time value of money encourages taxpayers to delay payment of taxes to the greatest extent possible. For example, if the taxpayer can delay a $1 tax payment from this year until next year, the present value cost of the tax has been reduced from $1 to about 91 cents (i.e., the taxpayer can set aside 91 cents today and still have enough money to pay the tax in the next year). If the taxpayer can delay the tax long enough — say, for ten or more years — this deferral may be nearly as advantageous as avoiding the tax altogether. Conversely, in the case of deductions or credits that reduce taxable income, the taxpayer has an incentive to take these items into account as soon as possible. The IRS will, of course, be on the opposite side in both cases, seeking to accelerate income and delay deductions whenever possible. Present value, or the time value of money, is merely a more precise way of measuring this effect.

Given the potentially immense value of tax deferral, it is not surprising that timing issues are among the principal themes of the course. For example, most tax shelters involve kinds of investments (oil and gas, real estate, etc.) that are designed to produce deductions in the early years and income, if at all, only after some years have passed. Pensions and other employee benefit plans are likewise designed to defer rather than avoid income tax; money deposited in these plans remains untaxed until withdrawn by the taxpayer many years after deposit. Timing issues are also important in the debate regarding an income and a consumption

---

[19] Because present values are dependent on interest rates, the time value of money becomes a greater concern when interest rates are high, as they were in the 1970s and early 1980s, and a somewhat lesser concern when interest rates are lower, as they have been throughout the past decade. For example, assuming a 5 percent (instead of a 10 percent) interest rate, $1 a year from now is worth about 95 cents (rather than 91 cents) today, and so on throughout the example. But it is still worth less than $1 today; the difference is one of degree, and not kind.

tax. Chapters 3, 4, and 8 of this book emphasize the deferral issue in these and similar contexts. But timing issues appear throughout the course, and it is useful to begin thinking in these terms from the very beginning.

C. The Significance of Accounting Methods

There tends to be less accounting than one anticipates in tax courses, which is probably just fine with law students. That said, you ought to know at least some terminology to make it through the material. Two principal distinctions are at stake here: the distinction between cash and accrual accounting, and that between tax accounting and accounting for "real world" business purposes.

The distinction between cash and accrual accounting is essentially a distinction between performance and payment. Say you go to the dentist in December, but don't pay the bill until January or February of the next year. The accrual method, which looks to the date on which the obligation to pay accrues (usually, the date on which goods are transferred or services performed), places this transaction in the first year when the trip to the dentist was made. Thus, assuming that you are both accrual basis taxpayers, the dentist has income in year 1 and you — assuming that you have a deduction, at all[20] — likewise receive it in year 1. By contrast, if you are both cash basis taxpayers, each of these consequences takes place in year 2 when the bill is finally paid. Where services are "prepaid," that is, where money is paid before the obligation accrues, the opposite result will obtain: the cash method will result in earlier income and deduction and the accrual method in a delay of both items.

Most observers believe that the accrual method measures income more accurately than the cash method, but that it is also somewhat more complicated. For this reason larger businesses, who can presumably handle the complexity, are generally required to use the accrual method, while most individuals and some small businesses continue to be cash basis taxpayers. There are also rules to prevent the deliberate use of inconsistent methods — for example, having our hypothetical dentist use the cash method and his patient the accrual method, resulting in an early deduction and later receipt of income — although these rules do not apply in all cases.

The issue of cash and accrual accounting suggests a broader point regarding differences between tax and financial accounting. Consider again our imaginary dentist. In addition to accounting for tax consequences, he must keep records for business purposes, to determine how much money he has made or lost in a given year and (perhaps) to provide information to creditors or others with a stake in the business. For these purposes he will have an incentive to accurately state or even overstate his income, so that the business will appear to be doing well and be able to attract new customers, suppliers, or lenders. But for tax purposes, he has an opposite incentive: to reduce taxable income so that he will pay as little tax as possible. Put differently, a taxpayer may have an incentive to describe the same reality in different ways for tax and nontax audiences.

---

[20] Medical and dental expenses are deductible only to the extent that they exceed 7.5 percent of adjusted gross income (AGI). I.R.C. § 213.

To reduce the potential for inconsistent statements, the Code generally requires that the taxpayer use the same accounting method for tax and nontax purposes.[21] But there are numerous exceptions. For example tax depreciation, that is, the deduction for machinery and other equipment with a limited useful life, is often more rapid than that required by business accounting principles. The Code also contains various provisions — for example, the rules pertaining to oil and gas wells, farmers, and research and development (R & D) expenditures — that permit taxpayers to treat specified events in a manner different from (and usually more generous than) that reflected in nontax bookkeeping entries. Together with other tax incentives, these accounting differences mean that it is possible for a business to report a large profit to its owners and a smaller profit, or even a loss, for tax purposes. In these cases it is sometimes said that the business's "effective tax rate," expressed as a percentage of its real-world income, is lower than the "nominal tax rate" contained in the Code. Like the realization requirement, the distinctions between tax and business accounting are often cited as a form of favoritism for business taxpayers, and are a frequent target for tax reformers.

IV.   PERSONAL VALUES AND ETHICS IN TAX PRACTICE

Often the biggest adjustment for tax students is not the terminology of business transactions, but the values that seem to go with them. Students learn quickly that the value of an item for tax purposes ("fair market value") is not its subjective or emotional value, but the amount that a rational — that is, economically oriented — person would pay for it. A distinction between business and personal activities pervades the course, with an implicit suggestion that the former are more productive and meaningful than the latter. Especially in older judicial decisions, there is often a condescending attitude toward women, childcare, and alternative lifestyles.[22] Poor people are shunted aside; everyone, everywhere, seems interested only in making money. The nightmare of the first year of law school, which many students find so culturally alienating, is thus often revisited in an introductory tax course.

The cultural issue also expresses itself in the moral or ethical side of contemporary tax practice. To appreciate this, a brief digression is necessary. Broadly speaking, tax lawyers engage in two kinds of work. The first is a counseling role: advising clients how to structure their personal and business affairs so as to reduce the payment of tax without sacrificing their other, nontax business goals. The second is a litigating role, representing a client who already has a tax problem before the IRS or the courts. Because of the prevalence of the case method, the second of these roles tends to get more attention in law school, although the first is by and large more important.

In both their counseling and litigating roles, tax lawyers are often called upon to render opinions, either less formally (as in verbal advice to a client) or more formally (as in an opinion letter or a tax return signed by the lawyer as return

---

[21] I.R.C. § 446(a).

[22] *See, e.g.*, Smith v. Comm'r, 40 B.T.A. 1038 (1939) (denying a deduction for "nursemaid" or child care expenses). The issue of women and the tax code is discussed further in Chapter 10.

preparer). In each of these cases there may be enormous pressure to take whatever position will save the client money, even when the argument for that position is weak or unconvincing. For example, clients frequently attempt to characterize personal expenses as business-related in order to claim a deduction that would be unavailable if a more honest description were made. Formal rules of ethics offer some, but little, protection in these cases: the rules are typically written by lawyers themselves, and sometimes seem more like guidelines for cheating than strictures for a genuinely ethical practice. For example, ethical rules generally permit a lawyer to represent multiple parties in a new business, so long as they mention the potential conflicts that may result.

There is probably not much a casebook can do to combat this kinds of cynicism; like Dorothy and the Ruby Slippers, you have to learn the lesson for yourself. But two points ought to be made. First, as a moral matter, you don't stop being a human being when you begin to practice tax (or any) law. That applies both to your readiness to take specific positions you don't really believe in, and to your broader willingness — one hopes unwillingness — to compromise your personal values in pursuit of material goals. Second, on a more practical level, it remains a fact that the best tax lawyers are not the most aggressive or unscrupulous, or the most willing to bend their principles to their clients' immediate goals. To the contrary, the best tax lawyers are notoriously conservative, constantly looking for weaknesses in their clients' position, for reasons a proposal will not fly. As one observer put it, the most important word in a tax lawyer's vocabulary is frequently "no."

None of this means that you need be indifferent to your clients' interests, or that you will not face pressure to make many compromises in tax or nontax legal practice. It does mean that the best lawyers acquire their reputations by being smart and hard-working, rather than conniving or facile, and that many have rich and rewarding lives outside of their legal practice.[23] On a more profound level it is important that you begin your legal career with at least some measure of idealism. The world will give you ample reasons to be cynical; try to start out with a healthy does of old-fashioned optimism.

V.   A DOSE OF REALITY: COMPLETING A FORM 1040

So much for introductions. To learn tax law, you have to start looking at real people's taxes. The best way to do that is to fill out a real tax return. This is in a sense a misleading exercise, since tax lawyers (as opposed to accountants) don't spend much time filling out returns, and many issues in the course don't really show up on them. Still, the return is the best single overview of the tax system, and the principal or only point of contact for millions of taxpayers. And knowing how to fill one out will make you very popular around April 15.

---

[23] At the risk of proselytizing, one advantage of tax as opposed to (say) litigation practice is that you tend to be valued for your expertise rather than as an interchangeable body; the hours thus tend to be somewhat more reasonable, and the work less repetitive, than in many other specialties. There is also a camaraderie among tax lawyers, and a sense of public responsibility, that exceeds that in most legal subjects. Tax lawyers work hard, but the good ones have a great deal beyond money to show for it.

Below are capsule descriptions of three different taxpayers: a single (and prosperous) young professional; a middle aged, working-to-middle class couple; and a retiree with a reasonable, but largely fixed, income. Pick one of the three taxpayers, and do your estimates and/or best to complete the appropriate income tax return, arriving at a reasonable estimate of taxable income and (to the extent you can complete it from section 1) of the tax owed in each case. At times, you will have to rely on intuition: if you knew all the answers, you wouldn't be taking the course. Think of it as an appetizer, the equivalent of the spelling pre-test in elementary school, or the pre-game predictions before the teams take the field. If you are not sure how to treat an item, make an educated guess. At various points in the course, we will revisit these issues and offer you a chance to see what you have learned in the interim.

In addition to getting your feet wet, the tax form provides a useful introduction to the course, or at least that portion which concerns the individual income tax (about the first ten weeks). Thus, Form 1040 begins by computing gross income; moves on to various nonitemized (bottom of page 1) and itemized (on Schedule A) deductions; and contains additional forms (Schedules B, C, and D) for dealing with interest and dividends, income from a trade or business, and capital gain and loss income. With some exceptions, this is roughly the same order that these issues come up in the course. Other income tax matters, like timing and income-shifting, are reflected indirectly on the 1040. So the organization of the course is not arbitrary or theoretical, but reflects the steps that real taxpayers must take to compute their annual tax liability.

A further benefit of comparing returns is that it gives us a kind of raw, bare knuckles look at tax policy and its effects. Consider the three taxpayers whose returns you have completed and that you have discussed (by now) in your class. Which of them is getting the best and the worst deal from the tax system? How would their relative positions be changed by a shift to a "flat tax" system, in which all taxpayers were taxed at (say) a flat 18 percent rate, with no deductions for home mortgages, charitable contributions, or other presently deductible items? What about a switch from an income to a consumption tax, in which all savings and investment was fully deductible, and one paid tax only on income consumed in the taxable year? Which of these three taxpayers would be likely to support one or both of these changes, or would they be largely indifferent to them? Moving from policy to (real-world) politics, which of the three do you think will be most effective in conveying their views? Why?

Taxpayer #1 — Yolanda Yuppie

Yolanda Yuppie is single, with no children, and lives in a rental apartment in the swank part of a major city. She has an income of $150,000 from her job as an associate at a high-powered law firm, together with about $1,500 of uncompensated expenses (telephone calls, magazine subscriptions, etc.) associated with her job. Her investments include a bank account, which paid $2,000 in interest during the calendar year, and stocks which paid $3,000 in dividends, together with a small number of tax-exempt bonds. Her expenses include $4,000 in State taxes, $10,000 in student loan interest, and $20,000 in rent, together with extensive amounts for food and entertainment.[24] During the year Yolanda also sold stock, which she had purchased five years earlier, at a $5,000 profit, and received a $10,000 gift from her parents, who seem reasonably happy at the way that she has turned out. Grateful for her good fortune, Yolanda also gave $7,500 to charity, and made an additional $1,000 in political contributions.

Taxpayer #2 — Mark Middle and Marcie Mode

Mark and Marcie are a middle-aged married couple with two small children and occupy a modest suburban home. They each earn $37,500 from their jobs as public school teachers for a combined income of $75,000. During the year they paid $12,000 on their home mortgage, virtually all of it for interest, together with $3,500 in State and local property taxes and a further $2,000 in State income tax. Mark and Marcie also had numerous expenses for food, clothing, etc. including $5,000 in day-care expenditures for which they received the maximum $960 tax credit.[25] The couple earned $1,500 in interest on their savings account, plus a net $2,500 in rental income from a small piece of real estate they share with other family members. During the year, they contributed $1,000 to an individual retirement account (IRA), and an additional $3,000 to their favorite charity.

Taxpayer #3 — Pam and Peter Pensioner

Pam and Peter are a married couple, both over the age of 65, and live in an apartment in a primarily senior citizen community. Peter is a retired car salesman and Pam is a retired housewife; their children are grown up and live in other States. Pam and Peter's income consists primarily of distributions from Peter's pension ($10,000) and the couple's IRA ($5,000), to which they made extensive tax-free contributions during the years Peter was working, plus $15,000 in social security distributions.[26] The couple supplemented this with $2,500 in taxable interest and dividends; an additional $2,500 interest on tax-free municipal bonds; and $2,500 Pam earned working part-time at a local library. Pam and Peter pay $30,000 in rent and other living expenses (their State has no state income tax) and have extensive medical and dental expenses although these are mostly covered by health insurance. During the year, the couple inherited $20,000 from a deceased relative, and made $2,500 in charitable contributions.

To assist you in this assignment, copies of Form 1040 and Schedule A thereto are included on the following pages.

---

[24] Student loan interest is generally deductible up to a limit of $2,500 per year, with this amount being ratably phased out as modified adjusted gross income ("MAGI") increases from $55,000 to $70,000 ($115,000 to $145,000 for married couples filing joint returns). These amounts are current for 2008 returns, and are adjusted for inflation. *See infra* Chapter 5, Section II.B. I.R.C. § 221.

[25] I.R.C. § 21(c).

[26] Distributions from previously untaxed pension and IRA funds are taxed at the couple's now-applicable regular tax rate. Social Security is subject to tax under a rather complex formula contained in section 86 of the Code. Under this rule, if the sum of the taxpayer's adjusted gross income ("AGI"), tax-exempt interest (if any), and one-half of Social Security benefits is greater than $25,000 ($32,000 for married couples filing jointly), then one-half of the excess up to an amount not exceeding 50 percent of Social Security benefits is subject to tax. For incomes above $34,000 ($44,000), the tax rate may be as high as 85 percent.

Form **1040**	Department of the Treasury—Internal Revenue Service **U.S. Individual Income Tax Return** 2009	(99)	IRS Use Only—Do not write or staple in this space.

For the year Jan. 1–Dec. 31, 2009, or other tax year beginning _____ , 2009, ending _____ , 20 ____ | OMB No. 1545-0074

Label
(See instructions on page 14.)
Use the IRS label.
Otherwise, please print or type.

L A B E L   H E R E

Your first name and initial | Last name | Your social security number

If a joint return, spouse's first name and initial | Last name | Spouse's social security number

Home address (number and street). If you have a P.O. box, see page 14. | Apt. no.

▲ You **must** enter your SSN(s) above. ▲

City, town or post office, state, and ZIP code. If you have a foreign address, see page 14.

Checking a box below will not change your tax or refund.

Presidential Election Campaign ▶ Check here if you, or your spouse if filing jointly, want $3 to go to this fund (see page 14) ▶ ☐ You ☐ Spouse

Filing Status
Check only one box.
1 ☐ Single
2 ☐ Married filing jointly (even if only one had income)
3 ☐ Married filing separately. Enter spouse's SSN above and full name here. ▶
4 ☐ Head of household (with qualifying person). (See page 15.) If the qualifying person is a child but not your dependent, enter this child's name here. ▶
5 ☐ Qualifying widow(er) with dependent child (see page 16)

Exemptions
6a ☐ **Yourself.** If someone can claim you as a dependent, **do not** check box 6a . . . . .
b ☐ **Spouse** . . . .
c **Dependents:**

(1) First name Last name	(2) Dependent's social security number	(3) Dependent's relationship to you	(4) ✓ if qualifying child for child tax credit (see page 17)
			☐
			☐
			☐
			☐

If more than four dependents, see page 17 and check here ▶ ☐

d Total number of exemptions claimed . . . .

Boxes checked on 6a and 6b ____
No. of children on 6c who:
• lived with you ____
• did not live with you due to divorce or separation (see page 18) ____
Dependents on 6c not entered above ____
Add numbers on lines above ▶ ☐

Income

Attach Form(s) W-2 here. Also attach Forms W-2G and 1099-R if tax was withheld.

If you did not get a W-2, see page 22.

Enclose, but do not attach, any payment. Also, please use Form 1040-V.

7	Wages, salaries, tips, etc. Attach Form(s) W-2	7
8a	Taxable interest. Attach Schedule B if required	8a
b	Tax-exempt interest. **Do not** include on line 8a . . .	8b	
9a	Ordinary dividends. Attach Schedule B if required	9a
b	Qualified dividends (see page 22)	9b	
10	Taxable refunds, credits, or offsets of state and local income taxes (see page 23) . .	10
11	Alimony received	11
12	Business income or (loss). Attach Schedule C or C-EZ	12
13	Capital gain or (loss). Attach Schedule D if required. If not required, check here ▶ ☐	13
14	Other gains or (losses). Attach Form 4797	14
15a	IRA distributions .	15a	b Taxable amount (see page 24)	15b
16a	Pensions and annuities	16a	b Taxable amount (see page 25)	16b
17	Rental real estate, royalties, partnerships, S corporations, trusts, etc. Attach Schedule E	17
18	Farm income or (loss). Attach Schedule F	18
19	Unemployment compensation in excess of $2,400 per recipient (see page 27)	19
20a	Social security benefits	20a	b Taxable amount (see page 27)	20b
21	Other income. List type and amount (see page 29) _____	21
22	Add the amounts in the far right column for lines 7 through 21. This is your **total income** ▶	22

Adjusted Gross Income

23	Educator expenses (see page 29)	23	
24	Certain business expenses of reservists, performing artists, and fee-basis government officials. Attach Form 2106 or 2106-EZ	24	
25	Health savings account deduction. Attach Form 8889 .	25	
26	Moving expenses. Attach Form 3903	26	
27	One-half of self-employment tax. Attach Schedule SE . .	27	
28	Self-employed SEP, SIMPLE, and qualified plans . .	28	
29	Self-employed health insurance deduction (see page 30)	29	
30	Penalty on early withdrawal of savings	30	
31a	Alimony paid b Recipient's SSN ▶ _____	31a	
32	IRA deduction (see page 31)	32	
33	Student loan interest deduction (see page 34) . .	33	
34	Tuition and fees deduction. Attach Form 8917 . .	34	
35	Domestic production activities deduction. Attach Form 8903	35	
36	Add lines 23 through 31a and 32 through 35	36
37	Subtract line 36 from line 22. This is your **adjusted gross income** . . . . . ▶	37

For Disclosure, Privacy Act, and Paperwork Reduction Act Notice, see page 97.   Cat. No. 11320B   Form **1040** (2009)

Form 1040 (2009)   Page **2**

Tax and Credits	38	Amount from line 37 (adjusted gross income)	38	
	39a	Check { ☐ **You** were born before January 2, 1945, ☐ Blind. } Total boxes If: { ☐ **Spouse** was born before January 2, 1945, ☐ Blind. } checked ► 39a		
Standard Deduction for— ● People who check any box on line 39a, 39b, or 40b or who can be claimed as a dependent, see page 35. ● All others: Single or Married filing separately, $5,700 Married filing jointly or Qualifying widow(er), $11,400 Head of household, $8,350	b	If your spouse itemizes on a separate return or you were a dual-status alien, see page 35 and check here ► 39b☐		
	40a	**Itemized deductions** (from Schedule A) **or** your **standard deduction** (see left margin) . .	40a	
	b	If you are increasing your standard deduction by certain real estate taxes, new motor vehicle taxes, or a net disaster loss, attach Schedule L and check here (see page 35) . ► 40b☐		
	41	Subtract line 40a from line 38	41	
	42	**Exemptions.** If line 38 is $125,100 or less and you did not provide housing to a Midwestern displaced individual, multiply $3,650 by the number on line 6d. Otherwise, see page 37 .	42	
	43	**Taxable income.** Subtract line 42 from line 41. If line 42 is more than line 41, enter -0-	43	
	44	**Tax** (see page 37). Check if any tax is from: **a** ☐ Form(s) 8814 **b** ☐ Form 4972	44	
	45	**Alternative minimum tax** (see page 40). Attach Form 6251	45	
	46	Add lines 44 and 45 . . . . ►	46	
	47	Foreign tax credit. Attach Form 1116 if required	47	
	48	Credit for child and dependent care expenses. Attach Form 2441	48	
	49	Education credits from Form 8863, line 29	49	
	50	Retirement savings contributions credit. Attach Form 8880	50	
	51	Child tax credit (see page 42)	51	
	52	Credits from Form: **a** ☐ 8396 **b** ☐ 8839 **c** ☐ 5695	52	
	53	Other credits from Form: **a** ☐ 3800 **b** ☐ 8801 **c** ☐	53	
	54	Add lines 47 through 53. These are your **total credits**	54	
	55	Subtract line 54 from line 46. If line 54 is more than line 46, enter -0- . . . . ►	55	
Other Taxes	56	Self-employment tax. Attach Schedule SE	56	
	57	Unreported social security and Medicare tax from Form: **a** ☐ 4137 **b** ☐ 8919	57	
	58	Additional tax on IRAs, other qualified retirement plans, etc. Attach Form 5329 if required . .	58	
	59	Additional taxes: **a** ☐ AEIC payments **b** ☐ Household employment taxes. Attach Schedule H	59	
	60	Add lines 55 through 59. This is your **total tax** . . . . ►	60	
Payments	61	Federal income tax withheld from Forms W-2 and 1099 . .	61	
	62	2009 estimated tax payments and amount applied from 2008 return	62	
If you have a qualifying child, attach Schedule EIC.	63	Making work pay and government retiree credits. Attach Schedule M	63	
	64a	**Earned income credit (EIC)**	64a	
	b	Nontaxable combat pay election **64b**		
	65	Additional child tax credit. Attach Form 8812	65	
	66	Refundable education credit from Form 8863, line 16 . .	66	
	67	First-time homebuyer credit. Attach Form 5405	67	
	68	Amount paid with request for extension to file (see page 72)	68	
	69	Excess social security and tier 1 RRTA tax withheld (see page 72)	69	
	70	Credits from Form: **a** ☐ 2439 **b** ☐ 4136 **c** ☐ 8801 **d** ☐ 8885	70	
	71	Add lines 61, 62, 63, 64a, and 65 through 70. These are your **total payments** . . . ►	71	
Refund Direct deposit? See page 73 and fill in 73b, 73c, and 73d, or Form 8888.	72	If line 71 is more than line 60, subtract line 60 from line 71. This is the amount you **overpaid**	72	
	73a	Amount of line 72 you want **refunded to you.** If Form 8888 is attached, check here . ► ☐	73a	
	► b	Routing number ＿＿＿＿＿＿＿＿＿ ► c Type: ☐ Checking ☐ Savings		
	► d	Account number ＿＿＿＿＿＿＿＿＿＿		
	74	Amount of line 72 you want **applied to your 2010 estimated tax** ► **74**		
Amount You Owe	75	**Amount you owe.** Subtract line 71 from line 60. For details on how to pay, see page 74 . ►	75	
	76	Estimated tax penalty (see page 74) **76**		
Third Party Designee		Do you want to allow another person to discuss this return with the IRS (see page 75)? ☐ **Yes.** Complete the following. ☐ **No**		
		Designee's name ► Phone no. ► Personal identification number (PIN) ►		

Sign Here
Joint return?
See page 15.
Keep a copy for your records.

Under penalties of perjury, I declare that I have examined this return and accompanying schedules and statements, and to the best of my knowledge and belief, they are true, correct, and complete. Declaration of preparer (other than taxpayer) is based on all information of which preparer has any knowledge.

Your signature	Date	Your occupation	Daytime phone number
Spouse's signature. If a joint return, **both** must sign.	Date	Spouse's occupation	

Paid Preparer's Use Only

Preparer's signature ►		Date	Check if self-employed ☐	Preparer's SSN or PTIN
Firm's name (or yours if self-employed), address, and ZIP code ►			EIN	
			Phone no.	

Form **1040** (2009)

SCHEDULE A (Form 1040)	Itemized Deductions	OMB No. 1545-0074

Department of the Treasury
Internal Revenue Service (99)

▶ **Attach to Form 1040.** ▶ **See Instructions for Schedule A (Form 1040).**

20**09**

Attachment
Sequence No. **07**

Name(s) shown on Form 1040

Your social security number

Medical and Dental Expenses

Caution. Do not include expenses reimbursed or paid by others.

1 Medical and dental expenses (see page A-1) . . . . . | 1 |

2 Enter amount from Form 1040, line 38 | 2 |

3 Multiply line 2 by 7.5% (.075) . . . . | 3 |

4 Subtract line 3 from line 1. If line 3 is more than line 1, enter -0- . . . . | 4 |

Taxes You Paid

(See page A-2.)

5 State and local **(check only one box):**
a ☐ Income taxes, **or**
b ☐ General sales taxes | 5 |

6 Real estate taxes (see page A-5) . . . . | 6 |

7 New motor vehicle taxes from line 11 of the worksheet on back. Skip this line if you checked box 5b . . . . . | 7 |

8 Other taxes. List type and amount ▶ _____ | 8 |

9 Add lines 5 through 8 . . . . | 9 |

Interest You Paid

(See page A-6.)

Note.
Personal interest is not deductible.

10 Home mortgage interest and points reported to you on Form 1098 | 10 |

11 Home mortgage interest not reported to you on Form 1098. If paid to the person from whom you bought the home, see page A-7 and show that person's name, identifying no., and address ▶

_____

_____ | 11 |

12 Points not reported to you on Form 1098. See page A-7 for special rules . . . . | 12 |

13 Qualified mortgage insurance premiums (see page A-7) . | 13 |

14 Investment interest. Attach Form 4952 if required. (See page A-8.) | 14 |

15 Add lines 10 through 14 . . . . | 15 |

Gifts to Charity

If you made a gift and got a benefit for it, see page A-8.

16 Gifts by cash or check. If you made any gift of $250 or more, see page A-8 . . . . | 16 |

17 Other than by cash or check. If any gift of $250 or more, see page A-8. You **must** attach Form 8283 if over $500 . . . | 17 |

18 Carryover from prior year . . . . | 18 |

19 Add lines 16 through 18 . . . . | 19 |

Casualty and Theft Losses

20 Casualty or theft loss(es). Attach Form 4684. (See page A-10.) . . . . | 20 |

Job Expenses and Certain Miscellaneous Deductions

(See page A-10.)

21 Unreimbursed employee expenses—job travel, union dues, job education, etc. Attach Form 2106 or 2106-EZ if required. (See page A-10.) ▶ _____ | 21 |

22 Tax preparation fees . . . . | 22 |

23 Other expenses—investment, safe deposit box, etc. List type and amount ▶ _____
_____ | 23 |

24 Add lines 21 through 23 . . . . | 24 |

25 Enter amount from Form 1040, line 38 | 25 |

26 Multiply line 25 by 2% (.02) . . . . | 26 |

27 Subtract line 26 from line 24. If line 26 is more than line 24, enter -0- . . . . . | 27 |

Other Miscellaneous Deductions

28 Other—from list on page A-11. List type and amount ▶ _____
_____ | 28 |

Total Itemized Deductions

29 Is Form 1040, line 38, over $166,800 (over $83,400 if married filing separately)?

☐ **No.** Your deduction is not limited. Add the amounts in the far right column for lines 4 through 28. Also, enter this amount on Form 1040, line 40a. ▶

☐ **Yes.** Your deduction may be limited. See page A-11 for the amount to enter. | 29 |

30 If you elect to itemize deductions even though they are less than your standard deduction, check here . . . . ▶ ☐

For Paperwork Reduction Act Notice, see Form 1040 instructions.   Cat. No. 17145C   Schedule A (Form 1040) 2009

Chapter 1

INTRODUCTION TO THE INCOME TAX: CLASSIC PROBLEMS IN THE DEFINITION OF INCOME

Although we will eventually reach other subjects, approximately the first ten chapters of this book are devoted to the domestic, federal income tax. This is reasonable, as the income tax remains — for all its limitations — the primary source of government revenues and the tax that most directly impinges on business and personal decisions. A knowledge of the federal income tax is also necessary to understand the additional topics (international tax, estate tax, and state and local taxes) discussed later in the book.

The first question to arise under the income tax is also the most obvious: what is income? This is both an easier and a harder question than first appears. The great majority of income consists of salaries, wages, and similar items, paid in cash or its equivalent, and with most or all of the tax withheld by the employer at the time of payment. Self-employed taxpayers, e.g., independent professionals or those operating their own business enterprises, are required to file estimated tax returns in place of wage withholding, but do so under the same basic system and subject to the same rules. Apart from a few tax protesters, no one seriously disputes that these items are subject to tax.

Things get interesting when the facts diverge from this pattern. This happens, for example, when employees are compensated with non-cash items (e.g., free goods and services, health or retirement insurance, or other fringe benefits), or when people receive money in various non-employment contexts, such as gifts, bequests, prizes, awards, scholarships and other similar items. In these cases, there may be arguments for eliminating or at least reducing the tax on the relevant item, because it is not "income" as commonly understood; because it is too administratively difficult to assign a value to the item; or because Congress decides to encourage the particular compensation or other activity in question. In still further cases, there may be no obvious reason for excluding an item, but the Code may exclude it anyway, for political or other reasons. This being (after all) law school, it should come as no surprise that we will devote most of our time to these unusual cases.

This chapter presents three classic problems in the definition of income: food and lodging provided "for the convenience of the employer"; gratuitous transfers (gifts, windfalls, and so forth); and the taxability of personal injury awards that compensate the taxpayer for physical or emotional damage. Each of these is an issue that attracted significant attention from Congress and the courts over the years; all three have played an important role in the development of income tax theory. Each presents a clash between different interpretive sources and competing tax policy goals. Although the issues may at times appear trivial, they are an important introduction to the themes and concepts that will stay with us throughout the course.

As the first substantive chapter, this chapter also introduces the analytical and reasoning skills that you will be expected to develop during the course. With this in mind, consider the following questions as you read the materials:

First, what are the sources of authority — Code, regulation, or judicial decisions — for the law in each of these areas? Section 61 of the Code provides that "Except as otherwise provided in this subtitle, gross income means all income from whatever source derived," and lists fifteen examples that suggest a broad if not all-inclusive definition of taxable income. That being the case, what is the argument for exclusion in each of our cases? To the extent that exceptions are created by judicial decisions, do the courts cite any statutory authority, or do they simply invent the exceptions out of thin air? Where exceptions are created by statute (i.e., by legislation), does Congress appear to have been responding to tax policy or political pressures, or was it simply codifying decisions already reached by the courts?

Second, what are the tax policy factors at issue in each case? This part of the course is often described as a clash between horizontal equity, which suggests taxation of most of the relevant items, and simplicity or administrability, which suggests that some of the items should go untaxed. Does this pattern fit all or most of the materials in this chapter? What is the role, if any, of vertical equity or economic efficiency in evaluating these issues? Given the ambiguity of the statute on many of these issues, do they wind up being decided largely on policy grounds?

Third, what if anything are the practical implications of the decisions the law makes in these areas? For example, how does the "convenience of the employer" rule affect the compensation of hotel and restaurant employees, and how do the personal injury rules affect the structuring of verdicts and settlements in this area? As a lawyer — now that you know the results of the cases — how would you balance your clients' tax and nontax goals in these areas, and avoid finding yourself in the next edition of this (or somebody else's) casebook?

I. EMPLOYER-PROVIDED MEALS AND LODGING: THE "CONVENIENCE OF THE EMPLOYER" DOCTRINE

BENAGLIA v. COMMISSIONER
Board of Tax Appeals
36 B.T.A. 838 (1937)

STERNHAGEN, J:

The Commissioner determined a deficiency in the petitioners' joint income tax for 1933 of $856.68, and for 1934 of $1,001.61, and they contest the inclusion in gross income each year of the alleged fair market value of rooms and meals furnished by the husband's employer.

FINDINGS OF FACT

The petitioners are husband and wife, residing in Honolulu, Hawaii, where they filed joint income tax returns for 1933 and 1934.

The petitioner has, since 1926 and including the tax years in question, been employed as the manager in full charge of the several hotels in Honolulu owned and operated by Hawaiian Hotels, Ltd., a corporation of Hawaii, consisting of the Royal Hawaiian, the Moana and bungalows, and the Waialae Golf Club. These are large resort hotels, operating on the American plan. Petitioner was constantly on duty, and, for the proper performance of his duties and entirely for the convenience of his employer, he and his wife occupied a suite of rooms in the Royal Hawaiian Hotel and received their meals at and from the hotel.

Petitioner's salary has varied in different years, being in one year $25,000. In 1933 it was $9,625, and in 1934 it was $11,041.67. These amounts were fixed without reference to his meals and lodging, and neither petitioner nor his employer ever regarded the meals and lodging as part of his compensation or accounted for them.

OPINION

The Commissioner has added $7,845 each year to the petitioner's gross income as "compensation received from Hawaiian Hotels, Ltd.," holding that this is "the fair market value of rooms and meals furnished by the employer." In the deficiency notice he cites article 52 [53], Regulations 77, and holds inapplicable *Jones v. United States*, 60 Ct.Cls. 552; I.T. 2232; G.C.M. 14710; and G.C.M. 14836. The deficiency notice seems to hold that the rooms and meals were not in fact supplied "merely as a convenience to the hotels" of the employer.

From the evidence, there remains no room for doubt that the petitioner's residence at the hotel was not by way of compensation for his services, not for his personal convenience, comfort or pleasure, but solely because he could not otherwise perform the services required of him. The evidence of both the employer and employee shows in detail what petitioner's duties were and why his residence in the hotel was necessary. His duty was continuous and required his presence at a moment's call. He had a lifelong experience in hotel management and operation in the United States, Canada, and elsewhere, and testified that the functions of the manager could not have been performed by one living outside the hotel, especially a resort hotel such as this. The demands and requirements of guests are numerous, various, and unpredictable, and affect the meals, the rooms, the entertainment, and everything else about the hotel. The manager must be alert to all these things day and night. He would not consider undertaking the job and the owners of the hotel would not consider employing a manager unless he lived there. This was implicit throughout his employment, and when his compensation was changed from time to time no mention was ever made of it. Both took it for granted. The corporation's books carried no accounting for the petitioner's meals, rooms, or service.

Under such circumstances, the value of meals and lodging is not income to the employee, even though it may relieve him of an expense which he would otherwise bear. In *Jones v. United States, supra*, the subject was fully considered in determining that neither the value of quarters nor the amount received as commutation of quarters by an Army officer is included within his taxable income. There is also a full discussion in the English case of *Tennant v. Smith*, H.L. (1892) App. Cas. 150, III British Tax Cases 158. A bank employee was required to live in quarters located in the bank building, and it was held that the value of such lodging was not taxable income. The advantage to him was merely an incident of the performance of his duty, but its character for tax purposes was controlled by the dominant fact that the occupation of the premises was imposed upon him for the convenience of the employer. The Bureau of Internal Revenue has almost consistently applied the same doctrine in its published rulings.

The three cases cited by the respondent, *Ralph Kitchen*, 11 B.T.A. 855; *Charles A. Frueauff*, 30 B.T.A. 449; and *Fontaine Fox*, 30 B.T.A. 451, are distinguishable entirely upon the ground that what the taxpayer received was not shown to be primarily for the need or convenience of the employer. Of course, as in the *Kitchen* case, it can not be said as a categorical proposition of law that, where an employee is fed and lodged by his employer, no part of the value of such perquisite is income. If the Commissioner finds that it was received as compensation and holds it to be taxable income, the taxpayer contesting this before the Board must prove by evidence that it is not income. In the *Kitchen* case the Board held that the evidence did not establish that the food and lodging were given for the convenience of the employer. In the present case the evidence clearly establishes that fact, and it has been so found.

The determination of the Commissioner on the point in issue is reversed.

Reviewed by the Board.

Judgment will be entered under Rule 50.

MURDOCK concurs only in the result.

ARNOLD, dissenting:

I disagree with the conclusions of fact that the suite of rooms and meals furnished petitioner and his wife at the Royal Hawaiian Hotel were entirely for the convenience of the employer and that the cash salary was fixed without reference thereto and was never regarded as part of his compensation.

Petitioner was employed by a hotel corporation operating two resort hotels in Honolulu — the Royal Hawaiian, containing 357 guest bed rooms, and the Moana, containing 261 guest bed rooms, and the bungalows and cottages in connection with the Moana containing 127 guest bed rooms, and the Waialae Golf Club. His employment was as general manager of both hotels and the golf club.

His original employment was in 1925, and in accepting the employment he wrote a letter to the party representing the employer, with whom he conducted the negotiations for employment, under date of September 10, 1925, in which he says:

> Confirming our meeting here today, it is understood that I will assume the position of general manager of both the Royal Waikiki Beach Hotel (now under construction) and the Moana Hotel in Honolulu, at a yearly

salary of $10,000.00, payable monthly, together with living quarters, meals, etc., for myself and wife. In addition I am to receive $20.00 per day while traveling, this however, not to include any railroad or steamship fares, and I to submit vouchers monthly covering all such expenses.

While the cash salary was adjusted from time to time by agreement of the parties, depending on the amount of business done, it appears that the question of living quarters, meals, etc., was not given further consideration and was not thereafter changed. Petitioner and his wife have always occupied living quarters in the Royal Hawaiian Hotel and received their meals from the time he first accepted the employment down through the years before us. His wife performed no services for the hotel company.

This letter, in my opinion, constitutes the basic contract of employment and clearly shows that the living quarters, meals, etc., furnished petitioner and his wife were understood and intended to be compensation in addition to the cash salary paid him. Being compensation to petitioner in addition to the cash salary paid him, it follows that the reasonable value thereof to petitioner is taxable income. *Cf. Ralph Kitchen*, 11 B.T.A. 855; *Charles A. Frueauff*, 30 B.T.A. 449.

Conceding that petitioner was required to live at the hotel and that his living there was solely for the convenience of the employer, it does not follow that he was not benefited thereby to the extent of what such accommodations were reasonably worth to him. His employment was a matter of private contract. He was careful to specify in his letter accepting the employment that he was to be furnished with living quarters, meals, etc., for himself and wife, together with the cash salary, as compensation for his employment. Living quarters and meals are necessities which he would otherwise have had to procure at his own expense. His contract of employment relieved him to that extent. He has been enriched to the extent of what they are reasonably worth.

The majority opinion is based on the finding that petitioner's residence at the hotel was solely for the convenience of the employer and, therefore, not income. While it is no doubt convenient to have the manager reside in the hotel, I do not think the question here is one of convenience or of benefit to the employer. What the tax law is concerned with is whether or not petitioner was financially benefited by having living quarters furnished to himself and wife. He may have preferred to live elsewhere, but we are dealing with the financial aspect of petitioner's relation to his employer, not his preference. He says it would cost him $3,600 per year to live elsewhere.

It would seem that if his occupancy of quarters at the Royal Hawaiian was necessary and solely for the benefit of the employer, occupancy of premises at the Moana would be just as essential so far as the management of the Moana was concerned. He did not have living quarters or meals for himself and wife at the Moana and he was general manager of both and both were in operation during the years before us. Furthermore, it appears that petitioner was absent from Honolulu from March 24 to June 8 and from August 19 to November 2 in 1933, and from April 8 to May 24 and from September 3 to November 1 in 1934 — about 5 months in 1933 and 3 1/2 months in 1934. Whether he was away on official business or not we do not know. During his absence both hotels continued in operation. The $20 per day travel allowance in his letter of acceptance indicates his duties were not confined to managing the hotels in Honolulu, and the entire letter indicates he was to receive maintenance, whether in Honolulu or elsewhere, in addition to his cash salary.

At most the arrangement as to living quarters and meals was of mutual benefit, and to the extent it benefited petitioner it was compensation in addition to his cash salary, and taxable to him as income.

The Court of Claims in the case of *Jones v. United States*, relied on in the majority opinion, was dealing with a governmental organization regulated by military law where the compensation was fixed by law and not subject to private contract. The English case of *Tennant v. Smith*, involved the employment of a watchman or custodian for a bank whose presence at the bank was at all times a matter of necessity demanded by the employer as a condition of the employment.

The facts in both these cases are so at variance with the facts in this case that they are not controlling in my opinion.

SMITH, TURNER, and HARRON agree with this dissent.

Understanding *Benaglia*

1. *Benaglia* was decided before enactment of present law (section 119) and the existing statute (section 22) did not directly address the issue. Instead, the court had to rely on more limited precedents, including cases holding that lodging received by an Army officer and a bank guard did not constitute taxable income. There was also a Regulation which excluded from tax "living quarters such as camps [that] are furnished to the employee for the convenience of the employer" but required tax where the lodging was intended as compensation. Do these precedents support the holding in *Benaglia*? Was Benaglia's situation really comparable to that of an army officer, or a person forced to sleep in a bank? How much deference should a court be required to show to (i) a regulation and (ii) the decision of a prior (in one case, a non-American) court?

2. The majority opinion asserts that Benaglia "was constantly on duty" and that the hotel "would not consider employing a manager unless he lived there." How then did he manage to run a second hotel where he didn't live, and to spend more than a third of the year (on average) out of town? Is the dissenting opinion correct that these facts cast doubt on the "convenience of the employer" rationale that is determinative of the case? What sort of factual evidence might we want before concluding that Benaglia was in fact "on call" at all hours?

3. Assume that the hotel did indeed force Benaglia to live on the premises, and that (left to his own devices) he would have preferred to live somewhere else. So what? Isn't he still better off, financially, than someone who received the same salary and had to pay for his own food and lodging? If so, doesn't horizontal equity require that Benaglia be taxed on these benefits? Could an employee at a competing hotel, who had to pay for his own food and lodging, claim a deduction for the cost of these items? If not, why should Benaglia be allowed to exclude them?

4. Perhaps the real problem here is valuation. The food and lodging received by Benaglia are obviously worth something, but their value to him may be less than to another customer, because of the forced nature of the consumption and because (given the choice) he would have preferred to spend the same money on other items. Thus it is not clear whether he should be taxed on the fair market value of the rooms and lodging ($7,845); on the amount that he would have spent on meals and lodging had they not been provided by the hotel ($3,600); on the employer's cost for providing the food and lodging (probably very low); or on a subjective amount, based on the forced consumption argument or other factors. Because it is administratively difficult to determine the amount of food and lodging subject to tax, the court does the next best thing and exempts them from tax, altogether.

Is this line of argument sensible? Wouldn't it be better to assign an arbitrary value to Benaglia's food and lodging than simply allow him to receive the benefits tax free? Is there (should there be) a general principle of excluding items from tax because they are difficult to value?

5. Do you think the hotel deducted the amount of Benaglia's room and board from its own taxable income? Does it matter?

Using the Sources

What would be the tax treatment of *Benaglia* under present law?

Law and Planning

1. How do you think that the IRS found out about Benaglia's free room and board and decided to challenge him on it?

2. If Benaglia had lost the case, and had to pay tax on his free room and board, what do you think he would have asked for at his next contract negotiation? Would the hotel have agreed to it? What if anything does this tell you about the result in the case?

3. Now that Benaglia has won, and avoided paying tax on the benefits, what do you think his employer (and other hotels) will do?

Politics and Policy

1. What are the horizontal and vertical equity implications of the *Benaglia* decision? Does the availability of tax-free food and lodging benefit primarily wealthy or poorer individuals? Or is it merely a quirk associated with a few businesses (hotels, hospitals, etc.) where one can argue that one's presence is required on a round-the-clock basis? Could a law firm argue that it required its associates to be on call 24 hours a day, and begin paying them with tax-free food and lodging instead of (taxable) cash compensation? Would it trouble you if they did?

2. As long as we're touching all bases, what about economic efficiency? Does the decision in *Benaglia* encourage more people to take jobs as hotel managers, night watchmen, etc., and make fewer of them available for other activities? Or will hotels

and similar industries, knowing their employees have this unusual tax break, simply pay them somewhat reduced salaries, so that the whole thing becomes a mild tax incentive for the hospitality industry and has relatively little effect on the employees, either way? Might the real message of *Benaglia* be "yes, we know it's an unfair tax break, but it's not that much money, it's an administrative nightmare, the market probably corrects the more glaring inequities, and it's simply not worth going after it?" Is that a good reason to exempt something from tax?

3. Assume that Benaglia had lost the case, and you were hired to lobby Congress for a bill restoring tax-free treatment of meals and lodging provided to hotel employees. How would you present this issue to a congressional committee? Would you emphasize the unfairness of the tax to managers like Benaglia, or to night watchmen and other lower-paid individuals? What unions or trade groups could you expect to assist in your efforts? Would it help or hurt your effort that hotel employees tend to be concentrated in a few large states (California, Florida, Hawaii) and are already organized for other purposes?

Section 119

Good idea or bad, the holding in *Benaglia* was adopted by Congress in section 119 of the Code, which remains in effect today. Section 119 provides that the value of meals or lodging furnished to an employee or her spouse or dependents, for the convenience of the employer, is excluded from gross income despite the more general language of section 61. It is one of several occasions in which the Code, having failed (quite understandably) to anticipate all of the issues arising under the income tax, essentially ratifies a previous judicial decision on the matter in question.

Because section 119 is the first Code provision you have encountered, it is worth examining in some detail. Of immediate interest are the separate tests contained in the provision, which require only that meals be furnished on the employer's business premises (§ 119(a)(1)), but in the case of lodging require both that (i) the lodging be located on the employer's business premises and (ii) that the employee is required to accept such lodging as a condition of her employment (§ 119(a)(2)). (The first part of section 119(a), which sets forth the convenience of the employer standard and other general rules, applies to both meals and lodging.) Why might Congress have decided to include a stricter rule for lodging than for meals? Would Benaglia and his wife meet the statutory standard, with respect to their meals, lodging, or both combined? What would be the relevance to Benaglia of section 119(b)(1), stating that the provisions of an employment contract shall not be not determinative of whether meals or lodging are intended as compensation? Why do you think that Congress decided to include this provision?

The enactment of section 119 did not end the litigation regarding the convenience of the employer rule. Numerous questions remain, including the scope of the underlying doctrine (how necessary must the employee's physical presence be in order to qualify for the exclusion?), the meaning of "business premises" (does it include an apartment or restaurant across the street from the employer, in the same neighborhood, or only at the actual business location?), and the form of benefit received (does a meal or lodging allowance, as opposed to direct, "in kind" provision of the relevant benefits, qualify for tax exemption?) But all of these questions now have as their starting point the language of section 119; in theory, at least, all are matters of statutory interpretation rather than free-ranging judicial or administrative discretion. The questions are thus the same as they were for Benaglia, but the style of argument is somewhat different.

The following case, *Commissioner v. Kowalski*, concerns the issue of meal allowances, probably the most significant question to arise under the convenience of the employer doctrine. As you read the case, consider to what degree (if any) the language of section 119 actually constrains the Court. Is the decision required by the statute, or does the Court merely use section 119 as a springboard for its own, independent analysis?

Is *Kowalski* consistent with *Benaglia*, or does it undermine part of its intended effect?

COMMISSIONER v. KOWALSKI
United States Supreme Court
434 U.S. 77 (1977)

OPINION:

Mr. Justice Brennan delivered the opinion of the Court.

This case presents the question whether cash payments to state police troopers, designated as meal allowances, are included in gross income under § 61(a) of the Internal Revenue Code of 1954, 26 U.S.C. § 61(a), and, if so, are otherwise excludable under § 119 of the Code, 26 U.S.C. § 119.

I

The pertinent facts are not in dispute. Respondent is a state police trooper employed by the Division of State Police of the Department of Law and Public Safety of the State of New Jersey. During 1970, the tax year in question, he received a base salary of $8,739.38, and an additional $1,697.54 designated as an allowance for meals.

The State instituted the cash meal allowance for its state police officers in July 1949. Prior to that time, all troopers were provided with midshift[1] meals in kind at various meal stations located throughout the State. A trooper unable to eat at an official meal station could, however, eat at a restaurant and obtain reimbursement. The meal-station system proved unsatisfactory to the State because it required troopers to leave their assigned areas of patrol unguarded for extended periods of time. As a result, the State closed its meal stations and instituted a cash-allowance

---

[1] [5] While on active duty, New Jersey troopers are generally required to live in barracks. Meals furnished in kind at the barracks before or after a patrol shift are not involved in this case. Nor is the meal allowance intended to pay for meals eaten before or after a shift in those instances in which the trooper is not living in the barracks. However, because of the duration of some patrols, a trooper may be required to eat more than one meal per shift while on the road.

system. Under this system, troopers remain on call in their assigned patrol areas during their midshift break. Otherwise, troopers are not restricted in any way with respect to where they may eat in the patrol area and, indeed, may eat at home if it is located within that area. Troopers may also bring their midshift meal to the job and eat it in or near their patrol cars.

The meal allowance is paid biweekly in advance and is included, although separately stated, with the trooper's salary. The meal-allowance money is also separately accounted for in the State's accounting system. Funds are never commingled between the salary and meal-allowance accounts. Because of these characteristics of the meal-allowance system, the Tax Court concluded that the "meal allowance was not intended to represent additional compensation." 65 T.C. 44, 47 (1975).

Notwithstanding this conclusion, it is not disputed that the meal allowance has many features inconsistent with its characterization as a simple reimbursement for meals that would otherwise have been taken at a meal station. For example, troopers are not required to spend their meal allowances on their midshift meals, nor are they required to account for the manner in which the money is spent. With one limited exception not relevant here,[2] no reduction in the meal allowance is made for periods when a trooper is not on patrol because, for example, he is assigned to a headquarters building or is away from active duty on vacation, leave, or sick leave. In addition, the cash allowance for meals is described on a state police recruitment brochure as an item of salary to be received in addition to an officer's base salary and the amount of the meal allowance is a subject of negotiations between the State and the police troopers' union. Finally, the amount of an officer's cash meal allowance varies with his rank[3] and is included in his gross pay for purposes of calculating pension benefits.

On his 1970 income tax return, respondent reported $9,066 in wages. That amount included his salary plus $326.45 which represented cash meal allowances reported by the State on respondent's Wage and Tax Statement (Form W-2).[4] The remaining amount of meal allowance, $1,371.09, was not reported. On audit, the Commissioner determined that this amount should have been included in respondent's 1970 income and assessed a deficiency.

Respondent sought review in the United States Tax Court, arguing that the cash meal allowance was not compensatory but was furnished for the convenience of the employer and hence was not "income" within the meaning of § 61(a) and that, in any case, the allowance could be excluded under § 119. In a reviewed decision, the Tax Court, with six dissents, held that the cash meal payments were income within the meaning of § 61 and, further, that such payments were not excludable under

---

[2] [6] The amount of the allowance is adjusted only when an officer is on military leave.

[3] [7] Troopers, such as respondent, and other noncommissioned officers received $1,740 per year; lieutenants and captains received $1,776, majors $1,848, and the Superintendent $2,136.

[4] [8] On October 1, 1970, the Division of State Police began to withhold income tax from amounts paid as cash meal allowances. No claim has been made that the change in the Division's withholding policy has any relevance for this case.

§ 119.[5] 65 T.C. 44 (1975). The Court of Appeals for the Third Circuit, in a per curiam opinion, held that its earlier decision in *Saunders v. Commissioner*, 215 F.2d 768 (1954), which determined that cash payments under the New Jersey meal-allowance program were not taxable, required reversal. 544 F.2d 686 (1976). We granted *certiorari* to resolve a conflict among the Courts of Appeals on the question. 430 U.S. 944 (1977). We reverse.

II

A

The starting point in the determination of the scope of "gross income" is the cardinal principle that Congress in creating the income tax intended "to use the full measure of its taxing power." *Helvering v. Clifford*, 309 U.S. 331, 334 (1940); *accord*, *Helvering v. Midland Mutual Life Ins. Co.*, 300 U.S. 216, 223 (1937); *Douglas v. Willcuts*, 296 U.S. 1, 9 (1935); *Irwin v. Gavit*, 268 U.S. 161, 166 (1925). In applying this principle to the construction of § 22(a) of the Internal Revenue Code of 1939 this Court stated that "Congress applied no limitations as to the source of taxable receipts, nor restrictive labels as to their [nature, but intended] to tax all gains except those specifically exempted." *Commissioner v. Glenshaw Glass Co.*, 348 U.S. 426, 429–430 (1955), citing *Commissioner v. Jacobson*, 336 U.S. 28, 49 (1949), and *Helvering v. Stockholms Enskilda Bank*, 293 U.S. 84, 87–91 (1934). Although Congress simplified the definition of gross income in § 61 of the 1954 Code, it did not intend thereby to narrow the scope of that concept. *See Commissioner v. Glenshaw Glass Co.*, *supra*, at 432, and n. 11; H.R. Rep. No. 1337, 83d Cong., 2d Sess., A18 (1954); S. Rep. No. 1622, 83d Cong., 2d Sess., 168 (1954). In the absence of a specific exemption, therefore, respondent's meal-allowance payments are income within the meaning of § 61 since, like the payments involved in *Glenshaw Glass Co.*, the payments are "undeniabl[y] accessions to wealth, clearly realized, and over which the [respondent has] complete dominion." *Commissioner v. Glenshaw Glass Co.*, *supra*, at 431. *See also Commissioner v. LoBue*, 351 U.S. 243, 247 (1956); *Van Rosen v. Commissioner*, 17 T.C. 834, 838 (1951).

Respondent contends, however, that § 119 can be construed to be a specific exemption covering the meal-allowance payments to New Jersey troopers. Alternatively, respondent argues that notwithstanding § 119 a specific exemption may be found in a line of lower-court cases and administrative rulings which recognize that benefits conferred by an employer on an employee "for the convenience of the employer" — at least when such benefits are not "compensatory" — are not income within the meaning of the Internal Revenue Code. In responding to these contentions, we turn first to § 119. Since we hold that § 119 does not cover cash payments of any kind, we then trace the development over several decades of the convenience-of-the-employer doctrine as a determinant

---

[5] [10] The Tax Court also determined that amount of meal allowance attributable to respondent's expenses while "away from home" as defined in § 162(a)(2) of the Code, were properly deducted from respondent's income as travel expenses. *See* United States v. Correll, 389 U.S. 299 (1967). The Commissioner did not appeal from this holding.

of the tax status of meals and lodging, turning finally to the question whether the doctrine as applied to meals and lodging survives the enactment of the Internal Revenue Code of 1954.

B

Section 119 provides that an employee may exclude from income "the value of any meals . . . furnished to him by his employer for the convenience of the employer, but only if . . . the meals are furnished on the business premises of the employer. . . ." By its terms, § 119 covers meals furnished by the employer and not cash reimbursements for meals. This is not a mere oversight. As we shall explain at greater length below, the form of § 119 which Congress enacted originated in the Senate and the Report accompanying the Senate bill is very clear: "Section 119 applies only to meals or lodging furnished in kind." S. Rep. No. 1622, 83d Cong., 2d Sess., 190 (1954). *See also* Treas. Reg. § 1.119-1(c)(2), 26 CFR § 1.119-1 (1977). Accordingly, respondent's meal-allowance payments are not subject to exclusion under § 119.

* * *

D

Even if we assume that respondent's meal-allowance payments could have been excluded from income under the 1939 Code pursuant to the doctrine we have just sketched, we must nonetheless inquire whether such an implied exclusion survives the 1954 recodification of the Internal Revenue Code. *Cf. Helvering v. Winmill*, 305 U.S. 79, 83 (1938). Two provisions of the 1954 Code are relevant to this inquiry: § 119 and § 120,[6] now repealed, which allowed police officers to exclude from income subsistence allowances of up to $5 per day.

In enacting § 119, the Congress was determined to "end the confusion as to the tax status of meals and lodging furnished an employee by his employer." H.R. Rep. No. 1337, 83d Cong., 2d Sess., 18 (1954); S. Rep. No. 1622, 83d Cong., 2d Sess., 19 (1954). However, the House and Senate initially differed on the significance that should be given the convenience-of-the-employer doctrine for the purposes of § 119. As explained in its Report, the House proposed to exclude meals from gross income "if they [were] furnished at the place of employment and the employee [was] required to accept them at the place of employment as a condition of his

---

[6] [25] "Sec. 120. STATUTORY SUBSISTENCE ALLOWANCE RECEIVED BY POLICE.

"(a) GENERAL RULE. — Gross income does not include any amount received as a statutory subsistence allowance by an individual who is employed as a police official. . . .

"(b) LIMITATIONS. —

"(1) Amounts to which subsection (a) applies shall not exceed $5 per day.

"(2) If any individual receives a subsistence allowance to which subsection (a) applies, no deduction shall be allowed under any other provision of this chapter for expenses in respect of which he has received such allowance, except to the extent that such expenses exceed the amount excludable under subsection (a) and the excess is otherwise allowable as a deduction under this chapter." 68A Stat. 39.

employment." H.R. Rep. No. 1337, *supra*, at 18; *see* H.R. 8300, 83d Cong., 2d Sess., § 119 (1954). Since no reference whatsoever was made to the concept, the House view apparently was that a statute "designed to end the confusion as to the tax status of meals and lodging furnished an employee by his employer" required complete disregard of the convenience-of-the-employer doctrine.

The Senate, however, was of the view that the doctrine had at least a limited role to play. After noting the existence of the doctrine and the Tax Court's reliance on state law to refuse to apply it in *Doran v. Commissioner*, *supra*, the Senate Report states:

> "Your committee believes that the House provision is ambiguous in providing that meals or lodging furnished on the employer's premises, which the employee is required to accept as a condition of his employment, are excludable from income whether or not furnished as compensation. Your committee has provided that the basic test of exclusion is to be whether the meals or lodging are furnished primarily for the convenience of the employer (and thus excludable) or whether they were primarily for the convenience of the employee (and therefore taxable). However, in deciding whether they were furnished for the convenience of the employer, the fact that a State statute or an employment contract fixing the terms of the employment indicate the meals or lodging are intended as compensation is not to be determinative. This means that employees of State institutions who are required to live and eat on the premises will not be taxed on the value of the meals and lodging even though the State statute indicates the meals and lodging are part of the employee's compensation." S. Rep. No. 1622, *supra*, at 19.

In a technical appendix, the Senate Report further elaborated:

> "Section 119 applies only to meals or lodging furnished in kind. Therefore, any cash allowances for meals or lodging received by an employee will continue to be includible in gross income to the extent that such allowances constitute compensation." *Id.* at 190–191.

After conference, the House acquiesced in the Senate's version of § 119. Because of this, respondent urges that § 119 as passed did not discard the convenience-of-the-employer doctrine, but indeed endorsed the doctrine shorn of the confusion created by Mim. 6472 and cases like *Doran*. Respondent further argues that, by negative implication, the technical appendix to the Senate Report creates a class of noncompensatory cash meal payments that are to be excluded from income. We disagree.

The Senate unquestionably intended to overrule *Doran* and rulings like Mim. 6472. Equally clearly the Senate refused completely to abandon the convenience-of-the-employer doctrine as the House wished to do. On the other hand, the Senate did not propose to leave undisturbed the convenience-of-the-employer doctrine as it had evolved prior to the promulgation of Mim. 6472. The language of § 119 quite plainly rejects the reasoning behind rulings like O.D. 514, which rest on the employer's characterization of the nature of a payment. This conclusion is buttressed by the Senate's choice of a term of art, "convenience of the employer," in describing one of the conditions for exclusion under § 119. In so choosing, the Senate obviously intended to adopt the meaning of that term as it had developed over time, except, of course, to the extent § 119 overrules decisions like *Doran*. As we have noted above, *Van Rosen v. Commissioner*, 17 T.C. 834 (1951), provided the controlling court definition at the time of the 1954 recodification and it expressly rejected the *Jones* theory of "convenience of the employer" — and by implication the theory of O.D. 514 — and adopted as the exclusive rationale the business-necessity theory. *See* 17 T.C., at 838–840. The business-necessity theory was also the controlling administrative interpretation of "convenience of the employer" prior to Mim. 6472. Finally, although the Senate Report did not expressly define "convenience of the employer" it did describe those situations in which it wished to reverse the courts and create an exclusion as those where "an employee must accept . . . meals or lodging in order properly to perform his duties." S. Rep. No. 1622, *supra*, at 190.

As the last step in its restructuring of prior law, the Senate adopted an additional restriction created by the House and not theretofore a part of the law, which required that meals subject to exclusion had to be taken on the business premises of the employer. Thus § 119 comprehensively modified the prior law, both expanding and contracting the exclusion for meals and lodging previously provided, and it must therefore be construed as its draftsmen obviously intended it to be — as a replacement for the prior law, designed to "end [its] confusion."

Because § 119 replaces prior law, respondent's further argument — that the technical appendix in the Senate Report recognized the existence under § 61 of an exclusion for a class of noncompensatory cash payments — is without merit. If cash meal allowances could be excluded on the mere showing that such payments served the convenience of the employer, as respondent suggests, then cash would be more widely excluded from income than meals in kind, an extraordinary result given the presumptively compensatory nature of cash payments and the obvious intent of § 119 to narrow the circumstances in which meals could be excluded. Moreover, there is no reason to suppose that Congress would have wanted to recognize a class of excludable cash meal payments. The two precedents for the exclusion of cash — O.D. 514 and *Jones v. United States* — both rest on the proposition that the convenience of the employer can be inferred from the characterization given the cash payments by the employer, and the heart of this proposition is undercut by both the language of § 119 and the Senate Report. *Jones* also rests on *Eisner v. Macomber*, 252 U.S. 189 (1920), but Congress had no reason to read *Eisner*'s definition of income into § 61 and, indeed, any assumption that Congress did is squarely at odds with *Commissioner v. Glenshaw Glass Co.*, 348 U.S. 426 (1955). *See id.* at 430–431. Finally, as petitioner suggests, it is much more reasonable to assume that the cryptic statement in the technical appendix — "cash allowances . . . will continue to be includable in gross income to the extent that such allowances constitute compensation" — was meant to indicate only that meal payments otherwise deductible under § 162 (a)(2) of the 1954 Code were not affected by § 119.

Moreover, even if we were to assume with respondent that cash meal payments made for the convenience of the employer could qualify for an exclusion notwithstanding the express limitations upon the doctrine embodied in § 119, there would still be no reason to allow the meal allowance here to be excluded. Under the pre-1954 convenience-of-the-employer doctrine respondent's allowance is indistinguishable from that in *Van Rosen v. Commissioner, supra*, and hence it is income. Indeed, the form of the meal allowance involved here has drastically changed from that passed on in *Saunders v. Commissioner*, 215 F.2d 768 (CA3 1954), relied on by the Third Circuit below, *see supra*, at 82, and in its present form the allowance is not excludable even under *Saunders'* analysis. In any case, to avoid the completely unwarranted result of creating a larger exclusion for cash than kind, the meal allowances here would have to be demonstrated to be necessary to allow respondent "properly to perform his duties." There is not even a suggestion on this record of any such necessity.

Finally, respondent argues that it is unfair that members of the military may exclude their subsistence allowances from income while respondent cannot. While this may be so, arguments of equity have little force in construing the boundaries of exclusions and deductions from income many of which, to be administrable, must be arbitrary. In any case, Congress has already considered respondent's equity argument and has rejected it in the repeal of § 120 of the 1954 Code. That provision as enacted allowed state troopers like respondent to exclude from income up to $5 of subsistence allowance per day. Section 120 was repealed after only four years, however, because it was "inequitable since there are many other individual taxpayers whose duties also require them to incur subsistence expenditures regardless of the tax effect. Thus, it appears that certain police officials by reason of this exclusion are placed in a more favorable position taxwise than other individual income taxpayers who incur the same types of expense. . . ." H.R. Rep. No. 775, 85th Cong., 1st Sess., 7 (1957).

Reversed.

MR. JUSTICE BLACKMUN, with whom THE CHIEF JUSTICE joins, dissenting.

More than a decade ago the United States Court of Appeals for the Eighth Circuit, in *United States v. Morelan*, 356 F.2d 199 (1966), held that the $3-per-day subsistence allowance paid Minnesota state highway patrolmen was excludable from gross income under § 119 of the Internal Revenue Code of 1954, 26 U.S.C. § 119. It held, alternatively, that if the allowance were includable in gross income, it was deductible as an ordinary and necessary meal-cost trade or business expense under § 162 (a)(2) of the Code, 26 U.S.C. § 162 (a)(2). I sat as a Circuit Judge on that case. I was happy to join Chief Judge Vogel's opinion because I then felt, and still do, that it was correct on both grounds. Certainly, despite the usual persistent government opposition in as many Courts of Appeals as were available, the ruling was in line with other authority at the appellate level at that time.[7] Two cases, *Magness v. Commissioner*, 247 F.2d 740 (CA5 1957), *cert. denied*, 355 U.S. 931 (1958), and *Hyslope v. Commissioner*, 21 T.C. 131 (1953), were distinguished. 356 F.2d at 207.

---

[7] [*] Saunders v. Commissioner, 215 F.2d 768 (CA3 1954); United States v. Barrett, 321 F.2d 911 (CA5 1963); Hanson v. Commissioner, 298 F.2d 391 (CA8 1962). As in *Morelan, certiorari* apparently was not sought in any of this line of cases up to that time.

On December 11, 1967, however, this Court by a 5-3 vote decided *United States v. Correll*, 389 U.S. 299, restricting to overnight trips the travel-expense deduction for meal costs under § 162(a)(2). That decision, of course, disapproved *Morelan's* alternative ground for decision. I am frank to say that had I been a Member of this Court at the time *Correll* was decided, I would have joined its dissent, 389 U.S. at 307, for I fully agree with Mr. Justice Douglas' observation there, joined by Justices Black and Fortas — an observation which, for me, is unanswerable and unanswered — that the Court, with a bow to the Government's argument for administrative convenience, and conceding an element of arbitrariness, *id.* at 303, read the word "overnight" into § 162(a)(2), a statute that speaks only in geographical terms.

The taxpayer in the present case, faced with *Correll*, understandably does not press the § 162(a)(2) issue, but confines his defense to §§ 61 and 119.

I have no particular quarrel with the conclusion that the payments received by the New Jersey troopers constituted income to them under § 61. I can accept that, but my stance in *Morelan* leads me to disagree with the Court's conclusion that the payments are not excludable under § 119. The Court draws an in-cash or in-kind distinction. This has no appeal or persuasion for me because the statute does not speak specifically in such terms. It does no more than refer to "meals . . . furnished on the business premises of the employer," and from those words the Court draws the in-kind consequence. I am not so sure. In any event, for me, as was the case in *Morelan*, the business premises of the State of New Jersey, the trooper's employer, are wherever the trooper is on duty in that State. The employer's premises are statewide.

The Court in its opinion makes only passing comment, with a general reference to fairness, on the ironical difference in tax treatment it now accords to the paramilitary New Jersey state trooper structure and the federal military. The distinction must be embarrassing to the Government in its position here, for the Internal Revenue Code draws no such distinction. The Commissioner is forced to find support for it — support which the Court in its opinion in this case does not stretch to find — only from a regulation, Treas. Reg. § 1.61-2(b), 26 CFR § 1.61-2(b) (1977), excluding subsistence allowances granted the military, and the general references in 37 U.S.C. § 101 (25) (1970 ed., Supp. V), added by Pub. L. 93-419, § 1, 88 Stat. 1152, to "regular military compensation" and "Federal tax advantage accruing to the aforementioned allowances because they are not subject to Federal income tax." This, for me, is thin and weak support for recognizing a substantial benefit for the military and denying it for the New Jersey state trooper counterpart.

I fear that state troopers the country over, not handsomely paid to begin with, will never understand today's decision. And I doubt that their reading of the Court's opinion — if, indeed, a layman can be expected to understand its technical wording — will convince them that the situation is as clear as the Court purports to find it.

[Annotation of references omitted.]

Understanding *Kowalski*

1.   *Kowalski* is, in theory, an interpretation of the first clause of section 119(a), which excludes from taxation meals or lodging "furnished" to an employee or his spouse for the convenience of the employer. According to the Supreme Court, the word "furnished" means the food or lodging must be provided directly to the employee, rather than a cash allowance which the employee uses to purchase the relevant items. Would most people interpret the word "furnished" that way? How persuasive is the Senate Report language, cited by the Court, stating that "Section 119 applies only to meals or lodging furnished in kind"? Is it significant that this language was contained only in a committee report, and may not have been ratified by the full Senate, the House of Representatives, or the President in signing the bill? How many congressmen do you think read the descriptive portions of a tax committee report? How do you think this particular language got in the report in the first place?

2.   Together with the statute, legislative history, etc., courts sometimes consider the practical effect of their decisions. In evaluating *Kowalski*, is it relevant that in-kind benefits are likely to be provided only by a limited category of employers (hotels, restaurants, etc.), whereas a cash allowance can be paid by virtually any employer? Is the Court afraid that, if it holds in favor of Kowalski, employers will simply recharacterize a portion of their salaries as food allowances, resulting in enormous potential revenue loss? Or could the IRS deal with this problem by aggressively enforcing the "business premises" requirement and by limiting the exemption to cases in which workers were genuinely "on call" for duty, without worrying about the "in kind" problem, at all? Should courts consider the revenue effect of their decisions in interpreting tax provisions?

3.   Why would the Supreme Court, which receives hundreds of *certiorari* petitions every year, decide to hear a case like *Kowalski*? What does your answer tell you about the Court's role in tax issues, and the allocation of its resources, generally?

Using the Sources

Under section 119 and *Kowalski*, what would be the tax treatment of the following items?

a. A meal allowance allowing police officers to charge their employer for meals eaten at any location;

b. The same allowance, if the police officers were limited to a prearranged list of times and restaurants, so as not to distract from their police activities; and

c. A subsidized cafeteria, in which the police officers were permitted to purchase food at a reduced charge. (*See* Treasury Regulations, § 1.119-1(a)(3).)

Law and Planning

1.   Suppose you were counsel to the National Union of Police Officers at the time of *Kowalski*. What would you advise the union to do after learning of the decision? Is there any practical way that meal allowances for police officers could be restructured so as to remain tax-exempt? What specific language would you recommend for inclusion in the next contract, in order to achieve this result? Or would it be better for the officers to take a higher cash salary, pay tax, and buy food with "after tax" income?

2.   How, if at all, do you think the decision in *Kowalski* will affect the budgets of state and local police departments?

3.   How, if at all, do you think the decision in *Kowalski* will affect people's decisions to become police officers?

Politics and Policy

What are the vertical equity implications of *Benaglia* and *Kowalski*? Is it fair to allow a well-paid manager to receive a luxurious hotel suite free of tax, while taxing police officers and firefighters on a $7-per-day meal allowance? Is it relevant that New Jersey tried to provide in-kind meals for police officers, but the system failed because the police were too busy to use it? Does *Kowalski* have the perverse effect of allowing tax-free benefits in the most abusive cases (full room and board in a single, comfortable location) but denying them in comparatively modest circumstances (a small lunch allowance for workers required to eat on the go)? Do you think that Congress, in drafting section 119, intended this result?

The Section 119 Regulations

Although judicial opinions attract more attention, the largest volume of tax guidance is provided at the administrative level. The most comprehensive sources of administrative guidance are the regulations, drafted by the Treasury Department with the assistance of the IRS, that accompany virtually every Code section. While the regulations vary in length and detail, they have three principle functions. First, the regulations restate the statute in a language that, while still technical, is usually somewhat more readable than the Code itself. Second, the regulations add meat to the statutory bones, answering questions left open by the statute and clarifying the relationship between different statutory provisions. Finally, the regulations often contained detailed examples that explain the application of the statute in various fact situations. Like anything else, there are more and less useful regulations, but (after the Code itself) they are nearly always the starting point for tax research.

Examine Treasury Regulations § 1.119-1, or the portion of it that is contained in your statutory supplement. How are the regulations organized, and what general functions are they designed to accomplish? Do the regulations resolve most of the remaining issues under section 119, or is much of what they say obvious, leaving the more difficult decisions to rulings, case law, or the taxpayer's own devices?

Using the Sources

Based on the statute and regulations, how would you advise a client as to the applicability of section 119 in the following situations? Be precise as to the specific portion of the statute or regulations you are relying upon.

1.   David Doctor lives in an apartment, supplied free of charge by the hospital at which he is employed, and located approximately five blocks from the hospital. David has a 9-5 weekday schedule, but is frequently called to the hospital on evenings and weekends to participate in emergency surgery or similar activities.

2.   The law firm of Workhard & Playhard provides its associates with a free cafeteria, hoping that the associates will eat quick lunches at the cafeteria rather than going to lunch at one of several nearby restaurants, and thereby increase the firm's profitability. If necessary, attorneys can be reached at the cafeteria by means of the firm's paging system. The firm also has a policy of paying "supper money" for any attorney who works past 9 p.m., even if the attorney leaves the office before eating.

3.   The Alaska Pipeline Corporation deducts $10,000 from each employee's annual compensation to cover costs of food and lodging at its construction sites. The construction sites are at least 15 miles from the nearest town and a majority of the workers live and eat at the sites.

Law and Planning

Your client, Anne Bianco, pays income tax at a 30 percent marginal rate. Anne is negotiating with Highrise Hotels for a job as manager of the company's Philadelphia hotel, with a base salary of $100,000 per year. In addition to this, the company has informally offered her the choice of one of three options:

(i) Free food and lodging for Anne and her husband at the hotel (and, if she is traveling, at any other Highrise location).

(ii) An apartment, a few blocks from the hotel, with a $15,000 annual rental value, which would be rent-free to Anne and her husband (Anne and her husband would be required to supply their own food).

(iii) A $20,000 meal and lodging allowance which Anne and her husband can spend as they wish (the couple would agree to live "in reasonable proximity" to the hotel).

The $20,000 is roughly equivalent to what Anne and her husband spend on food and housing in a typical year; by contrast, the hotel food and accommodations have a fair market value of about $40,000, although Anne thinks she would get tired of the hotel food after a while. Anne has a "beeper" and would be on call for large-scale emergencies regardless of where she lived.

Based on the materials above, which of these three options would you advise Anne to accept? What procedural steps, if any, would you urge her to take in order to make it more likely that her preferred option qualifies for tax exemption? Are there any additional facts that you would want to know in order make either of these decisions?

Politics and Policy

Examine the section 119 regulations. Do they appear, as a general rule, to tighten or relax the requirements of the statute? What is the process for drafting regulations (initial drafting, public comment, etc.), and how might this account for your answer?

II. GRATUITOUS TRANSFERS: WINDFALLS, PRIZES, AND GIFTS

The convenience of the employer doctrine arises in an employment context, where there is generally a strong expectation that the employee will pay tax on all compensation. The question is whether a particular benefit is so tied to the performance of the job, and perhaps so incapable of definite valuation, that it should be exempted from this general principle. (We will examine additional "fringe benefits" in Chapter 2.)

The issue of taxability becomes fuzzier when people receive money outside of a normal employment context. Suppose you find $100 lying in the street and keep it (assume that this is permitted under applicable law). You're $100 richer than you were before, but you didn't do anything to earn it, and most people probably would not call the $100 "income" in a colloquial sense. Besides, somebody else — i.e., the person who lost the money — probably paid tax on the same $100, already, so that taxing you looks a little bit like two taxes on the same money. Last but not least, enforcement is going to be difficult: who is going to know that you found the $100, and how will they possibly catch up with you if you don't pay the tax?

The arguments above create a strong temptation to exempt gratuitous transfers from the income tax. Yet such an exemption would have an odd, even perverse character. How can we justify taxing people who have worked long hours for their income, while exempting those who have been enriched without any effort? Would not such an exemption violate both horizontal equity (because both parties have the same economic benefit) and vertical equity (because the rich are likely to receive more gifts and other gratuitous transfers)? Could a distortion of this magnitude — potentially far broader than that at stake in *Benaglia* — be so easily explained?

The following cases consider the tax treatment of three types of gratuitous transfers — windfalls, prizes, and gifts — the treatment of the third category being (as we will see) significantly different from the first two. In comparison to section 119, this area of law has developed largely by means of judicial decisions, with relatively brief statutes that resolve only a few of the difficult issues involved. As you read the materials, consider how this has affected the nature of the law in this area. Does the (relative) absence of statutory guidance make the law less predictable and more quirky? Are practitioners encouraged to take aggressive positions, by arguing that their specific facts are different from those in previous cases? Does the law become more or less favorable to taxpayers as a result of this process? Does it become more or less consistent with horizontal equity and other policy norms?

A.   Windfalls, Prizes, and Awards

CESARINI v. UNITED STATES

United States District Court, Northern District of Ohio

296 F. Supp. 3 (N.D. Ohio 1969), *aff'd*, 428 F.2d 812 (6th Cir. 1970)

YOUNG, J:

This is an action by the plaintiffs as taxpayers for the recovery of income tax payments made in the calendar year 1964. Plaintiffs contend that the amount of $836.51 was erroneously overpaid by them in 1964, and that they are entitled to a refund in that amount, together with the statutory interest from October 13, 1965, the date in which they made their claim upon the Internal Revenue Service for the refund.

. . . Plaintiffs are husband and wife, and live within the jurisdiction of the United States District Court for the Northern District of Ohio. In 1957, the plaintiffs purchased a used piano at an auction sale for approximately $15.00, and the piano was used by their daughter for piano lessons. In 1964, while cleaning the piano, plaintiffs discovered the sum of $4,467.00 in old currency, and since have retained the piano instead of discarding it as previously planned. Being unable to ascertain who put the money there, plaintiffs exchanged the old currency for new at a bank, and reported the sum of $4,467.00 on their 1964 joint income tax return as ordinary income from other sources. On October 18, 1965, plaintiffs filed an amended return with the District Director of Internal Revenue in Cleveland, Ohio, this second return eliminating the sum of $4,467.00 from the gross income computation, and requesting a refund in the amount of $836.51, the amount allegedly overpaid as a result of the former inclusion of $4,467.00 in the original return for the calendar year of 1964. On January 18, 1966, the Commissioner of Internal Revenue rejected taxpayers' refund claim in its entirety, and plaintiffs filed the instant action in March of 1967.

Plaintiffs make three alternative contentions in support of their claim that the sum of $836.51 should be refunded to them. First, that the $4,467.00 found in the piano is not includable in gross income under Section 61 of the Internal Revenue Code. (26 U.S.C. § 61) Secondly, even if the retention of the cash constitutes a realization of ordinary income under Section 61, it was due and owing in the year the piano was purchased, 1957, and by 1964, the statute of limitations provided by 26 U.S.C. § 6501 had elapsed. And thirdly, that if the treasure trove money is gross income for the year 1964, it was entitled to capital gains treatment under Section 1221 of Title 26. The Government, by its answer and its trial brief, asserts that the amount found in the piano is includable in gross income under Section 61(a) of Title 26, U.S.C., that the money is taxable in the year it was actually found, 1964, and that the sum is properly taxable at ordinary income rates, not being entitled to capital gains treatment under 26 U.S.C. §§ 1201 et seq.

After a consideration of the pertinent provisions of the Internal Revenue Code, Treasury Regulations, Revenue Rulings, and decisional law in the area, this Court has concluded that the taxpayers are not entitled to a refund of the amount requested, nor are they entitled to capital gains treatment on the income item at issue.

The starting point in determining whether an item is to be included in gross income is, of course, Section 61(a) of Title 26 U.S.C., and that section provides in part:

> "Except as otherwise provided in this subtitle, *gross income means all income from whatever source derived*, including (but not limited to) the following items: . . ."

Subsections (1) through (15) of Section 61(a) then go on to list fifteen items specifically included in the computation of the taxpayer's gross income, and Part II of Subchapter B of the 1954 Code (Sections 71 et seq.) deals with other items expressly included in gross income. While neither of these listings expressly includes the type of income which is at issue in the case at bar, Part III of Subchapter B (Sections 101 et seq.) deals with items specifically *excluded* from gross income, and found money is not listed in those sections either. This absence of express mention in any of the code sections necessitates a return to the "all income from whatever source" language of Section 61(a) of the code, and the express statement there that gross income is "not limited to" the following fifteen examples. Section 1.61-1(a) of the Treasury Regulations, the corresponding section to Section 61(a) in the 1954 Code, reiterates this broad construction of gross income, providing in part:

> "Gross income means all income from whatever source derived, unless excluded by law. *Gross income includes income realized in any form*, whether in money, property, or services. . . ."

The decisions of the United States Supreme Court have frequently stated that this broad all-inclusive language was used by Congress to exert the full measure of its taxing power under the Sixteenth Amendment to the United States Constitution. *Commissioner of Internal Revenue v. Glenshaw Glass Co.*, 348 U.S. 426, 429 (1955); *Helvering v. Clifford*, 309 U.S. 331, 334 (1940); *Helvering v. Midland Mutual Life Ins. Co.*, 300 U.S. 216, 223 (1937); *Douglas v. Willcuts*, 296 U.S. 1, 9 (1935); *Irwin v. Gavit*, 268 U.S. 161, 166 (1925).

In addition, the Government in the instant case cites and relies upon an I.R.S. Revenue Ruling which is undeniably on point:

> "The finder of treasure trove is in receipt of taxable income, for Federal income tax purposes, to the extent of its value in United States currency, for the taxable year in which it is reduced to undisputed possession." Rev. Rul. 61, 1953-1, Cum. Bull. 17.

The plaintiffs argue that the above ruling does not control this case for two reasons. The first is that subsequent to the Ruling's pronouncement in 1953, Congress enacted Sections 74 and 102 of the 1954 Code, § 74 expressly *including* the value of prizes and gifts in gross income in most cases, and § 102 specifically *exempting* the value of gifts received from gross income. From this, it is argued that Section 74 was added because prizes might otherwise be construed as nontaxable gifts, and since no such section was passed expressly taxing treasure trove, it is therefore a gift which is non-taxable under Section 102. This line of reasoning overlooks the statutory scheme previously alluded to, whereby income from all sources is taxed unless the taxpayer can point to an express exemption. Not only have the taxpayers failed to list a specific exclusion in the instant case, but also the Government *has* pointed to express language covering the found money, even though it would not be required to do so under the broad language of Section 61(a) and the foregoing Supreme Court decisions interpreting it.

* * *

Understanding *Cesarini*

1.   The logic of *Cesarini* is essentially as follows: Congress has enacted section 61, which adopts (or has been interpreted to adopt) a broad definition of income; there is no applicable statutory exception; and, accordingly, the money found by the Cesarinis was taxable when they found it. As a matter of statutory interpretation, is this logic convincing? Would the dictionary definition of "income" encompass money found inside a second-hand piano, used car, or other unlikely location? If not, is there any evidence that Congress intended section 61 to take a broader view? Would it really be so inconsistent if the law required people to pay tax on salary and investment income, but not on found money and similarly unusual transactions?

2.   In support of its holding, the court cites an IRS ruling holding that "treasure trove" constitutes taxable income under section 61. The United States (and thus effectively the IRS) is also a party to *Cesarini* litigation. How persuasive is a document, written by one of the parties to a case, which discusses the very issue at stake in the same case? How, if at all, does your answer to the previous question change if the respective party responsible for the document is a government agency? Should the ruling be any more persuasive than a position in an IRS brief? Does it matter that the ruling (i) is more than ten years old, and (ii) was codified in a regulation adopted before the facts in *Cesarini* took place?

3.   Is *Cesarini* consistent with *Benaglia*? Why (or why not)?

Using the Sources

What would be the tax treatment of the following items?

a. Money found in the sleeve of a recently purchased book;[8]

b. Money misplaced in the attic and recently rediscovered; and

c. A prize for the best law school tax essay. (*See* § 74.)

---

[8] Something of this type was once attempted by a publisher who wanted to know how many people actually read, as opposed to merely purchased, its books. The answer was not flattering.

Law and Planning

1. Suppose you had clients who, instead of cash, found in their piano an old bracelet, which would cost $4,500 in a jewelry store, but for which they could get perhaps $2,500 for if they attempted to sell it, and which they are inclined to keep for sentimental reasons. Would you advise them to pay tax on $4,500; $2,500; or (following *Benaglia*) could you argue that the valuation problem suggests that the transaction should not be subject to tax, at all? Note that, if forced to pay tax (especially at the higher amount), your clients may be forced to sell the bracelet in order to pay tax, or else dip into their remaining assets to do so.

2. What do you think is the likelihood of the bracelet in item 1 being discovered by the IRS on audit, and would this affect the advice that you gave to your clients? Would it be legitimate for you to discuss this issue with the clients, at all?

3. What if the clients themselves asked you about the likelihood of an audit?

Politics and Policy

What are the horizontal and vertical equity implications of the *Cesarini* decision?

Although at first glance rather trivial, the issue in *Cesarini* is important because of its implications for the broader structure of the tax code. Somewhat oversimplified, the issue is this: will the Code adopt a "bottom up" definition of income, under which only items specified by Congress are subject to tax, or a "top down" definition, under which any enrichment is income unless there is a specific statutory exception? For a time, the former view predominated: in its decision in *Eisner v. Macomber*, 252 U.S. 189 (1920), the Supreme Court defined income as "the gain derived from capital, from labor, or from both combined," a formula which would appear to exclude prizes, awards, money found in old musical instruments, and other gratuitous receipts. By the 1950s, the Court had changed its mind, now holding that "Congress applied no limitations as to the source of taxable receipts" and referring to "the intention of Congress to tax all gains except those specifically exempted" by the Code. *Commissioner v. Glenshaw Glass Co.*, 348 U.S. 426, 429–30 (1955).[9] Under this latter formula, any measurable form of enrichment is likely to be taxed, unless there is a timing problem or else a specific exception (like section 119) applicable to the case. *Cesarini* is an example, if a small one, of this rule.

The adoption of a "top down" definition of income has two principal effects. The first is to put a great deal of pressure on the exceptions to this rule, whether they be of statutory origin or (in rarer cases) of a court-made variety. All of Code sections 101 through 150 are, *essentially*, exceptions to the broad definition of income contained in section 61, and the action in this area tends to focus on these exceptions rather than on the section 61 rule.

An expanded definition of income also tends to focus increased attention on the valuation issue. The normal tax rule is that items of income or deduction are taken

---

[9] The *Macomber* and *Glenshaw Glass* cases are discussed further in subsequent chapters.

into account at their "fair market value," which is usually defined as the prevailing retail price — that is, the price that you would pay for an object if you bought it, rather than the lower price for which you could sell the object if you were forced to do so.[10] This rule results in considerable hardship if a person receives an item that they don't really want: if they keep the object, they will derive less benefit than the fair market value suggests, but if they sell it they will be unlikely to realize anything like the fair market price. For example, the recipient of a used car with a list price of $10,000 can sell it for perhaps two-thirds of that, and may not need a car, at all; but they are nonetheless taxed on the full $10,000 of retail value.

In cases of employee compensation, courts typically adopt a hard-nosed attitude toward the valuation problem, on the theory that the employee has bargained for her compensation package and cannot now claim that she does not like the items she has received. The tendency in these cases is thus either to exempt the item from tax altogether (as in *Benaglia*) or else to insist on a rather rigid application of the fair market value rule. In cases involving treasure trove, prizes, and other gratuitous transfers, for which the recipient did not bargain and over which they exercise relatively little control, there is pressure to take a somewhat more forgiving view.

The following case, *Turner v. Commissioner*, arose in a prize or award context. Prizes and awards are plainly taxable, with limited exceptions for employee achievement awards and certain prizes that are contributed to charity (§ 74). Valuation is a somewhat trickier matter, as observed in the following item.

TURNER v. COMMISSIONER
United States Tax Court
T.C. Memo. 1954-38

Memorandum Findings of Fact and Opinion

The Commissioner determined a deficiency of $388.96 in the income tax of the petitioners for 1948. The only question for decision is the amount which should be included in income because of the winning by Reginald of steamship tickets by answering a question on a radio program.

Findings of Fact

The petitioners are husband and wife who filed a joint return for 1948 with the collector of internal revenue for the District of North Carolina. They reported salary of $4,535.16 for 1948.

Reginald, whose name had been selected by chance from a telephone book, was called on the telephone on April 18, 1948 and was asked to name a song that was

---

[10] The formal definition of fair market value is "the price at which the property would change hands between a willing buyer and a willing seller, neither being under any compulsion to buy or to sell and both having reasonable knowledge of relevant facts." Regulations, § 20.2031-1(a). The regulations generally define this to mean the price at which an object is sold in the most commonly available retail market.

being played on a radio program. He gave the correct name of the song and then was given the opportunity to identify a second song and thus to compete for a grand prize. He correctly identified the second song and in consideration of his efforts was awarded a number of prizes, including two round trip first-class steamship tickets for a cruise between New York City and Buenos Aires. The prize was to be one ticket if the winner was unmarried, but, if he was married, his wife was to receive a ticket also. The tickets were not transferable and were good only within one year on a sailing date approved by the agent of the steamship company.

The petitioners reported income on their return of $520, representing income from the award of the two tickets. The Commissioner, in determining the deficiency, increased the income from this source to $2,220, the retail price of such tickets.

Marie was born in Brazil. The petitioners had two sons. Reginald negotiated with the agent of the steamship company, as a result of which he surrendered his rights to the two first-class tickets, and upon payment of $12.50 received four round trip tourist steamship tickets between New York City and Rio de Janeiro. The petitioners and their two sons used those tickets in making a trip from New York City to Rio de Janeiro and return during 1948.

The award of the tickets to Reginald represented income to him in the amount of $1,400.

Opinion

MURDOCK, J: Persons desiring to buy round trip first-class tickets between New York and Buenos Aires in April 1948, similar to those to which the petitioners were entitled, would have had to pay $2,220 for them. The petitioners, however, were not such persons. The winning of the tickets did not provide them with something which they needed in the ordinary course of their lives and for which they would have made an expenditure in any event, but merely gave them an opportunity to enjoy a luxury otherwise beyond their means. Their value to the petitioners was not equal to their retail cost. They were not transferable and not salable and there were other restrictions on their use. But even had the petitioner been permitted to sell them, his experience with other more salable articles indicates that he would have had to accept substantially less than the cost of similar tickets purchased from the steamship company and would have had selling expenses. Probably the petitioners could have refused the tickets and avoided the tax problem. Nevertheless, in order to obtain such benefits as they could from winning the tickets, they actually took a cruise accompanied by their two sons, thus obtaining free board, some savings in living expenses, and the pleasure of the trip. It seems proper that a substantial amount should be included in their income for 1948 on account of the winning of the tickets. The problem of arriving at a proper fair figure for this purpose is difficult. The evidence to assist is meager, perhaps unavoidably so. The Court, under such circumstances, must arrive at some figure and has done so. *Cf. Cohan v. Commissioner*, 39 Fed. (2d) 540.

Decision will be entered under Rule 50.

Understanding *Turner*

1.   What is the source for the $1,400 value that the court ascribes to the Turners' cruise tickets? Is it based on the subjective value of the tickets to the couple, rather than their objective, fair market value? Would the valuation be different if (i) Reginald Turner voluntarily entered the contest, rather than being chosen out of the telephone book, or (ii) Marie Terrell Turner had been born in Brooklyn, rather than Brazil, and therefore derived less enjoyment out of a South American cruise? What are the fairness and administrability consequences of this sort of personalized valuation in tax cases?

2.   Suppose that, instead of a contest, Turner had obtained the cruise as a reward from his employer, with the catch that he and his wife had to spend the trip in the company of his coworkers. Should Turner now be taxed on (i) the fair market value of the cruise ($2,200); (ii) a reduced amount as in the actual *Turner* decision, or (iii) nothing, on the theory that it is now essentially a business trip and not compensation, at all? Are there any additional facts that you would want to know before making this decision?

3.   Would *Turner* be a valid decision under present law?

WADE v. COMMISSIONER
United States Tax Court
T.C. Memo 1988-118

SWIFT, J:

Respondent determined deficiencies in petitioners' Federal income tax liabilities as follows:

Year	Deficiency
1983	$1,162
1984	1,432
1985	659

Three issues remain for decision: (1) The fair market value of trips awarded to petitioner Nathan L. Wade, as a Subaru automobile dealer in Salt Lake City, Utah; (2) whether the imputed cost of one of the trips is deductible as an ordinary and necessary business expense under section 162; and (3) whether a claimed partnership loss is allowable. At the trial of this case in Salt Lake City on February 24, 1988, only the first two issues were tried. The third issue, if not settled, will be tried at a subsequent time. References to petitioner are to Nathan L. Wade.

FINDINGS OF FACT

Some of the facts have been stipulated and are so found. During the years in issue, petitioner owned and operated a Subaru automobile dealership in Salt Lake City, Utah. In order to promote the sale of automobiles, Subaru of Northern California, Inc., the regional distributor of Subaru automobiles (hereinafter

"Subaru"), contracted with local Salt Lake City television stations for advertising time. The television stations offered various incentive programs to increase the level of advertising by their clients. If advertising clients purchased a specified amount of advertising time, the stations awarded to the clients all-expense-paid trips to various international destinations. As advertising time reached higher and higher levels, multiple all-expense-paid trips were awarded.

The trips were arranged through travel agencies. Typically, the stations would negotiate group charters at discounted or wholesale prices, and the recipients of the awards would be required to travel with the charter groups for the portion of the trips paid by the stations.

In 1983, 1984, 1985, Subaru purchased a significant amount of advertising time from television stations KSL and KUTV in Salt Lake City. Under the advertising incentive programs described above, Subaru received a number of trip awards from the stations. Subaru, in turn, transferred the awards to the owners of Subaru automobile dealerships in the Salt Lake City intermountain area based on their respective annual sales of Subaru automobiles.

Petitioner's dealership sold sufficient Subaru automobiles for petitioner to receive five trip awards, as indicated below:

Year	Destination
1983	Acapulco
1983	Greece
1984	Monte Carlo
1985	Paris
1985	Israel

Petitioner was awarded two tickets for each trip. In each case, he and his wife used the tickets to fly with other individuals who had received the same trip awards. The groups stayed at specified hotels in each city. Breakfasts generally were provided. Each trip lasted 10 to 14 days with the exception of the trip of Israel which lasted 20 days.

On three of the trips, petitioners were joined by another couple. These were friends of petitioners who were not Subaru dealers, nor were they recipients of trip awards from the television stations. In order to make these trips, petitioners' friends located other individuals who had received trip awards but who did not wish to make the trips and who were willing to sell their awards. In each case, petitioners' friends apparently were able to buy two tickets for each of the three trips for $2,000 each. Their tickets included both airfare and land packages identical to petitioners. . . .

For Federal income tax reporting purposes, the TV stations determined their total actual direct costs of the charter flights and land packages for all award recipients and allocated those costs among all of the actual travelers on a pro rata basis. If, for example, there were 60 spaces reserved for a particular trip which cost the station $250,000, but only 50 individuals were able to make the trip, the station would allocate $5,000 of its total cost to each traveler (*i.e.*, $250,000 divided by 50 equals $5,000).

Petitioner reported as taxable income on his and his wife's Federal income tax returns the value of the trip awards they received each year based upon the amount their friends paid to purchase tickets to travel with petitioners (namely, $2,000 each). In his notices of deficiency, respondent treated as taxable income to petitioners the value of the trips as computed by the television stations.

OPINION

With certain exceptions not relevant here, gross income includes the fair market value of prizes and awards received by a taxpayer. Secs. 61 and 74; sec. 1.74-1(a), Income Tax Regs.; *Hornung v. Commissioner*, 47 T.C. 428 (1967); *McCoy v. Commissioner*, 38 T.C. 841 (1962). Petitioners do not dispute the taxability of the trip awards they received. They do, however, dispute the value of those awards as determined by respondent.

In valuing taxable prizes and awards for Federal income tax purposes, courts do not always adopt the same methodology. In some situations, the retail value of prizes and awards is used. In other situations, a wholesale or other discounted value is used. *See McCoy v. Commissioner*, *supra* at 844. Objective factors are emphasized, but subjective factors also are given weight in determining the value of prizes and awards to particular taxpayers. *See Turner v. Commissioner*, T.C. Memo. 1954-38.

In *Turner*, the value was determined of two round-trip, first class steamship tickets from New York City to Buenos Aires which the taxpayer received from a radio station as a promotional award. The Court commented as follows:

> The winning of the tickets did not provide [the taxpayers] with something which they needed in the ordinary course of their lives and for which they would have made an expenditure in any event, but merely gave them an opportunity to enjoy a luxury otherwise beyond their means. Their value to the petitioners was not equal to their retail cost. They were not transferable and not salable and there were other restrictions on their use. . . . [*Turner v. Commissioner*, *supra*, 13 T.C.M. 462, 463, 23 P-H Memo T.C. par. 54,142 at 54-465.]

In the context of valuation questions arising under section 61, courts have emphasized objective factors in determining the amount to be included in a taxpayer's income upon the receipt of property other than cash. *Baker v. Commissioner*, 88 T.C. 1282, 1289–1290 (1987). In *Rooney v. Commissioner*, 88 T.C. 523, 528 (1987), we state that —

> Section 61 requires an objective measure of fair market value. Under such standard, the [taxpayers] may not adjust the acknowledged retail price of the goods and services received merely because they decide among themselves that such goods and services were overpriced. [Citations and fn. ref. omitted.]

In *Koons v. United States*, 315 F.2d 542 (9th Cir. 1963), an employee received household moving services in partial payment for accepting employment at a new location. The Ninth Circuit in Koons rejected the argument that the amount of income charged to the employee with respect to the moving services should be measured on the basis of a subjective valuation thereof by the taxpayer. The Ninth Circuit stated that —

> The use of any such [subjective] measure of value as is suggested is contrary to the usual way of valuing either services or property, and would make the administration of the tax laws in this area depend upon a knowledge by the Commissioner of the state of mind of the individual taxpayer. We do not think that tax administration should be based upon anything so whimsical. . . . We think that sound administration of the tax laws requires that there be as nearly objective a measure of the value of services that are includible in income as possible, and only such objective measure . . . is fair market value. [*Koons v. United States, supra* at 545; Citations omitted.]

In *McCoy v. Commissioner, supra,* arguments similar to those made herein were addressed. The taxpayer argued that the value of a new Lincoln Continental received as an employee award should be controlled by the amount he realized on the sale of the automobile 10 days after he received it. Respondent contended that the employer's cost of the automobile should control. The Court rejected both approaches. The taxpayer's approach was rejected on the ground that the automobile in question had been driven by the taxpayer for 10 days before reselling it. Respondent's approach was rejected on the ground that a new car rarely can be resold at the same price for which it was purchased.

Taking into account the principles and policies described above, with emphasis on the objective factors established in this case, we must determine the value of the five international trip awards petitioner received in 1983, 1984, and 1985. Petitioner argues that even though he did not resell the trip awards he received, other award recipients did resell their awards, and his friends purchased those awards for the identical itinerary of his trips. Petitioner therefore argues that the price at which his friends purchased the awards (namely, $2,000 each) should control the value of the awards he received. Other than the fact of those isolated purchases, however, we know essentially nothing of the circumstances surrounding those transactions. Neither party to the transactions testified. We are not privy to the factors that may have affected the negotiations. We do not know if the transactions occurred at arm's length. We have only petitioner's brief hearsay testimony with regard to the transactions.

With regard to respondent's valuation of the awards based on the allocable portion of the television stations' total costs thereof, witnesses from both stations testified as to how the costs of the trips were negotiated with travel agencies on a group discount basis. The trips were purchased by the stations at a cost significantly below what their retail value was if they had been purchased individually. Under the circumstances of this case, the best measure of the fair market value of the awards is the allocable pro rata portion of the television stations' total direct costs of the trips.

* * *

Understanding *Wade*

1.   Why is the *Turner* court willing to accept a subjective valuation method (that is, the value of the tickets to the Turners rather than their nominal face value), but not the court in *Wade*? Is the difference that *Turner* arose in a quiz show context, and *Wade* in business surroundings? Or that it was more common for automobile dealers in the 1980s to go to Paris than for modest families in the 1950s to take cruises to Latin America? Why should any of this matter, if at all?

2.   One hates to be cruel, but if the trips were bought at a discount by the radio station, shouldn't the fair market value have been *higher* than what the station paid for them? If a new car would cost me $15,000, but only costs the dealer $12,000, isn't the fair market value $15,000 rather than $12,000? Did the court cut the Wades at least a partial break here?

3.   The Wades advanced a second argument — that the trip should be deductible as an ordinary trade or business expense. Is this really as crazy as it sounds? Would the argument have been more persuasive if the Wades had been accompanied on the trip by other Subaru dealers rather than by personal friends who had purchased their tickets? *See Rudolph v. United States*, 370 U.S. 269 (1962) (denying deduction for a business convention attended by insurance salesmen and their wives and a substantial portion of which was devoted to personal activities).[11]

Using the Sources

How would you go about determining the fair market value of the following items for income tax purposes?

a. A new car

b. A new house

c. A painting

d. Stock in General Motors

e. Stock in a family-owned company

f. A free year's rental of a New York City apartment

g. A free year's membership at the local country club

Would it matter, in any of these cases, if you had won the relevant item in a contest; been awarded it by your employer, in return for good performance; or negotiated for it as part of your regular contract? Why?

---

[11] Trade or business expenditures are discussed further in Chapter 6.

Law and Planning

1. The day after *Turner* is decided, you are approached by a client with essentially the same facts as in the *Turner* case. The client wants to know what value, if any, he should assign the cruise tickets on his tax return. What advice would you give him? Would it affect your answer if (i) your client lived in a different geographic region than the Turner family, or (ii) if the IRS had so far refused to acquiesce in (i.e., accept) the *Turner* decision?

2. What if the client came to you before accepting the steamship tickets, and wanted to know what to do?

3. How would you answer the above questions if the facts in *Wade*, rather than *Turner*, were at issue?

Politics and Policy

Do you think that the government should have fought the result in *Turner* more assertively, insisting on a full fair market value inclusion in all prize and award cases? Or are these cases simply too unusual to worry about? What if taxpayers, using *Turner* as precedent, began to argue that items of compensation (i.e., fringe benefits) should be taxed at less than fair market value?

Because of the administrative and other problems inherent in subjective valuation, cases like *Turner* have remained something of an anomaly, and courts have usually insisted on a stricter application of the fair market value rule, especially in a compensation or similar business context. Some of the flavor of *Turner* is present in the valuation of real estate, family businesses, and other items which have no easily determinable fair market value, and for which the value to one person may be different than that which would be assigned by an unfettered free market. For example, a farmer leaving a farm to his children may argue that it should be valued according to its use as a farm only, even though a developer might pay more to use the land as an office park or shopping center.[12] In other cases, everyone may agree on the fair market value standard, but disagree as to how to apply it. We will have occasion to revisit the valuation issue in our next chapter, regarding fringe benefits, and later in chapters on charitable contributions and on transfer pricing (in the international taxation area). Note that, for items such as fringe benefits, the taxpayer will tend to argue for reduced valuation, while for charitable contributions she will prefer a higher value, so that the law reflects an unusual clash of interests in this area.

B.   Gifts and Section 102

One thing that does not have to be valued, at least for income tax purposes, is gifts. Instead, section 102 of the Code provides that "[g]ross income does not include the value of property acquired by gift, bequest, devise, or inheritance," an exception that has been part of the Code for most of its history. Of all the provisions contained in the Code, the gift exception is perhaps the most difficult to

---

[12] *See* I.R.C. § 2032A.

explain. What is the point of including gratuitous receipts in income, if the largest category of these receipts (gifts and bequests) is excluded from tax, anyway? How can we possibly justify taxing a person who earns a $20,000 salary, but not one who receives an effortless, $2 million bequest? Doesn't this violate both horizontal and vertical equity, especially since recipients of large gifts are likely to have above average incomes?

Three arguments are typically made in favor of the gift exclusion. The first is that the money (or property) that is the subject of the gift has already been taxed, presumably when it was earned by the person now making the gift. But this is also true of windfalls, prizes, and other gratuitous receipts; yet these remain subject to tax.

A second argument is that a gift tax, entirely separate from the income tax, is imposed on transfers in excess of $10,000, so that imposing the income tax on these same transactions would (arguably) result in double taxation. But the gift tax is imposed on the donor rather than the donee; is paid only when the donor has made more than $1 million in lifetime gifts; and can often be reduced or avoided through various not-especially-difficult planning stratagems. In any case there is no general principle that two taxes cannot be imposed on the same money.

A third argument focuses less on theory than on practicality. As a practical matter — or so the argument goes — most gifts are between family members. Since we already ignore many intrafamily transfers (e.g., by taxing married couples at a unified tax rate), and since it is hard to police transactions between family members, the income tax simply lets the matter go, leaving the gift tax to catch exceptionally large or unusual transfers. This argument is sometimes buttressed by the notion that gifts are a good thing, since they (theoretically) transfer resources from people with more money to people with less of it, and the Code ought therefore to encourage them. Do these strike you as convincing arguments, or do they have the flavor of rationalization, buttressed by the obvious fact that gift givers (and receivers) tend to be wealthy and powerful people?

Whatever its logic, section 102 has led to enormous interpretive problems, especially when "gifts" are made outside the usual parental or family context. The most famous case, *Commissioner v. Duberstein*, considers two such situations: a transfer from one businessman to another in return for useful information, and a gratuitous payment to a departing employee. In evaluating *Duberstein*, consider whether these two situations are treated in a consistent manner; and whether a more specific rule, limiting gifts to a family or similar context, might have saved everyone a great deal of trouble.

COMMISSIONER v. DUBERSTEIN
United States Supreme Court
363 U.S. 278 (1960)

MR. JUSTICE BRENNAN delivered the opinion of the Court.

These two cases concern the provision of the Internal Revenue Code which excludes from the gross income of an income taxpayer "the value of property acquired by gift." They pose the frequently recurrent question whether a specific transfer to a taxpayer in fact amounted to a "gift" to him within the meaning of the statute. The importance to decision of the facts of the cases requires that we state them in some detail.

No. 376, *Commissioner v. Duberstein.* The taxpayer, Duberstein, was president of the Duberstein Iron & Metal Company, a corporation with headquarters in Dayton, Ohio. For some years the taxpayer's company had done business with Mohawk Metal Corporation, whose headquarters were in New York City. The president of Mohawk was one Berman. The taxpayer and Berman had generally used the telephone to transact their companies' business with each other, which consisted of buying and selling metals. The taxpayer testified, without elaboration, that he knew Berman "personally" and had known him for about seven years. From time to time in their telephone conversations, Berman would ask Duberstein whether the latter knew of potential customers for some of Mohawk's products in which Duberstein's company itself was not interested. Duberstein provided the names of potential customers for these items.

One day in 1951 Berman telephoned Duberstein and said that the information Duberstein had given him had proved so helpful that he wanted to give the latter a present. Duberstein stated that Berman owed him nothing. Berman said that he had a Cadillac as a gift for Duberstein, and that the latter should send to New York for it; Berman insisted that Duberstein accept the car, and the latter finally did so, protesting however that he had not intended to be compensated for the information. At the time Duberstein already had a Cadillac and an Oldsmobile, and felt that he did not need another car. Duberstein testified that he did not think Berman would have sent him the Cadillac if he had not furnished him with information about the customers. It appeared that Mohawk later deducted the value of the Cadillac as a business expense on its corporate income tax return.

Duberstein did not include the value of the Cadillac in gross income for 1951, deeming it a gift. The Commissioner asserted a deficiency for the car's value against him, and in proceedings to review the deficiency the Tax Court affirmed the Commissioner's determination. It said that "The record is significantly barren of evidence revealing any intention on the part of the payor to make a gift. . . . The only justifiable inference is that the automobile was intended by the payer to be remuneration for services rendered to it by Duberstein." The Court of Appeals for the Sixth Circuit reversed. 265 F.2d 28, 30.

No. 546, *Stanton v. United States.* The taxpayer, Stanton, had been for approximately 10 years in the employ of Trinity Church in New York City. He was comptroller of the Church corporation, and president of a corporation, Trinity Operating Company, the church set up as a fully owned subsidiary to manage its real estate holdings, which were more extensive than simply the church property. His salary by the end of his employment there in 1942 amounted to $22,500 a year. Effective November 30, 1942, he resigned from both positions to go into business for himself. The Operating Company's directors, who seem to have included the rector and vestrymen of the church, passed the following resolution upon his resignation: "BE IT RESOLVED that in appreciation of the services rendered by Mr. Stanton . . . a gratuity is hereby awarded to him of Twenty Thousand Dollars, payable to him in equal installments of Two Thousand Dollars at the end of each and every month commencing with the month of December, 1942; provided that, with the discontinuance of his services, the Corporation of Trinity Church is released from all rights and claims to pension and retirement benefits not already accrued up to November 30, 1942."

The Operating Company's action was later explained by one of its directors as based on the fact that, "Mr. Stanton was liked by all of the Vestry personally. He had a pleasing personality. He had come in when Trinity's affairs were in a difficult situation. He did a splendid piece of work, we felt. Besides that . . . he was liked by all of the members of the Vestry personally." And by another: "We were all unanimous in wishing to make Mr. Stanton a gift. Mr. Stanton had loyally and faithfully served Trinity in a very difficult time. We thought of him in the highest regard. We understood that he was going in business for himself. We felt that he was entitled to that evidence of good will."

On the other hand, there was a suggestion of some ill-feeling between Stanton and the directors, arising out of the recent termination of the services of one Watkins, the Operating Company's treasurer, whose departure was evidently attended by some acrimony. At a special board meeting on October 28, 1942, Stanton had intervened on Watkins' side and asked reconsideration of the matter. The minutes reflect that "resentment was expressed as to the 'presumptuous' suggestion that the action of the Board, taken after long deliberation, should be changed." The Board adhered to its determination that Watkins be separated from employment, giving him an opportunity to resign rather than be discharged. At another special meeting two days later it was revealed that Watkins had not resigned; the previous resolution terminating his services was then viewed as effective; and the Board voted the payment of six months' salary to Watkins in a resolution similar to that quoted in regard to Stanton, but which did not use the term "gratuity." At the meeting, Stanton announced that in order to avoid any such embarrassment or question at any time as to his willingness to resign if the Board desired, he was tendering his resignation. It was tabled, though not without dissent. The next week, on November 5, at another special meeting, Stanton again tendered his resignation which this time was accepted.

The "gratuity" was duly paid. So was a smaller one to Stanton's (and the Operating Company's) secretary, under a similar resolution, upon her resignation at the same time. The two corporations shared the expense of the payments. There was undisputed testimony that there were in fact no enforceable rights or claims to pension and retirement benefits which had not accrued at the time of the taxpayer's resignation, and that the last proviso of the resolution was inserted simply out of an abundance of caution. The taxpayer received in cash a refund of his contributions to the retirement plans, and there is no suggestion that he was entitled to more. He was required to perform no further services for Trinity after his resignation.

The Commissioner asserted a deficiency against the taxpayer after the latter had failed to include the payments in question in gross income. After payment of the deficiency and administrative rejection of a refund claim, the taxpayer sued the United States for a refund in the District Court for the Eastern District of New

York. The trial judge, sitting without a jury, made the simple finding that the payments were a "gift," and judgment was entered for the taxpayer. The Court of Appeals for the Second Circuit reversed. 268 F.2d 727.

The Government, urging that clarification of the problem typified by these two cases was necessary, and that the approaches taken by the Courts of Appeals for the Second and the Sixth Circuits were in conflict, petitioned for *certiorari* in No. 376, and acquiesced in the taxpayer's petition in No. 546. On this basis, and because of the importance of the question in the administration of the income tax laws, we granted *certiorari* in both cases. 361 U.S. 923.

The exclusion of property acquired by gift from gross income under the federal income tax laws was made in the first income tax statute passed under the authority of the Sixteenth Amendment, and has been a feature of the income tax statutes ever since. The meaning of the term "gift" as applied to particular transfers has always been a matter of contention. Specific and illuminating legislative history on the point does not appear to exist. Analogies and inferences drawn from other revenue provisions, such as the estate and gift taxes, are dubious. *See Lockard v. Commissioner*, 166 F.2d 409. The meaning of the statutory term has been shaped largely by the decisional law. With this, we turn to the contentions made by the Government in these cases.

First. The Government suggests that we promulgate a new "test" in this area to serve as a standard to be applied by the lower courts and by the Tax Court in dealing with the numerous cases that arise.[13] We reject this invitation. We are of opinion that the governing principles are necessarily general and have already been spelled out in the opinions of this Court, and that the problem is one which, under the present statutory framework, does not lend itself to any more definitive statement that would produce a talisman for the solution of concrete cases. The cases at bar are fair examples of the settings in which the problem usually arises. They present situations in which payments have been made in a context with business overtones — an employer making a payment to a retiring employee; a businessman giving something of value to another businessman who has been of advantage to him in his business. In this context, we review the law as established by the prior cases here.

The course of decision here makes it plain that the statute does not use the term "gift" in the common-law sense, but in a more colloquial sense. This Court has indicated that a voluntary executed transfer of his property by one to another, without any consideration or compensation therefore, though a common-law gift, is not necessarily a "gift" within the meaning of the statute. For the Court has shown that the mere absence of a legal or moral obligation to make such a payment does not establish that it is a gift. *Old Colony Trust Co. v. Commissioner*, 279 U.S. 716, 730. And, importantly, if the payment proceeds primarily from "the constraining force of any moral or legal duty," or from "the incentive of anticipated benefit" of an economic nature, *Bogardus v. Commissioner*, 302 U.S. 34, 41, it is not a gift. And, conversely, "where the payment is in return for services rendered, it is irrelevant

---

[13] [6] The government's proposed test is stated: "Gifts should be defined as transfers of property made for personal as distinguished from business reasons."

that the donor derives no economic benefit from it." *Robertson v. United States*, 343 U.S. 711, 714. A gift in the statutory sense, on the other hand, proceeds from a "detached and disinterested generosity," *Commissioner v. Lo Bue*, 351 U.S. 243, 246; "out of affection, respect, admiration, charity or like impulses." *Robertson v. United States, supra*, at 714. And in this regard, the most critical consideration, as the Court was agreed in the leading case here, is the transferor's "intention." *Bogardus v. Commissioner*, 302 U.S. 34, 43. "What controls is the intention with which payment, however voluntary, has been made." *Id.* at 45 (dissenting opinion).

The Government says that this "intention" of the transferor cannot mean what the cases on the common-law concept of gift call "donative intent." With that we are in agreement, for our decisions fully support this. Moreover, the *Bogardus* case itself makes it plain that the donor's characterization of his action is not determinative — that there must be an objective inquiry as to whether what is called a gift amounts to it in reality. 302 U.S. at 40. It scarcely needs adding that the parties' expectations or hopes as to the tax treatment of their conduct in themselves have nothing to do with the matter.

It is suggested that the *Bogardus* criterion would be more apt if rephrased in terms of "motive" rather than "intention." We must confess to some skepticism as to whether such a verbal mutation would be of any practical consequence. We take it that the proper criterion, established by decision here, is one that inquiries what the basic reason for his conduct was in fact — the dominant reason that explains his action in making the transfer. Further than that we do not think it profitable to go.

Second. The Government's proposed "test," while apparently simple and precise in its formulation, depends frankly on a set of "principles" or presumptions" derived from the decided cases, and concededly subject to various exceptions; and it involves various corollaries, which add to its detail. Were we to promulgate this test as a matter of law, and accept with it its various presuppositions and stated consequences, we would be passing far beyond the requirements of the cases before us, and would be painting on a large canvas with indeed a broad brush. The Government derives its test from such propositions as the following: That payments by an employer to an employee, even though voluntary, ought, by and large, to be taxable; that the concept of a gift is inconsistent with a payment's being a deductible business expense; that a gift involves "personal" elements; that a business corporation cannot properly make a gift of its assets. The Government admits that there are exceptions and qualifications to these propositions. We think, to the extent they are correct, that those propositions are not principles of law but rather maxims of experience that the tribunals which have tried the facts of cases in this area have enunciated in explaining their factual determinations. Some of them simply represent truisms: it doubtless is, statistically speaking, the exceptional payment by an employer to an employee that amounts to a gift. Others are overstatements of possible evidentiary inferences relevant to a factual determination on the totality of circumstances in the case: it is doubtless relevant to the over-all inference that the transferor treats a payment as a business deduction, or that the transferor is a corporate entity. But these inferences cannot be stated in absolute terms. Neither factor is a shibboleth. The taxing statute does not make nondeductibility by the transferor a condition on the "gift" exclusion; nor does it draw any distinction, in terms, between transfers by corporations and individuals, as to the availability of the "gift" exclusion to the transferee. The conclusion whether a transfer amounts to a "gift" is one that must be reached on consideration of all the factors.

Specifically, the trier of fact must be careful not to allow trial of the issue whether the receipt of a specific payment is a gift to turn into a trial of the tax liability, or of the propriety, as a matter of fiduciary or corporate law, attaching to the conduct of someone else. The major corollary to the Government's suggested "test" is that, as an ordinary matter, a payment by a corporation cannot be a gift, and, more specifically, there can be no such thing as a "gift" made by a corporation which would allow it to take a deduction for an ordinary and necessary business expense. As we have said, we find no basis for such a conclusion in the statute; and if it were applied as a determinative rule of "law," it would force the tribunals trying tax cases involving the donee's liability into elaborate inquiries into the local law of corporations or into the peripheral deductibility of payments as business expenses. The former issue might make the tax tribunals the most frequent investigators of an important and difficult issue of the laws of the several States, and the latter inquiry would summon one difficult and delicate problem of federal tax law as an aid to the solution of another. Or perhaps there would be required a trial of the vexed issue whether there was a "constructive" distribution of corporate property, for income tax purposes, to the corporate agents who had sponsored the transfer. These considerations, also, reinforce us in our conclusion that while the principles urged by the Government may, in nonabsolute form as crystallizations of experience, prove persuasive to the trier of facts in a particular case, neither they, nor any more detailed statement than has been made, can be laid down as a matter of law.

Third. Decision of the issue presented in these cases must be based ultimately on the application of the fact-finding tribunal's experience with the mainsprings of human conduct to the totality of the facts of each case. The nontechnical nature of the statutory standard, the close relationship of it to the data of practical human experience, and the multiplicity of relevant factual elements, with their various combinations, creating the necessity of ascribing the proper force to each, confirm us in our conclusion that primary weight in this area must be given to the conclusions of the trier of fact. *Baker v. Texas & Pacific R. Co.*, 359 U.S. 227; *Commissioner v. Heininger*, 320 U.S. 467, 475; *United States v. Yellow Cab Co.*, 338 U.S. 338, 341; *Bogardus v. Commissioner, supra,* at 45 (dissenting opinion).

This conclusion may not satisfy an academic desire for tidiness, symmetry and precision in this area, any more than a system based on the determinations of various fact-finders ordinarily does. But we see it as implicit in the present statutory treatment of the exclusion for gifts, and in the variety of forums in which federal income tax cases can be tried. If there is fear of undue uncertainty or overmuch litigation, Congress may make more precise its treatment of the matter by singling out certain factors and making them determinative of the matter, as it has done in one field of the "gift" exclusion's former application, that of prizes and awards. Doubtless diversity of result will tend to be lessened somewhat since federal income tax decisions, even those in tribunals of first instance turning on issues of fact, tend to be reported, and since there may be a natural tendency of professional triers of fact to follow one another's determinations, even as to factual matters. But the question here remains basically one of fact, for determination on a case-by-case basis.

One consequence of this is that appellate review of determinations in this field must be quite restricted. Where a jury has tried the matter upon correct instructions, the only inquiry is whether it cannot be said that reasonable men could reach differing conclusions on the issue. *Baker v. Texas & Pacific R. Co.,* *supra,* at 228. Where the trial has been by a judge without a jury, the judge's findings must stand unless "clearly erroneous." Fed. Rules Civ. Proc., 52 (a). "A finding is 'clearly erroneous' when although there is evidence to support it, the reviewing court on the entire evidence is left with the definite and firm conviction that a mistake has been committed." *United States v. United States Gypsum Co.,* 333 U.S. 364, 395. The rule itself applies also to factual inferences from undisputed basic facts, *id.* at 394, as will on many occasions be presented in this area. *Cf. Graver Tank & Mfg. Co. v. Linde Air Products Co.,* 339 U.S. 605, 609–610. And Congress has in the most explicit terms attached the identical weight to the findings of the Tax Court. I.R.C., § 7482 (a).

Fourth. A majority of the Court is in accord with the principles just outlined. And, applying them to the *Duberstein* case, we are in agreement, on the evidence we have set forth, that it cannot be said that the conclusion of the Tax Court was "clearly erroneous." It seems to us plain that as trier of the facts it was warranted in concluding that despite the characterization of the transfer of the Cadillac by the parties and the absence of any obligation, even of a moral nature, to make it, it was at bottom a recompense for Duberstein's past services, or an inducement for him to be of further service in the future. We cannot say with the Court of Appeals that such a conclusion was "mere suspicion" on the Tax Court's part. To us it appears based in the sort of informed experience with human affairs that fact-finding tribunals should bring to this task.

As to *Stanton,* we are in disagreement. To four of us, it is critical here that the District Court as trier of fact made only the simple and unelaborated finding that the transfer in question was a "gift."[14] To be sure, conciseness is to be strived for, and prolixity avoided, in findings; but, to the four of us, there comes a point where findings become so sparse and conclusory as to give no revelation of what the District Court's concept of the determining facts and legal standard may be. *See Matton Oil Transfer Corp. v. The Dynamic,* 123 F.2d 999, 1000–1001. Such conclusory, general findings do not constitute compliance with Rule 52's direction to "find the facts specially and state separately . . . conclusions of law thereon." While the standard of law in this area is not a complex one, we four think the unelaborated finding of ultimate fact here cannot stand as a fulfillment of these

---

[14] [14] The "Findings of Fact and Conclusions of Law" were made orally, and were simply: "The resolution of the Board of Directors of the Trinity Operating Company, Incorporated, held November 19, 1942, after the resignations had been accepted of the plaintiff from his positions as controller of the corporation of the Trinity Church, and the president of the Trinity Operating Company, Incorporated, whereby a gratuity was voted to the plaintiff, Allen [*sic*] D. Stanton, in the amount of $20,000 payable to him in monthly installments of $2,000 each, commencing with the month of December, 1942, constituted a gift to the taxpayer, and therefore need not have been reported by him as income for the taxable years 1942, or 1943."

requirements. It affords the reviewing court not the semblance of an indication of the legal standard with which the trier of fact has approached his task. For all that appears, the District Court may have viewed the form of the resolution or the simple absence of legal consideration as conclusive. While the judgment of the Court of Appeals cannot stand, the four of us think there must be further proceedings in the District Court looking toward new and adequate findings of fact. In this, we are joined by MR. JUSTICE WHITTAKER, who agrees that the findings were inadequate, although he does not concur generally in this opinion.

Accordingly, in No. 376, the judgment of this Court is that the judgment of the Court of Appeals is reversed, and in No. 546, that the judgment of the Court of Appeals is vacated, and the case is remanded to the District Court for further proceedings not inconsistent with this opinion.

It is so ordered.

MR. JUSTICE HARLAN concurs in the result in No. 376. In No. 546, he would affirm the judgment of the Court of Appeals for the reasons stated by MR. JUSTICE FRANKFURTER.

MR. JUSTICE WHITTAKER, agreeing with *Bogardus* that whether a particular transfer is or is not a "gift" may involve "a mixed question of law and fact," 302 U.S. at 39, concurs only in the result of this opinion.

MR. JUSTICE DOUGLAS dissents, since he is of the view that in each of these two cases there was a gift under the test which the Court fashioned nearly a quarter of a century ago in *Bogardus v. Commissioner*, 302 U.S. 34.

MR. JUSTICE BLACK concurring and dissenting.

I agree with the Court that it was not clearly erroneous for the Tax Court to find as it did in No. 376 that the automobile transfer to Duberstein was not a gift, and so I agree with the Court's opinion and judgment reversing the judgment of the Court of Appeals in that case.

I dissent in No. 546, *Stanton v. United States*. The District Court found that the $20,000 transferred to Mr. Stanton by his former employer at the end of ten years' service was a gift and therefore exempt from taxation under I.R.C. of 1939, § 22 (b)(3) (now I.R.C. of 1954, § 102 (a)). I think the finding was not clearly erroneous and that the Court of Appeals was therefore wrong in reversing the District Court's judgment. While conflicting inferences might have been drawn, there was evidence to show that Mr. Stanton's long services had been satisfactory, that he was well liked personally and had given splendid service, that the employer was under no obligation at all to pay any added compensation, but made the $20,000 payment because prompted by a genuine desire to make him a "gift," to award him a "gratuity." *Cf. Commissioner v. LoBue*, 351 U.S. 243, 246–247. The District Court's finding was that the added payment "constituted a gift to the taxpayer, and therefore need not have been reported by him as income. . . ." The trial court might have used more words, or discussed the facts set out above in more detail, but I doubt if this would have made its crucial, adequately supported finding any clearer. For this reason I would reinstate the District Court's judgment for petitioner.

MR. JUSTICE FRANKFURTER, concurring in the judgment in No. 376 and dissenting in No. 546.

As the Court's opinion indicates, we brought these two cases here partly because of a claimed difference in the approaches between two Courts of Appeals but primarily on the Government's urging that, in the interest of the better administration of the income tax laws, clarification was desirable for determining when a transfer of property constitutes a "gift" and is not to be included in income for purposes of ascertaining the "gross income" under the Internal Revenue Code. As soon as this problem emerged after the imposition of the first income tax authorized by the Sixteenth Amendment, it became evident that its inherent difficulties and subtleties would not easily yield to the formulation of a general rule or test sufficiently definite to confine within narrow limits the area of judgment in applying it. While at its core the tax conception of a gift no doubt reflected the non-legal, non-technical notion of a benefaction unentangled with any aspect of worldly requital, the divers blends of personal and pecuniary relationships in our industrial society inevitably presented niceties for adjudication which could not be put to rest by any kind of general formulation.

Despite acute arguments at the bar and a most thorough re-examination of the problem on a full canvass of our prior decisions and an attempted fresh analysis of the nature of the problem, the Court has rejected the invitation of the Government to fashion anything like a litmus paper test for determining what is excludable as a "gift" from gross income. Nor has the Court attempted a clarification of the particular aspects of the problem presented by these two cases, namely, payment by an employer to an employee upon the termination of the employment relation and non-obligatory payment for services rendered in the course of a business relationship. While I agree that experience has shown the futility of attempting to define, by language so circumscribing as to make it easily applicable, what constitutes a gift for every situation where the problem may arise, I do think that greater explicitness is possible in isolating and emphasizing factors which militate against a gift in particular situations.

Thus, regarding the two frequently recurring situations involved in these cases — things of value given to employees by their employers upon the termination of employment and payments entangled in a business relation and occasioned by the performance of some service — the strong implication is that the payment is of a business nature. The problem in these two cases is entirely different from the problem in a case where a payment is made from one member of a family to another, where the implications are directly otherwise. No single general formulation appropriately deals with both types of cases, although both involve the question whether the payment was a "gift." While we should normally suppose that a payment from father to son was a gift, unless the contrary is shown, in the two situations now before us the business implications are so forceful that I would apply a presumptive rule placing the burden upon the beneficiary to prove the payment wholly unrelated to his services to the enterprise. The Court, however, has declined so to analyze the problem and has concluded "that the governing principles are necessarily general and have already been spelled out in the opinions of this Court, and that the problem is one which, under the present statutory framework, does not lend itself to any more definitive statement that would produce a talisman for the solution of concrete cases."

The Court has made only one authoritative addition to the previous course of our decisions. Recognizing *Bogardus v. Commissioner*, 302 U.S. 34, as "the leading case here" and finding essential accord between the Court's opinion and the dissent in that case, the Court has drawn from the dissent in *Bogardus* for infusion into what will now be a controlling qualification, recognition that it is "for the triers of the facts to seek among competing aims or motives the ones that dominated conduct." 302 U.S. 34, 45 (dissenting opinion). All this being so in view of the Court, it seems to me desirable not to try to improve what has "already been spelled out" in the opinions of this Court but to leave to the lower courts the application of old phrases rather than to float new ones and thereby inevitably produce a new volume of exegesis on the new phrases.

Especially do I believe this when fact-finding tribunals are directed by the Court to rely upon their "experience with the mainsprings of human conduct" and on their "informed experience with human affairs" in appraising the totality of the facts of each case. Varying conceptions regarding the "mainsprings of human conduct" are derived from a variety of experiences or assumptions about the nature of man, and "experience with human affairs," is not only diverse but also often drastically conflicting. What the Court now does sets fact-finding bodies to sail on an illimitable ocean of individual beliefs and experiences. This can hardly fail to invite, if indeed not encourage, too individualized diversities in the administration of the income tax law. I am afraid that by these new phrasings the practicalities of tax administration, which should be as uniform as is possible in so vast a country as ours, will be embarrassed. By applying what has already been spelled out in the opinions of this Court, I agree with the Court in reversing the judgment in *Commissioner v. Duberstein*.

But I would affirm the decision of the Court of Appeals for the Second Circuit in *Stanton v. United States*. I would do so on the basis of the opinion of Judge Hand and more particularly because the very terms of the resolution by which the $20,000 was awarded to Stanton indicated that it was not a "gratuity" in the sense of sheer benevolence but in the nature of a generous lagniappe, something extra thrown in for services received though not legally nor morally required to be given. This careful resolution, doubtless drawn by a lawyer and adopted by some hardheaded businessmen, contained a proviso that Stanton should abandon all rights to "pension and retirement benefits." The fact that Stanton had no such claims does not lessen the significance of the clause as something "to make assurance doubly sure." 268 F.2d 728. The business nature of the payment is confirmed by the words of the resolution, explaining the "gratuity" as "in appreciation of the services rendered by Mr. Stanton as Manager of the Estate and Comptroller of the Corporation of Trinity Church throughout nearly ten years, and as President of Trinity Operating Company, Inc." The force of this document, in light of all the factors to which Judge Hand adverted in his opinion, was not in the least diminished by testimony at the trial. Thus the taxpayer has totally failed to sustain the burden I would place upon him to establish that the payment to him was wholly attributable to generosity unrelated to his performance of his secular business functions as an officer of the corporation of the Trinity Church of New York and the Trinity Operating Co. Since the record totally fails to establish taxpayer's claim, I see no need of specific findings by the trial judge.

Understanding *Duberstein*

1.   In *Duberstein*, the Supreme Court says that a transfer is a gift for income tax purposes only if it proceeds from "detached and disinterested generosity," arising "out of respect, admiration, charity, or like impulses (citations omitted)." Does anyone have such pure motives? Given the near impossibility of assessing individual mental states, is the decision likely to come down to more objective factors: the relationship between the parties, whether the transfer was of cash or property, whether there was a *quid pro quo* (i.e., consideration) for the transfer, and so forth? What do these factors tell you about the validity of the "gift" characterization on the *Duberstein* or *Stanton* facts? As in *Turner*, does the existence of a vague statute encourage taxpayers to take an aggressive position in close (and not-so-close) cases?

2.   Present law section 102(c) states that "[Section 102(a)] shall not exclude from gross income any amount transferred by or for an employer to, or for the benefit of, an employee." Had it been in effect earlier, would section 102(c) have changed the result in *Duberstein*? In *Stanton*? Why was the Court reluctant to adopt the rule eventually contained in section 102(c)?

3.   Is there still room for argument regarding the scope or applicability of section 102(c)? The Tenth Circuit has held that section 102(c) applies to deny gift treatment (i.e., to require taxability) even where the employer and employee were close personal friends and the "gifts" had been made regularly for several years. *Williams v. Commissioner*, 120 Fed. Appx. 289 (10th Cir. 2005). Should there be any situation in which a transfer from employer to employee can be considered a gift?

4.   Is it relevant that, in *Duberstein*, the payor deducted the supposed gift as a regular business expense? What about *Benaglia*, in which the hotel deducted the costs of Benaglia's room and lodging, but he did not account for them as income? In this context, note section 274(b) of present law, denying the transferor a deduction for most transfers that qualify as gifts to the recipient. Should this be replaced by a more general rule, requiring consistency in the treatment of an item by both parties to a given transaction? How could such a rule be enforced?

5.   After reading *Duberstein*, what do you think of the arguments for and against the section 102 gift exclusion, described in the preceding paragraphs?

As might be expected, the *Duberstein* case led to some confusion regarding what is and isn't a tax-exempt gift. Although section 102(c) denies gift treatment for transfers from employers to employees, a number of less obvious situations remain uncertain. An interesting example is the case of tips, i.e., gratuities paid by restaurant or other customers in return for good (or at least, not terribly bad) service. Tips have always been taxable income, although people don't always report them. But, under *Duberstein*, why should this be so? Couldn't the recipient argue that the payor was motivated by "detached and disinterested generosity," and leave the IRS to prove otherwise? Wouldn't this be especially attractive in cases where the customer became personally friendly with the waitperson, or left unusually large or unpredictable tips? What happens, of course, is that internal motivations are subordinated to external facts: we don't know what is on the mind of any individual tip-giver, but we know that tips are usually thought of as payment for services, and that many waiters and waitresses rely upon them as an integral part of their compensation package. So we impose the tax, even though a literal application of *Duberstein* would result in a more checkered pattern. It is interesting in this context to consider the so-called tip enforcement rule, under which tips are generally assumed to be equal to a specified percentage of restaurant receipts in the absence of contrary evidence.[15] Might this percent rule constitute an implicit recognition that tips have a mixed character, consisting primarily of compensation, but partly of a gift-like component that ought not to be subject to tax?

The gift exclusion also creates several technical problems. One particular issue concerns gifts, like a bank account or rental real estate, that continue to produce interest, rent, or other income after the gift has been transferred. Is this income part of the original gift, and therefore exempt from tax, or should it be taxed like any other interest or rental payments? This issue has generally been resolved against the taxpayer: section 102(b)(1) provides that there is no exclusion for income attributable to a gift property, and section 102(b)(2), reflecting the Supreme Court's decision in *Irwin v. Gavit*,[16] provides the same result for trusts and similar arrangements. A related issue, concerning gifts of appreciated property, is considered in Chapter 3.

If gifts are not taxable, what about transfer payments — welfare, social security, unemployment compensation — made by governmental agencies to vulnerable members of society? Are these properly treated as gifts, windfalls, income substitutes, or a special category that does not fit any of the usual descriptions? Is there any point in taxing such amounts, if the government will have to make up the amount of the tax, anyway, in the form of a larger transfer payment? The answers to these questions vary: welfare payments generally speaking are not taxed; unemployment compensation is; and social security is sometimes taxed, but only on a partial basis, and only if the recipient has other income that exceeds a specified amount.[17] All this is without even discussing employer-provided pension and retirement plans, which are subject to tax but on a deferred basis and frequently at lower rates than would have applied when the relevant income was earned.[18] What do you think is the vertical equity of a system that taxes unemployment compensation, but allows gifts and pensions to receive deferred or even tax-free treatment? Is the Code emphasizing abstract, hyper-technical distinctions, at the expense of a just social policy?

---

[15] I.R.C. § 6053.

[16] 268 U.S. 161 (1925).

[17] *See generally* Rev. Rul. 74-205, 1974-1 C.B. 20 (welfare payments); I.R.C. § 85 (unemployment compensation); I.R.C. § 86 (social security). Social security payments are discussed in Chapter 7.

[18] *See* Chapter 4, *infra*.

The following case considers the issue of gifts and transfer-type payments in greater detail. Does it make the distinctions in this area more, or even less, comprehensible?

UNITED STATES v. KAISER
United States Supreme Court
363 U.S. 299 (1960)

MR. JUSTICE BRENNAN announced the judgment of the Court, and delivered an opinion in which THE CHIEF JUSTICE, MR. JUSTICE BLACK, and MR. JUSTICE DOUGLAS join.

This case presents the questions whether a labor union's strike assistance, by way of room rent and food vouchers, furnished to a worker participating in a strike constitutes income to him under § 61(a) of the Internal Revenue Code of 1954; and whether the assistance furnished to this particular worker, who was in need, constituted a "gift" to him, and hence was excluded from income by § 102(a) of the Code.

The respondent was employed by the Kohler Company in Wisconsin. The bargaining representative at the Kohler plant was Local 833 of the United Automobile, Aircraft, and Agricultural Implement Workers of America, CIO (UAW). In April 1954, the Local, with the approval of the International Union of the UAW, called a strike against Kohler in support of various bargaining demands in connection with a proposed renewal of their recently expired collective bargaining contract. The respondent was not a member of the Union, but he went out on strike. He had been earning $2.16 an hour at his job. This was his sole source of income, and when he struck he soon found himself in financial need. He went to the Union headquarters and requested assistance. It was the policy of the Union to grant assistance to the many Kohler strikers simply on a need basis. It made no difference whether a striker was a union member. The Union representatives questioned respondent as to his financial resources, and his dependents. He had no other job and needed assistance with respect to the essentials of life. He was single during the period in question, and the Union provided him with a food voucher for $6 a week, redeemable in kind at a local store; the voucher was later increased to $7.50 a week. The Union also paid his room rent, which amounted to $9 a week. If in need, married strikers and married strikers with children received respectively larger food vouchers.[19] The over-all policy of the International Union was not to render strike assistance where strikers could obtain state unemployment compensation or local public assistance benefits. But the former condition does not prevail in Wisconsin, and local public assistance was available only on a showing of a destitution evidently deemed extreme by the Union.

The Union thought that strikers ought to perform picketing duty, but did not require, advise or encourage strikers who were receiving assistance to picket or

---

[19] [3] After the increase referred to, married strikers without children received a $15 weekly food voucher; those with one child, an $18 voucher.

perform any other activity in furtherance of the strike; but assistance ceased for strikers who obtained work. Respondent performed some picketing, though apparently no considerable amount. After receiving assistance for several months, he joined the Union. This had in no way been required of him or suggested to him in connection with the continued receipt of assistance.

The program of strike assistance was primarily financed through the strike fund of the International Union, which had been raised through crediting to it 25 cents of the $1.25 per capita monthly assessment the International required from the local unions. The Local also had a small strike fund built up through monthly credits of 5 cents of the local members' dues, and contributions were received in some degree, not contended to be substantial, from other unions and outsiders. The constitution of the International Union required that it be the authorizing agency for strikes, and imposed on it the general duty to render financial assistance to the members on strike.

During 1954, the Union furnished respondent assistance in the value of $565.54. In computing his federal income tax for the year, he did not include in gross income any amount in respect of the assistance. The District Director of Internal Revenue informed respondent that the $565.54 should have been added to his gross income and the tax due increased by $108 accordingly. Respondent paid this amount, and after administrative rejection of a refund claim, sued for a refund in the District Court for the Eastern District of Wisconsin. A jury trial was had, and the court submitted to the jury the single interrogatory whether the assistance rendered to respondent was a gift. The jury answered in the affirmative; but the court entered judgment for the Government, n.o.v., on the basis that as a matter of law the assistance was income to the respondent, and did not fall within the statutory exclusion for gifts. 158 F.Supp. 865.

By a divided vote, the Court of Appeals for the Seventh Circuit reversed. 262 F.2d 367. It held alternatively that the assistance was not within the concept of income of § 61(a) of the Code, and that in any event the jury's determination that the assistance was a gift, and hence excluded from gross income by § 102(a), had rational support in the evidence and accordingly was within its province as trier of the facts. We granted the Government's petition for *certiorari*, because of the importance of the issues presented. 359 U.S. 1010. Later, when the Government petitioned for *certiorari* in No. 376, *Commissioner v. Duberstein*, and acquiesced in the taxpayer's petition in No. 546, *Stanton v. United States*, it suggested that those cases be set down for argument with the case at bar, because they illustrated in a more general context the "gift" exclusion issues presented by this case. We agreed, and the cases were argued together. We conclude, on the basis of our opinion in the *Duberstein* case, that the jury in this case, as finder of the facts, acted within its competence in concluding that the assistance rendered here was a gift within § 102(a). Accordingly, we affirm the judgment of the Court of Appeals. Therefore, we think it unnecessary to consider or express any opinion as to whether the assistance in fact constituted income to the respondent within the meaning of § 61(a).

At trial, counsel for the Government did not make objection to any part of the District Court's charge to the jury or the "gift" exclusion. In this Court, the charge is belatedly challenged, and only as part of the Government's position that there should be formulated a new "test" for application in this area. We have rejected that contention in our opinion in *Duberstein*. In the absence of specific objection at trial, or of demonstration of any compelling reason for dispensing with such objection, we do not here notice any defect in the charge, in the light of the controlling legal principles as we have reviewed them in *Duberstein*.

We think, also, that the proofs were adequate to support the conclusion of the jury. Our opinion in *Duberstein* stresses the basically factual nature of the inquiry as to this issue. The factual inferences to be drawn from the basic facts were here for the jury. They had the power to conclude, on the record, taking into account such factors as the form and amount of the assistance and the conditions of personal need, of lack of other sources of income, compensation, or public assistance, and of dependency status, which surrounded the program under which it was rendered, that while the assistance was furnished only to strikers, it was not a recompense for striking. They could have concluded that the very general language of the Union's constitution, when considered with the nature of the Union as an entity and with the factors to which we have just referred, did not indicate that basically the assistance proceeded from any constraint of moral or legal obligation, of a nature that would preclude it from being a gift. And on all these circumstances, the jury could have concluded that assistance, rendered as it was to a class of persons in the community in economic need, proceeded primarily from generosity or charity, rather than from the incentive of anticipated economic benefit. We can hardly say that, as a matter of law, the fact that these transfers were made to one having a sympathetic interest with the giver prevents them from being a gift. This is present in many cases of the most unquestionable charity.

We need not stop to speculate as to what conclusion we would have drawn had we sat in the jury box rather than those who did. The question is one of the allocation of power to decide the question; and once we say that such conclusions could with reason be reached on the evidence, and that the District Court's instructions are not overthrown, our reviewing authority is exhausted, and we must recognize that the jury was empowered to render the verdict which it did.

Affirmed.

Mr. Justice Frankfurter, whom Mr. Justice Clark joins, concurring in the result.

In 1957 the Commissioner of Internal Revenue ruled that strike benefits paid by unions to strikers on the basis of need, without regard to union membership, were to be regarded as part of the recipient's gross income for income tax purposes. Rev. Rul. 57-1, 1957-1 Cum. Bull. 15. This ruling, if valid, governs this case. The taxpayer assails the ruling on three grounds. First, it is urged that in a series of rulings since 1920 the Commissioner has treated both public and private "subsistence relief" payments as not constituting gross income; that union strike benefits are not relevantly different from such "subsistence relief"; and that, with due regard to fair tax administration the Commissioner is constrained so to treat strike benefits in order to accord "equal treatment." Second, it is urged that both the Commissioner's rulings and court decisions have evolved an exclusion from the statutory category of "gross income," not explicitly stated in the statute, for "alleviative" receipts which do not result in any "enrichment," *i.e.*, "reparation" payments made in compensation for some loss or injury suffered by the recipient, and that strike benefits fall within this exclusion. Third, it is urged that strike benefits in general, or at least these strike benefits in particular, are to be deemed "gifts" within the meaning of the statutory exclusion from gross income of "gifts."

* * *

Finding these strike benefits not otherwise outside the statutory concept of "gross income," the decisive factor for me in this case is whether the strike benefits are to be deemed a "gift." As a matter of ordinary reading of language I could not conclude that all strike benefits are, as a matter of law, "gifts." I should suppose that a strike benefit does not fit the notion of "gift." A union surely has strong self-interest in paying such benefits to strikers. The implications arising out of the relationship between a union which calls a strike and its strikers are such that, without some special circumstances, it would be unrealistic for a court to conclude that payments made by the union for which only strikers qualify, even though based upon need, derive solely from the promptings of benevolence.

In this case, however, under instructions to the jury that

"the term 'gift' as here used denotes the receipt of financial advantage gratuitously, without obligation to make the payment, either legal or moral, and without the payment being made as remuneration for something that the Union wished done or omitted by the plaintiff. To be a gift, the payments must have been made with the intent that there be nothing of value received, or that they were not made to repay what was plaintiff's due but were bestowed only because of personal regard or pity or from general motives of philanthropy or charity. If the plaintiff received this assistance simply and solely because he and his family were in actual need and not because of any obligations, as above referred to, or any expectation of anything in return, then such payments were gifts,"

the jury found in a special verdict that the strike benefit payments to taxpayer were a "gift." These instructions certainly were not unfavorable to the Government.

* * *

. . . Although it is for me a very close question, I find sufficient evidence in the record to support the theory that in making these payments the union was exercising a wholly charitable function. On this view, restricted to the particular set of circumstances under which the special verdict was rendered, I would therefore hold the payment in this case to be a gift and would affirm the judgment below.

* * *

Mr. Justice Douglas, concurring.

While I join the opinion of my Brother Brennan, my view of the merits is so divergent from the rest that a word of explanation is needed. *Bogardus v. Commissioner*, 302 U.S. 34, 41, in holding payments by stockholders to employees were, on the facts there present, gifts, said:

> "There is entirely lacking the constraining force of any moral or legal duty as well as the incentive of anticipated benefit of any kind beyond the satisfaction which flows from the performance of a generous act."

. . . As the opinion of the Court points out, this striker (who became a union member without solicitation several months after he began receiving benefits) had no legal or moral duty to picket or to do any other act in furtherance of the strike. There is no evidence that the union made these payments to keep this striker in line. It is said that these strike payments serve the union's cause in promoting the strike. Yet the whole setting of the case indicates to me these payments were welfare, plain and simple. Unions, like employers, may have charitable impulses and incentives. Here only the needy got the relief. Yet since (so far as the present record shows) respondent acquiesced in the submission to the jury, the United States received more favored consideration than it could claim as of right.

Mr. Justice Whittaker, with whom Mr. Justice Harlan and Mr. Justice Stewart join, dissenting.

The question here is whether, in the light of the rule adopted by the Court today in *Commissioner v. Duberstein*, there is a reasonable basis in the evidence to support the jury's conclusion that the strike benefits paid to respondent by the union were nontaxable "gifts," within the meaning of § 102(a) of the 1954 Internal Revenue Code.

With deference, I am convinced that there was not, and that, to the contrary, the evidence compels the conclusion, as a matter of law, that those strike benefits were not "gifts" within the meaning of § 102(a), as construed by the Court in the *Duberstein* case.

* * *

. . . I find nothing in this record to indicate that the strike benefit payments by the union to respondent and other striking workers, while they were waging the strike, were made out of any "detached and disinterested generosity," or "out of affection, respect, admiration, charity or like impulses." To the contrary, it seems plain enough that those payments were made by the union to enable and encourage respondent and other striking workers to continue the strike which had been called or approved by the union, and were not motivated by benevolence. Those payments were therefore made in furtherance of one of the union's principal economic objectives — the winning of the strike — and hence proceeded primarily from " 'the incentive of anticipated benefit' of an economic nature" to the union, and from "the constraining force" of the union's promise to assist striking workers in winning the strike. *Duberstein*. Because of the economic advantages to be obtained by the union from winning the strike, the union had a manifest self-interest in financially sustaining the strikers while they carried on its strike. This shows, as a matter of law, that the payments were not made with the donative intent required to constitute "gifts" within the meaning of § 102(a) and of the *Bogardus* and *Duberstein* cases. Wholly apart from the immediate objective which the union sought to achieve by paying these strike benefits, they could qualify as "gifts," as the Court recognizes, only if they were made, as said in *Duberstein*, with a " 'detached and disinterested generosity,' " and this record shows that it was principally private business purposes, not detached and disinterested generosity, that prompted the union to make the payments in question.

Understanding *Kaiser*

1. *Kaiser* was decided immediately after *Duberstein* and had a similarly divided opinion. Are the two cases consistent with each other? Are strike payments made with "detached and disinterested generosity," supposedly the *Duberstein* standard for tax-free gifts? If not, why are they excludable? What is the relevance in *Kaiser* of the recipient's economic status or of the fact that he or she had no sources of income besides the union strike fund? Do these factors relate to the donor's state of mind, or (instead) to that of the recipient? What does your answer to this question tell you about the wisdom of the "detached and disinterested generosity" standard and its application in real-world cases?

2. Do you agree with the *Kaiser* court that the characterization of strike payments as a gift, rather than income, was within the competence of the jury? Is this determination properly treated as a finding of fact, a conclusion of law, or somewhere between the two? Should it matter?

3. Justice Frankfurter's concurrence and Justice Whittaker's dissent both make extensive reliance on the positions that the IRS has taken in previous Revenue Rulings and discuss whether the IRS's current position was consistent with those rulings. What is the authority of revenue rulings, and should the courts (or the IRS) be bound by previous rulings when faced with a new set of facts? What if regulations, rather than rulings, were at issue? What if the rulings were unpublished and directed only at one taxpayer (i.e., a private letter ruling)?

4. *Kaiser* was argued for the taxpayer by one of the leading civil rights attorneys in the country, with one of the then-most famous tax lawyers on the brief. Why was the case so important? What would be the practical consequences of a holding that strike benefits were taxable income, and how might it have affected union and management behavior in future crises? Should the tax system worry about these issues, or are they labor law problems?

Using the Sources

Under section 102, *Duberstein*, and the applicable regulations, do the following constitute taxable income or tax-free gifts?

a. A wedding gift from a corporation to its executive. (Does it matter if the gift is bought by other employees instead of the corporation?)

b. Money (or food) given to a homeless person by a thoughtful passerby.

c. A contribution to a political campaign.

d. A contribution to a charitable organization.

e. A reward for keeping a promise not to drink or smoke before age 21.

f. A Christmas bonus paid to the associates at a happy, successful law firm.

g. A one-night stay in the White House Lincoln Bedroom, given as a reward for supporting an embattled President.

Law and Planning

Your client, Isaac Industrious, is a young investment banker with the firm of Clinton & Bush (C & B). Isaac has been working extremely hard on a deal under the supervision of Mary Mentor, a senior partner at C & B. After the conclusion of the deal, there is a party at Mary's condominium to celebrate everyone's hard work. As Isaac is preparing to leave the party, Mary takes him aside and says, "I just want to thank you for all the work you've done on this deal. You're just like a son to me, really. I want to give you something special to thank you for all that you've done." With that, she thrusts into Isaac's hands a pair of season tickets to the local basketball team, with a cash value of $3,000, and hard to obtain even at that price without special connections.

Would you advise Isaac to report income on this transaction? Would it matter if he asked you for a written, signed opinion regarding the tax status of the tickets, or if he was merely asking your advice as to what position he should take on his return? What additional facts, if any, would help you to make this decision?

Politics and Policy

You are a tax advisor to the Russian Republic, which has had an unhappy experience with communism, but whose citizens are resentful of capitalist excesses, as well. Would you advise the Russians to include a gift exception, à la section 102, in their new income tax code? If so, would you limit the exception to transfers between family members, or give it a broader applicability? As long as we're on the subject, would it be advisable for Russia to implement (i) a progressive tax system, (ii) withholding on wages and salaries, and (iii) an estate or inheritance tax?

III. DAMAGES FOR PERSONAL INJURY

So far we have considered two problems in the definition of income: (i) employer provided meals and lodging and (ii) gifts and other gratuitous transfers. By this point two things should be clear. First, the language of the tax code, while it sets the terms for the debate, by no means resolves every tax issue. Instead a range of sources, including the statute, regulations, previous judicial decisions, and the practical consequences of alternate decisions, are brought to bear in even the simplest tax case. Second, the principles of tax policy — fairness, efficiency, simplicity or administrative feasibility — are often honored in the breach. While judges and legislators are sincere in their desire to improve the tax law, the goals of tax policy often clash with one another, and are frequently trumped by political or other less lofty concerns.

A further example of these contradictory tendencies is the tax treatment of damages for personal injury, under section 104(a)(2) of the Code. While this issue has been partially resolved by statutory amendment, its history tells us much about the clash of idealistic and cynical considerations that goes into the making of everyday tax law. The issue of personal injuries also provides a useful study of the interaction between tax and nontax law, and the role of tax law in planning and executing business strategies.

Suppose that you, or someone you know, is injured in an automobile accident. You sue the other driver, and the court awards you $1 million in damages, or you settle for the same amount before trial. Should the $1 million be included in income? On the one hand, you are $1 million richer than you were before the award, and also $1 million richer than another person who had a similar accident but was unable to recover for it. Moreover, the $1 million amount was likely calculated, at least in part, by reference to the income that you would have earned if you had not been injured; income that would, presumably, have been fully subject to the income tax.

Basic tax logic, and the principle of horizontal equity, may thus suggest that the award should be taxed. Yet the whole point of a damage award is to compensate you for your injuries and (so far as humanly possible) to put you back in the position that you would have been in if the injury had not taken place.[20] If you are, at best, being restored to your previous condition, why then should you pay any tax? And if you are forced to share a portion of the award with the IRS, will the compensation achieve its intended goal? These arguments are especially appealing if (as is likely) you received no deduction at the time of the injury; to tax you on the damage award effectively gives you the worst of both worlds, receiving no tax benefit for your injuries but incurring a tax cost when they are compensated. Taxing damage awards also has the flavor of kicking someone when they are down, and is likely to be politically unpopular.

For most of its history, the Code adopted the latter view. Thus section 104(a)(2), and its predecessors, have historically exempted "damages . . . on account of personal injuries" from the federal income tax. Until 1989, the statute made no distinction between physical and nonphysical injuries, or between compensatory and punitive damages.

What kept the issue lively were two distinct but related disputes. The first of these concerns nonphysical injuries, such as slander, libel, and other harm to reputation or personal standing. Since these injuries are theoretically "personal" in

---

[20] In tax terms, the damage award is a "return of capital," that is, a return of something you previously had and lost, rather than an additional form of enrichment. We will discuss the return of capital concept further in Chapter 3.

nature, section 104(a)(2) historically exempted them from taxation, even when the damages were measured by lost profits and other seemingly business-related criteria.[21] Taxpayers subsequently sought similar treatment for damages received under federal age and gender discrimination statutes, resulting in an increasingly arcane debate as to whether these statutes were more "tort-like" (i.e., covered by section 104(a)(2)) or "contract-like" (i.e., not covered) in nature.[22] To many observers, these cases seemed far removed from the original intention of section 104: a statute designed to deal with automobile accidents and slip-and-fall injuries was being extended to damages arising in a work context and measured largely, if not exclusively, by work-related amounts. Yet the language of the statute did not distinguish between physical and nonphysical injuries, and taxing awards in nonphysical injury cases would substantially reduce their benefit to the relevant plaintiffs.[23]

The second issue concerns the treatment of punitive damages. As any good torts student knows, damages for personal injury include both compensatory damages (lost wages, medical expenses, "pain and suffering," and so forth), and punitive damages, designed to punish tortfeasors and (arguably) reward successful claimants, but not specifically to compensate for any measurable injury. In many cases punitive damages are higher — sometimes much higher — than compensatory damages. Punitive damages have an odd character: while arising from the same injury as compensatory damages, they also have the flavor of a windfall, of something that does not merely restore the plaintiff to her original status, but rather makes her richer (sometimes, significantly richer) than she was before the injury occurred. For this and other reasons, the IRS was never entirely comfortable with the exclusion for punitive damages, and litigated the matter with mixed success in various courts.

The issues above occupied courts, commentators, and numerous law students for several decades, until Congress stepped in to end the drama. Like a parent disciplining an errant child, Congress acted in two distinct stages. First, in 1989, Congress decided that punitive damages should no longer be excludible in cases involving nonphysical injuries. Then, in 1996, the rule was further tightened: henceforth, for nonphysical injuries, no damages of any kind would be excluded, while even for physical injuries, only nonpunitive (that is, compensatory) damages would be excluded, with punitive damages now being fully taxable. Section 104(a)(2) now has the unusual distinction of having two parentheticals in the same sentence, excluding "the amount of any damages (other than punitive damages) received (whether by suit or agreement and whether as lump sums or as periodic payments) on account of personal physical injuries or physical sickness." The end result is to

---

[21] *See, e.g.*, Roemer v. Comm'r, 716 F.2d 693 (9th Cir. 1983).

[22] *See, e.g.*, United States v. Burke, 504 U.S. 229 (1992).

[23] This is particularly true if the effect of attorney's fees as well as taxes is taken into account. Consider a federal age discrimination suit, brought as a class action by a large group of plaintiffs, and settled for an aggregate of $10 million. If the lawyers take one-third of that amount (a reasonable estimate), and taxes take a remaining third, there may be relatively little left for the original plaintiffs. Of course, it is possible that judges and juries would become aware that damages were taxable and increase the amount of the awards to compensate for this problem; but the law makes no provision for such an adjustment, and it would be hard for plaintiffs to rely on such treatment.

resolve both of the borderline issues in favor of the government, with only the "core" of section 104(a)(2) (compensatory damages in traditional physical injury cases) remaining exempt from tax.[24]

Understanding Section 104

1.   A recurring argument in favor of taxing punitive damages is that such damages are intended solely to punish the wrongdoer and not to compensate the plaintiff. If that is true, why are the damages paid to the plaintiff and not to the government or other third party? Does (doesn't) the taxation of punitive damages decrease the plaintiff's incentive for bringing an otherwise meritorious claim? Does this matter?

2.   A distinction between compensatory and punitive damages may be difficult to administer because the allocation between these elements is often arbitrary in nature and can be manipulated by the parties so as to exaggerate the untaxed (i.e., compensatory) element. How serious is this concern? What about a rule which said simply that "the parties' allocation between compensatory and punitive damages will be respected in most cases, but may be challenged by IRS when there is reason to believe that the allocation does not accurately reflect the economic substance of the settlement, the burden of proof in such cases resting on the IRS to disprove the parties' original allocation"? In an important law review article, Professor Joseph Dodge suggested that only economic damages qualify for exemption, with damages for emotional distress — i.e., both pain and suffering and punitive damages — both being subject to tax. *See* Joseph M. Dodge, *Taxes and Torts*, 77 CORNELL L. REV. 143 (1992). Would this be a harder or easier line to draw than the line between compensatory and punitive damages? Would you recommend that the courts adopt such a test?

Cohen & Sager, *Why Civil Rights Lawyers Should Study Tax*
22 HARV. BLACKLETTER L.J. 1, 1, 2, 3, 8 (2006)[25]

INTRODUCTION

Civil rights and income taxation may seem as far apart as any two legal subjects could be, but they actually intersect in a surprising number of significant ways. Consider the following examples.

---

[24]   The United States Court of Appeals for the District Court of Columbia Circuit provided an unusual degree of entertainment with regard to section 104 in the case of *Murphy v. IRS*, **cite need for this case.** The court first attracted attention by holding that compensatory damages for nonphysical injuries were not income within the meaning of the Sixteenth Amendment — a decision which, if upheld, would have overturned the entire structure of section 104, and much else besides. Perhaps awestruck with the impact of its own decision, the court agreed to rehear the case and reversed itself, leaving the state of the law more or less what it was before. *Murphy* is one of a number of decisions in which the federal courts, after making a bold but perhaps ill-advised foray into the tax area, have reversed themselves under pressure from a combination of tax experts and government officials. The *Albertson's* case in Chapter 4 is another example of this process.

[25]   Copyright © 2006 Harvard BlackLetter Law Journal. All rights reserved. Reprinted by permission.

* * *

Since 1996, the Internal Revenue Code has drawn a sharp distinction between damages for physical and nonphysical injury. Under § 104(a)(2), damages for lost earnings or pain and suffering received on account of "personal physical injuries or physical sickness" are excluded from taxation. On the other hand, damages for lost earnings or pain and suffering received on account of a nonphysical injury are subject to the general rule of § 61(a) that "gross income [includes] all income from whatever source derived" and therefore are subject to taxation.

The dramatic difference in the treatment of such damages depending on whether the injury is physical or nonphysical seems arbitrary and unfair. The distinction is especially troubling because its principal effect is to impose a greater tax burden on victims of civil rights violations, including unlawful discrimination, than on victims of physical injury. It seems arbitrary and unfair, for example, that damages for sexual harassment are taxed if damages for a broken leg are tax-exempt.

* * *

From a tax policy perspective, the current tax treatment of personal injury damages is anomalous in two respects. First, lost earnings paid to the victim of a physical injury are excluded from taxation, although the earnings would have been taxable absent the physical injury and although lost earnings paid to the victim of a nonphysical injury are taxable. Second, damages for the emotional suffering caused by a nonphysical injury are taxable, although such damages compensate for a right that, absent the injury, would be enjoyed tax-free, and although damages for the pain and suffering of a physical injury remain tax-exempt.

* * *

The fact that § 104(a)(2), as interpreted by the IRS and the courts, makes such fine distinctions in the example above — between emotional distress caused by the physical contact and emotional distress caused by being fired and between lost wages attributable to the physical contact and lost wages attributable to being fired — reinforces the conclusion that the current tax rules make little sense and should be replaced. As indicated above, it would be more in keeping with the "in lieu of" principle, which governs the taxation of other damages, to abolish the distinction between physical and nonphysical injuries and to exempt from taxation all damages for pain and suffering (or emotional distress) while taxing all damages for lost wages. Whether such changes occur, civil rights lawyers need to remain attentive to how taxation affects the after-tax value of recoveries for unlawful discrimination.

Using the Sources

1. Under section 104, which of the following are included in taxable income?

    a. An award of lost income resulting from a serious automobile accident.

    b. An award for "pain and suffering" resulting from the same accident.

    c. Punitive damages resulting from the accident.

    d. Any of the same items in a slander or libel lawsuit. (Does it matter if the plaintiff's personal or business reputation was the subject of the slander or libel?)

2. The end of section 104(a) states as follows:

    "For purposes of paragraph (2), emotional distress shall not be treated as a physical injury or physical sickness. The preceding sentence shall not apply to an amount of damages not in excess of the amount paid for medical care . . . attributable to emotional distress."

What do these two sentences mean? Specifically, how would the language apply in each of the following cases?

    (i) A taxpayer who is awarded damages for psychiatrist's bills in connection with an automobile accident.

    (ii) A sexual harassment plaintiff, who became physically ill as a result of the harassment, and is awarded damages with respect to the physical and emotional damage resulting from the harassment.

    (iii) Same as item (ii), except that the plaintiff is hospitalized as a result of her symptoms.

Law and Planning

You are counsel to Peter Plaintiff in a lawsuit against Willy Laboratories, the makers of Gozac, an anti-depressant drug which has cured Peter's depression but at the cost of headaches, nausea, impotence, and other physical maladies that (or so he claims) have ruined his personal and professional life. You have a strong case but anticipate some difficulty proving damages, since Peter has a generous pension and has therefore sustained relatively limited financial loss; at most, you believe that you could win approximately $1 million in lost wages and other economic damages. The plaintiff is, however, in a sympathetic position and you believe that you could win up to $5 million in punitive damages, together with perhaps $2 million in pain and suffering, if you pursue these issues aggressively.

    (i) How, if at all, would the taxability of punitive damages affect your litigation strategy if the case above goes to trial? Would you emphasize compensatory as opposed to punitive damages, or would you pursue the best otherwise available litigation strategy without regard to tax issues?

    (ii) Suppose that the defendant offered a settlement in which it agreed to pay $1 million in compensatory damages, $2 million in punitive damages, and promised never to do it again. How would you respond to this settlement offer? Would the tax consequences affect your response?

(iii) How, if at all, would your answers to (i) and (ii) differ if you were representing a client in a small "slip and fall" litigation instead of a multimillion dollar case against a large pharmaceutical company?

Politics and Policy

1.   What do you think of the policy of distinguishing between physical and nonphysical injuries, and between compensatory and punitive damages, as exemplified by section 104(a)(2)? In particular, does present law discourage plaintiffs from bringing otherwise meritorious anti-discrimination, harassment, and similar "nonphysical" damage suits, as well as physical injury cases that involve large punitive damages? Should the tax law worry about this, or is it somebody else's problem?

2.   What do you think of the proposal in the Cohen and Sager excerpt that the distinction between physical and nonphysical injuries be replaced by a rule exempting from taxation all damages for pain and suffering while taxing all damages for lost wages? Would this rule be administrable? Would it be desirable?

3.   Do you agree that it is unfair that damages for sexual harassment are taxed while damages for a broken leg are tax-exempt? Is this the type of unfairness that tax policy should be concerned with? How would you balance this concern with fairness (or horizontal equity) against concerns about administrability?

IV.   APPLYING THE TAX LAW TO NEW DEVELOPMENTS: REPARATIONS FOR THE HOLOCAUST AND OTHER HUMAN RIGHTS ABUSES

To this point we have considered classic issues in the definition of income, issues which — although provoking a high degree of controversy — have mostly been settled for some time. Sometimes the tax system is called upon to resolve issues which do not fit so neatly into existing categories. Indeed, it is in these cases that tax law is the most interesting, and where tax lawyers' analytical and reasoning tools are likely to be most important.

An interesting example of such issues is the tax treatment of so-called reparations payments to victims of the Holocaust and other serious human rights abuses. As you probably know, such reparations have actually been paid in a number of cases, including Holocaust victims and Japanese-Americans,[26] and proposed in several other instances, most notably by African-American groups as compensation for slavery and later discrimination. Because reparation payments involve elements of compensation for lost property and personal suffering, while also serving to recognize the victims' suffering and provide a (modest) form of penitence for the oppressors, it is often difficult to categorize them exactly for tax purposes. Such

---

[26] The Japanese-American claims were based on deportations and loss of property during the Second World War.

mundane considerations might seem trivial when compared to the human suffering involved in these payments; yet the tax treatment of reparations payments has a substantial effect on the recipients, and involves important philosophical questions about the nature of the payments and society's attitude towards them. The reparations issue also provides a fascinating example of the balance between politics and policy that characterizes the making and interpretation of tax law.

The following items consider the reparations issue as it has played out at different times and in different fora. In reading the items, consider which, if any, of our previous cases are relevant to this new problem. Is the issue being decided on the basis of these precedents, or in response to political or other factors unique to this extraordinary phenomenon?

Revenue Ruling 56-518
1956-2 C.B. 25

Claims for compensation are authorized under certain laws of the Federal Republic of Germany to be filed by persons who, as former citizens of Germany, were persecuted because of anti-Nazi persuasion or for reasons of race, faith, or philosophy of life, by the National-Socialist (Nazi) regime and thereby suffered damage to life, body, health, liberty, rights of property or ownership, or to professional or economic advancement. *Held*, (1) the compensation paid by the Federal Republic of Germany to citizens or residents of the United States pursuant to claims filed under its laws on account of such persecution which resulted in damage to life, body, health, liberty, or to professional or economic advancement, are in the nature of reimbursement for deprivation of civil or personal rights and do not constitute taxable income to the recipients for Federal income tax purposes. *See* Rev. Rul. 55-132, C.B. 1955-1, 213. *Held further*, (2) where the right of property ownership is involved, payments which are measured by the value of property taken from persecuted taxpayers do not in any event constitute taxable income where the taxpayer has not recovered his basis. *See* G.C.M. 16166, C.B. XV-1, 175 (1936). In any case in which payments measured by the value of property exceed the cost or other basis of the property, the question whether the excess represents taxable income will be determined on the basis of the facts and circumstances of each case.

GRUNFEDER v. HECKLER
United States Court of Appeals, Ninth Circuit
748 F.2d 503 (1984)

[This case addressed the question of whether German reparations to Holocaust survivors should count as "income" in determining eligibility for supplemental security income ("SSI") under the Social Security Act, a question theoretically distinct but closely related to the treatment of the payments for Federal income tax purposes. The claimant, Felicia Grunfeder, had escaped as a small child from the Warsaw Ghetto and later developed severe psychological problems as a result of her wartime experiences. The Court of Appeals, by an 8-4 vote, held that the payments received by Grunfeder from the German government (about $228 per month) should not count in determining her eligibility for SSI payments. The concluding paragraphs of the court's opinion are reproduced below:]

In sum, even though Congress has not spoken directly on the matter, we conclude that Congress's historical concern for Holocaust victims and Congress's and the SSA's treatment of analogous payments, when considered in conjunction with principles of international comity, indicate a congressional intent to exclude German reparations payments from income in determining SSI eligibility.

This case requires us to resolve a conflict between the Government's interest in allocating a limited pool of funds to support the country's aged, blind, and disabled, and the Government's interest in restoring a semblance of normal existence to Holocaust survivors who are part of our society. In resolving the matter in favor of the latter, we follow the lead of Congress. Having recognized the great suffering of people like Felicia Grunfeder, and having consistently taken steps to ameliorate their plight, Congress could not have intended to undermine its own longstanding policy favoring their welfare by counting German reparations payments as income in determining eligibility for SSI benefits.

Today's decision is in harmony with Congress's desire to provide some solace to the victims of one of human history's terrible tragedies.

* * *

[Concurring opinion omitted. — Ed.]

———————

During the 1990s, the issue of the tax treatment of Holocaust reparations arose once again in the context of new claims against Germany, Switzerland, and other countries for wartime slave labor and for assets lost in bank or insurance accounts held by Holocaust victims. The legislation discussed below was enacted in response to these claims.

General Explanation of Tax Legislation
Enacted in the 107th Congress
Joint Committee on Taxation, Pub. L. 107-16 (2001)
(Jan. 24, 2003)

* * *

VII. OTHER PROVISIONS

C. Income Tax Treatment of Certain Restitution Payments to Holocaust Victims (sec. 803 of the Act)

Present and Prior Law

Under the Code, gross income means "income from whatever source derived" except for certain items specifically exempt or excluded by statute (section 61).

There is no explicit statutory exception from gross income provided for amounts received due to status as a Holocaust victim or heir thereof.

Explanation of Provision

EGTRRA provides that excludable restitution payments made to an eligible individual (or the individual's heirs or estate) are: (1) excluded from gross income; and (2) not taken into account for any provision of the Code which takes into account excludable gross income in computing adjusted gross income (*e.g.*, taxation of Social Security benefits).

The basis of any property received by an eligible individual (or the individual's heirs or estate) that is excluded under this provision is the fair market value of such property at the time of receipt by the eligible individual (or the individual's heirs or estate).

Eligible restitution payments are any payment or distribution made to an eligible individual (or the individual's heirs or estate) which: (1) is payable by reason of the individual's status as an eligible individual (including any amount payable by any foreign country, the United States, or any foreign or domestic entity of fund established by any such country or entity, any amount payable as a result of a final resolution of legal action, and any amount payable under a law providing for payments or restitution or property); (2) constitutes the direct or indirect return of, or compensation or reparation for, assets stolen or hidden, or otherwise lost to, the individual before, during, or immediately after World War II by reason of the individual's status as an eligible individual (including any proceeds of insurance under policies issued on eligible individuals by European insurance companies immediately before and during World War II); or (3) interest payable as part of any payment or distribution described in (1) or (2), above. An eligible individual is a person who was persecuted for racial or religious reasons or on the basis of physical or mental disability or sexual orientation by Nazi Germany, or any other Axis regime, or any other Nazi-controlled or Nazi-allied country.

EGTRRA also provides that interest earned by enumerated escrow or settlement funds are excluded from tax.

Effective Date

The provision is effective for any amounts received on or after January 1, 2000. No inference is intended with respect to the income tax treatment of any amount received before January 1, 2000.

Revenue Effect

The provision is estimated to reduce Federal fiscal year budget receipts by $3 million annually in 2003–2011.

Understanding Holocaust Claims

1.   Taxation of Holocaust damage payments is a complex issue, in part, because of the difficulty of fitting such extraordinary events into existing categories. Consider the following arguments:

a. The payments should not be taxed because they are similar to government transfer (e.g., welfare) payments.

b. The payments should not be taxed because they are similar to ordinary gifts.

c. The payments should not be taxed because they are compensation for losses sustained by the same individual, i.e., people receiving payments remain no better off — one would imagine, quite a bit worse off — than people who are not Holocaust survivors.

d. The payments should be taxed because they are similar to a windfall or an award (section 74).

e. The payments should be taxed because they are an accretion to income and not a gift or other historic tax exemption.

Which of these arguments strike you as the most convincing? On which do the 1956 revenue ruling, and the subsequent 2001 legislative history, rely? Is the eventual resolution of this issue — by and large, in the taxpayers' favor — a reflection of ordinary tax principles or of political pressure together with the entirely justified sympathy for the remaining survivors?

2.   Rev. Rul. 56-518, together with the 2001 legislation, refers specifically to compensation for confiscated property. According to the ruling, compensation that is less than the basis (cost) of the property will not be taxable, while the tax treatment of compensation that exceeds the basis will be determined on a "facts and circumstances" basis.[27] Under ordinary tax principles, is there any doubt that these latter cases ought to be taxed? Or is the policy of protecting the Holocaust survivors strong enough to overcome this presumption? What if a survivor received compensation for lost income (e.g., wages for slave labor) that would have been taxed if earned directly, but that would arguably be exempted under the new provision? Is this a serious inequity, or is it too trivial to consider under the circumstances?

3.   What do you make of the "international comity" argument in *Grunfeder*? Should this be a factor in domestic tax decisions? If the German government wanted to be sure the benefits carried a sufficient after-tax value, why didn't they simply make the awards bigger? Do you think they considered this issue? Should they have?

4.   Recall the *Kaiser* decision regarding the tax treatment of employee strike benefits. Would this case have been better resolved by emphasizing the recovery of capital or compensation for injury issues, as was done in Rev. Rul. 56-518, rather

---

[27]   This situation would exist, for example, if a taxpayer had purchased a house for $5,000 in (say) 1914, which had somehow appreciated to $50,000 in value by the time it was confiscated, and was lucky enough to receive compensation for all $50,000.

than the section 102 problem? How would you compare the decisions in these two cases?

5.   What do you think would be both the political and practical consequences of imposing tax on reparation payments?

On reparations for slavery, see Kevin Hopkins, *Forgive U.S. Our Debts? Righting the Wrongs of Slavery*, 89 Geo. L.J. 2531 (2001).

For a website making the case for reparations to African-Americans, see www.ncobra.com.

Additional Assignment — Chapter 1[28]

Although this casebook is largely self-contained, the real-world practice of tax law will require you to make extensive use of the tax library. The source materials for tax law differ in many ways from those for constitutional or common law subjects — contracts, torts, etc. — that you are familiar with from your first-year courses. This is true whether one relies primarily on "hard" copy materials or, as is increasingly the case, on the Lexis or Westlaw computer research systems. Many features of tax research are shared by other statutory fields such as environmental, corporate, securities, labor, and employment or anti-discrimination law, so that learning these skills will place you in good stead even if you do not become a tax lawyer.

The following exercise tests your skills in locating primary and secondary tax resources relating to issues (the gift exclusion and "convenience of the employer" rule) discussed in the preceding chapter. In some cases, you are asked to devise alternate strategies involving computer or hard copy research. All of these materials should be available in any law school library.[29]

Answer the following questions, using your law school library, Lexis or Westlaw computer services, or other sources as directed:

1. There is often more than one single way to approach a tax problem. Although section 119 does not generally apply to police officers' meal allowances, the case of *Christey v. United States*, 841 F.2d 809 (8th Cir. 1988), holds that, under certain circumstances, police officers may deduct the cost of their meals as a section 162 business expense.

   a. One place to find this case is, obviously, on page 809 of volume 841 of the Federal Reporter, 2d series. What are two other hard copy (i.e., not computer) citations for the case? (Hint: one of these citations will be in the U.S. Tax Cases (CCH) series, and the other in the American Federal Tax Reports, published by Prentice Hall/RIA.)

   b. *Christey* cited a Tax Court decision, *Cooper v. Commissioner*, which held that otherwise personal expenses may be deductible if the nature of the job gives them a predominantly business character. Who was (were) the judge(s) in the Cooper case, and on what page of what volume of what reporter did you find out?

2. Suppose that you were assigned to research the application of section 119 to airline or railroad employees who were given free food during their time in transit.

   a. Where could you find a hard copy annotation of cases and rulings pertaining to this topic? Please give precise volume and page citations, and name at least two relevant cases not previously mentioned. (Hint: One location should be in the CCH loose-leaf reporter, and the other in the RIA

---

[28] This assignment, although part of an odd-numbered chapter, is possibly best completed in writing, although the instructor may prefer to grade it on a pass-fail basis.

[29] The Background Chapter of this book contains an introduction to the sources of tax law and their significance.

United States Tax Reporter service (this is different from the Federal Tax Coordinator designed primarily for accountants' use).)

b. Describe in words (not more than three sentences) how you would conduct the same research using the Lexis or Westlaw computer system. Indicate specific libraries and files and specific search term(s) that you would use.

c. Do you think the research above would be more efficiently conducted by hard copy or by computer? Why? What if, instead of the above, the project concerned the valuation of prizes and awards under *Turner* and related cases? What if the assignment involved a memorandum explaining to the client the general treatment of personal injury awards?

3. Section 431 of the Economic Growth and Tax Relief Reconciliation Act of 2001 (EGTRRA) reinserted in the Code a limited deduction for higher education expenses. These expenses had previously been nondeductible although a credit was permitted under certain limited circumstances. This provision, which is located in section 222 of the Code, is discussed further in Chapter 6.

a. Suppose you needed to know the effective date or a transitional provision relating to the legislation above.[30] Where in the library could you find the actual statutory language of the provision, that is, the language as originally enacted by Congress before incorporation into the Internal Revenue Code? Give two (2) alternate citations, including precise volumes and page numbers, and describe the location in your library where these are found.

b. Where would one find the relevant committee report language explaining the reasons and purpose of the provision above? (Again, please give two alternate citations, including volumes, page numbers, and approximate physical location). If you did find it, how important would it be?

4. A well-known law professor wrote a 1996 article in the Tax Law Review that includes an extensive discussion of statutory interpretation in tax cases. While not focusing specifically on any of the issues above, it might conceivably be relevant to their resolution.

a. What is the exact citation for the article above, and on what pages does it discuss the parallels in interpreting the tax code and the UCC?

b. Provide the citations for at least two more recent articles on statutory interpretation in tax cases. (The Index to Federal Tax Articles, which should be available in your law library, is one possible way to track down these articles.)

5. In Chapter 8, Section I.A, of your casebook is reproduced Revenue Ruling 94-38, relating to the tax treatment of environmental clean-up facilities. (The principal issue, which will be discussed in Chapter 8, involves the timing of the deduction for such facilities). The citation indicates that this revenue ruling is found on volume 1, page 35 of the 1994 IRS Cumulative Bulletin.

---

[30] Transitory provisions of this nature are frequently not included in the Code.

a. What are the number and topic of the Revenue Ruling (or Revenue Procedure) immediately following Rev. Rul. 94-38 in the cumulative bulletin? Since the revenue rulings aren't in numerical order, how are they arranged?

b. How would one go about determining if Rev. Rul. 94-38 were still good law, i.e., that it hasn't been reversed or superseded by a subsequent ruling? For that matter, how would you do that with a case like *Christey*, above?

A Closing Thought

Now that you have completed your assignment, you have probably noticed there is no single, universal strategy for tax research. Instead there are different strategies for different problems. If you are researching a relatively narrow question, like the gift exclusion or the applicability of the fringe benefit rules, it probably makes the most sense to proceed directly to the computer or hard-copy loose-leaf service, identifying cases or rulings on the relevant issue and then using these materials in a manner similar to nontax research. This approach saves time and money for your clients, who will not wish to pay you to reinvent the wheel for each project.

If by contrast the project involves multiple questions or areas of tax law, so that you are not entirely sure what the question (let alone the answer) is, treatises and other secondary source materials are often extremely helpful. At best, these materials will help you to focus your research and guide you to the right primary sources. At worst, they provide you with some intellectual context, and the comfort that others have previously asked and answered the same questions you are now asking.

The point above leads once again to the choice — computers or hard copy — that is so important for beginning attorneys. My own sense is that computers have largely displaced the traditional tax library for the first kind of research described above, that is, focused research on specific provisions where the researcher already knows the general outline of the law in the relevant area. The speed of computers, and their ability to do pinpoint searches on specific Code sections ("368 and convertible debentures," "74 and quiz shows," etc.), usually outweighs the cost in this area. For the second, background type of research, many lawyers still prefer hard volumes, although even here the principal texts, together with cases, rulings and other primary materials, are increasingly available on CDs or similar databases. This is particularly true as clients may be reluctant to pay the cost of computer "browsing" before their particular problem has been identified. Even if you intend to rely primarily on computers, it is worth familiarizing yourself with the tax or other specialized library at your law firm or other law office. The computer is after all a search engine rather than an original source of knowledge, and research materials remain largely the same whether they are accessed on-line or by more traditional methods.

Chapter 2

NONCASH COMPENSATION AND FRINGE BENEFITS

In Chapter 1 we considered three problems in the definition of income: food and lodging provided "for the convenience of the employer" (section 119), the tax treatment of windfalls and gifts, and the issue of personal injury damage awards. Because each of these was to some extent a borderline issue, they provided important insights into the application of tax policy criteria, and into the use of sources (statutes, regulations, previous case law) by taxpayers and their lawyers. We have also begun to see the faint outlines of a broader system, in which any form of current enrichment is taxed under section 61, unless a specific statutory or case law exception has been provided. In the nature of an introduction, we have pursued these issues in only limited detail, and have yet to put much meat on the bones of our general theory.

Chapter 2 considers a single issue, the tax treatment of noncash compensation and fringe benefits, in greater detail. Fringe benefits include a wide range of items, ranging from health and life insurance to free air travel and company cars, which are provided by employers to employees free of charge or at a substantially reduced cost. In theory, all these items would be taxable under section 61, which states that "gross income means all income from whatever source derived" and specifically includes fringe benefits as an item subject to tax.[1] In practice, there are good reasons for excluding many or most of them. These include the difficulty of valuing fringe benefits,, enforcement problems, and the political unpopularity of taxing items that people consider "part of the job" and have never thought of as taxable compensation. Balancing against this is the horizontal inequity of allowing those who receive noncash benefits to avoid payment of tax, and the fear of extensive revenue loss if fringe benefits expand without limit. In short, this area involves many of the same issues first observed in the *Benaglia* case, but spread several times wider and involving a larger variety of situations. The amounts at stake are not trivial: a quarter or more of many employees' compensation consists of tax-free fringe benefits, and the amount would surely be larger if efforts to rein in these exemptions had not been made.

Most of the law regarding fringe benefits is statutory or regulatory in nature, and the provisions are often more complex than those in Chapter 1. This chapter will thus enable us to develop the skill of reading and interpreting the Code and Regulations in the manner of a real, practicing tax lawyer. Later in the chapter, we will consider two contemporary issues, involving frequent flyer mileage and college tuition discounts, in which the statute is (or historically has been) uncertain and in which there is strong political pressure to reduce or eliminate payment of tax. In

---

[1] *See also* Treas. Reg. § 1.61-2(d) ("if services are paid for in property, the fair market value of the property taken in payment must be included in income as compensation.")

such cases, the room for interpretation is wider, and political or other factors may trump sound tax policy and lead to surprising or inconsistent results.

Understanding fringe benefits requires an understanding of the real-world economics that lie behind the transaction in question. This chapter, accordingly, discusses both tax and nontax aspects of employee compensation, and concludes with a problem designed to test your planning and evaluation abilities in a fringe benefit context. The chapter also includes several problems that relate to fringe benefit tax policy, notably the choice between tax subsidies and direct spending — a recurring issue in this field.

I. THE FRINGE BENEFIT PROBLEM: SOME HISTORICAL BACKGROUND

In a modern society, the great majority of compensation takes the form of cash or cash-equivalents (bank deposits, electronic funds transfers, and so forth). This is true for several reasons. For one, it is simply clumsy to pay people in goods or services; imagine workers carting home piles of food or heating oil at the end of each regular pay period. (Something like this actually happens in countries, like post-Soviet Russia, in which the currency loses so much value as to become unreliable.) Employees also differ in their preferred uses of money: some spend more on housing, some on food and entertainment, and some prefer to save or invest their money rather than to immediately spend it. Paying people in cash allows them to make their own choices, and allows the economy to function in a more modern and efficient manner.

Why then does anyone pay noncash compensation? There appear to be three principal answers. The first is that there are many benefits which an employer can provide free or at reduced price to its employees without incurring any substantial additional cost, because it is already providing a much larger volume of the same benefits to its paying clients or customers. For example, an airline may provide free (or nearly free) flights to its employees, or a restaurant may allow its employees to eat a limited amount of free food, without costing the company much money, since the airline and the kitchen are going to be operating whether or not the employees use them. These "inherent" benefits may be an attractive way to improve employee morale and sweeten the compensation package without seriously affecting the employer's bottom line. Indeed, most employees probably don't think of these items as compensation at all, but merely "part of the job," and — like *Benaglia* in the previous section — are surprised to learn that they may be taxable in certain cases.

A second reason relates to the economic and political incentives for business employers. To remain competitive, businesses are often under pressure to reduce wages, or at least not to increase them beyond acceptable levels. At various times, notably during World War II and again during the 1970s, the federal government has imposed "wage and price controls," which forbid increasing wages beyond stated amounts. Increasing fringe benefits may be a convenient or even a deliberate strategy for evading such rules. A perception that fringe benefits are not taxable, even if this perception is not always accurate, may further encourage employers to substitute fringe benefits for cash compensation.

A third reason involves paternalism on the part of employers, the federal government, or both combined. While in theory employees should be free to spend money as they choose, there remains a fear that they will waste all or part of their income, failing to provide adequately for education, health, retirement, and other individual or family needs. Providing employees with, e.g., health insurance or pension benefits, in return for a somewhat reduced salary, may be a way of ensuring that these needs are met even by otherwise irresponsible or profligate individuals.

The Government has a particular interest in encouraging such benefits, both as a matter of general social policy and because governmental agencies might otherwise be called on to provide the same benefits through direct spending programs.

From a tax perspective, the issue of fringe benefits presents a classic conflict between the goals of equity, on the one hand, and simplicity or administrability, on the other. Allowing fringe benefits to go untaxed would appear to violate horizontal equity, since taxpayers with similar economic incomes would be taxed on different amounts. Vertical equity may also suffer if, as is frequently the case, the juicier benefits go to more highly paid employees. But taxing fringe benefits is an administrative nightmare: valuation is difficult or impossible, and the items don't usually show up on taxpayers' withholding slips or similar documents, so that it may be difficult even to determine who has taken advantage of fringe benefits and who hasn't. Encouraging employers to provide tax-free health care, retirement, and similar benefits may also be an attractive alternative to direct governmental assistance, especially if the cost of this subsidy is hidden from public view. These factors, together with political pressure, may encourage Congress and the IRS to leave many important fringe benefits untaxed.

II.   RESOLVING THE PROBLEM: THE FRINGE BENEFIT STATUTES

A.   "Inherent" Fringe Benefits: Section 132

The fringe benefit provisions reflect the competing pressures described above. For many years, the Code has contained special tax breaks designed to encourage employer-provided life insurance (section 79), health insurance (sections 104 and 105), pension and retirement benefits (section 401 et seq.), and other noncash compensation deemed to serve important social or policy goals. (We refer to these below, somewhat grandiosely, as "paternalistic" fringe benefits.) More recently these have been joined by provisions covering employer assistance for educational expenses, child care, and various other expenditures. While these programs are anything but fringe-like in character — it is estimated that the exclusion for health insurance alone costs the Government over half a trillion dollars in annual foregone tax revenues — they are politically popular and have been largely impervious to contemporary tax reform efforts.[2]

---

[2] Joel Slemrod & Jon Bakija, Taxing Ourselves: A Citizen's Guide to the Debate Over Taxes 34 (2008).

The issue of "inherent" or "part of the job" fringe benefits — free travel, employee discounts and so forth — took somewhat longer to resolve. Under section 61 of the Code, these items are plainly taxable, and should be included in the employee's income at their fair market value. Until the 1970s, this rule went unenforced: employees did not, by and large, report income on such items and the IRS, by and large, did not challenge this underreporting. During the 1970s, a demand for revenue, coupled with a sense that the fringe benefit bonanza had gotten out of hand, led the IRS to promulgate regulations subjecting most remaining categories of fringe benefits to tax. Congress blocked implementation of these regulations on at least two different occasions, but in 1984 legislated on the subject, enacting the provisions that became section 132 of the Code. These provisions essentially permitted the most popular categories of fringe benefits to remain untaxed, provided that they were not overgenerous and, in some cases, that they were provided to both higher- and lower-ranking employees on a more or less equal basis. Section 132 has remained in existence, with relatively minor changes, for over two decades, and appears to have become a relatively stable part of the tax law.

The materials that follow pose a number of questions regarding the present fringe benefit rules, beginning with section 132 and proceeding to other, more esoteric provisions. As you answer these questions, try to keep in mind the conflict between equity and administrability that characterizes the fringe benefit issue, and how this conflict plays itself out in individual tax rules. Keep in mind also the role being played by various Governmental authorities. Are the regulations consistent with the statute or legislative history, or have the Treasury Department and IRS effectively created their own law in this area? Finally, consider the effect of these rules on private businesses. Do the existing tax provisions encourage businesses to replace cash compensation with nontaxable fringe benefits, and if so, what is the effect on the companies and the people who work for them?

Understanding Section 132

Section 132, like section 119, is an exclusion provision, which exempts from tax various items that would otherwise be taxable under section 61 of the Code. Although they deal with different subjects, the structure of such exclusions tends to be rather similar. Typically they begin with a general statement, like 132(a), which states that one or more categories of benefits will be tax-exempt provided that they meet the rules contained in the remainder of the section. In section 132, these categories (section 132(a)(1) through (8)) include no-additional-cost service, qualified employee discount, working condition fringe, *de minimis* fringe, qualified transportation fringe, qualified moving expense reimbursement, qualified retirement planning services, and qualified military base realignment and closure fringe. The first four of these categories correspond, very roughly, to the inherent fringe benefits described in Part A above, i.e., fringe benefits that cost relatively little to the employer and/or are commonly thought of as "part of the job" by the recipient employees. (The remaining four categories, were later additions to the original statute.)

The statute next provides detailed definitions of each of the excluded fringe benefits, including numerical and other limitations for each category of benefit (section 132(b) through (g)). For example, section 132(c), which defines qualified employee discounts, contains rules limiting the amount of the permitted discount and subjecting excessive discounts to tax. Finally, there are rules of application that cut across the preceding categories, or that deal with situations not covered by the previous sections (section 132(h) through (k)). For example, section 132(h) concerns the treatment of employees' families, while section 132(j)(1) contains a requirement of "nondiscrimination" between higher- and lower-paid employees. Various combinations of these rules apply to each of the categories identified in section 132(a), so that reading the statute requires both applying the specific rules applicable to that type of fringe benefit and determining which, if any, of the general rules apply to that category.

Like any statute, section 132 answers only a small portion of the questions regarding fringe benefit taxation. The regulations (section 1.132-1 through -8) answer more questions, and provide examples of the more confusing provisions. Where the statute and regulations are not dispositive, the practitioner must consult cases, IRS rulings, or the broader policy of the statute in order to answer the question at hand. The practitioner's goal must thus be not only to know the technical provisions of the Code, but to discern their underlying logic, so as to answer questions not specifically addressed by the statutory language.

The following questions test your knowledge of section 132 and the section 132 regulations in some detail. Take your time in answering them; the answers will be more difficult to locate than in section 119, but they should all be there somewhere.

Using the Sources

1.   Under section 132 and the corresponding regulations, which of the following items are exempt from tax under section 132 and — if they are taxable — how might they be valued? Be sure to indicate the authority for your answer (i.e., the specific Code or Regulation section that you believe is applicable), and whether the answer appears clear-cut or requires further investigation.

   a. A nice office with a view of the river.

   b. The use of a company car for business purposes.

   c. The use of a company car for personal travel.

   d. Taxi fare and a free meal (not exceeding $35) to anyone who works after 8 p.m. What if everyone in the office works late (every day)?

   e. Free parking (cash value of $150 per month).

   f. A free subway pass (cash value of $15 per month).

   g. A subsidized (i.e., reduced price) company cafeteria. (What if there is a 100 percent subsidy (i.e., the food is free)?)

   h. Free standby flights, available to airline employees. (What if the airline company also owns a hotel chain, and the flights are available to hotel employees?)

i. A 15 percent discount on facials, made available to employees of a beauty parlor.

j. The sale "at cost" of stereo equipment to the employees of a music supply store. (Does each separate item have to be sold at no less than cost, or is it acceptable that, on average, the store covers its costs for all items?)

2.   For any of the items listed in Question 1 above, would it matter if the benefit was provided only to executive employees? If it were extended to the employee's family?

3.   Review your answers to each item in Question 1 above. Of the items that you believed might be subject to tax — that is, outside the scope of section 132 — how many were plainly taxable, and how many were difficult or borderline cases? Are there any cases in which you think the benefit is probably taxable, but there is a reasonable argument in favor of exclusion, so that you would encourage a client to take the latter position on his or her tax return? How, if at all, would your answer be affected by section 6662 of the Code, imposing a 20 percent penalty for understatements of tax where there was not "substantial authority" for the taxpayer's position?

Law and Planning

Your client, Consolidated Industries, operates three businesses: a bank, an airline, and a department store. The company — especially its banking division — is engaged in a fierce competition for executive talent, and thinks that section 132-type fringe benefits would be a way to attract such talent without significantly increasing its expenses. To reduce costs the company would prefer to restrict benefits to the smallest groups possible. It is aware of the nondiscrimination rule contained in section 132 but believes that it may be possible to "get around" this rule with creative tax planning.

1.   To what extent, if any, could the company achieve its goals by offering each of the following alternate fringe benefits?

a. Free travel on the company airline, which could be made available to all or a specified category of employees, e.g., only executive employees or only employees of one or more of the company's operating divisions. (Feel free to suggest what specific category or categories of employees would receive this benefit, and how this would advance the company's tax and business goals.)

b. Discount purchases at the company department store, which would be available to all or a specified category of the company's employees. (Once again, please indicate what category.)

c. Free parking and a free on-site athletic facility, to be available to all or a specified category of employees.

2.   Which of the above appears to be the best alternative, and why? How did you balance tax and nontax (business) motivations in making this choice? What, if

anything, do your answers to these questions tell you about the effectiveness of the section 132(j) nondiscrimination rule, and of section 132 generally?

3.   Did you have any ethical qualms in answering the preceding two questions?

Politics and Policy

1.   Now that you have read and applied section 132, how does it resolve the underlying policy issues (fairness vs. administrability, policy vs. politics, etc.) that characterize the fringe benefits area? Does the statute reflect a coherent policy at all, or does it allow a bunch of unrelated tax breaks to continue because nobody was courageous enough to get rid of them? What is the effect of provisions like sections 132(i) (regarding reciprocal agreements between employers) and 132(h)(3) (special rule for parents in the case of air transportation) on statutory coherence? What are these provisions doing here, anyway?

2.   Why do you suppose that the nondiscrimination rule (section 132(j)(1)) applies only to no-additional-cost services and qualified employee discounts? Is discrimination less of a problem for *de minimis* or working condition fringes? Or would it be too difficult to enforce such a rule in these cases?

3.   A frequent criticism of the fringe benefit rules — and other tax incentives — is that they put small businesses at a disadvantage compared to larger competitors. For example, section 132(j)(4) provides an exemption for on-premises athletic facilities, which are likely to be affordable only to large companies, but not for health club memberships or similar items that might be used by smaller employers. Is this a justified concern, or should small businesses just stop complaining?

4.   Assume that you were a lobbyist and wanted to encourage Congress to maintain or expand a number of existing fringe benefits under section 132. What policy arguments (horizontal and vertical equity, economic efficiency, and simplicity or administrability) would you make on behalf of each of the following provisions? On a political level, what entities (businesses, labor, consumers groups, etc.) would be likely to support you in protecting these fringe benefits, and how would you go about building a coalition in support of this outcome?

a. No additional cost services (e.g., standby travel).

b. Employee discounts (goods and services).

c. Qualified transportation fringes (§ 132(f)).

d. *De minimis* and working condition fringes.

Now assume you were a public interest lawyer and wanted to reduce the perceived abuse of fringe benefits and the resulting revenue loss. Which of these items would you emphasize, and how would you make your argument?

B.   Paternalistic Fringe Benefits: Health, Retirement, and Other Noble Purposes

The fringe benefits covered by section 132 tend to be limited in nature and are at least arguably inherent to the employee's job. For these reasons, it is perhaps inevitable that the Code would exclude them. The same cannot be said for life and health insurance, pensions, and numerous other benefits excluded from tax. There is nothing "fringe" about a multi-million dollar pension plan, or health insurance for tens of millions of workers. Nor is it particularly hard to measure these benefits: employers keep exacting records of their contributions to insurance and pension plans, and report the amounts to employees on their paychecks or similar statements.

Why then are these benefits exempt? Part of the reason is historical: such benefits were traditionally much smaller than they are today, and by the time they got larger a precedent for nontaxation had already been established. (It's harder to close an old loophole than it is to create a new one.) But there is also a paternalistic aspect to these provisions. In theory, people could simply be paid cash and, being reasonably intelligent, would be trusted to provide for their own health care and retirement needs. In practice this doesn't happen, and governments everywhere find themselves making some provision for health, retirement, and other public welfare needs. In most countries, this is accomplished by direct Government spending, e.g., national health insurance or national retirement plans.[3]

In the United States, for various reasons, we prefer to do the same things through private employers. Instead of direct spending, this is accomplished by means of tax incentives: by providing advantageous tax treatment, the Code encourages private employers to provide health, retirement, and other benefits that the Government would otherwise have to provide on its own. The fringe benefit provisions are thus good examples of the "tax expenditure" phenomenon, under which tax deductions, exclusions, and so forth are designed to advance goals that might otherwise be handled by government spending programs. A similar logic pertains to deductions for charitable contributions and other similar items.

The reliance on private initiative may be admirable, but it raises several questions. One obvious point is that it does nothing for people who are unemployed or work for companies that do not provide the relevant benefits. In particular many service employees, especially those working for smaller companies, receive little or no health insurance and similar benefits. A related problem is vertical equity: by providing tax advantages for those who are lucky enough to receive benefits, but nothing for those who don't, the Code may actually increase the distinction between higher- and lower-paid employees. This is corrected to some extent by nondiscrimination provisions,[4] requiring that, e.g., health and pension benefits be available across income categories, but like the section 132 anti-discrimination

---

[3] The United States has a national retirement plan in the form of Social Security and Medicare, the former providing a minimum level of retirement income and the latter health benefits for aged or disabled individuals; but these payments are widely viewed as inadequate to ensure a happy retirement, and are typically supplemented by pensions or equivalent private savings.

[4] See, e.g., I.R.C. § 105(b) (nondiscrimination provision with respect to self-insured medical expense

rules, these provisions are only incompletely effective. Finally there are the rules themselves, which tend to be technical and somewhat arbitrary, even by the standards of the tax code. For example, section 79 imposes a $50,000 limit on the tax exemption for the cost of group-term life insurance, while section 106 provides an unlimited exemption for accident or health insurance, without any obvious reason why these two items should be treated differently.

For practitioners, this is a largely "black-letter" subject, the principal challenge being to read the law carefully and ensure that benefit plans comply with the maze of technical rules that are applicable to them. This is a lot harder than it may sound. Unlike section 132, many of these laws were drafted in piecemeal fashion; even when they are well drafted, their significance depends on the interplay of different laws and regulations rather than a patient reading of any one provision. Paternalistic fringe benefits also present important challenges for tax and business planning, since the same fringe benefits may not be appealing to all employees, and management may be inclined (once again) to provide a different type or level of benefits to more highly compensated employees.

The following questions concern primarily benefits relating to health (sections 104-106) and life (section 79 and 101) insurance, together with the items that did not fit into any one category. (Pension benefits are considered in Chapter 4.) To ensure that you engage the statute, we will forego a lengthy introduction and jump right into the problems. One hint: sections 104, 105, and 106 constitute a unified (if not necessarily logical) approach to the health insurance problem, so you will have to read these sections together to answer the relevant questions. In particular, section 106(a) refers to an issue that comes, chronologically speaking, before the issue in section 105; so you may wish to read these sections "out of order" so as to increase your comprehension.

Using the Sources

Read sections 79, 101, and 104 through 106 of the Code and answer the following questions, indicating the specific section(s) or subsection(s) on which you are relying for your answer:

1.   A's employer, Washington Industries, purchases health insurance for A at a cost of $5,000 per year.

   a. Does A have income at the time that the employer purchases the health insurance?

   b. Suppose that A develops a serious illness and the health insurance, purchased by A's employer, pays $25,000 to cover A's medical expenses, as well as an additional $5,000, which is automatically paid to cover that kind of illness. Is A taxable on either or both of these amounts?

   c. Suppose that, in addition to the items described above, the insurance company pays A $50,000 in lost wages to cover the time A was absent from

---

reimbursement plans); I.R.C. § 401(a) (imposing minimum funding and nondiscrimination requirements on qualified pension plans).

work as a result of the illness.

d. Would your answer to any of the above questions be different if the employer is "self-insured," that is, compensates employee health claims out of its own money rather than by using an insurance company?

e. Would any of your answers be different if A (i.e., the employee) purchased the insurance using her own personal funds?

f. What if the employee and the employer split the cost of the insurance?

g. What additional facts, if any, would you need to know in order to answer any of the foregoing questions?

2.   In addition to health insurance, A's employer purchases $250,000 of group-term life insurance for each of its employees, with the employees being required to pay one-half of the cost and the employer paying the remaining half.[5] Is any amount included in A's income in the year the insurance is purchased? If A dies, is any of the $250,000 benefit taxable to A's estate? (Hint: You will need to look at more than one Code section in order to answer this question.)

3.   Explain, in plain English, what is happening in section 101(g). What kind of person might be interested in knowing about this provision? How would the provision help them?

Law and Planning

1.   Review the questions under "Using the Sources" above, and choose at least two cases in which you found the employee taxable on the benefit provided. If you were an employer designing a new fringe benefit package, is there anything you could do to avert (or at least reduce) this payment of tax, without sacrificing your broader business and financial goals? How important would tax, as opposed to business factors, be in making this decision?

2.   In general, how do you think that the tax laws affect the amount of health and life insurance that are offered to employees and the way that these plans are structured?

Politics and Policy

1.   What do you think is the policy reason for each of the following provisions?

a. The distinction between payments related to, and unrelated to, the period of absence from work (§ 105(c)).

b. The first clause of section 105(b) ("Except in the case of amounts attributable to (and not in excess of) deductions allowed under section 213 . . . for any prior taxable year . . .").

---

[5] The $250,000 here refers to the amount of the coverage (i.e., the amount that the insurer would pay on the death of the insured), rather than the cost of the insurance, which is presumably much lower.

c. The nondiscrimination rule for self-insured medical plans (§ 105(h)). (How, if at all, does this differ from the section 132 nondiscrimination rules?)

2.   The Code provides a limit on the amount of employee life insurance that can be provided tax free (section 79(a)), but there is no similar limit on health insurance plans. What is the justification, if any, for this difference? What would you think of a proposal to tax employer-provided health insurance in excess of a specified dollar amount, and use the funds to pay for health insurance for unemployed or otherwise uninsured individuals? What about an alternate proposal to retain an unlimited exclusion for employer-provided health insurance, and pay for expanded health coverage by increasing the tax rate on upper-income taxpayers?

3.   Consider further the proposals contained in the last sentence of item 2. What are the likely political constituencies in favor of and against these proposed changes? Suppose that you were (i) a public interest advocate trying to enact the proposal, and (ii) a lobbyist hired to oppose it. What arguments would you make in each case, and how successful do you think they would be?

III.   THE FRONTIERS OF FRINGE BENEFITS: FREQUENT FLYERS, SCRAPPY STUDENTS, AND THE PROBLEM OF IMPUTED INCOME

From the materials above, it might appear that fringe benefit taxation is a rather dry, open-and-shut proposition. Three examples serve to demonstrate that this is not always the case. The first, frequent flyer mileage, demonstrates the difficulty of determining fringe benefit (or other tax) tax outcomes by a purely mechanical reading of the statutory language, particularly when there are new factual developments not anticipated when the original language was drafted. The frequent flyer problem also demonstrates the incredible political pressure that is placed on the IRS to refrain from taxing popular benefits, especially those that benefit the "middle class" and its representatives. The second example, involving scholarships and other education tax incentives, demonstrates the interaction of fringe benefits with other tax provisions and the numerous planning challenges — not to mention near-incoherence of policy — that result from this interaction. Both examples provide a taste of the navigation between conflicting rules and interpretations that characterize the real world of the sophisticated tax practitioner.

A third example, involving the tax treatment of imputed or "psychic" income, explores the limits of fringe benefit taxation and the role of policy analysis in understanding even the most basic tax rules.

A.   Frequent Flyer Mileage

A good example of how the tax system functions — some would say malfunctions — in a changing world is the case of frequent flyer mileage. As you probably know, frequent flyer miles are a promotion employed by various airlines to encourage repeated use of the airline by business (or frequent vacation) travelers. Each time that a passenger flies on a particular airline, she receives a credit based on the number of miles in the flight she has taken. Once she accumulates sufficient credit, she is entitled to a free or reduced fare flight of a specified length on the same airline. For example, a total of 25,000 miles might entitle the passenger to a free domestic flight, while 50,000 miles might yield a free trip anywhere in the world. Many airlines participate in joint frequent flyer programs, so that a flight to Topeka might be the first step toward a free flight to Tokyo, or similarly exotic combinations. (Coffee bars and other businesses have adopted similar policies, although the airline programs remain the most famous.)

Frequent flyer mileage presents at least two tax issues. The first concerns miles which an individual accumulates by virtue of his or her own, self-financed personal travel. Are they best described as a windfall, taxable under section 61, or as a purchase price adjustment, which remains untaxed? For example, if a person bought $10,000 of airline tickets, and received $2,500 of free flights, should they be treated as having received a $2,500 windfall, or simply as having negotiated a 20 percent price reduction, paying $10,000 for a total of $12,500 in airline travel? This issue has generally been resolved in favor of the purchase price theory, so that an individual or company accumulating and using its own frequent flyer mileage usually pays no income tax.[6]

A second, more daunting problem involves business travelers who accumulate frequent flyer mileage on company-related travel and then convert the mileage to personal use. Suppose that Ernie Executive accumulates 25,000 in frequent flyer miles while conducting business trips for Continental Flange, Inc., for which he is a middle-level manager. Since the miles are in his name, and since the company is willing to pay full price for his future business trips, Ernie uses the credits to take himself and his wife on a free trip to Florida for the winter vacation. (Some employers don't permit this, but many others do.) Hasn't Ernie effectively received a fringe benefit, in the form of a free personal trip which would otherwise have cost him a substantial amount of money? Since the benefit is provided by Ernie's employer, and is outside the scope of section 132 — the service is not offered by Ernie's employer in the ordinary course of its trade or business and may violate the nondiscrimination or other provisions of the statute, as well — shouldn't this benefit be subject to tax? Or is this being overly literal, compulsive, and Scrooge-like?

The following materials consider frequent flyer taxation, and especially the fringe benefit issue, in greater detail. As you read the materials, consider how the various decision-making bodies apply the law to a new, largely unprecedented issue. To what extent do they rely on the statutory language; to what extent on amorphous policy concepts (fairness, efficiency, simplicity, etc.); and to what extent do they, well, drop the ball?

---

[6] These discounts are not provided by the employer and hence are not subject to the requirements of section 132(c).

CHARLEY v. COMMISSIONER
United States Court of Appeals, Ninth Circuit
91 F.3d 72 (9th Cir. 1996)

O'Scannlain, J:

Do travel credits converted to cash in a personal travel account established by an employer constitute gross income to the employee for federal income tax purposes?

I

Dr. Philip Charley and his wife Katherine Charley appeal the tax court's determination of an income tax deficiency for tax year 1988 in the amount of $882 and an addition to tax of $44 pursuant to Internal Revenue Code ("IRC") § 6653. We affirm on the merits and reverse the penalty.

During 1988, Truesdail Laboratories ("Truesdail") engaged in the testing business, including testing urine for horse racing activities and investigating the causes of industrial accidents. Philip was the President of Truesdail and, together with Katherine, owned 50.255% of its shares. Philip performed various services for Truesdail including inspecting mechanical devices suspected of failure.

Philip, in his capacity as an employee of Truesdail, traveled to various accident sites to inspect machinery. Truesdail had an "unwritten policy" that the frequent flyer miles that were earned during an employee's travel for Truesdail became the sole property of the employee.

During the year at issue, the following procedures were followed by Truesdail with respect to Philip's travel:

(1) A client would engage the services of Truesdail and would direct that Philip travel to a particular accident site;

(2) If Philip chose to travel to the site by air, Truesdail would bill the client for round-trip, first class air travel;

(3) Philip would instruct a travel agent, Archer Travel Services ("Archer"), to arrange for coach service to and from the site, but to charge Truesdail for first class travel;

(4) Philip then would use his frequent flyer miles (largely earned in connection with his business travel for Truesdail) to upgrade the coach ticket to first class; and

(5) Philip would instruct Archer to transfer funds to his personal travel account amounting to the difference in price between the first class ticket for which Truesdail was charged and the coach ticket, albeit upgraded, which Philip actually used.

Over the course of 1988, Archer maintained separate travel accounts for Philip and Truesdail. Philip took four business trips that year, and using the procedures outlined above, received $3,149.93 in his personal travel account from his "sale" of the frequent flyer miles.

The parties stipulated that Philip and Katherine did not know that the receipt of the travel credits was taxable income, and that they did not intend to conceal the process utilized to obtain the travel credits.

The tax court held that the travel credits constituted taxable income. The tax court also upheld imposition of an addition to tax by the Internal Revenue Service ("IRS") of $44 pursuant to former IRC § 6653(a)(1), which provided for an addition to tax if any part of an underpayment resulted from negligence or intentional disregard of rules and regulations.

The petitioners appeal both the tax court's determination of an income tax deficiency and its imposition of the addition to tax (penalty).

III

The statute at issue, IRC § 61, provides that gross income "means all income from whatever source derived." Gross income has been defined as an "undeniable accession[] to wealth, clearly realized, and over which the taxpayer[] [has] complete dominion." *Commissioner v. Glenshaw Glass*, 348 U.S. 426, 431 (1955). The tax court noted that there was no indication Philip could not use the travel credits for personal travel or redeem them for cash. Consequently, the tax court upheld the IRS' determination of deficiency on the ground that:

Whether we regard this fact situation as a straight "rip-off" by petitioner of his employer or a highly technical "sale" of his frequent flyer miles (which have zero basis) for the credits, the fact remains that petitioner was wealthier after the transaction than before. In such circumstances, the accretion of wealth is the receipt of income.

The Charleys do not dispute the tax court's finding that travel credits were Philip's to use for personal travel. Nor do they dispute the tax court's conclusion that Philip had sole control over the credits in his account. Rather, the Charleys argue that no taxable event occurred. We find this argument unpersuasive.

The Charleys argue that this case raises the question of whether, in the abstract, frequent flyer miles constitute gross income. We disagree and do not reach that issue.

As the tax court noted, the case can be analyzed in one of two ways. First, the travel credits which were converted to cash can be characterized as additional compensation. On this view, Philip received property from his employer in the form of an account upon which he could draw up to $3,149.93, which he did. This is so because Truesdail paid for first-class airfare and allowed Archer to credit Philip's account with the difference between the first-class price and the coach price. The funds constituting the difference came from Truesdail; Philip consequently received compensation in the amount of $3,149.93 from his employer. The fact that the travel credits were exchanged for frequent flyer miles simply is not relevant to the analysis.

In the alternative, if it is assumed that the frequent flyer miles were not given to Philip by Truesdail, but belonged to him all along, then the transaction can be viewed as a disposition of his own property. Gross income includes "gains derived from dealings in property." IRC § 61(a)(3). A gain from the disposition of property is equal to the "amount realized" from the disposition minus the property's adjusted basis. IRC § 1001(a). The amount realized from a disposition of property is the sum of any money received plus the fair market value of the property (other than money) received. IRC § 1001(b). The adjusted basis is generally determined by reference to cost. IRC § 1012.

Because Philip received the frequent flyer miles at no cost, he had a basis of zero. He then exchanged his frequent flyer miles for cash, resulting in a gain of $3,149.93 (the fair market value of the property received minus the adjusted basis of zero).

Thus, the funds credited to Philip's account are taxable, whether they are characterized as a gain from the disposition of property or as additional compensation, unless he can show that they qualify for an exclusion. Philip cannot maintain that the funds constituted a non-taxable gift because IRC § 102(c), concerning exclusions for gifts, provides that "subsection (a) shall not exclude from gross income any amount transferred by or for an employer to, or for the benefit of, an employee."

Philip argues the credits should be construed as a "no-additional-cost service," which is excludable pursuant to IRC § 132(a). However, in order to qualify for this exclusion, the service in question must, among other things, be "offered for sale to customers in the ordinary course of the line of business of the employer in which the employee is performing services." IRC § 132(b). Truesdail obviously did not offer frequent flyer miles to customers in the ordinary course of its business; thus, the travel credits at issue here cannot be deemed an excludable no-additional-cost service.

In sum, we hold that the tax court was correct in concluding that the travel credits under the facts of this case constituted taxable income.

IV

The IRS imposed an addition to tax in the amount of $44 pursuant to the former version of IRC § 6653, which provided for an addition to tax if any part of an underpayment is due to negligence or intentional disregard of rules or regulations.

Philip has the burden of proving that the underpayment was not due to negligence. *Allen v. Commissioner*, 925 F.2d 348, 353 (9th Cir. 1991). Former section 6653(a)(3) defined "negligence" as including "any failure to make a reasonable attempt to comply with the provisions of this title." Similarly, caselaw has defined "negligence" as the "lack of due care or the failure to do what a reasonable and prudent person would do under similar circumstances." *Allen*, 925 F.2d at 353.

We are persuaded that the tax court erred in sustaining the penalty. There is nothing in the record which would cause a reasonable person to conclude that the travel credit conversion would constitute taxable income. As the government conceded in its brief, "the tax treatment of frequent flyer bonus programs is still under consideration." There is no showing that the conventional personal use of frequent flyer miles in the late 1980s gave rise to taxable income under then-current IRS policy. Therefore, the penalty for negligent or intentional disregard of IRS rules was not warranted.

The decision of the tax court is AFFIRMED in part and REVERSED in part. Each party shall bear his or her own costs on appeal.

Understanding *Charley*

1.   The transaction in *Charley* was essentially as follows: assume a first class ticket to a particular destination cost $1,500, a coach ticket cost $900, and Charley had the equivalent of $600 in frequent flyer miles earned on previous business travel. The company would bill the client $1,500; buy Charley a $900 coach ticket, which he would then upgrade to first class using his frequent flyer mileage; and, following the above, direct the travel agent to credit $600 (i.e., the difference between the amount the client was billed and the amount spent on Charley's ticket) to Charley's personal travel account. When the dust cleared, $600 in frequent flyer mileage, earned primarily on business travel, had been converted to Charley's personal use.

Putting tax law aside for the moment, is this ethical business behavior? Would the client have paid $1,500 instead of $900 for the tickets, if it knew that this difference was effectively subsidizing Charley's personal travel? Is the Tax Court's decision affected by the arguably unsympathetic nature of Charley's conduct? Should it be?

2.   Suppose that an executive, less sophisticated than Charley, earns 100,000 frequent flyer miles on business travel and uses the mileage to take his family to Disney World. Does this constitute taxable income? How is this different from (say) an individual who gets a discounted bridge pass for use in business travel and uses the pass to drive over the same bridge, at reduced cost, on weekends? Or who gets better service in a restaurant because her company does business with its owner? Does every private advantage resulting from one's employment relationship give rise to taxable income, or only those that are extensive enough to constitute serious tax avoidance? Does it matter if the taxpayer negotiated for the arrangement as a form of compensation, or if it is simply a quirk of airline pricing that is largely outside his (or his employer's) control?

3.   Charley's arrangement with his accountant made it easy to measure the amount of his income from frequent flyer miles. Suppose that the taxpayer in the previous question, who converted business frequent flyer miles directly to personal use, were subject to income tax. How would the amount of income be measured? Suppose that the regular round-trip coach fare to Disney World was $1,500, but excursion fares ranged from $300 to $500 depending on the day of the flight, whether the ticket was purchased in advance, and so forth. Which, if any, of these figures would provide an accurate measure of income? What if the taxpayer could prove that she would not have gone to Disney World, at all, if she had not had the frequent flyer miles? And when would the income be taxable: when the miles were initially earned, when the ticket to Disney World was bought, or when the flight was

actually taken? Do the timing and valuation problems suggest that it is easier to exempt this kind of income from tax, altogether? Or is some, even an inexact, tax better than nothing?

The suggestion that frequent flyer miles might be subject to tax when used for personal travel led to considerable anxiety in the mid-1990s. As often happens when people — especially rich people — complain, the IRS begins quickly to backtrack. As also frequently happens, politicians sided with the taxpayers, introducing legislation to block the imposition of tax and allow tax-free conversion of business miles to proceed unabated. Scholars adopted a middle position, but were (as usual) ignored, although each side felt free to cite them when it suited their partisan interests.

The following are a series of administrative, legislative, and scholarly (or at very least, journalistic) responses to the frequent flyer controversy, in chronological order. As you read these materials, consider the nature of the arguments being made by the various parties, the fora in which they make them, and the quality of the sources they cite in support. Is there really a serious legal argument against taxing frequent flyer mileage, or did the IRS simply get cold feet in response to political pressure? Do you think that the protests would have been so strong if a benefit enjoyed by welfare recipients, rather than middle class businesspersons, were in question? How would you have handled the frequent flyer issue, if it had been up to you to decide?

Internal Revenue Service, Technical Advice Memorandum
Letter Ruling 9547001 (July 11, 1995)[7]

* * *

FACTS

The Taxpayer maintains several arrangements through which it reimburses its employees for official business expenses. We have been asked to determine whether three of those arrangements, the Non-Supervisors Automobile Expense Allowance Arrangement ("Non-Supervisors Auto Arrangement"), the Supervisors Automobile Expense Allowance Arrangement ("Supervisors Auto Arrangement"), and the Air Travel Allowance and Reimbursement Arrangement ("Air Travel Arrangement"), are "accountable plans" within the meaning of section 62(c) of the Code.

Each Auto Arrangement provides that, under certain circumstances, employees may be eligible for reimbursement of expenses incurred in using privately-owned vehicles for official purposes. Eligibility for reimbursements under each arrangement is determined by an "approving official," who must determine that the use of a privately-owned vehicle will be beneficial to the Taxpayer. Employees

---

[7] Letter rulings are addressed only to one taxpayer, and in theory have no precedential value, although in the absence of other guidance, lawyers frequently use them to determine the applicable law. *See* Background and Basic Themes, Section A, *supra*.

will be reimbursed for all mileage incurred for official business.

Under the Non-Supervisors Auto Arrangement, employees are required to supply odometer readings for purposes of calculating reimbursable mileage. Employees are reimbursed under this arrangement at the applicable "cents-per-mile rate" prescribed by the Service.

The Supervisors Auto Arrangement provides that supervisors:

"will be reimbursed at the rate of per day or the applicable cents-per-mile rate, whichever is greater, whenever privately-owned vehicle is used for business purposes. Odometer readings are not required on the respective claim forms; the integrity of the claim is the responsibility of the traveler. However, should the approving official have reason to question the claim, the claimant must provide evidence that supports the claim of distance traveled."

The Air Travel Arrangement sets forth the conditions under which the taxpayer pays the cost of employee air travel for official business. It requires employees to use the method of transportation that is most advantageous to the Taxpayer. Employees must consider per diem, overtime, and lost work time costs in addition to transportation costs. The Air Travel Arrangement instructs all employees who are denied seating on an overbooked flight to demand penalty payments. Employees are to request that the airline make the check payable to the Taxpayer. If the check is nonetheless made payable to the employee, the employee must endorse the check for payment to the Taxpayer. Until recently, the Air Travel Arrangement required employees to return certain airline incentives, including discount coupons for future air travel, to an appropriate official of the Taxpayer. The Air Travel Arrangement has been amended to provide that

"accumulated mileage/points obtained via participation in Frequent Flyer or Frequent Traveler programs sponsored by commercial airlines . . . may be retained and used by you for personal travel. However, official travel arrangements must be made using the most economical accommodations available, commensurate with the needs of the business."

APPLICABLE LAW

Section 62(a) of the Code lists the deductions from gross income allowed in computing "adjusted gross income." Section 62(a)(2)(A) includes among those deductions those allowed by part VI (section 161 through section 196), which consists of expenses paid or incurred by the taxpayer, in connection with his or her performance of services as an employee, under a reimbursement or other expense allowance arrangement with his or her employer. Section 62(c) of the Code provides that arrangements will not be treated as "reimbursement or other expense allowance arrangements" for purposes of section 62(a)(2)(A) unless (1) the arrangement requires the employee to substantiate the expenses covered by the arrangement to the person providing the reimbursement and (2) the arrangement requires the employee to return any amount in excess of the substantiated expenses covered under the arrangement. In enacting section 62(c) of the Code, Congress noted the sharp distinction it had drawn in the Tax Reform Act of 1986 between unreimbursed and reimbursed employee business expenses by subjecting unreimbursed employee expenses and other miscellaneous itemized deductions to the two-percent floor under section 67. The rationale for the limitation is that, under a true reimbursement arrangement, the employer has an incentive to require sufficient substantiation to ensure that the employee's allowance be limited to actual business expenditures. In the case of nonaccountable plans, however, there is no reason to allow the employee an above-the-line deduction. Such amounts more nearly resemble salary payments: the amount received by the employee is not necessarily determined by the actual amount of business expenses incurred by the employee, and the employee may retain amounts that are not spent for business purposes. The Conference Committee stated:

> "If an above-the-line deduction is allowed for expenses incurred pursuant to a nonaccountable plan, the two-percent floor enacted in the 1986 Act could be circumvented solely by restructuring the form of the employee's compensation so that the salary amount is decreased, but the employee receives an equivalent nonaccountable expense allowance."

See H.R. Conf. Rep. No. 998, 100th Cong., 2d Sess. 203 (1988).

Under section 1.62-2(c)(1) of the Income Tax Regulations, a reimbursement or other expense allowance arrangement satisfies the requirements of section 62(c) of the Code if it meets the three requirements of business connection, substantiation, and returning amounts in excess of expenses. These requirements are set forth in paragraphs (d), (e), and (f), respectively, of section 1.62-2 ("the three requirements").

An arrangement meets the business connection requirement of section 1.62-2(d) of the regulations if it provides advances, advances (including per diem allowances, allowances only for meals and incidental expenses, and mileage allowances), or reimbursements only for business expenses that are allowable as deductions under sections 161 through 196 of the Code, and that are paid or incurred by the employee in connection with the performance of services as an employee of the employer.

An arrangement meets the substantiation requirement of section 162-2(e) of the regulations if it requires each business expense to be substantiated to the payor (the employer, its agent or a third party) within a reasonable period of time. An arrangement that reimburses business expenses governed by section 274(d) of the Code meets this requirement if the information submitted to the payor sufficiently substantiates the requisite elements of each expenditure or use.

For example, section 1.274-5T(b)(6) of the regulations provides that the elements to be proved with respect to listed property, including passenger automobiles, are amount, time, and business purpose. The amount of business and total use of a passenger automobile must be substantiated based on mileage. Section 1.274-5T(b)(6)(i)(B). To meet the "adequate records" requirements of section 274(d), a taxpayer must maintain an account book, diary, log, statement of expense, trip sheets, or similar record. Section 1.274-5T(c)(1).

An arrangement meets the requirements of section 1.62-2(f) of the regulations if it requires the employee to return to the payor within a reasonable period of time any amount paid under the arrangement in excess of the expenses substantiated ("return of excess requirement"). The determination of whether an arrangement requires an employee to return amounts in excess of substantiated expenses will depend on the facts and circumstances. An arrangement under which money is advanced to an employee to defray expenses will satisfy this requirement only if the amount advanced is reasonably calculated not to exceed the amount of anticipated expenses.

Under section 1.62-2(f)(2) of the regulations, mileage allowances calculated at the applicable cents-per-mile rate are deemed substantiated. Thus, it is not necessary for an arrangement to require the employee to return any unused portion of the allowance calculated under this method.

Section 1.62-2(k) provides that, if a payor's reimbursement or other expense allowance arrangement evidences a pattern of abuse, all payments made under the arrangement will be treated as made under a nonaccountable plan.

DISCUSSION

Automobile Mileage Reimbursements

The Non-Supervisors Auto Arrangement provides that employees of the Taxpayer who occupy non-supervisory positions are reimbursed for official use of their privately-owned vehicles at the applicable cents-per-mile rate. The Non-Supervisors Auto Arrangement requires substantiation of the business use of privately-owned vehicles with mileage records and, thus, satisfies the substantiation requirement of section 1.62-2(e) of the regulations. Because non-supervisory employees are reimbursed at the applicable cents-per-mile rate, the return of excess requirement is deemed to be satisfied. Section 1.62-2(f)(2).

The Supervisors Auto Arrangement does not require supervisor employees to submit mileage records or return amounts in excess of substantiated expenses. This arrangement also establishes a different rate of reimbursement for supervisory employees. Reimbursements are calculated at the rate of per day or the applicable cents-per-mile rate, whichever is greater.

To meet the substantiation requirement of section 1.62-2(e)(2) of the regulations for passenger automobiles, an arrangement must require the submission of information sufficient to meet the requirements of section 1.274-5T to the payor. The Supervisors Auto Arrangement does not require the submission of mileage records and thus, does not meet the applicable substantiation requirements. In addition, the Automobile Arrangement provides for reimbursements at the rate of the greater of per day or the applicable cents-per- mile rate without requiring the return of amounts in excess of actual or deemed substantiated expenses. Accordingly, the Supervisors Auto Arrangement does not meet the substantiation or return of excess requirements of paragraphs (e) and (f) of section 1.62-2 of the regulations. Therefore, the Supervisors Auto Arrangement is a nonaccountable plan.

Air Travel Allowances and Reimbursements

Under the Air Travel Arrangement, the Taxpayer pays for its employees' official business travel. This arrangement requires all employees to return to the Taxpayer any compensation for involuntarily denied boarding on overbooked flights. By requiring the return of these excess amounts to the Taxpayer, the Air Travel Arrangement satisfies the return of excess requirement of section 1.62-2(f) of the regulations with respect to denied boarding compensation.

In contrast, the Air Travel Arrangement allows the Taxpayers' employees to retain mileage and awards accumulated on business travel. Mileage accrued toward awards constitutes a rebate in consideration of flying on a particular airline. Under generally accepted principles of tax law, a rebate is a purchase price adjustment, *i.e.*, it reduces the purchaser's cost of the property acquired. These purchase price adjustments constitute amounts in excess of the substantiated expenses covered under the Air Travel Arrangement. Accordingly, the Air Travel Arrangement's failure to require the return of such excess means that the Arrangement is a "nonaccountable plan" under section 1.62-2(c)(3)(i) of the regulations.

CONCLUSIONS

The Non-Supervisors Auto Arrangement meets the return of excess requirement of section 62(c)(2) of the Code and 1.62-2(f) of the regulations. The Supervisors Auto Arrangement, however, requires neither substantiation of business mileage nor the return of amounts in excess of substantiated expenses. Accordingly, the Supervisors Auto Arrangement is a nonaccountable plan.

The Air Travel Arrangement requires the Taxpayer's employees to return denied boarding compensation to the Taxpayer and, thus, satisfies the return of excess requirement of section 1.62-2(f) of the regulations with respect to those payments. However, because the Air Travel Arrangement allows employees to retain the purchase price adjustments, the Arrangement does not require the Taxpayer's employees to return amounts in excess of substantiated expenses and is, thus, a nonaccountable plan.

Frequent Flyer Miles Attributable to Business or Official Travel
I.R.S. Announcement 2002-18, 2002-1 C.B. 621 (March 11, 2002)

Most major airlines offer frequent flyer programs under which passengers accumulate miles for each flight. Individuals may also earn frequent flyer miles or other promotional benefits, for example, through rental cars or hotels. These promotional benefits may generally be exchanged for upgraded seating, free travel, discounted travel, travel-related services, or other services or benefits.

Questions may have been raised concerning the taxability of frequent flyer miles or other promotional items that are received as the result of business travel and used for personal purposes. There are numerous technical and administrative issues relating to these benefits on which no official guidance has been provided, including issues relating to the timing and valuation of income inclusions and the basis for identifying personal use benefits attributable to business (or official) expenditures versus those attributable to personal expenditures. Because of these unresolved issues, the IRS has not pursued a tax enforcement program with respect to promotional benefits such as frequent flyer miles.

Consistent with prior practice, the IRS will not assert that any taxpayer has understated his federal tax liability by reason of the receipt or personal use of frequent flyer miles or other in-kind promotional benefits attributable to the taxpayer's business or official travel. Any future guidance on the taxability of these benefits will be applied prospectively.

This relief does not apply to travel or other promotional benefits that are converted to cash, to compensation that is paid in the form of travel or other promotional benefits, or in other circumstances where these benefits are used for tax avoidable purposes.

* * *

Understanding Frequent Flyers

1. Under section 132(e), a *de minimis* fringe benefit means "any property or service the value of which (after taking into account the frequency with which similar fringes are provided by the employer to the employer's employees) is so small as to make accounting for it unreasonable or administratively impracticable." Using this definition, how convincing do you find the argument that frequent flyer mileage should be treated as a *de minimis* fringe? What about Regulations, § 1.61-21(a)(1), which specifically include "an employer-provided free or discounted commercial airline flight" on the list of taxable fringe benefits? Can the taxpayer escape this provision by arguing that the discount is provided by the airline rather than by the employer who consents to the personal use of frequent flyer mileage? Does it matter?[8]

2. Alternatively, how convincing would you find an argument that frequent flyer miles should not be taxable because they are not transferable by the employee and are subject to cancellation if the employee tries to sell them? Do these questions properly affect the taxability of frequent flyer miles, or do they merely suggest a lower valuation once they are included in income? Are these issues similar to or different from those in *Benaglia v. Commissioner*?

3. Some opponents of taxing frequent flyer miles argued that doing so would result in a myriad of administrative difficulties, raising questions such as timing, valuation, etc. How serious is the administrability argument against taxing frequent flyer miles, and what might the IRS do to reduce the scope of this problem?

4. What do you think caused the IRS to cave on the issue of frequent flyer miles

---

[8] With respect to the *de minimis* issue, a 1993 observer estimated that the airline industry's aggregate liability for frequent flyer benefits was approximately $3.5 billion and that roughly 3 percent of all airline traffic consisted of redemptions of frequent flyer miles. Today's totals are vastly higher. Lee A. Shepard, *News Analysis: Collecting the Tax on Frequent Flyer Benefits*, 93 TAX NOTES TODAY 115-4, at 2 (June 1, 1993) (quoting Helene Becker, airline analyst for Shearson Lehman).

in Announcement 2002-18, above? What in particular is the meaning of the somewhat odd language stating that "the IRS will not assert" taxability for frequent flyer miles and "any further guides . . . will be applied prospectively"? If frequent flyer miles are not taxable, why not say so directly? Would this language be enough to satisfy you as a practitioner, or would you want further clarification? How, if at all, could you get it?

Using the Sources

Based on the materials above, how would you advise your client to treat employer-provided frequent flyer miles for federal income tax purposes?

Law and Planning

1.   Suppose that you were a regular business traveler with a choice of several airlines, some of which had more and less attractive frequent flyer programs (use of miles, arrangements with other airlines, attractive destinations, etc.). Assume that the miles are not subject to income tax. How much would your choice of airline be affected by these programs, and would you be willing to sacrifice other factors (time of flight, small price differences, etc.) in order to accumulate more frequent flyer miles?

2.   Now assume that the miles were fully taxable when used for personal travel. Would you still be interested (or as interested) in collecting frequent flyer mileage? Why?

3.   By now, nearly all airlines have frequent flyer plans, which means that they should in theory cancel each other out (except for the lost air fares). So why do they have them, and what if anything should this tell you about the tax treatment?

Politics and Policy

1.   How would you rate the (effective) tax exemption for frequent flyer miles in terms of fairness (horizontal and vertical equity) and economic efficiency? If you had to make a case in favor of the exemption in front of a congressional tax writing committee, which of these factors would you emphasize, and what other points might you include in your presentation? What groups, if any, would you count on for political support? How, if at all, would your answer to these questions differ if you were (i) discussing the same issue with Treasury Department or IRS officials, or (ii) arguing the point in a judicial proceeding?

2.   Various fringe benefits, including employee discounts, no additional cost services, and some health and pension benefits, are subject to an antidiscrimination rule. Yet Announcement 2002-18 makes no mention of any such rule. Should it?

3.   Since September 11, 2001, the airline industry has suffered severe losses resulting from increasing energy costs, added security costs, a general fear of flying, and related problems. Some airlines have argued that they should be entitled to new tax breaks, ranging from faster depreciation to better treatment of business losses, to help them cope with this situation. Do airlines deserve this assistance, or

are industry's problems at least partially, well, its own fault? If the industry does deserve help, is it better provided by tax breaks or direct government spending? How might you design a tax package for the airline industry, to ensure that the money was used to address the industry's long-term problems and not simply to reward companies that had already failed?

B.   Scholarships, Tuition Assistance, and Tax Breaks for Education

Frequent flyer mileage is an intellectually fascinating but largely self-contained issue. More challenging for tax lawyers are situations that involve an interplay of different provisions, which may be inconsistent in nature and drafted at different times. Here the problem is not too little law, but too much: the lawyer, in approaching a problem, may not even be certain which provision is relevant, or whether the answer must be found in cases or rulings that lie outside the "Code and Regulations" framework. The proliferation of sources multiplies tax planning problems, and tempts taxpayers to make aggressive interpretations that undermine the spirit if not the letter of the statutory scheme. Finally, a proliferation of inconsistent tax rules may lead to incoherent or contradictory policy outcomes.

A good example of this problem — and one dear to the hearts of students — is the tax treatment of scholarships, tuition assistance, and other educational programs. Let's assume the Government believes education to be (generally speaking) a good thing, and wants to provide some tax subsidy for it. Students don't usually have lot of income, so the simplest solution — letting students deduct tuition and related expenditures — probably isn't going to get the job done. A tuition deduction might also be problematic for vertical equity reasons (there are still an awful lot of people who don't go to college) and because education has traditionally been viewed as a mixed personal and business expenditure, although students may tend to doubt this.[9]

What then are the alternatives? One possibility is to provide a tax benefit to a third party, most likely the student's parents or close relative, who assists the student with his or her tuition. Another possibility is generous tax treatment of grants or loans received by a student to fund educational expenses, or of savings or investment plans that have a similar objective. Still a third alternative is to provide tax breaks for employees whose companies pay all or part of an employee's educational expenses, although as a practical matter, this alternative is likely to benefit primarily part-time rather than full-time students. (Only the last of these items is, strictly speaking, an employee fringe benefit, although the others raise similar practical and policy issues.)

As might be expected, the Code has tried all these approaches, including tuition tax credits;[10] exclusion of scholarships from income;[11] deductions for student loan

---

[9] This issue, and the deductibility (or nondeductibility) of tuition expenditures, are discussed further in Chapter 6.

[10] I.R.C. § 25A. The tuition tax credit is actually two credits: the Hope Scholarship Credit and the so-called Lifetime Learning Credit, each of which is limited in time and amount and subject to phase-out

interest;[12] special tax treatment of educational retirement accounts (IRAs) and state-sponsored tuition savings plans; exclusion of qualified tuition program distributions from income;[13] and exclusion of employer-provided educational assistance plans.[14] The provisions above are logical on their own terms, but their policies as well as their mechanical application rules often clash with one another. For example, employer-provided educational assistance plans, together with tuition tax credits and the deduction for student loan interest, are nominally targeted to lower- and middle-income taxpayers, while scholarship assistance and most state tuition savings plans — which also rely heavily on federal tax benefits — are available to wealthier families, as well. There are also numerous differences in the level of education covered (college, graduate and professional school, etc.) and other technical aspects of the various different provisions. While it might seem logical to replace this patchwork with one or two streamlined, consistent provisions, each provision has its own political constituency who would presumably be unhappy to see "their" provision eliminated even if it were replaced by a single, more logical rule.

The existence of so many overlapping rules complicates tax planning and results in inconsistent policy. Assume that a student has the choice of attending school A or B, each of which charges annual tuition of $15,000 and similarly astronomical sums for room and board, supplies, etc. (i.e., $30,000 annual expenses). School A is more prestigious, and will offer $15,000 in student loans but no outright grants, with the remainder of the student's expenses to be funded by work-study or summer jobs (the income from which is fully taxable) and the student's or family's own funds. School B is slightly less prestigious, but will offer $10,000 in scholarship grants together with an additional $5,000 in loans. Even to evaluate the tax consequences of these alternatives — let alone balance these against other, real-world factors — requires knowledge of at least three different tax provisions (sections 117, 221, and 25A); the family's financial situation (two of the three provisions contain income-based phaseouts and the effect of all three is different at different incomes); and the possibility (indeed, the likelihood) that the law or the family's situation will change during the relevant period. The calculation becomes more complicated if

---

for higher income levels. *See infra* Chapter 6, Section III (Understanding Educational Costs).

[11] I.R.C. § 117(a). Qualified scholarships are limited to amounts used to cover tuition and fees at a qualifying educational organization, together with books, fees, etc. required for courses. Amounts to cover room and board, as well as amounts which represent payment for teaching, research, or other services are not exempt from tax.

[12] I.R.C. § 221. Section 221 allows a limited deduction for student loan interest, not exceeding $2,500 per year and phased out at higher income levels. *See infra* Chapter 6, Section III (Understanding Educational Costs).

[13] Section 529 excludes qualified tuition program distributions from income up to the amount of beneficiary's adjusted qualified education expenses.

[14] I.R.C. § 127. Educational assistance plans are excluded up to a limit of $5,250 per employee and are subject to various additional rules, including a general limitation to undergraduate courses and a requirement — similar to that under section 132 — that the program not discriminate in favor of highly compensated employees. A program is not to be found in violation of the nondiscrimination rules merely because of different "utilization rates" for the assistance offered under the program, which means that, in practice, the assistance may be used primarily by one category of employees so long as it is offered on an equal basis to everyone. The employee may not receive a deduction or credit for any amount excluded under the employee assistance provision.

the taxpayer qualifies for employer educational assistance (§ 127), or if decisions about college financing must be made before the relevant schools and their financial plans are fully known to the taxpayer. One could say "that's life" and be done with it, but it seems excessive that a person should need a professional tax advisor just to finance her college education, before even considering the real-world, practical tradeoffs that attend this decision.

A further problem with complex statutes is that they encourage practitioners to maneuver in the spaces between the provisions, thereby rewarding those with crafty tax advisors and creating still further complexity. An example of this phenomenon is the practice of tuition reductions for university employees and their families. To attract new employees (especially professors), universities frequently allow employees, their spouses, or children to attend for as little as 10 percent of the usual, inflated cost. In some cases, tuition reductions are also available at other, equivalent institutions, either by reciprocal agreement or because the employing university pays the tuition at the second school. Because they do not fit precisely within any of the statutes described above, for many years, the tax status of these arrangements was somewhat murky. Since they depend on an employment relationship, it is uncertain whether they qualify for tax exemption as ordinary scholarships (§ 117(b)). Nor do they appear to meet the requirements of educational assistance programs (§ 127), which cover assistance by a third-party payor, rather than the educational institution itself, and do not exempt payments for the employee's spouse or children. Arguably they are most similar to no additional cost services (e.g., standby flying) of section 132, but they are more likely to involve a cost in terms of foregone revenue and are far more valuable to employees than standby flights or similar items. In the absence of a special provision, the tax fate of such arrangements was uncertain, as seen in the following case:

KNAPP v. COMMISSIONER
United States Court of Appeals, Second Circuit
867 F.2d 749 (1989)

Winter, Circuit Judge:

Appellants Charles and Beverley Knapp appeal from a decision of the Tax Court determining a deficiency in their federal income tax for the year 1979. The dispute concerns the taxability of payments made by Mr. Knapp's employer, the New York University School of Law ("N.Y.U."), to educational institutions attended by the Knapps's children pursuant to a program in which N.Y.U. provided tuition assistance to the children of its faculty members. We hold that these payments did not fall within the scope of the exemption for scholarships provided in Section 117 of the Internal Revenue Code, 26 U.S.C. § 117 (as that section read in 1979). We also hold that the Tax Court's authority to redetermine deficiencies empowers that court to consider the provisions of the "Fringe Benefit Moratorium" ("Moratorium") enacted by Congress on October 7, 1978, Pub. L. No. 95-427, 92 Stat. 996 (1978). The Moratorium does not, however, affect the deficiency in question.

BACKGROUND

The relevant facts are not in dispute. N.Y.U. qualifies as an educational institution under I.R.C. § 170(b)(1)(A)(ii) and is exempt from taxation under I.R.C. § 501(c)(3). In 1976, its law school adopted a policy of providing tuition assistance to the children of its faculty members. This program was administered by the Law Center Foundation ("LCF"), an organization established by N.Y.U. and also exempt from taxation under I.R.C. § 501(c)(3).

In 1979 the LCF program was available to all children of full-time faculty members and administrators with the rank of director, assistant dean or associate dean. To qualify for assistance the child had to be enrolled in a private elementary school, a private secondary school or a college. Neither the child's academic record nor the family's financial resources were considered in providing assistance. The payments were made by LCF directly to the school attended by the child.

In 1979, Knapp was both a tenured professor and an associate dean of the N.Y.U. Law School. By virtue of his positions, his two daughters, Jennifer and Liza, were eligible for, and received, tuition assistance from the LCF. Jennifer attended Swarthmore College while Liza attended the Brearley School. As a result, LCF made the following tuition payments directly to the respective schools:

Date	School	Amount
January 4, 1979	Swarthmore	$2,200
January 4, 1979	Brearley	$1,420
August 14, 1979	Swarthmore	$2,350
August 14, 1979	Brearley	$2,280
	Total	$8,250

The Knapps did not report this $8,250 as income on their joint tax return filed for the year 1979. The Commissioner, however, determined that the tuition assistance constituted taxable income and issued a notice of deficiency to the Knapps. The Knapps then petitioned the Tax Court for a redetermination of the asserted deficiency. They claimed that: (i) the tuition assistance grants constituted non-taxable scholarships pursuant to I.R.C. § 117 and 26 C.F.R. § 1.117-3(a) (1979); and (ii) because taxes appear never to have been imposed on such payments, the Tax Commissioner was barred from taxing the tuition assistance grants by the "Fringe Benefit Moratorium" enacted by Congress, Act of October 7, 1978, Pub. L. No. 95-427, 92 Stat. 996 (1978), as extended. A majority of the Tax Court sustained the deficiency. In doing so, however, the majority was divided on the issue of whether the court had jurisdiction to enforce the Moratorium.

DISCUSSION

This appeal raises three issues: (i) whether the Tax Court erred by finding that the tuition payments made by LCF to Swarthmore and Brearley were taxable income to the Knapps; (ii) whether the Tax Court has jurisdiction to enforce the Fringe Benefit Moratorium; and (iii) whether the Fringe Benefit Moratorium bars the Commissioner from including in the Knapps's taxable income the tuition assistance grants received by the Knapps's daughters from LCF. We will address these issues seriatim.

In 1979, Section 61(a) of the Internal Revenue Code, 26 U.S.C. § 61(a), defined gross income as "all income from whatever source derived, including . . . compensation for services." "When assets are transferred by an employer to an employee to secure better services they are plainly compensation," *Commissioner v. Lo Bue*, 351 U.S. 243, 247, 100 L. Ed. 1142, 76 S. Ct. 800 (1956), and no party to this litigation argues that the tuition assistance grants extended by LCF do not constitute compensation for the purposes of the Internal Revenue Code. Instead, the Knapps argue that the tuition assistance provided by LCF falls within the scope of the exemption for educational scholarships set out in Section 117(a) (as it read in 1979), a provision enacted by Congress in 1954. Section 117(a) stated:

§ 117. *Scholarships and fellowship grants*

(a) General rule

In the case of an individual, gross income does not include —

(1) any amount received —

(A) as a scholarship at an educational organization described in section 170(b)(1)(A)(ii). . . .

Because Swarthmore and Brearley are undeniably "educational organizations," the only issue is whether the tuition assistance grants received by the Knapps's children constituted "scholarships" within the meaning of Section 117(a).

Section 117(a) does not exempt from income payments by employers generally for tuition assistance to the children of an employee as part of the employee's compensation. *Bingler v. Johnson*, 394 U.S. 741 (1969). Application of that general principle to LCF's tuition assistance payments would clearly render them taxable. Appellants contend, however, that where the employer is an educational institution, Congress intended to exempt such payments. This contention rests solely upon the following remarks found in both the Senate and House Reports accompanying Section 117(a):

If an educational institution . . . maintains or participates in a plan whereby the tuition of a child of a faculty member of any such institution is *remitted at* any other participating educational institution . . . attended by such child, the amount of tuition so remitted shall be considered to be an amount received as a scholarship under this section.

(emphasis added). H.R. Rep. No. 1337, 83d Cong., 2d Sess. A37, *reprinted in* 1954 U.S. Code Cong. & Admin. News. 4017, 4173–74; S. Rep. No. 1622, 83d Cong., 2d Sess. 188, *reprinted in* 1954 U.S. Code Cong. & Admin. News 4621, 4823.

The applicable Regulation, Section 1.117-3(a), 26 C.F.R. § 1.117-3(a), stated (and still states) in pertinent part that: "[a] scholarship generally means an amount paid or allowed to, or for the benefit of, a student, whether an undergraduate or a graduate, to aid such individual in pursuing his studies." The final sentence of Regulation 1.117-3(a), however, is at the heart of the dispute in this case. That sentence, taken from the above-quoted language from the Senate and House

Reports, provided for the exclusion from gross income of benefits provided under tuition remission arrangements between educational employers. It read as follows:

> If an educational institution maintains or participates in a plan whereby the tuition of a child of a faculty member of such institution is *remitted by* any other participating educational institution attended by such child, the amount of the tuition so remitted shall be considered to be an amount received as a scholarship.

26 C.F.R. § 1.117-3(a) (emphasis added).

By exempting only payments by the school attended by the students pursuant to a tuition assistance arrangement, this sentence by implication excludes from the definition of scholarship payments by the employing institution. The payments at issue in the present case are thus not scholarships under the Regulation and are taxable income.

The Knapps argue that Congress intended to treat all tuition assistance payments by educational institutions, including employing institutions, for the benefit of the children of faculty members as non-taxable. In support, they correctly note that the language of Regulation 1.117-3(a) differs from the language of the congressional reports in that the former refers to the tuition being "remitted *by*" the other institution while the latter refer to the tuition being "remitted *at*" the other institution. The phrase "remitted at," the Knapps argue, calls for a construction which encompasses a tuition assistance program like LCF because "remitted at," unlike "remitted by", specifies only the payee rather than the payor. The Knapps thus contend that Regulation 1.117-3(a) is invalid.

We disagree. Even if "remitted at" specifies only the payee school, the language of the committee reports does not unambiguously establish the non-taxable status of the LCF grants. "Remitted at" an educational institution may easily, if not inevitably, be read to mean "remitted by." Faced with this ambiguity, we are obliged to defer to the view taken by the Regulation so long as it embodies a reasonable interpretation of the statutory language and legislative history. *Chevron U.S.A. v. Natural Resources Defense Council*, 467 U.S. 837, 844 (1984) ("a court may not substitute its own construction of a statutory provision for a reasonable interpretation made by the administrator of an agency").

The Knapps asserts however, that the Regulation's construction of Section 117(a) treats similarly situated taxpayers differently and therefore makes no sense as tax policy. We are not persuaded. Scholarships are generally, although admittedly not always, provided by the institution attended by the child, and the Regulation in question exempts payments by such institutions. Moreover, the Regulation is clearly attempting to distinguish between tuition assistance payments that are a *quid pro quo* for a particular employee's services and those that are not. The Regulation exempts tuition payments where the paying institution receives no direct benefit from the services of the employee and the payments in question are not direct compensation. We cannot say this is a wholly irrational line to draw.

Moreover, exemptions from taxation are to be construed narrowly, *Bingler v. Johnson*, 394 U.S. 741, 751–52 (1969), and "exemptions from taxation are not to be implied; they must be unambiguously proved." *United States v. Wells Fargo Bank*,

485 U.S. 351 (1988). Appellants simply have not "unambiguously proved" that Congress intended grants extended by tuition assistance plans such as the LCF to be exempt from taxation. The language of the statute itself mentions only "scholarship[s] at . . . educational organizations." Nothing in this language constitutes a clearly stated intention on the part of Congress to provide a blanket tax exemption for the proceeds of tuition assistance programs by educational institutions that finance the education of the children of their faculty members at other schools. The ambiguous language of the committee reports is the only evidence of a legislative intent to exclude from taxation any and all tuition assistance programs educational institutions establish for the children of their faculty members attending other schools. We therefore conclude that taxation of the benefits the Knapps received from LCF was not precluded by Section 117(a).

Concluding that Section 117(a) does not exempt the grants the Knapps received from the LCF does not fully resolve this appeal. On October 7, 1978, Congress enacted what has come to be known as the Fringe Benefit Moratorium. The Moratorium states in pertinent part:

SECTION 1. FRINGE BENEFIT REGULATIONS.

(a) IN GENERAL. — No fringe benefit regulation shall be issued —

(1) in final form on or after May 1, 1978, and on or before December 31, 1979, or

(2) in proposed or final form on or after May 1, 1978, if such regulation has an effective date on or before December 31, 1979.

(b) DEFINITION OF FRINGE BENEFIT REGULATION. — For purposes of subsection (a), the term "fringe benefit regulation" means a regulation providing for the inclusion of any fringe benefit in gross income by reason of section 61 of the Internal Revenue Code of 1954.

Pub. L. No. 95-427, 92 Stat. 996 (1978). The Moratorium thus statutorily bars the Commissioner from issuing any new regulations concerning the tax status of a fringe benefit. Absent from the Moratorium, however, was a clause granting the Tax Court jurisdiction to enforce its terms. Consequently, the Commissioner argues that the Tax Court lacks authority to compel compliance with the Moratorium. We disagree.

The Tax Court is a court of limited jurisdiction, *see Taylor v. Commissioner*, 258 F.2d 89, 93 (2d Cir. 1958), possessing only those powers expressly conferred upon it by Congress. One of those powers, however, is the authority "to redetermine the correct amount of [a] deficiency" in income tax, 26 U.S.C. § 6214 (Supp. IV 1986), and to review both law and fact with respect to deficiencies. *Dobson v. Commissioner*, 320 U.S. 489, 501 (1943). As an incident to these functions, the Tax Court must hear challenges to the validity of regulations in redetermining deficiencies. *CSX Corp. v. Commissioner*, 89 T.C. 134, 143–46 (1987). Because the Moratorium clearly affects the validity of regulations promulgated after the specified dates, the Tax Court is not only empowered, but also obligated, to apply it when it is relevant to a redetermination of a challenged deficiency. In the present case, therefore, the

Tax Court should have considered the Moratorium's provisions when examining the Commissioner's assertion of a deficiency.

We now consider the impact of the Moratorium, if any, on the taxability of the LCF tuition assistance grants. As drafted, the Moratorium precludes the issuance of any regulations concerning fringe benefits after the specified dates. The present case, however, does not involve the promulgation of any such regulation. The Knapps claim, however, that the provisions of the Moratorium must be interpreted in light of the House Report accompanying its enactment which stated in pertinent part:

> While the provisions of this bill relate only to the issuance of regulations, it is the intent of the committee that the Treasury Department will not alter, or deviate from, in any significant way the historical treatment of fringe benefits through the issuance of revenue rulings or revenue procedures, etc.

H.R. Rep. No. 1232, 95th Cong., 2d Sess. 5, *reprinted in* 1978 U.S. Code Cong. & Admin. News 2508, 2510. The Knapps thus contend that Congress intended the Moratorium to freeze the administrative practice concerning the taxation of scholarships for faculty children as of October 1, 1977. Finally, the Knapps argue that as of October 1, 1977, the administrative *status quo* was that tuition assistance grants such as those extended by LCF were nontaxable. To support this contention the Knapps rely upon private letter rulings and technical advice memoranda.

It appears that tuition payments of the kind at issue here were not in practice taxed before the Moratorium — that is, the Commissioner never brought a proceeding to collect such a tax[15] — and that certain private letter rulings and technical advice memoranda support the Knapps's position. Nevertheless, we do not believe that the Moratorium applies. The Supreme Court "[has] repeatedly recognized that 'when . . . the terms of a statute [are] unambiguous, judicial inquiry is complete, except "in 'rare and exceptional circumstances.' " ' In the absence of a 'clearly expressed legislative intention to the contrary,' the language of the statute itself 'must ordinarily be regarded as conclusive.' " *United States v. James*, 478 U.S. 597, 606 (1986) (citations omitted).

The language of the Moratorium limiting its effect to the promulgation of new regulations could hardly be more plain. Indeed, the House Report in question concedes that the statutory language is so limited but goes on to state that the Committee does not agree with that language. We cannot infer, however, that the Senate also meant something other than what the statute said, or that the executive — the branch entrusted with authority to enforce the tax laws — also understood

---

[15] [1] It is not at all clear that the non-taxation of such payments has resulted from a deliberate forbearance by the Commissioner based on an interpretation of the meaning of Section 117(a) or from the failure of educational institutions and their employees to report such payments. We believe it self-evident that a failure to tax such payments resulting solely from a combination of lack of resources on the Commissioner's part and non-reporting by educational institutions and taxpayers does not constitute a frozen "historical treatment," even under the House Committee's view of the Moratorium. This particular problem does, however, illustrate the difficulty in substituting the language of the House Report — which includes, *inter alia*, as examples of "historical treatment" the word "etc." — for the language of the statute.

the statutory language to be in error. Moreover, I.R.C. § 6110(j)(3) provided that private rulings and technical advice memoranda were not to be cited or treated as precedent, a position quite at odds with the statement in the House Report and the contentions advanced by the Knapps.

Against these rulings and memoranda is the Regulation that preceded the Moratorium that, as explicated above, exempted only tuition assistance programs that are arranged between various schools. If Congress wanted the Moratorium to extend beyond existing regulations, it could have done so by expressly stating that intention in the statute. Congress, however, elected not to do so. Consequently, we will apply the statute as drafted. Because the instant case does not involve new regulations, the Moratorium is inapplicable.

We therefore affirm the Tax Court.

Understanding *Knapp*

1.   The regulations in effect at the time of *Knapp* (Treas. Reg. § 1.117-3(a)) stated that reciprocal arrangements allowing reduced tuition for children of faculty members were to be treated as tax-exempt scholarships, even though these arrangements were based on an employment relationship and were almost certainly thought of as a form of compensation by relevant faculty members. Is this regulation consistent with the statutory purpose of section 117, or is it an unwarranted giveaway? Why do you think that the NYU Law School, which presumably has good tax counsel, structured its program in the form of a grant to interested faculty members rather than as a reciprocal tuition reduction plan, which would have qualified under section 117?

2.   Could any or all of NYU's programs qualify as an educational assistance grant under section 127 of present law? What changes, if any, would have to be made in the programs in order to qualify for this provision? Would you recommend this as an alternate tax reduction strategy?

3.   What do you make of the court's suggestion that tax exemptions ought to be construed narrowly? Couldn't one argue the opposite: that the income tax itself is an interference with people's right to keep their own money, and so the tax itself, rather than the exceptions to it, ought to be narrowly construed?

4.   What are the fairness (horizontal and vertical equity) implications of the *Knapp* decision?

Perhaps tiring of cases like *Knapp*, Congress in 1984 added section 117(d) to the Code, providing a statutory exemption for qualified tuition reductions.[16] These are defined as "any reduction in tuition provided to an employee of an organization described in section 170(b)(1)(A)(ii) [regarding tax-exempt educational institutions] for . . . education (below the graduate level) at such organization or another organization described in section 170(b)(1)(A)(ii). . . ." The exemption applies to the employee and his spouse or dependent children, as defined in section 132(h). Section 117(d) also contains an antidiscrimination rule, similar to that in section 132,

---

[16] *Knapp* related to a taxable year before this provision took effect.

and a special rule for students engaged in teaching and research activities for an educational organization, who are permitted to qualify at the graduate as well as undergraduate level. Under these rules, most tuition reductions for university employees and their families qualify for tax exemption, but only if they meet the nondiscrimination and other rules of the statute and are structured as tuition reductions in the manner described by the Code. (Ironically, the arrangement in *Knapp* itself would not qualify, since it was structured as an employee payment rather than a tuition reduction. One presumes that it has since been adjusted.)

Take a close look at section 117(d). It is a good example of how Congress, in attempting to resolve existing problems, tends to create new ones. Among its dubious provisions are the allowance of exchange programs between different universities (section 117(d)(2)) (isn't this equivalent to providing the employee with cash which he then uses to pay tuition at the other institution?); the ambivalent treatment of graduate students (section 117(d)(5)); and the nondiscrimination rule contained in section 117(d)(3). The last of these is especially problematic. Assume that a university complies with this provision and makes tuition discounts available to all its employees, from the highest-paid professor to the lowest-paid secretary, on essentially equal terms. Aren't the children of professors more likely to be admitted to the university, and therefore take advantage of this provision, than the children of secretaries and custodial employees? Should this matter, so long as both groups have theoretically equal access, and there are at least some members of the latter group who take advantage of the program? Or should universities be required to adopt other means (e.g., affirmative action for students from disadvantaged backgrounds or an admissions preference for the children of lower- and middle-ranked employees) to make this concept more meaningful? What generally are the horizontal and vertical equity implications of the tax exemption for tuition reduction programs, and how do they compare to other fringe benefits we have studied? Does section 117(d) deal effectively with these problems, or does it merely adopt a cosmetic solution?

Using the Sources

Examine section 117(d) of the present law (including relevant cross-references) and answer the following questions:

1. Atlantic and Pacific universities are both private educational institutions described in section 170(b)(1)(a)(ii). The two universities have an agreement under which children of their employees may attend college at either university for 10 percent of the otherwise applicable tuition (i.e., a 90 percent discount).

a. Will the students, or their parents, be taxable under this arrangement?

b. Would your answer be different if the students received free tuition at the Atlantic or Pacific law schools?

c. What if the students were attending the Atlantic or Pacific graduate schools in economics and were required to work as teaching assistants in return for reduced tuition?

2.   Section 117(d)(3) requires that tuition reductions be made available to a "reasonable classification . . . which does not discriminate in favor of highly compensated employees. . . ." Suppose that a university wanted to provide tuition reductions for the children of all its professors, regardless of rank, but not for the children of clerical or administrative employees. Would this system qualify as a "reasonable classification" under section 117(d)(3)? Would you recommend that a university limit its program in this manner?

3.   What if, instead of the system described in item 2, a large state university provided tuition discounts to the children of all employees who worked at its most prestigious, four-year campus, but not to employees of other campuses or two-year (community) colleges?

4.   After answering the items above, how would you evaluate the effectiveness of the section 117(d) antidiscrimination rule?

Law and Planning

(Note: The following problem concerns educational tax incentives generally and is not limited to section 117(d).)

Suppose that you were a 25-year old secretary, single, earning approximately $40,000 per year and had recently been accepted to a private, four-year college. The college costs about $22,500 per year in tuition and fees and an additional $12,500 in room, board, and related expenses, for a total of $35,000 per year. The college offers you a scholarship grant of $20,000 per year and a student loan of an additional $10,000 at a favorable interest rate. The remainder ($5,000 per year) would be financed from your own, very limited savings.

Because of the financial strain involved in the previous alternative, you are also considering keeping your job and attending college at night at a slightly less prestigious, but still respectable, university. In this case, the aggregate expenses would be $25,000 per year, of which $5,000 would be covered by a student loan (there would be no grant available); $15,000 by a tax-free educational assistance program, to be provided by your employer; and $5,000 from your own funds. Part-time attendance would mean that it would take six instead of four years to earn your degree and the increased earnings would likely go with it; on the other hand, you would still have your current income during the interim period, and fewer loans to repay in the future.

a. Which of the following alternatives is most attractive, and why?

i. Take the scholarship and attend the fancier college on a full-time basis

ii. Keep working and attend the university part-time, using salary, loans, and employer assistance to finance your educational costs

iii. Forget (or at least delay) higher education and continue in your current job

b. Which specific tax provisions are relevant to your decision, and what role (if any) did they play in your answer, above?

c. What if anything does your answer tell you about current tax incentives for education and how they might be improved?

Politics and Policy

1.   How would you rate each of the following provisions according to the standards of vertical and horizontal equity, economic efficiency, and simplicity or administrability, as previously described?

a. The exclusion for scholarships that cover tuition, books, and supplies (section 117(a)).

b. The exclusion for employer-provided educational assistance programs (section 127).

c. The exclusion for college tuition reduction programs (section 117(d)).

d. The partial deduction for student loan interest payments (section 221).

e. Tuition tax credits (section25A).

f. The exclusion for Qualified Tuition Program distributions (section 529).

2.   Suppose that there was a proposal to provide a new tax credit for up to 50 percent of tuition or related expenditures, to be available to whomever (student, parents, etc.) paid the expenses (i.e., an expanded section 25A). All existing tax incentives for education would be repealed to make way for the new credit. Would you support this proposal? What groups or entities do you think would be likely to come out in favor of this concept, and which would be likely to oppose it? Why?

3.   What if the proposal were to eliminate all educational tax incentives, including the section 25A credit, and use the money to pay for direct (i.e., nontax) Governmental assistance to universities and their students?

C.   Imputed Income and the Uneasy Boundary Between Law and Policy

Tax law (what the law is) is usually distinct from tax policy (what somebody thinks it should be). But that doesn't mean that the second should be ignored. Even when tax reformers are unable to change one provision of the Code, their arguments often have an indirect impact, resulting in an enhanced understanding that ultimately affects the way other, even more important rules are conceptualized and changed.

An interesting example of this phenomenon is the tax treatment of imputed or psychic income. Suppose that two taxpayers each earn $50,000 in income, with the same fringe benefits and other contractual provisions. One works in a coal mine, while the other has a corner office overlooking the Brooklyn Bridge.[17] Isn't the second one better off than the first? Wouldn't any rational person take the second job over the first one? Should the tax system reflect this difference by taxing the

---

[17]   Or San Francisco Bay, or Lake Michigan, or . . .

second person on the imputed or psychic income resulting from his enjoyable working conditions, or else by allowing the first person a deduction for her more burdensome working conditions?

The answer, of course, is that the Code does not tax such imputed income, for a number of reasons. The most obvious is valuation: it is simply too subjective to determine how much enjoyment one derives from a large office, or a nice view, and the amount of enjoyment presumably differs between different people. (Some people might find living in New York more oppressive than working in a coal mine.) Enforcement would be nearly impossible: imagine a team of appraisers going from office to office assessing furniture, windows, and similar items for a possible tax. Finally, there may be a sense that the market corrects for imputed income by, e.g., paying coal miners a premium to compensate for their less attractive work environment, although this arguably makes things even worse, because the miners will now be taxed on a higher income while their office counterparts pay no tax on their compensating, nonmonetary advantages.

So imputed income is an interesting theoretical concept without much practical application. Why then should we bother to talk about it? One reason is that, while imputed income is nearly impossible to tax, the failure to tax it may tell us a great deal about other things that we can tax. Consider again our imaginary coal miner and office worker. Although it is probably impossible to tax the imputed income resulting from the office worker's more pleasant working conditions, identifying that income — and the tax system's failure to reach it — may make us more sympathetic to the coal miner when he asks for (say) a deduction for coal mining equipment, or contributions to a fund for research on Black Lung Disease, or another similar concept. More broadly, a recognition that wealthy individuals benefit from many forms of untaxed enjoyment (large offices, business travel, etc.) may make us more supportive of progressive tax rates and of "nondiscrimination" provisions, like that in section 132, that encourage employers to provide as many benefits as possible to less wealthy taxpayers. Or we may reject either of these arguments; but imputed income will remain part of the debate, increasing our understanding of tax policy and affecting the resolution of specific tax issues.[18]

The imputed income concept demonstrates the difficulty of separating "law" from "policy" in a tax context. Even in the most straightforward area, the law cannot fully be understood without understanding the policy issues that lie just beneath its surface. To put the matter in more flowery language, the statute constitutes the words of the law, but the policy is its music; to read one without the other is very likely to miss the point of both.

In addition to amorphous or psychic income, the term "imputed income" is also used to describe the economic benefit resulting from the self-performance of

---

[18] Imputed income resulting from pleasant employment conditions may at times overlap with working condition fringe benefits, as described in section 132(d) of the Code. For example, an office with a large picture window might be described as a working condition fringe benefit (because it would be deductible if the employee paid for with his own funds), or else as imputed income (because the benefit is largely psychological in nature and would not be taxed under the general principles of section 61). Because both imputed income and working condition fringe benefits are always exempt from tax, this is a largely academic distinction.

services that are available in the cash economy. For example, individuals who perform services for themselves (laundry, housework, etc.) are often said to have imputed income equal to the value of those services, as if they had earned additional income and paid it to themselves for performing the services. As in the employment context, no one really expects the imputed income from goods or services to be taxed, but the failure to do so may tell us something about the resolution of other tax issues. For example, consider the case of two families, each of whom earns $50,000, but the first of whom has one parent at home performing child care and similar services, while the second has both parents working and must pay $10,000 for equivalent services. We are unlikely to tax the first couple on $10,000 of imputed income; but the recognition that we haven't — that the first couple has arguably benefitted from an untaxed form of enrichment — may make us more sympathetic to the second couple when they ask for a child care or similar deduction. *See* Chapter 6, *infra*.

Finally, related issues arise in a number of contexts in which taxpayers receive benefits outside of a clear employment context. For example, in the case of *U.S. v. Gotcher*, 401 F.2d 118 (5th Cir. 1968), a taxpayer and his wife received a twelve-day expense-paid trip to Germany for the purpose of touring Volkswagen facilities. The trip was primarily paid for by the Volkswagen Company, which desired to expand its U.S. presence by offering expense-paid tours to prospective dealers — like Mr. Gotcher. The Service determined that Mr. Gotcher had income equal to the cost of the trip, but the Court held that the personal benefit to Mr. Gotcher was clearly subordinate and incidental to the concrete benefits to the Volkswagen Company, making the cost of Mr. Gotcher's trip excludable from income. In contrast, the Court ruled that Mrs. Gotcher's trip constituted a vacation and thus the cost for her trip was included in income.

The *Gotcher* case presents an example of where psychic income (or imputed income) arises outside of a clear employer-to-employee relationship. The case was decided using a variation of the convenience-to-the-employer test used in *Benaglia*, at the beginning of Chapter 1; but in *Gotcher* the test becomes whether or not the benefits to the taxpayer are *"incidental"* to the business purposes of the payor. As with other forms of imputed income, valuation and enforcement concerns warn against extending the scope of section 61 too far. Although courts frequently pay lip service to the notion that section 61 encompasses all forms of gain that are not explicitly excluded from income, it is not hard to find examples where benefits that should arguably be included in a broad notion of income nevertheless go untaxed.

As we conclude our discussion of the "what is income?" question in Chapters 1 and 2, we are left with both areas where statutory provisions supersede general principles and areas where case law applications of general principles remain our primary sources for guidance. This pattern will repeat itself throughout your study of tax law. Even (or perhaps especially) when faced with as detailed a statute as the Internal Revenue Code, many important questions remain which cannot be answered without considering the policy behind the Code.

Additional Assignment — Chapter 2[19]

Assume that you are an associate in the tax department of a prestigious law firm. A partner at the firm, Charles Benaglia, has sent you the following assigning memo:

"Our client, Trans Global Airlines (TGA), is concerned about the tax treatment of its frequent flyer program, particularly with respect to passengers who used miles earned working for their employers in order to take personal pleasure trips. TGA wishes to know the answer to this question, both for informational purposes and because it is concerned that negative tax consequences may make the program less popular. The company also wishes to be prepared for possible legislative changes in this area.

"Specifically, TGA wishes to ascertain the following:

"(1) Under present law, are passengers who earn frequent flyer miles on business travel, and use them for personal flights, likely to be assessed federal income tax? Is there a clear answer to this question, or does it remain in dispute?

"(2) TGA understands that there may be legislation proposed to clarify that the transactions described in item 1 are, in fact, subject to income tax. If such a tax were to be assessed, when would it most likely be assessed (i.e., at the time the miles are earned or when they are traded in), and how would the amount of tax likely be calculated?

"(3) TGA is considering the creation of a program under which — in addition to trading in their frequent flyer miles for free flights, etc. — individuals could sell them to the company for a specified price per mile. Under present law, what would be the likely tax consequences of this program?

"(4) Is there anything else that TGA should or should not do, in structuring its frequent flyer plan, in order to ensure favorable tax treatment of the program?

"Please write me a brief memorandum on this subject, not later than 5 p.m. yesterday afternoon. Because I will likely forward the memo (after my review) directly to the client, please try to make it as nontechnical as possible, although of course any substantive error will be the end of your career at the firm. Also, because the client is extremely sensitive about billing, please do not write more than three (3) double-spaced pages, and please limit yourself to the casebook and other course materials. And don't bother trying to reach me, I'm visiting a new Caribbean tax haven this weekend."

After you finish screaming, please provide Mr. Benaglia with his memorandum.

---

[19] This assignment, like those in all even-numbered chapters from here on, is intended for use as a short take-home writing assignment, although some instructors may prefer to use it as the basis for in-class discussion.

Chapter 3

TIMING I: THE BASIS CONCEPT AND THE
RELATIONSHIP BETWEEN TAXABLE YEARS

Thus far, our study has emphasized the question of taxability vs. tax exemption, without paying a great deal of attention to when an item is taxed, or how results in one taxable year affect those in another. In this chapter things get more interesting. In particular, we begin to consider the issue of timing. What happens when a taxpayer is promised a benefit, but has yet to receive it? What if she has received the benefit, but may be required to give it back? And what about investments that have increased in value, but which the taxpayer has not actually sold? The taxpayer will almost invariably prefer to delay tax on these items, while the IRS will usually prefer to accelerate them. (The opposite is true when dealing with tax deductions.) The significance of this issue increases with the length of time involved: a short delay may be relatively minor, while a delay of ten years or more is almost equivalent to complete avoidance of tax.[1] But it is nearly always important.

The question of timing leads to the further issue of accounting methods and taxable periods. Suppose that a taxpayer earns money in year one, loses it in year two, and finds it again in year three. Should she be taxed in the year that she finds it? Does it matter whether she received a deduction in year two, or whether (and to what extent) she was originally taxed in year one? Or should each taxable year be considered separately, without regard to events that took place in other periods? Is there a consistent answer to this question, or does it vary in different circumstances? Why do we need a taxable year at all, and what are its implications for other tax issues?

Finally, the matter of timing leads to a number of secondary issues, including loans, basis, and the special rules relating to capital gain income.

Accounting issues often appear technical in nature, but they have important policy implications. This is especially true of the tax rules regarding stocks, real estate, and other forms of investment property. Under the "realization" requirement of our tax system, property that has increased in value is generally not taxed unless the property has been sold or exchanged by the taxpayer. This means that people with relatively modest salaries must pay tax on their full income when it is earned, while those with vast investment gains may delay tax until they dispose of the investment. Is that a fair, or even a logical, result? Would it be so difficult for wealthy taxpayers to keep track of their investments, paying tax on a portion of the gain on their investment property? Or would such a system be administratively cumbersome and discourage people from making useful investments? What are the

---

[1] The precise computation depends upon the interest rate in effect during the relevant period. *See* Background and Basic Themes Chapter, Section C.2, *supra*.

tax reform implications of a system which taxes income from services immediately, but income from property later, if at all, and then often at preferential tax rates? How would a consumption tax or similar reform effort change these rules?

Timing rules also have an enormous impact on personal and business tax planning. Pension and employee benefit taxation is based almost entirely on timing issues, deferral of taxation being permitted for "qualified" pension plans but denied, or at least sharply restricted, for those that don't qualify. Much of corporate, partnership, and international tax planning involves efforts to delay, rather than avoid, tax on the increased value of a business investment. On the deduction side, tax-favored activities — oil and gas, farming, research and development (R & D) expenditures — are typically those that have not the largest number of deductions, but the deductions which may be taken most rapidly.

These issues, or an introduction to them, are the subject of the next few chapters. This chapter introduces the basis and realization concepts and considers essential problems in the timing of income and the relationship between taxable years. Chapter 4 covers realization in greater detail, together with deferred compensation and the possible transition to a consumption or cash-flow tax. Chapter 5 covers loans, interest, and debt-financed property; a separate subject but closely related to the timing rules laid out in the preceding materials.

I. BASIS AND PROPERTY TRANSACTIONS

A. General Rules: Sales and Exchanges of Property

Suppose that in September 2010, instead of spending your full paycheck, you bought $500 of stock in General Motors.[2] Two years later, in September 2012, you sold the stock for $600, *i.e.*, a $100 profit. How much income did you have at that point?

The answer — $100 — seems intuitive, probably because we are so used to the income tax that its general outlines are part of our broader economic worldview. But the answer is hardly inevitable. One can easily imagine a system in which the original $500 would have been deducted from your income in 2010, and the full $600 included in income two years later, on the theory that the money should be taxed only when it is withdrawn for consumption and not when it is invested in other assets. Indeed, one form of a "consumption" tax system would mandate this very calculation. One can also imagine a system that would have imposed incremental taxes based on the increased value of the stock in 20011 and 2012, so that you would have paid some tax even before the stock was sold, although this system might be more difficult to administer.

Under the existing Code, however, the answer is simple. There are no tax consequences in 2010 or 2011, and a tax on $100 of income is imposed in 2012, when the stock is finally sold. The same rule now applies to the new purchaser: if in a

---

[2] For an introduction to stocks, bonds, and similar concepts, see Background and Basic Themes Chapter, Section C.1, *supra*.

future year she sells the stock for an amount greater than $600, she will register taxable gain, and if for less than that, a deductible loss.

Although the rules above may seem intuitive, there is nevertheless a correct way to say them. In tax parlance, your adjusted basis for the stock is said to be $500, and your amount realized on the sale $600. The gain on the sale is $100, or the excess of the amount realized over the adjusted basis. I.R.C. § 1001(a). By contrast, if the adjusted basis exceeded the amount realized, you would have a loss equal to that latter excess. The increased value of stock, before it is sold, simply does not show up in the tax code. In tax parlance, it is most commonly referred to as "unrealized appreciation" or "unrealized gain," and is excluded from tax because of the realization requirement.

The basis concept is simple enough when dealing with stock, land, or other assets that do not depreciate or lose value after they have been purchased. For these assets, adjusted basis (section 1011) is generally the same as basis (section 1012), which in turn usually means the taxpayer's cost for the property. The situation is somewhat more complicated for assets on which the taxpayer is entitled to depreciation or depletion deductions, such as factory equipment or an oil well. We will discuss such assets in detail in later chapters; for now, you should understand that adjusted basis is reduced by the amount of depreciation or similar deductions, so that the taxpayer will not receive a double benefit on disposition of the asset.[3] Amount realized can likewise become more complicated where property as well as cash are received in a transaction, or where assets are subject to mortgages or other forms of debt. But in the simplest instance, basis is simply the (adjusted) cost of an asset, and the equation in section 1001(a) reflects the common-sense assumption that sales producing a profit should be subject to tax and those producing a loss should give rise to tax deductions.

B.   Special Rules: Gifts and Bequests

The rules above work well enough for sales, exchanges, or similar arm's-length transactions. What about gifts, bequests, and other gratuitous transfers? In Chapter 1, we learned that gifts and bequests are not included in the recipient's income under section 102 of the Code. Thus, if Mother gives Daughter $500, there is no income tax consequence for either person. (Gift taxes may be owed in some cases.[4])

What if, instead of cash, Mother gives Daughter stock that Mother bought previously for $10,000, but is now worth $50,000? Even assuming that the gift itself is nontaxable, shouldn't the Mother at least be taxed on the $40,000 in

---

[3] For example, if a taxpayer bought a factory for $1 million, and took $300,000 of depreciation, the adjusted basis of the factory would be reduced to $700,000. The total "recovery" of basis by the taxpayer ($300,000 depreciation plus $700,000 to be offset against the profits of any future sale) would thus not exceed $1 million or the taxpayer's original cost for the property. Depreciation is discussed further in Chapter 8.

[4] A gift tax, similar to the estate tax at death, is imposed on lifetime transfers that exceed the annual exclusion level ($13,000 in 2009), subject to a credit that (effectively) postpones payment of the tax until more than $1 million of cumulative gifts ($2 million for married couples) have been made.

appreciation? If the Daughter turns around and sells the stock for $55,000, one year later, how much tax should she pay?

The answer to these questions dates back to the holding in *Taft v. Bowers*, 278 U.S. 470 (1929), decided by the Supreme Court in 1929, and is today found in section 1015(a) of the Code. Under this rule, for gifts received after 1920, the recipient's basis "shall be the same as it would be in the hands of the donor or the last preceding owner by whom it was not acquired by gift. . . ." In other words, when Mother gives the appreciated stock to Daughter, nothing happens. No (income) tax is paid by Mother or Daughter, and Daughter takes the stock with a $10,000 basis that reflects the price Mother paid when she acquired the stock some years back. In tax parlance, the recipient receives a "carryover" or a "substituted" basis, and the transaction itself is a "nonrecognition" transaction, that is, one that does not require payment of tax on the appreciation built in to the property. If Daughter later sells the stock for $55,000, she pays tax on $45,000 of income ($55,000–$10,000), rather than the $5,000 which would be taxable to her if she had acquired the stock in a taxable transaction.[5]

Before moving on, two things should be noted about the discussion above. The first is that the entire issue is essentially a matter of timing: should the $40,000 in appreciation, which took place while Mother held the stock, be subject to tax now, at the time of the gift, or later, when Daughter sells the same stock? The answer to this question — not now, but later — is accomplished by avoiding tax at the time of the gift, and giving Daughter a basis that reflects the (lower) price when Mother acquired the stock rather than the (higher) price in effect when Daughter actually received it ($50,000). The carryover basis thus ensures that the untaxed income will "catch up" with Daughter on a subsequent sale of the stock.[6] This is the usual pattern of nonrecognition transactions: tax is delayed, but not avoided, by the mechanism of reducing (or refusing to increase) basis as would be the case in a taxable transaction.

A second interesting aspect relates to tax rates and simple tax planning. One reason people make gifts of appreciated property is precisely to avoid tax on the appreciation, or to have the tax paid by a younger family member who is likely to be in a lower tax bracket. The Code effectively permits this mechanism, by allowing (say) a parent to transfer appreciated stock to a child and have the full amount of the appreciation taxed at the child's lower tax rate.[7] Yet the same generous treatment is not extended to losses. Under the second clause of section 1015(a), "if [the adjusted] basis . . . is greater than the fair market value of the property at the time of the gift, then for purpose of determining loss the basis shall be such fair market value." Thus, if Father gave Son a gift of stock that Father had purchased

---

[5] If the transaction had been taxable, Mother would have paid tax on $40,000 of appreciation, but Daughter would have received a $50,000 basis, resulting in taxable gain of $5,000 on a later $55,000 sale. Under the carryover basis regime, there is no tax at the time of the gift; instead there is $45,000 of taxable income ($55,000 - $10,000) on the subsequent sale.

[6] *See* note 6 *supra*. Daughter may permanently avoid the tax if she dies without ever selling the stock, as discussed in the following pages.

[7] This example assumes that the child is over 18 years of age. *Cf.* I.R.C. § 1(g) (income of certain minor children taxed as if it were parents' income).

for $50,000, but which was worth $10,000 at the time of transfer, Son's basis for determining loss would be $10,000 rather than $50,000, effectively denying Son the $40,000 of "built-in" loss for tax purposes. Why do you suppose that Congress would enact a rule that permitted taxpayers to shift the taxation of built-in gains on gift property, but prevented them from doing the same thing for built-in losses? What are the equity and efficiency implications of a rule that requires gift recipients to pay tax on previous appreciation in the value of gift property, but prevents them from taking deductions for an equivalent decline in value?

C.   Section 1014 and the "Step-Up" of Basis at Death

For the most part, the basis rules are characterized by consistency. Basis may increase to reflect a taxable gain on the sale or exchange of property, decrease to reflect a deductible loss, or remain constant when a transfer has no tax consequences (as is the case for a lifetime gift). But basis does not, as a general rule, emerge from nowhere. One cannot usually have one's cake and eat it too, by avoiding tax on a transaction but still receiving an increased basis as if the tax had been paid.

Section 1014 is a major — almost literally fatal — exception to this principle. Under section 1014, the basis of property held at death is its fair market value on the date of death, even if the decedent bought it for a much lower price and even though no tax is paid on the appreciation that took place during the decedent's life. Thus, if the decedent bought stock for $50,000 in 1981, and the stock is worth $500,000 upon his death twenty years later, his children (or other inheritors) automatically receive a $500,000 basis for the stock, so that the $450,000 in appreciation will never be taxed — not now, not later, never.[8] Essentially, the tax and basis questions are both resolved in favor of the taxpayer. There is no tax at the time of death, but also no future "catch up" as in the case of lifetime transfers. According to recent estimates, the provision costs the Treasury more than $40 billion in annual revenues and the amount increases each year.

How can such a rule possibly be defended? Three arguments are usually made. The first relates to taxpayer bookkeeping. It would (or so the argument goes) be hard for the survivors to figure out the decedent's original purchase price for each asset, and it's easier to use the date of death value, which is likely to be more easily obtainable by the executors. But this problem appears to be exaggerated, and a reasonable estimate of the purchase price would still be more accurate than an automatic "step-up" to the date of death value. A second argument is sympathy: it seems harsh to hit the survivors with a tax at the moment of their grief, and frustrates the decedent's goal of keeping money within the family in the first place. But this humanitarian concern is rather unusual for the tax system, and arguably insulting to less wealthy families, who are presumably no less unhappy when relatives dies, but must make do without a substantial tax benefit to console them.

A third argument — really, a more sophisticated version of the second — relates to the interplay of the estate and income taxes. According to this argument,

---

[8] There is a rule (section 1014(e)) that prevents one from giving property to a dying person, just to benefit from the step-up. Anyone who asked this question has a good future as a tax lawyer.

simultaneous imposition of the estate and income taxes would, in the absence of section 1014, result in a near-confiscatory tax burden, especially if the assets in question had appreciated significantly in the decedent's lifetime. For example, if a decedent had $2 million in property for which she had paid $200,000, a 50 percent estate tax (creating a $1 million tax liability), together with a 40 percent tax on the lifetime appreciation (.40 × $1.8 million = a $0.72 million tax liability), would result in a combined tax rate of over 80 percent on the relevant property ($1.72 million combined tax liability / $2 million property value).[9] This is a more persuasive argument, but somewhat naive. The estate tax is imposed only on millionaires, and there are numerous ways for reducing or avoiding the tax by careful planning. The present law rules also result in a highly inconsistent policy: section 1014 applies to people who hold their property until death, but not to those selling property and passing on the resulting cash to their survivors, who remain subject to both the income and estate taxes on these amounts.[10]

In the year 2000, as part of a multiyear phase-out of the estate and gift taxes, Congress enacted a staged repeal of the section 1014 basis step-up. When and if completed, in 2010, the law would require recipients of inherited property to take a carryover basis in the property, just as section 1015 mandates for lifetime gifts. Even when the phase-out is completed — and assuming Congress does not change its mind again in the interim — the basis of property could still be increased by up to $1.3 million ($3.0 million for property passing to a surviving spouse) by the executor of any given estate. Thus, in one form or another, the basis step-up is likely to be with us for the foreseeable future.

Using the Sources

Using sections 1011 through 1015, explain the federal income tax consequences of the following transactions:

1. Smith buys 500 shares of stock at a total price of $50,000 and sells them, at a price of $75,000, three years later.

2. Jones buys a factory, at a price of $2 million, in 2005. She takes $500,000 of depreciation deductions and then, in 2010, sells the factory for a price of $1.8 million.

3. Mr. Goldberg bought stock for $10,000 in 1950. In 1980, when it was worth $50,000, he gave it as a gift to his daughter, Jane. In 2001, Jane sold the stock — which had continued to increase in value — for $100,000.

4. Mrs. Gonzalez bought stock for $50,000 in 1950. In 1970, when it had declined in value to $40,000, she gave it as a gift to her son, Juan. In 2001, Juan sold the stock

---

[9] The estate tax is imposed, usually at rates of 50 percent or higher, on the fair market value of the estate, determined in most cases as of the date of death. The gift tax is imposed on lifetime transfers. Both the gift and estate taxes are subject to an exclusion provision, the effect of which is to exempt a substantial portion of lifetime and death transfers from tax. The estate tax is currently scheduled to be eliminated in 2010 and to reappear in 2011.

[10] For example, had the individual in the text sold her stock for $2 million and allowed the resulting cash to pass through her estate, she would have been paid income tax on the appreciation ($1.8 million) and estate tax on the full $2 million, even allowing for the existence of section 1014.

for the same price ($40,000). What would your answer be if instead of $40,000, Juan sold the stock at a price of (a) $100,000, (b) $45,000?

5.   George Geezer died in 2001, owning stock which he had purchased twenty years earlier for $400,000, but that at the time of his death had a fair market value of $800,000. If his estate sells the stock at that same price three months later, how much gain or loss does it realize for income tax purposes? What if instead the sale price was $850,000 (or $750,000), reflecting changes in the stock's value after George's death?

Law and Planning

Whatever the logical merits of the gift and death basis rules, they make for fascinating planning opportunities. To appreciate these fully, one needs to know somewhat more about the estate tax, capital gain rules, and other issues in addition to income taxes. But it's never too soon to start thinking about these issues. Using your current knowledge, do your best to answer the questions below. (Assume the present law rules remain in effect in all cases; we'll discuss dealing with future changes in a moment.)

1.   Anne and Michael Wennington are 45 years old and have two children, Sarah (15) and Jonathan (10). Anne and Michael own stock in a family corporation which has a low basis (about $250,000) but a fair market value of $1 million. The corporation is doing well, so that Anne and Michael expect that the stock will continue to appreciate in value during the remainder of their lifetimes. The couple's goal is, eventually, to transfer the stock to their children with the lowest aggregate payment of tax.

a. Assuming the income tax was their only concern, would Anne and Michael be better off transferring the stock to their children now, as a gift, or holding the stock and letting it pass to their children at their death? What would be the likely income tax treatment, of themselves and their children, in either case?

b. Assume that, in addition to income taxes, Anne and Michael are concerned about the effect of estate and gift taxes. (For purposes of this question, assume that these taxes are imposed at a flat 50 percent rate and ignore the effect of any deductions, credits, and so forth). Since the estate and gift taxes are based on the fair market value of the property at the time of the gift (gift tax) or at the time of death (estate tax), in the case of appreciating property, the taxes are likely to be lower the sooner the transfer is made. How does this new consideration affect your answer to question one, above? Between the income tax, on the one hand, and the estate and gift taxes, on the other, which is likely to be the couple's predominant concern?

c. What effect would each of the following have on your answers to a and b above?

i. The family corporation is in a highly volatile field (*e.g.*, high technology) and the future performance of its stock is extremely difficult to predict.

    ii. Sarah and Jonathan are nice but not particularly responsible children, and show signs of growing into nice but not particularly responsible adults.

    iii. Anne and Michael are (alas) in poor health and uncertain of reaching old age.

2.   Assume now that your clients ask you to take into account the effect of possible future changes in the law: that is, the scheduled phase-out of the estate and gift tax and partial repeal of the section 1014 basis step-up. Both these phase-outs are scheduled to be completed by the year 2010, but Congress is notorious for changing its mind about such matters, and your clients have an awful lot of money riding on the correct answer. How would you deal with this uncertainty in answering any part of question one, above, and what steps (if any) would you advise your clients to take in order to "hedge" against the resulting legal uncertainty?

3.   What additional facts, if any, would you want to have in order to answer questions one or two more fully?

Politics and Policy

When Congress makes a major change in the law, such as the (eventual) repeal of the section 1014 basis step-up, is it obligated to provide transitional relief for people who entered into transactions before the change was adopted? For example, should people who bought property before 2000, on the assumption that the basis step-up would apply indefinitely, continue to qualify for this benefit even if other, later purchasers do not? If so, where should the line be drawn?

Most contemporary scholars seem to believe that there is no inherent "right" to transitional relief and, indeed, that such relief introduces more distortions and unfairness than it corrects. For these observers, changes in the law are not fundamentally different from changes in the economy, the weather, or anything else: you take your chances and a smart player plans for all eventualities. Yet taxpayers often consider it unfair to "change the rules in the middle of the game," and in practice most major tax changes are either delayed, like the section 1014 amendments, and/or made subject to extensive transitional relief. For a comprehensive tax change, such as the adoption of a consumption rather than income tax, the cost of transitional relief could run into the tens of billions of dollars.

On the issue of transitional relief, see Daniel Shaviro, *When Rules Change: An Economic and Political Analysis of Transition Relief and Retroactivity* (2000).

II. RETURN OF CAPITAL AND ITS EFFECT ON INCOME COMPUTATION

In essence, the basis rules are simply a way of ensuring that you don't pay tax twice on the same money. Thus, if a person buys stock for $100 and sells it for $500, he pays tax on only $400 of that amount. The first $100 — that is to say, his basis

— remains untaxed because it is a return ("recovery") of his original capital investment. Another way to say this is that the person was already taxed, at some previous point, when he earned the $100 in question; taxing it a second time would amount to double taxation, which the Code avoids at any (or at almost any) cost.

The underlying notion — that you shouldn't be taxed twice on the same money — recurs frequently in the tax code, but wears different disguises. Although we will study these items in more detail later on, a brief overview is useful.

At one extreme are expenditures, like salaries paid to the employees of a business, the benefits of which are used up within one year.[11] These kind of expenditures are usually deductible in the year paid; that is, the business gets to subtract them from its taxable income and pay tax on the excess of its income over these (and other similar) deductions. These deductions are dealt with in Chapter 6.

In a second category are expenditures for assets, like machinery or equipment, which last longer than one year, but not forever. These expenditures are recovered under a system, commonly known as depreciation, that prorates deductions over the "useful life" or some other period relating to the asset. For example, if a computer costs $10,000, and is expected to last five years, $2,000 (that is, one fifth) of the cost of the computer might be deducted against income for each of the next five years.[12] These items, and the distinctions between them and more immediately deductible expenses, are considered in Chapter 8.

A third category of expenditures relates to assets, like land or corporate stock, that have theoretically unlimited useful lives, *i.e.*, that (at least in theory) last forever. Since these expenditures are not being "used up" with the passage of time, there is no need to allow deductions or depreciation for them. Instead, the taxpayer simply takes a basis for the items and offsets that basis against the sale price when and if she decides to sell the property. This delayed recovery of basis is essentially the basis equivalent of the income realization rule, which delays taxation of gain until the asset has been sold or otherwise disposed of. It is with this third category of assets that we are primarily concerned in this chapter.

When an asset like land or stock is sold in its entirety, the issue of capital recovery is relatively simple. It becomes more interesting when the disposal is less clear-cut. For example, part but not all of the asset may be sold, requiring the basis to be allocated among different portions of the original property. Or the asset may be damaged but not destroyed in an accident or similar casualty, leading to the question of how much, if any, of the original basis should be offset against a recovery from the tortfeasor. In other cases, the taxpayer may receive payments that are related to, but not precisely the same as, previous investments in the same property. In all of these cases, the boundary between (taxable) income and (nontaxable) return of capital is elusive. Since unrecovered basis generally remains to offset income in later taxable years, these cases primarily raise timing issues: the taxpayer prefers an earlier recovery of capital for convenience purposes and

---

[11] Some salaries, like those of workers constructing a building, may give rise to multi-year benefits and their deductions may be accordingly delayed. *See* Chapter 8, *infra*.

[12] This example assumes that the computer is used for a valid business purpose. There is no deduction for computers or other items intended for personal use.

because of the time value of money, while the Government typically argues for delay. In some cases (*e.g.*, personal injury awards), unrecovered basis may be lost altogether, and the issue has a more all-or-nothing character.

The following cases raise the recovery of capital issue in its various forms. Try to focus on the conceptual issues that these items suggest. Exactly what kind of "capital" does the taxpayer claim to be recovering in each case, and is the argument convincing or not? Is the taxpayer trying to avoid taxation altogether, or merely trying to defer it, so that the case raises primarily timing issues? What broader issues, if any, are implicated by these decisions?

CLARK v. COMMISSIONER
Board of Tax Appeals
40 B.T.A. 333 (1939)

LEECH, J:

This is a proceeding to redetermine a deficiency in income tax for the calendar year 1934 in the amount of $10,618.87. The question presented is whether petitioner derived income by the payment to him of an amount of $19,941.10, by his tax counsel, to compensate him for a loss suffered on account of erroneous advice given him by the latter. The facts were stipulated and are so found. The stipulation, so far as material, follows:

* * *

3. The petitioner during the calendar year 1932, and for a considerable period prior thereto, was married and living with his wife. He was required by the Revenue Act of 1932 to file a Federal Income Tax Return of his income for the year 1932. For such year petitioner and his wife could have filed a joint return or separate returns.

4. Prior to the time that the 1932 Federal Income Tax return or returns of petitioner and/or his wife were due to be filed, petitioner retained experienced tax counsel to prepare the necessary return or returns for him and/or his wife. Such tax counsel prepared a joint return for petitioner and his wife and advised petitioner to file it instead of two separate returns. In due course it was filed with the Collector of Internal Revenue for the First District of California. . . .

5. Thereafter on or about the third day of February, 1934, a duly appointed revenue agent of the United States audited the aforesaid 1932 return and recommended an additional assessment against petitioner in the sum of $34,590.27, which was subsequently reduced to $32,820.14. This last mentioned sum was thereafter assessed against and was paid by petitioner to the Collector of Internal Revenue for the First District of California.

6. The deficiency of $32,820.14 arose from an error on the part of tax counsel who prepared petitioner's 1932 return. The error was that he improperly deducted from income the total amount of losses sustained on

the sale of capital assets held for a period of more than two years instead of applying the statutory limitation required by Section 101(b) of the Revenue Act of 1932.

7. The error referred to in paragraph six above was called to the attention of the tax counsel who prepared the joint return of petitioner and his wife for the year 1932. Recomputations were then made which disclosed that if petitioner and his wife had filed separate returns for the year 1932 their combined tax liability would have been $19,941.10 less than that which was finally assessed against and paid by petitioner.

8. Thereafter, tax counsel admitted that if he had not erred in computing the tax liability shown on the joint return filed by the petitioner, he would have advised petitioner to file separate returns for himself and his wife, and accordingly tax counsel tendered to petitioner the sum of $19,941.10, which was the difference between what petitioner and his wife would have paid on their 1932 returns if separate returns had been filed and the amount which petitioner was actually required to pay on the joint return as filed. Petitioner accepted the $19,941.10.

9. In his final determination of petitioner's 1934 tax liability, the respondent included the aforesaid $19,941.10 in income.

10. Petitioner's books of account are kept on the cash receipts and disbursements basis and his tax returns are made on such basis under the community property laws of the State of California.

* * *

The theory on which the respondent included the above sum of $19,941.10 in petitioner's gross income for 1934, is that this amount constituted taxes paid for petitioner by a third party and that, consequently, petitioner was in receipt of income to that extent. The cases of *Old Colony Trust Co. v. Commissioner*, 279 U.S. 716; *United States v. Boston & Maine Railroad*, 279 U.S. 732, are cited as authority for his position. Petitioner, on the contrary, contends that this payment constituted compensation for damages or loss caused by the error of tax counsel, and that he therefore realized no income from its receipt in 1934.

We agree with petitioner. The cases cited by the respondent are not applicable here. Petitioner's taxes were not paid for him by any person — as rental, compensation for services rendered, or otherwise. He paid his own taxes.

When the joint return was filed, petitioner became obligated to and did pay the taxes computed on that basis. *John D. Biggers*, 39 B.T.A. 480. In paying that obligation, he sustained a loss which was caused by the negligence of his tax counsel. The $19,941.10 was paid to petitioner, not *qua* taxes (*cf. T. G. Nicholson*, 38 B.T.A. 190), but as compensation to petitioner for his loss. The measure of that loss, and the compensation therefor, was the sum of money which petitioner became legally obligated to and did pay because of that negligence. The fact that such obligation was for taxes is of no moment here.

It has been held that payments in settlement of an action for breach of promise to marry are not income. *Lyde McDonald*, 9 B.T.A. 1340. Compromise payments in settlement of an action for damages against a bank on account of conduct impairing the taxpayer's goodwill by injuring its reputation are also not taxable. *Farmers & Merchants Bank of Catlettsburg, Ky. v. Commissioner*, 59 Fed.(2d) 912. The same result follows in the case of payments in settlement for injuries caused by libel and slander. *C.A. Hawkins*, 6 B.T.A. 1023. Damages for personal injury are likewise not income. *Theodate Pope Riddle*, 27 B.T.A. 1339.

The theory of those cases is that recoupment on account of such losses is not income since it is not "derived from capital, from labor or from both combined." *See Merchants Loan & Trust Co. v. Smietanka*, 255 U.S. 509; *United States v. Safety Car Heating & Lighting Co.*, 297 U.S. 88. And the fact that the payment of the compensation for such loss was voluntary, as here, does not change its exempt status. *Rice, Barton & Fales Inc. v. Commissioner*, 41 Fed.(2d) 339. It was, in fact, compensation for a loss which impaired petitioner's capital.

Moreover, so long as petitioner neither could nor did take a deduction in a prior year of this loss in such a way as to offset income for the prior year, the amount received by him in the taxable year, by way of recompense, is not then includable in his gross income. *Central Loan & Investment Co.*, 39 B.T.A. 981.

Decision will be entered for the petitioner.

Understanding *Clark*

1. *Clark* concerns a lawyer who compensated his client for the consequences of a tax planning error. That being the case, why do cases of libel, slander, and breach of promise to marry figure prominently in the opinion? Do the phrases "return of capital" or "impairment of capital" do anything to explain these seemingly misplaced citations? Are these convincing or relevant precedents?

2. The last paragraph of *Clark* notes, almost in passing, that Clark received no deduction for his lawyer's original mistake in filing his taxes. Suppose that taxpayers were permitted a deduction for bad legal advice and that Clark had taken advantage of this deduction upon discovering the mistake in 1933. Would the result of the case have been any different? What if tax rates doubled between 1933 and 1934, so that the deduction only saved Clark (say) $10,000, but including the item in income would cost him $20,000 in additional taxes? While we're on the subject, why couldn't Clark simply amend his 1932 tax return, and avoid the entire problem?

3. Can Clark's lawyer deduct the amount of the repayment? Is this relevant to Clark's treatment, or is it a separate issue?

RAYTHEON PRODUCTION CORP. v. COMMISSIONER
United States Court of Appeals, First Circuit
144 F.2d 110 (1944)

Before MAGRUDER, MAHONEY, and WOODBURY, CIRCUIT JUDGES.

MAHONEY, CIRCUIT JUDGE.

This case presents the question whether an amount received by the taxpayer in compromise settlement of a suit for damages under the Federal Anti-Trust Laws, 15 U.S.C.A. § 1 *et seq.*, is a non-taxable return of capital or income. If the recovery is non-taxable, there is a second question as to whether the Tax Court erred in holding that there was insufficient evidence to enable it to determine what part of the lump sum payment received by the taxpayer was properly allocable to compromise of the suit and what part was allocable to payment for certain patent license rights which were conveyed as a part of the settlement.

Petitioner, Raytheon Production Corporation, came into existence as a result of a series of what both parties as well as the Tax Court have treated as tax free reorganizations. Since we think such is the proper treatment, we shall simplify the facts by referring to any one of the original and successor companies as Raytheon. The original Raytheon Company was a pioneer manufacturer of a rectifying tube which made possible the operation of a radio receiving set on alternating current instead of on batteries. In 1926 its profits were about $450,000; in 1927 about $150,000; and in 1928, $10,000. The Radio Corporation of America had many patents covering radio circuits and claimed control over almost all of the practical circuits. Cross-licensing agreements had been made among several companies including R.C.A., General Electric Company, Westinghouse, and American Telephone & Telegraph Company. R.C.A. had developed a competitive tube which produced the same type of rectification as the Raytheon tube. Early in 1927, R.C.A. began to license manufacturers of radio sets and in the license agreement it incorporated "Clause 9," which provided that the licensee was required to buy its tubes from R.C.A. In 1928 practically all manufacturers were operating under R.C.A. licenses. As a consequence of this restriction, Raytheon was left with only replacement sales, which soon disappeared. When Raytheon found it impossible to market its tubes in the early part of 1929, it obtained a license from R.C.A. to manufacture tubes under the letters patent on a royalty basis. The license agreement contained a release of all claims of Raytheon against R.C.A. by reason of the illegal acts of the latter under Clause 9 but by a side agreement such claims could be asserted if R.C.A. should pay similar claims to others. The petitioner was informed of instances in which R.C.A. had settled claims against it based on Clause 9. On that ground it considered itself released from the agreement not to enforce its claim against R.C.A. and consequently, on December 14, 1931, the petitioner caused its predecessor, Raytheon, to bring suit against R.C.A. in the District Court of Massachusetts alleging that the plaintiff had by 1926 created and then possessed a large and valuable goodwill in interstate commerce in rectifying tubes for radios and had a large and profitable established business therein so that the net profit for the year 1926 was $454,935; that the business had an established prospect of large increases and that the business and goodwill thereof was of a value of exceeding $3,000,000; that by the beginning of 1927 the plaintiff was doing approximately 80% of the business of rectifying tubes of the entire United States; that the defendant conspired to destroy the business of the plaintiff and others by a monopoly of such business and did suppress and destroy the existing companies; that the manufacturers of radio sets and others ceased to purchase tubes from the plaintiffs; that by the end of 1927 the conspiracy had completely destroyed the profitable business and that by the early part of 1928 the tube business of the plaintiff and its property and goodwill had been totally destroyed at a time when it had a present value in excess of $3,000,000, and thereby the plaintiff was injured in its business and property in a sum in excess of $3,000,000. The action against R.C.A. was referred to an auditor who found that clause 9 was not the cause of damage to the plaintiff but that the decline in plaintiff's business was due to advancement in the radio art and competition. The auditor, however, also found that if it should be decided that Clause 9 had turned the development of the radio art away from plaintiff's type of tube, then the damages would be $1,000,000.

In the spring of 1938, after the auditor's report and just prior to the time for the commencement of the trial before a jury, the Raytheon affiliated companies began negotiations for the settlement of the litigation with R.C.A. In the meantime a suit brought by R.C.A. against the petitioner for the non-payment of royalties resulted in a judgment of $410,000 in favor of R.C.A. R.C.A. and the petitioner finally agreed on the payment by R.C.A. of $410,000 in settlement of the antitrust action. R.C.A. required the inclusion in the settlement of patent license rights and sublicensing rights to some thirty patents but declined to allocate the amount paid as between the patent license rights and the amount for the settlement of the suit. The agreement of settlement contained a general release of any and all possible claims between the parties.

The officers of the Raytheon companies testified that $60,000 of the $410,000 received from R.C.A. was the maximum worth of the patents, basing their appraisal on the cost of development of the patents and the fact that few of them were then being used and that no royalties were being derived from them. In its income tax return the petitioner returned $60,000 of the $410,000 as income from patent licenses and treated the remaining $350,000 as a realization from a chose in action and not as taxable income. The Commissioner determined that the $350,000 constituted income on the following ground contained in the statement attached to his notice of deficiency: "It is the opinion of this office that the amount of $350,000 constitutes income under § 22(a) of the Revenue Act of 1936. There exists no clear evidence of what the amount was paid for so that an accurate apportionment can be made as to a specific consideration for patent rights transferred to Radio Corporation of America and a consideration for damages. The amount of $350,000 has therefore been included in your taxable income."

Adverting to the question of whether that part of the $410,000 which was paid by R.C.A. to Raytheon to settle the antitrust suit was a return of capital or ordinary income, we must observe that the auditor's report is immaterial on that issue. Despite the fact that the auditor found that the loss was not caused by Clause 9, it was open to the jury to come to a different conclusion on the question of liability, and to avoid this R.C.A. settled the suit by compromise.

Damages recovered in an antitrust action are not necessarily nontaxable as a return of capital. As in other types of tort damage suits, recoveries which represent a reimbursement for lost profits are income. *Swastika Oil & Gas Co. v. Commissioner*, 6 Cir., 1941, 123 F.2d 382, *certiorari denied* 1943, 317 U.S. 639; *H. Liebes & Co. v. Commissioner*, 9 Cir., 1937, 90 F.2d 932; *Sternberg v. Commissioner*, 1935, 32 B.T.A. 1039. The reasoning is that since the profits would be taxable income, the proceeds of litigation which are their substitute are taxable in like manner.

Damages for violation of the anti-trust acts are treated as ordinary income where they represent compensation for loss of profits. *Commercial Electrical Supply Co. v. Commissioner*, 1927, 8 B.T.A. 986; *see Park v. Gilligan*, D.C.S.D. Ohio 1921, 293 F. 129, 130.

The test is not whether the action was one in tort or contract but rather the question to be asked is "In lieu of what were the damages awarded?" *Farmers' & Merchants' Bank v. Commissioner*, 6 Cir., 1932, 59 F.2d 912; *Swastika Oil & Gas Co. v. Commissioner, supra*; *Central R. Co. of New Jersey v. Commissioner*, 3 Cir., 1935, 79 F.2d 697, 101 A.L.R. 1448. *See United States v. Safety Car Heating & Lighting Co.*, 1936, 297 U.S. 88, 98. Plumb, *Income Tax on Gains and Losses in Litigation* (1940) 25 Cornell L.Q. 221. Where the suit is not to recover lost profits but is for injury to goodwill, the recovery represents a return of capital and, with certain limitations to be set forth below, is not taxable. *Farmers' & Merchants' Bank v. Commissioner, supra*. Plumb, *supra*, 25 Cornell L.Q. 221, 225. "Care must certainly be taken in such cases to avoid taxing recoveries for injuries to goodwill or loss of capital." 1 Paul and Mertens Law of Federal Income Taxation § 6.48.

Upon examination of Raytheon's declaration in its anti-trust suit we find nothing to indicate that the suit was for the recovery of lost profits. The allegations were that the illegal conduct of R.C.A. "completely destroyed the profitable interstate and foreign commerce of the plaintiff and thereby, by the early part of 1928, the said tube business of the plaintiff and the property goodwill of the plaintiff therein had been totally destroyed at a time when it then had a present value in excess of three million dollars and thereby the plaintiff was then injured in its business and property in a sum in excess of three million dollars." This was not the sort of antitrust suit where the plaintiff's business still exists and where the injury was merely for loss of profits. The allegations and evidence as to the amount of profits were necessary in order to establish the value of the goodwill and business since that is derived by a capitalization of profits. A somewhat similar idea was expressed in *Farmers' & Merchants' Bank v. Commissioner, supra*, 59 F.2d at page 913. "Profits were one of the chief indications of the worth of the business; but the usual earnings before the injury, as compared with those afterward, were only an evidential factor in determining actual loss and not an independent basis for recovery." Since the suit was to recover damages for the destruction of the business and goodwill, the recovery represents a return of capital. Nor does the fact that the suit ended in a compromise settlement change the nature of the recovery; "the determining factor is the nature of the basic claim from which the compromised amount was realized." Paul Selected Studies in Federal Taxation, Second Series, pp. 328–9, footnote 76; *Helvering v. Safe Deposit & Trust Co. of Baltimore*, 1941,

316 U.S. 56, 139 A.L.R. 1513; *Lyeth v. Hoey*, 1938, 305 U.S. 188,119 A.L.R. 410; *Central R. of New Jersey v. Commissioner, supra; Farmers' & Merchants' Bank v. Commissioner, supra; Megargel v. Commissioner*, 1944, 3 T.C. 238.

But, to say that the recovery represents a return of capital in that it takes the place of the business goodwill is not to conclude that it may not contain a taxable benefit. Although the injured party may not be deriving a profit as a result of the damage suit itself, the conversion thereby of his property into cash is a realization of any gain made over the cost or other basis of the goodwill prior to the illegal interference. Thus A buys Blackacre for $5,000. It appreciates in value to $50,000. B tortiously destroys it by fire. A sues and recovers $50,000 tort damages from B. Although no gain was derived by A from the suit, his prior gain due to the appreciation in value of Blackacre is realized when it is turned into cash by the money damages.

Compensation for the loss of Raytheon's goodwill in excess of its cost is gross income. *See* MAGIL TAXABLE INCOME, p. 339. 1 MERTENS, LAW OF FEDERAL INCOME TAXATION, § 5.21, footnote 82. Plumb, *supra*, 25 CORNELL L.Q. 225,6.

Since we assume with the parties that the petitioner secured the original Raytheon's assets through a series of tax free reorganizations, petitioner's basis or the goodwill is the same as that of the original Raytheon. As the Tax Court pointed out, the record is devoid of evidence as to the amount of that basis and "in the absence of evidence of the basis of the business and goodwill of Raytheon, the amount of any nontaxable capital recovery cannot be ascertained." 1 T.C. 952. *Cf. Sterling v. Commissioner*, 2 Cir., 1937, 93 F.2d 304.

Where the cost basis that may be assigned to property has been wholly speculative, the gain has been held to be entirely conjectural and not taxable. In *Strother v. Commissioner*, 4 Cir., 1932, 55 F.2d 626, *affirmed on other grounds*, 1932, 287 U.S. 308, a trespasser had taken coal and then destroyed the entries so that the amount of coal taken could not be determined. Since there was no way of knowing whether the recovery was greater than the basis for the coal taken, the gain was purely conjectural and not taxed. Magill explains the result as follows: "as the amount of coal removed could not be determined until a final disposition of the property, the computation of gain or loss on the damages must await that disposition." TAXABLE INCOME, pp. 339–340. The same explanation may be applied to *Farmers' & Merchants' Bank v. Commissioner, supra*, which relied on the *Strother* case in finding no gain. The recovery in that case had been to compensate for the injury to goodwill and business reputation of the plaintiff bank inflicted by defendant reserve banks' wrongful conduct in collecting checks drawn on the plaintiff bank by employing "agents who would appear daily at the bank with checks and demand payment thereof in cash in such a manner as to attract unfavorable public comment." Since the plaintiff bank's business was not destroyed but only injured and since it continued in business, it would have been difficult to require the taxpayer to prove what part of the basis of its goodwill should be attributed to the recovery. In the case at bar, on the contrary, the entire business and goodwill were destroyed so that to require the taxpayer to prove the cost of the goodwill is no more impractical than if the business had been sold.

Inasmuch as we conclude that the portion of the $410,000 attributable to the suit is taxable income, the second question as to allocation between this and the ordinary income from patent licenses is not present.

The decision of the Tax Court is affirmed.

Understanding *Raytheon*

1.   What is the significance of the distinction made by the taxpayer between royalty payments, on the one hand, and amounts received in settlement of an antitrust claim, on the other? Which of these does the taxpayer say should be nontaxable, and why? What if anything does this discussion have to do with the return of capital concept?

2.   The court appears to accept Raytheon's argument that a portion of its recovery is a nontaxable return of capital, but the taxpayer still loses the case. Why?

3.   What do you think was the likely effect of *Raytheon* on plaintiffs' willingness to bring antitrust lawsuits? Is this a legitimate tax issue, or is it somebody else's problem?

4.   *Raytheon* concerned only the compensatory as opposed to the punitive or "treble" damages portion of an antitrust recovery. Compensatory antitrust damages have consistently been held taxable as ordinary income, since they represent compensation for lost profits and other taxable income, although (as *Raytheon* suggests) they may be wholly or partially excludible if they can be characterized as a tax-free return of capital. Punitive or treble antitrust damages, *i.e.*, damages in excess of actual economic harm, were the occasion for some uncertainty until they were held taxable by the Supreme Court in *Commissioner v. Glenshaw Glass*, 348 U.S. 426 (1955). The various types of antitrust damages are thus now taxed in the same way, as compared to personal injury awards where a distinction is made between compensatory and punitive damages. What do you think accounts for this difference, and is the taxation of antitrust damages consistent with the underlying purpose of the antitrust laws?

REINKE v. COMMISSIONER
United States Tax Court
65 T.C.M. 2570 (1993)

TANNENWALD, JUDGE; Respondent determined the following deficiencies in, and additions to, petitioners' Federal income taxes:

Additions To Tax

Year	Deficiency	Sec. 6661
1985	$33,367.07	$8,432.00
1986	61,817.45	15,454.00
1987	16,904.90	4,226.00

After concessions, the main issue for decision is whether certain coal lease payments received by petitioners constitute ordinary income, recovery of capital, or proceeds from the sale of a capital asset. If respondent prevails on this issue, we must determine whether petitioners are liable for the additions to tax under section 6661.

This case was submitted fully stipulated pursuant to Rule 122(a). All the stipulated facts are found accordingly. The attached exhibits are incorporated by reference.

Petitioner Mary Reinke resided in Center, North Dakota, at the time she filed the petition in this case. For the 1985 taxable year, she filed a joint Federal income tax return with decedent. For the 1986 and 1987 taxable years, she filed individual Federal income tax returns.

During the years at issue, Ervin A. Reinke and/or Marion Reinke (hereinafter sometimes referred to as the Reinkes) owned the surface and mineral rights to the southeast quarter of section 26 of a tract of land in Oliver County, North Dakota, and the surface rights only to the southwest and northeast quarters of section 26. The bases in the surface rights to the southeast, southwest, and northeast quarters of section 26 were $22,424, $21,336, and $19,976, respectively. The basis in the mineral rights to the southeast quarter of section 26 was $25,411.

On August 2, 1961, the Reinkes entered into a coal lease agreement (1961 lease) with Lignite Electric Power Cooperative, Inc. (Lignite Electric), of Bismarck, North Dakota, in respect of the southeast quarter of section 26. The agreement provided in pertinent part as follows:

> THIS AGREEMENT, made and entered into . . . between Ervin A. Reinke and Marion Reinke . . . , Lessors, Parties of the first part, and Lignite Electric Coop. of Bismarck, North Dakota, Lessees, party of the second part:
>
> WITNESSETH, that the Lessors for and in consideration of the rents and royalties, covenants and agreements, hereinafter stated, and by the Lessees to be paid, kept and performed, have granted, demised, leased and let, and by these presents do grant, demise, lease and let unto the Lessees, all that certain real estate situated in Oliver County, North Dakota, more particularly described as follows, to-wit:
>
> The Southeast quarter (SE 1/4) of Section Twenty-six (26). . . .
>
> Together with the appurtenances and rights and privilege to remove any and all lignite coal, and the minerals that are an integral part thereof . . . from said premises by strip mining or otherwise, and to reduce and process the same, together with all the rights and privileges incident to mining and securing said coal. . . .
>
> IT IS AGREED that this lease shall remain in force for a term of 35 years from the date hereof, and as long thereafter as coal in an amount of not less than ten tons per acre per year of the land herein leased is being mined therefrom. . . .

IN CONSIDERATION of the premises the said Lessees covenant and agree:

1. To pay the Lessors, as royalty for coal, the sum of ten cents (10 cents) per ton, . . . for all coal removed from said land, and as rental payments and damages for any surface used, occupied or destroyed in the mining and removal of any coal in and underlying lessor's said lands. . . .

* * *

4. It is understood and agreed that the royalties and rentals thereinbefore set forth contemplate the ownership by the lessors of 100% of the coal mineral rights therein, but that if the Lessors own a less interest in the above described coal minerals under said land, then the royalties and rentals to be paid as herein provided shall be paid only in the proportion which lessor's interest bears to the whole and undivided ownership thereof.

On December 6, 1968, Lignite Electric assigned its rights under the above lease to Baukol-Noonan, Inc. (BNI).

On September 15, 1971, the Reinkes entered into a second coal lease agreement (1971 lease) with BNI in respect of the southwest and northeast quarters of section 26. The contractual provisions of the 1971 agreement were identical to those utilized in the 1961 agreement except that the following language was added to paragraph 4 (presumably in recognition of the fact that the Reinkes either owned or were expected to own less than 100 percent of the mineral rights and perhaps only the surface rights): "PROVIDED, However, that the royalty paid to the lessor herein shall never be less than 2 cents per ton of coal."

On October 3, 1979, the Reinkes entered into an "Agreement With Respect To Surface Use Payments" (surface use agreement) with BNI which clarified BNI's legal and financial obligations under the North Dakota Surface Owners Protection Act, N.D. Cent. Code secs. 38-18-01 to 38-18-08 (1987), in respect of the three leased quarters of section 26. The surface use agreement provided in relevant part:

By virtue of the North Dakota Surface Owners Protection Act there has arisen some uncertainties concerning the legal obligations between the parties to this agreement. That is, the act could be construed as requiring BN to pay to the surface owner surface damages for the use of the surface in the course of mining the real property covered by its coal lease, even though BN might not have been obligated to do so at all or to the same extent under the laws pertaining to contracts and real property in existence prior to the enactment of the act. . . .

In order to resolve this uncertainty . . . the parties do hereby agree as follows:

1. BN will pay to the surface owner ten cents a ton for every ton of coal actually mined and removed from the property on and after October 1, 1979, with the payments to be made on a monthly basis commencing on November 15, 1979.

2. The surface owner agrees that such payment by BN to him shall constitute all of the payments or damages to which he is entitled by virtue of NDCC 38-18-07(1) and NDCC 38-18-06(5).

* * *

On October 3, 1979, the Reinkes executed a Soil Stockpiling Agreement which granted BNI a "lease and license" to store soil from section 26 on land not owned by the Reinkes and to utilize that soil for reclamation purposes on other property so long as an equal amount of soil was respread on section 26 following the strip-mining process. This agreement provided that BNI was "required to reclaim the land which it mines."

On May 7, 1982, the Reinkes entered into an agreement with BNI which permitted BNI to "stockpile" coal extracted from the southeast quarter of section 26 under the 1961 lease.

Petitioner received the following amounts from BNI under the coal lease agreements and the surface use agreement in 1985, 1986, and 1987:

	1985	1986	1987
Surface/Mineral	$175,859	$91,519	$-0-
Stockpiled Coal	-0-	117,432	-0-
Surface Only	75,106	87,525	71,111
Lease Payments	3,245	1,430	1,100
Break of Lease Payment	-0-	7,911	-0-

The foregoing amounts were reported on the Federal income tax returns for 1985, 1986, and 1987, as follows:

Year	Capital Gains	Rents and Royalties
1985	$254,531	-0-
1986	296,796	$9,021
1987	71,431	780

BNI issued Forms 1099 to petitioner for the years at issue which characterized all the 1985 and 1986 payments as "Rents"; the 1987 payment was divided into a "Royalty" component ($71,111) and a "Lease" component ($1,100).

We must determine the correct tax treatment of payments received by petitioner during the years at issue under the 1961 and 1971 leases and the surface use agreement. The parties agree that the "lease payments" and "break of lease payments" constitute ordinary income. They further agree that, insofar as the payments relate to petitioner's ownership of the mineral rights, including the payments for "stockpiled coal," she is entitled to recover her basis in those rights and to treat the excess as capital gain. In this regard, respondent allocated one-half of the surface/mineral payments to petitioner's mineral rights, to which petitioner has raised no objection. Thus, it is with respect to the tax treatment of payments attributable to petitioner's surface rights that the parties disagree.

Petitioner contends that all payments received under the 1961 and 1971 leases and the surface use agreement in respect of her surface rights (hereinafter referred to as surface payments) represent compensation for damages BNI inflicted upon her land in the strip-mining process, and that she is therefore entitled to recover her basis in the land with any excess receiving capital gain treatment. She alternatively contends that the payments represent consideration for: (1) Granting BNI an easement, which constitutes the sale or exchange of a capital asset, or (2) the "exercise of the power of requisition" by BNI in respect of her rights in the surface land. Finally, petitioner maintains that the provisions of the North Dakota Surface Owners Protection Act are inapplicable because that Act was enacted after petitioner and BNI entered into the 1961 and 1971 lease agreements and that, even if the Act applied, its requirements were satisfied by the 1979 surface use agreement.

Respondent counters that petitioner has failed to show that BNI's strip-mining operations permanently damaged her land. Assuming that her land was actually damaged, respondent contends that BNI had a legal obligation to reclaim that land under the North Dakota Surface Owners Protection Act, and that that Act voided any waiver of that obligation, thus negating the 1979 surface use agreement. Insofar as petitioner's first alternative position is concerned, respondent claims that she had a right of reversion in the surface rights; thus, there was no sale or exchange of a capital asset. Finally, respondent contends that the parties never intended the payments to serve as remuneration for damages to petitioner's land. In this respect, respondent directs our attention to the Forms 1099 which characterize payments received under the leases as rental or royalty payments.

The burden of proof is on petitioner, Rule 142(a), and that burden is not lessened by the fact that this case was fully stipulated. *Borchers v. Commissioner*, 95 T.C. 82, 91 (1990), *affd.* 943 F.2d 22 (8th Cir. 1991).

* * *

We first address the issue whether the payments in question were for damages to petitioner's surface rights in the land. In contending that such was the case, petitioner relies upon *Inaja Land Co. v. Commissioner*, 9 T.C. 727 (1947). In that case, the taxpayer acquired land to be used by its member-shareholders as a private fishing club. Portions of the land were also leased to third parties to graze livestock. Shortly after the land was acquired, The Department of Water and Power of The City of Los Angeles started construction of a tunnel to carry waters diverted from a nearby basin to a point upstream from the taxpayer's land. Once the waters were emptied upstream, they would then flow over and through the taxpayer's land to a point downstream for diversion into the water supply of the City of Los Angeles. Throughout the construction phase, substantial amounts of polluted seepage water escaped from the tunnel onto the taxpayer's land killing its fish and interfering with the members' fishing activities. After the tunnel was completed, the natural flow of waters over and through the taxpayer's land was significantly increased, further damaging the fishing habitat and other portions of the property.

The taxpayer having threatened legal proceedings in respect of damages to its property rights, the city agreed to pay $50,000 for a release of all past, present, and future claims in respect of such damages. The taxpayer, with an adjusted basis in the property exceeding $50,000, treated such payment as a nontaxable return of capital. Respondent determined that $48,945 ($50,000–$1,085 in attorney's fees) was compensation for the loss of present and future income and, thus, taxable as ordinary income.

Based upon an analysis of the agreements and the actions of the taxpayer and the city, we first rejected respondent's contention and concluded that the $50,000 payment was to compensate the taxpayer for the conveyance of a right of way and easements as well as for damages to its land. *Inaja Land Co. v. Commissioner*, 9 T.C. at 735. We then went on to hold that, since it was not possible accurately to calculate the amount of the taxpayer's basis which should be apportioned to those rights and the damaged property, the taxpayer was entitled to treat the payment as a recovery of capital to the extent of its basis in the entire property. *Inaja Land Co. v. Commissioner*, 9 T.C. at 736. Since the $50,000 payment was less than the basis, we had no need to, nor did we, discuss the question whether, if there had been an excess over basis, it would have been entitled to capital gain treatment. In view of the fact that a perpetual easement was involved in Inaja Land, petitioner's reliance on that case as authority for her claim of capital gain treatment for land damage is clearly misplaced.

Petitioner's reliance on Inaja Land is further flawed. In that case, we were called upon to choose between alternative characterizations of the payments received. By way of contrast, in this case, we are faced with the question of whether the payments received should be allocated between two characterizations. The 1961 and 1971 lease agreements clearly describe the 10 cents per ton "as royalty . . . and as rental payments" as well as "damages . . . for any surface used, occupied or destroyed." To be sure, the 1979 surface use agreement appears to convert the 10 cents per ton into a damage payment, but we are not persuaded that this agreement was sufficient to obviate the multiple purposes of the originally specified payment and, in effect, confer upon BNI a gratuitous right to enter on the land and mine coal. Petitioner seeks to transpose the Court's unwillingness to allocate basis in Inaja Land into a mandate against making any allocation in order to determine the character of the payments against which the basis might have been applied.

We need not go as far as respondent urges so as to require petitioner to show that her surface rights were actually damaged. Although *Gilbertz v. United States*, 808 F.2d 1374, 1379–1380 (10th Cir. 1987), contains language suggesting that such proof may be required, we think the Court of Appeals did no more than indicate that proof of legally compensable damage was needed. At least for the purposes of this case, we are prepared to assume that strip mining necessarily results in such damage. *See Denise Coal Co. v. Commissioner*, 271 F.2d 930, 934 (3d Cir. 1959), *modifying* 29 T.C. 528, 551 (1957); *Rochez Bros. v. Duricka*, 97 A.2d 825, 826 (Pa. 1953). This is certainly true, during the years in issue, when the North Dakota Surface Owners Protection Act was in effect. In this connection, we note that although petitioner argued that that Act was inapplicable to the 1961 and 1971 leases executed before its enactment, petitioner furnished us with no authority in support of her position, and the fact of the matter is that a recent opinion of the Supreme Court of North Dakota indicates that petitioner's position may well be incorrect. *See Knife River Coal Mining Co. v. Neuberger*, 466 N.W.2d 606, 608 n.1 (N.D. 1991). Moreover, the

1979 surface use agreement indicates that petitioner and BNI thought that the Act might well be applicable to coal mined subsequent to its enactment.

In any event, the assumption that there was damage does not solve petitioner's problem because the record herein is totally lacking any evidence sufficient to permit us to make an estimate of the measure of such damage. Thus, we have no basis for applying the rule of *Cohan v. Commissioner*, 39 F.2d 540 (2d Cir. 1930). *See Norgaard v. Commissioner*, 939 F.2d 874, 879 (9th Cir. 1991), *affg. in part, revg. in part* T.C. Memo. 1989-390.

With respect to petitioner's first alternative position, we conclude that she did not grant BNI an easement to use her land. An easement is not a temporary right to use the land of another, as was given BNI in the 1961 and 1971 leases; it is a conveyance of an interest in property. Petitioner had a right of reversion in her surface ownership, which, under the leases, was to take effect at the later of (1) 35 years from the date the lease was executed, or (2) at such time thereafter that BNI ceased mining a minimum of 10 tons of coal per acre a year. Petitioner having retained a reversionary interest in the surface land, there was no "sale or exchange" of property. *See Fasken v. Commissioner*, 71 T.C. 650, 656 n.3 (1979); *Nay v. Commissioner*, 19 T.C. 114 (1952). The fact that BNI's use of petitioner's surface land could continue past the original 35-year-lease period does not negate the fact that BNI's rights to use the surface land eventually will revert to petitioner. *Vest v. Commissioner*, 481 F.2d 238, 245–246 (5th Cir. 1973), *affg. on this issue* 57 T.C. 128 (1971).

Gilbertz v. United States, supra, does not support petitioner's position. In that case, a pipeline company paid the taxpayer for "the right to construct, maintain, inspect, operate, protect, repair, or remove . . . pipeline and appurtenances" necessary to transport oil and other petroleum products across the taxpayer's land. *Gilbertz v. United States*, 808 F.2d at 1381. The court found that such rights were granted in perpetuity and therefore constituted an easement with the result that there was a sale or exchange of a capital asset. *Gilbertz v. United States*, 808 F.2d at 1381–1382. Petitioner, contending that the damage occasioned by the laying of pipeline is less severe than that caused by strip mining, maintains that she, like the taxpayer in *Gilbertz*, is entitled to treat BNI's payments as from the sale of a capital asset. We disagree. The circuit court's decision was premised not, as petitioner seems to conclude, upon the severity of damages; rather, it was based on the finding that the taxpayer granted an easement.

Petitioner's second alternative position, that BNI exercised a power of requisition in respect of her surface rights, is totally without merit. The power of requisition, as used in section 1231, refers to the action or threat of action by a governmental body to take a taxpayer's property without consent. *See Koziara v. Commissioner*, 86 T.C. 999, 1006–1007 (1986), *affd. without published opinion* 841 F.2d 1126 (6th Cir. 1988). It is clear on this record that petitioner consented to the strip mining. Beyond this, we have no basis for concluding that BNI was a governmental body.

* * *

Understanding *Reinke*

1.   *Inaja Land*, described in the *Reinke* decision, involved the characterization of payments in settlement of a damage suit as either (i) compensation for lost income (which would be fully taxable) or (ii) compensation for property damage together with an easement to continue engaging in the polluting activity (which would constitute nontaxable recovery of capital to the extent of the taxpayer's basis and capital gain to the extent of any excess). *Reinke* involved a similar allocation between lease payments (taxable as ordinary income) and compensation for damage caused by the strip-mining process (nontaxable or at worst capital gain). Why did Inaja win, and the Reinkes lose?

2.   What do you make of the court's argument that, even assuming there was damage to the Reinkes' property, there was no evidence as to the amount of damage and thus no way to measure the recovery of the capital component of the surface rights payments? Would it be that difficult to make a reasonable estimate? On the other hand, how convincing is it for a landowner to enter into a (profitable) mining agreement, and then claim that their land is being ruined by the agreement? Is this part of the answer to Question 1, above?

3.   What are the environmental implications, if any, of the decision in *Reinke*?

Reinke combines the recovery of capital issue with the issue of ordinary income and (reduced) capital gain tax rates. For now the most important point is that in a recovery of capital situation no tax at all is paid unless the amount of the recovery exceeds the taxpayer's basis for the relevant property and — even after that point — the tax that is paid is likely to be imposed at a substantially reduced rate. By contrast, if the doctrine does not apply, all of the money received by the taxpayer will be taxed at the regularly applicable ("ordinary") income tax rates.

Using the Sources

Note: Additional problems relating to these materials are found at the conclusion of Part III.

1. Which of the following fact patterns involve a return of capital issue?

a. Taxpayer buys a share of stock and sells it five years later at a modest profit.

b. Taxpayer earns $50,000 and spends it on business expenses.

c. Taxpayer earns $50,000 and spends it in Las Vegas.

d. Taxpayer buys an automobile for business use.

e. Taxpayer buys an automobile for personal use.

f. Taxpayer's property is damaged leading taxpayer to bring a successful tort suit.

g. Same as f, but the suit is for breach of contract.

h. Same as f, but in addition to the tort settlement, the taxpayer accepts $1 million from the tortfeasor in return for an easement permitting the tortious behavior to continue.

i. Same as h, but the settlement does not specify how much is being awarded for each purpose.

j. Taxpayer is injured in an automobile accident and receives damages.

Now focus on those items that did involve a return of capital issue. For each of these items, how would the relevant capital be "recovered" for tax purposes (i.e., as an immediate deduction, a deduction spread out over several years, or an offset against the tax to be paid when the property was sold)? Does this result strike you as reasonable?

Law and Planning

Suppose that your client is a landowner who wants to enter into an agreement with a surface mining company, under which the company would conduct mining operations on the property and the landowner would receive lease (royalty) or similar payments. After reading *Reinke*, how would you advise the landowner to structure the agreement in order to get the best possible tax treatment? Is there any similar advice that you would give to an antitrust plaintiff, based on *Raytheon*, or an unhappy professional client, based on the *Clark* decision? What if anything do your answers tell you about the validity of the return of capital doctrine and its application in different fact circumstances?

Politics and Policy

Now that we have studied the recovery of capital doctrine, we can reexamine the issue of personal injury awards, first considered in Chapter 1. A key argument against taxation of personal injury awards is that they constitute a return of the taxpayer's capital; that is, they compensate the taxpayer for the loss of something she already had, rather than increasing her overall wealth. Since the possession of the original item was not taxed (or so goes the argument), neither should its replacement. Indeed, the personal injury exclusion was mentioned in *Clark* — if somewhat clumsily — as a precedent for the court's holding.

Given what you now know about the return of capital doctrine, can the exclusion for personal injury awards be justified on this basis? What kind of "capital," if any, is being returned in these cases? Can this doctrine possibly be extended to punitive as well as compensatory damages? If an injured person, like Clark, could be given back exactly what they had lost — *i.e.*, could be restored to perfect physical health — it would seem clear to most people that they shouldn't pay any tax. Should it make a difference that, given the near impossibility of accomplishing this in the typical personal injury case, they are compensated with monetary benefits instead?

III.   ANNUAL ACCOUNTING AND ITS LIMITATIONS

A.   Scope and Origins of the Annual Accounting Concept

A perfect tax system, like the Gates of Repentance, would never be completely closed. There would always be some later event that might change the character of a previous item or require the adjustment of a previous return. In practice there is a somewhat greater demand for finality, in order to maintain administrative sanity and provide a more-or-less reliable flow of revenues. This finality is provided by the annual accounting system, which requires taxpayers to file returns on a once-a-year basis and assumes that — absent extraordinary events — the returns will be completed as filed.[13] For example, a taxpayer who received a $20,000 bonus in 2010 would be required to file a return reflecting that salary by April 15, 2010, even though it is at least theoretically possible that a mistake was made and the taxpayer was really entitled to a $10,000 (or a $30,000) bonus. Similarly, a taxpayer who has a deductible casualty loss with respect to stolen property is permitted to take that loss although it is possible (if unlikely) that the property will be returned in a later year. This inexactitude is tolerated in the name of administrative efficiency and, perhaps, a human desire to close out the past and move on. While past returns may be amended for errors and omissions, there is a limitation (usually three years) on this process and amendments must be based on mistakes pertaining to the taxable year in question rather than subsequent events.[14]

One problem with annual accounting is that real life does not always compress itself into neat, 365-day cycles. *Clark* is a modest example of this problem: the money returned by the lawyer would likely have been income on its own terms, but was excluded by reference to events that took place in an earlier taxable year. Other examples are less trivial. For example, in *Burnet v. Sanford & Brooks*, 282 U.S. 359 (1931), the taxpayer spent some $176,000 working under a dredging contract in the years 1913–15, only to discover that the Government had incorrectly described to it the character of the material that needed to be dredged, so that it was impossible for the taxpayer to complete the work as anticipated. The taxpayer sued the Government for breach of contract in 1920, and was awarded the $176,000 plus interest. The Court of Appeals ruled that the taxpayer could exclude the $176,000 from income, amend its earlier returns to give back deductions for work already completed on the contract, and call it a day.[15] But the Supreme Court — citing a rather strict version of the annual accounting concept — required the taxpayers to take the $176,000 into income in 1920. The taxpayer thus faced the unappetizing situation of paying tax on a transaction which had earned no net profit, with deductions limited to years in which they were of no or only partial use to it.

---

[13] The term "accounting" is used here in a limited sense to indicate the time period (one year, several years, etc.) in which income is computed. The issue of accounting methods generally (cash, accrual, and so forth) is considered separately.

[14] *See generally* I.R.C. § 6511.

[15] All parties agreed that the $16,000 in interest payments was taxable income.

Cases like *Sanford & Brooks* are troubling for two reasons. The first involves fairness to individual taxpayers. Strict adherence to annual accounting may require a taxpayer to pay tax when she (it) has not made any money on a transaction, because the taxpayer's gains and losses are realized in different years, and there is inadequate income against which to offset the losses. (Deductions in excess of income are generally not refunded to taxpayers.) This is especially likely for long-term projects, in which there may be a substantial outlay in the early years with profits coming only toward the end of the contract. Compounding this problem are differences in tax rates: even if deductions are usable, they may fail to offset taxes if the tax rate in the deduction year is lower than that when income is realized. For example, a $10,000 deduction at a 20 percent tax rate would save the taxpayer only $2,000 in taxes, while an offsetting $10,000 of income would result in $3,000 of taxes if the tax rate had meanwhile increased to 30 percent. (A declining tax rate has the opposite effect.)

Second, apart from the issue of fairness, it is conceptually inaccurate to conduct accounting on an inflexible annual basis. Consider the taxpayer in *Sanford & Brooks*. Had it really lost money in the first few years of the contract when it undertook the dredging operations? Would it suddenly have become richer, when and if the work was completed? More likely, the company would treat its initial outlay as a form of investment, to be recouped or (hopefully) exceeded when it began making money in the later years of the contract. Internally, the company would use a transactional or contractual method of accounting, which matched income from the project against expenditures for the same project. In a sense — although the comparison is imperfect — the company would take a basis in the project and pay tax only when its income from the project exceeded the amount invested in the activity. Should the tax system adopt a similar transactional perspective, rather than a strict annual accounting rule?

The immediate problem in *Sanford & Brooks* is today dealt with by section 172 of the Code, the so-called net operating loss provision. Section 172 allows taxpayers to carry unused business losses backward for up to two years and forward for up to twenty years. Such losses may be used against income from the same or different business projects. For example, if section 172 had existed in Sanford and Brooks' era, the company could have carried its 1913–15 losses forward to be used against its 1920 income, which would have fallen well within the 20-year carryover period.[16] Yet the problem of annual accounting and its limitations remains in many cases that, even today, would not be covered or would be covered only incompletely by the NOL rules. The following materials demonstrate several aspects of this ongoing problem.

B.   Claim of Right Doctrine

One persistent problem in annual accounting concerns money which has been earned by the taxpayer but for one reason or another may have to be returned in later years. When should such income be taxed, and what happens if the taxpayer is later forced to surrender it? The following cases consider this issue.

---

[16] Section 172 is further discussed below.

NORTH AMERICAN OIL CONSOL. v. COMMISSIONER
United States Supreme Court
286 U.S. 417 (1932)

MR. JUSTICE BRANDEIS delivered the opinion of the Court.

The question for decision is whether the sum of $171,979.22 received by the North American Oil Consolidated in 1917, was taxable to it as income of that year.

The money was paid to the company under the following circumstances. Among many properties operated by it in 1916 was a section of oil land, the legal title to which stood in the name of the United States. Prior to that year, the Government, claiming also the beneficial ownership, had instituted a suit to oust the company from possession; and on February 2, 1916, it secured the appointment of a receiver to operate the property, or supervise its operations, and to hold the net income thereof. The money paid to the company in 1917 represented the net profits which had been earned from that property in 1916 during the receivership. The money was paid to the receiver as earned. After entry by the District Court in 1917 of the final decree dismissing the bill, the money was paid, in that year, by the receiver to the company. *United States v. North American Oil Consolidated*, 242 Fed. 723. The Government took an appeal (without supersedeas) to the Circuit Court of Appeals. In 1920, that Court affirmed the decree. 264 Fed. 336. In 1922, a further appeal to this Court was dismissed by stipulation. 258 U.S. 633.

The income earned from the property in 1916 had been entered on the books of the company as its income. It had not been included in its original return of income for 1916; but it was included in an amended return for that year which was filed in 1918. Upon auditing the company's income and profits tax returns for 1917, the Commissioner of Internal Revenue determined a deficiency based on other items. The company appealed to the Board of Tax Appeals. There, in 1927 the Commissioner prayed that the deficiency already claimed should be increased so as to include a tax on the amount paid by the receiver to the company in 1917. The Board held that the profits were taxable to the receiver as income of 1916; and hence made no finding whether the company's accounts were kept on the cash receipts and disbursements basis or on the accrual basis. 12 B.T.A. 68. The Circuit Court of Appeals held that the profits were taxable to the company as income of 1917, regardless of whether the company's returns were made on the cash or on the accrual basis. 50 F.2d 752. This Court granted a writ of certiorari. 284 U.S. 614.

It is conceded that the net profits earned by the property during the receivership constituted income. The company contends that they should have been reported by the receiver for taxation in 1916; that if not returnable by him, they should have been returned by the company for 1916, because they constitute income of the company accrued in that year; and that if not taxable as income of the company for 1916, they were taxable to it as income for 1922, since the litigation was not finally terminated in its favor until 1922.

First. The income earned in 1916 and impounded by the receiver in that year was not taxable to him, because he was the receiver of only a part of the properties operated by the company. Under § 13(c) of the Revenue Act of 1916, receivers who "are operating the property or business of corporations" were obliged to make returns "of net income as and for such corporations," and "any income tax due" was to be "assessed and collected in the same manner as if assessed directly against the organization of whose business or properties they have custody and control." The phraseology of this section was adopted without change in the Revenue Act of 1918, 40 Stat. 1057, 1081, c. 18, § 239. The regulations of the Treasury Department have consistently construed these statutes as applying only to receivers in charge of the entire property or business of a corporation; and in all other cases have required the corporations themselves to report their income. Treas. Regs. 33, arts. 26, 209; Treas. Regs. 45, arts. 424, 622. That construction is clearly correct. The language of the section contemplates a substitution of the receiver for the corporation; and there can be such substitution only when the receiver is in complete control of the properties and business of the corporation. Moreover, there is no provision for the consolidation of the return of a receiver of part of a corporation's property or business with the return of the corporation itself. It may not be assumed that Congress intended to require the filing of two separate returns for the same year, each covering only a part of the corporate income, without making provision for consolidation so that the tax could be based upon the income as a whole.

Second. The net profits were not taxable to the company as income of 1916. For the company was not required in 1916 to report as income an amount which it might never receive. *See Burnet v. Logan,* 283 U.S. 404, 413. Compare *Lucas v. American Code Co.,* 280 U.S. 445, 452; *Burnet v. Sanford & Brooks Co.,* 282 U.S. 359, 363. There was no constructive receipt of the profits by the company in that year, because at no time during the year was there a right in the company to demand that the receiver pay over the money. Throughout 1916 it was uncertain who would be declared entitled to the profits. It was not until 1917, when the District Court entered a final decree vacating the receivership and dismissing the bill, that the company became entitled to receive the money. Nor is it material, for the purposes of this case, whether the company's return was filed on the cash receipts and disbursements basis, or on the accrual basis. In neither event was it taxable in 1916 on account of income which it had not yet received and which it might never receive.

Third. The net profits earned by the property in 1916 were not income of the year 1922 — the year in which the litigation with the Government was finally terminated. They became income of the company in 1917, when it first became entitled to them and when it actually received them. If a taxpayer receives earnings under a claim of right and without restriction as to its disposition, he has received income which he is required to return, even though it may still be claimed that he is not entitled to retain the money, and even though he may still be adjudged liable to restore its equivalent. *See Board v. Commissioner,* 51 F.2d 73, 75, 76. Compare *United States v. S. S. White Dental Mfg. Co.,* 274 U.S. 398, 403. If in 1922 the Government had prevailed, and the company had been obliged to refund the profits received in 1917, it would have been entitled to a deduction from the profits of 1922, not from those of any earlier year. Compare *Lucas v. American Code Co., supra.*

Affirmed.

UNITED STATES v. LEWIS
United States Supreme Court
340 U.S. 590 (1951)

MR. JUSTICE BLACK delivered the opinion of the Court.

Respondent Lewis brought this action in the Court of Claims seeking a refund of an alleged overpayment of his 1944 income tax. The facts found by the Court of Claims are: In his 1944 income tax return, respondent reported about $22,000 which he had received that year as an employee's bonus. As a result of subsequent litigation in a state court, however, it was decided that respondent's bonus had been improperly computed; under compulsion of the state court's judgment he returned approximately $11,000 to his employer. Until payment of the judgment in 1946, respondent had at all times claimed and used the full $22,000 unconditionally as his own, in the good faith though "mistaken" belief that he was entitled to the whole bonus.

On the foregoing facts the Government's position is that respondent's 1944 tax should not be recomputed, but that respondent should have deducted the $11,000 as a loss in his 1946 tax return. *See* G. C. M. 16730, XV-1 Cum. Bull. 179 (1936). The Court of Claims, however, relying on its own case, *Greenwald v. United States*, 57 F.Supp. 569, 102 Ct. Cl. 272, held that the excess bonus received "under a mistake of fact" was not income in 1944 and ordered a refund based on a recalculation of that year's tax. 91 F.Supp. 1017, 117 Ct. Cl. 336. We granted *certiorari*, 340 U.S. 903, because this holding conflicted with many decisions of the courts of appeals, *see, e.g., Haberkorn v. United States*, 173 F.2d 587, and with principles announced in *North American Oil v. Burnet*, 286 U.S. 417.

In the *North American Oil* case we said: "If a taxpayer receives earnings under a claim of right and without restriction as to its disposition, he has received income which he is required to return, even though it may still be claimed that he is not entitled to retain the money, and even though he may still be adjudged liable to restore its equivalent." 286 U.S. at 424. Nothing in this language permits an exception merely because a taxpayer is "mistaken" as to the validity of his claim. Nor has the "claim of right" doctrine been impaired, as the Court of Claims stated, by *Freuler v. Helvering*, 291 U.S. 35, or *Commissioner v. Wilcox*, 327 U.S. 404. The *Freuler* case involved an entirely different section of the Internal Revenue Code, and its holding is inapplicable here. 291 U.S. at 43. And in *Commissioner v. Wilcox*, *supra*, we held that receipts from embezzlement did not constitute income, distinguishing *North American Oil* on the ground that an embezzler asserts no "bona fide legal or equitable claim." 327 U.S. at 408.

Income taxes must be paid on income received (or accrued) during an annual accounting period. *Cf.* I.R.C., §§ 41, 42; *and see Burnet v. Sanford & Brooks Co.*, 282 U.S. 359, 363. The "claim of right" interpretation of the tax laws has long been used to give finality to that period, and is now deeply rooted in the federal tax system. *See* cases collected in 2 MERTENS, LAW OF FEDERAL INCOME TAXATION, § 12.103. We see no reason why the Court should depart from this well-settled interpretation merely because it results in an advantage or disadvantage to a taxpayer.[17]

Reversed.

Mr. Justice Douglas, dissenting.

The question in this case is not whether the bonus had to be included in 1944 income for purposes of the tax. Plainly it should have been because the taxpayer claimed it as of right. Some years later, however, it was judicially determined that he had no claim to the bonus. The question is whether he may then get back the tax which he paid on the money.

Many inequities are inherent in the income tax. We multiply them needlessly by nice distinctions which have no place in the practical administration of the law. If the refund were allowed, the integrity of the taxable year would not be violated. The tax would be paid when due; but the Government would not be permitted to maintain the unconscionable position that it can keep the tax after it is shown that payment was made on money which was not income to the taxpayer.

Understanding Claims of Right

1. *North American Oil* was exclusively a timing case. Everyone agreed that the money should be taxed, the only question being which year (1916, 1917, or 1922) the tax should fall in. That being the case, what is everyone so excited about? Why in particular does the taxpayer seem to prefer being taxed in an earlier year (1916) to a later year (1917), assuming that the remaining alternative (1922) is eliminated? What happened in 1917 that might explain this situation?

2. Doesn't common sense dictate that Justice Douglas's position in *Lewis* — that the taxpayer be permitted to recompute his 1944 taxes — is right? Yet how can this outcome be reconciled with the "claim of right" doctrine, as stated in *North American Oil*, or with the annual accounting concept? Does it matter if Lewis lost the $11,000 bonus as a result of facts that were (or should have been) known in 1944, or only as a result of facts which became known in later years? By the way, why does Lewis care whether the deduction falls in 1944 or 1946 — wouldn't an $11,000 deduction be worth the same amount in either year? Why did the Government bother to litigate this case?

3. Does it make a difference, in either case, if the taxpayer used the cash or accrual method of accounting?[18]

North American Oil is famous for the claim of right doctrine (contained in its last full paragraph), which remains, for whatever it is worth, good law. By contrast, *Lewis* was essentially overruled by section 1341 of the Code, which permits taxpayers in a like situation to choose between taking a deduction in the later year

---

[17] [*] It has been suggested that it would be more "equitable" to reopen respondent's 1944 tax return. While the suggestion might work to the advantage of this taxpayer, it could not be adopted as a general solution because, in many cases, the three-year statute of limitations would preclude recovery. I.R.C. § 322(b).

[18] *See* Background and Basic Themes Chapter, Section C.3, *supra.*

or recomputing the prior year's taxes as if the item had been excluded from income in the first place.[19] For example, had section 1341 applied to Lewis himself, he would have been permitted to recompute his 1944 taxes as if the $11,000 had not been included in income, and — assuming the reduction in taxes was worth more to him than a deduction in 1946 — would have been entitled to a refund of this larger amount. Thus, if Lewis had no other taxable income in 1946, or if tax rates had been reduced in the interim, he would still be permitted to offset his original "error" on a dollar-for-dollar basis; indeed, he would receive whichever treatment (1944 credit or 1946 deduction) was more favorable under the circumstances.

Examine the language of section 1341, especially subsections (a)(1) and (a)(2) thereof. Is it clear section 1341 would apply on the *Lewis* facts? At the end of 1944, did it "appea[r]" that the taxpayer had an unrestricted right to such item," as required by section 1341(a)(1)? What if the company had simply made a mathematical error in Lewis's favor, Lewis had (understandably) said nothing, and the company had discovered the error in 1945? Alternatively, what if there was an ongoing dispute about the computation of bonuses, and Lewis knew all along that there was a possibility that the bonus would be rescinded? For extra credit, what is the significance of section 1341(b)(1), and how might it be relevant to Lewis?

C.   The Tax Benefit Rule

Along with cases in which income is earned but then lost, the tax system may have to deal with the opposite situation, in which deductions are taken by taxpayers for money or property that is later returned to them. The following case deals with this problem and with the concept, the so-called "tax benefit rule," that was created to deal with it. Try your best to follow the case untutored; a longer description of the tax benefit concept follows.

HILLSBORO NATIONAL BANK v. COMMISSIONER
United States Supreme Court
460 U.S. 370 (1983)

JUSTICE O'CONNOR delivered the opinion of the Court.

These consolidated cases present the question of the applicability of the tax benefit rule to two corporate tax situations: the repayment to the shareholders of taxes for which they were liable but that were originally paid by the corporation; and the distribution of expensed assets in a corporate liquidation. We conclude that, unless a nonrecognition provision of the Internal Revenue Code prevents it, the tax benefit rule ordinarily applies to require the inclusion of income when events occur that are fundamentally inconsistent with an earlier deduction. Our examination of the provisions granting the deductions and governing the liquidation in these cases leads us to hold that the rule requires the recognition of income in the case of the liquidation but not in the case of the tax refund.

---

[19] Technically speaking, the reduction in the prior year's taxes is taken as a deduction in the later year, but the amount of the reduction is based on the prior year's tax computation.

I

In No. 81-485, *Hillsboro National Bank v. Commissioner*, the petitioner, Hillsboro National Bank, is an incorporated bank doing business in Illinois. Until 1970, Illinois imposed a property tax on shares held in incorporated banks. Ill. Rev. Stat., ch. 120, § 557 (1971). Banks, required to retain earnings sufficient to cover the taxes, § 558, customarily paid the taxes for the shareholders. Under § 164(e) of the Internal Revenue Code of 1954, 26 U.S.C. § 164(e), the bank was allowed a deduction for the amount of the tax, but the shareholders were not. In 1970, Illinois amended its Constitution to prohibit ad valorem taxation of personal property owned by individuals, and the amendment was challenged as a violation of the Equal Protection Clause of the Federal Constitution. The Illinois courts held the amendment unconstitutional in *Lake Shore Auto Parts Co. v. Korzen*, 49 Ill. 2d 137, 273 N.E.2d 592 (1971). We granted *certiorari*, 405 U.S. 1039 (1972), and, pending disposition of the case here, Illinois enacted a statute providing for the collection of the disputed taxes and the placement of the receipts in escrow. Ill. Rev. Stat., ch. 120, para. 676.01 (1979). Hillsboro paid the taxes for its shareholders in 1972, taking the deduction permitted by § 164(e), and the authorities placed the receipts in escrow. This Court upheld the state constitutional amendment in *Lehnhausen v. Lake Shore Auto Parts* Co., 410 U.S. 356 (1973). Accordingly, in 1973 the County Treasurer refunded the amounts in escrow that were attributable to shares held by individuals, along with accrued interest. The Illinois courts held that the refunds belonged to the shareholders rather than to the banks. *See Bank & Trust Co. of Arlington Heights v. Cullerton*, 25 Ill. App. 3d 721, 726, 324 N.E.2d 29, 32 (1975) (alternative holding); *Lincoln National Bank v. Cullerton*, 18 Ill. App. 3d 953, 310 N.E.2d 845 (1974). Without consulting Hillsboro, the Treasurer refunded the amounts directly to the individual shareholders. On its return for 1973, Hillsboro recognized no income from this sequence of events. The Commissioner assessed a deficiency against Hillsboro, requiring it to include as income the amount paid its shareholders from the escrow. Hillsboro sought a redetermination in the Tax Court, which held that the refund of the taxes, but not the payment of accrued interest, was includible in Hillsboro's income. On appeal, relying on its earlier decision in *First Trust and Savings Bank of Taylorville v. United States*, 614 F.2d 1142 (1980), the Court of Appeals for the Seventh Circuit affirmed. 641 F.2d 529, 531 (CA7 1981).

In No. 81-930, *United States v. Bliss Dairy, Inc.*, the respondent, Bliss Dairy, Inc., was a closely held corporation engaged in the business of operating a dairy. As a cash basis taxpayer, in the taxable year ending June 30, 1973, it deducted upon purchase the full cost of the cattle feed purchased for use in its operations, as permitted by § 162 of the Internal Revenue Code, 26 U.S.C. § 162. A substantial portion of the feed was still on hand at the end of the taxable year. On July 2, 1973, two days into the next taxable year, Bliss adopted a plan of liquidation, and, during the month of July, it distributed its assets, including the remaining cattle feed, to the shareholders. Relying on § 336, which shields the corporation from the recognition of gain on the distribution of property to its shareholders on liquidation, Bliss reported no income on the transaction. The shareholders continued to operate the dairy business in noncorporate form. They filed an election under § 333 to limit the gain recognized by them on the liquidation, and they therefore calculated their basis in the assets received in the distribution as provided in § 334(c). Under that provision, their basis in the assets was their basis in their stock in the liquidated corporation, decreased by the amount of money received, and increased by the amount of gain recognized on the transaction. They then allocated that total basis over the assets, as provided in the regulations, Treas. Reg. § 1.334-2, 26 CFR § 1.334-2 (1982), presumably taking a basis greater than zero in the feed, although the amount of the shareholders' basis is not in the record. They in turn deducted their basis in the feed as an expense of doing business under § 162. On audit, the Commissioner challenged the corporation's treatment of the transaction, asserting that Bliss should have taken into income the value of the grain distributed to the shareholders. He therefore increased Bliss' income by $60,000. Bliss paid the resulting assessment and sued for a refund in the District Court for the District of Arizona, where it was stipulated that the grain had a value of $56,565, *see* Pretrial Order, at 3. Relying on *Commissioner v. South Lake Farms, Inc.*, 324 F.2d 837 (CA9 1963), the District Court rendered a judgment in favor of Bliss. While recognizing authority to the contrary, *Tennessee-Carolina Transportation, Inc. v. Commissioner*, 582 F.2d 378 (CA6 1978), *cert. denied*, 440 U.S. 909 (1979), the Court of Appeals saw *South Lake Farms* as controlling and affirmed. 645 F.2d 19 (CA9 1981) (per curiam).

II

The Government in each case relies solely on the tax benefit rule — a judicially developed principle[20] that allays some of the inflexibilities of the annual accounting system. An annual accounting system is a practical necessity if the federal income tax is to produce revenue ascertainable and payable at regular intervals. *Burnet v. Sanford & Brooks Co.*, 282 U.S. 359, 365 (1931). Nevertheless, strict adherence to an annual accounting system would create transactional inequities. Often an apparently completed transaction will reopen unexpectedly in a subsequent tax year, rendering the initial reporting improper. For instance, if a taxpayer held a note that became apparently uncollectible early in the taxable year, but the debtor made an unexpected financial recovery before the close of the year and paid the debt, the transaction would have no tax consequences for the taxpayer, for the repayment of the principal would be recovery of capital. If, however, the debtor's financial recovery and the resulting repayment took place after the close of the taxable year, the taxpayer would have a deduction for the apparently bad debt in the first year under § 166(a) of the Code, 26 U.S.C. § 166(a). Without the tax benefit rule, the repayment in the second year, representing a return of capital, would not be taxable. The second transaction, then, although economically identical to the first, could, because of the differences in accounting, yield drastically different tax consequences. The Government, by allowing a deduction that it could not have known to be improper at the time, would be foreclosed[21] from recouping any of the tax saved because of the improper deduction. Recognizing and seeking to avoid the

---

[20] [8] Although the rule originated in the courts, it has the implicit approval of Congress, which enacted 26 U.S.C. § 111 as a limitation on the rule. *See* n.12, *infra*.

[21] [9] A rule analogous to the tax benefit rule protects the taxpayer who is required to report income received in one year under claim of right that he later ends up repaying. Under that rule, he is allowed

possible distortions of income, the courts have long required the taxpayer to recognize the repayment in the second year as income. [Citations omitted.][22]

The taxpayers and the Government in these cases propose different formulations of the tax benefit rule. The taxpayers contend that the rule requires the inclusion of amounts *recovered* in later years, and they do not view the events in these cases as "recoveries." The Government, on the other hand, urges that the tax benefit rule requires the inclusion of amounts previously deducted if later events are inconsistent with the deductions; it insists that no "recovery" is necessary to the application of the rule. Further, it asserts that the events in these cases are inconsistent with the deductions taken by the taxpayers. We are not in complete agreement with either view.

An examination of the purpose and accepted applications of the tax benefit rule reveals that a "recovery" will not always be necessary to invoke the tax benefit rule. The purpose of the rule is not simply to tax "recoveries." On the contrary, it is to approximate the results produced by a tax system based on transactional rather than annual accounting. [Citations omitted.] It has long been accepted that a taxpayer using accrual accounting who accrues and deducts an expense in a tax year before it becomes payable and who for some reason eventually does not have to pay the liability must then take into income the amount of the expense earlier deducted. *See, e.g., Mayfair Minerals, Inc. v. Commissioner*, 456 F.2d 622 (CA5 1972) (per curiam); *Bear Manufacturing Co. v. United States*, 430 F.2d 152 (CA7 1970), *cert. denied*, 400 U.S. 1021 (1971); *Haynsworth v. Commissioner*, 68 T.C. 703 (1977), *affirmance order*, 609 F.2d 1007 (CA5 1979); *G. M. Standifer Construction Corp. v. Commissioner*, 30 B.T.A. 184, 186–187 (1934), *petition for review dism'd*, 78 F.2d 285 (CA9 1935). The bookkeeping entry canceling the liability, though it increases the balance sheet net worth of the taxpayer, does not fit within any ordinary definition of "recovery." Thus, the taxpayers' formulation of the rule neither serves the purposes of the rule nor accurately reflects the cases that establish the rule. Further, the taxpayers' proposal would introduce an undesirable formalism into the application of the tax benefit rule. Lower courts have been able to stretch the definition of "recovery" to include a great variety of events. For instance, in cases of corporate liquidations, courts have viewed the corporation's receipt of its own stock as a "recovery," reasoning that, even though the instant

---

a deduction in the subsequent year. *See generally* 26 U.S.C. § 1341; 1 B. Bittker, Federal Taxation of Income, Estates and Gifts para. 6.3 (1981).

[22] [12] Even this rule did not create complete transactional equivalence. In the second version of the transaction discussed in the text, the taxpayer might have realized no benefit from the deduction, if, for instance, he had no taxable income for that year. Application of the tax benefit rule as originally developed would require the taxpayer to recognize income on the repayment, so that the net result of the collection of the principal amount of the debt would be recognition of income. Similarly, the tax rates might change between the two years, so that a deduction and an inclusion, though equal in amount, would not produce exactly offsetting tax consequences. Congress enacted § 111 to deal with part of this problem. Although a change in the rates may still lead to differences in taxes due, see Alice Phelan Sullivan Corp. v. United States, 381 F.2d 399, 180 Ct. Cl. 659 (1967), § 111 provides that the taxpayer can exclude from income the amount that did not give rise to some tax benefit. *See* Dobson v. Commissioner, 320 U.S. 489, 505–506 (1943). This exclusionary rule and the inclusionary rule described in the text are generally known together as the tax benefit rule. It is the inclusionary aspect of the rule with which we are currently concerned.

that the corporation receives the stock it becomes worthless, the stock has value as it is turned over to the corporation, and that ephemeral value represents a recovery for the corporation. *See, e.g., Tennessee-Carolina Transportation, Inc. v. Commissioner*, 582 F.2d at 382 (alternative holding). Or, payment to another party may be imputed to the taxpayer, giving rise to a recovery. *See First Trust and Savings Bank of Taylorville v. United States*, 614 F.2d, at 1146 (alternative holding). Imposition of a requirement that there be a recovery would, in many cases, simply require the Government to cast its argument in different and unnatural terminology, without adding anything to the analysis.

The basic purpose of the tax benefit rule is to achieve rough transactional parity in tax, *see* n. 12, *supra*, and to protect the Government and the taxpayer from the adverse effects of reporting a transaction on the basis of assumptions that an event in a subsequent year proves to have been erroneous. Such an event, unforeseen at the time of an earlier deduction, may in many cases require the application of the tax benefit rule. We do not, however, agree that this consequence invariably follows. Not every unforeseen event will require the taxpayer to report income in the amount of his earlier deduction. On the contrary, the tax benefit rule will "cancel out" an earlier deduction only when a careful examination shows that the later event is indeed fundamentally inconsistent with the premise on which the deduction was initially based. That is, if that event had occurred within the same taxable year, it would have foreclosed the deduction. In some cases, a subsequent recovery by the taxpayer will be the only event that would be fundamentally inconsistent with the provision granting the deduction. In such a case, only actual recovery by the taxpayer would justify application of the tax benefit rule. For example, if a calendar-year taxpayer made a rental payment on December 15 for a 30-day lease deductible in the current year under § 162(a)(3), *see* Treas. Reg. § 1.461-1(a)(1), 26 CFR § 1.461-1(a)(1) (1982); *e.g., Zaninovich v. Commissioner*, 616 F.2d 429 (CA9 1980), the tax benefit rule would not require the recognition of income if the leased premises were destroyed by fire on January 10. The resulting inability of the taxpayer to occupy the building would be an event not fundamentally inconsistent with his prior deduction as an ordinary and necessary business expense under § 162(a). The loss is attributable to the business and therefore is consistent with the deduction of the rental payment as an ordinary and necessary business expense. On the other hand, had the premises not burned and, in January, the taxpayer decided to use them to house his family rather than to continue the operation of his business, he would have converted the leasehold to personal use. This would be an event fundamentally inconsistent with the business use on which the deduction was based. In the case of the fire, only if the lessor — by virtue of some provision in the lease — had refunded the rental payment would the taxpayer be required under the tax benefit rule to recognize income on the subsequent destruction of the building. In other words, the subsequent recovery of the previously deducted rental payment would be the only event inconsistent with the provision allowing the deduction. It therefore is evident that the tax benefit rule must be applied on a case-by-case basis. A court must consider the facts and circumstances of each case in the light of the purpose and function of the provisions granting the deductions.

When the later event takes place in the context of a nonrecognition provision of the Code, there will be an inherent tension between the tax benefit rule and the nonrecognition provision. *See Putoma Corp. v. Commissioner*, 601 F.2d 734, 742 (CA5 1979); *id.* at 751 (Rubin, J., dissenting); *cf. Helvering v. American Dental Co.*, 318 U.S. 322 (1943) (tension between exclusion of gifts from income and treatment of cancellation of indebtedness as income). We cannot resolve that tension with a blanket rule that the tax benefit rule will always prevail. Instead, we must focus on the particular provisions of the Code at issue in any case.

The formulation that we endorse today follows clearly from the long development of the tax benefit rule. JUSTICE STEVENS' assertion that there is no suggestion in the early cases or from the early commentators that the rule could ever be applied in any case that did not involve a physical recovery, is incorrect. The early cases frequently framed the rule in terms consistent with our view and irreconcilable with that of the dissent. *See Barnett v. Commissioner*, 39 B.T.A. 864, 867 (1939) ("Finally, the present case is analogous to a number of others, where . . . [when] some event occurs which is *inconsistent* with a deduction taken in a prior year, adjustment may have to be made by reporting a balancing item in income for the year in which the change occurs") (emphasis added); *Estate of Block v. Commissioner*, 39 B.T.A. 338, 341 ("*When recovery or some other event which is inconsistent* with what has been done in the past occurs, adjustment must be made in reporting income for the year in which the change occurs") (emphasis added); *South Dakota Concrete Products Co. v. Commissioner*, 26 B.T.A. 1429, 1432 ("[When] an *adjustment* occurs which is *inconsistent* with what has been done in the past in the determination of tax liability, the adjustment should be reflected in reporting income for the year in which it occurs") (emphasis added). The reliance of the dissent on the early commentators is equally misplaced, for the articles cited in the dissent, like the early cases, often stated the rule in terms of inconsistent events.

Finally, JUSTICE STEVENS' dissent relies heavily on the codification in § 111 of the exclusionary aspect of the tax benefit rule, which requires the taxpayer to include in income only the amount of the deduction that gave rise to a tax benefit, *see* n. 12, *supra*. That provision does, as the dissent observes, speak of a "recovery." By its terms, it only applies to bad debts, taxes, and delinquency amounts. Yet this Court has held, *Dobson v. Commissioner*, 320 U.S. 489, 505–506 (1943), and it has always been accepted since, that § 111 does not *limit* the application of the exclusionary aspect of the tax benefit rule. On the contrary, it lists a few applications and represents a general endorsement of the exclusionary aspect of the tax benefit rule to other situations within the inclusionary part of the rule. The failure to mention inconsistent events in § 111 no more suggests that they do not trigger the application of the tax benefit rule than the failure to mention the recovery of a capital loss suggests that it does not, *see Dobson, supra*.

JUSTICE STEVENS also suggests that we err in recognizing transactional equity as the reason for the tax benefit rule. It is difficult to understand why even the clearest recovery should be taxed if not for the concern with transactional equity. Nor does the concern with transactional equity entail a change in our approach to the annual accounting system. Although the tax system relies basically on annual accounting, *see Burnet v. Sanford & Brooks Co.*, 282 U.S. 359, 365, the tax benefit rule eliminates some of the distortions that would otherwise arise from such a system. *See, e.g.*, Bittker & Kanner 268–270; Tye 350; Plumb 178, and n. 172. The limited nature of the rule and its effect on the annual accounting principle bears repetition: *only* if the occurrence of the event in the earlier year would have resulted in the disallowance of the deduction can the Commissioner require a compensating recognition of income when the event occurs in the later year. Our approach today is consistent with our decision in *Nash v. United States*, 398 U.S. 1 (1970). There, we rejected the Government's argument that the tax benefit rule required a taxpayer who incorporated a partnership under § 351 to include in income the amount of the bad debt reserve of the partnership. The Government's theory was that, although § 351 provides that there will be no gain or loss on the transfer of assets to a controlled corporation in such a situation, the partnership had taken bad debt deductions to create the reserve, *see* § 166(c), and when the partnership terminated, it no longer needed the bad debt reserve. We noted that the receivables were transferred to the corporation along with the bad debt reserve. *Id.* at 5, and n. 5. Not only was there no "recovery," *id.* at 4, but there was no inconsistent event of any kind. That the fair market value of the receivables was equal to the face amount less the bad debt reserve, *ibid.*, reflected that the reserve, and the deductions that constituted it, were still an accurate estimate of the debts that would ultimately prove uncollectible, and the deduction was therefore completely consistent with the later transfer of the receivables to the incorporated business. *See Citizens' Acceptance Corp. v. United States*, 320 F.Supp. 798 (Del. 1971), *rev'd on other grounds*, 462 F.2d 751 (CA3 1972); Rev. Rul. 78-279, 1978-2 Cum. Bull. 135; Rev. Rul. 78-278, 1978-2 Cum. Bull. 134; *see generally* O'Hare, *Statutory Nonrecognition of Income and the Overriding Principle of the Tax Benefit Rule in the Taxation of Corporations and Shareholders*, 27 Tax L. Rev. 215, 219–221 (1972).

In the cases currently before us, then, we must undertake an examination of the particular provisions of the Code that govern these transactions to determine whether the deductions taken by the taxpayers were actually inconsistent with later events and whether specific nonrecognition provisions prevail over the principle of the tax benefit rule.

III

In *Hillsboro*, the key provision is § 164(e). That section grants the corporation a deduction for taxes imposed on its shareholders but paid by the corporation. It also denies the shareholders any deduction for the tax. In this case, the Commissioner has argued that the refund of the taxes by the State to the shareholders is the equivalent of the payment of a dividend from Hillsboro to its shareholders. If Hillsboro does not recognize income in the amount of the earlier deduction, it will have deducted a dividend. Since the general structure of the corporate tax provisions does not permit deduction of dividends, the Commissioner concludes that the payment to the shareholders must be inconsistent with the original deduction and therefore requires the inclusion of the amount of the taxes as income under the tax benefit rule.

In evaluating this argument, it is instructive to consider what the tax consequences of the payment of a shareholder tax by the corporation would be without § 164(e) and compare them to the consequences under § 164(e). Without § 164(e), the corporation would not be entitled to a deduction, for the tax is not imposed on it. *See* Treas. Reg. § 1.164-1(a), 26 CFR § 1.164-1(a) (1982); *Wisconsin Gas & Electric Co. v. United States*, 322 U.S. 526, 527–530 (1944). If the corporation has earnings and profits, the shareholder would have to recognize income in the amount of the taxes, because a payment by a corporation for the benefit of its shareholders is a constructive dividend. *See* §§ 301(c), 316(a); *e.g.*, *Ireland v. United States*, 621 F.2d 731, 735 (CA5 1980); B. BITTKER & J. EUSTICE, FEDERAL INCOME TAXATION OF CORPORATIONS AND SHAREHOLDERS para. 7.05 (4th ed. 1979). The shareholder, however, would be entitled to a deduction since the constructive dividend is used to satisfy his tax liability. § 164(a)(2). Thus, for the shareholder, the transaction would be a wash: he would recognize the amount of the tax as income, but he would have an offsetting deduction for the tax. For the corporation, there would be no tax consequences, for the payment of a dividend gives rise to neither income nor a deduction. 26 U.S.C. § 311(a) (1976 ed., Supp. V).

Under § 164(e), the economics of the transaction of course remain unchanged: the corporation is still satisfying a liability of the shareholder and is therefore paying a constructive dividend. The tax consequences are, however, significantly different, at least for the corporation. The transaction is still a wash for the shareholder; although § 164(e) denies him the deduction to which he would otherwise be entitled, he need not recognize income on the constructive dividend, Treas. Reg. § 1.164-7, 26 CFR § 1.164-7 (1982). But the corporation is entitled to a deduction that would not otherwise be available. In other words, the only effect of § 164(e) is to permit the corporation to deduct a dividend. Thus, we cannot agree with the Commissioner that, simply because the events here give rise to a deductible dividend, they cannot be consistent with the deduction. In at least some circumstances, a deductible dividend is within the contemplation of the Code. The question we must answer is whether § 164(e) permits a deductible dividend in these circumstances — when the money, though initially paid into the state treasury, ultimately reaches the shareholder — or whether the deductible dividend is available, as the Commissioner urges, only when the money remains in the state treasury, as properly assessed and collected tax revenue.

Rephrased, our question now is whether Congress, in granting this special favor to corporations that paid dividends by satisfying the liability of their shareholders, was concerned with the *reason* the money was paid out by the corporation or with the *use* to which it was ultimately put. Since § 164(e) represents a break with the usual rules governing corporate distributions, the structure of the Code does not provide any guidance on the reach of the provision. This Court has described the provision as "prompted by the plight of various banking corporations which paid and voluntarily absorbed the burden of certain local taxes imposed upon their shareholders, but were not permitted to deduct those payments from gross income." *Wisconsin Gas & Electric Co. v. United States*, *supra*, at 531 (footnote omitted). The section, in substantially similar form, has been part of the Code since the Revenue Act of 1921, 42 Stat. 227. The provision was added by the Senate, but its Committee Report merely mentions the deduction without discussing it, *see* S.

Rep. No. 275, 67th Cong., 1st Sess., 19 (1921). The only discussion of the provision appears to be that between Dr. T.S. Adams and Senator Smoot at the Senate hearings. Dr. Adams' statement explains why the States imposed the property tax on the shareholders and collected it from the banks, but it does not cast much light on the reason for the deduction. Hearings on H. R. 8245 before the Committee on Finance, 67th Cong., 1st Sess., 250–251 (1921) (statement of Dr. T.S. Adams, tax advisor, Treasury Department). Senator Smoot's response, however, is more revealing:

> "I have been a director in a bank . . . for over 20 years. They have paid that tax ever since I have owned a share of stock in the bank. . . . I know nothing about it. I do not take 1 cent of credit for deductions, and the banks are entitled to it. *They pay it out.*" *Id.* at 251 (emphasis added).

The *payment* by the corporations of a liability that Congress knew was not a tax imposed on them gave rise to the entitlement to a deduction; Congress was unconcerned that the corporations took a deduction for amounts that did not satisfy their tax liability. It apparently perceived the shareholders and the corporations as independent of one another, each "[knowing] nothing about" the payments by the other. In those circumstances, it is difficult to conclude that Congress intended that the corporation have no deduction if the State turned the tax revenues over to these independent parties. We conclude that the purpose of § 164(e) was to provide relief for corporations making these payments, and the focus of Congress was on the act of payment rather than on the ultimate use of the funds by the State. As long as the payment itself was not negated by a refund to the corporation, the change in character of the funds in the hands of the State does not require the corporation to recognize income, and we reverse the judgment below.

IV

The problem in *Bliss* is more complicated. Bliss took a deduction under § 162(a), so we must begin by examining that provision. Section 162(a) permits a deduction for the "ordinary and necessary expenses" of carrying on a trade or business. The deduction is predicated on the consumption of the asset in the trade or business. *See* Treas. Reg. § 1.162-3, 26 CFR § 1.162-3 (1982) ("Taxpayers . . . should include in expenses the charges for materials and supplies only in the amount that they are *actually consumed and used in operation* in the taxable year . . .") (emphasis added). If the taxpayer later sells the asset rather than consuming it in furtherance of his trade or business, it is quite clear that he would lose his deduction, for the basis of the asset would be zero, *see, e.g., Spitalny v. United States*, 430 F.2d 195 (CA9 1970), so he would recognize the full amount of the proceeds on sale as gain. *See* §§ 1001(a), (c). In general, if the taxpayer converts the expensed asset to some other, nonbusiness use, that action is inconsistent with his earlier deduction, and the tax benefit rule would require inclusion in income of the amount of the unwarranted deduction. That nonbusiness use is inconsistent with a deduction for an ordinary and necessary business expense is clear from an examination of the Code. While § 162(a) permits a deduction for ordinary and necessary business expenses, § 262 explicitly denies a deduction for personal expenses. In the 1916 Act, the two provisions were a single section. *See* § 5(a)(First), 39 Stat. 756. The provision has been uniformly interpreted as providing a deduction only for those expenses attributable to the business of the taxpayer. *See, e.g., Kornhauser v. United States,* 276 U.S. 145 (1928); Hearings on Proposed Revision of Revenue Laws before the Subcommittee of the House Committee on Ways and Means, 75th Cong., 3d Sess., 54 (1938) ("a taxpayer should be granted a reasonable deduction for the direct expenses he has incurred *in connection with his income*") (emphasis added); *see generally,* 1 BITTKER, *supra* n. 9, para. 20.2. Thus, if a corporation turns expensed assets to the analog of personal consumption, as Bliss did here — distribution to shareholders — it would seem that it should take into income the amount of the earlier deduction.

That conclusion, however, does not resolve this case, for the distribution by Bliss to its shareholders is governed by a provision of the Code that specifically shields the taxpayer from recognition of gain — § 336. We must therefore proceed to inquire whether this is the sort of gain that goes unrecognized under § 336.

V

Thus, the legislative history of § 336, the application of other general rules of tax law, and the construction of the identical language in § 337 all indicate that § 336 does not permit a liquidating corporation to avoid the tax benefit rule. Consequently, we reverse the judgment of the Court of Appeals and hold that, on liquidation, Bliss must include in income the amount of the unwarranted deduction.

* * *

Bliss paid the assessment on an increase of $60,000 in its taxable income. In the District Court, the parties stipulated that the value of the grain was $56,565, but the record does not show what the original cost of the grain was or what portion of it remained at the time of liquidation. The proper increase in taxable income is the portion of the cost of the grain attributable to the amount on hand at the time of liquidation. In *Bliss,* then, we remand for a determination of that amount. In *Hillsboro,* the taxpayer sought a redetermination in the Tax Court rather than paying the tax, so no further proceedings are necessary, and the judgment of the Court of Appeals is reversed.

It is so ordered.

JUSTICE BRENNAN, concurring in No. 81-930 and dissenting in No. 81-485.

I join Parts I, II, and IV of the Court's opinion. For the reasons expressed in Part I of JUSTICE BLACKMUN's dissenting opinion, however, I believe that a proper application of the principles set out in Part II of the Court's opinion would require an affirmance rather than a reversal in No. 81-485.

JUSTICE STEVENS, with whom JUSTICE MARSHALL joins, concurring in the judgment in No. 81-485 and dissenting in No. 81-930.

These two cases should be decided in the same way. The taxpayer in each case is a corporation. In 1972 each taxpayer made a deductible expenditure, and in 1973 its shareholders received an economic benefit. Neither corporate taxpayer ever recovered any part of its 1972 expenditure. In my opinion, the benefits received by the shareholders in 1973 are matters that should affect their returns; those benefits should not give rise to income on the 1973 return of the taxpayer in either case.

* * *

JUSTICE BLACKMUN, dissenting.

These consolidated cases present issues concerning the so-called "tax benefit rule" that has been developed in federal income tax law. In No. 81-485, the Court concludes that the rule has no application to the situation presented. In No. 81-930, it concludes that the rule operates to the detriment of the taxpayer with respect to its *later* tax year. I disagree with both conclusions.

* * *

I have no difficulty in favoring some kind of "tax benefit" adjustment in favor of the Government for each of these situations. An adjustment should be made, for in each case the beneficial deduction turned out to be improper and undeserved because its factual premise proved to be incorrect. Each taxpayer thus was not entitled to the claimed deduction, or a portion of it, and this non-entitlement should be reflected among its tax obligations.

This takes me, however, to the difficulty I encounter with the second concern, that is, the unraveling or rectification of the situation. The Commissioner and the United States in these respective cases insist that the Bank and the Dairy should be regarded as receiving income in the very next tax year when the factual premise for the prior year's deduction proved to be incorrect. I could understand that position, if, in the interim, the bar of a statute of limitations had become effective or if there were some other valid reason why the preceding year's return could not be corrected and additional tax collected. But it seems to me that the better resolution of these two particular cases and others like them — and a resolution that should produce little complaint from the taxpayer — is to make the necessary adjustment, whenever it can be made, in the tax year for which the deduction was originally claimed. This makes the correction where the correction is due and it makes the amount of net income for each year a true amount and one that accords with the facts, not one that is structured, imprecise, and fictional. This normally would be accomplished either by the taxpayer's filing an amended return for the earlier year, with payment of the resulting additional tax, or by the Commissioner's assertion of a deficiency followed by collection. This actually is the kind of thing that is done all the time, for when a taxpayer's return is audited and a deficiency is asserted due to an overstated deduction, the process equates with the filing of an amended return.

The Dairy's case is particularly acute. On July 2, 1973, on the second day after the end of its fiscal year, the Dairy adopted a plan of liquidation pursuant to § 333 of the Code, 26 U.S.C. § 333. That section requires the adoption of a plan of liquidation; the making and filing, within 30 days, of written elections by the qualified electing shareholders; and the effectuation of the distribution in liquidation within a calendar month. § 333(a), (c), and (d). It seems obvious that the Dairy, its management, and its shareholders, by the end of the Dairy's 1973 fiscal year on June 30, and certainly well before the filing of its tax return for that fiscal year, all had conceived and developed the July 2, 1973, plan of liquidation and were resolved to carry out that plan with the benefits that they felt would be afforded by it. Under these circumstances, we carry the tax benefit rule too far and apply it too strictly when we utilize the unconsumed feed to create income for the Dairy for fiscal 1974 (the month of July 1973), instead of decreasing the deduction for the same feed in fiscal 1973. Any concern for the integrity of annual tax reporting should not demand that much. I thus would have the Dairy's returns adjusted in a realistic and factually true manner, rather than in accord with an inflexibly administered tax benefit rule.

Much the same is to be said about the Bank's case. The decisive event, this Court's decision in *Lehnhausen*, occurred on February 22, 1973, within the second month of the Bank's 1973 tax year. Indeed, it took place before the Bank's calendar year 1972 return would be overdue. Here again, an accurate return for 1972 should be preferred over inaccurate returns for both 1972 and 1973.

This, in my view, is the way these two particular tax controversies should be resolved. I see no need for anything more complex in their resolution than what I have outlined. Of course, if a statute of limitations problem existed, or if the facts in some other way prevented reparation to the Government, the cases and their resolution might well be different.

I realize that my position is simplistic, but I doubt if the judge-made tax benefit rule really was intended, at its origin, to be regarded as applicable in simple situations of the kind presented in these successive-tax-year cases. So often a judge-made rule, understandably conceived, ultimately is used to carry us further than it should.

I would vacate the judgment in each of these cases and remand each case for further proceedings consistent with this analysis.

Understanding *Hillsboro*

1.   What does Justice O'Connor appear to mean by the term "tax benefit rule," and how does she apply it to the cases at bar?[23] Do you find the difference in outcome between the two cases (*i.e.*, application of the rule in *Bliss Dairy* but not *Hillsboro*) convincing as a conceptual matter? Why (or why not)?

2.   What do you think of Justice Blackman's suggestion that — instead of including income in the later year — the taxpayers should simply amend their prior years' returns to eliminate the offending deduction. Is this consistent with the

---

[23] The tax treatment of dividends, at issue in Hillsboro, is discussed further in Chapter 11, *infra*.

annual accounting principle, described above? Is it practical? What would be the other advantages and disadvantages of adopting this alternate approach?

3. Why do you think that Bliss Dairy decided to distribute the remaining feed to its shareholders instead of (say) selling it to another company and then distributing the proceeds of the sale? Knowing the Supreme Court's decision, what would you advise a similarly situated company to do next time around? Would this advice make sense from a practical, as well as a tax, perspective?

The tax benefit rule is the converse of the rule in *Clark* and may be explained with a simple example. Suppose that somebody took a casualty loss deduction for a family heirloom that appeared to be stolen in 2001, but that, miraculously, reappeared two years later. (If you prefer a business context, assume that the same person took a legitimate bad debt deduction and that the debt in question was eventually repaid.)

It seems obvious that the taxpayer should have to "give back" the original deduction in some way; but how? It's too late (in most cases) to amend the previous year's return, and in any event nothing changed in the previous year: the change came only later, when the facts that gave rise to the original deduction came unstuck. Yet requiring someone to pay tax in the later year also has problems. What if the taxpayer received an incomplete benefit from the original deduction, because tax rates were lower or because she had insufficient income to make use of her deductions (*e.g.*, the same problems as in *United States v. Lewis*)? Or what if the returned property is worth less than the property originally "lost?" And how close does the relationship between the deduction and the later contradictory or inconsistent event have to be?

The tax law deals with this problem through a combination of judicial and statutory rules. First, case law established the principle that the return of property which was the subject of a previous deduction results in income to the taxpayer in the year of the return. That seems reasonable enough, but may result in unfairness if the taxpayer was unable to use the deduction in the previous year. Section 111 was accordingly added to the Code, providing that "gross income does not include income attributable to the recovery . . . of any amount deducted in any prior taxable year to the extent such amount did not reduce the amount of tax imposed by this chapter." For example, if the taxpayer took a $50,000 casualty loss in 2001, but was able to use only $30,000 of it — so that the remaining $20,000 was effectively "wasted" from the taxpayer's perspective — only $30,000 would be included in the taxpayer's income when and if the property was returned to her.[24] (Both the inclusion rule and the section 111 limitation are sometimes referred to as "the tax benefit rule," although the latter is more properly described as a restriction on that rule.)

Section 111 makes it sound as if the tax benefit rule is a sort of recapture doctrine: the taxpayer should have to give back only the actual amount of the

---

[24] This might happen, for example, if the taxpayer had extensive itemized deductions in 2001, so that her adjusted gross income (AGI) was high enough to support a large casualty deduction but her taxable income was too low to make full use of it. Casualty losses are generally deductible to the extent that they exceed 10 percent of AGI. *See* I.R.C. § 165(h).

deduction that he (erroneously) took in the original year. If so, what about changes in tax rates? The general rule is that these are ignored, that is, the taxpayer must take the amount of the "false" deduction into income, even if tax rates have increased in the interim, so that the actual tax paid on the income will be greater than the amount of the deduction taken in the earlier year.[25] (A taxpayer facing declining tax rates would receive an equivalent windfall.) This rule reflects a more general reluctance to adjust for changes in tax rates, and is consistent with the concept of separate accounting for taxable years that underlies most of the tax law. Yet there is an uneasy quality to the compromise: the law seems willing to look back at previous taxable years for some purposes, but not others, and it is often difficult to say where the line will be drawn. The tax benefit rule is thus a microcosm of the more general annual accounting problem: tax years are independent, but not always so, and the degree and nature of the exceptions vary according to the particular facts.

Statutory Fixes:
Net Operating Losses and Income Averaging Rules —
Net Operating Losses and Fairness for Businesses

While courts play an important role in tax law, they are ultimately subject to the will of the United States Congress, which has to be elected every two (or, in the Senate, every six) years. There is accordingly a marked tendency for harsh results to be softened by congressional action, especially if the "victims" are wealthy or visible enough to make themselves heard. We have observed this already in *Benaglia*, where Congress codified a pro-taxpayer holding, and again in *Lewis*, where it overturned a harsh (but not entirely unreasonable) anti-taxpayer decision. Each of these decisions was indeed helpful to taxpayers, although each raised potential new inconsistencies and created new interpretive problems, which remain features of the tax law today.

Sometimes Congress intervenes on a grander scale. An example is Section 172, the so-called net operating loss ("NOL") rules. As indicated above, section 172 allows excess business losses to be carried back to the two preceding and forward to the twenty following taxable years, thereby avoiding a situation in which the taxpayer has "mismatched" income and deductions and is forced to pay tax when it has little or no net taxable income. For example, assume that a business loses $1 million each year from 2003 through 2007, but begins to show a profit thereafter, registering $1 million of net income in 2008, $2 million in 2009, and $5 million in 2010 and all succeeding tax years. Under section 172(b), the company — assuming its losses met the definition of "net operating losses" in section 172(c) — would "carry forward" $5 million of aggregate losses into its 2008 tax year, which would be sufficient to eliminate its otherwise taxable income in 2008 ($1 million) and 2009 ($2 million) together with the first $3 million of income in its 2010 tax year. Only in 2010 would the company pay any tax (on its last $2 million of income), and only in 2011 would it begin to pay tax on its full $5 million of income. If the company made money

---

[25] For example, a taxpayer who took a $10,000 deduction in year one at a 20 percent tax rate, for a tax savings of $2,000, might later be required to take the same amount into income at a 50 percent rate, resulting in a $5,000 (albeit somewhat delayed) tax. *See* Alice Phelan Sullivan Corp. v. Comm'r, 381 F.2d 399 (Ct. Cl. 1967).

first and then lost it, it could likewise "carry back" losses against its earlier income, although only to the two preceding tax years. For example, a business that made $5 million annually from 2003 to 2005, but lost $25 million in 2006, could use that loss to eliminate its tax liability for 2004 and 2005, but not for 2003 or any previous year. (The remaining $15 million of losses could still be carried forward to later taxable years.)

The NOL provisions go a long way toward eliminating the problem in *Sanford & Brooks* and similar cases. But they raise significant issues. One particular issue concerns the payment (or more exactly, nonpayment) of interest on NOL carryforwards. Suppose a company registers losses for fifteen consecutive years but, owing to an eternally optimistic owner, remains in business and begins to earn a profit in year sixteen. Under section 172, it can carry forward its earlier losses against this income. But these losses are carried forward without interest, that is to say, a $1 million loss from year 1 offsets exactly $1 million of income in year 16, with no increase to make up for the lost time. By contrast, if the company borrowed $1 million in year 1 to cover its losses, it has probably paid $2 or $3 million in interest (albeit deductible interest) during the intervening period before it can repay the loan in year 16. If the purpose of NOL carryovers is to permit full use of accumulated losses — to adopt a "transactional" rather than "annual" accounting method — shouldn't interest be paid on NOL carryforwards?

The interest problem raises a related matter of timing and availability. Under the NOL regime, a company may have to wait as long as twenty years to deduct its excess business losses. Why should this long wait be necessary? Why shouldn't the Government simply write a check to companies that have excess losses, and let the companies reinvest the money in an effort to achieve future profits? Note that, for small start-up companies, the present law carryovers often come too late to prevent bankruptcy or business failure; the present law rules may thus add to the already existing disadvantage that they face in competing with larger, more established enterprises. Is this discrimination justified?

A third, related problem arises with NOL carrybacks. From the taxpayer's perspective, carrybacks are attractive because they provide immediate tax relief and avoid the delay problems highlighted above. But from the Government's perspective the situation is the reverse. While an NOL carryforward merely results in a foregone tax somewhere in the future, a carryback means that a taxpayer will receive a refund for taxes already paid — *i.e.*, the Government will effectively write a check to the taxpayer to cover their previous tax liability. For example, assume that an automobile company, owing to high demand and a (relative) absence of competition, makes $100 million in year 1 and year 2. In year 3, the car market is hit with heavy import competition and the company loses $200 million. Not only will the company not pay any tax in year 3, but the Government will refund it (albeit, without interest) the taxes paid in year 1 and year 2 — a subsidy of tens of millions of dollars to a company precisely because it failed to anticipate competition and accordingly lost large sums of money in the third year. At the same time, the company may have laid off thousands of workers who receive limited unemployment benefits and no equivalent tax assistance.

Because of the problems above, there is a tendency to restrict NOL carrybacks, which are presently limited to two years as opposed to the twenty year carryforward period. Skeptics have also noted that this policy puts revenue losses off in the future where the present Congress can escape blame for them. Several industries that have performed poorly for long stretches — usually because of their own bad management — have successfully lobbied Congress for an extended carryback period.

Finally, it goes without saying that the NOL provisions raise monstrous technical problems, including the definition of operating losses, the exclusion of capital losses from that definition, and the treatment of NOLs in mergers and other corporate acquisitions.

Income Averaging and Fairness for Individuals

If a multi-year perspective is available to businesses, what about individuals? Here the problem is not so much loss deductions as the effect of progressive tax rates, which tend to punish individuals whose income jumps up and down in different taxable years rather than remaining at a relatively constant level.[26] Should such individuals be allowed to combine the taxable periods in question, in order to avert this result?

For example, assume that an aspiring actress makes $75,000 in year 1; loses her job and accordingly made no money in year 2; finds a new, better job and earned $100,000 in year 3; but is forced to reduce her hours and accordingly earned only $25,000 in year 4. Because of the progressive rate system, she will be forced to pay tax at a relatively high rate in her "good" years (year 1 and year 3) and — although her taxes will obviously be lower in years 2 and 4 — the combined tax is still likely to be higher than that which would be paid on a flat income of $50,000 in each of the four years.[27] Is this a fair, or reasonable, outcome?

For many years, the effect above was mitigated by income averaging, which permitted qualifying individuals to spread out their income over a maximum four- or five-year period and thereby reduce the impact of progressivity on widely varying compensation. Through a complex set of calculations, the taxpayer was essentially allowed to pay tax on her median level of income ($50,000, in the example above) and avoid the unhappy result described in the preceding paragraph. The effects of annual accounting were thus ameliorated in a manner distinct from, but conceptually related to, NOL carryovers for business enterprises. Income averaging was particularly attractive to those (*e.g.*, farmers and fishermen) whose income

---

[26] Progressive tax rates also apply to corporations, but corporations with more than $75,000 of taxable income are taxed at a (nearly) flat rate.

[27] As an example, assume (only a slight simplification) that the tax rate was 15 percent on the first $25,000 of income and 28 percent thereafter, with no applicable deductions. A taxpayer who earned $50,000 would pay a total of $10,750 in tax ($3,750 on the first $25,000 and $7,000 on the second $25,000) in each taxable year or $43,000 over a four-year period. By contrast our aspiring actress would pay $17,750 ($3,750 + $14,000) in year one; nothing in year two; $24,750 ($3,750 + $21,000) in year three; and $3,750 in year four, for a total of $46,250 over the four-year period, while coping with substantially more economic uncertainty than a steady wage-earner. As incomes increase, pushing taxpayers into still higher percentage brackets, these differences become more pronounced.

tends to gyrate between different years, as well as to others (particularly women) who enter and leave the work force for reasons that may be beyond their control.

Income averaging was repealed in 1986, in order to save revenue and because the newly compressed rate structure appeared to some observers to render it super-fluous.[28] There was also a sense that income averaging was helping students and young professionals, whose income fluctuations were likely to be temporary in nature, more than its originally intended beneficiaries, *i.e.*, those whose income varied on a more ongoing basis. (NOLs remained part of the Code.) What do you think of these limitations and do they address the benefits for women and others with naturally fluctuating incomes resulting from an income averaging system?

Using the Sources

Based on the materials in the preceding three sections (*i.e.*, return of capital, net operating losses, and income averaging) what would be the tax consequences of each of the following hypothetical transactions?

Taxpayer lost property in Year One, found it in Year Two, and was not entitled to a casualty loss deduction at the time of the loss.[29] (For extra credit, what is the tax treatment of the person who finds the property?)

Taxpayer lost property in Year One, found it in Year Two, and took a casualty loss deduction at the time of the loss.

Taxpayer lost property in Year One, found it in Year Two, and was entitled to a casualty loss deduction in Year One but forgot to claim it.

Taxpayer finds $500 in a taxi and, believing it has been abandoned by its original owner, appropriates the money for her own use. Would it affect your answer if the taxpayer's right to keep the money was questionable under local law?

Same as d., except that the original owner of the $500 shows up two years later and the taxpayer is compelled to return the money to her (For extra credit, again, what is the tax treatment of the original owner?)

Same as d., except the original owner shows up during Year One and the taxpayer is engaged in litigation with her at the end of the year.

Pharaoh Industries, a corporation, has seven fat years (all gains) followed by seven lean years (all losses).

Pharaoh Industries, a corporation, has seven lean years (all losses) followed by seven fat years (all gains).

Taxpayer, who owns a hardware store, takes a deduction for a bad debt in Year One, but the debt is then paid during Year Two. What if the debt itself was never repaid, but the taxpayer made money on other transactions involving the same customer, so that (on balance) the loss from the bad debt was compensated for?

---

[28] On the repeal of income averaging, see generally Richard Schmalbeck, *Income Averaging after Twenty Years: A Failed Experiment in Horizontal Equity*, 1984 DUKE L.J. 509.

[29] I.R.C. § 165(c).

Taxpayer contributes a building to charity in the year 2011, at which time it was worth $100,000, and takes a deduction for that amount. In 2015, the charitable organization decides that it cannot use the property and returns it — now worth $250,000 — to the taxpayer. Would it make any difference to your answer (i) if the taxpayer had only $50,000 of gross income (and so could use only half of the deduction) in 2011, or (ii) if tax rates doubled between 2011 and 2015? Why?

Law and Planning

1.   Suppose that section 172 (net operating loss rules) did not exist. What effect would the annual accounting principle have on the willingness of businesses to embark on risky, long-term business projects? Does section 172 adequately address these concerns?

2.   Suppose that you were contributing property to a charity and wanted to avoid the problem described in item j under "Using the Sources," above, *i.e.*, a return of the property resulting in potential liability under the Tax Benefit Rule. How could you design the contribution so as to reduce or eliminate this problem? (Hint: think about potential limitations on the donation and how they might affect its value for charitable contribution purposes.)

3.   Suppose instead that you were a lawyer, à la Clark, who had made several mistakes and wanted to compensate your clients for those errors in order to protect your professional reputation. What could you do (i) to increase the chances that you would receive a personal tax deduction for your efforts, and (ii) to reduce the chance that your clients would be taxed on the return? Would tax law play a major role in your decision, or would it be peripheral to other considerations?

Politics and Policy

1.   What do you think of the idea of extending NOL carrybacks — say, from two to seven years — as a way of helping depressed industries? As a (somewhat weaker) alternative, what about the idea of keeping present law in place, but paying interest on NOL carryforwards? What would be the likely arguments for and against this proposal?

2.   Does it bother you that businesses can adopt a multiyear perspective by means of NOLs, when equivalent nonbusiness provisions (*e.g.*, income averaging) were repealed or never existed? Is there a difference between business and nonbusiness activities that justifies this different treatment? What other differences have we observed in tax treatment of businesses and individuals, and who usually winds up getting better treatment? Why?

3.   What do you think was the relative impact of the elimination of income averaging on (i) women and men, (ii) younger and older taxpayers, and (iii) the wealthy as compared to the poor and middle class? With respect specifically to gender differences, is income averaging a good way to promote equality, or is it likely to be ineffective? Do men and women have different life patterns that might reflect themselves in higher and lower tax liabilities for the same (net) income? Should the Code be concerned about this issue at all?

4.   Taken as a whole, what does this chapter tell you about the tax legislative process and the kinds of problems that it places a priority on fixing? What changes would you recommend in the lawmaking process in order to address these issues?

Additional Assignment — Chapter 3[30]

One of the more challenging aspects of tax practice occurs when a lawyer is asked to plan a business transaction "ex ante" (that is, before it happens), rather than simply applying the law to an already existing ("ex post") situation. This may involve situations as basic as planning for individual retirement or as complex as structuring the operations of a large, multinational corporation. In each of these cases the goal is to accomplish the client's tax goals — generally, to pay as little tax as possible — without sacrificing their real-world business objectives. (For example, telling a client to give all of her money to charity would be good tax advice, as it would avoid further income or estate tax, but probably not the most practical assistance.) Indeed, it is the tension between tax and nontax goals that defines the successful tax lawyer, who must typically be a good business lawyer as well as a technical tax expert.

With the above in mind, consider the following hypothetical. Your client, Long-Range Industries (LRI), is engaged in the manufacture and production of sophisticated computer technology having both civilian and military applications.[31] In particular LRI is considering a project to develop advanced Internet security software that — while most immediately the subject of a Government, national security-based contract — may also have implications for private businesses, families (e.g., protecting children from Internet-related pornography), and other peaceful purposes. Investments of this type are highly profitable, but risky, and take a long time to come to fruition; in this particular case LRI expects to have at least five years of losses on the new product before it generates positive net revenues. Throughout this period LRI will also be working on various other projects but none having the size or importance of the Internet security product.

LRI has come to you for advice regarding the tax consequences of the transaction described above. In particular, it has the following questions:

1. What will be the effect on LRI of the annual accounting principle, and to what degree will that effect be mitigated by the availability of net operating loss carryovers under section 172? (Be sure to distinguish between NOL carrybacks and carryforwards and the likelihood that each will be useful to LRI in improving its tax situation.)

2. What steps should LRI take, in negotiating its contract with the Government or in organizing its own internal operations, in order to mitigate the effect of the rules described in the preceding paragraph and achieve the most favorable tax result?

3. Suppose that, in the third year of the project, LRI had a copyright infringement claim against a competing company with respect to the Internet security project, which it believed to be a valid claim but which it could not be sure of until litigation. Would the tax principles in this chapter (annual accounting, claim

---

[30] This problem, like those in the succeeding odd-numbered chapters, is designed to be read by students at home and serve as the basis for in-class discussion.

[31] If you are uncomfortable with military applications, feel free to delete the last three words.

of right, tax benefit rule, etc.) have any effect on your decision whether or how to proceed with this potential lawsuit? If so, what would these effects be?

4. Suppose that LRI approached its congressperson (Senator) for assistance in changing the law to allow for contractual accounting on long-range technology projects.[32] How do you think this proposal would be received, and what would be the strongest arguments for and against it? Would you, as a congressperson, be likely to support this proposed legislation? Why (or why not)?

5. What additional facts, if any, would you want to know before answering any of the questions above?

---

[32] Contractual accounting is a system under which income is measured on a project-by-project rather than an annual accounting basis. For example, if a company invested $1 million in a particular project, no tax would be paid until it had earned back at least that amount from the same activity. The general effect of this system would be to delay payment of tax until a point at or near completion of the project.

Chapter 4

TIMING II: REALIZATION, RECOGNITION, AND THE PROBLEM OF DEFERRED COMPENSATION

Chapter 3 introduced the basics of tax timing, including the basis and realization concepts and the relationship between events occurring in different taxable years. This chapter builds further upon those ideas. First, the chapter considers several close cases in which gain or loss may or may not have been realized by the taxpayer, enabling us to develop a more complete understanding of the realization concept. Second, we will take a brief look at the so-called nonrecognition provisions, that is, situations in which gain has plainly been realized, but the Code elects not to recognize (*i.e.*, take into account) the gain for income tax purposes. Third, the chapter considers the use of deferral (*i.e.*, delay) of taxation as a tax reduction strategy. In particular, we will consider the nature and significance of deferred compensation schemes, including pensions, stock options, and restricted property transfers.

For the first time in the course, this chapter places a primary emphasis on tax planning. Tax planning is the intentional structuring of transactions so as to reduce tax and increase after-tax income. This means that we will devote an increasing amount of time to both the business and the tax logic of various financial arrangements. As you read the chapter, try to keep in mind the taxpayers' "real world" situations, as well as their tax situations. Notice when and how the tax system impinges on the taxpayers' achievement of their financial and business goals.

I. REALIZATION: WHAT IS, AND ISN'T, A REALIZATION EVENT?

A. Gains

HELVERING v. BRUUN
United States Supreme Court
309 U.S. 461 (1940)

MR. JUSTICE ROBERTS delivered the opinion of the Court.

The controversy had its origin in the petitioner's assertion that the respondent realized taxable gain from the forfeiture of a leasehold, the tenant having erected a new building upon the premises. The court below held that no income had been realized. Inconsistency of the decisions on the subject led us to grant *certiorari*.

The Board of Tax Appeals made no independent findings. The cause was submitted upon a stipulation of facts. From this it appears that on July 1, 1915, the respondent, as owner, leased a lot of land and the building thereon for a term of ninety-nine years.

The lease provided that the lessee might, at any time, upon giving bond to secure rentals accruing in the two ensuing years, remove or tear down any building on the land, provided that no building should be removed or torn down after the lease became forfeited, or during the last three and one-half years of the term. The lessee was to surrender the land, upon termination of the lease, with all buildings and improvements thereon.

In 1929 the tenant demolished and removed the existing building and constructed a new one which had a useful life of not more than fifty years. July 1, 1933, the lease was cancelled for default in payment of rent and taxes and the respondent regained possession of the land and building.

The parties stipulated "that as at said date, July 1, 1933, the building which had been erected upon said premises by the lessee had a fair market value of $64,245.68 and that the unamortized cost of the old building, which was removed from the premises in 1929 to make way for the new building, was $12,811.43, thus leaving a net fair market value as at July 1, 1933, of $51,434.25, for the aforesaid new building erected upon the premises by the lessee."

On the basis of these facts, the petitioner determined that in 1933 the respondent realized a net gain of $51,434.25. The Board overruled his determination and the Circuit Court of Appeals affirmed the Board's decision.

The course of administrative practice and judicial decision in respect of the question presented has not been uniform. In 1917 the Treasury ruled that the adjusted value of improvements installed upon leased premises is income to the lessor upon the termination of the lease. The ruling was incorporated in two succeeding editions of the Treasury Regulations. In 1919 the Circuit Court of Appeals for the Ninth Circuit held in *Miller v. Gearin*, 258 F. 225, that the regulation was invalid as the gain, if taxable at all, must be taxed as of the year when the improvements were completed.

The regulations were accordingly amended to impose a tax upon the gain in the year of completion of the improvements, measured by their anticipated value at the termination of the lease and discounted for the duration of the lease. Subsequently the regulations permitted the lessor to spread the depreciated value of the improvements over the remaining life of the lease, reporting an aliquot part each year, with provision that, upon premature termination, a tax should be imposed upon the excess of the then value of the improvements over the amount theretofore returned.

In 1935 the Circuit Court of Appeals for the Second Circuit decided in *Hewitt Realty Co. v. Commissioner*, 76 F.2d 880, that a landlord received no taxable income in a year, during the term of the lease, in which his tenant erected a building on the leased land. The court, while recognizing that the lessor need not receive money to be taxable, based its decision that no taxable gain was realized in that case on the fact that the improvement was not portable or detachable from the land, and if removed would be worthless except as bricks, iron, and mortar. It said (p. 884): "The question as we view it is whether the value received is embodied in something separately disposable, or whether it is so merged in the land as to become financially a part of it, something which, though it increases its value, has no value of its own when torn away."

This decision invalidated the regulations then in force.

In 1938 this court decided *M.E. Blatt Co. v. United States*, 305 U.S. 267. There, in connection with the execution of a lease, landlord and tenant mutually agreed that each should make certain improvements to the demised premises and that those made by the tenant should become and remain the property of the landlord. The Commissioner valued the improvements as of the date they were made, allowed depreciation thereon to the termination of the leasehold, divided the depreciated value by the number of years the lease had to run, and found the landlord taxable for each year's aliquot portion thereof. His action was sustained by the Court of Claims. The judgment was reversed on the ground that the added value could not be considered rental accruing over the period of the lease; that the facts found by the Court of Claims did not support the conclusion of the Commissioner as to the value to be attributed to the improvements after a use throughout the term of the lease; and that, in the circumstances disclosed, any enhancement in the value of the realty in the tax year was not income realized by the lessor within the Revenue Act.

The circumstances of the instant case differentiate it from the *Blatt* and *Hewitt* cases; but the petitioner's contention that gain was realized when the respondent, through forfeiture of the lease, obtained untrammeled title, possession and control of the premises, with the added increment of value added by the new building, runs counter to the decision in the *Miller* case and to the reasoning in the *Hewitt* case.

The respondent insists that the realty, — a capital asset at the date of the execution of the lease, — remained such throughout the term and after its expiration; that improvements affixed to the soil became part of the realty indistinguishably blended in the capital asset; that such improvements cannot be separately valued or treated as received in exchange for the improvements which were on the land at the date of the execution of the lease; that they are, therefore, in the same category as improvements added by the respondent to his land, or accruals of value due to extraneous and adventitious circumstances. Such added value, it is argued, can be considered capital gain only upon the owner's disposition of the asset. The position is that the economic gain consequent upon the enhanced value of the recaptured asset is not gain derived from capital or realized within the meaning of the Sixteenth Amendment and may not, therefore, be taxed without apportionment.

We hold that the petitioner was right in assessing the gain as realized in 1933.

We might rest our decision upon the narrow issue presented by the terms of the stipulation. It does not appear what kind of a building was erected by the tenant or whether the building was readily removable from the land. It is not stated whether the difference in the value between the building removed and that erected in its place accurately reflects an increase in the value of land and building considered as a single estate in land. On the facts stipulated, without more, we should not be warranted in holding that the presumption of the correctness of the Commissioner's determination has been overborne.

The respondent insists, however, that the stipulation was intended to assert that the sum of $51,434.25 was the measure of the resulting enhancement in value of the real estate at the date of the cancellation of the lease. The petitioner seems not to contest this view. Even upon this assumption we think that gain in the amount named was realized by the respondent in the year of repossession.

The respondent cannot successfully contend that the definition of gross income in § 22(a) of the Revenue Act of 1932 is not broad enough to embrace the gain in question. That definition follows closely the Sixteenth Amendment. Essentially the respondent's position is that the Amendment does not permit the taxation of such gain without apportionment amongst the states. He relies upon what was said in *Hewitt Realty Co. v. Commissioner, supra,* and upon expressions found in the decisions of this court dealing with the taxability of stock dividends to the effect that gain derived from capital must be something of exchangeable value proceeding from property, severed from the capital, however invested or employed, and received by the recipient for his separate use, benefit, and disposal. He emphasizes the necessity that the gain be separate from the capital and separately disposable. These expressions, however, were used to clarify the distinction between an ordinary dividend and a stock dividend. They were meant to show that in the case of a stock dividend, the stockholder's interest in the corporate assets after receipt of the dividend was the same as and inseverable from that which he owned before the dividend was declared. We think they are not controlling here.

While it is true that economic gain is not always taxable as income, it is settled that the realization of gain need not be in cash derived from the sale of an asset. Gain may occur as a result of exchange of property, payment of the taxpayer's indebtedness, relief from a liability, or other profit realized from the completion of a transaction. The fact that the gain is a portion of the value of property received by the taxpayer in the transaction does not negate its realization.

Here, as a result of a business transaction, the respondent received back his land with a new building on it, which added an ascertainable amount to its value. It is not necessary to recognition of taxable gain that he should be able to sever the improvement begetting the gain from his original capital. If that were necessary, no income could arise from the exchange of property; whereas such gain has always been recognized as realized taxable gain.

Judgment reversed.

THE CHIEF JUSTICE concurs in the result in view of the terms of the stipulation of facts.

MR. JUSTICE McREYNOLDS took no part in the decision of this case.

Understanding *Bruun*

1.   The realization requirement is generally interpreted as requiring some act — most frequently, a sale or taxable exchange — by which the owner severs the gain from the underlying property. *See, e.g., Eisner v. Macomber*, 252 U.S. 189, 207 (1920). So what does the *Bruun* Court mean when it says that "[i]t is not necessary to recognition of taxable gain that [the taxpayer] should be able to sever the improvement begetting the gain from his original capital"? If that's the case, why have a realization requirement at all? Bruun plainly could not separate the house from the underlying land and sell it to a new buyer without also selling the underlying land. Conceivably, he could recognize some interim economic benefit by living in the house himself or renting it to a new tenant, although in the second case it would seem appropriate to tax him later, when these things occur, rather than now, when they haven't. So in what sense has he "realized" anything? Isn't Bruun's original position — that he should be taxed only when he sells or disposes of the entire property — reasonable under the circumstances? Why does the Court reject it?

2.   Assume the Court is right and Bruun should be taxed sooner rather than later on the improvements. The Court suggests at least four different ways to accomplish this:

a. Tax him when the building was completed (1929), even though the lease was still running.

b. Tax him in 1929, but on a reduced amount, reflecting the facts that (i) the landlord would not take possession of the building until the lease was completed, and (ii) the building might have deteriorated and therefore been worth less at that later point. (This method would presumably involve some kind of present value calculation, together with an adjustment when the lease ended ahead of schedule in 1933.)

c. Tax him on the rental value of the building in each year of the lease. That is, tax him as though he was receiving a small amount of income in each year of the lease (of amount equal to the estimated rental value of the building), rather than receiving one large, lump-sum amount upon termination of the lease (of amount equal to the estimated value of the entire building).

d. Tax him on the full value of the building in 1933, when the lease was terminated (*i.e.*, the actual holding in the case).

Which of these makes the most sense from the perspectives of fairness or efficiency? Which is easiest to administer? Does the difficulty of deciding between these options make Bruun's own preferred alternative — no tax at all until such later year in which Bruun sells the underlying property — seem even more attractive?

3.   What was going on in the United States in the 1930s that might have made it hard for the tenant to pay Bruun his rent? How, if at all, does this affect your answers to questions one and two, above?

4.   Why does Bruun care if the tax is imposed now or later?

Whatever its theoretical merits, *Bruun* is a nasty result, taxing an unfortunate person in the middle of a bad situation not of his own making. It is thus not surprising that Congress overruled the case, enacting the rule that is now section 109 of the Code. Like section 1341 after *Lewis*, section 109 sets out a rule opposite to the holding of the Supreme Court, stating that "[g]ross income does *not* include income (other than rent) derived by a lessor of real property on the termination of a lease, representing the value of such property attributable to buildings erected or other improvements made by the lessee" (emphasis supplied). Thus, if section 109 had existed in 1933, Bruun would have paid no tax on the termination of the lease, the improvements being reflected in income only at such time (if ever) when he sold the entire underlying property.

To prevent a double benefit from accruing to the taxpayer, section 1019 provides that there is no basis increase in a section 109-type situation. For example, if Bruun's land had a basis and a fair market value equal to $100,000, and if the building constructed by his tenant increased the fair market value to $151,500, a subsequent sale for that price would result in $51,500 of income ($151,500 amount realized, minus $100,000 basis), thereby "catching up" — albeit much later in time — for the tax originally excluded upon termination of the lease. (There is no "catch-up" if the owner holds the property until death, resulting in a section 1014 basis step-up).

An interesting feature of section 109 is the parenthetical "other than rent", which suggests that the rule will not protect landlords who deliberately encourage tenants to construct buildings or other improvements as a sort of rent substitute. Section 109 does not elaborate on this exception, although the section 61 regulations state cryptically that "[w]hether or not improvements made by a lessee result in rental income to the lessor in a particular case depends upon the intention of the parties, which may be indicated either by the terms of the lease or by the surrounding circumstances." Treas. Reg. § 1.61-8(c). What circumstances might the IRS look for in establishing that improvements were, in fact, intended to be a substitute for rent? Why would anybody try to pay rent in such a roundabout fashion? If you were counsel to a landlord, and the lease permitted the tenant to construct improvements on the rental property, what steps might you take to ensure that the improvements were not treated as rent under the regulation, above?

JAMES v. UNITED STATES
United States Supreme Court
366 U.S. 213 (1961)

MR. CHIEF JUSTICE WARREN announced the judgment of the Court and an opinion in which MR. JUSTICE BRENNAN and MR. JUSTICE STEWART concur.

The issue before us in this case is whether embezzled funds are to be included in the "gross income" of the embezzler in the year in which the funds are misappropriated under § 22(a) of the Internal Revenue Code of 1939 and § 61(a) of the Internal Revenue Code of 1954.

The facts are not in dispute. The petitioner is a union official who, with another person, embezzled in excess of $738,000 during the years 1951 through 1954 from his employer union and from an insurance company with which the union was doing business.[1] Petitioner failed to report these amounts in his gross income in those years and was convicted for willfully attempting to evade the federal income tax due for each of the years 1951 through 1954 in violation of § 145(b) of the Internal Revenue Code of 1939 and § 7201 of the Internal Revenue Code of 1954. He was sentenced to a total of three years' imprisonment. The Court of Appeals affirmed. 273 F.2d 5. Because of a conflict with this Court's decision in *Commissioner v. Wilcox*, 327 U.S. 404, a case whose relevant facts are concededly the same as those in the case now before us, we granted *certiorari*. 362 U.S. 974.

In *Wilcox*, the Court held that embezzled money does not constitute taxable income to the embezzler in the year of the embezzlement under § 22(a) of the Internal Revenue Code of 1939. Six years later, this Court held, in *Rutkin v. United States*, 343 U.S. 130, that extorted money does constitute taxable income to the extortionist in the year that the money is received under § 22(a) of the Internal Revenue Code of 1939. In *Rutkin*, the Court did not overrule *Wilcox*, but stated:

> "We do not reach in this case the factual situation involved in *Commissioner v. Wilcox*, 327 U.S. 404. We limit that case to its facts. There embezzled funds were held not to constitute taxable income to the embezzler under § 22(a)." *Id.* at 138.

However, examination of the reasoning used in *Rutkin* leads us inescapably to the conclusion that *Wilcox* was thoroughly devitalized.

The basis for the *Wilcox* decision was "that a taxable gain is conditioned upon (1) the presence of a claim of right to the alleged gain and (2) the absence of a definite, unconditional obligation to repay or return that which would otherwise constitute a gain. Without some bona fide legal or equitable claim, even though it be contingent or contested in nature, the taxpayer cannot be said to have received any gain or profit within the reach of § 22(a)." *Commissioner v. Wilcox, supra*, at p. 408. Since Wilcox embezzled the money, held it "without any semblance of a bona fide claim of right," *ibid.*, and therefore "was at all times under an unqualified duty and

---

[1] [3] Petitioner has pleaded guilty to the offense of conspiracy to embezzle in the Court of Essex County, New Jersey.

obligation to repay the money to his employer," *ibid.*, the Court found that the money embezzled was not includible within "gross income." But, Rutkin's legal claim was no greater than that of Wilcox. It was specifically found "that petitioner had no basis for his claim . . . and that he obtained it by extortion." *Rutkin v. United States, supra,* at p. 135. Both Wilcox and Rutkin obtained the money by means of a criminal act; neither had a bona fide claim of right to the funds. Nor was Rutkin's obligation to repay the extorted money to the victim any less than that of Wilcox. The victim of an extortion, like the victim of an embezzlement, has a right to restitution. Furthermore, it is inconsequential that an embezzler may lack title to the sums he appropriates while an extortionist may gain a voidable title. Questions of federal income taxation are not determined by such "attenuated subtleties." *Lucas v. Earl,* 281 U.S. 111, 114; *Corliss v. Bowers,* 281 U.S. 376, 378. Thus, the fact that Rutkin secured the money with the consent of his victim, *Rutkin v. United States, supra,* at p. 138, is irrelevant. Likewise unimportant is the fact that the sufferer of an extortion is less likely to seek restitution than one whose funds are embezzled. What is important is that the right to recoupment exists in both situations.

Examination of the relevant cases in the courts of appeals lends credence to our conclusion that the *Wilcox* rationale was effectively vitiated by this Court's decision in *Rutkin*. Although this case appears to be the first to arise that is "on all fours" with *Wilcox*, the lower federal courts, in deference to the undisturbed *Wilcox* holding, have earnestly endeavored to find distinguishing facts in the cases before them which would enable them to include sundry unlawful gains within "gross income."

It had been a well-established principle, long before either *Rutkin* or *Wilcox*, that unlawful, as well as lawful, gains are comprehended within the term "gross income." Section IIB of the Income Tax Act of 1913 provided that "the net income of a taxable person shall include gains, profits, and income . . . from . . . the transaction of any *lawful* business carried on for gain or profit, or gains or profits and income derived from any source whatever. . . ." (Emphasis supplied.) 38 Stat. 167. When the statute was amended in 1916, the one word "lawful" was omitted. This revealed, we think, the obvious intent of that Congress to tax income derived from both legal and illegal sources, to remove the incongruity of having the gains of the honest laborer taxed and the gains of the dishonest immune. *Rutkin v. United States, supra,* at p. 138; *United States v. Sullivan,* 274 U.S. 259, 263. Thereafter, the Court held that gains from illicit traffic in liquor are includible within "gross income." *Ibid. See also Johnson v. United States,* 318 U.S. 189; *United States v. Johnson,* 319 U.S. 503. And, the Court has pointed out, with approval, that there "has been a widespread and settled administrative and judicial recognition of the taxability of unlawful gains of many kinds," *Rutkin v. United States, supra,* at p. 137. These include protection payments made to racketeers, ransom payments paid to kidnappers, bribes, money derived from the sale of unlawful insurance policies, graft, black market gains, funds obtained from the operation of lotteries, income from race track bookmaking and illegal prize fight pictures. *Ibid.*

The starting point in all cases dealing with the question of the scope of what is included in "gross income" begins with the basic premise that the purpose of Congress was "to use the full measure of its taxing power." *Helvering v. Clifford,*

309 U.S. 331, 334. And the Court has given a liberal construction to the broad phraseology of the "gross income" definition statutes in recognition of the intention of Congress to tax all gains except those specifically exempted. *Commissioner v. Jacobson*, 336 U.S. 28, 49; *Helvering v. Stockholms Enskilda Bank*, 293 U.S. 84, 87–91. The language of § 22(a) of the 1939 Code, "gains or profits and income derived from any source whatever," and the more simplified language of § 61(a) of the 1954 Code, "all income from whatever source derived," have been held to encompass all "accessions to wealth, clearly realized, and over which the taxpayers have complete dominion." *Commissioner v. Glenshaw Glass Co.*, 348 U.S. 426, 431. A gain "constitutes taxable income when its recipient has such control over it that, as a practical matter, he derives readily realizable economic value from it." *Rutkin v. United States, supra*, at p. 137. Under these broad principles, we believe that petitioner's contention, that all unlawful gains are taxable except those resulting from embezzlement, should fail.

When a taxpayer acquires earnings, lawfully or unlawfully, without the consensual recognition, express or implied, of an obligation to repay and without restriction as to their disposition, "he has received income which he is required to return, even though it may still be claimed that he is not entitled to retain the money, and even though he may still be adjudged liable to restore its equivalent." *North American Oil v. Burnet, supra*, at p. 424. In such case, the taxpayer has "actual command over the property taxed — the actual benefit for which the tax is paid," *Corliss v. Bowers, supra*. This standard brings wrongful appropriations within the broad sweep of "gross income"; it excludes loans. When a law-abiding taxpayer mistakenly receives income in one year, which receipt is assailed and found to be invalid in a subsequent year, the taxpayer must nonetheless report the amount as "gross income" in the year received. *United States v. Lewis, supra*; *Healy v. Commissioner, supra*. We do not believe that Congress intended to treat a law-breaking taxpayer differently. Just as the honest taxpayer may deduct any amount repaid in the year in which the repayment is made, the Government points out that, "If, when, and to the extent that the victim recovers back the misappropriated funds, there is of course a reduction in the embezzler's income." Brief for the United States, p. 24.

Petitioner contends that the *Wilcox* rule has been in existence since 1946; that if Congress had intended to change the rule, it would have done so; that there was a general revision of the income tax laws in 1954 without mention of the rule; that a bill to change it was introduced in the Eighty-sixth Congress but was not acted upon; that, therefore, we may not change the rule now. But the fact that Congress has remained silent or has re-enacted a statute which we have construed, or that congressional attempts to amend a rule announced by this Court have failed, does not necessarily debar us from re-examining and correcting the Court's own errors. *Girouard v. United States*, 328 U.S. 61, 69–70; *Helvering v. Hallock*, 309 U.S. 106, 119–122. There may have been any number of reasons why Congress acted as it did. *Helvering v. Hallock, supra*. One of the reasons could well be our subsequent decision in *Rutkin* which has been thought by many to have repudiated *Wilcox*. Particularly might this be true in light of the decisions of the Courts of Appeals which have been riding a narrow rail between the two cases and further distinguishing them to the disparagement of *Wilcox*.

We believe that *Wilcox* was wrongly decided and we find nothing in congressional history since then to persuade us that Congress intended to legislate the rule. Thus, we believe that we should now correct the error and the confusion resulting from it, certainly if we do so in a manner that will not prejudice those who might have relied on it. *Cf. Helvering v. Hallock, supra,* at 119. We should not continue to confound confusion, particularly when the result would be to perpetuate the injustice of relieving embezzlers of the duty of paying income taxes on the money they enrich themselves with through theft while honest people pay their taxes on every conceivable type of income.

But, we are dealing here with a felony conviction under statutes which apply to any person who "willfully" fails to account for his tax or who "willfully" attempts to evade his obligation. In *Spies v. United States,* 317 U.S. 492, 499, the Court said that § 145(b) of the 1939 Code embodied "the gravest of offenses against the revenues," and stated that willfulness must therefore include an evil motive and want of justification in view of all the circumstances. *Id.* at 498. Willfulness "involves a specific intent which must be proven by independent evidence and which cannot be inferred from the mere understatement of income." *Holland v. United States,* 348 U.S. 121, 139.

We believe that the element of willfulness could not be proven in a criminal prosecution for failing to include embezzled funds in gross income in the year of misappropriation so long as the statute contained the gloss placed upon it by *Wilcox* at the time the alleged crime was committed. Therefore, we feel that petitioner's conviction may not stand and that the indictment against him must be dismissed.

Since MR. JUSTICE HARLAN, MR. JUSTICE FRANKFURTER, and MR. JUSTICE CLARK agree with us concerning *Wilcox,* that case is overruled. MR. JUSTICE BLACK, MR. JUSTICE DOUGLAS, and MR. JUSTICE WHITTAKER believe that petitioner's conviction must be reversed and the case dismissed for the reasons stated in their opinions.

Accordingly, the judgment of the Court of Appeals is reversed and the case is remanded to the District Court with directions to dismiss the indictment.

It is so ordered.

* * *

MR. JUSTICE WHITTAKER, whom MR. JUSTICE BLACK and MR. JUSTICE DOUGLAS join, concurring in part and dissenting in part.

* * *

An embezzler, like a common thief, acquires not a semblance of right, title, or interest in his plunder, and whether he spends it or not, he is indebted to his victim in the full amount taken as surely as if he had left a signed promissory note at the scene of the crime. Of no consequence from any standpoint is the absence of such formalities as (in the words of the prevailing opinion) "the consensual recognition, express or implied, of an obligation to repay." The law readily implies whatever "consensual recognition" is needed for the rightful owner to assert an immediately ripe and enforceable obligation of repayment against the wrongful taker. These principles are not "attenuated subtleties" but are among the clearest and most easily applied rules of our law. They exist to protect the rights of the innocent victim, and we should accord them full recognition and respect.

The fact that an embezzler's victim may have less chance of success than other creditors in seeking repayment from his debtor is not a valid reason for us further to diminish his prospects by adopting a rule that would allow the Commissioner of Internal Revenue to assert and enforce a prior federal tax lien against that which "rightfully and completely belongs" to the victim. *Commissioner v. Wilcox, supra,* at 410. THE CHIEF JUSTICE's opinion quite understandably expresses much concern for "honest taxpayers," but it attempts neither to deny nor justify the manifest injury that its holding will inflict on those honest taxpayers, victimized by embezzlers, who will find their claims for recovery subordinated to federal tax liens. Statutory provisions, by which we are bound, clearly and unequivocally accord priority to federal tax liens over the claims of others, including "judgment creditors."

However, if it later happens that the debtor-creditor relationship between the embezzler and his victim is discharged by something other than full repayment, such as by the running of a Statute of Limitations against the victim's claim, or by a release given for less than the full amount owed, the embezzler at that time, but not before, will have made a clear taxable gain and realized "an accession to income" which he will be required under full penalty of the law to report in his federal income tax return for that year. No honest taxpayer could be harmed by this rule.

* * *

Understanding *James*

1.   If the product of embezzlement is not income in the year of the embezzlement, when — if ever — does it become income? What practical difference does the timing make to the embezzler? To the IRS? To the company that the embezzler works for? What is the fuss about?

2.   What do you think of the idea of taxing illegal income, generally? On the one hand, is it unfair for (say) a drug dealer to pay no tax while a successful lawyer might share over a third of her income with the federal and state tax authorities? On the other hand, is it realistic to expect anyone to file a return that lists their occupation as "drug dealer?" Isn't this really a law enforcement problem that the IRS should be loath to get involved in? Or does tax evasion, à la Al Capone, provide a good way to get at criminals who are otherwise impervious to arrest?

That illegal income should be taxed on the same basis as the legal variety is longstanding tax doctrine. The bigger problem arises when states or the Federal Government enact special taxes on illegal activities — which no one really expects to collect — as a further law-enforcement effort. This strategy was especially popular in the 1990s, when several states sold "marijuana tax stamps" which were supposed to be attached to bundles of, well, marijuana used or sold in the state. Most were apparently sold as offbeat souvenirs. Tax experts tend to be skeptical about the use of the tax system in this manner, as do some constitutional lawyers who see these provisions as an attempted end-run around the procedural and other protections in a normal criminal prosecution. But the provisions have political appeal and we are likely to see more of them in the future.

Using the Sources

1.   Which of the following constitutes a realization event resulting in the imposition of tax?

> a. Selling appreciated stock or (investment) real estate at a profit.

> b. Exchanging appreciated stock or real estate for other, dissimilar assets (*see* section 1031).

> c. Exchanging the stock or real estate for other, similar-type assets.

> d. Taking out a loan secured by the appreciated property.

> e. Contributing the property to a corporation in which you will be a sole or partial shareholder.

> f. Watching the property appreciate in value and feeling very, very happy about it.

> g. Embezzling money from your employer which you intend to repay just as soon as possible.

2.   Goldstar Properties leases a parcel of land to the Bourbon Development Company on a 25-year lease, for a rental payment equal to $100,000 per year. The lease further requires Bourbon to construct a state-of-the-art office building on the property, to be completed by the tenth year of the lease, and to become the property of the landlord upon completion of the lease. The terms of the lease specify that "the construction of the aforementioned office building is not intended as a substitute for rent and shall not be treated as such for any purposes." Office buildings have a useful life of 40 years for depreciation purposes but in fact last longer than that in most cases.

> a. Does the construction of the building, or the subsequent termination of the lease, result in tax to Goldstar under sections 61 and 1019 of the Code? If so, when would the tax be paid, and how much?

> b. Would it affect your answer to (i) above if construction of the building were not required by the terms of the lease, but Bourbon (the tenant) went ahead and built it, anyway?

> c. Would it affect your answer if construction of the building were not required by the lease, and the tenant demolished the building before the lease was over?

> d. What additional facts, if any, would you need in order to give a more definitive answer to a. through c., above?

3.   Suppose that Parent transfers to Child a painting which Parent bought several years earlier for $25,000, but which at the time of the transfer has a value

of $250,000. Although the transfer is intended as a gift, the Parent insists that the Child pay $50,000 to defray various expenses associated with the painting. Does this qualify as a full or partial realization event under section 1001? How much, if anything, is Parent taxed on, and what is Child's basis for the painting? How would your answer differ if the child had been required to pay $15,000 for the painting? $150,000? *See* Treas. Reg. § 1.1001-1(e).

Law and Planning

Consider question two under "Using the Sources," above. If you were counsel to Goldstar Properties, how would you advise modifying the lease so as to reduce the likelihood of taxation, without sacrificing the taxpayer's apparent business goals? Would you advise entering into this type of transaction at all?

Politics and Policy

What do you think are the horizontal and vertical equity implications of the *Bruun* and *James* decisions, and of section 109 of the Code?

B.   Losses

The following cases consider the issue of realization in situations involving losses rather than gains. Note that the parties' positions are (for obvious reasons) reversed in these cases: the taxpayers argue in favor of realization, and the government now argues against it. Note, likewise, the conflict this creates for government lawyers: in attempting to define realization narrowly for loss purposes, they may create precedents that are damaging to the IRS position when a gain is at stake.

CORRA RESOURCES, LTD. v. COMMISSIONER
United States Court of Appeals, Seventh Circuit
945 F.2d 224 (1991)

EASTERBROOK, J:

Corra Resources, an investment vehicle for Edwin Corra and his wife Genevieve, put some of its assets into a coal mining lease in 1978. (Corra Plumbing Co., which made the investment, sold its operating assets in 1980 and was renamed as it became an investment company.) Corra Resources obtained from Salem Minerals the right to mine coal in Pikeville, Kentucky (the "Pikeville Quadrangle" lease); it put down $77,500 as prepaid royalties and hired Hurricane Mining Co. to do the mining and Euran Energy to manage its interests. Corra Resources paid additional royalties by nonrecourse promissory note. Corra Resources made the last cash payment on January 20, 1980; thereafter it was entitled to sit back and collect any profits that exceeded the sums due under the note.

Corra was not in this alone. Salem assembled a number of investors with the promise of tax benefits. Corra Resources took deductions that produced more than

$250,000 in tax savings. These benefits depended, among other things, on coal being mined. Coal was not mined. Euran sent the investors reports explaining why. One year Euran said that bad weather and a weak market prevented mining; another year mild weather was to blame (less need for coal, you see). One report said that electrical utilities had built up large stockpiles of coal, so there was little market for new supplies; another report had it that reduced stockpiles were responsible for the lack of demand. In 1981 the IRS notified investors in the Pikeville Quadrangle that their returns were under examination. In 1984 the IRS assessed deficiencies against Corra Resources and the other investors in this venture. After filing a petition for review in the Tax Court, Corra Resources agreed to be bound by the outcome of a case testing the validity of deductions arising out of the Pikeville Quadrangle leases. The IRS prevailed, *Wiseman v. CIR*, 53 T.C.M. (CCH) 1432, T.C. Memo 1987-364 (1987), leaving Corra Resources searching for a way to salvage something from the debacle.

Leo Eatman, Edwin Corra's confidant and Corra Resources' accountant, concluded that something was fishy when the IRS notice was the first product to emerge from the Pikeville Quadrangle. He testified that after the promoters gave him the runaround, he advised Edwin Corra to have nothing further to do with the venture. Eatman was not an employee of Corra Resources, but Edwin Corra took Eatman's advice on financial matters, and we shall assume that Corra was agreeable to this recommendation. (Eatman wanted to testify that Corra approved his suggestion but a hearsay objection intervened; Corra himself did not give evidence.) After *Wiseman* foreclosed any effort to preserve the deductions Corra Resources actually took on its tax returns, the firm contended that it was entitled to deduct the $77,500 as the cost of an abandoned asset — the lease. *See* 26 U.S.C. § 165(a). According to Corra Resources, the abandonment took place in its 1981 fiscal year (which ended September 30, 1981), during which Eatman inquired, did not like what he found, and told Edwin Corra to wash his hands of the business. After a trial, Special Trial Judge Goldberg concluded that Corra Resources had not abandoned the lease in 1981, because it had not taken any step to dissociate itself from the venture. Judge Fay adopted this opinion, 59 T.C.M. (CCH) 102, T.C. Memo 1990-133 (1990), *see Freytag v. CIR*, 501 U.S. 868 (1991), and entered the judgment from which Corra Resources appeals.

Corra Resources concedes that it took no concrete step. It did not send Salem a letter repudiating the lease (and its notes) on the ground of non-performance by the promoters. It did not tell Hurricane to quit preparing to mine on its behalf. It did not adopt a corporate resolution jettisoning the lease. It did not raise the subject with the IRS until after the Tax Court decided *Wiseman* in 1987. Nonetheless, Corra Resources submits, it abandoned the asset in 1981. The lease was by then objectively worthless, and both Eatman and Edwin Corra mentally walked away from the investment. Corra Resources could not claim the $77,500 as an abandonment loss until 1987, when *Wiseman* stripped it of the deductions it had taken on other grounds. You can't deduct as a loss more than your adjusted basis in an asset; until *Wiseman* that basis was zero. What more does the Commissioner want, Corra Resources asks?

What the Commissioner wants — what the Tax Court held the Commissioner is entitled to demand — is some step that irrevocably cuts ties to the asset. In the words of Regulation 1.165-1(d)(1), the deduction is not available until "the loss occurs as evidenced by closed and completed transactions and as fixed by identifiable events occurring in [the] taxable year." *See also* Regulation 1.165-2(a). Investors would love to hold onto an asset in the hope that it will pay off despite long odds, while retaining the option of taking a deduction if it does not. A firm with surplus, and apparently worthless, inventory wants to write it off while keeping it in a warehouse to sell if demand picks up. *Thor Power Tool Co. v. CIR*, 439 U.S. 522, 531–46 (1979), disapproves of that maneuver, and *Rexnord, Inc. v. United States*, 940 F.2d 1094 (7th Cir. 1991), denies a deduction when a sale in practice does no more than move the inventory to a warehouse off the taxpayer's premises. Although these cases were decided under 26 U.S.C. §§ 446 and 471, they illustrate the principle that a taxpayer may not hedge bets at the Treasury's expense. *Thor Power Tool*, 439 U.S. at 545–46. A plea that a spare part (or a lease) has minuscule market value is not enough. Until some observable event (the burning of a warehouse, the sinking of a ship, the sale or scrapping of inventory, the repudiation of a lease) marks the loss, the taxpayer may try to recharacterize the transaction. *Laport v. CIR*, 671 F.2d 1028, 1031 (7th Cir. 1982); *John R. Thompson Co. v. United States*, 477 F.2d 164, 168 (7th Cir. 1973). Intra-corporate affairs (what Eatman said to Corra, what Corra said to Eatman, what either or both intended) do not generate signs visible to outside observers and therefore do not mark the crossing of the Rubicon. Perhaps Corra Resources would have returned a royalty check had one arrived in 1982, or 1983, or any other year through 1987 (when it first told the IRS that the lease had been abandoned). The Commissioner is entitled to more than the taxpayer's after-the-fact assurance that this is so.

Corra Resources has a legitimate point that it is not so clear how one abandons a mineral lease being managed by a third party — or why, tax considerations aside, a lessee that has no further obligations would want to. Corra Resources could not pull its equipment out of the mine; it had none there. The lease provided no means of termination or abandonment. And the expedient of withholding delay rentals (sums paid to keep the lease alive during non-mining periods), an observable act extinguishing any opportunity to receive future profits, an act that *Brountas v. CIR*, 692 F.2d 152, 162–63 (1st Cir. 1982), and *CRC Corp. v. CIR*, 693 F.2d 281, 283–84 (3d Cir. 1982), say would mark abandonment, was not available because Corra Resources made the last required cash installment in 1980 and had delivered in 1978 a nonrecourse note covering all royalties through 1985. Yet Corra Resources was not helpless. It could have sent letters to Salem, Hurricane, and Euran giving up the ghost, and in particular telling Hurricane and Euran to cease making efforts on its behalf. Until doing something of the sort, Corra Resources retained the option to reap the benefits if mining should commence. (As late as October 1981 Euran assured the investors that profitable production was just around the corner.) *Gulf Oil Corp. v. CIR*, 914 F.2d 396, 402 (3d Cir. 1990), holds that one who retains all rights to a favorable outcome of a mineral lease may not obtain an abandonment deduction. *See also Davis v. CIR*, 241 F.2d 701, 703–04 (7th Cir. 1957) (abandonment of a lease means expiration or termination).

The final sentence of Reg. 1.165-2(a) is not the solace Corra Resources seeks. It says that the "taxable year in which the loss is sustained is not necessarily the taxable year in which the overt act of abandonment, or the loss of title to the property, occurs." Corra Resources treats this as eliminating the need for an observable act of abandonment, which is hardly plausible given the requirement of Reg. 1.165-1(d)(1). We understand this language as addressed to a different problem: an asset becomes worthless but the taxpayer waits until an opportune moment (perhaps a year with large profits in search of a tax shield) to supply the act of abandonment. Regulation 1.165-2(a) reserves the Commissioner's right to reallocate this loss to the year in which the asset became worthless. *Laport*, 671 F.2d at 1031 n. 5; *A.J. Industries, Inc. v. United States*, 503 F.2d 660, 668–70 & n. 6b (9th Cir. 1974). It does not bestow the privilege that *Thor Power Tool* and Reg. 1.165-1(d)(1) are set against: allowing the investor to hold the asset in the hope of an upturn in its value while reserving the right to declare abandonment during this period of hopeful waiting. Corra Resources did not abandon the lease during 1981. The lease expired in 1986, making that the year in which the loss was realized.

Affirmed.

Understanding *Corra Resources*

1.   Section 165(a) of the Code provides for the deduction of "any loss sustained during the taxable year and not compensated for by insurance or otherwise." Treas. Reg. § 1.165-1(d)(1) provides that a deduction is permitted under section 165 only when the "the loss is evidenced by closed and completed transactions [and] fixed by identifiable events occurring in [the] taxable year." *Corra Resources* interprets this latter rule to require an action "that irrevocably cuts ties to the asset," such as a repudiation of the lease, abandonment of the property, or the equivalent.

One problem with the *Corra Resources* approach is that an oil well that is unprofitable at today's prices may become profitable again if prices increase. Encouraging drillers to abandon or "walk away" from such wells may make it harder for the driller to access them when and if the market rebounds.[2] Does this suggest that the case has perverse effects, and ought to be overruled? Or does the unpredictability of the oil market — the chance that today's unprofitable well may again turn profitable in the future — reinforce the Government's position that there is no "closed and completed" transaction until the well is closed down? Is energy policy an appropriate concern in tax lawmaking, or is it a nontax issue?

2.   Suppose that you had a client who had invested in a nonproducing oil well and who wanted to take a current tax deduction without jeopardizing their right to future income if the well eventually proved profitable. Knowing the result in *Corra Resources*, what would you advise the client to do? If the well has to be abandoned, can you suggest a strategy that would at least preserve your client's personal relationship with the promoters, in case there should be additional profitable wells in the same area?

3.   Is *Corra Resources* consistent with the gain realization cases (*Bruun* and *James*) discussed in the previous section? Should the Government be entitled to

---

[2]   For example, assume that it costs $15 per barrel to produce oil from a given well, owing to its depth, natural characteristics, and so forth. If oil is selling for $10 per barrel, the well is unprofitable. If oil were selling at $30 per barrel, it is (figuratively speaking), a gold mine.

apply a more stringent definition of the realization rule in loss than in gain cases? What might be the possible advantages and disadvantages of this strategy?

On the dilemma that Government lawyers sometimes face in litigating precedent-setting tax cases, see Kirk J. Stark, *The Unfulfilled Tax Legacy of Justice Robert H. Jackson*, 54 Tax L. Rev. 171 (2001).

COTTAGE SAVINGS ASSOCIATION v. COMMISSIONER
United States Supreme Court
499 U.S. 554 (1991)

Justice Marshall delivered the opinion of the Court:

The issue in this case is whether a financial institution realizes tax-deductible losses when it exchanges its interests in one group of residential mortgage loans for another lender's interests in a different group of residential mortgage loans. We hold that such a transaction does give rise to realized losses.

I

Petitioner Cottage Savings Association (Cottage Savings) is a savings and loan association (S & L) formerly regulated by the Federal Home Loan Bank Board (FHLBB).[3] Like many S & L's, Cottage Savings held numerous long-term, low-interest mortgages that declined in value when interest rates surged in the late 1970's. These institutions would have benefited from selling their devalued mortgages in order to realize tax-deductible losses. However, they were deterred from doing so by FHLBB accounting regulations, which required them to record the losses on their books. Reporting these losses consistent with the then-effective FHLBB accounting regulations would have placed many S & L's at risk of closure by the FHLBB.

The FHLBB responded to this situation by relaxing its requirements for the reporting of losses. In a regulatory directive known as "Memorandum R-49," dated June 27, 1980, the FHLBB determined that S & L's need not report losses associated with mortgages that are exchanged for "substantially identical" mortgages held by other lenders.[4] The FHLBB's acknowledged purpose for

---

[3] [1] Congress abolished the FHLBB in 1989. *See* § 401 of the Financial Institutions Reform, Recovery, and Enforcement Act of 1989, Pub. L. 101-73, 103 Stat. 354.

[4] [2] Memorandum R-49 listed 10 criteria for classifying mortgages as substantially identical.
"The loans involved must:
  "1. involve single-family residential mortgages,
  "2. be of similar type (*e.g.*, conventionals for conventionals),
  "3. have the same stated terms to maturity (*e.g.*, 30 years),
  "4. have identical stated interest rates,
  "5. have similar seasoning (*i.e.*, remaining terms to maturity),
  "6. have aggregate principal amounts within the lesser of 2 1/2% or $100,000 (plus or minus) on both sides of the transaction, with any additional consideration being paid in cash,
  "7. be sold without recourse,

Memorandum R-49 was to facilitate transactions that would generate tax losses but that would not substantially affect the economic position of the transacting S & L's.

This case involves a typical Memorandum R-49 transaction. On December 31, 1980, Cottage Savings sold "90% participation interests" in 252 mortgages to four S & L's. It simultaneously purchased "90% participation interests" in 305 mortgages held by these S & L's.[5] All of the loans involved in the transaction were secured by single-family homes, most in the Cincinnati area. The fair market value of the package of participation interests exchanged by each side was approximately $4.5 million. The face value of the participation interests Cottage Savings relinquished in the transaction was approximately $6.9 million. *See* 90 T.C. 372, 378–382 (1988).

On its 1980 federal income tax return, Cottage Savings claimed a deduction for $2,447,091, which represented the adjusted difference between the face value of the participation interests that it traded and the fair market value of the participation interests that it received. As permitted by Memorandum R-49, Cottage Savings did not report these losses to the FHLBB. After the Commissioner of Internal Revenue disallowed Cottage Savings' claimed deduction, Cottage Savings sought a redetermination in the Tax Court. The Tax Court held that the deduction was permissible. *See* 90 T.C. 372 (1988).

On appeal by the Commissioner, the Court of Appeals reversed. 890 F.2d 848 (CA6 1989). The Court of Appeals agreed with the Tax Court's determination that Cottage Savings had realized its losses through the transaction. *See id.* at 852. However, the court held that Cottage Savings was not entitled to a deduction because its losses were not "actually" sustained during the 1980 tax year for purposes of 26 U.S.C. § 165(a). *See* 890 F.2d at 855.

Because of the importance of this issue to the S & L industry and the conflict among the Circuits over whether Memorandum R-49 exchanges produce deductible tax losses, we granted certiorari. 498 U.S. 808 (1990). We now reverse.

II

Rather than assessing tax liability on the basis of annual fluctuations in the value of a taxpayer's property, the Internal Revenue Code defers the tax consequences of a gain or loss in property value until the taxpayer "realizes" the gain or loss. The realization requirement is implicit in § 1001(a) of the Code, 26 U.S.C. § 1001(a), which defines "the gain [or loss] from the sale or other disposition of property" as the difference between "the amount realized" from the sale or

---

"8. have similar fair market values,

"9. have similar loan-to-value ratios at the time of the reciprocal sale, and

"10. have all security properties for both sides of the transaction in the same state." Record, Exh. 72-BT.

[5] [3] By exchanging merely participation interests rather than the loans themselves, each party retained its relationship with the individual obligors. Consequently, each S & L continued to service the loans on which it had transferred the participation interests and made monthly payments to the participation-interest holders. *See* 90 T. C. 372, 381 (1988).

disposition of the property and its "adjusted basis." As this Court has recognized, the concept of realization is "founded on administrative convenience." *Helvering v. Horst*, 311 U.S. 112, 116 (1940). Under an appreciation-based system of taxation, taxpayers and the Commissioner would have to undertake the "cumbersome, abrasive, and unpredictable administrative task" of valuing assets on an annual basis to determine whether the assets had appreciated or depreciated in value. *See* 1 B. BITTKER & L. LOKKEN, FEDERAL TAXATION OF INCOME, ESTATES AND GIFTS ¶ 5.2, p. 5-16 (2d ed. 1989). In contrast, "[a] change in the form or extent of an investment is easily detected by a taxpayer or an administrative officer." R. MAGILL, TAXABLE INCOME 79 (rev. ed. 1945).

Section 1001(a)'s language provides a straightforward test for realization: to realize a gain or loss in the value of property, the taxpayer must engage in a "sale or other disposition of [the] property." The parties agree that the exchange of participation interests in this case cannot be characterized as a "sale" under § 1001(a); the issue before us is whether the transaction constitutes a "disposition of property." The Commissioner argues that an exchange of property can be treated as a "disposition" under § 1001(a) only if the properties exchanged are materially different. The Commissioner further submits that, because the underlying mortgages were essentially economic substitutes, the participation interests exchanged by Cottage Savings were not materially different from those received from the other S & L's. Cottage Savings, on the other hand, maintains that *any* exchange of property is a "disposition of property" under § 1001(a), regardless of whether the property exchanged is materially different. Alternatively, Cottage Savings contends that the participation interests exchanged were materially different because the underlying loans were secured by different properties.

We must therefore determine whether the realization principle in § 1001(a) incorporates a "material difference" requirement. If it does, we must further decide what that requirement amounts to and how it applies in this case. We consider these questions in turn.

A

Neither the language nor the history of the Code indicates whether and to what extent property exchanged must differ to count as a "disposition of property" under § 1001(a). Nonetheless, we readily agree with the Commissioner that an exchange of property gives rise to a realization event under § 1001(a) only if the properties exchanged are "materially different." The Commissioner himself has by regulation construed § 1001(a) to embody a material difference requirement:

> "Except as otherwise provided . . . the gain or loss realized from the conversion of property into cash, *or from the exchange of property for other property differing materially either in kind or in extent*, is treated as income or as loss sustained." Treas. Reg. § 1.1001-1, 26 CFR § 1.1001-1 (1990) (emphasis added).

Because Congress has delegated to the Commissioner the power to promulgate "all needful rules and regulations for the enforcement of [the Internal Revenue Code],"

26 U.S.C. § 7805(a), we must defer to his regulatory interpretations of the Code so long as they are reasonable, *see National Muffler Dealers Assn., Inc. v. United States*, 440 U.S. 472, 476–477 (1979).

We conclude that Treasury Regulations § 1.1001-1 *is* a reasonable interpretation of § 1001(a). Congress first employed the language that now comprises § 1001(a) of the Code in § 202(a) of the Revenue Act of 1924, ch. 234, 43 Stat. 253; that language has remained essentially unchanged through various reenactments. And since 1934, the Commissioner has construed the statutory term "disposition of property" to include a "material difference" requirement. As we have recognized, " 'Treasury regulations and interpretations long continued without substantial change, applying to unamended or substantially reenacted statutes, are deemed to have received congressional approval and have the effect of law.' " *United States v. Correll*, 389 U.S. 299, 305–306 (1967), quoting *Helvering v. Winmill*, 305 U.S. 79, 83 (1938).

Treasury Regulation § 1.001-1 is also consistent with our landmark precedents on realization. In a series of early decisions involving the tax effects of property exchanges, this Court made clear that a taxpayer realizes taxable income only if the properties exchanged are "materially" or "essentially" different. *See United States v. Phellis*, 257 U.S. 156, 173 (1921); *Weiss v. Stearn*, 265 U.S. 242, 253–254 (1924); *Marr v. United States*, 268 U.S. 536, 540–542 (1925); *see also Eisner v. Macomber*, 252 U.S. 189, 207–212 (1920) (recognizing realization requirement). Because these decisions were part of the "contemporary legal context" in which Congress enacted § 202(a) of the 1924 Act, *see Cannon v. University of Chicago*, 441 U.S. 677, 698–699 (1979), and because Congress has left undisturbed through subsequent reenactments of the Code the principles of realization established in these cases, we may presume that Congress intended to codify these principles in § 1001(a), *see Pierce v. Underwood*, 487 U.S. 552, 567 (1988); *Lorillard v. Pons*, 434 U.S. 575, 580–581 (1978). The Commissioner's construction of the statutory language to incorporate these principles certainly was reasonable.

B

Precisely what constitutes a "material difference" for purposes of § 1001(a) of the Code is a more complicated question. The Commissioner argues that properties are "materially different" only if they differ in economic substance. To determine whether the participation interests exchanged in this case were "materially different" in this sense, the Commissioner argues, we should look to the attitudes of the parties, the evaluation of the interests by the secondary mortgage market, and the views of the FHLBB. We conclude that § 1001(a) embodies a much less demanding and less complex test.

Unlike the question *whether* § 1001(a) contains a material difference requirement, the question of *what constitutes* a material difference is not one on which we can defer to the Commissioner. For the Commissioner has not issued an authoritative, pre-litigation interpretation of what property exchanges satisfy this requirement. Thus, to give meaning to the material difference test, we must look to the case law from which the test derives and which we believe Congress intended to codify in enacting and reenacting the language that now comprises § 1001(a). *See Lorillard v. Pons, supra*, at 580–581.

We start with the classic treatment of realization in *Eisner v. Macomber, supra.* In *Macomber*, a taxpayer who owned 2,200 shares of stock in a company received another 1,100 shares from the company as part of a pro rata stock dividend meant to reflect the company's growth in value. At issue was whether the stock dividend constituted taxable income. We held that it did not, because no gain was realized. *See id.* at 207–212. We reasoned that the stock dividend merely reflected the increased worth of the taxpayer's stock, *see id.* at 211–212, and that a taxpayer realizes increased worth of property only by receiving "something of exchangeable value *proceeding from* the property," *see id.* at 207.

In three subsequent decisions — *United States v. Phellis, supra; Weiss v. Stearn, supra;* and *Marr v. United States, supra* — we refined *Macomber's* conception of realization in the context of property exchanges. In each case, the taxpayer owned stock that had appreciated in value since its acquisition. And in each case, the corporation in which the taxpayer held stock had reorganized into a new corporation, with the new corporation assuming the business of the old corporation. While the corporations in *Phellis* and *Marr* both changed from New Jersey to Delaware corporations, the original and successor corporations in *Weiss* both were incorporated in Ohio. In each case, following the reorganization, the stockholders of the old corporation received shares in the new corporation equal to their proportional interest in the old corporation.

The question in these cases was whether the taxpayers realized the accumulated gain in their shares in the old corporation when they received in return for those shares stock representing an equivalent proportional interest in the new corporations. In *Phellis* and *Marr*, we held that the transactions were realization events. We reasoned that because a company incorporated in one State has "different rights and powers" from one incorporated in a different State, the taxpayers in *Phellis* and *Marr* acquired through the transactions property that was "materially different" from what they previously had. *United States v. Phellis*, 257 U.S. at 169–173; *see Marr v. United States, supra,* at 540–542 (using phrase "essentially different"). In contrast, we held that no realization occurred in *Weiss*. By exchanging stock in the predecessor corporation for stock in the newly reorganized corporation, the taxpayer did not receive "a thing really different from what he therefore had." *Weiss v. Stearn, supra,* at 254. As we explained in *Marr*, our determination that the reorganized company in *Weiss* was not "really different" from its predecessor turned on the fact that both companies were incorporated in the same State. *See Marr v. United States, supra,* at 540–542 (outlining distinction between these cases).

Obviously, the distinction in *Phellis* and *Marr* that made the stock in the successor corporations materially different from the stock in the predecessors was minimal. Taken together, *Phellis, Marr,* and *Weiss* stand for the principle that properties are "different" in the sense that is "material" to the Internal Revenue Code so long as their respective possessors enjoy legal entitlements that are different in kind or extent. Thus, separate groups of stock are not materially different if they confer "the same proportional interest of the same character in the same corporation." *Marr v. United States*, 268 U.S. at 540. However, they *are* materially different if they are issued by different corporations, *id.* at 541; *United States v. Phellis, supra,* at 173, or if they confer "different rights and powers" in the same corporation, *Marr v. United States, supra,* at 541. No more demanding a standard than this is necessary in order to satisfy the administrative purposes underlying the realization requirement in § 1001(a). *See Helvering v. Horst,* 311 U.S. at 116. For, as long as the property entitlements are not identical, their exchange will allow both the Commissioner and the transacting taxpayer easily to fix the appreciated or depreciated values of the property relative to their tax bases.

In contrast, we find no support for the Commissioner's "economic substitute" conception of material difference. According to the Commissioner, differences between properties are material for purposes of the Code only when it can be said that the parties, the relevant market (in this case the secondary mortgage market), and the relevant regulatory body (in this case the FHLBB) would consider them material. Nothing in *Phellis, Weiss,* and *Marr* suggests that exchanges of properties must satisfy such a subjective test to trigger realization of a gain or loss.

Moreover, the complexity of the Commissioner's approach ill serves the goal of administrative convenience that underlies the realization requirement. In order to apply the Commissioner's test in a principled fashion, the Commissioner and the taxpayer must identify the relevant market, establish whether there is a regulatory agency whose views should be taken into account, and then assess how the relevant market participants and the agency would view the transaction. The Commissioner's failure to explain how these inquiries should be conducted further calls into question the workability of his test.

Finally, the Commissioner's test is incompatible with the structure of the Code. Section 1001(c) of Title 26 provides that a gain or loss realized under § 1001(a) "shall be recognized" unless one of the Code's nonrecognition provisions applies. One such nonrecognition provision withholds recognition of a gain or loss realized from an exchange of properties that would appear to be economic substitutes under the Commissioner's material difference test. This provision, commonly known as the "like kind" exception, withholds recognition of a gain or loss realized "on the exchange of property held for productive use in a trade or business or for investment . . . for property of like kind which is to be held either for productive use in a trade or business or for investment." 26 U.S.C. § 1031(a)(1). If Congress had expected that exchanges of similar properties would *not* count as realization events under § 1001(a), it would have had no reason to bar recognition of a gain or loss realized from these transactions.

C

Under our interpretation of § 1001(a), an exchange of property gives rise to a realization event so long as the exchanged properties are "materially different" — that is, so long as they embody legally distinct entitlements. Cottage Savings' transactions at issue here easily satisfy this test. Because the participation interests exchanged by Cottage Savings and the other S & L's derived from loans that were made to different obligors and secured by different homes, the exchanged interests did embody legally distinct entitlements. Consequently, we conclude that Cottage Savings realized its losses at the point of the exchange.

The Commissioner contends that it is anomalous to treat mortgages deemed to be "substantially identical" by the FHLBB as "materially different." The anomaly, however, is merely semantic; mortgages can be substantially identical for Memorandum R-49 purposes and still exhibit "differences" that are "material" for purposes of the Internal Revenue Code. Because Cottage Savings received entitlements different from those it gave up, the exchange put both Cottage Savings and the Commissioner in a position to determine the change in the value of Cottage Savings' mortgages relative to their tax bases. Thus, there is no reason not to treat the exchange of these interests as a realization event, regardless of the status of the mortgages under the criteria of Memorandum R-49.

III

Although the Court of Appeals found that Cottage Savings' losses were realized, it disallowed them on the ground that they were not sustained under § 165(a) of the Code, 26 U.S.C. § 165(a). Section 165(a) states that a deduction shall be allowed for "any loss sustained during the taxable year and not compensated for by insurance or otherwise." Under the Commissioner's interpretation of § 165(a),

> "To be allowable as a deduction under section 165(a), a loss must be evidenced by closed and completed transactions, fixed by identifiable events, and, except as otherwise provided in section 165(h) and § 1.165-11, relating to disaster losses, actually sustained during the taxable year. Only a bona fide loss is allowable. Substance and not mere form shall govern in determining a deductible loss." Treas. Reg. § 1.165-1(b), 26 CFR § 1.165-1(b) (1990).

The Commissioner offers a minimal defense of the Court of Appeals' conclusion. The Commissioner contends that the losses were not sustained because they lacked "economic substance," by which the Commissioner seems to mean that the losses were not bona fide. We say "seems" because the Commissioner states the position in one sentence in a footnote in his brief without offering further explanation. *See* Brief for Respondent 34–35, n. 39. The only authority the Commissioner cites for this argument is *Higgins v. Smith*, 308 U.S. 473 (1939). *See* Brief for United States in No. 89-1926, p. 16, n. 11.

In *Higgins*, we held that a taxpayer did not sustain a loss by selling securities below cost to a corporation in which he was the sole shareholder. We found that the losses were not bona fide because the transaction was not conducted at arm's length and because the taxpayer retained the benefit of the securities through his wholly owned corporation. *See Higgins v. Smith, supra,* at 475–476. Because there is no contention that the transactions in this case were not conducted at arm's length, or that Cottage Savings retained *de facto* ownership of the participation interests it traded to the four reciprocating S & L's, *Higgins* is inapposite. In view of the Commissioner's failure to advance any other arguments in support of the Court of Appeals' ruling with respect to § 165(a), we conclude that, for purposes of this case, Cottage Savings sustained its losses within the meaning of § 165(a).

IV

For the reasons set forth above, the judgment of the Court of Appeals is reversed, and the case is remanded for further proceedings consistent with this opinion.

So ordered.

JUSTICE BLACKMUN, with whom JUSTICE WHITE joins, concurring in part and dissenting in part in No. 89-1926 and dissenting in No. 89-1965.

I agree that the early withdrawal penalties collected by Centennial Savings Bank FSB do not constitute "income by reason of the discharge . . . of indebtedness of the taxpayer," within the meaning of 26 U.S.C. § 108(a)(1) (1982 ed.), and that the penalty amounts are not excludable from Centennial's gross income. I therefore join Part III of the Court's opinion in No. 89-1926.

I dissent, however, from the Court's conclusions in these two cases that Centennial and Cottage Savings Association realized deductible losses for income tax purposes when each exchanged partial interests in one group of residential mortgage loans for partial interests in another like group of residential mortgage loans. I regard these losses as not recognizable for income tax purposes because the mortgage packages so exchanged were substantially identical and were not materially different.

The exchanges, as the Court acknowledges, were occasioned by Memorandum R-49, Record, Exh. 72-BT, issued by the Federal Home Loan Bank Board (FHLBB) on June 27, 1980, and by that Memorandum's relaxation of theretofore-existing accounting regulations and requirements, a relaxation effected to avoid placement of "many S & L's at risk of closure by the FHLBB" without substantially affecting the "economic position of the transacting S & L's." But the Memorandum, the Court notes, also had as a purpose the "facilitation of transactions that would generate tax losses." I find it somewhat surprising that an agency not responsible for tax matters would presume to dictate what is or is not a deductible loss for federal income tax purposes. I had thought that that was something within the exclusive province of the Internal Revenue Service, subject to administrative and judicial review. Certainly, the FHLBB's opinion in this respect is entitled to no deference whatsoever. *See United States v. Stewart*, 311 U.S. 60, 70 (1940); *Graff v. Commissioner*, 673 F.2d 784, 786 (CA5 1982) (concurring opinion). The Commissioner, of course, took the opposing position. *See* Rev. Rul. 85-125, 1985-2 Cum. Bull. 180; Rev. Rul. 81-204, 1981-2 Cum. Bull. 157.

It long has been established that gain or loss in the value of property is taken into account for income tax purposes only if and when the gain or loss is "realized," that is, when it is tied to a realization event, such as the sale, exchange, or other disposition of the property. Mere variation in value — the routine ups and downs of the marketplace — do not in themselves have income tax consequences. This is fundamental in income tax law.

In applying the realization requirement to an exchange, the properties involved must be materially different in kind or in extent. Treas. Reg. § 1.1001-1(a), 26 CFR

§ 1.10011(a) (1990). This has been the rule recognized administratively at least since 1935, *see* Treas. Regs. 86, Art. 111-1, issued under the Revenue Act of 1934, and by judicial decision. *See, e.g., Mutual Loan & Savings Co. v. Commissioner*, 184 F.2d 161 (CA5 1950). *See also Marr v. United States*, 268 U.S. 536, 541 (1925); *Weiss v. Stearn*, 265 U.S. 242, 254 (1924); *United States v. Phellis*, 257 U.S. 156 (1921). This makes economic as well as tax sense, for the parties obviously regard the exchanged properties as having equivalent values. In tax law, we should remember, substance rather than form determines tax consequences. *Commissioner v. Court Holding Co.*, 324 U.S. 331, 334 (1945); *Gregory v. Helvering*, 293 U.S. 465, 469–470 (1935); *Shoenberg v. Commissioner*, 77 F.2d 446, 449 (CA8), *cert. denied*, 296 U.S. 586 (1935). Thus, the resolution of the exchange issue in these cases turns on the "materially different" concept. The Court recognizes as much.

That the mortgage participation partial interests exchanged in these cases were "different" is not in dispute. The materiality prong is the focus. A material difference is one that has the capacity to influence a decision. *See, e.g., Kungys v. United States*, 485 U.S. 759, 770–771 (1988); *Basic Inc. v. Levinson*, 485 U.S. 224, 240 (1988); *TSC Industries, Inc. v. Northway, Inc.*, 426 U.S. 438, 449 (1976).

The application of this standard leads, it seems to me, to only one answer — that the mortgage participation partial interests released were not materially different from the mortgage participation partial interests received. Memorandum R-49, as the Court notes, lists 10 factors that, when satisfied, as they were here, serve to classify the interests as "substantially identical." These factors assure practical identity; surely, they then also assure that any difference cannot be of consequence. Indeed, non-materiality is the full purpose of the Memorandum's criteria. The "proof of the pudding" is in the fact of its complete accounting acceptability to the FHLBB. Indeed, as has been noted, it is difficult to reconcile substantial identity for financial accounting purposes with a material difference for tax accounting purposes. *See First Federal Savings & Loan Assn. of Temple v. United States*, 694 F. Supp. 230, 245 (WD Tex. 1988), *aff'd*, 887 F.2d 593 (CA5 1989), *cert. pending* No. 89-1927. Common sense so dictates.

This should suffice and be the end of the analysis. Other facts, however, solidify the conclusion: The retention by the transferor of 10% interests, enabling it to keep on servicing its loans; the transferor's continuing to collect the payments due from the borrowers so that, so far as the latter were concerned, it was business as usual, exactly as it had been; the obvious lack of concern or dependence of the transferor with the "differences" upon which the Court relies (as transferees, the taxpayers made no credit checks and no appraisals of collateral, *see* 890 F.2d 848, 849 (CA6 1989)); 90 T.C. 372, 382 (1988); 682 F. Supp. 1389, 1392 (ND Tex. 1988); the selection of the loans by a computer programmed to match mortgages in accordance with the Memorandum R-49 criteria; the absence of even the names of the borrowers in the closing schedules attached to the agreements; Centennial's receipt of loan files only six years after its exchange, *id.* at 1392, n. 5; the restriction of the interests exchanged to the same State; the identity of the respective face and fair market values; and the application by the parties of common discount factors to each side of the transaction — all reveal that any differences that might exist made no difference whatsoever and were not material. This demonstrates the real nature of the transactions, including nonmateriality of the claimed differences.

We should be dealing here with realities and not with superficial distinctions. As has been said many times, and as noted above, in income tax law we are to be concerned with substance and not with mere form. When we stray from that principle, the new precedent is likely to be a precarious beacon for the future.

I respectfully dissent on this issue.

Understanding *Cottage Savings*

1. *Cottage Savings* involves a deliberate attempt by a nontax agency (the Federal Home Loan Bank Board) to procure tax losses for its member banks without making them suffer any losses for banking (and real-world economic) purposes. Even by banking standards, isn't this taking cynicism to a new low? Should a nontax agency be able to make the tax system subsidize its constituents by means of artificial tax deductions, rather than by spending its own agency funds? Should taxpayers be allowed to use one set of books for tax purposes and another for business and accounting audiences? What if the Supreme Court said, "The banks can have these deductions, but only if they are reported as losses for FHLBB purposes also; otherwise, nothing doing." (There is some justice in the world: the FHLBB was abolished a few years after *Cottage Savings*, at least partially because shenanigans of this nature had undermined faith in the home loan banking industry. The IRS, although chastened, is still here.)

2. *Cottage Savings* rejects an "economic substance" test and holds that exchanges of property result in deductible losses so long as the new properties have different "legal entitlements" from the old ones. How could any taxpayer possibly flunk this test? If two real estate companies own identical office buildings on the opposite sides of the same highway, both of which have declined in value because of a depressed local real estate market, can they both realize losses by simply swapping the office buildings and otherwise continuing as before? Suppose that (as in *Cottage Savings*) they set up the transaction so that all of the same tenants remain in the same buildings, and nothing changes except the sign in the lobby? (Note that, in the office building case, there would actually be a bigger change than in *Cottage Savings*, since one office building might, in theory, prove better located or more structurally sound than the other; the vast number of properties in *Cottage Savings* spreads the risk so broadly that there is virtually no chance of this happening.)

3. Suppose that you were the head of tax litigation for the Federal Government and you wanted to argue for a rehearing of *Cottage Savings* before the Supreme Court. Which of the following flaws in the Court's decision would offer the most promising grounds for reversal?

> a. The Court failed to properly apply the section 1001 regulations requiring that exchanged property "diffe[r] materially either in kind or in extent" in order to realize a loss.

> b. The section 1001 regulations are themselves inconsistent with the statutory language.

    c. The loss is prohibited under section 165 and its supporting regulations, which require a closed and completed transaction in order to realize a deductible loss (*i.e.*, the Court of Appeals position).

    d. The Court's original opinion makes it too easy to deduct losses and would result in extensive revenue loss.

If you were counsel to the taxpayer in the case, how might you respond to each of these different arguments?

    4.   The Supreme Court's perceived failure in cases like *Cottage Savings* has caused some tax scholars to seek creation of a Federal Court of Tax Appeals, which would have exclusive jurisdiction over appellate tax cases. Does this strike you as a good idea, or would the dangers of such a proposal outweigh its purported advantages? Why?

    5.   Why do you think the Court was so hesitant to adopt an economic substance test in *Cottage Savings*?

Cottage Savings is one of a number of tax cases in which the Government appears to have been "outlitigated" and the taxpayers to have gotten away with an unjustified tax break. Yet one can appreciate the Court's position. Suppose that the Supreme Court had held against Cottage Savings, saying that the transaction lacked economic substance and denying a section 1001 (or section 165) loss deduction. What would have happened next? The banks would have probably come back with another transaction that had just a bit more economic substance — properties more different from each other, more variation in interest rates, perhaps a swap of actual mortgages instead of participation interests — and seen whether the IRS challenged the transactions and whether the courts backed up the IRS challenge. There would likely have ensued extensive litigation to determine how much "economic substance" was necessary to support a deduction, most or all of it conducted before courts that had little understanding of (and perhaps little interest in) the relevant tax and business issues. While it does not justify the result in the case, one can appreciate the Court's desire to avoid this inquiry, leaving to the IRS and Congress the problem of amending the law to prevent future abuses.

    One interesting aspect of *Cottage Savings* is the interplay between sections 1001 and 1031. As we will see momentarily, section 1031 prohibits the deduction of any losses on exchanges of like-kind property, the theory being that the taxpayer has changed the form but not the substance of her underlying investment. For various technical reasons, it is relatively easy to structure an exchange so as to avoid the section 1031 rules. (For example, two offsetting sales, as opposed to a formal exchange, are outside the section 1031 rules.) If it is similarly easy to "beat" section 1001, what is to stop any taxpayer from turning an unrealized loss into a realized loss by exchanging the loss property for something having the same substantive, but different formal, characteristics? And if taxpayers can selectively realize losses, while holding on to property that has increased in value, who will ever pay any tax? The fear of selective loss realization lies behind many different tax provisions, most notably the capital loss limitations and related rules; decisions like *Cottage Savings* threaten to undermine them.[6]

Using the Sources

Which of the following would result in realization of losses under existing law? (For purposes of this question only, you may ignore the existence of section 1031 and similar rules that provide for nonrecognition treatment of realized gains and losses.)

a. The sale of property at a loss.

b. The exchange of property that has declined in value for other, similar property.

c. The exchange of property that has declined in value for other, identical property.

d. Does it make any difference, in items a. and b., if the exchange is effected by taking cash and then buying the new property a short time later?

e. A store with six branches, three of which are performing poorly, but none of which has yet been closed.

f. A store with six branches which closes three of them down.

g. What if, in item f., the stores are drastically reduced in size instead of being completely closed down?

Law and Planning

You are a tax advisor to an oil company that has a large number of oil-producing properties, many of which have become unprofitable because of a continuing depression in oil prices. Faced with the choice of completely abandoning the wells or foregoing section 165 tax losses (see above), and having heard about *Cottage Savings*, you have hit upon a novel solution. Instead of capping the wells, you will swap them with another producer, who has similar loss properties and would also like to realize an immediate tax deduction.[7] Each company would become the owner of the other company's existing oil wells, which would be similar enough, in the aggregate, to minimize additional financial risk. To reduce administrative costs, each company would continue to manage its own previous wells — now owned by its competitor — under long-term management contracts. Both companies would plan to take an immediate tax deduction to the extent that the fair market value of the properties exceeds their adjusted basis.

---

[6] To limit the damage from *Cottage Savings*, the Treasury Department adopted a number of new regulations, although these deal primarily with financial instruments and don't directly address the holding in the case. *See, e.g.*, Treas. Reg. § 1.1001-3.

[7] To avoid section 1031, the deal could be structured as a reciprocal sale and purchase rather than as a formal exchange. A similar arrangement was used in *Cottage Savings*.

(i) Would the scheme described above work for tax purposes? Why or why not?

(ii) Assume that the president of the company asks you to evaluate three strategies for improving the company's tax situation without harming its long-term business objectives:

    a. The scheme above (swap the unprofitable wells)

    b. Sell the unprofitable wells to another company for cash

    c. Cap the unprofitable wells and take a deduction under section 165, with the possibility of uncapping the wells if oil prices increase in the future

Based on the facts above, which of these three strategies strikes you as the most promising? What additional facts would you need to know in order to make a more complete recommendation? For extra credit (real or imagined), what alternative strategies can you think of for reducing the company's taxes, without sacrificing its likely business objectives?

Politics and Policy

The following question is preceded by a few paragraphs of introduction (the question itself is on the following page):

Although the realization requirement raises interesting borderline cases, its principal function is to delay recognition of gain on appreciated property until the property is sold. Because rich people have more property than do poor people, this reduces the progressivity of the tax system and leads to some apparently incongruous results. For example, a person who invested $100,000 in stocks in 1980, and watched it grow to $1 million or more without any further effort on her part, would pay no tax until she sold the stock and thereby "realized" the underlying profit. By contrast, a person who earned $900,000 through years of backbreaking labor would pay tax on every (or almost every) penny. This is admittedly an improbable example, since most people with large investments also have significant salaries, interest, and so on, but it is a valid conceptual point, and the regressive impact of the realization requirement remains a serious concern. Scholars have also noted that African-Americans tend to own less property than Whites with similar incomes, so that the failure to tax income from property more effectively has a disproportionate racial impact. *See, e.g.*, Beverly I. Moran & William Whitford, *A Black Critique of the Internal Revenue Code*, 1996 WISC. L. REV. 751.

In order to fix this problem, some tax scholars have proposed a tax on unrealized appreciation, that is, the increased value of property still held by the original purchaser.[8] For example, a person who purchased stock for $100,000, whose stock increased in value to $150,000, would pay tax on the $50,000 of appreciation, even though she still held the stock and there had been no sale or other traditional realization event. To prevent double taxation, the basis for the stock would increase

---

[8] For a creative approach in this direction, see Mary Louise Fellows, *A Comprehensive Attack on Tax Deferral*, 88 MICH. L. REV. 722 (1990).

— in this case, to $150,000 — to reflect the amount of gain subject to tax. In effect, the law would assume an imaginary sale of appreciated assets in each year, followed by the repurchase of the assets at their new price, with any untaxed gain being subject to tax when the asset was sold.

While the proposal to tax unrealized appreciation is intellectually appealing, it faces serious practical problems. A first problem is valuation. While some items — *e.g.*, publicly traded stock — are relatively easy to value, others may be more difficult to quantify without benefit of a formal sale. Assets like real estate, family businesses, and "collectibles" (art, stamps, baseball cards, etc.) are especially subjective in value, which could result in an endless round of taxes and deductions as they bounced up and down in value.

A second problem relates to the source of tax payments. Whatever else the realization requirement accomplishes, it guarantees that the person paying tax will have money with which to pay it. The seller simply takes a portion of the sale proceeds and allocates them for the payment of tax. By contrast, in a tax on unrealized appreciation, the owner of property may be required to pay tax without having any readily available funds to do so. In some cases, the owner might even be forced to sell all or part of the property in order to pay the tax. This is arguably a dubious example, since most people with appreciated property have at least some liquid assets, but it raises the specter of confiscation and is likely to be extremely unpopular in some circles.

Imagine that, in a deep and dark nightmare, you find yourself counsel to the Joint Committee on Taxation, and are asked to evaluate three alternative proposals:

> 1. A proposal to impose a tax on all unrealized appreciation, *i.e.*, a full-blown alternative to the existing realization rule, as described above;

> 2. A proposal to tax unrealized appreciation, but only for stocks and other financial instruments, and excluding real estate, "collectibles" (*e.g.*, stamps and coins), and other more idiosyncratic forms of property; and

> 3. A proposal to tax unrealized appreciation, but only to the extent that it exceeded $100,000 per year for any individual ($200,000 for a joint return).

How would you advise the committee with regard to the above proposals? How do they stack up under the traditional tax policy criteria of fairness, efficiency, and simplicity or administrative ease? What is their likely political fallout? Is there any further information, about the tax system or the economy, that you would want to have in order to be able to make a more complete recommendation?

II. THE NONRECOGNITION PROVISIONS: WHEN, WHY, AND HOW

Realization and recognition are distinct, albeit closely related, concepts. Realization is both a tax and an economic (or at least, pseudo-economic) concept, referring to the existence of an event that severs gain or loss in some way from the underlying property. Recognition, by contrast, is the statement of a tax result: to say that gain or loss is recognized is merely to say that it is taken into account for tax purposes, and to say that it is unrecognized means it is not. Most of the time, these two go together, so that a realization event gives rise to a recognized gain or loss, and the absence of a realization event denies this possibility. But it is possible to have exceptions in either direction. For example, a tax on unrealized appreciation would (as its name suggests) result in recognition of gain even when there was no sale or other realization event. In the opposite direction, the "nonrecognition" provisions of the Code prevent recognition of gain or loss, even though they have been realized under normal tax rules. Although the importance of these latter provisions is sometimes exaggerated — their practical impact is largely limited to the real estate area — they are conceptually significant and introduce several concepts that recur in more advanced subjects.

The granddaddy of the nonrecognition rules is section 1031, the "like-kind exchange" provision, arguably one of the most confusing sections of the tax code. Section 1031 is difficult right from the start, providing that "[n]o gain or loss shall be recognized on the exchange of property held for productive use in a trade or business or for investment if such property is exchanged solely for property of like kind which is to be held either for productive use in a trade or business or for investment" (section 1031(a)(1)). This one sentence contains at least three different concepts: (i) that no gain or loss will be recognized on certain exchanges (but not sales and repurchases, mutual sales, etc.) of property; (ii) that both the property exchanged and that received must be held either for business or investment use, apparently excluding personal use property like a house, car, personal computer, and so forth; and (iii) that the two properties must be "of like kind" to each other, an undefined term that virtually guarantees substantial administrative confusion. Remaining provisions make the section even more complicated, stating that the section will not apply to exchanges of stocks and other securities, partnership interests, and "stock in trade or other property held primarily for sale" (section 1031(a)(2));[9] imposing procedural requirements designed to discourage taxpayer abuses (section 1031(a)(3), (f), (g), and (h)); and providing for the case of exchanges "not solely in kind," *i.e.*, in which a taxpayer exchanges her property partly for like-kind property but partly for money or property not covered by the provision (section 1031(b), (c), and (d)). Leaving no stone unturned, the statute further specifies that male and female livestock are not like kind property, a fact presumably well known to the livestock and now known to taxpayers, as well.

Why does section 1031 exist in the first place? The most common explanation is that a like-kind transfer changes the form, but not the substance, of one's investment, and is therefore an inappropriate occasion for the imposition of tax. One problem with this theory is that the definition of "like kind" property has little to do with the nature of the investment. For example, section 1031 excludes any stock or securities from nonrecognition treatment, even if the two companies are highly

---

[9] Thus section 1031 applies neither to personal use property, on the one hand, nor to business inventory, on the other, but only to investment type property or property held for productive use in a trade or business. For example, neither a personal residence nor real estate held by a real estate dealer would qualify under the provision. Real estate held by an investor, or used as a factory or similar productive facility, would qualify.

similar in nature, while permitting virtually any exchange of real estate to qualify, even if an apartment building is exchanged for a farm, or a shopping center for an unimproved vacant lot. *See* Treas. Reg. § 1.1031(a)-1(c).) Other definitional problems, such as whether Impressionist and Expressionist Art qualify as like-kind property, border on the absurd. This is without reaching the numerous abuses under section 1031, including three party exchanges, exchanges deliberately left uncompleted for long periods, and other shenanigans which various reform efforts have restricted but never wholly eliminated.

If like-kind exchanges are exempt from tax, what about situations in which a taxpayer sells one property and replaces it, within a relatively short period, with another similar property? The most common example is personal residences, which people regularly sell when they change locations or simply need more space, but which they typically replace with other residences at the same or a higher price. This situation is not covered by section 1031, because personal residences are not investment-type property and because it is usually too inconvenient to trade houses as opposed to selling and buying them in separate, independent transactions. Should it too be exempted from tax?

For many years the Code contained a rule providing for nonrecognition or "rollover" of gain on the sale of a personal residence.[10] Under this rule, if a taxpayer reinvested the proceeds from the sale of a personal residence in another equally or more expensive residence, the tax from any gain on the sale would be deferred until the sale of the second (or third or fourth) residence in the chain. For example, a taxpayer who bought an apartment for $100,000, sold it for $200,000, and bought a $250,000 house within a two-year period would avoid paying any tax on the sale, although the basis for the new residence would remain at $100,000, so that appreciation on the first residence would in theory "catch up" with the homeowner upon the sale of the second. (The purchase of a less expensive residence would result in a partial deferral.) Since the deferral could be repeated an unlimited number of times — and since the law further provided for exclusion of up to $125,000 of gain on sale of a personal residence by anyone over the age of 55 — in practice, only a limited number of taxpayers ever paid tax on such transactions.

In 1997, Congress consolidated the rollover and the age 55 provisions into a single rule. The Code now excludes up to $250,000 of gain ($500,000 for joint returns) on the sale of any principal residence, regardless of the taxpayer's age and regardless of whether the funds are reinvested in a new home.[11] The enactment of this provision effectively severs the link between the housing provisions and the like-kind exchange rule, and appears to be one of a series of special tax breaks for homeowners, rather than a consistent policy scheme.

The logic of the like-kind exchange provisions remains applicable in several other areas. Some prominent examples include section 1033, which deals with condemnations and other "involuntary conversions" of property, and section 1041, regarding transfers of property between spouses or incident to divorce. Although differing

---

[10] I.R.C. § 1034. The section was repealed and is no longer in effect.

[11] I.R.C. § 121. Old section 1034 remains relevant for calculating the basis of previously purchased residences (*See* I.R.C. § 121(g)).

in many respects, these provisions generally have a common policy of deferring tax, but at the cost of a carryover or substituted basis in the newly acquired property, so that the deferred tax will (theoretically) be paid when the new property is eventually disposed of. Section 1041 is discussed further in Chapter 10.

Using the Sources

1.   Which of the following items qualify for nonrecognition of gain under section 1031? If they do qualify, are both or only one of the parties entitled to nonrecognition treatment?

a. Kane trades an appreciated shopping center to Abel in return for Abel's farm, which has also increased substantially in value. Prior to the transaction both Kane and Abel held their respective properties as business investments.

b. Kane trades the same shopping center for Abel's palatial personal residence, which he (Kane) plans to hold as an investment. Abel will also hold his new shopping center as an investment, and plans to live somewhere else.

c. Same as a. above, except that Kane and Abel are brothers, and Kane plans to sell Abel's farm to an unrelated third party upon completion of the exchange.

d. Smith and Jones, prominent art collectors, exchange a Rembrandt and a Van Gogh.

e. Smith and Jones exchange stock in two corporations, both of which have extensive art-related investments.

2.   Assume that Nancy and Jane trade two farms in an exchange that qualifies for like-kind treatment under section 1031. Nancy's farm has a basis of $10,000 and a fair market value of $130,000, while Jane's farm has a basis of $20,000 and a fair market value of $100,000. To make the exchange even, Jane throws in an extra $30,000 of cash. *Nancy recognized §1031(b)   Jane- 1031(a)   Basis N: 1031(d)*

a. How much gain, if any, do Nancy and Jane recognize on the exchange, *J = 1031(d) + 1012* and what is each party's basis in her new farm at the end of the exchange?

b. How would your answer to any of these questions differ if, instead of $10,000, Nancy's basis for her original farm was (i) $100,000? (ii) $140,000?

c. In which of the situations above (Nancy's original basis equals $10,000, $100,000, or $140,000) would you have advised Nancy to enter into the exchange in the first place? Why?

Note to students: There is nothing wrong with your TV set; these are difficult problems. To answer them, read subsections (b), (c), and (d) of section 1031 carefully, and remember the purpose of the nonrecognition rule: to defer tax on gain that is reinvested in like-kind property, while recognizing gain to the extent that it is converted into money or other objects. Remember further that — with the exception of section 1014 — basis typically increases when gain is recognized, and remains constant when it is not. Finally, remember that any basis remaining to the taxpayer after a transaction must be allocated among all of the properties received in the transaction. Section 1031 is complicated, but it generally conforms to these rules.

A good way to check yourself is to imagine what would happen if, the day after the transaction, each of the parties sold the property acquired in the exchange at its fair market value in a taxable sale transaction. If you have made your computations correctly, the amount of gain on such a sale — that is, the fair market value minus the property's adjusted basis — should equal precisely the amount of gain deferred (*i.e.*, unrecognized) on the like-kind exchange.

3.   Suppose that Jules and Jim each own a parcel of investment real estate with a basis of $100,000 and a fair market value of $1,000,000. Each property is subject to a $300,000 unpaid mortgage (that is, Jules and Jim each owe the bank $300,000 on a loan to finance his respective property). If the parties exchange the two properties, subject to the existing mortgages, will the transaction qualify as a like-kind exchange under section 1031, and will either of the two parties recognize gain under section 1031(b)? What if Jules' original property was subject to a $300,000 mortgage, and Jim's property to a $500,000 mortgage, and Jules insisted that Jim pay him $200,000 in cash to compensate him for taking a property subject to higher debt? (*See* Treas. Reg. § 1.1031(b)-1(c).)

Law and Planning

Section 1031(a)(3) requires that, in order to qualify as a like-kind exchange, the property to be received in the exchange must be identified within 45 days after the taxpayer's property is transferred, and be received within 180 days of that date. For example, if A transfers Blackacre to B on July 1, B must indicate whether she plans to transfer Whiteacre, Greenacre, or some other property to A by August 15, and must actually complete the transfer by the next January 1 (or the due date for A's annual tax return, if earlier than Jan. 1). This rule was designed to prevent abuses in which exchanges were deliberately kept open for long periods, thereby approximating the effect of a sale for cash and a subsequent purchase of new property, while still technically falling within the like-kind provision. For example, in *Starker v. United States*, 602 F.2d 1341 (9th Cir. 1979), the taxpayers were found to be entitled to like-kind treatment, although the transaction remained open for two years and several of the exchanged properties were acquired from third parties while the exchange was already in progress.

Suppose Carol Creative owns an office building in the city which has appreciated substantially in value, but which is a management headache and is located in a marginal area. Carol would like to get rid of the property, but is concerned about high taxes that would result if she were to sell for cash. With this in mind, Carol approaches her friend Bob Brilliant, a suburban real estate investor, about the possibility of a like-kind exchange. Brilliant expresses interest in the concept, regretting that right now he has no property that would be suitable for an exchange, but expressing confidence that he will be able to acquire one soon.

What are the potential risks and advantages to Carol for each of the following strategies, and which would you recommend she adopt?

a. Transfer her property to Brilliant now, and allow him to identify a property of his choice in return within the 45-day statutory period.

b. Sit tight, wait until Brilliant or a competitor has acquired a property to her liking, and then immediately enter into the exchange.

c. Forget the whole exchange concept and sell the property, immediately, for cash.

What does your answer to this question tell you about the effectiveness of the section 1031(a)(3) restrictions, and of section 1031, in general?

Politics and Policy

A frequent theme in this course is the favorable — some might say too favorable — tax treatment accorded to real estate. We have seen examples of this in sections 1031, which allows a wide variety of real estate to qualify for nonrecognition treatment, and section 121, which excludes from tax up to $250,000 of gain ($500,000 for married couples) on the sale of a personal residence. More extensive examples include the deduction for home mortgage interest (section 163(h)); generous depreciation rules (investment real estate only); and many narrower provisions (credits, deductions, etc.) providing incentives for specific kinds of real estate investments.[12] Although these provisions have different scopes and purposes — section 1031 and the depreciation rules apply primarily to commercial (including rental) real estate, while sections 121 and 163(h) concern the taxpayer's personal residence — together, they amount to a range of tax benefits that is probably unparalleled in the tax code. Indeed, one of the major goals of tax reform has been to restrict the tax preferences for real estate and its owners.

Consider, in particular, section 121, an unusually blatant case of solicitude toward real estate investment. The arguments against this provision are easy enough to recite: it loses money, discriminates between homeowners and renters, and contains several arbitrary limitations ($250,000 limitation, 2-year occupancy rule, and so forth). Which of the following, if any, strikes you as a convincing argument in its favor?

a. Home ownership is an important goal for many families and we shouldn't punish them by imposing a large tax on the sale of a personal residence.

b. Taxpayers are not permitted to deduct losses on the sale of a home that declines in value, so they shouldn't have to pay tax if the home increases in value, either. (*See* section 262).

---

[12] *See, e.g.*, I.R.C. §§ 103, 141(e) & 142(a) (tax-exempt bonds for various types of real estate); 42 (credit for low-income housing); 168(e)(2) (depreciation provisions with respect to residential and nonresidential real property.)

c. A tax on home sales discourages people from selling their personal residence, even when they no longer need it, and therefore interferes with the smooth operation of the housing market.

Now consider the broader policy of tax incentives for homeowners, as reflected throughout the tax code. This policy is arguably unfair, because it discriminates between housing and other investments, and inefficient, because it encourages taxpayers to spend more on their personal residences and less on other items (clothing, health care, vacations, etc.) than they would in a completely free market. Are these negative consequences justified by an increase in social welfare or stability resulting from enhanced levels of home ownership? Do homeowners tend to be better citizens or more reliable neighbors than people who rent homes or live with their parents? Do they play a more active role in public affairs? Do they take better care of their property? Or is all of this a lot of nonsense concocted by the housing industry and its well-paid (and no doubt, well-housed) lobbyists?

Surveys usually show the United States to be near the top of industrial nations in our standard of housing, and lower in many other "quality of life" categories. Does this mean that the existing tax subsidies are effective, and ought to be a model for other countries? Or does it suggest that we might better spend the same money on other programs? If the money is to be spent on housing, are there any changes that you would recommend in order to target the incentives more effectively to their intended audience?

III. DEFERRAL AS DELIBERATE TAX PLANNING: THE PROBLEM OF DEFERRED COMPENSATION

Up to this point we have generally treated deferral as a consequence of a transaction rather than its original purpose. But this is only one part of the story. Since the long-term deferral of tax is nearly as good as tax avoidance, it is not surprising that taxpayers organize their affairs so as to deliberately defer as much tax for as long as possible. It is perhaps also not surprising that the Government, in providing tax incentives, uses deferral as often or more often than outright forgiveness of tax. Many of the most important (and costly) tax subsidies, ranging from business tax incentives to retirement and other individual tax benefits, are essentially deferral provisions. By contrast, much of the supposed "war" against tax shelters is a struggle against excessive deferral, rather than complete tax avoidance.

The following materials consider the issue of deferred compensation, one of the most important and familiar examples of deferral in the Internal Revenue Code. The first part of this section considers two forms of deferred compensation, stock options and restricted stock, which have historically been limited to highly paid executives, although they have become somewhat more widely dispersed in recent years. The second part concerns pension and employee benefit plans, which are more generally available, although they remain controversial on political and economic grounds. (Many of you will come face-to-face with this issue immediately upon graduation when you consider your employers' pension or similar plans.) Because deferred compensation is often characterized as a fringe benefit, these materials will enable us to tie together some of the legal and policy themes elaborated on in the last three chapters, and to observe once more the tension between individuals' tax and business goals.

A.   Stock Options

COMMISSIONER v. LOBUE
United States Supreme Court
351 U.S. 243 (1956)

Mr. Justice Black delivered the opinion of the Court.

This case involves the federal income tax liability of respondent LoBue for the years 1946 and 1947. From 1941 to 1947 LoBue was manager of the New York Sales Division of the Michigan Chemical Corporation, a producer and distributor of chemical supplies. In 1944 the company adopted a stock option plan making 10,000 shares of its common stock available for distribution to key employees at $5 per share over a 3-year period. LoBue and a number of other employees were notified that they had been tentatively chosen to be recipients of nontransferable stock options contingent upon their continued employment. LoBue's notice told him: "You may be assigned a greater or less amount of stock based entirely upon your individual results and that of the entire organization." About 6 months later he was notified that he had been definitely awarded an option to buy 150 shares of stock in recognition of his "contribution and efforts in making the operation of the Company successful." As to future allotments he was told "It is up to you to justify your participation in the plan during the next two years."

LoBue's work was so satisfactory that the company in the course of 3 years delivered to him 3 stock options covering 340 shares. He exercised all these $5 per share options in 1946 and in 1947, paying the company only $1,700 for stock having a market value when delivered of $9,930. Thus, at the end of these transactions, LoBue's employer was worth $8,230 less to its stockholders and LoBue was worth $8,230 more than before. The company deducted this sum as an expense in its 1946 and 1947 tax returns but LoBue did not report any part of it as income. Viewing the gain to LoBue as compensation for personal services the Commissioner levied a deficiency assessment against him, relying on § 22(a) of the Internal Revenue Code of 1939, 53 Stat. 9, as amended, 53 Stat. 574, which defines gross income as including "gains, profits, and income derived from . . . compensation for personal service . . . of whatever kind and in whatever form paid. . . ."

LoBue petitioned the Tax Court to redetermine the deficiency, urging that "The said options were not intended by the Corporation or the petitioner to constitute additional compensation but were granted to permit the petitioner to acquire a proprietary interest in the Corporation and to provide him with the interest in the successful operation of the Corporation deriving from an ownership interest." The Tax Court held that LoBue had a taxable gain if the options were intended as compensation but not if the options were designed to provide him with "a proprietary interest in the business." Finding after hearings that the options were granted to give LoBue "a proprietary interest in the corporation, and not as compensation for services" the Tax Court held for LoBue. 22 T.C. 440, 443. Relying on this finding the Court of Appeals affirmed, saying: "This was a factual issue which it was the peculiar responsibility of the Tax Court to resolve. From our examination of the evidence we cannot say that its finding was clearly erroneous." 223 F.2d 367, 371. Disputes over the taxability of stock option transactions such as this are longstanding. We granted certiorari to consider whether the Tax Court and the Court of Appeals had given § 22(a) too narrow an interpretation. 350 U.S. 893.

We have repeatedly held that in defining "gross income" as broadly as it did in § 22(a) Congress intended to "tax all gains except those specifically exempted." *See, e.g., Commissioner v. Glenshaw Glass Co.*, 348 U.S. 426, 429–430. The only exemption Congress provided from this very comprehensive definition of taxable income that could possibly have application here is the gift exemption of § 22(b)(3). But there was not the slightest indication of the kind of detached and disinterested generosity which might evidence a "gift" in the statutory sense. These transfers of stock bore none of the earmarks of a gift. They were made by a company engaged in operating a business for profit, and the Tax Court found that the stock option plan was designed to achieve more profitable operations by providing the employees "with an incentive to promote the growth of the company by permitting them to participate in its success." 22 T.C. at 445. Under these circumstances the Tax Court and the Court of Appeals properly refrained from treating this transfer as a gift. The company was not giving something away for nothing.

Since the employer's transfer of stock to its employee LoBue for much less than the stock's value was not a gift, it seems impossible to say that it was not compensation. The Tax Court held there was no taxable income, however, on the ground that one purpose of the employer was to confer a "proprietary interest." But there is not a word in § 22(a) which indicates that its broad coverage should be narrowed because of an employer's intention to enlist more efficient service from his employees by making them part proprietors of his business. In our view there is no statutory basis for the test established by the courts below. When assets are transferred by an employer to an employee to secure better services they are plainly compensation. It makes no difference that the compensation is paid in stock rather than in money. Section 22(a) taxes income derived from compensation "in whatever form paid." And in another stock option case we said that § 22(a) "is broad enough to include in taxable income any economic or financial benefit conferred on the employee as compensation, whatever the form or mode by which it is effected." *Commissioner v. Smith*, 324 U.S. 177, 181. LoBue received a very substantial economic and financial benefit from his employer prompted by the employer's desire to get better work from him. This is "compensation for personal service" within the meaning of § 22(a).

LoBue nonetheless argues that we should treat this transaction as a mere purchase of a proprietary interest on which no taxable gain was "realized" in the year of purchase. It is true that our taxing system has ordinarily treated an arm's length purchase of property even at a bargain price as giving rise to no taxable gain in the year of purchase. *See Palmer v. Commissioner*, 302 U.S. 63, 69. But that is not to say that when a transfer which is in reality compensation is given the form of a purchase the Government cannot tax the gain under § 22(a). The transaction here was unlike a mere purchase. It was not an arm's length transaction between strangers. Instead it was an arrangement by which an employer transferred valuable property to his employees in recognition of their services. We hold that LoBue realized taxable gain when he purchased the stock.[13]

A question remains as to the time when the gain on the shares should be measured. LoBue gave his employer promissory notes for the option price of the first 300 shares but the shares were not delivered until the notes were paid in cash.[14] The market value of the shares was lower when the notes were given than when the cash was paid. The Commissioner measured the taxable gain by the market value of the shares when the cash was paid. LoBue contends that this was wrong, and that the gain should be measured either when the options were granted or when the notes were given.

It is of course possible for the recipient of a stock option to realize an immediate taxable gain. *See Commissioner v. Smith*, 324 U.S. 177, 181-182. The option might have a readily ascertainable market value and the recipient might be free to sell his option. But this is not such a case. These three options were not transferable and LoBue's right to buy stock under them was contingent upon his remaining an employee of the company until they were exercised. Moreover, the uniform Treasury practice since 1923 has been to measure the compensation to employees given stock options subject to contingencies of this sort by the difference between the option price and the market value of the shares at the time the option is exercised. We relied in part upon this practice in *Commissioner v. Smith*, 324 U.S. 177, 324 U.S. 695. And in its 1950 Act affording limited tax benefits for "restricted stock option plans" Congress adopted the same kind of standard for measurement of gains. § 130A, Internal Revenue Code of 1939, as amended, 64 Stat. 942. *And see* § 421, Internal Revenue Code of 1954, 68A Stat. 142. Under these circumstances there is no reason for departing from the Treasury practice. The taxable gain to LoBue should be measured as of the time the options were exercised and not the time they were granted.

It is possible that a bona fide delivery of a binding promissory note could mark the completion of the stock purchase and that gain should be measured as of that date. Since neither the Tax Court nor the Court of Appeals passed on this question the judgment is reversed and the case is remanded to the Court of Appeals with instructions to remand the case to the Tax Court for further proceedings.

Reversed and remanded.

---

[13] [6] Since our view of the statute requires taxation of gain here it is unnecessary for us to rely on the Treasury Regulations to reach that conclusion. Apparently the present regulations were not applicable to all of the options. *See* 26 CFR, Rev. 1953, § 39.22(a)-1(c); 1939-1 Cum. Bull. 159; 1946-1 Cum. Bull. 15-18. And since the transactions in question here occurred prior to 1950, the 1950 statute establishing special tax treatment for "restricted stock option plans" has no relevance. *See* § 130A, Internal Revenue Code of 1939, as amended, 64 Stat. 942. *And see* § 421, Internal Revenue Code of 1954, 68A Stat. 142.

[14] [7] LoBue paid cash for the last 40 shares.

Mr. Justice Frankfurter and Mr. Justice Clark, concurring.

We join in the judgment of the Court and in its opinion on the main issue. However, the time when LoBue acquired the interest on which he is taxed was not in issue either before the Tax Court or the Court of Appeals. In the circumstances of this case, there certainly is no reason for departing from the general rule whereby this Court abstains from passing on such an issue in a tax case when raised here for the first time. *See Helvering v. Minnesota Tea Co.*, 296 U.S. 378, 380; *Helvering v. Tex-Penn Co.*, 300 U.S. 481, 498.

Mr. Justice Harlan, whom Mr. Justice Burton joins, concurring in part and dissenting in part.

In my view, the taxable event was the grant of each option, not its exercise. When the respondent received an unconditional option to buy stock at less than the market price, he received an asset of substantial and immediately realizable value, at least equal to the then-existing spread between the option price and the market price. It was at that time that the corporation conferred a benefit upon him. At the exercise of the option, the corporation "gave" the respondent nothing; it simply satisfied a previously-created legal obligation. That transaction, by which the respondent merely converted his asset from an option into stock, should be of no consequence for tax purposes. The option should be taxable as income when given, and any subsequent gain through appreciation of the stock, whether realized by sale of the option, if transferable, or by sale of the stock acquired by its exercise, is attributable to the sale of a capital asset and, if the other requirements are satisfied, should be taxed as a capital gain. Any other result makes the division of the total gains between ordinary income (compensation) and capital gain (sale of an asset) dependent solely upon the fortuitous circumstance of when the employee exercises his option.[15]

The last two options granted to respondent were unconditional and immediately exercisable, and thus present no further problems. The first option, however, was granted under somewhat different circumstances. Respondent was notified in January 1945 that 150 shares had been "allotted" to him, but he was given no right to purchase them until June 30, 1945, and his right to do so then was expressly made contingent upon his still being employed at that date. His right to purchase the first allotment of stock was thus not vested until he satisfied the stated condition, and it was not until then that he could be said to have received income, the measure of which should be the value of the option on that date.

Accordingly, while I concur in the reversal of the judgment below and in the remand to the Tax Court, I would hold the granting of the options to be the taxable events and would measure the income by the value of the options when granted.

---

[15] [2] Suppose two employees are given unconditional options to buy stock at $5, the current market value. The first exercises the option immediately and sells the stock a year later at $15. The second holds the option for a year, exercises it, and sells the stock immediately at $15. Admittedly the $10 gain would be taxed to the first as capital gain; under the Court's view, it would be taxed to the second as ordinary income because it is "compensation" for services. I fail to see how the gain can be any more "compensation" to one than it is to the other.

Understanding *LoBue*

1.   The Court considers three possible times for taxing LoBue's stock options:

    a. When the options were granted (1944), based on the fair market value (if any) of the options at that time.

    b. When the options were exercised (1946 and 1947), based on the difference between the option price and fair market value. Thus, a $1,700 stock purchase (340 shares @ $5 per share), when the fair market value of the same stock was $9,930, would result in $8,230 of income in the year of exercise. (Because he had been taxed on the full value of the stock, LoBue's basis for the stock would now be equal to its fair market value.)

    c. In some later year, when LoBue sells the stock at a (presumed) profit. Under this method, LoBue would pay no tax in 1944 or 1946, but would have a basis for the stock equal to his (reduced) purchase price, so that any future sale would result in income — presumably, capital gain — to the extent that the sale price exceeded this amount. For example, a future sale of the stock at a price of $10,000 would result in $8,300 of capital gain income ($10,000 – $1,700), while a sale for $1,000 would result in a $700 capital loss.

Examine the case from LoBue's perspective, as a litigant. Which of the three alternatives is best, from his perspective? Which is worst? Does you answer depend, in part, on additional facts regarding the company or LoBue's tax situation, and if so, what additional facts? Note that, if LoBue's tax is delayed, the company's deduction for amounts paid to LoBue (section 162) is likely to be delayed as well. Is this something that LoBue should be concerned about, or should he only be concerned about the timing of his own income?

2.   LoBue argued that he should pay no immediate tax (*i.e.*, Option c), because he had merely purchased an additional stake in his own company and had not "realized" income in cash or other readily disposable property. Isn't this a pretty good argument? Has an executive who plows back money into his own corporation, and is subject to the risks of that company's future performance, realized gain in any meaningful way? Wouldn't a more accurate measure of his income be the difference in the value of the stock when and if he sells it, as compared to the (admittedly reduced) price he paid upon the original purchase? Or are stock options merely a device for compensating highly paid executives on a tax-delayed basis, and worthy of no particular sympathy?

3.   Neither the majority nor the dissenting opinion accepts LoBue's argument, with the majority opting for Option b (tax on the exercise of the option), and the dissent making a strong argument for Option a (tax at the time of issue). The amount of tax under the majority's opinion is relatively easy to compute, being based upon the difference between the option price and fair market value at the time of exercise ($8,230 per share). How would tax be computed under the dissenting opinion? Does an option have a value before it is exercised? What if LoBue was taxed on the estimated fair market value of the option in 1944, but failed to exercise the option — should he be entitled to a discount, or a recomputation of his earlier taxes, at that point? What if the stock price increased dramatically

between 1944 and 1946, so that the option was in fact worth more than it appeared to be when granted? Do these practical considerations argue in favor of the majority's system, even if the dissent is more theoretically appealing?

Whatever the logic of *LoBue*, the reality is that very few people would use stock options if they were subject to immediate tax (Options a or b above). Some form of relief from *LoBue* has accordingly been available at most times. The current version is located in sections 421 and 422 of the Code, which provide for delayed imposition of tax — *i.e.*, the equivalent of Option c — if various conditions are met. One important condition is that the option price be not less than the fair market value of the stock at the time the option is granted (section 422(b)(4)). For example, if General Motors stock is selling at $50 per share on July 1, 1999, and the company issues an incentive stock option on that date, the option price may not be less than $50 per share. (The option may still be quite valuable, because the market price may be well over $50 by the time the option is exercised, or by the later date on which the executive sells the stock). Other conditions pertain to the time during which the option is exercisable; the period for which the stock must be held after exercise; and various other particulars.

Examine closely sections 421 and 422 and, especially, the requirements contained in subsections 422(a) and (b). Why do you think Congress included a requirement that, in order to qualify for deferral treatment, the option must not be exercisable for a period of more than ten years (section 422(b)(3))? What about the requirements that the stock option plan be approved by the shareholders of the corporation (section 422(b)(1)), and that options not be available to anyone owning more than 10 percent of the corporation (section 422(b)(6))? Why, for that matter, may the option price not be less than fair market value at the time the option is granted? Does the term "incentive" in the section title help to answer any of these questions? Exactly what incentive is being provided by section 422 stock options, and does this incentive component justify the generous tax treatment afforded to this kind of benefit?

Stock options have long been a popular form of executive compensation, but became especially so in the 1990s, because the rapid increase in stock prices meant that even a relatively small volume of options could be extremely profitable.[16] Not surprisingly, they have come in for their share of criticism. One frequent criticism is that — like other "incentive"-based compensation — stock options reward employees regardless of whether their own efforts contributed decisively to the company's performance. For example, a Microsoft employee may be permitted to buy stock at $10 per share that later sells for $100 or even $1,000 per share, although that particular employee's contribution to Microsoft's performance may have been negligible. Indeed, the entire company's performance may have had more to do with overall market trends than with any particular decision by Microsoft executives, even at the very top level. The "incentive" component of stock options may thus be highly tenuous in some cases.

---

[16] A further reason involves section 162(m), which forbids public corporations from deducting executive compensation in excess of $1 million, but does not apply to stock options and other "performance-based" compensation. *See* Chapter 6, *infra*.

A second criticism is that — assuming that the incentive does work — it may be the wrong, in some cases even a perverse, incentive. A frequent criticism of American managers is that they tend to adopt a short-term perspective rather than considering the long-term health of the corporation. Stock options may exacerbate this trend by encouraging executives to "run up" the share price (and thereby increase the value of their options), rather than focusing on longer-range objectives. According to this view, executives may be encouraged to take actions, like the sale of assets or the firing of employees, that increase overnight share values but have deleterious business (not to mention human) consequences over the long haul. Stock options are obviously only one part of this broader equation, but since they form an increasingly large percentage of executive compensation, they have a significant role.

Finally, of course, stock options tend to benefit wealthier individuals and thus raise serious vertical equity issues. Against these disadvantages must be weighed the incentives resulting from this provision and the advantages of a society with a marginally broader distribution of stock ownership.

Using the Sources

When and how would each of the following stock options be taxed?

a. A stock option that was granted but never exercised

b. An option to buy 1,000 shares of National Motors stock at $20 per share, which was granted to an executive in 2001, at which time the stock was selling at $30 per share, and exercised by her two years later, at which time the stock was selling at a price of $40 per share

c. Same as b. above, except the option price was $30 per share

d. What additional facts, if any, would you need to know in order to answer any of the preceding questions?

Law and Planning

Suppose that you were an employee of MacroHard Corporation, a computer software company that did very well in the 1990s and — while still growing — is showing signs of shakiness today. The company pays you a reasonable fixed salary but not enough to keep you from looking at other possibilities. As part of an effort to keep you working for the company, it offers you the following three alternatives:

a. A $10,000 one-time cash bonus;

b. An option to buy 1,000 shares of the company's stock at $35 per share, exercisable for up to ten years from the issue date, and set up so as to comply with the rules of section 422 (the company's stock is presently selling at precisely $35 per share, down from an all-time high of $50 two years ago, but still considerably higher than the 50 cents or so that it was worth a decade ago); or

c. $10,000 of tax-free health and retirement benefits.

Which of the three alternatives would you choose, and what role (if any) would tax factors play in making your decision?

Politics and Policy

Based on the above, do you think the incentive stock option provision (*i.e.*, section 422) makes sense from the perspective of tax and/or corporate policy? How would you evaluate this provision in terms of fairness (horizontal and vertical equity); simplicity or administrability; and economic efficiency? Do you think that it provides sound or unsound incentives, and (assuming there are at least some sound incentives) are these better provided by tax or other means? If you had the chance to change or abolish the existing rule, what kinds of changes would you be likely to make? For extra credit — and assuming that you have taken both tax and corporate law courses — which course did you like better, and why?

B.   Restricted Property and Section 83

Stock options tend to be used by larger, more established companies as a way of compensating executives and (they hope) encouraging better performance. For small start-up companies, the requirements of section 422, together with the complexities of administering an options program, may make this route unattractive. Instead, such companies frequently use restricted stock programs, in which employees are given stock either free or at a very low price, but with the proviso that they must return the stock (or sell it back at an equivalent discount) if they leave the company before a set date. For example, an executive of a small Internet firm might have been permitted to purchase the company's stock at $5 a share in 1999, even though the market price was probably more like $25 and might shortly have reached $250 or more if the company succeeded. (The market value of such stock is often highly speculative, which is one of the reasons the tax rules get so complicated.) The terms of the transfer would require that, if the executive left the company before (say) December 31, 2001, she would be required to sell the stock back to the company at the $5 price, thereby eliminating the benefit of the discount. But if she stayed past that date, she could keep the stock indefinitely; the more the stock went up in value — the more it diverged from the original $5 that she paid for it — the richer, and presumably happier, she would become. For its part, the employer would have provided its executive with an incentive to stay at the company and increase its share value, without the price and other limits applicable to an option plan.

When should this employee be taxed? To answer this question, a little bit of tax theory is necessary. It is axiomatic in the tax law that a mere promise — "I'll pay you $100 next year, if you're still here and I can find you" — is not taxable. But the receipt of money or property, pursuant to an apparently valid claim of right, *is* generally taxable, even though some unforeseen event might cause the money or property to be returned in the future. It has also been held that the receipt of property is taxable, even though the property consists of an annuity or similar contract that will not begin paying cash benefits until some point in the future.[17] How, then, should these principles apply to a conditional benefit, such as the transfer of stock in year 1, with the proviso that the stock be returned if the employee leaves before the end of year 3? Should the stock be taxed in year 1, when transferred, or at the end of year 3, when it can no longer be forfeited? Or should the tax be delayed until some later date — the equivalent of *LoBue's* Option C — when the stock is sold to a third party?[18]

The answers are provided by section 83, a short but maddening provision. Section 83 states that property transfers to employees become taxable at the point when either (i) the employee's rights in the property may be transferred to another person, or (ii) the employee's rights "are not subject to a substantial risk of forfeiture," *i.e.*, the employee has the property and is no longer in any serious danger of losing it. Since restricted stock is usually not transferable, this means that a conditional transfer will normally be taxed when the condition lapses, based on the difference between the then market price of the stock and the price paid by the employee. For example, in the hypothetical described above, our Internet executive would be taxed on December 31, 2001, based on the excess of the market price on that date over the price ($5 per share) she originally paid for the stock (section 83(a)). If she preferred, the employee could elect instead to pay tax in 1999, based on the (presumably lesser) excess of the market price over $5 at that point, although if she made this election she would receive no offsetting deduction were she to leave the firm and therefore be forced to resell the stock before 2001 (section 83(b)). Section 83 thus delays tax until the point at which the economic benefit has become definite and apparently irreversible, albeit with the option to pay an earlier (but presumably lower) tax if the employee wishes to do so.

Armed with the capsule description above, it is interesting to compare the advantages offered by incentive stock options and restricted stock plans.[19] Stock options offer the greater tax benefits, since tax is deferred until the date on which the stock is eventually sold (Option C), a date which may lie many years off in the future. By contrast, under a restricted stock plan, tax is imposed either at the point when the stock becomes nonforfeitable or, at the taxpayer's election, when the stock is originally received — the rough equivalent of Options B or A in a stock option context. On the other hand, restricted stock plans are considerably more flexible, since the purchase price for the stock may be set as low as the company wants — it may even be provided to employees free of charge — and the timing and other rules of section 422 are not applicable to such plans. The economic or nontax benefits may thus be greater in a restricted stock plan. Finally, the coercive aspect of restricted stock transfers (retracting benefits if an employee leaves

---

[17] United States v. Drescher, 179 F.2d 863 (2d Cir. 1950).

[18] Note that the problem of restricted property is related to, but conceptually distinct from, the "claim of right" issue in the preceding chapter. The difference is that in a claim of right situation, the taxpayer appears to have an unrestricted right to the property, and only later discovers that she may have to relinquish it. By contrast, in the case of restricted property, the conditional nature of ownership is known from the beginning. This tends to show up on a lot of exams.

[19] For a comparison of the policy issues, including incentive stock options and restricted stock, see generally David M. Schizer, *Executives and Hedging: The Fragile Legal Foundation of Incentive Compatibility*, 100 COLUM. L. REV. 440 (2000).

before a prescribed date) may be important for a new business, which can ill-afford to lose talent during its initial growth phase.

What all this boils down to is that stock options tend to be more popular with larger, more established companies, and restricted stock transfers with small, start-up companies, especially in high-tech or other risky fields. But this is a very broad generalization; the trade-off between tax and business advantages depends upon the facts of each company, and must be made separately in each individual case. Section 83 is thus a valuable lesson in good tax planning: one must always measure tax benefits against the real-world costs, and a tax savings that conflicts with business objectives may be no savings, at all.

Although employers usually make a deliberate choice between a section 83 and a section 422 compensation plan, there are occasions in which the two provisions overlap, especially when incentive stock options run afoul of the section 422 rules and find themselves subject to tax under section 83 rules. *See, e.g.,* T.C. Memo. 1990-551. Such situations are usually best avoided, and a clear choice made between one or the other incentive provision.

Using the Sources

How and when would the following items be taxed? (Unless otherwise stated, assume that there is no section 83(b) election.)

a. On June 30, 2001, Sam Screenhead buys 1,000 shares of his employer, ScrollLock Enterprises, at $10 per share (the fair market value of the stock is estimated at $50 per share). The conditions of the sale require that, if he leaves the company within three years of the purchase date (*i.e.,* June 30, 2004), he must sell the stock back to the company at $10 per share. As of midnight on June 30, 2004, Sam is still with the company, and the stock is selling at $500 per share.

b. Same as a., except that Sam has made an election under section 83(b).

c. Same as a., except Sam leaves the company in 2003.

d. What are the tax consequences to the employer in each of the above situations?

e. Based on the above, if you had a client in a restricted stock situation, would you advise them to make an election under section 83(b)?

Law and Planning

Hardball Enterprises is a new corporation that intends to provide consulting services to politicians involved in major personal scandals. Hardball intends to hire a mix of young lawyers, journalists, and public relations experts along with a handful of more senior Washington figures to give it an air of partial respectability (and also increase its consulting fees). The principals anticipate that it will take a few years to establish the company's reputation, but — given Washington's virtually unlimited appetite for scandal — it expects to do quite well thereafter.

Since it anticipates being short of cash, at least for a time, Hardball is looking for an alternate way to augment its compensation package.

a. Would you advise Hardball to institute a restricted stock program under section 83, an incentive stock option program under section 422, or both? Why?

b. How would your answer to item a. be affected by each of the following?

(i) The scandal consulting business is extremely competitive and it is difficult to predict the company's future performance.

(ii) Most of the company's employees are likely to receive offers from one or more competing firms.

(iii) The company's principal employees all have substantial savings and are likely to be in very high tax brackets.

c. What additional facts, if any, would you want to know before making any of the decisions above?

Politics and Policy

A common complaint is that the tax code has too many complex, overlapping provisions that apply to the same or similar transactions. The implication is that such complexity rewards people with clever tax advisers, rather than those deserving of aid. A related implication is that a comprehensive reform process, which eliminated duplicative provisions and stated tax rules in plain, simple language, might result in a fairer and more efficient, as well as a simpler, tax code.

From a tax policy perspective, what value is served by having two alternate incentive systems like sections 83 and 422? Would it be better to combine these rules into a single provision? What might that provision look like? Knowing what you now know about the tax legislative process, whose interests — large or small corporations, highly- or lowly-compensated employees, etc. — would be likely to have the most influence over this new drafting process? More generally, who has the most influence over tax reform, and is it likely to make the law better or worse than it was before the reform started?

C.　Pensions and Other Large-Scale Retirement Plans

Stock options and restricted property are largely restricted to executives or to the employees of small, rapidly growing companies. By contrast, pensions or similar retirement plans are available to a vast number of private and public sector employees. So vast has this industry become that the term "employee benefits" is often used interchangeably with pensions, a recognition of the degree to which retirement savings have dwarfed the other, more traditional kinds of fringe benefits discussed in Chapter 2.

The rise of the pension industry is, to a surprising degree, a uniquely American phenomenon. Until the middle of the last century, most people had no systematic form of retirement savings. They worked hard, saved what they could, and relied upon their children or other relatives to support them in their old age. Indeed, historians tell us, that's one reason they had so many children.

In the United States and other "advanced" countries, Social Security or similar Government-run systems appeared during the first half of the twentieth century, usually funded by a mix of payroll contributions and other tax revenues. In many countries, these systems shouldered the full burden of retirement savings. But here in the United States, there has long been a sense that Social Security is inadequate to provide for a full, happy retirement, particularly in today's world where people live longer and feel they can rely less on family and private charity to support them. This economic reality is coupled with a peculiarly American sense that it is unhealthy to be too reliant on Government, and that the private sector should accordingly shoulder some of the burden of retirement planning. These considerations, together with substantial tax benefits, gave rise to today's pension industry.

The tax side of pensions amounts to one simple paradigm and a welter of mind-numbing details. The paradigm can be summed up in one word: deferral. Money set aside for a "qualified" pension plan (section 401(a)) is immediately deductible to the employer, but is not included in the employee's income until the time — presumably, many years later — when it is withdrawn by the (now-retired) employee for personal use. This arrangement has two potentially huge benefits to both parties. The most obvious is timing: by allowing the employer a deduction, while delaying the employee's payment of tax, the statute permits the parties to "have their cake and eat it too," in a manner that is unusual, although not entirely unprecedented, in the tax law. (By contrast, both *LoBue* and section 83 require consistency in the timing of deductions and income.) What is more, by imposing tax when the employee is retired — and likely to be in a lower tax bracket — the law reduces the likely amount of tax, even apart from timing differences. Finally, qualified pension plans allow interest to build up without any current imposition of tax, thereby significantly increasing the effective rate at which the money will grow.[20]

To qualify for this advantageous tax treatment, the law imposes several requirements on pension plans and their beneficiaries. The most important tax rule is the concept of equity, or (yes, that word again) "nondiscrimination," which requires that a plan not be excessively stacked in favor of highly compensated employees within the meaning of the statute.[21] Other important principles include the minimum participation standards, which require that the plan be open to reasonable categories of employees as defined under the statute, and a series of funding requirements designed to ensure that the pension fund assets will, in fact, be available to the employees when they need them.[22] If these conditions are met,

---

[20] For example, assuming a 30% tax rate and 10% interest, money will grow at an after-tax rate of 7% per year, so that $1 deposited today will become approximately $7.61 30 years from now. A tax-free account, which will grow at the full 10% per year, will reach $17.45 in the same period. This interest, together with the amount of the original contribution, is taxable upon withdrawal by the beneficiary, but at a much later date and (depending upon the individual's tax situation) potentially a lower tax rate.

[21] I.R.C. § 401(a)(4).

[22] I.R.C. § 401(a)(3) and (a)(2), respectively.

the plan is denoted a "qualified plan," and the employer is permitted to deduct contributions while the employees delay recognition of income, as described above. If not, the plan is a "nonqualified plan," which — although it may possibly be advantageous on other grounds — is not permitted the advantageous tax treatment reserved for qualified plans. The Code also includes numerous additional provisions regarding salary deferral arrangements (section 401(k)),[23] Individual Retirement Accounts,[24] and other arrangements by which employees or (in some cases) self-employed individuals can supplement their social security and pension benefits, if any, in planning for their retirement; many of these have at least some elements in common with section 401 qualified plans. (Section 409A of the Code, added by the American Jobs Creation Act of 2004, provides further clarification regarding the treatment of nonqualified plans.)

As one might expect, a great deal of care and planning goes into the design and operation of qualified pension plans. Lawyers being lawyers, much of this effort goes into pressing the limits of the rules as far as possible, e.g., discriminating as much as possible in favor of highly compensated employees without technically violating the "nondiscrimination" rules, or else providing as little funding as possible without violating the so-called funding requirements. Essentially, this is a more sophisticated version of the fringe benefit problem already observed in Chapter 2, except that the amounts of money are far greater and the level of detail, correspondingly, more daunting. The technical challenge of the pension area is indeed so exquisite that it has become effectively an independent area of practice, with "pension tax" lawyers frequently separating themselves from the remainder of the tax field and practicing all, or mostly, in the pension area for the remainder of their natural lives. (One is tempted to say that pension tax lawyers are to tax lawyers as tax lawyers are to the rest of society; but this may be unfair to all parties.)

No case can possibly capture all the interpretation, planning, and cynical maneuvering that characterizes the pension tax area. But one case, *Albertson's, Inc. v. Commissioner*, 12 F.3d 1529 (9th Cir. 1993), comes close. *Albertson's* has a little bit of everything — statutory interpretation, tax policy, the interplay of tax and business issues — with the added excitement that, had the case gone the other way, it would have destroyed a good part of the existing pension tax system. The case is difficult, not in the least because the same court, in an original and rehearing decision, came out two ways on the same issue. It is worth the effort, both for its insight into the pension provisions and (more generally) into the way that courts of general jurisdiction attempt to resolve difficult tax issues. Do your best to follow the case; you will be rewarded (!) with a series of questions and problems at its conclusion.

---

[23] I.R.C. § 401(k) allows employees to place a portion of their own cash compensation in a tax-deferred account.

[24] IRAs are individual accounts which permit tax-free contributions and interest buildup (traditional IRAs) or only tax-free buildup (Roth IRAs) and thereby supplement other retirement plans.

ALBERTSON'S, INC. v. COMMISSIONER (ALBERTSON'S I)
United States Court of Appeals, Ninth Circuit
12 F.3d 1529 (1993)

REINHARDT, J:

I. OVERVIEW

Petitioner Albertson's, Inc. ("Albertson's")[25] appeals two decisions of the United States Tax Court. In the first decision, the Tax Court held that Albertson's was not entitled to claim work incentive tax credits ("WIN credits") retroactively for its past hiring of certain welfare recipients. *See Albertson's, Inc. v. Commissioner*, 1990 Tax Ct. Memo LEXIS 177, 59 T.C.M. (CCH) 186, 1990 T.C. Memo 153 (1990). In the second decision, the Tax Court held that Albertson's was not entitled to claim current deductions for interest-like obligations that had accrued under deferred compensation agreements ("DCAs") made with certain of its top executives and directors. *See Albertson's, Inc. v. Commissioner*, 95 T.C. 415 (1990).

Respondent Commissioner of Internal Revenue ("Commissioner") cross-appeals a third decision of the United States Tax Court. In the third decision, the Tax Court held that Albertson's was entitled to claim investment tax credits for its heating, ventilating, and air-conditioning ("HVAC") systems. *See Albertson's, Inc. v. Commissioner*, 1988 Tax Ct. Memo LEXIS 611, 56 T.C.M. (CCH) 928, 1988 T.C. Memo 582 (1988).

We affirm the Tax Court with respect to its judgment on the first issue (WIN credits). We reverse the Tax Court with respect to its judgment on the second issue (DCAs). We also reverse the Tax Court with respect to its judgment on the third issue (HVAC credits). We discuss each issue separately below.

* * *

B. Deferred Compensation Agreements

1. Background. Deferred compensation agreements ("DCAs") are agreements in which certain employees and independent contractors ("DCA participants") agree to wait a specified period of time ("deferral period") before receiving bonuses, salaries, or director's fees for services already rendered ("deferred compensation"). During the deferral period, the employer uses the deferred compensation as an inexpensive source of working capital. At the end of the deferral period, the employer pays the participating individuals the deferred compensation *and* an additional amount ("additional amount") for the time value of the deferred compensation.

---

[25] [1] Petitioner, a Delaware corporation, has its principal place of business in Boise, Idaho. Petitioner operates over 400 retail food and drug stores in the western, southern, and southeastern United States. Petitioner is an accrual basis taxpayer.

Prior to 1982, Albertson's entered into DCAs with eight of its top executives and one outside director. The parties agreed that they would be paid deferred compensation plus an additional amount as calculated by a predetermined formula.[26] The DCA participants would be eligible to receive the total sum (the deferred compensation plus the additional amount) upon their retirement or termination of employment with Albertson's. The DCA participants also had the option of deferring payment of the total sum for up to fifteen years thereafter. During that extra period, the additional amounts would continue to accrue on an annual basis.

In 1982, Albertson's requested permission from the IRS to deduct currently the additional amounts (but not the deferred compensation), instead of waiting until the end of the deferral period.[27] In 1983, the IRS granted Albertson's request. Accordingly, Albertson's claimed deductions of $667,142 for the additional amounts that had already accrued, even though it had not yet paid the DCA participants anything. In 1987, the IRS changed its mind, however, and sought a deficiency for those amounts. Albertson's filed a petition with the Tax Court, claiming that the additional amounts constituted "interest" and thus could be deducted as they accrued.

In a sharply divided opinion, the Tax Court rejected Albertson's position. The court found that the additional amounts were not interest, but rather compensation. Under section 404 of the Internal Revenue Code, compensation was not deductible until the end of the deferral period. Accordingly, the court prohibited Albertson's from deducting its expenses relating to the additional amounts until the end of the deferral period. *See Albertson's*, 95 T.C. at 430.[28] We

---

[26] [9] The terms of the eight executives' agreements were as follows:

3.1 The COMPANY agrees to defer payment of certain compensation earned by EMPLOYEE during each fiscal year, such deferred compensation to be paid to EMPLOYEE after EMPLOYEE'S employment is terminated. The compensation to be deferred shall be as set forth . . . below:

* * *

3.2 The COMPANY agrees to pay to EMPLOYEE a further sum of money equal to the amount of interest accrued which shall be calculated by applying a rate of interest to the total accumulated amount of deferred compensation including accrued interest compounded monthly. The rate to be used will be the weighted average of the COMPANY'S long term borrowing rate for that current fiscal year.

* * *

The outside director was paid on his additional amount at a rate equivalent to the rates for new certificates of deposit over $1,000,000 as published in the Wall Street Journal.

[27] [10] In light of the time value of money, it is clearly more advantageous for the taxpayer to take an earlier deduction. Such a deduction reduces the taxpayer's current tax obligations and accordingly allows the taxpayer to invest the assets that he would have otherwise paid to the IRS.

[28] [11] The nine-member majority held that the additional amount was not currently deductible because it was not interest. The four-member concurrence argued that the additional amount was interest, but that section 404's timing restrictions applied to *both* compensation and interest. The five-member dissent argued that the additional amount was interest and that section 404's timing restrictions applied *only* to compensation. One judge did not participate.

Oddly, one member of the court voted both in favor of the majority *and* in favor of the concurrence. This resulted in nine votes in favor of calling the additional amounts "compensation," and nine votes in favor of calling the additional amounts "interest." Because both parties agree that the former position is

reluctantly reverse the judgment of the Tax Court.

2. Discussion. This issue raises two related questions. First, we must decide whether the tax court erred in finding that the additional amounts were not "interest" within the meaning of the Code. Second, if so, we must decide whether section 404's restrictions against making deductions prior to the end of the deferral period (the "timing restrictions") applied to interest expenses. We answer the first question in the positive and the second in the negative.

a. Albertson's Additional Payments. Albertson's argues that the Tax Court erred in holding that the additional amounts were not "interest" within the definition of I.R.C. § 163. We agree. Section 163(a) allowed a deduction for "all interest paid or accrued within the taxable year on indebtedness." Although neither section 163 nor the regulations relating to it specifically defined "interest," the Supreme Court has held that interest is the measure of the value of the use of money over time. *See Dickman v. Commissioner*, 465 U.S. 330, 337 (1984). The additional amounts specified in the DCAs were a direct reflection of what Albertson's would have paid on the open market in order to borrow such amounts. *See* 2 B. BITTKER & L. LOKKEN, FEDERAL TAXATION OF INCOME, ESTATE AND GIFTS, Par. 60.2.1 (2d ed. 1990) (describing the interest component of DCAs, which "reflects the time value of money"). Accordingly, they were a fair measure of the time value of the monies loaned to Albertson's by the DCA participants, and they qualified as interest under the Code.

The Commissioner argues that the additional amounts were not interest because Albertson's never properly "borrowed" the deferred compensation from the DCA participants. According to the Commissioner, Albertson's could not have borrowed the deferred compensation because the DCA participants never had a "legal right to possess" such compensation until the end of the deferral period.[29] We disagree. As the Tax Court concurrence points out, this approach is "anachronistic." *Albertson's*, 95 T.C. at 431 (Halpern, J., concurring).[30] Circuit precedent clearly holds that a legal right to possession of the assets on which the additional amounts are earned is not necessary in order for those earnings to qualify as interest. For example, in *Starker v. United States*, 602 F.2d 1341 (9th Cir. 1979), we recognized interest that accrued in exchange for the ability to make deferred payments over a five-year period. We recognized interest in *Starker* even though the interest payee had no legal right to possess the deferred payments in full until the end of the five-year period. The controlling principle was not

---

the "majority" holding of the Tax Court, we accept their characterization throughout this section of the opinion.

[29] [13] This is because the DCA participants are on the cash method of accounting, which means that they do not include the additional amounts as income until it is paid to them at the end of the deferral period.

[30] [14] Indeed, in recent years Congress has aggressively attempted to identify many forms of "hidden" interest. *See, e.g.*, I.R.C. §§ 163(b), 467, 483, 1272, 7872. The Commissioner argues that those provisions can be distinguished in that they all seek to *prevent* tax avoidance. We reject this argument. The government cannot recognize interest when it results in more revenue, but deny it when it results in less. The Commissioner simply cannot have it both ways. Indeed, to deny an interest element in this transaction would be "to stand history on its head." *See Albertson's*, 95 T.C. at 433 n.4 (Fay, J., dissenting).

possession, but rather "compensation for the use or forbearance of money." *Id.* at 1356. We find this case indistinguishable from *Starker.* Accordingly, the Commissioner's argument fails.

The Commissioner further argues that the additional amounts were not interest, but rather additional deferred compensation. We disagree. The predetermined rate for calculating the additional amounts did not depend in any way upon the amount or type of services performed by the participants. The rate was simply a function of the time that had elapsed since the signing of the DCAs. Under the DCA, participating employees performed the same services and received the same salary as their non-participating colleagues. The only difference between the two groups was the delay in payment and the additional amount received at the end of the deferral period. Accordingly, the additional amounts were not additional compensation, and the Commissioner's argument fails.

Upon a participant's termination of employment with Albertson's, he could still elect to defer payment of the additional amount for up to fifteen years, even though he was no longer providing services to the corporation. Again, the participants were not required to perform any services in return for compensation. The additional amount was calculated at the same rate at which the interest had accrued prior to the employee's termination. Accordingly, the additional amounts were not compensation, and the Commissioner's argument fails.

The Commissioner finally argues that the additional amounts were not interest because they were not payments for true "indebtedness" by Albertson's. *See* I.R.C. § 163(a) (allowing interest only on payments for "indebtedness"). We disagree. The Tax Court has held that indebtedness is an "unconditional legally enforceable obligation for the payment of money." *Horn v. Commissioner,* 90 T.C. 908, 923 (1988). In this case, the DCAs were bona fide, non-forfeitable contracts, and Albertson's was unconditionally and legally obligated to pay the DCA participants for deferring their compensation upon the rendering of their services. Accordingly, the additional amounts were payment for indebtedness, and the Commissioner's argument fails.

b. Section 404 and Interest Expenses. Having held that the additional amounts are interest within the meaning of section 163, we now turn to the question whether the timing restrictions of section 404 applied to interest expenses — in other words, did section 404 prohibit Albertson's from deducting such expenses prior to the time the participants were required to recognize the additional amounts as income? Based on a plain-language reading of the statute in effect during the taxable year at issue, we conclude that the answer is no — the timing restrictions did *not* apply to interest expenses. Albertson's was therefore free to deduct such expenses as they accrued. Accordingly, we reverse the judgment of the Tax Court.

Prior to 1942, corporations were allowed to deduct DCA-related expenses as they accrued each year, even though employees did not recognize any income until a subsequent taxable year. In 1942, Congress abolished this preferential treatment for certain deductions relating to "unqualified" DCAs such as the ones at issue in this case.[31] In so doing, Congress forced employers to wait until the *end* of the deferral period before they could deduct expenses relating to their unqualified DCAs. *See* I.R.C. §§ 404(a)(5) & 404(d) (1983).[32] This is because section 404 of the Code prohibited an employer from deducting certain expenses until they were includible in the income of the DCA participants, which was usually not until the end of the deferral period.[33] *See id.*

In the taxable year at issue, the Code and regulations specified two categories of deductions to which the timing restrictions of section 404 applied. First, section 404 applied to section 162 deductions, *see* I.R.C. § 162, which included "all the ordinary and necessary expenses paid or incurred during the taxable year in carrying on any trade or business." *See* I.R.C. § 404(a)(5) (1983). Second, section 404 applied to section 212 deductions, *see* I.R.C. § 212, which included "all the ordinary and necessary expenses paid or incurred during the taxable year for the production or collection of income." *See id.*; *see generally* Treas. Reg. § 1.404(a)-1(b) (1983).[34]

The interest accrued under the DCAs in this case did not fall within either of the above categories. Interest deductions, which included "all interest paid or accrued within the taxable year on indebtedness," were covered by section 163 of the Code. *See* I.R.C. § 163. They were not subject to either section 162 or section 212. *Compare* I.R.C. § 163 (pertaining to interest) *with* I.R.C. §§ 162 & 212 (not pertaining to interest). Because we must not "add to or alter the words employed

---

[31] [17] Unqualified plans are those that, among other things, discriminate in favor of highly compensated employees. *See* I.R.C. § 401(a)(4). Albertson's concedes that the DCAs at issue in this case are not qualified plans.

[32] [18] The relevant provisions, at the time Albertson's filed its 1983 tax return, were as follows:

Sec. 404. Deduction for . . . compensation under a deferred-payment plan.

(a) General rule. — . . . If compensation is paid or accrued on account of any employee under a plan deferring the receipt of such compensation, such . . . compensation shall not be deductible under section 162 (relating to trade or business expenses) or section 212 (relating to expenses for the production of income); but if they satisfy the conditions of either of such sections, they shall be deductible . . .

(5) . . . in the taxable year in which an amount attributable to the contribution is includible in the gross income of employees participating in the plan. . . .

(d) Deductibility of payments of deferred compensation, etc., to independent contractors. — If a plan would be described [as above] . . . [the] compensation —

(1) shall not be deductible by the payor thereof under section 162 or 212, but

(2) shall . . . be deductible under this subsection for the taxable year in which an amount attributable to the . . . compensation is includible in the gross income of the persons participating in the plan.

Id.

[33] [19] Most individuals are on the cash accounting system and thus would not include the income from their DCAs until it is paid to them in full.

[34] [20] The relevant provisions were as follows:

(b) In order to be deductible under section 404(a), contributions must be expenses which would be deductible under section 162 (relating to trade or business expenses) or 212 (relating to expenses for production of income) if it were not for the provision in section 404(a) that they are deductible, if at all, only under section 404(a). Contributions may therefore be deducted under section 404(a) *only* to the extent that they are ordinary and necessary expenses [incurred] during the taxable year in carrying on the trade or business or for the production of income and are compensation for personal services actually rendered.

Id.

to effect a purpose which does not appear on the face of the statute," *Hanover Bank v. Commissioner*, 369 U.S. 672, 687 (1962), we hold that, in the taxable year at issue, the timing restrictions of section 404 were inapplicable to interest deductions.

The legislative history of section 404 lends support to our conclusion. There is absolutely no indication that Congress intended section 404 to apply to interest deductions. Section 404 was codified in its present form in 1954. At that time, Congress was fully aware of the differences between the predecessors to sections 162 (trade or business expenses), 163 (interest), and 212 (production of income expenses) of the Code. *See, e.g.*, H.R. Rep. No. 1337, 83d Cong., 2d Sess., *reprinted in* 1954 U.S.C.C.A.N. 4017, 4181 (discussing the relationship between the predecessors to sections 162, 163, and 212). If Congress had intended section 404 to govern the timing of interest deductions, it could have made specific reference to the predecessor of section 163 as well. *See, e.g.*, I.R.C. § 267 (1983) (explicitly referring to section 163 as well as sections 162 and 212). To the contrary, the legislative history of section 404 mentions only "compensation." *See, e.g.*, S. Rep. No. 1631, 77th Cong., 2d Sess. (1942), *reprinted in* 1942-2 Com. Bull. at 504, 607–09. Accordingly, there is no indication in the legislative history of section 404 that Congress intended it to apply to interest.

The Commissioner argues that a 1986 "clarifying" amendment to section 404, which eliminated the references to sections 162 and 212 in order to make clear the broad scope of the statute, evidenced Congressional intent, *ab initio*, to include interest under that section. We reject this argument. According to the legislative history of the 1986 amendment, it is true that Congress intended to clarify section 404 to include all forms of *compensation* for services rendered. However, there is insufficient indication that Congress intended to include anything *other* than *compensation*. *See, e.g.*, S. Rep. No. 313, 99th Cong., 2d Sess. 1, 1013 (1986) (referring repeatedly to compensation). n21 As we have noted, for DCA purposes, "compensation" and "interest" are two very different concepts. Accordingly, we reject the Commissioner's argument that the 1986 amendment evidenced an intent by Congress to include interest expenses under the timing restrictions of section 404.

The relevant provisions are as follows:

b. Clarification of the scope of the deduction-timing rules applicable to *deferred compensation* arrangements. . . .

Explanation of Provision

The bill clarifies that the deduction-timing rules for *deferred compensation* arrangements apply to any plan or method of deferring *compensation* regardless of the section under which the amounts might otherwise be deductible and that the amount shall be deductible under section 404(a)(5) and shall not otherwise be deductible under any other section. This clarification is necessary to prevent taxpayers from asserting that *deferred compensation* is attributable to capitalizable compensation expenses [*e.g.*, under section 263A enacted in 1986] and, thereby, accelerate the timing of the deduction for such *deferred compensation*.

Id. (emphasis added).

Finally, the Commissioner argues that, notwithstanding the plain language of the statute, Congress must have intended to include interest expenses within the scope of section 404 because Congress enacted timing restrictions with respect to compensation expenses. We do not agree that simply because Congress determined to treat compensation in a particular manner it necessarily intended to treat interest in that same manner. Congress' decisions with respect to tax policy do not always fit a neat and logical pattern. Sometimes they are even influenced by less-than-objective forces. Still, we sympathize with the Commissioner's "policy" arguments regarding Congress' intent. It is quite possible that, had Congress considered this problem in 1942 and 1986, it would have modified the wording of section 404 to cover deductions for interest as well as for compensation. Permitting the deduction of interest may simply have resulted from a glitch in the Code. Even if that is the case, however, Code changes are for Congress to make — not the courts.

In sum, we hold that the timing restrictions of section 404 do not apply to expenses relating to interest that is paid pursuant to a DCA. Accordingly, Albertson's may properly deduct such expenses as they accrue, and we reverse the Tax Court on this issue.

* * *

———

Following its decision in *Albertson's I*, the Ninth Circuit was deluged with response from the IRS and numerous tax commentators. Most of these argued that the court's decision, by allowing a "nonqualified" arrangement to achieve the same results (current deduction to the employer and deferred income to the employee) as a qualified plan, would effectively undo the policy of the entire pension provisions. Why, these commentators asked, would anyone bother to follow the nondiscrimination and other rules pertaining to qualified plans, when with a quick sleight of hand it could achieve the same results, anyway? Under a barrage of such pressure, the Ninth Circuit made a rare decision to rehear the same case a few months later. An excerpt from its second and final opinion follows.

ALBERTSON'S, INC. v. COMMISSIONER (ALBERTSON'S II)
United States Court of Appeals, Ninth Circuit
42 F.3d 537 (1994)

REINHARDT, J:

On December 30, 1993, we filed an opinion concerning various disputes between Albertson's and the Internal Revenue Service. 12 F.3d 539 (9th Cir. 1993). We granted the government's petition for rehearing as to Part II.B of the opinion, which concerned the appropriate tax treatment of deferred compensation agreements. Today we vacate Part II.B of the original opinion and affirm the Tax Court's decision.

I. *BACKGROUND*

Deferred compensation agreements ("DCAs") are agreements in which certain employees and independent contractors ("DCA participants") agree to wait a specified period of time ("deferral period") before receiving the annual bonuses, salaries, or director's fees that they would otherwise receive on a current basis. During the deferral period, the employer uses the basic amounts of deferred compensation ("basic amounts"), which accumulate on an annual basis, as a source of working capital. At the end of the deferral period, the employer pays the participating individuals the basic amounts and an additional amount for the time value of the deferred payments that have accumulated on the basic amounts ("additional amount"). The time-value-of-money sums are also computed on a yearly basis. The total of these basic amounts and the amounts attributable to compensation for the delay in payment of those amounts constitutes the whole of the deferred compensation ("deferred compensation"). The time-value-of-money component may be measured by interest rate indices, equity fund indices, or cost of living increases, or it may simply be included within a lump-sum payment.

Prior to 1982, Albertson's entered into DCAs with eight of its top executives and one outside director. The parties agreed that their deferred compensation would include the annual basic amounts plus additional amounts calculated annually in accordance with an established formula. *Albertson's, Inc. v. Commissioner*, 12 F.3d 1529, 1534 (9th Cir. 1993). The DCA participants would be eligible to receive the deferred compensation (the total sum) upon their retirement or termination of employment with Albertson's. The DCA participants also had the option of further deferring payment for up to fifteen years thereafter. During that extra period, the additional amounts would continue to accrue on an annual basis. *Id.* at 1535.

In 1982, Albertson's requested permission from the IRS to deduct the additional amounts (but not the basic amounts) during the year in which they accrued instead of waiting until the end of the deferral period. *Id.* In 1983, the IRS granted Albertson's request. Accordingly, Albertson's claimed deductions of $667,142 for the additional amounts that had already accrued, even though it had not yet paid the DCA participants any sums under the deferred compensation agreements. *Id.* In 1987, the IRS changed its policy, however, and sought a deficiency for the additional amounts, contending that all amounts provided for in the deferred compensation agreements were deductible only when received by Albertson's employees. Albertson's filed a petition with the Tax Court, claiming that the additional amounts constituted "interest" and thus could be deducted as they accrued. *Id.*

In a sharply divided opinion, the Tax Court rejected Albertson's position. *Albertson's, Inc. v. Commissioner*, 95 T.C. 415 (1990). The court found that the additional amounts represented compensation, not interest, and were therefore not deductible until the end of the deferral period under I.R.C. § 404(a)(5) & (d).

We reversed the decision of the Tax Court. *Albertson's, Inc. v. Commissioner*, 12 F.3d 1529 (9th Cir. 1993). We held that the additional amounts constituted interest within the definition of I.R.C. § 163(a) and that interest payments were not governed by the timing restrictions of section 404. The government petitioned for rehearing due to the significant fiscal impact of the panel's opinion which it estimates will cause a $7 billion loss in tax revenues.

II. *REHEARING*

We agreed to rehear this issue after lengthy consideration and reflection. In our original opinion, we stated that the plain language of the statute strongly supported Albertson's interpretation and, accordingly, we adopted it. Nevertheless, we expressed sympathy for the Commissioner's argument that Congress intended the timing restrictions of I.R.C. § 404 to apply to all payments made under a deferred compensation plan and recognized that our plain language interpretation seemed to undercut Congress' purpose.

We have now changed our minds about the result we reached in our original opinion and conclude that our initial decision was incorrect. The question is not an easy one, however. We have struggled with it unsuccessfully at least once, and it may, indeed, ultimately turn out that the United States Supreme Court will tell us that it is this opinion which is in error. This is simply one of those cases — and there are more of them than judges generally like to admit — in which the answer is far from clear and in which there are conflicting rules and principles that we are forced to try to apply simultaneously. Such accommodation sometimes proves to be impossible. In some cases, as here, convincing arguments can be made for both possible results, and the court's decision will depend on which of the two competing legal principles it chooses to give greater weight to in the particular circumstance. Law, even statutory construction, is not a science. It is merely an effort by human beings, albeit judges, to do their best with imperfect tools to arrive at a correct result.

There is a question whether, having once decided a case, we should change our decision when we are not entirely certain that the result we reached is wrong. One response is that, if the issue could be resolved with that degree of certainty, it is unlikely that we would have decided the case incorrectly the first time. Moreover, if certainty were the standard, we would probably never reverse ourselves. There is actually no clear set of rules that tells us when a case warrants our changing our decision on rehearing. We start with the premise that doing so is not generally desirable, and that it runs contrary to the sense of stability and finality that the law seeks to foster. We also know that it is often better to have a definitive answer, whatever it is, than to have continuing reexaminations or self-questioning.

On the other hand, we judges do not just bury our mistakes. We display them publicly in the Federal Reporters and, while we may then as individuals move on to more decision-making, the opinions we have published continue to haunt indefinitely not just the parties, but often numerous other persons whose affairs and fortunes will be governed by them. Because all of us make hundreds of difficult decisions a year involving complex legal questions, we know that we will make a certain number of errors. All that we can do is to try our best to hold them to a minimum. At the same time, if a rehearing is requested and we have a strong sense that we may have erred in the particular case, we should not hesitate to undertake a reexamination of the issue. This is particularly so when significant individual rights or interests are at stake or when a number of parties may be seriously affected by a decision that may be erroneous. Given all of this, our conclusion is that, while we should not ordinarily abandon the decisions we have just reached following full deliberation, we must be willing to take that unusual step — at least in cases of some significance — when ultimately we are fairly persuaded that our decision is in error. This is such a case.

In its petition for rehearing, the government, far more forcefully and clearly than it did originally, has articulated the purpose of the timing restrictions outlined in I.R.C. § 404: to encourage employers to invest in qualified compensation plans by requiring inclusions and deductions of income and expense to be "matched" for nonqualified plans. The matching principle, widely recognized to be the key to I.R.C. § 404, provides significant tax incentives for employers to invest in *qualified* deferred compensation plans, which are nondiscriminatory and ensure that employees receive the compensation promised to them. *See* 2 Boris I. Bittker & Lawrence Lokken, Federal Taxation of Income, Estates & Gifts Par. 60.1 (2d ed. 1990) (noting that the "matching principle" is "the most consistent feature of the rules for nonqualified plans."). As the Commissioner forcefully argues, our original interpretation of I.R.C. § 404 undercut the essential purpose of that provision by violating the matching principle and creating a taxation scheme that favors the type of plan that Congress intended to discourage. For this reason, we granted the Commissioner's petition for rehearing. We now withdraw the portion of our earlier opinion that dealt with deferred compensation agreements, published at 12 F.3d at 1534–1539, and affirm the Tax Court's decision, although not for the reasons upon which the Tax Court majority relied.

III. *ANALYSIS*

Albertson's again urges this court (1) to characterize the additional amounts as interest as defined by I.R.C. § 163(a), and (2) to find that such "interest" payments are deductible under I.R.C. § 404. However, we have now concluded that, notwithstanding the statutory language on which Albertson's relies, to hold the additional amounts to be deductible would contravene the clear purpose of the taxation scheme Congress created to govern deferred compensation plans. As the Supreme Court noted in *Bob Jones University v. United States*, 461 U.S. 574 (1983), a term in the Code "*must* be analyzed and construed within the framework of the Internal Revenue Code and against the background of the congressional purposes." *Id.* at 586 (emphasis added).

(a) GENERAL RULE. — There shall be allowed as a deduction all interest paid or accrued within the taxable year on indebtedness.

An examination of the differences between qualified and nonqualified plans is essential to an understanding of the purpose of the congressional scheme governing deferred compensation agreements. Congress has imposed few restrictions upon nonqualified deferred compensation plans. An employer may limit participation in a nonqualified plan to highly paid executives, and it need not guarantee equal benefits for all participants. In addition, the employer is not required to set aside any funds or provide any guarantees (beyond the initial contractual promise) that its employees will receive the compensation. Thus, promised benefits for unfunded, nonqualified plans are subject to the claims of the employer's general creditors.

Under a qualified plan, in contrast, an employer may not discriminate in favor of officers, shareholders, or highly compensated employees. I.R.C. § 401(a)(4) & (a)(5). In addition, a qualified plan must satisfy minimum participation and coverage standards concerning eligibility and actual rates of participation. I.R.C §§ 401(a)(2) & (a)(26), 410. The amounts which an employer may contribute to qualified plans and the benefits which qualified plans may provide are also restricted. I.R.C. §§ 401(a)(17), 415.

A qualified plan also provides significant guarantees that employees will receive the compensation promised to them. It generally must be funded through a trust. I.R.C. § 401(a). Neither the corpus nor the income of the trust may be diverted for any purpose; they can only be used for the exclusive benefit of the participants. I.R.C. § 401(a)(2). Under certain qualified plans, the employer's contributions must meet strict funding requirements, and minimum standards govern the vesting of participants' benefits. I.R.C. §§ 401(a)(1) & (a)(7), 411, 412; see also 29 U.S.C. § 1082.

It is clear that few employers would adopt a qualified deferred compensation plan, with all of its burdensome requirements, if the taxation scheme favored nonqualified plans or treated nonqualified and qualified plans similarly. Although qualified plans provide significant benefits to employees, they allow employers little flexibility in structuring a plan, require them to provide extensive coverage, prevent them from discriminating in favor of highly compensated employees, and involve a significant initial outlay of funds. Thus, the extensive regulations Congress has imposed upon qualified plans would serve little purpose unless employers had an incentive to adopt such plans. As we discuss in the next part, section 404 provides the incentive necessary to encourage employers to adopt qualified plans by providing significantly more favorable tax treatment of qualified plans than of nonqualified ones.

The most significant difference between the two types of plans, for purposes of tax deductibility, is that under a qualified plan the employer must turn over annually to a third party the basic amounts that are deferred and may not use those amounts for the employer's own benefit. Thus, the employer, in effect, is required to make the deferred payments at the time the employee is earning the compensation. It is only the employee's right to receive the funds that is delayed. In contrast, an employer with a nonqualified plan is not required to turn any funds over to anyone until the end of the deferred compensation period. Such an employer may use those funds for its own purposes for a period of many years. In a nonqualified plan, it is not only the employee's right to receive the funds that is deferred; the employer's obligation to part with the funds is deferred as well. If one could simply retain the funds and receive tax benefits similar to those one would receive if those amounts were paid out, there would clearly be little incentive to establish a qualified plan.

B. *The Purpose of Section 404*

Congress enacted section 23(p), the forerunner to section 404, in 1942. Prior to 1942, corporations were allowed to deduct DCA-related expenses as they accrued each year, even though employees did not recognize any income until a subsequent taxable year. In 1942, Congress eliminated this favorable treatment for deductions relating to "nonqualified" deferred compensation agreements, such as the DCAs at issue in this case.[35] In so doing, Congress forced employers who chose to retain their funds for their own use to wait until the *end* of the deferral period, when these amounts were includible in plan participants' taxable income, before they could take deductions for deferred compensation payments. However, employers who maintained a "qualified" plan that met the rigorous requirements of the Internal Revenue Code (and now ERISA), including turning over the sums involved to a trust fund (or purchasing an annuity), were allowed to continue to take the annual deductions even though their employees would not receive the deferred compensation until a later year. *See, e.g.,* I.R.C. §§ 404(a) & (d); 29 U.S.C. § 1082 (1988).

1. *The Matching Principle*

Congress provided a single explanation for the timing restrictions of section 404: to ensure matching of income inclusion and deduction between employee and employer under nonqualified plans. As both the House and Senate Reports note, "if an employer on the accrual basis defers paying any compensation to the employee until a later year or years . . . he will not be allowed a deduction until the year in which the compensation is paid." H.R. Rep. No. 2333, 77th Cong., 2d Sess. (1942), 1942-2 Cum. Bull. 372, 452; S. Rep. No. 1631, 77th Cong., 2d Sess. (1942), 1942-2 Cum. Bull. 504, 609.

Commentators have widely agreed that this "matching principle" is the key to section 404. As Boris Bittker and Lawrence Lokken have observed, "the most consistent feature for the rules for nonqualified plans is that the employer is ordinarily allowed no deduction for contribution, payments or benefits until they are taxed to the employee." 2 BORIS I. BITTKER & LAWRENCE LOKKEN, FEDERAL TAXATION OF INCOME, ESTATES & GIFTS Par. 60.1 (2d ed. 1990). Similarly, Daniel Halperin has noted that, in the case of deferred payment of compensation under nonqualified plans, Congress has imposed "a matching requirement, which denies an employer's deduction until the deferred amount is included in the employee's income." Daniel I. Halperin, *Interest in Disguise: Taxing the "Time Value of Money"*, 95 YALE L.J. 506, 520 (1986) (discussing section 404). David Davenport also cites section 404 as the primary proof that "current law follows a matching principle and defers the employer's deduction until the year of payment." David S. Davenport, *Education & Human Capital: Pursuing an Ideal Income Tax and a Sensible Tax Policy* 42 CASE W. RES. L. REV. 793, 865 (1992); *see also* MERTEN'S LAW OF FEDERAL INCOME TAXATION, Comm. § 404 (1990 & 1994 Supp.); Joseph L. Cummings, Jr., *The Silent Policies of*

---

[35] [6] The relevant provision is as follows:

§ 23 Deductions from gross income

* * *

(p) Contributions of an employer to an employees' trust or annuity plan and compensation under a deferred-payment plan.

(1) General Rule.

If . . . compensation is paid or accrued on account of any employee under a plan deferring the receipt of such compensation, such . . . compensation shall not be deductible under subsection (a) [business expenses] but shall be deductible, if deductible under subsection (1) without regard to this subsection, under this subsection.

I.R.C. § 23 (1942).

Conservation and Cloning of Tax Basis and Their Corporate Application, 48 TAX L. REV. 113, 162 n.245 (1992) (noting that the matching principle governs section 404); Noel B. Cunningham, *A Theoretical Analysis of the Tax Treatment of Future Costs*, 40 TAX L. REV. 577, 610 (1985) (same) Mark P. Gergen, *Reforming Subchapter K: Compensating Service Partnerships*, 48 TAX L. REV. 69, 97 n.91 (1992) (same).

2. *The Significance of the Matching Principle*

The significance of section 404's matching principle becomes evident when one compares the treatment of qualified and nonqualified plans under that section. Because section 404 requires employer deductions for contributions to nonqualified plans to be "matched," an employer cannot take tax deductions for payments to its employees until the DCA participants include those payments in their taxable income — that is, until the employees actually receive the compensation promised to them.

Qualified plans, in contrast, are *not* governed by the matching principle and consequently generate concurrent tax benefits to employers. Although employees are not taxed upon the benefits they receive from the plan until they actually receive them, an employer's contributions to a qualified plan are deductible when paid to the trust. I.R.C. §§ 402(a)(1) & 404(a). Thus, the employer may take an *immediate, unmatched* deduction for any contribution it makes to a qualified plan.[36]

By exempting contributions to qualified plans from the matching principle, Congress compensates employers for meeting the burdensome requirements associated with qualified plans by granting them favorable tax treatment. The current taxation scheme thus creates financial incentives for employers to contribute to qualified plans while providing no comparable benefits for employers who adopt plans that are unfunded or that discriminate in favor of highly compensated employees.

C. *The Effects of Albertson's Proposal*

Albertson's maintains that section 404 only requires that the basic amounts of compensation be matched; it argues that all additional amounts paid to compensate an employee for the time value of money represent "interest" payments for which an employer may take an immediate deduction. In light of the clear purpose underlying section 404 — to encourage employers to create qualified plans for their employees — we decline to ascribe such an intention to Congress.

First, Albertson's proposal appears to undermine the effectiveness of the timing restrictions by reducing the significance of the incentive structure created by section 404. In order to adopt Albertson's proposal and allow employers to take current deductions for additional "interest" payments, we would be required to conclude that Congress created a system in which employers could deduct a substantial portion of the nonqualified deferred compensation package long before its employees had received any of those funds. For example, when the additional

---

[36] [7] In addition, the earnings of a trust established by a qualified plan are not taxable to the trust. I.R.C. §§ 401(a) & 501(a).

amounts are calculated for a compensation package deferred over a fifteen-year period using an interest rate similar to that used by Albertson's, an employer can classify more than seventy percent of the deferred compensation package as "interest payments."[37] If the additional amounts were calculated at an eight percent interest rate, compounded annually, almost fifty percent of the compensation package could be characterized as "interest" under Albertson's approach. Even under a deferred compensation package with an interest rate one-third as high as Albertson's, one third of the amount paid to the employee at the end of a fifteen-year period would consist of "interest." Moreover, we note that, under Albertson's deferred compensation agreement, participants have the option of deferring payment of the total sum available to them upon retirement for an additional period of up to fifteen years. *All* payments during that additional period would also constitute "interest," and the deductible portion of the final compensation package would thus increase exponentially.

Albertson's has been unable to explain why Congress, in designing a taxation scheme to encourage the creation of qualified plans, would require an employer that maintains a nonqualified plan to defer taking a deduction on the basic amounts of a promised compensation package but nevertheless allow that employer to take current deductions on amounts that constitute a substantial portion of the compensation package, merely because that portion is classified as "interest." Given that the interest payments will often constitute the bulk of the total compensation package that an employee under a nonqualified plan ultimately receives, it would make little sense to impose a matching requirement upon "basic" payments but not upon "interest" payments. Albertson's interpretation of section 404 would seriously undermine the incentive structure designed by Congress to encourage employers to establish qualified plans.

An additional reason to reject Albertson's statutory interpretation of section 404 is that, in certain cases, Albertson's approach might actually create an incentive for employers to establish *nonqualified* plans. Whereas an employer who maintains a qualified plan may only take a current deduction for the basic amounts of promised compensation, an amount it actually has paid out, under Albertson's approach an employer that maintains a nonqualified plan could take current deductions for "interest" payments that substantially exceed the basic amounts even though it has paid out none of these funds. Moreover, the employer could take advantage of these tax benefits without being constrained by the burdensome requirements associated with qualified plans. For this reason, characterizing the additional amounts as deductible interest, as Albertson's suggest, would encourage employers to maintain nonqualified plans and thus directly contradict the statutory purpose underlying I.R.C. § 404.[38]

---

[37] [8] According to the record, it appears that Albertson's employees were compensated at a 14.8% interest rate, compounded monthly.

[38] [9] We also note the government's argument concerning the possible consequences of a finding in favor of Albertson's. According to the Commissioner, under a long-standing administrative practice, employees are currently not taxed upon the benefits they receive from deferred compensation plans until they actually receive them, precisely because employers have not taken deductions for those amounts. Because section 404 only exempts payments under qualified plans from the matching principle, were we to uphold Albertson's approach, the Commissioner suggests that we would be required to conclude that

Thus, Albertson's proposal runs counter to the congressional scheme. It undermines Congress' attempts to encourage employers to adopt qualified plans and, in some cases, directly contradicts the purpose of section 404 by creating an incentive to create nonqualified plans.

D. *Albertson's Response*

Albertson's has not been able to refute the argument that its interpretation of section 404 undercuts the provision's central purpose. Equally important, it offers us no reason why Congress would have wanted to treat the "interest" part of the deferred compensation package differently from the basic amounts for tax purposes.

Instead, Albertson's rests its argument upon its contention that, because the plain language of § 404 only refers to "compensation" rather than "interest," the employers have a statutory right to deduct the additional amounts as interest under § 163. In this connection, Albertson's points out that section 404 prohibits deduction under sections 162 and 212 but not under section 163, and it is the latter section that governs the deduction of interest. Albertson's argument as to the plain language of the statute is a strong one. We certainly agree that the additional payments resemble "interest" and that, under a literal reading of the statutory language, the deduction of interest is not affected by section 404. However, holding such payments to be deductible "interest" under section 404 would lead to an anomalous result: a taxation scheme designed to make nonqualified plans less attractive would in many cases provide incentives for adopting such plans, and a provision intended to apply the matching principle to nonqualified deferred compensation agreements would exempt substantial portions of DCA payments from its application.

In the end we are forced, therefore, to reject Albertson's approach. We may not adopt a plain language interpretation of a statutory provision that directly undercuts the clear purpose of the statute. In *Brooks v. Donovan*, 699 F.2d 1010 (9th Cir. 1983), we refused to adopt a plain language interpretation of a statute governing pension funds. We reasoned that the "court must look beyond the express language of a statute where a literal interpretation 'would thwart the purpose of the overall statutory scheme or lead to an absurd or futile result.'" *Brooks*, 699 F.2d at 1011 (quoting *International Tel. & Tel. Corp. v. General Tel. & Elec. Corp.*, 518 F.2d 913, 917–918 (9th Cir. 1975)). In reaching our conclusion, we followed the Supreme Court's approach in *United States v. American Trucking Ass'ns.*, 310 U.S. 534 (1940). There the Court noted that "when [a given] meaning has led to absurd results . . . this Court has looked beyond the words to the purpose of the act. Frequently, however, *even when the plain meaning did not produce absurd results but merely an unreasonable one 'plainly at variance with the policy of the legislation as a whole,' this Court has followed that purpose, rather than the literal*

---

employer deductions for interest accruing under nonqualified plans must be "matched" by the inclusion of those amounts in employees' current taxable income. As is clear from the foregoing discussion, such an unrealized addition to the employees' income for tax purposes would indeed be substantial and, as far as the employees are concerned, harshly inequitable. We express no opinion about the merits of the government's argument.

words." American Trucking Ass'ns., 310 U.S. at 543 (emphasis added; citations omitted).

The Supreme Court's decision in *Bob Jones University v. United States*, 461 U.S. 574 (1983), provides especially useful guidance in this regard. In *Bob Jones University*, the Supreme Court addressed the question of whether I.R.C. § 501(c)(3) — which provides that "corporations . . . organized and operated exclusively for religious, charitable . . . or educational purposes" are entitled to tax exemption — included educational institutions with racially discriminatory policies. Even though Congress had explicitly outlined eight categories of exempt organizations in section 501(c)(3) without making any mention of additional requirements beyond those outlined in the statute, the Supreme Court interpreted the statute to include an additional requirement: the organization in question must serve a valid charitable purpose. *Bob Jones University*, 461 U.S. at 592 n.19. Thus, the Court was willing to read additional language into the text of the statute because an alternative interpretation would undermine the fundamental purpose of the legislation. As the Court itself noted, "it is a well-established canon of statutory construction that a court should go beyond the literal language of a statute if reliance on that language would defeat the plain purpose of the statute." *Id.* at 586.

In rejecting Albertson's appeal, we take heed of the Supreme Court's instructions concerning the proper interpretation of the Internal Revenue Code when the plain language of the provision leads to an unreasonable result and directly contradicts its underlying purpose: the provision "*must* be analyzed and construed within the framework of the Internal Revenue Code and against the background of the congressional purposes." *Id.* (emphasis added). For the reasons we have expressed, we conclude that, despite the literal wording of the statute, Congress could not have intended to exclude interest payments, a substantial part of the deferred compensation package, from the rule prohibiting deductions until such time as the employee receives the benefits. Indeed, the matching principle would not be much of a principle if so substantial a part of the deferred compensation package were excluded from its operation.

IV. *CONCLUSION*

In sum, we decline to adopt Albertson's interpretation of I.R.C. § 404. Whether or not the additional amounts constitute interest, allowing Albertson's to deduct them prior to their receipt by their employees would contravene the clear purpose of the taxation scheme governing deferred compensation agreements. Accordingly, we vacate the portion of our original opinion dealing with deferred compensation agreements and affirm the Tax Court's holding that Albertson's may not currently deduct the additional amounts.

AFFIRMED

Understanding *Albertson's*

1. *Albertson's* involved the interplay of the qualified pension plan rules (specifically, section 404) with the rule allowing deduction of interest payments under section 163. The taxpayer argued that the plain language of section 163 permitted

deduction of the "additional sums" contributed to the deferred compensation arrangements. The Government argued that the sums were not appropriately considered interest and, even if they were, that deduction of these so-called interest payments was inconsistent with the policy of section 404 and related provisions. The Government's position had a particular urgency since, if other taxpayers could do what Albertson's did, they could achieve the advantageous treatment reserved for qualified plans without following the nondiscrimination or other rules pertaining to such plans.

As a question of statutory interpretation, which side had the better argument? Was Albertson's right that the "plain meaning" of the statute supported its interpretation? By contrast, how strong was the Government's argument based on the "purpose" or "policy" of the qualified pension plan rules? Is it so clear what the policy was, and if it was so obvious, why didn't the statute say so explicitly? Generally speaking, should a court ignore the plain meaning of a statute to reach a result consistent with its reading of the underlying legislative intent? Should this be more or less acceptable in tax, as opposed to (say) environmental or antitrust cases? Does anything in tax ever really have a plain meaning, anyway?

2. What do you think of the (successful) effort by professors and other experts to get the Court of Appeals to change its mind in *Albertson's*? Do professors have any real advantage over ordinary practitioners in interpreting laws of this kind? Should a law firm need to have a professor on staff in order to understand the meaning of the tax laws? How much would you have to pay to get one?

3. *Albertson's* involved an attempted "end run" around the nondiscrimination rules, in which a few highly paid executives would get tax-advantaged retirement benefits not available to other employees. Are you troubled by this possibility? Is it really any worse than stock options, section 83 stock, or just plain high salaries being paid to privileged employees? Why is the nondiscrimination principle so important in the pension area, and why do you think so many experts were mobilized to protect it?

4. How would you have decided the *Albertson's* case?

In recent years there have been numerous proposals to liberalize the pension and other retirement tax provisions, ranging from incremental proposals, like expansion of Individual Retirement Accounts (IRAs) or deferred salary arrangements (section 401(k)), to proposals for comprehensive overhaul of the entire retirement system. In part, these proposals result from a sense that Social Security and other Government assistance — even together with employer-provided plans, for those who have them — may be inadequate to provide long-term retirement security. This issue is compounded by demographic changes, including the extraordinary number of people who now live twenty-five years or longer after retiring, and by changes in life patterns, including the large number of divorced people (especially women) who may not have adequate retirement funding under their own or their ex-spouses' plans. There is also a strong political cast to the issue, with many conservatives believing that people should make their own retirement choices and not be dependent on the Government for their financial needs, and many liberals regarding this as a thinly veiled excuse for cutting back on workers' protection. Some, including former President Bush, have suggested that Social Security be "priv atized," in whole or part, by allowing individuals to invest a portion of their social security in private retirement accounts. Although it is not purely a tax issue, the Social Security problem demonstrates the interaction of tax policy with retirement security, health, and other public policy matters, and the difficulty of separating taxation from one's broader political views.

What do you think of the proposals to "privatize" all or a portion of Social Security, and can tax incentives take the place of some, or all, direct government spending in this area?

D.   Deferral, Tax Policy, and the Consumption Tax

When one studies any subject for the first time, there is a tendency to think that the rules are inevitable, that they couldn't possibly be any other way. One way to correct this is to take a "time out" at important junctures and consider significant tax reform proposals. (This also has the advantage of preparing you if the law changes a few years down the road, and your expensive textbook is suddenly an elegant doorstop.)

One major reform proposal involves the substitution of a consumption or cash-flow levy for the existing income tax. Although it sounds like an enormous change, a consumption tax is really just an extension of the pension/IRA concept to a more general exclusion of savings from the income tax base. Thus, under the income tax, a person who earns $50,000 and puts $10,000 in the bank is taxed on all $50,000, with limited exceptions for pensions and similar programs. (The money in the bank is also taxed a second time when it earns interest, the dreaded "double tax" on savings under the existing tax system.)

By contrast, under one form of a consumption tax, the taxpayer would receive a deduction for the full $10,000 in savings, and accordingly pay tax only on the remaining $40,000 that was available to be consumed (i.e., spent) in the year it was earned. What is more, the savings could earn tax-free interest, so long as it remained in the bank; the original $10,000, plus interest, would be taxed only when it was withdrawn from the bank and became available for individual spending purposes. A consumption tax thus resembles an income tax with a huge IRA or an unlimited, do-it-yourself pension plan, but without the various limitations that exist on these programs under present law.[39]

The major argument for a consumption tax is economic efficiency, together with the notion — perhaps just slightly paternalistic — that it would encourage saving and investment activity. The key objection involves fairness and, especially, vertical equity concerns. Put simply, most poor people do not save a lot of money, since they require a higher percentage of their income in order to meet day-to-day needs. This means that they would tend to derive less benefit from a consumption tax than

---

[39] A consumption tax may also be described arithmetically, starting with the Haig-Simons definition of income. According to Haig and Simons, income equals consumption (i.e., spending) plus accumulation (i.e., savings and investment) — the famous "I C + A" of tax policy lore. A consumption tax would tax the "C" but not the "A" component of this equation, deferring tax on the latter until it was withdrawn for consumption purposes. See generally HENRY C. SIMONS, PERSONAL INCOME TAXATION: THE DEFINITION OF INCOME AS A PROBLEM OF FISCAL POLICY (1938).

their wealthier fellow citizens. This concern, together with sheer inertia, has so far prevented the consumption tax from wholly displacing the income tax system. Yet there are already so many consumption tax elements contained in the existing income tax — pension plans, IRAs, even (arguably) the realization requirement — that it is probably more accurate to speak of present law as a hybrid income-and-consumption tax system than as a pure income tax.

Based on what you have observed in this chapter, does a consumption tax strike you as a good idea, or another excuse to reduce taxes on wealthy people? How could such a tax be designed so as to achieve its goals while addressing these underlying fairness (*i.e.*, vertical equity) concerns? Would you support such a tax as a replacement, in whole or in part, for the existing income tax?

Additional Assignment — Chapter 4

You are a law clerk to a United States Supreme Court Justice who has mixed feelings about the Ninth Circuit's second decision in *Albertson's II*, and would like to have the Court take the case. The remaining eight justices are, well, less than ecstatic about tax cases and would rather spend their time on something else. However, they have agreed to read a memorandum from your Justice, *not exceeding four (4) double-spaced pages in length*, explaining why the case is important enough for them to hear. Being Supreme Court Justices, they are interested in knowing not only the significance of the case for tax and pension law, but its importance for the interpretation of statutes in general. Specifically, they wish to know if *Albertson's II* is creating a new precedent for the reading of statutes contrary to their plain or literal meaning, which may come back to haunt them in other, weightier settings; or if it is a more parochial decision limited to the special circumstances of tax cases. The Justices are also interested in knowing whether the decision in *Albertson's II* was really necessary to preserve the entire pension system, or whether this could be accomplished in a less intrusive manner.

Write a draft of the memorandum. Please note that you need not convince the remaining Justices that *Albertson's* is incorrectly decided; merely, that there is an important national issue at stake in the case that justifies their attention. And don't offend them by exceeding their own page limit!

Chapter 5

LOANS, INTEREST, AND MORTGAGES

The subject of loans and interest is one of the classic topics in tax policy, both for its practical significance and for what it says about the nature of tax law and adjudication. The practical significance arises from the importance of debt financing in nearly all commercial and many personal activities. The legal significance relates to the role of unenacted, court-made rules — what is sometimes labeled "tax common law" — and their interplay with the written (but often incomplete) language of the Internal Revenue Code. Many of the most famous tax cases involve loans or mortgage transactions, and many of these cases, in turn, involve clashes between amorphous "tax theory" and the literal language of the Code.

The treatment of loans and interest includes two distinct but related issues. The first involves the tax treatment of loan proceeds and the discharge of indebtedness: what happens when a loan is taken out and repaid, or when, for some reason, a debtor is relieved of all or part of the responsibility for repayment. The second involves interest payments, in particular the distinction between business interest, which is generally deductible for tax purposes, and nonbusiness or personal interest, which generally is not deductible. The latter issue also suggests the problem of home mortgage interest, which appears to be personal in character and yet remains deductible under the Code for a combination of political and policy reasons.

Because debt financing is so important in business transactions, this chapter will give us a further opportunity to consider the commercial implications of tax policy and the role of tax factors in choosing among different kinds of investments. For the first time, we will encounter the concept of the tax shelter, a business investment that is undertaken largely, if not primarily, because of its attendant tax consequences. This chapter thus forms a bridge between the early part of the course, which is concerned primarily with the definition of income, and the middle part, which is concerned primarily with deductions and considers a wide range of tax planning and reduction strategies.

I. LOAN PROCEEDS AND DISCHARGE OF INDEBTEDNESS

Suppose that you take out a $1,000 loan from the bank, which you are required to pay back, with interest, over a three-year period.[1] The general tax rule is that you don't have any income resulting from this transaction, since the $1,000 cash you now

---

[1] Home mortgages, and some business loans, are typically repaid using a "level-payment" scheme, under which the borrower makes the same payment each month part of which goes to pay interest and the remainder of which goes to repay principal on the loan. Since the outstanding balance of the loan

have is precisely balanced by an obligation to repay the $1,000 at some time in the future. Nor does the repayment of loan "principal" — the $1,000 itself, independent of any interest payments — give rise to a tax deduction. (The interest may or may not be deductible, depending on the purpose of the loan.) Although this rule is hardly intuitive — a consumption tax, for example, might include the loan proceeds in income and allow a deduction for principal repayment — it has always been the rule for income tax purposes, and no one has seriously proposed it be changed.

If everyone repaid their loans that would be about it, and the subject of loans would occupy a small portion of a tax casebook. Things get interesting because they don't. Suppose that you go to the bank, offer to repay your loan, and the bank — in an inexplicably friendly mood — tells you not to bother repaying. What are your tax consequences? Clearly, you should be taxed on $1,000 of income, although explaining why may be a bit daunting. A layperson would probably say that you should be taxed because you now have a positive balance ($1,000) as compared to a zero or neutral balance before, when you still had to repay. A tax expert would be more likely to emphasize the elimination of a negative, explaining that you previously had a $1,000 debt which had now been forgiven by the bank and that the discharge or cancellation of indebtedness constituted a form of taxable income.[2] The Code adopts essentially the latter view, stating that income from discharge of indebtedness is a form of taxable income (section 61(a)(12)), albeit proceeding to provide numerous exceptions to this rule (section 108). Really, though, these are two ways of saying the same thing, and the taxation of debt forgiveness seems inevitable from the standpoint of pure tax theory.

The problem, of course, is that reality is never so simple. In the real world, debt cancellation takes place for two principal reasons. The most obvious reason is that the debtor is insolvent or otherwise incapable of repaying his debts; the lender is willing to take less than 100 cents on the dollar, or perhaps forgive the debt entirely, rather than try to get blood from a stone. This strikes many as a sympathetic situation, and the Code has provided several exceptions to section 61(a)(12) in such cases. Thus, section 108 exempts from tax income from the discharge of indebtedness if the discharge occurs in a title 11 (bankruptcy) case (section 108(a)(1)(A)), when the taxpayer is insolvent (108(a)(1)(B)), or in certain cases involving farmers, a group apparently regarded as sympathetic even if they do not meet the normal bankruptcy criteria (108(a)(1)(C)). To prevent taxpayers from taking advantage of these provisions, section 108(b) provides for a reduction of the "tax attributes" (NOLs, credits, basis, etc.) of anyone benefiting from these three rules, so that — if the taxpayer gets back on his feet — he will eventually pay tax on the amount excluded when he was down.

A second reason for debt forgiveness involves changes in interest rates. Recall the *Cottage Savings* case in Chapter 4, in which a bank had lent money at low

---

decreases over time, the percentage of each payment needed to cover interest charges decreases, and the percentage available to repay principal correspondingly increases, over the life of the loan. Many other business loans are repaid using a "balloon payment" scheme, in which interest only is paid on a yearly or monthly basis and the principal amount is repaid in one large (balloon) payment at the end of the loan term.

[2] *See, e.g.*, United States v. Kirby Lumber Co., 284 U.S. 1 (1931).

interest rates but had to pay higher rates to depositors in order to stay in business.[3] To escape this problem, Cottage Savings tried to "sell" its low-interest loans to another bank and take a large, one-time tax deduction. Suppose that, instead of this strategy, the bank had approached its borrowers with the following offer: "You owe us $100,000, on a thirty-year loan, at a 5 percent interest rate. That's a bad deal for you, because you have to repay the whole $100,000, and for us, because we're stuck with a low-interest, unprofitable loan. Why don't you pay us $75,000 now, forget the rest, and call it a day? You'll pay less, we'll make more money lending out the $75,000 at a 10 or 15 percent interest rate, and everyone goes home happy."

Under a literal application of debt forgiveness principles, borrowers who accept this offer would have $25,000 of immediate taxable income.[4] Yet such a result is likely to outrage the borrowers, who believe that they are repaying the loan to the bank's satisfaction, and make any similar arrangement impossible in the future. Wouldn't it be wiser and fairer to let the tax go?

You can see what is happening here: while most observers support taxation of debt discharge in theory, they are tempted to forego tax in many cases where it actually happens. A sense of ambivalence pervades the entire subject, with Congress and the courts vindicating the basic principle of taxation but carving out exceptions for the more popular real-world transactions. The air of confusion is compounded by the presence of an inclusion rule (section 61(a)(12)) and a separate exclusion provision (section 108), both of which deal with essentially the same subject but neither one of which makes any mention of the other.

The following cases explore this ambivalence in greater detail. The first case, *Zarin v. Commissioner*, refuses to apply the cancellation of indebtedness doctrine to an unusual, highly personal set of facts involving a casino's "forgiveness" of debts by a compulsive gambler. The second, *Rood v. Commissioner*, applies the doctrine to a similar set of facts. As you read these cases — especially *Zarin* — consider whether their outcomes can be explained by rigid tax principles, or whether human sympathy and emotion are not a large part of the equation.

ZARIN v. COMMISSIONER
United States Court of Appeals, Third Circuit
916 F.2d 110 (1990)

Cowen, J:

David Zarin ("Zarin") appeals from a decision of the Tax Court holding that he recognized $2,935,000 of income from discharge of indebtedness resulting from his gambling activities, and that he should be taxed on the income. This Court has jurisdiction to review the Tax Court's decision under section 7482 of the Internal

---

[3] Banks make money by charging higher interest on their loans than they pay to their depositors. For example, a healthy bank might pay 7 percent to its depositors, but charge 10 percent on its loans, using the 3 percent "spread" to pay salaries, taxes, and overhead with the remainder constituting after-tax income or profit. A bank that pays higher interest to its depositors than it charges on its loans has got to do something, fast.

[4] I.R.C. § 108(a)(1)(D) (exempting certain real estate debt, applies only to trade or business property).

Revenue Code (1954) (the "Code"). After considering the issues raised by this appeal, we will reverse.

I.

Zarin was a professional engineer who participated in the development, construction, and management of various housing projects. A resident of Atlantic City, New Jersey, Zarin occasionally gambled, both in his hometown and in other places where gambling was legalized. To facilitate his gaming activities in Atlantic City, Zarin applied to Resorts International Hotel ("Resorts") for a credit line in June, 1978. Following a credit check, Resorts granted Zarin $10,000 of credit. Pursuant to this credit arrangement with Resorts, Zarin could write a check, called a marker,[5] and in return receive chips, which could then be used to gamble at the casino's tables.

Before long, Zarin developed a reputation as an extravagant "high roller" who routinely bet the house maximum while playing craps, his game of choice. Considered a "valued gaming patron" by Resorts, Zarin had his credit limit increased at regular intervals without any further credit checks, and was provided a number of complimentary services and privileges. By November, 1979, Zarin's permanent line of credit had been raised to $200,000. Between June, 1978, and December, 1979, Zarin lost $2,500,000 at the craps table, losses he paid in full.

Responding to allegations of credit abuses, the New Jersey Division of Gaming Enforcement filed with the New Jersey Casino Control Commission a complaint against Resorts. Among the 809 violations of casino regulations alleged in the complaint of October, 1979, were 100 pertaining to Zarin. Subsequently, a Casino Control Commissioner issued an Emergency Order, the effect of which was to make further extensions of credit to Zarin illegal.

Nevertheless, Resorts continued to extend Zarin's credit limit through the use of two different practices: "considered cleared" credit and "this trip only" credit. Both methods effectively ignored the Emergency Order and were later found to be illegal.[6]

By January, 1980, Zarin was gambling compulsively and uncontrollably at Resorts, spending as many as sixteen hours a day at the craps table.[7] During April, 1980, Resorts again increased Zarin's credit line without further inquiries. That same month, Zarin delivered personal checks and counterchecks to Resorts which were returned as having been drawn against insufficient funds. Those dishonored checks totaled $3,435,000. In late April, Resorts cut off Zarin's credit.

Although Zarin indicated that he would repay those obligations, Resorts filed a New Jersey state court action against Zarin in November, 1980, to collect the $3,435,000. Zarin denied liability on grounds that Resort's claim was unenforceable

---

[5] [2] A "marker" is a negotiable draft payable to Resorts and drawn on the maker's bank.

[6] [4] On July 8, 1983, the New Jersey Casino Control Commission found that Resorts violated the Emergency Order at least thirteen different times, nine involving Zarin, and fined Resorts $130,000.

[7] [5] Zarin claims that at the time he was suffering from a recognized emotional disorder that caused him to gamble compulsively.

under New Jersey regulations intended to protect compulsive gamblers. Ten months later, in September, 1981, Resorts and Zarin settled their dispute for a total of $500,000.

The Commissioner of Internal Revenue ("Commissioner") subsequently determined deficiencies in Zarin's federal income taxes for 1980 and 1981, arguing that Zarin recognized $3,435,000 of income in 1980 from larceny by trick and deception. After Zarin challenged that claim by filing a Tax Court petition, the Commissioner abandoned his 1980 claim, and argued instead that Zarin had recognized $2,935,000 of income in 1981 from the cancellation of indebtedness which resulted from the settlement with Resorts.

Agreeing with the Commissioner, the Tax Court decided, eleven judges to eight, that Zarin had indeed recognized $2,935,000 of income from the discharge of indebtedness, namely the difference between the original $3,435,000 "debt" and the $500,000 settlement. *Zarin v. Commissioner*, 92 T.C. 1084 (1989). Since he was in the seventy percent tax bracket, Zarin's deficiency for 1981 was calculated to be $2,047,245. With interest to April 5, 1990, Zarin allegedly owes the Internal Revenue Service $5,209,033.96 in additional taxes. Zarin appeals the order of the Tax Court.

II.

The sole issue before this Court is whether the Tax Court correctly held that Zarin had income from discharge of indebtedness.[8] Section 108 and section 61(a)(12) of the Code set forth "the general rule that gross income includes income from the discharge of indebtedness." I.R.C. § 108(e)(1). The Commissioner argues, and the Tax Court agreed, that pursuant to the Code, Zarin did indeed recognize income from discharge of gambling indebtedness.

Under the Commissioner's logic, Resorts advanced Zarin $3,435,000 worth of chips, chips being the functional equivalent of cash. At that time, the chips were not treated as income, since Zarin recognized an obligation of repayment. In other words, Resorts made Zarin a tax-free loan. However, a taxpayer does recognize income if a loan owed to another party is cancelled, in whole or in part. I.R.C. §§ 61(a)(12), 108(e). The settlement between Zarin and Resorts, claims the Commissioner, fits neatly into the cancellation of indebtedness provisions in the Code. Zarin owed $3,435,000, paid $500,000, with the difference constituting income. Although initially persuasive, the Commissioner's position is nonetheless flawed for two reasons.

---

[8] [6] Subsequent to the Tax Court's decision, Zarin filed a motion to reconsider, arguing that he was insolvent at the time Resorts forgave his debt, and thus, under I.R.C. section 108(a)(1)(B), could not have income from discharge of indebtedness. He did, not, however, raise that issue before the Tax Court until after it rendered its decision. The Tax Court denied the motion for reconsideration. By reason of our resolution of this case, we do not need to decide whether the Tax Court abused its discretion in denying Zarin's motion.

III.

Initially, we find that sections 108 and 61(a)(12) are inapplicable to the Zarin/Resorts transaction. Section 61 does not define indebtedness. On the other hand, section 108(d)(1), which repeats and further elaborates on the rule in section 61(a)(12), defines the term as any indebtedness "(A) for which the taxpayer is liable, or (B) subject to which the taxpayer holds property." I.R.C. § 108(d)(1). In order to come within the sweep of the discharge of indebtedness rules, then, the taxpayer must satisfy one of the two prongs in the section 108(d)(1) test. Zarin satisfies neither.

Because the debt Zarin owed to Resorts was unenforceable as a matter of New Jersey state law,[9] it is clearly not a debt "for which the taxpayer is liable." I.R.C. § 108(d)(1)(A). Liability implies a legally enforceable obligation to repay, and under New Jersey law, Zarin would have no such obligation.

Moreover, Zarin did not have a debt subject to which he held property as required by section 108(d)(1)(B). Zarin's indebtedness arose out of his acquisition of gambling chips. The Tax Court held that gambling chips were not property, but rather, "a medium of exchange within the Resorts casino" and a "substitute for cash." Alternatively, the Tax Court viewed the chips as nothing more than "the opportunity to gamble and incidental services . . ." *Zarin*, 92 T.C. at 1099. We agree with the gist of these characterizations, and hold that gambling chips are merely an accounting mechanism to evidence debt.

Gaming chips in New Jersey during 1980 were regarded "solely as evidence of a debt owed to their custodian by the casino licensee and shall be considered at no time the property of anyone other than the casino licensee issuing them." N.J. Admin. Code tit. 19k, § 19:46-1.5(d) (1990). Thus, under New Jersey state law, gambling chips were Resorts' property until transferred to Zarin in exchange for the markers, at which point the chips became "evidence" of indebtedness (and not the property of Zarin).

Even were there no relevant legislative pronouncement on which to rely, simple common sense would lead to the conclusion that chips were not property in Zarin's hands. Zarin could not do with the chips as he pleased, nor did the chips have any

---

[9] [7] The Tax Court held that the Commissioner had not met its burden of proving that the debt owed Resorts was enforceable as a matter of state law. *Zarin*, 92 T.C. at 1090. There was ample evidence to support that finding. In New Jersey, the extension of credit by casinos "to enable [any] person to take part in gaming activity as a player" is limited. N.J. Stat. Ann. § 5:12-101(b) (1988). Under N.J. Stat. Ann. § 5:12-101(f), any credit violation is "invalid and unenforceable for the purposes of collection " In Resorts Int'l Hotel, Inc. v. Salomone, 178 N.J. Super. 598, 429 A.2d 1078 (App. Div. 1981), the court held that "casinos must comply with the Legislature's strict control of credit for gambling purposes. Unless they do, the debts reflected by players' checks will not be enforced. . . ." *Id.* at 607, 429 A.2d at 1082.

With regards to the extension of credit to Zarin after the Emergency Order of October, 1979, was issued, Resorts did not comply with New Jersey regulations. The Casino Control Commission specifically stated in 1983 "that Resorts was guilty of infractions, violations, improprieties, with the net effect that [Zarin] was encouraged to continue gambling long after, one, his credit line was reached, and exceeded; two, long after it became apparent that the gambler was an addicted gambler; three, long after the gambler had difficulty in paying his debts; and four, Resorts knew the individual was gambling when he should not have been gambling." Appendix at 325–326. It follows, therefore, that under New Jersey law, the $3,435,000 debt Zarin owed Resorts was totally unenforceable.

independent economic value beyond the casino. The chips themselves were of little use to Zarin, other than as a means of facilitating gambling. They could not have been used outside the casino. They could have been used to purchase services and privileges within the casino, including food, drink, entertainment, and lodging, but Zarin would not have utilized them as such, since he received those services from Resorts on a complimentary basis. In short, the chips had no economic substance.

Although the Tax Court found that theoretically, Zarin could have redeemed the chips he received on credit for cash and walked out of the casino, *Zarin*, 92 T.C. at 1092, the reality of the situation was quite different. Realistically, before cashing in his chips, Zarin would have been required to pay his outstanding IOUs. New Jersey state law requires casinos to "request patrons to apply any chips or plaques in their possession in reduction of personal checks or Counter Checks exchanged for purposes of gaming prior to exchanging such chips or plaques for cash or prior to departing from the casino area." N.J. Admin. Code tit. 19k, § 19:45-1.24(s) (1979) (currently N.J. Admin. Code tit. 19k, § 19:45-1.25(o) (1990) (as amended)). Since his debt at all times equaled or exceeded the number of chips he possessed, redemption would have left Zarin with no chips, no cash, and certainly nothing which could have been characterized as property.

Not only were the chips non-property in Zarin's hands, but upon transfer to Zarin, the chips also ceased to be the property of Resorts. Since the chips were in the possession of another party, Resorts could no longer do with the chips as it pleased, and could no longer control the chips' use. Generally, at the time of a transfer, the party in possession of the chips can gamble with them, use them for services, cash them in, or walk out of the casino with them as an Atlantic City souvenir. The chips therefore become nothing more than an accounting mechanism, or evidence of a debt, designed to facilitate gambling in casinos where the use of actual money was forbidden.[10] Thus, the chips which Zarin held were not property within the meaning of I. R.C. § 108(d)(1)(B).[11]

In short, because Zarin was not liable on the debt he allegedly owed Resorts, and because Zarin did not hold "property" subject to that debt, the cancellation of indebtedness provisions of the Code do not apply to the settlement between Resorts and Zarin. As such, Zarin cannot have income from the discharge of his debt.

---

[10] [8] Although, as noted above, Zarin would not have been able to leave the casino with cash or chips, and probably would not have used the chips for services, these facts do not change the character of the chips. Despite the aforementioned limitations upon Zarin's use of the chips, they remain an accounting mechanism or evidence of a debt. Resorts' increased interest in Zarin's chips does not rise to the level of a property interest, since Zarin still has dominion over the chips within the casino.

[11] [9] The parties stipulated before the Tax Court that New Jersey casino "chips are property which are not negotiable and may not be used to gamble or for any other purpose outside the casino where they were issued." It could be argued that we are bound by this stipulation to accept the proposition that chips are property. We do not dispute the notion that chips are property, but as discussed above, they are only property in the hands of the casino. The stipulation is consistent with this idea. In fact, both parties agreed in their briefs that chips are property of the casino. Moreover, during oral arguments, both parties agreed that chips were not property when held by the gambler.

IV.

Instead of analyzing the transaction at issue as cancelled debt, we believe the proper approach is to view it as disputed debt or contested liability. Under the contested liability doctrine, if a taxpayer, in good faith, disputed the amount of a debt, a subsequent settlement of the dispute would be treated as the amount of debt cognizable for tax purposes. The excess of the original debt over the amount determined to have been due is disregarded for both loss and debt accounting purposes. Thus, if a taxpayer took out a loan for $10,000, refused in good faith to pay the full $10,000 back, and then reached an agreement with the lender that he would pay back only $7000 in full satisfaction of the debt, the transaction would be treated as if the initial loan was $7000. When the taxpayer tenders the $7000 payment, he will have been deemed to have paid the full amount of the initially disputed debt. Accordingly, there is no tax consequence to the taxpayer upon payment.

The seminal "contested liability" case is *N. Sobel, Inc. v. Commissioner*, 40 B.T.A. 1263 (1939). In *Sobel*, the taxpayer exchanged a $21,700 note for 100 shares of stock from a bank. In the following year, the taxpayer sued the bank for rescission, arguing that the bank loan was violative of state law, and moreover, that the bank had failed to perform certain promises. The parties eventually settled the case in 1935, with the taxpayer agreeing to pay half of the face amount of the note. In the year of the settlement, the taxpayer claimed the amount paid as a loss. The Commissioner denied the loss because it had been sustained five years earlier, and further asserted that the taxpayer recognized income from the discharge of half of his indebtedness.

The Board of Tax Appeals held that since the loss was not fixed until the dispute was settled, the loss was recognized in 1935, the year of the settlement, and the deduction was appropriately taken in that year. Additionally, the Board held that the portion of the note forgiven by the bank "was not the occasion for a freeing of assets and that there was no gain. . . ." *Id.* at 1265. Therefore, the taxpayer did not have any income from cancellation of indebtedness.

There is little difference between the present case and *Sobel*. Zarin incurred a $3,435,000 debt while gambling at Resorts, but in court, disputed liability on the basis of unenforceability. A settlement of $500,000 was eventually agreed upon. It follows from *Sobel* that the settlement served only to fix the amount of debt. No income was realized or recognized. When Zarin paid the $500,000, any tax consequence dissolved.[12]

Only one other court has addressed a case factually similar to the one before us. In *United States v. Hall*, 307 F.2d 238 (10th Cir. 1962), the taxpayer owed an unenforceable gambling debt alleged to be $225,000. Subsequently, the taxpayer and the creditor settled for $150,000. The taxpayer then transferred cattle valued at $148,110 to his creditor in satisfaction of the settlement agreement. A jury held that the parties fixed the debt at $150,000, and that the taxpayer recognized income

---

[12] [10] Had Zarin not paid the $500,000 dollar settlement, it would be likely that he would have had income from cancellation of indebtedness. The debt at that point would have been fixed, and Zarin would have been legally obligated to pay it.

from cancellation of indebtedness equal to the difference between the $150,000 and the $148,110 value affixed to the cattle. Arguing that the taxpayer recognized income equal to the difference between $225,000 and $148,000, the Commissioner appealed.

The Tenth Circuit rejected the idea that the taxpayer had any income from cancellation of indebtedness. Noting that the gambling debt was unenforceable, the Tenth Circuit said, "The cold fact is that taxpayer suffered a substantial loss from gambling, the amount of which was determined by the transfer." *Id.* at 241. In effect, the Court held that because the debt was unenforceable, the amount of the loss and resulting debt cognizable for tax purposes were fixed by the settlement at $148,110. Thus, the Tenth Circuit lent its endorsement to the contested liability doctrine in a factual situation strikingly similar to the one at issue.

The Commissioner argues that *Sobel* and the contested liability doctrine only apply when there is an unliquidated debt; that is, a debt for which the amount cannot be determined. *See Colonial Sav. Ass'n v. Commissioner*, 85 T.C. 855, 862–863 (1985) (*Sobel* stands for the proposition that "there must be a liquidated debt"), *aff'd*, 854 F.2d 1001 (7th Cir. 1988). *See also N. Sobel, Inc. v. Commissioner*, 40 B.T.A. at 1265 (there was a dispute as to "liability and the amount" of the debt). Since Zarin contested his liability based on the unenforceability of the entire debt, and did not dispute the amount of the debt, the Commissioner would have us adopt the reasoning of the Tax Court, which found that Zarin's debt was liquidated, therefore barring the application of *Sobel* and the contested liability doctrine. *Zarin*, 92 T.C. at 1095 (Zarin's debt "was a liquidated amount" and "there is no dispute about the amount [received].").

We reject the Tax Court's rationale. When a debt is unenforceable, it follows that the amount of the debt, and not just the liability thereon, is in dispute. Although a debt may be unenforceable, there still could be some value attached to its worth. This is especially so with regards to gambling debts. In most states, gambling debts are unenforceable, and have "but slight potential. . . ." *United States v. Hall*, 307 F.2d 238, 241 (10th Cir. 1962). Nevertheless, they are often collected, at least in part. For example, Resorts is not a charity; it would not have extended illegal credit to Zarin and others if it did not have some hope of collecting debts incurred pursuant to the grant of credit.

Moreover, the debt is frequently incurred to acquire gambling chips, and not money. Although casinos attach a dollar value to each chip, that value, unlike money's, is not beyond dispute, particularly given the illegality of gambling debts in the first place. This proposition is supported by the facts of the present case. Resorts gave Zarin $3.4 million dollars of chips in exchange for markers evidencing Zarin's debt. If indeed the only issue was the enforceability of the entire debt, there would have been no settlement. Zarin would have owed all or nothing. Instead, the parties attached a value to the debt considerably lower than its face value. In other words, the parties agreed that given the circumstances surrounding Zarin's gambling spree, the chips he acquired might not have been worth $3.4 million dollars, but were worth something. Such a debt cannot be called liquidated, since its exact amount was not fixed until settlement.

To summarize, the transaction between Zarin and Resorts can best be characterized as a disputed debt, or contested liability. Zarin owed an unenforceable debt of $3,435,000 to Resorts. After Zarin in good faith disputed his obligation to repay the debt, the parties settled for $500,000, which Zarin paid. That $500,000 settlement fixed the amount of loss and the amount of debt cognizable for tax purposes. Since Zarin was deemed to have owed $500,000, and since he paid Resorts $500,000, no adverse tax consequences attached to Zarin as a result.[13]

V.

In conclusion, we hold that Zarin did not have any income from cancellation of indebtedness for two reasons. First, the Code provisions covering discharge of debt are inapplicable since the definitional requirement in I.R.C. section 108(d)(1) was not met. Second, the settlement of Zarin's gambling debts was a contested liability. We reverse the decision of the Tax Court and remand with instructions to enter judgment that Zarin realized no income by reason of his settlement with Resorts.

STAPLETON, J, dissenting.

I respectfully dissent because I agree with the Commissioner's appraisal of the economic realities of this matter.

Resorts sells for cash the exhilaration and the potential for profit inherent in games of chance. It does so by selling for cash chips that entitle the holder to gamble at its casino. Zarin, like thousands of others, wished to purchase what Resorts was offering in the marketplace. He chose to make this purchase on credit and executed notes evidencing his obligation to repay the funds that were advanced to him by Resorts. As in most purchase money transactions, Resorts skipped the step of giving Zarin cash that he would only return to it in order to pay for the opportunity to gamble. Resorts provided him instead with chips that entitled him to participate in Resorts' games of chance on the same basis as others who had paid cash for that privilege.[14] Whether viewed as a one or two-step transaction, however, Zarin received either $3.4 million in cash or an entitlement for which others would have had to pay $3.4 million.

Despite the fact that Zarin received in 1980 cash or an entitlement worth $3.4 million, he correctly reported in that year no income from his dealings with

---

[13] [12] The Commissioner argues in the alternative that Zarin recognized $3,435,000 of income in 1980. This claim has no merit. Recognition of income would depend upon a finding that Zarin did not have cancellation of indebtedness income solely because his debt was unenforceable. We do not so hold. Although unenforceability is a factor in our analysis, our decision ultimately hinges upon the determination that the "disputed debt" rule applied, or alternatively, that chips are not property within the meaning of I.R.C. section 108.

[14] [1] I view as irrelevant the facts that Resorts advanced credit to Zarin solely to enable him to patronize its casino and that the chips could not be used elsewhere or for other purposes. When one buys a sofa from the furniture store on credit, the fact that the proprietor would not have advanced the credit for a different purpose does not entitle one to a tax-free gain in the event the debt to the store is extinguished for some reason.

Resorts. He did so *solely* because he recognized, as evidenced by his notes, an offsetting obligation to repay Resorts $3.4 million in cash. *See, e.g., Vukasovich, Inc. v. Commissioner*, 790 F.2d 1409 (9th Cir. 1986); *United States v. Rochelle*, 384 F.2d 748 (5th Cir. 1967), *cert. denied*, 390 U.S. 946 (1968); Bittker and Thompson, *Income From the Discharged Indebtedness: The Progeny of* United States v. Kirby Lumber Co., 66 Calif. L. Rev. 159 (1978). In 1981, with the delivery of Zarin's promise to pay Resorts $500,000 and the execution of a release by Resorts, Resorts surrendered its claim to repayment of the remaining $2.9 million of the money Zarin had borrowed. As of that time, Zarin's assets were freed of his potential liability for that amount and he recognized gross income in that amount. *Commissioner v. Tufts*, 461 U.S. 300 (1983); *United States v. Kirby Lumber Company*, 284 U.S. 1 (1931); *Vukasovich, Inc. v. Commissioner*, 790 F.2d 1409 (9th Cir. 1986). *But see United States v. Hall*, 307 F.2d 238 (10th Cir. 1962).[15]

The only alternatives I see to this conclusion are to hold either (1) that Zarin realized $3.4 million in income in 1980 at a time when both parties to the transaction thought there was an offsetting obligation to repay or (2) that the $3.4 million benefit sought and received by Zarin is not taxable at all. I find the latter alternative unacceptable as inconsistent with the fundamental principle of the Code that anything of commercial value received by a taxpayer is taxable unless expressly excluded from gross income.[16] *Commissioner v. Glenshaw Glass Co.*, 348 U.S. 426 (1955); *United States v. Kirby Lumber Co., supra.* I find the former alternative unacceptable as impracticable. In 1980, neither party was maintaining that the debt was unenforceable and, because of the settlement, its unenforceability was not even established in the litigation over the debt in 1981. It was not until 1989 in this litigation over the tax consequences of the transaction that the unenforceability was first judicially declared. Rather than require such tax litigation to resolve the correct treatment of a debt transaction, I regard it as far preferable to have the tax consequences turn on the manner in which the debt is treated by the parties. For present purposes, it will suffice to say that where something that would otherwise be includable in gross income is received on credit in a purchase money transaction, there should be no recognition of income so long as the debtor continues to recognize an obligation to repay the debt. On the other hand, income, if not earlier recognized, should be recognized when the debtor no

---

[15] [2] This is not a case in which parties agree subsequent to a purchase money transaction that the property purchased has a value less than thought at the time of the transaction. In such cases, the purchase price adjustment rule is applied and the agreed-upon value is accepted as the value of the benefit received by the purchaser; *see, e.g.,* Commissioner v. Sherman, 135 F.2d 68 (6th Cir. 1943); N. Sobel, Inc. v. Commissioner, 40 B.T.A. 1263 (1939). Nor is this a case in which the taxpayer is entitled to rescind an entire purchase money transaction, thereby to restore itself to the position it occupied before receiving anything of commercial value. In this case, the illegality was in the extension of credit by Resorts and whether one views the benefit received by Zarin as cash or the opportunity to gamble, he is no longer in a position to return that benefit.

[16] [3] As the court's opinion correctly points out, this record will not support an exclusion under § 108(a) which relates to discharge of debt in an insolvency or bankruptcy context. Section 108(e)(5) of the Code, which excludes discharged indebtedness arising from a "purchase price adjustment" is not applicable here. Among other things, § 108(e)(5) necessarily applies only to a situation in which the debtor still holds the property acquired in the purchase money transaction. Equally irrelevant is § 108(d)'s definition of "indebtedness" relied upon heavily by the court. Section 108(d) expressly defines that term solely for the purposes of § 108 and not for the purposes of § 61(a)(12).

longer recognizes an obligation to repay and the creditor has released the debt or acknowledged its unenforceability.

In this view, it makes no difference whether the extinguishment of the creditor's claim comes as a part of a compromise. Resorts settled for 14 cents on the dollar presumably because it viewed such a settlement as reflective of the odds that the debt would be held to be enforceable. While Zarin should be given credit for the fact that he had to pay 14 cents for a release, I see no reason why he should not realize gain in the same manner as he would have if Resorts had concluded on its own that the debt was legally unenforceable and had written it off as uncollectible.[17]

I would affirm the judgment of the Tax Court.

Understanding *Zarin*

1. *Zarin* involved the cancellation of indebtedness under section 61(a)(12); the section 108 exemptions were not raised by the taxpayer and none appear to have applied. That being the case, why did the court conduct a lengthy analysis of the definition of "indebtedness of the taxpayer" under section 108(d)(1), which expressly applies "for purposes of this section" (*i.e.*, section 108) only? In the absence of a clear definition in section 61, was it legitimate to look at a parallel provision? Why do you think section 108(d)(1) was included in the statute in the first place, and what does this tell you about its relevance to the *Zarin* facts?

2. Why didn't Zarin assert from the beginning that he was insolvent within the meaning of section 108(a)(1)(B), and avoid tax on that basis? For that matter, what about section 108(e)(5), which treats a "purchase-money debt reduction" by a solvent debtor as a purchase price adjustment rather than a discharge of debt? Was (wasn't) Zarin a "purchaser of property" within the meaning of this latter rule? Do the majority and dissent deal adequately with this issue?

3. The dissent argues that Zarin's repayment obligation was either (i) unenforceable (in which case he should have had income as soon as he took out the non-enforceable $3.4 million "loan") or else (ii) enforceable (in which case he had income when a substantial portion of the loan was forgiven). The majority avoids this choice by asserting that the debt was a "contested liability," such as might occur if (*e.g.*) a store and a customer disagreed over the amount of a bill, and agreed that the customer pay 50% or 75% of the bill as a compromise solution. The rule in these cases is that the compromise is treated as a purchase price adjustment rather than as debt discharge income.

Is the contested liability doctrine really relevant to the *Zarin* facts? Was there a genuine dispute as to the amount of Zarin's debt, or was Zarin arguing that the debt was never really enforceable, so that (under the dissent's logic) he should have been taxed at the time of the original advance? Suppose that a bank and its borrower,

---

[17] [15] A different situation exists where there is a bona fide dispute over the amount of a debt and the dispute is compromised. Rather than require tax litigation to determine the amount of income received, the Commission treats the compromise figure as representing the amount of the obligation. I find this sensible and consistent with the pragmatic approach I would take.

anxious to avoid debt discharge income, developed a plan under which (a) the borrower refused to pay the full amount of his loan and (b) the bank agreed to a settlement under which the borrower repaid a prearranged portion of the loan and the rest of it remained unpaid. Would this constitute a contested liability, and if not, how does it differ from *Zarin*?

4.   Why couldn't Zarin concede that the debt cancellation was income, and use his gambling losses to wipe out tax on that income? *See* § 165(d) (allowing gambling losses only to the extent necessary to offset gambling income). What is the logic, if any, of this rule? Does the arbitrary nature of section 165(d) make Zarin's position somewhat more sympathetic, and the courts more willing to be creative in finding a way out for him?

5.   Why would a casino advance more than $3 million to a compulsive gambler in the first place? What, if anything, does your answer tell you about (i) the value of the chips as property in Zarin's hands, and (ii) the outcome of the *Zarin* case? Taking this into account, is *Zarin* such a bad decision, after all?

Zarin is probably the most celebrated tax case in the last twenty years, although more for its intellectual interest than its real-world applications. Especially interesting is the style of decision-making in the case. Although two Code sections (61(a)(12) and 108) and numerous subsections apply to the case, none of these are really dispositive, and they may even contradict one another. The case is, accordingly, decided not by reference to the statute, but by applying court-made doctrines — the contested liability doctrine, consistency in the treatment of loan proceeds, and so forth — to the facts at hand. Indeed, even these theories (as the dissent notes) do not adequately explain the result in the case; a fair amount of sympathy for Zarin, given the unusual circumstances of the case, appears to be at work as well. *Zarin* is thus an example of how statutes and regulations, case law, and "tax theory" mix with practical considerations and plain old common-sense in resolving difficult tax issues — and, perhaps, of how difficult cases can give rise to questionable precedents. Unlike *Albertson's*, it is not so much a matter of ignoring the statute as of "filling it in" with an eclectic variety of other sources. This process is obviously exaggerated in a case like *Zarin*, but to some extent it is present in all tax decisions.

On a narrower level, *Zarin* demonstrates (once again) the ambivalence surrounding cancellation of indebtedness income. While much of the law is stacked against Zarin, there is a rebellion against the idea of requiring a loser to pay a substantial tax, together with residual doubts as to whether compromise of a debt should give rise to taxable income in the first place. Yet, these elements — sympathy for a loser, the thin line between contested liability and debt cancellation, etc. — are likely to be present in a large percentage of debt discharge cases. *Zarin* thus exemplifies the difference between the experts' view (in which cancellation of indebtedness is always taxable income) and the laymen's or common sense view (in which the rule above must be tempered by the facts and circumstances of individual cases). In theory, the experts would win most such arguments, but in a democratic society, the outcome is likely to be more ambiguous.

Not all debtors are as fortunate (tax-wise) as Mr. Zarin. Consider the following:

ROOD v. COMMISSIONER
United States Tax Court
T.C. Memo. 1996-248

MEMORANDUM FINDINGS OF FACT AND OPINION

WELLS, JUDGE:

Respondent determined a deficiency of $60,457 in petitioner's 1988 Federal income tax. The only issue presented in the instant case is whether petitioner realized income from the cancellation of an allegedly disputed gambling debt written off by a casino. Unless otherwise indicated, all section references are to the Internal Revenue Code as in effect for the year in issue, and all Rule references are to the Tax Court Rules of Practice and Procedure.

FINDINGS OF FACT

Some of the facts and the exhibits have been stipulated for trial pursuant to Rule 91. The parties' stipulations are incorporated herein by reference and are found accordingly.

During 1988 and when the petition in the instant case was filed, petitioner resided in Tampa, Florida.

Petitioner is an attorney who was recognized in 1991 for 50 years of membership in the Florida Bar. He is a former president of the Association of Trial Lawyers of America, the Tampa and Hillsborough County Bar Associations, the Florida Academy of Trial Lawyers, and the Junior Bar of the State of Florida.

Prior to 1985, petitioner maintained a line of credit at Caesar's Palace (Caesar's or the casino), a casino in Las Vegas, Nevada, where he gambled.

To draw on a line of credit, typically, a customer would sign the credit instrument given in exchange for chips (marker), in the gambling pit or at the cashier's cage in the casino. A marker could be presented to a customer's bank by the casino for payment in the same manner as a check. If a customer wished to allow another to gamble on the customer's credit, the customer would sign the marker. If the gambler won money gambling on credit, he or she would be asked to redeem the marker in the pit, if it were still there. Otherwise, when the gambler sought to cash the chips won, the casino cashier would check to see whether there was a balance due for credit extended by the casino, and the gambler would be expected to apply the chips against the balance at that time.

When a payment is made on a customer's account at the casino cage, it is the casino's practice to give the payor a numbered receipt, a duplicate of which is kept in a receipt book and another duplicate of which is kept in the IOU envelope for the customer's account, in which Caesar's also files the customer's markers and correspondence. It is also Caesar's practice to record all contacts with a customer concerning the account on the IOU envelope. Receipts are consecutively numbered. A payment made that did not appear to have been credited to a customer's account could be traced through the receipt book.

Petitioner incurred gambling debts at Caesar's. On November 23, 1984, Caesar's extended $110,000 of credit to petitioner. Caesar's generally expected payment of the outstanding balance of petitioner's account at the end of one trip to the casino at the time of his next trip, holding the account up to 60 days. During at least January, February, and March of 1985, Caesar's repeatedly contacted petitioner concerning payment of the debt, which Caesar's stated was due March 21, 1985. Petitioner informed Caesar's that he would pay the debt during his next trip to the casino. The debt was paid by cash and personal check on May 4, 1985. On May 5, 1985, Caesar's extended $110,000 of credit to petitioner. On that date, a payment of $80,000 was made by personal check. On May 6, 1985, Caesar's extended an additional $80,000 of credit to petitioner. On that date, a payment of $80,000 was made by personal check drawn on a business account. On May 7, 1985, Caesar's extended additional credit of $80,000 to petitioner. Caesar's also paid petitioner's airfare for the May 1985 trip.

On October 11, 1985, a payment of $110,000 was made on petitioner's account by personal check. On October 12, 1985, Caesar's extended credit of $85,000 to petitioner. On that date, a payment of $75,000 was made on petitioner's account by personal check. On October 13, 1985, Caesar's extended $240,000 of credit to petitioner. Caesar's paid petitioner's airfare for his October 1985 trip to the casino.

Beginning no later than November 1985, Caesar's repeatedly contacted petitioner concerning repayment of the amounts owed. During October, November, and December 1985, the $110,000 and $75,000 checks were deposited by Caesar's, returned, redeposited, and returned again because of either a missing endorsement or insufficient funds. Caesar's posted the check for $110,000 as returned on December 9, 1985, and the check for $75,000 as returned on December 10, 1985, and increased the balance owed by petitioner from $250,000 to $435,000. That balance was attributable to credit extended by Caesar's prior to December 1985. When informed of the returns of the checks, petitioner promised to make arrangements to clear them and, subsequently, to send new checks. In the course of a contact with Caesar's concerning the returned check for $110,000, petitioner also inquired when the $250,000 balance of his account was due, and Caesar's informed him that it was due January 12, 1986. On December 23, 1985, Caesar's received a check for $110,000, which was returned due to insufficient funds on January 15, 1986.

During 1986, petitioner made the following payments on his account:

Date	Amount
May 13, 1986	$25,000
Aug. 11, 1986	$10,000
Dec. 3, 1986	$10,000

The IOU envelope for petitioner's account sets forth the following notation with respect to a contact with petitioner on January 8, 1987: "Got him [petitioner] straightened out about 25M pmt [payment] which we rec back in 5/13/86 — verified balance & pmts [payments] made & he agrees." Caesar's sent petitioner an account statement dated February 4, 1987, informing him that its executive committee had approved a lump-sum settlement in a reduced amount and inviting him to call its account representative for details. During 1987 and 1988, petitioner made payments on his account as follows:

Date	Amount
Apr. 2, 1987	$5,000
May 27, 1987	$5,000
July 16, 1987	$5,000
Aug. 22, 1987	$5,000
Oct. 27, 1987	$5,000
Dec. 29, 1987	$5,000
Mar. 13, 1988	$5,000

In statements addressed to petitioner acknowledging receipt of the foregoing payments or setting forth the outstanding balance of his account, Caesar's requested that petitioner make monthly payments of between $5,000 and $10,000 to enable the casino to continue to hold his account and reminding him that its settlement offer was still open. In the statement dated March 15, 1988, Caesar's informed petitioner that it could not retain accounts indefinitely and that a 50-percent lump-sum settlement previously presented to petitioner was open to discussion.

By March 1988, $80,000 of petitioner's $435,000 debt to the casino had been repaid, leaving a balance of $355,000, according to the casino's records. A letter dated April 20, 1988, from Caesar's general counsel to petitioner stated that the casino required petitioner to pay his account in full immediately and that, if he did not contact Caesar's account representative within 15 days, the casino would turn petitioner's account over to a law firm or a collection agency to institute legal proceedings against him if necessary. The letter further stated that (1) any suit commenced against petitioner would be filed in Nevada and (2) once judgment was obtained against petitioner, Caesar's would then have the judgment enforced against him by the courts of his home State. It was Caesar's usual practice to proceed in this manner in the event a lawsuit was instituted against a debtor.

A letter dated May 5, 1988, from Caesar's account representative to petitioner stated that the casino would accept a lump sum settlement of $142,000 in payment of petitioner's account, provided payment was made prior to June 5, 1988. Petitioner and the casino continued to negotiate a settlement after that offer. Petitioner subsequently signed an allowance receipt that was received by Caesar's on July 18, 1988, that requested $255,000 be written off his account balance to induce him to make payment on the account. In accordance with an agreement between Caesar's and petitioner, petitioner paid Caesar's $100,000 by check dated June 29, 1988, that was received by the casino on September 2, 1988.

Caesar's wrote off the $255,000 balance of petitioner's account in September 1988 and noted in its records that (1) no attempt should be made to collect that amount should petitioner return to the casino to gamble and (2) no credit would be extended to petitioner in the future due to the settlement.

Petitioner retained no records of his contacts with Caesar's concerning the repayment of his debts to the casino.

Petitioner was not insolvent during 1988. Petitioner did not report the $255,000 written off by Caesar's as income from the cancellation of indebtedness on his 1988 Federal income tax return.

OPINION

Section 61(a)(12) provides the general rule that gross income includes income from the cancellation of indebtedness. The amount of the income includable generally is the difference between the face value of the debt and the amount paid in satisfaction of the debt. *Babin v. Commissioner*, 23 F.3d 1032, 1034 (6th Cir. 1994), *affg.* T.C. Memo. 1992-673. The income is recognized in the year cancellation occurs. *Montgomery v. Commissioner*, 65 T.C. 511, 520 (1975). A frequently cited rationale for the rule is that the cancellation results in an accession to income by effecting a freeing of assets previously offset by the liability arising from the indebtedness. *United States v. Kirby Lumber Co.*, 284 U.S. 1, 3 (1931); *Cozzi v. Commissioner*, 88 T.C. 435, 445 (1987). If, however, the cancellation of all or part of a debt is made in settlement of a dispute concerning the debt, no income from cancellation of indebtedness arises. *N. Sobel, Inc. v. Commissioner*, 40 B.T.A. 1263, 1265 (1939); *Exchange Sec. Bank v. United States*, 345 F. Supp. 486, 490–491 (N.D. Ala. 1972), *revd. on other grounds*, 492 F.2d 1096 (5th Cir. 1974); *see also Colonial Sav. Association v. Commissioner*, 85 T.C. 855, 862–863 (1985), *affd.* 854 F.2d 1001 (7th Cir. 1988). Settlement in such circumstances does not occasion a freeing of assets and accession to income. *N. Sobel, Inc. v. Commissioner, supra* at 1265. Petitioner bears the burden of showing that the settlement with Caesar's did not result in income from the cancellation of indebtedness. Rule 142(a).

Petitioner, relying on *Zarin v. Commissioner*, 916 F.2d 110 (3d Cir. 1990), *revg.* 92 T.C. 1084 (1989), claims that he disputed his debt to Caesar's, that his payments to Caesar's were in settlement of the dispute, and that therefore he realized no income upon the cancellation of the $255,000 that Caesar's claimed it was owed by petitioner.[18] Petitioner bases his argument upon certain facts alleged by him which respondent disputes. Petitioner claims that during early December 1985, he hosted a charity golf tournament at Caesar's involving 12 players; that at a dinner on the evening before the tournament, he invited the players to gamble on his credit if they did not have credit with Caesar's; that several players obtained chips on his credit, including one who obtained $100,000 of such chips; that the players who gambled on petitioner's credit turned chips in to the casino cage, including the player who obtained the $100,000 of chips; and that the return of the chips was not reflected on petitioner's account by the casino employee in the cage. Petitioner contends that each player reported receiving a slip of paper when returning chips to the cage, but petitioner does not know what became of the receipts. Petitioner claims to have

---

[18] [2] Petitioner does not argue that the settlement constituted a purchase price adjustment pursuant to sec. 108(e)(5). In Zarin v. Commissioner, 916 F.2d at 1097–1100, we concluded that sec. 108(e)(5) was inapplicable to the settlement of gambling debts, and that conclusion was not disturbed or criticized by the Court of Appeals for the Third Circuit.

personally lost $80,000 gambling at Caesar's during the tournament.

Petitioner claims that, from the time Caesar's began attempting to collect from him, he had a "running telephone dispute" with Caesar's because of the foregoing events, but he neither put his claims in writing nor attempted to obtain statements from the tournament gamblers to prove his allegations to Caesar's. Petitioner claims that Caesar's accepted his word. He claims to have dealt with Mr. Roy Jones, Caesar's casino collection manager, and that, after the tournament, he asked Mr. Jones to look into the absence of payment records. Although petitioner states that he never heard specifically what had occurred at the cage, petitioner claims that Caesar's started to send him letters concerning settlement of his account soon thereafter. Petitioner asserts that Caesar's must have known or thought it probable that a cage employee had mishandled the chips and that Caesar's settled for that reason. Petitioner contends that he owed Caesar's only $180,000, the amount that he repaid, but petitioner offers no evidence that directly corroborates his testimony that he disputed his debt to Caesar's. Petitioner, however, did offer the testimony of a witness who corroborated his version of some of the events occurring at the time of the golf tournament.

After considering the record in the instant case, however, we conclude that petitioner has not established the factual predicate for the alleged dispute between himself and Caesar's concerning the amount of his debt to the casino; namely, the use of his credit by others during December 1985 and the failure of the casino to record repayments by those persons. The records of the casino in evidence concerning petitioner's account show that the extensions of credit that created the debts the casino sought to collect from petitioner occurred during May and October of 1985, not during December of that year as petitioner claims. Because the records show that the casino made no additional extensions of credit to petitioner subsequent to October 1985, there is no support in those records for petitioner's contention that his indebtedness to the casino arose as a result of events occurring during early December 1985. Furthermore, petitioner does not claim that there was any dispute concerning his liability for or the amount of any of his debts to Caesar's that arose prior to December 1985.

Moreover, nothing in those records supports petitioner's contention that he incurred a debt to Caesar's of $80,000 during the December 1985 tournament due to gambling losses, which losses formed the basis for a portion of the debt that he acknowledged that he owed Caesar's. As noted above, Caesar's records show no new debt arising during December 1985. In light of petitioner's claims, we are nonplussed by the failure of those records to even indicate that petitioner made a trip to Caesar's during December 1985. Thus, as far as Caesar's records are concerned, the payments made by petitioner were made with respect to liabilities arising in May and October 1985, not during December 1985, as petitioner contends. Consequently, any events occurring with respect to the tournament that petitioner alleged took place during December 1985 did not affect the debt that Caesar's sought to collect from petitioner and which was the subject of the settlement between them.

Furthermore, there is nothing in the records that indicates that petitioner communicated to Caesar's his dispute concerning the amount of the debt on the grounds he advanced at trial. According to the testimony of the representative from Caesar's, it is Caesar's policy to record all contacts with a debtor on the IOU envelope for the debtor's account. The contacts recorded on the IOU envelope for petitioner's account do not contain any reference to any of the circumstances forming the basis of petitioner's alleged dispute with the casino. Instead, the contacts recorded on the IOU envelope simply chronicle the casino's inquiries as to when payments would be made and its difficulties with collecting payment from petitioner. One contact record dated January 8, 1987, notes that Caesar's verified with petitioner both the balance of petitioner's account and the payments that had been made and that petitioner agreed with them. The contact record entry is evidence standing in direct contrast to petitioner's claim that he disputed the amount he owed the casino.

It seems likely that, if petitioner did not believe that he owed the full amount Caesar's claimed, he would have told one or more of the account representatives who contacted him and that his claim, which involved an allegation of serious wrongdoing by a casino employee, would have been noted on the IOU envelope during the more than 2-1/2 years that Caesar's attempted to collect the debt. Petitioner claims that, because the casino accepted his word on the matter, he made no effort to prove his claim concerning the repayments from the tournament gamblers by, for instance, obtaining statements from them or showing the casino the receipts they apparently received from the casino cage when chips were cashed. However, in the records of Caesar's that are in evidence, there is no indication of any such acceptance. Petitioner claims that neither he nor the casino wanted to put anything concerning the dispute in writing prior to the making of settlement offers, but petitioner offers no plausible explanation for such a desire.

Moreover, it seems to us that petitioner readily could have resolved any dispute by presenting the casino with evidence of payment, such as the receipts apparently received by the tournament gamblers, rather than conducting a "running telephone dispute" with the casino that lasted over 2-1/2 years. Instead, petitioner testified that although the players received "slips of paper" when they returned chips to the cage, he did not "remember what happened to them or why they would have been important." In light of petitioner's legal background, we find curious petitioner's plea of ignorance as to the importance of such evidence as a matter of proof of his claim.

Petitioner also claimed to have dealt, by telephone, with Mr. Jones, Caesar's collection manager, and denied dealing with other Caesar's employees whose names appeared on casino correspondence with him. However, the IOU envelope and Caesar's correspondence with petitioner indicate that petitioner dealt with a number of Caesar's employees, and there is nothing in the records of Caesar's contacts with petitioner that shows that petitioner informed Mr. Jones of any dispute with the casino. Accordingly, it seems that Mr. Jones' testimony would have been of value to petitioner in corroborating his claim. Petitioner did not call Mr. Jones to testify, claiming that he did not need his testimony and that, in his experience as a lawyer, he had not been able to subpoena someone from as far away as Las Vegas to appear at a trial, which, in the instant case, was held in Tampa, Florida.

* * *

Petitioner contends that the casino's efforts to settle the debt were the result of its realization that a cage employee had mishandled chips and the difficulty of winning a suit against petitioner for collection of the amount it claimed he owed. Petitioner points to nothing in any of the documents in the record that indicates that those considerations prompted Caesar's to settle with petitioner. Mr. Larry Gaddis, the casino's assistant collection manager, who testified at trial, offered the following considerations that would have induced Caesar's to settle petitioner's account for less than the outstanding balance: (1) The age of and minimal payments that had been received on petitioner's account; (2) the cost of collecting the remaining balance of his account were a suit instituted against petitioner; and (3) the benefit to the casino of receiving a lump sum in the amount of the settlement versus payments over a long period of time. Such considerations are not the result of concerns on the part of Caesar's as to the enforceability of petitioner's debt.[19]

Petitioner argues that the fact that the casino settled petitioner's debt indicates that the debt was disputed. We do not agree. As to petitioner's contention, we find useful the analysis in *Exchange Sec. Bank v. United States*, 345 F. Supp. at 491, which involved a cancellation of indebtedness resulting from the settlement of litigation to collect a debt. The District Court offered the following analysis of the effect of a settlement that has been made for some of the reasons advanced by Caesar's in the instant case:

> On the other hand . . . [the debtor] may actually owe the debt; and yet . . . [the creditor], confronted with a denial of liability, may be willing to settle, saving the time and expense of litigation, by accepting a much smaller payment than that actually owing. Where there are serious problems of proof or of collectibility, or when . . . [the creditor] is confronted with unusual policy considerations, he may even be willing to dismiss the suit without any payment. In such situations it seems clear that . . . [the debtor] would thereby realize cancellation of indebtedness income subject to the "insolvency" and "gift" exceptions.[20]

---

[19] [11] Respondent claims that petitioner's debt to Caesar's was legally enforceable against him. It was Caesar's practice to obtain judgment against a debtor in the Nevada courts and then to have the judgment enforced against the debtor by the courts of the debtor's home State. A gaming debt evidenced by a credit instrument was legally enforceable pursuant to Nevada law when petitioner incurred his debt to Caesar's. Nev. Rev. Stat. secs. 463.367, 463.368(1) (1985). A judgment obtained in the Nevada courts would have been enforceable against petitioner in Florida pursuant to the Full Faith and Credit Clause of the U.S. Constitution, art. IV, sec. 1, notwithstanding that petitioner's debt to Caesar's would not have been enforceable pursuant to Florida law. Fauntleroy v. Lum, 210 U.S. 230, 237–238 (1908); Trauger v. A.J. Spagnol Lumber Co., 442 So. 2d 182, 183–184 (Fla. Dist. Ct. App. 1983); M & R Invs. Co. v. Hacker, 511 So. 2d 1099, 1100–1101 (Fla. Dist. Ct. App. 1987); GNLV Corp. v. Featherstone, 504 So. 2d 63 (Fla. Dist. Ct. App. 1987). Petitioner essentially conceded in his petition that, had Caesar's obtained a Nevada judgment against him, the judgment would have been legally enforceable against him in Florida. Petitioner, however, alleged that such circumstance was not relevant because Caesar's did not file suit against petitioner because of a "legitimate dispute concerning the amount due."

[20] [12] Neither exception is relevant in the instant case. Petitioner was not insolvent during 1988, nor has he established any donative intent on the part of Caesar's in settling his debt. Moreover, although there is no express abolition of the gift exception in sec. 108, the legislative history of the Bankruptcy Tax Act of 1980, Pub. L. 96-589, 94 Stat. 3389, which amended sec. 108, states, in the course of discussing

The conclusion which must be reached is that the settlement of a disputed debt may or may not result in cancellation-type income. The institution of a collection suit by a purported creditor does not establish that a debt exists or has existed, but essentially is only evidence that the plaintiff so contends; likewise, a defendant's denial of liability does not establish that a debt does not exist or is no longer enforceable, but essentially is only evidence that the purported debtor so contends. The terms of the agreement settling the litigation are of probative value (though not conclusive) in determining the relative merits of the two parties' positions — for example, the payment of no or only nominal consideration by the purported debtor tends to support the conclusion that at least one of its defenses is well taken. [*Id.*[21]].

Consequently, although, given the fact that Caesar's settled with petitioner, one might infer the existence of a dispute concerning the debt, and the amount of the settlement might be an indicator of the relative merits of their respective positions, such circumstances are not conclusive of whether a debt is disputed in good faith for purposes of deciding whether or not a debtor has realized income from the cancellation of indebtedness as a result of the settlement.[22] If a settlement alone were sufficient to establish the disputed nature of a debt, a taxpayer whose liability for the full amount of a settled debt was not in question would reap a windfall in the form of an untaxed freeing of the assets previously offset by the liability represented by the debt. In contrast, in the case of a settlement of a truly disputed debt, the settlement does not give rise to an accession to income due to the freeing

---

provisions relating to the realization of cancellation of indebtedness income arising from contributions by a shareholder of debt to the capital of a corporation, that "it is intended that there will not be any gift exception in a commercial context (such as a shareholder-corporation relationship) to the general rule that income is realized on the discharge of indebtedness." H. Rept. 96-833, at 15 n.21 (1980); S. Rept. 96-1035, at 19 n.22 (1980), 1980-2 C.B. 620, 629. Consequently, there is at least a question whether the gift exception continues to be applicable to commercial transactions, such as the one in issue in the instant case.

[21] [13] The court in Exchange Sec. Bank v. United States, 345 F. Supp. 486, 491 (N.D. Ala. 1972), *revd. on other grounds* 492 F.2d 1096 (5th Cir. 1974), also stated that "the trial court in a tax case involving alleged cancellation-type income must, it appears, determine the underlying, critical facts, *e.g.*, the actual amount (if any) of the debt." We note that, in Zarin v. Commissioner, 916 F.2d at 115–116, the Court of Appeals for the Third Circuit held that a good faith dispute between a lender and borrower would cause a settlement not to give rise to an accession to income from cancellation of indebtedness. The Board of Tax Appeals also found that settlement of a dispute concerning a debt did not give rise to income from the cancellation of indebtedness where litigation concerning the taxpayer's liability was bona fide, and, because of the settlement of the litigation, it could not be said whether or not the litigation would have established the liability. N. Sobel, Inc. v. Commissioner, 40 B.T.A. 1263, 1265 (1939). Thus, the Board seems to have adopted a similar standard in deciding whether the disputed debt rule applies to a settlement.

Notwithstanding the correct standard to be applied, however, petitioner cannot prevail because he has not established either that the actual amount of his debt was less than the amount Caesar's claimed that he owed or that there was a good faith dispute concerning the amount.

[22] [14] We conclude, based on the record, that petitioner has not established the existence of any dispute concerning the enforceability of his debt to Caesar's on any of the grounds alleged by him. The issue as to the enforceability of a debt, which was a factor considered by the Court of Appeals for the Third Circuit in Zarin v. Commissioner, 916 F.2d at 115–116, is accordingly not present in the instant case.

of the debtor's assets because the amount of the assets that were offset by the debt is not clear.

In the instant case, there is no direct evidence other than petitioner's testimony that he disputed his debt to Caesar's prior to the institution of proceedings in the instant case. Although petitioner contends that his testimony concerning his dealings with the casino was uncontradicted, we need not accept such testimony at face value where it is improbable, unreasonable, or questionable. *Quock Ting v. United States*, 140 U.S. 417 (1891); *Archer v. Commissioner*, 227 F.2d 270, 273 (5th Cir. 1955), *affg.* a Memorandum Opinion of this Court dated February 18, 1954. We find the evidence supporting and refuting petitioner's claim concerning the alleged dispute with Caesar's, at best, to be in equipoise, a state which is insufficient to carry petitioner's burden of proof.

Accordingly, we hold that petitioner has not established by a preponderance of the evidence that the settlement of his account with Caesar's was of a disputed debt. Consequently, we further hold that petitioner realized income from the cancellation of indebtedness in the amount of the balance of that account written off by Caesar's; to wit, $255,000.

To reflect the foregoing,

Decision will be entered for respondent.

Understanding *Rood*

1. Both Zarin and Rood owed money, claimed that the debt was wholly or partially invalid, and were able to extract a settlement under which they made partial payment of the relevant debt. Yet Zarin successfully avoided tax under the contested liability doctrine, while Rood conspicuously failed to do so. Why?

2. If Rood did not have a valid argument against payment of the debt, as the court suggests, then why did Caesar's agree to settle with him? Isn't the amount of the settlement the best single indication of the value of the debt? Or would this rule essentially allow taxpayers to escape taxation for cancellation of indebtedness, without regard to the "good faith" of the taxpayer's claim? How does the Tax Court deal with this problem?

3. At the time the case arose, Rood had been an attorney for more than 50 years and had served as President of the Association of Trial Lawyers of America, as well as various Florida bar organizations. Do you think this had any effect on the court's decision? Should it have? Why do you think the Tax Court mentioned this fact in the first page of its opinion?

Using the Sources

What are the federal income tax consequences of the following transactions?

a. Taxpayer borrows $100,000 from the bank and repays it

b. Taxpayer borrows $100,000 and the bank forgives the loan

c. Taxpayer borrows $100,000, but the bank — thinking it could make better use of the money somewhere else — permits the taxpayer to repay only $80,000 and calls it a day

d. Taxpayer borrows $100,000 and, when the bank tries to collect on the loan, argues that the loan was made in violation of state banking laws; the bank and the taxpayer subsequently settle for a payment of $50,000.

e. Does it make any difference, in item d., if the taxpayer's argument under the state banking laws had any merit?

Law and Planning

Suppose you are a homeowner with a $200,000, thirty-year mortgage, bearing a five-percent interest rate: that is, you are required to pay the bank, each month for thirty years, an amount that (in the aggregate) reflects the original $200,000 debt principal, plus five percent interest on the unpaid balance each year. After ten years, when you still owe $180,000 in principal, the bank offers to forego all remaining mortgage payments in return for an immediate payment of $150,000. You are fortunate enough to have $150,000 in cash lying around, but suspicious of the bank's motives, and concerned about the tax consequences too: after all, if it's such a great deal, why are they offering it to you?

Would you accept the bank's offer, or advise a client to do so? What effect would it have on your decision if (i) the $30,000 of debt "forgiveness" is likely to be taxable under the Code, and (ii) the 5 percent interest payments are deductible home mortgage interest (see Section II, infra)? Would these tax issues be sufficient to discourage your acceptance, or would more practical considerations encourage you to accept the bank's offer? What additional facts would you want to know to make this decision?

The "Mortgage Forgiveness Debt Relief Act of 2007" excludes up to $2 million of gain from the discharge of qualified residence indebtedness from the definition of taxable income.[23] But — unless Congress extends the provision — this relief is only effective for discharge of indebtedness occurring between January 1, 2007 and January 1, 2013.[24] Would this legislation have a meaningful effect on your choices in the preceding problem?

Politics and Policy

Now suppose that you are a member of Congress, and a number of constituents come to you complaining of the negative tax consequences of mortgage loan forgiveness, like those described in the preceding paragraph(s). The constituents — or the more eloquent of them, anyway — make three principal arguments:

(1) Taxation of loan forgiveness is discouraging transactions that would be economically beneficial to both the homeowners and the banks (economic

---

[23] Public Law 110-142, Mortgage Forgiveness Debt Relief Act of 2007.

[24] Public Law 110-343 extended the relief granted by Public Law 110-142.

efficiency).

(2) Most ordinary people would not think of a mutually agreed debt reduction as a form of income, but rather as a purchase price reduction or similar transaction (fairness or administrability argument with *Zarin* thrown in for good measure).

(3) People will never report this income to the IRS, anyway, making honest taxpayers feel like saps if they do.

The constituents ask you to sponsor legislation eliminating the tax on this type of transaction (or, at least, making the relief provision of the "Mortgage Forgiveness Debt Relief Act of 2007" permanent, *see* the Law and Planning question above).

Would you agree to sponsor this legislation? Which, if any, of the constituents' arguments do you find persuasive, and do you think that there would be political pressure for or against the proposal? Does the requested exemption seem more or less reasonable than those provided by Congress in section 108, or by the courts in *Zarin* or similar cases? As a general rule, are gamblers less sympathetic than homeowners? Or does it depend upon which gambler (which homeowner) we're talking about?

II. DEDUCTIONS FOR INTEREST PAYMENTS

A. Section 163

The concept of interest sounds complicated to law students, but it is really nothing more than the percentage fee received or paid by individuals or organizations when they lend or borrow money; it is the economic equivalent of rent for the use of land, or royalties for the use of intellectual property (although no one has yet discovered a Napster to avoid interest payments). Historically, the tax treatment of interest was straightforward: if you received interest, you paid tax, and if you paid interest, you got a corresponding tax deduction.

The first half of the above statement remains true: interest received is fully taxable with the notable exception of tax-free municipal bonds. But since 1987, the tax treatment of interest payments has grown considerably more complicated. The deductibility of such payments now depends upon (*inter alia*) the source of the loan, its purpose, and the security for its repayment. These rules are neither intuitive nor even particularly logical, so that comprehending them is an exercise in technical competence as much as (or more than) intellectual deduction.

To understand the rules, look at section 163, a case study in how a basically good idea can lead to confusion. The original rule, providing an overall deduction for interest payments, remains in section 163(a). This is still the applicable rule for business interest, which is deductible without limitation. The most significant limitation is contained in section 163(h), which denies a deduction for any personal interest.[25] Under this rule, interest on credit card loans, car loans, and other loans for personal purposes is no longer deductible for income tax purposes.

---

[25] Investment interest is technically in a middle category, being deductible only to the extent of

But section 163(h) includes a significant exception to the disallowance for personal interest expenses. Under this rule, qualified residence (*i.e.*, home mortgage) interest remains deductible, even though it is plainly personal interest within the broader statutory definition (section 163(h)(3)). Qualified residence interest includes both acquisition indebtedness, which is the original loan used to finance the purchase or improvement of a home, and home equity indebtedness, which is a loan secured by the home but used for some other purpose (college, medical expenses, a weekend in Paris, etc.)[26] This distinction is important, because one can deduct the interest on acquisition indebtedness up to $1 million — a pretty nice house, even in California — but on home equity indebtedness only up to $100,000, which is enough to pay for two years at a fancy college, but probably not all four.[27] Qualified residences, for purposes of acquisition or home equity indebtedness, include the taxpayer's principal and one other (presumably vacation) residence, although not cars, boats, or other places the taxpayer may prefer to spend her time instead of being at home.

The deductibility of home mortgage interest raises at least two policy questions. The first is the question of horizontal equity (fairness). If personal interest generally is suspect, why should interest on a home be treated differently than interest on a car, boat, or other tangible asset, or for that matter on credit cards or other consumer debt? Why should this special treatment then be extended to home equity loans, which aren't even used to buy a home, but merely to let the homeowner borrow against his or her equity in order to finance some other activity? One could argue that homes are an investment rather than a form of consumption, or that home ownership encourages "citizenship externalities" like mowing the lawn, paying your taxes, and generally being a good, upstanding member of the community.[28] But these arguments are somewhat forced, and most people would probably buy the same or similar residences even if mortgage interest were not, or were only partially, deductible. More likely, the difference is political. Home mortgages are extremely popular with the middle class voters who decide most American elections, and accordingly were protected when other forms of personal interest were not.

In addition to these policy issues, there is a more practical problem with the interest disallowance rules. It's fine to say that "interest on a business loan shall be fully deductible" or "interest on a personal loan shall not be deductible unless it is for home mortgage purposes." But money is interchangeable: one dollar is the same as any other, and it is extremely difficult to tell which loan has been used for what purpose. Suppose that a wealthy individual wants to expand his Internet consulting business, but prefers not to contribute his own personal assets, which would require him to reduce personal spending (restaurants, vacations, etc.) and

---

investment income (section 163(d)), although this provision does not affect most taxpayers.

[26] Equity refers to the excess in value of a property over the debt attaching to that property. For example, a person owning a home worth $400,000, subject to a $150,000 mortgage, would be said to have $250,000 of equity. The equity concept is discussed further in connection with the *Crane* case, *infra*.

[27] Refinancing of acquisition indebtedness remains in that same category. The Code (section 221) also allows a limited deduction for student loan interest, despite its at least nominally personal character.

[28] *See generally* Edward Zelinsky, *Efficiency and Income Taxes: The Rehabilitation of Tax Incentives*, 64 Tex. L. Rev. 973 (1986).

otherwise cut back on his lifestyle. Instead, he instructs the business to borrow $500,000 and continues his high-priced lifestyle. Because the loan is for business purposes, the interest is deductible under section 163. But hasn't the loan, in purely economic terms, enabled the businessman to engage in more personal spending? Should a portion of the interest deduction be disallowed on this basis? What about people who simply commingle (mix) business and personal assets, so that it is difficult to tell what money is being spent for what purpose? Finally, what about hybrid arrangements, like home equity loans, where money is borrowed using housing as collateral, but potentially used for a different, unrelated purpose? In what category, if any, should this loan be placed?

To deal with these problems, the law has adopted an ungainly series of rules, many of which clash with each other and which produce some seemingly incongruous results. The rule in section 163(h) — the one that distinguishes business from personal interest — operates on a tracing basis. Interest on loans that are used for business purposes is deductible, while interest on loans used for personal purposes is not, even though a business loan might effectively "free up" other money to be used for personal spending (and vice-versa). By contrast, the deduction for interest on home equity loans (section 163(h)(3)(C)) relies exclusively on the security for the loan. Loans secured by a principal residence qualify for the deduction, regardless of whether the proceeds are used for business, personal, or indeed wholly disreputable purposes; what matters is not the purpose of the loan, but the security for its repayment. Acquisition indebtedness has elements of both systems, requiring that the loan be used to acquire, construct, or improve a principal residence, and also be secured by the residence (section 163(h)(2)(B)). Other rules rely on the taxpayer's subjective purpose in taking out a loan; allocate loans proportionately between a taxpayer's different assets; or employ some mix of these different methods.

Because two or more of these rules are often applicable to the same transaction, section 163 sometimes produces odd — or at least surprising — results, and places a premium on careful tax planning. The following problems ask you to consider these issues. The first considers a fairly straightforward application of section 163(h), and the others more complex situations. The policy issues relating to section 163, and especially home mortgage interest, are considered in subsequent problems.

Using the Sources

1. To what extent, if any, would interest on the following loans be deductible:

    a. A car loan (for a personal car) secured by business assets.

    b. A business loan secured by your car (you may assume that you don't live in the car).

    c. A business loan secured by your house.

    d. A car loan secured by your house.

    e. A car loan secured by your car.

Do these results suggest a logical pattern, or are they instead arbitrary and unfair? How might the rules be changed to create a more coherent pattern? Why aren't they?

2. Ashley Findley bought a $300,000 home, paying $50,000 in cash and taking out a $250,000, thirty-year mortgage. Ten years later, when the home had increased in value to $400,000, and she still owed $200,000 in principal on the first mortgage, she took out a second, home equity loan on the same property in the amount of $150,000. She used the proceeds of the second loan to finance purchase of a small vacation cottage.

a. How much interest, if any, can Ashley deduct on each of these loans?

b. Do you have any suggestions as to how she could get a larger deduction?

3. On July 1, Ben Harley opens a bank account, contributing $25,000 in cash and $75,000 in borrowed funds (Loan A). On July 10, he borrows an additional $50,000 (Loan B) and places it in the account, whose balance is now $150,000, plus a small amount of accrued interest. On August 1, Harley withdraws $50,000 from the account to buy supplies for his business, and on August 15 withdraws an additional $50,000 to cover personal expenses. On September 1, he borrows an additional $100,000 (Loan C) and deposits it in the account, bringing the account balance back to (approximately) $150,000.

a. How much interest, if any, can Harley deduct on his three loans?

b. Is there anything he could have done to get a larger deduction?

See Treas. Reg. § 1.163-8T.

Law and Planning

Since interest on most personal loans is currently nondeductible, while home equity loans are at least partially deductible, there is an obvious incentive to borrow against a home in order to finance other activities. For example, interest on a car loan is nondeductible, but a home equity loan, the proceeds of which are used to purchase a new car, results in deductible interest. On a grander scale, individuals may be tempted to borrow against their homes to finance educational or medical expenses, retirement needs, or other large-scale expenditures. Not surprisingly, banks and other lending institutions tend to be aggressive in pointing out these advantages.

There are at least two dangers in this sort of transaction. One is that people may exaggerate the benefits of tax deductions and take out loans that don't make much business sense. For example, a $250,000 loan, at 10 percent interest, has an interest cost of $25,000 per year. If the interest is deductible, and assuming a 40 percent tax bracket, the interest cost is reduced to $15,000 a year ($25,000 - $10,000 tax deduction) — a better deal, but still a very substantial interest cost, especially if the same family could finance the same expenses without borrowing. There is thus a possibility of people being talked into loans they don't need in order to secure relatively limited tax deductions.

A more serious danger is the possibility of default. People taking out home equity loans sometimes seem not to realize, or choose to ignore, that they are effectively second mortgages, with all the risks and liabilities that accompany an original mortgage loan. Put bluntly, a borrower who defaults on a home equity loan risks losing his house. This is especially significant, since many home equity borrowers are middle-aged people whose incomes may be static or declining during the repayment period.

Suppose that you were advising a married couple, both 55 years of age, who anticipated spending about $200,000 to finance their daughter's (an only child) education. The couple had $200,000 in savings, but were reluctant to exhaust this money in case they had their own medical or retirement needs. Owing to a booming real estate market, the couple also owned a home that was worth $500,000, on which they had paid off nearly all the original mortgage, leaving them with equity in excess of $450,000.

The couple was considering the following three alternatives for financing their daughter's education:

> a. Take out a home equity loan;
>
> b. have their daughter take out student loans;[29] and
>
> c. use up their existing cash savings.

What strategy or mix of strategies strikes you as the best method of accomplishing these objectives? What additional facts, if any, would you want to know in order to make this decision? Would the deductibility of interest on home equity loans (up to $100,000) be a major factor in your decision, or would others issues likely outweigh it? (For purposes of this question, you may ignore the effect of tuition tax credits (section 25A) and similar provisions that might be available without regard to the financing method.)

Politics and Policy

As noted above, the deduction for home mortgage interest is among the most frequently criticized of tax provisions. A majority of tax scholars see the provision as unfair to renters (who receive no equivalent deduction for rental payments) and to poorer taxpayers generally (who either do not own homes or cannot afford a home large enough to receive a significant deduction). Critics further note that the provision is regressive, providing larger deductions to wealthier persons, and overbroad, providing benefits to many individuals who would have bought houses even without the deduction.

Defenders of the deduction emphasize its role in encouraging home ownership and related social benefits, and in overcoming alleged "barriers to entry" in the housing market. They further argue that renters benefit from deductions and other tax subsidies available to landlords, who pass them on in the form of lower rent. All

---

[29] The tax treatment of student loans is discussed *infra*; for now, you may assume that — given the couples' high income — the interest on student loans would either be nondeductible or only deductible in small part.

agree that the deduction is expensive, costing almost $100 billion per year in lost revenues to the Government, according to one recent estimate.[30]

Do you approve of the home mortgage interest deduction? Is home ownership something that the government should encourage, perhaps because (as some argue) home owners become better citizens due to their greater investment in their communities? Even if we concede that promoting home ownership is desirable, is the tax code an appropriate vehicle for promoting social policy goals?

Once a decision has been made to promote a social policy goal — like home ownership — through the tax system, a separate set of questions arise regarding the targeting of the tax benefit. Targeting issues can be tricky, both for the mortgage interest deduction and for tax incentives, generally. It is difficult to know exactly who will buy a house at what level of subsidy; moreover, there tends to be more political support for a broad program than a narrow one, even if the narrow program scores better under traditional policy criteria. One effort to achieve better targeting is the low-income housing credit program (section 42), which provides a tax credit to investors who build rental housing projects suitable for low- (or at least, lower-) income residents. Unlike the mortgage interest deduction, this program is restricted to renters below specified income levels; the program also contains numerous restrictions regarding the nature and type of housing to be constructed, similar to those that might be found in a direct spending program. A drawback of the program is that — in order to provide housing for lower-income individuals — it must first provide a generous tax subsidy to wealthy real estate investors. Are you offended by this tax shelter potential, or is it a necessary price for encouraging good behavior? In general, does the housing issue seem better addressed by tax subsidies or by some form of direct governmental assistance?

B.   Student Loans and Section 265

Section 163 does not exhaust the tax rules relating to the deductibility of interest payments. Among the other issues that remain to be addressed is a matter of interest to many readers: student loans, the interest on which was fully deductible before 1987, but which has since been characterized as nondeductible "personal interest" under section 163(h) of the Code.

The issue of student loans — like all issues relating to educational expenses — is a difficult one because of the mix of personal and business elements in the education process. While educational expenditures are generally not deductible, the historic deduction for student loan interest, together with the at least partially business purpose of postsecondary (and especially professional school) education, have combined to create a strong momentum for at least some form of deduction. There is also political pressure to "do something" about education costs, which, with the possible exception of turnpike tolls and the cost of Major League baseball tickets, seem to increase faster than just about any other item in the economy.

---

[30] Tax Expenditures, Analytical Perspectives from Office of Management and Budget: Budget of the United States Government, Fiscal Year 2007.

Perhaps responding to this pressure, the Code now includes a rule permitting a deduction of up to $2,500 of student loan interest in any year, but with a phase-out for adjusted gross income between $50,000 and $100,000 ($65,000 and $130,000 for joint returns), above which no deduction is permitted at all.[31] This is consistent with the emerging pattern with respect to educational expenses, which qualify for various indirect tax subsidies, (tuition tax credits, exclusion for employer-provided educational assistance, etc.) but not for an outright deduction or similar benefit. (Educational expenditures are discussed further in Chapter 6.)

A more abstract, but no less important, issue is presented by section 265 of the Code, which restricts borrowing to finance tax-exempt activities (section 265(a)(1)) or to "purchase or carry" tax-exempt bonds (section 265(a)(2)). The idea here is a simple one: that the taxpayer should not be permitted to deduct his interest expense on the one hand and use the same money to earn tax-exempt income on the other. This is often viewed as the grandmother of tax shelters, and a rule prohibiting it has long been contained in the Code.

The problem comes when you try to enforce the section 265 rule. Almost anyone wealthy enough to own tax-exempt bonds has some kind of debt outstanding at the same time, whether a home mortgage or a consumer loan or (if the taxpayer is in business) loans to buy new supplies and equipment or simply to keep the business going from year to year. The general rule here is that loans with an independent business purpose are exempted from section 265, but all loans that do not meet this description are assumed to be used to purchase or carry tax-exempt obligations, even if the funds are not directly traceable from one source to another.[32] Where a taxpayer has a portfolio of taxable and tax-exempt investments, a fraction of which is tax-exempt, an equivalent fraction of her otherwise deductible interest expenditure is denied. Section 265 is thus different from the remaining interest provisions, in that it (i) denies a deduction even when there is no direct link between the loan proceeds and a forbidden use, and (ii) emphasizes the taxpayer's subjective mental state ("purpose") rather than a mechanical tracing or security rule. Essentially, the burden is on the taxpayer to demonstrate that he was not intending to evade the rule; if this burden is not met, a proportionate amount of the interest deduction is eliminated.

The following case demonstrates the strengths and limitations of the section 265 purpose approach, in a somewhat unusual context.

WISCONSIN CHEESEMAN, INC. v. UNITED STATES
United States Court of Appeals, Seventh Circuit
388 F.2d 420 (1968)

CUMMINGS, Circuit J:

This lawsuit involves the proper construction of Section 265(2) of the Internal Revenue Code. The question for resolution is whether the taxpayer may deduct

---

[31] I.R.C. § 221.

[32] Rev. Proc. 72-18, 1972-1 C.B. 740.

from its gross income the interest it paid on its mortgage and some of its short-term loans.

Taxpayer is located in Sun Prairie, Wisconsin, and is in the business of packaging fancy cheeses for sale as Christmas gifts. Its business is seasonal and is most active during the last three months of each calendar year. Its sales are solicited exclusively through a catalog mailed each October. It incurs high costs in the last three months of each calendar year. Funds are borrowed annually from September through early November to cover such costs.

During the three fiscal years ending July 31, 1960, 1961 and 1962, taxpayer obtained short-term bank loans to meet its recurring needs for working capital. These borrowings took place each fall and were repaid, from late November through January, out of the receipts of each year's sales. The balance of the receipts was used to purchase municipal bonds and treasury bills. The treasury bills were acquired with staggered maturity dates to meet the off-season needs of the business. They were reduced to cash by the middle of each July. The municipal bonds were used as collateral for the bank loans, enabling taxpayer to borrow almost 100% of their value. On August 1, 1959, taxpayer had municipal bond holdings of $138,168.29. By July 31, 1962, these holdings had increased to $218,542.70.

In the second of the fiscal years involved, in order to build a new plant, taxpayer borrowed $69,360 from a bank. This loan was secured by a mortgage upon its real estate. The proceeds of the loan were used to pay for construction and not directly to purchase municipal bonds.

For these taxable fiscal years, the Commissioner of Internal Revenue disallowed taxpayer's deductions of interest on the mortgage and on some of the short-term loans. The taxpayer paid the resulting assessments and later brought this refund suit against the United States.

The District Court held that taxpayer incurred the indebtedness to "carry obligations . . . the interest on which is wholly exempt" from Federal income tax within the meaning of Section 265(2) of the Internal Revenue Code. Therefore, judgment was entered for the United States. We agree as to the interest on the short-term loans but not as to the mortgage interest.

Interest on Short-Term Loans

During each fall in the years in question, taxpayer used its municipal bonds as collateral for short-term bank loans for essential working capital. Instead of resorting to bank loans, taxpayer could have sold its municipals to meet the high cost seasonal needs of its business. Because this alternative was available to taxpayer, the Government argues that the short-term indebtedness was automatically incurred in order to enable taxpayer to "carry [tax-exempt] obligations," so that the interest on this indebtedness would be non-deductible under Section 265(2) of the Internal Revenue Code. The District Court construed Section 265(2) as forbidding the deduction of interest on indebtedness incurred or continued "in order to" or "for the purpose of" carrying tax-exempt obligations. We approve this construction but do not believe deduction is forbidden whenever taxpayer has an alternative of liquidating tax-exempts in lieu of borrowing.

The taxpayer contends that the short-term loans were incurred for the purpose of meeting its heavy fall seasonal financing needs, whereas the Government contends that the indebtedness was incurred for the purpose of making it possible for taxpayer to carry its municipal securities. In holding that the interest on the short-term loans could not be deducted, the District Court stated:

> "To accomplish the purpose of obtaining cash to meet plaintiff's seasonal needs, it was not a condition precedent that indebtedness be incurred. To accomplish the purpose of carrying the municipal securities, it was a condition precedent that indebtedness be incurred."

In reaching its conclusion that no refund was due, the District Court construed the Congressional intent as not to grant a deduction for interest payments by a taxpayer who holds securities, the interest from which is not taxable. This is the double benefit prohibited by Section 265(2). Stated another way, Congress sought to prevent a taxpayer from requiring the United States to finance its investments. *United States v. Atlas Life Insurance Co.*, 381 U.S. 233, 247.

In our view, the taxpayer is not *ipso facto* deprived of a deduction for interest on indebtedness while holding tax-exempt securities. The Government has not convinced us that interest deduction can be allowed only where the taxpayer shows that he wanted to sell the tax-exempt securities but could not. For example, Congress certainly did not intend to deny deductibility to a taxpayer who holds salable municipals and takes out a mortgage to buy a home instead of selling the municipals. As the Court of Claims stated in *Illinois Terminal Railroad Company v. United States*, 375 F.2d 1016, 1021, 179 Ct. Cl. 674 (Ct. Cl. 1967):

> "It is necessary [for the Commissioner] to establish a sufficiently direct relationship of the continuance of the debt for the purpose of carrying the tax-exempt bonds."

This construction flows from the use of "to" in Section 265(2). In this case, this nexus or "sufficiently direct relationship" is established by the fact that the tax-exempt securities were used as collateral for the seasonal loans. Under Section 265(2), it is clear that a taxpayer may not deduct interest on indebtedness when the proceeds of the loan are used to buy tax-exempts. 4A MERTENS, LAW OF FEDERAL INCOME TAXATION (1966 ed.) § 26.13 and cases cited. Applying the rule that the substance of the transaction is controlling in determining the tax liability, the same result should follow when the tax-exempt securities are used as collateral for a loan. Surely one who borrows to buy tax-exempts and one who borrows against tax-exempts already owned are in virtually the same economic position. Section 265(2) makes no distinction between them.

In addition, our analysis of the statute and its legislative history convinces us that the deduction should not be allowed if a taxpayer could reasonably have foreseen at the time of purchasing the tax-exempts that a loan would probably be required to meet future economic needs of an ordinary, recurrent variety. This test would not permit this taxpayer to deduct the short-term loan interest, for its regular business pattern shows that it would have to go into debt each fall if it bought or kept municipals as a long-term investment.[33] This established course of conduct is convincing proof that the underlying reason for these recurring loans was to carry the municipals.

To support its position, taxpayer relies on subsequent legislative history. However, subsequent legislative history is rarely of persuasive weight. *United States v. United Mine Workers of America*, 330 U.S. 258, 282. Furthermore, subsequent legislative history only indicates that Section 265(2) was not intended to operate as a "mechanical rule." Here we are not applying a mechanical rule but are insisting upon a connection between the tax-exempt securities and the loans before interest deductibility is disallowed.

Taxpayer relies mainly on *R.B. George Machinery Co. v. Commissioner of Internal Revenue*, 26 B.T.A. 594 (1932), and *Sioux Falls Metal Culvert Co. v. Commissioner of Internal Revenue*, 26 B.T.A. 1324 (1932). Those cases are distinguishable since the securities were not salable. In the other cases relied upon by taxpayer, the Commissioner prevailed; those cases permit the deduction if the taxpayer's only purpose is to meet business needs. *Illinois Terminal Railroad Company v. United States*, 375 F.2d 1016, 1021, 179 Ct. Cl. 674 (Ct. Cl. 1967), required taxpayer to have "purity of purpose" to obtain the deduction.

As taxpayer contends, there should be no discrimination against seasonal businesses but neither should they be put in a preferred position. If a nonseasonal business borrowed to buy municipals, the interest on the loans would be nondeductible. There is no reason why a seasonal business should fare better.

Taxpayer had the burden of overcoming the presumption of validity of the Commissioner's determination of deficiencies (*Drybrough v. Commissioner of Internal Revenue*, 376 F.2d 350, 360 (6th Cir. 1967)). This taxpayer has failed to sustain that burden.

Interest on Mortgage

The $69,360 construction loan was secured by a ten-year 6% mortgage on taxpayer's real estate. No municipal bonds were put up as collateral. The mortgage was for a new plant to meet a growing demand. The entire $69,360 mortgage proceeds were used to pay for this plant. According to the uncontroverted testimony, if taxpayer had sold municipal bonds to pay for the plant, it would have had fewer liquid assets to meet seasonal needs and would have had difficulty in borrowing to meet those needs. Plant construction is undeniably a major, nonrecurrent expenditure and is usually financed over a long term. We cannot say that a reasonable person would sacrifice liquidity and security by selling municipals in lieu of incurring mortgage debt to finance a new plant. Business reasons dominated the mortgaging of the property. Therefore, we are unwilling to accept the Commissioner's view that taxpayer should have liquidated municipals instead of obtaining a real estate mortgage loan. There is an insufficient relationship between the mortgage indebtedness and the holding of the municipal bonds to justify denial

---

[33] [3] Under this test, the deduction would be disallowed here even if the municipals were not used as collateral for the short-term loans.

of deduction of the mortgage interest. For non-deductibility, we have seen that the Commissioner must establish a sufficiently direct relationship between the debt and the carrying of the tax-exempt bonds. That has not been done as to the mortgage, so that the mortgage interest deductions must be allowed under Section 163(a) of the Internal Revenue Code.

The judgment is affirmed in part and reversed in part and the cause is remanded.

Understanding *Wisconsin Cheeseman*

1. What do you think of the court's application of the "independent business purpose" requirement in *Wisconsin Cheeseman*? Is (isn't) it pretty clearly foreseeable that a Christmas-oriented business would need to make seasonal borrowings to finance its activities at other times of the year? On the other hand, should the company be forbidden from adopting a business strategy that was probably not motivated by an illicit, tax-avoidance purpose? What do you make of the court's distinction between loans to finance long-term plant construction and those to finance short-term business activities? Aren't both of these equally foreseeable, and isn't the tax avoidance essentially equivalent in both cases? If so, what is the basis for the distinction?

2. Aside from tax avoidance, what do you think was the taxpayer's reason for investing in tax-exempt obligations in *Wisconsin Cheeseman*? Would you advise it to continue doing so, now that it has lost the case? Why (or why not)?

3. Suppose that an individual had the following three kinds of loans outstanding, together with a small portfolio of tax-exempt municipal bonds:

     a. A regular home mortgage (acquisition indebtedness).

     b. A home equity loan.

     c. An unsecured loan, which the taxpayer used to fund a mix of business and personal expenditures.

Which of the loans would result in deductible interest, and on which would the deduction be wholly or partially disallowed under section 265?

4. Would you recommend substituting the section 265 purpose requirement for the tracing rules under section 163 of the Code?

III.   SALES OF DEBT-ENCUMBERED PROPERTY: *CRANE* AND *TUFTS*

So far we have observed what happens when a loan is taken out and repaid (not much, unless the debt is forgiven), and when interest is paid on a loan (a deduction for business and certain kinds of favored personal interest, but otherwise no tax effects). But loans also have other, more indirect tax consequences. Both business and personal property are frequently subject to mortgages or other forms of debt. It is not uncommon for such property to be transferred from one taxpayer to another while the underlying debt remains outstanding or otherwise unpaid. What happens in that situation, and how does it relate to the issues discussed above?

To understand this problem, it may be helpful to return to the discussion of debt forgiveness at the beginning of the chapter. Suppose that Bob Borrower owes $100,000 to a bank and can't pay it back. (For a moment, ignore interest payments). The bank won't forgive the debt, but Bob's mother, who keeps an eye out for this sort of thing, agrees to pay the debt for him. This transaction has no tax consequences for Bob's bank — as far as the bank is concerned, the loan was taken out and repaid like any normal indebtedness. But what about for Bob and his mother?

It should not be difficult to see that Bob's mother's payment of the debt is, effectively, a gift of $100,000 from her to him, much as if she had given him the cash and he had paid the debt directly. Since gifts are exempt from income tax,[34] no tax will be paid on this particular transaction. But we have established an important pattern: where a third-party satisfies a debtor's obligation to a creditor, it will be treated as if the debtor received cash and satisfied the obligation herself.

Now assume that Bob doesn't have such a generous mother, but still needs to repay his debt. Instead of a gratuitous transfer, he decides to sell Carol, an unrelated person, a piece of real estate that Bob purchased a few years ago for $10,000, but which now has a fair market value of $100,000. In return for the property, Bob asks that Carol satisfy his $100,000 debt to the bank. This transaction is also equivalent to the receipt of $100,000 in cash by Bob, except that this time it is not a gift, but the sale price of an asset with a basis of $10,000. So Bob is taxed on $90,000 of gain ($100,000 amount realized - $10,000 basis); Carol takes the asset with a basis of $100,000; and everyone goes home happy, including the tax collector, who receives the same tax that she would have gotten on a cash sale, only in a slightly different format.

Finally, assume that there is no bank, but that Bob holds a piece of real estate with a basis of $10,000 and a fair market value of $100,000, and subject to an unpaid $50,000 mortgage loan. He sells the real estate to Carol in return for $50,000 in cash and her assumption of responsibility for repaying the $50,000 loan. Has Bob realized $90,000 of gain, as in the preceding example? What if Bob is not personally liable on the mortgage (a so-called "nonrecourse" loan), so that he could (in theory) abandon the property without ever repaying the loan?[35] And what if the value of the property was rapidly declining, so that it was not merely possible, but likely, that the loan would never be repaid? Should any of this matter, or should relief from a loan always be treated as the equivalent of cash, without regard to other circumstances?

These questions are directly or indirectly addressed by the following case, *Crane v. Commissioner*, the classic decision regarding debt relief and the transfer of property. As you read it, consider first the mode of statutory interpretation in the opinion: is the Court faithful to the literal language of the Code, or does it create

---

[34] I.R.C.§ 102.

[35] Nonrecourse loans are a common type of financing, especially in a business context, where people may not wish to place their home, car, etc., at risk in each transaction. Such loans are frequently secured by the property that they finance, so that a default — although not bankrupting the debtor — will result in forfeiture of the underlying property.

new law to deal with a fascinating but unanticipated fact situation? Consider also the case's outcome: does the IRS really "win" *Crane*, or does it create a precedent that will come back to haunt it in other cases?

CRANE v. COMMISSIONER
United States Supreme Court
331 U.S. 1 (1947)

MR. CHIEF JUSTICE VINSON delivered the opinion of the Court.

The question here is how a taxpayer who acquires depreciable property subject to an unassumed mortgage, holds it for a period, and finally sells it still so encumbered, must compute her taxable gain.

Petitioner was the sole beneficiary and the executrix of the will of her husband, who died January 11, 1932. He then owned an apartment building and lot subject to a mortgage,[36] which secured a principal debt of $255,000.00 and interest in default of $7,042.50. As of that date, the property was appraised for federal estate tax purposes at a value exactly equal to the total amount of this encumbrance. Shortly after her husband's death, petitioner entered into an agreement with the mortgagee whereby she was to continue to operate the property — collecting the rents, paying for necessary repairs, labor, and other operating expenses, and reserving $200.00 monthly for taxes — and was to remit the net rentals to the mortgagee. This plan was followed for nearly seven years, during which period petitioner reported the gross rentals as income, and claimed and was allowed deductions for taxes and operating expenses paid on the property, for interest paid on the mortgage, and for the physical exhaustion of the building. Meanwhile, the arrearage of interest increased to $15,857.71. On November 29, 1938, with the mortgagee threatening foreclosure, petitioner sold to a third party for $3,000.00 cash, subject to the mortgage, and paid $500.00 expenses of sale.

Petitioner reported a taxable gain of $1,250.00. Her theory was that the "property" which she had acquired in 1932 and sold in 1938 was only the equity, or the excess in the value of the apartment building and lot over the amount of the mortgage. This equity was of zero value when she acquired it. No depreciation could be taken on a zero value.[37] Neither she nor her vendee ever assumed the mortgage, so, when she sold the equity, the amount she realized on the sale was the net cash received, or $2,500.00. This sum less the zero basis constituted her gain, of which she reported half as taxable on the assumption that the entire property was a "capital asset."[38]

---

[36] [1] The record does not show whether he was personally liable for the debt.

[37] [2] This position is, of course, inconsistent with her practice in claiming such deductions in each of the years the property was held. The deductions so claimed and allowed by the Commissioner were in the total amount of $25,500.00.

[38] [3] *See* § 117(a), (b), Revenue Act of 1938, c. 289, 52 Stat. 447. Under this provision only 50% of the gain realized on the sale of a "capital asset" needs be taken into account, if the property had been held more than two years.

The Commissioner, however, determined that petitioner realized a net taxable gain of $23,767.03. His theory was that the "property" acquired and sold was not the equity, as petitioner claimed, but rather the physical property itself, or the owner's rights to possess, use, and dispose of it, undiminished by the mortgage. The original basis thereof was $262,042.50, its appraised value in 1932. Of this value $55,000.00 was allocable to land and $207,042.50 to building. During the period that petitioner held the property, there was an allowable depreciation of $28,045.10 on the building, so that the adjusted basis of the building at the time of sale was $178,997.40. The amount realized on the sale was said to include not only the $2,500.00 net cash receipts, but also the principal amount of the mortgage subject to which the property was sold, both totaling $257,500.00. The selling price was allocable in the proportion, $54,471.15 to the land and $203,028.85 to the building. The Commissioner agreed that the land was a "capital asset," but thought that the building was not. Thus, he determined that petitioner sustained a capital loss of $528.85 on the land, of which 50% or $264.42 was taken into account, and an ordinary gain of $24,031.45 on the building, or a net taxable gain as indicated.

The Tax Court agreed with the Commissioner that the building was not a "capital asset." In all other respects it adopted petitioner's contentions, and expunged the deficiency. Petitioner did not appeal from the part of the ruling adverse to her, and these questions are no longer at issue. On the Commissioner's appeal, the Circuit Court of Appeals reversed, one judge dissenting. We granted certiorari because of the importance of the questions raised as to the proper construction of the gain and loss provisions of the Internal Revenue Code.

The 1938 Act, n12 § 111(a), defines the gain from "the sale or other disposition of property" as "the excess of the amount realized therefrom over the adjusted basis provided in section 113(b). . . ." It proceeds, § 111(b), to define "the amount realized from the sale or other disposition of property" as "the sum of any money received plus the fair market value of the property (other than money) received." Further, in § 113(b), the "adjusted basis for determining the gain or loss from the sale or other disposition of property" is declared to be "the basis determined under subsection (a), adjusted . . . [(1)(B)] . . . for exhaustion, wear and tear, obsolescence, amortization . . . to the extent allowed (but not less than the amount allowable). . . ." The basis under subsection (a) "if the property was acquired by . . . devise . . . or by the decedent's estate from the decedent," § 113(a)(5), is "the fair market value of such property at the time of such acquisition. "

Logically, the first step under this scheme is to determine the unadjusted basis of the property, under § 113(a)(5), and the dispute in this case is as to the construction to be given the term "property." If "property," as used in that provision, means the same thing as "equity," it would necessarily follow that the basis of petitioner's property was zero, as she contends. If, on the contrary, it means the land and building themselves, or the owner's legal rights in them, undiminished by the mortgage, the basis was $262,042.50.

We think that the reasons for favoring one of the latter constructions are of overwhelming weight. In the first place, the words of statutes — including revenue acts — should be interpreted where possible in their ordinary, everyday senses. The only relevant definitions of "property" to be found in the principal standard dictionaries are the two favored by the Commissioner, *i.e.*, either that "property" is the physical thing which is a subject of ownership, or that it is the aggregate of the owner's rights to control and dispose of that thing. "Equity" is not given as a synonym, nor do either of the foregoing definitions suggest that it could be correctly so used. Indeed, "equity" is defined as "the value of a property . . . above the total of the liens. . . ." The contradistinction could hardly be more pointed. Strong countervailing considerations would be required to support a contention that Congress, in using the word "property," meant "equity," or that we should impute to it the intent to convey that meaning.

In the second place, the Commissioner's position has the approval of the administrative construction of § 113(a)(5). With respect to the valuation of property under that section, Reg. 101, Art. 113(a)(5)-1, promulgated under the 1938 Act, provided that "the value of property as of the date of the death of the decedent as appraised for the purpose of the Federal estate tax . . . shall be deemed to be its fair market value. . . ." The land and building here involved were so appraised in 1932, and their appraised value — $262,042.50 — was reported by petitioner as part of the gross estate. This was in accordance with the estate tax law and regulations, which had always required that the value of decedent's property, undiminished by liens, be so appraised and returned, and that mortgages be separately deducted in computing the net estate. As the quoted provision of the Regulations has been in effect since 1918, and as the relevant statutory provision has been repeatedly reenacted since then in substantially the same form, the former may itself now be considered to have the force of law.

Moreover, in the many instances in other parts of the Act in which Congress has used the word "property," or expressed the idea of "property" or "equity," we find no instances of a misuse of either word or of a confusion of the ideas. In some parts of the Act other than the gain and loss sections, we find "property" where it is unmistakably used in its ordinary sense. On the other hand, where either Congress or the Treasury intended to convey the meaning of "equity," it did so by the use of appropriate language.

A further reason why the word "property" in § 113(a) should not be construed to mean "equity" is the bearing such construction would have on the allowance of deductions for depreciation and on the collateral adjustments of basis.

Section 23(l) permits deduction from gross income of "a reasonable allowance for the exhaustion, wear and tear of property. . . ." Sections 23(n) and 114(a) declare that the "basis upon which exhaustion, wear and tear . . . are to be allowed" is the basis "provided in section 113(b) for the purpose of determining the gain upon the sale" of the property, which is the § 113(a) basis "adjusted . . . for exhaustion, wear and tear . . . to the extent allowed (but not less than the amount allowable). . . ."

Under these provisions, if the mortgagor's equity were the § 113(a) basis, it would also be the original basis from which depreciation allowances are deducted. If it is, and if the amount of the annual allowances were to be computed on that value, as would then seem to be required, they will represent only a fraction of the cost of the corresponding physical exhaustion, and any recoupment by the mortgagor of the remainder of that cost can be effected only by the reduction of his taxable gain in the year of sale. If, however, the amount of the annual allowances were to be computed on the value of the property, and then deducted from an equity basis, we would in some instances have to accept deductions from a minus basis or deny deductions altogether.[39] The Commissioner also argues that taking the mortgagor's equity as the § 113(a) basis would require the basis to be changed with each payment on the mortgage, and that the attendant problem of repeatedly recomputing basis and annual allowances would be a tremendous accounting burden on both the Commissioner and the taxpayer. Moreover, the mortgagor would acquire control over the timing of his depreciation allowances.

Thus it appears that the applicable provisions of the Act expressly preclude an equity basis, and the use of it is contrary to certain implicit principles of income tax depreciation, and entails very great administrative difficulties.[40] It may be added that the Treasury has never furnished a guide through the maze of problems that arise in connection with depreciating an equity basis, but, on the contrary, has consistently permitted the amount of depreciation allowances to be computed on the full value of the property, and subtracted from it as a basis. Surely, Congress' long-continued acceptance of this situation gives it full legislative endorsement.

We conclude that the proper basis under § 113(a)(5) is the value of the property, undiminished by mortgages thereon, and that the correct basis here was $262,042.50. The next step is to ascertain what adjustments are required under § 113(b). As the depreciation rate was stipulated, the only question at this point is whether the Commissioner was warranted in making any depreciation adjustments whatsoever.

Section 113(b)(1)(B) provides that "proper adjustment in respect of the property *shall in all cases be made* . . . for exhaustion, wear and tear . . . to the extent allowed (but not less than the amount allowable). . . ." (Italics supplied.) The Tax Court found on adequate evidence that the apartment house was property of a kind subject to physical exhaustion, that it was used in taxpayer's trade or business, and consequently that the taxpayer would have been entitled to a depreciation allowance under § 23(1), except that, in the opinion of that Court, the basis of the property was zero, and it was thought that depreciation could not be taken on a zero basis. As we have just decided that the correct basis of the property was not zero, but $262,042.50, we avoid this difficulty, and conclude that an adjustment should be made as the Commissioner determined.

Petitioner urges to the contrary that she was not entitled to depreciation deductions, whatever the basis of the property, because the law allows them only to one who actually bears the capital loss, and here the loss was not hers but the mortgagee's. We do not see, however, that she has established her factual premise.

---

[39] [28] So long as the mortgagor remains in possession, the mortgagee cannot take depreciation deductions, even if he is the one who actually sustains the capital loss, as § 23(l) allows them only on property "used in the trade or business."

[40] [30] Obviously we are not considering a situation in which a taxpayer has acquired and sold an equity of redemption only, *i.e.*, a right to redeem the property without a right to present possession. In that situation, the right to redeem would itself be the aggregate of the taxpayer's rights and would undoubtedly constitute "property" within the meaning of § 113(a). No depreciation problems would arise. *See* note 28.

There was no finding of the Tax Court to that effect, nor to the effect that the value of the property was ever less than the amount of the lien. Nor was there evidence in the record, or any indication that petitioner could produce evidence, that this was so. The facts that the value of the property was only equal to the lien in 1932 and that during the next six and one-half years the physical condition of the building deteriorated and the amount of the lien increased, are entirely inconclusive, particularly in the light of the buyer's willingness in 1938 to take subject to the increased lien and pay a substantial amount of cash to boot. Whatever may be the rule as to allowing depreciation to a mortgagor on property in his possession which is subject to an unassumed mortgage and clearly worth less than the lien, we are not faced with that problem and see no reason to decide it now.

At last we come to the problem of determining the "amount realized" on the 1938 sale. Section 111(b), it will be recalled, defines the "amount realized" from "the sale . . . of property" as "the sum of any money received plus the fair market value of the property (other than money) received," and § 111(a) defines the gain on "the sale . . . of property" as the excess of the amount realized over the basis. Quite obviously, the word "property," used here with reference to a sale, must mean "property" in the same ordinary sense intended by the use of the word with reference to acquisition and depreciation in § 113, both for certain of the reasons stated heretofore in discussing its meaning in § 113, and also because the functional relation of the two sections requires that the word mean the same in one section that it does in the other. If the "property" to be valued on the date of acquisition is the property free of liens, the "property" to be priced on a subsequent sale must be the same thing. Starting from this point, we could not accept petitioner's contention that the $2,500.00 net cash was all she realized on the sale except on the absurdity that she sold a quarter-of-a-million dollar property for roughly one per cent of its value, and took a 99 per cent loss. Actually, petitioner does not urge this. She argues, conversely, that because only $2,500.00 was realized on the sale, the "property" sold must have been the equity only, and that consequently we are forced to accept her contention as to the meaning of "property" in § 113. We adhere, however, to what we have already said on the meaning of "property," and we find that the absurdity is avoided by our conclusion that the amount of the mortgage is properly included in the "amount realized" on the sale.

Petitioner concedes that if she had been personally liable on the mortgage and the purchaser had either paid or assumed it, the amount so paid or assumed would be considered a part of the "amount realized" within the meaning of § 111(b). The cases so deciding have already repudiated the notion that there must be an actual receipt by the seller himself of "money" or "other property," in their narrowest senses. It was thought to be decisive that one section of the Act must be construed so as not to defeat the intention of another or to frustrate the Act as a whole, and that the taxpayer was the "beneficiary" of the payment in "as real and substantial [a sense] as if the money had been paid it and then paid over by it to its creditors. Both these points apply to this case. The first has been mentioned already. As for the second, we think that a mortgagor, not personally liable on the debt, who sells the property subject to the mortgage and for additional consideration, realizes a benefit in the amount of the mortgage as well as the boot.[41] If a purchaser pays boot, it is immaterial as to our problem whether the mortgagor is also to receive money from the purchaser to discharge the mortgage prior to sale, or whether he is merely to transfer subject to the mortgage — it may make a difference to the purchaser and to the mortgagee, but not to the mortgagor. Or put in another way, we are no more concerned with whether the mortgagor is, strictly speaking, a debtor on the mortgage, than we are with whether the benefit to him is, strictly speaking, a receipt of money or property. We are rather concerned with the reality that an owner of property, mortgaged at a figure less than that at which the property will sell, must and will treat the conditions of the mortgage exactly as if they were his personal obligations. If he transfers subject to the mortgage, the benefit to him is as real and substantial as if the mortgage were discharged, or as if a personal debt in an equal amount had been assumed by another.

Therefore we conclude that the Commissioner was right in determining that petitioner realized $257,500.00 on the sale of this property.

The Tax Court's contrary determinations, that "property," as used in § 113(a) and related sections, means "equity," and that the amount of a mortgage subject to which property is sold is not the measure of a benefit realized, within the meaning of § 111(b), announced rules of general applicability on clear-cut questions of law. The Circuit Court of Appeals therefore had jurisdiction to review them.

Petitioner contends that the result we have reached taxes her on what is not income within the meaning of the Sixteenth Amendment. If this is because only the direct receipt of cash is thought to be income in the constitutional sense, her contention is wholly without merit. If it is because the entire transaction is thought to have been "by all dictates of common sense . . . a ruinous disaster," as it was termed in her brief, we disagree with her premise. She was entitled to depreciation deductions for a period of nearly seven years, and she actually took them in almost the allowable amount. The crux of this case, really, is whether the law permits her to exclude allowable deductions from consideration in computing gain.[42] We have already showed that, if it does, the taxpayer can enjoy a double deduction, in effect, on the same loss of assets. The Sixteenth Amendment does not require that result any more than does the Act itself.

Affirmed.

---

[41] [37] Obviously, if the value of the property is less than the amount of the mortgage, a mortgagor who is not personally liable cannot realize a benefit equal to the mortgage. Consequently, a different problem might be encountered where a mortgagor abandoned the property or transferred it subject to the mortgage without receiving boot. That is not this case.

[42] [42] In the course of the argument some reference was made, as by analogy, to a situation in which a taxpayer acquired by devise property subject to a mortgage in an amount greater than the then value of the property, and later transferred it to a third person, still subject to the mortgage, and for a cash boot. Whether or not the difference between the value of the property on acquisition and the amount of the mortgage would in that situation constitute either statutory or constitutional income is a question which is different from the one before us, and which we need not presently answer.

MR. JUSTICE JACKSON, dissenting.

The Tax Court concluded that this taxpayer acquired only an equity worth nothing. The mortgage was in default, the mortgage debt was equal to the value of the property, any possession by the taxpayer was forfeited and terminable immediately by foreclosure, and perhaps by a receiver *pendente lite*. Arguments can be advanced to support the theory that the taxpayer received the whole property and thereupon came to owe the whole debt. Likewise it is argued that when she sold she transferred the entire value of the property and received release from the whole debt. But we think these arguments are not so conclusive that it was not within the province of the Tax Court to find that she received an equity which at that time had a zero value. *Dobson v. Commissioner*, 320 U.S. 489; *Commissioner v. Scottish American Investment Co., Ltd.*, 323 U.S. 119. The taxpayer never became personally liable for the debt, and hence when she sold she was released from no debt. The mortgage debt was simply a subtraction from the value of what she did receive, and from what she sold. The subtraction left her nothing when she acquired it and a small margin when she sold it. She acquired a property right equivalent to an equity of redemption and sold the same thing. It was the "property" bought and sold as the Tax Court considered it to be under the Revenue Laws. We are not required in this case to decide whether depreciation was properly taken, for there is no issue about it here.

We would reverse the Court of Appeals and sustain the decision of the Tax Court.

MR. JUSTICE FRANKFURTER and MR. JUSTICE DOUGLAS join in this opinion.

Understanding *Crane*

1. *Crane* involves two separate computations: the basis of the property that was inherited by Mrs. Crane (sections 1011 and 1014 of present law) and the amount realized on the sale of the property (section 1001(b)). The Court makes the first issue sound easy: the basis of inherited property equals the fair market value of the property without any offset for mortgage or other debt, *i.e.*, without regard to the owner's equity in the property. Is this really so clear? If an ordinary person inherited a $30,000 building, subject to a loan of precisely the same amount, would they think of themselves as having inherited a property worth $30,000, or a property whose net value was (for all intents and purposes) zero? Is Mrs. Crane arguing common sense economics, while the Government advances a technically appealing but excessively complex theory? Why does the Government take this position?

2. The second *Crane* computation concerns the amount realized on the sale of the property, which the statute defines as "the sum of any money received plus the fair market value of the property (other than money) received."[43] The Government's (and the Court's) position is that this amount includes the unpaid balance of the loan

---

[43] I.R.C. § 1001(b). The amount of gain realized is equal to the excess of the amount realized over the adjusted basis of the property (section 1001(a)).

to which the property is subject. Does this position make sense? Would most people call a mortgage assumption "property," particularly when the seller was not personally liable for the mortgage, and could (at least in theory) have abandoned the property without ever paying the mortgage? Once again, is the court deciding the case according to the actual words of the statute, or its own sense of appropriate tax policy? If the latter reading, is it correct in doing so?

3.   If Mrs. Crane had won the case, her basis at the time of the inheritance would in theory have been zero. What then would have happened when she tried to take depreciation deductions on the property? Would her basis in the property have been reduced to a negative number? Or would someone else — presumably, the bank holding the mortgage — have been entitled to depreciation until her equity increased to the point where she had a positive basis? Who would make this allocation, and how? Is the fear of negative basis one reason that the Court rejects Mrs. Crane's version of the case?

4.   Toward the end of its decision, the Court refers to "the reality that an owner of property, mortgaged at a figure less than that at which the property will sell, must and will treat the conditions of the mortgage exactly as if they were his personal obligations." In other words, since the building was still worth more than the amount of the mortgage, Mrs. Crane — like most borrowers on nonrecourse loans — would eventually have paid the mortgage rather than abandoning the property. Relief from the debt was therefore a tangible benefit to her that should be reflected in her taxable income.

Is the logic argument above really as convincing as the Court suggests? For one thing, how do we know that the property is worth more than the amount of the mortgage? Is it possible that the buyer's $3,000 cash payment was merely a sweetener designed to make the transaction more palatable to Mrs. Crane, rather than a judgment that the property was worth more than the mortgage? Even if the property had been worth less than the mortgage, wouldn't the underlying logic of the case — that relief from debt is equivalent to the receipt of cash — been essentially the same? Or would different facts have produced a different outcome?

5.   If you were on the Supreme Court, how would you have voted in *Crane*?

Crane is fascinating in that the taxpayer and the IRS offered two completely different, internally consistent descriptions of the same series of transactions. The taxpayer's view was that the amount of the loan should be excluded both at the "front" end of the transaction (*i.e.*, the computation of basis) and the "back" end (*i.e.*, the computation of gain on sale of the property). Under this view of the case, the taxpayer's basis was zero (*i.e.*, her equity in the property); the amount realized was $2,500 ($3,000 cash - $500 sale expenses); and there was a total of $2,500 gain on the sale. The IRS argued that the amount of the loan should be included in both computations: thus, the basis at the time of inheritance was approximately $262,000 (*i.e.*, the value of the property without any offset for debt financing), which was reduced by depreciation to about $234,000; the amount realized was $257,500 ($2,500 cash + $255,000 debt relief); and the amount of gain was approximately $23,500.

In thinking about these differences, it may be useful to distinguish between practical and philosophical issues. The practical difference is that the IRS version required the taxpayer to "recapture" depreciation deductions taken while she was owner of the property, while the taxpayer's version allowed her to escape that result. This accounts for the $20,000-plus difference in the resulting tax liabilities.

The philosophical difference is significantly broader. The IRS argued — and the Supreme Court eventually held — that a taxpayer's basis in property is determined without regard to how the property is financed — cash, debt, or a combination of the two — and without further regard to whether the debt is recourse, nonrecourse, or somewhere in between. All that matters is the price paid for the property, or (in the case of inherited property) the fair market value at the time of inheritance. A taxpayer may thus finance a property primarily or exclusively with borrowed funds and receive the same basis — and the same depreciation deductions — as if she had put down her own cash. There is a cost, to be sure, in that the unpaid balance of the loan will be included in the amount realized on a later sale of the property; to say otherwise would let the taxpayer benefit from inconsistent treatment of the same item. But this is likely to seem a long way off at the beginning of the transaction, and it may never happen, at all. In the meantime the taxpayer gets the benefit of depreciation and other deductions flowing from the inflated basis, while her actual economic stake in the property may be relatively low.

Although nominally an IRS victory, *Crane* was thus a favorable precedent for many taxpayers. One particular beneficiary was the tax shelter industry. Under the taxpayer's version of *Crane*, an investor who wanted to take (say) $200,000 of depreciation deductions would have had to come up with $200,000 of his own money. By contrast, under the Court's holding, the same individual could put down $20,000 of his own money, together with $180,000 in borrowed funds, and be entitled to the same benefits. These depreciation deductions are in addition to the interest and other deductions that are available for business or investment property.[44] *Crane* thus helped to make possible the "two-to-one," "three-to-one," and even "ten-to-one" writeoffs that characterize the tax shelter industry. While recent legislation has restricted these possibilities,[45] it has not eliminated them, and *Crane* remains a vital precedent for understanding the tax shelter phenomenon.

Although it had immediate and widespread significance, *Crane* left an important question unanswered. What would be the holding in a *Crane*-like case if the value of the property were less than the amount of the outstanding nonrecourse mortgage — if, in other words, the *Crane* court's analysis of the taxpayer's "economic" motivation no longer applied? Only a generation later was this question answered in the case that follows.

---

[44] I.R.C. § 163.

[45] *See* I.R.C. §§ 465 (limiting deductions to the amount "at risk" in a transaction); 469 (restricting use of passive activity losses).

COMMISSIONER v. TUFTS
United States Supreme Court
461 U.S. 300 (1983)

Justice Blackmun delivered the opinion of the Court.

Over 35 years ago, in *Crane v. Commissioner*, 331 U.S. 1 (1947), this Court ruled that a taxpayer, who sold property encumbered by a nonrecourse mortgage (the amount of the mortgage being less than the property's value), must include the unpaid balance of the mortgage in the computation of the amount the taxpayer realized on the sale. The case now before us presents the question whether the same rule applies when the unpaid amount of the nonrecourse mortgage exceeds the fair market value of the property sold.

I

On August 1, 1970, respondent Clark Pelt, a builder, and his wholly owned corporation, respondent Clark, Inc., formed a general partnership. The purpose of the partnership was to construct a 120-unit apartment complex in Duncanville, Tex., a Dallas suburb. Neither Pelt nor Clark, Inc., made any capital contribution to the partnership. Six days later, the partnership entered into a mortgage loan agreement with the Farm & Home Savings Association (F&H). Under the agreement, F&H was committed for a $1,851,500 loan for the complex. In return, the partnership executed a note and a deed of trust in favor of F&H. The partnership obtained the loan on a nonrecourse basis: neither the partnership nor its partners assumed any personal liability for repayment of the loan. Pelt later admitted four friends and relatives, respondents Tufts, Steger, Stephens, and Austin, as general partners. None of them contributed capital upon entering the partnership.

The construction of the complex was completed in August 1971. During 1971, each partner made small capital contributions to the partnership; in 1972, however, only Pelt made a contribution. The total of the partners' capital contributions was $44,212. In each tax year, all partners claimed as income tax deductions their allocable shares of ordinary losses and depreciation. The deductions taken by the partners in 1971 and 1972 totaled $439,972. Due to these contributions and deductions, the partnership's adjusted basis in the property in August 1972 was $1,455,740.

In 1971 and 1972, major employers in the Duncanville area laid off significant numbers of workers. As a result, the partnership's rental income was less than expected, and it was unable to make the payments due on the mortgage. Each partner, on August 28, 1972, sold his partnership interest to an unrelated third party, Fred Bayles. As consideration, Bayles agreed to reimburse each partner's sale expenses up to $250; he also assumed the nonrecourse mortgage.

On the date of transfer, the fair market value of the property did not exceed $1,400,000. Each partner reported the sale on his federal income tax return and indicated that a partnership loss of $55,740 had been sustained.[46] The Commissioner of Internal Revenue, on audit, determined that the sale resulted in a partnership capital gain of approximately $400,000. His theory was that the partnership had realized the full amount of the nonrecourse obligation.[47]

Relying on *Millar v. Commissioner*, 577 F.2d 212, 215 (CA3), *cert. denied*, 439 U.S. 1046 (1978), the United States Tax Court, in an unreviewed decision, upheld the asserted deficiencies. 70 T.C. 756 (1978). The United States Court of Appeals for the Fifth Circuit reversed. 651 F.2d 1058 (1981). That court expressly disagreed with the *Millar* analysis, and, in limiting *Crane v. Commissioner, supra*, to its facts, questioned the theoretical underpinnings of the *Crane* decision. We granted *certiorari* to resolve the conflict. 456 U.S. 960 (1982).

II

Section 752(d) of the Internal Revenue Code of 1954, 26 U.S.C. § 752(d), specifically provides that liabilities involved in the sale or exchange of a partnership interest are to "be treated in the same manner as liabilities in connection with the sale or exchange of property not associated with partnerships." Section 1001 governs the determination of gains and losses on the disposition of property. Under § 1001(a), the gain or loss from a sale or other disposition of property is defined as the difference between "the amount realized" on the disposition and the property's adjusted basis. Subsection (b) of § 1001 defines "amount realized": "The amount realized from the sale or other disposition of property shall be the sum of any money received plus the fair market value of the property (other than money) received." At issue is the application of the latter provision to the disposition of property encumbered by a nonrecourse mortgage of an amount in excess of the property's fair market value.

A

In *Crane v. Commissioner, supra*, this Court took the first and controlling step toward the resolution of this issue. Beulah B. Crane was the sole beneficiary under the will of her deceased husband. At his death in January 1932, he owned an apartment building that was then mortgaged for an amount which proved to be equal to its fair market value, as determined for federal estate tax purposes. The widow, of course, was not personally liable on the mortgage. She operated the building for nearly seven years, hoping to turn it into a profitable venture; during that period, she claimed income tax deductions for depreciation, property taxes, interest, and operating expenses, but did not make payments upon the mortgage

---

[46] [1] The loss was the difference between the adjusted basis, $1,455,740, and the fair market value of the property, $1,400,000. On their individual tax returns, the partners did not claim deductions for their respective shares of this loss. In their petitions to the Tax Court, however, the partners did claim the loss.

[47] [2] The Commissioner determined the partnership's gain on the sale by subtracting the adjusted basis, $1,455,740, from the liability assumed by Bayles, $1,851,500. Of the resulting figure, $395,760, the Commissioner treated $348,661 as capital gain, pursuant to § 741 of the Internal Revenue Code of 1954, 26 U.S.C. § 741, and $47,099 as ordinary gain under the recapture provisions of § 1250 of the Code. The application of § 1250 in determining the character of the gain is not at issue here.

principal. In computing her basis for the depreciation deductions, she included the full amount of the mortgage debt. In November 1938, with her hopes unfulfilled and the mortgagee threatening foreclosure, Mrs. Crane sold the building. The purchaser took the property subject to the mortgage and paid Crane $3,000; of that amount, $500 went for the expenses of the sale.

Crane reported a gain of $2,500 on the transaction. She reasoned that her basis in the property was zero (despite her earlier depreciation deductions based on including the amount of the mortgage) and that the amount she realized from the sale was simply the cash she received. The Commissioner disputed this claim. He asserted that Crane's basis in the property, under § 113(a)(5) of the Revenue Act of 1938, 52 Stat. 490 (the current version is § 1014 of the 1954 Code, as amended, 26 U.S.C. § 1014 (1976 ed. and Supp. V)), was the property's fair market value at the time of her husband's death, adjusted for depreciation in the interim, and that the amount realized was the net cash received plus the amount of the outstanding mortgage assumed by the purchaser.

In upholding the Commissioner's interpretation of § 113(a)(5) of the 1938 Act, the Court observed that to regard merely the taxpayer's equity in the property as her basis would lead to depreciation deductions less than the actual physical deterioration of the property, and would require the basis to be recomputed with each payment on the mortgage. 331 U.S. at 9–10. The Court rejected Crane's claim that any loss due to depreciation belonged to the mortgagee. The effect of the Court's ruling was that the taxpayer's basis was the value of the property undiminished by the mortgage. *Id.* at 11.

The Court next proceeded to determine the amount realized under § 111(b) of the 1938 Act, 52 Stat. 484 (the current version is § 1001(b) of the 1954 Code, 26 U.S.C. § 1001(b)). In order to avoid the "absurdity," *see* 331 U.S. at 13, of Crane's realizing only $2,500 on the sale of property worth over a quarter of a million dollars, the Court treated the amount realized as it had treated basis, that is, by including the outstanding value of the mortgage. To do otherwise would have permitted Crane to recognize a tax loss unconnected with any actual economic loss. The Court refused to construe one section of the Revenue Act so as "to frustrate the Act as a whole." *Ibid.*

Crane, however, insisted that the nonrecourse nature of the mortgage required different treatment. The Court, for two reasons, disagreed. First, excluding the nonrecourse debt from the amount realized would result in the same absurdity and frustration of the Code. *Id.* at 13–14. Second, the Court concluded that Crane obtained an economic benefit from the purchaser's assumption of the mortgage identical to the benefit conferred by the cancellation of personal debt. Because the value of the property in that case exceeded the amount of the mortgage, it was in Crane's economic interest to treat the mortgage as a personal obligation; only by so doing could she realize upon sale the appreciation in her equity represented by the $2,500 boot. The purchaser's assumption of the liability thus resulted in a taxable economic benefit to her, just as if she had been given, in addition to the boot, a sum of cash sufficient to satisfy the mortgage.

In a footnote, pertinent to the present case, the Court observed:

"Obviously, if the value of the property is less than the amount of the mortgage, a mortgagor who is not personally liable cannot realize a benefit equal to the mortgage. Consequently, a different problem might be encountered where a mortgagor abandoned the property or transferred it subject to the mortgage without receiving boot. That is not this case." *Id.* at 14, n.37.

B

This case presents that unresolved issue. We are disinclined to overrule *Crane*, and we conclude that the same rule applies when the unpaid amount of the nonrecourse mortgage exceeds the value of the property transferred. *Crane* ultimately does not rest on its limited theory of economic benefit; instead, we read *Crane* to have approved the Commissioner's decision to treat a nonrecourse mortgage in this context as a true loan. This approval underlies *Crane*'s holdings that the amount of the nonrecourse liability is to be included in calculating both the basis and the amount realized on disposition. That the amount of the loan exceeds the fair market value of the property thus becomes irrelevant.

When a taxpayer receives a loan, he incurs an obligation to repay that loan at some future date. Because of this obligation, the loan proceeds do not qualify as income to the taxpayer. When he fulfills the obligation, the repayment of the loan likewise has no effect on his tax liability.

Another consequence to the taxpayer from this obligation occurs when the taxpayer applies the loan proceeds to the purchase price of property used to secure the loan. Because of the obligation to repay, the taxpayer is entitled to include the amount of the loan in computing his basis in the property; the loan, under § 1012, is part of the taxpayer's cost of the property. Although a different approach might have been taken with respect to a nonrecourse mortgage loan,[48] the Commissioner has chosen to accord it the same treatment he gives to a recourse mortgage loan. The Court approved that choice in *Crane*, and the respondents do not challenge it here. The choice and its resultant benefits to the taxpayer are predicated on the assumption that the mortgage will be repaid in full.

We express no view as to whether such an approach would be consistent with the statutory structure and, if so, and *Crane* were not on the books, whether that approach would be preferred over *Crane*'s analysis. We note only that the *Crane*

---

[48] [5] The Commissioner might have adopted the theory, implicit in Crane's contentions, that a nonrecourse mortgage is not true debt, but, instead, is a form of joint investment by the mortgagor and the mortgagee. On this approach, nonrecourse debt would be considered a contingent liability, under which the mortgagor's payments on the debt gradually increase his interest in the property while decreasing that of the mortgagee. Note, *Federal Income Tax Treatment of Nonrecourse Debt*, 82 COLUM. L. REV. 1498, 1514 (1982); Lurie, *Mortgagor's Gain on Mortgaging Property for More than Cost Without Personal Liability*, 6 TAX L. REV. 319, 323 (1951); *cf.* Brief for Respondents 16 (nonrecourse debt resembles preferred stock). Because the taxpayer's investment in the property would not include the nonrecourse debt, the taxpayer would not be permitted to include that debt in basis. Note, 82 COLUM. L. REV. at 1515; *cf.* Gibson Products Co. v. United States, 637 F.2d 1041, 1047–1048 (CA5 1981) (contingent nature of obligation prevents inclusion in basis of oil and gas leases of nonrecourse debt secured by leases, drilling equipment, and percentage of future production).

Court's resolution of the basic issue presumed that when property is purchased with proceeds from a nonrecourse mortgage, the purchaser becomes the sole owner of the property. 331 U.S. at 6. Under the *Crane* approach, the mortgagee is entitled to no portion of the basis. *Id.* at 10, n.28. The nonrecourse mortgage is part of the mortgagor's investment in the property, and does not constitute a coinvestment by the mortgagee. *But see* Note, 82 COLUM. L. REV. at 1513 (treating nonrecourse mortgage as coinvestment by mortgagee and critically concluding that *Crane* departed from traditional analysis that basis is taxpayer's investment in property).

When encumbered property is sold or otherwise disposed of and the purchaser assumes the mortgage, the associated extinguishment of the mortgagor's obligation to repay is accounted for in the computation of the amount realized. *See United States v. Hendler*, 303 U.S. 564, 566–567 (1938). Because no difference between recourse and nonrecourse obligations is recognized in calculating basis,[49] *Crane* teaches that the Commissioner may ignore the nonrecourse nature of the obligation in determining the amount realized upon disposition of the encumbered property. He thus may include in the amount realized the amount of the nonrecourse mortgage assumed by the purchaser. The rationale for this treatment is that the original inclusion of the amount of the mortgage in basis rested on the assumption that the mortgagor incurred an obligation to repay. Moreover, this treatment balances the fact that the mortgagor originally received the proceeds of the nonrecourse loan tax-free on the same assumption. Unless the outstanding amount of the mortgage is deemed to be realized, the mortgagor effectively will have received untaxed income at the time the loan was extended and will have received an unwarranted increase in the basis of his property. The Commissioner's interpretation of § 1001(b) in this fashion cannot be said to be unreasonable.

C

The Commissioner in fact has applied this rule even when the fair market value of the property falls below the amount of the nonrecourse obligation. Treas. Reg. § 1.1001-2(b), 26 CFR § 1.1001-2(b) (1982); Rev. Rul. 76-111, 1976-1 Cum. Bull. 214. Because the theory on which the rule is based applies equally in this situation, *see Millar v. Commissioner*, 67 T.C. 656, 660 (1977), *aff'd on this issue*, 577 F.2d 212, 215–216 (CA3), *cert. denied*, 439 U.S. 1046 (1978); *Mendham Corp. v. Commissioner*, 9 T.C. 320, 323–324 (1947); *Lutz & Schramm Co. v. Commissioner*, 1 T.C. 682, 688–689 (1943), we have no reason, after *Crane*, to question this treatment.[50]

---

[49] [7] The Commissioner's choice in *Crane* "laid the foundation stone of most tax shelters," Bittker, *Tax Shelters, Nonrecourse Debt, and the* Crane *Case*, 33 TAX L. REV. 277, 283 (1978), by permitting taxpayers who bear no risk to take deductions on depreciable property. Congress recently has acted to curb this avoidance device by forbidding a taxpayer to take depreciation deductions in excess of amounts he has at risk in the investment. Pub. L. 94-455, § 204(a), 90 Stat. 1531 (1976), 26 U.S.C. § 465; Pub. L. 95-600, §§ 201–204, 92 Stat. 2814–2817 (1978), 26 U.S.C. § 465(a) (1976 ed., Supp. V). Real estate investments, however, are exempt from this prohibition. § 465(c)(3)(D) (1976 ed., Supp. V). Although this congressional action may foreshadow a day when nonrecourse and recourse debts will be treated differently, neither Congress nor the Commissioner has sought to alter *Crane*'s rule of including nonrecourse liability in both basis and the amount realized.

[50] [11] Professor Wayne G. Barnett, as *amicus* in the present case, argues that the liability and property portions of the transaction should be accounted for separately. Under his view, there was a

Although this indeed could be a justifiable mode of analysis, it has not been adopted by the Commissioner. Nor is there anything to indicate that the Code requires the Commissioner to adopt it. We note that Professor Barnett's approach does assume that recourse and nonrecourse debt may be treated identically.

Respondents received a mortgage loan with the concomitant obligation to repay by the year 2012. The only difference between that mortgage and one on which the borrower is personally liable is that the mortgagee's remedy is limited to foreclosing on the securing property. This difference does not alter the nature of the obligation; its only effect is to shift from the borrower to the lender any potential loss caused by devaluation of the property. If the fair market value of the property falls below the amount of the outstanding obligation, the mortgagee's ability to protect its interests is impaired, for the mortgagor is free to abandon the property to the mortgagee and be relieved of his obligation.

This, however, does not erase the fact that the mortgagor received the loan proceeds tax-free and included them in his basis on the understanding that he had an obligation to repay the full amount. *See Woodsam Associates, Inc. v. Commissioner*, 198 F.2d 357, 359 (CA2 1952); Bittker, *supra* n. 7, at 284. When the obligation is canceled, the mortgagor is relieved of his responsibility to repay the sum he originally received and thus realizes value to that extent within the meaning of § 1001(b). From the mortgagor's point of view, when his obligation is assumed by a third party who purchases the encumbered property, it is as if the mortgagor first had been paid with cash borrowed by the third party from the mortgagee on a nonrecourse basis, and then had used the cash to satisfy his obligation to the mortgagee.

Moreover, this approach avoids the absurdity the Court recognized in *Crane*. Because of the remedy accompanying the mortgage in the nonrecourse situation, the depreciation in the fair market value of the property is relevant economically only to the mortgagee, who by lending on a nonrecourse basis remains at risk. To permit the taxpayer to limit his realization to the fair market value of the property would be to recognize a tax loss for which he has suffered no corresponding economic loss. Such a result would be to construe "one section of the Act . . . so as . . . to defeat the intention of another or to frustrate the Act as a whole." 331 U.S. at 13.

In the specific circumstances of *Crane*, the economic benefit theory did support the Commissioner's treatment of the nonrecourse mortgage as a personal obligation. The footnote in *Crane* acknowledged the limitations of that theory when applied to a different set of facts. *Crane* also stands for the broader proposition, however, that a nonrecourse loan should be treated as a true loan. We therefore hold that a taxpayer must account for the proceeds of obligations he has received tax-free and included in basis. Nothing in either § 1001(b) or in the Court's prior decisions requires the Commissioner to permit a taxpayer to treat a sale of encumbered property asymmetrically, by including the proceeds of the nonrecourse

---

transfer of the property for $1.4 million, and there was a cancellation of the $1.85 million obligation for a payment of $1.4 million. The former resulted in a capital loss of $50,000, and the latter in the realization of $450,000 of ordinary income. Taxation of the ordinary income might be deferred under § 108 by a reduction of respondents' bases in their partnership interests.

obligation in basis but not accounting for the proceeds upon transfer of the encumbered property. *See Estate of Levine v. Commissioner*, 634 F.2d 12, 15 (CA2 1980).

* * *

IV

When a taxpayer sells or disposes of property encumbered by a nonrecourse obligation, the Commissioner properly requires him to include among the assets realized the outstanding amount of the obligation. The fair market value of the property is irrelevant to this calculation. We find this interpretation to be consistent with *Crane v. Commissioner*, 331 U.S. 1 (1947), and to implement the statutory mandate in a reasonable manner. *National Muffler Dealers Assn. v. United States*, 440 U.S. 472, 476 (1979).

The judgment of the Court of Appeals is therefore reversed.

It is so ordered.

JUSTICE O'CONNOR, concurring.

I concur in the opinion of the Court, accepting the view of the Commissioner. I do not, however, endorse the Commissioner's view. Indeed, were we writing on a slate clean except for the decision in *Crane v. Commissioner*, 331 U.S. 1 (1947), I would take quite a different approach — that urged upon us by Professor Barnett as *amicus*.

Crane established that a taxpayer could treat property as entirely his own, in spite of the "coinvestment" provided by his mortgagee in the form of a nonrecourse loan. That is, the full basis of the property, with all its tax consequences, belongs to the mortgagor. That rule alone, though, does not in any way tie nonrecourse debt to the cost of property or to the proceeds upon disposition. I see no reason to treat the purchase, ownership, and eventual disposition of property differently because the taxpayer also takes out a mortgage, an independent transaction. In this case, the taxpayer purchased property, using nonrecourse financing, and sold it after it declined in value to a buyer who assumed the mortgage. There is no economic difference between the events in this case and a case in which the taxpayer buys property with cash; later obtains a nonrecourse loan by pledging the property as security; still later, using cash on hand, buys off the mortgage for the market value of the devalued property; and finally sells the property to a third party for its market value.

The logical way to treat both this case and the hypothesized case, is to separate the two aspects of these events and to consider, first, the ownership and sale of the property, and, second, the arrangement and retirement of the loan. Under *Crane*, the fair market value of the property on the date of acquisition — the purchase price — represents the taxpayer's basis in the property, and the fair market value on the date of disposition represents the proceeds on sale. The benefit received by the taxpayer in return for the property is the cancellation of a mortgage that is worth no more than the fair market value of the property, for that is all the mortgagee can expect to collect on the mortgage. His gain or loss on the disposition of the property equals the difference between the proceeds and the cost of acquisition. Thus, the taxation of the transaction *in property* reflects the economic fate of the *property*. If the property has declined in value, as was the case here, the taxpayer recognizes a loss on the disposition of the property. The new purchaser then takes as his basis the fair market value as of the date of the sale. *See, e.g., United States v. Davis*, 370 U.S. 65, 72 (1962); *Gibson Products Co. v. United States*, 637 F.2d 1041, 1045, n.8 (CA5 1981) (dictum); *see generally* Treas. Reg. § 1.1001-2(a)(3), 26 CFR § 1.1001-2(a)(3) (1982); 2 B. BITTKER, FEDERAL TAXATION OF INCOME, ESTATES AND GIFTS para. 41.2.2., pp. 41–10 to 41–11 (1981).

In the separate borrowing transaction, the taxpayer acquires cash from the mortgagee. He need not recognize income at that time, of course, because he also incurs an obligation to repay the money. Later, though, when he is able to satisfy the debt by surrendering property that is worth less than the face amount of the debt, we have a classic situation of cancellation of indebtedness, requiring the taxpayer to recognize income in the amount of the difference between the proceeds of the loan and the amount for which he is able to satisfy his creditor. 26 U.S.C. § 61(a)(12). The taxation of the financing transaction then reflects the economic fate of the loan.

The reason that separation of the two aspects of the events in this case is important is, of course, that the Code treats different sorts of income differently. A gain on the sale of the property may qualify for capital gains treatment, §§ 1202, 1221 (1976 ed. and Supp. V), while the cancellation of indebtedness is ordinary income, but income that the taxpayer may be able to defer. §§ 108, 1017 (1976 ed., Supp. V). Not only does Professor Barnett's theory permit us to accord appropriate treatment to each of the two types of income or loss present in these sorts of transactions, it also restores continuity to the system by making the taxpayer-seller's proceeds on the disposition of property equal to the purchaser's basis in the property. Further, and most important, it allows us to tax the events in this case in the same way that we tax the economically identical hypothesized transaction.

Persuaded though I am by the logical coherence and internal consistency of this approach, I agree with the Court's decision not to adopt it judicially. We do not write on a slate marked only by *Crane*. The Commissioner's longstanding position, Rev. Rul. 76-111, 1976-1 Cum. Bull. 214, is now reflected in the regulations. Treas. Reg. § 1.1001-2, 26 CFR § 1.1001-2 (1982). In the light of the numerous cases in the lower courts including the amount of the unrepaid proceeds of the mortgage in the proceeds on sale or disposition, *see, e.g., Estate of Levine v. Commissioner*, 634 F.2d 12, 15 (CA2 1980); *Millar v. Commissioner*, 577 F.2d 212 (CA3), *cert. denied*, 439 U.S. 1046 (1978); *Estate of Delman v. Commissioner*, 73 T.C. 15, 28-30 (1979); *Peninsula Properties Co., Ltd. v. Commissioner*, 47 B.T.A. 84, 92 (1942), it is difficult to conclude that the Commissioner's interpretation of the statute exceeds the bounds of his discretion. As the Court's opinion demonstrates, his interpretation is defensible. One can reasonably read § 1001(b)'s reference to "the amount realized *from* the sale or other disposition of property" (emphasis added) to permit the Commissioner to collapse the two aspects of the transaction. As long as his view is a reasonable reading of § 1001(b), we should defer to the regulations promulgated by the agency charged with interpretation of the statute. *National Muffler Dealers*

Assn. v. United States, 440 U.S. 472, 488–489 (1979); *United States v. Correll*, 389 U.S. 299, 307 (1967); *see also Fulman v. United States*, 434 U.S. 528, 534 (1978). Accordingly, I concur.

Understanding *Tufts*

1.   *Tufts* differs from *Crane* in that the fair market value of the property at the time of sale ($1.4 million) was less than the amount of the nonrecourse mortgage ($1.85 million). The taxpayer argued that relief from a nonrecourse mortgage, secured by a $1.4 million property, could not possibly be worth more than $1.4 million, since the worst that could happen under the mortgage was that the taxpayer would default and surrender the property. Thus, under the logic of *Crane*, the taxpayer had an $0.05 million loss ($1.4 million amount realized — $1.45 million adjusted basis in the property). By contrast, the IRS argued that the face value of the loan ($1.85 million) should be taken into account, resulting in an $0.4 million gain.

As in the previous cases, isn't the taxpayer's position in *Tufts* more persuasive? How can a taxpayer possibly be relieved of an amount of debt larger than that they would be required to pay? Or does the logic of *Crane* require that — as the price of including loans in basis — any loan relief must similarly be included in the amount realized on disposition of the property, regardless of the loan's nonrecourse status and regardless of the property's value? Note that the statute (section 1001(b)) refers to the "fair market value of the property (other than money)" received in the transaction; is the Court's holding consistent with this language, or did it "massage" the statute to reach its preferred result?

2.   The taxpayer in *Tufts* argued that the property was worth only $1.4 million, which was significantly less than the value of the outstanding mortgage. If that's true, why would anyone buy it? Is it consistent to argue that "this property was worth $1.4 million, but we found a buyer who was willing to take it subject to a $1.85 million (albeit nonrecourse) mortgage"? Is it possible that the valuations in the case were, well, uncertain, and that this encouraged the Court to stick with a stricter, anti-taxpayer rule?

3.   In contrast to Mrs. Crane, who inherited a used building, the taxpayers in *Tufts* were sophisticated tax shelter investors, who had used debt financing to generate depreciation and interest deductions and now sought to abandon the property with no "back-end" tax consequences. (They were even clever enough to get federal mortgage insurance.) Does this less-than-sympathetic behavior affect the outcome of the case? Should it?

4.   Nonrecourse loans involve no personal liability on the part of the borrowers: if they default, they surrender any property securing the loan, but are not required to repay the loan from their personal assets. Why do people lend money on a nonrecourse basis, and why are such debts — notwithstanding their nonrecourse status — usually repaid by the borrowers? Does your answer tell you anything about the results in *Crane* and *Tufts*? Generally speaking, should the tax law distinguish between recourse and nonrecourse debts, or is this too tenuous and manipulable a distinction to rely on?

5. *Tufts* was one of the most closely watched tax cases of its generation, and the Government (together with various tax scholars) invested substantial energy in arguing it. Why? How would you have voted in the *Tufts* case?

Tufts is typically described as the completion of *Crane*, holding that relief from a *bona fide* loan will result in taxable income regardless of the value of the underlying property. The third prong of *Crane*, regarding Mrs. Crane's incentive to repay the loan, is thus seen as dictum rather than a vital part of the original *Crane* holding. Interestingly, not all tax scholars saw the issue that way prior to *Tufts*, although the case was probably consistent with most expert opinion on the subject.

Tufts may also be seen as a triumph of tax logic or policy over the statutory language. The Court, prodded by the IRS, accepted a principal of consistency in the tax treatment of loan proceeds: loans would thus be included in basis (and would not result in taxable income) at the time they were taken out, but relief from a loan would similarly result in taxable income regardless of fair market value and other factors. This principle appears nowhere in the Code, and was to a degree violated in *Zarin* and other cases. But it struck the Court, together with most commentators, as a good rule, and to enforce it they were willing to read the statute in a non-literal but logically appealing way.

Arguably the most interesting aspect of *Tufts* is Justice O'Connor's concurrence, in which she (with apologies to Prof. Wayne Barnett) argues for "bifurcation" of the case into component parts. According to this view, the taxpayers would have had an $0.05 million loss on the real property transaction ($1.4 million amount realized — $1.45 million adjusted basis), but $0.5 million of cancellation of indebtedness income, since they were satisfying a $1.85 million loan by transferring $1.4 million of property.[51] This description is conceptually more pleasing than the majority opinion, but the full Court, perhaps put off by its complexity, refused to endorse it. *Tufts* thus suggests there are limits to tax policy: courts will occasionally strong-arm statutory language but will do so in a way that does minimal damage to existing precedents and, not coincidentally, is understandable to a lay (nontax) audience. Professors influence courts, but — with apologies to *Albertson's* — rarely control them.

Using the Sources

Carol Chavez bought a $2 million piece of real estate investment property, which she financed with $0.2 million in cash and a $1.8 million nonrecourse mortgage. During the next seven years, Carol paid $0.3 million of principal and a substantial amount of interest on the loan. During this same period she also took $0.5 million in depreciation deductions. After the seven years were up, Carol sold the property to Daniel Dershowitz, subject to the mortgage, for $1 million.

1. What is Carol's basis for the property immediately after she acquires it?

---

[51] The combined result would have been similar to the majority opinion (net $0.45 million of income), except that the cancellation of indebtedness would likely have been treated as ordinary income rather than capital gain, resulting in a higher tax rate. Capital gain is discussed in Chapter 9.

2.   What is her gain (or loss) when she sells the property, and how did you compute it?

3.   What would be the result in 2. above, if the property had declined in value, and Carol transferred the property to Dershowitz, subject to the mortgage, but without any payment of cash?

4.   Do you think it would have made any difference, to any of your answers, if Carol had first bought the property for cash and later (in year 3) taken out a $1.8 million mortgage? (*See Woodsam v. Commissioner*, 198 F.2d 357 (2d Cir. 1952)).

5.   What would be Dershowitz's basis for the property in questions 2. and 3., above? Does this result make sense?

6.   How much interest, if any, would be deductible on the loan described in the preceding hypothetical?

Law and Planning

Suppose that your client was offered an opportunity to invest in a real estate venture under the following terms: A partnership would be formed to purchase a new office building, paying a small amount of cash and taking out a large, nonrecourse loan. The partnership would take interest and depreciation deductions which the investors would use to "shelter" other income from tax. After several years, assuming the building had increased in value, the partnership would sell it at a considerable profit. If it had declined in value, the partnership would attempt to "unload" the building on a third party, subject to the mortgage, on terms similar to those described in the *Tufts* case. (For purposes of this question, assume that the client would be entitled to deductions despite the passive loss rules and other tax shelter restrictions.)

Would you recommend this investment to your client? What effect, if any, would the holding in *Tufts* have on your evaluation, and how would you balance this consideration against the tax and practical benefits of the investment? What additional facts might you want to know before answering any of these questions?

Politics and Policy

Zarin and *Tufts* were very different cases, but had a number of similar elements. In both cases, a taxpayer was allowed to take out a large initial loan without tax consequences, on the theory that the loan was offset by an equal repayment obligation. In each case, the taxpayer avoided repaying all or part of the loan: Zarin, because the casino "forgave" part of the debt, and Tufts, because a third-party purchaser took the property subject to the mortgage. In both cases, the Government argued for taxation on similar grounds: that it was inconsistent to allow tax-free treatment of loan proceeds without imposing tax if the loan was not repaid. Indeed, the *Zarin* dissent cited *Tufts* for this proposition.

Why did Zarin win and Tufts lose, and what does your answer tell you about the logic (or illogic) of tax policy in this area?

Additional Assignment — Chapter 5

The persistence of the deduction for home mortgage interest, when other forms of personal interest are nondeductible, is one of the most controversial issues in tax policy. The issue is fascinating, because it is so difficult to separate the traditional tax policy arguments from broader issues of social and housing policy. Mortgage interest also has important political connotations, since home ownership is viewed almost as a right by many Americans and there would likely be strong opposition to elimination or serious restriction of the deduction.

Pretend, for one day, that the class is the United States Senate and has been assigned to debate the continued existence of the mortgage interest deduction. (In some classes this may take less pretending than others.) Divide the class into two equal-sized factions, one of which will present the case for abolishing the deduction and the other of which will argue for its retention. If the class is large, you may divide into smaller, evenly sized groups.

Each side should receive approximately 15 minutes to present its arguments, with an equivalent period left for rebuttal and open-ended discussion. Although the exact presentation is up to each of the participants, you will probably wish to consider at least the following arguments:

Arguments in favor of abolition

1. The deduction is horizontally inequitable because it distinguishes between home loans and loans for other good purposes, and between renters and homeowners.

2. The deduction is vertically inequitable, because most homeowners tend to be relatively well off, and bigger homeowners get a larger deduction.

3. The deduction is inefficient because it encourages people to over-invest in housing and under-invest in other activities; it also has a substantial revenue cost that increases taxes for everybody else.

Arguments in favor of retention

1. The tax code frequently encourages desirable activities (*e.g.*, education, health care, R & D, etc.); home ownership is a part of "The American Dream" and entitled to no less support.

2. Homeowners have more of a stake in the community and tend to take better care of their property; indeed, home ownership stimulates the economy to such an extent that it may actually increase tax revenues.

3. The vertical equity argument is exaggerated, since many homeowners are modest, middle-class people and the really big fish are eliminated by the $1 million limit in present law. If people are worried about abuse, they should perhaps reduce this limitation, but not eliminate the entire deduction.

Now, in the few minutes remaining in class, step back and consider the nature of the arguments made by both sides. How many of the arguments were presented in traditional tax policy terms — fairness, efficiency, simplicity or administrability, etc. — and how many in more overtly "political" or social policy terms? What type of argument do you think would be most convincing to what type of Senator (Republican, Democrat, urban and rural states, etc.), and is there even a meaningful distinction between the different types of arguments? If there is not — if "politics" and "policy" are hopelessly mixed — what does this tell you about tax policy in general, and what is the contribution that tax scholars can make to large-scale discussions as opposed to narrow, technical debates? Should they even keep on trying?

Chapter 6

DEDUCTIONS I: BUSINESS AND PERSONAL EXPENSES AND THE LINE-DRAWING PROBLEM

In the first five chapters we have observed the measurement of income on increasingly complex transactions: fringe benefits, sales of property, and loans and loan-related transactions. In the next several chapters we turn our attention to the deduction side of the ledger. We have seen a hint of deductions in our discussion of tax exemptions, which sometimes have a similar logic, and the return of capital, which can be recovered as an offset to gain on the sale of property or (for wasting assets) as a depreciation or similar tax deduction. We have also discussed the interest deduction as a part of our general treatment of loans and property transactions. It is now time to consider these issues more systematically.

The basic rule surrounding deductions is simple. Business-related expenditures are generally deductible from taxable income, on the theory that tax should be imposed on net income — the amount left after subtracting the costs of earning the income — rather than on a gross amount. For example, a person who earns $100,000 selling apples, but pays $40,000 for the apples and other legitimate expenses, is taxed on $60,000 rather than $100,000. By contrast, personal and living expenses are not deductible, on the theory that they are not a cost of earning income and — more cynically — that no one would pay much tax if they were. Thus, if our hypothetical salesperson spends the remaining $60,000 on food, clothing, shelter, or rock music videos, he or she will not be entitled to a tax deduction; although no doubt enjoyable, they will be treated as a form of income consumption rather than as a cost of earning the income in the first place. These basic rules are stated in Code sections 162 (allowing a deduction for ordinary and necessary business expenses) and 262 (denying an equivalent deduction for personal and living expenses), although other provisions also get into the act.

Two problems arise very quickly. The first is that there is no clear boundary between business and personal life. Suppose that our apple-seller, in addition to paying $40,000 for apples, spends $5,000 a year commuting to the job from a home in the suburbs, together with $5,000 in child care expenses and a significant amount of state and local taxes. In a purely economic sense, these expenditures plainly reduce the amount of income produced by the job. Should they reduce it for tax purposes, as well? Or are the decisions to live in the suburbs, have children, and live in a high-tax state simply forms of consumption that should have no bearing on taxable income? And how should these questions be decided: by means of a "but for" causation test (any expense caused by the job is automatically deductible), or on a more intuitive, everyday sense of what the terms business and personal mean? What role, if any, should be played by changing lifestyles, in a society in which an increasing number of women (and men) work at home or are regularly called away from the office to deal with child-care and other supposedly "personal" issues?

A second problem concerns expenses that are personal in nature, but which the Code wishes to encourage for various social or policy reasons. A good example is home mortgage interest, which is personal in nature and yet remains deductible under section 163(h). Further examples include charitable contributions (section 170), excessive medical and casualty losses (sections 213 and 165), and state and local income and real property taxes (section 164). These provisions are sometimes called exceptions to the rule providing for the nondeductibility of personal expenses; but it is probably more accurate to say that they occupy a middle category, involving expenses that are either sufficiently business-related or have sufficient public purpose to make them deductible in spite of their superficially personal nature. This category is interesting for its own sake, but also casts doubt on the consistency of the more general business vs. personal distinction.

The following chapters consider these issues in turn. This chapter considers four classic issues in the distinction between business and personal expenditures: travel and entertainment deductions, including the famous problem of the "three martini lunch"; commuting, child care, and similar indirect expenses that are occasioned by business employment; home offices; and educational expenditures, which present a seemingly indivisible aggregate of business and personal aspects. Chapter 7 considers personal expenses that are deductible under specific statutory provisions, emphasizing charitable contributions and (to a lesser extent) the deduction for large medical expenses. In both chapters, we will balance legal and practical considerations, taking a hard look at how lawyers advise clients in uncertain cases and at the ethics of playing the "audit lottery" in a developing, fluid area of law. We will likewise devote substantial attention to policy issues, emphasizing in particular the gender and lifestyle implications of the business vs. personal distinction and the unique role that private charitable organizations play in the American political and cultural landscape.

I. TRAVEL AND ENTERTAINMENT: CLASSIC CASES AND THE PERILS OF INCREMENTAL TAX REFORM

Perhaps the most famous example of business deductions is the case of travel and entertainment expenses. Section 162 does not specifically mention such expenses, but permits their deduction as a subdivision of general trade and business expenditures.[1] The problem is where to draw the line. Several well-known tax cases, together with extensive popular folklore, document the use of "t and e" deductions to finance what most people would consider to be essentially personal expenditures. Like fringe benefits in Chapter 2, this area presents a conflict between different tax policy goals, with the goal of horizontal equity (travel and entertainment should be deductible on the same basis as other business expenses) clashing with vertical equity (since wealthy people tend to take most aggressive advantage of these deductions) and the problem of administrability (since it is extremely difficult to audit these cases and taxpayers may be tempted to take aggressive positions on their tax returns). Because these cases frequently involve people who are lying, or

---

[1] In deference to popular usage, this section is labeled "travel and entertainment" expenditures although it concerns largely the meals and entertainment part of such expenses. Away-from-home business travel is discussed in the following section.

at least exaggerating the business nature of their expenditures, they tend to be rather entertaining and provide an antidote to some of the dryer material in a tax course.

To understand the travel and entertainment area, it is useful to divide the issue into a substantive component (what expenses are sufficiently business-related to qualify for an income tax deduction) and a procedural component (what does the taxpayer have to do to substantiate this business relationship and what are the consequences if he or she doesn't). The first issue corresponds, roughly speaking, to section 162 of the Code, and the second to section 274, which was added in the 1960s and expanded in the 1980s when Congress concluded that many taxpayers were, well, prevaricating a bit with respect to these expenses. As you will quickly see, the substantive and procedural issues frequently overlap.

A.   "My Business is My Pleasure": What Is a Deductible Business Expense?

MOSS v. COMMISSIONER
United States Court of Appeals, Seventh Circuit
758 F.2d 211 (1985)

POSNER, CIRCUIT JUDGE.

The taxpayers, a lawyer named Moss and his wife, appeal from a decision of the Tax Court disallowing federal income tax deductions of a little more than $1,000 in each of two years, representing Moss's share of his law firm's lunch expense at the Cafe Angelo in Chicago. 80 T.C. 1073. The Tax Court's decision in this case has attracted some attention in tax circles because of its implications for the general problem of the deductibility of business meals. *See, e.g.,* McNally, *Vulnerability of Entertainment and Meal Deductions Under the* Sutter *Rule,* 62 TAXES 184 (1984).

Moss was a partner in a small trial firm specializing in defense work, mostly for one insurance company. Each of the firm's lawyers carried a tremendous litigation caseload, averaging more than 300 cases, and spent most of every working day in courts in Chicago and its suburbs. The members of the firm met for lunch daily at the Cafe Angelo near their office. At lunch the lawyers would discuss their cases with the head of the firm, whose approval was required for most settlements, and they would decide which lawyer would meet which court call that afternoon or the next morning. Lunchtime was chosen for the daily meeting because the courts were in recess then. The alternatives were to meet at 7:00 a.m. or 6:00 p.m., and these were less convenient times. There is no suggestion that the lawyers dawdled over lunch, or that the Cafe Angelo is luxurious.

The framework of statutes and regulations for deciding this case is simple, but not clear. Section 262 of the Internal Revenue Code (Title 26) disallows, "except as otherwise expressly provided in this chapter," the deduction of "personal, family, or living expenses." Section 119 excludes from income the value of meals provided by an employer to his employees for his convenience, but only if they are provided on the employer's premises; and section 162(a) allows the deduction of "all the ordinary and necessary expenses paid or incurred during the taxable year in carrying on any trade or business, including — . . . (2) traveling expenses (including amounts expended for meals . . .) while away from home. . . ." Since Moss was not an employee but a partner in a partnership not taxed as an entity, since the meals were not served on the employer's premises, and since he was not away from home (that is, on an overnight trip away from his place of work, *see United States v. Correll*, 389 U.S. 299 (1967)), neither section 119 nor section 162(a)(2) applies to this case. The Internal Revenue Service concedes, however, that meals are deductible under section 162(a) when they are ordinary and necessary business expenses (provided the expense is substantiated with adequate records, see section 274(d)) even if they are not within the express permission of any other provision and even though the expense of commuting to and from work, a traveling expense but not one incurred away from home, is not deductible. Treasury Regulations on Income Tax § 1.262-1(b)(5); *Fausner v. Commissioner*, 413 U.S. 838 (1973) (per curiam).

The problem is that many expenses are simultaneously business expenses in the sense that they conduce to the production of business income and personal expenses in the sense that they raise personal welfare. This is plain enough with regard to lunch; most people would eat lunch even if they didn't work. Commuting may seem a pure business expense, but is not; it reflects the choice of where to live, as well as where to work. Read literally, section 262 would make irrelevant whether a business expense is also a personal expense; so long as it is ordinary and necessary in the taxpayer's business, thus bringing section 162(a) into play, an expense is (the statute seems to say) deductible from his income tax. But the statute has not been read literally. There is a natural reluctance, most clearly manifested in the regulation disallowing deduction of the expense of commuting, to lighten the tax burden of people who have the good fortune to interweave work with consumption. To allow a deduction for commuting would confer a windfall on people who live in the suburbs and commute to work in the cities; to allow a deduction for all business-related meals would confer a windfall on people who can arrange their work schedules so they do some of their work at lunch.

Although an argument can thus be made for disallowing *any* deduction for business meals, on the theory that people have to eat whether they work or not, the result would be excessive taxation of people who spend more money on business meals because they are business meals than they would spend on their meals if they were not working. Suppose a theatrical agent takes his clients out to lunch at the expensive restaurants that the clients demand. Of course he can deduct the expense of their meals, from which he derives no pleasure or sustenance, but can he also deduct the expense of his own? He can, because he cannot eat more cheaply; he cannot munch surreptitiously on a peanut butter and jelly sandwich brought from home while his client is wolfing down tournedos Rossini followed by souffle au grand marnier. No doubt our theatrical agent, unless concerned for his longevity, derives personal utility from his fancy meal, but probably less than the price of the meal. He would not pay for it if it were not for the business benefit; he would get more value from using the same money to buy something else; hence the meal confers on him less utility than the cash equivalent would. The law could require him to pay tax on the fair value of the meal to him; this would be (were it not for costs of administration) the economically correct solution. But the government does not attempt this difficult measurement; it once did, but gave up the attempt as not worth the cost, *see United States v. Correll, supra,* 389 U.S. at 301 n.6. The taxpayer is permitted to deduct the whole price, provided the expense is "different from or in excess of that which would have been made for the taxpayer's personal purposes." *Sutter v. Commissioner,* 21 T.C. 170, 173 (1953).

Because the law allows this generous deduction, which tempts people to have more (and costlier) business meals than are necessary, the Internal Revenue Service has every right to insist that the meal be shown to be a real business necessity. This condition is most easily satisfied when a client or customer or supplier or other outsider to the business is a guest. Even if Sydney Smith was wrong that "soup and fish explain half the emotions of life," it is undeniable that eating together fosters camaraderie and makes business dealings friendlier and easier. It thus reduces the costs of transacting business, for these costs include the frictions and the failures of communication that are produced by suspicion and mutual misunderstanding, by differences in tastes and manners, and by lack of rapport. A meeting with a client or customer in an office is therefore not a perfect substitute for a lunch with him in a restaurant. But it is different when all the participants in the meal are coworkers, as essentially was the case here (clients occasionally were invited to the firm's daily luncheon, but Moss has made no attempt to identify the occasions). They know each other well already; they don't need the social lubrication that a meal with an outsider provides — at least don't need it daily. If a large firm had a monthly lunch to allow partners to get to know associates, the expense of the meal might well be necessary, and would be allowed by the Internal Revenue Service. *See Wells v. Commissioner,* T.C. Memo 1977-419, 1977 T.C. Memo 419, 36 T.C.M. (CCH) 1698, 1699 (1977), *aff'd without opinion,* 626 F.2d 868 (9th Cir. 1980). But Moss's firm never had more than eight lawyers (partners and associates), and did not need a daily lunch to cement relationships among them.

It is all a matter of degree and circumstance (the expense of a testimonial dinner, for example, would be deductible on a morale-building rationale); and particularly of frequency. Daily — for a full year — is too often, perhaps even for entertainment of clients, as implied by *Hankenson v. Commissioner,* T.C. Memo 1984-200, 1984 T.C. Memo 200, 47 T.C.M. 1567, 1569 (1984), where the Tax Court held nondeductible the cost of lunches consumed three or four days a week, 52 weeks a year, by a doctor who entertained other doctors who he hoped would refer patients to him, and other medical personnel.

We may assume it was necessary for Moss's firm to meet daily to coordinate the work of the firm, and also, as the Tax Court found, that lunch was the most convenient time. But it does not follow that the expense of the lunch was a necessary business expense. The members of the firm had to eat somewhere, and the Cafe Angelo was both convenient and not too expensive. They do not claim to have incurred a greater daily lunch expense than they would have incurred if there had been no lunch meetings. Although it saved time to combine lunch with work, the meal itself was not an organic part of the meeting, as in the examples we gave earlier where the business objective, to be fully achieved, required sharing a meal.

The case might be different if the location of the courts required the firm's members to eat each day either in a disagreeable restaurant, so that they derived less value from the meal than it cost them to buy it, *cf. Sibla v. Commissioner*, 611 F.2d 1260, 1262 (9th Cir. 1980); or in a restaurant too expensive for their personal tastes, so that, again, they would have gotten less value than the cash equivalent. But so far as appears, they picked the restaurant they liked most. Although it must be pretty monotonous to eat lunch at the same place every working day of the year, not all the lawyers attended all the lunch meetings and there was nothing to stop the firm from meeting occasionally at another restaurant proximate to their office in downtown Chicago; there are hundreds.

An argument can be made that the price of lunch at the Cafe Angelo included rental of the space that the lawyers used for what was a meeting as well as a meal. There was evidence that the firm's conference room was otherwise occupied throughout the working day, so as a matter of logic Moss might be able to claim a part of the price of lunch as an ordinary and necessary expense for work space. But this is cutting things awfully fine; in any event Moss made no effort to apportion his lunch expense in this way.

AFFIRMED.

Understanding *Moss*

1.   Judge Posner describes the deductibility of business meals as a clash between horizontal equity (the meals may not be as enjoyable as the price suggests because of the element of forced consumption and, perhaps, the quality of the guests) and vertical equity (allowing a deduction tends to favor wealthier people who are better positioned to mix their business and personal activities). Do you think that this is an accurate description of the case? Between the two arguments, which strikes you as more convincing? How much sympathy do you think that an industrial worker, who paid tax at the statutory rate with no business deductions, would have for the business executive who derives incomplete enjoyment from a dinner at a fancy restaurant? Or is a little bit of tax-assisted camaraderie a small price to pay for "greasing the wheels" of the U.S. economy?

2.   What would have been the effect, if any, of the following fact changes in *Moss*?

   a. The lawyers met at Cafe Angelo, not every day, but once a week to discuss ongoing cases.

   b. The lawyers met every day, but at various different restaurants, and with a different mix of lawyers showing up for each meeting.

   c. Clients, as well as lawyers, regularly attended the meetings.

3.   If a larger Chicago law firm had a daily Litigation Department lunch, catered by a local restaurant and held in the firm's conference room, would the firm be able to deduct the cost under section 162? Section 119? Would the lawyers be likely to include the value of the lunch in taxable income? Are your answers to these questions consistent with the result in Cafe Angelo? If not, are you bothered by the apparent inconsistency?

4.   Why was substantiation (section 274 as opposed to 162) not an issue in *Moss*?

B.   Section 274: Substantiation Problems and the "Three Martini Lunch"

Moss provided a sophisticated discussion of the law of travel and entertainment deductions. However, most "t and e" cases are almost entirely fact-sensitive. Suppose that a businesswoman shows up, at the end of the year, with $3,000 of Visa and MasterCard receipts for lunches or dinners at local restaurants. She claims that $2,500 were for meals with real or prospective customers, and deducts that amount from her taxes. In the majority of cases, the IRS will not even audit the taxpayer, and the story will end right there. Even if it does audit her, under section 162, it would be the taxpayer's word against that of the IRS with respect to the business or personal nature of each meal. Most likely, the taxpayer would settle with the IRS for (say) one-half or one-third of her original deduction, encouraging later taxpayers to play the "audit lottery" on the belief that, if caught, they would still survive with a substantial portion of their deduction intact. Indeed, this was precisely what happened until the 1960s, when section 162 was the only applicable law in this area.

In situations like this, where taxpayers control the facts and it is difficult or impossible to audit all cases, Congress is often tempted to seek a legislative solution. Concern over the deductibility of so-called "three martini lunches" spurred Congress toward reforms in 1962, during the (liberal) administration of President John F. Kennedy, and again in 1986, during the (conservative) administration of President Ronald Reagan. Although these reforms have done much to eliminate the abuse of travel and entertainment deductions, they raise new and difficult issues, and demonstrate how hard it is to separate the good and bad cases in this area.

The current rules, contained mostly in section 274, have three principal aspects. The first, in section 274(a), restricts the deduction for entertainment and amusement activities to items "directly related to . . . the active conduct of the taxpayer's trade or business." The idea is to eliminate deductions for background or "goodwill" entertainment, as when a shoe salesman entertains his friends and neighbors on the theory that they all have feet and might, eventually, want to come in and purchase some shoes. (Don't laugh; this actually happens.) The effect of this rule is somewhat mitigated by the intermediate clause of section 274(a), which states that in the case of items directly preceding or following a substantial and bona fide business discussion, the expenditure must merely be "associated with," rather than directly related to, the taxpayer's trade or business; thus an evening at the opera or a Yankee game, or even an entire convention, is deductible as long as some reasonable portion of the time is (theoretically) devoted to business discussions. These rules are difficult to enforce: it's impossible to know if people really talked about business at a given luncheon or other meeting, so the law essentially assumes that they did if the timing and context make it believable, and leaves it at that. Famous in this area is the so-called "floor show" rule in Treasury Regulations, which denies deductions under the directly related standard "if the entertainment occurred under circumstances where there was little or no possibility of engaging in the active conduct of trade or business," including night clubs, theaters, sporting events, and cocktail parties; these events could presumably still be deducted if they were proceeded or followed by another, less distracted business discussion.[2]

A second, and more famous, reform is the substantiation requirement in section 274(d). This rule requires that the taxpayer keep detailed records regarding the amount, time and place, and business purpose of each entertainment-related activity, as well as travel and gift expenses, together with the business relationship between the taxpayer and the person being entertained.[3] If the taxpayer is audited, and fails to produce such documentation, he loses the entire deduction for the relevant items, and will in all likelihood be audited for previous years, as well, with the likelihood of interest and penalties on both these and the original taxable year. What this means is that a taxpayer who wants to lie about his business deductions must be willing to do so systematically and in writing, rather than simply making an "estimate" at the end of the year and being prepared to compromise if he should be unlucky enough to be audited. No doubt this still happens quite often, but the substantiation rule has at least changed the culture surrounding travel and entertainment expenses and reduced many of the more extreme types of noncompliance.

Finally, in 1986, Congress — frustrated by the persistence of real or perceived abuses — added a number of additional, tougher rules. The harshest of these is section 274(n), which denies 50 percent of meal and entertainment deductions, even if the substantive and procedural standards above are satisfied.[4] This rule applies to whoever actually pays for the item, *i.e.*, an employee who is compensated $200 by her employer for a business meal does not have any net income from the transaction, but the employer may deduct only $100 for the item. Additional rules restrict deductions for overseas conventions, cruises, and other exotic expenditures. These rules are arbitrary and unfair — a lawyer could take ten surly clients to dinner and be permitted to deduct only half the cost — but they are, in their way, effective; it's hard to plan around a 50 percent reduction, and if nothing else, the rules reduce the revenue loss associated with travel and entertainment deductions.

The ensuing materials include one case decided before the addition of section 274; a second case decided after its enactment; and excerpts from the legislative history of the 1962 amendments, which provide additional perspective on the problem and its ramifications. As you read these materials, consider whether section 274 successfully addresses the travel and entertainment issue, or whether it merely creates a new, more complex set of challenges.

---

[2] Treas. Reg. § 1.274-2(c)(7).

[3] A small *per diem* amount can be deducted without substantiation.

[4] This rule applies to all food and beverage expenses not exempted by the statute, as well as entertainment-related expenses of the type covered by section 274(a). For example, a meal eaten by the taxpayer on a business trip would be subject to the 50 percent disallowance, even if the trip did not constitute entertainment and was thus outside the substantive rules of section 274(a). The section 274(d) substantiation rules similarly apply both to entertainment and away-from home travel expenditures, as well as gifts and other "listed property" (section 274(d)(4)). Got it?

COHAN v. COMMISSIONER
United States Court of Appeals, Second Circuit
39 F.2d 540 (1930)

L. HAND, J:

* * *

In the production of his plays Cohan was obliged to be free-handed in entertaining actors, employees, and, as he naively adds, dramatic critics. He had also to travel much, at times with his attorney. These expenses amounted to substantial sums, but he kept no account and probably could not have done so. At the trial before the Board he estimated that he had spent eleven thousand dollars in this fashion during the first six months of 1921, twenty-two thousand dollars, between July first, 1921, and June thirtieth, 1922, and as much for his following fiscal year, fifty-five thousand dollars in all. The Board refused to allow him any part of this, on the ground that it was impossible to tell how much he had in fact spent, in the absence of any items or details. The question is how far this refusal is justified, in view of the finding that he had spent much and that the sums were allowable expenses. Absolute certainty in such matters is usually impossible and is not necessary; the Board should make as close an approximation as it can, bearing heavily if it chooses upon the taxpayer whose inexactitude is of his own making. But to allow nothing at all appears to us inconsistent with saying that something was spent. True, we do not know how many trips Cohan made, nor how large his entertainments were; yet there was obviously some basis for computation, if necessary by drawing upon the Board's personal estimates of the minimum of such expenses. The amount may be trivial and unsatisfactory, but there was basis for some allowance, and it was wrong to refuse any, even though it were the traveling expenses of a single trip. It is not fatal that the result will inevitably be speculative; many important decisions must be such. We think that the Board was in error as to this and must reconsider the evidence.

* * *

Revenue Act of 1962
S. REP. No. 1881, 87th Cong. 2d Sess. (Aug. 16, 1960)

* * *

IV. Disallowance of Certain Entertainment, Etc., Expenses
(Sec. 4 of the bill and sec. 274 of the Code)

A. *Reasons for provision*

The Treasury brought to the attention of Congress that widespread abuses have developed through the use of the expense account. In his tax message to the

Congress last year, the President stated his conviction that entertainment and related expenses, even though having a connection with the needs of business, confer substantial tax-free personal benefits on the recipients, and that in many instances deductions are obtained by disguising personal expenses as business expenses. He recommended that the cost of such business entertainment and the maintenance of entertainment facilities be disallowed in full as a tax deduction and that restrictions be imposed on the deductibility of business gifts and travel expenses.

Much of the abuse described by the President can be traced to the broad judicial and administrative interpretation given to the term "ordinary and necessary" which has resulted in many entertainment expenses being allowed as deductions where their connection with a trade or business is quite remote. Under present law, where a business purpose, however slight, exists, then the entertainment expenses generally are fully deductible if they are "ordinary and necessary" business expenses.

After careful consideration of the proposal, your committee has concluded that deductions for entertainment and traveling expenses and business gifts should be restricted to prevent abuses. The committee agrees that this abuse of the tax law should not be condoned, but on the other hand it does not believe that complete disallowance as recommended by the President is the proper solution to the problem. Rather, your committee is convinced that expenses incurred for valid business purposes should not be discouraged since such expenses serve to increase business income, which in turn produces additional tax revenues for the Treasury. If valid business expenses were to be disallowed as a deduction (particularly expenses associated with selling functions), there might be a substantial loss of revenue where business transactions are discouraged, or where they fail to be consummated. Moreover, the entertainment industry employs large numbers of service personnel, most of whom are unskilled workers who would find it difficult to obtain new employment in other fields if the disallowance of entertainment expenses created considerable unemployment in the entertainment industry. In such cases, taxes now paid by these workers would be lost to the Treasury.

B. Comparison of committee amendment with House provision

The House bill provides rules which in general would: (1) disallow a deduction with respect to entertainment activities, except to the extent that the expense is directly related to the active conduct of a trade or business; (2) disallow a deduction with respect to entertainment facilities, unless the facility is used primarily for the furtherance of the taxpayer's trade or business and the expense is directly related to the active conduct of the trade or business; (3) abolish the Cohan rule by requiring the taxpayer to substantiate, by adequate records or by sufficient evidence corroborating his own statement, all expenditures for entertainment and related facilities, and for travel and gifts; and (4) limit the deduction for gifts to $25 per year per recipient.

Your committee's bill to a considerable degree retains the basic structure of the House bill. However, the effect of the principal provision (the disallowing of a deduction for certain entertainment expenses) has been modified to permit the deduction of expenses for goodwill where a close association is established between the expense and the active conduct of a trade or business.

* * *

Understanding Section 274

1. *Cohan v. Commissioner* is famous for its "fudge" rule permitting the deduction of an estimated amount of business expenses, even though the taxpayer could not substantiate the expenditures with detailed, contemporaneous documentation. By contrast, section 274 denies a deduction for meal and entertainment expenses unless such documentation is present. How effective do you suppose this rule is? If people are willing to lie at the end of the year, will they be equally willing to lie in a daily report, claiming that friends are "business" acquaintances and that personal entertainment is really a form of business promotion? Or does the requirement of specificity deter all but the most hard-core finaglers? Note that the necessary documentation need not be attached to your return, but must be produced on audit by an IRS agent; if the documentation is not present at that point, you lose the deduction and have probably earned yourself an audit of several prior year tax returns, as well. Treas. Reg. § 1.274-5T.

2. The 1962 act was supposed to address a whole range of tax reform issues, but wound up emphasizing the travel and entertainment issue, summed up in the catchphrase "the three martini lunch" and considered a paradigm of tax abuse. Was this something of a wimping out on Congress's part? How much revenue do you suppose is lost from high-priced business lunches as opposed to (say) the exclusion of fringe benefits or tax shelter investments? Or is there something especially galling about rich people dining at your expense, while you pay 40 percent of your income in taxes? Taken together, do the 1962 and 1986 tax reforms solve the problem of exaggerated entertainment expenses, or do they leave you (so to speak) hungry for more?

3. What would happen to Cohan today?

Using the Sources

Under present law, which of the following items give rise to valid business deductions, and to what extent (if any) are the deductions subject to the 50 percent disallowance contained in section 274(n)?

a. An executive at the Continental Flange Co. takes a client to lunch to discuss business matters.

b. The same executive takes the same client to a professional basketball game, with seats perched between Spike Lee and Jerry Seinfeld, and then for a brief meal and business discussion.

c. Same as a., but no one really talks much about business.

d. An investment adviser invites ten of her neighbors to dinner in order to build personal friendships and maybe, just maybe, convince them to someday be clients.

Would it affect your answer if (i) the dinner took place in the adviser's home, rather than a restaurant, and (ii) if spouses were present?

e. What substantiation, if any, would be required in each of the above cases? If the expenses were compensated by the individual's employer, would the employer be entitled to a deduction, and would the employee have any taxable income? What Code provision(s), if any, support this result?

f. For the items above that do not give rise to *valid* business deductions, do you think it likely that many taxpayers would claim the deductions anyway, and how effective do you think the IRS is likely to be in preventing taxpayers from claiming these deductions? What about taxpayers who are willing to take extremely aggressive reporting positions or even to lie on their tax returns?

Law and Planning

Assume you are a business executive in charge of your company's travel and entertainment policy and recognize that the 50 percent disallowance rule is likely to remain in effect for the foreseeable future. What sorts of adjustments, if any, would you recommend that the company make in order to cope with the disallowance rule? In particular, how would you evaluate the following three alternatives?

a. Cut back on meal and entertainment expenses; they are too expensive without the deduction.

b. Continue entertaining, but look for less expensive restaurants and do more videoconferencing.

c. Keep eating until you're not hungry anymore.

Now suppose that you were a restaurant owner faced with declining sales because of the 50 percent rule. What, if anything, might you do to adjust?

Politics and Policy

If you were a lobbyist, hired to restore a 100 percent deduction for meal and entertainment expenses, how would you encourage Congress to do so? Consider in particular the following elements of your strategy:

a. What policy arguments you would make against the current disallowance rule (horizontal and vertical equity, economic efficiency, administrability, etc.)?

b. What political support would you enlist, *i.e.*, what kinds of people (executives, restaurant owners, waiters and bellboys) would you want to have testify in front of the relevant congressional committees, and what business or labor groups could you enlist as part of your lobbying effort?

c. How would you deal with the perception — by no means an outlandish one — that your proposal would mostly benefit wealthy, over-indulged people?

Now pretend you are a staff member at a public interest tax organization (yes, there is such a thing), and your organization is dead set against the proposal. What kind of arguments would you make to refute the above, and who or what interest groups would you attempt to mobilize in your support?

II. INCREASED PERSONAL EXPENDITURES RESULTING FROM BUSINESS EMPLOYMENT: THE DISTINCTION BETWEEN "HOME" AND "OFFICE" AND THE RELEVANCE OF SOCIAL CHANGE

Less famous than the travel and entertainment issue, but more intellectually challenging, is the problem of increased personal expenditures that are occasioned by business employment. A person who takes on a new job does not simply add income and continue to have the same personal expenses. Rather, her personal expenditures are likely to increase in several ways: directly, to encompass commuting and other costs occasioned by the new job; and indirectly, because she will now be required to pay for services (child care, household assistance, etc.) that she would otherwise have provided on her own. The new job may also occasion a messy overlap between business and personal expenditures, as when a bedroom or living room becomes a so-called "home office" for the exercise of nighttime, weekend, and even 9-to-5 chores. The choice of the female pronoun is not accidental here: women in our society continue to bear the lion's share of child care and household responsibilities, and the non-deductibility of these expenses has been cited as a major factor in discouraging them from entering the paid labor force.

The following materials consider the commuting, child care, and home office issues, together with opinions of important commentators and proposals for future change. As you read them, keep in mind the social and political contexts in which these rules arose, and whether the rules are consistent with the way in which most women and men view their business and personal responsibilities in today's world. Do the rules derive from immutable tax principles, or are they provisional arrangements that are likely to mutate as the world changes around them?

A.   Commuting and "Away From Home" Travel Expenses

COMMISSIONER v. FLOWERS
United States Supreme Court
326 U.S. 465 (1946)

Mr. Justice Murphy delivered the opinion of the Court.

This case presents a problem as to the meaning and application of the provision of § 23(a)(1)(A) of the Internal Revenue Code[5] allowing a deduction for income tax

---

[5] [1] 26 U.S.C. § 23(a)(1)(A), as amended, 56 Stat. 819.

"§ 23. DEDUCTIONS FROM GROSS INCOME.

"In computing net income there shall be allowed as deductions:

"(a) *Expenses.* —

"(1) *Trade or Business Expenses.* —

purposes of "traveling expenses (including the entire amount expended for meals and lodging) while away from home in the pursuit of a trade or business."

The taxpayer, a lawyer, has resided with his family in Jackson, Mississippi, since 1903. There he has paid taxes, voted, schooled his children and established social and religious connections. He built a house in Jackson nearly thirty years ago and at all times has maintained it for himself and his family. He has been connected with several law firms in Jackson, one of which he formed and which has borne his name since 1922.

In 1906 the taxpayer began to represent the predecessor of the Gulf, Mobile & Ohio Railroad, his present employer. He acted as trial counsel for the railroad throughout Mississippi. From 1918 until 1927 he acted as special counsel for the railroad in Mississippi. He was elected general solicitor in 1927 and continued to be elected to that position each year until 1930, when he was elected general counsel. Thereafter he was annually elected general counsel until September, 1940, when the properties of the predecessor company and another railroad were merged and he was elected vice president and general counsel of the newly formed Gulf, Mobile & Ohio Railroad.

The main office of the Gulf, Mobile & Ohio Railroad is in Mobile, Alabama, as was also the main office of its predecessor. When offered the position of general solicitor in 1927, the taxpayer was unwilling to accept it if it required him to move from Jackson to Mobile. He had established himself in Jackson both professionally and personally and was not desirous of moving away. As a result, an arrangement was made between him and the railroad whereby he could accept the position and continue to reside in Jackson on condition that he pay his traveling expenses between Mobile and Jackson and pay his living expenses in both places. This arrangement permitted the taxpayer to determine for himself the amount of time he would spend in each of the two cities and was in effect during 1939 and 1940, the taxable years in question.

The railroad company provided an office for the taxpayer in Mobile but not in Jackson. When he worked in Jackson his law firm provided him with office space, although he no longer participated in the firm's business or shared in its profits. He used his own office furniture and fixtures at this office. The railroad, however, furnished telephone service and a typewriter and desk for his secretary. It also paid the secretary's expenses while in Jackson. Most of the legal business of the railroad was centered in or conducted from Jackson, but this business was handled by local counsel for the railroad. The taxpayer's participation was advisory only and was no different from his participation in the railroad's legal business in other areas.

"(A) *In General.* — All the ordinary and necessary expenses paid or incurred during the taxable year in carrying on any trade or business, including a reasonable allowance for salaries or other compensation for personal services actually rendered; traveling expenses (including the entire amount expended for meals and lodging) while away from home in the pursuit of a trade or business; and rentals or other payments required to be made as a condition to the continued use or possession, for purposes of the trade or business, of property to which the taxpayer has not taken or is not taking title or in which he has no equity."

The taxpayer's principal post of business was at the main office in Mobile. However, during the taxable years of 1939 and 1940, he devoted nearly all of his time to matters relating to the merger of the railroads. Since it was left to him where he would do his work, he spent most of his time in Jackson during this period. In connection with the merger, one of the companies was involved in certain litigation in the federal court in Jackson and the taxpayer participated in that litigation.

During 1939 he spent 203 days in Jackson and 66 in Mobile, making 33 trips between the two cities. During 1940 he spent 168 days in Jackson and 102 in Mobile, making 40 trips between the two cities. The railroad paid all of his traveling expenses when he went on business trips to points other than Jackson or Mobile. But it paid none of his expenses in traveling between these two points or while he was at either of them.

The taxpayer deducted $900 in his 1939 income tax return and $1,620 in his 1940 return as traveling expenses incurred in making trips from Jackson to Mobile and as expenditures for meals and hotel accommodations while in Mobile.[6] The Commissioner disallowed the deductions, which action was sustained by the Tax Court. But the Fifth Circuit Court of Appeals reversed the Tax Court's judgment, 148 F.2d 163, and we granted certiorari because of a conflict between the decision below and that reached by the Fourth Circuit Court of Appeals in *Barnhill v. Commissioner*, 148 F.2d 913.

The portion of § 23(a)(1)(A) authorizing the deduction of "traveling expenses (including the entire amount expended for meals and lodging) while away from home in the pursuit of a trade or business" is one of the specific examples given by Congress in that section of "ordinary and necessary expenses paid or incurred during the taxable year in carrying on any trade or business." It is to be contrasted with the provision of § 24(a)(1) of the Internal Revenue Code disallowing any deductions for "personal, living, or family expenses." And it is to be read in light of the interpretation given to it by § 19.23(a)-2 of Treasury Regulations 103, promulgated under the Internal Revenue Code. This interpretation, which is precisely the same as that given to identical traveling expense deductions authorized by prior and successive Revenue Acts, is deemed to possess implied legislative approval and to have the effect of law. *Helvering v. Winmill*, 305 U.S. 79; *Boehm v. Commissioner*, 326 U.S. 287. In pertinent part, this interpretation states that

> "Traveling expenses, as ordinarily understood, include railroad fares and meals and lodging. If the trip is undertaken for other than business purposes, the railroad fares are personal expenses and the meals and lodging are living expenses. If the trip is solely on business, the reasonable and necessary traveling expenses, including railroad fares, meals, and lodging, are business expenses. . . . Only such expenses as are reasonable

---

[6] [2] No claim for deduction was made by the taxpayer for the amounts spent in traveling from Mobile to Jackson. He also took trips during the taxable years to Washington, New York, New Orleans, Baton Rouge, Memphis and Jackson (Tenn.), which were apparently in the nature of business trips for which the taxpayer presumably was reimbursed by the railroad. No claim was made in regard to them.

and necessary in the conduct of the business and directly attributable to it may be deducted. . . . Commuters' fares are not considered as business expenses and are not deductible."

Three conditions must thus be satisfied before a traveling expense deduction may be made under § 23(a)(1)(A):

(1) The expense must be a reasonable and necessary traveling expense, as that term is generally understood. This includes such items as transportation fares and food and lodging expenses incurred while traveling.

(2) The expense must be incurred "while away from home."

(3) The expense must be incurred in pursuit of business. This means that there must be a direct connection between the expenditure and the carrying on of the trade or business of the taxpayer or of his employer. Moreover, such an expenditure must be necessary or appropriate to the development and pursuit of the business or trade.

Whether particular expenditures fulfill these three conditions so as to entitle a taxpayer to a deduction is purely a question of fact in most instances. *See Commissioner v. Heininger*, 320 U.S. 467, 475. And the Tax Court's inferences and conclusions on such a factual matter, under established principles, should not be disturbed by an appellate court. *Commissioner v. Scottish American* Co., 323 U.S. 119; *Dobson v. Commissioner*, 320 U.S. 489.

In this instance, the Tax Court without detailed elaboration concluded that "The situation presented in this proceeding is, in principle, no different from that in which a taxpayer's place of employment is in one city and for reasons satisfactory to himself he resides in another." It accordingly disallowed the deductions on the ground that they represent living and personal expenses rather than traveling expenses incurred while away from home in the pursuit of business. The court below accepted the Tax Court's findings of fact but reversed its judgment on the basis that it had improperly construed the word "home" as used in the second condition precedent to a traveling expense deduction under § 23(a)(1)(A). The Tax Court, it was said, erroneously construed the word to mean the post, station or place of business where the taxpayer was employed — in this instance, Mobile — and thus erred in concluding that the expenditures in issue were not incurred "while away from home." The court below felt that the word was to be given no such "unusual" or "extraordinary" meaning in this statute, that it simply meant "that place where one in fact resides" or "the principal place of abode of one who has the intention to live there permanently." 148 F.2d at 164. Since the taxpayer here admittedly had his home, as thus defined, in Jackson and since the expenses were incurred while he was away from Jackson, the court below held that the deduction was permissible.

The meaning of the word "home" in § 23(a)(1)(A) with reference to a taxpayer residing in one city and working in another has engendered much difficulty and litigation. 4 Mertens, Law of Federal Income Taxation (1942) § 25.82. The Tax Court and the administrative rulings have consistently defined it as the equivalent of the taxpayer's place of business. *See Barnhill v. Commissioner*, *supra* (C.C.A. 4). On the other hand, the decision below and *Wallace v. Commissioner*, 144 F.2d 407 (C.C.A. 9), have flatly rejected that view and have confined the term to the taxpayer's actual residence. *See also Coburn v. Commissioner*, 138 F.2d 763 (C.C.A. 2).

We deem it unnecessary here to enter into or to decide this conflict. The Tax Court's opinion, as we read it, was grounded neither solely nor primarily upon that agency's conception of the word "home." Its discussion was directed mainly toward the relation of the expenditures to the railroad's business, a relationship required by the third condition of the deduction. Thus even if the Tax Court's definition of the word "home" was implicit in its decision and even if that definition was erroneous, its judgment must be sustained here if it properly concluded that the necessary relationship between the expenditures and the railroad's business was lacking. Failure to satisfy any one of the three conditions destroys the traveling expense deduction.

Turning our attention to the third condition, this case is disposed of quickly. There is no claim that the Tax Court misconstrued this condition or used improper standards in applying it. And it is readily apparent from the facts that its inferences were supported by evidence and that its conclusion that the expenditures in issue were non-deductible living and personal expenses was fully justified.

The facts demonstrate clearly that the expenses were not incurred in the pursuit of the business of the taxpayer's employer, the railroad. Jackson was his regular home. Had his post of duty been in that city the cost of maintaining his home there and of commuting or driving to work concededly would be non-deductible living and personal expenses lacking the necessary direct relation to the prosecution of the business. The character of such expenses is unaltered by the circumstance that the taxpayer's post of duty was in Mobile, thereby increasing the costs of transportation, food and lodging. Whether he maintained one abode or two, whether he traveled three blocks or three hundred miles to work, the nature of these expenditures remained the same.

The added costs in issue, moreover, were as unnecessary and inappropriate to the development of the railroad's business as were his personal and living costs in Jackson. They were incurred solely as the result of the taxpayer's desire to maintain a home in Jackson while working in Mobile, a factor irrelevant to the maintenance and prosecution of the railroad's legal business. The railroad did not require him to travel on business from Jackson to Mobile or to maintain living quarters in both cities. Nor did it compel him, save in one instance, to perform tasks for it in Jackson. It simply asked him to be at his principal post in Mobile as business demanded and as his personal convenience was served, allowing him to divide his business time between Mobile and Jackson as he saw fit. Except for the federal court litigation, all of the taxpayer's work in Jackson would normally have been performed in the headquarters at Mobile. The fact that he traveled frequently between the two cities and incurred extra living expenses in Mobile, while doing much of his work in Jackson, was occasioned solely by his personal propensities. The railroad gained nothing from this arrangement except the personal satisfaction of the taxpayer.

Travel expenses in pursuit of business within the meaning of § 23(a)(1)(A) could arise only when the railroad's business forced the taxpayer to travel and to live temporarily at some place other than Mobile, thereby advancing the interests of the railroad. Business trips are to be identified in relation to business demands and the traveler's business headquarters. The exigencies of business rather than the personal conveniences and necessities of the traveler must be the motivating factors. Such was not the case here.

It follows that the court below erred in reversing the judgment of the Tax Court.

Reversed.

Mʀ. Jᴜꜱᴛɪᴄᴇ Jᴀᴄᴋꜱᴏɴ took no part in the consideration or decision of this case.

Mʀ. Jᴜꜱᴛɪᴄᴇ Rᴜᴛʟᴇᴅɢᴇ, dissenting.

I think the judgment of the Court of Appeals should be affirmed. When Congress used the word "home" in § 23 of the Code, I do not believe it meant "business headquarters." And in my opinion this case presents no other question.

Congress allowed the deduction for "traveling expenses (including the entire amount expended for meals and lodging) while away from home in the pursuit of a trade or business." Treasury Regulations 103, § 19.23(a)-1, are to the same effect, with the word "solely" added after "home." Section 19.23(a)-2 also provides: "Commuters' fares are not considered as business expenses and are not deductible." By this decision, the latter regulation is allowed, in effect, to swallow up the deduction for many situations where the regulation has no fit application.

Respondent's home was in Jackson, Mississippi, in every sense, unless for applying § 23. There he maintained his family, with his personal, political and religious connections; schooled his children; paid taxes, voted, and resided over many years. There too he kept hold upon his place as a lawyer, though not substantially active in practice otherwise than to perform his work as general counsel for the railroad. This required his presence in Mobile, Alabama, for roughly a third of his time. The remainder he spent in Jackson at the same work, except for the time he was required to travel to points other than Mobile.

* * *

I agree with the Court of Appeals that if Congress had meant "business headquarters," and not "home," it would have said "business headquarters." When it used "home" instead, I think it meant home in everyday parlance, not in some twisted special meaning of "tax home" or "tax headquarters." I find no purpose stated or implied in the Act, the regulations or the legislative history to support such a distortion or to use § 23 as a lever to force people to move their homes to the locality where their employer's chief business headquarters may be, although their own work may be done as well in major part at home. The only stated purpose, and it is clearly stated, not in words of art, is to relieve the tax burden when one is away from home on business.

By construing "home" as "business headquarters"; by reading "temporarily" as "very temporarily" into § 23; by bringing down "ordinary and necessary" from its first sentence into its second; by finding "inequity" where Congress has said none exists; by construing "commuter" to cover long-distance, irregular travel; and by conjuring from the "statutory setting" a meaning at odds with the plain wording of the clause, the Government makes over understandable ordinary English into highly technical tax jargon. There is enough of this in the tax laws inescapably, without adding more in the absence of either compulsion or authority. The arm of the tax-gatherer reaches far. In my judgment it should not go the length of this case. Congress has revised § 23 once to overcome niggardly construction. It should not have to do so again.

Understanding *Flowers*

1.   From the language of what is now section 162(a)(2), the Court derives a three-part test for deductibility of away-from-home expenses: the expense must be reasonable and necessary, must be made while "away from home," and must be incurred for business rather than personal reasons. Since Flowers' commuting expenses in *Flowers* fail the third (business purpose) test, the majority does not reach the question of the location of his tax home. Is this move a little too clever? If Flowers' tax home was his principal residence, in Jackson — as the dissent vociferously argues — the expenses in Mobile would appear to be away from home and (arguably) incurred for business reasons, since his office was in Mobile and he had no other, personal reason for being there. By contrast, if his tax home is his principal place of business, in Mobile, the trips to Jackson look more like personal expenditures, Flowers having had the option to live near his place of business and chosen, for personal reasons, to live elsewhere. Is the court, without quite saying so, adopting a rule that one's home for tax purposes is his place of business, rather than his personal residence? If so, do you agree with this rule?

2.   Suppose that, instead of his Mobile expenses, Flowers had tried to deduct a portion of the cost of his home in Jackson, together with transportation expenses and miscellaneous costs (food, laundry, etc.) associated with his Jackson residence. Would he have been more successful? As a strategic matter, why do you think that Flowers attempted to deduct his Mobile, rather than Jackson, expenditures?

3.   Just out of curiosity, why did Flowers, who was a railroad employee, have to pay for his rail travel? Suppose that his employer, after hearing of the Supreme Court's decision, decides henceforth to provide Flowers with free travel on its Mobile-Jackson route. What would be the tax consequences to Flowers, and might the IRS find it more difficult to police arrangements of this sort than the actual arrangement in the *Flowers* case?

Although *Flowers* sidesteps the issue, the usual rule is that a taxpayer's tax home is her principal place of business — that is, her office — rather than her personal residence, so that commuting between home and office becomes a personal rather than business expense and is (generally speaking) not deductible from income. Another way of saying this is that the taxpayer's business day begins when she arrives at work: expenses like commuting, child care, or work clothing may well be caused by her job, but retain their personal character with some very limited exceptions.[7] Following this analysis, Flowers was simply a long-distance commuter: whether he chose to live in Mobile, a Mobile suburb, or in another state, his travel expenditures were nondeductible unless he showed a good business purpose for leaving the Mobile area.

Apart from its philosophical implications, the home-is-where-the-office-is rule raises a number of daunting practical problems. One obvious problem is that an increasing number of taxpayers work all or part of the time at home, so that the distinction between business and personal locations becomes essentially meaningless in these cases. The question arises whether these taxpayers should be entitled to deduct the costs (depreciation, utilities, etc.) associated with a "home office," and — if they have both a home office and other business locations — the costs of travel between these (supposedly) different business locations. These questions are discussed in Section C., below.

A somewhat narrower problem involves the changing of tax homes, even by a taxpayer who does most of his or her work at the office. Suppose that Flowers, tired of the whole Mobile scene, takes a job in Minneapolis-St. Paul. If he moves his family with him, buying a house in a Minneapolis suburb, the answer is: Flowers' tax home would move with him, and his commute between Minneapolis and its suburbs, together with any return trips to see old friends in Mississippi, would be nondeductible personal expenses. But suppose that Flowers is on temporary assignment to Minneapolis, or has been given a six-month tryout at a new job, and — being a prudent sort — decides to live out of a suitcase in Minneapolis, keeping his family in Mississippi and coming home weekends and holidays. Can it be argued that his (permanent) tax home remains in Mobile, or in Jackson, and that the Minneapolis adventure is essentially just a long business trip, so that Flowers should be entitled to deduct his Minneapolis living expenses, together with the rail (or more likely, plane fares) between Minneapolis and his original home? Should the answer depend upon Flowers' mental state, *i.e.*, whether he honestly intends to return from Minneapolis to the Deep South in the foreseeable future, or on whether he actually does so? Note that a large amount of money is at stake here: deducting all travel and living expenses may be sufficient to wipe out a large portion of taxable income, while the loss of deductions may force the taxpayer to have duplicative expenses without any immediate tax relief.

As might be expected, taxpayers have been anything but shy about exploiting the "temporary assignment" concept. One famous case involved a Harvard law student who attempted to deduct the costs of her New York apartment and shuttle air fares while working as a summer intern at a New York law firm, on the theory that she was temporarily away from her Boston tax home and would be returning at the end of the summer.[8] (She lost, and now teaches legal philosophy.) A more successful, if equally dubious, stratagem involves professors who "visit" at other universities for one or two semesters at a time, deducting travel and living expenses on the theory

---

[7] Although commuting by train, car, etc., is generally nondeductible, employer-provided van pools, transit passes, etc. — together with free employee parking — may be excludible from income in certain cases (section 132(f)). For an interesting discussion of the commuting issue, see Marvin A. Chirelstein, *Federal Income Taxation* (9th ed. 2002).

[8] Hantzis v. Comm'r, 638 F.2d 248 (1st Cir.).

that they will be returning to their home school, which usually has to take them, when they have completed the visit. Congress cracked down, a bit, in 1992, limiting temporary employment to positions not more than one year in duration (§ 162); but a year is a pretty long time, and the statute does not prevent a taxpayer from taking a series of temporary positions in different locations with the accompanying tax advantages.

The following cases consider the scope of the temporary employment doctrine in two rather different settings.

ANDREWS v. COMMISSIONER
United States Court of Appeals, First Circuit
931 F.2d 132 (1991)

CAMPBELL, J:

Edward W. Andrews and his wife, Leona J. Andrews, brought this action in the Tax Court for a redetermination of an income tax deficiency that the Commissioner had assessed for the tax year 1984. At issue is Andrews' deduction of travel expenses, including meals and costs associated with maintaining a second home at Lighthouse Point, Florida, as "traveling expenses . . . while away from home in the pursuit of a trade or business." Internal Revenue Code of 1954, 26 U.S.C. § 162(a)(2). Personal living expenses are generally not deductible. 26 U.S.C. § 262. The Tax Court sustained the Commissioner's disallowance of the deduction on the grounds that Andrews was not "away from home" when these expenses were incurred. *Andrews v. Commissioner*, 60 T.C.M. (CCH) 277, T.C. Memo 1990-391. Andrews appeals to this court pursuant to 26 U.S.C. § 7482.

Background

We summarize the Tax Court's findings only to the extent helpful in understanding this decision. Andrews was president and chief executive officer of Andrews Gunite Co., Inc. ("Andrews Gunite"), which is engaged in the swimming pool construction business in New England, a seasonal business. His salary in 1984 was $108,000. Beginning in 1964, during the off-season, Andrews, establishing a sole proprietorship known as Andrews Farms, began to race and breed horses in New England, and in 1972 moved his horse business to Pompano, Florida. Andrews' horse business proliferated and prospered.

In 1974, Andrews Gunite diversified by establishing a Florida-based division, known as Pilgrim Farms, to acquire horses to breed with two of Andrews Farms' most successful horses and to develop a racing stable similar to Andrews Farms. By 1975, Andrews Farms had 130 horses, and by 1984 Pilgrim Farms had twenty to thirty horses. Andrews was responsible, in 1984, for managing and training Pilgrim Farms horses and Andrews Farms horses, though he was compensated for his services to Pilgrim Farms only by payment of his airfare to Florida. While in Florida during racing season, Andrews worked at the racetrack from seven in the morning until noon, and he returned to the track to solicit sales of his horses and watch the races on four nights per week.

Also, in 1983, Andrews' son, who had worked for Andrews Gunite, sought to establish a pool construction business in Florida. Andrews, along with his brother and son, formed a corporation, originally known as East Coast Pools by Andrews, Inc. and renamed Pools by Andrews, Inc., to purchase the assets of a troubled pool business in Florida. Andrews owned one-third of Pools by Andrews, Inc. in 1984. Andrews assisted his son in the Florida pool business, but drew no salary for his services. By the time of trial, this pool business was one of the biggest, if not the biggest builder of pools in Florida, with offices in West Palm Beach and Orlando and plans for a third office in Tampa.

Andrews resided in Lynnfield, Massachusetts with his wife prior to and during 1984. During this period, the expansion of the horse business required Andrews to make an increasing number of trips to Florida. In order to reduce travel costs and facilitate lodging arrangements, Andrews purchased a condominium in Pompano Beach, Florida in 1976, which he used as a residence when in Florida during the racing season. The neighborhood around the condominium became unsafe, and Andrews decided to move, purchasing a single family home with a swimming pool in Lighthouse Point, Florida in 1983. The home was closer than the condominium to the Pompano Beach Raceway, where Andrews maintained, trained, and raced many of the Andrews Farms and Pilgrim Farms horses. Andrews used the Florida house as his personal residence during the racing season.

The Tax Court concluded that in 1984 Andrews worked in Florida primarily in his horse business for six months, from January through April and during November and December, and that Andrews worked primarily in his pool construction business in Massachusetts for six months, from May to October. On his 1984 amended return, Andrews claimed one hundred percent business usage on his Florida house, and claimed depreciation deductions on the furniture and house in connection with his horse racing business. He also characterized tax, mortgage interest,[9] utilities, insurance, and other miscellaneous expenses as "lodging expenses," which he deducted in connection with the Florida pools and horse racing businesses, along with expenses for meals while he was in Florida.

Discussion

The Tax Court correctly stated: "The purpose of the section 162(a)(2) deduction is to mitigate the burden upon a taxpayer who, because of the exigencies of his trade or business, must maintain two places of abode and thereby incur additional living expenses." *See Hantzis v. Commissioner*, 638 F.2d 248, 256 (1st Cir.), *cert. denied*, 452 U.S. 962 (1981); *Dilley v. Commissioner*, 58 T.C. 276 (1972); *Kroll v. Commissioner*, 49 T.C. 557, 562 (1962). The Tax Court then stated its general rule that "a taxpayer's home for purposes of section 162(a) is the area or vicinity of his principal place of business." Responding thereafter to the Commissioner's contention that during the horse racing season Florida was Andrews' "tax home,"

---

[9] [4] The Commissioner conceded in the Tax Court that real estate taxes and mortgage interest expenses on the Lighthouse Point, Florida house were independently deductible under 26 U.S.C. §§ 163–64, to the extent they were substantiated. The deductibility of these expenses is therefore not at issue in this appeal.

rendering Andrews' Florida meals and lodging expenses personal and nondeductible living expenses under sections 262 and 162(a)(2), the Tax Court concluded that Andrews had two "tax homes" in 1984. The Tax Court, without further elaboration, based its decision on an observation that Andrews' business in Florida between January and mid-April and during November and December of each year was recurrent with each season, rather than temporary.

On appeal, the Commissioner who, while maintaining its ongoing position that the taxpayer's home for purposes of section 162(a)(2) is his principal place of business and that Andrews' principal place of business was in Florida, agrees with Andrews that the Tax Court erred in finding that he had more than one tax home and urges that we remand for the Tax Court to determine the location of Andrews' principal place of business. For the reasons that follow, we hold that the Tax Court erred in determining that Andrews had two "tax homes" in this case.

As we have previously stated, section 162 provides a category of deductible business expenses which reflects "a fundamental principle of taxation: that a person's taxable income should not include the cost of producing that income." *Hantzis*, 638 F.2d at 249. A specific example of a deductible cost of producing income is section 162(a)(2) travel expenses. *Id.* The Supreme Court first construed the meaning of the travel expense deduction provision in *Commissioner v. Flowers*, 326 U.S. 465 (1946). In *Flowers*, the Court construed this provision to mean that travel expenses are deductible only if: (1) "reasonable and necessary"; (2) "incurred 'while away from home' "; and (3) incurred "in pursuit of business." *Id.* at 470.

The issue of the reasonableness or necessity of Andrews' Florida expenses is not presented in this appeal. Rather, the Tax Court based its decision on a holding that Andrews did not satisfy the second *Flowers* requirement for deduction of his Florida expenses; as the Tax Court determined Andrews' home in 1984 was in both Massachusetts and Florida, he was not away from home when these expenses were incurred. We turn, then, to interpret the meaning of the "away from home" language of section 162(a)(2). The question here is whether, within the meaning of "home" in section 162(a)(2), Andrews could have had two homes in 1984.

The Supreme Court, in *Flowers*, noted: "The meaning of the word 'home' in [the travel expense deduction provision] with reference to a taxpayer residing in one city and working in another has engendered much difficulty and litigation." *Id.* at 471; *see also Commissioner v. Stidger*, 386 U.S. 287, 292 (1967). The Internal Revenue Service has consistently taken the position that a taxpayer's home for purposes of section 162(a) is the area or vicinity of his principal place of employment. Rev. Rul. 75-432, 1975-2 C.B. 60; Rev. Rul. 63-82, 1963-1 C.B. 33; Rev. Rul. 61-67, 1961-1 C.B. 25. The Tax Court in this case acknowledged the general validity of that rule, as have a number of courts of appeals. *See, e.g., Coombs v. Commissioner*, 608 F.2d 1269, 1275 (9th Cir. 1979); *Markey v. Commissioner*, 490 F.2d 1249, 1255 (6th Cir. 1974). Judge Friendly, writing for the Second Circuit, however, reasoned that Congress intended that "home" should be accorded its natural non-technical ordinary meaning of primary residence in a tax statute. *Rosenspan v. United States*, 438 F.2d 905, 911 (2d Cir.), *cert. denied*, 404 U.S. 864 (1971).

This court, in *Hantzis*, after reviewing cases addressing this issue, declined in that case to focus upon the "principal place of business" or "primary residence" definitions of "home," and suggested a "functional definition of the term," 638 F.2d at 253. Effectuation of the travel expense provision must be guided by the policy underlying the provision that costs necessary to producing income may be deducted from taxable income. *Id.* at 251. Where business necessity requires that a taxpayer maintain two places of abode, and thereby incur additional and duplicate living expenses, such duplicate expenses are a cost of producing income and should ordinarily be deductible. We believe it continues to be the case that, "whether it is held in a particular decision that a taxpayer's home is his residence or his principal place of business, the ultimate allowance or disallowance of a deduction is a function of the court's assessment of the reason for a taxpayer's maintenance of two homes." *Id.* "The exigencies of business rather than the personal conveniences and necessities of the traveler must be the motivating factors." *Flowers*, 326 U.S. at 474. The Commissioner and courts have adhered consistently to this policy that living expenses duplicated as a result of business necessity are deductible, whereas those duplicated as a result of personal choice are not.

The principle — that living expenses are deductible to the extent business necessity requires that they be duplicated — is also reflected in cases concerning temporary and itinerant workers. The courts and the Commissioner have agreed that a taxpayer cannot be expected to relocate her primary residence to a place of temporary employment. Hence, duplicate living expenses incurred at the place of temporary employment (if different from the place of usual abode), result from business exigency in satisfaction of the third prong of the *Flowers* test. An exception to the "principal place of business" definition of "tax home" is made where the business assignment is only temporary. *See Peurifoy v. Commissioner*, 358 U.S. 59 (1958) (per curiam); *Yeates v. Commissioner*, 873 F.2d 1159, 1160 (8th Cir. 1989) (per curiam); *Hantzis*, 638 F.2d at 254–55; *Six v. United States*, 450 F.2d 66 (2d Cir. 1971); *Harvey v. Commissioner*, 283 F.2d 491 (9th Cir. 1960). Moreover, an "itinerant" worker who has no principal place of business and has no permanent place of abode ordinarily does not bear duplicate living expenses at all, and no deduction is generally allowable. *See Deamer v. Commissioner*, 752 F.2d 337, 339 (8th Cir. 1985) (per curiam); *Rosenspan*, 438 F.2d at 912; *Duncan v. Commissioner*, 47 F.2d 1082 (2d Cir. 1931); Rev. Rul. 60-189, 1960-1, C.B. 60.

Here, we face a situation where the Tax Court found that the taxpayer, Andrews, had two businesses which apparently required that he spend a substantial amount of time in each of two widely separate places in 1984. However, the Tax Court's conclusion — that Andrews had two "tax homes" — is inconsistent with the well-settled policy underlying section 162(a)(2): that duplicated living expenses necessitated by business are deductible. We have previously said that "a taxpayer who is required to travel to get to a place of secondary employment which is sufficiently removed from his place of primary employment is just as much within the [travel expense deduction] provision as an employee who must travel at the behest of his employer." *Chandler v. Commissioner*, 226 F.2d 467, 469 (1st Cir. 1955), *disapproved on other grounds, Commissioner v. Bagley*, 374 F.2d 204, 208 n.11 (1st Cir. 1967), *cert. denied*, 389 U.S. 1046 (1968). On the facts the Tax Court has found, it appears that Andrews, due to his geographically disparate horse and pool construction businesses, was required to incur duplicate living expenses. The Tax Court found that Andrews maintained at least the Massachusetts house throughout the year, and duplicate expenses were seemingly incurred by maintaining the Florida house, at least in part attributable to business exigency. If so, Andrews could have had only one "home" for purposes of section 162(a)(2) in 1984; duplicate living expenses while on business at the other house were a cost of producing income.[10]

We do not seek to instruct the Tax Court how to determine which house in 1984, in Florida or in Massachusetts, was Andrews' "tax home," and which house gave rise to deductible duplicate living expenses while "away from home in pursuit of a trade or business," for purposes of section 162(a)(2). The guiding policy must be that the taxpayer is reasonably expected to locate his "home," for tax purposes, at his "major post of duty" so as to minimize the amount of business travel away from home that is required; a decision to do otherwise is motivated not by business necessity but by personal considerations, and should not give rise to greater business travel deductions. The length of time spent engaged in business at each location should ordinarily be determinative of which is the taxpayer's "principal place of business" or "major post of duty."[11] Defining that location as the taxpayer's "tax home" should result in allowance of deductions for duplicate living expenses incurred at the other "minor post of duty." Business necessity requires that living expenses be duplicated only for the time spent engaged in business at the "minor post of duty," whether that is the "primary residence" or not. See Montgomery v.

---

[10] [9] In support of its decision that Andrews had two "tax homes" in 1984, the Tax Court cited Regan v. Commissioner, 54 T.C.M. (CCH) 846, T.C. Memo 1987-512. In Regan, the taxpayer was employed near Tampa, Florida from January through June, and in the vicinity of Gainesville, Florida from July through December. The taxpayer argued that his home was in Tampa, and he continued to pay rent on his Tampa apartment when he was in Gainesville. Unpersuaded, the Tax Court found that the taxpayer spent an equal amount of time, engaged in an equal amount of business, derived an equal amount of income from his activities, and "merely rented an apartment" in both places. The Tax Court concluded from these facts that the taxpayer's principal place of business, and hence "tax home," was in Tampa from January to June, and in Gainesville from July through December. On this basis, the Tax Court sustained the disallowance of the taxpayer's deduction of travel expenses for his time in Gainesville. We doubt this decision was correct, as the taxpayer appears to have incurred duplicate lodging expenses, including at least rent, as a result of business exigency. We note that prior memorandum decisions of the Tax Court are not treated by that court as binding precedent. Newman v. Commissioner, 68 T.C. 494, 502 n.4 (1977).

This is not to say we could not imagine a rare case where a finding of "two tax homes" would be appropriate and would fit within the policies underlying section 162(a)(2). A taxpayer, spending six months of the year engaged in business in each of two different places, and maintaining a permanent home in neither place (for example, living in hotels at both places), might not incur duplicate expenses. Such a taxpayer, whether viewed in the nature of an "itinerant," see supra, or as having two "tax homes," should not generally be allowed to deduct meals and lodging as business travel deductions under section 162(a)(2). This, however, is not the case here.

[11] [10] the Sixth Circuit has established an "objective test" to determine the situs of a taxpayer's "major post of duty," including three factors: (1) the length of time spent at the location; (2) the degree of activity in each place; and (3) the relative portion of taxpayer's income derived from each place. Markey, 490 F.2d at 1255. The first factor would ordinarily be the most important, since the time spent as a business necessity at the location is a reasonable proxy for the amount of living expenses that business requires be incurred in each place. See Markey, 490 F.2d at 1252; Sherman v. Commissioner, 16 T.C. 332 (1951) (amount of income derived from activity at each location not controlling); Rev. Rul. 82, 1963-1 C.B. 33; Rev. Rul. 67, 1961-1 C.B. 25. We recognize, however, that other factors might be considered or even found determinative under appropriate circumstances.

Commissioner, 532 F.2d 1088 (6th Cir. 1976); *Markey, supra*, 490 F.2d at 1252; *Sherman v. Commissioner*, 16 T.C. 332 (1951).

Vacated and remanded for further proceedings consistent with this opinion.

YEATES v. COMMISSIONER
United States Court of Appeals, Eighth Circuit
873 F.2d 1159 (1989)

Per Curiam

Raymond and Donna Yeates appeal pro se from the tax court decision determining that expenses incurred by Raymond during 1983 for meals, lodging and transportation while employed in the Chicago, Illinois area were not deductible under 26 U.S.C. § 162(a)(2) as business travel expenses. We affirm.

The facts, as stipulated by the parties and accepted by the tax court, are as follows. Raymond Yeates has worked as a journeyman electrician since 1941. Prior to 1975 the taxpayers lived primarily in the Chicago, Illinois area, where Raymond regularly received job assignments from Local 134 of the International Brotherhood of Electrical Workers (IBEW). Local 134 assigned available jobs on the basis of seniority, and as Raymond had been a member of the union since 1951, he was able to work regularly in the Chicago area.

In 1975 the taxpayers moved to Arkansas and, Raymond obtained employment there through IBEW Local 700. In 1979, however, Raymond began having trouble finding work in Arkansas. From January 1980 to April 1981 the taxpayers lived in southern California where Raymond obtained employment through IBEW Local 569 in San Diego and IBEW Local 11 in Los Angeles.

In April 1981 the taxpayers acquired their present home in Rogers, Arkansas. From that date to the present, the taxpayers have maintained their legal residence in Rogers, Arkansas, although Raymond has not worked in the state during this time period.

Raymond continued to work in southern California until September 1981. In October 1981 he worked in the Chicago area through IBEW Local 134 and continued to obtain employment in Chicago through Local 134 during the following time periods: September 1982 to November 1982; January 19, 1983 to July 14, 1983; July 20, 1983 to December 16, 1983; January 1984 to December 1984; January 1985 to May 1985; and the entire year in 1986 except for a two-week period in California and a three-week period in Missouri. During the tax year in question, 1983, Raymond worked for 10 1/2 months in the Chicago area through Local 134. His family, however, continued to reside in Arkansas. Raymond retired on March 1, 1987.

On their joint federal tax return for 1983, the taxpayers claimed a deduction of $16,156.25 in employee business expenses, representing the traveling and living expenses (meals, lodging and transportation) incurred by Raymond in traveling to and working in the Chicago area during that year. *See* 26 U.S.C. § 162(a)(2) (allowing deduction of business traveling expenses). The Commissioner disallowed the deduction on the ground that the Chicago area was Raymond's "tax home" and that, consequently, the expenses he incurred in that area for meals, lodging and transportation constituted nondeductible personal expenses under section 262 of the Internal Revenue Code.

Following a trial, the tax court issued its decision that Raymond's employment in the Chicago area during 1983 was indefinite, rather than temporary, and Chicago was therefore his tax home. Accordingly, Raymond's living expenses of $16,156.25 were nondeductible under section 162(a) and the taxpayers had an income tax deficiency of $2,772.00 for the 1983 tax year. In reaching this result, the tax court noted that Raymond was assured of fairly steady employment in the Chicago area due to his seniority in Local 134.[12]

The taxpayers appeal contending that Raymond's employment in Chicago during 1983 was temporary as he was contracted to ten different employers for short job assignments of predetermined duration and tried repeatedly to find work near his permanent residence in Rogers, Arkansas. The taxpayers further argue that Raymond never expected to continue working in the Chicago area, that it would have been unreasonable for him to have moved his family there, and that he made himself available for work in areas besides Chicago during the year in question.

Living and traveling expenses are generally nondeductible personal expenses. 26 U.S.C. § 262; *Ellwein v. United States*, 778 F.2d 506, 509 (8th Cir. 1985). Section 162(a)(2) allows a deduction, however, where the taxpayer incurs expenses while away from home in the pursuit of his trade or business. "For purposes of section 162(a), the taxpayer's 'home' is his principal place of business, and the taxpayer is 'away from home' when required to travel to a vicinity other than his principal place of business for temporary work." *Walraven v. Commissioner*, 815 F.2d 1246, 1247 (8th Cir. 1987) (per curiam) (citing *Ellwein v. United States*, 778 F.2d at 509). The "away from home" requirement is considered "in light of the further requirement that the expense be the result of business exigencies," and if a taxpayer maintains his permanent residence at a different locale than his employment for personal reasons, a deduction is not allowed. *Hantzis v. Commissioner*, 638 F.2d 248, 253–54 (1st Cir.), *cert. denied*, 452 U.S. 962 (1981).

This court has construed the exception in section 162(a)(2) to include living and traveling expenses incurred when it appears that a taxpayer's employment away from home will be temporary as opposed to indeterminate or indefinite. *See Walraven*, 815 F.2d at 1247–48; *Ellwein*, 778 F.2d at 509–510; *Frederick v. United States*, 603 F.2d 1292, 1294–1295 (8th Cir. 1979). Employment is considered indefinite if the job prospects in the new location are likely to result in a substantial amount of time, whereas employment is temporary "if its termination could be reasonably foreseen within a short time." *Ellwein*, 778 F.2d at 509. The taxpayer bears the burden of proving that his employment was temporary, *Kasun v. United States*, 671 F.2d 1059, 1063 (7th Cir. 1982), and determination of whether a job is

---

[12] [3] Although Raymond was not entitled to deduct his traveling and living expenses while in Chicago, the tax court allowed him to deduct moving expenses of $307.50 for the costs of moving there to procure new employment. Raymond was also able to deduct $574.00 claimed for air fare incurred as a result of job hunting trips.

temporary or indefinite is a factual question. *Peurifoy v. Commissioner*, 358 U.S. 59, 61 (1958).

In *Frederick*, this court rejected the "reasonableness" test advanced by taxpayers and made an objective determination of "the taxpayer's prospects for continued employment." 603 F.2d at 1295–96; *see also Dahood v. United States*, 747 F.2d 46, 49 (1st Cir. 1984). Courts have also uniformly rejected, in the construction industry context, the contention that work is *temporary* if it involves traveling to various worksites. *See Dahood*, 747 F.2d at 49; *Kasun*, 671 F.2d at 1062.

With these considerations, we affirm the tax court's determination that Raymond Yeates' employment in Chicago was indefinite rather than temporary. Based on his seniority status in IBEW Local 134, the tax court reasonably found that Raymond's prospects for continued employment there were good and, in fact, Local 134 provided him with relatively continuous employment from 1981 through 1986 in the Chicago area. *Cf. Frederick*, 603 F.2d at 1296–97 (construction worker's employment found temporary where employment at projects was seasonal and workers knew they would be laid off during the winter).

Accordingly, we affirm.

Understanding *Andrews* and *Yeates*

1. Andrews made a business decision to have two separate enterprises, one in Massachusetts and one in Florida, together with two residences that he traveled between on a predictable schedule.

Is this really a "temporary" arrangement, akin to a short business trip, or is it more like a permanent system of living in two separate locations? If the problem was duplicative living expenses, why couldn't he simply rent his Massachusetts home out when he was in Florida, and his Florida home when he was up north? What if a New Yorker, who spent winters in South Florida, decided to open a part-time art gallery in his Florida condominium, and proceeded to deduct his Florida living expenses on the grounds that he was "away from home" in pursuit of his Florida business? Is this different from *Andrews*, or is it just a matter of degree?

2. The *Yeates* court's holding suggests that Yeates should have brought his family to Chicago — a city he already left and in which he never had permanent employment — or else pay tax on an amount which is likely to be vastly greater than his net income after deducting travel expenses. Is that a fair result? Is it consistent with the statute? Is the court saying that Yeates' tax home is Chicago, or that as an itinerant electrician he has no single tax home and therefore cannot be away from it? What exactly is the court saying?

3. Yeates appeared *pro se*, that is, he did not have a lawyer, while Andrews was represented by two apparently quite competent and presumably well-paid Boston attorneys. What effect, if any, do you think this had on the outcomes? What do you think are the vertical equity implications of *Andrews* and *Yeates* and of the "away from home" concept, in general?

Using the Sources

Angela Accountant works in the Los Angeles office of Ernst & Young, a "Big Four" accounting firm. What amounts, if any, would be deductible by Angela as "away-from-home" business expenses under section 162 of the Code?

1.   Angela is assigned for 90 days to her firm's San Francisco office, staying in San Francisco Monday-Friday each week during this period and flying home on weekends.

2.   Angela is assigned to the San Francisco office for as long as it takes to complete an audit of two prominent clients, again flying home to Los Angeles every weekend. (Does it matter, in this case, if Angela expects the audit to be completed in less than one year? If it actually is?)

3.   Angela is assigned permanently to the San Francisco office, but continues to spend weekends and holidays in Los Angeles, where her husband is a prominent attorney. (Would it change your answer if Angela saw clients at her Los Angeles home, one day a week?)

4.   Instead of San Francisco, Angela is assigned for 90 days to AHPW's San Diego office, which is within a (long) day's driving distance of her Los Angeles home, and drives back and forth each day between Los Angeles and San Diego.

5.   What happens in 3, above, if Angela leaves her San Francisco office on Wednesday morning for a trip to the firm's Seattle office, flying home to Los Angeles on Friday to spend the weekend with her family?

(Note: For the East Coasters among you, Seattle is about an hour's flying time north of San Francisco, which is an hour's flight north of Los Angeles, which is approximately 100 miles north of San Diego; beyond that are Canada and Mexico, which have their own tax laws.)

Law and Planning

Imagine you are a law professor and are offered a visiting position at another, equally prestigious university for a period not exceeding one year. Under existing tax law, the visit appears to qualify as a temporary assignment, allowing you to deduct travel and living expenses (food, lodging, etc.) for the duration of the appointment.

(i) All other things being equal, how big a factor would this tax treatment be in your decision to accept, or reject, the visiting offer? Would you actually "come out ahead" as a result of the favorable tax treatment, or would it merely help you to minimize the economic cost associated with the maneuver? Would the answer to this question vary if you were single with no close personal ties, or (alternatively) married with two young and boisterous children?

(ii) Suppose that the law school you were visiting offered you the choice of two inducements in order to accept the visit: (i) $15,000 in additional salary, or (ii) a $10,000 allowance for food and other living expenses which would have to be documented by appropriate receipts, etc. Which of these would you pick, and why?

In answering this question, note that uncompensated business expenses are deductible only to the extent that they are in excess of 2 percent of adjusted gross income (AGI) (§ 67). What incentives are created by this rule, and how would they affect your decision in this case?

Politics and Policy

The deduction for "away-from-home" travel expenses is usually justified on the grounds of duplicative expense. That is, the taxpayer incurs food and lodging (as well as transportation) expenses at the temporary site while still making mortgage or rental payments and watching food go rotten in their refrigerator at their permanent location. This is why food, lodging, and other usually nondeductible expenses become deductible when the taxpayer is away from home in pursuit of a trade or business, and also why the deduction applies to temporary but not permanent changes of employment, which do not involve such duplication.

In an era when many executives eat in restaurants even in their home city, how persuasive is the "duplication" argument, especially for meals? Note that the 50 percent cutback in meal and entertainment deductions (§ 274(n)) applies to meals eaten away from home in pursuit of the trade or business, as well as meals and entertainment — typically with clients or customers — that are deductible even if incurred in the taxpayer's home base. Is the 50 percent cutback a recognition that the duplication problem may be exaggerated, and that there is a large component of personal enjoyment in most purportedly business travel? How logical is it to deny deductions for commuting to work from the suburbs, but permit deductions for conventions and similar trips that may have a large or even preponderant personal aspect?

B.   Child-Care and Housework Expenditures

SMITH v. COMMISSIONER
Board of Tax Appeals
40 B.T.A. 1038 (1939)

OPPER, J:

Respondent determined a deficiency of $23.62 in petitioner's 1937 income tax. This was due to the disallowance of a deduction claimed by petitioners, who are husband and wife, for sums spent by the wife in employing nursemaids to care for petitioners' young child, the wife, as well as the husband, being employed. The facts have all been stipulated and are hereby found accordingly.

Petitioners would have us apply the "but for" test. They propose that but for the nurses the wife could not leave her child; but for the freedom so secured she could not pursue her gainful labors; and but for them there would be no income and no tax. This thought evokes an array of interesting possibilities. The fee to the doctor, but for whose healing service the earner of the family income could not leave his sickbed; the cost of the laborer's raiment, for how can the world proceed about its business unclothed; the very home which gives us shelter and rest and the food which provides energy, might all by an extension of the same proposition be construed as necessary to the operation of business and to the creation of income. Yet these are the very essence of those "personal" expenses the deductibility of which is expressly denied. Revenue Act of 1936, section 24(a).

We are told that the working wife is a new phenomenon. This is relied on to account for the apparent inconsistency that the expenses in issue are now a commonplace, yet have not been the subject of legislation, ruling, or adjudicated controversy. But if that is true it becomes all the more necessary to apply accepted principles to the novel facts. We are not prepared to say that the care of children, like similar aspects of family and household life, is other than a personal concern. The wife's services as custodian of the home and protector of its children are ordinarily rendered without monetary compensation. There results no taxable income from the performance of this service and the correlative expenditure is personal and not susceptible of deduction. *Rosa E. Burkhart*, 11 B.T.A. 275. Here the wife has chosen to employ others to discharge her domestic function and the services she performs are rendered outside the home. They are a source of actual income and taxable as such. But that does not deprive the same work performed by others of its personal character nor furnish a reason why its cost should be treated as an offset in the guise of a deductible item.

We are not unmindful that, as petitioners suggest, certain disbursements normally personal may become deductible by reason of their intimate connection with an occupation carried on for profit. In this category fall entertainment, *Blackmer v. Commissioner*, 70 Fed.(2d) 255 (C.C.A., 2d Cir.), and traveling expenses, *Joseph W. Powell*, 34 B.T.A. 655; *affd.*, 94 Fed.(2d) 483 (C.C.A., 1st Cir.), and the cost of an actor's wardrobe, *Charles Hutchison*, 13 B.T.A. 1187. The line is not always an easy one to draw nor the test simple to apply. But we think its principle is clear. It may for practical purposes be said to constitute a distinction between those activities which, as a matter of common acceptance and universal experience, are "ordinary" or usual as the direct accompaniment of business pursuits, on the one hand; and those which though they may in some indirect and tenuous degree relate to the circumstances of a profitable occupation, are nevertheless personal in their nature, of a character applicable to human beings generally, and which exist on that plane regardless of the occupation, though not necessarily of the station in life, of the individuals concerned. *See Welch v. Helvering*, 290 U.S. 111.

In the latter category, we think, fall payments made to servants or others occupied in looking to the personal wants of their employers. *David Sonenblick*, 4 B.T.A. 986. And we include in this group nursemaids retained to care for infant children.

Decision will be entered for the respondent.

Understanding *Smith*

1.   The *Smith* court rejects the taxpayer's claim by a sort of *reductio ad absurdum* argument, suggesting that a deduction for child-care expenditures would require a deduction for food, clothing, shelter and similar personal expenses. Does this necessarily follow? Wouldn't a stay-at-home spouse still have to eat and wear clothing, whereas child-care expenditures are caused directly by the decision to go to work? Or does the statutory language, which refers to "ordinary and necessary" business expenses, imply that personal-type expenses should never be deductible, even if they are caused by a business exigency? Exactly what test is the court applying here?

2.   Towards the middle of its opinion, the court compares a working couple like the Smiths with a couple having at least one stay-at-home spouse:

> The wife's services as custodian of the home and protector of its children are ordinarily rendered without monetary compensation. There results no taxable income from the performance of this service and the correlative expenditure is personal and not susceptible of deduction.

Couldn't one make the opposite argument: that a couple with a stay-at-home spouse receives a significant benefit because the imputed income from the spouse's services goes untaxed, and a couple who has to pay for child care should receive an equivalent benefit in the form of a deduction for child care expenditures?[13] Suppose that the Smiths had $10,000 of income and spent $3,000 of it on child care, while the Joneses, who lived next door, earned $7,000 with one spouse staying at home. Both couples finish the year with $7,000 and happy, well-fed children. Is it fair to tax the Smiths on $10,000 of income, and the Joneses on only $7,000, as the court's opinion suggests? Or is this an unfair, or at least misleading, comparison?

3.   What do you make of the ironic tone that pervades the court's opinion? Did judges in 1940 — virtually all of whom were male — really take seriously the problems of the "working wife" and mother? Faced with an opinion like this, sixty years later, should courts change their mind and decide the issue on the basis of our contemporary, presumably more open-minded, attitudes? Or should changes of this type be left to Congress and other elected officials, most of whom are probably men, anyway? What if anything do contemporary theories of statutory interpretation have to say about this problem?

The child care issue presents one of the classic examples of the clash between tax law and broader social policy. Although cloaked in neutral language, decisions like *Smith* plainly have the effect of discouraging "second earners" — still heavily women — from seeking gainful outside employment. This is especially true when tax and nontax factors are considered together. Thus, a woman working outside the home is already subject to tax at her husband's (typically higher) marginal tax rate, beginning from her first dollar of income. In addition, she is likely to incur numerous additional expenses, including child care, commuting, and assorted household items, most or all of which will be nondeductible for federal income tax purposes. This is before even considering Social Security, Medicare, and state and

---

[13]   *See* Chapter 2, *supra.*

local taxes, or the emotional stress of finding suitable childcare and balancing work and personal activities. Although taxes are only one element in this equation, they play a significant role.

The following two excerpts consider child care and related issues from two different "critical" perspectives. The first, by Grace Blumberg, is a 1970s-era feminist critique of the *Smith* case and the ideology underlying it. The second excerpt, by Nancy Staudt, emphasizes the taxation of imputed income from self-provided household services, rather than a deduction for equivalent amounts paid to outsiders; in Staudt's view, such taxation would recognize the market value of household services, and would result in additional retirement income for those who had worked primarily in the home. Do you find either of these views convincing, and what do you think is the most likely future direction of the tax law in this area?

Grace Blumberg, *Sexism in the Code:*
A Comparative Study of Income
Taxation of Working Wives and Mothers
21 BUFFALO L. REV. 49 (1971)[14]

I. INTRODUCTION

Close scrutiny of the Internal Revenue Code reveals a strong pattern of work disincentive for married women and inequitable treatment of the two-earner family. The nature and scope of discriminatory treatment cannot be fully appreciated without consideration of alternative systems of income taxation: those in effect in other countries and those that have been proposed here and abroad. This paper will consider the nature of American taxation of working wives and mothers in the comparative context of other national systems; the propriety of work disincentive as an instrument of social control; and the social and political desirability of neutral taxation for married women.

The Code will be examined in its current social context. Thus, the observation that American working wives are predominantly secondary family earners is not intended to express a social ideal. It merely reflects a contemporary social reality. Women workers generally earn substantially less than their male counterparts. Working wives earn less than their employed husbands. The American wife's working career is likely to be broken by child-bearing and rearing. Unless prompted by economic necessity, her return to work is generally considered discretionary. Even when she is earning a substantial salary, her husband is unlikely to view his employment as discretionary. Thus, the American working wife should properly be understood as a secondary family earner for the purpose of determining the work disincentive effect of various Code provisions.

* * *

[Professor Blumberg proceeds to discuss the system of combined tax rates on married couples and other provisions, which she believes discourages paid work

---

outside the home by "secondary" earners (most commonly women).]

* * *

D. Deduction of Child Care Expenses

1. *Smith v. Commissioner.* Deductibility of child care expenses incurred for the purpose of enabling a taxpayer to work was initially considered in the context of two Code provisions:

> There shall be allowed as a deduction all ordinary and necessary expenses paid or incurred during the taxable year in carrying on any trade or business. . . .

> Except as otherwise expressly provided in this chapter, no deduction shall be allowed for personal, living, or family expenses.

In her 1937 tax return, Mrs. Smith deducted the cost of wages paid to nursemaids who cared for her child while she was gainfully employed. The Commissioner disallowed the deduction and assessed a deficiency of $23.62, giving rise to *Smith v. Commissioner*, a case frequently cited to support disallowance of certain employment-related expenses. The Board of Tax Appeals refused to allow the deduction for two reasons: the expenditure was essentially "personal", and a deduction could not be made for an expense that was a substitute for imputed non-taxable income, the value of a housewife's services. The opinion is eloquent but unpersuasive:

> Petitioners would have us apply the "but for" test. They propose that but for the nurses the wife could not leave her child; but for the freedom so secured she could not pursue her gainful labors; and but for them there would be no income and no tax. This thought evokes an array of interesting possibilities.

The fee to the doctor, but for whose healing service the earner of the family income could not leave his sickbed; the cost of the laborer's raiment, for how can the world proceed about its business unclothed; the very home which gives us shelter and rest and the food which provides energy, might all by an extension of the same proposition be construed as necessary to the operation of business and to the creation of income. Yet these are the very essence of those "personal" expenses the deductibility of which is expressly denied.

The cost of child care necessary to enable a parent to pursue gainful employment is not analogous to the cost of medical care, food and shelter. One does not seek medical care, food or shelter in order to be gainfully employed, but rather to sustain one's corporal existence. Child care, on the other hand, is an expense that Mrs. Smith need not have incurred had she not been employed. It is not a *sine qua non* of human survival or comfort but an expense which necessarily arises only when both parents are employed. Nor is expenditure for child care analogous, as the Board suggests, to expenditure for personal servants. Employment of household servants generally represents a discretionary expense unrelated to (or at least not required by) the fact of the taxpayer's employment. A working mother's provision for child care is a nondiscretionary expense directly related to the fact of her employment.

The Board's second argument is somewhat abstruse. A wife's housekeeping services do not give rise to income, or rather give rise to nontaxable, that is, imputed, income. If the services are not taxable, a deduction for them is not allowable. Pursuing the Board's analysis to its logical end leads to a different conclusion. If a wife's housekeeping services do give rise to nontaxable income and the two-earner family thus loses a windfall, the effective substitute, a wife's earned income from employment, should not be taxable either, at least not to the extent that it replaces lost imputed income. Indeed, this is one argument for a special earned income allowance for working wives. It would give them parity with housewives who stay at home and provide the family with nontaxable service income.

Additionally, while it is true that Mrs. Smith's performance of child care duties would not have given rise to taxable income, she hired nursemaids to perform those services for her. The nursemaids have taxable income and Mrs. Smith is deducting the nursemaids' income rather than her own loss of imputed income. The Board's imputed income argument would thus seem to lead to the conclusion that either the nursemaids' income is nontaxable because it is a substitute for Mrs. Smith's lost imputed income, or that all or part of Mrs. Smith's employment income is nontaxable because it has replaced her nontaxable imputed income.

The Board's injection of the imputed income argument is regrettable on two grounds. It was clearly not dispositive of the issue and drew the Board away from the functional approach it should have taken. A proper analysis of borderline expenses that might be characterized as either business or personal should entail a careful inquiry into the nature of the expense. Would it have been incurred absent gainful employment? If so, it is not deductible. This criterion would eliminate food, shelter and medical expenses.

Was it a discretionary expense? Discretionary expenditures which are not incurred in the actual course of the taxpayer's work should not be deductible. Under this criterion most commuting expenses would be nondeductible. While the ordinary wage earner must incur some commuting expenses, substantial expenditure usually represents a discretionary choice of housing location.

To be deductible, expenses must be readily and accurately ascertainable. Some necessary nondiscretionary employment-related expenses are not. For example, many employees are implicitly required to purchase a larger and more expensive wardrobe than they would acquire if left to follow their own taste and inclination. But the differential between what they have purchased and what they would have purchased cannot be determined with certainty or accuracy. Child care expenses can, however, be ascertained and itemized with absolute accuracy.

A final possible, although questionable, criterion, expressing general policy rather than individual equity considerations, might require frequent incidence of the employment expense. Do many people incur this type of employment-related nondiscretionary expense? Highly particularized expenses might be disallowed because they arise from the taxpayer's unusual or unique circumstances rather than from any common socially predictable pattern of living. For example, nondeductible particularized expenses might include lawyer's fees incurred to get a taxpayer out of the Navy and back to his work, or the cost of usually frequent haircuts required by a fastidious employer. But the 10.6 million women workers with children under eighteen should be allowed to deduct their child care expenses.

A reargument of *Smith* would also include reference to the existence, in 1937, of an earned income allowance which could reasonably have been understood to absorb many employment-related expenses. Furthermore, when *Smith* was decided, taxation was individual rather than aggregate. In the absence of any general work disincentive for Mrs. Smith, policy considerations did not dictate that she be allowed child care deductions. Now, however, absent an earned income allowance and in light of the aggregation disincentive, a working woman ought to be allowed to deduct the cost of necessary child care.

Unfortunately, *Smith* is no longer subject to reargument. Congress, in 1954, provided for extremely limited child care deductions. By creating a limited exception to the rule of *Smith*, Congress appears to have expressed its approval of the Board's general disallowance of child care deductions.

Nancy C. Staudt, *Taxing Housework*
84 Geo. L.J. 1571, 1571–74, 1618–19 (1996)[15]

* * *

INTRODUCTION

Many features of the Federal Income Tax Code reflect the assumption that our society is composed of heterosexual married couples, with men occupying the "public" sphere and women occupying the "private" domestic sphere. Social security benefits funded through the payroll taxes, for example, offer spousal benefits only to legally married couples, and only heterosexual couples can obtain the tax benefits under the joint return provisions. Once married, many provisions encourage women to undertake a traditional caretaking role in the home to the exclusion of work in the paid labor force. By providing only a limited childcare subsidy, for example, the Tax Code provides financial incentives for women to work in the home after bearing children.

It is not surprising that the tax laws reflect an image of men as public actors earning a wage in the market, and that the laws assume women do not and should not have such roles. Congress devised the Tax Code in 1913 when many perceived waged labor as a male endeavor and household labor as a distinctly female activity associated with the social, but not economic, maintenance of the family. Many commentators have noted these underlying assumptions and the manner in which the Tax Code contributes to women's economic insecurity by encouraging reliance on men for financial support. Accordingly, tax analysts almost uniformly propose tax reform intended to enable women to move more easily into the market. Many

---

argue that by lowering the tax costs associated with participating in the waged labor market, women will be encouraged to substitute marketwork for housework, thereby gaining access to the wages and benefits tied to traditional market labor.

The prevailing "market-oriented" approach to women's economic subordination is based on the belief that housework can be both isolating and demoralizing. These tax analysts argue that waged labor in the market promotes self-reliance and individual success, while unwaged labor in the home might leave women disempowered socially and individually. In short, tax reformers have focused on the perceived oppressive nature of women's caring and nurturing role in the home and the possibility of using tax incentives to enable escape from this devalued role.

The market-oriented approach to women's equality and liberation acknowledges the material costs associated with performing unpaid labor and the role it plays in preventing women from obtaining the level of wages and benefits that men receive in the market. To remedy this problem, the market-oriented scholars have devised practical solutions that would, in effect, provide women with greater returns on their market labor. Although this has worthy distributional effects, focusing only upon women's work outside of the home ignores important aspects of women's lives. Indeed, by failing to acknowledge the productive nature of women's work in the home, tax scholars might contribute to the false and gendered distinction between paid work outside of the home and unpaid work inside of it.

Additionally, market-oriented incentives will not enable women to choose freely between caretaking responsibilities in the home and a career in the market. In 1994, the majority of women of all races and classes were working in the market; nevertheless, women continued to be responsible for seventy to eighty percent of housework responsibilities. Providing market opportunities, therefore, does not cause a corresponding decrease in the level of women's housework. The market-oriented approach to tax policy also fails to acknowledge that many women do not seek to exchange their household responsibilities for a greater level of market participation. Many women of color, for example, believe that in light of health hazards disproportionately suffered by communities of color, caretaking services that ensure the family's survival can be personally satisfying and politically important.

Characterizing household labor as demeaning, isolating, and oppressive, thus, ignores the valuable and productive aspects of the labor that many women, perhaps women of color in particular, find important. The only general assumptions that can and should be made concerning nonmarket labor are that (1) women, and not men, do the work, and (2) this work does not entitle women to wages or other economic benefits tied to traditional market employment.

In this article, I argue that rather than maintaining the invisibility of housework, feminists should encourage society to value the productive and political nature of women's labor both in the home and in the market. A recognition of the importance of women's work, regardless of the setting, would more accurately reflect women's valuable contributions to the economy. Once formally recognized, society is likely to value nonmarket housework activities similarly to market activities, thereby entitling women to social welfare benefits that are currently tied only to waged labor in the market.

* * *

[Professor Staudt's article proceeds to propose a tax on the imputed value of household services, to be used to support claims for social security or similar benefits, with a credit designed to prevent vertical inequity for poorer women.]

* * *

IV. VALUING AND TAXING WOMEN'S HOUSEHOLD LABOR

The previous discussion demonstrates that past efforts to increase women's economic security through tax reform have had limited success. Women, for a variety of reasons, have not responded to incentives aimed at encouraging their market participation. As a result, feminist scholars must shift their attention to other means for achieving the goal of economic independence.

In particular, scholars must seriously consider the advantages of broadening the tax base to include the benefits of women's unwaged labor. As discussed above, taxation provides access to substantial, independent social welfare benefits in retirement and disability. Tying the benefits to household labor as well as market labor would ensure greater resources for women and would represent a congressional recognition of caretaking responsibilities as valuable and productive labor. Broadening the tax base to include nonmarket labor, therefore, is an attempt to ignore the market/nonmarket dichotomy that, in effect, labels household endeavors simply as gratuitous acts undertaken by women out of love and commitment to their families.

This tax reform proposal builds on the traditional conception of income, which theoretically includes all increases in the taxpayer's economic wealth. By refusing to make a distinction between labor performed in the private and public spheres, Congress would recognize the value of household labor and the individual laborers regardless of the location of the labor. Rather than viewing women only as nurturing caregivers providing gratuitous services to the home out of love, duty, and custom, women would be treated as autonomous individuals with economic rights. Finally, by taxing household labor, Congress would follow the lead of other areas of law in which the public/private distinction has been seen as both false and problematic.

* * *

———————

Underlying the child care debate is the question whether the tax code should try to be "neutral" with respect to different races, genders, etc., or whether it should affirmatively intervene to help those in a weaker position. For instance, Edward McCaffery has argued that the code should try consciously to equalize the roles of men and women in the labor market by (for example) taxing the income of second-earners at a rate lower than that of the highest earner in the family.[16] Does this sort of positive intervention make sense to you, or is it better done somewhere outside the tax code? Given the difficulty of identifying a neutral position in this area, should we at least err on the side of those in a weaker position? Or does this analysis itself reflect a value judgment that the tax law is unable or unwilling to make?

Statutory Compromises: Sections 21 and 129

One problem with the "leave it to Congress" attitude is that Congress has a tendency to avoid contentious issues, or resolve them in a confused, unsatisfactory manner. The child care issue is a good example of this phenomenon. After experimenting with various limited deductions, Congress in 1976 enacted a credit for "household and dependent care services necessary for gainful employment" (§ 21), which remains in effect in slightly modified form today. The expenses qualifying for the credit cannot exceed $3,000 if there is one qualifying dependent, or $6,000 if there are two or more qualifying dependents, while the credit percentage begins at 35 percent and phases down to 20 percent as the taxpayer's adjusted gross income increases from $15,000 to $43,000. Thus the highest possible credit is $2,100 (35 percent × $6,000) for a taxpayer with $15,000 or less of AGI and $1,200 (20 percent × $6,000) for a taxpayer with AGI in excess of $43,000. These amounts are obviously nowhere near enough to cover the full costs of child care for two or more children, but they provide at least symbolic assistance to working families and recognize, at least implicitly, the mixed business and personal nature of the relevant expenses. The choice of a credit rather than deduction is designed to provide an equal benefit to richer and poorer families, although one wonders how people with $15,000 of income could afford to pay $6,000 for child care even with the credit. Section 21 credit is distinct from the so-called "child tax credit" in section 24, which applies regardless of the presence of paid child care, but is limited to $1,000 per child and is phased out for upper-income taxpayers.

Also significant is the provision for dependent care assistance programs (Code section 129), which allows employees to receive up to $5,000 tax-free from their employers for child care and similar purposes. This is one of a number of targeted fringe benefit rules added in recent decades, which allow tax-free benefits in lieu of additional salary for statutorily approved purposes (education, child care, etc.) and which, not coincidentally, tend to be quite politically popular. Like other fringe benefit provisions, section 129 contains anti-discrimination rules which require that the benefits be made available to both higher- and lower-paid employees, although the ambivalence behind these rules is suggested by section 129(d)(8)(B), which substantially relaxes the rules in the case of salary reduction agreements.[17] Amounts covered by a dependent care plan to do not qualify for the section 21

---

[16] EDWARD J. McCAFFERY, TAXING WOMEN (1997).

[17] A salary reduction agreement means that the amounts in question are deducted from the salary otherwise payable to the employee, rather than being paid by the employer in addition to the salary. The advantage to the employee lies in the untaxed nature of the amounts in the salary reduction agreement. Some benefits (*e.g.*, retirement plans) are funded by a combination of salary reductions and direct employer contributions.

credit, so an employee who received the highest amount of section 129 assistance ($5,000) would never have occasion to claim the credit.

One interesting feature of sections 21 and 129 is that the creditable or excludable amounts are in both cases limited to the lesser of the two spouses' income.[18] This rule appears to be based on the theory that it would be irrational for someone to incur (say) $15,000 of child care expenses in order to take a job paying $10,000; or, at least, that the last $5,000 of such expenses could not reasonably be "necessary for gainful employment" in that case. Does this limitation make sense? Might the psychological and other benefits from working outside the home justify someone taking a job even if it led to a net financial loss? What about stay at home parents, who don't have a job outside the home at all? Aren't they "working" too, and don't they (or their families) deserve some equivalent kind of assistance? Many conservatives have argued that an expanded personal exemption, which provided benefits to both dual-earner and single-earner households, would be superior to the child care credit on this basis. (The personal exemption, together with other deductions and credits based on personal circumstances, is discussed further in the next chapter.)

Using the Sources

Assuming that it met the remaining statutory requirements, what is the largest credit that a married couple would be entitled to under section 21, in each of the following circumstances?

a. Three qualifying individuals (section 21(b)(1)), adjusted gross income (AGI) of $115,000

b. Two qualifying individuals, AGI of $20,000

c. One qualifying individual, AGI of $10,000

d. Would either of the following make any difference to your answers above?

(i) The amounts were paid for day care rather than in-home child care services.

(ii) One of the members of the couple stayed home with the children, and the relevant amounts were expended for maids and housecleaning activities instead of child care *per se*.

e. What happens, under section 21, if the amount of the credit exceeded the amount of tax otherwise owed by the taxpayer in question? Is this a serious problem?

Law and Planning

Suppose that your employer offered you a choice of three different benefits:

---

[18] I.R.C. §§ 21(d), 129(b).

a. $5,000 worth of employer-provided dependent care assistance, which you could easily spend on day care for your two small children. (If you chose this option, you would have to forfeit any available section 21 credit.)

b. $5,000 in employer contributions to a medical savings account (MSA) (sections 106 and 220), which you could probably make use of, but were somewhat less certain about.

c. $5,000 in cash.

Which alternative would you choose? What additional facts might help you to make the decision?

Politics and Policy

Imagine that you are counsel to a conservative organization, which believes that the child care credit discriminates against families with one stay-at-home parent, and wants to substitute a provision providing benefits to both single- and dual-earner families. What kind of arguments would you make to Congress on behalf of this change? Would you limit yourself to arguments based on horizontal equity (*i.e.*, the credit discriminates between otherwise similar families who have one or two working parents), or can you think of vertical equity and economic efficiency considerations on behalf of this change? What role would moral factors (*i.e.*, the alleged advantages of having a stay-at-home parent) play in your presentation, or would these arguments cost you more support than they gained? As always, what group or groups in the broader population would you try to organize on your behalf?

Now assume that you represent an organization that wishes to preserve or expand the existing child care credit. How would you argue on behalf of this position, and how would you refute the arguments made by your adversary above?

C.   Home Offices and Section 280A

A particularly striking example of the business-personal dichotomy involves taxpayers who try to deduct the costs of their homes, or part of them, as a business expense. Most frequently, these taxpayers argue that one or more rooms of their house — a basement, a converted bedroom, etc. — constitutes a "home office" which is deductible on the same terms as a more conventional, outside business location. The taxpayers then proceed to claim depreciation on a portion of their home's purchase price together with deductions for the portion of utilities (heating, air conditioning, etc.) and other costs pertaining to the alleged business space. Often these are combined with deductions for computers, fax machines, and other equipment in the home office, resulting in a substantial tax savings for the individuals concerned. The IRS is understandably suspicious of these claims, but an increasing number of people work at home and are no less assertive in suggesting the deductibility of their expenses.

The history of home offices follows a pattern similar to the other deductions in this chapter. Pursuant to this pattern, taxpayers first claim deductions under the general language of section 162, with the IRS losing key decisions or simply lacking the resources to audit all the relevant cases. Congress then adds a newer statutory requirement designed to make it more difficult for taxpayers to claim the deduction. Taxpayers then stretch the limits of the new statute, sometimes forcing new legislation, as the cat and mouse game proceeds to a new stage. A similar pattern prevailed for travel and entertainment expenses and (to some degree) for away-from-home business travel. One difference is that while not everyone travels, almost everyone has some sort of home. The potential revenue losses are thus particularly large in the home office area and the IRS is particularly keen to control them.

The following materials trace the history of the home office doctrine and of section 280A, which was intended to curb abuse in this area. Consider whether it has accomplished this goal, or has simply created new and unnecessary complications without resolving the underlying issue it was designed to deal with. Consider further the "line-drawing" problem: does section 280A prevent only abuses, or does it also prevent other, more legitimate kinds of deductions? What implications for the fairness of the overall tax system?

COMMISSIONER v. SOLIMAN
United States Supreme Court
506 U.S. 168 (1993)

Justice Kennedy delivered the opinion of the Court.

We address in this decision the appropriate standard for determining whether an office in the taxpayer's home qualifies as his "principal place of business" under 26 U.S.C. § 280A(c)(1)(A). Because the standard followed by the Court of Appeals for the Fourth Circuit failed to undertake a comparative analysis of the various business locations of the taxpayer in deciding whether the home office was the principal place of business, we reverse.

I

Respondent Nader E. Soliman, an anesthesiologist, practiced his profession in Maryland and Virginia during 1983, the tax year in question. Soliman spent 30 to 35 hours per week with patients, dividing that time among three hospitals. About 80 percent of the hospital time was spent at Suburban Hospital in Bethesda, Maryland. At the hospitals, Soliman administered the anesthesia, cared for patients after surgery, and treated patients for pain. None of the three hospitals provided him with an office.

Soliman lived in a condominium in McLean, Virginia. His residence had a spare bedroom which he used exclusively as an office. Although he did not meet patients in the home office, Soliman spent two to three hours per day there on a variety of tasks such as contacting patients, surgeons, and hospitals by telephone; maintaining billing records and patient logs; preparing for treatments and presentations; satisfying continuing medical education requirements; and reading medical journals and books.

On his 1983 federal income tax return, Soliman claimed deductions for the portion of condominium fees, utilities, and depreciation attributable to the home office. Upon audit, the Commissioner disallowed those deductions based upon his determination that the home office was not Soliman's principal place of business. Soliman filed a petition in the Tax Court seeking review of the resulting tax deficiency.

The Tax Court, with six of its judges dissenting, ruled that Soliman's home office was his principal place of business. 94 T.C. 20 (1990). After noting that in its earlier decisions it identified the place where services are performed and income is generated in order to determine the principal place of business, the so-called "focal point test," the Tax Court abandoned that test, citing criticism by two Courts of Appeals. *Id.* at 24–25 (noting *Meiers v. Commissioner*, 782 F.2d 75 (CA7 1986); *Weissman v. Commissioner*, 751 F.2d 512 (CA2 1984); and *Drucker v. Commissioner*, 715 F.2d 67 (CA2 1983)). Under a new test, later summarized and adopted by the Court of Appeals, the Tax Court allowed the deduction. The dissenting opinions criticized the majority for failing to undertake a comparative analysis of Soliman's places of business to establish which one was the principal place. 94 T.C. at 33, 35.

The Commissioner appealed to the Court of Appeals for the Fourth Circuit. A divided panel of that court affirmed. 935 F.2d 52 (1991). It adopted the test used in the Tax Court and explained it as follows:

> "[The] test . . . provides that where management or administrative activities are essential to the taxpayer's trade or business and the only available office space is in the taxpayer's home, the 'home office' can be his 'principal place of business,' with the existence of the following factors weighing heavily in favor of a finding that the taxpayer's 'home office' is his 'principal place of business:' (1) the office in the home is essential to the taxpayer's business; (2) he spends a substantial amount of time there; and (3) there is no other location available for performance of the office functions of the business." *Id.* at 54.

For further support, the Court of Appeals relied upon a proposed IRS regulation related to home office deductions for salespersons. Under the proposed regulation, salespersons would be entitled to home office deductions "even though they spend most of their time on the road as long as they spend 'a substantial amount of time on paperwork at home.'" *Ibid.* (quoting proposed Treas. Reg. § 1.280A-2(b)(3), 45 Fed. Reg. 52399 (1980), as amended, 48 Fed. Reg. 33320 (1983)). While recognizing that the proposed regulation was not binding on it, the court suggested that it "evinced a policy to allow 'home office' deductions for taxpayers who maintain 'legitimate' home offices, even if the taxpayer does not spend a majority of his time in the office." 935 F.2d at 55. The court concluded that the Tax Court's test would lead to identification of the "true headquarters of the business." *Ibid.* Like the dissenters in the Tax Court, Judge Phillips in his dissent argued that the plain language of § 280A(c)(1)(A) requires a comparative analysis of the places of business to assess which one is principal, an analysis that was not undertaken by the majority. *Ibid.*

Although other Courts of Appeals have criticized the focal point test, their approaches for determining the principal place of business differ in significant ways from the approach employed by the Court of Appeals in this case, see *Pomarantz v. Commissioner*, 867 F.2d 495, 497 (CA9 1988); *Meiers v. Commissioner, supra*, at 79; *Weissman v. Commissioner, supra*, at 514–516; *Drucker v. Commissioner, supra*, at 69. Those other courts undertake a comparative analysis of the functions performed at each location. We granted *certiorari* to resolve the conflict. 503 U.S. 935 (1992).

II

A

Section 162(a) of the Internal Revenue Code allows a taxpayer to deduct "all the ordinary and necessary expenses paid or incurred . . . in carrying on any trade or business." 26 U.S.C. § 162(a). That provision is qualified, however, by various limitations, including one that prohibits otherwise allowable deductions "with respect to the use of a dwelling unit which is used by the taxpayer . . . as a residence." § 280A(a). Taxpayers may nonetheless deduct expenses attributable to the business use of their homes if they qualify for one or more of the statute's exceptions to this disallowance. The exception at issue in this case is contained in § 280A(c)(1):

> "Subsection (a) shall not apply to any item to the extent such item is allocable to a portion of the dwelling unit which is exclusively used on a regular basis —
>
> "(A) [as] *the principal place of business for any trade or business of the taxpayer*[,]
>
> "(B) as a place of business which is used by patients, clients, or customers in meeting or dealing with the taxpayer in the normal course of his trade or business, or
>
> "(C) in the case of a separate structure which is not attached to the dwelling unit, in connection with the taxpayer's trade or business.
>
> "In the case of an employee, the preceding sentence shall apply only if the exclusive use referred to in the preceding sentence is for the convenience of his employer." (Emphasis added.)

Congress adopted § 280A as part of the Tax Reform Act of 1976. Pub. L. 94-455, 94th Cong., 2d Sess. Before its adoption, expenses attributable to the business use of a residence were deductible whenever they were "appropriate and helpful" to the taxpayer's business. *See, e.g., Newi v. Commissioner*, 432 F.2d 998 (CA2 1970). This generous standard allowed many taxpayers to treat what otherwise would have been nondeductible living and family expenses as business expenses, even though the limited business tasks performed in the dwelling resulted in few, if any, additional or incremental costs to the taxpayer. H. R. Rep. No. 94-658, p. 160 (1975); S. Rep. No. 94-938, p. 147 (1976). Comparing the newly enacted section with the previous one, the apparent purpose of § 280A is to provide a narrower scope for the deduction, but Congress has provided no definition of "principal place of business."

In interpreting the meaning of the words in a revenue Act, we look to the " 'ordinary, everyday senses' " of the words. *Malat v. Riddell*, 383 U.S. 569 (1966) (per curiam) (quoting *Crane v. Commissioner*, 331 U.S. 1, 6 (1947)). In deciding whether a location is "the principal place of business," the commonsense meaning of "principal" suggests that a comparison of locations must be undertaken. This view is confirmed by the definition of "principal," which means "most important, consequential, or influential." WEBSTER'S THIRD NEW INTERNATIONAL DICTIONARY 1802 (1971). Courts cannot assess whether any one business location is the "most important, consequential, or influential" one without comparing it to all the other places where business is transacted.

Contrary to the Court of Appeals' suggestion, the statute does not allow for a deduction whenever a home office may be characterized as legitimate. *See* 935 F.2d at 55. That approach is not far removed from the "appropriate and helpful" test that led to the adoption of § 280A. Under the Court of Appeals' test, a home office may qualify as the principal place of business whenever the office is essential to the taxpayer's business, no alternative office space is available, and the taxpayer spends a substantial amount of time there. *See* 935 F.2d at 54. This approach ignores the question whether the home office is more significant in the taxpayer's business than every other place of business. The statute does not refer to the "principal office" of the business. If it had used that phrase, the taxpayer's deduction claim would turn on other considerations. The statute refers instead to the "principal place" of business. It follows that the most important or significant place for the business must be determined.

B

In determining the proper test for deciding whether a home office is the principal place of business, we cannot develop an objective formula that yields a clear answer in every case. The inquiry is more subtle, with the ultimate determination of the principal place of business being dependent upon the particular facts of each case. There are, however, two primary considerations in deciding whether a home office is a taxpayer's principal place of business: the relative importance of the activities performed at each business location and the time spent at each place.

Analysis of the relative importance of the functions performed at each business location depends upon an objective description of the business in question. This preliminary step is undertaken so that the decision maker can evaluate the activities conducted at the various business locations in light of the particular characteristics of the specific business or trade at issue. Although variations are inevitable in case-by-case determinations, any particular business is likely to have a pattern in which certain activities are of most significance. If the nature of the trade or profession requires the taxpayer to meet or confer with a client or patient or to deliver goods or services to a customer, the place where that contact occurs is often an important indicator of the principal place of business. A business location where these contacts occur has sometimes been called the "focal point" of the business and has been previously regarded by the Tax Court as conclusive in ascertaining the principal place of business. *See* 94 T.C. at 24–25. We think that phrase has a metaphorical quality that can be misleading, and, as we have said, no one test is determinative in every case. We decide, however, that the point where goods and services are delivered must be given great weight in determining the place where the most important functions are performed.

Section 280A itself recognizes that the home office gives rise to a deduction whenever the office is regularly and exclusively used "by patients, clients, or customers in meeting or dealing with the taxpayer in the normal course of his trade or business." § 280A(c)(1)(B). In that circumstance, the deduction is allowed whether or not the home office is also the principal place of business. The taxpayer argues that because the point of delivery of goods and services is addressed in this provision, it follows that the availability of the principal place of business exception does not depend in any way upon whether the home office is the point of delivery. We agree with the ultimate conclusion that visits by patients, clients, and customers are not a required characteristic of a principal place of business, but we disagree with the implication that whether those visits occur is irrelevant. That Congress allowed the deduction where those visits occur in the normal course even when some other location is the principal place of business indicates their importance in determining the nature and functions of any enterprise. Though not conclusive, the point where services are rendered or goods delivered is a principal consideration in most cases. If the nature of the business requires that its services are rendered or its goods are delivered at a facility with unique or special characteristics, this is a further and weighty consideration in finding that it is the delivery point or facility, not the taxpayer's residence, where the most important functions of the business are undertaken.

Unlike the Court of Appeals, we do not regard the necessity of the functions performed at home as having much weight in determining entitlement to the deduction. In many instances, planning and initial preparation for performing a service or delivering goods are essential to the ultimate performance of the service or delivery of the goods, just as accounting and billing are often essential at the final stages of the process. But that is simply because, in integrated transactions, all steps are essential. Whether the functions performed in the home office are necessary to the business is relevant to the determination of whether a home office is the principal place of business in a particular case, but it is not controlling. Essentiality, then, is but part of the assessment of the relative importance of the functions performed at each of the competing locations.

We reject the Court of Appeals' reliance on the availability of alternative office space as an additional consideration in determining a taxpayer's principal place of business. While that factor may be relevant in deciding whether an employee taxpayer's use of a home office is "for the convenience of his employer," § 280(c)(1), it has no bearing on the inquiry whether a home office is the principal place of business. The requirements of particular trades or professions may preclude some taxpayers from using a home office as the principal place of business. But any taxpayer's home office that meets the criteria here set forth is the principal place of business regardless of whether a different office exists or might have been established elsewhere.

In addition to measuring the relative importance of the activities undertaken at each business location, the decision-maker should also compare the amount of time spent at home with the time spent at other places where business activities occur. This factor assumes particular significance when comparison of the importance of the functions performed at various places yields no definitive answer to the principal place of business inquiry. This may be the case when a taxpayer performs income-generating tasks at both his home office and some other location.

The comparative analysis of business locations required by the statute may not result in every case in the specification of which location is the principal place of business; the only question that must be answered is whether the home office so qualifies. There may be cases when there is no principal place of business, and the courts and the Commissioner should not strain to conclude that a home office qualifies for the deduction simply because no other location seems to be the principal place. The taxpayer's house does not become a principal place of business by default.

Justice Cardozo's observation that in difficult questions of deductibility "life in all its fullness must supply the answer to the riddle," *Welch v. Helvering*, 290 U.S. 111, 115 (1933), must not deter us from deciding upon some rules for the fair and consistent interpretation of a statute that speaks in the most general of terms. Yet we accept his implicit assertion that there are limits to the guidance from appellate courts in these cases. The consequent necessity to give considerable deference to the trier of fact is but the law's recognition that the statute is designed to accommodate myriad and ever-changing forms of business enterprise.

III

Under the principles we have discussed, the taxpayer was not entitled to a deduction for home office expenses. The practice of anesthesiology requires the medical doctor to treat patients under conditions demanding immediate, personal observation. So exacting were these requirements that all of respondent's patients were treated at hospitals, facilities with special characteristics designed to accommodate the demands of the profession. The actual treatment was the essence of the professional service. We can assume that careful planning and study were required in advance of performing the treatment, and all acknowledge that this was done in the home office. But the actual treatment was the most significant event in the professional transaction. The home office activities, from an objective standpoint, must be regarded as less important to the business of the taxpayer than the tasks he performed at the hospital.

A comparison of the time spent by the taxpayer further supports a determination that the home office was not the principal place of business. The 10 to 15 hours per week spent in the home office measured against the 30 to 35 hours per week at the three hospitals are insufficient to render the home office the principal place of business in light of all of the circumstances of this case. That the office may have been essential is not controlling.

The judgment of the Court of Appeals is reversed.

It is so ordered.

Justice Blackmun, concurring.

I join the Court's opinion but add these few words primarily to fortify my own conclusions:

This case concerns § 280A(c)(1)(A) of the Internal Revenue Code, 26 U.S.C. § 280A(c)(1)(A). A deduction from gross income is a matter of grace, not of right, *Commissioner v. Sullivan*, 356 U.S. 27, 28 (1958); *Commissioner v. Tellier*, 383 U.S. 687, 693 (1966), so that our analysis starts with an assumption of non-deductibility. Precise exceptions to this are then provided by the statute.

Although he is a licensed physician who treats patients, respondent finds no solace in subsection (B) of § 280A(c)(1). Subsection (B) requires that the place of business be "used by patients . . . in meeting or dealing with the taxpayer," a factual element that is lacking here unless the physician-taxpayer's papers, records, and telephone calls are to be deemed to personify the patient in the office. Such an interpretation, in my view, would stretch the statute too far.

Respondent is thus confined to subsection (A), which uses the vital words "principal place of business." As Justice Kennedy points out, this phrase invites and compels a comparison, an exercise the Court of Appeals did not undertake. When comparison is made, this taxpayer loses his quest for a deduction. The bulk of his professional time and performance is spent in the hospitals. By any measure, the greater part of his remuneration is generated and earned there. His home office well may be important, even essential, to his professional activity, but it is not "principal." The fact that it is his primary, perhaps his only, office is not in itself enough.

This result is compelled by the language of the statute. Congress must change the statute's words if a different result is desired as a matter of tax policy.

Justice Thomas, with whom Justice Scalia joins, concurring in the judgment.

Today the Court announces that there is "no one test" to determine whether a home office constitutes a taxpayer's "principal place of business" within the meaning of 26 U.S.C. § 280A(c)(1)(A), and concludes that whether a taxpayer will be entitled to a home office deduction will be "dependent upon the particular facts of each case." The Court sets out two "primary considerations" to guide the analysis — the importance of the functions performed at each business location and the time spent at each location. I think this inquiry, "subtle" though it may be, will unnecessarily require the lower courts to conduct full-blown evidentiary hearings each time the Commissioner challenges a deduction under § 280A(c)(1)(A). More-over, as structured, the Court's "test" fails to provide clear guidance as to how the two-factor inquiry should proceed. Specifically, it is unclear whether the time element and importance-of-the-functions element are of equal significance. I write separately because I believe that in the overwhelming majority of cases (including the one before us), the "focal point" test — which emphasizes the place where the taxpayer renders the services for which he is paid or sells his goods — provides a clear, reliable method for determining whether a taxpayer's home office is his "principal place of business." I would employ the totality-of-the-circumstances inquiry, guided by the two factors discussed by the Court, only in the small minority of cases where the home office is one of several locations where goods or services are delivered, and thus also one of the multiple locations where income is generated.

I certainly agree that the word "principal" connotes " 'most important,' " but I do not agree that this definition requires courts in every case to resort to a totality-of-the-circumstances analysis when determining whether the taxpayer is entitled to a home office deduction under § 280A(c)(1)(A). Rather, I think it is logical to assume that the single location where the taxpayer's business income is generated — *i.e.*, where he provides goods or services to clients or customers — will be his principal place of business. This focal point standard was first enunciated in *Baie v. Commissioner*, 74 T.C. 105 (1980),[19] and has been consistently applied by the Tax Court (until the present case) in determining whether a taxpayer's home office is his principal place of business.

Indeed, if one were to glance quickly through the Court's opinion today, one might think the Court was in fact adopting the focal point test. At two points in its opinion the Court hails the usefulness of the focal point inquiry: It states that the place where goods are delivered or services rendered must be given "great weight in determining the place where the most important functions are performed," and that "the point where services are rendered or goods delivered is a principal consideration in most cases." In fact, the Court's discomfort with the focal point test seems to rest on two fallacies — or perhaps one fallacy and a terminological obstinacy. First, the Court rejects the focal point test because "no one test is determinative in every case." But the focal point test, as I interpret it, is *not* always determinative: Where it provides no single principal place of business, the "totality of the circumstances" approach is invoked. Second, the Court rejects the focal point test because its name has a "metaphorical quality that can be misleading." But rechristening it the "place of sale or service test" — or whatever label the Court would find less confusing — is surely a simple matter.

The Commissioner's quarrel with the focal point test is that "it ignores management functions." Tr. of Oral Arg. 24. To illustrate this point, the Commissioner at oral argument presented the example of a sole proprietor who runs a rental car company with many licensees around the country, and who manages the licensees from his home, advising them on how to operate the businesses. Yet the Commissioner's unease is unfounded, since the focal point inquiry easily resolves this example. The taxpayer derives his income from *managing* his licensees, and he performs those services at his home office. Thus, his home office would be his "principal place of business" under § 280A(c)(1)(A). On the other hand, if the taxpayer owned several car dealerships and used his home office to do the dealership's bookkeeping, he would not be entitled to deduct the expenses of his home office even if he spent the majority of his time there. This is because the focal points of that business would be the dealerships where the cars are sold — *i.e.*,

---

[19] [1] In *Baie*, the taxpayer operated a hot dog stand. She prepared all the food in the kitchen at her home and transferred it daily to the stand for sale. She also used another room in her house exclusively for the stand's bookkeeping. The Tax Court denied the taxpayer a home office deduction under § 280A(c)(1)(A), recognizing that although "preliminary preparation may have been beneficial to the efficient operation of petitioner's business, both the final packaging for consumption and sales occurred on the premises of the [hot dog stand]." 74 T.C. at 109-110. Thus, the court concluded that the hot dog stand was the "focal point of [the taxpayer's] activities." *Id.* at 109.

where the taxpayer sells the goods for which he is paid.

There will, of course, be the extraordinary cases where the focal point inquiry will provide no answer. One example is the sole proprietor who buys jewelry wholesale through a home office, and sells it both at various craft shows and through mail orders out of his home office. In that case, the focal point test would yield more than one location where income is generated, including the home. Where the taxpayer's business involves multiple points of sale, a court would need to fall back on a totality-of-the-circumstances analysis. That inquiry would be rationally guided, of course, by the two factors set out in the Court's opinion: an analysis of the relative importance of the functions performed at each business location and the time spent at each. The error of the Tax Court's original construction of the focal point test was the implicit view that the test allowed no escape valve. Clearly it must. Nevertheless, since in the vast majority of cases the focal point inquiry will provide a quick, objective, and reliable method of ascertaining a taxpayer's "principal place of business," I think the Court errs today in not unequivocally adopting it.

The difficulty with the Court's two-part test can be seen in its application to the facts of this case. It is uncontested that the taxpayer is paid to provide one service — anesthesiology. It is also undisputed that he performs this service at several different hospitals. At this juncture, under the focal point test, a lower court's inquiry would be complete: On these facts, the taxpayer's home office would not qualify for the § 280A(c)(1)(A) deduction. Yet under the Court's formulation, the lower court's inquiry has only just begun. It would need to hear evidence regarding the types of business activities performed at the home office and the relative amount of time the taxpayer spends there. It just so happens that in this case the taxpayer spent 30 to 35 hours per week at the hospitals where he worked. But how would a court answer the § 280A(c)(1)(A) question under the standard announced today if the facts were altered slightly, so that the taxpayer spent 30 to 35 hours at his home office and only 10 hours actually performing the service of anesthesiology at the various hospitals? Which factor would take precedence? The importance of the activities undertaken at the home compared to those at the hospitals? The number of hours spent at each location? I am at a loss, and I am afraid the taxpayer, his attorney, and a lower court would be as well.

We granted *certiorari* to clarify a recurring question of tax law that has been the subject of considerable disagreement. Unfortunately, this issue is no clearer today than it was before we granted certiorari. I therefore concur only in the Court's judgment.

JUSTICE STEVENS, dissenting.

Respondent is self-employed. He pays the ordinary and necessary expenses associated with the operation of his office in McLean, Virginia; it is the only place of business that he maintains. In my opinion the Tax Court and the Court of Appeals correctly concluded that respondent is entitled to an income tax deduction for the cost of maintaining that office. This Court's contrary conclusion misreads the term "principal place of business" in § 280A of the Internal Revenue Code, deviates from Congress' purpose in enacting that provision, and unfairly denies an intended benefit to the growing number of self-employed taxpayers who manage their businesses from a home office.

* * *

The test applied by the Tax Court, and adopted by the Court of Appeals, is both true to the statute and practically incapable of abuse. In addition to the requirements of exclusive and regular use, those courts would require that the taxpayer's home office be essential to his business and be the only office space available to him. 935 F.2d 52, 54 (CA4 1991); 94 T.C. at 29. Respondent's home office is the only place where he can perform the administrative functions essential to his business. Because he is not employed by the hospitals where he works, and because none of those hospitals offers him an office, respondent must pay all the costs necessary for him to have any office at all. In my judgment, a principal place of business is a place maintained *by* or (in the rare case) *for* the business. As I would construe the statute in this context, respondent's office is not just the "principal" place of his trade or business; it is the *only* place of *his* trade or business.[20]

Nothing in the history of this statute provides an acceptable explanation for disallowing a deduction for the expense of maintaining an office that is used exclusively for business purposes, that is regularly so used, and that is the only place available to the taxpayer for the management of his business. A self-employed person's efficient use of his or her resources should be encouraged by sound tax policy. When it is clear that no risk of the kind of abuse that led to the enactment of § 280A is present, and when the taxpayer has satisfied a reasonable, even a strict, construction of each of the conditions set forth in § 280A, a deduction should be allowed for the ordinary cost of maintaining his home office.

In my judgment, the Court's contrary conclusion in this case will breed uncertainty in the law,[21] frustrate a primary purpose of the statute, and unfairly penalize deserving taxpayers. Given the growing importance of home offices, the result is most unfortunate.

I respectfully dissent.

Understanding *Soliman*

1.   One can understand the suspicion of home offices, but isn't the Court being a little hard on Soliman? Where else could someone in his position do their paperwork, etc., other than in their home? Does the Court's decision put Soliman at a disadvantage as compared to an employee of one single, large hospital, who is

---

[20] [16] If his tax form asked for the address of his principal place of business, respondent would certainly have given his office address (he did, of course, give that address as his business address on the relevant tax forms). It borders on the absurd to suggest that he should have identified a place over which he has no control or dominion as *his* place.

[21] [17] Most, if not all, of the uncertainty in cases debating the relative merits of the "focal point" test and the "facts and circumstances" test, as well as the uncertainty that today's opinion is sure to generate, would be eliminated by defining the term "place of business" to encompass only property that is owned or leased by the taxpayer or his employer.

provided with a regular office in which to accomplish these and similar functions? Would allowing him a deduction have provided him with an unfair advantage?

2. On a more technical level, what do you make of the Court's interpretation of section 280A? Does the term "principal place of business" mean that the taxpayer must spend 50 percent of her time there, or merely that she spend more time there than at any other single business location? Does it require the actual performance of the job in question (meeting customers, clients, etc.) as opposed to paperwork or other administrative activity? If so, why are subparagraphs (A) and (B) of section 280A(c)(1) phrased in a disjunctive ("or" rather than "and") manner? Is this a mere oversight, or did the Court get the statute backward?

3. Do you believe Soliman was telling the truth regarding the amount of time that he spends in his home office? Do you think the Court believed him?

Congress overrode much of *Soliman* in 1997 when it added the final sentence to section 280A(c)(1), stating that the term "principal place of business" includes a location used for administrative or management activities "if there is no other fixed location of such trade or business where the taxpayer conducts substantial administrative or management activities . . ." While resolving the Soliman problem, this change leaves several unanswered questions, including the meaning of "fixed" location and what constitutes "substantial" administrative or management activities. But for the moment, the taxpayers are ahead, at least on this narrow issue.

POPOV v. COMMISSIONER
United States Court of Appeals, Ninth Circuit
246 F.3d 1190 (2001)

HAWKINS, J:

This case concerns the continuing problem of the home office deduction. We conclude, on the facts of this case, that a professional musician is entitled to deduct the expenses from the portion of her home used exclusively for musical practice.

Facts and Procedural Background

Katia Popov is a professional violinist who performs regularly with the Los Angeles Chamber Orchestra and the Long Beach Symphony. She also contracts with various studios to record music for the motion picture industry. In 1993, she worked for twenty-four such contractors and recorded in thirty-eight different locations. These recording sessions required that Popov be able to read scores quickly. The musicians did not receive the sheet music in advance of the recording sessions; instead, they were presented with their parts when they arrived at the studio, and recording would begin shortly thereafter. None of Popov's twenty-six employers provided her with a place to practice.

Popov lived with her husband Peter, an attorney, and their four-year-old daughter Irina, in a one-bedroom apartment in Los Angeles, California. The apartment's living room served as Popov's home office. The only furniture in the living room consisted of shelves with recording equipment, a small table, a bureau for storing sheet music, and a chair. Popov used this area to practice the violin and to make recordings, which she used for practice purposes and as demonstration tapes for orchestras. No one slept in the living room, and the Popovs' daughter was not allowed to play there. Popov spent four to five hours a day practicing in the living room.

In their 1993 tax returns, the Popovs claimed a home office deduction for the living room and deducted forty percent of their annual rent and twenty percent of their annual electricity bill. The Internal Revenue Service ("the Service") disallowed these deductions, and the Popovs filed a petition for redetermination in the Tax Court.

The Tax Court concluded that the Popovs were not entitled to a home office deduction. Although "practicing at home was a very important component to [Popov's] success as a musician," the court found that her living room was not her "principal place of business." In the court's view, her principal places of business were the studios and concert halls where she recorded and performed, because it was her performances in these places that earned her income.

The Popovs filed this timely appeal.[22] We have jurisdiction under 26 U.S.C. § 7482.

Analysis

The Internal Revenue Code allows a deduction for a home office that is exclusively used as "the principal place of business for any trade or business of the taxpayer." 26 U.S.C. § 280A(c)(1)(A). The Code does not define the phrase "principal place of business."

A. The *Soliman* Tests

Our inquiry is governed by *Commissioner v. Soliman*, 506 U.S. 168 (1993), the Supreme Court's most recent treatment of the home office deduction. In *Soliman*, the taxpayer was an anesthesiologist who spent thirty to thirty-five hours per week with patients at three different hospitals. None of the hospitals provided Soliman with an office, so he used a spare bedroom for contacting patients and surgeons, maintaining billing records and patient logs, preparing for treatments, and reading medical journals.

The Supreme Court denied Soliman a deduction for his home office, holding that the "statute does not allow for a deduction whenever a home office may be characterized as legitimate." *Id.* at 174. Instead, courts must determine whether the home office is the taxpayer's principal place of business. Although the Court could not "develop an objective formula that yields a clear answer in every case," the Court stressed two primary considerations: "the relative importance of the

---

[22] [2] The Popovs also challenge the Tax Court's denial of their deductions for long-distance phone calls, meal expenses, and clothing. We find no merit in these claims. The Popovs did not adequately establish the business purpose of the phone calls or the meal expenses. *See* Welch v. Helvering, 290 U.S. 111, 115 (1933). The Tax Court did not err in finding that most of Katia Popov's concert attire was adaptable to general usage as ordinary clothing. *See* Pevsner v. Comm'r, 628 F.2d 467, 469 (5th Cir. 1980).

activities performed at each business location and the time spent at each place." *Id.* at 174–75. We address each in turn.

1. Relative Importance

The importance of daily practice to Popov's profession cannot be denied. Regular practice is essential to playing a musical instrument at a high level of ability, and it is this level of commitment that distinguishes the professional from the amateur.[23] Without daily practice, Popov would be unable to perform in professional orchestras. She would also be unequipped for the peculiar demands of studio recording: The ability to read and perform scores on sight requires an acute musical intelligence that must be constantly developed and honed. In short, Popov's four to five hours of daily practice lay at the very heart of her career as a professional violinist.

Of course, the concert halls and recording studios are also important to Popov's profession. Without them, she would have no place in which to perform. Audiences and motion picture companies are unlikely to flock to her one-bedroom apartment. In *Soliman*, the Supreme Court stated that, although "no one test is determinative in every case," "the point where goods and services are delivered must be given great weight in determining the place where the most important functions are performed." *Id.* at 175. The Service places great weight on this statement, contending that Popov's performances should be analogized to the "service "of delivering anesthesia that was at issue in *Soliman*; these "services" are delivered in concert halls and studios, not in her apartment.

We agree with Popov that musical performance is not so easily captured under a "goods and services" rubric. The German poet Heinrich Heine observed that music stands" halfway between thought and phenomenon, between spirit and matter, a sort of nebulous mediator, like and unlike each of the things it mediates — spirit that requires manifestation in time, and matter that can do without space."[24] Heinrich Heine, Letters on the French Stage (1837), *quoted in* Words about Music: A Treasury of Writings 2 (John Amis & Michael Rose eds., 1989). Or as Harry Ellis Dickson of the Boston Symphony Orchestra explained more concretely:

> A musician's life is different from that of most people. We don't go to an office every day, or to a factory, or to a bank. We go to an empty hall. We don't deal in anything tangible, nor do we produce anything except sounds. We saw away, or blow, or pound for a few hours and then we go home. It is a strange way to make a living!

Harry Ellis Dickson, Gentlemen, More Dolce Please (1969), quoted in *Drucker v. Comm'r*, 715 F.2d 67, 68–69 (2d Cir. 1983).

It is possible, of course, to wrench musical performance into a "delivery of services" framework, but we see little value in such a wooden and unblinking

---

[23] [3] One who doubts this might consult George Bernard Shaw's famous observation that "hell is full of musical amateurs." George Bernard Shaw, Man and Superman act 3 (1903).

[24] [4] Although not, perhaps, without practice space.

application of the tax laws. Soliman itself recognized that in this area of law "variations are inevitable in case-by-case determinations." 506 U.S. at 175. We believe this to be such a case. We simply do not find the "delivery of services" framework to be helpful in analyzing this particular problem. Taken to extremes, the Service's argument would seem to generate odd results in a variety of other areas as well. We doubt, for example, that an appellate advocate's primary place of business is the podium from which he delivers his oral argument, or that a professor's primary place of business is the classroom, rather than the office in which he prepares his lectures.

We therefore conclude that the "relative importance" test yields no definitive answer in this case, and we accordingly turn to the second prong of the *Soliman* inquiry.

2. Amount of Time

Under *Soliman*, "the decisionmaker should . . . compare the amount of time spent at home with the time spent at other places where business activities occur." *Id.* at 177. "This factor assumes particular significance when," as in this case, "comparison of the importance of the functions performed at various places yields no definitive answer to the principal place of business inquiry." *Id.*[25] In *Soliman*, the taxpayer spent significantly more time in the hospitals than he did in his home office. In this case, Popov spent significantly more time practicing the violin at home than she did performing or recording.[26]

This second factor tips the balance in the Popovs' favor.

They are accordingly entitled to a home office deduction for Katia Popov's practice space, because it was exclusively used as her principal place of business.

B. *Drucker*

The result we reach in this case harmonizes with that of the Second Circuit in *Drucker v. Comm'r*, 715 F.2d 67 (2d Cir. 1983). *Drucker* involved concert musicians employed by the Metropolitan Opera Association, which did not provide its musicians with practice facilities. Each musician instead devoted a portion of his or

---

[25] [5] Justices Thomas and Scalia concurred in *Soliman*, but noted that the Court provided no guidance if the taxpayer "spent 30 to 35 hours at his home office and only 10 hours" at the hospitals. 506 U.S. at 184 (Thomas, J., concurring) "Which factor would take precedence? The importance of the activities undertaken at home . . . ? The number of hours spent at each location? I am at a loss, and I am afraid the taxpayer, his attorney, and a lower court would be as well." *Id.*

[26] [6] The Service argues that the evidence is unclear as to "how much time Mrs. Popov spent practicing at home as opposed to the time she spent performing outside of the home." It is true that the evidence is not perfectly clear and that the Tax Court made no specific comparative findings. However, the Tax Court found that she practiced four to five hours a day in her apartment. If we read this finding in the light most generous to the Service and assume that she only practiced four hours a day 300 days a year, Popov would still have practiced 1200 hours in a year. She testified that she performed with two orchestras for a total of 120–140 hours. If she spent a similar amount of time recording, she would still be spending about five hours practicing for every hour of performance or recording. The only plausible reading of the evidence is that Popov spent substantially more time practicing than she did performing or recording.

her apartment exclusively to musical study and practice, and spent approximately thirty hours a week practicing. *Id.* at 68. The musicians sought to deduct a portion of the rent and electricity allocable to the practice area. The Service denied the deduction. The Tax Court agreed with the Service, holding that off-premises practice was not a requirement of the musicians' jobs and that the musicians' principal place of business was Lincoln Center.

The Second Circuit reversed. The court first rejected as clearly erroneous the Tax Court's conclusion that practice was not a "requirement or condition of employment." *Id.* at 69. The court then concluded that the musicians' principal place of business was their home practice studios, finding that this was "the rare situation in which an employee's principal place of business is not that of his employer." *Id.* Both "in time and in importance, home practice was the 'focal point' of the appellant musicians' employment-related activities." *Id.* Accordingly, the musicians were entitled to a deduction for home office expenses. The facts in this case are even more compelling. In *Drucker*, the musicians had only one employer; here Popov worked for twenty-six different employers and recorded in thirty-eight different locations.

We are unpersuaded by the Service's contention that *Drucker* is no longer good law. The Service has not directed us to any decision that has ever called *Drucker* into question.

The Supreme Court cited *Drucker* twice in *Soliman*, but never suggested that it was overruling *Drucker*'s result. *Soliman*, 506 U.S. at 171, 172. Although the particular "focal point test" employed by the Second Circuit may no longer be valid, we are unwilling to conclude that the Supreme Court sub silentio overruled a long-standing precedent of the Second Circuit. "Uniformity of decision among the circuits is vitally important on issues concerning the administration of tax laws. Thus the tax decisions of other circuits should be followed unless they are demonstrably erroneous or there appear cogent reasons for rejecting them." *Unger v. Comm'r*, 290 U.S. App. D.C. 259, 936 F.2d 1316, 1320 (D.C. Cir. 1991) (quoting *Keasler v. United States*, 766 F.2d 1227, 1233 (8th Cir. 1985)).

C. Conclusion

For the foregoing reasons, the Tax Court's denial of the Popovs' home office deduction is reversed.

Understanding *Popov*

1.   *Popov* was decided under the *Soliman* test, *i.e.*, before the 1997 amendments to the statute. Why then does it come out differently? Is it because music is known to require a lot of practice; because the Popovs seemed to live modestly; or some other reason? How is Popov different from (say) an athlete who does push-ups in his living room, or an Italian professor who lines his study with books that no one else in the family can read? Do you think they would be permitted an equivalent deduction?

2.   Just out of curiosity, do you believe that the Popov's daughter was really prohibited from playing in the living room, as the case suggests? Was her husband

subject to the same rule? Are these trivial points, or do they relate directly to the section 280A requirements and whether they were satisfied?

In *Weissman v. Commissioner*, 751 F.2d 512 (2d Cir. 1984), the Second Circuit allowed a home office deduction to a professor who claimed to spend 80 percent of his time at home — a ten-room apartment of which two rooms were used "exclusively" for research and writing — rather than at his City College office. The court held that Weissman's principal place of business was his home office and that he worked at home for the "convenience of his employer" within the meaning of section 280A, because as a professor, it was impossible to conduct research at his campus office. The dissent stated that City College was the "focal point" of Professor Weissman's job, regardless of the time spent at home and would have denied a deduction. Is *Weissman* still good law, or is it effectively pre-empted by *Soliman* and the subsequent statutory changes?

Using the Sources

Patricia Pennywise is an architect who is employed by SpaceSolutions, Inc., a leading architectural firm. Which of the following would be deductible to her, in whole or in part, under section 280A(c)(1)?

a. A living room which she uses partly for work and partly for personal reflection

b. An home office which she uses exclusively (well, almost exclusively) for work-related activities

c. Same as in b, except the office is also used frequently to meet clients who are not available during regular business hours

d. Would it affect any of your answers above if Patricia were self-employed rather than an employee?

e. Would it affect any of your answers if Patricia's office were located in a separate structure adjacent to her home?

Law and Planning

Donald Devious is a tax professor who would like to get a deduction for his home office, but has been frustrated by section 280A, especially the principal place of business rule and the "convenience of the employer" requirement in section 280A(c)(1). Please evaluate the following three possible strategies that Donald has come up with for achieving his goal:

a. Have his employer purchase the home office and lease it back to him, and then deduct the rent.

b. Argue that the writing of casebooks, hornbooks, etc., constituted a separate and distinct trade or business from his job as a tax professor, for which his home office was the principal location.

c. Make a *Soliman*-type argument that his regular law school office was unsuitable requiring him to perform research and similar activities at his home.

This argument is complicated for Devious, since — unlike Prof. Weissman — he has a large office at the law school; but the quarrelsome nature of law students and professors ensures he gets little if any work done there.

Politics and Policy

Beyond the technical issues in cases like *Soliman*, the home office issue is pervaded by a sense of illegitimacy. The statute seems to assume that anyone who takes the deduction is lying, and the rules make it as difficult as possible to claim one. Indeed, the treatment of home offices is in some respect harsher than that of travel and entertainment deductions, which are presumed to be legitimate if the taxpayer offers adequate documentation.

Is this skepticism justified? In an era of faxes, e-mail, and palm pilots, is it really so surprising that people would work at home and claim a deduction for work-related expenses? What particularly is the effect of section 280A on women, who bear the brunt of child care responsibilities and must frequently "telecommute" even when they have a real office? Compare the treatment of home offices with the treatment of travel and entertainment expenses. What does the contrast tell you about the Code's attitude toward gender and (more specifically) about the boundary between business and personal concerns in people's day-to-day lives?

III.   EDUCATION AND THE "INSEPARABLE AGGREGATE" PROBLEM

Together with travel, child care and home offices, the borderline between business and personal expenses manifests itself in an area familiar to all of you: the tax treatment of educational expenditures, including the course you are enjoying at this very moment. We hinted at this issue in Chapter 2, when we discussed scholarships and educational assistance, and in Chapter 5, when we discussed student loans. Before considering it further, a bit of background is useful.

Suppose that you invested $50,000 a year, for seven or eight years, in a machine that would produce income over the next fifty years. Under present tax law, you would be entitled to a depreciation deduction for the cost of machine; that is, you would deduct a portion of the machine's cost in each taxable year, and offset it against the income you made in that year.[27] Assuming an aggregate $400,000 expenditure, and a 50-year, straight-line recovery period, the deduction would be equal to $8,000 per year. If the machine produced $50,000 of income in any given year, with no other significant expenditures, you would be taxed on $42,000. The purpose of this deduction is to "match" the costs of the machine with income resulting from it, and provide as accurate a measure as possible of the taxpayer's net income.

Now assume that, instead of buying a machine, you invest $400,000 in the cost of your college and law school education, and proceed to earn money on the basis of that education.

---

[27] Depreciation is discussed further in Chapter 8.

Shouldn't you be able to deduct or depreciate those costs, too? After all, your investment in education is economically similar to a business's investment in plants and equipment: you (or your parents) lay out a ton of money now, in hopes of earning back a larger amount later on. Indeed, it may take several years of working before you even earn back your tuition and get back to where you would have been (economically) if you went to work after high school. So why can a business deduct these costs; but you, as a general rule, cannot?

The legal answer is easy: because the IRS says so. Treasury Regulations make clear that an educational expense is deductible only if it (1) maintains or improves skills required by the individual in his employment or other trade or business, or (2) meets the express requirements of the employer (or applicable law or regulations) in order to retain an established employment relationship (Treas. Reg. § 1.162-5(a)). Educational expenditures are not deductible if they enable an individual to meet the minimum educational requirements for qualification in her employment or other trade or business, or are part of a program of study that will lead to qualification in a new trade or business (Treas. Reg. § 1.162-5(b)). Thus, refresher or "continuing education" courses taken by lawyers, accountants, and other professionals are typically deductible, as perhaps are courses designed to develop expertise in a new area of law. But the costs of a J.D. program, or of (say) medical school for a lawyer who is thinking about changing fields, are not deductible, as they constitute the underlying requirements of a new field and not maintenance or improvement of an existing one. Undergraduate college is even more clearly nondeductible. Since these regulations have been around for a long time, and never successfully challenged, they have an authority close to that of statutory law.[28]

The policy rationale is more complicated, and consists of three principal parts. The first part — found in the Regulations themselves — is that college or professional school is either personal in nature or (alternatively) constitutes an "inseparable aggregate" of business and personal expenditures. According to this view, you go to college only partly to train for a career, but also to improve yourself as a person, learn a few social graces, and (if you are lucky) meet that one special person who will make the rest of your life bearable. Since it's hard to know how much time you will spend preparing for a career, as opposed to hanging out at the Student Union, it's safest to make nothing deductible. This has always struck us as a somewhat elitist view, and seems particularly odd when applied to professional schools, where personal enjoyment appears to be relatively low on the list of most student achievements. (The only couple we know of to survive law school is Bill and Hillary Clinton, and look what happened to them.) But it is difficult to draw a sharp line here, and perhaps the rule is a wise one for that practical if not entirely convincing reason.

A second answer relates to timing concerns. A building or a machine depreciates at a more or less predictable rate. People are harder to predict. What would happen, for example, if a lawyer received fifty year amortization (depreciation) for her law school tuition, but practiced for only ten years? What if he simply couldn't find any

---

[28] A limited deduction for educational expenses, together with an even more restricted "tuition tax credit," is now provided by sections 222 and 25A of the Code; but such expenses remain nondeductible under section 162. These provisions are discussed further, *infra*.

368 DEDUCTIONS I: BUSINESS AND PERSONAL EXPENSES CH. 6

clients? Would an unsuccessful lawyer be treated like a dry oil well, and entitled to deduct any remaining unrecovered educational costs in his last year? (Imagine the debate over "capping" or abandoning a dried-out lawyer in order to receive a deduction.) What if he worked longer than originally anticipated? These questions are hardly insurmountable — the law makes simplifying assumptions in many more difficult cases — but they suggest the difficulty of treating a human being as a tangible asset even if, in purely economic terms, she is.

Finally, there is a vertical equity issue, namely, that people who attend college and professional school — as oppressed as they may sometimes feel — usually make more money than people who go straight to work after High School. Providing doctors and lawyers with an ongoing tax deduction, not shared by their less fortunate fellow citizens, might be difficult for even a creative politician (or candidate) to explain.

For all these reasons, educational expenditures have generally remained nondeductible under section 162 of the Code. Yet the issue of educational expenses remains a fascinating one, because of its combination of policy elements and the number of borderline legal issues that it raises. The following items consider these issues, together with additional Code provisions that deal with the education problem. As you read these materials, keep in mind the comparison between investments in machinery and "human capital" (horizontal equity), but also the contrast between those individuals who can afford many years of educational training and those who cannot (vertical equity), together with the likely economic and social impact of a deduction or non-deduction for educational expenditures. Which of these criteria strikes you as most valid, and what does it tell you about the validity of deducting educational expenditures, both in general and in specific cases?

GREENBERG v. COMMISSIONER
United States Court of Appeals, First Circuit
367 F.2d 663 (1966)

COFFIN, CIRCUIT JUDGE.

The sole question in this case is whether the Tax Court erred in denying a deduction claimed by petitioner, a psychiatrist, as an "ordinary and necessary" business expense, for the cost of his own analysis as part of an extensive training program in psychoanalysis.

The availability of the deduction claimed under 26 U.S.C. § 162(a) depends upon the pertinent 1954 Treasury Regulations, which are set forth in the margin. The critical question raised by these regulations is whether petitioner's psychoanalytic studies, including his own analysis, were undertaken to improve his skills as a psychiatrist or were for the purposes of obtaining a new position, obtaining a substantial advancement in position, or fulfilling his general educational aspirations.

The facts found by the Tax Court, apart from stipulated data concerning the profession of psychiatry and the purpose of the Boston Psychoanalytic Institute, covered the psychiatric education and experience of petitioner and his undertaking a six or seven year training program at the Boston Institute. In these respects the facts are very similar to those in *Arnold Namrow*, 1959, 33 T.C. 419, *aff'd*, 4 Cir., 1961, 288 F.2d 648, *cert. denied*, 368 U.S. 914, and *Grant Gilmore*, 1962, 38 T.C. 765.

In this case, as in those, a psychiatrist, having completed medical school, internship, and at least one year of psychiatric residency, qualified for the practice of psychiatry, and, while engaging in such practice, pursued a lengthy institute-sponsored training program in psychoanalysis. Such a program consisted of several years of the taxpayer's own analysis, seminars and courses in psychoanalytical theory, and the supervised handling of several patients over a lengthy period. On the satisfactory completion of such a program, the psychiatrists would be eligible for membership in the particular psychoanalytical institute and recognized as full-fledged psychoanalysts. In all three cases the taxpayer unsuccessfully claimed that the training in psychoanalysis was undertaken primarily to improve his skills as a psychiatrist, the Tax Court holding that the dominant purpose was to prepare for the practice of a separate specialty, psychoanalysis.

Omitted from the findings of fact in this case is the considerable testimony of petitioner, the only witness, relating to his purpose in taking extended training in psychoanalysis. Since the regulations above quoted in footnote 1 make purpose of the taxpayer central in the determination of such questions, since the judge who heard this testimony found it not only "uncontradicted" but "believable", and since it goes substantially beyond such evidence in *Namrow* and *Gilmore*, it is appropriate to summarize it briefly.

Petitioner, even while in medical school, became interested in the application of psychoanalytical thinking to neurophysiological data, writing a paper on the subject. Although he had resolved, during his time in medical school, to become a psychiatrist, he postponed his psychiatric residency one year to allow him to study neurology, which he felt to be important to his future work as a psychiatrist. He then took two succeeding years of psychiatric residency. These two years, together with his year in neurology, met the minimum psychiatric board requirement. He did not seek additional years of psychiatric residency because, he said, he then had in mind obtaining psychoanalytic training as "a continuation of my psychiatric training".

As he began his practice as a psychiatrist with the Boston Veterans Administration Hospital, he also applied for admission to the Boston Psychoanalytic Society and Institute, writing in his application, "At this point, my choice of psychiatry as a specialty seems a happy one. . . . I feel that with psychoanalytic training, I may be able to gain more understanding of the function of the mind and also will be able to help emotionally ill patients achieve a better living adjustment."

In defending this purpose as not being unusual, petitioner testified that over 90 per cent of those associated with the Boston Institute spend "more or less of their time" teaching psychiatric residents, teaching psychiatry to medical students, and doing psychiatric research. He referred to articles in professional journals on the place of psychoanalysis in psychiatric training; a foundation grant to train young psychiatrists in psychoanalysis to further their work in psychiatric research; and

National Institute of Health career fellowships in psychiatry, which included psychoanalytic training.

Petitioner gave testimony at length on the connection of each part of the psychoanalytic training program to the work of a psychiatrist. Personal analysis helped, he said, to remove one's own "blind spots" and to work more easily with a patient. The study of basic psychoanalytical theory, covered only sparsely in medical school and psychiatric residencies, was "one of the basic sciences in psychiatric thinking" and, more particularly, was useful in his own work in teaching psychiatric residents and as a prerequisite to research. The supervised handling of several cases in depth and at length, petitioner testified, was "one of the main dividends," giving insights into the problems of other patients he would see in the course of his regular work.

As to petitioner's future plans, he testified that he would continue to work part-time at the Boston Veterans Administration Hospital, where he teaches and does research, and to continue to conduct a private practice. He would apply psychoanalytical methods, either "classical" or "modified" as the needs of the patient indicated. As to referrals, he testified, "I think in terms of my being a better psychiatrist, for having this training, that the referrals will come."

Finally, respondent's counsel, at the conclusion of his cross-examination, asked: "Is it your position in this case that you undertook the analytic training and the supervised clinical work and the theoretical instruction to improve your field [sic] as a psychiatrist?" To which petitioner answered, "That is right."

The opinion of the Tax Court majority cited *Namrow* and *Gilmore* where the pursuit of a lengthy program of psychoanalytic training was held to be for the purpose of acquiring a new specialty or a new skill, and not the sharpening of a skill already possessed. It went on to say that these two cases could not be rationally distinguished from that of petitioner. It further pointed out (1) that, while petitioner had stated his reason as that of improving his skills as a psychiatrist, he did not say that this was his "primary" reason; (2) that he did not say that he did not intend to practice psychoanalysis upon graduation; (3) that in fact petitioner's testimony indicated his intention to treat some patients with psychoanalysis; and (4) that it is a reasonable inference that when petitioner testified about hoped-for referrals, he meant referrals for psychoanalytic treatment. From these specific observations the Tax Court arrives at its final conclusion, phrased in the negative: "This record would hardly warrant a finding that petitioner did not intend to hold himself out as a practicing psychoanalyst when he completed his six-year course at the Institute."

We reverse. We have set forth the substance of petitioner's testimony and the Tax Court's opinion at some length to illuminate our difficulty. For we do not take issue either with any specific finding of fact or with any inference drawn therefrom except the final conclusion. Our action is based on our conviction that, reviewing the entire evidence, "a mistake has been committed". *Commissioner v. Duberstein*, 1960, 363 U.S. 278, 291; *United States v. United States Gypsum Co.*, 1948, 333 U.S. 364, 395.

The error lies in the automatic assumption, which contravenes the overwhelming weight of the evidence in this case, that the acquisition of a "specialty" is inconsistent with the improvement of skills required for the practice of a preexisting profession. To put the difficulty in terms of the facts of this case, the Tax Court majority deemed it sufficient to ask only two questions: is psychoanalysis a specialty? and is it reasonable to infer that the petitioner intended to use the knowledge and methods which he was learning? Affirmative answers to both questions effectively disposed of the case. The question unasked was: did the petitioner have a primary (and reasonable) purpose of using the lore of this new specialty in improving his skills as a practicing and teaching psychiatrist? Since this is the question required by existing regulations, the failure to answer it in the light of the evidence constitutes reversible error.

What is involved in the improvement of skills of a taxpayer in his employment, trade, or business reflects the complexity and variety of our society itself. Perhaps the worker tightening bolts on an assembly line may be said to require only one skill. But most occupations require a bundle of skills. And, to the extent that one is engaged in a learned profession, he must employ a multiplicity of skills. The fact that what is newly acquired by a taxpayer may be recognized as a "skill" or a "specialty" — or, as is usually the case, another group of skills — is irrelevant if the taxpayer's primary purpose is to add to his equipment in carrying on his preexisting vocation. Some of the cases cited in the margin have gone quite far in allowing deductions for training of less proximate relevance than that indicated by the testimony in this case. Most of them involved a new "specialty."

The regulations attempt to delineate the area of deductible education not only by the positive language referring to improving skills but by proscriptive language. Education pursued primarily to obtain "a new position or substantial advancement in position" and to satisfy "general educational aspirations or other personal purposes" is beyond the pale. Most of the cases holding against the taxpayer do so, not on the ground that he was studying another field of learning, but on the ground that his intent was to change the direction or nature of his career or to qualify for a specific job opportunity.

Of the cases which have come to our attention, only *Namrow* and *Gilmore* seem out of harmony with this parallel line of cases. These decisions may have stemmed from insufficient evidence of the reasons why a psychiatrist would consider psychoanalytic knowledge as helpful in his psychiatric practice. In any event the holdings have hardened into what we consider the unrealistic doctrine that, since psychoanalysis is a specialty (and is practiced exclusively by some), it cannot be considered as an improvement in skills for a psychiatrist who will, depending on his patient's needs, utilize whatever combination of drug, chemical, hypnosis, occupational, industrial, insulin, shock, and psychoanalytical therapy seems to be indicated.

Primary purpose under the quoted regulations is to be determined by the facts of each case. The petitioner testified at length on the interrelationship of psychoanalytic knowledge and methods and the work of one engaged in practicing psychiatry, teaching psychiatric residents, and doing psychiatric research. There was no evidence to the contrary.

The unrebutted testimony even went so far as to indicate that it was not unusual for other members of petitioner's profession to undertake such education. Under the regulations, if customary conduct is proved, ". . . the taxpayer will ordinarily be considered to have undertaken this education for the purposes [of improving skills]. . . ." While the evidence on this point might not compel a finding of custom, it at least forecloses any inferences which might be drawn from unusual conduct.

There was no evidence that petitioner had any other "position" in mind than that of continuing his part-time work at the Boston VA Hospital and his part-time psychiatric practice. There was no hint of any purpose to secure a "substantial advancement in position," except the obvious aim to increase in stature in his profession. Nor could it be said that the six or seven year program was to fulfill his general educational aspirations or other personal purposes.

The Tax Court's difficulty seems to stem from its appropriate findings and inferences that petitioner intended to apply what he was learning when it was applicable. Without addressing itself to the question required by the regulations, i.e., whether or not the petitioner had succeeded in showing that he was motivated principally to improve his skills as a psychiatrist, it took a long leap in concluding that petitioner's primary purpose was to hold himself out as a practicing psychoanalyst. If this means that petitioner intended wholly or substantially to abandon his practice of psychiatry and his position at the Hospital, there is no support whatsoever in the evidence. If this means that petitioner would, in the course of his practice, administer psychoanalysis in varying degrees without having to refer patients to others, it does not support the court's decision under the regulations.

Without making any generalizations as to how far the Tax Court can, with propriety, disregard uncontradicted evidence, we believe in this case that if the court's decision did not reflect an erroneous application of the regulations, it reflected an unjustified rejection of unimpeached and credible testimony. In either case, the decision must be reversed.

Jay Katz, *The Deductibility of Educational Costs: Why Does Congress Allow the IRS to Take Your Education So Personally?*
17 Va. Tax Rev. 1, 4-7, 101-02 (1997)[29]

* * *

A. Prelude to Inequitable Tax Treatment of Educational Costs

Because the Service treats educational costs differently than other business expenses, very few educational costs are deductible. Generally, business expenses are deductible if there is a direct and proximate relationship between the benefit or use of the expense and the taxpayer's trade or business. However, the Service does not apply this business standard to most educational costs; instead, they are

---

characterized as nondeductible "personal" expenses.

Ironically, as compared to other business expenses, educational costs characterized by the Service as "personal" are often the most significant business-related expense a taxpayer is likely to incur in her entire career and, therefore, present the most compelling argument for deductibility. For example, an aspiring physician must attend medical school to obtain the necessary license and training to practice medicine. Yet, the Service treats the cost of medical school as a nondeductible personal expense for that very reason — it qualifies the taxpayer to practice medicine. This result is illogical because without a medical degree, the taxpayer could not practice medicine. Without a medical practice, the taxpayer would not have a business in which to incur such deductible expenses as office rent and utilities. In spite of the compelling significance of a medical degree to the taxpayer's practice, the cost of medical school is the only business-related expense that the taxpayer may never deduct.

Another instance of the Service's improper treatment of educational costs occurs when a taxpayer established in a profession decides to pursue education to maintain or improve her work skills. Regardless of the extent to which this education enhances the taxpayer's work skills, the Service treats its cost as a nondeductible personal expense if it also qualifies her for a new trade or business (even if the taxpayer never enters into such trade or business). For example, many non-legal professionals, such as accountants, corporate administrators, and doctors who testify as expert witnesses, may routinely deal with legal matters. Suppose that such a professional decides to attend law school to improve her legal skills. If she attends an accredited law school because it provides a better legal education, the Service would deny her a deduction for its cost, on the theory that as a graduate of an accredited law school she could potentially become a licensed attorney. On the other hand, if the professional attends non-accredited law school of lesser quality, the Service would allow a deduction for its cost, because a graduate of a non-accredited law school cannot qualify to become a lawyer.

Finally, in the midst of nonsensical rules which deny a deduction for most educational costs, there are special rules that, for no apparent reason, allow teachers to deduct certain educational costs that other taxpayers may not deduct. For example, a certified teacher in one state may deduct the cost of college courses necessary to become a certified teacher in a second state. This is because under the Service's rules all teaching is considered to be one trade or business. Therefore, the cost of the education necessary to become certified to teach in a second state is deductible because it does not qualify the taxpayer for a new trade or business.

In contrast, any other professional licensed to render services in one state may not deduct the cost of education necessary or helpful to become licensed to render those same services in another state. This is because the Service considers professionals (other than teachers) of the same discipline licensed in different states to be separate trades or business. Thus a lawyer licensed in one state may not deduct the cost of a bar review course taken to prepare for the bar examination of a second state.

In the final analysis, without any authority from the underlying Code sections, the Service inappropriately departs from basic tax principles to wrongfully deny a deduction for most educational costs. Specifically, a taxpayer may not deduct the cost of education necessary to enter into a trade or business or to maintain or improve skills in an existing one (if the underlying education also qualifies the taxpayer for a new trade or business). In addition, for no apparent reason, the Service discriminates in favor of teachers, allowing a deduction for certain educational costs that non-teachers cannot deduct.

* * *

In the final analysis, "regulatory" tax law discriminates against investments in education. By treating educational costs as inherently personal expenses, the section 262 regulations set the stage for the Current Regulations to impose an additional layer of restrictive rules, eliminating the deductibility of most educational costs, regardless of their connection with the taxpayer's trade or business. These additional restrictive rules go beyond those applied to other business expenses. Ultimately, the Current Regulations deny a deduction for those educational costs which often bear the most compelling business relationship to the taxpayer's trade or business than do any other business expense.

The most direct way to correct the inequitable treatment of educational costs is to treat them like any other business expense. The courts could accomplish this by declaring the Current Regulations void. Since the underlying statutes do not discriminate against the deductibility of educational costs, the courts could declare the Current Regulations invalid because they are "unreasonable and plainly inconsistent with the revenue statutes." Unfortunately, such judicial interpretation is unlikely to occur because the courts have consistently upheld the validity of the Current Regulations.

Finally, because the Service and the courts inappropriately continue to treat educational costs as personal expenses, any change would require legislative intervention. However, in spite of recent legislation providing limited tax relief, the nation's large current budget deficit makes the more ambitious repeal of the Current Regulations prohibitive. Thus, the only practical alternatives are to (1) accept the limited educational tax relief provided by the recent legislation; or (2) eliminate some currently deductible expenses and/or other tax benefits so as to allow the more liberal deductibility of educational costs. The author advocates that a debate should now begin on the second alternative.

Understanding Educational Costs

1. In *Sharon v. Commissioner*, 66 T.C. 515 (1976), the taxpayer was denied a deduction for his college and law school tuition as well as bar review courses. He was, however, permitted to amortize various licensing fees, etc., which, assuming that he had a 50-year life expectancy, would result in a deduction of less than $25 per year. In support of its holding, the Tax Court stated that college and law school "provided him [Sharon] with a general education which will be beneficial to him in a number of ways." Since when is law school part of a general humanistic education? Can this argument possibly be extended to a bar review course? How much personal growth have you experienced as a law student, and what role did this anticipated

personal pleasure play in your decision to attend? Are the regulations, which deny a deduction for most professional schools, consistent with the statute in this area?

Conversely, the Tax Court permitted a deduction for business school (M.B.A.) tuition paid by a salesman for a sporting goods company in *Allemeier v. Commissioner*, T.C. Memo. 2005-207. The employee argued successfully that he had not learned a new trade or business and was more or less doing the same kind of things after the M.B.A. as before. Why then did he bother? Do you agree with this decision?

2.   If law school is too personal for a deduction, how could Greenberg possibly argue that his own psychoanalysis was for primarily business purposes? Which do you suppose is more personally satisfying, analysis or the first year of law school? Pursuing this same logic, what do you make of the First Circuit's distinction between "psychiatry," which was Greenberg's existing profession, and "psychoanalysis," which would have been a new profession but which Greenberg was found not to be entering? Suppose that, after the first year of law school, you received a "Bachelor of General Laws" degree and then studied two further years in order to qualify in a subspecialty (tax, litigation, public law, etc.) Would the last two years of law school now be deductible because they were "improving" your skills in an existing profession? How is this different from *Greenberg*?

3.   What do you think of Professor Katz's critique of the existing section 1.162-5 regulations? In particular, how convincing is his argument that educational expenses are akin to other, more tangible forms of business expenditures, like depreciation of business equipment or depletion of a mineral resource? What are some possible objections to this argument?

Although educational expenses are not deductible under section 162, the Code does encourage them in a number of less direct ways. Two of these, the exclusion for employer-provided educational assistance and the limited deduction for student loan interest, have already been discussed in previous chapters. Another important provision is the so-called tuition tax credit, added in the 1990s and found in section 25 of the Code. The tuition tax credit is actually two different credits: the so-called Hope Scholarship Credit, which provides a credit for the first $1,000 and 50 percent of the second $1,000 of eligible tuition and related expenses, but limited to the first two years of postsecondary education and phased out as Adjusted Gross Income (AGI) increases from $40,000 to $80,000 ($80,000 to $160,000 for joint returns); and a Lifetime Learning Credit, which is equal to 20 percent of tuition and related expenses not exceeding $10,000 and is subject to a similar income phaseout. Finally, in 2001, Congress added section 222 which provided for a deduction of up to $3,000 in qualifying educational expenditures in 2002 and 2003 and $4,000 after 2003. The original statute was supposed to expire Dec. 31, 2005, but it has been since extended twice. The statute currently in effect is due to expire December 31, 2009. This provision is also subject to a phaseout for higher-income taxpayers as well as to the sunset provisions described above. (Both credits, or the credit and the deduction, may not be claimed by the same taxpayer in the same taxable year.) These provisions reflect some of the same ambivalence as the deduction for student loan interest (section 221), which is similarly limited to $2,500 per year and phased out between $50,000 and $65,000 of AGI ($100,000 and $130,000 on joint returns, and in section 127 relating to employer-provided educational assistance programs, described in Chapter 2. Like the section 21 child care credit, these rules are probably best seen as in-between measures, allowing a partial deduction or credit for items that have traditionally been considered personal in nature, but are necessary for full participation in many attractive, income-earning activities. The provisions also exemplify the trend toward "targeting" tax benefits to low or middle-income taxpayers: a tendency that is easy to criticize but that, taken in the aggregate, contributes substantially to the progressivity of the tax system.

Using the Sources

Under present law, which of the following would be deductible or amortizable as an educational expense, under section 162 or (for amortization) 167? If amortizable, what would be the relevant recovery period?

a. Undergraduate college

b. Law school, attended by someone who wanted to be a lawyer

c. Law school, attended by an accountant or journalist who planned to return to her original profession

d. Law school refresher ("continuing education") programs, taken by an already practicing attorney. (Does it matter if the attorney or her law firms pays for the course?)

e. Medical school courses taken by an already practicing attorney who wishes to improve his skill in defending malpractice cases

f. Same as e., except the medical school is in Tahiti, and meets only in the winter

g. Summer travel to England by a law professor who wanted to appreciate the Anglo-Saxon legal tradition more fully

Law and Planning

Imagine that you are a second or third year law student and were considering an LL.M. program in tax or environmental law upon graduation. LL.M. programs are useful, but expensive, and you would like if at all possible to make the cost tax-deductible. Which of the following seems like the best strategy?

a. Do the LL.M. right after law school, assert that it is deductible because it improves or enhances your skill in an existing trade or business, and deduct the cost against your summer or other taxable income (particularly advantageous if the LL.M. "straddles" two different taxable years).

b. Work two or three years and then break one year to complete the LL.M., making it more likely that the I.R.S. will buy the "existing trade or business" argument.

c. Find an employer who will pay for your LL.M. studies and let them worry about the tax consequences. (Is there any chance that you would have taxable income as a result of this last arrangement?)

Politics and Policy

Self-interest aside, are you troubled by the lack of a full-blown deduction for education-related expenses? Do you think such a deduction would actually encourage anyone to undertake higher education that they would not have otherwise attended? Or would it be more like a "freebie" for those who would have gone anyway? As between various forms of tax subsidy — an expanded tuition tax credit, student loan interest deduction, or amortization of expenditures over (say) a twenty- or thirty-year period, which strikes you as the most effective, and how do any of these compare with federal grants, loans, and other forms of direct (*i.e.*, nontax) assistance? How would each of these proposals rate under traditional tax policy criteria, and which would be most likely to achieve its intended goal?

Finally, if you believe that there should be some broader form of educational expense deduction, would you extend this deduction only to graduate and professional schools or to undergraduate and (perhaps) private secondary schools, as well? What about less conventional institutions like beauty schools, vocational training, or the kinds of things that used to be found on the back of matchbook covers? What are the arguments in favor of and against extending tax benefits to these institutions?

Additional Assignment — Chapter 6

Your client, Leona Loophole, has come to your firm with a problem relating to the deduction for home offices (section 280A). It seems that Leona, who recently graduated from a prestigious public policy school, works three days a week for the state health department and an additional one or two days as a consultant to private HMOs who need help in navigating the legal and economic minefield of health regulation. (No credit for questioning the ethics of the HMO and related industries.) Leona and her husband, Leon, also have two small children and accordingly she likes to work at home when she can, at the very least on the days when she is doing her consulting work, but sometimes "telecommuting" on the days when she is working for the state health department, as well.

Leona comes to you with advice regarding the following questions:

1. There is a room in her house that is used "exclusively" by Leona for her state health department and consulting work ("my husband has another office and I chase the kids out any time they come near the place"). Leona's consulting clients also occasionally visit her in this office although most of this work is conducted on the road. Leona would like to know if she can deduct anything with respect to this office, and if so, what.

2. There is a computer in the office which Leona again insists is used exclusively for her work although in checking her e-mail she inevitably comes across some personal messages. When pressed, she admits the children have loaded "one or two" video games on the computer but promises to remove them immediately. (Note: you have not studied section 280F, regarding computers and other "listed" property, but should be able to figure out its basic principles pretty quickly.)

3. Leona often commutes by car either to the state health department or to one of her consulting locations. When her schedule demands, she sometimes makes a "triangular" trip in which she goes directly from the health department to a consulting site, or vice-versa, returning home later in the evening. She wishes to know how much, if any, of these travel costs (automobile mileage, meals and tolls, etc.) is deductible.

4. Can you offer any suggestions to Leona as to how she might increase her deductions, without sacrificing important business or personal goals?

Please write a memorandum to Leona, *not exceeding five (5) double-spaced pages*, explaining the likely tax treatment of items 1. through 3. above and any suggestions you have with respect to item 4. Please also specify what further information, if any, you would need in order to answer these questions.

Note: A memorandum to a client is not an official opinion letter, but it is not quite the same as spoken advice either, since a written record exists and might be cited by the client if they are later audited by IRS. This is sometimes a good reason to avoid writing them. But clients often request written advice, if only to justify the lawyer's bill, so it cannot always be avoided. The key skills here are (i) to state the law accurately but in nontechnical terms (remember it is a nonlawyer who will likely be reading it), (ii) to be fair and balanced but remember that you are an advocate and not a judge (*i.e.*, the client may wish to take an aggressive position on a particular issue but it is your job to inform them of the risks and probability of success of this or alternative positions), and (iii) to do all this without getting yourself into trouble if the memo is eventually "discovered" in litigation. Since some internal law firm memos are eventually forwarded to clients, it is not a bad idea to observe many of the same guidelines when drafting internal firm memos.

Chapter 7

DEDUCTIONS II: CHARITABLE CONTRIBUTIONS AND OTHER ITEMIZED DEDUCTIONS

If there is a simple rule for deductibility, it is that business expenditures are deductible, and personal expenditures are not. But nothing is ever that simple. As you might expect, the Code permits a large number of items to be deducted despite their seemingly personal nature. Several of these — home mortgage interest, charitable contributions, state and local taxes — are among the most important and popular deductions in the Code.

This chapter considers the rules that apply to these deductions and the policies that support them. At a practical level, these items correspond roughly to Schedule A, the first and most common schedule attached to the 1040 income tax form. We will devote the majority of our time to the charitable contribution deduction (secs. 170 and 501), spending somewhat less time on the medical, casualty, and other Schedule A items. (The interest deduction was previously discussed in Chapter 5.) The discussion of charitable contributions will also provide us with an opportunity to discuss the broader issue of tax-exempt organizations and the unique role these organizations play in American society. The chapter concludes with a brief discussion of personal exemptions and a number of other deductions and credits of special interest to older and poorer taxpayers.

A word of background is in order before beginning this section. Most personal deductions are available only if the taxpayer elects to "itemize" deductions on Schedule A, rather than taking a fixed "standard deduction" as provided in section 63.[1] Since the standard deduction for 2009 was $5,700 for individuals ($11,400 for joint returns), taxpayers with a large volume of deductions — especially home mortgage interest, state and local taxes, and charitable contributions — are likely to itemize in most cases. However, many taxpayers, especially those with more modest incomes, do not itemize, so these deductions are essentially worthless to them. Together with their ostensibly personal nature, the fact that itemized deductions are effectively limited to one category of taxpayers puts them in an unusual category and makes them a perennial target of tax reformers, as we will see in the following pages.

---

[1] A limited charitable deduction for "nonitemizers" (*i.e.*, taxpayers who use the standard deduction) was in effect for part of the 1980s, but has since been repealed.

I. PERSONAL DEDUCTIONS: INCOME MEASUREMENT AND "INCENTIVE" PROVISIONS

Why should personal expenditures ever be deductible? One possible answer is that they are not quite as personal, or, at any rate, not as voluntary, as they might seem. Consider a family that earns $30,000 of income, but has a $20,000, wholly unforeseen (and wholly uninsured) medical or casualty expense. It seems reasonable to say that the family has improved its economic lot by only $10,000, rather than $30,000, and tax them on this lower amount. This argument becomes more difficult if the medical expense was elective in nature, like plastic surgery or therapy for self-improvement, or if the casualty was avoidable, as in the case of families who continue to build exposed beachfront properties without buying adequate flood insurance. But for truly unavoidable expenditures, it remains a reasonably persuasive argument.

A second reason is that — even for voluntary expenditures — we might wish to provide some kind of subsidy. A good example is charitable contributions, which support organizations (*e.g.*, universities, hospitals, museums) that would otherwise have to be supported by governmental or quasi-governmental agencies. Home mortgage interest is arguably in a similar category.[2] The arguments for such incentives often mix tax policy with constitutional law. Thus, federalism remains an important factor in the evaluation of state and local taxes, and the separation of church and state accounts for much of the earlier history of the charitable contribution deduction. Some people believe that the church has a right to a fraction of their income before it even reaches their pockets, and that a deduction of this amount from taxable income is merely a recognition of this already established fact.

Although theoretically distinct, the "income measurement" and "incentive" arguments tend to merge in practice, so that the argument for the charitable deduction becomes a curious mixture of public policy, church and state concerns, and the simple political clout of religious and charitable organizations, not to mention their numerous and well-placed donors. Indeed, the appeal of these arguments may sometimes obscure important, countervailing factors. Among these are the regressive nature of itemized deductions, which tend to be concentrated among wealthier taxpayers, thus providing a larger deduction to people in higher tax brackets;[3] the absence of any deduction for non-itemizing taxpayers; and the subsidy provided to many borderline activities, like elective medical treatment or extremist charitable organizations, that would be unlikely to receive direct government assistance. These features have made many important tax scholars critical of such deductions.

The following are excerpts from a well-known debate on itemized deductions, conducted by a then-middle aged, mainstream professor and an *enfant terrible* with ties to the critical legal studies movement. In evaluating this discussion, think about the arguments used by the participants, and their underlying values. To what extent

---

[2] *See* Chapter 5, *supra.*

[3] For example, a $10,000 deduction is worth $4,000 to a taxpayer in the 40 percent tax bracket, but only $1,500 to a taxpayer in the 15 percent bracket, and nothing at all to a taxpayer who does not itemize deductions.

are the two participants debating, and to what extent are they merely talking past one another?

William D. Andrews, *Personal Deductions in an Ideal Income Tax*
86 HARV. L. REV. 309, 309–15, 335–56 (1972)[4]

* * *

A variety of provisions in the income tax law are now described as tax expenditures and evaluated as if they involved direct government expenditures equivalent in amount and distribution to the revenue reduction they produce. The medical expense deduction, for example, is described as the equivalent of a direct expenditure program by which the federal government provides partial reimbursement for extraordinary medical expenses. So viewed, of course, the provision seems to reflect an upside-down idea of policy because the rate of reimbursement is the taxpayer's marginal tax rate; this results in relatively generous rates of reimbursement for the well-to-do, while it provides nothing at all for the very poor who presumably have the greatest need.

Similarly, the charitable contribution deduction has been described as a kind of government matching gift program for the support of taxpayers' charities. Again the distribution of matching grants is effectively skewed to favor the charities of the wealthy because of their higher marginal tax rates: in the 70% bracket, for example, the Government contributes $70 to match the taxpayer's $30 contribution, while in the 20% bracket the Government's matching grant is only $20 for each $80 contributed by the taxpayer. Furthermore, there are other difficulties. Presumably, we would not permit direct government expenditures to provide matching gifts for churches. And if we were to have programs of direct support for other charities, it seems likely that we would insist upon a much more rigorous evaluation of priorities than the tax expenditure mechanism provides.

These are devastating criticisms. If they are correct, it seems to me the provisions in question are indefensible. But my feeling is that the criticisms are somehow overstated and that more sense can be made out of these two provisions than tax expenditure analysis immediately indicates. To be sure, there are other provisions of the tax law, like the exclusion of municipal bond interest, with respect to which I think the tax expenditure analysis is completely valid. But its application to the medical expense and charitable contribution deductions seems to me somehow to miss the mark.

* * *

In general I will argue that an ideal personal income tax is one in which tax burdens are accurately apportioned to a taxpayer's aggregate personal consumption and accumulation of real goods and services and claims thereto — the uses to which income is typically put rather than the sources from which it is derived. This formulation is suggested by Henry Simons' definition of personal income as the sum of personal consumption and accumulation. More importantly, it is consistent with the primary, intended, real effect of the tax, which is to reduce private consumption and accumulation in order to free resources for public use. The practical operating base on which the tax is computed consists of income transactions, but the ultimate object of the tax is to lay a uniform graduated burden on aggregate consumption and accumulation.

This formulation of an ideal does not provide clear or easy answers to all specific questions of income determination because it incorporates the ambiguities implicit in the concepts of consumption and accumulation. Consumption in particular is not a self-defining term. In practice we start from a tentative definition that includes whatever people spend their money for. However, that is only a convenient starting point from which to try to move toward a more refined concept defined ultimately in terms of real goods and services. To make taxable income conform with this more refined concept ideally requires, as Simons clearly recognized, an addition to cash income for goods and services included in the refined consumption concept but not purchased. It also requires, though this has not been so widely recognized, a deduction for expenditures for items not included either in the refined consumption concept or in accumulation. The central question about any particular deduction provision is whether there is good reason, in refining the concept of personal consumption as a component of taxable income, to exclude the particular goods or services for which the deductible expenditure is made.

Thus, in evaluating the medical expense deduction the underlying question is whether medical services should be included or excluded in the refined concept of personal consumption for tax purposes. For many purposes, of course, medical services are properly classed as personal consumption. But for purposes of interpersonal comparisons of taxable capacity there are persuasive reasons for excluding medical services. As between two people with otherwise similar patterns of personal consumption and accumulation, a greater utilization of medical services by one is likely not to reflect any greater material well-being or taxable capacity, but rather only greater medical need. Ultimately the question of excluding medical services from the tax base is a question of judgment. But there is a rational argument to be made for it, in terms that are quite germane to the elaboration of an ideal personal tax base, not extraneous objectives. This is the basis on which the medical expense deduction should be primarily evaluated.

Evaluating the charitable contribution deduction is considerably more complex. Should personal consumption, as a component in our base for distributing or allocating income tax burdens, reflect the provision by churches, schools, museums, and other charities of collective goods and services financed largely by voluntary contributions? And if so, how can the value of such goods and services be measured and on whose return should they be reported — the recipient of the services or the contributor who pays for them? In the case of many charitable contributions the material goods or services purchased with the contributed funds inure entirely to the benefit of persons other than the donor, and the donor enjoys only the nonmaterial satisfaction of making a gift. Even in the case of charities like churches which provide some service to their donors, the benefits received by the donor have many of the marks of free or collective goods, which are generally not reflected in our tax base. In the case of food, clothing, housing, and other divisible goods the price system operates to make what one pays an accurate measure of what he gets. Therefore, a tax on income spent for these items will be apportioned in fair relation to consumption. But in the case of collective goods financed with contributions there is no such correspondence between what one contributes and what he receives.

A good argument can be made that taxable personal consumption should be defined to include divisible, private goods and services whose consumption by one household precludes enjoyment by others, but not collective goods whose enjoyment is nonpreclusive or the nonmaterial satisfactions that arise from making contributions. Whether to accept this argument and where to draw the required lines are matters of policy choice and judgment rather than logical demonstration, but again the question is one that is intrinsic to the elaboration of an ideal personal tax base. It is primarily on this basis that the charitable contribution deduction should be evaluated.

In summary, there are substantial arguments in favor of both these personal deduction provisions that are intrinsic arguments of tax policy germane to the basic question of how to achieve a fair distribution of personal tax burdens. Moreover, these are arguments that illuminate the concept of an ideal personal tax base, as well as the particular deduction provision in question, and make the elaboration of the former bear on the evaluation of the latter and vice versa.

* * *

Mark G. Kelman, *Personal Deductions Revisited: Why They Fit Poorly in an "Ideal" Income Tax and Why They Fit Worse in a Far From Ideal World*
31 STAN. L. REV. 831 (1979)[5]

This article is an extended comment on Professor William Andrews' *Personal Deductions in an Ideal Income Tax*. Professor Andrews essentially argues that the tax base should take into account the different *uses* to which people put their money, and that the tax system ought to treat taxpayers who use their money for charitable contributions or medical care as if they had never received that money at all.

Professor Andrews rejects the common argument for building a concept of uses into the tax base that relies on social or economic purposes "extrinsic" to the tax system. Under that view, if Congress favors charity and health, it can use tax law to *encourage* charitable giving or purchases of medical care, or *finance* charitable giving or medical expenditures that would occur regardless of the tax laws. Though Congress could encourage or finance charitable or medical services through direct grants to the proper parties, it can achieve the same goals, perhaps at lower administrative cost, by allowing taxpayers to deduct the amount they spend on such favored uses. For example, if a 40 percent marginal-rate taxpayer makes a

---

medical expenditure that costs $10,000 pretax, it will cost her only $6,000 after tax: The government might believe that the prospect of such savings will encourage the taxpayer to purchaser a higher, more desirable level of medical care, or simply might be willing to finance the medical expenditure to the extent of $4,000. The $4,000 that the deduction scheme takes away from the government is called a "tax expenditure" to distinguish it from a direct grant to the favored party.

The shortcomings of supporting social and economic goals through "tax expenditures" rather than direct grants are now familiar. As a way of *encouraging* the purchase of medical care, for example, the deduction scheme is irrational: To encourage low-income taxpayers to purchase more medical care, the government has wasted a great deal of money by setting the price for richer taxpayers lower than necessary to encourage *them* to purchase an appropriate amount of medical care. As a way of *financing* medical care, the scheme is simply unfair. If A, a 50 percent bracket taxpayer, and B, a 20 percent bracket taxpayer, each spend $10,000 on doctors, the government will support A's expenditure by $5,000 and B's by only $2,000. It is hard to imagine Congressmen advocating a *direct* welfare spending program that would reward people for being rich.

In place of the tax expenditure concept, Professor Andrews approves the charitable and medical deductions for reasons "intrinsic" to the tax system: The government can measure the taxpayer's very capacity to pay taxes, and the extent of the claims the tax system can justly make on her, only after excluding certain categories of uses from the tax base. My basic dispute with Professor Andrews concerns what constitutes the appropriate tax base.

Professor Andrews relies on Henry Simon's well-accepted principle that taxpayers ought to be taxed on *income* which equals the sum of consumption and accumulation (or savings). But Professor Simons's definition does not illuminate my difference with Professor Andrews. My view is that a taxpayer's net receipts, receipts minus the cost of obtaining the receipts, *tautologically* consists of consumption plus savings. The critical problem is to define "consumption" (using money to obtain satisfaction).

Professor Andrews has narrowed the meaning of consumption and, in effect, has identified certain uses of money which are strictly neither savings nor consumption. A use is not consumption unless it is "private preclusive appropriation" of resources. And even uses that *are* private preclusive appropriations will not constitute consumption unless they improve the taxpayer's position beyond a baseline psychic condition of tax-free health. Thus, charitable donations are not consumption, even though they may give the donor as much personal satisfaction as ordinary spending, because the donor does not appropriate goods or services for her private preclusive use. Medical expenditures, even though they clearly involve the private preclusive appropriation of goods and services, are not consumption because they simply restore the level of health that the taxpayer enjoyed, tax-free, before illness or injury occurred.

I hope to demonstrate that Professor Andrews' notion of private preclusive appropriation is unconvincing, and in any event would not logically justify the charitable deduction. And while *some* deduction for medical care might be supportable, Professor Andrews's argument, which allows deduction for *all actual* expenditures on what is conventionally deemed medical care (and which falls back on a dubious assumption that Congress can alter rates to correct vertical inequities caused by the deduction) is ultimately unpersuasive. Moreover, Professor Andrews regularly makes unfounded empirical assumptions to suppress the weaknesses of his case, and these assumptions consistently contravene progressivity and ignore the effect of differences in economic class on the nature of charitable and medical spending.

I will affirmatively argue that a net receipts tax base would respond to two major concerns in designing a tax system: The tax system ought to measure inequality in earnings capacity, and yet respect a taxpayer's decision not to fulfill her earnings capacity. While the tax system should not force a taxpayer to take dominion over as many resources as she is able, once she voluntarily takes control of resources, her particular subsequent uses of those resources are irrelevant to tax law.

* * *

Conclusion

Ultimately, I suspect that my support of a net receipts tax and Professor Andrews's support of use-oriented deductions reflect the different ideological lenses through which we view reality.

The economic stratification in our society is extreme. Given citizens of widely divergent talent and background and a hierarchical wage structure in which people respond to wage signals in choosing what work to do, no tax system could eliminate this stratification. But progressive taxation may help to mitigate it.

A tax system whose goal is redistribution must look to the taxpayers' relative abilities to pay. But I do not advocate a direct tax on ability to earn to achieve this goal, because I both recognize its administrative difficulties and think the tax system's respect for a taxpayer's refusal to treat potentially marketable resources as commodities represents a desirable anti-capitalist strain in a market-obsessed culture. But I believe that once people deliberately exercise their earning power in the market, the tax system should measure their relative positions as prelude to redistribution.

My opposition to the charitable donation is bolstered by my sense that charitable donors are the same as everyone else in an individualist culture: They use their money for their own relative benefit. Even the most sincere altruist buys the scarce resource of looking altruistic.

My hostility to an expenditure-oriented medical care deduction is sharpened by my feeling that a capitalist system encourages its members to disguise their ability to pay in order to avoid taxes. Government spending benefits everyone, regardless of individual tax payment; but each person's tax payment reduces her ability to make private appropriations. And as long as the taxpayer's sense of "utility" is grounded in private consumption, she will assume an adversarial role with respect to the tax system. The government inevitably exacerbates the problem by putting the tax law in terms of "rules" rather than "standards." A taxpayer can manipulate a "rule" ("deduct medical expenditures") by imbedding as much consumption as she can into an imprecise legal definition of a nontaxable transaction. The government can observe only the flow of money — it is largely bound by the taxpayer's initial characterization of her expenditure. While the government could interpret a "standard" ("deduct *reasonable* medical expenditures") to serve the ultimate purpose of measuring true ability to pay, standards are inevitably nonadministrable and prejudicially enforced.

If the purpose of defining a tax base is to determine relative abilities to pay *and* if earnings capacity best measures ability to pay *and* if net receipts best measure earnings capacity (given the desirable side constraint of respecting the decision not to enter the market), as income tax that ignores different uses of received income is presumptively just. There are a number of arguments for accounting for *one* sort of use in picking a tax base, exempting funds "used" to save — but one ought to be wary of such focuses on uses, particularly when taxpayers in higher income classes are more prone to use their funds to make exempt purchases. Use distinctions *among* consumption items should be particularly suspect: Andrews' distinctions between either charitable or medical care spending and other forms of taxed spending are tenuous; ultimately, one would be very likely to adopt them unless one's goal were to reduce the progressivity of the tax system or increase its complexity.

Understanding the Andrews-Kelman Debate

1.   Prof. Andrews' argument emphasizes the role of the medical and charitable deductions in accurate income measurement: a person who makes these expenditures has less income to spend on herself, and should, accordingly pay fewer taxes. This is probably true of at least some medical expenditures, but does it really work for charitable deductions? Isn't a charitable contribution a voluntary decision, like consumption, saving, or other uses of money? Or does the selfless nature of a charitable contribution, and the lack of private consumption resulting from it, make it a special case? (Incidentally, isn't Kelman just a little bit cynical in suggesting that (essentially) "everything is a form of consumption"? Don't people, even lawyers, sometimes do things for noble reasons? Don't you?)

2.   In the then-prevalent style of critical legal studies, Kelman takes Andrews to task for emphasizing petty issues of horizontal equity over the vertical equity consequences of personal deductions — that is, their tendency to provide much larger benefits to wealthy rather than poorer taxpayers. Is this argument really fair? If the charitable deduction were eliminated tomorrow, who do you think would complain most loudly: wealthy individuals, or more modest middle class taxpayers and the institutions (especially churches) they support with their contributions? Statistics repeatedly demonstrate that many poor and working class people give a surprising percentage of their incomes to charitable organizations, especially churches and other religious organizations, although, presumably, most do not itemize their deductions. Purely as a philosophical matter, are these figures consistent with Kelman's argument? Even if Kelman is right, doesn't the redistributive aspect of charitable contributions compensate, to some degree, for its

upside-down nature? Does it depend on what kind of charitable organizations — museums, hospitals, homeless food kitchens — we are talking about?

3. Just out of curiosity, what did you make of Andrew's and Kelman's argumentative styles? If you were debating tax policy, would you make your case in such abstract, rhetorical terms, or would you point to more real-world evidence (i.e. the number of lives saved by voluntary medical procedures, the work done by charitable tax-exempt organizations, and so forth)? One frequent criticism of legal scholarship is that it tends to be highly argumentative and formalistic, with relatively little application to real-world, empirical facts. This is a problem that probably begins in law school, where wise guys (and girls) are rewarded, and students do relatively little research outside the law library. *See* Michael A. Livingston, *Reinventing Tax Scholarship: Lawyers, Economists, and the Role of the Legal Academy*, 83 CORNELL L. REV. 365 (1998) (calling, in abstract and highly nonempirical rhetoric, for a less rhetorical and more empirical tax scholarship).

II. CHARITABLE CONTRIBUTIONS: POLICY AND PRACTICE

A.   Tax Exemptions and Public Policy: What Is a Charitable Organization?

BOB JONES UNIVERSITY v. UNITED STATES
United States Supreme Court
461 U.S. 574 (1983)

CHIEF JUSTICE BURGER delivered the opinion of the Court.

We granted *certiorari* to decide whether petitioners, nonprofit private schools that prescribe and enforce racially discriminatory admissions standards on the basis of religious doctrine, qualify as tax-exempt organizations under § 501(c)(3) of the Internal Revenue Code of 1954.

I

A

Until 1970, the Internal Revenue Service granted tax-exempt status to private schools, without regard to their racial admissions policies, under § 501(c)(3) of the Internal Revenue Code, 26 U.S.C. § 501(c)(3), and granted charitable deductions for contributions to such schools under § 170 of the Code, 26 U.S.C. § 170.

On January 12, 1970, a three-judge District Court for the District of Columbia issued a preliminary injunction prohibiting the IRS from according tax-exempt status to private schools in Mississippi that discriminated as to admissions on the basis of race. *Green v. Kennedy*, 309 F.Supp. 1127, *appeal dism'd sub nom. Cannon v. Green*, 398 U.S. 956 (1970). Thereafter, in July 1970, the IRS concluded that it could "no longer legally justify allowing tax-exempt status [under § 501(c)(3)] to private schools which practice racial discrimination." IRS News Release, July 7, 1970, reprinted in App. in No. 81-3, p. A235. At the same time, the IRS announced that it could not "treat gifts to such schools as charitable deductions for income tax purposes [under § 170]." *Ibid.* By letter dated November 30, 1970, the IRS formally notified private schools, including those involved in this litigation, of this change in policy, "applicable to all private schools in the United States at all levels of education." *See id.* at A232.

On June 30, 1971, the three-judge District Court issued its opinion on the merits of the Mississippi challenge. *Green v. Connally*, 330 F. Supp. 1150, *summarily aff'd sub nom. Coit v. Green*, 404 U.S. 997 (1971). That court approved the IRS's amended construction of the Tax Code. The court also held that racially discriminatory private schools were not entitled to exemption under § 501(c)(3) and that donors were not entitled to deductions for contributions to such schools under § 170. The court permanently enjoined the Commissioner of Internal Revenue from approving tax-exempt status for any school in Mississippi that did not publicly maintain a policy of nondiscrimination.

The revised policy on discrimination was formalized in Revenue Ruling 71-447, 1971-2 Cum. Bull. 230:

> "Both the courts and the Internal Revenue Service have long recognized that the statutory requirement of being 'organized and operated exclusively for religious, charitable, . . . or educational purposes' was intended to express the basic common law concept [of 'charity']. . . . All charitable trusts, educational or otherwise, are subject to the requirement that the purpose of the trust may not be illegal or contrary to public policy."

Based on the "national policy to discourage racial discrimination in education," the IRS ruled that "a [private] school not having a racially nondiscriminatory policy as to students is not 'charitable' within the common law concepts reflected in sections 170 and 501(c)(3) of the Code." *Id.* at 231.

The application of the IRS construction of these provisions to petitioners, two private schools with racially discriminatory admissions policies, is now before us.

B

No. 81-3, Bob Jones University v. United States

Bob Jones University is a nonprofit corporation located in Greenville, S.C. Its purpose is "to conduct an institution of learning . . . , giving special emphasis to the Christian religion and the ethics revealed in the Holy Scriptures." Certificate of Incorporation, Bob Jones University, Inc., of Greenville, S.C., reprinted in App. in No. 81-3, p. A119. The corporation operates a school with an enrollment of approximately 5,000 students, from kindergarten through college and graduate school. Bob Jones University is not affiliated with any religious denomination, but is dedicated to the teaching and propagation of its fundamentalist Christian religious beliefs. It is both a religious and educational institution. Its teachers are required to be devout Christians, and all courses at the University are taught according to the Bible. Entering students are screened as to their religious beliefs, and their public and private conduct is strictly regulated by standards promulgated by University authorities.

The sponsors of the University genuinely believe that the Bible forbids interracial dating and marriage. To effectuate these views, Negroes were completely excluded until 1971. From 1971 to May 1975, the University accepted no applications from unmarried Negroes,[6] but did accept applications from Negroes married within their race.

Following the decision of the United States Court of Appeals for the Fourth Circuit in *McCrary v. Runyon*, 515 F.2d 1082 (1975), *aff'd*, 427 U.S. 160 (1976), prohibiting racial exclusion from private schools, the University revised its policy. Since May 29, 1975, the University has permitted unmarried Negroes to enroll; but a disciplinary rule prohibits interracial dating and marriage. That rule reads:

"There is to be no interracial dating.

"1. Students who are partners in an interracial marriage will be expelled.

"2. Students who are members of or affiliated with any group or organization which holds as one of its goals or advocates interracial marriage will be expelled.

"3. Students who date outside of their own race will be expelled.

"4. Students who espouse, promote, or encourage others to violate the University's dating rules and regulations will be expelled." App. in No. 81-3, p. A197.

The University continues to deny admission to applicants engaged in an interracial marriage or known to advocate interracial marriage or dating. *Id.* at A277.

Until 1970, the IRS extended tax-exempt status to Bob Jones University under § 501(c)(3). By the letter of November 30, 1970, that followed the injunction issued in *Green v. Kennedy*, 309 F.Supp. 1127 (DC 1970), the IRS formally notified the University of the change in IRS policy, and announced its intention to challenge the tax-exempt status of private schools practicing racial discrimination in their admissions policies.

After failing to obtain an assurance of tax exemption through administrative means, the University instituted an action in 1971 seeking to enjoin the IRS from revoking the school's tax-exempt status. That suit culminated in *Bob Jones University v. Simon*, 416 U.S. 725 (1974), in which this Court held that the Anti-Injunction Act of the Internal Revenue Code, 26 U.S.C. § 7421(a), prohibited the University from obtaining judicial review by way of injunctive action before the assessment or collection of any tax.

Thereafter, on April 16, 1975, the IRS notified the University of the proposed revocation of its tax-exempt status. On January 19, 1976, the IRS officially revoked the University's tax-exempt status, effective as of December 1, 1970, the day after

---

[6] [5] Beginning in 1973, Bob Jones University instituted an exception to this rule, allowing applications from unmarried Negroes who had been members of the University staff for four years or more.

the University was formally notified of the change in IRS policy. The University subsequently filed returns under the Federal Unemployment Tax Act for the period from December 1, 1970, to December 31, 1975, and paid a tax totaling $21 on one employee for the calendar year of 1975. After its request for a refund was denied, the University instituted the present action, seeking to recover the $21 it had paid to the IRS. The Government counterclaimed for unpaid federal unemployment taxes for the taxable years 1971 through 1975, in the amount of $489,675.59, plus interest.

The United States District Court for the District of South Carolina held that revocation of the University's tax-exempt status exceeded the delegated powers of the IRS, was improper under the IRS rulings and procedures, and violated the University's rights under the Religion Clauses of the First Amendment. 468 F.Supp. 890, 907 (1978). The court accordingly ordered the IRS to pay the University the $21 refund it claimed and rejected the IRS's counterclaim.

The Court of Appeals for the Fourth Circuit, in a divided opinion, reversed. 639 F.2d 147 (1980). Citing *Green v. Connally*, 330 F. Supp. 1150 (DC 1971), with approval, the Court of Appeals concluded that § 501(c)(3) must be read against the background of charitable trust law. To be eligible for an exemption under that section, an institution must be "charitable" in the common-law sense, and therefore must not be contrary to public policy. In the court's view, Bob Jones University did not meet this requirement, since its "racial policies violated the clearly defined public policy, rooted in our Constitution, condemning racial discrimination and, more specifically, the government policy against subsidizing racial discrimination in education, public or private." 639 F.2d at 151. The court held that the IRS acted within its statutory authority in revoking the University's tax-exempt status. Finally, the Court of Appeals rejected petitioner's arguments that the revocation of the tax exemption violated the Free Exercise and Establishment Clauses of the First Amendment. The case was remanded to the District Court with instructions to dismiss the University's claim for a refund and to reinstate the IRS's counterclaim.

* * *

We granted *certiorari* in both cases, 454 U.S. 892 (1981),[7] and we affirm in each.

---

[7] [9] After the Court granted *certiorari*, the Government filed a motion to dismiss, informing the Court that the Department of the Treasury intended to revoke Revenue Ruling 71-447 and other pertinent rulings and to recognize § 501(c)(3) exemptions for petitioners. The Government suggested that these actions were therefore moot. Before this Court ruled on that motion, however, the United States Court of Appeals for the District of Columbia Circuit enjoined the Government from granting § 501(c)(3) tax-exempt status to any school that discriminates on the basis of race. Wright v. Regan, No. 80-1124 (Feb. 18, 1982) (per curiam order). Thereafter, the Government informed the Court that it would not revoke the Revenue Rulings and withdrew its request that the actions be dismissed as moot. The Government continues to assert that the IRS lacked authority to promulgate Revenue Ruling 71-447, and does not defend that aspect of the rulings below.

II

A

In In Revenue Ruling 71-447, the IRS formalized the policy, first announced in 1970, that § 170 and § 501(c)(3) embrace the common-law "charity" concept. Under that view, to qualify for a tax exemption pursuant to § 501(c)(3), an institution must show, first, that it falls within one of the eight categories expressly set forth in that section, and second, that its activity is not contrary to settled public policy.

Section 501(c)(3) provides that "[corporations] . . . organized and operated exclusively for religious, charitable . . . or educational purposes" are entitled to tax exemption. Petitioners argue that the plain language of the statute guarantees them tax-exempt status. They emphasize the absence of any language in the statute expressly requiring all exempt organizations to be "charitable" in the common-law sense, and they contend that the disjunctive "or" separating the categories in § 501(c)(3) precludes such a reading. Instead, they argue that if an institution falls within one or more of the specified categories it is automatically entitled to exemption, without regard to whether it also qualifies as "charitable." The Court of Appeals rejected that contention and concluded that petitioners' interpretation of the statute "tears section 501(c)(3) from its roots." 639 F.2d at 151.

It is a well-established canon of statutory construction that a court should go beyond the literal language of a statute if reliance on that language would defeat the plain purpose of the statute:

> "The general words used in the clause . . . , taken by themselves, and literally construed, without regard to the object in view, would seem to sanction the claim of the plaintiff. But this mode of expounding a statute has never been adopted by any enlightened tribunal — because it is evident that in many cases it would defeat the object which the Legislature intended to accomplish. And it is well settled that, in interpreting a statute, the court will not look merely to a particular clause in which general words may be used, *but will take in connection with it the whole statute . . . and the objects and policy of the law . . . .*" *Brown v. Duchesne,* 19 How. 183, 194 (1857) (emphasis added).

Section 501(c)(3) therefore must be analyzed and construed within the framework of the Internal Revenue Code and against the background of the congressional purposes. Such an examination reveals unmistakable evidence that, underlying all relevant parts of the Code, is the intent that entitlement to tax exemption depends on meeting certain common-law standards of charity — namely, that an institution seeking tax-exempt status must serve a public purpose and not be contrary to established public policy.

This "charitable" concept appears explicitly in § 170 of the Code. That section contains a list of organizations virtually identical to that contained in § 501(c)(3). It is apparent that Congress intended that list to have the same meaning in both sections.[8] In § 170, Congress used the list of organizations in defining the term "charitable contributions." On its face, therefore, § 170 reveals that Congress' intention was to provide tax benefits to organizations serving charitable purposes. The form of § 170 simply makes plain what common sense and history tell us: in enacting both § 170 and § 501(c)(3), Congress sought to provide tax benefits to charitable organizations, to encourage the development of private institutions that serve a useful public purpose or supplement or take the place of public institutions of the same kind.

Tax exemptions for certain institutions thought beneficial to the social order of the country as a whole, or to a particular community, are deeply rooted in our history, as in that of England. The origins of such exemptions lie in the special privileges that have long been extended to charitable trusts.

More than a century ago, this Court announced the caveat that is critical in this case:

> "[It] has now become an established principle of American law, that courts of chancery will sustain and protect . . . a gift . . . to public charitable uses, *provided the same is consistent with local laws and public policy. . . .*" *Perin v. Carey*, 24 How. 465, 501 (1861) (emphasis added).

Soon after that, in 1877, the Court commented:

> "A charitable use, *where neither law nor public policy forbids,* may be applied to almost any thing *that tends to promote the well-doing and well-being of social man.*" *Ould v. Washington Hospital for Foundlings*, 95 U.S. 303, 311 (emphasis added).

See also, e.g., Jackson v. Phillips, 96 Mass. 539, 556 (1867). In 1891, in a restatement of the English law of charity[9] which has long been recognized as a leading authority in this country, Lord MacNaghten stated:

> " 'Charity' in its legal sense comprises four principal divisions: trusts for the relief of poverty; *trusts for the advancement of education;* trusts for the advancement of religion; and trusts for *other purposes beneficial to the*

---

   [8] [10] The predecessor of § 170 originally was enacted in 1917, as part of the War Revenue Act of 1917, ch. 63, § 1201(2), 40 Stat. 330, whereas the predecessor of § 501(c)(3) dates back to the income tax law of 1894, Act of Aug. 27, 1894, ch. 349, 28 Stat. 509, *see* n. 14, *infra.* There are minor differences between the lists of organizations in the two sections, *see generally* Liles & Blum, *Development of the Federal Tax Treatment of Charities*, 39 Law & Contemp. Prob. 6, 24–25 (No. 4, 1975) (hereinafter Liles & Blum). Nevertheless, the two sections are closely related; both seek to achieve the same basic goal of encouraging the development of certain organizations through the grant of tax benefits. The language of the two sections is in most respects identical, and the Commissioner and the courts consistently have applied many of the same standards in interpreting those sections. *See* 5 J. Mertens, Law of Federal Income Taxation § 31.12 (1980); 6 *id.,* §§ 34.01-34.13 (1975); B. Bittker & L. Stone, Federal Income Taxation 220–222 (5th ed. 1980). To the extent that § 170 "aids in ascertaining the meaning" of § 501(c)(3), therefore, it is "entitled to great weight," United States v. Stewart, 311 U.S. 60, 64–65 (1940). *See* Harris v. Commissioner, 340 U.S. 106, 107 (1950).

   [9] [13] The draftsmen of the 1894 income tax law, which included the first charitable exemption provision, relied heavily on English concepts of taxation; and the list of exempt organizations appears to have been patterned upon English income tax statutes. *See* 26 Cong. Rec. 584–588, 6612–6615 (1894).

community, not falling under any of the preceding heads." *Commissioners v. Pemsel*, [1891] A.C. 531, 583 (emphasis added).

See, e.g., 4 A. SCOTT, LAW OF TRUSTS § 368, pp. 2853–2854 (3d ed. 1967) (hereinafter SCOTT). These statements clearly reveal the legal background against which Congress enacted the first charitable exemption statute in 1894: charities were to be given preferential treatment because they provide a benefit to society.

What little floor debate occurred on the charitable exemption provision of the 1894 Act and similar sections of later statutes leaves no doubt that Congress deemed the specified organizations entitled to tax benefits because they served desirable public purposes. *See, e.g.*, 26 Cong. Rec. 585–586 (1894); *id.* at 1727. In floor debate on a similar provision in 1917, for example, Senator Hollis articulated the rationale:

> "For every dollar that a man contributes for these public charities, educational, scientific, or otherwise, the public gets 100 per cent." 55 Cong. Rec. 6728.

See also, e.g., 44 Cong. Rec. 4150 (1909); 50 Cong. Rec. 1305–1306 (1913). In 1924, this Court restated the common understanding of the charitable exemption provision:

> "Evidently the exemption is made in recognition of the benefit which the public derives from corporate activities of the class named, and is intended to aid them when not conducted for private gain." *Trinidad v. Sagrada Orden*, 263 U.S. 578, 581.

In enacting the Revenue Act of 1938, ch. 289, 52 Stat. 447, Congress expressly reconfirmed this view with respect to the charitable deduction provision:

> "The exemption from taxation of money or property devoted to charitable and other purposes is based upon the theory that the Government is compensated for the loss of revenue by its relief from financial burdens which would otherwise have to be met by appropriations from other public funds, and by the benefits resulting from the promotion of the general welfare." H.R. Rep. No. 1860, 75th Cong., 3d Sess., 19 (1938).[10]

A corollary to the public benefit principle is the requirement, long recognized in the law of trusts, that the purpose of a charitable trust may not be illegal or violate established public policy. In 1861, this Court stated that a public charitable use must be "consistent with local laws and public policy," *Perin v. Carey*, 24 How. at 501.

---

[10] [16] The common-law requirement of public benefit is universally recognized by commentators on the law of trusts. For example, the Bogerts state:

> "In return for the favorable treatment accorded charitable gifts which imply some disadvantage to the community, the courts must find in the trust which is to be deemed 'charitable' some real advantages to the public which more than offset the disadvantages arising out of special privileges accorded charitable trusts." G. BOGERT & G. BOGERT, LAW OF TRUSTS AND TRUSTEES § 361, p. 3 (rev. 2d ed. 1977) (hereinafter BOGERT).

For other statements of this principle, *see, e.g.*, 4 SCOTT § 348, at 2770; RESTATEMENT (SECOND) OF TRUSTS § 368, Comment *b* (1959); E. FISCH, D. FREED, & E. SCHACHTER, CHARITIES AND CHARITABLE FOUNDATIONS § 256 (1974).

Modern commentators and courts have echoed that view. *See, e.g.*, RESTATEMENT (SECOND) OF TRUSTS § 377, Comment *c* (1959); 4 SCOTT § 377, and cases cited therein; BOGERT § 378, at 191–192.

When the Government grants exemptions or allows deductions all taxpayers are affected; the very fact of the exemption or deduction for the donor means that other taxpayers can be said to be indirect and vicarious "donors." Charitable exemptions are justified on the basis that the exempt entity confers a public benefit — a benefit which the society or the community may not itself choose or be able to provide, or which supplements and advances the work of public institutions already supported by tax revenues. History buttresses logic to make clear that, to warrant exemption under § 501(c)(3), an institution must fall within a category specified in that section and must demonstrably serve and be in harmony with the public interest. The institution's purpose must not be so at odds with the common community conscience as to undermine any public benefit that might otherwise be conferred.

B

We are bound to approach these questions with full awareness that determinations of public benefit and public policy are sensitive matters with serious implications for the institutions affected; a declaration that a given institution is not "charitable" should be made only where there can be no doubt that the activity involved is contrary to a fundamental public policy. But there can no longer be any doubt that racial discrimination in education violates deeply and widely accepted views of elementary justice. Prior to 1954, public education in many places still was conducted under the pall of *Plessy v. Ferguson*, 163 U.S. 537 (1896); racial segregation in primary and secondary education prevailed in many parts of the country. *See, e.g.*, SEGREGATION AND THE FOURTEENTH AMENDMENT IN THE STATES (B. Reams & P. Wilson eds. 1975).[11] This Court's decision in *Brown v. Board of Education*, 347 U.S. 483 (1954), signaled an end to that era. Over the past quarter of a century, every pronouncement of this Court and myriad Acts of Congress and Executive Orders attest a firm national policy to prohibit racial segregation and discrimination in public education.

An unbroken line of cases following *Brown v. Board of Education* establishes beyond doubt this Court's view that racial discrimination in education violates a most fundamental national public policy, as well as rights of individuals.

---

[11] [20] In 1894, when the first charitable exemption provision was enacted, racially segregated educational institutions would not have been regarded as against public policy. Yet contemporary standards must be considered in determining whether given activities provide a public benefit and are entitled to the charitable tax exemption. In Walz v. Tax Comm'n, 397 U.S. 664, 673 (1970), we observed:

> "Qualification for tax exemption is not perpetual or immutable; some tax-exempt groups lose that status when their activities take them outside the classification and new entities can come into being and qualify for exemption."

Charitable trust law also makes clear that the definition of "charity" depends upon contemporary standards. *See, e.g.*, RESTATEMENT (SECOND) OF TRUSTS § 374, Comment *a* (1959); BOGERT § 369, at 65–67; 4 SCOTT § 368, at 2855–2856.

> "The right of a student not to be segregated on racial grounds in schools
> . . . is indeed so fundamental and pervasive that it is embraced in the
> concept of due process of law." *Cooper v. Aaron*, 358 U.S. 1, 19 (1958).

In *Norwood v. Harrison*, 413 U.S. 455, 468–469 (1973), we dealt with a nonpublic
institution:

> "[A] private school — even one that discriminates — fulfills an important
> educational function; *however*, . . . [that] legitimate educational function
> cannot be isolated from discriminatory practices. . . . [Discriminatory]
> treatment exerts a pervasive influence on the entire educational process.*"
> (Emphasis added.)

See also Runyon v. McCrary, 427 U.S. 160 (1976); *Griffin v. County School Board*,
377 U.S. 218 (1964).

Congress, in Titles IV and VI of the Civil Rights Act of 1964, Pub. L. 88-352, 78
Stat. 241, 42 U.S.C. §§ 2000c, 2000c-6, 2000d, clearly expressed its agreement that
racial discrimination in education violates a fundamental public policy. Other
sections of that Act, and numerous enactments since then, testify to the public
policy against racial discrimination. [Citations omitted].

The Executive Branch has consistently placed its support behind eradication of
racial discrimination. Several years before this Court's decision in *Brown v. Board
of Education, supra*, President Truman issued Executive Orders prohibiting racial
discrimination in federal employment decisions, Exec. Order No. 9980, 3 CFR 720
(1943-1948 Comp.), and in classifications for the Selective Service, Exec. Order No.
9988, 3 CFR 726, 729 (1943-1948 Comp.). In 1957, President Eisenhower employed
military forces to ensure compliance with federal standards in school desegregation
programs. Exec. Order No. 10730, 3 CFR 389 (1954-1958 Comp.). And in 1962,
President Kennedy announced:

> "[The] granting of Federal assistance for . . . housing and related facilities
> from which Americans are excluded because of their race, color, creed, or
> national origin is unfair, unjust, and inconsistent with the public policy of
> the United States as manifested in its Constitution and laws." Exec. Order
> No. 11063, 3 CFR 652 (1959-1963 Comp.).

These are but a few of numerous Executive Orders over the past three decades
demonstrating the commitment of the Executive Branch to the fundamental policy
of eliminating racial discrimination. [Citations omitted].

Few social or political issues in our history have been more vigorously debated
and more extensively ventilated than the issue of racial discrimination, particularly
in education. Given the stress and anguish of the history of efforts to escape from
the shackles of the "separate but equal" doctrine of *Plessy v. Ferguson*, 163 U.S. 537
(1896), it cannot be said that educational institutions that, for whatever reasons,
practice racial discrimination, are institutions exercising "beneficial and stabilizing
influences in community life," *Walz v. Tax Comm'n*, 397 U.S. 664, 673 (1970), or
should be encouraged by having all taxpayers share in their support by way of
special tax status.

There can thus be no question that the interpretation of § 170 and § 501(c)(3) announced by the IRS in 1970 was correct. That it may be seen as belated does not undermine its soundness. It would be wholly incompatible with the concepts underlying tax exemption to grant the benefit of tax-exempt status to racially discriminatory educational entities, which "[exert] a pervasive influence on the entire educational process." *Norwood v. Harrison, supra,* at 469. Whatever may be the rationale for such private schools' policies, and however sincere the rationale may be, racial discrimination in education is contrary to public policy. Racially discriminatory educational institutions cannot be viewed as conferring a public benefit within the "charitable" concept discussed earlier, or within the congressional intent underlying § 170 and § 501(c)(3).

C

Petitioners contend that, regardless of whether the IRS properly concluded that racially discriminatory private schools violate public policy, only Congress can alter the scope of § 170 and § 501(c)(3). Petitioners accordingly argue that the IRS overstepped its lawful bounds in issuing its 1970 and 1971 rulings.

Yet ever since the inception of the Tax Code, Congress has seen fit to vest in those administering the tax laws very broad authority to interpret those laws. In an area as complex as the tax system, the agency Congress vests with administrative responsibility must be able to exercise its authority to meet changing conditions and new problems. Indeed as early as 1918, Congress expressly authorized the Commissioner "to make all needful rules and regulations for the enforcement" of the tax laws. Revenue Act of 1918, ch. 18, § 1309, 40 Stat. 1143. The same provision, so essential to efficient and fair administration of the tax laws, has appeared in Tax Codes ever since, *see* 26 U.S.C. § 7805(a); and this Court has long recognized the primary authority of the IRS and its predecessors in construing the Internal Revenue Code, *see, e.g., Commissioner v. Portland Cement Co. of Utah,* 450 U.S. 156, 169 (1981); *United States v. Correll,* 389 U.S. 299, 306–307 (1967); *Boske v. Comingore,* 177 U.S. 459, 469–470 (1900).

Congress, the source of IRS authority, can modify IRS rulings it considers improper; and courts exercise review over IRS actions. In the first instance, however, the responsibility for construing the Code falls to the IRS. Since Congress cannot be expected to anticipate every conceivable problem that can arise or to carry out day-to-day oversight, it relies on the administrators and on the courts to implement the legislative will. Administrators, like judges, are under oath to do so.

In § 170 and § 501(c)(3), Congress has identified categories of traditionally exempt institutions and has specified certain additional requirements for tax exemption. Yet the need for continuing interpretation of those statutes is unavoidable. For more than 60 years, the IRS and its predecessors have constantly been called upon to interpret these and comparable provisions, and in doing so have referred consistently to principles of charitable trust law. In Treas. Regs. 45, Art. 517(1) (1921), for example, the IRS's predecessor denied charitable exemptions on the basis of proscribed political activity before the Congress itself added such conduct as a disqualifying element. In other instances, the IRS has denied charitable exemptions to otherwise qualified entities because they served too limited a class of people and thus did not provide a truly "public" benefit under the common-law test. *See, e.g., Crellin v. Commissioner*, 46 B.T.A. 1152, 1155–1156 (1942); *James Sprunt Benevolent Trust v. Commissioner*, 20 B.T.A. 19, 24–25 (1930). *See also* Treas. Reg. § 1.501(c)(3)-1(d)(1)(ii) (1959). Some years before the issuance of the rulings challenged in these cases, the IRS also ruled that contributions to community recreational facilities would not be deductible and that the facilities themselves would not be entitled to tax-exempt status, unless those facilities were open to all on a racially nondiscriminatory basis. *See* Rev. Rul. 67-325, 1967-2 Cum. Bull. 113. These rulings reflect the Commissioner's continuing duty to interpret and apply the Internal Revenue Code. *See also Textile Mills Securities Corp. v. Commissioner*, 314 U.S. 326, 337–338 (1941).

Guided, of course, by the Code, the IRS has the responsibility, in the first instance, to determine whether a particular entity is "charitable" for purposes of § 170 and § 501(c)(3). This in turn may necessitate later determinations of whether given activities so violate public policy that the entities involved cannot be deemed to provide a public benefit worthy of "charitable" status. We emphasize, however, that these sensitive determinations should be made only where there is no doubt that the organization's activities violate fundamental public policy.

On the record before us, there can be no doubt as to the national policy. In 1970, when the IRS first issued the ruling challenged here, the position of all three branches of the Federal Government was unmistakably clear. The correctness of the Commissioner's conclusion that a racially discriminatory private school "is not 'charitable' within the common law concepts reflected in . . . the Code," Rev. Rul. 71-447, 1971-2 Cum. Bull., at 231, is wholly consistent with what Congress, the Executive, and the courts had repeatedly declared before 1970. Indeed, it would be anomalous for the Executive, Legislative, and Judicial Branches to reach conclusions that add up to a firm public policy on racial discrimination, and at the same time have the IRS blissfully ignore what all three branches of the Federal Government had declared.[12] Clearly an educational institution engaging in practices affirmatively at odds with this declared position of the whole Government cannot be seen as exercising a "beneficial and stabilizing [influence] in community life," *Walz v. Tax Comm'n*, 397 U.S. at 673, and is not "charitable," within the meaning of § 170 and § 501(c)(3). We therefore hold that the IRS did not exceed its authority when it announced its interpretation of § 170 and § 501(c)(3) in 1970 and 1971.[13]

---

[12] [23] JUSTICE POWELL misreads the Court's opinion when he suggests that the Court implies that "the Internal Revenue Service is invested with authority to decide which public policies are sufficiently 'fundamental' to require denial of tax exemptions." The Court's opinion does not warrant that interpretation. JUSTICE POWELL concedes that "if any national policy is sufficiently fundamental to constitute such an overriding limitation on the availability of tax-exempt status under § 501(c)(3), it is the policy against racial discrimination in education." Since that policy is sufficiently clear to warrant JUSTICE POWELL'S concession and for him to support our finding of longstanding congressional acquiescence, it should be apparent that his concerns about the Court's opinion are unfounded.

[13] [24] Many of the *amici curiae*, including *amicus* William T. Coleman, Jr. (appointed by the Court), argue that denial of tax-exempt status to racially discriminatory schools is independently required by the equal protection component of the Fifth Amendment. In light of our resolution of this litigation, we do not reach that issue. *See, e.g.,* United States v. Clark, 445 U.S. 23, 27 (1980); NLRB v. Catholic Bishop of Chicago, 440 U.S. 490, 504 (1979).

D

The actions of Congress since 1970 leave no doubt that the IRS reached the correct conclusion in exercising its authority. It is, of course, not unknown for independent agencies or the Executive Branch to misconstrue the intent of a statute; Congress can and often does correct such misconceptions, if the courts have not done so. Yet for a dozen years Congress has been made aware — acutely aware — of the IRS rulings of 1970 and 1971. As we noted earlier, few issues have been the subject of more vigorous and widespread debate and discussion in and out of Congress than those related to racial segregation in education. Sincere adherents advocating contrary views have ventilated the subject for well over three decades. Failure of Congress to modify the IRS rulings of 1970 and 1971, of which Congress was, by its own studies and by public discourse, constantly reminded, and Congress' awareness of the denial of tax-exempt status for racially discriminatory schools when enacting other and related legislation make out an unusually strong case of legislative acquiescence in and ratification by implication of the 1970 and 1971 rulings.

Ordinarily, and quite appropriately, courts are slow to attribute significance to the failure of Congress to act on particular legislation. *See, e.g., Aaron v. SEC*, 446 U.S. 680, 694, n. 11 (1980). We have observed that "unsuccessful attempts at legislation are not the best of guides to legislative intent," *Red Lion Broadcasting Co. v. FCC*, 395 U.S. 367, 382, n. 11 (1969). Here, however, we do not have an ordinary claim of legislative acquiescence. Only one month after the IRS announced its position in 1970, Congress held its first hearings on this precise issue. Equal Educational Opportunity: Hearings before the Senate Select Committee on Equal Educational Opportunity, 91st Cong., 2d Sess., 1991 (1970). Exhaustive hearings have been held on the issue at various times since then. These include hearings in February 1982, after we granted review in this case. Administration's Change in Federal Policy Regarding the Tax Status of Racially Discriminatory Private Schools: Hearing before the House Committee on Ways and Means, 97th Cong., 2d Sess. (1982).

Nonaction by Congress is not often a useful guide, but the nonaction here is significant. During the past 12 years there have been no fewer than 13 bills introduced to overturn the IRS interpretation of § 501(c)(3). Not one of these bills has emerged from any committee, although Congress has enacted numerous other amendments to § 501 during this same period, including an amendment to § 501(c)(3) itself. Tax Reform Act of 1976, Pub. L. 94-455, § 1313(a), 90 Stat. 1730. It is hardly conceivable that Congress — and in this setting, any Member of Congress — was not abundantly aware of what was going on. In view of its prolonged and acute awareness of so important an issue, Congress' failure to act on the bills proposed on this subject provides added support for concluding that Congress acquiesced in the IRS rulings of 1970 and 1971. [Citations omitted].

The evidence of congressional approval of the policy embodied in Revenue Ruling 71-447 goes well beyond the failure of Congress to act on legislative proposals. Congress affirmatively manifested its acquiescence in the IRS policy when it enacted the present § 501(i) of the Code, Act of Oct. 20, 1976, Pub. L. 94-568, 90 Stat. 2697. That provision denies tax-exempt status to social clubs whose charters or policy statements provide for "discrimination against any person on the basis of race, color, or religion."[14] Both the House and Senate Committee Reports on that bill articulated the national policy against granting tax exemptions to racially discriminatory private clubs. S. Rep. No. 94-1318, p. 8 (1976); H.R. Rep. No. 94-1353, p. 8 (1976).

Even more significant is the fact that both Reports focus on this Court's affirmance of *Green v. Connally*, 330 F. Supp. 1150 (DC 1971), as having established that "discrimination on account of race is inconsistent with an *educational institution's* tax-exempt status." S. Rep. No. 94–1318, *supra*, at 7–8, and n.5; H.R. Rep. No. 94-1353, *supra*, at 8, and n. 5 (emphasis added). These references in congressional Committee Reports on an enactment denying tax exemptions to racially discriminatory private social clubs cannot be read other than as indicating approval of the standards applied to racially discriminatory private schools by the IRS subsequent to 1970, and specifically of Revenue Ruling 71-447.[15]

* * *

Petitioner Bob Jones University, however, contends that it is not racially discriminatory. It emphasizes that it now allows all races to enroll, subject only to its restrictions on the conduct of all students, including its prohibitions of association between men and women of different races, and of interracial marriage. Although a ban on intermarriage or interracial dating applies to all races, decisions of this Court firmly establish that discrimination on the basis of racial affiliation and association is a form of racial discrimination, *see, e.g., Loving v. Virginia*, 388 U.S. 1 (1967); *McLaughlin v. Florida*, 379 U.S. 184 (1964); *Tillman v. Wheaton-Haven Recreation Assn.*, 410 U.S. 431 (1973). We therefore find that the IRS properly applied Revenue Ruling 71-447 to Bob Jones University.[16]

The judgments of the Court of Appeals are, accordingly,

Affirmed.

---

[14] [26] Prior to the introduction of this legislation, a three-judge District Court had held that segregated social clubs were entitled to tax exemptions. McGlotten v. Connally, 338 F. Supp. 448 (DC 1972). Section 501(i) was enacted primarily in response to that decision. *See* S. Rep. No. 94-1318, pp. 7–8 (1976); H.R. Rep. No. 94-1353, p. 8 (1976).

[15] [27] Reliance is placed on scattered statements in floor debate by Congressmen critical of the IRS's adoption of Revenue Ruling 71-447. *See, e.g.*, Brief for Petitioner in No. 81-1, pp. 27–28. Those views did not prevail. . . .

[16] [31] This argument would in any event apply only to the final eight months of the five tax years at issue in this case. Prior to May 1975, Bob Jones University's admissions policy was racially discriminatory on its face, since the University excluded unmarried Negro students while admitting unmarried Caucasians.

* * *

JUSTICE REHNQUIST, dissenting.

The Court points out that there is a strong national policy in this country against racial discrimination. To the extent that the Court states that Congress in furtherance of this policy could deny tax-exempt status to educational institutions that promote racial discrimination, I readily agree. But, unlike the Court, I am convinced that Congress simply has failed to take this action and, as this Court has said over and over again, regardless of our view on the propriety of Congress' failure to legislate we are not constitutionally empowered to act for it.

In approaching this statutory construction question the Court quite adeptly avoids the statute it is construing. This I am sure is no accident, for there is nothing in the language of § 501(c)(3) that supports the result obtained by the Court. Section 501(c)(3) provides tax-exempt status . . . [text of statute omitted. — Ed.].

With undeniable clarity, Congress has explicitly defined the requirements for § 501(c)(3) status. An entity must be (1) a corporation, or community chest, fund, or foundation, (2) organized for one of the eight enumerated purposes, (3) operated on a nonprofit basis, and (4) free from involvement in lobbying activities and political campaigns. Nowhere is there to be found some additional, undefined public policy requirement.

The Court first seeks refuge from the obvious reading of § 501(c)(3) by turning to § 170 of the Internal Revenue Code, which provides a tax deduction for contributions made to § 501(c)(3) organizations. In setting forth the general rule, § 170 states:

> "There shall be allowed as a deduction any charitable contribution (as defined in subsection (c)) payment of which is made within the taxable year. A charitable contribution shall be allowable as a deduction only if verified under regulations prescribed by the Secretary." 26 U.S.C. § 170(a)(1).

The Court seizes the words "charitable contribution" and with little discussion concludes that "[on] its face, therefore, § 170 reveals that Congress' intention was to provide tax benefits to organizations serving charitable purposes," intimating that this implies some unspecified common-law charitable trust requirement.

The Court would have been well advised to look to subsection (c) where, as § 170(a)(1) indicates, Congress has defined a "charitable contribution":

> "For purposes of this section, the term 'charitable contribution' means a contribution or gift to or for the use of . . . [a] corporation, trust, or community chest, fund, or foundation . . . organized and operated exclusively for religious, charitable, scientific, literary, or educational purposes, or to foster national or international amateur sports competition (but only if no part of its activities involve the provision of athletic facilities or equipment), or for the prevention of cruelty to children or animals; . . . no part of the net earnings of which inures to the benefit of any private shareholder or individual; and . . . which is not disqualified for tax exemption under section 501(c)(3) by reason of attempting to influence

legislation, and which does not participate in, or intervene in (including the publishing or distributing of statements), any political campaign on behalf of any candidate for public office." 26 U.S.C. § 170(c).

Plainly, § 170(c) simply tracks the requirements set forth in § 501(c)(3). Since § 170 is no more than a mirror of § 501(c)(3) and, as the Court points out, § 170 followed § 501(c)(3) by more than two decades, *ante*, n. 10, it is at best of little usefulness in finding the meaning of § 501(c)(3).

Making a more fruitful inquiry, the Court next turns to the legislative history of § 501(c)(3) and finds that Congress intended in that statute to offer a tax benefit to organizations that Congress believed were providing a public benefit. I certainly agree. But then the Court leaps to the conclusion that this history is proof Congress intended that an organization seeking § 501(c)(3) status "must fall within a category specified in that section *and must demonstrably serve and be in harmony with the public interest.*" (emphasis added). To the contrary, I think that the legislative history of § 501(c)(3) unmistakably makes clear that *Congress has decided* what organizations are serving a public purpose and providing a public benefit within the meaning of § 501(c)(3) and has clearly set forth in § 501(c)(3) the characteristics of such organizations. In fact, there are few examples which better illustrate Congress' effort to define and redefine the requirements of a legislative Act.

[JUSTICE REHNQUIST tracks the long-term legislative history of section 501(c)(3) in an effort to demonstrate the lack of congressional intent to include a racial discrimination test in the statute. — Ed.]

One way to read the opinion handed down by the Court today leads to the conclusion that this long and arduous refining process of § 501(c)(3) was certainly a waste of time, for when enacting the original 1894 statute Congress intended to adopt a common-law term of art, and intended that this term of art carry with it all of the common-law baggage which defines it. Such a view, however, leads also to the unsupportable idea that Congress has spent almost a century adding illustrations simply to clarify an already defined common-law term.

Another way to read the Court's opinion leads to the conclusion that even though Congress has set forth *some* of the requirements of a § 501(c)(3) organization, it intended that the IRS additionally require that organizations meet a higher standard of public interest, not stated by Congress, but to be determined and defined by the IRS and the courts. This view I find equally unsupportable. Almost a century of statutory history proves that Congress itself intended to decide what § 501(c)(3) requires. Congress has expressed its decision in the plainest of terms in § 501(c)(3) by providing that tax-exempt status is to be given to any corporation, or community chest, fund, or foundation that is organized for one of the eight enumerated purposes, operated on a nonprofit basis, and uninvolved in lobbying activities or political campaigns. The IRS certainly is empowered to adopt regulations for the enforcement of these specified requirements, and the courts have authority to resolve challenges to the IRS's exercise of this power, but Congress has left it to neither the IRS nor the courts to select or add to the requirements of § 501(c)(3).

The Court suggests that unless its new requirement be added to § 501(c)(3), nonprofit organizations formed to teach pickpockets and terrorists would necessarily acquire tax-exempt status. *Ante*, n. 18. Since the Court does not challenge the characterization of *petitioners* as "educational" institutions within the meaning of § 501(c)(3), and in fact states several times in the course of its opinion that petitioners *are* educational institutions, it is difficult to see how this argument advances the Court's reasoning for disposing of petitioners' cases.

But simply because I reject the Court's heavyhanded creation of the requirement that an organization seeking § 501(c)(3) status must "serve and be in harmony with the public interest," does not mean that I would deny to the IRS the usual authority to adopt regulations further explaining what Congress meant by the term "educational." The IRS has fully exercised that authority in Treas. Reg. § 1.501(c)(3)-1(d)(3), 26 CFR § 1.501(c)(3)-1(d)(3) (1982), . . . [text of regulation omitted. — Ed.].

I have little doubt that neither the "Fagin School for Pickpockets" nor a school training students for guerrilla warfare and terrorism in other countries would meet the definitions contained in the regulations.

[JUSTICE REHNQUIST traces the recent legislative history, arguing that it is dangerous to find "ratification through inaction" of the IRS decisions denying tax-exemption to racially discriminating institutions. — Ed.]

I have no disagreement with the Court's finding that there is a strong national policy in this country opposed to racial discrimination. I agree with the Court that Congress has the power to further this policy by denying § 501(c)(3) status to organizations that practice racial discrimination.[17] But as of yet Congress has failed to do so. Whatever the reasons for the failure, this Court should not legislate for Congress.[18]

Petitioners are each organized for the "instruction or training of the individual for the purpose of improving or developing his capabilities," 26 CFR § 1.501(c)(3)-1(d)(3) (1982), and thus are organized for "educational purposes" within the meaning of § 501(c)(3). Petitioners' nonprofit status is uncontested. There is no indication that either petitioner has been involved in lobbying activities or political campaigns. Therefore, it is my view that unless and until Congress affirmatively amends § 501(c)(3) to require more, the IRS is without authority to deny petitioners § 501(c)(3) status. For this reason, I would reverse the Court of Appeals.

---

[17] [3] I agree with the Court that such a requirement would not infringe on petitioners' First Amendment rights.

[18] [4] Because of its holding, the Court does not have to decide whether it would violate the equal protection component of the Fifth Amendment for Congress to grant § 501(c)(3) status to organizations that practice racial discrimination. I would decide that it does not. The statute is facially neutral; absent a showing of a discriminatory purpose, no equal protection violation is established. Washington v. Davis, 426 U.S. 229, 241–244 (1976).

Understanding *Bob Jones*

1.   The statute at stake in *Bob Jones University* (section 501(c)(3)) exempts from tax "corporations . . . organized and operated exclusively for religious, charitable, scientific, . . . literary, or educational purposes," provided that no net earnings inure to the benefit of any private individual and the organization respects certain limitations on its political activities.[19] The statute makes no reference to racial or other discrimination and, since it is phrased in the alternative, does not even require that an educational organization be "charitable" in nature to qualify for tax exemption. That being the case, what is the source of the court's position that an organization must behave in a manner consistent with public policy — and specifically must refrain from racial discrimination — to qualify as tax-exempt? Would the Congress in 1913, when the predecessor of section 501 was enacted, have insisted upon such a requirement? Or should the question be resolved by reference to what a well-informed, public-spirited member of Congress would do at the time the case was decided? Is Justice Rehnquist simply being crotchety by dissenting, or does he have a good argumentative point?

2.   In an omitted concurring opinion, Justice Powell argues that the "public benefit" standard would result in excessive conformity by tax-exempt institutions. What do you make of this argument? If the Government is providing (effectively) a tax subsidy to tax-exempt organizations, why doesn't it have the right to determine what sort of organizations will qualify? Or is there something different between tax expenditures and direct Government spending, which requires the former to take in a much wider range of institutions? Numerous organizations, notably churches and other religious bodies, qualify for tax exemption, although they do not (and constitutionally could not) receive direct governmental assistance. Is this a flaw in the system, or simply neutral tax policy?

3.   Toward the end of its opinion, the Court notes that Congress was aware that the IRS was revoking tax exemptions for racially discriminatory institutions and took no action to halt such revocations. According to the Court, this suggests that Congress has acquiesced to the IRS policy. Is this a convincing line of argument? Does Congress's failure to act suggest that it agreed with the IRS policy, or that it simply did not want to get involved in a messy, politically divisive issue? Is it relevant that the tax code is the subject of frequent legislation, giving Congress numerous chances to reverse IRS decisions, as opposed to a rarely amended statute?

4.   As a general matter, should the tax law be interpreted in the same way as other Federal statutes, or does it have unique features that require a special interpretive style? What are these special features, and what sort of interpretation (literal, figurative, etc.) do they generally call for?

A leading scholar on statutory interpretation, William Eskridge, has described *Bob Jones University* as an example of "dynamic" interpretation, in which a court

---

[19] Section 501 deals with the tax-exemption for an organization itself, while section 170 concerns the tax deduction for contributions to the organization. Many, but not all, organizations qualifying for tax-exemption under section 501 are also entitled to receive tax-deductible contributions under section 170, and the two sections share many parallel provisions.

construes a statute consistently with the society's prevailing values at the time of the decision, rather than the date of original enactment. While agreeing with the Court's holding, Eskridge calls for greater candor in acknowledging the dynamic nature of the decision and (what is essentially the same thing) the possibility that the meaning of a statute can change over the course of time:

William N. Eskridge, Jr., *Dynamic Statutory Interpretation*
135 U. PA. L. REV. 1479, 1479–82, 1547–49 (1987)[20]

Federal judges interpreting the Constitution typically consider not only the constitutional text and its historical background, but also its subsequent interpretational history, related constitutional developments, and current societal facts. Similarly, judges interpreting common law precedents normally consider not only the text of the precedents and their historical context, but also their subsequent history, related legal developments, and current societal context. In light of this, it is odd that many judges and commentators believe judges should consider only the text and historical context when interpreting statutes, the third main source of law. Statutes, however, should — like the Constitution and the common law — be interpreted "dynamically," that is, in light of their present societal, political, and legal context.

Traditional doctrine teaches that statutes should not be interpreted dynamically. Prevailing approaches to statutory interpretation treat statutes as static texts. Thus, the leading treatise states that "[f]or the interpretation of statutes, 'intent of the legislature' is the criterion that is most often cited." This "intentionalist" approach asks how the legislature originally intended the interpretive question to be answered, or would have intended the question to be answered had it thought about the issue when it passed the statute. A "modified intentionalist" approach uses the original purpose of the statute as a surrogate for original intent, especially when the latter is uncertain; the proper interpretation is the one that best furthers the purpose the legislature had in mind when it enacted the statute.

Theoretically, these "originalist" approaches to statutory interpretation assume that the legislature fixes the meaning of a statute on the date the statute is enacted. The implicit claim is that a legislator interpreting the statute at the time of enactment would render the same interpretation as a judge interpreting the same statute fifty years later. This implication seems counterintuitive. Indeed, the legal realists argued this point earlier in the century. For example, gaps and ambiguities exist in all statutes, typically concerning matters as to which there was little legislative deliberation and, hence, no clear intent. As society changes, adapts to the statute, and generates new variations of the problem which gave rise to the statute, the unanticipated gaps and ambiguities proliferate. In such circumstances, it seems sensible that "the quest is not properly for the sense originally intended by the statute, [or] for the sense sought originally to be put into it, but rather for the sense which can be quarried out of it in the light of the new situation." Moreover, as time passes, the legal and constitutional context of the statute may

---

change. Should not an interpreter "ask [her]self not only what the legislation means abstractly, or even on the basis of legislative history, but also what it ought to mean in terms of the needs and goals of our present day society[?]"

The purpose of this Article is to explore the thesis that statutes, like the Constitution and the common law, should be interpreted dynamically. Part I sets forth a cautious model of dynamic statutory interpretation. It uses specific examples of dynamic interpretation to show how the model works. The Article accepts the traditional assumptions that a functioning representative democracy exists in our polity, that the legislature is the primary lawmaking body, and that in many cases statutory language will be sufficiently determinate to resolve a given case. Even under these conventional assumptions, however, original legislative expectations should not always control statutory meaning. This is especially true when the statute is old and generally phrased and the societal or legal context of the statute has changed in material ways.

Part II demonstrates that no good reason compels adherence to traditional originalist doctrine. Three major types of arguments have been invoked in favor of statutory intentionalism or modified intentionalism: (1) the formalist argument that the Constitution vests Congress with the exclusive power to create law or policy, leaving courts with no role but to carry out the intent (or purpose) of Congress; (2) the economic argument that statutes are contracts between interest groups and legislatures and as such must be enforced by judges (the "agents" of the legislature) according to their original terms and intent; and (3) the legal process argument that it is illegitimate for nonelected judges to make policy in a majoritarian political system by expanding upon the original meaning of statutes. None of these arguments, however, justifies unexceptioned statutory intentionalism when circumstances have changed and the statutory language is not determinate.

Part III describes the advantages of the proposed model of dynamic statutory interpretation over other current approaches to statutory interpretation. The Article argues that this model depicts what the Supreme Court typically does when it interprets statutes and that the model's descriptive power is superior to that of the models traditionally invoked by the Court — intentionalism and the progressive modified intentionalism of Henry Hart's and Albert Sacks's legal process materials. I do not contend that the model here is always, or usually, easier to apply than the intentionalist or modified intentionalist approaches. I only contend that it explains the results of the Supreme Court's cases better and is a more candid analysis of what the Court does. Finally, the Article contrasts my dynamic interpretation model with the more ambitious approach posited by Professor Ronald Dworkin. Dworkin, too, argues for dynamic interpretation, in which statutes change as "law's integrity" develops and changes. My approach is more cautious and conventional than that of Dworkin. He envisions judges performing the truly herculean task of reading magisterial coherence into the law. I envision judges as diplomats, whose ordering authority is severely limited but who must often update their orders to meet changing circumstances.

* * *

Bob Jones is a classic case in which the Hart and Sacks approach is invoked by the Court as a substitute for careful analysis. The Court obviously created new law in this case, going well beyond what Congress had done. Can it be justified? The best justification is the dynamic, deliberative one suggested by the concurring opinion of Justice Powell. The statutory language is open-ended and the original history of the statute is of little relevance because circumstances have changed radically. Hence, the evolutive perspective is critical. Our current attitudes about giving tax breaks to racially discriminatory institutions are decisively influenced by the public deliberation in which we have engaged since *Brown* and the various civil rights statutes. To the extent we have policymaking discretion, we should exercise it to penalize discrimination. Probably for this reason, the Internal Revenue Service, the agency charged with implementing section 501, adopted the antidiscrimination policy in 1970, which triggered a far-reaching policy debate in Congress during the 1970's. Ultimately, Congress rejected all efforts to overturn the agency's action and Justice Powell found some evidence that informed opinion embraced the agency's new interpretation. The Court's result capped a decade of deliberation on this public issue by putting the antidiscrimination exception in the statute.

One may disagree with this dynamic policy analysis, but it is more edifying than the obfuscating Hart and Sacks approach to the statute posited by the Court. At least it is honest: the Court's commitment to the public value of a nondiscriminatory society is important enough to influence its interpretation of an ambiguous statute. Congress may compromise that public value, within certain constitutional limits, but until it does so the Court should continue the uniquely public deliberative process that it started in *Brown*.

The broader point to be drawn from this analysis is that the Supreme Court often purports to rely on original legislative purposes in interpreting statutes, while in fact using the Hart and Sacks purpose analysis to bend statutory language to satisfy current policy goals. This typically leads to a sharp dissenting opinion that dredges up historical background material to disprove the Court's assertions about the historical understanding. The Court, in turn, often responds with its own historical material. What is too often lost in such an exchange of historical arcana is a careful analysis of the statutory text, the evolving policies currently of importance to the statute, and even the facts of the case. What I urge — and what the Court often displays — is candor about the marginal importance of the historical perspective. Then, rigorous deliberation can be given to the pertinent policy choices that the Court must make.

* * *

Do you agree with Eskridge's critique, and with the broader notion that statutes should be interpreted according to contemporary values? Is the gauging of popular sentiment an appropriate role for the courts, or is it better left to Congress and other elected officials? Suppose (not too fantastically) that Congress became more conservative and began to be less concerned about discrimination by private institutions. Do you think we would find Justice Rehnquist more willing to engage in dynamic interpretation, and Eskridge and other liberals less so?

An important question in *Bob Jones* is the nature of the public benefit that an organization is required to provide in order to qualify for tax exemption. This issue frequently expresses itself in a clash between an essentialist view, in which certain activities (education, health care, etc.) are considered inherently charitable in nature, and a more contextual approach in which one must examine the recipients of the services as well as the nature of the services provided to them. The law leans toward the former approach, although with elements of both aspects present, depending upon what kind of activity and organization is involved.

The following items consider this problem in the context of health care and hospitals, where it has been the most controversial. These materials are interesting, both for the specific issues they involve and for the inevitable clash of viewpoints between the tax and health policy worldviews that they represent. Try to get beyond the standing and other procedural matters in these cases and focus on the underlying policy issues.

Revenue Ruling 69-545
1969-2 C.B. 117 (1969)

Examples illustrate whether a nonprofit hospital claiming exemption under section 501(c)(3) of the Code is operated to serve a public rather than a private interest; Revenue Ruling 56-185 modified.

Advice has been requested whether the two nonprofit hospitals described below qualify for exemption from Federal income tax under section 501(c)(3) of the Internal Revenue Code of 1954. The articles of organization of both hospitals meet the organizational requirements of (3)-1 section 1.501(c)(3)-1(b) of the Income Tax Regulations, including the limitation of the organizations' purposes to those described in section 501(c)(3) of the Code and the dedication of their assets to such purposes.

Situation 1. Hospital *A* is a 250-bed community hospital. Its board of trustees is composed of prominent citizens in the community. Medical staff privileges in the hospital are available to all qualified physicians in the area, consistent with the size and nature of its facilities. The hospital has 150 doctors on its active staff and 200 doctors on its courtesy staff. It also owns a medical office building on its premises with space for 60 doctors. Any member of its active medical staff has the privilege of leasing available office space. Rents are set at rates comparable to those of other commercial buildings in the area.

The hospital operates a full time emergency room and no one requiring emergency care is denied treatment. The hospital otherwise ordinarily limits admissions to those who can pay the cost of their hospitalization, either themselves, or through private health insurance, or with the aid of public programs such as Medicare. Patients who cannot meet the financial requirements for admission are ordinarily referred to another hospital in the community that does serve indigent patients.

The hospital usually ends each year with an excess of operating receipts over operating disbursements from its hospital operations. Excess funds are generally applied to expansion and replacement of existing facilities and equipment, amortization of indebtedness, improvement in patient care, and medical training, education, and research.

Situation 2. Hospital B is a 60-bed general hospital which was originally owned by five doctors. The owners formed a nonprofit organization and sold their interests in the hospital to the organization at fair market value. The board of trustees of the organization consists of the five doctors, their accountant, and their lawyer. The five doctors also comprise the hospital's medical committee and thereby control the selection and the admission of other doctors to the medical staff. During its first five years of operations, only four other doctors have been granted staff privileges at the hospital. The applications of a number of qualified doctors in the community have been rejected.

Hospital admission is restricted to patients of doctors holding staff privileges. Patients of the five original physicians have accounted for a large majority of all hospital admissions over the years. The hospital maintains an emergency room, but on a relatively inactive basis, and primarily for the convenience of the patients of the staff doctors. The local ambulance services have been instructed by the hospital to take emergency cases to other hospitals in the area. The hospital follows the policy of ordinarily limiting admissions to those who can pay the cost of the services rendered. The five doctors comprising the original medical staff have continued to maintain their offices in the hospital since its sale to the nonprofit organization. The rental paid is less than that of comparable office space in the vicinity. No office space is available for any of the other staff members.

Section 501(c)(3) of the Code provides for exemption from Federal income tax of organizations organized and operated exclusively for charitable, scientific, or educational purposes, no part of the net earnings of which inures to the benefit of any private shareholder or individual.

Section 1.501(c)(3)-1(d)(1)(ii) of the regulations provides that an organization is not organized or operated exclusively for any purpose set forth in section 501(c)(3) of the Code unless it serves a public rather than a private interest.

Section 1.501(c)(3)-1(d)(2) of the regulations states that the term "charitable" is used in section 501(c)(3) of the Code in its generally accepted legal sense.

To qualify for exemption from Federal income tax under section 501(c)(3) of the Code, a nonprofit hospital must be organized and operated exclusively in furtherance of some purpose considered "charitable" in the generally accepted legal sense of that term, and the hospital may not be operated, directly or indirectly, for the benefit of private interests.

In the general law of charity, the promotion of health is considered to be a charitable purpose. RESTATEMENT (SECOND), TRUSTS, sec. 368 and sec. 372; IV SCOTT ON TRUSTS (3rd ed. 1967), sec. 368 and sec. 372. A nonprofit organization whose purpose and activity are providing hospital care is promoting health and may, therefore, qualify as organized and operated in furtherance of a charitable purpose. If it meets the other requirements of section 501(c)(3) of the Code, it will qualify for exemption from Federal income tax under section 501(a).

Since the purpose and activity of Hospital A, apart from its related educational and research activities and purposes, are providing hospital care on a nonprofit basis for members of its community, it is organized and operated in furtherance of a purpose considered "charitable" in the generally accepted legal sense of that term. The promotion of health, like the relief of poverty and the advancement of education and religion, is one of the purposes in the general law of charity that is deemed beneficial to the community as a whole even though the class of beneficiaries eligible to receive a direct benefit from its activities does not include all members of the community, such as indigent members of the community, provided that the class is not so small that its relief is not of benefit to the community. RESTATEMENT (SECOND), TRUSTS, sec. 368, comment (b) and sec. 372, comments (b) and (c); IV SCOTT ON TRUSTS (3rd ed. 1967), sec. 368 and sec. 372.2. By operating an emergency room open to all persons and by providing hospital care for all those persons in the community able to pay the cost thereof either directly or through third party reimbursement, Hospital A is promoting the health of a class of persons that is broad enough to benefit the community.

The fact that Hospital A operates at an annual surplus of receipts over disbursements does not preclude its exemption. By using its surplus funds to improve the quality of patient care, expand its facilities, and advance its medical training, education, and research programs, the hospital is operating in furtherance of its exempt purposes.

Furthermore, Hospital A is operated to serve a public rather than a private interest. Control of the hospital rests with its board of trustees, which is composed of independent civic leaders. The hospital maintains an open medical staff, with privileges available to all qualified physicians. Members of its active medical staff have the privilege of leasing available space in its medical building. (See Rev. Rul. 69-464, page 132, this Bulletin.) It operates an active and generally accessible emergency room. These factors indicate that the use and control of Hospital A are for the benefit of the public and that no part of the income of the organization is inuring to the benefit of any private individual nor are any private interest being served.

Accordingly, it is held that Hospital A is exempt from Federal income tax under section 501(c)(3) of the Code.

Hospital B is also providing hospital care. However, in order to qualify under section 501(c)(3) of the Code, an organization must be organized and operated *exclusively* for one or more of the purposes set forth in that section. Hospital B was initially established as a proprietary institution operated for the benefit of its owners. Although its ownership has been transferred to a nonprofit organization, the hospital has continued to operate for the private benefit of its original owners who exercise control over the hospital through the board of trustees and the medical committee. They have used their control to restrict the number of doctors admitted to the medical staff, to enter into favorable rental agreements with the hospital, and to limit emergency room care and hospital admission substantially to their own patients. These facts indicate that the hospital is operated for the private benefit of its original owners, rather than for the exclusive benefit of the public. *See*

Sonora Community Hospital v. Commissioner, 46 T.C. 519 (1966), *aff'd.* 397 F.2d 814 (1968).

Accordingly, it is held that Hospital *B* does not qualify for exemption from Federal income tax under section 501(c)(3) of the Code. In considering whether a nonprofit hospital claiming such exemption is operated to serve a private benefit, the Service will weigh all of the relevant facts and circumstances in each case. The absence of particular factors set forth above or the presence of other factors will not necessarily be determinative.

Even though an organization considers itself within the scope of *Situation* 1 of this Revenue Ruling, it must file an application on Form 1023, Exemption Application, in order to be recognized by the Service as exempt under section 501(c)(3) of the Code. The application should be filed with the District Director of Internal Revenue for the district in which is located the principal place of business or principal office of the organization. See section 1.501(a)-1 of the regulations.

Revenue Ruling 56-185, C.B. 1956-1, 202, sets forth requirements for exemption of hospitals under section 501(c)(3) more restrictive than those contained in this Revenue Ruling with respect to caring for patients without charge or at rates below cost. In addition, the fourth requirement of Revenue Ruling 56-185 is ambiguous in that it can be read as implying that the possibility of "shareholders" or "members" sharing in the assets of a hospital upon its dissolution will not preclude exemption of the hospital as a charity described in section 501(c)(3) of the Code. Section 1.501(c)(3)-1(b)(4) of the regulations promulgated subsequent to Revenue Ruling 56-185 makes it clear, however, that an absolute dedication of assets to charity is a precondition to exemption under section 501(c)(3) of the Code.

Revenue Ruling 56-185 is hereby modified to remove therefrom the requirements relating to caring for patients without charge or at rates below cost. Furthermore, requirement four has been modified by section 1.501(c)(3)-1(b)(4) of the regulations.

Together with an interesting example of the law of tax-exempt organizations, the problem of "charitable" hospitals provides a fascinating example of tax procedure. In *Simon v. Eastern Kentucky Welfare Rights Organization*, 426 U.S. 26 (1976), a public interest organization brought suit against the IRS, arguing that Revenue Ruling 69-545 was inconsistent with the Internal Revenue Code because it permitted tax exemption to hospitals that offered only emergency room services to indigent people. The Supreme Court dismissed the claim, finding that the plaintiffs, whose own tax status was in question, lacked standing to pursue the claim. While the holding is understandable on the merits — the Court was plainly unenthusiastic about a spate of "public interest" cases challenging IRS policy with regard to other taxpayers — the results are troubling on several levels. Particularly dubious is the Court's assertion that plaintiffs had demonstrated only a "speculative" link between the Rev. Rul. 69-545 and various hospitals' provision (or nonprovision) of indigent health care. If the effect of the ruling was so speculative, why did tax-exempt hospitals lobby so forcefully in favor of its adoption? Moreover, if neither public or private litigants have standing to challenge the ruling, how can it possibly be challenged? Note that Rev. Rul. 69-545 specifically modified a preexisting revenue ruling (56-185) to eliminate the requirement of caring for patients at a reduced cost, and was subsequently modified to eliminate even the emergency room requirement in some cases. Rev. Rul. 83-157, 1983-2 C.B. 94. Why do you think these things happened, and who do you think was most likely to benefit (and lose) as a result of the change?

While hospitals have tended to be rather forceful in defending their tax exemptions, the new wave of health maintenance organizations (HMOs), which are required or encouraged by many employers as an alternative to traditional health insurance plans, have not always met with equivalent success. The following case considers this issue.

GEISINGER HEALTH PLAN v. COMMISSIONER
United States Court of Appeals, Third Circuit
985 F.2d 1210 (1993)

LEWIS, CIRCUIT JUDGE.

The Commissioner of the Internal Revenue Service ("Commissioner" or "IRS") appeals from a Tax Court decision granting appellee Geisinger Health Plan ("GHP") tax-exempt status under 26 U.S.C. § 501(c)(3). This case requires us to decide whether a health maintenance organization (an "HMO") which serves a predominantly rural population, enrolls some Medicare subscribers, and which intends to subsidize some needy subscribers but, at present, serves only its paying subscribers, qualifies for exemption from federal income taxation under 26 U.S.C. § 501(c)(3). We hold that it does not.

We will remand this case to the Tax Court on a subsidiary issue, however. On remand, the Tax Court is to determine whether GHP should be considered an integral part of the health care system to which it belongs so as to qualify for tax-exempt status based upon the status of entities related to it.

This court's review of the Tax Court's decision, involving as it does a determination of the purpose of an entity applying for tax-exempt status based upon stipulated facts, is plenary. *Presbyterian and Reformed Publishing Co. v. Commissioner*, 743 F.2d 148, 158 n.9 (3d Cir. 1984). The Tax Court had jurisdiction over this case based upon 26 U.S.C. §§ 7428(a)(1)(A) and 7442, and this court's jurisdiction is based upon 26 U.S.C. § 7482(a)(1).

I.

GHP, which qualifies as an HMO under both Pennsylvania and federal law, operates as part of a system of health care organizations in northeastern and north central Pennsylvania (the "Geisinger System"). Under Pennsylvania law, an HMO is "an organized system which combines the delivery and financing of health care and which provides basic health services to voluntarily enrolled subscribers for a fixed prepaid fee." Pa. Stat. Ann. tit. 40, § 1552 (Supp. 1991). *See also* 42 U.S.C. § 300e (1991). GHP was formed as a nonprofit corporation in 1984 and, by March

31, 1988, had enrolled 4,396 individuals and 448 groups (accounting for another 66,441 individual subscribers).

The Geisinger System consists of GHP and eight other nonprofit entities. All are involved in some way in promoting health care in 27 counties in northeastern and northcentral Pennsylvania. They include: the Geisinger Foundation (the "Foundation"); Geisinger Medical Center ("GMC"); the Geisinger Clinic (the "Clinic"); Geisinger Wyoming Valley Medical Center ("GWV"); Marworth; Geisinger System Services ("GSS") and two professional liability trusts. Each of these entities is exempt from federal income taxation under one or more sections of the Internal Revenue Code (the "Code").

In order to provide cost-effective delivery of health care to areas it had identified as medically underserved, GMC experimented with a pilot prepaid health plan between 1972 and 1985. The results were sufficiently favorable that the Geisinger System formed GHP to provide its own prepaid health plan. GHP's service area encompasses 17 predominantly rural counties within the area served by the Geisinger System. As of November 30, 1987, according to a finding of a bureau of the federal Department of Health and Human Services, 23 percent of GHP's subscribers resided in medically underserved areas while 65 percent resided in counties containing medically underserved areas.

GHP's articles of incorporation provide that it was incorporated "for the purpose of conducting exclusively charitable, scientific and educational activities within the meaning of Section 501(c)(3) of the Internal Revenue Code," and list a number of specific purposes relating to the provision of health care through a prepaid fee arrangement. Its articles also prohibit GHP from lobbying, participating in political campaigns and engaging in activity that would invalidate its tax-exempt status. No earnings or profit may inure to the benefit of its members, directors, officers or other private persons; upon its dissolution, GHP's board of directors must pay any assets that remain to a tax-exempt charitable organization.

Any person, whether or not a resident of Pennsylvania, may serve on GHP's board of directors. GHP's president and the senior officers of the Geisinger Foundation, the Geisinger System's umbrella organization, automatically serve as directors. The remaining directors are elected by GHP's members, who can be directors themselves. Pennsylvania law requires that at least one-third of GHP's directors be GHP subscribers.

GHP has two types of subscribers. First, it is open to all adult individuals who reside in its service area and satisfactorily complete a routine questionnaire regarding their medical history. From its inception through June 30, 1987, GHP accepted all but 11 percent of its individual applicants. Second, it enrolls group subscribers. Any individual who resides in GHP's service area and belongs to a group of at least 100 eligible enrollees may enroll as a group subscriber without completing a health questionnaire. Individual applicants belonging to groups of less than 100 eligible enrollees must usually complete the questionnaire required of individual subscribers, however.

GHP describes itself as "providing health services." In reality, it contracts with other entities in the Geisinger System (at least one of which will contract with physicians from outside the Geisinger System) to provide services to GHP's subscribers. It also contracts with entities such as pharmacies to provide medical and hospital services to its subscribers in exchange for compensation. Under the terms of these contracts, GHP reimburses the hospitals and clinics by paying a negotiated per diem charge for inpatient services and a discounted percentage of billed charges for outpatient services. For the fiscal year ended June 30, 1987, the Clinic and GWV provided 80 percent of all hospital services to GHP subscribers. The remaining 20 percent were provided by other hospitals.

All physician services are provided to GHP subscribers pursuant to a contract between GHP and the Clinic. The contract requires the Clinic to open its emergency rooms to all GHP subscribers, regardless of ability to pay, just as the Clinic's emergency rooms are open to all members of the public, regardless of ability to pay. The Clinic will contract with unaffiliated physicians to provide required services, but for the year ended June 30, 1987, more than 84 percent of the physician services which the Clinic provided to GHP's subscribers were performed by physicians who were employees of the Clinic. GHP compensates the Clinic for the physicians' services by paying a fixed amount per subscriber.

Generally, both GHP's group and individual subscribers are required to pay for hospital services on the basis of a community rating system. This system balances high-risk subscribers against low-risk subscribers. The subscribers must also make copayments for certain goods and services. Individual subscribers pay an additional amount which group subscribers do not pay. This amount covers the additional costs associated with handling individual subscriberships. If a subscriber fails to pay an amount due to GHP or fails to make a required copayment, the subscriber's coverage is terminated upon 30 days written notice, unless payment is made within the 30 days.

GHP has adopted a subsidized dues program which has not yet been implemented. The program would establish a fund comprised of charitable donations and operating funds to subsidize GHP subscribers who are unable to pay their premiums. The fund would, in GHP's view, "add to the security of [subscribers], any of whom may at some time suffer financial misfortune due to loss of employment, physical or mental disability or other causes beyond their control and which impute no dishonor to the [subscriber]." Appendix at 165. Although the program makes reference to subsidizing people who are already subscribers, GHP's submissions indicate that it also intends to admit people who require subsidization at the time they apply.

Despite GHP's initial projection that it would fund the program by raising $125,000 in contributions over its first three years of operation, it has been unable to do so, it claims, because potential donors cannot be assured that contributions will be deductible on their federal income tax returns until GHP receives recognition of tax-exempt status under section 501(c)(3). GHP has likewise been unable to support the program with operating funds because it operated at a loss from its inception through the time the record in this case closed.

GHP enrolls some subscribers who are covered by Medicare and Medicaid. As of March 31, 1988, it had enrolled 1,064 Medicare recipients at a reduced rate on a wraparound basis, meaning that it will cover what Medicare does not. It also has enrolled a small number of Medicaid recipients in a few exceptional situations. Generally, however, GHP cannot offer coverage to Medicaid recipients until and unless it contracts with the Pennsylvania Department of Welfare, which administers Pennsylvania's Medicaid program. GHP has negotiated with the department to obtain such a contract, but efforts to reach agreement have thus far been unsuccessful.

II.

Shortly after its incorporation, GHP applied to the IRS for recognition of exemption. The Commissioner ruled that GHP was not exempt because (1) it was not operated exclusively for exempt purposes under section 501(c)(3); and (2) it could not vicariously qualify for exemption as an "integral part" of the Geisinger System.

GHP filed suit in Tax Court, requesting a declaratory judgment that it was exempt. The parties submitted the case to the Tax Court on a stipulated administrative record. The Tax Court reversed the Commissioner's ruling in an opinion dated December 30, 1991, which was made final by an order dated February 20, 1992. On May 15, 1992, the Commissioner appealed.

III.

The first issue is whether GHP, standing alone, is entitled to tax-exempt status under section 501(c)(3). The Code provides in part:

> (a) Exemption from taxation. — An organization described in subsection (c) . . . shall be exempt from taxation. . . .

* * *

> [(c)](3) Corporations . . . organized and operated exclusively for religious, charitable, scientific, testing for public safety, literary, or educational purposes, . . . no part of the net earnings of which inures to the benefit of any private shareholder or individual, no substantial part of the activities of which is carrying on propaganda, or otherwise attempting, to influence legislation . . . and which does not participate in, or intervene in . . . any political campaign on behalf of (or in opposition to) any candidate for public office.

26 U.S.C. § 501 (Supp. 1992). Taxpayers claiming exemption bear the burden of proving entitlement to exemption. *Living Faith, Inc. v. Commissioner*, 950 F.2d 365, 370 (7th Cir. 1991) (citing cases).

An organization must be both organized and operated exclusively for a charitable purpose to qualify for exemption under section 501(c)(3). IRS regulations provide:

(a) Organizational and operational tests. (1) In order to be exempt as an organization described in section 501(c)(3), an organization must be both organized and operated exclusively for one or more of the purposes specified in such section. If an organization fails to meet either the organizational test or the operational test, it is not exempt.

Organizations desire section 501(c)(3) status because it facilitates fundraising. An organization may qualify as tax-exempt under several sections of the Code. *See* 26 U.S.C. §§ 501(c)(1)–(25). Section 501(c)(3) status, however, carries with it the concomitant benefit of encouraging donors to contribute since such contributions are deductible for purposes of computing their federal income tax and estate and gift tax liability. *Compare* 26 U.S.C. § 170(c) *with* 26 U.S.C. § 501(c). *See Bob Jones University v. United States*, 461 U.S. 574, 577–78 nn.1 & 2 (1983).

Generally, "charitable exemptions are justified on the basis that the exempt entity confers a public benefit — a benefit which the society or the community may not itself choose or be able to provide, or which supplements and advances the work of public institutions already supported by tax revenues." *Bob Jones*, 461 U.S. at 591 (footnote omitted). Thus, charitable exemptions from income taxation constitute a quid pro quo: the public is willing to relieve an organization from paying income taxes because the organization is providing a benefit to the public.

The parties' dispute flows directly from an application of the second prong of the test set forth in the IRS regulations, the so-called "operational test." This test mandates that, in addition to being organized exclusively for exempt purposes, GHP must be operated exclusively for exempt purposes to qualify for tax-exempt status under section 501(c)(3). *See Presbyterian*, 743 F.2d at 154.

An organization is operated exclusively for exempt purposes "only if it engages primarily in activities which accomplish one or more of such exempt purposes specified in section 501(c)(3). An organization will not be so regarded if more than an insubstantial part of its activities is not in furtherance of an exempt purpose." 26 C.F.R. § 1.501(c)(3)-1(c). *See also Better Business Bureau v. United States*, 326 U.S. 279, 283 (1945) (when construing a similar provision of the Social Security Act, "the presence of a single [non-exempt] purpose, . . . substantial in nature, will destroy the exemption.").

As we stated in Presbyterian,

> Any exploration of unarticulated or illicit purpose necessarily involves courts in difficult and murky problems. When the legality of an action depends not upon its surface manifestation but upon the undisclosed motivation of the actor, similar acts can lead to diametrically opposite legal consequences.

* * *

The difficulties inherent in any legal standard predicated upon the subjective intent of an actor are further compounded when that actor is a corporate entity. . . . In reviewing the decision of the Tax Court . . . , therefore, the question is whether the proper indicia were relied upon in concluding that [the entity applying for exemption] was animated by a purpose alien to the statutory exemption of § 501(c)(3).

Presbyterian, 743 F.2d at 155. The only guidance offered in the IRS regulations is found at 26 C.F.R. § 501(c)(3)-1(d)(ii). *Id.* at 156 n.6. This regulation provides that even if the organization seeking exemption ostensibly serves a charitable purpose, it "is not organized or operated exclusively for one or more of the [listed exempt] purposes unless it serves a public rather than a private interest."

GHP argues that it qualifies for exemption because it serves the charitable purpose of promoting health in the communities it serves. There are no published revenue rulings and only one previously litigated case addressing whether an HMO may qualify for exemption under section 501(c)(3). The sole case on this issue is a Tax Court case, *Sound Health Association v. Commissioner*, 71 T.C. 158 (1978), acq. 1981-2 C.B. 2.

Thus, we face what is apparently a case of first impression among the United States Courts of Appeals. Under these circumstances, our task necessarily involves both outlining the proper test to be applied in determining whether an HMO may qualify for tax-exempt status and applying that test to the facts at hand.

A. The Appropriate Test

In *Sound Health*, the Tax Court applied the law pertaining to nonprofit hospitals as charitable entities in measuring an HMO's claim for exemption. Although this case does not involve a hospital, neither the IRS nor GHP argue that this distinction rendered inappropriate the Tax Court's reliance upon *Sound Health* in examining GHP's request for exemption. To the contrary, in fact, the IRS concedes that GHP's stated purpose, like a hospital's stated purpose, is to promote health; it simply argues that *Sound Health* and the hospital precedents require more than mere promotion of health in order to qualify for tax exemption. The IRS argues that the relevant precedents require at least some "indicia of charity" in the form of serving the public and providing some services free of charge.

While we are not bound by any approach taken by the Tax Court, we find no reason to conclude that the Tax Court erred in applying hospital precedent to its analysis of GHP's exempt status. Accordingly, in light of the parties' and the Tax Court's reliance on the law regarding the tax-exempt status of nonprofit hospitals in formulating the test to be applied to HMOs seeking exemption under section 501(c)(3), we will measure GHP's tax-exempt status against that standard. In doing so, we recognize that courts are to give weight to IRS revenue rulings but may disregard them if they conflict with the statute they purport to interpret or its legislative history, or if they are otherwise unreasonable. *Threlkeld v. Commissioner*, 848 F.2d 81, 84 (6th Cir. 1988); *Brook, Inc. v. Commissioner*, 799 F.2d 833, 836 n.4 (2d Cir. 1986); *Strick Corp. v. United States*, 714 F.2d 1194, 1197 (3d Cir. 1983); *Carle Foundation v. United States*, 611 F.2d 1192, 1195 (7th Cir. 1979).

1. Nonprofit Hospitals as Tax-Exempt Entities

Initially, the IRS required that nonprofit hospitals provide some free care in order to qualify for tax exemption under section 501(c)(3). *See* Rev. Rul. 56-185, 1956

C.B. 202. This reflected an early view that hospitals and other health care institutions were only exempt as "charitable" if they both provided relief to the poor and promoted health. *See* Mancino, *Income Tax Exemption of the Contemporary Nonprofit Hospital*, 32 St. Louis U.L.J. 1015, 1038 (1988) (hereinafter "Mancino").

In 1969, however, the IRS modified that requirement and established an alternative "community benefit" standard for hospitals seeking exempt status. Thus, in Rev. Rul. 69-545, the IRS modified Rev. Rul. 56-185 to remove "the requirements relating to caring for patients without charge or at rates below cost." Rev. Rul. 69-545, 1969-2 C.B. 117. It did so in the context of a hospital which provided emergency care to all, regardless of ability to pay.

In Rev. Rul. 69-545, the IRS stated that "the promotion of health is a charitable purpose." Indeed, the word "charitable" is used in its generally accepted legal sense in section 501(c)(3), 26 C.F.R. § 1.501(c)(3)-1(d)(2), and promotion of health has long been considered a charitable purpose under the traditional law of charitable trusts. *See Sound Health*, 71 T.C. at 178; *see generally* Bromberg, *The Charitable Hospital*, 20 Cath. U. L. Rev. 237 (1970) (hereinafter "Bromberg").

By issuing Rev. Rul. 69-545, however, the IRS did not abolish entirely the requirement that nonprofit hospitals provide free care. Shortly after it was issued, the United States Court of Appeals for the District of Columbia Circuit held that Rev. Rul. 69-545 did not overrule Rev. Rul. 56-185, but that it

> simply provided an alternative method whereby a nonprofit hospital can qualify as a tax exempt charitable organization. That method entails the operation of an emergency room open to all regardless of their ability to pay and providing hospital services to those able to pay the cost either directly or through third party reimbursement. Thus, to qualify as a tax exempt charitable organization, a hospital must still provide services to indigents.

Eastern Kentucky Welfare Rights Organization v. Simon, 165 U.S. App. D.C. 239, 506 F.2d 1278, 1289 (D.C. Cir. 1974), *vacated on other grounds*, 426 U.S. 26 (1976). *See also Sound Health*, 71 T.C. at 181 n.9.

In 1983, the IRS went a step further, issuing Rev. Rul. 83-157, in which it ruled that a nonprofit hospital need not even maintain an emergency room open to all, regardless of ability to pay, if doing so would result in needless duplication of services in the area. This ruling made clear, however, that other "significant factors" demonstrating that the hospital operated "exclusively to benefit the community" must be present to dispense with the requirement that the hospital need not maintain an open emergency room. Rev. Rul. 83-157, 1983-2 C.B. 94. But the ruling did not provide complete illumination; it did not explain, for example, what was meant by the word "benefit" or, more importantly for purposes of this appeal, who or what would constitute the "community." There have been no further pronouncements in the form of revenue rulings or regulations.

In sum, no clear test has emerged to apply to nonprofit hospitals seeking tax exemptions. Instead, a nonprofit hospital will qualify for tax-exempt status if it primarily benefits the community. One way to qualify is to provide emergency room services without regard to patients' ability to pay; another is to provide free care to indigents. A hospital may also benefit the community by serving those who pay their bills through public programs such as Medicaid or Medicare. For the most part, however, hospitals must meet a flexible "community benefit" test based upon a variety of indicia.[21]

2. HMOs as Tax-Exempt Entities

Overlaid against this background is *Sound Health*. In *Sound Health*, the Tax Court applied the hospital precedents in ruling that an HMO was exempt from taxation.

The *Sound Health* HMO resembled GHP in many ways. Its articles of incorporation listed a number of charitable purposes relating to the promotion of health. Like GHP's subscribers, its subscribers paid for services based upon a community rating system, and a subsidized dues program assisted those who could not afford subscribership. Subscribers also had to satisfy eligibility requirements similar to GHP's. *Sound Health*, 71 T.C. at 168–69, 172–73.

Unlike GHP, however, the *Sound Health* HMO provided health care services itself rather than simply arranging for others to provide them to its subscribers.[22] It also employed doctors, health care providers and medical personnel who were not affiliated with the HMO to provide health care to its subscribers. Significantly, the *Sound Health* HMO provided services to both subscribers and members of the general public through an outpatient clinic which it operated and at which it treated all emergency patients, subscribers or not, and regardless of ability to pay. *Id.* at 172. It also adjusted rates for and provided some free care to patients who were not subscribers. It offered public educational programs regarding health.

The court described the IRS' approach to tax exemptions for health care providers, as embodied in the hospital precedents, as reflecting a 'community benefit' approach. A charity will benefit the community if the class served is not so small that its relief is not of benefit to the community. This concept has been stated as follows:

> A trust is not a charitable trust if the persons who are to benefit are not of a sufficiently large or indefinite class so that the community is interested

---

[21] [13] *See generally* Mancino, 32 St. Louis U. L.J. at 1073; Bromberg, 20 Cath. U. L. Rev. at 248, 257–58 (Rev. Rul. 69-545 set forth an "existential requirement designed to make certain that the charitable hospital does, in fact, benefit the community").

[22] [4] GHP is, in fact, a different type of HMO than the HMO in *Sound Health*. HMOs had traditionally owned or provided hospital services themselves for a set, prepaid fee. In the late 1970's and early 1980's, however, Individual Practice Association (IPA) HMOs proliferated. "Unlike the traditional group practice or staff model HMOs, IPA-type HMOs do not directly own or provide hospital services. Rather, they arrange for the provision of hospital services by contracting with existing hospitals on a fee for service, capitation, per diem, or other basis." Mancino, 32 St. Louis U. L.J. at 1034. GHP appears to fall within the IPA-HMO category.

Also in the 1980's, nonprofit hospitals themselves began to form, purchase and contract with alternative delivery systems such as HMOs to vertically integrate and to maintain control over patient admissions. Mancino, 32 St. Louis U. L.J. at 1035. The Geisinger System's formation of GHP fits perfectly into this pattern.

in the enforcement of the trust. This is true even though the purpose of the trust is to promote health. . . .

The requirement that the community must benefit from a charity's activities has, as its natural corollary, that private interests must not so benefit in any substantial degree.

Sound Health, 71 T.C. at 181, *quoting* 4A SCOTT, SCOTT ON TRUSTS, § 372.2 at 2897.

The *Sound Health* court went to great lengths to find a benefit to the community rather than simply a benefit to the HMO's subscribers. It rejected the argument that the HMO at issue benefited only its subscribers, finding:

The most important feature of the Association's [subscribership] form of organization is that the class of persons eligible for [subscribership], and hence eligible to benefit from the Association's activities, is practically unlimited. The class of possible [subscribers] of the Association is, for all practical purposes, the class of members of the community itself. The major barrier to [subscribership] is lack of money, but a subsidized dues program demonstrates that even this barrier is not intended to be absolute. . . . It is safe to say that the class of persons potentially benefitted [sic] by the Association is not so small that its relief is of no benefit to the community.

Id. at 185.

As we have observed, however, the court listed several factors in addition to open subscribership as indications that the *Sound Health* HMO was operated for charitable purposes. Chief among these were the HMO's operation of an emergency room open to all persons, subscribers or not, and regardless of ability to pay; rendering some free care to both subscribers and those who did not subscribe; conducting research; and offering an educational program. *Id.* at 184. GHP refers to these as "marketing techniques," but, as the *Sound Health* court noted, the HMO benefited the community by engaging in these activities.

Thus, the *Sound Health* court did not entirely dispense with the requirement that an entity seeking tax exemption must benefit the community, either by providing services to those who cannot afford to pay or otherwise. *Sound Health* was decided before Rev. Rul. 83-157 was issued, but provision of emergency care was only one of the factors relied upon in holding that the HMO was exempt from taxation under section 501(c)(3). The HMO in *Sound Health* demonstrated that it benefited the community in several ways beyond merely providing emergency services regardless of ability to pay.

3. The Resulting Test

In administrative proceedings in this case, the IRS contended that GHP had to meet a strict, fourteen-factor test based upon the facts of *Sound Health* in order to qualify for tax-exempt status. Upon review, we cannot agree that any strict, multi-factor test is appropriate when determining whether an HMO qualifies for tax-exempt status under section 501(c)(3). Rather, the determination must be based upon the totality of the circumstances, with an eye toward discerning whether the HMO in question benefits the community in addition to its subscribers.

B. GHP's Status as a Tax-Exempt Entity

Viewed in this light, GHP standing alone does not merit tax-exempt status under section 501(c)(3). GHP cannot say that it provides any health care services itself. Nor does it ensure that people who are not GHP subscribers have access to health care or information about health care. According to the record, it neither conducts research nor offers educational programs, much less educational programs open to the public. It benefits no one but its subscribers.

GHP argues that the *Sound Health* requirement that an HMO seeking exemption must provide an emergency room open to all is rendered obsolete by Rev. Rul. 83-157. This may indeed be the case. Under the logic of Rev. Rul. 83-157, GHP need not provide an emergency room if doing so would unnecessarily duplicate services offered elsewhere in the area. Because the Clinic and other Geisinger System facilities provide emergency care to GHP's subscribers, requiring GHP to operate an emergency room may be unnecessarily duplicative and wasteful.

This conclusion would not, however, automatically bestow upon GHP an entitlement to tax-exempt status. The test remains one of community benefit, and GHP cannot demonstrate that it benefits anyone but its subscribers.

It is true that GHP is open to anyone who can afford to pay and that, like the HMO in *Sound Health*, GHP apparently intends to lower, or even to remove, this potential economic barrier to subscribing through its subsidized dues program. As we explain below, however, the mere presence of the subsidized dues program does not necessarily invite a conclusion that GHP benefits the community.

First, the *Sound Health* court ventured too far when it reasoned that the presence of a subsidized dues program meant that the HMO in question served a large enough class that it benefited the community. The court ruled that because there was no economic barrier to subscribership, "the class of persons potentially benefitted [sic] by the Association is not so small that its relief is of no benefit to the community." *Sound Health*, 71 T.C. at 185. In doing so, however, the court misconstrued the relevant inquiry by focusing on whether the HMO benefited the community at all rather than whether it primarily benefited the community, as an entity must in order to qualify for tax-exempt status.

The mere fact that a person need not pay to belong does not necessarily mean that GHP, which provides services only to those who do belong, serves a public purpose which primarily benefits the community. The community benefited is, in fact, limited to those who belong to GHP since the requirement of subscribership remains a condition precedent to any service. Absent any additional indicia of a charitable purpose, this self-imposed precondition suggests that GHP is primarily benefiting itself (and, perhaps, secondarily benefiting the community) by promoting subscribership throughout the areas it serves.

There may be circumstances in which an HMO will be able to demonstrate that the purpose of self-promotion is not so "substantial in nature" that it should not be accorded section 501(c)(3) status, even though access to service is premised upon membership. *See Better Business Bureau*, 326 U.S. at 283. *Cf. Presbyterian*, 743 F.2d at 155 (when legality of an action depends on the actor's motivation, "similar acts can lead to diametrically opposite legal consequences"). In this case, however, self-promotion appears to be the primary purpose for requiring membership. We are unaware of, and GHP has not identified, evidence which would lead to any other conclusion. Under these circumstances, we conclude that the presence of a subsidized dues program does not, in and of itself, primarily benefit the community sufficiently to enable GHP to qualify for tax-exempt status.

Second, the *Sound Health* court need not have gone as far as it did. The presence of a subsidized dues program was not the only factor it considered when deciding that the HMO in question qualified for tax-exempt status. For example, the HMO in *Sound Health* "in effect, [ran] a substantial outpatient clinic as an important ingredient of its medical care services." *Id.* It also provided free care even to persons who did not subscribe and offered educational programs to the public.

Finally, even considering the subsidized dues program, the amount of benefit GHP intends to confer on people other than paying subscribers is minuscule. GHP anticipates subsidizing approximately 35 people. We cannot say that GHP operates primarily to benefit the community at large rather than its subscribers by arranging for health care for only 35 people, who would not otherwise belong, as compared to more than 70,000 paying subscribers. GHP argues that the HMO in *Sound Health* had provided only $158.50 in subsidies when it was granted tax-exempt status. This is true, but, as previously noted, the HMO in that case also benefited the community in other ways, most notably by providing free or reduced-cost care to people who were not subscribers. An HMO must primarily benefit the community, not its subscribers plus a few people, in order to qualify for tax-exempt status under section 501(c)(3).

In sum, GHP does not qualify for tax-exempt status under section 501(c)(3) since it does no more than arrange for its subscribers, many of whom are medically underserved, to receive health care services from health care providers. This is so even though it has a program designed to subsidize the subscribership of those who might not be able to afford the fees required of all other subscribers. Arranging for the provision of medical services only to those who "belong" is not necessarily charitable, particularly where, as here, the HMO has arranged to subsidize only a small number of such persons. GHP, standing alone, is not entitled to tax-exempt status under section 501(c)(3).

IV.

Alternatively, GHP argues that it is entitled to tax-exempt status under section 501(c)(3) because it is an integral part of the Geisinger System. The integral part doctrine provides a means by which organizations may qualify for exemption vicariously through related organizations, as long as they are engaged in activities which would be exempt if the related organizations engaged in them, and as long as those activities are furthering the exempt purposes of the related organizations. *Texas Learning Technology Group v. Commissioner*, 958 F.2d 122, 126 (5th Cir. 1992). The integral part doctrine has been applied in the context of several Code sections. *See, e.g., Squire v. Students Book Corp.*, 191 F.2d 1018 (9th Cir. 1951); *Brundage v. Commissioner*, 54 T.C. 1468 (1970), acq. 1970-2 C.B. xix; Rev. Rul. 81-19, 1981-1 C.B. 30; Rev. Rul. 75-282, 1975-2 C.B. 201.

We decline to address the merits of the integral part doctrine at this stage, and instead remand the question of its application to this case to the Tax Court for clarification. *Cf. Garden State Bar Association v. Middlesex County Ethics Committee*, 687 F.2d 801, 802–03 (3d Cir. 1982). It is possible that the Tax Court, in ruling that GHP was entitled to exemption under section 501(c)(3), silently intermingled the roles played by GHP and other entities in the Geisinger System, thus effectively grounding its decision in the integral part doctrine. Its recitation of a great many facts regarding other entities in the Geisinger System suggests that it may have done just that. If that is the case, the Tax Court is in the best position to clarify this matter on remand.

V.

In conclusion, we will reverse the Tax Court's decision that GHP, standing alone, qualifies for tax-exempt status under 26 U.S.C. § 501(c)(3) because GHP does not demonstrate the community benefit required to satisfy the operational test. We will, however, remand this case to the Tax Court for a determination of whether GHP qualifies for tax-exempt status under section 501(c)(3) because it is an integral part of the Geisinger System.

Understanding the Public Benefit Concept

1.   Rev. Rul. 69-545 states that a hospital can be tax-exempt if it admits indigent patients to the emergency room and limits the remainder of the hospital to paying customers. In any place except the tax code, would this be considered a "charitable" organization? Suppose that a Wall Street law firm opened a small street-level law clinic with a sign, "Free help with your legal emergencies. No one turned away." Would the law firm now qualify as a tax-exempt charitable organization under section 501(c)(3)? Or is health care an inherently charitable function that should qualify as tax-exempt as long as it is made available to some reasonable portion of the population, even if they are mostly well-heeled? What do you think is the effect on health care in this country of having the emergency room be the only facility available to millions of people for health care?

2.   Suppose that a hospital complies with the requirements of Rev. Rul. 69-545 but deliberately places itself in a wealthy neighborhood where it knows that it will be inaccessible to poor people, even in its emergency room. Does the hospital qualify for tax exemption? Would a more stringent application of this and other rules result in the provision of more health care services to indigent people? Or would the affected hospitals simply become taxable, for-profit entities that do not even pretend to serve the poor?

3.   *Geisinger* holds that an HMO is not tax-exempt merely because it serves a primarily rural population and has (or intends to have) a program to subsidize needy subscribers. Is this consistent with the treatment of tax-exempt hospitals, or are the courts applying an inconsistent standard? If there is not to be a national health care system, as seems probable, should the tax code not at least encourage HMOs to provide as much indigent care as possible? Or would this create a further

boondoggle in which HMOs provided a de minimis amount of indigent assistance and otherwise continued as before?

4.   We have observed the relationship between tax and health care policy in at least two different contexts (fringe benefits and charitable deductions). Based on this experience, what do you think is the likelihood that the tax code can promote good policy in the health care area? What are some of the differences between the tax and health care "worldviews" that might make this a difficult task? What changes could make for a healthier (pardon the pun) relationship?

Revenue Ruling 69-545 refers to the traditional tests for tax exemption under section 501(c)(3): that an entity be organized and operated exclusively for religious, charitable, scientific, or educational purposes and that no part of its net earnings inure to the benefit of any private individual. To these requirements was subsequently added the limitations on political activity contained at the end of the subsection — "no substantial part of the activities of which is carrying on propaganda, or otherwise attempting, to influence legislation . . . , and which does not participate in, or intervene in (including the publishing or distributing of statements) any political campaign on behalf of (or in opposition to) any candidate for public office." The rules thus contain an absolute ban on participation in political election campaigns but — perhaps in a concession to reality — a ban only on excessive ("substantial") lobbying activities. The latter are further defined in section 501(h), which provides a series of quantitative tests under which various categories of tax-exempt organizations (but not churches) may be deemed to have avoided substantial lobbying or "grass roots" political activity during the relevant period. (The constitutionality of the political activity limitations was upheld in *Regan v. Taxation With Representation of Washington*, 461 U.S. 540 (1983).)

The political activity limitations were designed primarily to tame liberal interest groups (*e.g.*, environmental and other "public interest" organizations) that were thought to be engaging in excessive lobbying activity. However, the provisions also strike at religious and conservative political organizations and have been criticized by both sides as inconsistent with free speech and related societal values. (What good is it to litigate for the environment if Congress then rewrites all the laws?) The effect of the rules is somewhat mitigated by the existence of other tax-exemption provisions, *e.g.*, section 501(c)(4), which permit a wider degree of political activity without sacrificing one's tax-exempt status. Despite being exempt from taxation on their own organizational activity, section 501(c)(4) organizations do not qualify to receive tax-deductible contributions under section 170 of the Code. Hence, their parent organizations must sometimes make the unenviable choice between restricting their political activities, on the one hand, or foregoing the right to receive tax-free contributions, on the other.

A particularly famous application (or non-application) of the political action rules was *In re United States Catholic Conference*, 885 F.2d 1020 (2d Cir. 1989). Plaintiffs, consisting of nine organizational and twenty individual supporters of abortion rights, challenged the tax-exempt status of the Roman Catholic Church on the grounds that its anti-abortion activities, and specifically its alleged support for anti-abortion candidates, constituted a violation of the political action rules. Taking a page from *Eastern Kentucky* and other precedents, the Court of Appeals found that the plaintiffs lacked standing and dismissed the suit. The case was particularly noteworthy for the participation of several (Protestant) ministries and (Jewish) rabbis as plaintiffs, which may not represent a high point of ecumenical efforts, but accurately reflects the emotions and values on both sides of this argument.

Like *Eastern Kentucky, In re United States Catholic Conference* raises a number of disturbing issues regarding both the substance and procedure of the tax-exempt organization provisions. The Court of Appeals is understandably reluctant to allow competing organizations to challenge each other's tax exemptions, particularly for an organization as venerable as the Roman Catholic Church. But if they don't, who will? Is it realistic to think that any president would permit the IRS to challenge the Church's tax exemption? Many statutes, notably in environmental law, permit individual citizens to serve as "private attorneys general" by bringing suits that the Government lacks the resources or inclination to bring. Might this be a thought for the tax code, as well?

The case further raises difficult issues of "line-drawing" on the political-religious continuum. Plaintiffs accused the Catholic Church of violating the terms of its exemption by engaging in political activity with respect to abortion and other issues. Is it realistic to think that an organization that believes abortion is murder should refrain from saying so at every available occasion? Or is the argument simply that the Church, if it wishes to lobby such issues, should do so under the same rules that apply to everyone else? What if liberal Protestant pastors were prohibited from participating in demonstrations for world peace, or rabbis from making television appearances in which they supported (or in some cases, criticized) Israel? Does the difficulty of drawing lines in this area suggest that we should be extremely circumspect about regulating the behavior of religious leaders in this way? Does it cast doubt on the wisdom, or even the enforceability, of the political action rules in the first place?

The political activities of charitable organizations tend to be an especially hot issue at election time. This was particularly true in 2004, when the Bush Administration attempted to involve more conservative churches in its reelection campaign, and liberal organizations (including churches) responded in kind. The IRS has since warned charities against direct or indirect participation in political campaigns, emphasizing the potential loss of tax exemption if these activities are not curtailed. *See Charities Again Cautioned Against Political Campaign Activities*, 2004 TAX NOTES TODAY 11-22 (June 10, 2004).

Using the Sources

Based on the decisions above, which of the following do you think would or should qualify for tax exemption under section 501(c)(3)?

1. A college that admits only men.

2. A college that admits only women.

3. An environmental organization that annually ranks members of Congress based on their support for or opposition to environmental legislation but does not participate directly in election campaigns.

4. A similar organization that runs television commercials, close to election time, urging voters to support environment-friendly candidates.

5. A Jewish or Islamic elementary school, which requires that all students observe traditional religious laws and — while admitting both boys and girls — puts them in different classes and insists that they remain physically separate at all times.

Law and Planning

Suppose that you were tax counsel for an environmental or similar organization whose members wanted to be involved directly in political campaigns but (understandably) did not want the organization to compromise its tax-exempt status. What strategy or strategies would you recommend to them, and what would be the advantages or disadvantages of each option?

Politics and Policy

One argument on behalf of the charitable deduction is that it encourages private organizations to perform many of the functions that, in other countries, would be performed by governmental units. This formula, it is said, encourages a higher level of civic involvement than exists in those other societies, while preserving individual freedom and restricting the size of the Federal and State bureaucracies. A similar argument is made on behalf of tax subsidies for retirement savings, health care, and other types of expenditures, which are supported by a mix of tax incentives and direct spending programs.

Based on the preceding materials, is the "private initiative" argument a convincing one? What consequences, positive and negative, flow from the decision to subsidize private bodies in the performance of important public functions, and how do these differ from the consequences that would result from direct governmental provision of the benefits in question? Consider, in particular, the following kinds of institutions:

1. Tax-exempt (*i.e.*, private) universities.

2. Tax-exempt (*i.e.*, private) nonprofit hospitals.

3. Museums and other cultural organizations.

What are the quality and the distribution of the services provided by these institutions, and how do they differ from the services that would likely be provided by governmental entities?

B.   Reciprocal Benefits and Quid Pro Quos: What Is a Charitable Contribution?

Once an organization is tax-exempt, there remains the question of whether individuals and corporations may deduct contributions to the organization from their own taxes. Unlike the tax-exemption issue, which is covered by section 501, the issue of deductibility is dealt with by section 170, which contains numerous rules regarding the kinds of organizations that qualify to receive tax-deductible contributions and the amount and type of donations that may be deducted. There is also a sort of "common law" of charitable donations, emphasizing the question of what qualifies as a tax-deductible contribution and what is, instead, an effective purchase of goods or services from the charitable organization. We consider this last issue first.

HERNANDEZ v. COMMISSIONER
United States Supreme Court
490 U.S. 680 (1989)

Justice Marshall delivered the opinion of the Court.

Section 170 of the Internal Revenue Code of 1954 (Code), 26 U.S.C. § 170, permits a taxpayer to deduct from gross income the amount of a "charitable contribution." The Code defines that term as a "contribution or gift" to certain eligible donees, including entities organized and operated exclusively for religious purposes. We granted *certiorari* to determine whether taxpayers may deduct as charitable contributions payments made to branch churches of the Church of Scientology (Church) in order to receive services known as "auditing" and "training." We hold that such payments are not deductible.

I

Scientology was founded in the 1950's by L. Ron Hubbard. It is propagated today by a "mother church" in California and by numerous branch churches around the world. The mother Church instructs laity, trains and ordains ministers, and creates new congregations. Branch churches, known as "franchises" or "missions," provide Scientology services at the local level, under the supervision of the mother Church. *Church of Scientology of California v. Commissioner*, 823 F.2d 1310, 1313 (CA9 1987), *cert. denied*, 486 U.S. 1015 (1988).

Scientologists believe that an immortal spiritual being exists in every person. A person becomes aware of this spiritual dimension through a process known as "auditing." Auditing involves a one-to-one encounter between a participant (known as a "preclear") and a Church official (known as an "auditor"). An electronic device, the E-meter, helps the auditor identify the preclear's areas of spiritual difficulty by measuring skin responses during a question and answer session. Although auditing sessions are conducted one on one, the content of each session is not individually tailored. The preclear gains spiritual awareness by progressing through sequential levels of auditing, provided in short blocks of time known as "intensives." 83 T.C. 575, 577 (1984), *aff'd*, 822 F.2d 844 (CA9 1987).

The Church also offers members doctrinal courses known as "training." Participants in these sessions study the tenets of Scientology and seek to attain the qualifications necessary to serve as auditors. Training courses, like auditing sessions, are provided in sequential levels. Scientologists are taught that spiritual gains result from participation in such courses. 83 T.C. at 577.

The Church charges a "fixed donation," also known as a "price" or a "fixed contribution," for participants to gain access to auditing and training sessions. These charges are set forth in schedules, and prices vary with a session's length and level of sophistication. In 1972, for example, the general rates for auditing ranged from $625 for a 12 1/2-hour auditing intensive, the shortest available, to $4,250 for a 100-hour intensive, the longest available. Specialized types of auditing required higher fixed donations: a 12 1/2-hour "Integrity Processing" auditing intensive cost $750; a 12 1/2-hour "Expanded Dianetics" auditing intensive cost $950. This system of mandatory fixed charges is based on a central tenet of Scientology known as the "doctrine of exchange," according to which any time a person receives something he must pay something back. *Id.* at 577–578. In so doing, a Scientologist maintains "inflow" and "outflow" and avoids spiritual decline. 819 F.2d 1212, 1222 (CA1 1987).

The proceeds generated from auditing and training sessions are the Church's primary source of income. The Church promotes these sessions not only through newspaper, magazine, and radio advertisements, but also through free lectures, free personality tests, and leaflets. The Church also encourages, and indeed rewards with a 5% discount, advance payment for these sessions. 822 F.2d at 847. The Church often refunds unused portions of prepaid auditing or training fees, less an administrative charge.

Petitioners in these consolidated cases each made payments to a branch church for auditing or training sessions. They sought to deduct these payments on their federal income tax returns as charitable contributions under § 170. Respondent Commissioner, the head of the Internal Revenue Service (IRS), disallowed these deductions, finding that the payments were not charitable contributions within the meaning of § 170.

Petitioners sought review of these determinations in the Tax Court. That court consolidated for trial the cases of the three petitioners in No. 87-1616: Katherine Jean Graham, Richard M. Hermann, and David Forbes Maynard. The petitioner in No. 87-963, Robert L. Hernandez, agreed to be bound by the findings in the consolidated *Graham* trial, reserving his right to a separate appeal. Before trial, the Commissioner stipulated that the branch churches of Scientology are religious organizations entitled to receive tax-deductible charitable contributions under the relevant sections of the Code. This stipulation isolated as the sole statutory issue whether payments for auditing or training sessions constitute "contribution[s] or gift[s]" under § 170.

The Tax Court held a 3-day bench trial during which the taxpayers and others testified and submitted documentary exhibits describing the terms under which the Church promotes and provides auditing and training sessions. Based on this record, the court upheld the Commissioner's decision. 83 T.C. 575 (1984). It observed first that the term "charitable contribution" in § 170 is synonymous with the word "gift," which case law had defined "as a *voluntary transfer* of property by the owner to another *without consideration* therefore." *Id.* at 580, quoting *DeJong v. Commissioner*, 36 T.C. 896, 899 (1961) (emphasis in original), aff'd, 309 F.2d 373 (CA9 1962). It then determined that petitioners had received consideration for their payments, namely, "the benefit of various religious services provided by the

Church of Scientology." 83 T.C. at 580. The Tax Court also rejected the taxpayers' constitutional challenges based on the Establishment and Free Exercise Clauses of the First Amendment.

The Courts of Appeals for the First Circuit in petitioner Hernandez's case, and for the Ninth Circuit in Graham, Hermann, and Maynard's case, affirmed. The First Circuit rejected Hernandez's argument that under § 170, the IRS' ordinary inquiry into whether the taxpayer received consideration for his payment should not apply to "the return of a commensurate *religious* benefit, as opposed to an *economic or financial* benefit." 819 F.2d at 1217 (emphasis in original). The court found "no indication that Congress intended to distinguish the religious benefits sought by Hernandez from the medical, educational, scientific, literary, or other benefits that could likewise provide the *quid* for the *quo* of a nondeductible payment to a charitable organization." *Ibid.* The court also rejected Hernandez's argument that it was impracticable to put a value on the services he had purchased, noting that the Church itself had "established and advertised monetary prices" for auditing and training sessions, and that Hernandez had not claimed that these prices misstated the cost of providing these sessions. *Id.* at 1218.

Hernandez's constitutional claims also failed. Because § 170 created no denominational preference on its face, Hernandez had shown no Establishment Clause violation. *Id.* at 1218-1221. As for the Free Exercise Clause challenge, the court determined that denying the deduction did not prevent Hernandez from paying for auditing and training sessions and thereby observing Scientology's doctrine of exchange. Moreover, granting a tax exemption would compromise the integrity and fairness of the tax system. *Id.* at 1221–1225.

The Ninth Circuit also found that the taxpayers had received a "measurable, specific return . . . as a quid pro quo for the donation" they had made to the branch churches. 822 F.2d at 848. The court reached this result by focusing on "the external features" of the auditing and training transactions, an analytic technique which "serves as an expedient for any more intrusive inquiry into the motives of the payor." *Ibid.* Whether a particular exchange generated secular or religious benefits to the taxpayer was irrelevant, for under § 170 "[i]t is the structure of the transaction, and not the type of benefit received, that controls." *Id.* at 849.

The Ninth Circuit also rejected the taxpayers' constitutional arguments. The tax deduction provision did not violate the Establishment Clause because § 170 is "neutral in its design" and reflects no intent "to visit a disability on a particular religion." *Id.* at 853. Furthermore, that the taxpayers would "have less money to pay to the Church, or that the Church [would] receive less money, [did] not rise to the level of a burden on appellants' ability to exercise their religious beliefs." *Id.* at 851. Indeed, because the taxpayers could still make charitable donations to the branch church, they were "not put to the choice of abandoning the doctrine of exchange or losing the government benefit, for they may have both." *Ibid.* Finally, the court noted that the compelling governmental interest in "the maintenance of a sound and uniform tax system" counseled against granting a free exercise exemption. *Id.* at 852–853.

We granted *certiorari*, 485 U.S. 1005 (1988); 486 U.S. 1022 (1988), to resolve a Circuit conflict concerning the validity of charitable deductions for auditing and training payments. We now affirm.

II

For over 70 years, federal taxpayers have been allowed to deduct the amount of contributions or gifts to charitable, religious, and other eleemosynary institutions. *See* 2 B. BITTKER, FEDERAL TAXATION OF INCOME, ESTATES AND GIFTS para. 35.1.1 (1981) (tracing history of charitable deduction). Section 170, the present provision, was enacted in 1954; it requires a taxpayer claiming the deduction to satisfy a number of conditions. The Commissioner's stipulation in this case, however, has narrowed the statutory inquiry to one such condition: whether petitioners' payments for auditing and training sessions are "contribution[s] or gift[s]" within the meaning of § 170.

The legislative history of the "contribution or gift" limitation, though sparse, reveals that Congress intended to differentiate between unrequited payments to qualified recipients and payments made to such recipients in return for goods or services. Only the former were deemed deductible. The House and Senate Reports on the 1954 tax bill, for example, both define "gifts" as payments "made with no expectation of a financial return commensurate with the amount of the gift." S. Rep. No. 1622, 83d Cong., 2d Sess., 196 (1954); H. Rep. No. 1337, 83d Cong., 2d Sess., A44 (1954). Using payments to hospitals as an example, both Reports state that the gift characterization should not apply to "a payment by an individual to a hospital *in consideration of* a binding obligation to provide medical treatment for the individual's employees. It would apply only if there were no expectation of any quid pro quo from the hospital." S. Rep. No. 1622, *supra*, at 196 (emphasis added); H. Rep. No. 1337, *supra*, at A44 (emphasis added).

In ascertaining whether a given payment was made with "the expectation of any quid pro quo," S. Rep. No. 1622, *supra*, at 196; H. Rep. No. 1337, *supra*, at A44, the IRS has customarily examined the external features of the transaction in question. This practice has the advantage of obviating the need for the IRS to conduct imprecise inquiries into the motivations of individual taxpayers. The lower courts have generally embraced this structural analysis. *See, e.g., Singer Co. v. United States*, 449 F.2d 413, 422–423 (Ct. Cl. 1971) (applying this approach and collecting cases), cited in *United States v. American Bar Endowment*, 477 U.S. 105, 117 (1986); *see also* 2 B. BITTKER, *supra*, at para. 35.1.3 (collecting cases). We likewise focused on external features in *United States v. American Bar Endowment, supra*, to resolve the taxpayers' claims that they were entitled to partial deductions for premiums paid to a charitable organization for insurance coverage; the taxpayers contended that they had paid unusually high premiums in an effort to make a contribution along with their purchase of insurance. We upheld the Commissioner's disallowance of the partial deductions because the taxpayers had failed to demonstrate, at a minimum, the existence of comparable insurance policies with prices lower than those of the policy they had each purchased. In so doing, we stressed that "[t]he *sine qua non* of a charitable contribution is a transfer of money or property *without adequate consideration*." *Id.* at 118 (emphasis added in part).

In light of this understanding of § 170, it is readily apparent that petitioners' payments to the Church do not qualify as "contribution[s] or gift[s]." As the Tax

Court found, these payments were part of a quintessential *quid pro quo* exchange: in return for their money, petitioners received an identifiable benefit, namely, auditing and training sessions. The Church established fixed price schedules for auditing and training sessions in each branch church; it calibrated particular prices to auditing or training sessions of particular lengths and levels of sophistication; it returned a refund if auditing and training services went unperformed; it distributed "account cards" on which persons who had paid money to the Church could monitor what prepaid services they had not yet claimed; and it categorically barred provision of auditing or training sessions for free. Each of these practices reveals the inherently reciprocal nature of the exchange.

Petitioners do not argue that such a structural analysis is inappropriate under § 170, or that the external features of the auditing and training transactions do not strongly suggest a *quid pro quo* exchange. Indeed, the petitioners in the consolidated *Graham* case conceded at trial that they expected to receive specific amounts of auditing and training in return for their payments. 822 F.2d at 850. Petitioners argue instead that they are entitled to deductions because a *quid pro quo* analysis is inappropriate under § 170 when the benefit a taxpayer receives is purely religious in nature. Along the same lines, petitioners claim that payments made for the right to participate in a religious service should be automatically deductible under § 170.

We cannot accept this statutory argument for several reasons. First, it finds no support in the language of § 170. Whether or not Congress could, consistent with the Establishment Clause, provide for the automatic deductibility of a payment made to a church that either generates religious benefits or guarantees access to a religious service, that is a choice Congress has thus far declined to make. Instead, Congress has specified that a payment to an organization operated exclusively for religious (or other eleemosynary) purposes is deductible *only* if such a payment is a "contribution or gift." 26 U.S.C. § 170(c). The Code makes no special preference for payments made in the expectation of gaining religious benefits or access to a religious service. *Foley v. Commissioner*, 844 F.2d 94, 98 (CA2 1988) (Newman, J., dissenting), *cert. pending*, No. 88-102. The House and Senate Reports on § 170, and the other legislative history of that provision, offer no indication that Congress' failure to enact such a preference was an oversight.

Second, petitioners' deductibility proposal would expand the charitable contribution deduction far beyond what Congress has provided. Numerous forms of payments to eligible donees plausibly could be categorized as providing a religious benefit or as securing access to a religious service. For example, some taxpayers might regard their tuition payments to parochial schools as generating a religious benefit or as securing access to a religious service; such payments, however, have long been held not to be charitable contributions under § 170. *Foley*, *supra*, at 98, citing *Winters v. Commissioner*, 468 F.2d 778 (CA2 1972); *see id.* at 781 (noting Congress' refusal to enact legislation permitting taxpayers to deduct parochial school tuition payments). Taxpayers might make similar claims about payments for church-sponsored counseling sessions or for medical care at church-affiliated hospitals that otherwise might not be deductible. Given that, under the First Amendment, the IRS can reject otherwise valid claims of religious benefit only on the ground that a taxpayers' alleged beliefs are not sincerely held, but not on the ground that such beliefs are inherently irreligious, *see United States v. Ballard*, 322 U.S. 78 (1944), the resulting tax deductions would likely expand the charitable contribution provision far beyond its present size. We are loath to effect this result in the absence of supportive congressional intent. *Cf. United States v. Lee*, 455 U.S. 252, 259–261 (1982).

Finally, the deduction petitioners seek might raise problems of entanglement between church and state. If framed as a deduction for those payments generating benefits of a religious nature for the payor, petitioners' proposal would inexorably force the IRS and reviewing courts to differentiate "religious" benefits from "secular" ones. If framed as a deduction for those payments made in connection with a religious service, petitioners' proposal would force the IRS and the judiciary into differentiating "religious" services from "secular" ones. We need pass no judgment now on the constitutionality of such hypothetical inquiries, but we do note that "pervasive monitoring" for "the subtle or overt presence of religious matter" is a central danger against which we have held the Establishment Clause guards. *Aguilar v. Felton*, 473 U.S. 402, 413 (1985); *see also Widmar v. Vincent*, 454 U.S. 263, 272, n. 11 (1981) ("[T]he University would risk greater 'entanglement' by attempting to enforce its exclusion of 'religious worship' and 'religious speech'" than by opening its forum to religious as well as nonreligious speakers); *cf. Thomas v. Review Bd. of Indiana Employment Security Div.*, 450 U.S. 707, 716 (1981).

Accordingly, we conclude that petitioners' payments to the Church for auditing and training sessions are not "contribution[s] or gift[s]" within the meaning of that statutory expression.

III

We turn now to petitioners' constitutional claims based on the Establishment Clause and the Free Exercise Clause of the First Amendment.

A

Petitioners argue that denying their requested deduction violates the Establishment Clause in two respects. First, § 170 is said to create an unconstitutional denominational preference by according disproportionately harsh tax status to those religions that raise funds by imposing fixed costs for participation in certain religious practices. Second, § 170 allegedly threatens governmental entanglement with religion because it requires the IRS to entangle itself with religion by engaging in "supervision of religious beliefs and practices" and "valuation of religious services." Brief for Petitioners 44.

Our decision in *Larson v. Valente*, 456 U.S. 228 (1982), supplies the analytic framework for evaluating petitioners' contentions. *Larson* teaches that, when it is claimed that a denominational preference exists, the initial inquiry is whether the law facially differentiates among religions. If no such facial preference exists, we proceed to apply the customary three-pronged Establishment Clause inquiry derived from *Lemon v. Kurtzman*, 403 U.S. 602 (1971).

Thus analyzed, § 170 easily passes constitutional muster. The line which § 170 draws between deductible and nondeductible payments to statutorily qualified organizations does not differentiate among sects. Unlike the Minnesota statute at issue in *Larson*, which facially exempted from state registration and reporting requirements only those religious organizations that derived more than half their funds from members, § 170 makes no "explicit and deliberate distinctions between different religious organizations," 456 U.S. at 246–247, n. 23, applying instead to all religious entities.

Section 170 also comports with the *Lemon* test. First, there is no allegation that § 170 was born of animus to religion in general or Scientology in particular. *Cf. Larson, supra*, at 254–255 (history of Minnesota restriction reveals hostility to "Moonies" and intent to "get at . . . people that are running around airports"). The provision is neutral both in design and purpose.

Second, the primary effect of § 170 — encouraging gifts to charitable entities, including but not limited to religious organizations — is neither to advance nor inhibit religion. It is not alleged here that § 170 involves "[d]irect government action endorsing religion or a particular religious practice." *Wallace v. Jaffree*, 472 U.S. 38, 69 (1985) (O'CONNOR, J., concurring in judgment). It may be that a consequence of the *quid pro quo* orientation of the "contribution or gift" requirement is to impose a disparate burden on those charitable and religious groups that rely on sales of commodities or services as a means of fundraising, relative to those groups that raise funds primarily by soliciting unilateral donations. But a statute primarily having a secular effect does not violate the Establishment Clause merely because it "happens to coincide or harmonize with the tenets of some or all religions." *McGowan v. Maryland*, 366 U.S. 420, 442 (1961); *see also Bob Jones University v. United States*, 461 U.S. 574, 604, n. 30 (1983).

Third, § 170 threatens no excessive entanglement between church and state. To be sure, ascertaining whether a payment to a religious institution is part of a *quid pro quo* transaction may require the IRS to ascertain from the institution the prices of its services and commodities, the regularity with which payments for such services and commodities are waived, and other pertinent information about the transaction. But routine regulatory interaction which involves no inquiries into religious doctrine, *see Presbyterian Church in U.S. v. Mary Elizabeth Blue Hull Memorial Presbyterian Church*, 393 U.S. 440, 451 (1969), no delegation of state power to a religious body, *see Larkin v. Grendel's Den, Inc.*, 459 U.S. 116 (1982), and no "detailed monitoring and close administrative contact" between secular and religious bodies, *see Aguilar*, 473 U.S. at 414, does not of itself violate the nonentanglement command. *See Tony and Susan Alamo Foundation v. Secretary of Labor*, 471 U.S. 290, 305–306 (1985) (stating that nonentanglement principle "does not exempt religious organizations from such secular governmental activity as fire inspections and building and zoning regulations" or the recordkeeping requirements of the Fair Labor Standards Act) (citation omitted). As we have observed, it is petitioners' interpretation of § 170, requiring the Government to distinguish between "secular" and "religious" benefits or services, which may be "fraught with the sort of entanglement that the Constitution forbids." *Lemon, supra*, at 620.

Nor does the application of § 170 to religious practices require the Government to place a monetary value on particular religious benefits. As an initial matter, petitioners' claim here raises no need for valuation, for they have alleged only that their payments are fully exempt from a *quid pro quo* analysis — not that some portion of these payments is deductible because it exceeds the value of the acquired service. *Cf. American Bar Endowment*, 477 U.S. at 117 (describing "dual character" payments) (citing, *inter alia*, Rev. Rul. 68-432, 1968-2 Cum. Bull. 104, 105); *see* n. 10, *supra*. In any event, the need to ascertain what portion of a payment was a purchase and what portion was a contribution does not ineluctably create entanglement problems by forcing the Government to place a monetary value on a religious benefit. In cases where the economic value of a good or service is elusive — where, for example, no comparable good or service is sold in the marketplace — the IRS has eschewed benefit-focused valuation. Instead, it has often employed as an alternative method of valuation an inquiry into the cost (if any) to the donee of providing the good or service. *See, e.g., Oppewal v. Commissioner*, 468 F.2d 1000, 1002 (CA1 1972) (cost of providing a "religiously-oriented" education); *Winters v. Commissioner*, 468 F.2d 778 (CA2 1972) (same); *DeJong v. Commissioner*, 309 F.2d 373 (CA9 1962) (same). This valuation method, while requiring qualified religious institutions to disclose relevant information about church costs to the IRS, involves administrative inquiries that, as a general matter, "bear no resemblance to the kind of government surveillance the Court has previously held to pose an intolerable risk of government entanglement with religion." *Tony and Susan Alamo Foundation, supra*, at 305; *cf. Lemon*, 403 U.S. at 621–622 (school-aid statute authorizing government inspection of parochial school records created impermissible "intimate and continuing relationship between church and state" because it required State "to determine which expenditures are religious and which are secular").

B

Petitioners also contend that disallowance of their § 170 deductions violates their right to the free exercise of religion by "plac[ing] a heavy burden on the central practice of Scientology." Brief for Petitioners 47. The precise nature of this claimed burden is unclear, but it appears to operate in two ways. First, the deduction disallowance is said to deter adherents from engaging in auditing and training sessions. Second, the deduction disallowance is said to interfere with observance of the doctrine of exchange, which mandates equality of an adherent's "outflow" and "inflow."

The free exercise inquiry asks whether government has placed a substantial burden on the observation of a central religious belief or practice and, if so, whether a compelling governmental interest justifies the burden. *Hobbie v. Unemployment Appeals Comm'n of Fla.*, 480 U.S. 136, 141–142 (1987); *Thomas v. Review Bd. of Indiana Employment Security Div.*, 450 U.S. at 717–719; *Wisconsin v. Yoder*, 406 U.S. 205, 220–221 (1972). It is not within the judicial ken to question the centrality of particular beliefs or practices to a faith, or the validity of particular litigants' interpretations of those creeds. *Thomas, supra*, at 716. We do, however, have doubts whether the alleged burden imposed by the deduction disallowance on the Scientologists' practices is a substantial one. Neither the payment nor the receipt of taxes is forbidden by the Scientology faith generally, and Scientology does not proscribe the payment of taxes in connection with auditing or training sessions specifically. *Cf. United States v. Lee*, 455 U.S. at 257. Any burden imposed on auditing or training therefore derives solely from the fact that, as a result of the deduction denial, adherents have less money available to gain access to such sessions. This burden is no different from that imposed by any public tax or fee; indeed, the burden imposed by the denial of the "contribution or gift" deduction would seem to pale by comparison to the overall federal income tax burden on an adherent. Likewise, it is unclear why the doctrine of exchange would be violated by a deduction disallowance so long as an adherent is free to equalize "outflow" with "inflow" by paying for as many auditing and training sessions as he wishes. *See* 822 F.2d at 850–853 (questioning substantiality of burden on Scientologists); 819 F.2d at 1222–1225 (same).

In any event, we need not decide whether the burden of disallowing the § 170 deduction is a substantial one, for our decision in *Lee* establishes that even a substantial burden would be justified by the "broad public interest in maintaining a sound tax system," free of "myriad exceptions flowing from a wide variety of religious beliefs." 455 U.S. at 260. In *Lee*, we rejected an Amish taxpayer's claim that the Free Exercise Clause commanded his exemption from Social Security tax obligations, noting that "[t]he tax system could not function if denominations were allowed to challenge the tax system" on the ground that it operated "in a manner that violates their religious belief." *Ibid.* That these cases involve federal income taxes, not the Social Security system, is of no consequence. *Ibid.* The fact that Congress has already crafted some deductions and exemptions in the Code also is of no consequence, for the guiding principle is that a tax "must be uniformly applicable to all, except as *Congress* provides explicitly otherwise." *Id.* at 261 (emphasis added). Indeed, in one respect, the Government's interest in avoiding an exemption is more powerful here than in *Lee*; the claimed exemption in *Lee* stemmed from a specific doctrinal obligation not to pay taxes, whereas petitioners' claimed exemption stems from the contention that an incrementally larger tax burden interferes with their religious activities. This argument knows no limitation. We accordingly hold that petitioners' free exercise challenge is without merit.

IV

We turn, finally, to petitioners' assertion that disallowing their claimed deduction is at odds with the IRS' longstanding practice of permitting taxpayers to deduct payments made to other religious institutions in connection with certain religious practices. Through the appellate stages of this litigation, this claim was framed essentially as one of selective prosecution. The Courts of Appeals for the First and Ninth Circuits summarily rejected this claim, finding no evidence of the intentional governmental discrimination necessary to support such a claim. 822 F.2d at 853 (no showing of "the type of hostility to a target of law enforcement that would support a claim of selective enforcement"); 819 F.2d at 1223 (no "discriminatory intent" proved).

In their arguments to this Court, petitioners have shifted emphasis. They now make two closely related claims. First, the IRS has accorded payments for auditing and training disparately harsh treatment compared to payments to other churches and synagogues for their religious services: Recognition of a comparable deduction for auditing and training payments is necessary to cure this administrative inconsistency. Second, Congress, in modifying § 170 over the years, has impliedly acquiesced in the deductibility of payments to these other faiths; because payments for auditing and training are indistinguishable from these other payments, they fall within the principle acquiesced in by Congress that payments for religious services are deductible under § 170.

Although the Commissioner demurred at oral argument as to whether the IRS, in fact, permits taxpayers to deduct payments made to purchase services from other churches and synagogues, Tr. of Oral Arg. 30-31, the Commissioner's periodic revenue rulings have stated the IRS' position rather clearly. A 1971 ruling, still in effect, states: "Pew rents, building fund assessments, and periodic dues paid to a church . . . are all methods of making contributions to the church, and such payments are deductible as charitable contributions within the limitations set out in section 170 of the Code." Rev. Rul. 70-47, 1970-1 Cum. Bull. 49 (superseding A.R.M. 2, Cum. Bull. 150 (1919)). We also assume for purposes of argument that the IRS also allows taxpayers to deduct "specified payments for attendance at High Holy Day services, for tithes, for torah readings and for memorial plaques." *Foley v. Commissioner*, 844 F.2d at 94, 96.

The development of the present litigation, however, makes it impossible for us to resolve petitioners' claim that they have received unjustifiably harsh treatment compared to adherents of other religions. The relevant inquiry in determining whether a payment is a "contribution or gift" under § 170 is, as we have noted, not whether the payment secures religious benefits or access to religious services, but whether the transaction in which the payment is involved is structured as a *quid pro quo* exchange. To make such a determination in this case, the Tax Court heard testimony and received documentary proof as to the terms and structure of the auditing and training transactions; from this evidence it made factual findings upon which it based its conclusion of nondeductibility, a conclusion we have held consonant with § 170 and with the First Amendment.

Perhaps because the theory of administrative inconsistency emerged only on appeal, petitioners did not endeavor at trial to adduce from the IRS or other sources any specific evidence about other religious faiths' transactions. The IRS' revenue rulings, which merely state the agency's conclusions as to deductibility and which have apparently never been reviewed by the Tax Court or any other judicial body, also provide no specific facts about the nature of these other faiths' transactions. In the absence of such facts, we simply have no way (other than the wholly illegitimate one of relying on our personal experiences and observations) to appraise accurately whether the IRS' revenue rulings have correctly applied a *quid pro quo* analysis with respect to any or all of the religious practices in question. We do not know, for example, whether payments for other faiths' services are truly obligatory or whether any or all of these services are generally provided whether or not the encouraged "mandatory" payment is made.

The IRS' application of the "contribution or gift" standard may be right or wrong with respect to these other faiths, or it may be right with respect to some religious practices and wrong with respect to others. It may also be that some of these payments are appropriately classified as partially deductible "dual payments." With respect to those religions where the structure of transactions involving religious services is established not centrally but by individual congregations, the proper point of reference for a *quid pro quo* analysis might be the individual congregation, not the religion as a whole. Only upon a proper factual record could we make these determinations. Absent such a record, we must reject petitioners' administrative consistency argument.

Petitioners' congressional acquiescence claim fails for similar reasons. Even if one assumes that Congress has acquiesced in the IRS' ruling with respect to "[p]ew rents, building fund assessments, and periodic dues," Rev. Rul. 70-47, 1970-1 Cum. Bull. 49, the fact is that the IRS' 1971 ruling articulates no broad principle of deductibility, but instead merely identifies as deductible three discrete types of payments. Having before us no information about the nature or structure of these three payments, we have no way of discerning any possible unifying principle, let alone whether such a principle would embrace payments for auditing and training sessions.

V

For the reasons stated herein, the judgments of the Courts of Appeals are hereby

Affirmed.

JUSTICE O'CONNOR, with whom JUSTICE SCALIA joins, dissenting.

The Court today acquiesces in the decision of the Internal Revenue Service (IRS) to manufacture a singular exception to its 70-year practice of allowing fixed payments indistinguishable from those made by petitioners to be deducted as charitable contributions. Because the IRS cannot constitutionally be allowed to select which religions will receive the benefit of its past rulings, I respectfully dissent.

* * *

When a taxpayer claims as a charitable deduction part of a fixed amount given to a charitable organization in exchange for benefits that have a commercial value, the allowable portion of that claim is computed by subtracting from the total amount paid the value of the physical benefit received. If at a charity sale one purchases for $1,000 a painting whose market value is demonstrably no more than $50, there has been a contribution of $950. The same would be true if one purchases a $1,000 seat at a charitable dinner where the food is worth $50. An identical calculation can be made where the *quid* received is not a painting or a meal, but an intangible such as entertainment, so long as that intangible has some market value established in a noncontributory context. Hence, one who purchases a ticket to a concert, at the going rate for concerts by the particular performers, makes a charitable contribution of zero even if it is announced in advance that all proceeds from the ticket sales will go to charity. The performers may have made a charitable contribution, but the audience has paid the going rate for a show.

It becomes impossible, however, to compute the "contribution" portion of a payment to a charity where what is received in return is not merely an intangible, but an intangible (or, for that matter a tangible) that is not bought and sold except in donative contexts so that the only "market" price against which it can be evaluated is a market price that always includes donations. Suppose, for example, that the charitable organization that traditionally solicits donations on Veterans Day, in exchange for which it gives the donor an imitation poppy bearing its name, were to establish a flat rule that no one gets a poppy without a donation of at least $10. One would have to say that the "market" rate for such poppies was $10, but it would assuredly not be true that everyone who "bought" a poppy for $10 made no contribution. Similarly, if one buys a $100 seat at a prayer breakfast — receiving as the *quid pro quo* food for both body and soul — it would make no sense to say that no charitable contribution whatever has occurred simply because the "going rate" for all prayer breakfasts (with equivalent bodily food) is $100. The latter may well be true, but that "going rate" *includes* a contribution.

Confronted with this difficulty, and with the constitutional necessity of not making irrational distinctions among taxpayers, and with the even higher standard of equality of treatment among *religions* that the First Amendment imposes, the Government has only two practicable options with regard to distinctively religious *quids pro quo:* to disregard them all, or to tax them all. Over the years it has chosen the former course.

* * *

There can be no doubt that at least some of the fixed payments which the IRS has treated as charitable deductions, or which the Court assumes the IRS would allow taxpayers to deduct are as "inherently reciprocal" as the payments for auditing at issue here. In exchange for their payment of pew rents, Christians receive particular seats during worship services. *See* ENCYCLOPEDIC DICTIONARY OF RELIGION 2760 (1979). Similarly, in some synagogues attendance at the worship services for Jewish High Holy Days is often predicated upon the purchase of a general admission ticket or a reserved seat ticket. *See* J. FELDMAN, H. FRUHAUF, & M. SCHOEN, TEMPLE MANAGEMENT MANUAL, ch. 4, p. 10 (1984). Religious honors such as publicly reading from Scripture are purchased or auctioned periodically in some synagogues of Jews from Morocco and Syria. *See* H. DOBRINSKY, A TREASURY OF SEPHARDIC LAWS AND CUSTOMS 164, 175–177 (1986). Mormons must tithe their income as a necessary but not sufficient condition to obtaining a "temple recommend," *i.e.*, the right to be admitted into the temple. *See* THE BOOK OF MORMON, 3 Nephi 24:7-12 (1921); REORGANIZED CHURCH OF JESUS CHRIST OF LATTER-DAY SAINTS, BOOK OF DOCTRINE AND COVENANTS § 106:1b (1978); *Corporation of Presiding Bishop of Church of Jesus Christ of Latter-day Saints v. Amos*, 483 U.S. 327, 330, n. 4 (1987). A Mass stipend — a fixed payment given to a Catholic priest, in consideration of which he is obliged to apply the fruits of the Mass for the intention of the donor — has similar overtones of exchange. According to some Catholic theologians, the nature of the pact between a priest and a donor who pays a Mass stipend is "a bilateral contract known as *do ut facias*. One person agrees to give while the other party agrees to do something in return." 13 NEW CATHOLIC ENCYCLOPEDIA, *Mass Stipend*, p. 715 (1967). A finer example of a *quid pro quo* exchange would be hard to formulate.

This is not a situation where the IRS has explicitly and affirmatively reevaluated its longstanding interpretation of § 170 and decided to analyze *all* fixed religious contributions under a *quid pro quo* standard. There is no indication whatever that the IRS has abandoned its 70-year practice with respect to payments made by those other than Scientologists. In 1978, when it ruled that payments for auditing and training were not charitable contributions under § 170, the IRS did not cite — much less try to reconcile — its previous rulings concerning the deductibility of other forms of fixed payments for religious services or practices. *See* Rev. Rul. 78-189, 1978-1 Cum. Bull. 68 (equating payments for auditing with tuition paid to religious schools).

Nevertheless, respondent now attempts to reconcile his previous rulings with his decision in these cases by relying on a distinction between direct and incidental benefits in exchange for payments made to a charitable organization. This distinction, adumbrated as early as the IRS' 1919 ruling, recognizes that even a deductible charitable contribution may generate certain benefits for the donor. As long as the benefits remain "incidental" and do not indicate that the payment was actually made for the "personal accommodation" of the donor, the payment will be deductible. It is respondent's view that the payments made by petitioners should not be deductible under § 170 because the "unusual facts in these cases . . . demonstrate that the payments were made primarily for 'personal accommodation.'" Brief for Respondent 41. Specifically, the Solicitor General asserts that "the rigid connection between the provision of auditing and training services and payment of the fixed price" indicates a *quid pro quo* relationship and "reflect[s] the value that petitioners expected to receive for their money." *Id.* at 16.

There is no discernible reason why there is a more rigid connection between payment and services in the religious practices of Scientology than in the religious practices of the faiths described above. Neither has respondent explained why the benefit received by a Christian who obtains the pew of his or her choice by paying a rental fee, a Jew who gains entrance to High Holy Day services by purchasing a ticket, a Mormon who makes the fixed payment necessary for a temple recommend, or a Catholic who pays a Mass stipend, is incidental to the real benefit conferred on the "general public and members of the faith," BNA Daily Report, at J-3, while the benefit received by a Scientologist from auditing is a personal accommodation. If the perceived difference lies in the fact that Christians and Jews worship in congregations, whereas Scientologists, in a manner reminiscent of Eastern religions, *see* App. 78-83 (testimony of Dr. Thomas Love), gain awareness of the "immortal spiritual being" within them in one-to-one sessions with auditors, such a distinction would raise serious Establishment Clause problems. *See Wallace v. Jaffree*, 472 U.S. 38, 69–70 (1985) (O'Connor, J., concurring in judgment); *Lynch v. Donnelly*, 465 U.S. 668, 687–689 (1984) (concurring opinion). The distinction is no more legitimate if it is based on the fact that congregational worship services "would be said anyway," Brief for Respondent 43, without the payment of a pew rental or stipend or tithe by a particular adherent. The relevant comparison between Scientology and other religions must be between the Scientologist undergoing auditing or training on one hand and the congregation on the other. For some religions the central importance of the congregation achieves legal dimensions. In Orthodox Judaism, for example, certain worship services cannot be performed and Scripture cannot be read publicly without the presence of at least 10 men. 12 ENCYCLOPEDIA JUDAICA, *Minyan*, p. 68 (1972). If payments for participation occurred in such a setting, would the benefit to the 10th man be only incidental while for the personal accommodation of the 11th? In the same vein, will the deductibility of a Mass stipend turn on whether there are other congregants to hear the Mass? And conversely, does the fact that the payment of a tithe by a Mormon is an absolute prerequisite to admission to the temple make that payment for admission a personal accommodation regardless of the size of the congregation?

Given the IRS' stance in these cases, it is an understatement to say that with respect to fixed payments for religious services "the line between the taxable and the immune has been drawn by an unsteady hand." *United States v. Allegheny County*, 322 U.S. 174, 176 (1944) (Jackson, J.). This is not a situation in which a governmental regulation "happens to coincide or harmonize with the tenets of some or all religions," *McGowan v. Maryland*, 366 U.S. 420, 442 (1961), but does not violate the Establishment Clause because it is founded on a neutral, secular basis. *See Bob Jones University v. United States*, 461 U.S. 574, 604, n. 30 (1983). Rather, it involves the differential application of a standard based on constitutionally impermissible differences drawn by the Government among religions. As such, it is best characterized as a case of the Government "put[ting] an imprimatur on [all but] one religion." *Gillette v. United States*, 401 U.S. 437, 450 (1971). That the Government may not do.

* * *

On a more fundamental level, the Court cannot abjure its responsibility to address serious constitutional problems by converting a violation of the Establishment Clause into an "administrative consistency argument," with an inadequate record. It has chosen to ignore both longstanding, clearly articulated IRS practice, and the failure of respondent to offer any cogent, neutral explanation for the IRS' refusal to apply this practice to the Church of Scientology. Instead, the Court has pretended that whatever errors in application the IRS has committed are hidden from its gaze and will, in any event, be rectified in due time.

In my view, the IRS has misapplied its longstanding practice of allowing charitable contributions under § 170 in a way that violates the Establishment Clause. It has unconstitutionally refused to allow payments for the religious service of auditing to be deducted as charitable contributions in the same way it has allowed fixed payments to other religions to be deducted. Just as the Minnesota statute at issue in *Larson v. Valente*, 456 U.S. 228 (1982), discriminated against the Unification Church, the IRS' application of the *quid pro quo* standard here — and only here — discriminates against the Church of Scientology. I would reverse the decisions below.

Understanding *Hernandez*

1.   At first glance, the "auditing" provided by the Church of Scientology to its members may appear sufficiently outside normal religious practices that the denial of a deduction is unsurprising. But is it really so unusual? As the dissent notes, members of churches and other religious bodies regularly receive all manner of benefits — preferential seating, religious education, personal and spiritual counseling, etc. — in return for their financial support of the organization. Although in theory the charitable deduction should be reduced by the amount of these benefits, many of them are extremely difficult to value, and it is fair to say that most people make little, if indeed any, such reduction. Why do these people (typically) win, while the Scientologists lose?

2.   Suppose that a church offered a weekend course on "Christian ethics in the practice of law," for which it charged a flat fee of $250. The course flyer indicated that the course would help participants become not only better Christians, but also better lawyers, because clients (or so the materials said) tend to like lawyers who bring a more spiritual approach to their work. Would the cost of this course be deductible as a charitable contribution? What about as a business expense? Would it matter if, instead of a separate charge, church members were permitted to take an unlimited number of such courses (together with other benefits) in return for an annual church membership fee? What if the Scientologists had used this sort of annual fee system instead of charging for individual tutoring sessions?

3.   What is the significance, if any, of the court's placement of Scientologist terminology in quotation marks ("auditing," "training," etc.) throughout the opinion? Is this merely done for the sake of accuracy, or does it give you some idea where the Court is going? Would the court put "Resurrection" in quotation marks if dealing with a Christian church, or "Passover Seder" for a synagogue? What is the difference?

The IRS subsequently entered into a confidential agreement with the Church of Scientology that, according to media reports, permitted the deduction of many of the amounts at stake in the *Hernandez* decision. This turn of events predictably led others to seek similar treatment, including the deduction of religious school tuition which (so the litigants argued) was equivalent in nature to the deductions now being permitted to Scientologists. One interesting example of this phenomenon was the Sklar family of Los Angeles, which has repeatedly tried, so far without success, to obtain a deduction for tuition to a Jewish school.

Most reciprocal benefit arrangements are considerably less elevated than that involved in *Hernandez*. A favorite ploy is to have an individual buy a ticket for a dinner, concert, or other event from a charitable organization, for an amount somewhat in excess of the actual value of the event — say, $100 for a concert ticket otherwise worth $40, or $200 for a $100 dinner. A related gambit, favored by public television stations, is to distribute free prizes — tote bags, CDs, videos of purple dinosaurs — in return for contributions to the station. The rule in these cases is clear: the contributor is entitled to deduct only the excess of the contribution over the value of any item received in return. Thus, if one contributes $100 to the local public television station, and receives a $36 tote bag, one should deduct only $64, *i.e.*, the remaining $36 being considered (essentially) a cash purchase rather than a charitable donation. But tote bags and purple dinosaurs (not to mention charity dinners) are notoriously difficult to value, and there is a strong temptation to deduct the entire amount, which may be enhanced by a sense that the dinners, gifts, etc., are merely a "recognition" of the contribution and not items of value received in exchange.[23] Charities themselves have frequently encouraged such behavior by stating that "amounts contributed are deductible to the extent permitted by law," or similar language?a clever tautology that seems plainly to encourage the aggressive interpretations/tax evasion activities cited above.

Since 1986, the IRS has added a number of new reporting requirements designed to limit abuse in the charitable contribution area. The most significant of these requires that, when providing a reciprocal benefit to a donor, the organization must state the value of the benefit and the value of the contribution in excess of this amount, with only the latter being deductible to the donor. Additional rules require the detailed listing and appraisal of contributions of property over specified amounts. These rules significantly restrict, although by no means eliminate, the tax avoidance schemes and dodges described above.[24]

A related question concerns individuals and corporations that receive intangible benefits in return for charitable contributions. These range from the purely psychic benefits of seeing one's name on buildings, plaques, and so forth, to the more tangible publicity resulting from association of the individual or corporate name with museum exhibits, high-class television, and the like. One donor to a university attended by one of the authors demanded, as a condition of his gift, that the library be floodlit whenever he was in the same city. Given the difficulty of valuing such items, it seems unlikely that they could be offset against the valuation of charitable contributions; but the problem of psychic benefits suggests the strange calculus of charitable donations and the difficulty of making normal tax principles apply in this supposedly selfless world.

C.   Appreciated Property and Charitable Tax Planning

The most hotly contested of all charitable contribution issues is the valuation of the items contributed. Valuation is always an entertaining issue, both because people tend to lie about it, and because the taxpayer and the IRS may be on different sides of the issue depending what provision is involved. Thus, the same taxpayer who argues for a low valuation for purposes of the estate tax or fringe benefit provisions is likely to seek the highest value when a charitable contribution is involved. In most of these cases, it is the taxpayer's word against the IRS's,

---

[23] The dangers of this behavior, which may seem trivial in the case of tote bags, become less trivial as the amounts become bigger. Assume that the combined deduction for a $100 charitable contribution, under Federal and State taxes, is about $50. This means that even an honest taxpayer, in making a $100 contribution, would be contributing $50 of her own money and $50 of Government funds. If the individual is simultaneously allowed to receive $36 in value from the charitable donee, she is (effectively) forcing a $50 Government contribution in return for $14 of her own money. If the item received were worth $50, the individual and the charity would have conspired to force a $50 Government contribution in return for no net transfer between them.

[24] *See generally* I.R.C. § 6115 (disclosure relating to quid pro quo contributions); Treas. Reg. § 1.170A-13 (reporting and record-keeping requirements with respect to charitable contributions).

although the regulations (especially for the estate tax) contain a multitude of valuation principles, and charitable donations in excess of a statutory minimum now require at least some form of expert appraisal.

An especially sticky issue concerns donations of appreciated property. The general rule is that the amount of a contribution equals the value of the money or property contributed at the time of the contribution (Treas. Reg. § 1.170A-1(c)). Thus, shares of stock purchased several years ago for $100,000, which are now worth $500,000, can be contributed to charity and deducted at their $500,000 value. Assuming a 40 percent tax bracket, this will result in a deduction worth $200,000 to the taxpayer, or twice the original purchase price — and probably higher, if state and local taxes (not to mention Federal estate taxes) are added in. What is more, the appreciation in value of the stock, from $100,000 to $500,000, will permanently escape income tax. Note that this result would not apply if the taxpayer had sold the stock, and then contributed $500,000 in cash to the charity, in which case there would have been a $500,000 deduction but also a capital gain tax on the appreciation. Indeed the combination of a high basis and no capital gain tax usually cannot be achieved by any means except death, an event surely somewhat more conclusive, if not necessarily more unpleasant, than giving one's wealth away.

The system above means that contributions of appreciated property are extremely attractive to charities and their contributors. It also makes it inevitable that Congress would, at least partially, crack down. The crackdown is found in section 170(e) of the Code, somewhat mysteriously labeled "certain contributions of ordinary income and capital gain property."

Take a look at the first paragraph of this provision (section 170(e)(1)) and see if you can figure out what is happening. Do these rules deal adequately with the appreciated property problem described in the preceding paragraphs, or do they simply provide new tricks to be mastered by clever taxpayers? What might be a better, or more complete, way to deal with the problem? (For the purposes of these questions, it should suffice to know that "long-term capital gain" consists of gain on investment-type property held for more than one year, while "ordinary income" consists of gain on property created by the taxpayer, or held for sale in the taxpayer's trade or business. More complete definitions are found in sections 1221 and 1222 of the Code.)

In addition to the limits on appreciated property, the Code contains overall limitations on the amount of the charitable deduction in any year, restricting the deduction to 50 percent of the taxpayer's contribution base (a slightly modified version of adjusted gross income), with a 30 percent sublimit for contributions to private foundations and other subsidiary limitations. Contributions exceeding these amounts can be carried over to later taxable years, subject to the same limitations in those years. Since relatively few people give half their income to charity, these limitations affect a small number of taxpayers, but they do demonstrate that some charities are more equal than others for tax purposes, and highlight the importance of careful tax planning, even for the more generous (and wealthy) among us. One popular technique is to set up a trust, in which one's actual stocks, bonds, etc., are transferred to a university or other tax-exempt institution, and the institution pays you a portion of the income (dividends, interest, etc.) from the securities each remaining year of your life, thereby providing you with sufficient funds to continue your (presumably luxurious) lifestyle and the university with unfettered use of the assets upon your inevitable demise. In addition to favorable tax treatment, arrangements of this type convey the psychological pleasure of aiding one's favorite charity without inordinate sacrifice, and are aggressively marketed by alumni magazines, museum circulars, and similar elite publications with just these advantages in mind.

Using the Sources

1.   Are the following items fully deductible, nondeductible, or partially deductible subject to an offset for benefits provided to the donor?

a. A donation to a university, which entitles the donor to have a building named in her and her husband's honor and ceaseless fawning by university officials.

b. A donation to a university, which provides the donor with the right to purchase courtside seats at university basketball games (see section 170(l) before answering).

c. Annual church or synagogue dues, which entitle its payers to reserved seats on major holidays and the same type of fawning referred to in a., above.

d. Annual church or synagogue dues, which include reserved seats on holidays and the provision of free day-care services, which are available at a fee to non-members.

e. A "sustaining membership" at a museum, which entitles the holder (*inter alia*) to free museum admission, attendance at exclusive previews, and the chance to rub shoulders with famous artists.

f. A church or synagogue pilgrimage to the Holy Land, at a cost of $5,000, which includes numerous tourist activities but at the cost of enduring ceaseless indoctrination as to why one's own sect is virtuous and all others are flawed.

g. A raffle ticket, sponsored by the local Police Benevolent Association, entitling one to a 1-in-5,000 chance of winning a late-model police car.

Consider now the items that you concluded were either not, or not completely, deductible. If you were the IRS commissioner, in which areas would you make a major effort at enforcement, and which would you more likely leave alone? What do you think happens in the real world?

2.   How large a deduction would be permitted under section 170(e)(1) in each of the following cases? (Try to be specific about what portion of the statute you are relying on.)

a. A painting purchased by an art collector five years ago for $10,000 and contributed to a museum at a time when it was worth $100,000.

b. A painting purchased by a professional art dealer five years ago for $10,000 and contributed to a museum at a time when it was worth $100,000.

c. A manuscript donated by its own author to the National Archives, having a fair market value of $1 million.

d. Same as a. above, except that the painting was donated to a tax-exempt hospital.

e. Stock in a Fortune 500 company which was purchased by an investor five years ago for $25,000 and contributed to a university at a time when it was worth $250,000.

3.   Other than the obvious answer — "because the statute says so" — can you state a good policy reason for the results in a. through e., above? Is there a method to the madness behind this statute?

4.   The hypotheticals above assume that the value of the contributed objects is known with reasonable certainty. In actual practice, what sort of evidence would the taxpayer have to provide regarding fair market value, and how likely would the IRS be to challenge that evidence? Would your answer be any different for (say) the paintings and manuscript or the stock and other financial products?

Law and Planning

Suppose that you were 55 years old and had three assets — cash, appreciated stock, and appreciated artwork — each of them worth $500,000. The stock had a basis of $250,000, and the artwork, $100,000.[25] Both the stock and the artwork were held as investments, and each had been in your possession for a period of at least five years. You anticipated that you would need one of the three assets to live on, together with social security and other retirement benefits. Of the remaining two assets, you wanted to give one to your favorite university and the other to the local museum.

Which of the three assets would you put to each use, and why? What additional facts, if any, would you want to know before you made this decision?

Politics and Policy

1.   Based on what you now know about the charitable deduction, what do you think of the debate between Andrews and Kelman, reported at the beginning of this chapter? How does the charitable deduction measure up under the tax policy criteria of horizontal and vertical equity, economic efficiency, and simplicity or administrability effects? Who would stand to lose the most if the deduction were eliminated? Who, if anyone, would gain? Are there any changes that would make the deduction less offensive to Kelman and his supporters?

2.   How do you feel about the tax avoidance potential arising from section 170 charitable contributions? In particular, how would you feel about a proposal to limit

---

[25] The basis of cash always equals its fair market value (*i.e.*, $500,000).

all charitable contributions to the taxpayer's basis in the property (*i.e.*, a revised and stronger version of the current section 170(e)(1))? What are the arguments in favor of and against this proposal, and who would be likely to support or oppose it?

III.   OTHER ITEMIZED DEDUCTIONS: MEDICAL AND CASUALTY LOSSES AND THE TREATMENT OF STATE AND LOCAL TAXES

The charitable deduction, together with the deduction for home mortgage interest (discussed in Chapter 5), is probably the most famous of the "Schedule A" deductions. Approaching these in political impact is the deduction for state and local taxes, of particular interest to those (like your authors) who live in relatively high-tax states. The deduction for state and local taxes has overtones of federalism — one branch of government should not touch the revenue source for another — but may also be seen as a form of subsidy to high-tax jurisdictions, since it effectively reduces the costs of living in a high-tax state and (indirectly) requires higher federal taxes on those who live in other locations. Like the mortgage interest deduction, the deduction for state and local taxes is rather arbitrary, having historically been limited to income and property taxes, thus denying a deduction for sales taxes and other levies. There is now an option to deduct state sales taxes instead of income taxes, thereby advantaging residents of states with only an income or a sales tax, at the expense of residents of states with both forms of taxation. The deduction for state income taxes is paralleled in the exemption for interest on state and local ("municipal") bonds, although the latter has been severely restricted by Congress, and the Supreme Court has held it a matter of legislative grace, rather than a constitutional requirement.[26]

Two remaining provisions — the deduction for medical expenditures (section 213) and for casualty losses (section 165(c)(3)) — are of more limited import, although (in a rather perverse way) more entertaining. The casualty loss deduction is an exception to the general principle that nonbusiness losses are not deductible for income tax purposes. The idea appears to be that some personal losses — the statute refers poetically to losses from "fire, storm, shipwreck, or other casualty, or from theft," — are so dramatic and unexpected that it seems only fair to reflect them in computing taxable income. There are a number of quirky cases in these areas, emphasizing the issue of whether losses were sufficiently sudden and unexpected to merit a deduction, or were instead the culmination of long periods of wear and tear which (at least for nonbusiness assets) do not merit a tax deduction.[27] Many of these cases involve water erosion or termite damage which was in fact occurring for several years, but was unknown to the victims until their rooms or houses collapsed — from their perspective, quite suddenly — at the end of the process. Taxpayers tend to lose more of these cases than they win, although they

---

[26]   South Carolina v. Baker, 485 U.S. 505 (1988). In addition to the deductions discussed in this chapter a number of "miscellaneous" deductions, notably unreimbursed employee business expenses, are permitted on Schedule A, but only where they exceed (in the aggregate) two percent of AGI.

[27]   The casualty loss rules call to mind the late Arthur Leff's definition of an "Act of God" as "something that no reasonable God would do."

are helped along by section 165(k), which creates a presumption of a casualty loss if a home in a federal Disaster Area is ordered abandoned as a result of the disaster. The scope of the casualty loss provision is reduced significantly by section 165(h), which eliminates from consideration any loss of $100 or less, and allows a deduction only to the extent that total uninsured casualties exceed 10 percent of the taxpayer's adjusted gross income.[28] This limitation has eliminated much of the petty litigation regarding lost jewelry, household items, etc., and ensured that the provision will be used only for large, uninsured losses.

Similar in policy, although somewhat broader in scope, is the deduction for extraordinary medical expenses (section 213). Section 213 provides a deduction for uncompensated medical expenses of the taxpayer, her spouse, or dependents, to the extent that such expenses exceed 7.5 percent of the taxpayer's adjusted gross income. Together with doctor and hospital bills, medical expenses include amounts paid for prescription drugs or insulin, but not for over-the-counter medications (section 213(b)). Medical expenses also include premiums paid for health insurance (section 213(d)(1)(D)), although it is unlikely that these premiums would approach 7.5 percent of AGI unless combined with other, much larger expenditures. The policy of section 213 appears to be a mixture of sympathy for individuals with large, unanticipated medical expenses (à la the casualty loss deduction) and a subsidy for a constructive, unselfish expenditure (à la the charitable contribution provisions), although the 7.5 percent rule significantly undercuts these objectives.

Because of the percentage floor — and because section 213 applies only to uninsured medical expenses — most litigation under this statute applies to unusual, even bizarre, expenditures, rather than the normal run of medical costs. Much of the litigation turns on section 213(d)(1)(A), which defines medical care as "amounts paid for the diagnosis, cure, mitigation, treatment, or prevention of disease, or for the purpose of affecting any structure or function of the body," together with "transportation primarily for and essential to medical care referred to in subparagraph (A)" (section 213(d)(1)(B)). Almost anything could fit this definition, and much has, from long-term physical therapies to indoor ramps and elevators to taxpayers who have attempted — generally without success — to deduct vacations, golf, and even lawn-mowing services on the grounds that these will enhance (or at least avoid aggravating) their existing state of health. Travel has been a particular problem, the statute having been amended several times to clarify the difference between ordinary vacations and genuinely health-related expenditures.

Although section 213 benefits many taxpayers, it also points out some of the inequities in the tax treatment of health care expenditures. For example, individuals who receive health care from their employers have this benefit excluded under sections 104-106 of the Code, while those who do not have insurance (or whose health problems are not covered by their insurance plans) have to settle for a rather narrowly defined deduction that applies only to expenditures in excess of 7.5 percent of their adjusted gross income. Section 106, regarding Medical Savings

[28] For example, a taxpayer who had uninsured casualty losses of $100, $500, and $5,000, and adjusted gross income of $50,000, would first reduce each individual item by $100, leaving an aggregate of $5,300 in deductible casualty losses ($0 + $400 + $4,900), and then deduct the excess of this aggregate over 10 percent of AGI ($5,300 − $5,000 = $300).

Accounts, is perhaps a limited effort at redressing this inequity. This provision, loosely modeled on individual retirement accounts (IRAs), allows the taxpayer to make tax-deductible contributions to an account for uninsured medical expenses and thereby pay a portion of these expenses with pre-tax dollars. 2003 tax legislation added so-called Health Savings Accounts (HSAs), which provide similar treatment for a wider variety of health-related expenditures.

IV.   EXEMPTIONS, CREDITS, AND THE TREATMENT OF OLDER AND POORER TAXPAYERS

Tax courses tend to emphasize younger, better-off taxpayers. Problems typically assume an income of $50,000 or $100,000 and up, and everyone seems to own plenty of business and personal assets with no sign of having done much work to acquire them. Children, except those with trust funds, are all but invisible. Yet most people are not that rich or that young, and the taxation of poorer and older taxpayers — not to mention working families and their children — is a major issue in tax policy. On a practical level, many of your clients may be in this category, so knowing something about their tax problems is an important part of your professional training.

One issue that applies to all taxpayers, but which is especially important for those with more modest means, is the matter of personal exemptions under sections 151 and 152 of the Code.[29] Personal exemptions are theoretically intended to compensate the taxpayer for the additional costs inherent in having more family members and other dependents living off the same income. (One could argue that having children was just another kind of consumption, but probably not many parents would be sympathetic to that argument.) Generally speaking, a taxpayer is entitled to one exemption each for himself, his spouse, any minor children living with the taxpayer, and certain other categories covered by section 152. In cases of divorce, separation, etc., the exemption generally goes to the custodial parent unless a written agreement to the contrary is negotiated between the two parties.

Since the exemption for 2009 returns was equal to $3,650, it is obviously insufficient to cover the additional costs of a new child, and we have yet to hear of anyone who enlarged their family specifically to qualify for this benefit. It is therefore probably best to think of the exemption as a symbolic recognition of the costs inherent in raising children and a modest helping hand, together with the child care credit and other provisions, for people who do so. Yet these amounts may still be significant, especially for working- or lower-class taxpayers, and the allocation of exemptions in a divorce or separation agreement may be an important issue between the parties. From a policy standpoint, an increased personal exemption is frequently proposed as a means of helping large families, particularly those with one stay-at-home parent who would not benefit from a child-care deduction or credit.

---

[29] The personal exemption is available to all taxpayers and should not be confused with the standard deduction, which is available only to taxpayers who choose not to itemize their deductions on Schedule A.

One entertaining aspect of section 151 is the treatment of full-time students, who may be treated as dependents up to the age of 23 instead of the age of 18 that applies to other individuals (presumably on the theory that students cannot support themselves financially, rather than any presumed immaturity attached to the educational experience). Also noteworthy is the phase-out of personal exemptions for taxpayers having more than approximately $159,950 of AGI in 2008 ($239,950 for joint returns). This provision introduces a note of progressivity into the personal exemptions, but — since everyone has at least one personal exemption — it is also a clever way of sneaking in a higher tax rate on wealthy individuals without it appearing in the regular tax tables.

In the past few decades, the personal exemption has been supplemented by an increasing number of new provisions designed to compensate taxpayers for the costs of caring for children and other relatives and (one suspects) to make a political statement in favor of "family values" and other causes popular at election time. We have seen examples of this phenomenon in the child and dependent care credit (section 21) and the various tax breaks for education — including tuition tax credits, partial deduction for educational expenditures, exclusion for employer-provided educational assistance, and a partial deduction for student loan interest — that have appeared at various places in the text. The Code also includes tax breaks for merely having children (*i.e.*, regardless of child care expenses[30]), for care of elderly and disabled taxpayers, and for various other noble purposes. Because these tax breaks are at least theoretically aimed at working- or middle-class taxpayers, they tend to be designed as credits rather than deductions, thereby providing the same benefit per dollar of expenditure to a poor or a rich individual. This is frequently combined with a phase-out or "cutoff" provision that denies the benefit outright to people above a defined income level. Tax scholars tend to dislike these provisions, which are enormously complex and have dubious effects on behavior (i.e., would parents refuse to educate their children or care for sick relatives, in the absence of a modest tax credit?), but they are politically popular and may provide an added boost to families who would otherwise have difficulty meeting the costs of the activity in question. Like the personal exemption, they are perhaps best seen as a form of symbolic assistance to a (supposedly) beleaguered working and middle class, rewarding good behavior and providing just enough of a subsidy to make a difference in very close cases. It is also noteworthy that — in the aggregate — these provisions have substantially increased the progressivity of the tax system.

Perhaps the most important innovation in this area has been the advent of the earned income credit (EIC) in section 32, a rare provision that is actually aimed at poorer rather than effectively middle class taxpayers. The EIC is intended to reduce the tax on the working poor and thereby increase the incentive to seek employment as opposed to welfare or other public assistance programs. (Many other provisions, including Social Security taxes and the loss of health or welfare benefits, tend to discourage people from working in these conditions.) To accomplish this goal, the EIC provides a credit against the tax liability of individuals with modified adjusted gross incomes below a specified threshold level, which is higher

---

[30] I.R.C. § 24. The child tax credit is a maximum of $1,000 per qualifying child and is phased out for upper-income taxpayers.

for taxpayers with children than those without, although the latter may still qualify for the credit. The actual amount of the credit depends upon the taxpayer's income and the number of qualifying children (zero, one, or two or more), with the credit phasing down to zero at higher income levels. The EIC thus functions as a sort of negative income tax or, if one prefers, as an indirect refund of Social Security and other employment taxes on lower-income taxes; as such, it has attracted wide support from both liberal and conservative lawmakers.

One interesting aspect of the EIC is that — unlike most tax credits — it is fully refundable; that is, if the amount of the credit exceeds income tax liability, the Government will write a check to the individual for the difference, making the EIC a sort of hybrid between a tax credit and a direct spending program. Given the extent of this benefit, it is frustrating that many people eligible for the EIC do not claim it, resulting from lack of knowledge and (one suspects) fear of Government in poor, especially immigrant, communities. A major publicity effort is in progress to reverse this unfortunate trend. Also unfortunate are repeated reports of cheating with respect to the EIC, a problem ironically magnified by the speed and efficiency of electronic tax filing systems; a substantial effort has likewise been made to combat this problem.[31]

If child-care and similar credits are important to middle-income families, and the EIC to the working poor, what about older and retired taxpayers? Generally speaking, the composition of spending programs — Social Security, Medicare, and so forth — is more important to senior older citizens than purely tax issues. Two important exceptions are the tax rules pertaining to pensions and retirement plans, described in Chapter 4, and the taxation of Social Security payments. Until the 1980s, Social Security income was exempt from direct or indirect tax. Since then, a portion of Social Security income has been subject to tax for some individuals. This provision is less than enthralling to most senior citizens, who find it odd for the Government to be distributing retirement benefits with one hand and taxing away part of them with another.[32] Yet taxation of at least a portion of Social Security benefits is probably necessary to achieve a measure of fairness between generations as well as between wealthier and poorer senior citizens, a distinction that tends to be overlooked in the retirement debate, but that remains very real. Like the EIC and other tax credits, the debate on social security taxation illustrates the inevitable politicization of tax issues, and the necessity to coordinate tax policy with spending, regulatory, and other policies affecting the same constituency.

---

[31] *See, e.g.,* Anne L. Alstott, *The Earned Income Tax Credit and the Limitations of Tax-Based Welfare Reform,* 108 HARV. L. REV. 533 (1995); Jonathan Barry Forman, *Improving the Delivery of Benefits to the Working Poor: Proposals to Reform the Earned Income Tax Credit Program,* 11 AM J. TAX POL'Y 225 (1994). The child tax credit (section 24) is also partially refundable.

[32] The precise formula for inclusion is described in footnote 26 of the Background and Basic Themes Chapter.

Using the Sources

1. Which of the following qualify for a personal exemption under sections 151 and 152 of the Code?

    a. The taxpayer's 10-year-old daughter.

    b. The taxpayer's 25-year-old daughter who lives at home and is supported primarily by scholarships and a summer job.

    c. The taxpayer's 85-year-old father who lives with the taxpayer and is supported primarily by Social Security and pension distributions.

    d. An adopted child who remains a citizen of a foreign country and resides for most of the year in that country.

    e. A child of divorced parents who lives with his mother but receives more than half his support from his father.

2. What would be the approximate amount of the earned income credit under section 32 in each of the following cases? (You may state a general range if it is too difficult to make a precise computation.)

    a. An individual with no qualifying children and earned income of $7,500.

    b. An individual with one qualifying child and earned income of $12,500.

    c. A married couple with two qualifying children and earned income of $15,000.

What, if anything, do your answers say about the policy behind the earned income credit and how well it works in actual practice?

3. Section 3507 of the Code provides for advanced payment of the EIC by the taxpayer's employer in some cases. Why does this provision exist, and who do you think would benefit from it?

4. Look over tax forms 1040 and Schedule A at the end of the Background and Basic Themes Chapter. See if you can answer the following questions based only on reviewing the tax forms.

    a. If a taxpayer wants to claim the standard deduction, on which line of the forms would they do so? Can you see how the forms make taxpayers choose between either claiming the standard deduction or itemized deductions?

    b. If a taxpayer wants to claim a charitable contribution deduction, where on the forms would they do so?

    c. If a taxpayer wants to claim a deduction for paid state and local taxes, where on the forms would they do so?

    d. Where on the forms would a taxpayer claim and calculate personal exemptions?

    e. Based solely on examining the forms, can you identify two personal deductions that need to be itemized (below-the-line deductions) and two that do not (above-the-line deductions)?

f. Which credits are refundable (can lead to a negative income tax liability), and how do the forms enact the distinction between refundable and non-refundable credits?

Law and Planning

1.   Suppose that you were counsel to Karen Kaminsky, who was in the process of getting divorced from her husband, Karl, and expected to receive custody of the couple's two children, Kenneth and Katelin. Karen's cash income was likely to be in the vicinity of $50,000 per year and Karl's about two or three times that; accordingly, Karl was to pay some alimony and a substantial amount of child support, and have visitation rights with respect to each child.

What options do Karen and Karl have regarding the allocation of future personal exemptions for Kenneth and Katelin, and which of these different options would you advise them to pursue? What additional facts, if any, would you want to know in order to make a more effective decision? (*See* § 152(e).)

2.   Now suppose you were working in a tax clinic, and you asked your first client how many children he had. "Three," he replied, "and I love them very much and try to help out whenever I can, but I have very little money, and, to be honest, I haven't seen much of them or their mother lately."

How would you advise him to handle personal exemptions on his tax return?

Politics and Policy

In dealing with less-wealthy taxpayers, one notices quickly the interplay of tax and non-tax factors, and the need to coordinate policy in these different areas. Consider five alternatives for assisting poor or middle-class taxpayers, each of which we will assume to bear the same revenue cost:

a. Increase the personal exemption, retaining the phase-out for wealthy taxpayers.

b. Increase the section 21, 24, and similar tax credits.

c. Increase the earned income credit.

d. Reduce the tax rate on the lowest income bracket below 10 percent.

e. Increase the minimum wage (no immediate revenue cost).

Which of the above strikes you as the preferred alternative for assisting the group in question? Why?

Additional Assignment — Chapter 7

You are a Washington-based tax lawyer with a specialty in creating and advising tax-exempt, section 501(c)(3) organizations. You are approached by an old friend, Dana Dogood, with the following proposition: Dana believes that there are too many organizations out there promoting the opposite sides of the Middle East (Arab-Israeli) conflict and would like to start a new charitable organization to encourage peacemaking and other "outreach" efforts. Although the exact parameters have yet to be mapped out, at a minimum, the organization would engage in the following activities:

1. The organization would conduct its own programs, including speakers, seminars, educational forums, and the like, to encourage understanding between Israelis and Arabs and their American supporters, and thereby counteract some of the more hostile attitudes emerging from both sides.

2. The organization would make grants to individuals or other charitable organizations for projects designed to promote understanding between the two sides, including exchange programs and scholarly research projects designed to promote a peaceful resolution of the conflict.

3. The organization, or a subsidiary, would engage in lobbying efforts designed to encourage an "enlightened" attitude toward the Middle East on the part of the United States Congress and Administration.

4. To fund items 1 through 3 above, the organization would seek to raise money from like-minded individuals through income tax-deductible contributions to the extent possible.

Dana is somewhat idealistic, but also has a lot of money, as do many of her friends; accordingly, she cannot be completely ignored, at least not by her own lawyer.

What advice can you offer Dana regarding the tax and (where relevant) practical aspects of her proposal? In particular, under what Code section or sections could Dana's proposed organization qualify for tax-exemption, and would you recommend that she create a single or two or more separate organizations to conduct her project? What additional questions, if any, would you want to ask her before deciding? Try to be as specific as possible about the various Code provisions and their effect upon your recommendations. (Note: In addition to the materials above, you may wish to have a quick look at section 509, regarding private foundations, and the parts of sections 170 and 501 that refer to it.)

Chapter 8

CAPITALIZATION, DEPRECIATION, AND TAX AVOIDANCE

Chapter 7 discussed expenditures that, despite their non-business character, are permitted a whole or a partial deduction. This chapter returns to business expenditures, emphasizing the question of when, rather than whether, the items in question are deductible. This issue is in many respects similar to the timing of income, but with a significant role reversal: since deductions are at stake, it will now be taxpayers who argue for faster realization and recognition events, while the IRS will seek to delay deductions until some later date. The issue also involves a broader clash of philosophies, with the IRS tending to favor deductions that correspond to the economic reality of a business, while taxpayers seek faster deductions in order to provide an "incentive" for favored kinds of investment. Because the amounts of money are large — the timing of deductions can make a difference between a good or bad investment and a successful or unsuccessful project — this issue is especially hard fought, involving large numbers of cases, IRS rulings, and frequent (and sometimes inconsistent) congressional action.

This chapter is also important for tax planning purposes. Because of the prevalence of tax incentives, many business transactions produce rapid tax deductions while producing slower — if any — real economic losses, and are accordingly attractive targets for tax shelter investments. Especially attractive are investments which generate excess deductions — that is, deductions in excess of taxable income — that can be used to reduce tax on one's salary or other income. Tax shelters can be as simple as inflated charitable deductions, or as complex as an overseas financing scheme, but the classic tax shelters typically involved investments in tangible, depreciable assets — oil and gas, real estate, industrial equipment, etc. — that generated deductions in the early years and taxable income, if at all, only much later on. This chapter is thus a good opportunity to begin investigating the economic, moral, and tax dimensions of the entire tax shelter problem (an investigation we will later continue as part of our discussion of business and international taxation in Chapters 11 and 12). We will also consider anti-tax shelter mechanisms, notably the passive activity loss rules (section 469), and ask whether these provisions are effective solutions to the tax shelter problem or have merely resulted in new, different kinds of unfairness.

Before beginning this chapter, we should clarify some terminology. Virtually all the expenses in this chapter are business-related and therefore deductible, in the sense that nearly all can be subtracted from taxable income at some point in time. The question, as suggested above, is when.

A large category of business expenditures — *e.g.*, pens, paper, rent for an office building, most employees' salaries — give rise to an immediate benefit and hence are deductible when paid (or, for an accrual taxpayer, when they accrue). These expenses are said to be "currently deductible," "immediately deductible," or (somewhat confusingly) "deductible under section 162," in order to distinguish them from expenditures, the deduction of which is delayed or denied by the Code.

A second category — *e.g.*, buildings, equipment, and intangible assets like a patent or copyright — provide benefits for more than one year but not forever. The deduction for these benefits is spread out over a five-, ten-, fifteen-, or other multi-year period which is theoretically designed to match the period over which income is being produced. These incremental deductions are most frequently called "depreciation," although the term "amortization" is often applied to intangibles, and some people have given up altogether and call both categories "cost recovery" (although this tells you nothing about the actual method used). As the Code has become more and more generous, the "cost recovery" term has been modified to "accelerated cost recovery," "moderated cost recovery," and other exotic phrases, perhaps recognizing that the system has more to do with politics than with a serious attempt to measure the depreciation or decline in value of a particular asset.

Finally, a large category of assets — notably stock and undeveloped land — do not necessarily lose value over time, and thus result in neither immediate nor delayed deductions. Instead, the taxpayer takes a basis in the asset when purchased and offsets that basis against the amount realized on the asset later on. The costs of these assets are often said to be "capitalized" rather than deducted, although the term "capitalization" is also applied to the second (depreciation) category in order to distinguish it from those expenditures which qualify for immediate deduction. Aggravating this confusion is section 263 of the Code, which makes clear that certain long-range expenditures are not immediately deductible, but does not always specify if they fit in category 2 (depreciation-style deductions) or category 3 (no deductions either now or over time, instead only basis offsets upon realization).

There are thus two steps to the question of when a deduction (or basis offset) can be taken for business-related expenses. The first asks: *Is the expense currently deductible, or must the expense be capitalized (by adding the amount of the expense to basis)?* The second step only applies for capitalized expenses, and asks: *Can depreciation or amortization deductions be taken, or are no deductions allowed until basis offset upon realization?*

It is useful to consider these questions in turn, beginning with the first question: *When are expenses currently deductible, and when must they be capitalized?*

I.   CURRENT AND CAPITAL EXPENDITURES

A.   Repairs and Improvements

MIDLAND EMPIRE PACKING COMPANY v. COMMISSIONER
United States Tax Court
14 T.C. 635 (1950)

This case involves deficiencies in declared value excess profits tax in the amount of $321.34 and excess profits tax in the amount of $4,092.72 for the taxable year ended November 30, 1943. The issue presented for decision is whether or not the sum of $4,868.81 expended by the petitioner in oilproofing the basement of its meat-packing plant during the taxable year 1943 is deductible as an ordinary and necessary business expense under section 23(a) of the Internal Revenue Code, or, in the alternative, as a loss sustained during the year and not compensated for by insurance or otherwise under section 23(f) of the Internal Revenue Code.

The case has been submitted on a partial stipulation of facts, documentary evidence, and oral testimony.

FINDINGS OF FACT

The petitioner, herein sometimes referred to as Midland, is a Montana corporation and the owner of a meat-packing plant which is located adjacent to the city of Billings, Yellowstone County, State of Montana. Its returns for the period here involved were filed with the collector of internal revenue for the district of Montana. Its books of account and its tax returns were, during the taxable year and at all other times, kept on the accrual basis of accounting. Petitioner's returns were based on a fiscal year ending November 30.

The basement rooms of petitioner's plant were used by it in its business for the curing of hams and bacon and for the storage of meat and hides. These rooms have been used for such purposes since the plant was constructed in about 1917. The original walls and floors, which were of concrete, were not sealed against water. There had been seepage for many years and this condition became worse around 1943. At certain seasons of the year, when the water in the Yellowstone River was high, the underground water caused increased seepage in the plant. Such water did not interfere with petitioner's use of the basement rooms. They were satisfactory for their purpose until 1943.

The Yale Oil Corporation, sometimes referred to herein as Yale, was the owner of an oil-refining plant and storage area located some 300 yards upgrade from petitioner's meat-packing plant. The oil plant was constructed some years after petitioner had been in business in its present location. Yale expanded its plant and storage from year to year and oil escaping from the plant and storage facilities was carried to the ground surrounding the plant of petitioner. In 1943 petitioner found that oil was seeping into its water wells and into water which came through the concrete walls of the basement of its packing plant. The water would soon drain out through the sump, leaving a thick scum of oil on the basement floor. Such oil gave off a strong odor, which permeated the air of the entire plant. The oil in the basement and fumes therefrom created a fire hazard. The Federal meat inspectors advised petitioner to oilproof the basement and discontinue the use of the water wells or shut down the plant.

As soon as petitioner discovered that oil had begun to seep into its water wells and into the basement of its plant, its officers conferred with the officers of the Yale Oil Corporation and informed Yale that they intended to hold it liable for all damage caused by the oil which had saturated the ground around its packing plant. They informed the officials of Yale that they believed this condition constituted a legal nuisance, which condition they expected would continue to exist for future years, and that they were discontinuing the use of their water wells. The officials of Yale were also informed that the Federal inspectors were requiring petitioner to oilproof the basement.

[The opinion proceeds here to describe, at some length, the negotiations between Midland and Yale's attorneys, noting, *inter alia*, that the defendant's attorneys believe Midland's claims to be valid and that (unknown to Midland) Yale had insurance coverage for such instances. — Ed.]

The original walls and floor of petitioner's plant were of concrete construction. For the purpose of preventing oil from entering its basement, petitioner added concrete lining to the walls from the floor to a height of about four feet, and also added concrete to the floor of the basement. Since the walls and floor had been thickened, petitioner now had less space in which to operate. Petitioner had this work done by independent contractors, supervised by [a construction company — Ed.], in the fiscal year ended November 30, 1943, at a cost of $4,868.81. Petitioner paid for this work during that year.

The oilproofing work was effective in sealing out the oil. While it has served the purposes for which it was intended down to the present time, it did not increase the useful life of the building or make the building more valuable for any purpose than it had been before the oil had come into the basement. The primary object of the oilproofing operation was to prevent the seepage of oil into the basement so that the petitioner could use the basement as before in preparing and packing meat for commercial consumption.

After the oilproofing was completed and prior to the close of the petitioner's taxable year ended November 30, 1943, negotiations for settlement were again conducted between representatives of petitioner and the Yale Oil Corporation, at which time Yale offered to pay petitioner in cash the sum of approximately $7,500 in satisfaction of all claims asserted by Midland against Yale, provided Midland would execute a general release to Yale. Because Midland was unwilling and refused to give such release for the payment offered, no amount was in fact paid to petitioner by Yale in that year. Petitioner continued to maintain that it was entitled to a much larger amount for the general damage done to the plant by this nuisance. Negotiations had reached this point in the fiscal year ended November 30, 1943.

The petitioner thereafter filed suit against Yale, on April 22, 1944, in a cause of action sounding in tort and on November 30, 1944, joined as a defendant in such action Yale's successor, the Carter Oil Co., which had acquired the properties of Yale Oil Corporation. This action was to recover damages for the nuisance created by the oil seepage. In those proceedings the defendants demurred to the joinder of parties in the petitioner's complaint. On appeal, the Montana Supreme Court sustained the demurrer.

Petitioner subsequently settled its cause of action against Yale for $11,659.49 and gave Yale a complete release from all liability. This release was dated October 23, 1946. The recovery of the cost of the waterproofing only was reported in its excess profits and income tax returns for the year ended November 30, 1946.

The petitioner is still making claim upon the Carter Oil Co. and is endeavoring to settle that claim without suit.

Midland charged the $4,868.81 to repair expense on its regular books and deducted that amount on its tax returns as an ordinary and necessary business expense for the fiscal year 1943. The Commissioner, in his notice of deficiency, determined that the cost of oilproofing was not deductible, either as an ordinary and necessary expense or as a loss in 1943.

OPINION

The issue in this case is whether an expenditure for a concrete lining in petitioner's basement to oilproof it against an oil nuisance created by a neighboring refinery is deductible as an ordinary and necessary expense under section 23(a) of the Internal Revenue Code, on the theory it was an expenditure for a repair, or, in the alternative, whether the expenditure may be treated as the measure of the loss sustained during the taxable year and not compensated for by insurance or otherwise within the meaning of section 23(f) of the Internal Revenue Code.

The respondent has contended, in part, that the expenditure is for a capital improvement and should be recovered through depreciation charges and is, therefore, not deductible as an ordinary and necessary business expense or as a loss.

It is none too easy to determine on which side of the line certain expenditures fall so that they may be accorded their proper treatment for tax purposes. Treasury Regulations 111,[1] from which we quote in the margin, is helpful in distinguishing between an expenditure to be classed as a repair and one to be treated as a capital outlay. In *Illinois Merchants Trust Co., Executor*, 4 B.T.A. 103, at page 106, we discussed this subject in some detail and in our opinion said:

It will be noted that the first sentence of the article [now Regulations 111, sec. 29.23(a)-4] relates to repairs, while the second sentence deals in effect with replacements. In determining whether an expenditure is a capital one

---

[1] [*] Section 29.23(a)-4. Repairs. — The cost of incidental repairs which neither materially add to the value of the property nor appreciably prolong its life, but keep it in an ordinarily efficient operating condition, may be deducted as expense, provided the plant or property account is not increased by the amount of such expenditures. Repairs in the nature of replacements, to the extent that they arrest deterioration and appreciably prolong the life of the property, should be charged against the depreciation reserve if such account is kept. (*See* sections 29.23(l)-1 to 29.23(l)-10, inclusive.)

or is chargeable against operating income, it is necessary to bear in mind the purpose for which the expenditure was made. To repair is to restore to a sound state or to mend, while a replacement connotes a substitution. A repair is an expenditure for the purpose of keeping the property in an ordinarily efficient operating condition. It does not add to the value of the property, nor does it appreciably prolong its life. It merely keeps the property in an operating condition over its probable useful life for the uses for which it was acquired. Expenditures for that purpose are distinguishable from those for replacements, alterations, improvements, or additions which prolong the life of the property, increase its value, or make it adaptable to a different use. The one is a maintenance charge, while the others are additions to capital investment which should not be applied against current earnings.

It will be seen from our findings of fact that for some 25 years prior to the taxable year petitioner had used the basement rooms of its plant as a place for the curing of hams and bacon and for the storage of meat and hides. The basement had been entirely satisfactory for this purpose over the entire period in spite of the fact that there was some seepage of water into the rooms from time to time. In the taxable year it was found that not only water, but oil, was seeping through the concrete walls of the basement of the packing plant and, while the water would soon drain out, the oil would not, and there was left on the basement floor a thick scum of oil which gave off a strong odor that permeated the air of the entire plant, and the fumes from the oil created a fire hazard. It appears that the oil which came from a nearby refinery had also gotten into the water wells which served to furnish water for petitioner's plant, and as a result of this whole condition the Federal meat inspectors advised petitioner that it must discontinue the use of the water from the wells and oilproof the basement, or else shut down its plant.

To meet this situation, petitioner during the taxable year undertook steps to oilproof the basement by adding a concrete lining to the walls from the floor to a height of about four feet and also added concrete to the floor of the basement. It is the cost of this work which it seeks to deduct as a repair. The basement was not enlarged by this work, nor did the oilproofing serve to make it more desirable for the purpose for which it had been used through the years prior to the time that the oil nuisance had occurred. The evidence is that the expenditure did not add to the value or prolong the expected life of the property over what they were before the event occurred which made the repairs necessary. It is true that after the work was done the seepage of water, as well as oil, was stopped, but, as already stated, the presence of the water had never been found objectionable. The repairs merely served to keep the property in an operating condition over its probable useful life for the purpose for which it was used.

While it is conceded on brief that the expenditure was "necessary," respondent contends that the encroachment of the oil nuisance on petitioner's property was not an "ordinary" expense in petitioner's particular business. But the fact that petitioner had not theretofore been called upon to make a similar expenditure to prevent damage and disaster to its property does not remove that expense from the classification of "ordinary" for, as stated in *Welch v. Helvering*, 290 U.S. 111, "ordinary in this context does not mean that the payments must be habitual or normal in the sense that the same taxpayer will have to make them often. . . . the expense is an ordinary one because we know from experience that payments for such a purpose, whether the amount is large or small, are the common and accepted means of defense against attack. *Cf. Kornhauser v. United States*, 276 U.S. 145. The situation is unique in the life of the individual affected, but not in the life of the group, the community, of which he is a part." Steps to protect a business building from the seepage of oil from a nearby refinery, which had been erected long subsequent to the time petitioner started to operate its plant, would seem to us to be a normal thing to do, and in certain sections of the country it must be a common experience to protect one's property from the seepage of oil. Expenditures to accomplish this result are likewise normal.

In *American Bemberg Corporation*, 10 T.C. 361, we allowed as deductions, on the ground that they were ordinary and necessary expenses, extensive expenditures made to prevent disaster, although the repairs were of a type which had never been needed before and were unlikely to recur. In that case the taxpayer, to stop cave-ins of soil which were threatening destruction of its manufacturing plant, hired an engineering firm which drilled to the bedrock and injected grout to fill the cavities where practicable, and made incidental replacements and repairs, including tightening of the fluid carriers. In two successive years the taxpayer expended $734,316.76 and $199,154.33, respectively, for such drilling and grouting and $153,474.20 and $79,687.29, respectively, for capital replacements. We found that the cost (other than replacement) of this program did not make good the depreciation previously allowed, and stated in our opinion:

> In connection with the purpose of the work, the Proctor program was intended to avert a plant-wide disaster and avoid forced abandonment of the plant. The purpose was not to improve, better, extend, or increase the original plant, nor to prolong its original useful life. Its continued operation was endangered; the purpose of the expenditures was to enable petitioner to continue the plant in operation not on any new or better scale, but on the same scale and, so far as possible, as efficiently as it had operated before. The purpose was not to rebuild or replace the plant in whole or in part, but to keep the same plant as it was and where it was.

The petitioner here made the repairs in question in order that it might continue to operate its plant. Not only was there danger of fire from the oil and fumes, but the presence of the oil led the Federal meat inspectors to declare the basement an unsuitable place for the purpose for which it had been used for a quarter of a century. After the expenditures were made, the plant did not operate on a changed or larger scale, nor was it thereafter suitable for new or additional uses. The expenditure served only to permit petitioner to continue the use of the plant, and particularly the basement for its normal operations.

In our opinion, the expenditure of $4,868.81 for lining the basement walls and floor was essentially a repair and, as such, it is deductible as an ordinary and necessary business expense. This holding makes unnecessary a consideration of petitioner's alternative contention that the expenditure is deductible as a business loss, nor need we heed the respondent's argument that any loss suffered was compensated for by "insurance or otherwise."

Decision will be entered under Rule 50.

MT. MORRIS DRIVE-IN THEATRE CO. v. COMMISSIONER
United States Tax Court
25 T.C. 272 (1955)

KERN, J:

The Commissioner determined a deficiency in the petitioner's income and excess profits tax for 1950 in the amount of $3,150.13. The only issue for decision is whether the amount of $8,224 spent by the petitioner in 1950 to construct a drainage system was deductible either as an ordinary or necessary business expense or as a loss, as contended by the petitioner, or whether it was a nondepreciable capital expenditure, as determined by the Commissioner. An alternative issue raised by the petitioner that the cost of the drainage system should be amortized over a period of at least 5 years was expressly abandoned by it at the hearing.

FINDINGS OF FACT

The petitioner is an Ohio corporation with its principal offices in Cleveland, Ohio. It filed an original and an amended Federal income and excess profits tax return for the calendar year 1950 with the collector of internal revenue for the eighteenth district of Ohio.

In 1947 petitioner purchased 13 acres of farm land located on the outskirts of Flint, Michigan, upon which it proceeded to construct a drive-in or outdoor theatre. Prior to its purchase by the petitioner the land on which the theatre was built was farm land and contained vegetation. The slope of the land was such that the natural drainage of water was from the southerly line to the northerly boundary of the property and thence onto the adjacent land, owned by David and Mary D. Nickola, which was used both for farming and a trailer park. The petitioner's land sloped sharply from south to north and also sloped from the east downward towards the west so that most of the drainage from the petitioner's property was onto the southwest corner of the Nickolas' land. The topography of the land purchased by petitioner was well known to petitioner at the time it was purchased and developed. The petitioner did not change the general slope of its land in constructing the drive-in theatre, but it removed the covering vegetation from the land, slightly increased the grade, and built aisles or ramps which were covered with gravel and were somewhat raised so that the passengers in the automobiles would be able to view the picture on the large outdoor screen.

As a result of petitioner's construction on and use of this land rain water falling upon it drained with an increased flow into and upon the adjacent property of the Nickolas. This result should reasonably have been anticipated by petitioner at the time when the construction work was done.

The Nickolas complained to the petitioner at various times after petitioner began the construction of the theatre that the work resulted in an acceleration and concentration of the flow of water which drained from the petitioner's property onto the Nickolas' land causing damage to their crops and roadways. On or about October 11, 1948, the Nickolas filed a suit against the petitioner in the Circuit Court for the County of Genesee, State of Michigan, asking for an award for damages done to their property by the accelerated and concentrated drainage of the water and for a permanent injunction restraining the defendant from permitting such drainage to continue. Following the filing of an answer by the petitioner and of a reply thereto by the Nickolas, the suit was settled by an agreement dated June 27, 1950. This agreement provided for the construction by the petitioner of a drainage system to carry water from its northern boundary across the Nickolas' property and thence to a public drain. The cost of maintaining the system was to be shared by the petitioner and the Nickolas, and the latter granted the petitioner and its successors an easement across their land for the purpose of constructing and maintaining the drainage system. The construction of the drain was completed in October 1950 under the supervision of engineers employed by the petitioner and the Nickolas at a cost to the petitioner of $8,224, which amount was paid by it in November 1950. The performance by the petitioner on its part of the agreement to construct the drainage system and to maintain the portion for which it was responsible constituted a full release of the Nickolas' claims against it. The petitioner chose to settle the dispute by constructing the drainage system because it did not wish to risk the possibility that continued litigation might result in a permanent injunction against its use of the drive-in theatre and because it wished to eliminate the cause of the friction between it and the adjacent landowners, who were in a position to seriously interfere with the petitioner's use of its property for outdoor theatre purposes. A settlement based on a monetary payment for past damages, the petitioner believed, would not remove the threat of claims for future damages.

On its 1950 income and excess profits tax return the petitioner claimed a deduction of $822.40 for depreciation of the drainage system for the period July 1, 1950, to December 31, 1950. The Commissioner disallowed without itemization $5,514.60 of a total depreciation expense deduction of $19,326.41 claimed by the petitioner. In its petition the petitioner asserted that the entire amount spent to construct the drainage system was fully deductible in 1950 as an ordinary and necessary business expense incurred in the settlement of a lawsuit, or, in the alternative, as a loss, and claimed a refund of part of the $10,591.56 of income and excess profits tax paid by it for that year.

The drainage system was a permanent improvement to the petitioner's property, and the cost thereof constituted a capital expenditure.

The stipulation of facts and the exhibits annexed thereto are incorporated herein by this reference.

OPINION

When petitioner purchased, in 1947, the land which it intended to use for a drive-in theatre, its president was thoroughly familiar with the topography of this land which was such that when the covering vegetation was removed and graveled ramps were constructed and used by its patrons, the flow of natural precipitation on the lands of abutting property owners would be materially accelerated. Some provision should have been made to solve this drainage problem in order to avoid annoyance and harassment to its neighbors. If petitioner had included in its original construction plans an expenditure for a proper drainage system no one could doubt that such an expenditure would have been capital in nature.

Within a year after petitioner had finished its inadequate construction of the drive-in theatre, the need of a proper drainage system was forcibly called to its attention by one of the neighboring property owners, and under the threat of a lawsuit filed approximately a year after the theatre was constructed, the drainage system was built by petitioner who now seeks to deduct its cost as an ordinary and necessary business expense, or as a loss.

We agree with respondent that the cost to petitioner of acquiring and constructing a drainage system in connection with its drive-in theatre was a capital expenditure.

Here was no sudden catastrophic loss caused by a physical "fault" undetected by the taxpayer in spite of due precautions taken by it at the time of its original construction work as in *American Bemberg Corporation*, 10 TC 361; no unforeseeable external factor as in *Midland Empire Packing Co.*, 14 TC 635; and no change in the cultivation of farm property caused by improvements in technique and made many years after the property in question was put to productive use as in *J.H. Collingwood*, 20 TC 937. In the instant case it was obvious at the time when the drive-in theatre was constructed, that a drainage system would be required to properly dispose of the natural precipitation normally to be expected, and that until this was accomplished, petitioner's capital investment was incomplete. In addition, it should be emphasized that here there was no mere restoration or rearrangement of the original capital asset, but there was the acquisition and construction of a capital asset which petitioner had not previously had, namely, a new drainage system.

That this drainage system was acquired and constructed and that payments therefore were made in compromise of a lawsuit is not determinative of whether such payments were ordinary and necessary business expenses or capital expenditures. "The decisive test is still the character of the transaction which gives rise to the payment." *Hales-Mullaly v. Commissioner*, 131 F.2d 509, 511, 512.

In our opinion the character of the transaction in the instant case indicates that the transaction was a capital expenditure.

Decision will be entered for the respondent.

RAUM, J., concurring:

The expenditure herein was plainly capital in nature, and, as the majority opinion points out, if provision had been made in the original plans for the construction of a drainage system there could hardly be any question that its cost would have been treated as a capital outlay. The character of the expenditure is not changed merely because it is made at a subsequent time, and I think it wholly irrelevant whether the necessity for the drainage system could have been foreseen, or whether the payment therefore was made as a result of the pressure of a law suit.

RICE, J., dissenting:

It seems to me that *JH Collingwood*, 20 TC 937 (1953), *Midland Empire Packing Co.*, 14 TC 635 (1950), *American Bemberg Corporation*, 10 TC 361 (1948), *affd.* 177 F.2d 200 (C.A. 1949), and *Illinois Merchants Trust Co. Executor*, 4 BTA 103 (19267), are ample authority or the conclusion that the expenditure which petitioner made was an ordinary and necessary business expense, which did not improve, better, extend, increase, or prolong the useful life of its property. The expenditure did not cure the original geological defect of the natural drainage onto the Nickolas' land, but only dealt with the intermediate consequence thereof. The majority opinion does not distinguish those cases adequately. And since those cases and the result reached herein do not seem to me to be able to "live together," I cannot agree with the majority that the expenditure here was capital in nature.

Understanding *Midland Empire* and *Mt. Morris*

1.   *Midland Empire* and *Mt. Morris* involved similar fact patterns: A new facility caused a leak that damaged a neighbor's property. The leak was plugged. The neighbor was unhappy. So why did the *Midland Empire* taxpayer win, and the *Mt. Morris* taxpayer lose? In answering this question, consider the following differences between the two cases:

   a. The taxpayer in *Midland Empire* was the "good guy" — that is, the party whose property was being damaged — while the taxpayer in *Mt. Morris* was the party that had caused the original damage.

   b. The flooding caused by the drive-in theater in *Mt. Morris* was foreseeable at the time the drive-in was constructed, so that the costs of correcting this problem should be depreciated as part of the overall cost of the facility, while the damage in *Midland Empire* was unanticipated and unforeseeable.

   c. The methods used to deal with the groundwater problem in *Mt. Morris* gave rise to longer-term benefits than the methods used to protect the vaults in *Midland Empire*.

Which if any of these factors explains the outcomes? Or are the cases inconsistent? If *Mt. Morris* had been identical to *Midland Empire*, but the polluter (instead of the victim) had been required to correct the problem, how do you think the case would have come out? Why?

2.   Under Treasury Regulations, section 1.162-4, repairs are currently deductible if they "neither materially add to the value of the property nor appreciably prolong its [useful] life. . . ." Does any serious repair really pass this test? Aren't the *Mt. Morris* and *Midland Empire* facilities both worth more with the new adjustments than without them? Or is the key word "materially" — *i.e.*, a repair is currently deductible so long as it does not add too much value, or so long as the value added (or the extension of useful life) is relatively small compared to the

repair or maintenance function? What is the policy reason for distinguishing repairs and improvements, and how effectively do the Regulations advance that policy?

The deductibility of repairs but not improvements results in a strange incentive: for some tax purposes, it is better to make a mess and clean it up than to prevent the mess from happening in the first place. This incentive is especially inconsistent with environmental policy, which quite reasonably prefers the prevention of environmental damage to the remediation of an already existing problem. A taxpayer who follows this good (environmental) advice may wind up with delayed, potentially useless tax deductions.

A further example of the inconsistency between tax and environmental law involves the deductibility of fines and other penalties in environmental litigations. Suppose that the Dustex Chemical Corporation has been sued for polluting a major river in a case brought under the Federal environmental laws. As part of a settlement Dustex agrees (i) to cease further pollution and (ii) to pay $10 million to local governments and environmental organizations to clean up existing damages and re-establish the natural habitats and water resources that existed before the pollution began. If this $10 million is characterized as a fine or penalty under the Code (section 162(f)), it is nondeductible to Dustex, meaning that it will cost $10 million of Dustex' own money (!) to meet the terms of the settlement agreement. By contrast, if the payment is categorized as a voluntary contribution to an environmental recovery fund, it is likely to be deductible for tax purposes, meaning that approximately one-third of the settlement would effectively be charged to the Federal treasury.[2] Can the parties avoid section 162(f) by characterizing the payment in this creative way? Note that, in the preceding problem, both plaintiffs and Dustex have an interest in making the payment deductible, since Dustex will save money on its taxes but will also (precisely because of this fact) be more willing to make the same, or an even larger, payment; the only loser is the Federal Government which is being asked to subsidize a desirable but costly cleanup through the tax system. Does this situation make sense to you, or would it be better if tax policy stayed out of this issue and the costs of environmental decisions were passed directly to polluters or else reflected in the budget of the relevant environmental agencies?

The following materials consider the clash of tax and environmental policies in somewhat greater detail. As you read them, consider whether the outlooks of the two fields are wholly irreconcilable in nature or whether there is some middle ground.

---

[2] Assuming a 35 percent corporate tax rate, which would reduce the company's net cost to $6.5 million ($10 million payment — $3.5 million tax saving). The Feds would pay the rest in reduced tax revenues.

TRUE v. UNITED STATES

United States Court of Appeals, Tenth Circuit

894 F.2d 1197 (1990)

SEYMOUR, CIRCUIT JUDGE.

Plaintiff taxpayers, a husband, wife, and their four adult children and spouses, were owners of True Oil Company, a general partnership organized under Wyoming's Uniform Partnership Act, and the sole shareholders of Belle Fourche Pipeline Company, an electing corporation under subchapter S of the 2 Internal Revenue Code, 26 U.S.C. § 1361. Plaintiffs brought five suits seeking income tax refunds for the taxable years 1973 through 1975. The actions were consolidated and the numerous issues variously decided by summary judgment, by directed verdict, and in a jury trial. The district court entered judgment for plaintiffs awarding them income tax refunds plus interest. *True v. United States*, 603 F. Supp. 1370 (D. Wyo. 1985). The Government has appealed. We affirm in part, reverse in part, and remand for further proceedings consistent with this opinion.

* * *

II.

The Government also appeals the district court's finding that Belle Fourche could deduct a civil penalty it paid. The facts relating to this issue are not in dispute. Belle Fourche paid a civil penalty in the amount of $1,200.00 during the fiscal year ending March 31, 1975. The penalty, assessed under section 311(b)(6) of the Federal Water Pollution Control Act ("FWPCA" or "Act"), 33 U.S.C. § 1321(b)(6) (Supp. II 1972),[3] was imposed because oil leaked from some of Belle Fourche's pipelines in violation of section 311(b)(3) of the Act, 33 U.S.C. § 1321(b)(3). Belle Fourche deducted this payment under I.R.C. § 162(a), but the Commissioner disallowed the deduction under the exception for any "fine or similar penalty" in section 162(f) of the Code, 26 U.S.C. § 162(f), and Treasury Regulation section 1.162-21 (1975).

---

[3] [10] At the time of the oil discharge in this case, section 311(b)(6) read:

"Any owner or operator of any vessel, onshore facility, or offshore facility from which oil or a hazardous substance is discharged in violation of paragraph (3) of this subsection shall be assessed a civil penalty by the Secretary of the department in which the Coast Guard is operating of not more than $5,000 for each offense. No penalty shall be assessed unless the owner or operator charged shall have been given notice and opportunity for a hearing on such charge. Each violation is a separate offense. Any such civil penalty may be compromised by such Secretary. In determining the amount of the penalty, or the amount agreed upon in compromise, the appropriateness of such penalty to the size of the business of the owner or operator charged, the effect on the owner or operator's ability to continue in business, and the gravity of the violation, shall be considered by such Secretary. The Secretary of the Treasury shall withhold at the request of such Secretary the clearance required by section 91 of Title 46 of any vessel the owner or operator of which is subject to the foregoing penalty. Clearance may be granted in such cases upon the filing of a bond or other surety satisfactory to such Secretary."

Code section 162(a) permits deduction of "all the ordinary and necessary expenses paid or incurred during the taxable year in carrying on any trade or business." Section 162(f) excepts from this general rule "any fine or similar penalty paid to a government for the violation of any law." Treasury Regulation section 1.162-21, implementing section 162(f), defines the statutory language "fine or similar penalty" to include moneys "paid as a civil penalty imposed by Federal, State, or local law." Treas. Reg. § 1.162-21(b)(1)(ii). The regulation provides several examples of civil penalties not deductible under section 162(f), including one which both parties acknowledge is dispositive of the issue before this court:

> "A civil penalty under 33 U.S.C. 1321(b)(6) of $5,000 was assessed against N Corp. with respect to the discharge [of oil in violation of 33 U.S.C. § 1321(b)(3)]. N Corp paid $5,000 to the Coast Guard in payment of the civil penalty. Section 162(f) precludes N Corp. from deducting the $5,000 penalty."

* * *

The court's role in reviewing Treasury Department regulations is very limited.

> "Congress has delegated to the Commissioner, not to the courts, the task of prescribing 'all needful rules and regulations for the enforcement' of the Internal Revenue Code. 27 U.S.C. § 7805(a). In this area of limitless factual variations 'it is the province of Congress and the Commissioner, not the courts, to make the appropriate adjustments.' The rule [sic] of the judiciary in cases of this sort begins and ends with assuring that the Commissioner's regulations fall within his authority to implement the congressional mandate in some reasonable manner."

United States v. Correll, 389 U.S. 299, 307 (1967) (citation omitted). As a general rule, Treasury regulations " 'must be sustained unless unreasonable and plainly inconsistent with the revenue statutes.' " *United Telecommunications, Inc. v. Commissioner*, 589 F.2d 1383, 1387 (10th Cir. 1978), *cert. denied*, 442 U.S. 917 (1979).

"In determining whether a particular regulation carries out the congressional mandate in a proper manner, [courts] look to see whether the regulation harmonizes with the plain language of the statute, its origin, and its purpose." *National Muffler Dealers Ass'n v. United States*, 440 U.S. 472, 477 (1979). Accordingly, we first analyze the scope of section 162(f).

Just what Congress intended by the words "fine or similar penalty" in section 162(f) is not immediately obvious. A common sense reading indicates to us that the addition of the words "similar penalty" reflects an intent to include more than just criminal fines, but not all penalties. The section's legislative history bears out this reading of the section's plain language.

The history of section 162(f)'s enactment in the Tax Reform Act of 1969 § 902(a), Pub. L. No. 91-172, 83 Stat. 711 (codified at I.R.C. § 162(f)), reveals that Congress intended to codify the "general court position" disallowing the deduction of fines and penalties.[4] At the time, the Supreme Court had declared in two cases concerning fines under penal statutes that no deduction was allowable for a fine or penalty if allowing the deduction would severely frustrate a sharply defined national policy. *See Tank Truck Rentals v. Commissioner*, 356 U.S. 30, 35 (1958) (test of nondeductibility is severity and immediacy of policy frustration from allowance of deduction); *Hoover Express Co. v. United States*, 356 U.S. 38, 40 (1958) (fine for violation of strict liability maximum weight statute held not deductible). This rule was also applied to civil penalties. *See, e.g., A.D. Juilliard & Co., Inc. v. Johnson*, 259 F.2d 837, 844 (2d Cir. 1958) (treble damages for Emergency Price Control Act civil penalty not deductible), *cert. denied*, 359 U.S. 942 (1959); *McGraw-Edison Co. v. United States*, 300 F.2d 453, 456, 156 Ct. Cl. 590 (1962) (no deduction for payment to U.S. in settlement of breach of agreement providing "penalty" for employing child labor); *Tunnel Ry. of St. Louis v. Commissioner*, 61 F.2d 166, 174–75 (8th Cir. 1932) (civil penalties under Safety Appliance Act not deductible), *cert. denied*, 288 U.S. 604 (1933).

Although this language deals expressly only with the disallowance of criminal fines, courts have interpreted the reference to the "general court position" to mean that the disallowance of civil penalties was intended as well. *See, e.g., Colt Indus., Inc. v. United States*, 880 F.2d 1311, 1313 (Fed. Cir. 1989) (section 162(f) codified case law disallowing deductions for civil penalties); *Adolf Meller Co. v. United States*, 600 F.2d 1360, 1362, 220 Ct. Cl. 500 (1979). *See also Mason & Dixon Lines, Inc. v. United States*, 708 F.2d 1043, 1046 (6th Cir. 1983); *Southern Pac. Transp. Co. v. Commissioner*, 75 T.C. 497, 652 (1980).

In 1971, two years after the enactment of section 162(f), the IRS issued its proposed regulations which, consistent with the extant case law, defined "fine or similar penalty" to include civil penalties. *See* 36 Fed. Reg. 9637–39 (May 27, 1971). That same year, proposed amendments to section 162 were considered as part of the Revenue Act of 1971. Section 162(f) remained untouched, although the Senate Finance Committee responded to questions concerning the proposed regulations and took the opportunity to clarify the meaning of a "fine or similar penalty":

> "In approving the provisions dealing with fines and similar penalties in 1969, it was the intention of the committee to disallow deductions for payments of sanctions which are imposed under civil statutes but which in general terms serve the same purpose as a fine exacted under a criminal statute."

S. Rep. No. 437, 92nd Cong., 1st Sess., *reprinted in* 1971 U.S. Code Cong. & Admin. News 1918, 1980. The Committee tried to illustrate its point with examples:

---

[4] [14] The Senate Finance Committee Report commented that

"the committee amendments provide that no deduction is to be allowed for any fine or similar penalty paid to a government for the violation of any law. This provision is to apply to any case in which the taxpayer is required to pay a fine because he is convicted of a crime (felony or misdemeanor) in a full criminal proceeding in an appropriate court. This represents a codification of the *general court position* in this respect."

S. Rep. No. 552, 91st Cong., 1st Sess., *reprinted in* 1969 U.S. Code Cong. & Admin. News 2027, 2311–12 (emphasis added).

"The provision was intended to apply, for example, to penalties provided for under the Internal Revenue Code in the form of . . . assessable penalties (subchapter B of chapter 68) as well as to additions to tax under the internal revenue laws (subchapter A of chapter 68) in these cases where the government has the fraud burden of proof. . . . It was also intended that this rule should apply to similar type payments under the laws of a state or other jurisdiction.

"On the other hand, it was not intended that deductions be denied in the case of sanctions imposed to encourage prompt compliance with require-ments of law. Thus, many jurisdictions impose 'penalties' to encourage prompt compliance with filing or other requirements which are really more in the nature of late filing charges or interest charges than they are fines. . . . In this area, the committee did not intend to liberalize the law in the case of fines and penalties."

Id.[5]

These comments, along with the prior case law which the 1969 report incorpo-rated, indicate that section 162(f) encompasses fines and penalties exacted to sanction or punish conduct which some well-defined state policy seeks to proscribe. Whether the statute is determined to be "criminal" or "civil" is not conclusive. Rather, the nondeductibility exception for "fines and similar penalties" includes criminal fines and any similar retributive civil penalty intended to sanction conduct the state specifically seeks to prohibit. It follows implicitly that compensatory or remedial payments are beyond the scope of section 162(f). In addition, civil penalties for the violation of reporting requirements, filing deadlines, and other procedural failings which do not frustrate the primary purpose of the statutory scheme also remain deductible.

Having determined the intent and scope of section 162(f), our next task is to determine whether Treasury Regulation section 1.162-21(b)(1)(ii), defining "fine or similar penalty," and the specific example provided in Treasury Regulation section 1.162-21(c)(2), are "unreasonable and plainly inconsistent" with section 162(f). *See United Telecommunications*, 589 F.2d at 1387. Plaintiffs argue that the regulation is invalid because it necessarily includes *all* civil penalties, not just the "similar" penalties contemplated in section 162(f). Taken literally and in isolation, we agree with plaintiffs that the regulation could be so interpreted. But plaintiffs ignore the exception in Treasury Regulation section 1.162-21(b)(4)[6] which provides that "compensatory damages . . . paid to a government do not constitute a fine or penalty." Thus, the regulation is consistent with the statute since civil sanctions compensatory in nature remain deductible.[7] We therefore conclude that section

---

[5] [15] We rely on subsequent legislative history in construing section 162(f) for several reasons. First, the section was reenacted without change in 1971 by substantially the same Senate Finance Committee that had proposed it in 1969 (only two of sixteen members had changed). Second, the Committee's subsequent statement is consistent with its stated intention in 1969 to adopt the "general court position" in this area.

[6] [17] Currently section 1.162-21(b)(2).

[7] [18] The regulatory definition of "fine or similar penalty" could perhaps be interpreted to include the

1.162-21(b)(2), properly construed, is reasonable and consistent with the statute.[8]

The question remains whether the dispositive example of a "fine or similar penalty" in the regulation concerning the same civil penalty at issue in this case, *see* Treas. Reg. § 1.162-21(c)(2), is "unreasonable and plainly inconsistent" with section 162(f). Plaintiffs argue that the example is inconsistent with section 162(f) because it is primarily compensatory rather than punitive. While the district court did not discuss the impact of the Treasury Regulation, it agreed with plaintiffs and concluded that the civil penalty in section 311(b)(6), 33 U.S.C. § 1321(b)(6) (Supp. II 1972), is primarily remedial and compensatory and therefore beyond the scope of section 162(f). In its opinion, the district court relied on the statute's strict liability standard and the Government's use of the proceeds to pay for administering the Act and financing oil cleanup. *True*, 603 F. Supp. at 1374.

If the civil penalty in section 311(b)(6) is primarily compensatory, then it is "plainly inconsistent" with section 162(f), and thus would invalidate the regulatory example. But we cannot accept the district court's conclusion that the civil penalty in section 311(b)(6) is essentially compensatory. Although the civil penalty in the FWPCA employs a strict liability standard, the legislative history of section 162(f) reflects that some penalties for violations of strict liability statutes may be nondeductible. In *Hoover Motor Express Co.*, for example, the Supreme Court concluded that a fine paid for violation of a state maximum weight requirement was not deductible "even assuming that petitioner acted with all due care and without willful intent." 356 U.S. at 40. The Court's discussion in *Hoover* illustrates that no necessary relationship exists between strict liability and a compensatory scheme. Moreover, the Court's decision in *Hoover* comprised part of the "general court position" to which the Senate Finance Committee referred in discussing section 162(f). We therefore cannot say that the strict liability standard makes the section 311(b)(6) penalty "plainly inconsistent" with section 162(f). Rather, the legislative history indicates that Congress intended to incorporate the judicial view that some strict liability penalties are nondeductible.

The district court also relied on several cases characterizing the FWPCA as a compensatory scheme to shift the costs of pollution from the public to the polluters. *See, e.g., United States v. Ward*, 448 U.S. 242, 249 (1980) (holding section 311(b)(6) penalties not sufficiently "criminal" to attract constitutional procedural safeguards for criminal defendants); *United States v. Marathon Pipe Line* Co., 589 F.2d 1305, 1309 (7th Cir. 1978) (application of strict liability standard to section 311(b)(6) penalties does not violate substantive due process); *United States v. Tex-Tow, Inc.*, 589 F.2d 1310, 1315 (7th Cir. 1978) (same).

---

procedural violations Congress had intended to exclude from section 162(f). But because the penalty assessed against plaintiffs in this case is not even remotely similar to a payment resulting from the type of procedural infraction specifically excluded by the Finance Committee we do not need to address this issue.

[8] [19] The court in *Adolf Meller Co.*, 600 F.2d at 1363, also rebuffed an attack on the validity of the definition of "fine or similar penalty." The court there upheld Treasury Regulation section 1.162-21(1)(b)(iii), which included amounts paid in settlement of actual or potential liability for a civil or criminal penalty. As we have done in this case, the *Meller* court construed the regulation in light of the legislative history of the statute it implements. *Id.* at 1362–64.

The Supreme Court's holding in *Ward* is of little consequence in the present case, since section 162(f) indisputably applies both to civil and criminal penalties. We also believe that the district court ascribed undue importance to dicta in a concurrence by two Justices in *Ward*, concerning constitutional criminal procedure, to determine the Supreme Court's hypothetical view on an unrelated tax law question.

We agree with the conclusion in *Marathon* and *Tex-Tow*, the other cases the district court cited, that a purpose of section 311(b)(6) *could* be compensatory and remedial. *Cf. Williamson v. Lee Optical*, 348 U.S. 483 (1955) (rational relation between actual evil and conceivable legislative purpose in addressing it enough to validate economic legislation under due process clause). In fact, employment of the proceeds from section 311(b)(6) to administer the Act and to finance cleanup costs actually does serve a remedial purpose. These facts, when viewed in context, do not suffice to justify a conclusion that the section 311(b)(6) example in the Treasury regulations is "plainly inconsistent" with the "fines and similar penalties" clause in section 162(f). To the contrary, the civil penalty in section 311(b)(6) strikes us on balance as serving a deterrent and retributive function similar to a criminal fine. For example, the maximum penalty for a particular violation of five thousand dollars has no bearing on the cleanup costs incurred by the Government or the amount of damage caused.[9] Instead, a wholly independent provision in the Act authorizing the Government to recoup costs incurred in oil cleanup operations appears to be the primary compensatory or remedial mechanism in the FWPCA. *See* 33 U.S.C. § 1321(f). The penalty in section 311(b)(6) consequently must serve as an *additional* sanction to deter and punish, not to compensate or remedy.

Moreover, section 311(b)(6) requires that the Coast Guard consider three factors in determining the size of the penalty: "the appropriateness of such penalty to the size of the business of the owner or operator charged, the effect on the owner or operator's ability to continue in business, and the gravity of the violation." 33 U.S.C. § 1321(b)(6) (Supp. II 1972). Only the last factor arguably relates to the amount of damage caused, but even that factor could relate as plausibly to the degree of fault of the party charged.[10] The first two factors unambiguously concern the degree of retributive impact on the violator.

Finally, the civil penalty in section 311(b)(6) sanctions conduct or consequences therefrom comprising the primary evil the FWPCA was enacted to prevent: water pollution. Section 311(b)(1) "declares that it is the policy of the United States that there should be no discharges of oil or hazardous substances into or upon the

---

[9] [20] Coast Guard policy for applying civil penalties in section 311(b)(6) of the FWPCA states that the amount of the penalty is "entirely unrelated to the subsequent removal responsibility for which the discharger must bear the expense. . . . In no case may a responsible party avoid or reduce a civil penalty by removing the discharged oil." United States v. LeBeouf Bros. Towing Co., 377 F. Supp. 558, 569–70 (E.D. La. 1974), *rev'd on other grounds*, 537 F.2d 149 (5th Cir. 1976), *cert. denied*, 430 U.S. 987 (1977).

[10] [21] Coast Guard policy as of 1973 provided:

"A number of considerations may be made in determining the gravity of a violation, such as the degree of culpability associated with the violation, the prior record of the responsible party, and the amount of oil discharged. Substantial intentional discharges should result in severe penalties, as should cases of gross negligence, and so on."

LeBeouf Bros., 377 F. Supp. at 569.

navigable waters of the United States." 33 U.S.C. § 1321(b)(1). This is an urgent and sharply defined national policy.

Far from being "'unreasonable and plainly inconsistent with the revenue statutes,'" *United Telecommunications, Inc.*, 589 F.2d at 1387, *quoting Fulman v. United States*, 434 U.S. 528, 533 (1978), we conclude that the section 311(b)(6) example in Treasury Regulation § 1.162(c)(2) is fully consistent with the "fines and similar penalties" clause in section 162(f). The regulation is therefore valid and, accordingly, we reverse the district court's conclusion that the penalty is deductible under section 162(a) of the Code.

* * *

Revenue Ruling 94-38
1994-1 C.B. 35

Environmental clean up costs of land. Costs incurred to clean up land and to treat groundwater that a taxpayer contaminated with hazardous waste from its business are deductible by the taxpayer as ordinary and necessary business expenses under section 162 of the Code. Costs properly allocable to constructing groundwater treatment facilities are capital expenditures under section 263. Rev. Rul. 88-57 modified.

ISSUE

Are the costs incurred to clean up land and to treat groundwater that a taxpayer contaminated with hazardous waste from its business deductible by the taxpayer as business expenses under § 162 of the Internal Revenue Code, or must they be capitalized under § 263?

FACTS

X, an accrual basis corporation, owns and operates a manufacturing plant. *X* built the plant on land that it had purchased in 1970. The land was not contaminated by hazardous waste when it was purchased by *X*. *X*'s manufacturing operations discharge hazardous waste. In the past *X* buried this waste on portions of its land.

In 1993, in order to comply with presently applicable and reasonably anticipated federal, state, and local environmental requirements ("environmental requirements"), *X* decided to remediate the soil and groundwater that had been contaminated by the hazardous waste, and to establish an appropriate system for the continued monitoring of the groundwater to ensure that the remediation had removed all hazardous waste. Accordingly, *X* began excavating the contaminated soil, transporting it to appropriate waste disposal facilities, and backfilling the excavated areas with uncontaminated soil. These soil remediation activities started in 1993 and will be completed in 1995. *X* also began constructing groundwater treatment facilities which included wells, pipes, pumps, and other equipment to extract, treat, and monitor contaminated groundwater. Construction of these groundwater treatment facilities began in 1993, and the facilities will remain in operation on X's land until the year 2005. During this time, X will continue to monitor the groundwater to ensure that the soil remediation and groundwater treatment eliminate the hazardous waste to the extent necessary to bring X's land into compliance with environmental requirements.

The effect of the soil remediation and groundwater treatment will be to restore X's land to essentially the same physical condition that existed prior to the contamination. During and after the remediation and treatment, X will continue to use the land and operate the plant in the same manner as it did prior to the cleanup except that X will dispose of any hazardous waste in compliance with environmental requirements.

LAW AND ANALYSIS

Section 162 generally allows a deduction for the ordinary and necessary expenses paid or incurred during the taxable year in carrying on any trade or business. Even though a particular taxpayer may incur an expense only once in the lifetime of its business, the expense may qualify as ordinary and necessary if it is appropriate and helpful in carrying on that business, is commonly and frequently incurred in the type of business conducted by the taxpayer, and is not a capital expenditure. *Commissioner v. Tellier*, 383 U.S. 687 (1966); *Deputy v. du Pont*, 308 U.S. 488 (1940); *Welch v. Helvering*, 290 U.S. 111 (1933). Section 162 has been applied to allow business expense deductions for the costs of removing and disposing of waste materials produced in a taxpayer's business. *See H.G. Fenton Material Co. v. Commissioner*, 74 T.C. 584 (1980).

Section 263 generally prohibits deductions for capital expenditures. Section 263(a)(1) provides that no deduction shall be allowed for any amounts paid out for new buildings or for permanent improvements or betterments made to increase the value of any property. Section 263(a)(2) provides that no deduction shall be allowed for any amount expended in restoring property or in making good the exhaustion thereof for which an allowance has been made in the form of a deduction for depreciation, amortization, or depletion. Section 1.263(a)-1(b) of the Income Tax Regulations provides that capital expenditures include amounts paid or incurred (1) to add to the value, or substantially prolong the useful life, of property owned by the taxpayer, such as plant or equipment, or (2) to adapt property to a new or different use. Section 1.263(a)-2(a) provides that capital expenditures include the cost of acquisition, construction, or erection of buildings, machinery and equipment, furniture and fixtures, and similar property having a useful life substantially beyond the taxable year.

Section 263A provides that the direct costs and indirect costs properly allocable to real or tangible personal property produced by the taxpayer shall be capitalized. Section 263A(g)(1) provides that, for purposes of section 263A, the term produce includes construct, build, install, manufacture, develop, or improve.

Pursuant to section 461(h), in determining whether an amount has been incurred for any item during the taxable year for an accrual method taxpayer, the all events test shall not be treated as met any earlier than when economic performance occurs.

Through provisions such as §§ 62(a), 263(a), and related sections, the Internal Revenue Code generally endeavors to match expenses with the revenues of the taxable period to which the expenses are properly attributable, thereby resulting in a more accurate calculation of net income for tax purposes. *See, e.g., INDOPCO, Inc. v. Commissioner*, 503 U.S. 79 (1992); *Commissioner v. Idaho Power Co.*, 418 U.S. 1, 16 (1974). Moreover, as the Supreme Court has specifically recognized, the "decisive distinctions [between capital and ordinary expenditures] are those of degree and not of kind," and a careful examination of the particular facts of each case is required. *Welch v. Helvering*, 290 U.S. at 114; *Deputy v. du Pont*, 308 U.S. at 496. In determining whether current deduction or capitalization is the appropriate tax treatment for any particular expenditure, it is important to consider the extent to which the expenditure will produce significant future benefits. *See INDOPCO, Inc. v. Commissioner*, 112 S. Ct. at 1044–45.

The groundwater treatment facilities constructed by *X* have a useful life substantially beyond the taxable year in which they are constructed and, thus, the costs of their construction are capital expenditures under §§ 263(a) and 1.263(a)-2(a). Moreover, because the construction of these facilities constitutes production within the meaning of § 263A(g)(1), *X* is required to capitalize under § 263A the direct costs and a proper share of allocable indirect costs of constructing these facilities. The costs of the groundwater treatment facilities are recoverable under applicable law (*e.g.*, § 168).

Under these facts, *X*'s soil remediation expenditures and ongoing groundwater treatment expenditures (*i.e.*, the groundwater treatment expenditures other than the expenditures to construct the groundwater treatment facilities) do not produce permanent improvements to *X*'s land within the scope of § 263(a)(1) or otherwise provide significant future benefits. Under the facts of this ruling, the appropriate test for determining whether the expenditures increase the value of property is to compare the status of the asset after the expenditure with the status of that asset before the condition arose that necessitated the expenditure (*i.e.*, before the land was contaminated by *X*'s hazardous waste). *See Plainfield-Union Water Co. v. Commissioner*, 39 T.C. 333, 338 (1962), *nonacq. on other grounds*, 1964-2 C.B. 8. *X*'s soil remediation and ongoing groundwater treatment expenditures do not result in improvements that increase the value of *X*'s property because *X* has merely restored its soil and groundwater to their approximate condition before they were contaminated by *X*'s manufacturing operations.

No other aspect of § 263 requires capitalization of *X*'s ongoing soil remediation or ongoing groundwater treatment expenditures. These expenditures do not prolong the useful life of the land, nor do they adapt the land to a new or different use. Moreover, since the land is not subject to an allowance for depreciation, amortization, or depletion, the amounts expended to restore the land to its original condition are not subject to capitalization under § 263(a)(2). Accordingly, the expenses incurred by *X* for the soil remediation and ongoing groundwater treatment do not constitute capital expenditures under § 263.

The soil remediation and ongoing groundwater treatment expenditures incurred by X represent ordinary and necessary business expenses within the scope of § 162. They are appropriate and helpful in carrying on X's business and are commonly and frequently required in X's type of business. Therefore, the costs incurred by X to evaluate and remediate its soil and groundwater contamination (other than the costs of constructing the groundwater treatment facilities) constitute ordinary and necessary business expenses that are deductible under § 162.

HOLDING

Under the circumstances described above, costs incurred (within the meaning of the economic performance rules of § 461(h)) to clean up land and to treat groundwater that a taxpayer contaminated with hazardous waste from its business (other than the costs attributable to the construction of groundwater treatment facilities) are deductible by the taxpayer as ordinary and necessary business expenses under § 162. Costs properly allocable to constructing the groundwater treatment facilities, as determined under § 263A and the regulations thereunder, are capital expenditures under § 263. These results are applicable whether the taxpayer plans to continue its manufacturing operations that discharge the hazardous waste or to discontinue those manufacturing operations and hold the land in an idle state.

EFFECT ON OTHER REVENUE RULINGS

Revenue Ruling 88-57, 1988-2 C.B. 36, is modified to the extent it implies that the value test applied by the Tax Court in *Plainfield-Union Water Co. v. Commissioner* cannot be an appropriate test in any case other than one in which there is sudden and unanticipated damage to an asset.

DRAFTING INFORMATION

The principal author of this revenue ruling is Merrill D. Feldstein of the Office of Assistant Chief Counsel (Income Tax and Accounting). For further information regarding this revenue ruling, contact Ms. Feldstein on (202) 622-4960 (not a toll-free call).

Jeffrey M. Gaba, *Tax Deduction of Hazardous Waste Cleanup Costs: Harmonizing Federal Tax and Environmental Policies*
20 HARV. ENVTL. L. REV. 61 (1996)[11]

I. INTRODUCTION

Two things in life are certain: enormous hazardous waste cleanup costs and taxes. Despite the obvious significance of the tax consequences of the billions of

---

dollars in cleanup costs spent in the United States, the federal tax treatment of these costs remains uncertain. Perhaps the most basic question — whether cleanup expenses may be immediately deducted or must be capitalized — remains an issue that the Internal Revenue Service ("IRS") has been unable to resolve.

In the past few years, the IRS has issued a series of controversial opinions that have given little clear guidance on the proper tax treatment of cleanup costs. In several Technical Advice Memoranda ("TAM") issued in 1992 and 1993, the IRS suggested that most cleanup costs would not be deductible as ordinary expenses. In 1994, however, the IRS issued Revenue Ruling 94-38, which held that expenses incurred by a taxpayer to clean up its own property contaminated in the course of its business activities were generally deductible as ordinary expenses. The ruling, although limited in scope and sparse in logic or analysis, was hailed by some as an indication that the IRS would generally give favorable tax treatment to cleanup costs. Revenue Ruling 94-38 addressed a relatively simple situation, however, and its logic (or lack thereof) gave little guidance on how the IRS would deal with more complex situations. In a TAM issued in 1995, the IRS apparently reversed course once again, and it now appears to be stating that most cleanup costs (including the investigation and legal fees associated with a cleanup) cannot be deducted.

The IRS continues to struggle with the problem, and, as discussed below, analysis of the current tax treatment of the most common types of remediation expenses produces no clear answers. In analyzing the same set of facts, the IRS and taxpayers can legitimately reach conflicting conclusions.

Perhaps the basic problem is that traditional tests used to distinguish capital expenditures from ordinary and necessary business expenses are inappropriate for environmental remediation expenses. It makes little sense to ask whether remediation, essentially the cleaning up of dirt, is more like a "repair" or an "improvement." The current approach of the IRS not only creates uncertainty and complicates tax planning, but also has the potential to perversely influence the selection of cleanup standards and technology based upon an inappropriate consideration of tax consequences. The IRS, in attempting to apply traditional tax analysis to the complex requirements of environmental remediation, may be making both bad tax policy and bad environmental policy.

* * *

It is time to adopt a clear and consistent rule that resolves the tax treatment of remediation expenses. Such a rule should ideally be easy to apply, consistent in its treatment of remediation expenses, generally consistent with existing tax law on deductions and, at a minimum, eliminate tax considerations from selection of remediation objectives and techniques. A rule that promoted environmentally responsible efforts should also be a national objective.

Most of these objectives can be attained by adoption of a relatively simple approach to tax treatment of remediation expenses. In general, the IRS, through adoption of a treasury regulation, or Congress, through amendment to the Internal Revenue Code, should adopt a provision of general applicability; such a provision should provide for the deduction as ordinary expenses (in the year in which economic performance occurs) of all costs that are incurred to remediate hazardous substances or hazardous or solid wastes under the requirements of federal and state laws or pursuant to federal or state regulations that authorize the recovery of such expenses from private parties.

In addition to a general standard of compliance with federal and state environmental laws, such a provision should specifically provide that remediation expenses are deductible if these costs:

(1) would be recoverable under section 107(a)(4)(B) of CERCLA,

(2) are incurred to comply with corrective action obligations under section 3004(u), 3008(h) of RCRA,

(3) are incurred to comply with the corrective action obligations applicable to Underground Storage Tanks under section 9003 of RCRA, or

(4) are incurred for remediation of petroleum, hazardous substances or hazardous wastes under state laws comparable to CERCLA or RCRA.

Expenses that do not meet these criteria would be judged under the general approach currently being developed by the IRS. Most remediation expenses that are incurred in an environmentally appropriate manner would, however, qualify for treatment as ordinary expenses.

* * *

Understanding Environmental Cleanups

1.   *True* holds a civil penalty under the Federal Water Pollution Control Act nondeductible because the penalty was partly remedial (*i.e.*, punitive) and not wholly compensatory in purpose. Isn't this a rather easily manipulable test? Suppose that the EPA, under pressure from State officials, agreed to a settlement in which (a) Belle Fourche paid $2,000 as "compensation" for local cleanup costs and (b) in return, EPA withheld imposition of the $1,200 Federal fine.[12] Would a deduction be permitted under these new circumstances? What do you think is the policy of section 162(f), and does it make sense in environmental clean-up cases?

2.   What do you make of the use of source materials (Code, regulations, etc.) by the *True* court? Is the court too hesitant to overturn a regulation that may not make much policy sense? What about the "legislative history" employed by the court — does it really demonstrate legislative intent, or is it more likely that Congress never thought about the issue very much? Does it matter?

3.   Revenue Ruling 94-38 holds that costs incurred to clean up already polluted groundwater are currently deductible, while the costs of constructing groundwater treatment facilities must be capitalized under section 263. In other words, expenditures for preventing future pollution are, generally speaking, treated less

---

[12] The company would presumably agree to make a higher payment if it knew that the payment was to be tax deductible.

favorably than those for "curing" past omissions. Isn't this a perverse way of doing things, environmentally speaking? Or is the IRS afraid that, if it allowed current deduction of treatment facilities, taxpayers would describe every capital project as a form of environmental protection? Suppose that a current deduction were permitted for environmental treatment facilities, and an oil company tried to deduct a new refinery on the grounds that it polluted less than the refinery that it was replacing. Or that I tried to deduct my new car on the grounds that it made less noise and gave off fewer noxious fumes than my old one. Are these serious dangers, or is the "slippery slope" argument being overstated by these hypotheticals?

4.   What do you think of Professor Gaba's suggestion that IRS resolve the problem by providing a current deduction for all cleanup-related costs? Is this a reasonable solution, or another taxpayer giveaway? How would you draft such a proposal to avoid the "slippery slope" problem referred to in the preceding question?

5.   Are hazardous waste cleanups a public or a private responsibility, and how does this affect your answers to the preceding questions?

B.   The "Separate and Distinct" Asset Test

The repair vs. improvement issue is simply one example of the broader policy of sections 162 and 263, together with the latter's stepchild, section 263A. The idea — an eminently reasonable one — is to distinguish between expenditures that give rise to purely current benefits and those which give rise to benefits lasting more than one year; or, in the more poetic language of section 263, which are "paid out for new buildings or for permanent improvements or betterments made to increase the benefit of any property or estate." According to this rule, the former category of expenses would be currently deductible, while the latter would be capitalized and perhaps deducted over a longer period, reflecting the longer period over which they provided benefits to the taxpayer. This in turn would result in the "matching" of income and deductions and the most accurate possible measurement of the taxpayer's net income. For example, a taxpayer who purchased a machine that cost $10 million and lasted for exactly 10 years, while producing $1.5 million of income in each year, would in theory take a $1 million depreciation deduction in each year, resulting in $0.5 million of taxable income for each year during the relevant period.[13] This contrasts with the underreporting of income in the early years that would result from a current deduction of the $10 million, or the overreporting that would result if the entire deduction were delayed until year 10.

The problem is that, taken literally, almost any expenditure provides some benefit beyond the first year. Take, for example, the salary paid to an associate at a large law firm. Most of the salary probably goes to produce items (briefs, memos, carrying partners' briefcases) that benefit the firm on an immediate basis. But if the firm is intelligently organized, at least some of this work provides value that lives on into future years. For example, a brief written in one case, although directed primarily at the facts in that case, may be useful in cases that raise similar

---

[13] This example assumes straight-line depreciation, and an absence of other deductions. For further discussion of depreciation, see Section II, *infra*.

issues in future years. Yet it seems draconian to require capitalization of associates' salaries, and also administratively impossible: no one could reasonably measure the useful life of each memorandum, and — given a large enough number of projects — the effects of a depreciation system might not be terribly different from that of current deductibility, anyway.[14] There is, accordingly, need for a formula that will distinguish those cases involving substantial continuing benefits from those that are incidental or trivial in nature.

To deal with this problem, the Supreme Court in *Commissioner v. Lincoln Savings & Loan*, 403 U.S. 345 (1971), developed what has become known as the "separate and distinct asset" concept. According to this concept, an expenditure that gives rise to a clearly identifiable asset, having a useful life greater than one year's duration, must be capitalized. By contrast, an expenditure that does not result in a separate and distinct asset — even if it gives rise to some benefit beyond the current year — may (perhaps) be deducted in year one. The nature and evolution of this concept are suggested by the following case.

INDOPCO, INC. v. COMMISSIONER
United States Supreme Court
503 U.S. 79 (1992)

JUSTICE BLACKMUN delivered the opinion of the Court.

In this case we must decide whether certain professional expenses incurred by a target corporation in the course of a friendly takeover are deductible by that corporation as "ordinary and necessary" business expenses under § 162(a) of the Internal Revenue Code.

I

Most of the relevant facts are stipulated. *See* App. 12, 149. Petitioner INDOPCO, Inc., formerly named National Starch and Chemical Corporation and hereinafter referred to as National Starch, is a Delaware corporation that manufactures and sells adhesives, starches, and specialty chemical products. In October 1977, representatives of Unilever United States, Inc., also a Delaware corporation (Unilever),[15] expressed interest in acquiring National Starch, which was one of its suppliers, through a friendly transaction. National Starch at the time had outstanding over 6,563,000 common shares held by approximately 3,700 shareholders. The stock was listed on the New York Stock Exchange. Frank and Anna Greenwall were the corporation's largest shareholders and owned approximately 14.5% of the common. The Greenwalls, getting along in years and concerned about their estate plans, indicated that they would transfer their shares to Unilever only if a transaction tax free for them could be arranged.

---

[14] For example, a lawyer who was depreciating five memos — one from five years ago, one from four years ago, etc. — might yield a combined deduction not terribly different from the immediate deductibility of her current projects.

[15] [1] Unilever is a holding company. Its then principal subsidiaries were Lever Brothers Co. and Thomas J. Lipton, Inc.

Lawyers representing both sides devised a "reverse subsidiary cash merger" that they felt would satisfy the Greenwalls' concerns. Two new entities would be created — National Starch and Chemical Holding Corp. (Holding), a subsidiary of Unilever, and NSC Merger, Inc., a subsidiary of Holding that would have only a transitory existence. In an exchange specifically designed to be tax free under § 351 of the Internal Revenue Code, 26 U.S.C. § 351, Holding would exchange one share of its nonvoting preferred stock for each share of National Starch common that it received from National Starch shareholders. Any National Starch common that was not so exchanged would be converted into cash in a merger of NSC Merger, Inc., into National Starch.

In November 1977, National Starch's directors were formally advised of Unilever's interest and the proposed transaction. At that time, Debevoise, Plimpton, Lyons & Gates, National Starch's counsel, told the directors that under Delaware law they had a fiduciary duty to ensure that the proposed transaction would be fair to the shareholders. National Starch thereupon engaged the investment banking firm of Morgan Stanley & Co., Inc., to evaluate its shares, to render a fairness opinion, and generally to assist in the event of the emergence of a hostile tender offer.

Although Unilever originally had suggested a price between $65 and $70 per share, negotiations resulted in a final offer of $73.50 per share, a figure Morgan Stanley found to be fair. Following approval by National Starch's board and the issuance of a favorable private ruling from the Internal Revenue Service that the transaction would be tax free under § 351 for those National Starch shareholders who exchanged their stock for Holding preferred, the transaction was consummated in August 1978.[16]

Morgan Stanley charged National Starch a fee of $2,200,000, along with $7,586 for out-of-pocket expenses and $18,000 for legal fees. The Debevoise firm charged National Starch $490,000, along with $15,069 for out-of-pocket expenses. National Starch also incurred expenses aggregating $150,962 for miscellaneous items — such as accounting, printing, proxy solicitation, and Securities and Exchange Commission fees — in connection with the transaction. No issue is raised as to the propriety or reasonableness of these charges.

On its federal income tax return for its short taxable year ended August 15, 1978, National Starch claimed a deduction for the $2,225,586 paid to Morgan Stanley, but did not deduct the $505,069 paid to Debevoise or the other expenses. Upon audit, the Commissioner of Internal Revenue disallowed the claimed deduction and issued a notice of deficiency. Petitioner sought redetermination in the United States Tax Court, asserting, however, not only the right to deduct the investment banking fees and expenses but, as well, the legal and miscellaneous expenses incurred.

The Tax Court, in an unreviewed decision, ruled that the expenditures were capital in nature and therefore not deductible under § 162(a) in the 1978 return as "ordinary and necessary expenses." *National Starch and Chemical Corp. v.*

---

[16] [2] Approximately 21% of National Starch common was exchanged for Holding preferred. The remaining 79% was exchanged for cash. App. 14.

Commissioner, 93 T.C. 67 (1989). The court based its holding primarily on the long-term benefits that accrued to National Starch from the Unilever acquisition. *Id.* at 75. The United States Court of Appeals for the Third Circuit affirmed, upholding the Tax Court's findings that "both Unilever's enormous resources and the possibility of synergy arising from the transaction served the long-term betterment of National Starch." *National Starch & Chemical Corp. v. Commissioner*, 918 F.2d 426, 432–433 (1990). In so doing, the Court of Appeals rejected National Starch's contention that, because the disputed expenses did not "create or enhance . . . a separate and distinct additional asset," *see Commissioner v. Lincoln Savings & Loan Assn.*, 403 U.S. 345, 354 (1971), they could not be capitalized and therefore were deductible under § 162(a). 918 F.2d at 428–431. We granted certiorari to resolve a perceived conflict on the issue among the Courts of Appeals.[17] 500 U.S. 914 (1991).

II

Section 162(a) of the Internal Revenue Code allows the deduction of "all the ordinary and necessary expenses paid or incurred during the taxable year in carrying on any trade or business." 26 U.S.C. § 162(a). In contrast, § 263 of the Code allows no deduction for a capital expenditure — an "amount paid out for new buildings or for permanent improvements or betterments made to increase the value of any property or estate." § 263(a)(1). The primary effect of characterizing a payment as either a business expense or a capital expenditure concerns the timing of the taxpayer's cost recovery: while business expenses are currently deductible, a capital expenditure usually is amortized and depreciated over the life of the relevant asset, or, where no specific asset or useful life can be ascertained, is deducted upon dissolution of the enterprise. *See* 26 U.S.C. §§ 167(a) and 336(a); Treas. Reg. § 1.167(a), 26 CFR § 1.167(a) (1991). Through provisions such as these, the Code endeavors to match expenses with the revenues of the taxable period to which they are properly attributable, thereby resulting in a more accurate calculation of net income for tax purposes. *See, e.g., Commissioner v. Idaho Power Co.*, 418 U.S. 1, 16 (1974); *Ellis Banking Corp. v. Commissioner*, 688 F.2d 1376, 1379 (CA11 1982), *cert. denied*, 463 U.S. 1207 (1983).

In exploring the relationship between deductions and capital expenditures, this Court has noted the "familiar rule" that "an income tax deduction is a matter of legislative grace and that the burden of clearly showing the right to the claimed deduction is on the taxpayer." *Interstate Transit Lines v. Commissioner*, 319 U.S. 590, 593 (1943); *Deputy v. Du Pont*, 308 U.S. 488, 493 (1940); *New Colonial Ice Co. v. Helvering*, 292 U.S. 435, 440 (1934). The notion that deductions are exceptions to

---

[17] [3] Compare the Third Circuit's opinion, 918 F.2d at 430, with NCNB Corp. v. United States, 684 F.2d 285, 293–294 (CA4 1982) (bank expenditures for expansion-related planning reports, feasibility studies, and regulatory applications did not "create or enhance separate and identifiable assets," and therefore were ordinary and necessary expenses under § 162(a)), and Briarcliff Candy Corp. v. Commissioner, 475 F.2d 775, 782 (CA2 1973) (suggesting that *Lincoln Savings* "brought about a radical shift in emphasis," making capitalization dependent on whether the expenditure creates or enhances a separate and distinct additional asset). *See also* Central Texas Savings & Loan Assn. v. United States, 731 F.2d 1181, 1184 (CA5 1984) (inquiring whether establishment of new branches "creates a separate and distinct additional asset" so that capitalization is the proper tax treatment).

the norm of capitalization finds support in various aspects of the Code. Deductions are specifically enumerated and thus are subject to disallowance in favor of capitalization. *See* §§ 161 and 261. Nondeductible capital expenditures, by contrast, are not exhaustively enumerated in the Code; rather than providing a "complete list of nondeductible expenditures," *Lincoln Savings*, 403 U.S. at 358, § 263 serves as a general means of distinguishing capital expenditures from current expenses. *See Commissioner v. Idaho Power Co.*, 418 U.S. at 16. For these reasons, deductions are strictly construed and allowed only "as there is a clear provision therefor." *New Colonial Ice Co. v. Helvering*, 292 U.S. at 440; *Deputy v. Du Pont*, 308 U.S. at 493.

The Court also has examined the interrelationship between the Code's business expense and capital expenditure provisions. In so doing, it has had occasion to parse § 162(a) and explore certain of its requirements. For example, in *Lincoln Savings*, we determined that, to qualify for deduction under § 162(a), "an item must (1) be 'paid or incurred during the taxable year,' (2) be for 'carrying on any trade or business,' (3) be an 'expense,' (4) be a 'necessary' expense, and (5) be an 'ordinary' expense." 403 U.S. at 352. *See also Commissioner v. Tellier*, 383 U.S. 687, 689 (1966) (the term "necessary" imposes "only the minimal requirement that the expense be 'appropriate and helpful' for 'the development of the [taxpayer's] business,' " quoting *Welch v. Helvering*, 290 U.S. 111, 113 (1933)); *Deputy v. Du Pont*, 308 U.S. at 495 (to qualify as "ordinary," the expense must relate to a transaction "of common or frequent occurrence in the type of business involved"). The Court has recognized, however, that the "decisive distinctions" between current expenses and capital expenditures "are those of degree and not of kind," *Welch v. Helvering*, 290 U.S. at 114, and that because each case "turns on its special facts," *Deputy v. Du Pont*, 308 U.S. at 496, the cases sometimes appear difficult to harmonize. *See Welch v. Helvering*, 290 U.S. at 116.

National Starch contends that the decision in *Lincoln Savings* changed these familiar backdrops and announced an exclusive test for identifying capital expenditures, a test in which "creation or enhancement of an asset" is a prerequisite to capitalization, and deductibility under § 162(a) is the rule rather than the exception. Brief for Petitioner 16. We do not agree, for we conclude that National Starch has overread *Lincoln Savings*.

In *Lincoln Savings*, we were asked to decide whether certain premiums, required by federal statute to be paid by a savings and loan association to the Federal Savings and Loan Insurance Corporation (FSLIC), were ordinary and necessary expenses under § 162(a), as Lincoln Savings argued and the Court of Appeals had held, or capital expenditures under § 263, as the Commissioner contended. We found that the "additional" premiums, the purpose of which was to provide FSLIC with a secondary reserve fund in which each insured institution retained a pro rata interest recoverable in certain situations, "serve to create or enhance for Lincoln what is essentially a separate and distinct additional asset." 403 U.S. at 354. "As an inevitable consequence," we concluded, "the payment is capital in nature and not an expense, let alone an ordinary expense, deductible under § 162(a)." *Ibid.*

Lincoln Savings stands for the simple proposition that a taxpayer's expenditure that "serves to create or enhance . . . a separate and distinct" asset should be capitalized under § 263. It by no means follows, however, that *only* expenditures that create or enhance separate and distinct assets are to be capitalized under § 263. We had no occasion in *Lincoln Savings* to consider the tax treatment of expenditures that, unlike the additional premiums at issue there, did not create or enhance a specific asset, and thus the case cannot be read to preclude capitalization in other circumstances. In short, *Lincoln Savings* holds that the creation of a separate and distinct asset well may be a sufficient, but not a necessary, condition to classification as a capital expenditure. *See General Bancshares Corp. v. Commissioner*, 326 F.2d 712, 716 (CA8) (although expenditures may not "result in the acquisition or increase of a corporate asset, . . . these expenditures are not, because of that fact, deductible as ordinary and necessary business expenses"), *cert. denied*, 379 U.S. 832 (1964).

Nor does our statement in *Lincoln Savings*, 403 U.S. at 354, that "the presence of an ensuing benefit that may have some future aspect is not controlling" prohibit reliance on future benefit as a means of distinguishing an ordinary business expense from a capital expenditure.[18] Although the mere presence of an incidental future benefit — "*some* future aspect" — may not warrant capitalization, a taxpayer's realization of benefits beyond the year in which the expenditure is incurred is undeniably important in determining whether the appropriate tax treatment is immediate deduction or capitalization. *See United States v. Mississippi Chemical Corp.*, 405 U.S. 298, 310 (1972) (expense that "is of value in more than one taxable year" is a nondeductible capital expenditure); *Central Texas Savings & Loan Assn. v. United States*, 731 F.2d 1181, 1183 (CA5 1984) ("While the period of the benefits may not be controlling in all cases, it nonetheless remains a prominent, if not predominant, characteristic of a capital item"). Indeed, the text of the Code's capitalization provision, § 263(a)(1), which refers to "permanent improvements or betterments," itself envisions an inquiry into the duration and extent of the benefits realized by the taxpayer.

III

In applying the foregoing principles to the specific expenditures at issue in this case, we conclude that National Starch has not demonstrated that the investment banking, legal, and other costs it incurred in connection with Unilever's acquisition of its shares are deductible as ordinary and necessary business expenses under § 162(a).

Although petitioner attempts to dismiss the benefits that accrued to National Starch from the Unilever acquisition as "entirely speculative" or "merely incidental," Brief for Petitioner 39–40, the Tax Court's and the Court of Appeals' findings that the transaction produced significant benefits to National Starch that

---

[18] [4] Petitioner contends that, absent a separate-and-distinct-asset requirement for capitalization, a taxpayer will have no "principled basis" upon which to differentiate business expenses from capital expenditures. Brief for Petitioner 37–41. We note, however, that grounding tax status on the existence of an asset would be unlikely to produce the bright-line rule that petitioner desires, given that the notion of an "asset" is itself flexible and amorphous. *See* Johnson, 53 TAX NOTES, at 477–478.

extended beyond the tax year in question are amply supported by the record. For example, in commenting on the merger with Unilever, National Starch's 1978 "Progress Report" observed that the company would "benefit greatly from the availability of Unilever's enormous resources, especially in the area of basic technology." App. 43. *See also id.* at 46 (Unilever "provides new opportunities and resources"). Morgan Stanley's report to the National Starch board concerning the fairness to shareholders of a possible business combination with Unilever noted that National Starch management "feels that some synergy may exist with the Unilever organization given a) the nature of the Unilever chemical, paper, plastics and packaging operations . . . and b) the strong consumer products orientation of Unilever United States, Inc." *Id.* at 77–78.

In addition to these anticipated resource-related benefits, National Starch obtained benefits through its transformation from a publicly held, freestanding corporation into a wholly owned subsidiary of Unilever. The Court of Appeals noted that National Starch management viewed the transaction as " 'swapping approximately 3500 shareholders for one.' " 918 F.2d at 427; *see also* App. 223. Following Unilever's acquisition of National Starch's outstanding shares, National Starch was no longer subject to what even it terms the "substantial" shareholder-relations expenses a publicly traded corporation incurs, including reporting and disclosure obligations, proxy battles, and derivative suits. Brief for Petitioner 24. The acquisition also allowed National Starch, in the interests of administrative convenience and simplicity, to eliminate previously authorized but unissued shares of preferred and to reduce the total number of authorized shares of common from 8,000,000 to 1,000. *See* 93 T.C. at 74.

Courts long have recognized that expenses such as these, "incurred for the purpose of changing the corporate structure for the benefit of future operations are not ordinary and necessary business expenses." *General Bancshares Corp. v. Commissioner,* 326 F.2d at 715 (quoting *Farmers Union Corp. v. Commissioner,* 300 F.2d 197, 200 (CA9), *cert. denied,* 371 U.S. 861 (1962)). *See also* B. Bittker & J. Eustice, Federal Income Taxation of Corporations and Shareholders 5-33 to 5-36(5th ed. 1987) (describing "well-established rule" that expenses incurred in reorganizing or restructuring corporate entity are not deductible under § 162(a)). Deductions for professional expenses thus have been disallowed in a wide variety of cases concerning changes in corporate structure. Although support for these decisions can be found in the specific terms of § 162(a), which require that deductible expenses be "ordinary and necessary" and incurred "in carrying on any trade or business," courts more frequently have characterized an expenditure as capital in nature because "the purpose for which the expenditure is made has to do with the corporation's operations and betterment, sometimes with a continuing capital asset, for the duration of its existence or for the indefinite future or for a time somewhat longer than the current taxable year." *General Bancshares Corp. v. Commissioner,* 326 F.2d at 715. *See also Mills Estate, Inc. v. Commissioner,* 206 F.2d 244, 246 (CA2 1953). The rationale behind these decisions applies equally to the professional charges at issue in this case.

IV

The expenses that National Starch incurred in Unilever's friendly takeover do not qualify for deduction as "ordinary and necessary" business expenses under § 162(a). The fact that the expenditures do not create or enhance a separate and distinct additional asset is not controlling; the acquisition-related expenses bear the indicia of capital expenditures and are to be treated as such.

The judgment of the Court of Appeals is affirmed.

It is so ordered.

Understanding the Separate and Distinct Asset Test

1. *Lincoln Savings*, as cited in *INDOPCO*, states that an expenditure which gives rise to a "separate and distinct asset" must be capitalized and recovered over the useful life of the asset. By contrast, an expenditure not giving rise to a separate asset — even if it creates benefits over a multiyear period — may be currently deductible. Is that a reasonable distinction, or is too abstract to be workable? Suppose I am a real estate tycoon who spends my days buying and selling commercial buildings in sufficient volume that I can barely remember their names or locations. Are all of my administrative expenses currently deductible because it is unclear what distinct assets they are associated with? What would be the effects of such a rule on competition between me and a local management company, whose efforts were limited to one or two buildings and who would presumably have to capitalize their costs on this basis? *See NCNB Corporation v. United States*, 684 F.2d 285 (4th Cir. 1982) (allowing current deduction to a banking conglomerate under facts similar to the above).

2. *INDOPCO* modifies *Lincoln Savings* to hold that the presence of a separate and distinct asset is a sufficient, but not a necessary, condition for capitalization treatment. That is, an expense must be capitalized, even if no new asset is created, if the expense results in substantial enough benefits to the taxpayer over a multi-year period. If that is the rule, what doesn't have to be capitalized? Must a law firm now capitalize ordinary associates' salaries, because they result in some work that will be useful beyond the current year? Or does the requirement of a more than "incidental" benefit place a common-sense limit on such rules? Is it odd for the IRS to argue that the presence of a separate and distinct asset will always result in capitalization treatment, but that in the absence of such an asset, we may argue for capitalization anyway? Isn't this a bit of a "heads we win, tails you lose" argument?

3. *INDOPCO* involved expenses relating to a friendly takeover, which were incurred by the target of the takeover attempt. What if the same expenses were incurred in an effort to defend a company — either successfully or unsuccessfully — from a hostile takeover attempt? Or if there were a friendly takeover, but the expenses were incurred by the acquiring rather than the target company? Would it make a difference if the acquiring company's principal business consisted of mergers and acquisitions, so that the costs of merger and acquisition activity were (from its perspective) "ordinary" business expenses? What would be the competitive effects of this new, hypothetical rule?

4.	What do you make of the court's suggestion that deductions are a matter of "legislative grace" and ought to be interpreted in the narrowest way possible? Could you make an opposite presumption that people should be entitled to keep their own money, so that the income tax itself should be interpreted narrowly and provisions reducing the tax (deductions, credits, and so forth) should be given the broadest range possible? *See generally* BORIS I. BITTKER & LAWRENCE LOKKEN, FEDERAL TAXATION OF INCOME, ESTATES, AND GIFTS ¶ 4.2.1 (2d ed. 1989) (explaining the historic difficulty of applying a general interpretive presumption in tax cases).

5.	How, if at all, would *INDOPCO* affect your decision whether to enter into a merger or acquisition agreement?

Lincoln Savings and *INDOPCO* are the two most important cases on capitalization decided within the past few decades. But the rules governing capitalization have developed through new statutory provisions and regulations, as much as through judicial decisions.

In 2004, the Treasury Department issued extensive regulations meant to clarify the considerable uncertainty regarding capitalization of intangibles that remained after *INDOPCO*.[19] These regulations are generally viewed as being "taxpayer-favorable," at least as compared to the *INDOPCO* decision and to later developments based on that decision.[20] In other words, the regulations constricted "the class of cases in which capitalization is required as compared with prior law."[21] The 2004 regulations can be explained as the Treasury prioritizing administrative simplicity over revenue collection. As such, the regulations primarily serve to clarify that specified classes of expenditures are currently deductible, even though the expenditures might have been required to be capitalized following only the *INDOPCO* holding.

In addition to the evolution of the capitalization rules traced through *Lincoln Savings* and *INDOPCO* and the 2004 Treasury regulations, another major development came from Congressional enactment of Code section 263A in 1986.[22] Section 263A provides that the cost of property produced by the taxpayer, or acquired for resale, must be capitalized unless one of a series of exceptions listed in the statute applies. The costs subject to capitalization include the direct costs of the property (section 263A(a)(2)(B)) and a proper share of indirect costs (*e.g.*, rents, salaries, taxes) allocable to the property. There is an exception for resale property in the hands of taxpayers having gross receipts of $10 million or less, together with more specific exemptions for farmers, oil and gas wells, and other industries who are either well-connected or were able to present unusually convincing sob stories (more on this last point in a moment).

At first glance, section 263A appears to be somewhat redundant, since its

---

[19]	TD 9107, 69 Fed. Reg. 436 (Jan. 5, 2004), promulgating Reg. §§ 1.263(a)-4.

[20]	Ethan Yale, *The Final* INDOPCO *Regulations*, 105 TAX NOTES 435, 436 (2004).

[21]	*Id.*

[22]	A capital "A" or "B" following a section number indicates a section that was added after the other surrounding numbers were used up. This is distinct from a parenthetical letter (*e.g.*, section 263(a)), which indicates an ordinary subsection. The presence of a capital letter is usually a good sign that the previous rules didn't work properly, and some additional guidance was accordingly necessary.

underlying principle — that the costs of producing assets which last more than one year should be capitalized — was already stated in prior law. The difference is one of intensity: the general rules of section 263 were often flouted by taxpayers, while section 263A makes painfully clear what categories of expenses must be capitalized and what specific exceptions are contemplated. Yet section 263A, for all its complexity, still requires that there be some identifiable asset ("property") in order for capitalization to be required. Thus a taxpayer engaged in a general service business, like our hypothetical law firm above, may still escape capitalization if it does not produce identifiable pieces of property subject to the section 263A rules. To put the matter more systematically, expenses must be capitalized if they are subject to section 263A, or if (although not subject to section 263A) they result in the creation of "separate and distinct assets" under *Lincoln Savings* and similar precedents; but, under *INDOPCO*, other expenditures may be subject to capitalization, as well, if they result in more-than-incidental benefits over a more than one-year period and neither the Treasury regulations nor another provision applies to make them nonetheless currently deductible. (And you wondered why tax lawyers make so much money.)

One entertaining (literally) aspect of section 263A is subsection (h), enticingly labeled "Exemption for free-lance authors, photographers, and artists." The origins of this provision lie in the legislative history to the 1986 act, which suggested that the capitalization rules that already applied to the rest of the population should also apply to artists and writers who (say) deducted the cost of two years in Tuscany as part of the "research" for their next book. (Note here that we are not talking about actually denying these deductions, merely spreading them out over the useful life of the books (if any) that the authors actually produced.) Various artists and writers complained about this provision — rather eloquently, it must be conceded — and section 263A(h) was duly enacted, allowing current deduction of "qualified creative expenses" that would otherwise be subject to the section 263A rules. As befits such a creative group, this provision is perhaps the model of a specially targeted tax provision. Particularly entertaining are section 263A(h)(3)(C)(ii), which requires the IRS to evaluate the "originality and uniqueness" of the relevant art works together with the "predominance of aesthetic value over utilitarian value" contained therein, and the last sentence of section 263A(h)(2), which states that movies and videos will not be considered creative under any circumstances. On a more serious level, it is noteworthy that the provision applies to individuals and not corporations or other businesses; thus, Picasso's (or Jerry Garcia's) creative expenses might qualify for the provision, but not those of their production or distribution companies, a small blow for individual creativity in an increasingly conformist world.

C.   "Good Will" and Related Intangible Assets

1.   Self-Created Good Will

The issue of cost recovery is particularly challenging with respect to good will and related intangible items. "Good will" refers to the value of a business in excess of the value of its assets, which generally results from the firm's name, reputation, and the loyalty of customers or clients built up over a substantial period. Because good will has no obvious useful life — and because its value may be highly speculative in some cases — its tax treatment has been the subject of dispute. The following case considers the tax treatment of "self-created" good will; following this there is a discussion of good will that is acquired as part of a purchase or similar transaction.

WELCH v. HELVERING
United States Supreme Court
290 U.S. 111 (1933)

MR. JUSTICE CARDOZO delivered the opinion of the Court.

The question to be determined is whether payments by a taxpayer, who is in business as a commission agent, are allowable deductions in the computation of his income if made to the creditors of a bankrupt corporation in an endeavor to strengthen his own standing and credit.

In 1922 petitioner was the secretary of the E.L. Welch Company, a Minnesota corporation, engaged in the grain business. The company was adjudged an involuntary bankrupt, and had a discharge from its debts. Thereafter the petitioner made a contract with the Kellogg Company to purchase grain for it on a commission. In order to reestablish his relations with customers whom he had known when acting for the Welch Company and to solidify his credit and standing, he decided to pay the debts of the Welch business so far as he was able. In fulfillment of that resolve, he made payments of substantial amounts during five successive years. In 1924, the commissions were $18,028.20, the payments $3,975.97; in 1923, the commissions $31,377.07, the payments $11,968.20; in 1926, the commissions $20,925.25, the payments $12,815.72; in 1927, the commissions $22,119.61, the payments $7,379.72; and in 1928, the commissions $26,177.56, the payments $11,068.25. The Commissioner ruled that these payments were not deductible from income as ordinary and necessary expenses, but were rather in the nature of capital expenditures, an outlay for the development of reputation and good will. The Board of Tax Appeals sustained the action of the *Commissioner* (25 B.T.A. 117), and the Court of Appeals for the Eighth Circuit affirmed. 63 F.2d 976. The case is here on *certiorari*.

"In computing net income there shall be allowed as deductions . . . all the ordinary and necessary expenses paid or incurred during the taxable year in carrying on any trade or business." Revenue Act of 1924, c. 234, 43 Stat. 253, 269, § 214; 26 U.S.C. § 955; Revenue Act of 1926, c. 27, 44 Stat. 9, 26, § 214; 26 U.S.C. App. § 955; Revenue Act of 1928, c. 852, 45 Stat. 791, 799, § 23; cf. Treasury Regulations 65, Arts. 101, 292, under the Revenue Act of 1924, and similar regulations under the Acts of 1926 and 1928.

We may assume that the payments to creditors of the Welch Company were necessary for the development of the petitioner's business, at least in the sense that they were appropriate and helpful. *McCulloch v. Maryland*, 4 Wheat. 316. He certainly thought they were, and we should be slow to override his judgment. But the problem is not solved when the payments are characterized as necessary. Many necessary payments are charges upon capital. There is need to determine whether they are both necessary and ordinary. Now, what is ordinary, though there must always be a strain of constancy within it, is nonetheless a variable affected by time and place and circumstance. Ordinary in this context does not mean that the payments must be habitual or normal in the sense that the same taxpayer will have to make them often. A lawsuit affecting the safety of a business may happen once in a lifetime. The counsel fees may be so heavy that repetition is unlikely. Nonetheless, the expense is an ordinary one because we know from experience that payments for such a purpose, whether the amount is large or small, are the common and accepted means of defense against attack. *Cf. Kornhauser v. United States*, 276 U.S. 145. The situation is unique in the life of the individual affected, but not in the life of the group, the community, of which he is a part. At such times there are norms of conduct that help to stabilize our judgment, and make it certain and objective. The instance is not erratic, but is brought within a known type.

The line of demarcation is now visible between the case that is here and the one supposed for illustration. We try to classify this act as ordinary or the opposite, and the norms of conduct fail us. No longer can we have recourse to any fund of business experience, to any known business practice. Men do at times pay the debts of others without legal obligation or the lighter obligation imposed by the usages of trade or by neighborly amenities, but they do not do so ordinarily, not even though the result might be to heighten their reputation for generosity and opulence. Indeed, if language is to be read in its natural and common meaning (*Old Colony R. Co. v. Commissioner*, 284 U.S. 552, 560; *Woolford Realty Co. v. Rose*, 286 U.S. 319, 327), we should have to say that payment in such circumstances, instead of being ordinary is in a high degree extraordinary. There is nothing ordinary in the stimulus evoking it, and none in the response. Here, indeed, as so often in other branches of the law, the decisive distinctions are those of degree and not of kind. One struggles in vain for any verbal formula that will supply a ready touchstone. The standard set up by the statute is not a rule of law; it is rather a way of life. Life in all its fullness must supply the answer to the riddle.

The Commissioner of Internal Revenue resorted to that standard in assessing the petitioner's income, and found that the payments in controversy came closer to capital outlays than to ordinary and necessary expenses in the operation of a business. His ruling has the support of a presumption of correctness, and the petitioner has the burden of proving it to be wrong. *Wickwire v. Reinecke*, 275 U.S. 101; *Jones v. Commissioner*, 38 F.2d 550, 552. Unless we can say from facts within our knowledge that these are ordinary and necessary expenses according to the ways of conduct and the forms of speech prevailing in the business world, the tax must be confirmed. But nothing told us by this record or within the sphere of our judicial notice permits us to give that extension to what is ordinary and necessary. Indeed, to do so would open the door to many bizarre analogies. One man has a family name that is clouded by thefts committed by an ancestor. To add to his own standing he repays the stolen money, wiping off, it may be, his income for the year. The payments figure in his tax return as ordinary expenses. Another man conceives the notion that he will be able to practice his vocation with greater ease and profit if he has an opportunity to enrich his culture. Forthwith the price of his education becomes an expense of the business, reducing the income subject to taxation. There is little difference between these expenses and those in controversy here. Reputation and learning are akin to capital assets, like the good will of an old partnership. *Cf. Colony Coal & Coke Corp. v. Commissioner*, 52 F.2d 923. For many, they are the only tools with which to hew a pathway to success. The money spent in acquiring them is well and wisely spent. It is not an ordinary expense of the operation of a business.

Many cases in the federal courts deal with phases of the problem presented in the case at bar. To attempt to harmonize them would be a futile task. They involve the appreciation of particular situations, at times with borderline conclusions. Typical illustrations are cited in the margin. [Citations omitted]

The decree should be

Affirmed.

Understanding *Welch v. Helvering*

1. Cardozo was awfully bright, but did he understand the issue in *Welch v. Helvering*? Was the case about the "ordinary and necessary" character of Welch's payments, or about the timing of the deduction for them? If the latter, why did Cardozo devote so much time to the previous issue? Or was he simply recognizing the fact that amortization over a sufficiently long term would have been economically similar to losing the deduction altogether, so the case — although nominally a timing dispute — was effectively a deduction vs. no deduction issue? If you were Welch's lawyer, after reading the case, when, if at all, would you advise him to deduct his original expenditures? What if anything would you advise him to do differently next time, if he wanted to ensure better tax treatment?

2. Even applying Cardozo's "ordinary and necessary" standards, was Welch's conduct really all that extraordinary? Who would do business with a salesman whose previous employer had failed to pay any of his bills? Absent clear malfeasance, shouldn't a businessperson's judgment be respected in such matters, or does "ordinary and necessary" imply a more demanding standard?

3. What is the proper tax treatment of the people who received Welch's payments?

2. Purchased or Acquired Good Will

Welch v. Helvering established that expenditures to create goodwill — with the notable exception of advertising expenses — were generally not deductible. What about the purchase of a company with existing good will? Suppose that you become wealthy enough to purchase an existing department store, or newspaper, or baseball team. Part of the purchase price will reflect the tangible, physical assets held by the company that you acquire. But part (sometimes, a larger part) will reflect less tangible items. A store, or a newspaper, will have customers or subscribers who have a loyalty to the company and an established pattern of buying its products. A baseball team has an existing fan base and a maze of contractual rights (player contracts, television deals, the right to participate in an annual draft of new talent) quite apart from its offices, stadium, and so forth. This intangible value of a business, in excess of its actual physical assets, is indeed the very definition of good will. What is the proper characterization of these items, and how should they be treated for tax purposes?

Until 1993, the law in these cases was rather confusing. Purchased good will, like the self-created variety, remained nondeductible for tax purposes. But if a purchaser could manage to "carve off" some distinct asset from good will, and ascribe to it a measurable useful life, she could amortize (*i.e.*, depreciate) the cost of the asset even if it was logically indistinguishable from the underlying goodwill. As one might expect, purchasers exercised considerable creativity in identifying assets — subscription lists, contracts with key personnel, etc. — which were arguably separate from goodwill and accordingly resulted in better tax treatment. One purchaser went so far as to conduct a study which demonstrated that the average football player depreciated, or otherwise wore out, in approximately five years' time, and sought to amortize a portion of the team's purchase price on this basis. The incentive to litigate was unusually high in these cases, since the stakes were enormous and — even if one lost — the worst that could happen was to revert to the same nondepreciable goodwill that one had, in the first place.

In 1993 Congress, tiring of the goodwill lottery, enacted section 197 of the Code. Section 197 ends the argument by providing 15-year amortization for purchased goodwill and for most of the items — workforce, trademarks, customer and supplier lists, etc. — previously used as goodwill substitutes. The statute emphasizes that the fifteen-year rule is exclusive: even if a taxpayer can demonstrate that its customer list, etc., has a shorter useful life, the fifteen-year recovery period remains in force. Section 197 has ended the litigation about the tax treatment of purchased goodwill, although at the cost of new inequity between purchased and self-created goodwill and a maze of technical problems.[23]

Examine closely the wording of section 197. In everyday language, what is this provision trying to accomplish, and why do you suppose the list of section 197 intangibles (section 197(d)(1)) is as long and complicated as it is? What specifically is meant by a "customer-based intangible" (section 197(d)(2)) and a "supplier-based intangible" (section 197(d)(3)), and what might be examples of these items in the real world? For extra credit, what is the purpose of the "anti-churning" rules (section 197(f)(9)), and do you think that they are likely to achieve their intended purpose?

Using the Sources

Under present law, which of the following would be currently deductible, and which would have to be capitalized? If capitalized, what is the likely recovery period?

a. A salary paid to a law school professor.

b. A salary paid to a construction worker.

c. A fee paid to an outside business consultant to research possible mergers.

---

[23] The American Jobs Creation Act of 2004 later extended the section 197 rules to sports franchises and related assets.

d. A fee paid to an advertising agency.

e. The costs of adding asbestos to an existing building to prevent fires.

f. The costs of removing the same asbestos twenty years later.

g. The costs of acquiring a new baseball franchise.

h. The costs of acquiring an existing baseball franchise.

i. The costs of acquiring a competing newspaper which you plan to close down immediately and use only its subscription list.

j. Living expenses for a year in Provence during which you research your next novel.

Law and Planning

1.   Suppose that you were the tax adviser to a company that had been sued for releasing chemical substances that had contaminated the local groundwater. The company has identified four principal alternatives for resolving this problem:

    a. Reach a settlement with the people and businesses affected by the contamination, paying them a fixed sum in return for a release from all civil and criminal liability in the case.

    b. Construct a new "scrubber" system that will reduce the percentage of contaminating substances in the runoff from the company's plants.

    c. Construct a new, cleaner factory that will eliminate the pollution problem.

    d. Do nothing and let the victims (or the Government) come after us.

Which of these alternatives makes the most sense to you, and what role would tax factors play in your decision?

2.   Now suppose that the same company wished to enter the Internet bookselling business, and could do so in one of three ways:

    a. Buy an existing company with a strong reputation and customer base as well as a developed technical capacity (each of which will be reflected in the price of the company).

    b. Invest the same money in an effort to develop its own "good will" and customer loyalty, together with its own technical skills.

    c. Same as b. above, except that a large portion of the development activity would be "farmed out" to an outside consultant.

Again, which of these alternatives would you recommend, and what role (if any) would tax factors play in your decision?

3.   Think about your answers to questions 1. and 2. above. Did the tax system create logical incentives, or did it make it more difficult to pursue an intelligent business strategy? How if at all could the system be changed to create more rational incentives?

Politics and Policy

1.   Suppose that a member of Congress was unhappy with the current rules on capitalization of expenses and wanted to make things easier for the affected businesses. To accomplish this, she introduced a bill which contained all of the following provisions:

a. Section 263A would be repealed outright.

b. Expenditures for both self-created and purchased good will would be deductible over a five-year statutory period.

c. The *INDOPCO* decision would be overruled, that is, expenses incurred in takeovers and similar transactions would be currently deductible unless they resulted in creation of a separate and distinct asset.

d. For good measure, all environmental cleanup-related costs would be currently deductible, regardless of whether they constituted "repairs" or improvements under existing law.

The sponsor of the bill, upon introducing it, stated:

The IRS is discouraging businesses from making otherwise attractive investments, because they are unable to recover their costs in a fair and reasonable manner. If a company invests in its future, it should be able to deduct its costs as quickly as possible, unless it is certain that the expenditures will give rise to benefits over a longer period. Ties should go to the taxpayer.

What are the arguments for and against this proposal, and would you support it if it came to a vote?

2.   What do you think are the implications of the present law capitalization rules on competition between large and small companies? If there is an imbalance, how do you propose to correct it?

3.   What do you think are the vertical equity implications (that is, the effect on rich and poor taxpayers) of the capitalization rules?

II.   DEPRECIATION, ACRS, AND THE ROLE OF TAX INCENTIVES

A.   General Rules: Accelerated Cost Recovery and Section 168

The issue of cost recovery arises most dramatically in the case of tangible (*i.e.*, physical) assets. Suppose that a company invests in a new computer, which costs $1 million and which the company expects to use for five years. One obvious answer is to let the company deduct the cost ratably over a five-year period ($200,000 per year). Not so fast, says the company. First of all, we don't really know how long the computer will last: technology changes overnight, and what looks like a five-year investment today may wind up a hunk of metal in ninety days. Even if it does last for five years, the computer is likely to lose most of its value in the first year or two, the way a new car loses one-third of its value after you drive it home from the showroom. Finally, the company may argue, we need an incentive to invest in new plant and equipment and keep our country ahead of Europe, Japan, China, and other competitors we haven't identified, yet. (Why businesses need an incentive to do what businesses do anyway is not quite clear, but politicians seem to believe it and there is probably enough evidence to allow one to think either way.)

Given the arguments above — not to mention the clout of business lobbyists — it is probably not surprising that depreciation rules tend to be more generous than economic reality. This is reflected in two principal ways. First, the recovery periods for depreciable assets tend to be shorter than their actual useful lives. This is plainly visible in section 168, which prescribes the recovery periods and methods for most tangible property.[24] Compare, in particular, the left- and right-hand columns of section 168(e)(1), which classifies property for depreciation purposes. Do you see what is happening? In almost every category, the property's statutory classification is significantly shorter than its estimated class (*i.e.*, useful) life: property having a 4- to 10-year class life is classified as 5-year property; property having a 10- to 16-year class life is classified as 7-year property; and so on down the line. Only in the case of residential and nonresidential real property are the recovery periods more realistic, and even here, one can argue that many buildings gain rather than lose value and should not be subject to depreciation, at all. So the statute plainly adopts a policy of recovery periods shorter than an asset's real useful life: given the time value of money, that's a clear advantage for the investors in such assets, and results in the payment of less tax than they would otherwise pay.

A second issue pertains to recovery methods. Recall our argument that assets lose value disproportionately in the early years. This assumption is reflected in so-called accelerated cost recovery, which allows a disproportionate amount of depreciation deductions to be taken in those early years.[25] The most popular method, the 200 percent or "double declining balance" method, is described in section 168(b)(1). Under this method, the taxpayer's deduction, in each of the early years, is equal to twice the deduction that the taxpayer would receive under the equivalent straight-line method. For example, assume a taxpayer, on April 15, 2006, places in service a new machine that cost $10,000 and was classified as 5-year property under section 168. (The 2006 date is chosen to avoid certain temporary provisions applicable in earlier years.) Under the half-year convention applicable to such assets (section 168(d)(1)), the property would be deemed to be placed in

---

[24] Tangible assets include real property (*i.e.*, buildings) and personal property (*i.e.*, plant and equipment), the depreciation for each of which is specified by section 168. Amortization of intangibles, for which there is less specific statutory guidance, is covered by section 167 (and in the case of goodwill, section 197). No depreciation or amortization is provided for land, stock, or other assets deemed to have indefinite useful lives.

[25] A straight-line method applies to real property and some other assets (section 168(b)(3)). An additional first-year depreciation allowance, equal to 50 percent of the adjusted basis, applies to certain categories of property — generally, those with shorter recovery periods — that are acquired before 2005.

service on midnight of July 1. If a straight-line method were employed, the taxpayer's recovery percentage would be 20 percent per year, and its depreciation deductions would be as follows:

Year	Deduction
2006	$1,000 (20 percent × one-half year)
2007	$2,000 (20 percent)
2008	$2,000 (20 percent)
2009	$2,000 (20 percent)
2010	$2,000 (20 percent)
2011	$1,000 (20 percent × one-half year)

By contrast, under the double declining balance method, the recovery percentage is 40 percent and the deductions would be more heavily weighted to the early years:

Year	Deduction
2006	$2,000 (40 percent × 10,000 × one-half year; leaves balance of 8,000)
2007	$3,200 (40 percent × 8,000; leaves balance of 4,800)
2008	$1,920 (40 percent 4,800; leaves balance of 2,880)
2009	$1,152 (40 percent × 2,880, leaves balance of 1,768)

Of course, this method cannot continue indefinitely, since (as someone named Xeno noted) applying the same percentage to a declining number will never reach your ultimate goal.[26] The Code recognizes this, and allows the taxpayer to switch to the straight-line method at the point when this method will yield the larger deduction (section 168(b)(1)(B)).[27] But the real point is in the early years: by allowing a 40 rather than a 20 percent recovery percentage, the Code has allowed the taxpayer to recover more than one-half the cost in the first 18 months, even though the asset is nominally five-year property and its actual economic life (as we observed) may be significantly longer than that. While the same aggregate amount ($5,000) is recovered, the timing difference makes the accelerated method far more attractive from the taxpayer's point of view.

The issue may seem rather technical, but its significance is difficult to overstate. Since businesses are always investing in something, the ability to depreciate the cost of new assets at an accelerated pace goes a long way to reducing or even eliminating their tax liability. During the early 1980s, depreciation allowances were

---

[26] Actually, Xeno's Paradox states that no one can ever arrive at a different place, since to get there they would have to go half way (50 percent), then another half (total 75 percent), then another (87.5 percent), and so on in ever smaller steps that never quite reached their destination. Yet people get places all the time, so Xeno was obviously wrong. The flaw is that you do indeed cover smaller and smaller distances, but at an ever increasing rate, so that you are eventually covering infinitely small distances at an infinitely high speed. For a good laugh, try this on your younger siblings.

[27] Actually, the Code says that you switch in the first taxable year "for which using the straight line method with respect to the adjusted basis of the beginning of such year will yield a larger allowance." So, in our example, one would switch in the year 2010, recovering two-thirds of the remaining balance ($1152) in 2005 and one-third ($576) in the first half of 2011. By contrast, the 40 percent declining balance method would yield a deduction of $691 in 2010, and fail to reach the $5,000 limit in 2011.

so generous that it was estimated a real estate project could be abandoned immediately upon completion and still be profitable to the owners because of the associated tax deductions. Depreciation (especially for real property) has become somewhat less generous since then, but remains extraordinarily generous, and is the single biggest reason for the relative decline in business taxes over the past generation.

If buildings and equipment are subsidized, what about "high-tech" industries that invest in new technologies rather than new physical structures? Have no fear; the tax code takes care of them too. In addition to a current deduction for research and development (R & D) expenditures (section 174), the Code provides a credit for a substantial amount of these expenses (section 41): that is, a dollar-for-dollar reduction in tax liability for each dollar spent on R & D subject to the limitations contained in the provision.[28] Although there is no doubt a good argument for R & D subsidies — a company that invests in a new technology may not be able to capture all of the returns pertaining to the technology, and the patent system provides only partial protection — most original scientific research is in fact conducted by the Government or section 501(c)(3) organizations that are not subject to the income tax, anyway. The R & D credit thus winds up subsidizing largely development work, like taking a new pharmaceutical breakthrough and developing it into a safe, marketable pill, or a new automotive technology and developing it for public use. In other words, the credit winds up subsidizing pretty much the same things that a competent business would probably be doing, anyway. Whether that's any worse than accelerated depreciation is a fair question, but it's surely not much better, and the credit is probably best seen as an indirect tax cut for high-tech businesses, compensating them for the lack of depreciation and similar deductions that remain available to the more old-fashioned, "smokestack" industries.

B.   Recapture, Characterization, and the Seeds of the Tax Shelter Problem

"In the long run," said Keynes, "we are all dead." So, one might say, do many or most tax consequences even out in the long run. Assume, as in our depreciation example above, that a company buys a piece of equipment for $10,000, and takes $10,000 of depreciation deductions over a five-year period. Assume further that the equipment has actually increased in value and the company is able to sell it, at the end of the 5-year period, for its original $10,000 price. While this tax treatment might seem unduly generous, it will ultimately "even out": the deductions will reduce the company's basis in the property down to 0, so that when it sells the property, it will have to pay tax on $10,000 of gain ($10,000 amount realized – 0 adjusted basis), effectively wiping out the advantage that it got from the unjustified or false depreciation in the earlier years. Indeed, the "recapture" rule of section 1245 requires that such gain, to the extent of precious depreciation deductions, be treated as ordinary income rather than capital gain, thus avoiding a situation in

---

[28] The credit and deduction cannot be claimed for the same amounts.

which the taxpayer gets deductions at a high tax rate and income only at a reduced, lower rate.[29] What, then, is the problem here?

The answer, yet again, is timing. Even if we assume that the company disposes of the property in a taxable sale, the tax on that transaction will come only on the date of sale. Meanwhile, the company has taken depreciation deductions that reduced taxable income for a five-, ten-, fifteen-year or longer period. This is in addition to interest or other deductions arising from the same transaction. It is as if the IRS offered taxpayers a loan, the proceeds of which could be used today, but which had to be repaid (if at all) only much later and without any interest payments. If the taxpayers are middle-aged or older when they enter the transaction — and if the property is held for an extensive period — the danger of such repayment may seem particularly remote.

The timing or "deferral" element associated with such investments in depreciable property is an important aspect of the tax shelter problem, as we shall see, below.

Using the Sources

1.   Over what period, and using what method (straight-line, accelerated, etc.) would the cost of the following be recovered? (*See* I.R.C. § 168.)

   a. An automobile used in the taxpayer's trade or business.

   b. A new business computer.

   c. An apartment building which you owned and rented to others.

   d. An apartment that you and your family lived in.

   e. A patent or copyright (or the costs of acquiring same).

   f. A list of customers and suppliers, stored on a (top secret) computer disk, and which is part of the assets of a new business that you just acquired.

   g. Same as f., except there is no disk and the information exists only in the minds of the business' employees and business contacts.

2.   Refer back to the example above (Section II.A.) involving a taxpayer who purchases a $10,000 machine (five-year property) on April 15, 2006. Suppose that the taxpayer sold the same machine, on August 15, 2009, for $11,000. How much income would the taxpayer have, and how much of it would be ordinary income and/or capital gain? How would these answers vary, if the sale were for $8,000?

3.   Examine carefully section 179 of the Code. What is this provision about, and to what taxpayers and in what situations might it be helpful? What do you think is the policy behind this provision, and does it make sense to you or not?

---

[29]   I.RC. § 1245(a). A similar rule applies to real property, but only to the extent the taxpayer has used an accelerated depreciation method; since accelerated depreciation no longer applies to real estate, this rule is relevant only for older properties. I.R.C. § 1250. The terms "capital gain" and "ordinary income" are explained further in Chapter 9.

Law and Planning

Suppose that you were interested in buying an (unincorporated) medical or dental practice from another practitioner. What would be the principal assets that you were acquiring, and how would the costs of these be recovered for tax purposes? Is there anything you could do, in structuring the purchase, to make the tax consequences more attractive? Would the seller agree willingly to these terms or would he demand some form of compensation for doing so? How important, if at all, would the tax issue be in your decision to buy the practice?

Politics and Policy

1.   Like buildings and equipment which benefit from accelerated depreciation, and high-tech industries which benefit from the R&D tax credit, the oil and gas industry benefits from various tax subsidies, including accelerated deductions for so-called intangible drilling costs; favorable methods of depletion (a sort of depreciation equivalent that applies to mineral deposits); and similar benefits. Suppose that you were an industry lobbyist and had to argue the case for oil and gas tax incentives before Congress or the Treasury Department. Which of the following do you think you would emphasize?

a. Oil and gas is a risky business, and the recovery methods for related expenditures should compensate for this increased risk.

b. Domestic production frees us from dependence on unreliable foreign suppliers, so oil and gas tax incentives are important for national security.

c. Other industries have similar tax breaks (*e.g.*, accelerated depreciation and the R & D credit), so the energy industry should get something too.

If you were an environmental or similar lobbyist, opposed to oil and gas tax breaks, how would you respond to these arguments? Who, if anyone, would you expect to be convinced by them?

2.   As a general rule, do you think that the tax system encourages or discourages taxpayers from making risky investments? What changes would you like to see in the Code in order to deal with these issues more effectively? (Hint: Think about deductions as well as income and timing provisions before answering this question.)

III.   TAX SHELTERS AND ANTI-TAX SHELTER MECHANISMS

A.   Tax Shelters and Tax Avoidance

The issue of tax incentives brings us to the broader subject of tax shelters and tax avoidance methods. "Tax shelter" is the most emotionally charged term in the tax lexicon, conjuring up images of shady deals in obscure resort islands that permit the wealthy to avoid tax while you and I pay through the nose. While there is something to this image, most tax shelters are considerably less dramatic, involving nothing more than the intentional use of perfectly legal tax provisions to reduce tax on an individual's (or corporation's) salary or other income. Well, not perfectly legal; there is an inevitable tendency to push the envelope in designing and marketing tax shelters, and ethical issues come to the fore frequently in the field. Yet the bulk of tax shelters are considerably less exotic than most people think, and the line between legitimate and shady transactions is extraordinarily difficult to draw.

Begin with definitions. In a sense, any investment that is made with an eye to tax consequences could be called a tax shelter. Consider an individual who buys a tax-exempt (*i.e.*, municipal) bond instead of a corporate bond or other security. A major reason for doing so is, clearly, that interest on the former is tax-exempt, while interest on the latter would be taxed as ordinary income. But most people would call this a "tax-free" or a "tax-advantaged" investment, rather than a full-blown tax shelter. For a tax-free bond, or fringe benefit, does not really protect ("shelter") any other income from tax; the item is itself free from tax, but the taxpayer continues to pay at the appropriate tax rate on everything else.

A genuine tax shelter goes further, by producing excess deductions or credits that can be used to reduce tax on salary or other income. Sometimes this results from aggressive manipulation of facts, rather than creative legal strategies. Consider a taxpayer who buys a diamond or other gem stone for $5,000. Three years later, the taxpayer donates the gem stone to a section 501(c)(3) charitable organization, claiming a valuation of $50,000.[30] Assuming that the taxpayer is in the 40 percent tax bracket, the deduction saves him $20,000 in taxes — a 4-to-1 write-off as compared to his initial investment, and likely more when state and local taxes are taken into account. The problem, of course, is that the taxpayer is (probably) lying: very few gem stones increase ten-fold in value over three years, and when they do, people usually don't give them to charity. But it's hard to police this sort of individualized, fact-based issue; there is really no substitute for case-by-case audit and litigation, and while interest and penalties will undoubtedly deter some taxpayers, others may be willing to take their chances.[31]

Or consider a personal favorite of your authors, the so-called "master" recording or lithograph tax shelter. In this transaction, the buyer would acquire the rights to a music or art composition authored by someone this side of Picasso, putting down (say) $0.2 million and financing the remainder of the purchase with a nonrecourse, $1.8 million loan provided by the seller of the property. (The tangible property (*e.g.*, master disk) was necessary to qualify for section 168 treatment.) The buyer would then take depreciation deductions based on a $2 million purchase price, which — together with the then-available "investment tax credit," equal to 15 percent of the investment in the first year — would provide tax benefits many times in excess of

---

[30] This example assumes that the taxpayer is entitled to a full fair market value deduction under section 170(e)(1), as in the case of an organization that could use the gem stone in performing its exempt function (section 170(e)(1)(B)). It also assumes that the taxpayer met the appropriate record-keeping requirements (section 170(f)(8)), which is probably not too difficult. Charitable contributions are discussed further in Chapter 7.

[31] A sizable portion of the Tax Court docket has historically been devoted to gem stone or similar valuation cases.

the original cash investment.[32] Of course, the matter of repaying the loan would remain, but in many or most cases the seller would fail to collect it, and enforcing the tax on cancellation of indebtedness for a loan of this nature would be an extraordinarily difficult task. Even if the loan were repaid, or the tax on debt cancellation enforced, the taxpayer would benefit from an enormous timing advantage, getting deductions and credits "up front" and paying the piper only at a much later date, if at all.

The examples above have the flavor of cheating, of manipulating facts and law in a manner not intended by the authors of the tax code. But many tax shelters are much more "legitimate" in nature. Consider in this vein the typical 1980s-era real estate tax shelter, of a type which with a few small modifications might still be effective today.[33] Such a tax shelter was frequently based on the transfer of tax benefits to those in high tax brackets rather than the creation of new deductions.

Say that a retailer owned several supermarkets that generated depreciation and other deductions that were not particularly useful to the retailer, either because it was in a low tax bracket or because it already had other deductions, credits, and exclusions which had reduced its taxable income to a low level. These deductions might however be quite useful to doctors, lawyers, and other high income individuals with no other obvious way to reduce taxes on that income. A tax shelter promoter, with the assistance of a law or accounting firm, would bundle these "investors" into a limited partnership or similar entity created for the express purposes of acquiring the properties in question and their attendant tax benefits. The partnership would buy the properties and immediately lease them back to their original owner (*i.e.*, the retailer) for a thirty-year or similarly extended period. Meanwhile, the partnership and its investors would be the owners of the property for tax purposes and would qualify for depreciation and other deductions which, at least until the advent of the passive loss rules, might substantially reduce their taxes on salary and other income. If the property was a good investment, the same investors might make a further profit on the sale of the property — either to its original owner or a third party — at the end of the 30-year period, so that they would effectively be deducting tax losses on a property which was at the same time increasing in real world value. (The cleverer among you may have noticed that this game will eventually "catch up" with the investors, who will have to pay tax on the difference between the sale price (which they hope will be high) and the basis of the property (which has been reduced to a small number by depreciation) at the time of the sale, or else (if they default on the loan) will be hit with a substantial tax on cancellations of indebtedness income. But these consequences are many years in the future and may not mean much to a 55- or 60-year old investor looking for a quick tax fix. In the meantime, the investors have registered a major tax advantage.)

---

[32] The investment tax credit was (mercifully) repealed in 1986.

[33] This example dates from a period before the passive loss rules. It would remain attractive today to those investors who had adequate passive income, which could be used to "soak up" deductions resulting from the shelter, or who could manage to be actively involved in the shelter activity within the section 469 definition.

Before evaluating this tax shelter, it is important to understand how it works. The key benefits of a tax shelter are often said to consist of three elements: deferral, leverage, and conversion. Deferral, as you remember from Chapter 4, refers to the delay of tax liability to a later year, which is valuable because of the time value of money and (sometimes) because the taxpayer hopes to be in a lower tax bracket in the subsequent year. Whereas pensions and IRAs achieve deferral by delaying the receipt of taxable income, a tax shelter achieves the same effect by generating excess deductions that are used to reduce tax on salary or other current income of the taxpayer. For example, in the tax shelter above, depreciation and other deductions were available from year one whereas gain (if any) on the sale or property was many years in the future.

Leverage means simply that the tax effects of the investment are magnified by the extensive reliance on borrowed funds. For example, under *Crane*, a taxpayer could put down only $20,000 of a $200,000 tax shelter investment, borrow the remaining $180,000, and take depreciation and other deductions based on the higher figure while also deducting interest payments under section 163(a) (business interest). It is this ability to inflate deductions by means of borrowed money that enables taxpayers to achieve 2:1, 3:1, and other deductions in excess of the amount actually invested.[34]

Conversion means that, while deductions resulting from tax shelters can generally be used to reduce the taxpayer's ordinary income, the subsequent gain on sale of a tax shelter asset is sometimes taxed at lower, capital gain rates. The present law recapture rules (section 1245 and 1250) restrict but do not eliminate this possibility, especially not with respect to real estate.

Tax shelters are not magic: taxpayers can still lose money if (say) the value of the purchased property collapses, and a bad investment should never be made solely because of the tax benefits. But a good tax shelter can take an otherwise, well, marginal investment and make it extremely attractive to people who have the right characteristics and are situated in the right tax brackets. For example, the investment described in the preceding prospectus would probably be of limited interest to someone who was not interested in the tax deductions, but was obviously quite attractive to many who were. Many investments, if not solely tax-driven, would clearly not be undertaken if not for the additional tax advantages.

Having explained how one tax shelter works, the question remains: is anything wrong with it? A surprising number of tax experts would answer: no. According to this view, Congress, by enacting accelerated depreciation and other tax benefits for real estate investments, was making a conscious decision to encourage investment in this industry rather than other economic sectors. All the sale-leaseback is doing is transferring these tax benefits from the original owner, who for some reason doesn't need them, to a partnership of (presumably wealthy) individuals who do.[35]

---

[34] The at risk rules restrict, although they do not eliminate, this possibility, at least with respect to nonrecourse debt. For the classic treatment of the role of leverage in tax shelters, see George Cooper, *The Taking of the Shield: Identifying and Controlling Income Tax Avoidance*, 85 COLUM. L. REV. 657 (1985).

[35] As in so many areas, the interplay between tax and other (especially securities) laws is important

In other words, the "deferral" resulting from real estate, oil and gas, or other tax shelters might seem unfair to the layman, but was part of Congress' plan in encouraging investment in these industries, in the first place. The "leverage" and "conversion" aspects, likewise, amount to nothing more than taxpayers taking advantage of the *Crane* rule, which allows borrowed funds to be included in the basis of property, and the capital gain provisions, which intentionally provide lower rates on investment-type income. The results might seem unfair in the short run, but in the long run, everyone gains.

The arguments above have some force, but strike many people as rationalizations. For one thing, it is not clear that many new assets are constructed as a result of sale-leaseback and similar arrangements, which often involve already existing properties. For another, tax shelters tend to make a hash of the distributional tables, resulting in numerous horror stories of wealthy individuals paying little or no tax while the average working Joe or Jane pays higher and higher taxes on a stagnant personal income. (Try explaining to a steel worker why it's a good thing that his boss pays less tax than he does.) Finally, it just doesn't seem right for so many tax liabilities to change based on what were, in essence, paper transactions. In the 1970s and 1980s, arguments like this led to a strong political, if not intellectual, argument for reforming the tax shelter industry.

The change came in several phases. First, in 1969, Congress added the alternative (originally "add-on") minimum tax to require some tax payments even from those individuals and corporations with numerous tax reduction strategies.[36] The 1976 and 1978 reform acts added further provisions, notably the at risk rules (section 465), a sort of partial repeal of the *Crane* rule that eliminated nonrecourse debt from basis in certain instances.[37] These were coupled, over the years, with various ethical standards regarding tax shelters and aggressive enforcement and penalty provisions for tax shelter promoters.[38] Finally, in 1986, Congress adopted the passive loss rules (section 469), which restricted the ability to use tax shelter losses against salary or other active income of the taxpayer. (The passive loss rules are discussed further, below.)

---

for tax shelters. For example, Securities and Exchange Commission (SEC) regulations have historically permitted limited partnership interests to be marketed to small numbers of wealthy sophisticated investors without the reporting and other requirements that would normally apply under the securities laws, thus reducing substantially the administrative and "paperwork" costs associated with such investments.

[36] The alternative minimum tax essentially requires taxpayers to make a separate calculation, based on the assumption of a lower tax rate but a more stringent tax base (*i.e.*, one that provided fewer exclusions from income, less generous deductions and depreciation, etc.). If the tax calculated under the "AMT" is higher than that under the regular tax system, the taxpayer is required to pay this higher amount. Originally intended to reach a few individuals and corporations with extensive tax shelter activities, the AMT now affects a relatively large number of taxpayers, particularly in the higher income brackets.

[37] The basic idea of the at risk rules is to limit loss deductions to the amount a taxpayer actually stands to lose (*i.e.*, has "at risk") in the transaction. Because there is no clear line between recourse and nonrecourse debt, and because taxpayers became adept at the use of grantees and other arrangements designed to create an artificial risk of loss, the rules have never been completely effective. Real estate was not subject to the at risk rules until 1986.

[38] *See* Section II.C, *infra*.

Before considering the passive loss rules, it may be worthwhile to consider the failed attempt to limit tax shelters by means of litigation, which reached its peak in the late 1970s and early 1980s. The following is the most famous case of this era, *Frank Lyon Co. v. United States*, which involved an unsuccessful attack on a real estate tax avoidance scheme. *Frank Lyon* is in many respects an odd case: it involved a bank seeking financing for a new building, rather than a partnership or other typical tax shelter investor; even if the Government were successful, it would have affected primarily real estate sale-leaseback transactions, rather than the entire tax shelter industry. Yet the case became a sort of poster child for the failure to deal successfully with tax shelters, and helped create the situation in which more draconian rules were deemed necessary. Read it and see if you can understand why.

FRANK LYON CO. v. UNITED STATES
United States Supreme Court
435 U.S. 561 (1978)

MR. JUSTICE BLACKMUN delivered the opinion of the Court.

This case concerns the federal income tax consequences of a sale-and-leaseback in which petitioner Frank Lyon Company (Lyon) took title to a building under construction by Worthen Bank & Trust Company (Worthen) of Little Rock, Ark., and simultaneously leased the building back to Worthen for longterm use as its headquarters and principal banking facility.

I

The underlying pertinent facts are undisputed. They are established by stipulations, App. 9, 14, the trial testimony, and the documentary evidence, and are reflected in the District Court's findings.

A

Lyon is a closely held Arkansas corporation engaged in the distribution of home furnishings, primarily Whirlpool and RCA electrical products. Worthen in 1965 was an Arkansas-chartered bank and a member of the Federal Reserve System. Frank Lyon was Lyon's majority shareholder and board chairman; he also served on Worthen's board. Worthen at that time began to plan the construction of a multistory bank and office building to replace its existing facility in Little Rock. About the same time Worthen's competitor, Union National Bank of Little Rock, also began to plan a new bank and office building. Adjacent sites on Capitol Avenue, separated only by Spring Street, were acquired by the two banks. It became a matter of competition, for both banking business and tenants, and prestige as to which bank would start and complete its building first.

Worthen initially hoped to finance, to build, and to own the proposed facility at a total cost of $9 million for the site, building, and adjoining parking deck. This was to be accomplished by selling $4 million in debentures and using the proceeds in the acquisition of the capital stock of a wholly owned real estate subsidiary. This subsidiary would have formal title and would raise the remaining $5 million by a conventional mortgage loan on the new premises. Worthen's plan, however, had to be abandoned for two significant reasons:

1. As a bank chartered under Arkansas law, Worthen legally could not pay more interest on any debentures it might issue than that then specified by Arkansas law. But the proposed obligations would not be marketable at that rate.

2. Applicable statutes or regulations of the Arkansas State Bank Department and the Federal Reserve System required Worthen, as a state bank subject to their supervision, to obtain prior permission for the investment in banking premises of any amount (including that placed in a real estate subsidiary) in excess of the bank's capital stock or of 40% of its capital stock and surplus. *See* Ark. Stat. Ann. § 67-547.1 (Supp. 1977); 12 U.S.C. § 371d (1976 ed.); 12 CFR § 265.2(f)(7) (1977). Worthen, accordingly, was advised by staff employees of the Federal Reserve System that they would not recommend approval of the plan by the System's Board of Governors.

Worthen therefore was forced to seek an alternative solution that would provide it with the use of the building, satisfy the state and federal regulators, and attract the necessary capital. In September 1967 it proposed a sale-and-leaseback arrangement. The State Bank Department and the Federal Reserve System approved this approach, but the Department required that Worthen possess an option to purchase the leased property at the end of the 15th year of the lease at a set price, and the federal regulator required that the building be owned by an independent third party.

Detailed negotiations ensued with investors that had indicated interest, namely, Goldman, Sachs & Company; White, Weld & Co.; Eastman Dillon, Union Securities & Company; and Stephens, Inc. Certain of these firms made specific proposals.

Worthen then obtained a commitment from New York Life Insurance Company to provide $7,140,000 in permanent mortgage financing on the building, conditioned upon its approval of the titleholder. At this point Lyon entered the negotiations and it, too, made a proposal.

Worthen submitted a counterproposal that incorporated the best features, from its point of view, of the several offers. Lyon accepted the counterproposal, suggesting, by way of further inducement, a $21,000 reduction in the annual rent for the first five years of the building lease. Worthen selected Lyon as the investor. After further negotiations, resulting in the elimination of that rent reduction (offset, however, by higher interest Lyon was to pay Worthen on a subsequent unrelated loan), Lyon in November 1967 was approved as an acceptable borrower by First National City Bank for the construction financing, and by New York Life, as the permanent lender. In April 1968 the approvals of the state and federal regulators were received.

In the meantime, on September 15, before Lyon was selected, Worthen itself began construction.

B

In May 1968 Worthen, Lyon, City Bank, and New York Life executed complementary and interlocking agreements under which the building was sold by Worthen to Lyon as it was constructed, and Worthen leased the completed building back from Lyon.

1. Agreements between Worthen and Lyon. Worthen and Lyon executed a ground lease, a sales agreement, and a building lease.

Under the ground lease dated May 1, 1968, App. 366, Worthen leased the site to Lyon for 76 years and 7 months through November 30, 2044. The first 19 months were the estimated construction period. The ground rents payable by Lyon to Worthen were $50 for the first 26 years and 7 months and thereafter in quarterly payments:

12/1/94 through 11/30/99 (5 years)	$100,000 annually
12/1/99 through 11/30/04 (5 years)	$150,000 annually
12/1/04 through 11/30/09 (5 years)	$200,000 annually
12/1/09 through 11/30/34 (25 years)	$250,000 annually
12/1/34 through 11/30/44 (10 years)	$10,000 annually

Under the sales agreement dated May 19, 1968, *id.* at 508, Worthen agreed to sell the building to Lyon, and Lyon agreed to buy it, piece by piece as it was constructed, for a total price not to exceed $7,640,000, in reimbursements to Worthen for its expenditures for the construction of the building.[39]

Under the building lease dated May 1, 1968, *id.* at 376, Lyon leased the building back to Worthen for a primary term of 25 years from December 1, 1969, with options in Worthen to extend the lease for eight additional 5-year terms, a total of 65 years. During the period between the expiration of the building lease (at the latest, November 30, 2034, if fully extended) and the end of the ground lease on November 30, 2044, full ownership, use, and control of the building were Lyon's, unless, of course, the building had been repurchased by Worthen. *Id.* at 369. Worthen was not obligated to pay rent under the building lease until completion of the building. For the first 11 years of the lease, that is, until November 30, 1980, the stated quarterly rent was $145,581.03 ($582,324.12 for the year). For the next 14 years, the quarterly rent was $153,289.32 ($613,157.28 for the year), and for the option periods the rent was $300,000 a year, payable quarterly. *Id.* at 378–379. The total rent for the building over the 25-year primary term of the lease thus was $14,989,767.24. That rent equaled the principal and interest payments that would amortize the $7,140,000 New York Life mortgage loan over the same period. When the mortgage was paid off at the end of the primary term, the annual building rent, if Worthen extended the lease, came down to the stated $300,000. Lyon's net rentals from the building would be further reduced by the increase in ground rent Worthen

---

[39] [2] This arrangement appeared advisable and was made because purchases of materials by Worthen (which then had become a national bank) were not subject to Arkansas sales tax. *See* Ark. Stat. Ann. § 84-1904(*l*) (1960); First Agricultural Nat. Bank v. Tax Comm'n, 392 U.S. 339 (1968). Sales of the building elements to Lyon also were not subject to state sales tax, since they were sales of real estate. *See* Ark. Stat. Ann. § 84-1902(c) (Supp. 1977).

would receive from Lyon during the extension.[40]

The building lease was a "net lease," under which Worthen was responsible for all expenses usually associated with the maintenance of an office building, including repairs, taxes, utility charges, and insurance, and was to keep the premises in good condition, excluding, however, reasonable wear and tear.

Finally, under the lease, Worthen had the option to repurchase the building at the following times and prices:

11/30/80 (after 11 years)	$6,325,169.85
11/30/84 (after 15 years)	$5,432,607.32
11/30/89 (after 20 years)	$4,187,328.04
11/30/94 (after 25 years)	$2,145,935.00

These repurchase option prices were the sum of the unpaid balance of the New York Life mortgage, Lyon's $500,000 investment, and 6% interest compounded on that investment.

2. Construction financing agreement. By agreement dated May 14, 1968, *id.* at 462, City Bank agreed to lend Lyon $7,000,000 for the construction of the building. This loan was secured by a mortgage on the building and the parking deck, executed by Worthen as well as by Lyon, and an assignment by Lyon of its interests in the building lease and in the ground lease.

3. Permanent financing agreement. By Note Purchase Agreement dated May 1, 1968, *id.* at 443, New York Life agreed to purchase Lyon's $7,140,000 6 3/4% 25-year secured note to be issued upon completion of the building. Under this agreement Lyon warranted that it would lease the building to Worthen for a noncancelable term of at least 25 years under a net lease at a rent at least equal to the mortgage payments on the note. Lyon agreed to make quarterly payments of principal and interest equal to the rentals payable by Worthen during the corresponding primary term of the lease. *Id.* at 523. The security for the note was a first deed of trust and Lyon's assignment of its interests in the building lease and in the ground lease. *Id.* at 527, 571. Worthen joined in the deed of trust as the owner of the fee and the parking deck.

In December 1969 the building was completed and Worthen took possession. At that time Lyon received the permanent loan from New York Life, and it discharged the interim loan from City Bank. The actual cost of constructing the office building and parking complex (excluding the cost of the land) exceeded $10,000,000.

---

[40] [3] This, of course, is on the assumption that Worthen exercises its option to extend the building lease. If it does not, Lyon remains liable for the substantial rents prescribed by the ground lease. This possibility brings into sharp focus the fact that Lyon, in a very practical sense, is at least the ultimate owner of the building. If Worthen does not extend, the building lease expires and Lyon may do with the building as it chooses.

The Government would point out, however, that the net amounts payable by Worthen to Lyon during the building lease's extended terms, if all are claimed, would approximate the amount required to repay Lyon's $500,000 investment at 6% compound interest. Brief for United States 14.

C

Lyon filed its federal income tax returns on the accrual and calendar year basis. On its 1969 return, Lyon accrued rent from Worthen for December. It asserted as deductions one month's interest to New York Life; one month's depreciation on the building; interest on the construction loan from City Bank; and sums for legal and other expenses incurred in connection with the transaction.

On audit of Lyon's 1969 return, the Commissioner of Internal Revenue determined that Lyon was "not the owner for tax purposes of any portion of the Worthen Building," and ruled that "the income and expenses related to this building are not allowable . . . for Federal income tax purposes." App. 304–305, 299. He also added $2,298.15 to Lyon's 1969 income as "accrued interest income." This was the computed 1969 portion of a gain, considered the equivalent of interest income, the realization of which was based on the assumption that Worthen would exercise its option to buy the building after 11 years, on November 30, 1980, at the price stated in the lease, and on the additional determination that Lyon had "loaned" $500,000 to Worthen. In other words, the Commissioner determined that the sale-and-leaseback arrangement was a financing transaction in which Lyon loaned Worthen $500,000 and acted as a conduit for the transmission of principal and interest from Worthen to New York Life.

All this resulted in a total increase of $497,219.18 over Lyon's reported income for 1969, and a deficiency in Lyon's federal income tax for that year in the amount of $236,596.36. The Commissioner assessed that amount, together with interest of $43,790.84, for a total of $280,387.20.

Lyon paid the assessment and filed a timely claim for its refund. The claim was denied, and this suit, to recover the amount so paid, was instituted in the United States District Court for the Eastern District of Arkansas within the time allowed by 26 U.S.C. § 6532(a)(1).

After trial without a jury, the District Court, in a memorandum letter-opinion setting forth findings and conclusions, ruled in Lyon's favor and held that its claimed deductions were allowable. 75-2 USTC para. 9545 (1975), 36 AFTR 2d para. 75-5059 (1975); App. 296–311. It concluded that the legal intent of the parties had been to create a bona fide sale-and-leaseback in accordance with the form and language of the documents evidencing the transactions. It rejected the argument that Worthen was acquiring equity in the building through its rental payments. It found that the rents were unchallenged and were reasonable throughout the period of the lease, and that the option prices, negotiated at arm's length between the parties, represented fair estimates of market value on the applicable dates. It rejected any negative inference from the fact that the rentals, combined with the options, were sufficient to amortize the New York Life loan and to pay Lyon a 6% return on its equity investment. It found that Worthen would acquire equity in the building only if it exercised one of its options to purchase, and that it was highly unlikely, as a practical matter, that any purchase option would ever be exercised. It rejected any inference to be drawn from the fact that the lease was a "net lease." It found that Lyon had mixed motivations for entering into the transaction, including the need to diversify as well as the desire to have the benefits of a "tax shelter." App. 296, 299.

The United States Court of Appeals for the Eighth Circuit reversed. 536 F.2d 746 (1976). It held that the Commissioner correctly determined that Lyon was not the true owner of the building and therefore was not entitled to the claimed deductions. It likened ownership for tax purposes to a "bundle of sticks" and undertook its own evaluation of the facts. It concluded, in agreement with the Government's contention, that Lyon "totes an empty bundle" of ownership sticks. *Id.* at 751. It stressed the following: (a) The lease agreements circumscribed Lyon's right to profit from its investment in the building by giving Worthen the option to purchase for an amount equal to Lyon's $500,000 equity plus 6% compound interest and the assumption of the unpaid balance of the New York Life mortgage.[41] (b) The option prices did not take into account possible appreciation of the value of the building or inflation.[42] (c) Any award realized as a result of destruction or condemnation of the building in excess of the mortgage balance and the $500,000 would be paid to Worthen and not Lyon.[43] (d) The building rental payments during the primary term were exactly equal to the mortgage payments.[44] (e) Worthen retained control over the ultimate disposition of the building through its various options to repurchase and to renew the lease plus its ownership of the site.[45] (f) Worthen enjoyed all benefits and bore all burdens incident to the operation and ownership of the building so that, in the Court of Appeals' view, the only economic advantages accruing to Lyon, in the event it were considered to be the true owner of the property, were income tax savings of approximately $1.5 million during the first 11 years of the arrangement.[46] *Id.* at 752–753.[47] The court concluded, *id.* at 753, that the transaction was "closely akin"

---

[41] [5] Lyon here challenges this assertion on the grounds that it had the right and opportunities to sell the building at a greater profit at any time; the return to Lyon was not insubstantial and was attractive to a true investor in real estate; the 6% return was the minimum Lyon would realize if Worthen exercised one of its options, an event the District Court found highly unlikely; and Lyon would own the building and realize a greater return than 6% if Worthen did not exercise an option to purchase.

[42] [6] Lyon challenges this observation by pointing out that the District Court found the option prices to be the negotiated estimate of the parties of the fair market value of the building on the option dates and to be reasonable. App. 303, 299.

[43] [7] Lyon asserts that this statement is true only with respect to the total destruction or taking of the building on or after December 1, 1980. Lyon asserts that it, not Worthen, would receive the excess above the mortgage balance in the event of total destruction or taking before December 1, 1980, or in the event of partial damage or taking at any time. *Id.* at 408–410, 411.

[44] [8] Lyon concedes the accuracy of this statement, but asserts that it does not justify the conclusion that Lyon served merely as a conduit by which mortgage payments would be transmitted to New York Life. It asserts that Lyon was the sole obligor on the New York Life note and would remain liable in the event of default by Worthen. It also asserts that the fact the rent was sufficient to amortize the loan during the primary term of the lease was a requirement imposed by New York Life, and is a usual requirement in most long-term loans secured by a long-term lease.

[45] [9] As to this statement, Lyon asserts that the Court of Appeals ignored Lyon's right to sell the building to another at any time; the District Court's finding that the options to purchase were not likely to be exercised; the uncertainty that Worthen would renew the lease for 40 years; Lyon's right to lease to anyone at any price during the last 10 years of the ground lease; and Lyon's continuing ownership of the building after the expiration of the ground lease.

[46] [10] In response to this, Lyon asserts that the District Court found that the benefits of occupancy Worthen will enjoy are common in most long-term real estate leases, and that the District Court found that Lyon had motives other than tax savings in entering into the transaction. It also asserts that the net cash after-tax benefit would be $312,220, not $1.5 million.

[47] [11] Other factors relied on by the Court of Appeals, 536 F.2d at 752, were the allocation of the

to that in *Helvering v. Lazarus & Co.*, 308 U.S. 252 (1939): "In sum, the benefits, risks, and burdens which [Lyon] has incurred with respect to the Worthen building are simply too insubstantial to establish a claim to the status of owner for tax purposes. . . . The vice of the present lease is that all of [its] features have been employed in the same transaction with the cumulative effect of depriving [Lyon] of any significant ownership interest." 536 F.2d at 754.

We granted *certiorari*, 429 U.S. 1089 (1977), because of an indicated conflict with *American Realty Trust v. United States*, 498 F.2d 1194 (CA4 1974).

II

This Court, almost 50 years ago, observed that "taxation is not so much concerned with the refinements of title as it is with actual command over the property taxed — the actual benefit for which the tax is paid." *Corliss v. Bowers*, 281 U.S. 376, 378 (1930). In a number of cases, the Court has refused to permit the transfer of formal legal title to shift the incidence of taxation attributable to ownership of property where the transferor continues to retain significant control over the property transferred. *E.g.*, *Commissioner v. Sunnen*, 333 U.S. 591 (1948); *Helvering v. Clifford*, 309 U.S. 331 (1940). In applying this doctrine of substance over form, the Court has looked to the objective economic realities of a transaction rather than to the particular form the parties employed. The Court has never regarded "the simple expedient of drawing up papers," *Commissioner v. Tower*, 327 U.S. 280, 291 (1946), as controlling for tax purposes when the objective economic realities are to the contrary. "In the field of taxation, administrators of the laws, and the courts, are concerned with substance and realities, and formal written documents are not rigidly binding." *Helvering v. Lazarus & Co.*, 308 U.S. at 255. *See also Commissioner v. P.G. Lake, Inc.*, 356 U.S. 260, 266–267 (1958); *Commissioner v. Court Holding Co.*, 324 U.S. 331, 334 (1945). Nor is the parties' desire to achieve a particular tax result necessarily relevant. *Commissioner v. Duberstein*, 363 U.S. 278, 286 (1960).

In the light of these general and established principles, the Government takes the position that the Worthen-Lyon transaction in its entirety should be regarded as a sham. The agreement as a whole, it is said, was only an elaborate financing scheme designed to provide economic benefits to Worthen and a guaranteed return to Lyon. The latter was but a conduit used to forward the mortgage payments, made under the guise of rent paid by Worthen to Lyon, on to New York Life as mortgagee. This, the Government claims, is the true substance of the transaction as viewed under the microscope of the tax laws. Although the arrangement was case in sale-and-leaseback form, in substance it was only a financing transaction, and the terms of the repurchase options and lease renewals so indicate. It is said that Worthen could reacquire the building simply by satisfying the mortgage debt and paying Lyon its $500,000 advance plus interest, regardless of the fair market value of the building at the time; similarly, when the mortgage was paid off, Worthen could extend the

---

investment credit to Worthen, and a claim that Lyon's ability to sell the building to a third party was "carefully circumscribed" by the lease agreements. The investment credit by statute is freely allocable between the parties, § 48(d) of the 1954 Code, 26 U.S.C. § 48(d), and the Government has not pressed either of these factors before this Court.

lease at drastically reduced bargain rentals that likewise bore no relation to fair rental value but were simply calculated to pay Lyon its $500,000 plus interest over the extended term. Lyon's return on the arrangement in no event could exceed 6% compound interest (although the Government conceded it might well be less, Tr. of Oral Arg. 32). Furthermore, the favorable option and lease renewal terms made it highly unlikely that Worthen would abandon the building after it in effect had "paid off" the mortgage. The Government implies that the arrangement was one of convenience which, if accepted on its face, would enable Worthen to deduct its payments to Lyon as rent and would allow Lyon to claim a deduction for depreciation, based on the cost of construction ultimately borne by Worthen, which Lyon could offset against other income, and to deduct mortgage interest that roughly would offset the inclusion of Worthen's rental payments in Lyon's income. If, however, the Government argues, the arrangement was only a financing transaction under which Worthen was the owner of the building, Worthen's payments would be deductible only to the extent that they represented mortgage interest, and Worthen would be entitled to claim depreciation; Lyon would not be entitled to deductions for either mortgage interest or depreciation and it would not have to include Worthen's "rent" payments in its income because its function with respect to those payments was that of a conduit between Worthen and New York Life.

The Government places great reliance on *Helvering v. Lazarus & Co., supra*, and claims it to be precedent that controls this case. The taxpayer there was a department store. The legal title of its three buildings was in a bank as trustee for land-trust certificate holders. When the transfer to the trustee was made, the trustee at the same time leased the buildings back to the taxpayer for 99 years, with option to renew and purchase. The Commissioner, in stark contrast to his posture in the present case, took the position that the statutory right to depreciation followed legal title. The Board of Tax Appeals, however, concluded that the transaction between the taxpayer and the bank in reality was a mortgage loan and allowed the taxpayer depreciation on the buildings. This Court, as had the Court of Appeals, agreed with that conclusion and affirmed. It regarded the "rent" stipulated in the leaseback as a promise to pay interest on the loan, and a "depreciation fund" required by the lease as an amortization fund designed to pay off the loan in the stated period. Thus, said the Court, the Board justifiably concluded that the transaction, although in written form a transfer of ownership with a leaseback, was actually a loan secured by the property involved.

The *Lazarus* case, we feel, is to be distinguished from the present one and is not controlling here. Its transaction was one involving only two (and not multiple) parties, the taxpayer-department store and the trustee-bank. The Court looked closely at the substance of the agreement between those two parties and rightly concluded that depreciation was deductible by the taxpayer despite the nomenclature of the instrument of conveyance and the leaseback. *See also Sun Oil Co. v. Commissioner*, 562 F.2d 258 (CA3 1977) (a two-party case with the added feature that the second party was a tax-exempt pension trust).

The present case, in contrast, involves three parties, Worthen, Lyon, and the finance agency. The usual simple two-party arrangement was legally unavailable to Worthen. Independent investors were interested in participating in the alternative available to Worthen, and Lyon itself (also independent from Worthen) won the privilege. Despite Frank Lyon's presence on Worthen's board of directors, the transaction, as it ultimately developed, was not a familial one arranged by Worthen, but one compelled by the realities of the restrictions imposed upon the bank. Had Lyon not appeared, another interested investor would have been selected. The ultimate solution would have been essentially the same. Thus, the presence of the third party, in our view, significantly distinguishes this case from *Lazarus* and removes the latter as controlling authority.

III

It is true, of course, that the transaction took shape according to Worthen's needs. As the Government points out, Worthen throughout the negotiations regarded the respective proposals of the independent investors in terms of its own cost of funds. *E.g.*, App. 355. It is also true that both Worthen and the prospective investors compared the various proposals in terms of the return anticipated on the investor's equity. But all this is natural for parties contemplating entering into a transaction of this kind. Worthen needed a building for its banking operations and other purposes and necessarily had to know what its cost would be. The investors were in business to employ their funds in the most remunerative way possible. And, as the Court has said in the past, a transaction must be given its effect in accord with what actually occurred and not in accord with what might have occurred. *Commissioner v. National Alfalfa Dehydrating & Milling Co.*, 417 U.S. 134, 148–149 (1974); *Central Tablet Mfg. Co. v. United States*, 417 U.S. 673, 690 (1974).

There is no simple device available to peel away the form of this transaction and to reveal its substance. The effects of the transaction on all the parties were obviously different from those that would have resulted had Worthen been able simply to make a mortgage agreement with New York Life and to receive a $500,000 loan from Lyon. Then *Lazarus* would apply. Here, however, and most significantly, it was Lyon alone, and not Worthen, who was liable on the notes, first to City Bank, and then to New York Life. Despite the facts that Worthen had agreed to pay rent and that this rent equaled the amounts due from Lyon to New York Life, should anything go awry in the later years of the lease, Lyon was primarily liable.[48] No matter how the transaction could have been devised otherwise, it remains a fact that as the agreements were placed in final form, the obligation on the notes fell squarely on Lyon.[49] Lyon, an ongoing enterprise, exposed its very business well-being to this real and substantial risk.

The effect of this liability on Lyon is not just the abstract possibility that something will go wrong and that Worthen will not be able to make its payments. Lyon has disclosed this liability on its balance sheet for all the world to see. Its financial position was affected substantially by the presence of this long-term debt,

---

[48] [12] New York Life required Lyon, not Worthen, to submit financial statements periodically. *See* Note Purchase Agreement, App. 453–454, 458–459.

[49] [13] It may well be that the remedies available to New York Life against Lyon would be far greater than any remedy available to it against Worthen, which, as lessee, is liable to New York Life only through Lyon's assignment of its interest as lessor.

despite the offsetting presence of the building as an asset. To the extent that Lyon has used its capital in this transaction, it is less able to obtain financing for other business needs.

In concluding that there is this distinct element of economic reality in Lyon's assumption of liability, we are mindful that the characterization of a transaction for financial accounting purposes, on the one hand, and for tax purposes, on the other, need not necessarily be the same. *Commissioner v. Lincoln Savings & Loan Assn.*, 403 U.S. 345, 355 (1971); *Old Colony R. Co. v. Commissioner*, 284 U.S. 552, 562 (1932). Accounting methods or descriptions, without more, do not lend substance to that which has no substance. But in this case accepted accounting methods, as understood by the several parties to the respective agreements and as applied to the transaction by others, gave the transaction a meaningful character consonant with the form it was given. Worthen was not allowed to enter into the type of transaction which the Government now urges to be the true substance of the arrangement. Lyon and Worthen cannot be said to have entered into the transaction intending that the interests involved were allocated in a way other than that associated with a sale-and-leaseback.

Other factors also reveal that the transaction cannot be viewed as anything more than a mortgage agreement between Worthen and New York Life and a loan from Lyon to Worthen. There is no legal obligation between Lyon and Worthen representing the $500,000 "loan" extended under the Government's theory. And the assumed 6% return on this putative loan — required by the audit to be recognized in the taxable year in question — will be realized only when and if Worthen exercises its options.

The Court of Appeals acknowledged that the rents alone, due after the primary term of the lease and after the mortgage has been paid, do not provide the simple 6% return which, the Government urges, Lyon is guaranteed, 536 F.2d at 752. Thus, if Worthen chooses not to exercise its options, Lyon is gambling that the rental value of the building during the last 10 years of the ground lease, during which the ground rent is minimal, will be sufficient to recoup its investment before it must negotiate again with Worthen regarding the ground lease. There are simply too many contingencies, including variations in the value of real estate, in the cost of money, and in the capital structure of Worthen, to permit the conclusion that the parties intended to enter into the transaction as structured in the audit and according to which the Government now urges they be taxed.

It is not inappropriate to note that the Government is likely to lose little revenue, if any, as a result of the shape given the transaction by the parties. No deduction was created that is not either matched by an item of income or that would not have been available to one of the parties if the transaction had been arranged differently. While it is true that Worthen paid Lyon less to induce it to enter into the transaction because Lyon anticipated the benefit of the depreciation deductions it would have as the owner of the building, those deductions would have been equally available to Worthen had it retained title to the building. The Government so concedes. Tr. of Oral Arg. 22–23. The fact that favorable tax consequences were taken into account by Lyon on entering into the transaction is no reason for disallowing those consequences.[50] We cannot ignore the reality that the tax laws affect the shape of nearly every business transaction. *See Commissioner v. Brown*, 380 U.S. 563, 579–580 (1965) (Harlan, J., concurring). Lyon is not a corporation with no purpose other than to hold title to the bank building. It was not created by Worthen or even financed to any degree by Worthen.

The conclusion that the transaction is not a simple sham to be ignored does not, of course, automatically compel the further conclusion that Lyon is entitled to the items claimed as deductions. Nevertheless, on the facts, this readily follows. As has been noted, the obligations on which Lyon paid interest were its obligations alone, and it is entitled to claim deductions therefore under § 163 (a) of the 1954 Code, 26 U.S.C. § 163(a).

As is clear from the facts, none of the parties to this sale-and-leaseback was the owner of the building in any simple sense. But it is equally clear that the facts focus upon Lyon as the one whose capital was committed to the building and as the party, therefore, that was entitled to claim depreciation for the consumption of that capital. The Government has based its contention that Worthen should be treated as the owner on the assumption that throughout the term of the lease Worthen was acquiring an equity in the property. In order to establish the presence of that growing equity, however, the Government is forced to speculate that one of the options will be exercised and that, if it is not, this is only because the rentals for the extended term are a bargain. We cannot indulge in such speculation in view of the District Court's clear finding to the contrary. We therefore conclude that it is Lyon's capital that is invested in the building according to the agreement of the parties, and it is Lyon that is entitled to depreciation deductions, under § 167 of the 1954 Code, 26 U.S.C. § 167. *Cf. United States v. Chicago B. & Q. R. Co.*, 412 U.S. 401 (1973).

IV

We recognize that the Government's position, and that taken by the Court of Appeals, is not without superficial appeal. One, indeed, may theorize that Frank Lyon's presence on the Worthen board of directors; Lyon's departure from its principal corporate activity into this unusual venture; the parallel between the payments under the building lease and the amounts due from Lyon on the New York Life mortgage; the provisions relating to condemnation or destruction of the property; the nature and presence of the several options available to Worthen; and the tax benefits, such as the use of double declining balance depreciation, that accrue to Lyon during the initial years of the arrangement, form the basis of an argument that Worthen should be regarded as the owner of the building and as the recipient of nothing more from Lyon than a $500,000 loan.

---

[50] [15] Indeed, it is not inevitable that the transaction, as treated by Lyon and Worthen, will not result in more revenues to the Government rather than less. Lyon is gambling that in the first 11 years of the lease it will have income that will be sheltered by the depreciation deductions, and that it will be able to make sufficiently good use of the tax dollars preserved thereby to make up for the income it will recognize and pay taxes on during the last 14 years of the initial term of the lease and against which it will enjoy no sheltering deduction.

We, however, as did the District Court, find this theorizing incompatible with the substance and economic realities of the transaction: the competitive situation as it existed between Worthen and Union National Bank in 1965 and the years immediately following; Worthen's undercapitalization; Worthen's consequent inability, as a matter of legal restraint, to carry its building plans into effect by a conventional mortgage and other borrowing; the additional barriers imposed by the state and federal regulators; the suggestion, forthcoming from the state regulator, that Worthen possess an option to purchase; the requirement, from the federal regulator, that the building be owned by an independent third party; the presence of several finance organizations seriously interested in participating in the transaction and in the resolution of Worthen's problem; the submission of formal proposals by several of those organizations; the bargaining process and period that ensued; the competitiveness of the bidding; the bona fide character of the negotiations; the three-party aspect of the transaction; Lyon's substantiality[51] and its independence from Worthen; the fact that diversification was Lyon's principal motivation; Lyon's being liable alone on the successive notes to City Bank and New York Life; the reasonableness, as the District Court found, of the rentals and of the option prices; the substantiality of the purchase prices; Lyon's not being engaged generally in the business of financing; the presence of all building depreciation risks on Lyon; the risk, borne by Lyon, that Worthen might default or fail, as other banks have failed; the facts that Worthen could "walk away" from the relationship at the end of the 25-year primary term, and probably would do so if the option price were more than the then-current worth of the building to Worthen; the inescapable fact that if the building lease were not extended, Lyon would be the full owner of the building, free to do with it as it chose; Lyon's liability for the substantial ground rent if Worthen decides not to exercise any of its options to extend; the absence of any understanding between Lyon and Worthen that Worthen would exercise any of the purchase options; the nonfamily and nonprivate nature of the entire transaction; and the absence of any differential in tax rates and of special tax circumstances for one of the parties — all convince us that Lyon has far the better of the case.[52]

In so concluding, we emphasize that we are not condoning manipulation by a taxpayer through arbitrary labels and dealings that have no economic significance. Such, however, has not happened in this case.

In short, we hold that where, as here, there is a genuine multiple-party transaction with economic substance which is compelled or encouraged by business or regulatory realities, is imbued with tax-independent considerations, and is not

---

[51] [17] Lyon's consolidated balance sheet on December 31, 1968, showed assets of $12,225,612, and total stockholders' equity of $3,818,671. Of the assets, the sum of $2,674,290 represented its then investment in the Worthen building. App. 587–588.

[52] [18] Thus, the facts of this case stand in contrast to many others in which the form of the transaction actually created tax advantages that, for one reason or another, could not have been enjoyed had the transaction taken another form. *See, e.g.*, Sun Oil Co. v. Commissioner, 562 F.2d 258 (CA3 1977) (sale-and-leaseback of land between taxpayer and tax-exempt trust enabled the taxpayer to amortize, through its rental deductions, the cost of acquiring land not otherwise depreciable). Indeed, the arrangements in this case can hardly be labeled as tax-avoidance techniques in light of the other arrangements being promoted at the time. *See, e.g.*, Zeitlin, *Tax Planning in Equipment-Leasing Shelters*, 1969 So. Cal. Tax Inst. 621; Marcus, *Real Estate Purchase-Leasebacks as Secured Loans*, 2 Real Estate L.J. 664 (1974).

shaped solely by tax-avoidance features that have meaningless labels attached, the Government should honor the allocation of rights and duties effectuated by the parties. Expressed another way, so long as the lessor retains significant and genuine attributes of the traditional lessor status, the form of the transaction adopted by the parties governs for tax purposes. What those attributes are in any particular case will necessarily depend upon its facts. It suffices to say that, as here, a sale-and-leaseback, in and of itself, does not necessarily operate to deny a taxpayer's claim for deductions

The judgment of the Court of Appeals, accordingly, is reversed.

It is so ordered.

MR. JUSTICE WHITE dissents and would affirm the judgment substantially for the reasons stated in the opinion in the Court of Appeals for the Eighth Circuit. 536 F.2d 746 (1976).

MR. JUSTICE STEVENS, dissenting.

In my judgment the controlling issue in this case is the economic relationship between Worthen and petitioner, and matters such as the number of parties, their reasons for structuring the transaction in a particular way, and the tax benefits which may result, are largely irrelevant. The question whether a leasehold has been created should be answered by examining the character and value of the purported lessor's reversionary estate.

For a 25-year period Worthen has the power to acquire full ownership of the bank building by simply repaying the amounts, plus interest, advanced by the New York Life Insurance Company and petitioner. During that period, the economic relationship among the parties parallels exactly the normal relationship between an owner and two lenders, one secured by a first mortgage and the other by a second mortgage.[53] If Worthen repays both loans, it will have unencumbered ownership of the property. What the character of this relationship suggests is confirmed by the economic value that the parties themselves have placed on the reversionary interest.

All rental payments made during the original 25-year term are credited against the option repurchase price, which is exactly equal to the unamortized cost of the financing. The value of the repurchase option is thus limited to the cost of the financing, and Worthen's power to exercise the option is cost free. Conversely, petitioner, the nominal owner of the reversionary estate, is not entitled to receive *any* value for the surrender of its supposed rights of ownership.[54] Nor does it have

---

[53] [1] "[Where] a fixed price, as in *Frank Lyon Company*, is designed merely to provide the lessor with a predetermined fixed return, the substantive bargain is more akin to the relationship between a debtor and creditor than between a lessor and lessee." Rosenberg & Weinstein, *Sale-leasebacks: An analysis of these transactions after the* Lyon *decision*, 45 J. TAX. 146, 149 (1976).

[54] [2] It is worth noting that the proposals submitted by two other potential investors in the building did contemplate that Worthen would pay a price above the financing costs for acquisition of the leasehold interest. For instance, Goldman, Sachs & Company proposed that, at the end of the lease's primary term, Worthen would have the option to repurchase the property for either its fair market value or 20% of its

any power to control Worthen's exercise of the option.[55]

"It is fundamental that 'depreciation is not predicated upon ownership of property *but rather upon an investment in property.*' No such investment exists when payments of the purchase price in accordance with the design of the parties yield no equity to the purchaser." *Estate of Franklin v. Commissioner*, 544 F.2d 1045, 1049 (CA9 1976) (citations omitted; emphasis in original). Here, the petitioner has, in effect, been guaranteed that it will receive its original $500,000 plus accrued interest. But that is all. It incurs neither the risk of depreciation,[56] nor the benefit of possible appreciation. Under the terms of the sale-leaseback, it will stand in no better or worse position after the 11th year of the lease — when Worthen can first exercise its option to repurchase — whether the property has appreciated or depreciated.[57] And this remains true throughout the rest of the 25-year period.

Petitioner has assumed only two significant risks. First, like any other lender, it assumed the risk of Worthen's insolvency. Second, it assumed the risk that Worthen might *not* exercise its option to purchase at or before the end of the original 25-year term.[58] If Worthen should exercise that right *not* to repay, perhaps it would *then* be appropriate to characterize petitioner as the owner and Worthen as the lessee. But speculation as to what might happen in 25 years cannot justify the *present* characterization of petitioner as the owner of the building. Until Worthen has made a commitment either to exercise or not to exercise its option,[59] I think the

---

original cost, whichever was the greater. *See* Brief for United States 8 n. 7. A repurchase option based on fair market value, since it acknowledges the lessor's equity interest in the property, is consistent with a lessor-lessee relationship. *See* Breece Veneer & Panel Co. v. Commissioner, 232 F.2d 319 (CA7 1956); LTV Corp. v. Commissioner, 63 T.C. 39, 50 (1974); *see generally* Comment, *Sale and Leaseback Transactions*, 52 N.Y.U. L. REV. 672, 688–689, n. 117 (1977).

[55] [3] The situation in this case is thus analogous to that in Corliss v. Bowers, 281 U.S. 376, where the Court held that the grantor of a trust who retains an unrestricted cost-free power of revocation remains the owner of the trust assets for tax purposes. Worthen's power to exercise its repurchase option is similar; the only restraints upon it are those normally associated with the repayment of a loan, such as limitations on the timing of repayment and the amount due at the stated intervals.

[56] [4] Petitioner argues that it bears the risk of depreciation during the primary term of the lease, because the option price decreases over time. Brief for Petitioner 29-30. This is clearly incorrect. Petitioner will receive $500,000 plus interest, and no more or less, whether the option is exercised as soon as possible or only at the end of 25 years. Worthen, on the other hand, does bear the risk of depreciation, since its opportunity to make a profit from the exercise of its repurchase option hinges on the value of the building at the time.

[57] [5] After the 11th year of the lease, there are three ways that the lease might be terminated. The property might be condemned, the building might be destroyed by act of God, or Worthen might exercise its option to purchase. In any such event, if the property had increased in value, the entire benefit would be received by Worthen and petitioner would receive only its $500,000 plus interest. *See* Reply Brief for Petitioner 8–9, n. 2.

[58] [6] The possibility that Worthen might not exercise its option is a risk for petitioner because in that event petitioner's advance would be amortized during the ensuing renewal lease terms, totaling 40 years. Yet there is a possibility that Worthen would choose not to renew for the full 40 years or that the burdens of owning a building and paying a ground rental of $10,000 during the years 2034 through 2044 would exceed the benefits of ownership.

[59] [7] In this case, the lessee is not "economically compelled" to exercise its option. *See* American Realty Trust v. United States, 498 F.2d 1194 (CA4 1974). Indeed, it may be more advantageous for Worthen to let its option lapse since the present value of the renewal leases is somewhat less than the price of the option to repurchase. *See* Brief for United States 40 n. 26. But whether or not Worthen is

Government is correct in its view that petitioner is not the owner of the building for tax purposes. At present, since Worthen has the unrestricted right to control the residual value of the property for a price which does not exceed the cost of its unamortized financing, I would hold, as a matter of law, that it is the owner.

In effect, Worthen has an option to "put" the building to petitioner if it drops in value below $500,000 plus interest. Even if the "put" appears likely because of bargain lease rates after the primary terms, that would not justify the present characterization of petitioner as the owner of the building.

I therefore respectfully dissent.

Understanding *Frank Lyon*

1.   The Court offered a number of reasons for the taxpayer's victory in *Frank Lyon*, including (i) the fact that there were more than two parties to the transaction, (ii) the presence of credible nontax motives for the transaction, and (iii) the possibility that Lyon could lose money if Worthen had defaulted on all or a portion of the lease. Are any of these convincing reasons? As Justice Stevens suggests, a lender in a financing scheme (the IRS characterization of the case) would still face the possibility of losing money, but would not have the right to depreciation or other deductions as the owner of the property. Given the "matching" of the rents paid to Lyon with the interest that Lyon was required to pay each year to New York Life, as a practical matter, how much risk did Lyon undertake in the transaction? Would it really have entered into the transaction without regard to the tax factors?

2.   Under the taxpayer's characterization of the transaction (a loan from New York Life to Lyon and a separate sale-leaseback between Worthen and Lyon), the tax consequences would be essentially as follows: Worthen would get deductions for rental payments; Lyon would have income from the rental payments and an approximately equal deduction for interest paid to New York Life; and New York Life would have income in the amount of the interest payments. According to the IRS recharacterization (a financing transaction with Lyon as "middleman" between Worthen and New York Life), Worthen would have a similar deduction, albeit labeled interest rather than rent; Lyon would again have no net income; and New York Life would be treated more or less the same.[60] The only real difference is that, under the taxpayer's description, Lyon would receive depreciation as the owner of the property; in contrast, under the IRS recharacterization, Worthen would remain the owner and be entitled to these deductions. So what's the big deal, then? Why might it be important to the taxpayers who gets the depreciation, and why might it be important to the IRS?

3.   Why do you think that *Frank Lyon* was watched so closely by the tax shelter industry? Do you think the Supreme Court understood the broader implications of

---

likely to exercise the option, as long as it retains its unrestricted cost-free power to do so, it must be considered the owner of the building. *See* Sun Oil Co. v. Commissioner, 562 F.2d 258, 267 (CA3 1977) (repurchase option enabling lessee to acquire leased premises by repaying financing costs indicative of lessee's equity interest in those premises).

[60]   For explanatory purposes, the descriptions ignore the relatively small amount of money put up by Lyon itself.

its decision? What does the case tell you about the Court's general role in tax cases, and the advantages of creating a specialized appeals court for tax cases?

Frank Lyon is fascinating in that, like several famous tax cases — *Crane* in particular comes to mind — it involves two essentially different characterizations of the same transaction. The taxpayers described the transaction as a sale of the property from Worthen to Lyon, followed by a lease of the same property from Lyon to Worthen, and the loan from New York Life to Lyon as an essentially separate transaction. A pictorial representation of the transaction might look something like this:

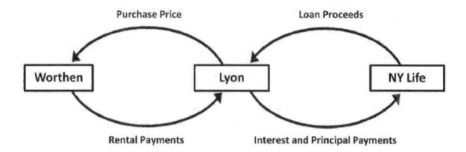

By contrast, the IRS saw the transaction as a loan from New York Life to Worthen, with Lyon serving as essentially a pass-through entity, *i.e.*, something like this:

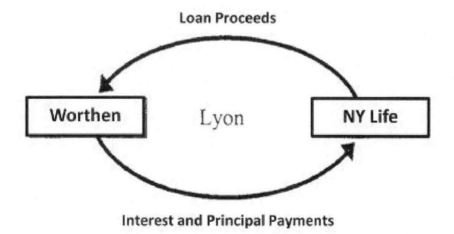

Frank Lyon is a premiere example of the "form and substance" doctrine, under which the tax system supposedly treats transactions according to their real-world economic substance rather than the legal form adopted by the taxpayers. According to this view, the Supreme Court's failure to invoke the substance-over-form concept in *Frank Lyon*, and its decision to instead respect the form adopted by the taxpayers, allowed the taxpayers to "get away" with an unseemly shifting of tax benefits and set the stage for still other, more aggressive tax shelters in the future. The last paragraph of the Court's opinion ("so long as the lessor retains significant and genuine attributes of the traditional lessor status, the form of the transaction adopted by the parties governs for tax purposes") was so common in early 1980s tax shelter opinions that many young tax associates could recite it by heart.

Although the Supreme Court (arguably) did not particularly distinguish itself in *Frank Lyon*, it is easy to understand its predicament. Suppose that the Court had taken a tougher line and said, effectively, "No; we're not fools; we know a pass-through transaction when we see one. Sorry, but the taxpayer loses." What would have happened next time? Presumably, some aggressive promoter would have tried a transaction that had just a little bit more economic substance and tried to build a tax shelter around it. Perhaps the rents and interest payments would have been less perfectly matched. Perhaps the excess of the ground lease over the sale-leaseback (known affectionately as a "shirt-tail" in the industry) would have been extended from 10 to 20 years. One way or another, the Court would likely have seen a series of borderline cases in which it had little intellectual interest and which distracted it from other, more significant matters. Like the decision in *Cottage Savings*, and perhaps *Crane* itself, the Court's decision at least had the merit of making the problem go away, or more likely, requiring somebody else to resolve it.

B. The Passive Loss Rules

The passive loss rules developed out of the ongoing failure to control tax shelters and, more immediately, from an article by a publicly spirited New York tax lawyer.[61] The laws were based on a deceptively simple distinction between active and passive activities. The losses from any business in which the taxpayer actively participated — the farmer's farm, the oil man's well, the doctor's or lawyer's professional practice — would be deductible without any restriction. But losses from a "passive" activity — say, an oil well owned by a dentist, or a real estate tax shelter owned by anyone not in the day-to-day real estate business — would have a second-tier status. These losses could be used against income from other passive activities, but not against the taxpayer's salary or other "active" income. Since the whole point of tax shelters is to reduce tax on one's salary and other active income, this would effectively shut down a large part of the tax shelter industry. The provision would, not entirely coincidentally, reduce the tax cut for rich people that might otherwise have rendered tax reform legislation politically unpalatable. Happy to find a way to resolve these various problems, a weary Congress adopted the passive loss rules as part of the 1986 tax reform act.[62]

[61] *See* Donald Schapiro, *Sheltering the Revenue from Shelters: A Legislative Proposal Involving the Minimum Tax and Accounting Provisions*, 22 TAX NOTES 811 (1984).

[62] For an interesting, if perhaps apocryphal, account of the genesis of the 1986 tax act, see JEFFREY H. BIRNBAUM & ALAN S. MURRAY, SHOWDOWN AT GUCCI GULCH: LAWMAKERS, LOBBYISTS, AND THE UNLIKELY TRIUMPH OF TAX REFORM 204-33 (1987) (describing genesis of the tax bill in a "two pitcher lunch" between

The passive loss rules are hard to justify in traditional tax policy terms. From an economist's perspective, it makes little difference if an individual invests her time or money in an activity: the taxpayer's risk from, and contribution to, an activity may be equally great in either case. The rules also hit particularly hard against some industries, notably real estate, in which it is common to own properties without being involved with them on a day-to-day basis. (For example, anyone who keeps their old apartment and rents it to a new tenant is potentially subject to the passive loss rules, albeit with the partial exemption provided by section 469(i).) Yet the rules do have the advantage of effectiveness — it's hard to find a tax shelter that keeps you actively involved on a day-to-day basis — and a certain intuitive charm: not everyone can understand the *Crane* case, but anyone can tell the difference between being a farmer in Iowa and a farmer in your New York City apartment. Perhaps for these reasons, the rules have had a much longer shelf life than was originally anticipated, and have become an accepted if still unloved portion of the tax landscape.

Because the passive loss rules were drafted as a unit, and have at least some doctrinal coherence, they provide a good opportunity for an exercise in statute reading and interpretation. (If you're like most students, you probably could use a statutory refresher at this point, anyway.) Refer to section 469 and the "material participation" regulations (Treas. Reg. section 1.469-5T) promulgated thereunder, and do your best to answer the immediately following questions. Following these questions, you will be asked to consider a few of the planning and policy issues that arise under section 469, which should give you a broader perspective on the provision and (as President Clinton might have said) help you to "feel the pain" of the lawyers and accountants who labor thereunder.

Using the Sources

1.   Under section 469, and the regulations issued thereunder, what is the definition of the following terms? In what part of the statute or regulations did you find them?

   a. passive activity.

   b. material participation.

   c. "regular, continuous, and substantial."

Does this language enable you to distinguish a passive from a nonpassive activity, or is it all a big circle? The regulations define material participation, in most cases, as involving 500 hours or more of participation during the taxable year (Treas. Reg. section 1.469-5T). Is this rule consistent with the statutory language, and what success might a taxpayer have in challenging these regulations?

2.   In each of the following, what are the tax consequences from engaging in the listed activities?

___

Senator Bob Packwood and his chief staff aide). At least some intellectual work, together with beer, went into the 1986 act.

a. Taxpayer, a suburban lawyer, owns one passive activity which produces $50,000 in income and an offsetting $100,000 in losses (*i.e.*, a net $50,000 loss).

b. The same taxpayer owns one passive activity which produces a net $50,000 in losses and a second passive activity which produces a net $25,000 of gain.

c. The same taxpayer owns one passive activity which produces a net $50,000 in losses and one nonpassive ("active") activity which produces a net $25,000 of gain.

d. The same taxpayer owns one passive activity producing a $50,000 net loss; one active activity producing a net $25,000 gain; and an investment portfolio producing $50,000 in interest, dividends, and capital gains.

e. The same taxpayer owns a limited partnership interest which produces $50,000 in net annual losses. Does it make any difference how much the taxpayer participates in the activities of the partnership?

3. Suppose that a taxpayer operates ten different dry cleaning stores, all of which seem to be losing money. She puts 100 hours a year into each of the stores, so that each would, on its own, qualify as a passive business, but an aggregate of 1,000 hours into all ten, which would easily meet the definition of material participation. The taxpayer would like to deduct her dry cleaning losses against her salary and other active income.

Can the taxpayer combine her dry cleaning stores for purposes of the material participation rules, or is she (once again) out of luck?

Law and Planning

1. Suppose that you owned an oil well that produced $50,000 in passive activity losses under section 469 of the Code.[63] You wanted to make use of these losses for tax purposes, but without jeopardizing your real-world business interests, and without undue complication. In making this decision, you were offered the following three alternatives:

a. Find some way to put 500 hours a year into the activity (hey, that's only ten hours a week).

b. Find another passive investment that generates positive taxable income, and offset the losses from the first property against the income from the second.

c. Sell the original (passive) property and use the losses under section 469(g).

Which of these alternatives strikes you as most attractive, and what tax and business factors would go into your decision?

---

[63] Assume that the property did not qualify as a working interest under section 469(c)(3).

2. Suppose you were planning to sell your apartment and move to a new home. A friend suggests that, instead of selling, you hold on to the apartment as an investment, *i.e.*, rent it out to a new occupant and try to make money from a combination of (i) the anticipated cash flow from the apartment (*i.e.*, the excess of rents over mortgage interest, taxes, and other costs associated with ownership of a housing unit), and (ii) the appreciation in price of the unit over a multiyear period. According to the same friend, you could use excess deductions (especially depreciation) resulting from the apartment against your salary or other active income.

Is your friend right, and what additional facts would you need to know in order to make this determination? *See* I.R.C. § 469(i).

3. Would section 469 affect your decision to investment in a corporation, partnership, or limited liability company (LLC)? What about investment in real estate or other types of assets? Why?

Politics and Policy

1. The passive loss rules have largely achieved their intended purpose — shutting down a considerable portion of the form of tax shelters that were common in the late 1970s and early 1980s following the *Frank Lyon* decision. Yet the Passive Loss Rules are a blunt enforcement instrument. Taxpayers engaging in "passive" businesses are denied deductions even when their businesses generate real losses and when the taxpayers entered into these businesses without any tax avoidance (or tax sheltering) motives. Is it fair for Congress to codify tax preferences like accelerated depreciation that create the demand for tax shelters, and then to combat the (excessive) use of these preferences through instruments like the passive loss rules? Should Congress instead focus its efforts on reforming the Code so that it better measures true economic income? Or are blunt tools like the passive loss rules required if the government is to have any real hope of containing the tax shelter problem?

2. Because of their inherently aggressive nature, tax shelters result in special ethical problems for lawyers, accountants, and other tax practitioners. One problem relates to the written opinions that lawyers provide in connection with tax shelter transactions. Assume that a tax shelter has only a 50-50 chance of working, that is, there is a 50 percent chance that the IRS, on audit, would deny the tax benefits associated with the transaction. Assume further (and realistically) that there is less than a 10 percent chance of being audited, so that the real-world chance of losing the tax benefits becomes 5 percent (10 percent × 50 percent) or less. Should the lawyer write an opinion in this situation? Should he hedge the opinion, by saying that the tax benefits are "more likely than not" to be granted, or by attaching a special notice to the taxpayer's return? For its part, should the IRS allow tax shelters to be marketed with hedged or otherwise dubious opinions, or should it impose penalties on tax shelter investors and promoters that would compensate for its unwillingness or inability to audit all or most tax shelter transactions?

This chapter has focused on classical tax shelters, of the form that were particularly common in the late 1970s and early 1980s. Modern tax shelters are often far more aggressive than their early progenitors, and typically rely on exploiting "loopholes" in the rules governing, corporate, partnership, and cross-border taxation, as well as the taxation of financial products. We will consider examples of these modern tax shelters in Chapters 11 and 12 as part of our examination of business taxation and international taxation.

Additional Assignment — Chapter 8

Imagine that you are special counsel to the Joint Committee on Taxation, United States Congress, with an assignment to research new legislation on tax shelters. Congress is frustrated that the existing tax shelter legislation, and especially the passive activity loss rules, are inadequate to deal with the continuing tax shelter problem. This is partly a problem of appearances — it doesn't look good for rich people to avoid paying taxes, when so many others are in difficult economic straits — but also a matter of substance, as tax shelters result in substantial loss of revenue to the Federal Government.

As a means of restricting tax shelters, Congress is considering three main approaches:[64]

a. A rule that would prohibit the use of losses arising in other activity — whether active or passive in nature — against income arising from a person's principal trade or business (*i.e.*, a strengthening of the general approach contained in the current passive loss rules).

b. A new, severe penalty on tax shelter promoters, to be equal to the greater of $100,000 or 100 percent of any false tax savings which they advertised to investors.

c. Substantive changes in specific laws that are exploited for tax shelter purposes, including a repeal of the *Crane* rule including borrowed funds in basis and a lengthening of the depreciation periods for real and personal property.

You have been asked to write a memorandum, *not exceeding five double-spaced pages*, which addresses the following issues:

1. Generally speaking which of the three approaches identified above strikes you as most promising for restricting tax shelters, and why? (This part should not exceed one page.)

2. Choose a specific approach and draft model statutory language that accomplishes the changes that you recommend, indicating where in the Code you would place the language, and defining terms that are indeterminate or unclear. (This part should not exceed two pages.)

3. Add a very brief explanation of the new statutory language and how it differs from present law (not exceeding two additional pages).

In drafting statutory language, you need not worry about formal drafting instructions ("strike everything after the third comma on the fourth page," etc.); simply indicate where in the Code your proposed language would go, what if anything it would replace, and draft it. But do try to use real legislative language rather than a mere paraphrase, and be as precise as possible in your choice of words and their relationship to other statutes. Whether or not you ever become a tax specialist, drafting — of legislation, contracts, etc. — will be important to you as a real lawyer; you might as well begin now.

---

[64] Because you have studied primarily individual taxes, these proposals concern primarily individual as opposed to corporate tax shelters. A significant portion of newer tax shelters involve tax evasion by corporations and other business entities, see the discussion of corporate tax shelters in Chapter 11.

Chapter 9

CAPITAL GAIN AND LOSS

The preceding chapters have considered income and deductions in the computation of taxable income. This chapter considers what might be called a hybrid problem: the case of capital gains, which are subject to tax, but usually at a lower rate than other ("ordinary") income. The reasons for reduced taxation of capital gain income are diffuse and not always convincing. They range from the sources of such income (much of nominal capital gain results from inflation and therefore should not be subject to tax) to practical consequences (high capital gain taxes would result in excessive "bunching" of income taxes and discourage people from selling unwanted investments) to a more straightforward argument for tax incentives (lower capital gain taxes encourage investment and risk-taking and thereby build a stronger economy). Perhaps because of the uneasy character of these arguments, the differential between the maximum ordinary income and capital gain tax rates has varied substantially over time. From a difference of 50 percentage points (70% vs. 20%, respectively) a few decades ago, the spread has declined to 20 percentage points (35% vs. 15%) as this edition goes to press,[1] following a brief period in the 1980s during which the maximum ordinary income and capital gain tax rates were identical (no differential, at all). Yet some differential seems likely to remain in force for the foreseeable future, and the incentive for taxpayers to "convert" ordinary income into capital gain, if not quite as great as it once was, remains an important feature of tax planning and policy.

This chapter considers the practical and policy aspects of the capital gain preference in some detail. The chapter begins with a brief description of the relevant statutory provisions (section 1201 *et seq.*), followed by discussion of some of the more forceful arguments made on behalf of, and against, this provision. These in turn are followed by several of the more important cases that have attempted to define the boundary between capital and ordinary income, especially as it relates to three "borderline" issues: housing sales, sale or termination of a small business, and commodity "hedging" transactions. The chapter concludes with an examination of the impact of capital gain taxes on stock and other capital markets, and how the U.S. and other countries have attempted to deal with this problem.

Together with the preference for capital gains, the Code also imposes limitations on the use of capital losses, generally allowing them to offset capital gains but not salary or other types of ordinary income.[2] These limitations — in many ways similar to the passive loss rules, but older and more encompassing — is an important part

---

[1] As this edition goes to press, the highest capital gains tax rate for the year 2010 is 15 percent, but this rate is scheduled to expire beginning in 2011, with the highest capital gains rate then becoming 20 percent (assuming no further Congressional action).

[2] More precisely, for individuals, the Code allows only $3,000 of capital losses to be used against

of both individual and business tax planning. Because they involve the same definitional issues, we will consider capital losses together with capital gains, but pause at times to consider the special importance of the loss limitation rules.

A note on terminology: although they are related in an economic sense, capital gain and loss are distinct concepts from "capitalization" or "capital expense" as used in the preceding chapters. For example, many business endeavors give rise to capital expenses, but result in ordinary income when and if they are profitable. For the time being, it's probably best to think of "capital gain" as a single defined term, and leave the more complex interactions until we have mastered the basics.

I. UNDERSTANDING THE RULES: THE CAPITAL GAIN AND LOSS PROVISIONS

A. Capital Gain

The first step in understanding any tax provision is to read the relevant Code sections. In the capital gain area, this is easier said than done. Difficult enough to begin with, the capital gain provisions have been made more convoluted through several sets of amendments, to the point where it is almost impossible to read them without outside assistance. The following may make the Code sections somewhat easier to understand.

The capital gain preference for individual taxpayers currently takes the form of a maximum, special tax rate rather than a percentage reduction in the tax rate on ordinary income. It is accordingly found in section 1(h) of the Code, rather than with the remaining capital gain and loss rules, which are found at section 1201, *et seq.* A book could easily be written about section 1(h) alone, which features, *inter alia*, a 15 percent maximum tax rate on most capital gain income of individuals; a lower rate on gain from certain capital assets held for more than five years;[3] a higher rate on certain "collectible" items (coins, stamps, baseball cards, etc.); and a maze of transitional and other rules that only an accountant, preferably one with a good computer, could love.

In addition to section 1(h), there are a bevy of additional rules found in the traditional capital gain portion of the Code. These include section 1202, which provides a 50 percent exclusion (and hence a still further reduced tax rate) on the sale of stock in certain small businesses, provided that (i) the taxpayer was the original holder of the stock, (ii) the aggregate gross assets of the corporation at the time the stock was issued did not exceed $50 million, (iii) the corporation is engaged in an active trade or business; and (iv) the amount excluded does not exceed the greater of $10 million or ten times the adjusted basis of the stock in question. This is not to be confused with section 1201, which imposes a 35 percent

---

ordinary income in any tax year, with unused gains being carried forward for use in future tax years. (*See* Code section 1211).

[3] The standard (*i.e.*, reduced) capital gain rate requires only that the asset be held more than one year (section 1222). The current capital gain tax rates are, in theory, of temporary duration, although it is likely that the matter will be revisited, probably more than once, before the relevant phase-outs are concluded.

maximum on capital gain incurred by corporations themselves; this is frequently the same as the ordinary income tax rate for corporations but may be lower in certain situations that we won't get into here. Like section 1(h), these provisions are complemented by a vast array of transitional and other rules applying to specific fact patterns.

The most important provision for law students is probably section 1221, which defines the term "capital asset" and hence delimits the boundary of what is, and is not, capital gain. What is most interesting about this definition is its perverse, counterintuitive character. Since capital gains are an exception to normal tax treatment, one might suppose that they would be narrowly defined by the statute. Instead, the statute begins with an extremely broad definition of capital asset, to include any "property held by the taxpayer (whether or not connected with his trade or business)," and then lists a series of exceptions to that definition. By far the most important exception is contained in section 1221(1), which excludes from capital gain status "stock in trade of the taxpayer or other property of a kind which would properly be included in the inventory of the taxpayer if on hand at the close of the taxable year, or property held by the taxpayer primarily for sale to customers in the ordinary course of his trade or business." This not-quite-Shakespearean language appears intended to exclude items sold in the everyday course of business — a shoemaker's shoes, a real estate dealer's real estate, and so forth — from capital gain status, while including more purely investment-type items (stocks and bonds, real estate in the hands of a nonprofessional investor, etc.) in the capital gain definition. The only problem is that it never quite says this, preferring to come at the issue in three different ways (inventory, stock in trade, held for sale to customers) in a sufficiently confusing manner to provoke two generations of litigation and controversy. The bulk of capital gain litigation concerns these brief but confusing phrases.

Most of the remaining paragraphs of section 1221 (paragraphs 3, 4, and 5) concern narrower items that Congress wished for various reasons to exclude from capital asset treatment. Of special historical interest is paragraph (3), which holds Presidential papers and similar materials in the hands of their creators to be ordinary income rather than capital asset items. (This also has the affect of denying a fair market value charitable deduction for these items, as described in Chapter 7, above.) Paragraph 2 provides a middle category, consisting of depreciable property (*e.g.*, a factory) used in a trade or business, but not held for sale to customers. This category — corresponding roughly to section 1231 of the Code — gets a "best of both worlds" treatment, qualifying for capital gain and ordinary loss treatment, a situation which dates back to World War II when the Government wished to encourage (or at very least, not discourage) the sale of factories to more productive users. As you probably realize by now, it's relatively easy to add such provisions, and a good deal harder to delete them once the initial crisis is over.

B.   Capital Loss

Simpler, but no less important, are the restrictions on capital losses. For individuals, the basic rule is contained in section 1211, which allows capital losses to offset (i) capital gains, and (ii) no more than $3,000 of ordinary income in any taxable year. For example, an individual who had $10,000 of capital gain and $15,000 of capital loss could use the losses to wipe out any tax on her capital gain together with the tax on $3,000 of ordinary income. The remaining $2,000 of capital loss would be carried over to the next taxable year, when the individual could once again use her aggregate capital losses (including those carried forward from the prior year) against any capital gain and up to $3,000 of ordinary income. The loss disallowance rule applies to both short- and long-term capital gains, as opposed to reduced rates, which apply only to gain on items held for more than one year. Corporations face a similar rule, but without the $3,000 allowance and with somewhat different carryover provisions.

Since $3,000 is a pretty small number for a big investor, the rule amounts essentially to a "schedular" approach to capital gains — that is, an approach allowing capital losses to reduce tax on capital gains but not, as a rule, to affect the tax on salary or other ordinary income items. The usual rationalization for this rule is the problem of "selective realization" or "loss farming." Without a loss limitation, it is argued, individuals who had large investment portfolios would simply sell enough loss items each year to reduce or eliminate their tax liability, while holding on to their appreciated assets which escaped tax until they were sold. There is also a vague sense that the tax code should not "subsidize losers" by continuing to provide a benefit for people who lose money on their investments, year after year. For these reasons, the capital loss limitation is a perennial feature of the tax code, and has remained in place even when the capital gain preference has been modified or repealed.

One interesting aspect of the capital loss limitation is that it puts the Government on different sides of the capital gain/ordinary income issue in different cases. In capital gain cases, the Government will, not surprisingly, tend to argue that the transaction in question requires ordinary income (that is, higher tax) treatment. In loss cases, however, the Government will argue for capital asset treatment so as to prevent the loss from reducing tax on the taxpayer's ordinary income. There is thus a strong tendency for the IRS position in one case to come back and haunt it in another — a tendency which is indeed a principal theme in capital gain litigation.

II. TAX POLICY: WHY SHOULD CAPITAL GAIN QUALIFY FOR A LOWER TAX RATE?

One of the hardest things to explain in a basic tax course is why capital gain income should qualify for a reduced tax rate. A number of arguments have been advanced, many of them heatedly and some of them even making a good deal of sense. Yet the arguments have serious limitations, and even proponents of reduced tax rates have been forced to concede the flaws in the statutory logic.

A frequent argument for reduced rates is that capital gain is in some way different from ordinary income, so that imposing a full tax on it — while apparently a neutral measure — would actually be unfair to the holders of capital assets.[4] For

---

[4] For a summary of the historic capital gain debate, see below.

example, the increased price of an asset may result from inflation rather than an increase in the asset's relative worth as opposed to other items. Many observers have argued that tax rates should be reduced in order to compensate for this effect. Capital gain is also said to have a "bunching" effect, pushing the taxpayer into an unnaturally high tax bracket in the year of sale, as opposed to ordinary income which tends to be spread out over a multi-year period. This too (or so it is argued) requires compensation in the form of a lower tax rate. These arguments have some validity, but are rather selective in nature. Inflation distorts the tax treatment of many items, but only in the case of capital gain is it an argument for special treatment. The bunching problem is really a general argument for income averaging, rather than a specific argument for a capital gain preference. Yet these arguments have at least some residual persuasiveness, and — especially when inflation is high — may be an important factor in the capital gain equation.

A second argument relates to tax incentives, especially for risky (or allegedly risky) investments. According to this argument, investments in stocks, real estate,[5] and similar assets are risky in nature, but good for the overall economy; the Code should accordingly encourage them with preferential tax rates. This is often coupled with the argument that high tax rates will "lock in" investors to their existing portfolio and discourage them from making sales and purchases that would make sense from a purely economic perspective. The incentive argument is probably the principal argument for reduced tax rates, and is supported by colorful imagery of start-up and other entrepreneurial ventures alleged to be strangled by high tax rates and bureaucratic red tape. The problem here is one of targeting: reduced rates apply to all capital assets, regardless of how risky, while many organizations engaging in risky investments (*e.g.*, universities and pension funds) are not subject to the individual income tax, anyway. There is also no obvious reason to distinguish between portfolio investments (*e.g.*, individuals buying stocks and bonds for personal investment purposes), which do qualify for reduced tax rates, and project investments (*e.g.*, a business undertaking a risky venture or building a risky facility), which do not qualify, although they may benefit from accelerated depreciation and other related tax benefits. The increasing compartmentalization of capital gain, including specially reduced rates for stock in qualified start-up corporations, is a partial effort to deal with this problem.

Finally, some observers support a low tax rate on realized appreciation (*i.e.*, capital gain) in order to balance the tax-free status of unrealized appreciation, although one might argue that the current system is doubly unfair because it allows both these benefits.

If the arguments for reduced tax rates are somewhat complex, the arguments against them are relatively simple. The principal point, made most famously by Henry Simons, pertains to horizontal equity: all income should be taxed at the same rate, regardless of its source or nature.[6] A second argument pertains to vertical equity and the (alleged) regressive impact of capital gain preferences. This

---

[5] The argument here pertains primarily to investment real estate properties. Up to $250,000 of gain ($500,000 for married couples) on personal residences is exempt from tax, altogether. I.R.C. § 121.

[6] HENRY SIMONS, PERSONAL INCOME TAXATION: THE DEFINITION OF INCOME AS A PROBLEM OF FISCAL POLICY (1938).

argument has become somewhat less powerful with the increasing dispersion of stock and other capital asset ownership, although a high percentage of stock continues to be owned by a relatively small number of wealthy investors.

One curious aspect of the capital gain debate is the assumption that high tax rates, without special relief, will invariably discourage risky activities. Actually, when deductions are taken into account, high taxes may well encourage risk. This results because the tax system — while reducing the return on a successful investment — also reduces the loss from an unsuccessful effort. Consider, for example, an investment that costs $100,000 but has a one-in-five chance of producing a $1 million (pre-tax) payoff. Although this investment has an expected return greater than zero, a risk-averse investor may shun the investment because he simply cannot afford the potential $100,000 loss. Now assume that there is a 50 percent tax rate with unlimited deductibility of losses (*i.e.*, a $100,000 loss will result in $50,000 of tax savings that can be used to reduce tax on the taxpayer's other income). The trade-off is now a $50,000 (after tax) loss against a one-in-five chance of $500,000 in income — still a risky investment, but less than before, and one a risk-averse investor might be more likely to make. Put differently, a 50 percent tax makes the Government (effectively) a 50 percent partner in every taxable venture, thereby encouraging taxpayers to take risks they would otherwise avoid.[7]

If the Government really wishes to encourage risk, it might accordingly think about liberalizing the rules regarding capital losses, rather than providing reduced rates for capital gain. (This has been done to a limited extent in section 1244, which provides up to $100,000 of ordinary loss treatment on small business stock.) The reason this has not happened more often is, in part, psychological: winners are more appealing than losers, and no one wants to run for office on a platform of helping companies whose stock keeps going down. ("We lost 20,000 jobs in my district last year, and with this new legislation, we hope to lose even more!") An unlimited loss deduction would also raise the selective realization (aka, "loss farming") problem discussed in the preceding pages. Yet this discussion highlights an important point about the capital gain debate: much of the law in this and other areas results from perception rather than reality, and it is difficult to separate the rhetoric of risk and incentive from the more complex and contradictory reality.

The following are two excerpts, the first of which discusses the normative arguments regarding the capital gain issue, and the second of which discusses some of the economic "facts" behind the discussion. Which, if either, of these excerpts do you find convincing, and what is your overall conclusion regarding the propriety of a reduced capital gain tax rate? Is the existing preference based on sound policy logic, or merely an old idea that no one (especially the wealthy) has an incentive to get rid of?

---

[7] Due to the existence of the loss limitation rules, this argument only holds to the extent the taxpayer has other capital income against which the capital losses can be used (or to the extent of the $3,000 of capital losses usable against ordinary income in the case of individual taxpayers).

Proposals and Issues Relating to
Taxation of Capital Gains and Losses (JCS-10-90)
U.S. Congress Joint Committee on Taxation
Mar. 23, 1990

1. Arguments for reduced tax on capital gains

Lock-in. — Many argue that higher tax rates discourage sales of assets. For individual taxpayers, this lock-in effect is exacerbated by the rules which allow a step-up in basis at death and defer or exempt certain gains on sales of homes. The legislative history suggests that this lock-in effect was an important consideration in Congress' decision to lower capital gains taxes in 1978. As an example of what is meant by the lock-in effect, suppose a taxpayer paid $500 for a stock which now is worth $1,000, and that the stock's value will grow by an additional 10 percent over the next year with no prospect of further gain thereafter. Assuming a 28-percent tax rate, if the taxpayer sells the stock one year or more from now, he or she will receive $932 after payment of $168 tax on the gain of $600. With a tax rate on gain of 28 percent, if the taxpayer sold this stock today, he or she would have, after tax of $140 on the gain of $500, $860 available to reinvest. The taxpayer would not find it profitable to switch to an alternative investment unless that alternative investment would earn a total pre-tax return in excess of 11.6 percent. Preferential tax rates impose a smaller tax on redirecting monies from older investments to projects with better prospects, in that way contributing to a more efficient allocation of capital.

A preferential tax rate on capital gains would both lower the tax imposed when removing monies from old investments and increase the after-tax return to redirecting those monies to new investments. Some have suggested that the lock-in effect could be reduced without lowering taxes on old investments. For example, eliminating the step-up in basis upon death would reduce lock-in. Alternatively, preferential tax rates only for gains on newly acquired assets would increase the after-tax return to new investments, thereby making reallocation of investment funds more attractive than currently is the case. On the other hand, taxpayers would not necessarily redirect their funds to new investments when their monies in older investments are unlocked. Taxpayers might instead choose to consume the proceeds.

Some have argued that the lock-in effect should not be as strong for capital gains accrued on assets held by corporations as on assets held by individual taxpayers, because corporations do not receive the benefit of step-up in basis. They also observe that most corporate assets do not represent portfolio investments, but rather are held in furtherance of the corporation's business activity. Therefore, there is likely to be less discretion in timing of realization of corporate assets. Proponents of a preferential tax rate on corporate capital gains counter that lock-in occurs because of the ability to defer realization and that consequently corporations can be subject to substantial lock-in effects.

Incentives for equity investments. — A second argument for preferential capital gains tax rates is that they encourage investors to buy corporate stock, and especially to provide venture capital for new companies, stimulating investment in productive business activities. This argument was important in the 1978 debate over capital gains taxes, and there has been a large growth in the availability of venture capital since 1978. Proponents argue that the preference provides an incentive for investment and capital formation, with particular mention of venture capital and high technology projects.

Others argue that the capital gains preference may be an inefficient mechanism to promote the desired capital formation. They argue that a preferential capital gains tax rate is not targeted toward any particular type of equity investment although promotion of high technology venture capital is apparently a goal. Furthermore, a broad capital gains preference affords capital gains treatment to non-equity investments such as gains on municipal bonds and certain other financial instruments.

To the extent that potential sources of venture capital or other equity investment, or secondary purchasers of corporate stock, are tax-exempt or partially tax-exempt (for example, pension funds and certain insurance companies and foreign investors), a tax preference could have a small incentive effect on investment. Since 1978, tax-exempt entities (pension funds and non-profit institutions) have constituted the fastest growing source of new venture capital funds. On the other hand, proponents argue that capital gains treatment for venture capitalists who are taxable has importance. They argue that this is particularly acute for the entrepreneur who often contributes more in time and effort than in capital.

Opponents of a capital gains preference argue that creating a preference for capital gains could encourage the growth of debt and the reduction of equity throughout the economy. When debt is used in a share repurchase program or leveraged buyout transaction the taxpayers who hold the original equity securities must realize any gain that they might have. A lower tax rate on gains could make holders of equity more likely to tender their shares in a leveraged buyout transaction or share repurchase program.

Competitiveness. — Related to the argument that preferential capital gains tax rates encourage investment is the argument that a lower capital gains tax rate will improve the international competitive position of the United States. Proponents of a reduction in capital gain tax rates observe that many of our major trading partners have lower marginal tax rates on the realization of capital gains than does the United States. For example, prior to this year, all gains on stocks, bonds, and unit trusts were exempt from tax in Japan. The recent Japanese tax reform imposes a tax at the taxpayer's discretion of either one percent of the gross proceeds or 20 percent of the gain, a rate still below the maximum U.S. rate. In West Germany, all long-term gains are exempt from tax.

Others point out that the issue of the effect of capital gains taxes on international competitiveness is really one of the cost of capital of domestic firms compared to that of their competitors. Corporate income taxes, individual income taxes on interest and dividends, net wealth taxes, as well as taxes on capital gains, all may affect the cost of capital. Opponents of a capital gains preference argue that the fact that marginal tax rates on capital gains are higher in the United States than in other countries does not imply automatically that American firms are at a competitive disadvantage. Moreover, because of the ability to defer gains, to receive step-up at death, and because of substantial holding of corporate equity by tax-exempt institutions, the effective tax rate on gains, which helps determine the cost of capital, may be substantially below the statutory rate. For example, one recent study calculated that prior to 1987 the effective marginal tax rate on capital gains, including State taxes, was less than 6 percent.

On the other hand, proponents of a capital gains tax reduction contend that any reduction in a tax on capital may reduce the cost of capital.

Bunching. — Because capital gain is generally not taxed until a disposition, taxpayers can face large jumps in taxable income when the gain is realized. With graduated tax rates, such bunching could lead to a higher tax burden than if the gain were taxed as it accrued. If the benefit of deferral is not enough to compensate for the extra tax in some of those cases, then the additional benefit of a preferential tax rate helps to achieve parity (although its availability is not limited to such cases).

Some analysts have argued that the flattened marginal tax rate schedule of present law diminishes the amount of bunching and so, presumably, reduces the need for a preferential tax rate as a remedy for it. These analysts have stated that the most significant bunching problems under present law would now befall those tax-payers in the 15-percent marginal tax bracket whose gains could push them into the 28-percent bracket. However, they point out that relatively few taxpayers who realize gains are in these circumstances.

Inflation. — Another argument for preferential tax treatment of capital gain is that part of the gain represents the effects of inflation and does not constitute real income. This argument was also important in 1978. Proponents observe that the preference may provide to taxpayers some rough compensation for inflation.

Others claim that a preferential tax rate is a very crude adjustment for inflation. For example, since 1978 the price level approximately has doubled. Thus, an asset purchased in 1978 for $1,000 and sold today for $2,000 would have a purely inflationary gain. Even with a preferential rate, this gain would be taxed. On the other hand, for an individual who purchased an asset in 1986 for $1,000 and sold it today for $2,000, a reduction in the tax rate from 28 percent to 19.6 percent would more than offset the effects of inflation over the past three years. A preferential rate also does not account for the impact of inflation on debt-financed assets, where inflation reduces the cost of repaying the debt.

Double taxation of corporate earnings. — Theorists have suggested that capital gains treatment on a disposition of corporate stock might be viewed as ameliorating the double taxation of corporate earnings. The first step of double taxation occurs at the corporate level; the second step occurs at the shareholder level as dividends are paid or as shares which have presumably increased in value by retained earnings are sold. However, other theorists have argued that preferential capital gains treatment is a very inexact means of accomplishing any such benefit. Among other things, the capital gains holding period requirement is unrelated to earnings. Also, any relief that a capital gains preference provides from the burden of double taxation applies only to retained corporate earnings. Distributed earnings would be still generally subject to double taxation.

2. Arguments against reduced tax on capital gains

Measurement of income. — Opponents of reduced tax on capital gains argue that appreciating assets already enjoy a tax benefit from the deferral of tax on accrued appreciation until the asset is sold, which benefit reduces in whole or in part any bunching or inflationary effects. In addition, if capital assets are debt-financed, inflation will reduce the real cost of borrowing to the extent interest rates do not rise to compensate for the reduced value of principal repayments and interest is deductible. Thus, debt financing may further tend to offset any adverse impact of inflation. Some opponents of the preference have contended that a direct basis adjustment by indexing for inflation would be more accurate and would reduce uncertainty regarding the eventual effective rate of tax on investments that might impair capital formation.

On the other hand, proponents of a preference for capital gains contend that the benefit of deferral is insufficient to make up for more than very modest inflation. Moreover, they argue that indexing may be viewed as too complex to implement.

Neutrality. — To the extent that preferential rates may encourage investments in stock, opponents have argued that the preference tilts investment decisions toward assets that offer a return in the form of asset appreciation rather than current income such as dividends or interest. Furthermore, because the individual capital gains preference is accomplished by a deduction (or exclusion) from income, it provides a greater benefit to high-income than to middle- or low-income taxpayers. On the other hand, it is argued that neutrality is not an appropriate goal because risky investments that produce a high proportion of their income in the form of capital gains may provide a social benefit not adequately recognized by investors in the marketplace.

Reduction of "conversion" opportunities. — Opponents of the preferential capital gains rate contend that it not only provides a reduced tax rate on gains from the preferred assets but also encourages taxpayers to enter transactions designed to convert other, ordinary, income to capital gains.

Conversion can also occur through debt-financing the cost of assets eligible for capital gains rates. For example, if a taxpayer borrows $100 at 10 percent annual interest to acquire a capital asset that is sold for $110 a year later, and repays the borrowing with sales proceeds, the taxpayer has an interest deduction of $10 that can reduce ordinary income 24 and a capital gain of $10 subject to preferential rates. The taxpayer thus has a net after-tax positive cash flow even though on a pre-tax basis the transaction was not profitable.

On the other hand, it is argued that such "conversion" opportunities are simply an additional tax incentive for types of investments the capital gains preference is intended to encourage. In addition, it is argued that the passive loss limitations of present law limit taxpayers' ability to "convert" ordinary income to capital gains.

Simplification and consistent treatment of taxpayers. — Opponents of the preferential capital gains rate point out that the application of different tax rates to different sources of income inevitably creates disputes over which assets are entitled to, the preferential rate and encourages taxpayers to mischaracterize their income as derived from the preferred source. Litigation involving holding period, sale or exchange treatment, asset allocation, and many other issues has been extensive in the past. A significant body of law, based both in the tax code and in judicial rules, has developed in response to conflicting taxpayer and Internal Revenue Service positions in particular cases. Its principles are complicated in concept and application, typically requiring careful scrutiny of the facts in each case and leaving opportunities for taxpayers to take aggressive tax return positions. It has been argued that the results derived in particular cases lack even rough consistency, notwithstanding the substantial resources consumed in this process by taxpayers and the Internal Revenue Service. Elimination of the preferential rates on capital gains has obviated the incentive for many such disputes. It has also obviated the need for such complex provisions as the collapsible corporation and collapsible partnership rules, which have been criticized for apparent inconsistencies in application, and certain aspects of the varying recapture provisions for different types of assets.

On the other hand, it is argued that so long as a limitation on deductions of capital or investment loss is retained, some areas of uncertainty and dispute continue to exist (for example, whether property was held primarily for sale to customers in the ordinary course of business, and the application of the Corn Products and related doctrines). Since (as discussed further below) limitations on the deductibility of capital or investment losses may be desirable to limit the selective realization of losses without realization of gains, the amount of simplification and consistency that has occurred as a result of eliminating the preference for long term capital gains has been limited somewhat.

James M. Poterba, *Capital Gains Tax Policy Toward Entrepreneurship*
42 NAT'L TAX J. 375, 375 (1989)[8]

The need to subsidize risky new ventures is frequently cited as a reason for taxing capital gains at rates below other types of income. This paper investigates the efficacy of lowering individual capital gains tax rates as a device for subsidizing such ventures, particularly those which are funded through the organized venture capital process.

The paper makes two central points. First, more than three quarters of the funds that are invested in start-up firms are provided by investors *who are not subject to the individual capital gains tax*. Funds committed by untaxed investors, notably pension funds, have expanded more rapidly than funds from taxable investors in the years since the 1978 capital gains tax cut. A significant fraction of the funds supplied to venture firms is therefore unaffected by the individual capital gains tax.

Second, the overwhelming majority of taxable capital gains results from investments in activities *other* than start-up firms. Less than one third of reported gains are the result of appreciation of corporate equity, and only a small fraction of the gains on equity are related to venture capital investments. An across-the-board capital gains tax cut is therefore a relatively blunt device for encouraging venture investment. If policymakers wish to subsidize venture investments, some form of targeted capital gains reduction would be a more attractive option.

* * *

Using the Sources

1.   Under present law, what is the maximum rate at which gain on each of the following items would be taxed? (Assume the item in question has been held by the taxpayer for more than one year. If any other variable would affect the tax treatment, please specify.)

  a. Stock in General Motors, held by a private investor.

  b. Stock in General Motors, held by a brokerage firm.

  c. Stock in a small start-up company (capitalization $5 million), held by a private investor who is its original owner.

  d. Same as c., but the initial capitalization is only $1 million.

  e. A factory building owned by an industrial company.

  f. A painting held by the painter.

  g. A painting held by someone other than the painter.

2.   Now assume that each of the items in item 1., above, was sold at a loss. Which of the losses would be subject to the capital loss limitation, and which would be ordinary losses?

Law and Planning

1.   Imagine your client has a long-term investment portfolio containing some stocks that have done well (aggregate appreciation of $1 million), and some that haven't done so well (aggregate decline in value of $0.5 million). The stock market is generally appreciating, so she expects the stocks to increase in value in the near future, although you can never be sure. Her salary and other income are approximately $100,000 per year and expected to stay there in the near future.

Based on tax consequences alone, would you advise your client to sell all or some of the appreciated and/or depreciated stock? What other information would you need in order to make a more complete recommendation?

2.   Suppose that your brother-in-law asks you to buy stock in his new restaurant, which is being set up in a traditional corporate form. You like your brother-in-law, but you know that most restaurants fail sooner or later, so you are

concerned about the tax treatment if the stock goes up and (alas) if it goes down or becomes worthless.

What sorts of questions might you ask him before deciding to invest in the restaurant? (Hint: Take a close look at section 1244, together with the more glamorous gain provisions.)

Politics and Policy

1.   How convincing do you find each of the following arguments in favor of a reduced capital gain tax rate? (Don't be afraid to disagree with the authors.)

   a. The inflation and bunching effects make it unfair to tax capital gains at the ordinary income rate.

   b. Society should encourage risk-taking by investing in capital assets.

   c. A reduced capital gain rate will encourage more trading in capital assets and thereby increase economic efficiency without losing (and perhaps gaining) new revenue

If you were lobbying Congress for a reduced tax rate, which of these points would you emphasize, and why? If you were opposed to a reduced rate, how would you respond?

2.   The higher — or, if you prefer, less reduced — tax rate on "collectibles" (section 1(h)(5)) appears to be part of a policy, in which the most generous treatment is provided for investments (e.g., new business stock) deemed to be most socially and economically productive, and less generous treatment for investments (stamps, coins, baseball cards) deemed to be less productive. This logic reaches its extreme in the treatment of gambling transactions, which — although undoubtedly risky — are subjected to unusually negative tax treatment. Not only are gambling winnings taxable as ordinary income, but gambling losses may be used only to offset gambling gains (section 165(d)), and special reporting requirements are applied to gambling transactions.

Does this sort of paternalism make sense in today's world? If people sell stamps and coins at a profit, doesn't this mean that society values these items no less than stocks, real estate, and other capital assets? If so, why should one qualify for better treatment than the other? Is gambling inherently less valuable than investment, because it produces no new assets, or does this evaluation depend on what specific type of activity is involved? Note that some investments may actually constitute gambling in economic terms, since their anticipated return is negative and people buy them in the small hope of a very large return. *See generally* Michael A. Livingston, *Risky Business: Economics, Culture, and the Taxation of High-Risk Activities*, 48 TAX L. REV. 163 (1993) (young tax professor risks career in attempt to demonstrate non-economic side of business taxation).

3.   What do you think of the favoritism for small, start-up companies as reflected in Code section 1202? Do most major innovations come from small business, or is this an outdated, romantic illusion? Are there other benefits (independence, creativity, personal satisfaction) that are more likely to be achieved by them? How

does the tax policy compare to other laws — notably antitrust statutes — that deal with the "big" vs. "small" issue, and which is more likely to achieve its goals?

III. THE CASE LAW: DELINEATING THE BOUNDARIES OF THE CAPITAL GAIN PREFERENCE

A. Basic Principles and the Inventory Exception

MALAT v. RIDDELL
United States Supreme Court
383 U.S. 569 (1966)

PER CURIAM:

Petitioner was a participant in a joint venture which acquired a 45-acre parcel of land, the intended use for which is somewhat in dispute. Petitioner contends that the venturers' intention was to develop and operate an apartment project on the land; the respondent's position is that there was a "dual purpose" of developing the property for rental purposes or selling, whichever proved to be the more profitable. In any event, difficulties in obtaining the necessary financing were encountered, and the interior lots of the tract were subdivided and sold. The profit from those sales was reported and taxed as ordinary income.

The joint venturers continued to explore the possibility of commercially developing the remaining exterior parcels. Additional frustrations in the form of zoning restrictions were encountered. These difficulties persuaded petitioner and another of the joint venturers of the desirability of terminating the venture; accordingly, they sold out their interests in the remaining property. Petitioner contends that he is entitled to treat the profits from this last sale as capital gains; the respondent takes the position that this was "property held by the taxpayer primarily for sale to customers in the ordinary course of his trade or business," and thus subject to taxation as ordinary income.

The District Court made the following finding:

> "The members of [the joint venture], as of the date the 44.901 acres were acquired, intended either to sell the property or develop it for rental, depending upon which course appeared to be most profitable. The venturers realized that they had made a good purchase price-wise and, if they were unable to obtain acceptable construction financing or rezoning . . . which would be prerequisite to commercial development, they would sell the property in bulk so they wouldn't get hurt. The purpose of either selling or developing the property continued during the period in which [the joint venture] held the property."

The District Court ruled that petitioner had failed to establish that the property was not held *primarily* for sale to customers in the ordinary course of business, and thus rejected petitioner's claim to capital gain treatment for the profits derived from the property's resale. The Court of Appeals affirmed, 347 F.2d 23. We granted *certiorari* (382 U.S. 900) to resolve a conflict among the courts of appeals with regard to the meaning of the term "primarily" as it is used in § 1221(1) of the Internal Revenue Code of 1954.

The statute denies capital gain treatment to profits reaped from the sale of "property held by the taxpayer *primarily* for sale to customers in the ordinary course of his trade or business." (Emphasis added.) The respondent urges upon us a construction of "primarily" as meaning that a purpose may be "primary" if it is a "substantial" one.

As we have often said, "the words of statutes — including revenue acts — should be interpreted where possible in their ordinary, everyday senses." *Crane v. Commissioner*, 331 U.S. 1, 6. *And see Hanover Bank v. Commissioner*, 369 U.S. 672, 687–688; *Commissioner v. Korell*, 339 U.S. 619, 627–628. Departure from a literal reading of statutory language may, on occasion, be indicated by relevant internal evidence of the statute itself and necessary in order to effect the legislative purpose. *See, e.g., Board of Governors v. Agnew*, 329 U.S. 441, 446–448. But this is not such an occasion. The purpose of the statutory provision with which we deal is to differentiate between the "profits and losses arising from the everyday operation of a business" on the one hand (*Corn Products Co. v. Commissioner*, 350 U.S. 46, 52) and "the realization of appreciation in value accrued over a substantial period of time" on the other. (*Commissioner v. Gillette Motor* Co., 364 U.S. 130, 134.) A literal reading of the statute is consistent with this legislative purpose. We hold that, as used in § 1221(1), "primarily" means "of first importance" or "principally."

Since the courts below applied an incorrect legal standard, we do not consider whether the result would be supportable on the facts of this case had the correct one been applied. We believe, moreover, that the appropriate disposition is to remand the case to the District Court for fresh fact-findings, addressed to the statute as we have now construed it.

Vacated and remanded.

Mr. Justice Black would affirm the judgments of the District Court and the Court of Appeals.

Mr. Justice White took no part in the decision of this case.

SUBURBAN REALTY COMPANY v. UNITED STATES
United States Court of Appeals, Fifth Circuit
615 F.2d 171 (1980)

Goldberg, J:

We must today answer the riddle at once adumbrated and apparently foreclosed by the false dichotomy created by the United States Supreme Court in *Malat v. Riddell*, 383 U.S. 569, 572 (1966) (per curiam): when profits have "aris[en] from the [ordinary] operation of a business" on the one hand and are also "the realization of appreciation in value over a substantial period of time" on the other, are these profits treated as ordinary income or capital gain? Lacking any clear guidance but the language of the capital asset statute itself, we turn to that language for the answer. Before we can arrive at this interesting and important question, however, we must once again tramp along (but not trample on) that time- and precedent-worn path which separates capital gains from ordinary income. By the time we emerge into the light at the far edge of the forest, we will find that the *Riddell* riddle has seemingly answered itself, and all that will remain will be a brief reassessment of our answer. In our peregrinations, we of necessity wander into virgin territory. We hope that we shed new light onto this murky terrain; at the least, we think we have neither riddled the cases nor muddled the issues.

I.

Suburban Realty Company was formed in November, 1937 to acquire an undivided one-fourth interest in 1,742.6 acres of land located in Harris County, Texas ("the property"). Suburban received its interest in the property in exchange for all of its stock from four individuals who had themselves acquired the property in a foreclosure proceeding brought against the property as a result of a default in the payment of certain bonds, the payment of which was secured by the property. Suburban's corporate charter states that it was formed to erect or repair any building or improvement, and to accumulate and lend money for such purposes, and to purchase, sell, and subdivide real property, and to accumulate and lend money for that purpose.

The five transactions whose characterization is in dispute here concern six tracts of unimproved real estate sold from the property by Suburban between 1968 and 1971. On its tax returns, Suburban originally reported profits from these sales, as well as all of its other real estate sales, as ordinary income. Later, Suburban filed a claim for refund asserting that these six tracts, as well as three similar tracts sold later, were capital assets, and that profits from these sales were entitled to capital gain treatment. The Internal Revenue Service denied Suburban's claim as to the sales here in issue. Suburban then instituted this action for a refund of $102,754.50. The district court, in a non-jury trial, rendered a decision against Suburban and entered a judgment dismissing Suburban's complaint. Suburban appealed.

Date	Acreage	Sales Price
December 31, 1968	4.5	$56,250
July 31, 1969	6.25	93,285
July 31, 1969	6.0225	90,225
July 31, 1969	17.50	262,282
1970 [sic]	5.6944	39,799
April 14, 1971	4.375	65,675

The parties' legal contentions are closely bound to the facts. It is undisputed that, at the time of sale, the tracts at issue here were subject to a grass lease which apparently covered much of the property. Except for this grass lease, the six tracts, as well as much of the rest of the property, were never put to any substantial use. However, certain other portions of the property were the subject of greater activity. The parties disagree to some degree concerning the extent of, and appropriate characterization of, the activities conducted relating to these other portions of the property, and they fundamentally dispute the weight such activities carry in properly characterizing the sales at issue here. We will first discuss Suburban's overall activities with respect to the entire property, and then turn to those portions of the property singled out by the parties as being the subject of greater activity.

A. Overall Activities.

1. Total Sales Activity From the Property.

Between 1939 and 1971, Suburban made at least 244 individual sales of real estate out of the property. Of these, approximately 95 sales were unplatted and unimproved property legally suitable for commercial development for any other purpose,[9] and at least 149 sales were from platted property restricted to residential development. In each of these 33 years, Suburban concluded at least one sale; in most years, there were four or more sales. Suburban's total proceeds from real estate sales over this period were $2,353,935. Proceeds from all other sources of income amounted to $474,845. Thus, eighty-three percent of Suburban's proceeds emanated from real estate sales; only seventeen percent flowed from all other sources.

2. North Loop Freeway.

In 1957, the Texas Highway Department proposed that the limited access superhighway now known as the North Loop would be located from east to west across the property. In 1959 and 1960, Suburban sold at least two parcels out of the property to the Texas Highway Department for the purpose of constructing this highway. The location of the highway had a dramatic effect on the price of land in the area. Land which had been selling for between three and five thousand dollars per acre prior to announcement of the highway rose in value to between seven and twelve thousand dollars per acre.

3. Corporate Discussions and Investments.

Starting not later than 1959, Suburban's officers, directors and stockholders began discussing liquidation of the corporation. Many of these discussions occurred after 1961, when Rice University became a stockholder of Suburban and the Treasurer of Rice University became a member of the board of directors. Because Rice University desired investments in income-producing assets rather than raw land, discussions concerning liquidation of Suburban's real estate holdings and the possibility of a partition of its holding among its stockholders were common. Starting in 1966, Suburban made substantial investments in stocks and bonds and began receiving substantial income from these investments.

---

[9] [6] There is no zoning in the City of Houston. Land use restrictions are ordinarily accomplished by placing restrictive covenants in the chain of title to the land.

B. Specific portions.

1. Houston Gardens.

In 1938, Suburban and the other owners of the property formed a separate corporation, Houston Gardens Annex, Inc. ("Houston Gardens"), to plat and sell a parcel in the northeast quadrant of the property. The stock ownership in Houston Gardens was in the same proportion as ownership interests in the property *i.e.*, Suburban and Mrs. Talbot each owned one-quarter of the stock of Houston Gardens; Mr. Hamman owned one-half of the stock. Houston Gardens owned approximately 200 or 250 lots, which were generally sold in bulk to builders. These sales covered as many as 20, 30, or even 50 lots at a time. By 1961, Houston Gardens had sold all but two of its lots, and it was then liquidated. Houston Gardens never engaged in advertising, used brokers or real estate agents, or employed a sales organization at any time during its existence.

2. Homestead Addition.

Certain portions of the property, located near its center, were designated as Homestead Addition Sections One, Two, Three, and Four. Little was done with Homestead Addition Section One except for platting it and running a few utility lines up to it.

Homestead Addition Section Two, however, was the primary subject of Suburban's activities. In July, 1948, Suburban acquired 100 percent ownership of Homestead Addition Section Two by exchanging cash and other land for the other owners' interests. Immediately thereafter, Suburban commenced development of Homestead Addition Section Two. The area was platted, streets and sewers were put in, and a sewage disposal plant was built nearby. Suburban also built a lumberyard in Section Two. At the instance of one of the individuals whom Suburban hired to collect water bills and notes on houses and to manage the lumberyard, Suburban also built eleven houses in Section Two in the early 1950's. The last was built by 1955, and none was sold later than 1958. Between 1948 and 1966, Suburban sold 252 subdivided lots out of Section Two. About half of these lots were sold in bulk to builders 10, 15, or 20 lots at a time.

Homestead Addition Sections Three and Four were platted for residential use by Suburban in 1951. This area was never developed by Suburban, however. In 1961 the plats were withdrawn and cancelled. This had the effect of eliminating restrictions which prevented commercial use of the land. Subsequently, the real estate within Sections Three and Four was sold to commercial and industrial users.

3. Other Parcels.

The remainder of the property appears to have been treated as one undifferentiated bulk by Suburban. It is from this undifferentiated, undeveloped remainder that the sales at issue here were made. There are no specific findings by the trial court, and there appears to be no evidence of record from which we could ourselves make findings, concerning the number and frequency of sales of real estate from other parts of the property. Rather, the evidence concerning annual sales groups all sales made by Suburban, including sales from the Homestead Addition Sections, together. However, it is clear that throughout the period 1939-1971, sales were being made from the remainder of the property.

II.

Our analysis of this case must begin with *Biedenharn Realty Co., Inc. v. United States*, 526 F.2d 409 (5th Cir.) (en banc), *cert. denied*, 429 U.S. 819 (1976). *Biedenharn* is this Court's latest (and only) en banc pronouncement concerning the characterization of profits of a real estate business as ordinary income or capital gain. The decision answers the characterization question by evaluating certain "factors" often present in cases of this ilk.[10] *Biedenharn* attempts to guide the analysis in this area by assigning different levels of importance to various of the "factors." Substantiality and frequency of sales is called the most important factor. *Biedenharn*, 526 F.2d at 416. Improvements to the land, solicitation and advertising efforts, and brokerage activities also play an important part in the *Biedenharn* analysis.

The question before us today, put into the *Biedenharn* framework, can be stated as follows: when a taxpayer engages in frequent and substantial sales over a period of years, but undertakes no development activity with respect to parts of a parcel of land, and engages in no solicitation or advertising efforts or brokerage activities, under what circumstances is income derived from sales of undeveloped parts of the parcel ordinary income?

The *Biedenharn* framework allows us to ask the question, but gives us little guidance in answering it. In the principal recent cases, there has always been a conjunction of frequent and substantial sales with development activity relating to the properties in dispute. *See, e.g., Houston Endowment, Inc. v. United States*, 606 F.2d 77, 82 (5th Cir. 1979), *Biedenharn*, 526 F.2d at 417; *United States v. Winthrop*, 417 F.2d 905, 911 (5th Cir. 1969). The conjunction of these two factors "will usually conclude the capital gains issue against [the] taxpayer." *Biedenharn*, 526 F.2d at 418. Judge Wisdom has recently written that "ordinary income tax rates usually apply when dispositions of subdivided property over a period of time are continuous and substantial rather than few and isolated." *Houston Endowment*, 606 F.2d at 81. Also, it has been explicitly stated that the factor which will receive greatest emphasis is frequency and substantiality of sales over an extended time period. *See Biedenharn*, 526 F.2d at 417. However, substantial and frequent sales activity, standing alone, has never been held to be automatically sufficient to trigger ordinary income treatment. In fact, we have continual reminders of the fact that

---

[10] [16] In the United States v. Winthrop, 417 F.2d 905, 910 (5th Cir. 1969), the following factors were enumerated:

   (1) The nature and purpose of the acquisition of the property and the duration of the ownership; (2) the extent and nature of the taxpayer's efforts to sell the property; (3) the number, extent, continuity and substantiality of the sales; (4) the extent of subdividing, developing, and advertising to increase sales; (5) the use of a business office for the sale of the property; (6) the character and degree of supervision or control exercised by the taxpayer over any representative selling the property; and (7) the time and effort the taxpayer habitually devoted to the sales.

"specific factors, or combinations of them are not necessarily controlling," *Biedenharn*, 526 F.2d at 415, quoting *Thompson v. Commissioner*, 322 F.2d 122, 127 (5th Cir. 1963), quoting *Wood v. Commissioner*, 276 F.2d 586, 590 (5th Cir. 1960).

Each of the parties invites us to look back to a case from long ago for guidance. Suburban points to *Alabama Mineral Land Co. v. Commissioner*, 250 F.2d 870 (5th Cir. 1957). The Government points to *Thompson, supra.* Each claims that the case it cites is substantially identical on its facts to the one before us. Each is essentially correct. However, we again decline, as have the earlier cases, to attempt a case-by-case distinction. *See Houston Endowment*, 606 F.2d at 82, *Biedenharn*, 526 F.2d at 421; *Thompson*, 322 F.2d at 127. We merely note that the Alabama Mineral decision contains no analysis of whether "the antiquated purpose" (liquidation of property holdings) was "overborne by later, but substantial and frequent selling activity." *Biedenharn*, 526 F.2d at 421. Rather, the court simply characterized taxpayer's purpose for acquiring the property as "liquidation," and concluded that sales made in liquidation result in capital gain rather than ordinary income. *Alabama Mineral*, 250 F.2d at 872. *Biedenharn* tells us, however, that "investment purpose has no built-in perpetuity nor a guarantee of capital gains forever more (sic)." 526 F.2d at 421. Thus, the method of analysis used in *Alabama Mineral* has not survived *Biedenharn*.

Today, we must go into territory as yet unmapped in this Circuit. Suburban's case is at once more favorable to the taxpayer than Biedenharn's and less so. It is more favorable because, with respect to the particular parcels of land here at issue, it is undisputed that Suburban undertook no development or subdivision activity. It is less favorable because Biedenharn was continually engaged in business activities other than real estate sales, whereas Suburban was for many years doing little else. Following the *Biedenharn* framework alone, we would be left with yet another essentially ad hoc decision to be made. We could justify a decision for either party, yet remain confident that we were being fully consistent with the analysis in *Biedenharn*. However, although there will always remain a certain irreducible ad hoc-ishness in this area, we are now firmly convinced that the uncertainty can be substantially reduced by turning to the divining rod of capital gains versus ordinary income — the statute itself.

III.

The jurisprudence of the "real estate capital gains-ordinary income issue" in this Circuit has at times been cast somewhat loose of its statutory mooring. The ultimate inquiry in cases of this nature is whether the property at issue was "property held by the taxpayer primarily for sale to customers in the ordinary course of his trade or business." 26 U.S.C.A. § 1221(1) (West 1967). In our focus on the "tests" developed to resolve this question, we have on occasion almost lost sight entirely of the statutory framework. The "tests" or "factors," whether they be counted to number seven, *see Winthrop*, 417 F.2d at 910, or to number four, *see Houston Endowment*, 606 F.2d at 81, have seemingly acquired an independent meaning of their own, only loosely tied to their statutory pier. Some years ago, Judge Brown cautioned us against this tendency:

> Essential as they are in the adjudication of cases, we must take guard lest we be so carried away by the proliferation of tests that we forget that the statute excludes from capital assets "property held by the taxpayer primarily for sale to customers in the ordinary course of his trade or business."

Thompson, 322 F.2d at 127. *See Biedenharn*, 526 F.2d at 424 (Roney, J., specially concurring).

The tendency to overemphasize the independent meaning of the "factors" has been accompanied by, perhaps even caused by, a tendency to view the statutory language as posing only one question: whether the property was held by the taxpayer "primarily for sale to customers in the ordinary course of his trade or business." This determination was correctly seen as equivalent to the question whether the gain was to be treated as ordinary or capital. However, probably because the question "is the gain ordinary" is a single question which demands an answer of yes or no, the courts have on occasion lost sight of the fact that the statutory language requires the court to make not one determination, but several separate determinations. In statutory construction cases, our most important task is to ask the proper questions. In the context of cases like the one before us, the principal inquiries demanded by the statute are:

1) was taxpayer engaged in a trade or business, and, if so, what business?

2) was taxpayer holding the property primarily for sale in that business?

3) were the sales contemplated by taxpayer "ordinary" in the course of that business?

We by no means intend to suggest that we disagree with anything decided by the recent Fifth Circuit decisions. *Biedenharn* guides our decision-making process. But after the relevant three independent statutory inquiries are pried apart, it becomes apparent that the central dispute in *Biedenharn* was a narrow one: was Biedenharn Realty Company holding the land in dispute "primarily for sale"? The majority, applying the *Winthrop* factors, decided this question in the affirmative. The dissent, emphasizing the continuing farming activities being conducted by Biedenharn, *see Biedenharn*, 526 F.2d at 425 & n.5, 426 (dissenting opinion), disagreed as to this conclusion.

In fact, once the inquiry is redirected towards the statutory inquiries, the ultimate relevance of the *Biedenharn* factors becomes apparent. It will remain true that the frequency and substantiality of sales will be the most important factor. But the reason for the importance of this factor is now clear: the presence of frequent and substantial sales is highly relevant to each of the principal statutory inquiries listed above. A taxpayer who engages in frequent and substantial sales is almost inevitably engaged in the real estate business. The frequency and substantiality of sales are highly probative on the issue of holding purpose because the presence of frequent sales ordinarily belies the contention that property is being held "for investment" rather than "for sale." And the frequency of sales may often be a key factor in determining the "ordinariness" question.

The extent of development activity and improvements is highly relevant to the question of whether taxpayer is a real estate developer. Development activity and improvements may also be relevant to the taxpayer's holding purpose, but, standing alone, some degree of development activity is not inconsistent with holding property for purposes other than sale. The extent of development activity also seems to be only peripherally relevant to the "ordinariness" question. Thus, under the statutory framework, as under *Biedenharn*, the extent of development activity and improvements, although an important factor, is less conclusive than the substantiality and frequency of sales.

Solicitation and advertising efforts are quite relevant both to the existence of a trade or business and to taxpayer's holding purpose. Thus, their presence can strengthen the case for ordinary income treatment. *See Biedenharn*, 526 F.2d at 418. However, in cases like *Biedenharn*, their absence is not conclusive on either of these statutory questions for, as we noted there, "even one inarguably in the real estate business need not engage in promotional exertions in the face of a favorable market." *Id.*

We need not comment individually on each of the other *Biedenharn-Winthrop* factors. It should be apparent that each factor is relevant, to a greater or lesser extent, to one or more of the questions posed by the statute along the path to the ultimate conclusion.

IV.

Having laid the framework for the requisite analysis, we must now apply that framework to the facts here. We must decide whether Suburban was engaged in a trade or business, and, if so, what business; whether Suburban was holding the properties at issue here primarily for sale; and whether Suburban's contemplated sales were "ordinary" in the course of Suburban's business.

Before we commence this analysis, we must ascertain the appropriate standard of appellate review. Unfortunately, the hidden supposition that the statutory language poses only one question has caused great confusion concerning whether the appropriate standard is "clearly erroneous" or "plenary review." This Circuit has often faced the question whether the characterization of property as "primarily held for sale to customers in the ordinary course of [taxpayer's] trade or business" is a question of law or a question of fact. This characterization is of course crucial to the outcome of many cases if the characterization is a question of fact, the factfinder's answer must be accepted unless clearly erroneous, but, if a question of law is presented, plenary review on appeal is appropriate. Unfortunately, there are two independent lines of authority in this Circuit on this issue. One line has its genesis in *Galena Oaks Corporation v. Scofield*, 218 F.2d 217 (5th Cir. 1954), and holds that the characterization "is inherently a question of law." *United States v. Winthrop*, 417 F.2d 905, 910 (5th Cir. 1969). The other line traces its roots to *Thompson v. Commissioner*, 322 F.2d 122, 127 (5th Cir. 1963), and can be followed through *United States v. Temple*, 355 F.2d 67, 68 (5th Cir. 1966), to *United States v. Burket*, 402 F.2d 426, 429 (5th Cir. 1968), and *Huxford v. United States*, 441 F.2d 1371, 1375 (5th Cir. 1971). This line holds that "the question of whether certain properties were held by a taxpayer "primarily for sale to customers in the ordinary course of [his] trade or business' is essentially a question of fact." *Burket*, 402 F.2d at 429. *See Commissioner v. Tri-S Corp.*, 400 F.2d 862, 864 (10th Cir. 1968) (question is "essentially a question of fact"); *Maddux Construction Co.*, 54 T.C. 1278, 1284 (1970) ("question is purely a factual question").

We need not here psychoanalyze the nightmares of characterization that have fascinated professors of civil procedure: the distinctions between historical, evidentiary, subsidiary, and ultimate facts are too fine for useful discussion. Once it is perceived that the ultimate legal conclusion of capital gain or ordinary income involves several independent determinations, it can be easily seen that some of the determinations are predominantly legal conclusions or are "mixed questions of fact and law," whereas others are essentially questions of fact. Thus, the question of taxpayer's purpose or purposes for holding the property is primarily factual, as is the question of which purpose predominates. Similarly, the "ordinariness" of the contemplated sales is mainly a fact question. The question of whether taxpayer was engaged in a trade or business involves the application of legal standards concerning what constitutes a trade or business to the facts concerning taxpayer's activities, and therefore is best characterized as a "mixed question of fact and law." The ultimate legal conclusion, based on these factual and legal conclusions, of whether the property was "held primarily for sale to customers in the ordinary course of his trade or business" cannot be appropriately characterized in this scheme at all because, as noted above, there are several subsidiary questions which, separately answered, lead to the ultimate conclusion.

A. Was Suburban in the Real Estate Business?

This is a relatively simple issue. The question is whether taxpayer has engaged in a sufficient quantum of focused activity to be considered to be engaged in a trade or business. The precise quantum necessary will be difficult to establish, and cases close to the line on this issue will arise.

Happily, we need not here define that line. It is clear to us that Suburban engaged in a sufficient quantity of activity to be in the business of selling real estate. Suburban's sales were continuous and substantial. It completed at least 244 sales transactions over the 33-year period 1939-1971. This averages to over 7 transactions per year. Proceeds from these sales exceeded 2.3 million dollars.

Suburban does not claim to have been engaged in any business other than real estate; rather, it claims that during the periods at issue it simply "did not carry on a trade or business." Br. for Appellee at 20. Were additional support necessary for our conclusion, we would point to Suburban's own statements on its tax returns over the years that its principal business activity was "development and sales of real estate." These statements are by no means conclusive of the issue. *See Thomas v. Commissioner*, 254 F.2d 233, 236–37 (5th Cir. 1958). However, we believe they show at least that if Suburban is engaged in a trade or business, that business is real estate. And Suburban's activities over the years were sufficient to convince us that it cannot sustain its contention that it was never engaged in any "trade or business" at all.

Suburban relies heavily on the insignificance of its subdivision and development activity and the total absence of any advertising or sales solicitation activity on its part. However, the first two absences do not concern us at all. We need not decide whether its subdivision and development activities were sufficient to compel the conclusion that Suburban was in the real estate development business. We rely solely on Suburban's real estate sales business.

The presence of any sales solicitation or advertising activity would certainly be relevant to the issue of whether Suburban was in the business of selling real estate. Strenuous, but largely unsuccessful, attempts to sell might compel the conclusion that a taxpayer with very few sales transactions was nonetheless in the business of selling. But the absence of such activity does not compel the opposite conclusion. *See Thompson*, 322 F.2d at 126.

Suburban also seeks solace from the fact that it never purchased any additional real estate to replenish acreage it sold. As is the case with the presence of sales activity, the presence of such purchases tends to demonstrate that a taxpayer is engaged in a real estate business, but their absence is not conclusive:

> The fact that [taxpayer] bought no additional lands during this period does not prevent his activity being a business. [Taxpayer] merely had enough land to do a large business without buying any more.

Biedenharn, 526 F.2d at 417, quoting *Snell v. Commissioner*, 92 F.2d 891 (5th Cir. 1938).

Additionally, Suburban points to its commencement of an investment program in securities in 1966. By itself, this cannot affect our conclusion that Suburban was in the real estate business. It merely demonstrates that, commencing in 1966, Suburban was also engaged in investing in securities. As stated earlier, the presence of other types of activities does not prevent taxpayer's real estate activities from being considered a business.

Suburban also contends that, if it was ever in the real estate business, it had exited that business long before 1968, the time of the first transaction here at issue. Even if this is true, it cannot affect our ultimate conclusion. The statutory language does not demand that property actually be sold while a taxpayer is still actively engaged in its trade or business for ordinary income treatment to be required. Rather, it demands that the property have been held primarily for sale in that business. To that inquiry we now turn.

B. What Was Suburban's Primary Purpose for Holding the Properties Whose Characterization Is Here in Dispute?

Put into the framework being used here, Suburban's contention concerning holding purpose is two-fold. Principally, it argues that, at the time of the sales in dispute, the properties were not being held for sale. Alternatively, it contends that it "originally acquired its property as an investment . . . , and it continued to hold it for investment purposes." Br. for Appellant at 7.

We reject Suburban's statement of the legal principle upon which its first argument is premised. It simply cannot be true that "the decisive question is the purpose for which [the property] 'primarily' was held when sold." Br. for Appellant at 15 (emphasis omitted). At the very moment of sale, the property is certainly being held "for sale." The appropriate question certainly must be the taxpayer's primary holding purpose at some point before he decided to make the sale in dispute.

There is language in the cases that supports the proposition we are here rejecting. For example, the Tax Court has stated explicitly that "the determining factor is the purpose for which the property is held at the time of sale." *Eline Realty Co.*, 35 T.C. 1, 5 (1960). *See Maddux Construction Co.*, 54 T.C. 1278, 1286 (1970).

However, neither party has cited any Supreme Court or Fifth Circuit precedent which states the proposition that the relevant holding purpose is that existing at the moment of sale. Suburban relies on *Malat v. Riddell*, 383 U.S. 569 (1966), and *Fahs v. Crawford*, 161 F.2d 315 (5th Cir. 1947). Malat does not address this issue at all, but concerns the meaning of the word "primarily" in 26 U.S.C. § 1221(1). *See* 389 U.S. at 571–572. *Fahs* merely acknowledges the possibility that a taxpayer's holding purpose for an asset may change, *see* 161 F.2d at 317, a concept we wholeheartedly approve. The Government points to *Ridgewood Land Co., Inc. v. Commissioner*, 477 F.2d 135 (5th Cir. 1973) (per curiam). There, as in *Fahs*, we see no more than a holding that a taxpayer's purpose for holding an asset may change, so that his intentions at the time of acquisition of the asset do not control the characterization of the proceeds of its sale. *See* 477 F.2d at 136.

Actually, although we are exceedingly hesitant to tell other courts that they do not mean precisely what they have said, the Tax Court cases cited above are not inconsistent with our approach. In *Eline Realty, supra*, the court found that taxpayer's holding purpose for the particular parcel at issue changed "from one of sale to one of investment" long before the parcel was sold. *Id.*, 35 T.C. at 6. Similarly, *Maddux Construction, supra*, stands for the proposition that a taxpayer can abandon prior to sale his initial purpose for acquiring the property. *Id.*, 54 T.C. at 1286.

The "holding purpose" inquiry may appropriately be conducted by attempting to trace the taxpayer's primary holding purpose over the entire course of his ownership of the property. *See Malat v. Riddell*, 383 U.S. 569 (1966); *Devine v. Commissioner*, 558 F.2d 807 (5th Cir. 1977). Thus, the inquiry should start at the time the property is acquired. We seek to divine the taxpayer's primary purpose for acquiring the property. In this case, we are willing to assume, as Suburban argues, that the property was acquired principally as an investment. We then seek evidence of a change in taxpayer's primary holding purpose. Here, such evidence is plentiful and convincing.

The property was acquired in December, 1937. Houston Gardens Annex, Inc. was formed in 1938 to plat and sell a portion of the property. Sales commenced by 1939, and sales were transacted in each year thereafter. From 1946 through 1956, approximately 17 sales per year occurred. Proceeds from sales exceeded $8,500 each year, and were as high as $69,000 (in 1952). Also during this period, the development activity pertaining to Homestead Addition Two was occurring. This development activity clearly contemplated, and was accompanied by, sales.

552 CAPITAL GAIN AND LOSS CH. 9

All of these factors convince us that, by the mid-1940's at the latest, and probably much earlier, Suburban's primary holding purpose was "for sale." We need not decide the precise moment. Were it necessary to our decision, we quite likely would be unwilling to accept Suburban's contention that the property was initially acquired for investment.

With its primary holding purpose through the 1940's and 1950's fixed at "for sale," Suburban is then entitled to show that its primary purpose changed to, or back to, "for investment." Suburban claims that this shift occurred either in 1959, when its officers and directors discussed liquidation; in 1961, when Rice University became a stockholder of Suburban, further liquidation discussions were held, and the plats were withdrawn; or, at the latest, in 1966, when further liquidation discussions were held and Suburban began investing in securities.

We view this determination to be a closer call than any of the others in this case. The frequency of sales did drop off after the late 1950's. Suburban had discontinued its development activities. Also, 1961 was the year the plats for Homestead Additions Three and Four were withdrawn.

This withdrawal of plats could be quite significant. Unlike liquidation discussions, which were apparently a dime a dozen for Suburban, withdrawal of the plats was an action taken by Suburban which may evince a different relationship to its land. The critical question is whether this withdrawal indicated that henceforth the land was being held principally as an investment or simply showed that Suburban was attempting to maximize sales profits by selling to commercial users.

The continuing sales activity is strong evidence that the latter interpretation is the correct one. Moreover, the trial court found that the withdrawal evinced "an attempt to maximize profits from the sale of real estate and to capitalize on the new North Loop Freeway which would cross [Suburban's] property." Thus, we conclude that Suburban's primary purpose for holding the property remained "for sale" at the time of the transactions here disputed.

Suburban does not explicitly contend that its primary purpose for holding the specific parcels at issue here was different from its purpose for holding the property as a whole. However, it does attempt to rely to some degree on the lack of development activity relating to the parcels here at issue. Although in some circumstances a taxpayer in the real estate business may be able to establish that certain parcels were held primarily for investment, the burden is on the taxpayer to establish that the parcels held primarily for investment were segregated from other properties held primarily for sale. The mere lack of development activity with respect to parts of a large property does not sufficiently separate those parts from the whole to meet the taxpayer's burden. *Cf. Houston Endowment*, 606 F.2d at 81 (pattern of sales activity with respect to entire tract determines characterization of individual sales). The lack of development activity with respect to the parts of the property here at issue is at least equally consistent with a primary motivation to maximize immediate sales profits as it is with a primary motivation to hold for investment.

C. Were the Sales Contemplated by Suburban "Ordinary" in the Course of Suburban's Business?

We need say no more on this question than quote from the discussion of this issue in *Winthrop, supra*:

> The concept of normalcy requires for its application a chronology and a history to determine if the sales of lots to customers were the usual or a departure from the norm. History and chronology here combine to demonstrate that [taxpayer] did not sell his lots as an abnormal or unexpected event. [Taxpayer] began selling shortly after he acquired the land; he never used the land for any other purpose; and he continued this course of conduct over a number of years. Thus, the sales were . . . ordinary.

417 F.2d at 912. The same is true here.

V.

Having relied on the language of § 1221 itself to determine that the assets here at issue were not capital assets, we must return for a moment to the query posed at the outset. In this case, as we have demonstrated, sales of the type here in dispute were precisely what Suburban's business was directed towards. In other words, the profits garnered from these sales arose from the ordinary operation of Suburban's business.

At the same time, however, these profits did not arise principally from the efforts of Suburban. Rather, they arose from the same historical, demographic, and market forces that have caused the City of Houston to grow enormously during the years Suburban held the land. Shrewdly, Suburban held on to much of its land. It only sold relatively small portions year by year. Thus, by 1968, market forces and the location of the North Loop Freeway had driven up the value of Suburban's land. We must decide whether the policies motivating lower tax rates on capital gains and the controlling precedents expressing those policies require that we ignore the plain language of § 1221 and hold for Suburban.

The key cases we must explore here number three. *First is Malat v. Riddell*, 383 U.S. 569 (1966) (per curiam). It lends us no aid. As we have previously stated, it suggests that profits cannot arise from both "the [ordinary] operation of a business" and "appreciation in value accrued over a substantial period of time." Yet here we have profits which fall squarely into both categories.

We thus turn to the two cases from which the *Malat* court quotations are taken, *Commissioner v. Gillette Motor Transport, Inc.*, 364 U.S. 130 (1960), and *Corn Products Refining Company v. Commissioner*, 350 U.S. 46 (1955). In *Gillette*, the Supreme Court said:

> This Court has long held that the term "capital asset" is to be construed narrowly in accordance with the purpose of Congress to afford capital-gains treatment only in situations typically involving the realization of appreciation in value accrued over a substantial period of time, and thus to ameliorate the hardship of taxation and the entire gain in one year.

364 U.S. at 134. We note that the quoted language does not state that all gains emanating from appreciation in value over a substantial period of time are to be treated as capital gains. Rather, it states the logical converse of that proposition; *i.e.*, that capital gain treatment will be proper only if the gain emanates from appreciation in value. Instances of gain emanating from appreciation being treated as ordinary income are not inconsistent with this proposition.

We also note the Supreme Court's recognition of the attempt by Congress to avoid taxing income earned over a period of years in one year. In Suburban's case, although it is true that with respect to each individual parcel of land there is a "bunching" effect, taxation of the overall gains from the property as a whole has been spread over a long period of years. Thus, the "bunching" effect has been minimized. Last, we note the Supreme Court's admonition to construe the term "capital asset" narrowly. *Id.*

Further support for a narrow construction of the term "capital asset" and a broad interpretation of its exclusions comes from *Corn Products*, the third key case in this area. *See Corn Products*, 76 S. Ct. at 24. More importantly, the Supreme Court in *Corn Products* squarely stated:

> Congress intended that profits and losses arising from the everyday operation of a business be considered as ordinary income or loss rather than capital gain or loss.

Id. It is this type of profit that is before us today.

We thus conclude that § 1221(1) should be construed in accord with its plain meaning, and that, if the other requirements of § 1221(1) are met, when the ordinary business of a business is to make profits from appreciation in value caused by market forces, those profits are to be treated as ordinary income. Such is the case here.

VI.

Our journey over, we have nothing more to add. The decision of the district court dismissing Suburban's complaint is AFFIRMED.

Understanding the Section 1221 Cases

1. *Malat* requires an inquiry into the taxpayer's "primary purpose" in holding a particular piece of property, with capital gain treatment if the primary purpose was investment and ordinary income if it was sale to customers in the ordinary course of a trade or business. Is this a realistic, or even a particularly logical, test? What if someone, like the Malats, buys property with the hope of dividing it into saleable units, but is perfectly happy to sell in bulk if it can make a better profit (or at least, take a smaller loss) in this way? Is the purpose to be judged at the time the property was originally purchased, when it was sold, or some intermediate point? Based on your reading of the opinion, what do you think the Malats' purpose was, and should they have been taxed at ordinary income or capital gain rates? Why?

Note: Malat won the case on remand to the District Court.

2. *Suburban Realty* considers a slightly different version of the same problem: what happens when the taxpayer's purpose in holding a property changes because of new economic or other conditions? This issue was particularly complicated because there were at least two possible changes: first, when Suburban initially realized that it could profit by subdividing the tracts for residential and commercial development (investment to trade or business purpose), and second, when it realized that it could sell unimproved lots at a higher profit because of the pattern of highway development (an arguable shift back to investment purpose). The court effectively finessed this issue by saying that it was concerned with the taxpayer's purpose over a "substantial period of time," and holding that this was primarily trade or business in nature. Do you find this outcome convincing? While we're at it, what do you think of the court's reluctance to separate the sales of certain unimproved lots from others involving smaller, more heavily improved tracts that would plainly be taxed at ordinary income rates? Can't a taxpayer have one purpose with respect to a particular lot of properties, and another purpose with respect to another? Why (or why not)?

3. Consider the following factors that were relevant to the court's decision in *Suburban Realty*:

    a. The frequency of sales;

    b. The size of each lot and the level of "improvements" attached to it; and

    c. The presence or absence of advertising and other marketing activities.

What is the significance of each of these items for the capital gain/ordinary income issue, and do you think each of them is applied correctly by the court? Are there any other factors, not mentioned in the decision, that might have been as or more significant?

4. Is the capital gain issue a problem of fact or of law? As a purely practical matter, why is this distinction important?

One interesting aspect of *Suburban Realty* is the difficulty of applying tax or other legal rules in a period of rapid economic change. Many people bought what was then rural real estate before World War II and found themselves sitting on a suburban gold mine in the postwar years. Were they long-term investors who had simply made a good investment, or were they now in the trade or business of selling real estate to consumers, and therefore deserving of ordinary income treatment? Should it matter if they undertook subdivisions, improvements, etc., on their own or sold property to someone else to do these things for them? *Suburban Realty* tries its best to deal with this problem, but in a sense, it remains insoluble: the capital gain vs. ordinary income distinction remains largely an artificial one, and only with difficulty is it imposed on the day-to-day decisions of real-world businesspeople.

Also of note is the role of mental images or "paradigms" in the application of tax law. When people think of ordinary income, they tend to picture a store or similar enterprise in which items (books, apples, television sets) are purchased in bulk and then individually displayed and sold, at a profit, to the general public. By contrast, capital gain conjures up images of passive investors, not particularly involved in the activity on a day-to-day basis, who are simply waiting and hoping for the relevant property to increase in value.[11] There is thus a tendency to take the activities that one associates with the former paradigm — subdivision, marketing, advertising — and read them into the ordinary income/capital gain distinction, even though they are nowhere to be found in the statute and may not be particularly relevant in individual cases. Whether this makes for good law is uncertain, but it provides at least some handle on an otherwise intractable (please pardon the pun) issue, and is likely to remain a feature of jurisprudence in this area.

Using the Sources

Which of the following would result in capital gain, and which in ordinary income?

a. The sale of real property by a real estate developer.

b. The sale of real property by a real estate investor.

c. The sale of a personal residence (be careful).

d. The sale of coins, stamps, or baseball cards by an aging adolescent collector. Does it matter if he (she) advertises in trade publications or sells individual items as opposed to complete sets? What other facts might you want to know, before answering this question?

e. The conversion of a rental apartment building into a co-op or condominium.

Law and Planning

Suppose that you owned undeveloped land in an outlying, still primarily rural area, which you believed was likely to appreciate in value as the suburbs drew ever closer. The land was purchased for $100,000 several years ago and is now worth at least five times that ($500,000), with the probability — although one can never be sure — of continued increases in the near future. Indeed, you were recently offered this price by a developer who expects, within the next three to five years, to begin constructing residential units on the property. The price of the units would depend on the size of the lots, the state of the housing market, and so forth, but houses in comparable areas have sold for $200,000 to $300,000 each, at least ten percent of which constitutes profit for the developers; and the land is large enough to support perhaps a hundred such units total.

You are presently considering four possible alternatives with respect to the property:

a. Accept the offer and sell for $500,000.

b. Divide the property into smaller, still undeveloped lots which would be sold to individual homeowners to develop on their own terms.

c. Hire a builder and start to develop the property; sell the developed lots to individual homeowners.

---

[11] The word "passive" is used here in its colloquial sense and not as a defined term in section 469.

d. Hold the property as is, and wait for a better price.

Which of these options strikes you as the most attractive, and what role, if any, would tax factors play in your decision? What additional facts, if any, would you want to know before making your decision?

Politics and Policy

Reduced capital gain rates are supposed to encourage long-term investment, prevent "lock-in," and (perhaps) protect taxpayers from the effects of inflation, bunching, and other associated horrors. Would any of these purposes be served by extending capital gain treatment to real estate speculators in *Malat, Suburban Realty*, or similar cases? Shouldn't capital gain treatment, as an exception to "ordinary" tax treatment, at least be interpreted narrowly? Or should the presumption be the opposite: that the taxpayers get to keep their own money unless the Government can prove convincingly otherwise? (Note that, when these cases arose, the capital gain rate was less than half that on ordinary income, so that the cases — had they been won by the taxpayers — would have resulted in something approaching complete avoidance of tax.)

B.   Everyday Business Operations and the Hedging Problem

CORN PRODUCTS REFINING CO. v. COMMISSIONER
United States Supreme Court
350 U.S. 46 (1955)

MR. JUSTICE CLARK delivered the opinion of the Court.

This case concerns the tax treatment to be accorded certain transactions in commodity futures.[12] In the Tax Court, petitioner Corn Products Refining Company contended that its purchases and sales of corn futures in 1940 and 1942 were capital-asset transactions under § 117(a) of the Internal Revenue Code of 1939. It further contended that its futures transactions came within the "wash sales" provisions of § 118. The 1940 claim was disposed of on the ground that § 118 did not apply, but for the year 1942 both the Tax Court and the Court of Appeals for the Second Circuit, 215 F.2d 513, held that the futures were not capital assets under § 117. We granted *certiorari*, 348 U.S. 911, because of an asserted conflict with holdings in the Courts of Appeal for the Third, Fifth, and Sixth Circuits. Since we hold that these futures do not constitute capital assets in petitioner's hands, we do not reach the issue of whether the transactions were "wash sales."

Petitioner is a nationally known manufacturer of products made from grain corn. It manufactures starch, syrup, sugar, and their by-products, feeds and oil. Its

---

[12] [1] A commodity future is a contract to purchase some fixed amount of a commodity at a future date for a fixed price. Corn futures, involved in the present case, are in terms of some multiple of five thousand bushels to be delivered eleven months or less after the contract. *Cf.* Hoffman, Future Trading (1932), 118.

average yearly grind of raw corn during the period 1937 through 1942 varied from thirty-five to sixty million bushels. Most of its products were sold under contracts requiring shipment in thirty days at a set price or at market price on the date of delivery, whichever was lower. It permitted cancellation of such contracts, but from experience it could calculate with some accuracy future orders that would remain firm. While it also sold to a few customers on long-term contracts involving substantial orders, these had little effect on the transactions here involved.

In 1934 and again in 1936 droughts in the corn belt caused a sharp increase in the price of spot corn. With a storage capacity of only 2,300,000 bushels of corn, a bare three weeks' supply, Corn Products found itself unable to buy at a price which would permit its refined corn sugar, cerelose, to compete successfully with cane and beet sugar. To avoid a recurrence of this situation, petitioner, in 1937, began to establish a long position in corn futures "as a part of its corn buying program" and "as the most economical method of obtaining an adequate supply of raw corn" without entailing the expenditure of large sums for additional storage facilities. At harvest time each year it would buy futures when the price appeared favorable. It would take delivery on such contracts as it found necessary to its manufacturing operations and sell the remainder in early summer if no shortage was imminent. If shortages appeared, however, it sold futures only as it bought spot corn for grinding.[13] In this manner it reached a balanced position with reference to any increase in spot corn prices. It made no effort to protect itself against a decline in prices.

In 1940 it netted a profit of $680,587.39 in corn futures, but in 1942 it suffered a loss of $109,969.38. In computing its tax liability Corn Products reported these figures as ordinary profit and loss from its manufacturing operations for the respective years. It now contends that its futures were "capital assets" under § 117 and that gains and losses there should have been treated as arising from the sale of a capital asset. In support of this position it claims that its futures trading was separate and apart from its manufacturing operations and that in its futures transactions it was acting as a "legitimate capitalist." *United States v. New York Coffee & Sugar Exchange*, 263 U.S. 611, 619. It denies that its futures transactions were "hedges" or "speculative" dealings as covered by the ruling of General Counsel's Memorandum 17322, XV-2 Cum. Bull. 151, and claims that it is in truth "the forgotten man" of that administrative interpretation.

Both the Tax Court and the Court of Appeals found petitioner's futures transactions to be an integral part of its business designed to protect its

---

[13] [2] The dispositions of the corn futures during the period in dispute were as follows:

	Sales of futures thousand bushels	Delivery under futures thousand bushels
1938	17,400	4,975
1939	14,180	2,865
1940	14,595	250
1941	2,545	2,175
1942	5,695	4,460

manufacturing operations against a price increase in its principal raw material and to assure a ready supply for future manufacturing requirements. Corn Products does not level a direct attack on these two-court findings but insists that its futures were "property" entitled to capital-asset treatment under § 117 and as such were distinct from its manufacturing business. We cannot agree.

We find nothing in this record to support the contention that Corn Products' futures activity was separate and apart from its manufacturing operation. On the contrary, it appears that the transactions were vitally important to the company's business as a form of insurance against increases in the price of raw corn. Not only were the purchases initiated for just this reason, but the petitioner's sales policy, selling in the future at a fixed price or less, continued to leave it exceedingly vulnerable to rises in the price of corn. Further, the purchase of corn futures assured the company a source of supply which was admittedly cheaper than constructing additional storage facilities for raw corn. Under these facts it is difficult to imagine a program more closely geared to a company's manufacturing enterprise or more important to its successful operation.

Likewise the claim of Corn Products that it was dealing in the market as a "legitimate capitalist" lacks support in the record. There can be no quarrel with a manufacturer's desire to protect itself against increasing costs of raw materials. Transactions which provide such protection are considered a legitimate form of insurance. *United States v. New York Coffee & Sugar Exchange*, 263 U.S. at 619; *Browne v. Thorn*, 260 U.S. 137, 139–140. However, in labeling its activity as that of a "legitimate capitalist" exercising "good judgment" in the futures market, petitioner ignores the testimony of its own officers that in entering that market the company was "trying to protect a part of [its] manufacturing costs"; that its entry was not for the purpose of "speculating and buying and selling corn futures" but to fill an actual "need for the quantity of corn [bought] . . . in order to cover . . . what [products] we expected to market over a period of fifteen or eighteen months." It matters not whether the label be that of "legitimate capitalist" or "speculator"; this is not the talk of the capital investor but of the far-sighted manufacturer. For tax purposes petitioner's purchases have been found to "constitute an integral part of its manufacturing business" by both the Tax Court and the Court of Appeals, and on essentially factual questions the findings of two courts should not ordinarily be disturbed. *Comstock v. Group of Investors*, 335 U.S. 211, 214.

Petitioner also makes much of the conclusion by both the Tax Court and the Court of Appeals that its transactions did not constitute "true hedging." It is true that Corn Products did not secure complete protection from its market operations. Under its sales policy petitioner could not guard against a fall in prices. It is clear, however, that petitioner feared the possibility of a price rise more than that of a price decline. It therefore purchased partial insurance against its principal risk, and hoped to retain sufficient flexibility to avoid serious losses on a declining market.

Nor can we find support for petitioner's contention that hedging is not within the exclusions of § 117(a). Admittedly, petitioner's corn futures do not come within the literal language of the exclusions set out in that section. They were not stock in trade, actual inventory, property held for sale to customers or depreciable property used in a trade or business. But the capital-asset provision of § 117 must not be so broadly applied as to defeat rather than further the purpose of Congress. *Burnet v. Harmel*, 287 U.S. 103, 108. Congress intended that profits and losses arising from the everyday operation of a business be considered as ordinary income or loss rather than capital gain or loss. The preferential treatment provided by § 117 applies to transactions in property which are not the normal source of business income. It was intended "to relieve the taxpayer from . . . excessive tax burdens on gains resulting from a conversion of capital investments, and to remove the deterrent effect of those burdens on such conversions." *Burnet v. Harmel*, 287 U.S. at 106. Since this section is an exception from the normal tax requirements of the Internal Revenue Code, the definition of a capital asset must be narrowly applied and its exclusions interpreted broadly. This is necessary to effectuate the basic congressional purpose. This Court has always construed narrowly the term "capital assets" in § 117. *See Hort v. Commissioner*, 313 U.S. 28, 31; *Kieselbach v. Commissioner*, 317 U.S. 399, 403.

The problem of the appropriate tax treatment of hedging transactions first arose under the 1934 Tax Code revision. Thereafter the Treasury issued G.C.M. 17322, *supra*, distinguishing speculative transactions in commodity futures from hedging transactions. It held that hedging transactions were essentially to be regarded as insurance rather than a dealing in capital assets and that gains and losses therefrom were ordinary business gains and losses. The interpretation outlined in this memorandum has been consistently followed by the courts as well as by the Commissioner. While it is true that this Court has not passed on its validity, it has been well recognized for 20 years; and Congress has made no change in it though the Code has been re-enacted on three subsequent occasions. This bespeaks congressional approval. *Helvering v. Winmill*, 305 U.S. 79, 83. Furthermore, Congress has since specifically recognized the hedging exception here under consideration in the short-sale rule of § 1233(a) of the 1954 Code.

We believe that the statute clearly refutes the contention of Corn Products. Moreover, it is significant to note that practical considerations lead to the same conclusion. To hold otherwise would permit those engaged in hedging transactions to transmute ordinary income into capital gain at will. The hedger may either sell the future and purchase in the spot market or take delivery under the future contract itself. But if a sale of the future created a capital transaction while delivery of the commodity under the same future did not, a loophole in the statute would be created and the purpose of Congress frustrated.

The judgment is

Affirmed.

MR. JUSTICE HARLAN took no part in the consideration or decision of this case.

Understanding *Corn Products*

1.   With slightly simplified numbers, the facts in *Corn Products* were as follows. A company used raw corn to make corn syrup, a popular sweetener, and other finished products. In order to ensure itself of a supply of corn at a fixed price, it

purchased corn futures contracts, giving it the right to buy corn at a fixed price at some future date. For example, assume that the price of corn was now $15 per unit; that it cost Corn Products $10 in other expenditures (labor, machinery, etc.) to turn this into an equivalent amount of corn syrup; and that it could sell the finished Corn Syrup at $30 per unit. By assuring itself of a future supply of corn at $15 per unit, the company would protect its profit margin of $5 per unit ($30 – $25), regardless of changes in the price of corn during the interim period. In the absence of this mechanism, an increase in the price of corn — say, from $15 to $20 per unit — would be sufficient to wipe out the profit margin and eventually destroy the company, assuming that market forces made it impossible to simply raise the price of corn syrup every time corn became more expensive. (Since corn syrup competes with sugar and other artificial sweeteners, that's probably a fair assumption.) The futures contract would also prevent the company from making even more money, if the price of corn decreased to (say) $10 per unit, because it would still be obligated to buy corn at $15; but the company might be willing to accept this limitation in order to ensure that it had at least some profit on the transaction.

The only wrinkle in the above is that commodity traders don't actually take delivery of the commodities in most cases. (You can't fit very much corn in the elevators at the Chicago Board of Trade.) Instead, the transactions are reflected on paper: if corn prices go up from $15 to $20 per unit, you register a $5 profit, since the right to buy a $20 item for $15 is worth, well, $5. So, if this happened to Corn Products, they would register a zero profit on their corn syrup business ($30 sale price — $20 for fresh corn — $10 other expenditures), but would have a $5 profit as corn futures traders. That indeed was the whole point of the transaction: to protect the company's profit margin in the event corn prices increased before their corn syrup orders had been filled. The same profit would be realized, but in a slightly different way.

Given this economic reality, isn't the Court right that income on the futures contract, which was effectively a substitute for income on the corn syrup business, should be taxed the same way as the corn syrup business, *i.e.*, as ordinary income? Or are commodity futures inherently an "investment" activity that gives rise to capital gain income? Suppose that Corn Products had losses instead of gains on the futures contracts, and argued that these should be treated as ordinary losses because of their relationship to the company's every day business — *i.e.*, the same argument that the Government used successfully in the *Corn Products* case. Do you think that the Court would have bought this argument? Why (or why not)?

2.   The taxpayer's position in *Corn Products* was weakened by the close relationship between the futures contracts and the company's principal business. (It's tough to argue that you're not in the corn business when your first name is "corn.") Suppose the link was less obvious. For example, imagine that a luxury car manufacturer bought stock in an oil company, because it had determined that fewer people bought luxury cars when gasoline prices were high, and wanted to protect its profit margin in the event of this contingency. Would gain on the oil company stock qualify as ordinary income under the *Corn Products* "everyday operation" doctrine? Or should the case be read as a limited holding regarding inventory-type purchases, rather than as a broader statement regarding hedging and other integrated economic activities? (*See infra.*)

3. In support of its holding, the Court states that "Congress intended that profits and losses arising from the everyday operation of a business be considered as ordinary income or loss rather than capital gain or loss." If so, why didn't they say it? Does the statutory provision at issue (section 1221(1)) say anything about the *Corn Products* issue, or does the Court simply rewrite the statute in order to achieve a desired result? Is there a way that the Court could have reached the same result, while staying closer to the actual legislative language?

Corn Products provides a good example of the trouble courts can get in when they create broad, well-meaning doctrines unsupported by the statutory language. The "everyday operation" concept was particularly dangerous, since the identical doctrine could be applied by taxpayers in loss cases, resulting in ordinary losses (which are deductible without limitation) rather than capital losses (which other than a small allowance can be used only against capital gains). In the decades following *Corn Products*, taxpayers made full use of the "everyday operation" logic, arguing that losses were ordinary in nature because the company in question provided a supply of paper to a newspaper company, or commodities to an agricultural firm, or because it somehow "hedged" or protected the taxpayer against losses in its primary business. This resulted in something of a "lose-lose" situation for the IRS, since taxpayers with a gain would (like Corn Products) tend to take the position that the gain was capital in nature, resulting in a reduced tax rate, while those with losses would tend to discover (or invent) a link to their everyday operations which permitted them to take unlimited ordinary losses. While the IRS won a large percentage of these cases, it is likely that many others escaped audit, and the IRS was required to expend significant resources on what was at best a break-even situation.

The game ended, or at least slowed down, only with the Supreme Court's holding in *Arkansas Best*, decided (like *Tufts* after *Crane*) a full generation after *Corn Products*. As you read *Arkansas Best*, consider how it is responding to the *Corn Products* problem, and whether it amounts to an interpretation or an effective overruling of the earlier decision.

ARKANSAS BEST CORPORATION v. COMMISSIONER
United States Supreme Court
485 U.S. 212 (1988)

JUSTICE MARSHALL delivered the opinion of the Court.

The issue presented in this case is whether capital stock held by petitioner Arkansas Best Corporation (Arkansas Best) is a "capital asset" as defined in § 1221 of the Internal Revenue Code regardless of whether the stock was purchased and held for a business purpose or for an investment purpose.

I

Arkansas Best is a diversified holding company. In 1968 it acquired approximately 65% of the stock of the National Bank of Commerce (Bank) in Dallas, Texas. Between 1969 and 1974, Arkansas Best more than tripled the number of shares it owned in the Bank, although its percentage interest in the Bank remained relatively stable. These acquisitions were prompted principally by the Bank's need for added capital. Until 1972, the Bank appeared to be prosperous and growing, and the added capital was necessary to accommodate this growth. As the Dallas real estate market declined, however, so too did the financial health of the Bank, which had a heavy concentration of loans in the local real estate industry. In 1972, federal examiners classified the Bank as a problem bank. The infusion of capital after 1972 was prompted by the loan portfolio problems of the bank.

Petitioner sold the bulk of its Bank stock on June 30, 1975, leaving it with only a 14.7% stake in the Bank. On its federal income tax return for 1975, petitioner claimed a deduction for an ordinary loss of $9,995,688 resulting from the sale of the stock. The Commissioner of Internal Revenue disallowed the deduction, finding that the loss from the sale of stock was a capital loss, rather than an ordinary loss, and that it therefore was subject to the capital loss limitations in the Internal Revenue Code.

Arkansas Best challenged the Commissioner's determination in the United States Tax Court. The Tax Court, relying on cases interpreting *Corn Products* held that stock purchased with a substantial investment purpose is a capital asset which, when sold, gives rise to a capital gain or loss, whereas stock purchased and held for a business purpose, without any substantial investment motive, is an ordinary asset whose sale gives rise to ordinary gains or losses. The court characterized Arkansas Best's acquisitions through 1972 as occurring during the Bank's " 'growth' phase," and found that these acquisitions "were motivated primarily by investment purpose and only incidentally by some business purpose." The stock acquired during this period therefore constituted a capital asset, which gave rise to a capital loss when sold in 1975. The court determined, however, that the acquisitions after 1972 occurred during the Bank's " 'problem' phase," and, except for certain minor exceptions, "were made exclusively for business purposes and subsequently held for the same reasons." These acquisitions, the court found, were designed to preserve petitioner's business reputation, because without the added capital the Bank probably would have failed. The loss realized on the sale of this stock was thus held to be an ordinary loss.

The Court of Appeals for the Eighth Circuit reversed the Tax Court's determination that the loss realized on stock purchased after 1972 was subject to ordinary-loss treatment, holding that all of the Bank stock sold in 1975 was subject to capital-loss treatment. The court reasoned that the Bank stock clearly fell within the general definition of "capital asset" in, and that the stock did not fall within any of the specific statutory exceptions to this definition. The court concluded that Arkansas Best's purpose in acquiring and holding the stock was irrelevant to the determination whether the stock was a capital asset. We granted *certiorari*, and now affirm.

II

Section 1221 of the Internal Revenue Code defines "capital asset" broadly, as "property held by the taxpayer (whether or not connected with his trade or business)," and then excludes five specific classes of property from capital-asset status. In the statute's present form,[14] the classes of property exempted from the broad definition are (1) "property of a kind which would properly be included in the inventory of the taxpayer"; (2) real property or other depreciable property used in the taxpayer's trade or business; (3) "a copyright, a literary, musical, or artistic composition," or similar property; (4) "accounts or notes receivable acquired in the ordinary course of trade or business for services rendered" or from the sale of inventory; and (5) publications of the Federal Government. Arkansas best acknowledges that the Bank stock falls within the literal definition of capital asset in § 1221, and is outside of the statutory exclusions. It asserts, however, that this determination does not end the inquiry. Petitioner argues that in this Court rejected a literal reading of § 1221, and concluded that assets acquired and sold for ordinary business purposes rather than for investment purposes should be given ordinary-asset treatment. Petitioner's reading of *Corn Products* finds much support in the academic literature[15] and in the courts.[16] Unfortunately for petitioner, this broad reading finds no support in the language of § 1221.

In essence, petitioner argues that "property held by the taxpayer (whether or not connected with his trade or business)" does not include property that is acquired and held for a business purpose. In petitioner's view an asset's status as "property" thus turns on the motivation behind its acquisition. This motive test, however, is not only nowhere mentioned in § 1221, but it is also in direct conflict with the parenthetical phrase "whether or not connected with his trade or business." The broad definition of the term "capital asset" explicitly makes irrelevant any consideration of the property's connection with the taxpayer's business, whereas petitioner's rule would make this factor dispositive.[17]

---

[14] [2] In 1975, when petitioner sold its Bank stock, § 1221 contained a different exception (5), which excluded certain federal and state debt obligations. *See* 26 U.S.C. § 1221(5) (1970 ed.). That exception was repealed by the Economic Recovery Tax Act of 1981, Pub. L. 97-34, § 505(a), 95 Stat. 331. The present exception (5) was added by the Tax Refund act of 1976, Pub. L. 94-455, § 2132(a), 90 Stat. 1925. These changes have no bearing on this case.

[15] [3] *See, e.g.*, 2 B. Bittker, Federal Taxation of Income, Estates and Gifts para. 51.10.3, p. 51-62 (1981); Chirelstein, *Capital Gain and the Sale of a Business Opportunity: The Income Tax Treatment of Contract Termination Payments*, 49 Minn. L. Rev. 1, 41 (1964); Troxell & Noall, *Judicial Erosion of the Concept of Securities as Capital Assets*, 19 Tax L. Rev. 185, 187 (1964); Note, *The* Corn Products *Doctrine and Its Application to Partnership Interests*, 79 Colum. L. Rev. 341, and n. 3 (1979).

[16] [4] *See, e.g.*, Campbell Taggart, Inc. v. United States, 744 F.2d 442, 456-458 (CA5 1984); Steadman v. Commissioner, 424 F.2d 1, 5 (CA6), *cert. denied*, 400 U. S. 869 (1970); Booth Newspapers, Inc. v. United States, 303 F.2d 916, 920-921, 157 Ct. Cl. 886, 893-896 (1962); W.W. Windle Co. v. Commissioner, 65 T.C. 694, 707-713 (1976).

[17] [5] Petitioner mistakenly relies on cases in which this Court, in narrowly applying the general definition of capital asset, has "construed 'capital asset' to exclude property representing income items or accretions to the value of a capital asset themselves properly attributable to income," even though these items are property in the broad sense of the word. United States v. Midland-Ross Corp., 381 U.S. 54, 57 (1965). *See, e.g.*, Commissioner v. Gillette Motor Co., 364 U.S. 130 (1960) ("capital asset" does not include compensation awarded taxpayer that represented fair rental value of its facilities); Commissioner v. P.G. Lake, Inc., 356 U.S. 260 (1958) ("capital asset" does not include proceeds from sale of oil payment rights); Hort v. Commissioner, 313 U.S. 28 (1941) ("capital asset" does not include payment to lessor for cancellation of unexpired portion of a lease). This line of cases, based on the premise that § 1221 "property" does not include claims or rights to ordinary income, has no application in the present context. Petitioner sold capital stock, not a claim to ordinary income.

In a related argument, petitioner contends that the five exceptions listed in § 1221 for certain kinds of property are illustrative, rather than exhaustive, and that courts are therefore free to fashion additional exceptions in order to further the general purposes of the capital-asset provisions. The language of the statute refutes petitioner's construction. Section 1221 provides that "capital asset" means "property held by the taxpayer[,] . . . but does not include" the five classes of property listed as exceptions. We believe this locution signifies that the listed exceptions are exclusive. The body of § 1221 establishes a general definition of the term "capital asset," and the phrase "does not include" takes out of that broad definition only the classes of property that are specifically mentioned. The legislative history of the capital asset definition supports this interpretation, *see* H.R. Rep. 704, 73d Cong., 2d Sess., 31 (1934) ("The definition includes all property, except as specifically excluded"); H.R. Rep. 1337, 83d Cong., 2d Sess., A273 (1954) ("[A] capital asset is property held by the taxpayer with certain exceptions"), as does the applicable Treasury regulation, see (1987) ("The term 'capital assets' includes all classes of property not specifically excluded by section 1221").

Petitioner's reading of the statute is also in tension with the exceptions listed in § 1221. These exclusions would be largely superfluous if assets acquired primarily or exclusively for business purposes were not capital assets. Inventory, real or depreciable property used in the taxpayer's trade or business, and accounts or notes receivable acquired in the ordinary course of business, would undoubtedly satisfy such a business-motive test. Yet these exceptions were created by Congress in separate enactments spanning 30 years. Without any express direction from Congress, we are unwilling to read § 1221 in a manner that makes surplusage of these statutory exclusions.

In the end, petitioner places all reliance on its reading of *Corn Products* — a reading we believe is too expansive. In *Corn Products*, the Court considered whether income arising from a taxpayer's dealings in corn futures was entitled to capital-gains treatment. The taxpayer was a company that converted corn into starches, sugars, and other products. After droughts in the 1930's caused sharp increases in corn prices, the company began a program of buying corn futures to assure itself an adequate supply of corn and protect against price increases. The company "would take delivery on such contracts as it found necessary to its manufacturing operations and sell the remainder in early summer if no shortage was imminent. If shortages appeared, however, it sold futures only as it bought spot corn for grinding." The Court characterized the company's dealing in corn futures as "hedging." As explained by the Court of Appeals in *Corn Products*, "hedging is a method of dealing in commodity futures whereby a person or business protects itself against price fluctuations at the time of delivery of the product which it sells or buys." In evaluating the company's claim that the sales of corn futures resulted in capital gains and losses, this Court stated:

"Nor can we find support for petitioner's contention that hedging is not within the exclusions of [§ 1221]. Admittedly, petitioner's corn futures do not come within the literal language of the exclusions set out in that section. They were not stock in trade, actual inventory, property held for sale to customers or depreciable property used in a trade or business. But the capital-asset provision of [§ 1221] must not be so broadly applied as to

defeat rather than further the purpose of Congress. Congress intended
that profits and losses arising from the everyday operation of a business be
considered as ordinary income or loss rather than capital gain or
loss. . . . Since this section is an exception from the normal tax requirements of the Internal Revenue Code, the definition of a capital asset must
be narrowly applied and its exclusions interpreted broadly." (citations
omitted).

The Court went on to note that hedging transactions consistently had been
considered to give rise to ordinary gains and losses, and then concluded that the
corn futures were subject to ordinary-asset treatment.

  The Court in *Corn Products* proffered the oft-quoted rule of construction that
the definition of capital asset must be narrowly applied and its exclusions
interpreted broadly, but it did not state explicitly whether the holding was based on
a narrow reading of the phrase "property held by the taxpayer," or on a broad
reading of the inventory exclusion of § 1221. In light of the stark language of § 1221,
however, we believe that *Corn Products* is properly interpreted as involving an
application of § 1221's inventory exception. Such a reading is consistent both with
the Court's reasoning in that case and with § 1221. The Court stated in *Corn
Products* that the company's futures transactions were "an integral part of its
business designed to protect its manufacturing operations against a price increase
in its principal raw material and to assure a ready supply for future manufacturing
requirements." The company bought, sold, and took delivery under the futures
contracts as required by the company's manufacturing needs. As Professor Bittker
notes, under these circumstances, the futures can "easily be viewed as surrogates
for the raw material itself." 2 B. Bittker, Federal Taxation of Income, Estates and
Gifts para. 51.10.3, p. 51–62 (1981). The Court of Appeals for the Second Circuit in
Corn Products clearly took this approach. That court stated that when commodity
futures are "utilized solely for the purpose of stabilizing inventory cost[,] . . . [they]
cannot reasonably be separated from the inventory items," and concluded that
"property used in hedging transactions properly comes within the exclusions of
[§ 1221]." This Court indicated its acceptance of the Second Circuit's reasoning
when it began the central paragraph of its opinion, "Nor can we find support for
petitioner's contention that hedging is not within the exclusions of [§ 1221]." In the
following paragraph, the Court argued that the Treasury had consistently viewed
such hedging transactions as a form of insurance to stabilize the cost of inventory,
and cited a Treasury ruling which concluded that the value of a manufacturer's
raw-material inventory should be adjusted to take into account hedging transactions in futures contracts. This discussion, read in light of the Second Circuit's
holding and the plain language of § 1221, convinces us that although the corn
futures were not "actual inventory," their use as an integral part of the taxpayer's
inventory-purchase system led the Court to treat them as substitutes for the corn
inventory such that they came within a broad reading of "property of a kind which
would properly be included in the inventory of the taxpayer" in § 1221.

  Petitioner argues that by focusing attention on whether the asset was acquired
and sold as an integral part of the taxpayer's everyday business operations, the
Court in *Corn Products* intended to create a general exemption from capital-asset
status for assets acquired for business purposes. We believe petitioner misunder

stands the relevance of the Court's inquiry. A business connection, although irrelevant to the initial determination of whether an item is a capital asset, is relevant in determining the applicability of certain of the statutory exceptions, including the inventory exception. The close connection between the futures transactions and the taxpayer's business in *Corn Products* was crucial to whether the corn futures could be considered surrogates for the stored inventory of raw corn. For if the futures dealings were not part of the company's inventory-purchase system, and instead amounted simply to speculation in corn futures, they could not be considered substitutes for the company's corn inventory, and would fall outside even a broad reading of the inventory exclusion. We conclude that *Corn Products* is properly interpreted as standing for the narrow proposition that hedging transactions that are an integral part of a business' inventory-purchase system fall within the inventory exclusion of § 1221.[18] Arkansas Best, which is not a dealer in securities, has never suggested that the Bank stock falls within the inventory exclusion. *Corn Products* thus has no application to this case.

It is also important to note that the business-motive test advocated by petitioner is subject to the same kind of abuse that the Court condemned in *Corn Products*. The Court explained in *Corn Products* that unless hedging transactions were subject to ordinary gain and loss treatment, taxpayers engaged in such transactions could "transmute ordinary income into capital gain at will." The hedger could garner capital-asset treatment by selling the future and purchasing the commodity on the spot market, or ordinary-asset treatment by taking delivery under the future contract. In a similar vein, if capital stock purchased and held for a business purpose is an ordinary asset, whereas the same stock purchased and held with an investment motive is a capital asset, a taxpayer such as Arkansas Best could have significant influence over whether the asset would receive capital or ordinary treatment. Because stock is most naturally viewed as a capital asset, the Internal Revenue Service would be hard pressed to challenge a taxpayer's claim that stock was acquired as an investment, and that a gain arising from the sale of such stock was therefore a capital gain. Indeed, we are unaware of a single decision that has applied the business-motive test so as to require a taxpayer to report a gain from the sale of stock as an ordinary gain. If the same stock is sold at a loss, however, the taxpayer may be able to garner ordinary-loss treatment by emphasizing the business purpose behind the stock's acquisition. The potential for such abuse was evidenced in this case by the fact that as late as 1974, when Arkansas Best still hoped to sell the Bank stock at a profit, Arkansas Best apparently expected to report the gain as a capital gain.

---

[18] [7] Although congressional inaction is generally a poor measure of congressional intent, we are given some pause by the fact that over 25 years have passed since *Corn Products* was initially interpreted as excluding assets acquired for business purposes from the definition of capital asset, *see* Booth Newspapers, Inc. v. United States, 303 F.2d 916, 157 Ct. Cl. 886 (1962), without any sign of disfavor from Congress. We cannot ignore the unambiguous language of § 1221, however, no matter how reticent Congress has been. If a broad exclusion from capital-asset status is to be created for assets acquired for business purposes, it must come from congressional action, not silence.

III

We conclude that a taxpayer's motivation in purchasing an asset is irrelevant to the question whether the asset is "property held by a taxpayer (whether or not connected with his business)" and is thus within § 1221's general definition of "capital asset." Because the capital stock held by petitioner falls within the broad definition of the term "capital asset" in § 1221 and is outside the classes of property excluded from capital-asset status, the loss arising from the sale of the stock is a capital loss. which we interpret as involving a broad reading of the inventory exclusion of § 1221, has no application in the present context. Accordingly, the judgment of the Court of Appeals is affirmed.

It is so ordered.

JUSTICE KENNEDY took no part in the consideration or decision of this case.

———————

Following *Arkansas Best*, the Treasury promulgated extensive regulations on hedging transactions in 1994. Treas. Reg. § 1.1221-2. These regulations were further supplemented by the addition of Code section 1221(a)(6) in 1999, which excludes from capital asset status "any hedging transaction which is clearly identified as such before the close of the day on which it was acquired, originated, or entered into. . . ."

Understanding *Arkansas Best*

1. Justice Marshall was arguably the most important lawyer of his generation, which means that he could sometimes convince you of something that isn't entirely true. Is he being just a bit disingenuous in pretending to uphold rather than overrule the *Corn Products* doctrine? Is it true that *Corn Products* "is properly interpreted as standing for the narrow proposition that hedging transactions that are an integral part of a business's inventory-purchase system fall within the inventory exclusion of sec. 1221?" What about the reference, in *Corn Products*, to "profits and losses arising from the everyday operation of a business," which (according to the case) are treated as ordinary income? If *Arkansas Best* were decided under the "everyday operation" standard, how do you think it would have come out?

2. Does *Arkansas Best* resolve the hedging issue effectively? Suppose that, instead of being concerned for its reputation, Arkansas Best purchased stock in another corporation because that corporation had assets that Arkansas Best needed for use in its business. Could this situation be squeezed into the inventory exception of section 1221, and thereby qualify for ordinary loss treatment? Or is this precisely the "motive" test that *Arkansas Best* seeks to avoid? Does it matter if the relationship to inventory is a very direct one, as in *Corn Products*, or a more indirect one, as in some of the later supply cases?

3. If Arkansas Best had registered gain on the National Bank of Commerce stock, how do you think it would have reported it?

Using the Sources

Under present law, which of the following would be characterized as ordinary, and which as capital, assets?

a. The purchase of corn futures by a corporation that made corn syrup. (What if it purchased raw corn, instead?)

b. An investment in a lumber and paper pulp company by a big-city newspaper.

c. The purchase of oil futures by an automobile manufacturer, on the theory that — if high oil prices depressed car sales — the company would make back part of its loss on the oil futures.

d. The purchase of oil futures by a supermarket chain, on the theory that — if high oil prices depressed the entire economy — the company would make back part its loss on the oil futures.

e. The purchase of oil futures by an oil company.

Law and Planning

Suppose that you found yourself in a situation similar to that of Arkansas Best between 1972 and 1975 — that is, you or your company had made an investment in a subsidiary that had gone well until recently, but was beginning to sour.[19] Like Arkansas Best, you faced conflicting pressures: on the one hand, you did not want to absorb the reputational and other damages that would result from abandoning the investment; on the other hand, you did not want to throw more good money after bad. Unlike Arkansas Best, you knew that, if the investment were later sold at a loss, both your original and any later losses would be nondeductible capital losses.

How long would you keep pumping money into the subsidiary, and what role (if any) would tax factors play in your decision?

Politics and Policy

The *Corn Products* issue suggests an interesting dilemma for Government tax lawyers. Winning the case required the Government to make a creative interpretation of the statute (the "everyday operations" doctrine) that would prevent tax avoidance on the immediate facts. Yet the same doctrine would likely result in substantial revenue reduction in capital loss cases. Indeed, if we make the (reasonable) assumption that taxpayers would be more likely to claim "ordinary income" treatment in loss than in gain cases, these revenue reductions might well outweigh the revenue increases resulting from the new doctrine.

If you were the Government's chief tax litigator, and a case like *Corn Products* arose, how aggressively would you pursue it? Does the IRS have a responsibility to argue each case as zealously as it can, or should it sometimes sacrifice individual

---

[19] Assume that the subsidiary did not manufacture anything of use to the parent, so that the losses were plainly capital in nature under the *Arkansas Best* decision.

cases for the big picture? Would the answer be different if the same question were posed to the taxpayer's lawyer? What are the ethical responsibilities of an attorney faced with this situation, and are they (should they be) different for a private or Government attorney?[20]

C.   Sale of a Business

One fascinating aspect of the capital gain/ordinary income distinction is that it requires first identifying an individual asset or assets to which the distinction can be applied.

Suppose that the owner of a local clothing store decides, after thirty years in the business, to retire and sell the business to someone else. (The concept of a local clothing store may seem quaint to some of you, but we're told there are a few still around.) What exactly is he or she selling, and how should the ordinary vs. capital gain (or loss) distinction apply in this case?

There are at least two ways to answer this question. The first is to take all of the individual items that make up the business — the building, the inventory, the equipment, any accounts receivable, and (if it is a successful business) its reputation with customers and suppliers — and allocate a portion of the purchase price to each item. The purchase price for each item could then be compared with its basis and gain or loss computed on each separate part of the business, with ordinary income or capital gain treatment depending upon the particular item in question. For example, the gain on a business's inventory or accounts receivable would receive ordinary income treatment (section 1221(1)), while gain on its building or equipment would likely qualify for capital gain status (section 1231), as would that portion of gain attributable to goodwill.

A second way is to treat the whole business as a combined entity and calculate the gain or loss on that entity, which would presumably be capital in nature, without regard to separate, individual items. This method seems consistent with business reality — most people probably think of a business as a combined entity rather than a collection of individual parts — and avoids the problem of often arbitrary allocations between bookkeeping categories. An aggregate method has its own dangers, however, and may allow its own inconsistency if businesses receive identical treatment despite varying amounts of ordinary income and capital gain items.

The following case considers the capital gain/ordinary income issue in the context of the sale of a sole proprietorship — *i.e.*, a business owned and operated by one person in his or her own personal name. After the case, we will consider the same issue in the context of corporations and other business entities, and how this difference might affect the choice between different forms of business entity.

---

[20] For an interesting discussion of the ethical issue, in the context of *Crane* and other cases of the era, see Kirk Stark, *The Unfulfilled Tax Legacy of Justice Robert H. Jackson*, 54 TAX L. REV. 171 (2001).

WILLIAMS v. McGOWAN
United States Court of Appeals, Second Circuit
152 F.2d 570 (1945)

L. Hand, J:

This is an appeal from a judgment dismissing the complaint in an action by a taxpayer to recover income taxes paid for the year 1940. Of the two questions involved the first is whether $700 which the plaintiff paid to attorneys to secure the refund of his taxes paid for the years 1936 and 1937, was a proper deduction under Sec. 23(a)(2) of the Internal Revenue Code as amended by Sec. 121 of the Act of 1942, 26 U.S.C.A. Int. Rev. Code, § 23(a)(2). Since the judgment below was entered the Supreme Court has decided that such expenses are deductible. *Trust of Bingham v. Commissioner*, 325 U.S. 365. It is true that that case, as its title implies, concerned a trust, but the Tax Court has held that this was not a controlling consideration (*Cammack v. Commissioner*, 5 T.C. 467); and even a casual reading of the Supreme Court's opinion shows that nothing turned upon the circumstance. We may therefore dispose of this question summarily, and proceed to the second, as to which the facts were as follows.

Williams, the taxpayer, and one Reynolds, had for many years been engaged in the hardware business in the City of Corning, New York. On the 20th of January, 1926, they formed a partnership, of which Williams was entitled to two-thirds of the profits, and Reynolds, one-third. They agreed that on February 1, 1925, the capital invested in the business had been $118,082.05, of which Reynolds had a credit of $29,029.03, and Williams, the balance — $89,053.02. At the end of every business year, on February 1st, Reynolds was to pay to Williams, interest upon the amount of the difference between his share of the capital and one-third of the total as shown by the inventory; and upon withdrawal of one party the other was to have the privilege of buying the other's interest as it appeared on the books. The business was carried on through the firm's fiscal year, ending January 31, 1940, in accordance with this agreement, and thereafter until Reynolds' death on July 18th of that year. Williams settled with Reynolds' executrix on September 6th in an agreement by which he promised to pay her $12,187.90, and to assume all liabilities of the business; and he did pay her $2,187.98 in cash at once, and $10,000 on the 10th of the following October. On September 17th of the same year, Williams sold the business as a whole to the Corning Building Company for $63,926.28 — its agreed value as of February 1, 1940 — 'plus an amount to be computed by multiplying the gross sales of the business from the first day of February, 1940 to the 28th day of September, 1940,' by an agreed fraction. This value was made up of cash of about $8100, receivables of about $7000, fixtures of about $800, and a merchandise inventory of about $49,000, less some $1000 for bills payable. To this was added about $6,000 credited to Williams for profits under the language just quoted, making a total of nearly $70,000. Upon this sale Williams suffered a loss upon his original two-thirds of the business but he made a small gain upon the one-third which he had bought from Reynolds' executrix; and in his income tax return he entered both as items of 'ordinary income,' and not as transactions in 'capital assets.' This the Commissioner disallowed and recomputed the tax accordingly;

Williams paid the deficiency and sued to recover it in this action. The only question is whether the business was 'capital assets' under Sec. 117(a)(1) of the Internal Revenue Code, 26 U.S.C.A. Int. Rev. Code, § 117(a)(1).

It has been held that a partner's interest in a going firm is for tax purposes to be regarded as a 'capital asset.' *Stilgenbaur v. United States*, 9 Cir., 115 F.2d 283; *Commissioner v. Shapiro*, 6 Cir., 125 F.2d 532, 114 A.L.R. 349. We too accepted the doctrine in *McClellan v. Commissioner*, 2 Cir., 117 F.2d 988, although we had held the opposite in *Helvering v. Smith*, 2 Cir., 90 F.2d 590, 591, where the partnership articles had provided that a retiring partner should receive as his share only his percentage of the sums 'actually collected' and 'of all earnings . . . for services performed.' Such a payment, we thought, was income; and we expressly repudiated the notion that the Uniform Partnership Act had, generally speaking, changed the firm into a juristic entity. *See also Doyle v. Commissioner*, 4 Cir., 102 F.2d 86. If a partner's interest in a going firm is 'capital assets' perhaps a dead partner's interest is the same. New York Partnership Law Secs. 61, 62(4), Consol. Laws N.Y. c. 39. We need not say. When Williams bought out Reynolds' interest, he became the sole owner of the business, the firm had ended upon any theory, and the situation for tax purposes was no other than if Reynolds had never been a partner at all, except that to the extent of one-third of the 'amount realized' on Williams' sale to the Corning Company, his 'basis' was different. The judge thought that, because upon that sale both parties fixed the price at the liquidation value of the business while Reynolds was alive, 'plus' its estimated earnings thereafter, it was as though Williams had sold his interest in the firm during its existence. But the method by which the parties agreed upon the price was irrelevant to the computation of Williams' income. The Treasury, if that served its interest, need not heed any fiction which the parties found it convenient to adopt; nor need Williams do the same in his dealings with the Treasury. We have to decide only whether upon the sale of a going business it is to be comminuted into its fragments, and these are to be separately matched against the definition in Sec. 117(a)(1), or whether the whole business is to be treated as if it were a single piece of property.

Our law has been sparing in the creation of juristic entities; it has never, for example, taken over the Roman 'universitas facti';[21] and indeed for many years it fumbled uncertainly with the concept of a corporation.[22] One might have supposed that partnership would have been an especially promising field in which to raise up an entity, particularly since merchants have always kept their accounts upon that basis. Yet there too our law resisted at the price of great continuing confusion; and, even when it might be thought that a statute admitted, if it did not demand, recognition of the firm as an entity, the old concepts prevailed. *Francis v. McNeal*, 228 U.S. 695. And so, even though we might agree that under the influence of the Uniform Partnership Act a partner's interest in the firm should be treated as indivisible, and for that reason a 'capital asset' within Sec. 117(a)(1), we should be chary about extending further so exotic a jural concept. Be that as it may, in this

---

[21] [1] 'By universitas facti is meant a number of things of the same kind which are regarded as a whole; *e.g.* a herd, a stock of wares.' Mackeldey, Roman Law § 162.

[22] [2] 'To the 'church' modern law owes its conception of a juristic person, and the clear line that it draws between 'the corporation aggregate' and the sum of its members.' Pollack & Maitland, Vol. 1, 489.

instance the section itself furnishes the answer. It starts in the broadest way by declaring that all 'property' is 'capital assets,' and then makes three exceptions. The first is 'stock in trade . . . or other property of a kind which would properly be included in the inventory'; next comes 'property held . . . primarily for sale to customers'; and finally, property 'used in the trade or business of a character which is subject to *** allowance for depreciation.' In the face of this language, although it may be true that a 'stock in trade,' taken by itself, should be treated as a 'universitas facti,' by no possibility can a whole business be so treated; and the same is true as to any property within the other exceptions. Congress plainly did mean to comminute the elements of a business; plainly it did not regard the whole as 'capital assets.'

As has already appeared, Williams transferred to the Corning Company 'cash,' 'receivables,' 'fixtures' and a 'merchandise inventory.' 'Fixtures' are not capital because they are subject to a depreciation allowance; the inventory, as we have just seen, is expressly excluded. So far as appears, no allowance was made for 'good-will'; but, even if there had been, we held in *Haberle Crystal Springs Brewing Company v. Clarke, Collector*, 2 Cir., 30 F.2d 219, that good-will was a depreciable intangible. It is true that the Supreme Court reversed that judgment — 280 U.S. 384 — but it based its decision only upon the fact that there could be no allowance for the depreciation of 'good-will' in a brewery, a business condemned by the Eighteenth Amendment. There can of course be no gain or loss in the transfer of cash; and, although Williams does appear to have made a gain of $1072.71 upon the 'receivables,' the point has not been argued that they are not subject to a depreciation allowance. That we leave open for decision by the district court, if the parties cannot agree. The gain or loss upon every other item should be computed as an item in ordinary income.

Judgment reversed.

FRANK, CIRCUIT JUDGE (dissenting in part).

I agree that it is irrelevant that the business was once owned by a partnership. For when the sale to the Corning Company occurred, the partnership was dead, had become merely a memory, a ghost. To say that the sale was of the partnership's assets would, then, be to indulge in animism.

But I do not agree that we should ignore what the parties to the sale, Williams and the Corning Company, actually did. They did not arrange for a transfer to the buyer, as if in separate bundles, of the several ingredients of the business. They contracted for the sale of the entire business as a going concern. Here is what they said in their agreement: 'The party of the first part agrees to sell and the party of the second part agrees to buy, all of the right, title and interest of the said party of the first part in and to the hardware business now being conducted by the said party of the first part, including cash on hand and on deposit in the First National Bank & Trust Company of Corning in the A. F. Williams Hardware Store account, in accounts receivable, bills receivable, notes receivable, merchandise and fixtures, including two G.M. trucks, good will and all other assets of every kind and description used in and about said business. . . . Said party of the first part agrees not to engage in the hardware business within a radius of twenty-five miles from the City of Corning, New York, for a period of ten years from the 1st day of October 1940.'

To carve up this transaction into distinct sales — of cash, receivables, fixtures, trucks, merchandise, and good will — is to do violence to the realities. I do not think Congress intended any such artificial result. In the Senate Committee Report on the 1942 amendment to Sec. 117, it was said: 'It is believed that this Senate amendment will be of material benefit to businesses which, due to depressed conditions, have been compelled to dispose of their plant or equipment at a loss. The bill defines property used in a trade or business of a character which is subject to the allowance for depreciation, and real property held for more than six months which is not properly includible in the inventory of the taxpayer if on hand at the close of the taxable year or property held by the taxpayer primarily for sale to customers in the ordinary course of his trade or business. If a newspaper purchased the plant and equipment of a rival newspaper and later sold such plant and equipment, being subject to depreciation, would constitute property used in the trade or business within the meaning of this section.' These remarks show that what Congress contemplated was not the sale of a going business but of its dismembered part. Where a business is sold as a unit, the whole is greater than its parts. Businessmen so recognize; so, too, I think, did Congress. Interpretation of our complicated tax statutes is seldom aided by saying that taxation is an eminently practical matter (or the like). But this is one instance where, it seems to me, the practical aspects of the matter should guide our guess as to what Congress meant. I believe Congress had those aspects in mind and was not thinking of the nice distinctions between Roman and Anglo-American legal theories about legal entities.

Understanding *Williams v. McGowan*

1.   *Williams v. McGowan* had a pretty distinguished panel, but did the majority spend too much time showing off their knowledge of different business assets? Isn't Judge Frank's dissent correct, that the parties were selling a combined business rather than separate bunches of assets? If they wanted to sell each of the assets separately, why didn't they?

2.   The court's decision requires an allocation of the business sale price between goodwill, on the one hand, and various tangible assets (buildings, inventories, etc.) on the other. How trustworthy is the taxpayer's allocation likely to be in such matters? Is there a mathematical formula that can be applied to such cases, or should the seller's allocation be respected in the absence of obvious misstatement? What if the seller allocates most of the purchase price to items that qualify for capital gain treatment, while the buyer allocates the bulk of the same purchase price to items that result in favorable tax or accounting treatment for her? *See* I.R.C. § 1060 (requiring consistency in the allocation of the purchase price on certain asset acquisitions); *cf.* I.R.C. § 197 (allowing 15-year amortization for purchased goodwill).

3.   What is the significance of the court's observation that the building fixtures had previously been subject to a depreciation allowance? Would the case have come out differently if this had not been the case? Why?

One interesting aspect of *Williams v. McGowan* is the difference it creates in the treatment of different forms of business entity. The sale of stock in a corporation, assuming that it has been held for more than one year, generally qualifies for capital gain treatment, as does the sale of a partnership interest, although the latter may result in ordinary income to the extent it is attributable to certain unrealized receivables or inventory items (section 751). By contrast, under *Williams*, the sale of a sole proprietorship results in a mix of ordinary income and capital gain treatment depending on the nature of the particular business in question. What is more, the allocation between assets in this latter case may be arbitrary (subject to the limitations of section 1060) and may not accurately reflect the economic reality of the entity being sold. Thus, the tax treatment of two identical sole proprietorships may be different both from each other and from an otherwise similarly situated corporation or partnership — hardly an unprecedented difference, but arguably inconsistent with the horizontal equity principle.

The treatment of sales and liquidations is but one example of the varying treatment accorded different forms of business entity by the tax code — in many cases, a key factor in the choice between those forms of entity. At this point, it is sufficient to note that the same factors that help the taxpayer in some cases may be harmful in others. For example, the capital gain treatment afforded to corporate stock, while an advantage in the case of a successful company, may be a source of frustration for one that has declined in value, since (with limited exceptions) the losses on such stock may not be deducted against ordinary income. Tax considerations must also be balanced against regular business goals; for example, a sole proprietorship is useful for deducting losses, but may also be administratively unwieldy, and will subject the owner to unlimited liability for the business's debts. A good tax planner must attempt to reduce her client's taxes without sacrificing these other, non-tax objectives. These and other aspects of business taxation will be discussed further in Chapter 12.

A further interesting aspect is the consistency in reporting rule contained in section 1060 of the Code, and alluded to above. This rule requires parties to an "applicable asset acquisition" to furnish information to the IRS regarding the allocation to section 197 intangibles and other specified items in the acquisition price. Unless rejected by the IRS, this allocation is binding on both the purchaser and seller for tax purposes. Although one might expect that the parties to a transaction would report it in the same way, in most cases there is no guarantee that this will happen, nor is it by any means clear that the normal audit process is capable of ferreting out inconsistencies. The fear of "whipsaw" — a colorful and entirely inscrutable term used to describe a situation in which the Government loses tax revenues by means of inconsistent reporting — thus remains alive and well and continues to be a significant concern for the government in making and enforcing tax law.

Using the Sources

What do you think would be the likely impact of *Williams v. McGowan* on each of the following businesses? How much of the gain on each business is likely to be attributable to ordinary income items (inventory, accounts receivable, etc.) and how much to capital gain assets? (Assume that all three businesses are operated as sole proprietorships.)

a. A clothing store.

b. A professional service business, such as a doctor or one-person law firm.

c. A small manufacturing company (*e.g.*, a furniture or clothing manufacturer).

Law and Planning

Suppose that you were starting up a business in each of the three areas described above, and knew in advance of the likely tax consequences upon sale of the business as described above. Would this affect your decision to operate as a sole proprietorship, or would it encourage you to choose a corporation or some alternate business form? How important would the sale of the business — which is after all a long way off — be compared to the tax consequences in the early years of business operation? Remember that capital gain treatment, although advantageous in the sale of a successful business, may make it more difficult to deduct losses on a business that has lost, or is losing, money. Do most new businesses generally expect to make or lose money, and how would you balance these considerations in choosing between different entity forms?

Politics and Policy

1. Do you think that the rules for computing gain on sale of a business should be standardized between different forms of entity (corporations, partnerships, sole proprietorships), or is some measure of taxpayer choice appropriate? If the rules should be consistent, what should the standard rule be? What do you think are the likely consequences of the inconsistency in today's Code, for choice of entity and other matters? Are you troubled by them?

2. Do you believe that the parties to a transaction such as the sale of a business should be required to report the transaction in the same manner? What other transactions can you imagine the rule being extended to, and how would you propose to enforce it?

3. Having read the cases above, does the capital gain preference make more or less sense to you than it did at the beginning of the chapter? Do the distinctions in the principal capital gain cases — fruits vs. trees, hedges vs. supply contracts, the sale of a sole proprietorship vs. the sale of a partnership or corporation — strike you as reasonable distinctions, consistent with a broad, general policy of favoring long-term investment over alternate uses of money? Or do they seem more like an arbitrary and archaic hodge-podge, rewarding clever lawyers rather than advancing any coherent tax policy? What are the vertical equity implications of a provision that taxes investment returns at a lower rate than salary or other earned income? Can these vertical equity problems be compensated by better targeting efforts or by the argument that, in encouraging increased investment, the rules ultimately benefit all segments of society? If you were drafting a new tax system from scratch, would you include some version of the capital gain/ordinary income distinction, or would you

replace it with some other, better targeted mechanism designed to achieve the same or similar goals? What form (if any) would this new mechanism take, and how would it differ from present law?

D.   Inflation, Indexing, and the Consumption Tax: Alternate Perspectives on the Capital Gain Problem

In evaluating the capital gain provisions, it is also interesting to consider some of the possible alternatives. One oft-proposed reform is to replace or supplement capital gain tax rates with an "indexing" system, under which the basis of capital assets was adjusted for inflation taking place while the asset was held. For example, assume that A purchased a parcel of investment real estate in the year 2000, at a cost of $200,000. Assume further that the price level during the next ten years increased by 40 percent, so that a bundle of items that cost $200,000 in the year 2000 would cost approximately $280,000 in 2010. If A sold her hypothetical real estate in the year 2010, at a cost of $320,000, she would be taxed only on the amount of $40,000 ($320,000 – $280,000), rather than on the nominal profit of $120,000 as would be the case today. The idea behind the proposal would be to tax A only on the amount that represents an actual increase in the value of the asset, as opposed to that which represents the effect of inflation and thereby does not bring her a true economic benefit. Presumably, this accounting for inflation would eliminate one of the major arguments in favor of a reduced capital gain tax rate. A number of foreign countries use some sort of indexing system, for all or select categories of assets, although administrative and political problems — the prime beneficiaries of the system would be wealthier individuals — have as yet prevented it from being enacted here.

The capital gain problem has also been cited as an argument in favor of a consumption, rather than income, tax.[23] Under a consumption tax, a deduction would be allowed for the purchase of any capital asset, which by definition would not be consumed in the year it was acquired. By contrast, the full sale price of the asset, without basis offset, would be taken into income in the year it was sold. For example, in the case described above, A would receive a $200,000 deduction in the year 2000 and be taxed on $320,000 in the year 2010, with no intermediate calculations, of basis or otherwise, required. Since the $200,000 deduction would be taken in 2000 (*i.e.*, pre-inflation) dollars, and the $320,000 would be taxed in 2010 (post-inflation) currency, the inflation problem would be "self-correcting" and not require an indexing system of the type suggested above. Of course, this is not necessarily an argument for a consumption tax, which may be objectionable on vertical equity or other grounds. But it does suggest the interrelationship of tax issues, and the difficulty of "fixing" any one part of the system without changing other and more complicated aspects, as well.

---

[23] *See* Chapter 4, *supra.*

Additional Assignment — Chapter 9

One of the challenging aspects of tax planning is the need to keep various provisions simultaneously in mind when adopting a new tax strategy. An idea that works brilliantly for capital gain purposes may make little sense if it prevents the use of related capital losses, or if it results in estate or gift tax problems. Likewise a good tax strategy is useless if it undermines the client's business or personal goals. Like a good chess player, the tax planner is always thinking two or three steps ahead, considering the effects of his or her decisions tomorrow as well as today.

With this in mind, consider the situation of our clients, Rydal and Bala Cheltenham, whom we will see more of in the following two chapters. The Cheltenhams are a fairly typical, prosperous American couple in their mid-to-late 40s with two teenage children. Rydal is a partner at a local law firm while Bala has a consulting business, which she runs mostly out of their home. With the help of a few mild sedatives, they are very, very happy.

The Cheltenhams' problems begin, although they certainly do not end, with some interesting capital gain issues. Among the couples' many assets are the following three items:

a. A stock portfolio, including stocks bought several years ago which have by and large increased in value (aggregate appreciation of $100,000), and a smaller number purchased more recently which have, alas, declined in value since purchase (for an aggregate decline of approximately $50,000 in value). About half of this decline is accounted for by stock in a family-owned restaurant business, which was started by Bala's brother, and which (as they say) has not been going as originally planned. The rest of the stocks are Fortune 500 companies.

b. A personal residence, which the Cheltenhams purchased for $200,000 about 15 years ago, and which is now worth approximately twice that amount ($400,000). The Cheltenhams financed the house with $50,000 in cash and a $150,000, 30-year mortgage, of which $100,000 in principal and a large amount of interest remains unpaid.

c. A piece of investment real estate, located in an industrial park a few miles from the Cheltenhams' home, which is occupied by various tenants and managed for the couple by a real estate management company. This investment has a cash value of approximately $500,000, but has a tendency to lose money, especially when depreciation is taken into account, and (unlike some other investments) has little emotional value to the couple.

In addition to these items the Cheltenhams have the usual run of cars, furniture, memorabilia, and toys and clothing that their children have long since outgrown.

As I said, you will see more of the Cheltenhams in the near future; but for now, you may content yourselves with the following questions:

1. The Cheltenhams have been thinking about selling stock in the next few years, particularly as they begin to run into college expenses for their two children. This

has led them to be concerned about capital gain and loss consequences of the possible transactions. Specifically, they want to know about the following tax reduction strategies:

a. To what extent, if any, can they offset potential gains on the sale of their appreciated stock by selling stock that has declined in value? Assuming that they can, does this make sense from a business as well as a tax angle? Why (or why not)?

b. The couple is being pressed to invest more money in Bala's brother's restaurant, to avoid harm to the family reputation if the business should fail. What are the tax (and especially the capital gain or loss) implications of such an investment, and how important should these be as compared to business or family considerations?

c. Are there any other ways in which the stock in the restaurant business might be treated differently for tax purposes than the rest of the Chelthenhams' investment portfolio, and what specific facts would be relevant to this determination?

2. The prospect of paying for college, together with a general sense that they are no longer children, has got the Cheltenhams thinking about their long-term financial strategy and its tax implications. Aside from the capital gain issues discussed above, what additional tax-related issues should the Cheltenhams be thinking about, and what steps if any can they take to improve their overall tax situation?

3. What additional facts, if any, would you want to have in order to answer the questions above?

Chapter 10

TAXATION OF THE FAMILY UNIT

Up to this point in the course, we have focused on questions related to whether, when, and how much tax should be paid. This chapter introduces an additional question — who or whom should be the taxable unit? Should tax liabilities be assessed solely at the individual level, or should families sometimes be the appropriate unit for taxation?

An important reason why the choice of taxable unit matters arises because many taxpayers are subject to tax at different rates. The chapter begins with a discussion of the income-shifting or assignment-of-income problem, wherein taxpayers facing higher marginal rates attempt to have a portion of their income assigned to taxpayers facing lower marginal rates. This problem was extremely important a generation ago, when tax rates ranged from 11 to 70 percent, and shifting the tax burden from one person to another could result in enormous tax savings. Today, tax rates are more flat, ranging from 10 to about 40 percent, and many common income-shifting techniques — in particular those using trusts or minor children — are prohibited by statute. Yet "who is the taxpayer" remains an important question, most notably within family groups, where there may be both tax and nontax reasons for attempting to transfer income among different family members.

Following a discussion of the assignment of income problem, the chapter considers events — marriage, divorce, and death — that are uniquely personal or familial in nature. While hardly anyone marries or divorces for tax reasons, and presumably no one dies for them, these events are often the occasion for significant, long-term tax planning. The chapter thus discusses marriage and divorce tax issues, including the tax treatment of alimony and the distinction between alimony, child support, and pre- or post-nuptial payments. The chapter finishes with a brief policy-oriented overview of the estate and gift taxes. These issues are of vital importance not only for the wealthy or powerful, but for ordinary taxpayers, as well.

Questions related to the taxation of the family unit necessarily raise the issue of who is married. Accordingly, this chapter will consider the effect of the tax laws on unmarried, gay, and other "nontraditional" couples, yet a further intersection between tax law and broader social policy.

I. ASSIGNMENT OF INCOME AND THE "WHO IS THE TAXPAYER?" PROBLEM

A. The Motivation for Income-Shifting and the Anti-Assignment Rule

The concern over income-shifting is almost exclusively a function of tax rates. Because of the progressive rate structure, it is usually more advantageous to split the same income between two or more taxpayers than to have the entire amount taxed to one person. Consider a simple example, in which A and B agree to pool their resources, A earning $100,000 in taxable income, and B providing untaxed household and other services. (To avoid offending anyone, we'll keep A and B genderless for the time being.) Let's assume further that the tax rate is 15 percent of the first $26,000, 28 percent up to $64,000, and 31 percent for the remaining income up to $100,000, which happens to have been roughly the rates on single taxpayers before Congress began major rate reductions and other changes in 2001 (explained as relevant below).

If all of the income is taxed to A, the aggregate income tax will be $25,700, computed as follows:

15% × 26,000 =	$3,900
28 % × 38,000 (64,000 – 26,000) =	$10,640
31% × 36,000 (100,000 – 64,000) =	$11,160
Total Tax =	$25,700

By contrast, if the income could be split 50-50 — $50,000 to A and $50,000 to B — the tax would be significantly lower, with each individual paying only $10,620 in tax, for a combined total of $21,240:

15% × 26,000 =	$3,900
28% × 24,000 (50,000 – 26,000) =	$6,720
Total tax (A or B) =	$10,620
Combined tax (A plus B) =	$21,240

Because A and B have now been permitted to split their income equally, they are in effect making two separate "trips" up the progressive rate scale, with twice the amount of income ($52,000 vs. $26,000) being taxed at the lowest, 15 percent rate, and the highest applicable rate (31 percent) now being avoided altogether. This effect is likely to be still greater when the effect of personal deductions, exemptions, and so forth is figured in. If A and B had two children, and were permitted to split the income four ways (*i.e.*, $25,000 each), the tax would be lower still, with all the income now being taxed solely at the 15 percent rate:

15% × 25,000 =	$3,750
Total Tax (A, B, C, or D) =	$3,750
Combined Tax (A, B, C, and D) =	$15,000

It should be noted that none of the above is an accident, but rather the inevitable result of the combination of progressive taxation with a (largely) individual tax system. The whole point of progressivity is to tax high incomes more than low ones: one person earning $100,000 is considered to have more tax-paying capacity than four people earning $25,000 each, who have the same aggregate income but four times as many mouths to feed and (presumably) more other expenses, as well. In this view it is only fair that "divided" income should be taxed less than the unified sort. Yet it seems bizarre to allow such facile, manipulative tax reduction. To prevent such a result, the courts long ago developed a rule preventing "anticipatory assignments of income"; or, in plain English, requiring that income be taxed to the person who earns the income rather than to its recipient. Over time, there have arisen numerous exceptions to this principle — most notably, joint returns by married couples — and much of this area is now covered by statutes instead of case law. But the basic principles remain valid, and many of the newer statutes were written with the old, classic cases in mind.

LUCAS v. EARL
United States Supreme Court
281 U.S. 111 (1930)

Mr. Justice Holmes delivered the opinion of the Court.

This case presents the question whether the respondent, Earl, could be taxed for the whole of the salary and attorney's fees earned by him in the years 1920 and 1921, or should be taxed for only a half of them in view of a contract with his wife which we shall mention. The Commissioner of Internal Revenue and the Board of Tax Appeals imposed a tax upon the whole, but their decision was reversed by the Circuit Court of Appeals, 30 F.2d 898. A writ of *certiorari* was granted by this Court.

By the contract, made in 1901, Earl and his wife agreed "that any property either of us now has or may hereafter acquire . . . in any way, either by earnings (including salaries, fees, etc.), or any rights by contract or otherwise, during the existence of our marriage, or which we or either of us may receive by gift, bequest, devise, or inheritance, and all the proceeds, issues, and profits of any and all such property shall be treated and considered and hereby is declared to be received, held, taken, and owned by us as joint tenants, and not otherwise, with the right of survivorship." The validity of the contract is not questioned, and we assume it to be unquestionable under the law of the State of California, in which the parties lived. Nevertheless we are of opinion that the Commissioner and Board of Tax Appeals were right.

The Revenue Act of 1918 approved February 24, 1919, c. 18, §§ 210, 211, 212(a), 213(a), 40 Stat. 1057, 1062, 1064, 1065, imposes a tax upon the net income of every individual including "income derived from salaries, wages, or compensation for personal service . . . of whatever kind and in whatever form paid," § 213(a). The provisions of the Revenue Act of 1921, c. 136, 42 Stat. 227, in sections bearing the same numbers are similar to those of the above. A very forcible argument is presented to the effect that the statute seeks to tax only income beneficially received, and that taking the question more technically the salary and fees became the joint property of Earl and his wife on the very first instant on which they were received. We well might hesitate upon the latter proposition, because however the matter might stand between husband and wife he was the only party to the contracts by which the salary and fees were earned, and it is somewhat hard to say that the last step in the performance of those contracts could be taken by anyone but himself alone. But this case is not to be decided by attenuated subtleties. It turns on the import and reasonable construction of the taxing act. There is no doubt that the statute could tax salaries to those who earned them and provide that the tax could not be escaped by anticipatory arrangements and contracts however skillfully devised to prevent the salary when paid from vesting even for a second in the man who earned it. That seems to us the import of the statute before us and we think that no distinction can be taken according to the motives leading to the arrangement by which the fruits are attributed to a different tree from that on which they grew.

Judgment reversed.

THE CHIEF JUSTICE took no part in this case.

Understanding *Earl*

1. Mr. and Mrs. Earl entered into their income-sharing arrangement in 1901, at a time when there was as yet no income tax. (The income tax was enacted in 1913.) Why do you think they did so, and what relevance, if any, does this have for the case?

2. Justice Holmes' opinion says that income should be taxed to the person who earned it rather than its beneficial recipient. Could it be argued that Mrs. Earl, by providing traditional household services, had contributed to earning the income as well as spending it? If her contribution was in fact worthless, why did the couple get married, and why did Mr. Earl agree to the income-sharing arrangement in the first place?

3. *Lucas v. Earl*, together with numerous other tax cases, uses a "fruit and tree" metaphor to describe the difference between income and its underlying sources. What is the significance of this metaphor, and how helpful did you find it in understanding the case? What might be some of its practical, not to say linguistic, limitations?

POE v. SEABORN
United States Supreme Court
282 U.S. 101 (1930)

MR. JUSTICE ROBERTS delivered the opinion of the Court.

Seaborn and his wife, citizens and residents of the State of Washington, made for the year 1927 separate income tax returns as permitted by the Revenue Act of 1926, c. 27, § 223 (U.S.C. App., Title 26, § 964).

During and prior to 1927 they accumulated property comprising real estate, stocks, bonds and other personal property. While the real estate stood in his name alone, it is undisputed that all of the property, real and personal, constituted community property and that neither owned any separate property or had any separate income.

The income comprised Seaborn's salary, interest on bank deposits and on bonds, dividends, and profits on sales of real and personal property. He and his wife each returned one-half the total community income as gross income and each deducted one-half of the community expenses to arrive at the net income returned.

The Commissioner of Internal Revenue determined that all of the income should have been reported in the husband's return, and made an additional assessment against him. Seaborn paid under protest, claimed a refund, and on its rejection, brought this suit.

The District Court rendered judgment for the plaintiff (32 Fed. 2d 916); the Collector appealed, and the Circuit Court of Appeals certified to us the question whether the husband was bound to report for income tax the entire income, or whether the spouses were entitled each to return one-half thereof. This Court ordered the whole record to be sent up.

The case requires us to construe Sections 210(a) and 211(a) of the Revenue Act of 1926 (U.S.C. App., Tit. 26, §§ 951 and 952), and apply them, as construed, to the interests of husband and wife in community property under the law of Washington. These sections lay a tax upon the net income of every individual. The Act goes no farther, and furnishes no other standard or definition of what constitutes an individual's income. The use of the word "of" denotes ownership. It would be a strained construction, which, in the absence of further definition by Congress, should impute a broader significance to the phrase.

The Commissioner concedes that the answer to the question involved in the cause must be found in the provisions of the law of the State, as to a wife's ownership of or interest in community property. What, then, is the law of Washington as to the ownership of community property and of community income, including the earnings of the husband's and wife's labor?

The answer is found in the statutes of the State, and the decisions interpreting them.

These statutes provide that, save for property acquired by gift, bequest, devise or inheritance, all property however acquired after marriage, by either husband or wife, or by both, is community property. On the death of either spouse, his or her interest is subject to testamentary disposition, and failing that, it passes to the issue of the decedent and not to the surviving spouse. While the husband has the management and control of community personal property and like power of disposition thereof as of his separate personal property, this power is subject to restrictions which are inconsistent with denial of the wife's interest as co-owner. The wife may borrow for community purposes and bind the community property (*Fielding v. Ketler*, 86 Wash. 194). Since the husband may not discharge his separate obligation out of community property, she may, suing alone, enjoin collection of his separate debt out of community property (*Fidelity & Deposit Co.*

v. Clark, 144 Wash. 520). She may prevent his making substantial gifts out of community property without her consent (*Parker v. Parker*, 121 Wash. 24). The community property is not liable for the husband's torts not committed in carrying on the business of the community (*Schramm v. Steele*, 97 Wash. 309).

The books are full of expressions such as "the personal property is just as much hers as his" (*Marston v. Rue*, 92 Wash. 129); "her property right in it [an automobile] is as great as his" (92 Wash. 133); "the title of one spouse . . . was a legal title as well as that of the other" (*Mabie v. Whittaker*, 10 Wash. 656, 663).

Without further extending this opinion it must suffice to say that it is clear the wife has, in Washington, a vested property right in the community property, equal with that of her husband; and in the income of the community, including salaries or wages of either husband or wife, or both. A description of the community system of Washington and of the rights of the spouses, and of the powers of the husband as manager, will be found in *Warburton v. White*, 176 U.S. 484.

The taxpayer contends that if the test of taxability under Sections 210 and 211 is ownership, it is clear that income of community property is owned by the community and that husband and wife have each a present vested one-half interest therein.

The Commissioner contends, however, that we are here concerned not with mere names, nor even with mere technical legal titles; that calling the wife's interest vested is nothing to the purpose, because the husband has such broad powers of control and alienation, that while the community lasts, he is essentially the owner of the whole community property, and ought so to be considered for the purposes of Sections 210 and 211. He points out that as to personal property the husband may convey it, may make contracts affecting it, may do anything with it short of committing a fraud on his wife's rights. And though the wife must join in any sale of real estate, he asserts that the same is true, by virtue of statutes, in most States which do not have the community system. He asserts that control without accountability is indistinguishable from ownership, and that since the husband has this, *quoad* community property and income, the income is that "of" the husband under Sections 210–211 of the income tax law.

We think, in view of the law of Washington above stated, this contention is unsound. The community must act through an agent. This Court has said with respect to the community property system (*Warburton v. White*, 176 U.S. 484) that "property acquired during marriage with community funds became an acquet of the community and not the sole property of the one in whose name the property was bought, although by the law existing at the time the husband was given the management, control and power of sale of such property. This right being vested in him, not because he was the exclusive owner, but because by law, he was created the agent of the community."

In that case, it was held that such agency of the husband was neither a contract nor a property right vested in him, and that it was competent to the legislature which created the relation to alter it, to confer the agency on the wife alone, or to confer a joint agency on both spouses, if it saw fit, — all without infringing any property right of the husband. *See, also, Arnett v. Reade*, 220 U.S. 311 at 319.

The reasons for conferring such sweeping powers of management on the husband are not far to seek. Public policy demands that in all ordinary circumstances, litigation between wife and husband during the life of the community should be discouraged. Law-suits between them would tend to subvert the marital relation. The same policy dictates that third parties who deal with the husband respecting community property shall be assured that the wife shall not be permitted to nullify his transactions. The powers of partners, or of trustees of a spendthrift trust, furnish apt analogies.

The obligations of the husband as agent of the community are no less real because the policy of the State limits the wife's right to call him to account in a court. Power is not synonymous with right. Nor is obligation coterminous with legal remedy. The law's investiture of the husband with broad powers by no means negatives the wife's present interest as a co-owner.

We are of opinion that under the law of Washington the entire property and income of the community can no more be said to be that of the husband, than it could rightly be termed that of the wife.

We should be content to rest our decision on these considerations. Both parties have, however, relied on executive construction and the history of the income tax legislation as supporting their respective views. We shall, therefore, deal with these matters.

The taxpayer points out that, following certain opinions of the Attorney General, the Decisions and Regulations of the Treasury have uniformly made the distinction that while under California law the wife's interest in community property amounts to a mere expectancy contingent on her husband's death and does not rise to the level of a present interest, her interest under the laws of Washington, Arizona, Texas and some other states is a present vested one. They have accordingly denied husband and wife the privilege of making separate returns of one-half the community income in California, but accorded that privilege to residents of such other states.

He relies further upon the fact that Congress has thrice, since these Decisions and Regulations were promulgated, re-enacted the income tax law without change of the verbiage found in §§ 210(a) and 211(a), thus giving legislative sanction to the executive construction. He stands also on the fact that twice the Treasury has suggested the insertion of a provision,[1] which would impose the tax on the husband in respect of the whole community income, and that Congress has not seen fit to adopt the suggestion.

On the other hand the Commissioner says that, granted the truth of these assertions, a different situation has been created as respects 1926 and subsequent years. For in the 1926 Act there was inserted a section which plainly indicated an

---

[1] [6] The provision desired by the Treasury was as follows: "Income received by any community shall be included in the gross income of the spouse having management and control of the community property." This clause was in the 1921 Act as passed by the House. It was stricken out in the Senate. When the 1924 Act was introduced it contained the same provision, which was stricken out by the Ways and Means Committee and not re-inserted.

intent to leave this question open for the future in States other than California, while closing it for past years.

We attribute no such intent to the section as is ascribed to it by the Commissioner. We think that although Congress had twice refused to change the wording of the Act, so as to tax community income to the husband in Washington and certain other states, in view of our decision in *United States v. Robbins*, 269 U.S. 315, it felt we might overturn the executive construction and assimilate the situation in Washington to that we had determined existed in California. Section 1212 therefore was merely inserted to prevent the serious situation as to resettlements, additional assessments and refunds which would follow such a decision.

The same comments apply to the Joint Resolution No. 88, 71st Congress, on which the Commissioner relies.

It is obvious that this resolution was intended to save the Government's right of resettlement, in event that the proposed test suits, of which this is one, should be decided in favor of the Government's present contention. See the Report of the Ways and Means Committee on the resolution (Cong. Record, June 11, 1930, pp. 10923–10925).

On the whole, we feel that, were the matter less clear than we think it is, on the words of the income tax law as applied to the situation in Washington, we should be constrained to follow the long and unbroken line of executive construction, applicable to words which Congress repeatedly reemployed in acts passed subsequent to such construction, (*New York v. Illinois*, 278 U.S. 367; *National Lead Co. v. United States*, 252 U.S. 140; *United States v. Farrar*, 281 U.S. 624), re-enforced, as it is, by Congress' refusal to change the wording of the Acts to make community income in states whose law is like that of Washington returnable as the husband's income.

The Commissioner urges that we have, in principal, decided the instant question in favor of the Government. He relies on *United States v. Robbins*, 269 U.S. 315; *Corliss v. Bowers*, 281 U.S. 376, and *Lucas v. Earl*, 281 U.S. 111.

In the *Robbins* case, we found that the law of California, as construed by her own courts, gave the wife a mere expectancy and that the property rights of the husband during the life of the community were so complete that he was in fact the owner. Moreover, we there pointed out that this accorded with the executive construction of the Act as to California.

The *Corliss* case raised no issue as to the intent of Congress, but as to its power. We held that where a donor retains the power at any time to revest himself with the principal of the gift, Congress may declare that he still owns the income. While he has technically parted with title, yet he in fact retains ownership, and all its incidents. But here the husband never has ownership. That is in the community at the moment of acquisition.

In the *Earl* case a husband and wife contracted that any property they had or might thereafter acquire in any way, either by earnings (including salaries, fees, etc.), or any rights by contract or otherwise, "shall be treated and considered and hereby is declared to be received held taken and owned by us as joint tenants. . . ." We held that, assuming the validity of the contract under local law, it still remained true that the husband's professional fees, earned in years subsequent to the date of the contract, were his individual income, "derived from salaries, wages, or compensation for personal services" under §§ 210, 211, 212(a) and 213 of the Revenue Act of 1918. The very assignment in that case was bottomed on the fact that the earnings would be the husband's property, else there would have been nothing on which it could operate. That case presents quite a different question from this, because here, by law, the earnings are never the property of the husband, but that of the community.

Finally the argument is pressed upon us that the Commissioner's ruling will work uniformity of incidence and operation of the tax in the various states, while the view urged by the taxpayer will make the tax fall unevenly upon married people. This argument cuts both ways. When it is remembered that a wife's earnings are a part of the community property equally with her husband's, it may well seem to those who live in states where a wife's earnings are her own, that it would not tend to promote uniformity to tax the husband on her earnings as part of his income. The answer to such argument, however, is, that the constitutional requirement of uniformity is not intrinsic, but geographic. *Billings v. United States*, 232 U.S. 261, Treas. Dec. 34429; *Head Money Cases*, 112 U.S. 580; *Knowlton v. Moore*, 178 U.S. 41. And differences of state law, which may bring a person within or without the category designated by Congress as taxable, may not be read into the Revenue Act to spell out a lack of uniformity. *Florida v. Mellon*, 273 U.S. 12.

The District Court was right in holding that the husband and wife were entitled to file separate returns, each treating one-half of the community income as his or her respective income, and its judgment is

Affirmed.

THE CHIEF JUSTICE and MR. JUSTICE STONE took no part in the consideration or decision of this case.

Understanding *Seaborn*

1.   *Poe v. Seaborn* allows the taxpayers to achieve essentially the same result that was prohibited in *Lucas v. Earl*, because the division of their income takes place pursuant to state law (the community property statute) rather than private agreement. Is this a relevant difference? How does the *Seaborn* Court distinguish *Earl*, and do you find this distinction convincing?

2.   The Court takes considerable pains to analyze the Washington statute and its alleged protection of women on financial and other grounds. Is any of this relevant to the assignment of income problem? Or could one argue that, by enacting a "progressive" measure designed to provide women with at least some financial independence, Washington and other states had earned a lower rate of tax on

married couples?[2] How do you think that the remaining, separate property states would have responded to this argument?

3. What is the purpose of community property laws, and how (if at all) does that relate to the issue in the case?

The issue of separate vs. community property states is now resolved by the existence of joint returns for married couples, as described in the succeeding materials. Under this rule, married couples may (and typically do) elect to be treated as a unit for income tax purposes, and are subject to a special set of tax rates designed specifically for that purpose. However, the rule against anticipatory assignments of income remains important with respect to other family members and in alternate contexts.

Using the Sources

Under the rules above, which of the following situations would constitute an anticipatory assignment of income, the income remaining taxable to the assignor, and which would result in a successful shifting of tax to the assignee?

a. An agreement by a mother to split income with her husband and the couple's three adult children.

b. Same as a., but the children are minors and the money is for their support.

c. An account receivable ("IOU") from a customer for services already rendered, which a businessman assigns to an adult member of his family.

d. Same as c., except five years have passed since the services were rendered.

e. A piece of income-producing real estate, which a mother assigns to her adult son, who supports himself with the income.

f. The copyright for his new book, which a father assigns to his adult daughter in the expectation that she will use it to receive royalty income.

g. Same as f., except that the father has already entered into a contract with a publishing company, and assigns his daughter the right to income under the contract.

h. Same as g., except that the father makes a prospective assignment of "the copyrights from any books that I may produce during the next five years and any royalty income arising from such copyrights."

Law and Planning

Suppose that you were the Earls' tax lawyer, immediately following the Supreme Court's decision in the case bearing your name. The Earls are stubborn people and would like to find another way to reduce their tax burden without sacrificing their personal goals. What might you advise them to do in order to

---

[2] Today's community property laws tend to provide a higher degree of equality between the spouses than that observed in *Poe v. Seaborn*.

reduce their tax burden, and do you think it would withstand the likely IRS scrutiny? (Hint: See Question b. under "Using the Sources," above.)

Politics and Policy

The issue of separate vs. community property states comes up frequently under the income, estate, and gift taxes. Not surprisingly, the community property states, most of which are west of the Mississippi, tend to say that community property should be respected when it results in a lower aggregate tax burden, and ignored when it results in higher taxes. The remaining states are equally self-interested.

What approach to community property makes the most sense to you, or should the answer depend upon the circumstances of the particular case? What is the reason for community property in the first place, and what if anything does this tell you about its tax treatment? As a general rule, should federal tax courts be bound by state decisions on non-tax legal issues, or should they be free to make their own decisions without regard to State law on marriage, property, and other similar matters? Why?

B.   Joint Returns, the "Kiddie Tax," and the Issue of Unmarried and Gay Couples

The holdings in *Lucas v. Earl* and *Poe v. Seaborn* created a situation in which vastly different taxes were paid by otherwise similar couples who happened to reside in different States. Whatever the policy merits, it was politically untenable to maintain this system indefinitely. The only real question was which system would apply for everybody: a system that regarded a husband and wife as two distinct taxpayers or one which treated them as a combined taxable unit. After experimenting with various solutions, Congress in 1948 adopted the current joint return system, which essentially allowed everyone the advantage that had previously been available only in community property jurisdictions.

Since 1948, the tax brackets applying to married couples have been larger than — but not necessarily twice as large as — the tax brackets that apply to unmarried persons.[3] For example, for the 2000 calendar year, the 28 (as opposed to 15) percent tax bracket began for single individuals at $26,250, but for married couples at $43,850. Under this system, if one person earning $53,500 married another person with no cash income, their taxes would decline, since $43,850 rather than $26,250 would qualify for tax at the lower, 15 percent level. However, if two wage-earners married each other, there was a substantial possibility that their combined income taxes would increase, since they previously benefited from the right to tax $53,500 (*i.e.*, 2 × $26,250) at a 15 percent rate, but would henceforth have the same benefit for about $10,000 less of income. At higher incomes, this effect might be more pronounced. One may object that two-earner, middle-class couples are not

---

[3] In addition to the single and married rates there is a "head of household" category, with rates somewhere between the single and married level, for people who are not married but have the responsibility of supporting children or other dependents. There is also the option for married people to file separate returns although the tax brackets in this case are so set up that there will rarely be a tax advantage in filing a separate return.

the most oppressed group in American society, or that married couples benefit from many other advantageous tax provisions, but the so-called "marriage penalty" struck many people as unfair and even perverse in a society that purports to encourage marriage as a social institution. And, needless to say, many such people vote.

In 2001, as part of a broader, phased-in tax reduction, the Republican-controlled Congress enacted legislation that significantly reduced the supposed marriage penalty. The 2001 legislation set the married tax brackets for the 10 percent and 15 percent rate brackets to kick in at exactly twice the amounts for the equivalent single taxpayers, thus mostly eliminating the marriage penalty for low-income taxpayers. The legislation also reduced the marriage penalty for higher-income taxpayers, but to a lesser extent. As this edition goes to press, many elements of the 2001 tax legislation — including those that reduced the marriage penalty — are scheduled to expire beginning in 2011. It remains to be seen to what extent Congress and the Obama Administration will actually allow these tax cuts to expire. But regardless of what happens in 2011, if history is a guide, the relative tax treatment of married and single taxpayers will be changed frequently in the decades to come.

If joint returns are provided for married couples, what about gay or (for that matter) heterosexual couples who live together without benefit of marriage? The historic IRS position has been to allow joint return tax treatment only for legally married, heterosexual couples. As various states (*e.g.*, Vermont) begin to recognize homosexual marriages, do you expect this situation to change? Should it?

DRUKER v. COMMISSIONER
United States Court of Appeals, Second Circuit
697 F.2d 46 (1982)

FRIENDLY, CIRCUIT JUDGE:

We have here an appeal by taxpayers and a cross-appeal by the Commissioner from a judgment after trial before Chief Judge Tannenwald of the Tax Court, Chief Judge Tannenwald of the Tax Court, 77 T.C. 867 (1981).

I.

The principal issue on the taxpayers' appeal is the alleged unconstitutionality of the so-called "marriage penalty." The issue relates to the 1975 and 1976 income tax returns of James O. Druker and his wife Joan. During the tax years in question James was employed as a lawyer, first by the United States Attorney for the Eastern District of New York and later by the District Attorney of Nassau County, New York, and Joan was employed as a computer programmer. For each of the two years they filed separate income tax returns, checking the status box entitled "married filing separately". In computing their respective tax liabilities, however, they applied the rates in I.R.C. § 1(c) for "Unmarried individuals" rather than the higher rates prescribed by § 1(d) for "Married individuals filing separate returns." Prior to undertaking this course of action, James consulted with the United States

Attorney for the Eastern District and with members of the Intelligence Division of the IRS, explaining that he and his wife wanted to challenge the constitutionality of the "marriage penalty" without incurring liability for fraud or willfulness. Following these conversations they filed their returns as described, attaching to each return a letter explaining that, although married, they were applying the tax tables for single persons because they believed that the "income tax structure unfairly discriminates against working married couples" in violation of the equal protection clause of the fourteenth amendment. The Tax Court rejected this constitutional challenge, sustaining the Commissioner's determination that the Drukers were subject to tax at the rates provided in § 1(d) for married persons filing separately.

Determination of the proper method for federal taxation of the incomes of married and single persons has had a long and stormy history. *See generally*, Bittker, *Federal Income Taxation and the Family*, 27 STAN. L. REV. 1389, 1399–1416 (1975). From the beginning of the income tax in 1913 until 1948 each individual was taxed on his or her own income regardless of marital status. Thus, as a result of the progressive nature of the tax, two married couples with the same aggregate income would often have very different tax liabilities — larger if most of the income belonged to one spouse, smaller as their incomes tended toward equality. The decision in *Poe v. Seaborn*, 282 U.S. 101 (1930), that a wife was taxable on one half of community income even if this was earned solely by the husband, introduced a further element of geographical inequality, since it gave married couples in community property states a large tax advantage over similarly situated married couples with the same aggregate income in common law states.

After *Poe* the tax status of a married couple in a community property state differed from that of a married couple in a common law state in two significant respects. First, each community property spouse paid the same tax as an unmarried person with one-half the aggregate community income, whereas each common law spouse paid the same tax as an unmarried person with the same individual income. Consequently, marriage usually reduced a couple's tax burden if they resided in a community property state but was a neutral tax event for couples in common law states. Second, in community property states all married couples with the same aggregate income paid the same tax, whereas in common law states a married couple's tax liability depended on the amount of income each spouse earned. *See* Bittker, *supra*, 27 STAN. L. REV. at 1408.

The decision in *Poe* touched off something of a stampede among common law states to introduce community property regimes and thereby qualify their residents for the privilege of income splitting. The Supreme Court's subsequent decision in *Commissioner v. Harmon*, 323 U.S. 44 (1944), that the income-splitting privileges did not extend to couples in states whose community property systems were elective, slowed but did not halt this movement. The result was considerable confusion and much upsetting of expectations founded on long experience under the common law. Congress responded in 1948 by extending the benefits of "income splitting" to residents of common law as well as community property states. Revenue Act of 1948, ch. 168, 62 Stat. 110. Pursuant to this Act, every married couple was permitted to file a joint return and pay twice the tax that a single individual would pay on one-half of their total income. This in effect taxed a married couple as if they were two single individuals each of whom earned half of the couple's combined income. The Act not only reduced the tax burden on married couples in common law states; it also ensured that all married couples with the same aggregate income paid the same tax regardless of the state in which they lived ("geographical uniformity") and regardless of the relative income contribution of each spouse ("horizontal equity").

While the 1948 Act was good news for married couples, it placed singles at a serious disadvantage. The tax liability of a single person was now sometimes as much as 41% greater than that of a married couple with the same income. S. Rep. No. 552, 91st Cong., 1st Sess. 260 (1969). Although constitutional challenges to the "singles' penalty" were uniformly rejected, [Citations omitted] the single taxpayer obtained some relief from Congress. The Tax Reform Act of 1969, Pub. L. No. 91-172, 83 Stat. 487 (1969), increased the number of tax schedules from two to four: § 1(a) for married couples filing jointly; § 1(b) for unmarried heads of households; § 1(c) for unmarried individuals; and § 1(d) for married individuals filing separately.[4] The schedules were set so that a single person's tax liability under § 1(c) would never be more than 120% that of a married couple with the same income filing jointly under § 1(a). See S. Rep. No. 552, supra, at 260–62.

The 1969 reform spawned a new class of aggrieved taxpayers — the two wage-earner married couple whose combined tax burden, whether they chose to file jointly under § 1(a) or separately under § 1(d), was now greater than it would have been if they had remained single and filed under § 1(c). It is this last phenomenon which has been characterized, in somewhat loaded fashion, as the "marriage penalty" or "marriage tax."[5] Here, again, while constitutional attack has been unavailing, [Citations omitted] as well as the decision here under review, Congress has acted to provide relief. The Economic Recovery Tax Act of 1981, Pub. L. No. 97-34, § 103, 95 Stat. 172, 187, allows two-earner married couples a deduction from gross income, within specified limits, equal to 10% of the earnings of the lesser-earning spouse.

Subsequent to the decisions in *Johnson* and *Mapes*, the Supreme Court made explicit in *Zablocki v. Redhail*, 434 U.S. 374 (1978), what had been implicit in earlier decisions, that the right to marry is "fundamental." The Court, however, citing *Califano v. Jobst*, 434 U.S. 47 (1977), took care to explain that it did "not mean to suggest that every state regulation which relates in any way to the incidents of or prerequisites for marriage must be subjected to rigorous scrutiny. To the contrary, reasonable regulations that do not significantly interfere with decisions to enter into the marital relationship may be legitimately imposed." 434 U.S. at 386. Whereas differences in race, religion, and political affiliation are almost

---

[4] [1] The rates set under § 1(d) were the pre-1969 rates for single taxpayers. So disadvantageous is this schedule that only about 1% of married couples file separately. Staff of the Joint Committee on Taxation, Report on the Income Tax Treatment of Married Couples and Single Persons, 96th Cong., 2d Sess. 48 (1980). As a general rule, married taxpayers file separately only when they are so estranged from one another that they do not wish to sign a joint return or when separate filing enables one spouse to exceed the 7.5% of AGI floor for medical deductions.

[5] [2] Not all married couples are so "penalized." For the couple whose income is earned primarily or solely by one partner, marriage still offers significant tax savings.

always irrelevant for legislative purposes, "a distinction between married persons and unmarried persons is of a different character." *Jobst, supra,* 434 U.S. at 53. "Both tradition and common experience support the conclusion that marriage is an event which normally marks an important change in economic status." *Id.*

We do not doubt that the "marriage penalty" has some adverse effect on marriage; indeed, James Druker stated at argument that, having failed thus far in the courts, he and his wife had solved their tax problem by divorcing but continuing to live together. The adverse effect of the "marriage penalty", however, like the effect of the termination of social security benefits in *Jobst,* is merely "indirect"; while it may to some extent weigh the choice whether to marry, it leaves the ultimate decision to the individual. *See generally, Developments in Law — The Constitution and the Family,* 93 HARV. L. REV. 1156, 1255 (1980). The tax rate structure of I.R.C. § 1 places "no direct legal obstacle in the path of persons desiring to get married". *Zablocki, supra,* 434 U.S. at n. 12. Nor is anyone "absolutely prevented" by it from getting married, *id.* at 387. Moreover, the "marriage penalty" is most certainly not "an attempt to interfere with the individual's freedom [to marry]". *Jobst, supra,* 434 U.S. at 54. It would be altogether absurd to suppose that Congress, in fixing the rate schedules in 1969, had any invidious intent to discourage or penalize marriage — an estate enjoyed by the vast majority of its members. Indeed, as has been shown, the sole and express purpose of the 1969 reform was to provide some relief for the single taxpayer. *See* S. Rep. No. 552, *supra,* at 260–261. Given this purpose Congress had either to abandon the principle of horizontal equity between married couples, a principle which had been established by the 1948 Act and the constitutionality of which has not been challenged, or to impose a "penalty" on some two-earner married couples. It was put to this hard choice because, as Professor Bittker has shown, *supra,* 27 STAN. L. REV. at 1395–96, 1429–31, it is simply impossible to design a progressive tax regime in which all married couples of equal aggregate income are taxed equally and in which an individual's tax liability is unaffected by changes in marital status.[6] *See also* Tax Treatment of Single Persons and Married Persons Where Both Spouses Are Working: Hearings Before the House Committee on Ways and Means, 92d Cong., 2d Sess. 78–79 (1972) (Statement of Edwin S. Cohen, Assistant Secretary for Tax Policy) ("No algebraic equation, no matter how sophisticated, can solve this dilemma. Both ends of a seesaw cannot be up at the same time."); Note, *The Case for Mandatory Separate Filing by Married Persons,* 91 YALE L.J. 363, 365 n.6 (1982) (mathematical proof of the logical inconsistency among progressivity, marriage neutrality, and horizontal equity between married couples). Faced with this choice, Congress in 1969 decided to hold fast to horizontal equity, even at the price of imposing a "penalty" on two-earner married couples like the Drukers. There is nothing in the equal protection clause that required a different choice. Since the objectives sought by the 1969 Act — the maintenance of horizontal equity

---

[6] [3] Professor Bittker puts it thus, 27 STAN. L. REV. at 1430–31:

Another way to describe this collision of objectives is that the tax paid by a married couple must be (a) greater than they paid before marriage, in which event they are subject to a marriage penalty, (b) less than they paid before marriage, in which event unmarried persons are subject to a singles penalty, or (c) unchanged by marriage, in which event equal-income married couples are subject to unequal taxes.

and progressivity, and the reduction of the differential between single and married taxpayers — were clearly compelling, the tax rate schedules in I.R.C. § 1 can survive even the "rigorous scrutiny" reserved by *Zablocki* for measures which "significantly interfere" with the right to marry. *Cf. Johnson, supra*, 422 F. Supp. at 973–74. Clearly, the alternative favored by the Drukers, that married persons be permitted to file under § 1(c) if they so wish, would entail the loss of horizontal equity.

In the area of family taxation every legislative disposition is "virtually fated to be both over-inclusive and under-inclusive when judged from one perspective or another." The result, as Professor Bittker has well said, is that there "can be no peace in this area, only an uneasy truce." 27 STAN. L. REV. at 1443. Congress must be accorded wide latitude in striking the terms of that truce. The history we have reviewed makes clear that Congress has worked persistently to accommodate the competing interests and accomplish fairness. While we could elaborate still further, we think that this, along with the discussion in *Johnson, Mapes*, and in Chief Judge Tannenwald's opinion below, is sufficient to show that what the Drukers choose to call the "marriage penalty" deprived them of no constitutional right. Whether policy considerations warrant a further narrowing of the gap between the schedules applied to married and unmarried persons is for Congress to determine in light of all the relevant legislative considerations.

MUELLER v. COMMISSIONER
United States Tax Court
T.C. Memo 2000-132 (2000)

LARO, J:

On July 6, 1998, respondent issued a notice of deficiency to petitioner determining deficiencies in and additions to his Federal income taxes for the years and in the amounts as follows:

		Additions to Tax	
Year	Deficiency	Sec. 6651(a)(1)	Sec. 6654
1986	$12,067	$1,284	$165
1987	6,675	1,172	225
1988	28,231	7,058	1,816
1989	25,087	6,272	1,697
1990	32,125	8,031	2,103
1991	33,841	8,460	1,934
1992	32,282	8,071	1,408
1993	31,642	7,587	1,265
1994	23,751	4,617	928
1995	23,426	4,503	944

The issues for decision are:

(1) Whether petitioner is entitled to a filing status other than "single" in recognition of his claim that he has an "economic partnership" with a same-sex individual with whom he resided from 1989 to 1996; (2) whether petitioner is liable for the additions to tax determined by respondent under section 6651(a)(1); and (3) whether petitioner is liable for the additions to tax determined by respondent under section 6654. We hold for respondent on all issues.

Unless otherwise stated, section references are to the Internal Revenue Code in effect for the years in issue, and Rule references are to the Tax Court Rules of Practice and Procedure. Dollar amounts are rounded to the nearest dollar.

FINDINGS OF FACT

Petitioner resided in Chicago, Illinois, when he petitioned the Court. Petitioner did not file Federal income tax returns for any of the taxable years 1986 through 1995. During these years petitioner earned the bulk of his income by working as a computer programmer/consultant for various companies and hospitals. Petitioner also had small amounts of interest and capital gain income in 1987.

Petitioner made no estimated tax payments to the Internal Revenue Service with respect to any of the years in issue. However, petitioner had the following amounts withheld from his wages:

Year	Withholding
1987	$1,986
1993	$1,295
1994	$5,283
1995	$5,413

Petitioner is homosexual. In 1989, petitioner began a relationship with another man whom petitioner describes as his roommate and partner. From 1989 through 1995 petitioner and his partner resided together and shared assets and income. Petitioner was not married (to his partner or anyone else) as of December 31 for any of the taxable years 1986 through 1995. In the notice of deficiency mailed to petitioner, respondent determined that petitioner's proper filing status for income tax purposes for each year before the Court was single. Accordingly, respondent calculated the deficiencies and additions to tax using the tax rates applicable to unmarried individuals pursuant to section 1(c).

OPINION

Petitioner does not challenge the facts on which respondent's determinations are based.[7] Petitioner's sole claim in this case is that he should be accorded married, rather than single, filing status on his tax returns for the years 1989 to 1995. Petitioner does not claim to have ever been married. Rather, petitioner argues that

---

[7] [1] At trial petitioner alleged for the first time that he had suffered several theft losses during the years at issue. However, petitioner failed to substantiate any such losses and abandoned the argument on brief.

he had an "economic partnership" with his roommate and that he was unconstitutionally denied the opportunity to file a joint tax return with him in recognition of such partnership. Petitioner references a number of constitutional provisions, but we understand the crux of petitioner's constitutional claim to be that the tax code's unequal or differential treatment between married taxpayers and unmarried persons in an economic partnership constitutes a violation of the due process notions implicit in the Fifth Amendment and of the equal protection standards incorporated thereunder.[8]

We have consistently denied constitutional challenges to marital classifications in the tax code. These have included challenges brought by disadvantaged married taxpayers,[9] [citations omitted], as well as by disadvantaged singles. [Citations omitted.] Other Federal courts have similarly upheld marital classifications in the tax code. [Citations omitted.]

Petitioner seeks to add a new gloss to these old challenges by identifying singles who share assets and income (whom he labels "economic partners") as a distinct class of taxpayers disadvantaged by marital classifications. For the reasons set forth below, we hold the tax code's distinctions between married taxpayers and unmarried economic partners to be constitutionally valid.

In evaluating whether a statutory classification violates equal protection, we generally apply a rational basis standard. *See Regan v. Taxation With Representation*, 461 U.S. 540, 547 (1983). We apply a higher standard of review only if it is found that the statute (1) impermissibly interferes with the exercise of a fundamental right or (2) employs a suspect classification, such as race. *See, e.g., id.; Harris v. McRae*, 448 U.S. 297, 322 (1980). Neither of these exceptions applies.

Petitioner does not directly identify any fundamental right impeded by the use of marital classifications in the tax code. Petitioner cites commentary addressing the right to marry. However, a law is considered to burden the right to marry only where the obstacle to marriage imposed by the law operates to preclude marriage entirely for a certain class of persons. *See DeMars v. Commissioner, supra* at 250. The classifications at issue in this case are a consequence, not a cause, of petitioner's non-married status, and thus do not burden the right to marry. *See Druker v. Commissioner*, 697 F.2d 46 at 50.

The marital classifications at issue also do not affect petitioner as a member of a suspect class. Petitioner claims discrimination not as a homosexual but as a person who shares assets and income with someone who is not his legal spouse. Petitioner therefore places himself in a class that includes non-married couples of the opposite

---

[8] [2] The equal protection principles of the Fourteenth Amendment are encompassed within the Fifth Amendment as applied to Federal legislation. *See, e.g.*, Weinberger v. Wiesenfeld, 420 U.S. 636, 638 n.2 (1975); Hamilton v. Commissioner, 68 T.C. 603, 606 (1977).

[9] [3] Being accorded married status under the tax code is not always favorable. *See* U.S. General Accounting Office, Income Tax Treatment of Married and Single Individuals (Pub. No. GAO/GGD-96-175) (1996) (describing provisions in the tax code favoring single taxpayers over married taxpayers and vice versa); *see also* Cohen & Morris, *Tax Issues From* Father Knows Best *To* Heather Has Two Mommies, 84 TAX NOTES 1309 (Aug. 30, 1999) (describing the tax advantages and tax planning opportunities available to nonmarried couples).

sex, family members, and friends. We are aware of no authority that would render such group a suspect class.[10]

Under the rational basis standard, a challenged classification is valid if rationally related to a legitimate governmental interest. *See City of Cleburne v. Cleburne Living Ctr., Inc.*, 473 U.S. 432, 440 (1985); *City of New Orleans v. Dukes*, 427 U.S. 297, 303 (1976). In *Kellems v. Commissioner*, 58 T.C. 556 (1972), *affd.* 474 F.2d 1399 (2d Cir. 1973), we addressed the constitutionality of the application of single return rates without the income-splitting benefit available to married taxpayers. We held therein that the classification between married and single taxpayers is founded upon a rational basis and was a permissible attempt to account for the greater financial burdens of married taxpayers and to equalize geographically their tax treatment.[11] *See id.* at 558–559.

Our holding in *Kellems* is of no less application here. Congress had a rational basis for adopting marital classifications in the tax code. That conclusion is not altered by petitioner's claim that there are additional classifications that could have been made. Undoubtedly, certain inequalities persisted between married taxpayers and unmarried economic partners following the enactment of the joint filing provisions. However, legislatures have especially broad latitude in creating classification and distinctions in tax statutes. *See Regan v. Taxation With Representation, supra* at 547. Moreover, "reform may take one step at a time, addressing itself to the phase of the problem which seems most acute to the legislative mind." *Williamson v. Lee Optical Co.*, 348 U.S. 483, 489 (1955).

While petitioner makes several arguments on policy and sociological grounds, in the face of the cases cited above to the contrary, they have no legal bearing on the issues in this case. Whether policy considerations warrant narrowing of the gap between the tax treatment of married taxpayers and homosexual and other non-married economic partners is for Congress to determine in light of all the relevant legislative considerations. *See Druker v. Commissioner*, 697 F.2d at 51.

Accordingly, we sustain the deficiencies determined by respondent.[12]

---

[10] [4] Petitioner claims that the Federal tax laws specifically began to target homosexuals as a group after the enactment of the Defense of Marriage Act (DOMA), Pub. L. 104-199, 110 Stat. 2419 (1996). That law defines "marriage" in any act of Congress (which would include the Federal tax code) as a legal union "between one man and one woman" as husband and wife. The DOMA also defines the word "spouse" to mean only a person of the "opposite sex" who is a husband or wife. We decline to pass on the constitutionality of the DOMA because it was not effective for the years at issue in this case.

[11] [5] Prior to 1948 each individual was taxed on his or her own income regardless of marital status. However, under the Supreme Court's decision in Poe v. Seaborn, 282 U.S. 101 (1930), married couples in community property States were permitted to split their community income evenly for Federal tax purposes regardless of the amounts each actually earned. *See* Kellems v. Commissioner, 58 T.C. 556, 558–559 (1972), *affd. per curiam* 474 F.2d 1399 (2d Cir. 1973).

[12] [6] We also note that petitioner, as a nonfiler, would not be entitled to the relief he now seeks even if he had been married at the relevant times. Married taxpayers who fail to file returns are not entitled to application of the married filing jointly tax rates. [Citations omitted].

ADDITION TO TAX UNDER SECTION 6651(a)(1)

Respondent determined additions to tax under section 6651(a) for petitioner's failure to file his 1986 through 1995 Federal income tax returns. In order to avoid this addition to tax, petitioner must prove that his failure to file was: (1) Due to reasonable cause and (2) not due to willful neglect. *See* sec. 6651(a); Rule 142(a); *United States v. Boyle*, 469 U.S. 241, 245 (1985); *United States v. Nordbrock*, 38 F.3d 440 (9th Cir. 1994). A failure to file a timely Federal income tax return is due to reasonable cause if the taxpayer exercised ordinary business care and prudence and, nevertheless, was unable to file the return within the prescribed time. *See* sec. 301.6651-1(c)(1), Proced. & Admin. Regs. Willful neglect means a conscious, intentional failure to file or reckless indifference. See *United States v. Boyle, supra* at 245.

Petitioner has offered no evidence to show that his failure to file was due to reasonable cause and not willful neglect. The evidence is clear that petitioner's actions were deliberate, intentional, and in complete disregard of the statutes and respondent's regulations. Petitioner made no attempt to file an authentic tax return for any of the years at issue.

Petitioner offers the "excuse" that his non-filing was as an act of "non-violent civil disobedience" on a "human rights issue". As we stated in *Klunder v. Commissioner*, T.C. Memo 1991-489: "Petitioner wants the best of both worlds, to civilly disobey and also to be absolved of the additions to tax." Whether or not petitioner considers his non-filing an act of civil disobedience, he must accept the consequences of actions knowingly taken. *See Kahn v. United States*, 753 F.2d 1208, 1215–1216 (3d Cir. 1985); *United States v. Malinowski*, 472 F.2d 850, 857 (3d Cir. 1973); *Reiff v. Commissioner*, 77 T.C. 1169, 1177, 1180 (1981).

Accordingly, we sustain respondent's determination under section 6651(a)(1) for the taxable years in issue.

ADDITION TO TAX UNDER SECTION 6654(a)

Respondent further determined an addition to tax under section 6654(a) for each of the years in issue, asserting that petitioner failed to pay estimated tax. Section 6654(a) provides for an addition to tax "in the case of any underpayment of estimated tax by an individual." Estimated income tax payments are used to provide for current payment of income taxes not collected through withholding. Generally, this addition to tax is mandatory, and there is no exception for reasonable cause. See *Recklitis v. Commissioner*, 91 T.C. 874, 913 (1988); *Grosshandler v. Commissioner*, 75 T.C. 1, 20–21 (1980). However, no addition to tax is imposed if one of the exceptions contained in section 6654 is met. *See Recklitis v. Commissioner, supra* at 913.

Petitioner has offered no evidence to show that any of the statutory exceptions apply. Accordingly, we sustain respondent's determination under section 6654(a) for the taxable years in issue.

We have reviewed petitioner's other arguments and find them to be irrelevant or without merit.

Decision will be entered for respondent.

Understanding *Druker* and *Mueller*

1.   Do you agree with the *Druker* court's conclusion that higher tax rates do not constitute a significant impediment to marriage? Do you think the couple's decision to divorce (or so they say) in response to the higher tax rates was a normal response to this problem? How high would the tax difference have to be in order to affect such decisions, and would it matter if (say) the couple were a pair of high-flying stockbrokers, two young assistant professors, or a couple of middle-aged parents barely squeezing by on their "middle class" income? Which couple do you think would have been affected most by the so-called marriage penalty, and why?

2.   The logic of *Mueller* appears to be first that the taxpayer is not entitled to joint filing status since he made a voluntary decision not to marry, and second, that even if he had married his partner the marriage would not be recognized for Federal tax purposes under the Defense of Marriage Act.[13] What do you think of this logic? Does it create a sort of Catch-22 situation, in which gay couples are prohibited from marrying and then punished for their unmarried status? From the perspective of tax policy, is the logic behind joint returns (shared expenses, pooling of resources, etc.) any less relevant to a homosexual than a heterosexual ("straight") couple? Should it matter if the couple is married under local law, or simply living together and otherwise sharing their financial and other resources? If the latter, where would you draw the line between qualifying couples and others who were just friends?

3.   What do you make of the tax penalty issue in *Mueller*?

Because the issue of joint returns touches so directly on questions of morality and changing lifestyles, scholarship on this issue has probably changed more in the past generation than (say) writing on like-kind exchanges or the claim of right doctrine. Consider in this context the following excerpt.

Patricia A. Cain, *Heterosexual Privilege and the Internal Revenue Code*
34 U.S.F. L. Rev. 465 (2000)[14]

Stephanie Wildman has written persuasively about "privilege," with a focus on the invisible systems of privilege people enjoy on the basis of their race, gender, or sexual orientation. In a 1995 article, she said: "Heterosexuality is privileged over any other relationships. The words we use, such as marriage, husband, and wife, are not neutral, but convey this privileging of heterosexuality."

Laws that recognize only heterosexual marriage privilege heterosexuals by indicating their relationships are more valuable than same-sex relationships. Gary

---

[13] The IRS has reiterated that it will not accept joint tax returns filed by same-sex couples, even if gay marriage is recognized by their home state, citing the Defense of Marriage Act. *See* Allen Kenney, *IRS: Joint Filing Not Allowed for Same-Sex Married Couples*, 103 Tax Notes 1466 (June 21, 2004).

[14] Copyright © 2000. All rights reserved. Reprinted by permission.

Spitko has written about this expressive function of law in the case of intestacy statutes that fail to recognize any connection between lifetime partners of the same sex. Such laws cause harm that extends beyond the denial of a possible economic benefit, including the harm of stigmatization caused by the negative message.

The Internal Revenue Code ("Code") treats spouses differently from unmarried life partners. This is true no matter how financially and emotionally intertwined the unmarried partners are. This disparate treatment of unmarried partners, however, is not always negative when assessing immediate economic benefits. Indeed, the tax treatment of spouses can often be worse than the treatment of unmarried couples in terms of the resulting economic benefits or burdens. The marriage penalty is a prime example of how tax rules can sometimes burden married couples as compared with unmarried couples who are similarly situated. However, the difference in treatment between married and unmarried couples, whether the economic effect is beneficial to one class or the other, always carries stigmatic harm to the extent that the message heard by gay and lesbian taxpayers is that their relationships do not count. Closely related to this stigmatic harm is another hidden burden the Code has created in its privileging of heterosexual marriage. The Code presumes that persons are either married or live their lives with a fair degree of financial separation from others. The reality is that many same-sex, committed couples do not live in a world of financial separation. The tax laws, in effect, force them into a reporting stance that is not reflective of their day-to-day lives.

Thus, there are at least three separately identifiable harms that same-sex unmarried couples experience as a result of the Internal Revenue Code's privileging of heterosexual marriage. They are:

1) Denial of specific tax benefits granted to married couples;

2) Stigmatic harm from failing to accord recognition of same-sex relation-ships; and

3) Consequential harms or burdens caused by rules that either ignore same-sex relationships or presume that same-sex relationships do not exist.

This article will describe and elaborate on each of these types of harms. In offering these descriptions, I intend to make more visible some of the hidden privileges embodied in current tax laws. Too often, scholars tend to focus only upon the denial of benefits category. In debating whether or not the Code discriminates against same-sex couples, tax scholars have focused only on the first type of harm — the denial of specific tax benefits. Professor Steve Johnson, for example, has argued that to make a claim that the Code discriminates against same-sex couples, one must first add up the individual benefits and burdens imposed upon all same-sex couples before one can conclude legitimately that discrimination exists. While I do not intend my explanations in this article to serve as definitive proof of class-based discrimination, I do hope that the further explanations I offer about the harms caused will dispel the notion that discrimination in tax law should be viewed merely as a comparison of direct economic benefits and burdens.

* * *

I. Marital Status, Tax Benefits, and Tax Burdens

Marital status is important under the current federal tax law. Being married can create tax benefits or burdens. The marriage tax penalty, discussed below, is perhaps the most well-known potential burden imposed upon married couples. The way the tax rates are structured, married couples sometimes experience marriage bonuses and marriage penalties. Recent reports indicate that approximately half the married couples filing tax returns report bonuses and half report penalties.

Other burdens married couples may experience as a result of the tax law's treatment of spouses include burdens stemming from: (1) the constructive ownership of stock; (2) the limitations on qualified mortgage interest deductions; (3) the non-recognition of gains on sales or exchanges between spouses; and (4) the non-recognition of losses on sales or exchanges between spouses.

These burdens, as well as the marriage penalty burden caused by the joint return rates, are often cited as examples of benefits to unmarried couples. Thus, when discussing the Code's denial of benefits to same-sex couples, it is necessary to consider these possible benefits resulting from Code provisions that burden spouses and other related parties.

* * *

Summary of Burdens Imposed on Married Couples

Thus, there are two types of burdens created by the current tax laws on married couples: anti-abuse rules and rules that presume a traditional one-earner family. The anti-abuse rules can be viewed as creating benefits for unmarried couples to the extent they can manipulate the tax rules to their benefit. However, to do so requires them to deny the reality that they do in fact operate as a couple, as a unit, and to run the risk they will in fact be treated as related parties under special tax rules or sham transaction theories. Thus, to claim that same-sex couples benefit from the related party rules is to overstate the benefit.

The other marriage burdening rules stem from the fact Congress has, over the years, enacted tax laws that presume a traditional one-earner family. While such tax rules deny benefits to married individuals as compared with their unmarried counterparts, heterosexual couples have the ability to opt out of the archaic model by electing not to marry. Those who do not opt out will continue to experience a loss of benefit until these rules are amended. So long as some married couples experience these burdens, all similarly-situated, unmarried couples can be viewed as experiencing a benefit. But the benefit is available to all unmarried couples, whether heterosexual or same-sex. The heterosexual privilege, in this case, is the privilege of choice.

* * *

———————

Whatever their political merits, joint returns at least eliminated the problem of assignments of income between husbands and wives, as observed in *Earl* and similar cases. Assignments between parents and children took a good deal longer to tackle.

The shifting of income to minor children is an obvious temptation under the tax laws. With the exception of a few rock bands and some very aggressive Internet users, most young children are likely to be in relatively low tax brackets. Assigning income to children — who, as any parent knows, are eventually going to wind up with it anyway — may thus result in a lower tax payment without any serious economic cost. This is particularly true if the assignment is made by means of trusts or similar arrangements which allow the parents at least some role in determining how the funds will be used.

Given the obvious benefits, it is somewhat surprising how long Congress let such arrangements go on. Only in 1986 did it enact section 1(g) of the Code, affectionately known as the "kiddie tax," which provided that most unearned income of children below age fourteen was to be taxed at their parents' tax rate. The "kiddie tax" was extended to children under 18 (as opposed to 14) years of age by the Tax Increase Prevention and Reconciliation Act of 2005. Additional legislation further extended the tax to 18 year olds as well as to all students under age 24, but in each case only if the child's earned income does not exceed one-half of his or her financial support.

This provision is a good example of how complicated even a relatively simple tax rule can be. First, the provision requires that a distinction be made between unearned (interest, dividends, etc.) and earned (Spice Girls-type) income, presumably on the theory that the former originated with the parents but the latter properly belongs to the individual, even a small one, who produced it. Second, there is a fairly substantial exemption amount, which is usually $500 but may be higher if the child has itemized deductions as well as income for the taxable year in question. (The provision imposes tax at the parents' tax rate, but the tax is still technically imposed on the child herself.) There is additionally the question of which parent's tax rate to impose in the case of divorce, separation, or similar conditions, which is usually resolved by using the tax rate of the custodial parent.

What about trusts, which are generally taxed separately from the individuals who created them, and may provide an attractive way to beat the kiddie tax and similar rules? Don't worry: Congress thought of that, too. Since 1986, the tax rates on trust income have generally been conformed to the rates on individual income, with a special rule combining different trusts that have substantially similar beneficiaries (section 643(f)). Additional rules (section 671 *et seq.*) provide for direct taxation of the grantor (*i.e.*, the individual creating the trust) if he or she retains excessive power over distribution of trust assets.

Using the Sources

What are the present law income tax advantages (if any) of each of the following? (Be as specific as possible; if you would need more facts, indicate what they would be.)

a. An assignment of income between spouses.

b. An assignment of income to a child under the age of 18.

c. A transfer of income-producing property (*e.g.*, stocks and bonds) to a child under the age of 18.

d. A transfer of income-producing property (*e.g.*, stocks and bonds) to a child over the age of 24.

e. A transfer of income-producing property (*e.g.*, stocks and bonds) to a trust for the benefit of family members.

Law and Planning

1. Your clients, Desmond and Mollie, are 35 years old and have approximately the same income. Desmond and Mollie are interested in getting married but are afraid to do so because of the so-called marriage penalty, which was reduced in 2001 but could soon reappear. Do you suggest that they see a psychiatrist, or is this a legitimate concern? If it is a concern, what if anything can they do to ameliorate it? What if the couple's names are Desmond and Marco, a gay couple who are thinking of being married in a state that recognizes gay marriages?

2. Twenty years have gone by and the (now married) couple have two children, Maxwell (age 19) and Rita (age 12), for whom they would like to begin to develop investment portfolios. In either or both cases, would it make sense for the parents to hold the investments in their own name or would it be preferable to transfer them to the children? What effect, if any, would section 1(g) have on your answer? (Consider only the income tax for the time being; ignoring any implications of the gift tax or estate taxes.)

3. Present law sharply restricts the benefits of married couples filing separately, by halving most of the benefits that would be applicable to married couples (*see, e.g.*, I.R.C. § 1(d)). Accordingly the overwhelming majority of married couples currently files joint returns. Under what circumstances, if any, would you counsel a married person to file a separate return? (Hint: Think about the couple's personal as well as tax situation.)

4. Under California's Domestic Registered Partner Laws, established in 1999 and more commonly known as "civil unions," registered same sex couples are subject to community property laws (in addition to receiving many of the other legal rights and responsibilities of marriage). Imagine you are giving tax advice to Desmond and Marco (a gay couple registered as domestic partners in California). Desmond makes $100,000 a year of income as a corporate lawyer, and Marco $20,000 a year as a bartender. How should they file their federal income taxes? Might the *Poe v. Seaborn* case be relevant to their situation?

Politics and Policy

1.   Assume you were tax advisor to a gay rights organization that had decided — notwithstanding the (sometime) tax advantages of unmarried status — to seek "joint return" status for gay couples, at least in states that recognized some form of gay marriage. How would you present this argument to Congress, the IRS, and the public? Consider the following arguments:

> a. Basic tax principles suggest that the Code should be neutral as between different personal choices and should not "legislate morality" by favoring one lifestyle over another.

> b. The logic underlying joint returns (shared expenses, joint pool of resources, etc.) is equally applicable to straight and gay couples.

> c. The general societal trend is toward acceptance of gay couples and the tax law should keep up with this trend.

Which of these arguments would you emphasize, and which do you think is most likely to be successful with each different audience? Do you think it would be a better strategy to request joint return treatment only for married gay couples, or would you extend your argument to all "unmarried" couples, whether homosexual or heterosexual in nature? Who do you think would be likely to support or oppose you in this effort?

Now assume that you were counsel to a conservative organization that sought to block the changes described above. How would you respond to these arguments, and what further points would you make on behalf of your position?

2.   A principal effect of joint returns is to tax the second (*i.e.*, lower) earner in a married couple at a rate which reflects the income of the higher earner (this effect is not changed by the 2001 amendments). What do you think is the likely effect of this on spouses — most frequently, women — who try to re-enter the job market after taking time off to have children? Would you favor a system of individual, separate tax returns as a way to deal with this problem?

C.   "Slices" of Income and the Fruits and Trees Problem

The fruit and tree analysis of *Lucas v. Earl* assumes a sharp distinction between income and property. If A gives B a piece of property — land, or stocks, or a bank account — the transfer itself will be exempt from income tax under section 102, and the income from the property will henceforth be taxed to B, rather than A. But if A tries to transfer income to B, without a transfer of any underlying property, the assignment is unsuccessful, and A continues to be taxed on the relevant income. (There may be a gift tax in both cases, but that's a different story.) This is indeed the essence of the "fruit and tree" analogy: one must transfer the underlying property (*i.e.*, the tree) in order to escape taxation, while the effort to strip away the income (*i.e.*, the fruit), without transferring the underlying tree that it grows upon, is not respected for tax purposes. Theoretically speaking, these same principles apply both to transfers of unearned income (rent, interest, dividends) and to salary and other earned income, although in the earned income case the metaphorical tree — *i.e.*, the assignor's earning capacity — would as a practical matter be all but impossible to transfer, anyway.

The fruit and tree analogy is problematic enough when one is dealing with naturally existing sources of income as in the foregoing materials. It becomes harder when people create artificial interests that deliberately straddle the income/property distinction. For example, in many trust arrangements, it is common to divide a piece of property into two interests, one of which represents the income from the property for some defined period (*i.e.*, a life estate or an estate for years) and the other of which represents the right to receive the property after that period is up (*i.e.*, the remainder interest). Sometimes these interests are divided even further, by assigning a fraction of the income interest to each of two or three people, or by distributing the income in some years to one person and in other years to another. In these situations, where the property interest itself consists of the right to receive income, the fruit and tree analogy starts to break down altogether. The problem is further complicated by the highly technical, esoteric terminology used in such arrangements, which frequently assigns different labels to the same underlying transaction.

The difficulties above are demonstrated by a celebrated pair of Supreme Court cases, *Blair* and *Horst*, that involve a similar issue but were decided in opposite fashion.

BLAIR v. COMMISSIONER
United States Supreme Court
300 U.S. 5 (1937)

Mr. Chief Justice Hughes delivered the opinion of the Court.

This case presents the question of the liability of a beneficiary of a testamentary trust for a tax upon the income which he had assigned to his children prior to the tax years and which the trustees had paid to them accordingly.

The trust was created by the will of William Blair, a resident of Illinois who died in 1899, and was of property located in that State. One-half of the net income was to be paid to the donor's widow during her life. His son, the petitioner Edward Tyler Blair, was to receive the other one-half and, after the death of the widow, the whole of the net income during his life. In 1923, after the widow's death, petitioner assigned to his daughter, Lucy Blair Linn, an interest amounting to $6000 for the remainder of that calendar year, and to $9000 in each calendar year thereafter, in the net income which the petitioner was then or might thereafter be entitled to receive during his life. At about the same time, he made like assignments of interests, amounting to $9000 in each calendar year, in the net income of the trust to his daughter Edith Blair and to his son, Edward Seymour Blair, respectively. In later years, by similar instruments, he assigned to these children additional interests, and to his son William McCormick Blair other specified interests, in the net income. The trustees accepted the assignments and distributed the income directly to the assignees.

The question first arose with respect to the tax year 1923 and the Commissioner of Internal Revenue ruled that the income was taxable to the petitioner. The Board of Tax Appeals held the contrary. 18 B. T. A. 69. The Circuit Court of Appeals reversed the Board, holding that under the law of Illinois the trust was a spendthrift trust and the assignments were invalid. *Commissioner v. Blair*, 60 F.2d 340. We denied *certiorari*. 288 U.S. 602.

Thereupon the trustees brought suit in the Superior Court of Cook County, Illinois, to obtain a construction of the will with respect to the power of the beneficiary of the trust to assign a part of his equitable interest and to determine the validity of the assignments he had made. The petitioner and the assignees were made defendants. The Appellate Court of Illinois, First District, after a review of the Illinois decisions, decided that the trust was not a spendthrift trust and upheld the assignments. *Blair v. Linn*, 274 Ill. App. 23. Under the mandate of the appellate court, the Superior Court of Cook County entered its decree which found the assignments to be "voluntary assignments of a part of the interest of said Edward Tyler Blair in said trust estate" and as such adjudged them to be valid.

At that time, there were pending before the Board of Tax Appeals proceedings involving the income of the trust for the years 1924, 1925, 1926 and 1929. The Board received in evidence the record in the suit in the state court and, applying the decision of that court, the Board overruled the Commissioner's determination as to the petitioner's liability. 31 B. T. A. 1192. The Circuit Court of Appeals again reversed the Board. That court recognized the binding effect of the decision of the state court as to the validity of the assignments but decided that the income was still taxable to the petitioner upon the ground that his interest was not attached to the corpus of the estate and that the income was not subject to his disposition until he received it. *Commissioner v. Blair*, 83 F.2d 655, 662.

Because of an asserted conflict with the decision of the state court, and also with decisions of circuit courts of appeals, we granted *certiorari*. October 12, 1936.

* * *

Third. The question remains whether, treating the assignments as valid, the assignor was still taxable upon the income under the federal income tax act. That is a federal question.

Our decisions in *Lucas v. Earl*, 281 U.S. 111, and *Burnet v. Leininger*, 285 U.S. 136, are cited. In the *Lucas* case the question was whether an attorney was taxable for the whole of his salary and fees earned by him in the tax years or only upon one-half by reason of an agreement with his wife by which his earnings were to be received and owned by them jointly. We were of the opinion that the case turned upon the construction of the taxing act. We said that "the statute could tax salaries to those who earned them and provide that the tax could not be escaped by anticipatory arrangements and contracts however skillfully devised to prevent the same when paid from vesting even for a second in the man who earned it." That was deemed to be the meaning of the statute as to compensation for personal service, and the one who earned the income was held to be subject to the tax. In *Burnet v. Leininger*, *supra*, a husband, a member of a firm, assigned future partnership income to his wife. We found that the revenue act dealt explicitly with the liability of partners as such. The wife did not become a member of the firm; the act specifically taxed the distributive share of each partner in the net income of the firm; and the husband by the fair import of the act remained taxable upon his distributive share. These cases are not on point. The tax here is not upon earnings which are taxed to the one who earns them. Nor is it a case of income attributable to a taxpayer by reason of the application of the income to the discharge of his obligation. *Old Colony Trust Co. v. Commissioner*, 279 U.S. 716; *Douglas v. Willcuts*, 296 U.S. 1, 9; *Helvering v. Stokes*, 296 U.S. 551; *Helvering v. Schweitzer*, 296 U.S. 551; *Helvering v. Coxey*, 297 U.S. 694. *See, also, Burnet v. Wells*, 289 U.S. 670, 677. There is here no question of evasion or of giving effect to statutory provisions designed to forestall evasion; or of the taxpayer's retention of control. *Corliss v. Bowers*, 281 U.S. 376; *Burnet v. Guggenheim*, 288 U.S. 280.

In the instant case, the tax is upon income as to which, in the general application of the revenue acts, the tax liability attaches to ownership. *See Poe v. Seaborn*, *supra*; *Hoeper v. Tax Commission*, 284 U.S. 206.

The Government points to the provisions of the revenue acts imposing upon the beneficiary of a trust the liability for the tax upon the income distributable to the beneficiary. But the term is merely descriptive of the one entitled to the beneficial interest. These provisions cannot be taken to preclude valid assignments of the beneficial interest, or to affect the duty of the trustee to distribute income to the owner of the beneficial interest, whether he was such initially or becomes such by valid assignment. The one who is to receive the income as the owner of the beneficial interest is to pay the tax. If under the law governing the trust the beneficial interest is assignable, and if it has been assigned without reservation, the assignee thus becomes the beneficiary and is entitled to rights and remedies accordingly. We find nothing in the revenue acts which denies him that status.

The decision of the Circuit Court of Appeals turned upon the effect to be ascribed to the assignments. The court held that the petitioner had no interest in the corpus of the estate and could not dispose of the income until he received it. Hence it was said that "the income was *his*" and his assignment was merely a direction to pay over to others what was due to himself. The question was considered to involve "the date when the income became transferable." 83 F.2d p. 662. The Government refers to the terms of the assignment, — that it was of the interest in the income "which the said party of the first part now is, or may hereafter be, entitled to receive during his life from the trustees." From this it is urged that the assignments "dealt only with a right to receive the income" and that "no attempt was made to assign any equitable right, title or interest in the trust itself." This construction seems to us to be a strained one. We think it apparent that the conveyancer was not seeking to limit the assignment so as to make it anything less than a complete transfer of the specified interest of the petitioner as the life beneficiary of the trust, but that with ample caution he was using words to effect such a transfer. That the state court so construed the assignments appears from the final decree which described them as voluntary assignments of interests of the petitioner "in said trust estate," and it was in that aspect that petitioner's right to make the assignments was sustained.

The will creating the trust entitled the petitioner during his life to the net income of the property held in trust. He thus became the owner of an equitable interest in the corpus of the property. *Brown v. Fletcher*, 235 U.S. 589, 598, 599; *Irwin v. Gavit*, 268 U.S. 161, 167, 168; *Senior v. Braden*, 295 U.S. 422, 432, 433; *Merchants' Loan & Trust Co. v. Patterson*, 308 Ill. 519, 530; 139 N.E. 912. By virtue of that interest he was entitled to enforce the trust, to have a breach of trust enjoined and to obtain redress in case of breach. The interest was present property alienable like any other, in the absence of a valid restraint upon alienation. *Commissioner v. Field*, 42 F.2d 820, 822; *Shanley v. Bowers*, 81 F.2d 13, 15. The beneficiary may thus transfer a part of his interest as well as the whole. *See* RESTATEMENT OF THE LAW OF TRUSTS, §§ 130, 132 *et seq.* The assignment of the beneficial interest is not the assignment of a chose in action but of the "right, title and estate in and to property." *Brown v. Fletcher, supra*; *Senior v. Braden, supra. See* BOGERT, TRUSTS AND TRUSTEES, vol. 1, § 183, pp. 516, 517; 17 COLUMBIA LAW REVIEW, 269, 273, 289, 290.

We conclude that the assignments were valid, that the assignees thereby became the owners of the specified beneficial interests in the income, and that as to these interests they and not the petitioner were taxable for the tax years in question. The judgment of the Circuit Court of Appeals is reversed and the cause is remanded with direction to affirm the decision of the Board of Tax Appeals.

Reversed.

HELVERING v. HORST
United States Supreme Court
311 U.S. 112 (1940)

MR. JUSTICE STONE delivered the opinion of the Court.

The sole question for decision is whether the gift, during the donor's taxable year, of interest coupons detached from the bonds, delivered to the donee and later in the year paid at maturity, is the realization of income taxable to the donor.

In 1934 and 1935 respondent, the owner of negotiable bonds, detached from them negotiable interest coupons shortly before their due date and delivered them as a gift to his son who in the same year collected them at maturity. The Commissioner ruled that under the applicable § 22 of the Revenue Act of 1934, the interest payments were taxable, in the years when paid, to the respondent donor who reported his income on the cash receipts basis. The Circuit Court of Appeals reversed the order of the Board of Tax Appeals sustaining the tax. We granted *certiorari*, because of the importance of the question in the administration of the revenue laws and because of an asserted conflict in principle of the decision below with that of *Lucas v. Earl*, 281 U.S. 111, and with that of decisions by other circuit courts of appeals. *See Bishop v. Commissioner*, 54 F.2d 298; *Dickey v. Burnet*, 56 F.2d 917, 921; *Van Meter v. Commissioner*, 61 F.2d 817.

The court below thought that as the consideration for the coupons had passed to the obligor, the donor had, by the gift, parted with all control over them and their payment, and for that reason the case was distinguishable from *Lucas v. Earl*, *supra*, and *Burnet v. Leininger*, 285 U.S. 136, where the assignment of compensation for services had preceded the rendition of the services, and where the income was held taxable to the donor.

The holder of a coupon bond is the owner of two independent and separable kinds of right. One is the right to demand and receive at maturity the principal amount of the bond representing capital investment. The other is the right to demand and receive interim payments of interest on the investment in the amounts and on the dates specified by the coupons. Together they are an obligation to pay principal and interest given in exchange for money or property which was presumably the consideration for the obligation of the bond. Here respondent, as owner of the bonds, had acquired the legal right to demand payment at maturity of the interest specified by the coupons and the power to command its payment to others, which constituted an economic gain to him.

Admittedly not all economic gain of the taxpayer is taxable income. From the beginning the revenue laws have been interpreted as defining "realization" of income as the taxable event, rather than the acquisition of the right to receive it. And "realization" is not deemed to occur until the income is paid. But the decisions and regulations have consistently recognized that receipt in cash or property is not the only characteristic of realization of income to a taxpayer on the cash receipts basis. Where the taxpayer does not receive payment of income in money or property realization may occur when the last step is taken by which he obtains the fruition of the economic gain which has already accrued to him. *Old Colony Trust Co. v. Commissioner*, 279 U.S. 716; *Corliss v. Bowers*, 281 U.S. 376, 378. *Cf. Burnet v. Wells*, 289 U.S. 670.

In the ordinary case the taxpayer who acquires the right to receive income is taxed when he receives it, regardless of the time when his right to receive payment accrued. But the rule that income is not taxable until realized has never been taken to mean that the taxpayer even on the cash receipts basis, who has fully enjoyed the benefit of the economic gain represented by his right to receive income, can escape taxation because he has not himself received payment of it from his obligor. The rule, founded on administrative convenience, is only one of postponement of the tax to the final event of enjoyment of the income, usually the receipt of it by the taxpayer, and not one of exemption from taxation where the enjoyment is consummated by some event other than the taxpayer's personal receipt of money or property. *Cf. Aluminum Castings Co. v. Routzahn*, 282 U.S. 92, 98. This may occur when he has made such use or disposition of his power to receive or control the income as to procure in its place other satisfactions which are of economic worth. The question here is, whether because one who in fact receives payment for services or interest payments is taxable only on his receipt of the payments, he can escape all tax by giving away his right to income in advance of payment. If the taxpayer procures payment directly to his creditors of the items of interest or earnings due him, *see Old Colony Trust Co. v. Commissioner, supra*; *Bowers v. Kerbaugh-Empire Co.*, 271 U.S. 170; *United States v. Kirby Lumber Co.*, 284 U.S. 1, or if he sets up a revocable trust with income payable to the objects of his bounty, §§ 166, 167, Revenue Act of 1934; *Corliss v. Bowers, supra*; *cf. Dickey v. Burnet*, 56 F.2d 917, 921, he does not escape taxation because he did not actually receive the money. *Cf. Douglas v. Willcuts*, 296 U.S. 1; *Helvering v. Clifford*, 309 U.S. 331.

Underlying the reasoning in these cases is the thought that income is "realized" by the assignor because he, who owns or controls the source of the income, also controls the disposition of that which he could have received himself and diverts the payment from himself to others as the means of procuring the satisfaction of his wants. The taxpayer has equally enjoyed the fruits of his labor or investment and obtained the satisfaction of his desires whether he collects and uses the income to procure those satisfactions, or whether he disposes of his right to collect it as the means of procuring them. *Cf. Burnet v. Wells, supra.*

Although the donor here, by the transfer of the coupons, has precluded any possibility of his collecting them himself, he has nevertheless, by his act, procured payment of the interest as a valuable gift to a member of his family. Such a use of his economic gain, the right to receive income, to procure a satisfaction which can be obtained only by the expenditure of money or property, would seem to be the enjoyment of the income whether the satisfaction is the purchase of goods at the corner grocery, the payment of his debt there, or such nonmaterial satisfactions as may result from the payment of a campaign or community chest contribution, or a gift to his favorite son. Even though he never receives the money, he derives money's worth from the disposition of the coupons which he has used as money or money's worth in the procuring of a satisfaction which is procurable only by the expenditure of money or money's worth. The enjoyment of the economic benefit accruing to him by virtue of his acquisition of the coupons is realized as completely as it would have been if he had collected the interest in dollars and expended them for any of the purposes named. *Burnet v. Wells, supra.*

In a real sense he has enjoyed compensation for money loaned or services rendered, and not any the less so because it is his only reward for them. To say that one who has made a gift thus derived from interest or earnings paid to his donee has never enjoyed or realized the fruits of his investment or labor, because he has assigned them instead of collecting them himself and then paying them over to the donee, is to affront common understanding and to deny the facts of common experience. Common understanding and experience are the touchstones for the interpretation of the revenue laws.

The power to dispose of income is the equivalent of ownership of it. The exercise of that power to procure the payment of income to another is the enjoyment, and hence the realization, of the income by him who exercises it. We have had no difficulty in applying that proposition where the assignment preceded the rendition of the services, *Lucas v. Earl, supra*; *Burnet v. Leininger, supra*, for it was recognized in the *Leininger* case that in such a case the rendition of the service by the assignor was the means by which the income was controlled by the donor and of making his assignment effective. But it is the assignment by which the disposition of income is controlled when the service precedes the assignment, and in both cases it is the exercise of the power of disposition of the interest or compensation, with the resulting payment to the donee, which is the enjoyment by the donor of income derived from them.

This was emphasized in *Blair v. Commissioner*, 300 U.S. 5, on which respondent relies, where the distinction was taken between a gift of income derived from an obligation to pay compensation and a gift of income-producing property. In the circumstances of that case, the right to income from the trust property was thought to be so identified with the equitable ownership of the property, from which alone the beneficiary derived his right to receive the income and his power to command disposition of it, that a gift of the income by the beneficiary became effective only as a gift of his ownership of the property producing it. Since the gift was deemed to be a gift of the property, the income from it was held to be the income of the owner of the property, who was the donee, not the donor — a refinement which was unnecessary if respondent's contention here is right, but one clearly inapplicable to gifts of interest or wages. Unlike income thus derived from an obligation to pay interest or compensation, the income of the trust was regarded as no more the income of the donor than would be the rent from a lease or a crop raised on a farm after the leasehold or the farm had been given away. *Blair v. Commissioner, supra*, 12, 13 and cases cited. *See also Reinecke v. Smith*, 289 U.S. 172, 177. We have held without deviation that where the donor retains control of the trust property the income is taxable to him although paid to the donee. *Corliss v. Bowers, supra. Cf. Helvering v. Clifford, supra.*

The dominant purpose of the revenue laws is the taxation of income to those who earn or otherwise create the right to receive it and enjoy the benefit of it when paid. *See Corliss v. Bowers, supra*, 378; *Burnet v. Guggenheim*, 288 U.S. 280, 283. The tax laid by the 1934 Revenue Act upon income "derived from . . . wages, or compensation for personal service, of whatever kind and in whatever form paid, . . . ; also from interest . . ." therefore cannot fairly be interpreted as not applying to income derived from interest or compensation when he who is entitled to receive it makes use of his power to dispose of it in procuring satisfactions which he would otherwise procure only by the use of the money when received.

It is the statute which taxes the income to the donor although paid to his donee. *Lucas v. Earl, supra; Burnet v. Leininger, supra*. True, in those cases the service which created the right to income followed the assignment, and it was arguable that in point of legal theory the right to the compensation vested instantaneously in the assignor when paid, although he never received it; while here the right of the assignor to receive the income antedated the assignment which transferred the right and thus precluded such an instantaneous vesting. But the statute affords no basis for such "attenuated subtleties." The distinction was explicitly rejected as the basis of decision in *Lucas v. Earl*. It should be rejected here; for no more than in the *Earl* case can the purpose of the statute to tax the income to him who earns, or creates and enjoys it be escaped by "anticipatory arrangements however skillfully devised" to prevent the income from vesting even for a second in the donor.

Nor is it perceived that there is any adequate basis for distinguishing between the gift of interest coupons here and a gift of salary or commissions. The owner of a negotiable bond and of the investment which it represents, if not the lender, stands in the place of the lender. When, by the gift of the coupons, he has separated his right to interest payments from his investment and procured the payment of the interest to his donee, he has enjoyed the economic benefits of the income in the same manner and to the same extent as though the transfer were of earnings, and in both cases the import of the statute is that the fruit is not to be attributed to a different tree from that on which it grew. *See Lucas v. Earl, supra*, 115.

Reversed.

The separate opinion of MR. JUSTICE McREYNOLDS.

The facts were stipulated. In the opinion of the court below the issues are thus adequately stated — "The petitioner owned a number of coupon bonds. The coupons represented the interest on the bonds and were payable to bearer. In 1934 he detached unmatured coupons of face value of $25,182.50 and transferred them by manual delivery to his son as a gift. The coupons matured later on in the same year, and the son collected the face amount, $25,182.50, as his own property. There was a similar transaction in 1935. The petitioner kept his books on a cash basis. He did not include any part of the moneys collected on the coupons in his income tax returns for these two years. The son included them in his returns. The Commissioner added the moneys collected on the coupons to the petitioner's taxable income and determined a tax deficiency for each year. The Board of Tax Appeals, three members dissenting, sustained the Commissioner, holding that the amounts collected on the coupons were taxable as income to the petitioner." The decision of the Board of Tax Appeals was reversed and properly so, I think.

The unmatured coupons given to the son were independent negotiable instruments, complete in themselves. Through the gift they became at once the absolute property of the donee, free from the donor's control and in no way dependent upon ownership of the bonds. No question of actual fraud or purpose to defraud the revenue is presented.

Neither *Lucas v. Earl*, 281 U.S. 111, nor *Burnet v. Leininger*, 285 U.S. 136, support petitioner's view. *Blair v. Commissioner*, 300 U.S. 5, 11, 12, shows that neither involved an unrestricted completed transfer of property.

Helvering v. Clifford, 309 U.S. 331, 335, 336, decided after the opinion below, is much relied upon by petitioner, but involved facts very different from those now before us. There no separate thing was absolutely transferred and put beyond possible control by the transferor. The Court affirmed that Clifford, both conveyor and trustee, "retained the substance of full enjoyment of all the rights which previously he had in the property." "In substance his control over the corpus was in all essential respects the same after the trust was created, as before." "With that control in his hands he would keep direct command over all that he needed to remain in substantially the same financial situation as before."

The general principles approved in *Blair v. Commissioner*, 300 U.S. 5, are applicable and controlling. The challenged judgment should be affirmed.

The CHIEF JUSTICE and MR. JUSTICE ROBERTS concur in this opinion.

Understanding *Blair* and *Horst*

1.   On their face, *Blair* and *Horst* appear to involve similar facts. In *Blair*, a father created a trust, paying income to his son for life, with the remainder presumably going to his grandchildren (the case does not specify). The son then assigned (re-assigned) specified fractions of the income to the various grandchildren in each year, without touching any of the underlying remainder interest. In *Horst*, a father owned a bond which, like the trust in *Blair*, was split into an income interest (the coupons) and a remainder interest (the underlying bond or principal). He too distributed some of the income interest coupons to his son, without transferring the remainder interest. In purely economic terms, both cases involved assignment of a portion of income from a larger property, without affecting the ownership of the property itself.

So why did the Court hold Blair's assignment to be successful, and Horst's, not? Is the distinction made in *Horst*, emphasizing the different legal status of the interests in the two cases, convincing? If not, what would a more convincing distinction be?

2.   *Blair* too ascribes considerable importance to the legal form of the assignment, which suggested that a property rather than an income interest was being transferred. Is this line of argument convincing? As a general rule, should tax courts defer to state law in defining property rights, or should they make their own determination?

3.   Focus now on the substantive economic rights held by Blair's and Horst's donees, respectively. Does either one of them hold something more substantial than the other, and (if so) does this justify the difference in tax treatment? What about the interests retained by the donors?

The most common effort to reconcile *Blair* and *Horst* involves the concept of horizontal and vertical slices. According to this interpretation, *Blair* involved a horizontal division of property — that is, a division by space rather than time — in which each of the transferees' interests lasted for as long as the transferor's own interest in the property. Because there was no reversion (return) of the property to the transferor, and because he retained no power to reallocate the transfers once given, this amounted to a completed transfer of property and subsequent income from the property was accordingly taxed to the donees. By contrast, *Horst* involved a vertical division of property — *i.e.*, a division by time rather than space — with income in some years being given to the recipient, but in later years being retained by the transferor. Because the property reverted to the transferor, and because he retained the (implicit) power to reallocate income in later years, this was an invalid assignment and resulted in tax to the transferor.[15]

The concept of horizontal and vertical slices is an intriguing one, but leaves

---

[15] For a pithy discussion of *Blair* and *Horst*, see MARVIN CHIRELSTEIN, FEDERAL INCOME TAXATION: A STUDENT'S GUIDE TO THE LEADING CASES AND CONCEPTS ¶ 8.03 (9th ed. 2002).

several questions unanswered. For one thing, it makes a great deal of tax consequence ride on what appears, at least superficially, to be a rather arbitrary distinction. For another, its application depends heavily on the perspective one brings to the case. For example, in *Blair*, the taxpayer had no reversionary interest and thus (or so the argument goes) "permanently" transferred a portion of his interest in the trust property. But that interest was itself temporary in nature, having been carved off from the underlying trust property by Blair's father (the grandfather) when he created the original trust. Likewise, in *Horst*, the coupons were "temporary" (a so-called vertical slice) from the father's perspective, since he also held the coupons for later years, but might well be considered permanent to the son, who held only those coupons he received from the father. A subsequent transfer of the coupons from the son to (say) a grandson or granddaughter might well be respected for tax purposes, even though the coupons represented a vertical slice from an earlier, larger piece of property. The horizontal and vertical distinction, like the fruit and trees concept before it, thus places great importance on formal characteristics in lieu of underlying economic realities, and may be as confusing as it is helpful in some cases.

Using the Sources

Under *Blair* and *Horst*, in which of the following cases is income taxed to the transferor, and in which to the transferee?

a. A mother, who owns an outright (fee) interest in a piece of real property, transfers the rents to her daughter for a ten-year period.

b. A mother, who owns a ten-year interest in a piece of real property, transfers her daughter one-half of the rents for the full ten-year period.

c. A mother, who owns a ten-year interest in a piece of real property, transfers her daughter the rents for years 1-5 only.

d. A mother, who owns a ten-year interest in a piece of real property, transfers her daughter the rents for years 6-10 only.

e. In each of items b., c., and d., what happens if the daughter now transfers her complete interest to her son (the grandson of the original transferor)?

f. Suppose that a father is in a high tax bracket and — hoping to reduce the tax on a sale of real estate — transfers it to his son who then completes the sale and pays a lower tax. Who is taxed, the father or son? Who should be?

Law and Planning

Suppose you were a parent with a large number of income-producing properties — bonds, real estate, etc. — and a trio of independent-minded children aged 16 to 25. You wanted to transfer each of them some of the income for a short period, but did not quite trust them enough to make a long-term assignment. Because you have taken a basic income tax course, you are aware that temporary or "vertical" slices result in tax to the assignor, although you are not sure how important that should be compared to your more practical concerns.

a. What are your options in this situation, and which would be the best choice? Why?

b. How would your answers differ, if the children were (i) all under 15 years of age, or (ii) all 25 years of age or older?

c. Would it make any difference, in a. or b., what kind of property was involved?

Politics and Policy

Under section 1(g) of the Code (the so-called "kiddie tax"), most unearned income of children under the age of 14 is taxed at the parents' tax rate. What would you think of extending this limit to (say) age 18 or 25? Would this measure help to prevent further tax avoidance, or are children over 18 (25) sufficiently independent that transfers to them should be considered complete for tax purposes? What other effects, good and bad, do you think that such a change would have?

II.   TAX ISSUES IN MARRIAGE AND DIVORCE

A.   Alimony Payments and the Deductibility Issue

One of the major themes of this chapter is that the income tax — for all the talk about its individual nature — is largely a tax upon family units. This results most prominently from the existence of joint returns, but also from the "kiddie tax," and (going back to Chapter 1) the exclusion for intrafamily gifts and bequests under section 102 of the Code. There are inevitably questions as to where the family begins and ends, but for a majority of Americans, the income tax is a tax upon households rather than on their individual members.

The emphasis on family units leaves the interesting question of what to do when such units are created or, less happily, destroyed. The issue is more complicated than one might think. Suppose that the marriage of two people is accompanied by a transfer of property from one spouse to another, pursuant to a prenuptial or similar agreement. Or, at the other end of things, suppose that a divorce or separation agreement is accompanied by a similar transfer of property, or else by an ongoing alimony or similar payment from the higher-earning to the lower-earning spouse. Should these transactions be treated as transactions between people who are already married (in the case of divorce, still married) to each other, and hence have no immediate tax consequences? Or are they better treated as arms-length transactions between two not yet (or no longer) related parties, and hence subject to tax on the same basis as other similar agreements? Note that this question is actually two questions: first, whether the recipient will be taxed on the receipt of the alimony or other property, with the payor receiving a deduction for an equivalent amount; and second, whether the payor will be taxed on any appreciation in value of the property at the time of the transfer. For example, if a divorcing husband transfers stock to the wife with a basis of $100,000, but a fair market value of $500,000, the question arises of whether the wife will be taxed on $500,000 and, no less importantly, whether the husband must pay tax on $400,000 of (presumably) capital gain on the transfer. (A cash payment would involve the first, but not the second, of these issues.)

The first of these questions is easier to answer, at least in the divorce situation. Under sections 71 and 215 of the Code, alimony and separate maintenance payments are treated as income to the recipient spouse (that is, former spouse), but deductible to the payor. By contrast, child support and property settlements have no tax consequences; the recipient pays no tax, but neither is a deduction permitted to the payor. In other words, for income tax purposes, child support and property transfers are treated something like an intrafamily gift, while alimony is treated more like a business transaction between unrelated parties. Alimony is defined as any cash payment received by or on behalf of a spouse under a divorce or separation agreement, where the payee and payor are not members of the same household, and there is no liability to continue the payments for any period after the death of the payee spouse (section 71(b)(1)(A)). There are also additional rules designed to prevent the camouflaging of child support or property settlements as alimony payments. For example, section 71(c) denies alimony treatment for any payment that is reduced when a child reaches a specified age or other milestone (graduation, marriage, etc.), the assumption being that such an amount (or the relevant part thereof) was really a child support rather than alimony payment. Similarly, section 71(f) denies alimony treatment for excessively "front-loaded" payments — generally, those which decrease by more than $15,000 per year during the first three post-divorce years — on the reasonable assumption that these payments were a disguised property settlement rather than genuine alimony payments. The parties may also voluntarily agree to treat alimony payments as resulting in no income or deductions to either parties (section 71(b)(1)(B)), although this election must be consistent between the two parties, and there is no concomitant allowance to "elect in" to the alimony provisions.

The alimony provisions raise two interesting problems. The first is whether alimony payments should have tax consequences, at all. If the purpose of alimony is to protect the more economically vulnerable of the two spouses, why impose tax on that spouse, while allowing a deduction to the wealthier, less vulnerable party? The answer appears to lie in the historic conception of alimony as a long-term, judicially imposed responsibility on the payor spouse (typically, the husband) who was forced to support his no-longer-wife and accordingly suffered a reduction in disposable income while the ex-wife's income increased by an equivalent amount. In today's world, where two-earner couples are the norm and alimony is usually a short-term, temporary arrangement, this view may be somewhat outdated. Many foreign countries treat alimony as a nontaxable transaction — effectively, a division of marital income — and the U.S. is something of an outlier in this area.

A second problem relates to enforcement. Since the payor is likely to be in a higher tax bracket than the recipient spouse, both may have an interest in exaggerating the amount of alimony payments, since the deduction to the payor will tend to outweigh the tax paid by the recipient party.[16] Thus, if an ex-wife pays

---

[16] For example, assume that an ex-wife is willing to pay her ex-husband $40,000 per year in child support or a property settlement. Assume further that the wife is a 40 percent tax bracket and the husband's marginal tax rate is 15 percent. If the payment is instead structured as alimony, the wife can

her former husband both alimony and child support, there is an incentive to overstate the alimony portion, so that the couple will receive an increased tax benefit without any real change in the underlying economic arrangement. A similar logic applies to property settlements, which may be difficult to distinguish from alimony payments. The rules in section 71(c) and (f) reduce, but do not eliminate, these possibilities, and may be easy to avoid with careful tax planning.

The following problems consider the alimony tax rules in greater detail. Consider whether the present law rules make sense as a matter of policy, and also whether they achieve their intended purpose; or whether the level of complexity exceeds the significance of the problem being addressed.

Using the Sources

What would be the treatment of each of the following items under section 71?

1.   Alimony paid in property (*e.g.*, stock or real estate) rather than in cash.

2. $50,000 in alimony, to be paid every year that the recipient spouse is alive, and to her children for five years after her death.

3. $50,000 in alimony, to be reduced to $20,000 in five years, which happens to be the time at which the oldest child graduates from college.

4.   Alimony payments of $100,000 in year one; $50,000 in year two; and zero in all subsequent years. (State the general rule that applies; extra credit for a precise calculation for each year.)

5.   A handshake agreement between the two parties to pay alimony for a set period. (Does it matter if this agreement is registered with the local court?)

Law and Planning

Freddie and Frieda Fastlane are planning to divorce and want the settlement to proceed as amicably (but also as cheaply) as possible. The couple has agreed that Freddie will pay Frieda $50,000 per year in alimony plus an additional $20,000 for support of each of the couple's two children, Felipe and Fatima (*i.e.*, a total of $40,000 per year), with payments to each child terminating upon the child's college graduation or marriage, whichever comes first. Freddie will also transfer to Frieda a $500,000 bank account as part of a broader property settlement. Felipe and Fatima are 15 and 12 years old, respectively. Freddie has a substantial income which places him in the 40 percent tax bracket, and substantial investment assets, while Frieda's tax bracket (independent of the transfers) is not anticipated to exceed 15 percent.

---

increase her payment to $50,000 and still come out ahead ($50,000 payment – $20,000 tax deduction = net $30,000 payment), while the husband will now receive a net of $42,500 ($50,000 – $7,500 tax payment), again in excess of the amount he would have received under a more honest arrangement. Effectively, the Government is being asked to subsidize the couple's divorce by allowing alimony payments to be deducted at a high tax rate and included in income at a lower percentage.

What steps might you advise the couple to take in order to improve the tax treatment of their divorce, and how confident would you feel about taking them?

Politics and Policy

A recurring problem in tax policy is whether the tax laws should be consistent with policy in other areas. With this in mind, consider the following excerpt:

Wendy Gerzog Shaller, *On Public Policy Grounds, A Limited Tax Credit for Child Support and Alimony*
11 Am. J. Tax Pol'y 321 (1994)[17]

INTRODUCTION

Currently, alimony payments to an ex-spouse are deductible from gross income while child support payments are nondeductible. While there is no cogent theoretical reason to deduct either alimony or child support, there are public policy reasons to eliminate the distinctions between them and to allow a limited credit for both types of payments. With the enactment of a limited credit statute applicable to both alimony and child support, furthermore, the abuse of income shifting already afforded the wealthy under the present alimony provision would be curtailed.

This Article will review the historical and theoretical reasons for the current treatment of alimony and child support, the manipulations afforded by the current statute defining alimony, the social need to enact a credit for child support payments, and will propose a limited credit statute that recognizes a social policy justification for encouraging both alimony and child support payments without permitting the wealthy to shift inappropriately the incidence of taxation.

* * *

I therefore propose a limited credit for both alimony and child support payments. The proposed credit would be computed at the 15 percent rate on the sum of alimony and child support up to $15,000. An alternative way of stating the limit is 15 percent of alimony and child support, not to exceed a credit of $2250. For 1990, the average alimony deducted by taxpayers with adjusted gross incomes of between $100,000 and $200,000 was $12,113; between $200,000 and $500,000 was $20,770; between $500,000 and $1 million was $31,312; of $1 million or more was $52,556. If there were a $15,000 limit placed on the amount used to determine the credit for alimony and child support payments and if the credit were determined at the 15 percent rate, the increased burden would fall on those taxpayers with adjusted gross incomes of $200,000 or more. By making the current deduction into a credit, all taxpayers would benefit at the same rate regardless of their particular tax brackets.

In contrast, all alimony and child support (not merely those amounts up to $15,000) would be includible in the recipient's income to reflect the greater wealth

---

[17] Copyright © 1994. All rights reserved. Reprinted by permission.

of the recipient as compared with a taxpayer who does not receive such support. A limited exclusion section could be enacted for low-income recipients of child support and alimony; however, this objective could be better accomplished by lowering income tax rates on low-income individuals, raising the threshold income subject to taxation, or by increasing the earned income tax credit. These steps would treat all low-income taxpayers with the same resources in the same way without regard to the source of their resources.

Further, adopting such a proposal would eliminate the need for the complex and counterproductive recapture rules currently applicable to the alimony deduction. The recapture provisions were enacted in 1984 and revised in 1986 to distinguish alimony from property settlements since the new statute eliminated the requirements that alimony be in the nature of support and that the payments be periodic. As originally legislated, the recapture provision called for the payment of alimony over a six-year period with recapture as income to the payor and a deduction to the payee of amounts that were reduced by more than $10,000 during those six "post separation" years. In 1986, in order to make the rules less complicated, Congress reduced the time period for the application of the recapture rules to three years and defined recapture as applying to reductions of alimony payments by more than $15,000 over this time frame.

The alimony recapture provisions have been criticized as adding to the Code's complexity and as an inadequate response to differentiating alimony from property settlements. Indeed, converting nondeductible property settlements into deductible alimony is a device currently used by most wealthy taxpayers. The recapture provisions, furthermore, have been criticized as a poor means of dealing with rehabilitative alimony which is a popular type of alimony in usage today.

With a tax credit for child support and alimony limited to apply to a total of $15,000 per year, there would be no need for the currently problematic alimony recapture provisions, which apply only to reductions that exceed $15,000. It would be impossible for a taxpayer to convert large property settlements into deductible alimony under such a restricted credit.

* * *

Does the author make a convincing case that U.S. tax policy is inconsistent with emerging trends in divorce and family law in this area? If so, should the tax laws be changed, or should lawyers simply get used to the tax rules and plan around them? Given that everyone is aware of the taxability of divorce payments, and can compensate by increasing the amount of such payments, is this a serious problem or simply another imperfection in the tax system without serious real-world effects?

B. Property Transfers and the Appreciation Problem

Section 71(a) makes clear that transfers of property other than cash do not qualify as deductible alimony payments. That doesn't mean that they don't raise any tax issues. One important issue concerns the treatment of appreciation on divorce or separation transfers. Suppose that Carol, on divorcing Bob, transfers him stock that she bought years ago for $500,000, but which is now worth three times that amount ($1.5 million). Should this transaction be treated like a sale of property, with Carol required to pay tax on the $1 million appreciation, and Bob taking a basis equal to the fair market value of the stock? Or should it be taxed like a gift or other non-recognition transaction, with Bob taking a carryover basis and payment of tax being delayed until his later sale of the stock? Is the answer the same in all cases, or might it depend upon the facts of the particular situation — for example, where the property came from, or what if anything Bob transferred to Carol in return for it?

As in so many areas of the course, there has been more than one answer to this question. The principal case in the area, *United States v. Davis*, treated the transaction as a sale of property and imposed tax; but this holding was effectively overridden by section 1041 of the Code, which imposes a largely non-recognition regime. Section 1041 itself contains limits which may result in different (and sometimes surprising) results in some cases. We consider these items in turn.

UNITED STATES v. DAVIS
United States Supreme Court
370 U.S. 65 (1962)

MR. JUSTICE CLARK delivered the opinion of the Court.

These cases involve the tax consequences of a transfer of appreciated property by Thomas Crawley Davis[18] to his former wife pursuant to a property settlement agreement executed prior to divorce, as well as the deductibility of his payment of her legal expenses in connection therewith. The Court of Claims upset the Commissioner's determination that there was taxable gain on the transfer but upheld his ruling that the fees paid the wife's attorney were not deductible. 287 F.2d 168, 152 Ct. Cl. 805. We granted *certiorari* on a conflict in the Court of Appeals and the Court of Claims on the taxability of such transfers. 368 U.S. 813. We have decided that the taxpayer did have a taxable gain on the transfer and that the wife's attorney's fees were not deductible.

In 1954 the taxpayer and his then wife made a voluntary property settlement and separation agreement calling for support payments to the wife and minor child in addition to the transfer of certain personal property to the wife. Under Delaware law all the property transferred was that of the taxpayer, subject to certain statutory marital rights of the wife including a right of intestate succession and a right upon divorce to a share of the husband's property. Specifically as a "division in settlement of their property" the taxpayer agreed to transfer to his wife, inter alia, 1,000 shares of stock in the E. I. du Pont de Nemours & Co. The then Mrs. Davis agreed to accept this division "in full settlement and satisfaction of any and all claims and rights against the husband whatsoever (including but not by way of limitation, dower and all rights under the laws of testacy and

---

[18] [1] Davis' present wife, Grace Ethel Davis, is also a party to these proceedings because a joint return was filed in the tax year in question.

intestacy). . . ." Pursuant to the above agreement which had been incorporated into the divorce decree, one-half of this stock was delivered in the tax year involved, 1955, and the balance thereafter. Davis' cost basis for the 1955 transfer was $74,775.37, and the fair market value of the 500 shares then transferred was $82,250. The taxpayer also agreed orally to pay the wife's legal expenses, and in 1955 he made payments to the wife's attorney, including $2,500 for services concerning tax matters related to the property settlement.

I.

The determination of the income tax consequences of the stock transfer described above is basically a two-step analysis: (1) Was the transaction a taxable event? (2) If so, how much taxable gain resulted therefrom? Originally the Tax Court (at that time the Board of Tax Appeals) held that the accretion to property transferred pursuant to a divorce settlement could not be taxed as capital gain to the transferor because the amount realized by the satisfaction of the husband's marital obligations was indeterminable and because, even if such benefit were ascertainable, the transaction was a nontaxable division of property. *Mesta v. Commissioner*, 42 B. T.A. 933 (1940); *Halliwell v. Commissioner*, 44 B.T.A. 740 (1941). However, upon being reversed in quick succession by the Courts of Appeals of the Third and Second Circuits, *Commissioner v. Mesta*, 123 F.2d 986 (C.A. 3d Cir. 1941); *Commissioner v. Halliwell*, 131 F.2d 642 (C.A. 2d Cir. 1942), the Tax Court accepted the position of these courts and has continued to apply these views in appropriate cases since that time. [Citations omitted]. In *Mesta* and *Halliwell* the Courts of Appeals reasoned that the accretion to the property was "realized" by the transfer and that this gain could be measured on the assumption that the relinquished marital rights were equal in value to the property transferred. The matter was considered settled until the Court of Appeals for the Sixth Circuit, in reversing the Tax Court, ruled that, although such a transfer might be a taxable event, the gain realized thereby could not be determined because of the impossibility of evaluating the fair market value of the wife's marital rights. *Commissioner v. Marshman*, 279 F.2d 27 (1960). In so holding that court specifically rejected the argument that these rights could be presumed to be equal in value to the property transferred for their release. This is essentially the position taken by the Court of Claims in the instant case.

II.

We now turn to the threshold question of whether the transfer in issue was an appropriate occasion for taxing the accretion to the stock. There can be no doubt that Congress, as evidenced by its inclusive definition of income subject to taxation, *i.e.*, "all income from whatever source derived, including . . . gains derived from dealings in property," intended that the economic growth of this stock be taxed. The problem confronting us is simply *when* is such accretion to be taxed. Should the economic gain be presently assessed against taxpayer, or should this assessment await a subsequent transfer of the property by the wife? The controlling statutory language, which provides that gains from dealings in property are to be taxed upon "sale or other disposition," is too general to include or exclude conclusively the transaction presently in issue. Recognizing this, the Government and the taxpayer argue by analogy with transactions more easily classified as within or without the ambient of taxable events. The taxpayer asserts that the present disposition is comparable to a nontaxable division of property between two co-owners,[19] while the Government contends it more resembles a taxable transfer of property in exchange for the release of an independent legal obligation. Neither disputes the validity of the other's starting point.

In support of his analogy the taxpayer argues that to draw a distinction between a wife's interest in the property of her husband in a common-law jurisdiction such as Delaware and the property interest of a wife in a typical community property jurisdiction would commit a double sin; for such differentiation would depend upon "elusive and subtle casuistries which . . . possess no relevance for tax purposes," *Helvering v. Hallock*, 309 U.S. 106, 118 (1940), and would create disparities between common-law and community property jurisdictions in contradiction to Congress' general policy of equality between the two. The taxpayer's analogy, however, stumbles on its own premise, for the inchoate rights granted a wife in her husband's property by the Delaware law do not even remotely reach the dignity of co-ownership. The wife has no interest — passive or active — over the management or disposition of her husband's personal property. Her rights are not descendable, and she must survive him to share in his intestate estate. Upon dissolution of the marriage she shares in the property only to such extent as the court deems "reasonable." 13 Del. Code Ann. § 1531(a). What is "reasonable" might be ascertained independently of the extent of the husband's property by such criteria as the wife's financial condition, her needs in relation to her accustomed station in life, her age and health, the number of children and their ages, and the earning capacity of the husband. *See, e.g., Beres v. Beres*, 52 Del. 133, 154 A.2d 384 (1959).

This is not to say it would be completely illogical to consider the shearing off of the wife's rights in her husband's property as a division of that property, but we believe the contrary to be the more reasonable construction. Regardless of the tags, Delaware seems only to place a burden on the husband's property rather than to make the wife a part owner thereof. In the present context the rights of succession and reasonable share do not differ significantly from the husband's obligations of support and alimony. They all partake more of a personal liability of the husband than a property interest of the wife. The effectuation of these marital rights may ultimately result in the ownership of some of the husband's property as

---

[19] [6] Any suggestion that the transaction in question was a gift is completely unrealistic. Property transferred pursuant to a negotiated settlement in return for the release of admittedly valuable rights is not a gift in any sense of the term. To intimate that there was a gift to the extent the value of the property exceeded that of the rights released not only invokes the erroneous premise that every exchange not precisely equal involves a gift but merely raises the measurement problem discussed in Part III, *infra*. Cases in which this Court has held transfers of property in exchange for the release of marital rights subject to gift taxes are based not on the premise that such transactions are inherently gifts but on the concept that in the contemplation of the gift tax statute they are to be taxed as gifts. Merrill v. Fahs, 324 U.S. 308 (1945); Commissioner v. Wemyss, 324 U.S. 303 (1945); *see* Harris v. Commissioner, 340 U.S. 106 (1950). In interpreting the particular income tax provisions here involved, we find ourselves unfettered by the language and considerations ingrained in the gift and estate tax statutes. *See* Farid-Es-Sultaneh v. Commissioner, 160 F.2d 812 (C.A. 2d Cir. 1947).

it did here, but certainly this happenstance does not equate the transaction with a division of property by co-owners. Although admittedly such a view may permit different tax treatment among the several States, this Court in the past has not ignored the differing effects on the federal taxing scheme of substantive differences between community property and common-law systems. *E.g., Poe v. Seaborn*, 282 U.S. 101 (1930). To be sure Congress has seen fit to alleviate this disparity in many areas, *e.g.*, Revenue Act of 1948, 62 Stat. 110, but in other areas the facts of life are still with us.

Our interpretation of the general statutory language is fortified by the long-standing administrative practice as sounded and formalized by the settled state of law in the lower courts. The Commissioner's position was adopted in the early 40's by the Second and Third Circuits and by 1947 the Tax Court had acquiesced in this view. This settled rule was not disturbed by the Court of Appeals for the Sixth Circuit in 1960 or the Court of Claims in the instant case, for these latter courts in holding the gain indeterminable assumed that the transaction was otherwise a taxable event. Such unanimity of views in support of a position representing a reasonable construction of an ambiguous statute will not lightly be put aside. It is quite possible that this notorious construction was relied upon by numerous taxpayers as well as the Congress itself, which not only refrained from making any changes in the statutory language during more than a score of years but re-enacted this same language in 1954.

III.

Having determined that the transaction was a taxable event, we now turn to the point on which the Court of Claims balked, *viz.*, the measurement of the taxable gain realized by the taxpayer. The Code defines the taxable gain from the sale or disposition of property as being the "excess of the amount realized therefrom over the adjusted basis. . . ." I. R. C. (1954) § 1001(a). The "amount realized" is further defined as "the sum of any money received plus the fair market value of the property (other than money) received." I. R. C. (1954) § 1001(b). In the instant case the "property received" was the release of the wife's inchoate marital rights. The Court of Claims, following the Court of Appeals for the Sixth Circuit, found that there was no way to compute the fair market value of these marital rights and that it was thus impossible to determine the taxable gain realized by the taxpayer. We believe this conclusion was erroneous.

It must be assumed, we think, that the parties acted at arm's length and that they judged the marital rights to be equal in value to the property for which they were exchanged. There was no evidence to the contrary here. Absent a readily ascertainable value it is accepted practice where property is exchanged to hold, as did the Court of Claims in *Philadelphia Park Amusement Co. v. United States*, 126 F. Supp. 184, 189, 130 Ct. Cl. 166, 172 (1954), that the values "of the two properties exchanged in an arms-length transaction are either equal in fact, or are presumed to be equal." *Accord, United States v. General Shoe Corp.*, 282 F.2d 9 (C.A. 6th Cir. 1960); *International Freighting Corp. v. Commissioner*, 135 F.2d 310 (C.A. 2d Cir. 1943). To be sure there is much to be said of the argument that such an assumption is weakened by the emotion, tension and practical necessities involved in divorce negotiations and the property settlements arising therefrom. However, once it is recognized that the transfer was a taxable event, it is more consistent with the general purpose and scheme of the taxing statutes to make a rough approximation of the gain realized thereby than to ignore altogether its tax consequences. *Cf. Helvering v. Safe Deposit & Trust Co.*, 316 U.S. 56, 67 (1942).

Moreover, if the transaction is to be considered a taxable event as to the husband, the Court of Claims' position leaves up in the air the wife's basis for the property received. In the context of a taxable transfer by the husband,[20] all indicia point to a "cost" basis for this property in the hands of the wife.[21] Yet under the Court of Claims' position her cost for this property, *i.e.*, the value of the marital rights relinquished therefore, would be indeterminable, and on subsequent disposition of the property she might suffer inordinately over the Commissioner's assessment which she would have the burden of proving erroneous, *Commissioner v. Hansen*, 360 U.S. 446, 468 (1959). Our present holding that the value of these rights is ascertainable eliminates this problem; for the same calculation that determines the amount received by the husband fixes the amount given up by the wife, and this figure, *i.e.*, the market value of the property transferred by the husband, will be taken by her as her tax basis for the property received.

Finally, it must be noted that here, as well as in relation to the question of whether the event is taxable, we draw support from the prior administrative practice and judicial approval of that practice. We therefore conclude that the Commissioner's assessment of a taxable gain based upon the value of the stock at the date of its transfer has not been shown erroneous.

IV.

The attorney-fee question is much simpler. It is the customary practice in Delaware for the husband to pay both, his own and his wife's legal expenses incurred in the divorce and the property settlement. Here petitioner paid $5,000 of such fees in the taxable year 1955 earmarked for tax advice in relation to the property settlement. One-half of this sum went to the wife's attorney. The taxpayer claimed that under § 212(3) of the 1954 Code, which allows a deduction for the "ordinary and necessary expenses paid . . . in connection with the determination, collection, or refund of any tax," he was entitled to deduct the entire $5,000. The Court of Claims allowed the $2,500 paid taxpayer's own attorney but denied the like amount paid the wife's attorney. The sole question here is the deductibility of the latter fee; the Government did not seek review of the amount taxpayer paid his own attorney, and we intimate no decision on that point. As to the deduction of the

---

[20] [7] Under the present administrative practice, the release of marital rights in exchange for property or other consideration is not considered a taxable event as to the wife. For a discussion of the difficulties confronting a wife under a contrary approach, see Taylor and Schwartz, *Tax Aspects of Marital Property Agreements*, 7 Tax L. Rev. 19, 30 (1951); Comment, *The Lump Sum Divorce Settlement as a Taxable Exchange*, 8 U.C.L.A. L. Rev. 593, 601–602 (1961).

[21] [8] Section 1012 of the Internal Revenue Code of 1954 provides that: "The basis of property shall be the cost of such property, except as otherwise provided in this subchapter and subchapters C (relating to corporate distributions and adjustments), K (relating to partners and partnerships), and P (relating to capital gains and losses). . . ."

wife's fees, we read the statute, if applicable to this type of tax expense, to include only the expenses of the taxpayer himself and not those of his wife. Here the fees paid her attorney do not appear to be "in connection with the determination, collection, or refund" of any tax of the taxpayer. As the Court of Claims found, the wife's attorney "considered the problems from the standpoint of his client alone. Certainly then it cannot be said that . . . [his] advice was directed to plaintiff's tax problems. . . ." 152 Ct. Cl. at 805, 287 F.2d at 171. We therefore conclude, as did the Court of Claims, that those fees were not a deductible item to the taxpayer.

Reversed in part and affirmed in part.

Mr. Justice Frankfurter took no part in the decision of these cases.

Mr. Justice White took no part in the consideration or decision of these cases.

Understanding *Davis*

1. The Court's decision in *Davis* relies heavily upon the intricacies of Delaware property law, which (it suggests) give the wife a subsidiary interest in her husband's property, but not an active ownership role. This suggests that the results — like those in *Lucas v. Earl* and *Poe v. Seaborn* — might be different in common law and community property jurisdictions, or in states that simply had different rules regarding control of marital property. Does this sort of difference make sense, or should the rules be the same in all states? Viewed in economic terms, does the transaction in *Davis* strike you as more similar to a gift, a sale, or a division of property, and with what income tax implications? How do you think most non-lawyers would view this transaction?

2. To make its sale analogy work, the court must assume that Mrs. Davis surrendered rights exactly equal to the fair market value of the stock; gain on the sale is thus simply the fair market value minus Mr. Davis's basis in the same property. But suppose that Mr. Davis was either a shrewd negotiator or an extremely unpleasant husband, and convinced his wife to surrender $1 million in legal rights in return for a relatively small amount of stock, just to get rid of him? Would he then have $925,000 ($1 million – $75,000) of taxable gain? Or what if he was a pushover, and gave up the stock in return for no legal concession? Would he then have a deductible loss? Does this line of questioning demonstrate a problem in the Court's analysis?

3. The divorce agreement specified that the transfer of stock was a "division in settlement of [the Davis's] property," although adding somewhat confusingly that Mrs. Davis accepted the property in satisfaction of her legal claims. Should this self-description have any weight in the Court's determination? Or should the Court be free to make its own analysis? What other practical (*i.e.*, nontax) effects might the couple's description of the transaction have, and are these consequences significant enough that the Court should respect the description for tax purposes, too?

4. After the *Davis* decision, but prior to the enactment of Code section 1041 in 1984, a number of courts held that property divisions incident to divorce were not taxable for spouses who have joint ownership interests in marital property, such as spouses in community property states. The Service agreed with this holding in Rev. Rul. 81-292, 1981-2 C.B. 158: "An approximately equal division of the total value of jointly owned property . . . under a divorce settlement agreement that provides for transferring some assets in their entirety to one spouse or the other, is a non-taxable division and does not result in the realization of gain or loss." Section 1041 (discussed below) by its terms only applies to spouses and not to registered domestic partners. (As this edition goes to press, California, Washington, and Nevada have all passed registered domestic partner laws). Might the pre-Section 1041 cases and/or the 1981 Revenue Ruling apply to registered domestic partners in community property states? For instance, how would registered domestic partners in a community property sate be taxed where there is only one earner and he or she pays to the other partner at dissolution a cash settlement of one million dollars which is half of the value of all assets acquired during the relationship? Does Code section 1041 apply to these taxpayers? What if the taxpayers transfer property in a transaction related to the cessation of their marriage (or registered domestic partnership), but their transfer would not qualify for non-recognition under the framework of Code section 1041? What about a cohabiting couple in a state that does not recognize their relationship? If all the assets were acquired by one partner and at dissolution they agree to split the assets equally, how should they be taxed?[22]

The holding in *Davis* was predictably unpopular with taxpayers and did not remain in effect for long. Section 1041(a) now provides an opposite answer to the *Davis* problem, stating simply that "[n]o gain or loss shall be recognized on a transfer of property from an individual to . . . (1) a spouse, or (2) a former spouse, but only if the transfer is incident to the divorce." Section 1041(b) makes the gift analogy explicit, providing that the transferee spouse takes a carryover basis in the property, so that tax will be paid when (if ever) the transferee disposes of the property in an otherwise taxable transaction. For example, if a divorcing husband transferred to his wife stock with a basis of $100,000 and a value of $1,000,000, no tax would be paid on the transfer but the stock would have $900,000 of "built-in" appreciation which would be taxed to the wife, together with any appreciation subsequent to the transfer, upon a lifetime sale of the property. Presumably, a well-advised transferee would take this factor into account, and demand a larger transfer to compensate for this future tax liability.

An interesting aspect of section 1041 is its definition of transfers which are "incident to the divorce," and which accordingly qualify for non-recognition treatment. Under section 1041(c), these include any transfer occurring within one year after the marriage ends (section 1041(c)) as well as any other transfer which, although outside the one-year window, is nonetheless "related to the cessation of the marriage" (section 1041(c)(2)). The regulations (Treas. Reg. Section 1.1041-1T(a)) state that this latter requirement is satisfied "if the transfer is pursuant to a divorce

---

[22] A discussion of the issues underlying this question can be found in Patricia Cain, *Taxing Families Fairly*, 48 SANTA CLARA L. REV. 805, 824 (2008).

or separation instrument . . . and the transfer occurs not more than 6 years after the date on which the marriage ceases." Transfers which fail to satisfy either of these requirements — that is, which occur more than 6 years after termination of the marriage or which are not pursuant to the original divorce or separation agreement — may still qualify if it is demonstrated that the transfer "was made to effect the division of property owned by the former spouses at the time of the cessation of the marriage."

The effect is to create a three-tiered system: an automatic tax benefit for transfers within one year of divorce; a presumption in favor of transfers between year one and year six; and a stronger (but still rebuttable) presumption against extending the benefit to transfers occurring after more than six years after marriage. This system is typical of the way the Code combines a bright-line test ("safe harbor"), under which transactions within a certain category are undisputedly acceptable, with a more subjective test for transactions, which although sympathetic, do not meet the bright-line provision. It may also be noteworthy that the section 1041 regulations continue to bear a "T," for "temporary," after more than fifteen years, suggesting that someone is either unsure about the regulations or at the very least in no great hurry to complete them.

YOUNG v. COMMISSIONER
United States Court of Appeals, Fourth Circuit
240 F.3d 369 (4th Cir. 2001)

DIANA GRIBBON MOTZ, Circuit J:

This case presents two tax questions arising from the settlement of a property dispute between former spouses. The first is whether a 1992 transfer of land from a husband to his former wife constitutes a transfer "incident to" their 1988 divorce for purposes of the non-recognition of gain rules. The second is whether the wife must include within her gross income the contingent fees paid directly to her attorneys from the proceeds of her subsequent sale of that land. We agree with the Tax Court's holding that both questions must be answered in the affirmative.

I.

Louise Young[23] and John Young married in 1969 and divorced in 1988. The following year they entered into a Mutual Release and Acknowledgment of Settlement Agreement ("1989 Settlement Agreement") to resolve "their Equitable Distribution [of] Property claim and all other claims arising out of the marital relationship." Pursuant to this agreement, Mr. Young delivered to Mrs. Young a promissory note for $1.5 million, payable in five annual installments plus interest, which was secured by a deed of trust on 71 acres of property that Mr. Young received as part of the same 1989 Settlement Agreement.

---

[23] [1] After her divorce from John Young, Louise married James Ausman, another appellant, and became Louise Ausman. Although it is not reflected in the caption of the case, Louise has since divorced and remarried and is now named Louise Rice. To remain consistent with the parties' stipulated facts before the Tax Court, however, we continue to refer to Louise Young.

In October 1990, Mr. Young defaulted on his obligations under the 1989 Settlement Agreement; the next month Mrs. Young brought a collection action in state court in North Carolina. On May 1, 1991, that court entered judgment for Mrs. Young, awarding her principal, interest, and reasonable attorneys' fees. Mr. Young paid only $160,000 toward satisfaction of that judgment, thus prompting Mrs. Young to initiate steps to execute the judgment. Before execution, however, Mr. and Mrs. Young entered into a Settlement Agreement and Release ("1992 Agreement"), which provided that Mr. Young would transfer to Mrs. Young, in full settlement of his obligations, a 59-acre tract of land (42.3 of the 71 acres that had collaterized his $1.5 million note and 16.7 acres adjoining that tract). Pursuant to the 1992 Agreement, Mr. Young retained an option to repurchase the land for $2.2 million before December 1992. Mr. Young assigned the option to a third party, who exercised the option and bought the land from Mrs. Young for $2.2 million.

On her 1992 and 1993 federal income tax returns, Mrs. Young reported no capital gain from the sale of the property nor the $300,606 portion of the $2.2 million that went directly to pay her attorneys' fees. At the same time, Mr. Young did not report any gain from his transfer of property, in which he had a $130,794 basis, to satisfy his then almost $2.2 million obligation to Mrs. Young. Thus, the appreciation of this property went untaxed despite the occurrence of a taxable event, *i.e.*, the transfer or the sale.

The Commissioner asserted deficiencies against both Mr. Young and Mrs. Young. Each then petitioned the Tax Court, which consolidated the two cases. After trial, the Tax Court ruled that the capital gain was properly taxable to Mrs. Young under 26 U.S.C. § 1041(a)(2) (1994), which provides that "no gain or loss shall be recognized on a transfer of property . . . to . . . a former spouse, . . . if the transfer is incident to the divorce." *See Young v. Commissioner*, 113 T.C. 152, 156 (1999). Because the Tax Court held that the 1992 property transfer was "incident to the divorce," it concluded that Mr. Young realized no gain through his transfer of this property to his former spouse. *Id.* Rather, according to the Tax Court, Mrs. Young took Mr. Young's adjusted basis in the land and should have recognized a taxable gain upon the subsequent sale of that property. In addition, the Tax Court held that the portion of the proceeds from the sale, which was paid directly to her attorneys, must be included in Mrs. Young's gross income. As a result of these holdings, the Tax Court ruled that Louise Young and her then husband, James Ausman, owed $206,323 in additional income tax in 1992, and Louise alone owed $262,657 in additional income tax in 1993.

Mrs. Young and James Ausman appeal both rulings. The Commissioner files a protective cross-appeal on the § 1041 issue, urging that if we do not agree with the Tax Court's conclusion that Mrs. Young (and Mr. Ausman) realized taxable capital gains, we also reverse its holding with respect to Mr. Young so that he is required to recognize the gain.

II.

We first consider the Tax Court's ruling involving § 1041, which provides that no taxable gain or loss results from a transfer of property to a former spouse if the transfer is "incident to the divorce." 26 U.S.C. § 1041(a)(2). Section 1041 further provides that "a transfer of property is incident to the divorce" if it is "related to the cessation of the marriage." 26 U.S.C. § 1041(c)(2). The statute does not further define the term "related to the cessation of the marriage," but temporary Treasury regulations provide some guidance. Those regulations extend a safe harbor to transfers made within six years of divorce if also "pursuant to a divorce or separation instrument, as defined in § 71(b)(2)." Temp. Treas. Reg. § 1.1041-1T(b) (2000). Section 71(b)(2) defines a "divorce or separation instrument" as a "decree of divorce or separate maintenance or a written instrument incident to such a decree." 26 U.S.C. § 71(b)(2) (1994). A property transfer not made pursuant to a divorce instrument "is presumed to be not related to the cessation of the marriage." Temp. Treas. Reg. § 1.1041-1T(b). This presumption may be rebutted "by showing that the transfer was made to effect the division of property owned by the former spouses at the time of the cessation of the marriage." *Id.*

The Tax Court held that the 1992 transfer from Mr. Young to Mrs. Young was "related to the cessation of the marriage," thus neither party recognized a gain or loss on the transfer, and Mrs. Young took the same basis in the land that the couple had when they were married. *Young*, 113 T.C. at 156. The court applied the regulatory safe harbor provision, but also found that the transfer "completed the division of marital property" and, regardless of the safe harbor provision, it "satisfied the statutory requirement that the transfer be 'related to the cessation of the marriage.' " *Id.* We agree with the Tax Court that the 1992 land transfer was "related to the cessation of the marriage," finding that it "effected the division of marital property." Temp. Treas. Reg. § 1.1041-1T(b).

The factual underpinnings of this case are not questioned. It is undisputed that the parties formulated and entered into the 1989 Settlement Agreement to resolve their "respective claims for equitable distribution of property" and "all other claims arising out of the marital relationship." The parties also agree that the 1992 Agreement was to resolve disputes arising from that 1989 Settlement Agreement. In fact, an entire section of the 1992 Agreement details the marital background of the dispute, beginning with the Youngs' divorce and subsequent execution of the 1989 Settlement Agreement, and expressly provides that the 1992 Agreement was to "fully settle all claims under the Judgment and Deed of Trust" that arose out of the 1989 Settlement Agreement. Not surprisingly then, the Tax Court explicitly found that the 1992 transfer "completed the division of marital property." *Young*, 113 T.C. at 156.[24]

Nonetheless, Mrs. Young challenges the Tax Court's finding and argues that the 1992 transfer did not "effect the division of [marital] property." In support of her contention, Mrs. Young notes that she was a judgment creditor when she entered into the 1992 Agreement. But the only status relevant for § 1041 purposes is "spouse" or "former spouse." Beyond her position as a former spouse, Mrs. Young's status makes no difference when determining whether the transfer is taxable; § 1041 looks to the character of and reason for the transfer, not to the status of the transferee as a creditor, lien-holder, devisee, trust beneficiary, or otherwise.

---

[24] [2] Whether the transfer effected the division of marital property is an issue of fact, and we cannot reverse the Tax Court's "subsidiary and ultimate findings on this factual issue" unless they are clearly erroneous. . . .

Indeed, in *Barnum v. Commissioner*, 19 T.C. 401, 407–08 (1952), although the former wife had obtained a judgment against her husband for alimony arrearage, the Tax Court found the resulting settlement to be "incident to a divorce" because, like the 1992 Agreement in this case, it settled the "dispute over obligations arising from a divorce decree." *Id.*

Additionally, Mrs. Young's reliance on a private letter ruling issued to another taxpayer is misplaced. P.L.R. 9306015 (Feb. 12, 1993). In that case, the divorce decree contemplated a sale of the former marital house, in which each spouse owned a one-half interest, to a third party. The IRS ruled that the husband's subsequent sale of his one-half interest in the house to his former wife instead of a third party was an "arm's-length transaction between two parties that happen to be former spouses," and thus did not "effect the division" of marital property pursuant to § 1041 and its regulations. *Id.* Because the husband in the private letter ruling had no obligation stemming from the divorce decree to sell his half interest in the home to his wife, the fact that the parties were former spouses truly had no bearing on the sale except as the means of their association. In contrast, Mr. Young transferred the 59 acres to satisfy an obligation that originated from the dissolution of the Youngs' marriage. Mr. Young's transfer of this land was not an independent decision "unrelated to the cessation of the marriage." And Mrs. Young did not just "happen" to be Mr. Young's "former spouse." Instead, the transaction occurred only because she was his former spouse enforcing her rights growing out of the dissolution of their marriage.

Mrs. Young's argument based on state court jurisdiction is no more persuasive. She asserts that the 1992 Agreement could not have effectuated the division of marital property, because the judgment that precipitated the 1992 Agreement was rendered by a North Carolina Superior Court, and not a North Carolina District Court, which "is the proper division . . . for . . . the enforcement of separation or property settlement agreements between spouses, or recovery for the breach thereof." N.C. Gen Stat. § 7A-244. Whatever the merits of this argument as to the jurisdiction of North Carolina courts, it cannot be the basis for a decision as to the federal tax consequences of a transfer of property. The Commissioner does not contend that the suit upon which the 1992 Agreement was based was for "recovery for the breach" of a property settlement agreement under North Carolina law, but only that the 1992 Agreement completed "the division" of marital property under § 1041 of the Internal Revenue Code.

Nor do we find Mrs. Young's "fairness" argument compelling. She points out that under the 1989 Settlement Agreement she was to receive $1.5 million plus interest, but if forced to pay the capital gains tax she will receive a lesser amount. For this reason, she argues that application of § 1041 to the 59-acre transfer would "result in a radical and unfair re-division of the Young's [sic] marital property." Brief of Appellant at 29. But, this argument overlooks the fact that Mrs. Young agreed to accept the 59 acres in lieu of enforcing her judgment against Mr. Young and receiving a cash payment. For whatever reason — and the record is silent as to Mrs. Young's motivations — she chose not to follow the latter route. In addition, if Mrs. Young had agreed to accept land in 1989, as she ultimately did in 1992, the resulting transfer would unquestionably have "effected the division of [marital] property" and been within § 1041. That the transfer occurred three years later, does not alter its "effect," or its treatment under § 1041.

The sole reason for the 1992 Agreement was to resolve the disputes that arose from the Youngs' divorce and subsequent property settlement. Had the Youngs reached this settlement at the time of their divorce, there is no question that this transaction would have fallen under § 1041. There is no reason for the holding to differ here where the same result occurred through two transactions instead of one.

The policy animating § 1041 is clear. Congress has chosen to "treat a husband and wife [and former husband and wife acting incident to divorce] as one economic unit, and to defer, but not eliminate, the recognition of any gain or loss on interspousal property transfers until the property is conveyed to a third party outside the economic unit." *Blatt v. Commissioner*, 102 T.C. 77, 80 (1994) (emphasis added). *See also* H.R. Rep. No. 98-432, at 1491 (1984), *reprinted in* 1984 U.S.C.C.A.N. 1134. Thus, no taxable event occurred and no gain was realized by either Mr. or Mrs. Young until Mrs. Young sold the 59 acres to a third party.

Indeed, holding otherwise would contradict the very purpose of § 1041. Congress enacted that statute to "correct the[problems" caused by *United States v. Davis*, 370 U.S. 65 (1962), in which "the Supreme Court had ruled that a transfer of appreciated property to a spouse (or former spouse) in exchange for the release of marital claims results in the recognition of gain to the transferor." H.R. Rep. No. 98-432, at 1491–92 (1984), reprinted in 1984 U.S.C.C.A.N. 1134–35. Congress found this result "inappropriate," *id.*, and thus amended the tax code in 1984 to add § 1041. Given this history, to impute a gain to Mr. Young on his transfer of "appreciated property . . . in exchange for the release of [Mrs. Young's] marital claims" would abrogate clear congressional policy. *Id.*

The dissent's contention that the result we reach here is not supported by equitable considerations misses the point. Congress has already weighed the equities and established a policy that no gain or loss will be recognized on a transfer between former spouses incident to their divorce. Thus, anytime former spouses transfer appreciated property incident to their divorce, the transferee spouse will bear the tax burden of the property's appreciated value after selling it and receiving the proceeds. Although this rule will undoubtedly work a hardship in some cases, the legislature has clearly set and codified this policy. We cannot disregard that choice to satisfy our own notions of equity.

In so concluding, we do not suggest that the boundaries defining when a transfer is "related to the cessation of the marriage" or made "to effect the division of [marital] property" are always clear. We cannot, however, on the facts of this case hold that Mr. Young's "interspousal property transfer" was a taxable event, when the purpose behind Mr. Young's transfer was to satisfy his obligations arising from the "cessation of the marriage." To do so would, we believe, contravene the language, purpose, and policy of § 1041 and the regulations promulgated pursuant thereto.

* * *

WILKINS, Circuit Judge, concurring in part and dissenting in part:

The majority affirms the determination of the Tax Court that the 1992 property transfer from John Young to his former wife Louise was "incident to" the Young's divorce and that Louise must include as her income the contingent fees paid directly to her attorneys from the sale of the land transferred. I concur regarding the contingency fee issue but respectfully dissent regarding whether the 1992 property transfer was incident to the Young's divorce. I would conclude that a property transfer made between former spouses to satisfy a judgment is not made "incident to" the parties' divorce merely because the lawsuit that produced the judgment was for default on a promissory note obtained in the parties' divorce property settlement.

I.

The issue in dispute here is which former spouse is responsible for paying capital gains taxes as a result of the substantial appreciation of the transferred property that occurred prior to the time John used the property to satisfy his debt to Louise.[25] The answer to that question depends on whether the 1992 transfer was a taxable event. If it was, then John owed capital gains taxes and Louise received a basis that reflected the fact that the property had appreciated substantially prior to her receiving it. If it was not, then John owed no capital gains taxes and Louise took the property at John's previous, much lower basis. I believe the applicable law demonstrates that the 1992 transfer was a taxable event and therefore capital gains taxes were due and payable by John as a result of this transaction.

The parties agree that the 1992 property transfer was a taxable event unless 26 U.S.C.A. § 1041 applies. That section provides that "no gain or loss shall be recognized on a transfer of property . . . to . . . a former spouse . . . if the transfer is incident to the divorce." 26 U.S.C.A. § 1041(a)(2) (West Supp. 2000). A transfer is "incident to the divorce" if it either "occurs within 1 year after the date on which the marriage ceases" or "is related to the cessation of the marriage." *Id.* § 1041(c). A temporary Treasury regulation interpreting § 1041 in turn provides, in pertinent part, that a transfer is deemed "related to the cessation of the marriage" when made within six years of the divorce and "pursuant to a divorce or separation agreement." Temp. Treas. Reg. § 1.1041-1T(b) (2000). On the other hand, "any transfer not pursuant to a divorce or separation instrument . . . is presumed to be not related to the cessation of the marriage." *Id.* The regulation further states that "this presumption may be rebutted only by showing that the transfer was made to effect the division of property owned by the former spouses at the time of the cessation of the marriage." *Id.*

---

[25] [1] John's basis in the property was $130,794. He transferred the land to Louise to satisfy a debt totaling $2,153,845, including $1,500,000 in principal, $344,938 in interest, $300,606.08 in attorney's fees, and $8,300 in collection costs. John reported no capital gain from his use of the appreciated property to satisfy his debt. Louise sold the property for $2,265,000 and reported a $100,000 short-term capital gain and $356,500 in interest income.

The majority does not address the question of whether the 1992 agreement to satisfy the judgment was a "divorce or separation instrument," but concludes that the Government met its burden of proving that the property transfer "was made to effect the division of [marital] property." I will briefly explain why I believe the property transfer was not a "divorce or separation instrument" and then explain why I believe it is incorrect to conclude that the property transfer "was made to effect the division of [marital] property."

A.

The term "divorce or separation instrument" appears in 26 U.S.C.A. § 71, which pertains to alimony and separate maintenance payments. That section defines "divorce or separation instrument," as pertinent here, as "a decree of divorce or separate maintenance or a written instrument incident to such a decree." 26 U.S.C.A. § 71(b)(2)(A) (West 1988). It is undisputed that the settlement agreement is not a decree of divorce or separate maintenance. Accordingly, it qualifies as a "divorce or separation instrument" only if it is "a written instrument incident to" "a decree of divorce or separate maintenance."

Words not defined in a statute are given their ordinary meaning. *See Scrimgeour v. Internal Revenue*, 149 F.3d 318, 327 (4th Cir. 1998). "Incident" means "dependent upon, appertaining or subordinate to, or accompanying something else of greater or principal importance." Black's Law Dictionary 762 (6th ed. 1990). Here, the 1992 agreement did not bear such a close relationship to the divorce decree. Instead, the 1988 divorce decree and the 1992 agreement were connected only indirectly: The 1992 agreement settled a dispute that arose out of the 1989 division of property that occurred as a result of the parties' 1988 divorce. Nothing in the divorce decree or the property division compelled the land transfer contemplated in the 1992 agreement. Accordingly, the settlement document does not fit the definition of a "divorce or separation instrument."

B.

The determination that the 1992 settlement agreement is not a "divorce or separation instrument," as that term is defined in § 71, gives rise to a presumption that the property transfer was not related to the cessation of the marriage. In order to rebut that presumption, the Government was required to show "that the transfer was made to effect the division of [marital] property." Temp. Treas. Reg. § 1.1041-1T(b). Because the division of marital property was completed years before the property transfer — when the parties released their marital claims against one another and Louise accepted the promissory note — I would hold that the Government failed to make the necessary showing.

A property transfer is not made for the purpose of effecting a marital property division when the marital property division has already been completed.[26] The Youngs completed this division when John delivered the promissory note to Louise.

---

[26] [2] The majority states that the statement made by the Tax Court that the 1992 transfer "completed the division of marital property" was a finding of fact that we must accept unless clearly

His payments on the note did not transfer marital property; the note itself accomplished that. Neither were the payments inherently marital, as alimony is. Instead, John's obligations on the note were the obligations of a debtor to a creditor and were no more intimate than a mortgage. Accordingly, although the judgment arising from John's default on the note was causally related to the marital property division, that division had been completed and the marital economic ties between the Youngs had been severed before the 1992 transfer occurred. The 1992 property transfer was made simply to satisfy a judgment between them, for reasons bearing no relationship to the fact that the parties were previously married. In other words, John owed a debt to Louise because of the marriage, but they did not agree to settle the debt by a land transfer because of the marriage.

Indeed, the fact that the parties' status as former spouses did not affect their decision to make the transfer in question was also the basis for private letter ruling 9306015. *See* Priv. Ltr. Rul. 9306015 (Feb. 12, 1993). There, the divorce decree contemplated a sale to a third party of the former marital house, in which each spouse owned an interest. Nevertheless, eight years after the parties' divorce, the husband sold his interest in the home to his former wife. The IRS ruled that because the sale was simply "an arm's-length transaction between two parties that happen to be former spouses," the transfer was not made to effect the division of marital property. *Id.* The majority attempts to distinguish this ruling by asserting that, unlike the parties in the private letter ruling, the Youngs were not simply "two parties that happen to be former spouses" because the circumstances that led John to make the 1992 transfer were created by the marital property division. Clearly, however, the IRS' characterization of the parties in the private letter ruling as "happening to be former spouses" did not refer to the history of the circumstances leading to the sale; indeed, the sale was the direct result of circumstances arising from the marriage. Rather, the characterization referred to the husband's purpose in making the transfer. Regardless of whether the husband's shared interest in the house arose from his prior marriage, that history did not affect his decision to sell his interest to his joint owner. The same principle applies here. Regardless of the fact that John's status as a judgment debtor arose from his prior marriage, that history did not affect his decision to satisfy the judgment by making the 1992 transfer. Accordingly, as in the private letter ruling, the 1992 transfer was simply "an arm's-length transaction between two parties that happen to be former spouses," and it cannot be said that the 1992 transfer was "made to effect the division of [marital] property."

The majority concludes that the 1992 property transfer should not be treated as a taxable event because that would have been the result had Louise agreed to the property transfer as part of the 1989 divorce settlement.[27] Although like transactions should indeed receive like treatment under the tax code, the hypothetical transaction offered by the majority and the transaction that actually occurred are not alike. In fact, they differ in the most critical way: In the

---

erroneous. *See ante* at n.2. Clearly, however, the statement was a conclusion of law, not a finding of fact. . . .

[27] [4] Of course, Louise did not agree to this. She agreed to receive from John $1.5 million tax free to her over a five-year period.

hypothetical, Louise would have obtained the property as a means of severing her economic union with her former spouse, thereby justifying treatment of the transfer as if it were made within a single economic unit, whereas in the actual transaction, the property was transferred after the Youngs' economic union had already been completely severed. *See* H.R. Rep. No. 98-432, at 1491–92 (1984), *reprinted in* 1984 U.S.C.C.A.N. 697, 1134 (noting that the reason that transfers between spouses are not taxed is "that a husband and wife are a single economic unit"). Accordingly, the hypothetical transfer would have been "made to effect the division of [marital] property," while the actual transaction was not. In contrast, John's transfer of the property to Louise to satisfy a judgment should not be treated differently from a sale by John to Louise of the property. Each property transfer is simply an arm's-length exchange of property for valuable consideration between people who happen to be former spouses, and no valid tax policy would justify treating these like transactions differently.[28]

If the words "made to effect the division of marital property" were interpreted in a vacuum, the majority's interpretation might be plausible, but when one considers the anomalous results produced by the majority's interpretation, its incorrectness becomes apparent. It is wrong to conclude that the Treasury Department intended to treat differently two arm's-length property transfers between former spouses based on the fact that in one the transferee pays cash for the property and in the other she allows the transfer to satisfy a judgment. It is therefore just as wrong to conclude that the Treasury Department intended that the line between transfers "made to effect the division of [marital] property" and transfers not made to effect such a division would be drawn where the majority draws it today.

One final aspect of this case deserves mention. From the majority's decision to interpret the applicable regulation in a manner that is supported neither by the language of the regulation nor by any valid tax policy, one might infer that unmentioned equitable considerations weigh in favor of the majority's result. Just the opposite is true, however. By holding that the 1992 transfer was a § 1041 transaction, the majority provides a substantial windfall of several hundred thousand dollars to a defaulting debtor while at the same time punishing a creditor who accepted a settlement instead of litigating her claims (which would have resulted in a satisfaction of the judgment without the tax burden she now faces).[29]

For all of these reasons, I believe that the 1992 transfer was not "incident to the divorce," and thus the transfer of the property was a taxable event to John. I respectfully dissent from the majority's conclusion to the contrary.

---

[28] [5] Indeed, the premise that the sale of the property to Louise would have been a taxable event but the transfer of the property in satisfaction of the judgment was not, leads to the strange result that the tax treatment of the 1992 transaction could have been changed simply by structuring the transaction as a sale of the property to Louise, with the proceeds to be used to satisfy the judgment.

[29] [6] The majority misunderstands my discussion of fairness. I do not suggest that equitable considerations should trump the language of § 1041 or the applicable regulation. Rather, I only point out that in addition to the fact that the majority's holding appears unguided by any coherent tax principle and produces anomalous results, it yields a tremendously unfair result for Louise Young.

Understanding *Young*

1. *Young* holds that a later settlement agreement, necessitated by the ex-husband's failure to meet the terms of the divorce agreement, is "incident to the divorce" within the meaning of section 1041. Is this really what the statute and regulations had in mind? What do you make of the dissent's argument, that the division of property was completed in 1989 and the 1992 settlement was a separate agreement necessitated only by Mr. Young's subsequent default? What is the purpose of section 1041, and is it advanced or contradicted by the court's decision?

2. In addition to its statutory interpretation argument, the dissent makes the following point about equity: "By holding that the 1992 transfer was a sec. 1041 transaction, the majority provides a substantial windfall of several hundred thousand dollars to a defaulting debtor while at the same time punishing a creditor who accepted a settlement instead of litigating her claims. . . ." Indeed the result of the decision is that Mrs. Young, who more or less fulfilled her end of the divorce agreement, will wind up paying more tax and having less money than she expected at the time of the divorce, while Mr. Young, who defaulted, will wind up with more. Is this a fair, or even a reasonable, result? Should courts apply this kind of equity argument in tax cases, or is it simply Mrs. Young's fault for not hiring a more clever lawyer, or one more attuned to tax issues? Why do you think that she didn't have one?

3. Even before the litigation began, Mr. and Mrs. Young took inconsistent positions regarding the relevant transactions, Mr. Young claiming he had no gain on the 1992 settlement (*i.e.*, that the transaction was within section 1041) and Mrs. Young reporting no capital gain on her subsequent sale of the property (because the settlement was outside section 1041 and hence resulted in a basis step-up for capital gain purposes). Regardless of the merits, should this sort of inconsistent reporting ever be permitted in a marriage and divorce situation? What do you think of a rule that said, "Take the position that you want, but at least, make it the same position." *Cf.* section 1060 (requiring consistent treatment by the seller and buyer in certain business acquisitions). Could such a rule be enforced, and would it solve the problems in *Young* and similar cases?

4. How would the decision in *Young* affect your strategy in a future divorce negotiation?

The need to plan extremely carefully in the alimony area is dramatized by the decision in *Hawley v. Commissioner*, 94 Fed. Appx. 126 (3d Cir. 2004), in which the court refused to allow a deduction for any portion of a support payment which did not clearly differentiate between the amount intended for the surviving spouse's needs and that intended for child support. The court refused to apply retroactively an amendment to Pennsylvania law providing that, in the absence of a specification to the contrary, the payments in such cases would terminate upon the death of the surviving spouse. According to the court, even if the payments were so terminated, a Pennsylvania court could be expected to require a substitute payment of some amount of child support following the spouse's death. For a further example of the confusion that may result from a failure clearly to distinguish alimony from child support payments, see *Kean v. Commissioner*, 407 F. 3d 186 (3d Cir. 2005) (holding that unallocated support payments pursuant to a divorce should be treated as alimony payments); *cf. Lovejoy v. Commissioner*, 293 F. 3d 1208 (10th Cir. 2002) (equivalent payments should not be treated as alimony).

Using the Sources

What is the treatment, under section 1041 and Treas. Reg. section 1.1041-1T, of the following transfers?

a. A transfer of appreciated real property, with a basis of $250,000 and a fair market value of $1 million, from a divorcing wife to her husband.

b. Same as a., except that the property is subject to a $500,000 mortgage, which the husband takes over on the transfer.

c. Same as a., except that the property is transferred directly by the divorcing wife to the couple's daughter, of whom the husband has custody, at the request of the husband.

d. A trust, the corpus of which consisted of appreciated property, and which was created by the wife to support the husband after the divorce.

e. Does it matter, in any of the above hypotheticals, when the transfer is made (*i.e.*, how long after the divorce)?

Law and Planning

1.   Suppose that you were counsel to Diana whose husband, Charles, had agreed to transfer her $500,000 in cash and cash equivalents as part of a divorce settlement. At the last minute, Charles proposes that, instead of cash, he will transfer Diana stock in a Fortune 500 company, which has a basis to him of $50,000 but a cash value of $500,000. "It's the least I can do," he explains.

As Diana's lawyer, what would be your response to this proposal? Would it matter if the proposal was advanced for the first time three years after the divorce was completed (*i.e.*, the $500,000 in stock were to be substituted for $500,000 in cash under the original divorce agreement)? Finally, what difference if any would it make if the stock were in Charles's family business, rather than in a large, publicly traded company?

2.   What effect would section 71 (as well as 1041) have on your answer to 1., above?

3.   Section 1041 does not address the issue of transfers occurring before marriage (*i.e.*, prenuptial agreements). According to the most prominent case in this area, prenuptial transfers — or at least, those made in consideration of a promise to marry — are treated as sales rather than gifts for income tax purposes, resulting in tax on any built-in appreciation at the time of transfer.[30] In other words, the rule in these cases remains similar to that enunciated by the Supreme Court in *United States v. Davis*, but this time without the provisions of section 1041 to protect you.

---

[30] Farid-es-Sultaneh v. Commissioner, 160 F.2d 812 (2d Cir. 1947).

Suppose that you are the lawyer for a prospective married couple that is concluding a prenuptial agreement. The couple is adamant that the marriage take place only upon a substantial transfer of assets from the wife to the husband, but is equally adamant that the transfer should avoid imposition of tax. (It's as easy to love a tax-free person as a taxable one, if all other things are equal, which they're usually not.)

How would you advise the couple to proceed?

Politics and Policy

The rule permitting deductibility of alimony payments seem to be based on the assumption that divorced spouses are dealing at arm's length with each other, that is, that they are no longer part of a combined economic and social unit. By contrast, section 1041 appears to assume that — at least for some intermediate period — the couple remains just such a combined unit. Are these rules consistent with each other and, if not, which should change?

III. THE ESTATE AND GIFT TAXES

A discussion of marriage and divorce inevitably leads one to consider birth, death, and the remaining life cycle events. While it is difficult to plan for one's own birth, planning for one's death has an honored place in the tax field. This results in large measure from the existence of the estate tax.

The estate tax has an odd position in the tax field. A relatively small number of people — essentially, millionaires and their spouses — pay the estate tax, and compared to the income tax it raises relatively little money. Yet its significance remains high, for it shapes the entire structure by which wealth is held and transmitted in our society. The estate tax and its lifetime equivalent, the gift tax, also make an important contribution to the progressivity of the federal tax system. As we have seen, income tax provisions regarding gifts, basis, capital gains, and many other subjects are impossible to understand without at least a rudimentary understanding of the estate tax.

Even a cursory discussion of the mechanics and legal rules underlying the estate and gift taxes is beyond the scope of this casebook. Instead, the following materials will briefly introduce the estate and gift taxes, with a focus on the policy issues underlying the current debate about whether the estate tax should be abolished.

"Don't tax death" is the rallying cry for estate tax opponents, and it has a certain ring to it, although it isn't clear that taxing dead people (who after all can't really complain about it) is necessarily such a bad idea. (When we asked a colleague why estate lawyers kept such short hours, he replied: "Because our clients are already dead.") The arguments in favor of estate taxation are a curious admixture of the usual arguments for progressivity, coupled with a fear of wealth concentration and a sense that people should earn, rather than inherit, their economic and social advantage.[31] By contrast, the arguments against the tax tend to emphasize private

---

[31] More general arguments in favor of progressivity can be found in any number of law review articles

property rights (it's our money and we should be able to keep it), coupled with arguments that estate taxes discourage saving, destroy small business, and result in double taxation of income that (at worst) should be taxed only once. In other words, the estate tax raises many of the same issues as income taxation, but with the added emotion that goes with a potentially very high, one-time tax that is imposed primarily on the upper stratum of society.

The following are excerpts from arguments in favor of and against estate taxes, together with an article by Professor Langbein that questions whether — even with the best intentions — an estate tax can be effective under modern conditions. Note that one of the articles critical of the estate tax (by Professor McCaffery) comes from a liberal perspective, suggesting that estate taxation is a matter of tax and social philosophy rather than a simple left-right issue.

Edward J. McCaffrey, *The Uneasy Case for Wealth Transfer Taxation*
104 YALE L.J. 283, 284–86, 288–89 (1994)[32]

I. INTRODUCTION

Privately held wealth and its unequal distribution, and perhaps especially the transmission of such wealth across generations, have long been thought to pose particularly pernicious influences in a liberal democratic state. Thus, some form of a wealth transfer tax — most commonly an estate or an inheritance tax — has typically been a part of real-world and theoretically supported comprehensive tax systems. As our ideas about the role of other taxes have shifted, both in practice and in theory, our intellectual allegiance to a system of wealth transfer taxation in the United States has remained more or less fixed. The present estate tax is similar, in its essential form, to the initial estate tax implemented in 1916, and scholarly support for some type of wealth transfer tax, although far from universal, remains strong. Recently, some scholars have even called for a confiscatory estate tax, or an abolition of inheritance altogether.

But times have changed since 1916. Our political-philosophical ideas have evolved. The federal income tax has grown from a relatively small surcharge on the highest incomes into a massive, broad-based tax system. Corresponding to this expansion in breadth, we have shifted, both in theory and in practice, from an income toward a consumption tax model. Over three-quarters of a century of experience with both estate taxes and nominal income taxation has strengthened our understanding of the possibilities and limitations of tax systems, all during a period of continued inequality of wealth, income, and consumption.

Meanwhile, the estate tax does not, in fact, appear to be working. It does not raise significant revenue. It is and has always been riddled with large exceptions, exemptions, and exclusions. Most striking is the fact that the tax has never been

---

or other academic publications. *See, e.g,* Joseph Bankman & Thomas Griffith, *Social Welfare and the Rate Structure, a New Look at Progressive Taxation*, 75 CAL. L. REV. 1905 (1987).

and is not now popular. At the same time, a more sophisticated tax scholarship has given us a wider range of policy options than our untutored imaginations put forth eight decades ago. These changes, in theory and in practice, make the case for the estate tax more uneasy than initial intuitions might otherwise suggest.

What is most surprising in my analysis is that unease over the estate tax arises specifically on *liberal* grounds. The linkage between liberalism and some form of wealth transfer tax has been so strong that severing this connection seems deeply counterintuitive, and thus highlights the wisdom of rethinking basic theoretic approaches, not just to issues of taxation, but also to social theory in general. Indirectly, at least, this Article is an exercise in how tax policy analysis and political theory can learn from each other.

* * *

My argument follows three basic steps: (1) The current gift and estate tax does not work, is in deep tension with liberal egalitarian ideals, and lacks strong popular or political support. (2) While the failure of the status quo may suggest a stronger wealth transfer tax as an alternative, such an answer suffers from two distinct problems: (a) a stronger tax is neither practical nor popular, and (b) given the many imperfections of the real world and the likely consequences of a strengthened transfer tax, such as reduced work, reduced savings, and increased inequality in consumption, a stronger wealth transfer tax may not be preferable even on ideal liberal grounds. (3) Motivated by the first two points to think through matters more deeply, we can arrive at alternative tax systems that both comport better with liberal first principles and fit well with the implicit spirit of our actual practices and beliefs, without any form of estate tax at all.

This argument leads naturally to a proposal for comprehensive tax reform, specifically a progressive consumption-without-estate tax. By responding to our objective preferences for work and savings while giving institutional form to our suspicions over the large-scale private use of wealth, such a tax system indeed fits best with liberal principles and with the often-inchoate spirit of our actual practices. To those who would immediately object that the private possession of wealth alone is a distinct liberal concern, not reached by a progressive consumption-without-estate tax, I hasten to add that the altered tax regime changes the very meaning, and hence the risks and dangers, of the "private possession" of wealth. The meaning of this phrase is not a constant, but rather depends on the legal rules in place. A liberal society's reasonable concerns over possession alone reduce largely to dual concerns over possession *qua* potential or actual use; the ability to use one's wealth, the threat of doing so, or the actual ongoing use of wealth as consumptive investment is what ought to concern the liberal. But a progressive consumption-without-estate tax, designed under a political theory of tax, changes matters by redefining property rights. In the end, it appears that our practices may be moving toward a better place, on strictly liberal grounds, than any answers that our most rarefied political theory alone could produce.

* * *

Anne L. Alstott, *The Uneasy Liberal Case Against Income and Wealth Transfer Taxation: A Response to Professor McCaffery*
51 Tax Law Rev. 363, 363–68 (1996)[33]

I. Introduction

In two recent articles, Professor Edward McCaffery argues that the United States should repeal its federal income and estate taxes and replace them with a progressive tax on consumption. The basic proposal is familiar: The progressive consumption tax has a long and distinguished academic lineage, and consumption taxation in a variety of forms currently is enjoying renewed political popularity. Professor McCaffery's novel claim is that his proposal is grounded in liberal egalitarian political theory, particularly that of John Rawls. In this Article, I argue that Professor McCaffery's argument, although provocative and interesting, is not persuasive. Professor McCaffery's articles make an important contribution because they seek to apply liberal egalitarian political theory to taxation. Professor McCaffery's particular recommendations, however, rest on normative claims that are in tension with basic liberal principles and on empirical predictions that rely on a strained reading of the available economic evidence.

To understand the nature of Professor McCaffery's surprising claim, one must understand both the traditional liberal justification for the estate and income taxes and the nature of consumption taxation. Traditionally, Rawls and other liberal egalitarians have considered an estate tax and, under some conditions, a progressive income tax, to be central to a liberal regime. In Rawls' theory, the estate tax is an important means of correcting disparities in the distribution of wealth and power that tend to undermine important principles of justice — the fair value of political liberty and fair equality of opportunity. Rawls also argues that progressive income taxation may be appropriate under conditions of extreme and continuing economic inequality, a condition that arguably is met in the United States today. Professor McCaffery, in contrast, argues that neither an estate tax nor an income tax is a prerequisite for distributive justice in a liberal egalitarian regime. Instead, he contends, a progressive consumption tax would best promote liberal objectives.

The defining characteristic of a consumption tax is that it removes from the tax base income that is saved or invested (for example, in financial investments like stocks or bonds or in real investments like plant and equipment). A consumption tax, by definition, taxes only income spent on current, personal consumption (for example, on cars, food and travel). By deferring tax on saved income until the money is spent, a proportional consumption tax essentially exempts the earnings on the investment from taxation. A progressive consumption tax of the kind Professor McCaffery advocates would offer significant tax benefits to savers while penalizing those with high levels of consumption spending. In contrast, an income

---

[33] Copyright © 1996. All rights reserved. Reprinted by permission.

tax encompasses both consumed and saved income, and an estate tax taxes all inherited wealth, whether saved or consumed.

Professor McCaffery's argument differs significantly from prior scholarship advocating a consumption tax. Many previous proposals for consumption taxation have been framed in explicitly utilitarian terms: Economists, in particular, have long argued that a consumption tax, relative to an income tax, would promote aggregate well-being by increasing economic efficiency. Other advocates have argued that the consumption tax would avoid the considerable administrative challenge of measuring income from capital. Some prominent proponents of consumption taxation have recommended an additional tax on wealth, for instance, an estate tax, in order to preclude an undue advantage for the rich, who own a disproportionate share of capital and income from capital. In contrast, Professor McCaffery's case for a progressive consumption tax does not rely on utilitarian norms, but instead on the principles of liberal egalitarian political theory, and his argument rejects not only the income tax but also the estate tax.

In this Article, I argue that Professor McCaffery's argument is untenable at three key points. First, Professor McCaffery contends that traditional liberal theory has ignored an important distinction between the possession and the use of wealth, and that it is primarily the use, or consumption, of wealth that is objectionable on grounds of equality of opportunity or political liberty. Thus, he concludes, a tax on consumed income is ideally suited to a liberal tax regime. A closer examination shows that Professor McCaffery's argument discounts the significant political, economic and social power that possession of wealth confers. His claim ultimately turns on an ethically unconvincing characterization of private savings and investment as liberal values. In attempting to reconcile private power with public benefit, Professor McCaffery advances institutional innovations that are both unworkable and in tension with the premises of his argument.

Professor McCaffery's second argument concerns the economic effects of the estate and income taxes. He argues that liberal society appropriately values work and savings, which a consumption tax would encourage but which income and estate taxation discourage. In addition, he claims, the economic gains created by repeal of the income and estate taxes would tend to increase, rather than reduce, economic equality. Professor McCaffery's economic case rests on an overly optimistic account of the relevant empirical evidence and relies on comparisons of an idealized consumption tax with the flawed, real-world income and estate taxes.

Finally, Professor McCaffery defends his interpretation of liberal egalitarian principles by reference to current social practices. He argues that liberal political theory has inappropriately ignored public opposition to the estate tax and contends that, in this case, public opinion is an appropriate guide to liberal egalitarian ideals. Social interpretation is, however, a tricky business, and Professor McCaffery's overly simple reading of public opinion and political rhetoric comes dangerously close to equating illiberal sentiments with liberal principles.

Although this Article challenges Professor McCaffery's conclusions, his work is important and well worth attention because it appropriately pushes us to consider how to fill in the significant institutional gaps in Rawlsian theory. Rawls provides a basic normative framework for thinking about just institutions but intentionally (and wisely) leaves unanswered many concrete questions about the nature of taxation in a liberal regime. Rawls' initial institutional recommendations regarding taxation are sketched in a few brief pages, and in a later work, Rawls acknowledges that matters of equitable distribution "rest on complicated inferences and intuitive judgments that require us to assess complex social and economic information about topics poorly understood." Assessing these complicated issues is a difficult task, but those who study tax policy and public finance and who are committed to liberal goals have a responsibility to bring to bear the best available information, to use it critically and to apply it responsibly to craft a taxing regime that best serves liberal goals.

These fundamental issues of justice in taxation are particularly important today, when already-large inequalities in income and wealth in the United States continue to grow and there is renewed debate in political circles about the propriety and economic costs of redistributive taxation and transfers. Although Professor McCaffery apparently does not intend a general attack on redistribution from richer to poorer, his moral and economic arguments bear an uncomfortable resemblance to familiar claims made by opponents of redistribution. Left unanswered, Professor McCaffery's arguments could offer unwarranted (though unintended) theoretical support for an illiberal political agenda. Although liberal egalitarian principles may be, as a practical matter, a thin defense against the powerful currents of politics, they provide important reasons for tempering prevalent concerns about aggregate economic output with a modicum of distributional fairness.

* * *

John H. Langbein, *The Twentieth-Century Revolution in Family Wealth Transmission*
86 MICH. L. REV. 722, 722–24, 750–51 (1988)[34]

The ancient field of trust-and-estate law has entered upon a period of serious decline. In some law firms, even seasoned practitioners have begun to diversify away from the field. In leading circles of the trust-and-estate bar, there is now open discussion of diminishing clientele, difficulty in billing for legal services at rates comparable to the rates for other specialties, and the reluctance of new associates to enter the field.

Although it has been fashionable to attribute this decline to the dramatic 1981 revision of the federal transfer taxes, which effectively relieved the middle classes from entanglement with the estate tax, the theme of this article is that the phenomenon has causes far more profound. The decline of the probate bar reflects the decline of probate. The decline of probate has two quite different dimensions. One is the much-remarked rise of the nonprobate system. Financial intermediaries operate a noncourt system for transferring account balances and other property on death with little or no lawyerly participation. I shall recur to that subject in Part IV.

The decline of probate has another dimension that has not been well understood. Fundamental changes in the very nature of wealth have radically altered traditional patterns of family wealth transmission, increasing the importance of lifetime transfers and decreasing the importance of wealth transfer on death.

In this article I shall be concerned with private-sector wealth. Into the eighteenth century, land was the dominant form of wealth. The technological forces that broke up older family-centered modes of economic organization called forth two new forms of private-sector wealth. One category is what we today call *financial assets* — that is, stocks, bonds, bank deposits, mutual fund shares, insurance contracts, and the like — which now comprise the dominant form of wealth. The other great form of modern wealth is what the economists call *human capital.* It is the skills and knowledge that lie at the root of advanced technological life.

The main purpose of this article is to sound a pair of themes about the ways in which these great changes in the nature of wealth have become associated with changes of perhaps comparable magnitude in the timing and in the character of family wealth transmission. My first theme, developed in Part II, concerns human capital. Whereas of old, wealth transmission from parents to children tended to center upon major items of patrimony such as the family farm or the family firm, today for the broad middle classes, wealth transmission centers on a radically different kind of asset: *the investment in skills.* In consequence, intergenerational wealth transmission no longer occurs primarily upon the death of the parents, but rather, when the children are growing up, hence, during the parents' lifetimes.

My other main theme, developed in Part III, arises from the awesome demographic transformation of modern life. For reasons that I shall explore, those same parents who now make their main wealth transfer to their children inter vivos are also living much longer. The need to provide for the parents in their lengthy old age has put a huge new claim on family wealth, a claim that necessarily reduces the residuum that would otherwise have passed to survivors. A new institution has arisen to help channel the process of saving and dissaving for old age: *the pension fund.* The wealth of the private pension system consists almost entirely of financial assets. I shall emphasize a distinctive attribute of pension wealth, namely, the bias toward annuitization. When wealth is annuitized, virtually nothing is left for transfer on death.

Thus, wealth transfer on death is ever less characteristic of family wealth transmission. Part IV relates these great changes in family property relations to the residual process of wealth transfer on death.

At the outset, I must emphasize a pair of exclusions from the trends being described in this article. I shall be talking about the patterns of wealth transmission that characterize the broad generality of American wealth-holders — roughly, the upper third to upper half of the populace. I mean, in short, the middle and especially the upper-middle classes, which is to say, the mostly white-collar, technical, managerial, and professional cohort. These people propel the knowledge-based economy of our post-industrial age, and they command much of its wealth. The trends I shall be discussing have had less influence upon the wealth transmission practices at the extremes of our society — among the very rich and among the poor.

The modes of gratuitous transfer have never had much relevance to the poor or near-poor. If you lack appreciable wealth, you will face many problems in life, but one problem that you will be spared is the question of how to transmit the wealth that you do not have.

At the other end of the spectrum, among those who populate the uppermost tail of the wealth distribution — people somewhere within the top one percent of wealth-holders — the trends that I shall be discussing have also not been of great significance. I shall have more to say about why the great forces canvassed in this article are largely spent before they touch dynastic wealth.

* * *

V. CONCLUSION

Increasingly, estate planning services for the middle and upper-middle classes have the quality of contingency planning. The client is motivated largely by concern to make arrangements for his family in the unlikely event that he should die prematurely. He does not expect property actually to pass under the instrument he executes. In this sense, he views his estate plan somewhat like his term life insurance policy. It is catastrophe insurance, worth having even though it is unlikely to be needed.

The modern expectation is that for middle-class wealth, the main intergenerational transfer will occur in mid-life, in the form of educational expenditures. The characteristic wealth of later years, the income streams from the public and private pension systems, do not give rise to heirship. Thus, wealth transfer on death is ever less important to the middle classes; and when it does occur, it is ever more likely to be channeled through the nonprobate system. These are the great forces that underlie the decline of the trust-and-estate bar.

So long as the carriage trade abides, the trust-and-estate bar will not go the way of the blacksmith, but the precipitous decline of the middle-class market is likely to continue. From the revolutionary changes that have affected the family property relations of the middle and upper-middle classes, only table scraps remain for the trust-and-estate lawyer. The days of routine, lawyer-guided wealth-transfer-on-death for the middle classes have largely passed.

Politics and Policy

1. How convincing do you find each of the following arguments in favor of, and opposed to, the existence of the estate tax?

a. (For) The estate tax is necessary in order to preserve some measure of tax progressivity, the income tax being insufficiently progressive and largely ineffective in reaching inherited wealth as opposed to earned income.

b. (For) The estate tax helps to break up large concentrations of wealth, which are dangerous to a democracy.

c. (For) It is inherently unfair for some people to start life with an advantage over others — they're lucky we don't confiscate inheritances, altogether.

d. (Against) The estate tax places an unfair burden on small (especially family) businesses, which must often be sold in order to pay the tax.

e. (Against) The estate tax discourages savings, since people who save their money rather than spend it will have to give back half of it in estate taxes, anyway.

f. (Against) The main reason people work hard is so they can leave money to their children: the estate tax breaks this vital link and thereby undermines the whole moral basis of our free enterprise society.

2. Supposing that you accepted Professor Langbein's thesis about the limitations of the estate tax, and wanted to propose a tax that reached the "new" forms of wealth transmission mentioned in his article. What kind of tax would you propose, and how would it measure up under the criteria of fairness, efficiency, and simplicity discussed earlier in this casebook? What do you think would be the likelihood of its adoption?

3. If the estate tax were repealed, what changes might you recommend in the income tax to compensate for its loss?

Additional Assignment — Chapter 10

Refer to the assignment following Chapter 9, concerning the capital gain and other tax problems of a well-meaning but slightly confused American couple, and consider the following additional facts:

As time goes on, the Cheltenhams have become dissatisfied with the conventional strategies outlined in Chapter 9, and are considering still more dramatic action in order to reduce their taxes. With the help of a rather aggressive accountant, they are considering the following schemes:

a. Entering into an income-sharing arrangement in which one-third of the parents' income would be transferred to each of their two children, Fred (19) and Wilma (12), on an indefinite basis.

b. Giving the children generous employment contracts with their mother (Bala's) consulting business.

c. Transferring $100,000 worth of stock to each of the children, which they would be expected to sell later on in order to finance their college educations or similar constructive pursuits. The idea would be to reduce the income tax on the sale as well as any dividends earned in the intervening years, and (perhaps) to teach a little responsibility to the children along the way. The children would be expected to consult with the parents regarding investment decisions. (Note: You may ignore estate and gift tax consequences.)

d. Firing the accountant and going back to Chapter 9.

Please prepare a memorandum to the couple, not to exceed three double-spaced pages, discussing the above possibilities.

What is the likelihood that each of these strategies would accomplish the Cheltenhams' tax and non-tax goals, and which if any would you recommend they consider adopting? Are adjustments necessary with respect to any of the three options, in order to achieve these goals? Finally — a question you are probably getting used to by now — what additional facts, if any, would you want to know before offering this advice?

Chapter 11

BUSINESS TAXATION AND THE CHOICE OF BUSINESS ENTITY

When one asks why tax is an important "building block" course the answer is often because of its importance to business transactions. Although a full treatment of business tax issues must await another course (or more likely courses), it seems a pity to complete a basic tax course without understanding the rudiments of business taxation. Even if you don't take another tax course, these materials will place you in better stead in other business or commercial courses, and enable you to appreciate the tax strategies that so often drive decisions in these areas.

Because of its condensed nature, this chapter takes a somewhat more practical focus than the preceding materials. We will attempt to quickly get to the basic questions: what are the differences in tax treatment of the basic forms of business entity (corporation, partnership, and limited liability company (LLC)), and how do these affect the choice between different entity forms? How do tax factors interact with other planning goals, like raising adequate capital and preserving management flexibility, and when must tax savings be compromised to accomplish these other goals? What are the basic tax choices that face an already existing business, with regard to distributions, operations, and (ultimately) sale or liquidation, and how do these differ for different entity forms? The emphasis will be on the application of tax principles for the general practitioner, leaving to a later course the intricacies of various sophisticated transactions and planning strategies.

After covering the basic elements of corporate and partnership taxation, the chapter discusses an example of a modern corporate tax shelter and the substance-over-form rules that have been relied on in combating modern tax shelters. Finally, the chapter concludes with a brief discussion of tax reform proposals, including prospects for the "integration" of corporate and individual income taxes.

In 2003, Congress passed legislation that "temporarily" reduced the tax rate on corporate dividends from almost 40 to just 15 percent, with still lower tax rates (and occasionally, no tax at all) applying in some cases. The dividend tax rate reduction was originally scheduled to expire in 2008, but in 2005 Congress and the Bush administration acted to extend the rate reduction through 2010. As this edition goes to press, the dividend tax rates are scheduled to return to their pre-2001 levels beginning in 2011, but there remains considerable political uncertainty about whether (or, to what extent) Congress and the Obama administration will allow the reduced tax rates to expire. The materials below attempt to discuss business tax planning dynamics under both the pre-2001 (and post-2010?) rate structure and the reduced rate structure enacted in 2003. Although the passing of time will eventually reveal the outcome of this particular political controversy, the broader lesson that tax rates change over time, and that different rate structures lead to different tax planning dynamics, provides an important insight into the development of tax law and policy.

I. CORPORATE TAXATION AND THE CHOICE OF ENTITY PROBLEM

Suppose that Amy, Ben, and Charles get together and form a new business to market Amy's new discovery, a pill that makes teenagers behave in a socially acceptable manner with no discernible side effects. Should this business be taxed as a separate, independent entity, or merely as an aggregate of the three individuals who formed it? If the business makes (or loses) money, should it reflect that amount on its own independent tax return, or should a fraction of the gain or loss be reflected on the individual tax returns of each of the three main participants? And what if the business, having already paid a separate, independent tax, decides to distribute some of its earnings to one or more of the individual owners? Should this be an occasion for a second tax on those individuals, or should they be credited (directly or indirectly) for taxes already paid by the entity?

Under the American tax system, the answer is . . . it depends. Under long-standing precedents, a corporation is generally treated as a separate legal entity, which is responsible for its own taxes and files its own separate and distinct tax returns. Distributions of income to shareholders, commonly called dividends, are then taxable a second time on those individuals' tax returns. This is consistent with the general treatment of corporations as separate legal entities, although of course it may be a disadvantage when considered from a tax standpoint.

By contrast, partnerships and limited liability companies (LLCs) are treated as aggregates for tax purposes and — although they file returns for information purposes — do not pay federal income tax. Instead, the tax is paid by the individual partners or LLC members in proportion to their ownership interest.[1] Thus, if Amy, Ben, and Charles were each one-third owners of the business described above, one-third of each year's income would be taxed to each of them, whether or not that income was distributed or otherwise made available for their personal use. A proportionate amount of the business' losses would likewise "pass through" to their individual tax returns. (Because income has already been taxed to the individual participants, a distribution by a partnership or LLC does not result in a second level of tax.).

The differences in corporate and partnership (or LLC) taxation are striking in magnitude and — even after the recent legislative changes — can result in significant differences in after-tax income for an otherwise similar company. Assume that Amy, Ben, and Charles decide to conduct their business as a corporation, to be known as ABC Enterprises, Inc. Assume further that the

---

[1] Under Subchapter S of the Internal Revenue Code, electing corporations are permitted to be taxed under a single-tax regime similar to that used by a partnership or LLC. However, such corporations are limited to 75 shareholders, may not issue preferred stock, and are subject to other conditions that make the election unattractive to many corporations. Unless otherwise indicated, this chapter generally uses the term "corporation" to refer to a standard, *i.e.*, subchapter C, corporation, which is subject to the regular corporate income tax.

company earns $100,000 of net income in its first year, which it plans to distribute in equal dividends to its three shareholders. Finally, assume that a maximum corporate tax rate of 35 percent applies to the corporation and a maximum individual rate of 35 percent (15 percent for dividends) applies to each of its three shareholders.[2] The corporation would first pay a $35,000 (35 percent) corporate income tax, leaving $65,000 for distribution to the three shareholders. The shareholders would then pay a combined $9,500 (15 percent) tax on the dividend distributions, so that an aggregate of about $54,500 of the original $100,000 would be available to them (*i.e.*, a $45,500 tax payment). The combination of the $35,000 (35 percent) corporate level tax and the $9,500 (15 percent of the remaining funds) shareholder level tax constitutes the dreaded "double tax" that is the bane of corporate tax lawyers' existence.[3] (If the 2003 dividend tax rate reductions are allowed to expire, the 15 percent tax rate on dividends may rise to as high as near 40 percent, thus dramatically increasing the magnitude of the "double tax.")

By contrast, in a partnership or LLC, Amy, Ben, and Charles would pay one tax (an aggregate of $35,000) at the individual level, but no entity-level tax so that $65,000 would remain in their hands at year's end — a hefty 35 percent tax rate, but still better than the combined rate of closer to 50 percent in the corporate hypothetical. (This difference was more significant for prior tax years, when the combined corporate and dividend tax rate was about 60 percent). Perhaps more significantly, the partnership or LLC would also permit the participants to use the business's tax losses (if any) against their individual income; in a corporation such losses could only be carried back or forward against corporate income.

So why does anyone choose to operate in the corporate form? One reason is that the tax bite may not always be as dramatic as that described in the preceding paragraph. For example, ABC Corporation may decide to reinvest its earnings in the business, rather than distributing them to shareholders, in which case it will pay the corporate (35 percent), but not individual dividend (15 percent), income tax. (The shareholders would still have to pay a capital gain tax on a later sale of their appreciated shares, but that may be well off in the future.) Or, the corporation may pay salaries to one or more of the participants, in which case it would receive a deduction wiping out all or part of the corporate level tax, although leaving the individual tax essentially in place. If it wanted to be truly aggressive, the corporation might even eliminate some of its stock holdings and replace them with bonds or other forms of debt, resulting in interest payments that (unlike corporate dividends) are deductible at the corporate level. Of course each of these stratagems has its costs: the shareholders may not want to reinvest all the income and salary or interest payments may cause serious cash-flow problems for a new start-up business. There is also the danger that — if the tax planning is too aggressive — the IRS will recharacterize interest or salary payments as disguised dividends and reinstate the original double-tax treatment. But each of these strategies offers the

---

[2] The corporate income tax is actually imposed on a graduated scale, although a 34 percent rate is reached rather quickly (at $75,000 of taxable income) and the 35 percent rate at $10 million of taxable income. I.R.C. § 11. As we are assuming the maximum rate for individual taxes, it seems reasonable to do similarly for the corporate tax. The 15 percent tax rate on dividends was enacted in 2003.

[3] The "double tax" is reduced, but not eliminated, by the 2003 changes (see below).

possibility of avoiding (or at least delaying) a second tax level, thus significantly reducing the disadvantages associated with corporate status.

A second reason for the popularity of corporations is that — although tax lawyers sometimes claim otherwise — not everything in life is taxes. Put simply, there are numerous non-tax business factors that go into the choice of entity and that are often more important than the issues described above. One big issue is limited liability, which is available in a corporation or LLC but (except for limited partners) not in a typical partnership. A second factor is financing, in which corporations have an advantage because of the existence of large capital markets (the New York Stock Exchange, NASDAQ, etc.) which have no precise equivalent in the partnership or LLC field. (This is a more important factor for large, publicly owned entities than small family businesses.)

Third, there are numerous structural differences between corporations and other entities, which may favor one entity or another in different circumstances, but are often more pressing than the long-range tax consequences. For example, a corporation is characterized by a separation of ownership and control, in which a Board of Directors (or more realistically, a cadre of professional managers) manages the corporation with only sporadic interference from the actual share-holders. In contrast, a partnership or LLC traditionally contemplates a somewhat higher degree of involvement from its participants. The capital structure of these entities also differs. Corporations may raise money by issuing stock, bonds, or preferred stock — a sort of hybrid entity which has some features of each of the two preceding options.[4] Partnerships likewise may issue partnership interests or debt (the equivalent of corporate stock and bonds), but also have the ability to make "special allocations" to individual partners, providing, e.g., that Partner A shall have a 1/3 interest in profits but a 2/3 interest in losses, or that her share of profits will change after the passage of a specified period of time or the occurrence of specified events. There are also differing presumptions regarding length and termination of the entity, transferability of interests, and other business particulars. As a very general rule, these factors tend to favor corporations for a large business and partnerships or LLCs for a small one; but there is no universal pattern and which factor predominates depends very much on the particular fact situation.

What all this means is that the choice of entity comes down to a balancing of tax and business factors or — what amounts to the same thing — to trying to reduce taxes without sacrificing any practical goals that one or more parties is unwilling to compromise. For a small business, which anticipates losses in the early years and expects to distribute at least some of its income should it become more profitable, tax factors are likely to be a major factor in entity selection. For this kind of business, avoiding the double tax may be an essential goal, and the question may be what type of single tax-entity (partnership, LLC, or electing subchapter S corporation) best meets its needs. Most new businesses probably fall into this category.

The situation may be different for businesses which anticipate retaining most earnings or that can reduce the corporate level tax by making extensive salary or

---

[4] Subchapter S corporations are forbidden to issue preferred stock.

interest payments. For such businesses, tax factors may be somewhat less pressing and the company may be free to choose its form of entity based on liability, fundraising, or other non-tax factors. An example of this might be a start-up company funded primarily by "venture capitalists," who primarily seek capital appreciation (that is, an increase in the value of their stock) and who are not particularly interested in dividends or similar distributions. Such businesses may decide that they have to incorporate in order to have access to the relevant capital markets and simply swallow the corporate double tax — which applies only to distributed income anyway — as the price of achieving this goal. In a study of "Silicon Valley" start-ups, Joseph Bankman found that a surprisingly large number elected to do business as standard, subchapter C corporations, apparently oblivious to tax factors or else deciding that they were outweighed by more immediate business concerns.[5] Large businesses may find it organizationally clumsy to operate as a partnership or LLC and choose to be a corporation for that reason.

The problems below consider the determination of tax and the issue of entity selection under a number of different fact patterns. In approaching the choice of entity problems, consider both the role of tax factors (including single vs. double tax, attribution of losses, and ability to reduce the double tax by means of salary or interest payments) and non-tax issues (including limited liability, managerial structure, and financing needs). Which of these factors appears most important to you in each fact pattern and how did you "balance" the factors against each other in making your decision?

Using the Sources

1.   What is the aggregate tax rate (*i.e.*, combined entity level tax, if any, and individual income tax) in each of the following cases? Assume a 35 percent corporate tax rate, 35 percent individual tax rate (except dividends), and a 15 percent tax rate on dividends received by an individual taxpayer. For extra credit, recompute the aggregate tax rate based on a 35 percent individual rate with no exception for dividends (*i.e.*, assuming that the current special treatment of dividends was eventually repealed).

   a. A corporation (subchapter C) that distributes all its income in dividends.

   b. A corporation (subchapter C) that distributes none of its income, preferring to reinvest profits in the corporation. What if the participants plan to sell their stock in the company five years later?

   c. A partnership or LLC that distributes all of its income to its partners (LLC members).

   d. A partnership or LLC that distributes none of its income to its partners (LLC members).

   e. A subchapter S corporation.

---

[5] *See* Joseph Bankman, *The Structure of Silicon Valley Start-Ups*, 41 UCLA L. REV. 1737 (1994).

2.   Describe three strategies for reducing taxes in a subchapter C corporation and their practical limitations.

3.   Suppose that a business has losses in excess of its income for the taxable year. (This can't go on forever, but happens with some regularity.) What is the tax treatment of these losses in (i) a subchapter C corporation, (ii) a subchapter S corporation, and (iii) a partnership or LLC? Can you cite specific statutory support for each of your answers? (The subchapter S provisions are found at section 1361 *et seq.* of the Code.)

Law and Planning

1.   What would be the most appropriate form(s) of entity in each of the following three hypothetical cases?

a. The business described in the preceding pages, in which Amy, Ben and Charles pool their resources to market a new pill discovered by Amy in her laboratory. Amy is a research scientist who will work full-time on research and product development; Ben is a financial wizard who will manage the business end of the company; and Charles is a retired businessman who will help supervise the company but will not be involved on a day-to-day basis. Amy and Ben will contribute their labor together with Amy's patent (worth $1 million) and real estate previously owned by Ben (also $1 million), while Charles will contribute $1 million in cash. Amy and Ben, who are both in their mid-30s, are putting most of their resources into the business, while Charles (age 55) has substantial outside investments.

b. A new restaurant, to be operated Fred and Kayla Rice and specializing in a mixture of Jewish, Asian, and African-American cuisine. The business is to be partially funded ($500,000) by the couple themselves and partially ($1,500,000) by friends and relatives that they have encouraged to invest, none of whom will work at the restaurant and no single one of whom is investing more than $250,000. Fred and Kayla plan to manage the business and do most of the cooking themselves, but would likely hire a number of employees as waiters, assistant chefs, and other positions.

c. A company being formed by George Gush and Al Bore, two retired politicians, to develop and market a new vote-counting mechanism that has a 100 percent accuracy rate and would accordingly avoid, well, you know what. The company is to have an initial capitalization of $10 million, of which the bulk is to be raised from outside investors; if the business goes well, a public offering of interests is anticipated. The company further expects that it will hire a substantial number of employees (including professional managers) and will reinvest any profits earned during the first ten years with a goal of expanding the company and increasing its long-term performance.

2.   Having chosen a form of entity in each case, what additional policies would you plan to pursue in order further to reduce taxes, without sacrificing any of your underlying business goals? Consider, among others, the business management

structure, salaries and other forms of compensation, and non-compensatory distributions to the business owners.

3.   What additional facts, if any, would you want to have in order to answer any of the preceding questions?

4.   How, if at all, would your answers to the questions above differ depending on whether the maximum tax rate on corporate dividends is 15 percent or near 40 percent?

Politics and Policy

If you've been paying even casual attention, you have probably noticed that the rules regarding taxation of business entities are inconsistent and (all too often) arbitrary in nature. Is there any need for this confusion? Would a uniform regime, providing the same tax treatment regardless of corporate partnership or LLC status really be so difficult to design?

LLCs and the "Check a Box" Problem

Sometimes, when the pace of tax reform is too slow, aggressive lawyers engage in a sort of do it yourself reform, pressing the limits of existing law until a new regime is effectively created. An example of this phenomenon is the rise of the limited liability company (LLC) during the past decade. The LLC arose in response to practitioners' demands for an entity that combined the best features of corporations (especially limited liability) with the best aspects of partnerships (notably single-level taxation and the right to use losses against the participants' outside income). Entities of this type had long existed in most European countries, but until the 1990s, American practitioners generally had to choose between limited liability and a single-tax loss allowance regime. These benefits could be combined in a subchapter S corporation, but a "Sub S" was subject to a limit of 35 (now 75) shareholders and had various other limitations that made it unsuitable for many businesses.

Enter the creative practitioners. In the late 1980s and early 1990s, some aggressive lawyers began organizing businesses as "limited liability companies," a form of entity that had existed for some time in several states, but which had generally been avoided because of fear of negative tax consequences. The practitioners asked the IRS to rule that these "LLCs" were partnerships, rather than corporations, and hence subject to only one level of tax on their distributed income. At that time, the IRS generally applied a "four-factor" test to entity classification, holding an entity taxable as a corporation if it had three or more of the principle four corporate characteristics (limited liability, centralized management, continuity of life, and free transferability of membership interests). Since LLCs by definition have limited liability, and since many of them are likely to have centralized management, in practice this meant an LLC would have to "flunk" both the continuity of life and free transferability tests in order to retain its partnership status and provide the tax and business benefits that the practitioners sought.

The IRS eventually gave the practitioners what they wanted, albeit in a two-stage process that made the issue considerably more complicated than it needed to be. First, it issued a series of rulings providing partnership status to LLCs that purported to lack both continuity of life and free transferability of interests, even though these entities were, in substance, not terribly different from equivalent corporations. (For example, LLCs were treated as partnerships if they required a vote of the full membership to approve a new owner, or to continue the entity if one or more members die.) This led a number of states to enact "bulletproof" LLC statutes designed specifically to comply with the IRS rules, while others enacted more liberal statutes under which an LLC — depending on its particular organizational structure — might or might not comply.

Faced with these inconsistencies, in 1996 the IRS gave up altogether and adopted the so-called "check-the-box" rules with respect to entity classification. Under these rules, an LLC could effectively choose to be taxed as a partnership or a corporation, regardless of the old four-factor test and regardless of whether it was substantively more similar to a corporation, a partnership, or a hybrid of these two entities.[6] For example, an LLC could theoretically have a board of directors, the equivalent of common and preferred stock, and other quintessentially corporate characteristics and continue to be taxed like a partnership so long as it was not called a corporation under the relevant state statute. Indeed, many states proceeded to adopt "permissive" LLC statutes that allowed businesses to do this, or something very close to it, without sacrificing their partnership tax status.

The history of LLCs exemplifies the dynamic character of tax law, in which practitioners frequently initiate new developments and the IRS finds itself in a reactive mode. But LLCs — for all their attractiveness — also pose difficult planning problems. For example, many state statutes permit an LLC to be organized as a "member-managed" entity — that is, something like a general partnership — or else to be run by professional managers, like a traditional business corporation. The former raises the question of what members should have veto powers over what decisions (sales and mergers, admission of new members, etc.), while the latter involves the surrender of substantial power to non-members and may cause the entity to be treated like a corporation for securities and other non-tax purposes. LLCs, like partnerships, also permit special (*i.e.*, disproportionate) allocations of income and losses to individual members, which increases the flexibility of tax planning, but also means that there are more things to argue about at the organizational and later stages. So the LLC is in many respects a mixed blessing: while rapidly becoming the entity of choice for new businesses, it presents a bevy of planning challenges more easily avoided in simpler times.

The LLC also raises anew the question of the two-level tax on corporations and what policy function it serves. If LLCs can elect whether to be taxed on one or two levels, why not permit the same election to a corporation? And what function (if any) is served by Subchapter S corporations, now that the LLC performs many of

---

[6] An LLC might elect to be taxed like a corporation if, *e.g.*, it planned to retain all or most of its earnings, or was sure that it could eliminate its corporate tax liability by interest or salary payments. The vast majority of LLCs choose to be taxed under the partnership rules.

the same functions in a more flexible way? These questions remain unanswered, but the general trend toward elective taxation appears irreversible and it would not be surprising to see some version of "check-the-box" treatment eventually extended to a wider range of tax issues.

II.   CAPITAL STRUCTURE AND THE DEBT/EQUITY ISSUE

The importance of tax issues does not end with the choice of a business entity. Many important decisions, ranging from the choice of capital structure to decisions regarding sales, distributions, and other business transactions, have significant tax consequences and are indeed often "driven" by tax as much as business considerations. In the interests of time, we will focus primarily on decisions that need to be made early in the business life cycle, *i.e.*, at the same time as the choice of entity or shortly thereafter. This section discusses a few basic tax issues in forming a new corporation; the ensuing section deals with similar issues in a partnership or LLC.

Perhaps the most important issue facing a new corporation is the choice of capital structure, that is, what kind of interests will the participants get in return for what kinds of contributions. The two principal kinds of interests are equity (*i.e.*, stock) or debt (*i.e.*, bonds or other evidence of indebtedness by the corporation to the debt holders). Stock, or equity, represents an ownership interest in the corporation and typically carries with it the right to participate in choosing the Board of Directors and (although the significance of this right varies) at least some right to vote on mergers and other major corporate transactions. Debt represents a contractual agreement between the corporation and its creditors, not unlike that which might exist between (say) a private borrower and a bank or other lending institution, and does not normally involve a management role.[7] Equity is generally considered a riskier investment than debt, since the stock may decline in value and there is no legal requirement to pay dividends or other distributions; but it has a higher upside potential, since stock of a successful corporation may be worth many times its original price, while the interest paid on debt will usually be about the same every year. (There is some risk in debt as well, as the corporation may go bankrupt and fail to pay its creditors, but this can to some degree be ameliorated by requiring security for the loan or simply by charging a higher interest rate).

The tax differences between debt and equity are most pronounced in a standard, subchapter C corporation. The difference is a simple one: interest payments on debt are deductible by the corporation, while dividends on stock — the economic equivalent of interest — are in most cases nondeductible.[8] Thus, distributions to debt holders result in only one tax payment, while those to stockholders in a double tax. For example, assume Quicksilver Corporation earns $1 million of income and distributes all $1 million to its shareholders, in Year One, in the form of dividend payments. As suggested above, the combined tax rate will be something in the vicinity of 45 percent, assuming a 35 percent corporate rate and the reduced 15 percent tax rate on dividends received by individual taxpayers. By contrast, if the

---

[7] A third type of interest, preferred stock, has elements of both debt and equity but is officially classified as an equity interest.

[8] An exception is provided when the shareholder is another corporation.

shareholders were transformed into creditors and the corporation distributed the same $1 million in the form of interest payments, the corporate tax would be eliminated, leaving $0.65 million ($1 million income–$0.35 million individual tax) in the hands of the recipients, or a combined 35 percent tax. The same tax result would be obtained if the shareholders were paid salaries as employees of the corporation or rents for property that they made available for corporate use. This difference is obviously less dramatic than it was before 2003, but remains significant, particularly if the relevant individual has deductions, etc., that may further reduce his or her effective tax rate. Note that these tax reductions schemes do not require that the corporation reinvest its income, or that it change to a partnership or LLC form, but merely that it make economically equivalent distributions in a different legal way.

So why doesn't everyone substitute debt for equity, leaving stock holdings as small as they can get away with? One answer is that the IRS isn't stupid and created a rule that deals with just this situation. Under section 385 of the Code, the Treasury Department is authorized to issue regulations that determine whether an interest is debt or equity — in other words, that recharacterize purported debt as equity for tax purposes — in appropriate situations. While these regulations have never been finalized, section 385 lists a number of factors that might go into the determination, including the conditional or unconditional nature of the payment obligation (a more conditional payment or an uncertain payment date, suggesting equity rather than real debt was at issue); whether there is subordination or preference between the different types of corporate debt (subordinated debt, or debt that is to repaid only after other obligations of the corporation, sounds suspiciously like equity and is liable to be labeled as such); the corporation's debt-equity ratio (an excessively high ratio is unusual and therefore suggests that some of the debt is really disguised equity); and other relevant factors. Courts have developed additional factors through caselaw. If too many of these factors are present, the tax advantages of issuing debt may not be realized and purported interest payments recharacterized as ordinary, double-taxed dividend distributions. Similar factors may be used to recharacterize "unreasonable" salaries or rentals as disguised dividend payments.[9]

A second reason relates to non-tax concerns. Although debt is a good tax strategy, it may be a business disaster. A company with large stock holdings may elect whether or not to pay dividends in any year. By contrast, debt or salary payments must be made annually, regardless of whether the corporation is making or losing money and regardless of the extent of its cash or other reserves. If these payments or not made, the corporation may be subject to lawsuits by its creditors or employees, and (if the failures are systematic) may find its debt recharacterized as equity under section 385, above. Meeting its debt payments is likely to be especially difficult if the company owes money to other businesses (banks, suppliers, etc.) and must make payments on this "outside" debt as well as the "inside" debt to its shareholders and other investors. So debt is a two-edged sword: a good tax and business strategy as long as things are going well, but a potential cash-flow disaster the minute things start to slow down.

---

[9] I.R.C. § 162(a)(1).

What all this means is that in determining capital structure — just as in choosing the form of entity — a good lawyer must balance tax and business concerns. The following problems deal with this issue in a relatively simple, "C" corporation, context.[10] As you answer these questions, consider the relative importance of tax and non-tax factors, and how much business danger you would be willing to place the corporation in to accomplish a significant level of potential tax savings. As a general matter, should tax factors ever "drive" underlying business decisions or do they become important only after these decisions are made?

Using the Sources

Under section 385, which of the following is likely to qualify as a debt instrument and which is likely to be reclassified as equity?

1.   A 30-year, $100,000 bond, with interest payable at a fixed 8 percent rate (*i.e.*, $8,000 of interest) every July 1 and principal to be repaid at the end of the 30-year period.

2.   Same as 1., except that the interest rate varies according to market conditions (*e.g.*, the rate on Government-issued securities).

3.   Same as 1., except that the bond indenture (documents) provides that interest will not be paid in any year that the company does not earn a net profit.

4.   Same as 1., except the bond indenture provides that interest will be paid only if the company's profits exceed $10 million per year.

5.   Same as 1., except that the company has five times as much debt as equity and the principal shareholders hold debt in the same proportion as their stock holdings.

Law and Planning

Suppose that you are general counsel to Mississippi.Com, a new corporation that planned to market law school and other textbooks over the Internet.[11] The three principal participants are Nathaniel Nerd, a law professor who was to lead the "educational" end of the business; Gina Grafetta, a financial expert who was to direct business operations; and Mary Moneybags, a slightly older investor who was to contribute $2.5 million but not participate in day-to-day business operations. Nerd and Grafetta will make relatively modest capital contributions ($1.25 million each) although their principal contribution will be in the form of services. The company also plans to borrow $10 million from a bank for a total initial capitalization of $15 million; later, if business goes well, a public offering of stock is contemplated. Internet businesses are extremely volatile (as if you didn't know) and the corporation may have several years of net losses before it becomes profitable.

---

[10] The debt-equity problems also exist in other forms of entity (partnership, LLC, and subchapter S corporation), albeit without the double tax problem, described above.

[11] Assume that the corporation has not made a subchapter S election.

Your initial draft of a capital and compensation structure is as follows:

Nerd	$1.25 million stock; $75,000 annual salary
Grafetta	$1.25 million stock; $75,000 annual salary
Moneybags	$1.25 million stock; $1.25 million 15-year, 7% bonds; no salary payments[12]
Bank	$10 million, 15-year loan (8%)

Before the deal is finalized, an aggressive (non-tax) member of your firm suggests that you are being too cautious. He suggests you rearrange the deal so that each participant will hold only $0.50 million in stock (*i.e.*, the same percentages as before, but with only one-fifth the aggregate stock holdings). The remainder of the parties' initial interests ($0.75 million each for Nerd and Grafetta, $2 million for Moneybags) would now be held in the form of debt. Your friend also suggests that you consider raising the salaries of Nerd and Grafetta and paying a modest salary to Moneybags, as further tax-reduction mechanisms. "If it works," he says, "you'll have the same economic structure and you'll pay much less tax. "If it doesn't work, the worst that can happen is you wind up back where you started."

What do you think of your friend's advice and would you recommend that your clients follow it?

Politics and Policy

Based on the above, what purpose is served by a rule that treats interest and dividend payments differently for tax purposes? Is the distinction actively perverse, encouraging people to make bad business decisions (*i.e.*, to issue excessive debt) in order to engender tax deductions? Or is the tax issue likely to be marginal to business decisions, so that the debt-equity problem is best addressed in some other, non-tax way? Would you recommend that a business increase its debt-equity ratio (*i.e.*, issue more debt and less equity) in order to achieve a higher deduction? Why or why not?

Although the materials above emphasize small businesses, the issue of debt and equity is also important in the context of large corporations, especially transactions that use sizeable amounts of debt to fund takeovers of large companies by a relatively small number of investors. The role of the interest deduction in encouraging such "leveraged buyouts" has long been a controversial issue in tax and corporate law policy. Excessive debt, and its encouragement by the tax system, has further been alleged to be (partially) responsible for increasing the level of risk in the economy and making it more vulnerable to a potential slowdown.

How concerned are you by the incentives the tax code creates for large companies and private equity investors to rely on debt financing? Do you think these tax incentives might have played a role in the 2008-2009 financial crisis?

---

[12] This is shorthand for bonds that will pay 7 percent interest each year, with the final interest payment and the original principal due at the end of 15 years.

Some scholars believe that — while excessive debt is obviously dangerous — a healthy level of debt may actually encourage better performance by executives who have to manage their companies in such a way so as to satisfy their debt payments. Do you agree that a high level of debt is likely to make managers more efficient, or is it more likely to focus their attention on short-term results rather than long-term performance and thereby damage the economy in the long run? How could we go about finding answers to these question, or are they largely questions of faith?

III. PARTNERSHIP TAXATION AND THE SPECIAL ALLOCATION PROBLEM

For an increasing number of small businesses, the entity of choice is a partnership or LLC, which is typically taxed in the same manner rather than a corporation. Among businesses that choose the corporate form, many will make a subchapter S election that provides "flow-through" tax treatment that is similar (although not identical) to a partnership or LLC. In many cases, this choice will be motivated by tax factors, although flexibility of operations and limited liability (especially for an LLC) are also important reasons.

The choice of a partnership or LLC format does not mean an end to tax planning. Although there is no double tax to worry about, partnership tax[13] involves a broad range of planning issues that are in many respects more challenging and complicated than their corporate equivalents. Indeed, there is a sense that partnership taxation, together with sophisticated corporate and international transactions are the "big leagues" of tax practice: if you like this, as the joke goes, you'll love being a tax lawyer.

The most lucrative issue in partnerships involves the question of income allocations. Say that Mississippi.Com, described in the preceding section, was organized as a partnership rather than a corporation. Because there is no stock in a partnership, the partnership is free to allocate income and losses in any way that the parties see fit. One possible way to do this would be proportional. Under this system, Nerd, Grafetta, and Moneybags would each receive one-third partnership interests, valued at $1.25 million each, entitling them each to one-third of all partnership tax items (gains, losses, etc.) realized in any year. To round out the picture, Moneybags could also be provided $1.25 million of debt, and Nerd and Grafetta a $75,000 (or higher) salary, just as in the corporate example. Under this system, if the partnership earned $1.5 million of income in a given year, each of the three participants would report $0.5 million on their individual tax return, together with any interest or salary payments. Any losses realized would be divided in a similar, proportional manner.

Now suppose that the parties wanted to be more creative. Suppose, for example, that Moneybags was in a higher tax bracket and needed deductions more than Nerd and Grafetta, who had limited outside income. Or suppose that Nerd and Grafetta,

---

[13] To avoid repetition, we will refer in this section to "partnership" taxation, with the knowledge that similar rules apply to an LLC.

who would be most responsible for the project's success or failure, wanted a higher percentage of income if the project exceeded $10 million in cumulative income, for which they were willing to compensate Moneybags with a disproportionate amount of income up to that point.[14] Alternatively, suppose that the parties wanted to allocate a particular kind of income or deduction to a particular individual; say, income from patent sales or royalty agreements to Nerd, or from certain business transactions to Grafetta, for a one-year or longer period.

Under the partnership agreement, the partners are free to make arrangements of this type and they are generally respected for tax purposes so long as they correspond to economic reality; or, as section 704(b) puts it, so long as they have "substantial economic effect." For example, the Mississippi.Com participants might decide on the following formula for allocating net income between the three original partners:

	Nerd	Grafetta	Moneybags
Net losses	20%	20%	60%
First $5 m net income	25%	25%	50%
$5 million-$10 million	33%	33%	33%
Above $10 million	40%	40%	20%

The effect of this allocation would be to give Moneybags a higher initial return with Nerd and Grafetta — whose efforts would be largely responsible for the company's success — receiving a higher share as the company became more successful. The parties might also decide that one or another of them was to be allocated income or losses that corresponded to their particular area of expertise, or to particular property that they had contributed to the business (*e.g.*, depreciation on a building or equipment or amortization of a patent or copyright interest). So long as these allocations were done for non-tax business reasons and reflected in the partnership's books, they would likely be noncontroversial.

The problem arises when allocations are manipulated to produce an artificial tax benefit without any obvious real-world impact. For example, assume that the partnership decides to allocate all net losses during the first five years to Moneybags, who is in the highest tax bracket and therefore can make the most use of the losses for tax purposes. Moneybags would prefer that this allocation remain essentially a bookkeeping trick; the tax loss will be scant comfort, if she is required to contribute money equivalent to her "losses," or if the losses are charged against her future share of income once the partnership becomes more profitable. In essence, she would like the partnership to keep two sets of accounts, one for tax purposes, and the other for purposes of internal partnership accounting. Yet if this is permitted, there is virtually no end to the potential tax savings and partnerships may be created for the express purpose of shifting income and losses to those in more favorable tax positions — the essence of the tax shelter phenomenon discussed in previous chapters.

---

[14] This arrangement would technically be referred to as a "shifting" rather than a "special" allocation, although the two are similar in effect.

To prevent this sort of thing, the partnership tax regulations contain some hundred-odd pages of highly technical rules, although it is not clear after reading them that one knows terribly much more about the subject than one knew at the beginning.[15] On a broad conceptual level, the rules break into two parts. The first, the "economic effect" test, requires that an allocation be reflected in the partner's capital account (*i.e.*, the books that measure the partner's share of partnership assets), so that a partner who leaves the partnership after taking a large number of deductions will receive a reduced share of partnership assets and, if her capital account balance is negative, will in theory be required to make up the difference to the other partners (Treas. Reg. section 1.704-1(b)(2)(ii)(b)).[16] For example, if Moneybags were to be allocated all losses during the first five years of the partnership, she would have to face the possibility that she might actually lose real money in return for this privilege.

The second part, the "substantiality" test, requires that there must be "a reasonable possibility that the allocation (or allocations) will affect substantially the dollar amounts to be received by the partners from the partnership, independent of tax consequences" (Treas. Reg. section 1.704-1(b)(2)(iii)(a)). For example, if one partner were allocated ordinary income and another partner capital gain, it would have to be demonstrated that these two numbers would (or at least, that there was a reasonable possibility that they would) differ from each other over the course of the partnership so that allocating income in this manner would carry risks as well as benefits for the partners involved. This is designed to prevent a situation in which, *e.g.*, a business tends to produce equal amounts of ordinary income and capital gain on a fairly predictable basis and the capital gain is simply allocated to the partner who — because she has capital losses or equivalent capital loss carryovers — would not pay tax on it anyway.

As one might expect, the name of the game in partnership allocations is to allocate items to those who need them the most for tax purposes, while giving the allocations just enough economic substance to pass the substantial economic effect test. The problems below test your skill in this sophisticated if cynical endeavor and in some of the simpler applications of section 704 regulations, generally. This material is hard — it's supposed to be hard — but it is worth at least a brief look to give you a taste of what real-world tax lawyers do on an everyday basis. Following these technical problems, we will consider whether the whole matter might not be a bit out of hand and whether or what kind of reforms might be useful in this area.

---

[15] At one point, the regulations say that in order to have a substantial economic effect, an allocation must have an economic effect, and that effect must be substantial (Treas. Reg. § 1.704-1(b)(2)(i)). It would seem difficult to deny this premise.

[16] The words "in theory" are important here: as you might expect, there are a variety of mechanisms for ensuring that the possibility of a deficit payback remains relatively remote. One favorite technique is to begin allocating more income to a partner whenever they come within striking distance of a negative capital account. Another popular gambit is to create situations in which a partner could theoretically lose money, but is as a practical matter unlikely to, so that the economic effect appears more "substantial" than it really is. *See* 2 McKee, Nelson & Whitmire, Federal Taxation of Partnerships and Partners ¶ 10.02 (2nd ed. 1990) (discussing the section 704(b) regulations).

Using the Sources

1. Which of the following allocations would have substantial economic effect under the section 704 regulations? (Try to be at least reasonably specific about the provision or provisions that you are relying on; if you can't state a precise regulation, give a broader citation or state the underlying concept.)

> a. An allocation of "bottom line" income among Partners A, B, and C, with the percentage allocations changing in each year and all allocations reflected in the respective partners' capital accounts.

> b. A special allocation of losses to Partner A, with the proviso that this allocation will be ignored for purposes of determining her capital account.

> c. A special allocation of losses to Partner B, to be reflected in his capital account, but with the proviso that — should Partner B leave the partnership with a negative capital account — the remaining partners will transfer sufficient assets to make up the difference.

> d. An allocation of deductions to Partner B, to be reflected in his capital account, but with the proviso that, should Partner B's capital account fall below zero, he will be allotted an additional percentage of partnership income until the account becomes positive again.

> e. An allocation of ordinary losses to Partner A (who has mostly ordinary income) and capital losses to Partner B (who has primarily capital gains), each allocation to be reflected in the partners' capital accounts. Does it matter if the ratio of capital gains to ordinary income produced by the partnership is generally predictable, or if it varies from year to year?

> f. An allocation of foreign income to A (who has a large number of foreign tax credits) and domestic income to B (who has domestic deductions, but no foreign tax credit). Assume for purposes of this question that, (i) the ratio of foreign to domestic income is more or less predictable on an annual basis, and (ii) both A and B are equally involved in the domestic and international aspects of the partnership's business.

2. Review your answers to question 1., and consider any cases in which the allocation might lack substantial economic effect. Is there any way you could change the allocation, consistent with the taxpayer's goals, so as to achieve substantial economic effect and thus have the allocation recognized for tax purposes?

3. Because "money" partners are frequently passive investors — and because they frequently are most eager to be allocated tax losses — the passive loss rules have an important effect on partnership tax planning. Consider once more the Mississippi.Com hypothetical earlier in this section. What effect would the passive loss rules have on Nerd, Grafetta, and Moneybags, respectively, and what steps (if any) might you take to deal with this problem?

Law and Planning

Go back further and consider the new business to be started by Amy, Ben, and Charles involving the exploitation of Amy's discovery of a new teenage behavior pill and described in item 1.a. of the Law and Planning section above. Suppose that the participants in this endeavor decided to do business as a partnership or LLC instead of a corporation and came to you for tax advice.

What capital structure (including general and limited partnership interests and debt holdings, if any) would you choose for this partnership and what percentage of income and loss would you allocate to each partner, in order to achieve these goals? Be sure to consider the possibility of both (i) shifting allocations (that is, allocations of bottom-line income that change from year to year) and (ii) special allocations (that is, allocations of particular kinds of income or loss to particular partners). What special allocations might you wish to make to Charles in particular and how would you ensure that these allocations were respected for tax purposes without sacrificing your underlying business goals? Would the other partners agree to these special allocations, and if not, could they be compensated in order to make them do so? How?

Politics and Policy

The substantial economic effect rules are essentially a partnership version of the substance over form concept, that is, the idea that transactions must have economic substance and not merely legal form in order to be respected for tax purposes. The problem is that taxpayers can manipulate the facts in order to give an appearance of economic substance that is greater than reality. There is a sort of inevitable degradation in this process, since lawyers who play by the book are likely to lose business to those who will "sign off" on transactions that are closer and closer to the line. The complexity of such transactions, and the mismatch in manpower between sophisticated law firms and the IRS, makes it difficult for tax administrators to reverse this process.

One possible response is to adopt an all-purpose interpretive principle, which permits the IRS to recharacterize transactions that meet the letter of the law, but are inconsistent with its overall purpose, whatever that may be. An interesting example of this phenomenon is found in Treas. Reg. section 1.701-2, the so-called partnership "anti-abuse" rule. This regulation provides that the IRS may "recast" a transaction, even if it literally complies with the partnership tax rules, in order to achieve a result that more accurately complies with the statutory purpose as divined by IRS. This may include the disregarding of the partnership's very existence (Treas. Reg. section 1.701-2(b)(1)); the reallocation of income or loss (Treas. Reg. section 1.701-2(b)(4)); and other similar measures. For example, the IRS might (in theory) disregard the existence of a partnership that it believed was created simply to shift income between different partners, even though the partnership complied with the literal requirements of section 704 and other applicable rules.

Although understandably popular with tax administrators, the anti-abuse rule is anathema to many practitioners who believe that the law should mean what it says and that the Government should not get a second chance to rewrite the statute if it does not like the original result. These arguments curiously replicate the traditional arguments against the use of legislative history, which was asserted to be unavailable to the average practitioner, although this argument was probably overstated in most cases.

What would you think of a general anti-abuse rule, which allowed the IRS to strike down transactions inconsistent with the spirit of any part of the tax law? What do you think would be the response of U.S. tax practitioners to a rule of this type, and do you think it would help or hinder the fair administration of the tax laws? Should such a rule, if adopted, be limited to tax law, or should it be applicable — with the possible exception of criminal statutes — as a more general jurisprudential concept? What might be the constitutional, as well as more purely political, objections to such a concept?[17]

IV. DISTRIBUTIONS, SALES, AND MERGERS: LATER PHASES OF THE BUSINESS LIFE CYCLE

Although much of the tax lawyer's work takes place at the business formation stage, by no means are all issues resolved at that point. Among the corporate transactions involving significant tax consequences are the distribution of cash or assets to shareholders; the "buy-out" of shareholders who wish (or who the remaining shareholders wish) to depart from the business; and the liquidation, sale or merger of the entity at the conclusion of its corporate existence. The same or similar issues are raised at equivalent stages of the partnership or LLC life cycle.[18] Even more than the choice of business entity, these transactions tend to be driven heavily by their tax consequences, so that the tax lawyer may also be the key business advisor in these cases.

While a complete description is beyond the scope of this book, a few basic principles are worth repeating. With respect to corporate distributions, the key issue is how to distribute earnings without resulting in the dreaded "double tax" on dividend payments. A common tactic is to attempt to characterize a distribution as the redemption (purchase) of all or a portion of the shareholder's stock rather than as a corporate dividend. If this tactic is successful, the shareholder will be taxed at a capital gain rather than an ordinary income rate, and — what is frequently more important — will be able to offset all or part of the basis in their stock against the amount of the money or property received.[19] (The 2003 legislation, which essentially conformed the dividend tax rate to the existing tax rate for capital gain, eliminated

---

[17] Canadian tax law includes a concept similar to the partnership anti-abuse rule but applicable to the entire tax system. *See generally* DAVID G. DUFF, CANADIAN INCOME TAX LAW 169-83 (2003). Section 482 of the (United States) tax law allows IRS to reallocate income and deductions between related companies if necessary to prevent tax evasion or otherwise clearly reflect income, although this is a slightly different and less ideologically ambitious concept. Section 482 is discussed further in the context of international pricing agreements. *See* Chapter 12, *infra*.

[18] In order to maintain your sanity, the remainder of this section focuses on corporations.

[19] For example, a taxpayer with a $20,000 basis for her shares, whose shares were redeemed for $50,000, would pay tax on only $30,000 rather than $50,000, in addition to paying a lower tax rate on this amount.

the first but not the second of these tax planning differences.)

Section 302 of the Code restricts this gambit by generally allowing capital gain treatment only for complete buy-outs of a shareholder's interest, or for those buy-outs which — although not retiring 100 percent of the shareholder's stock — are "substantially disproportionate" with respect to that shareholder.[20] The idea is that, if a transaction is to be regarded as a genuine purchase rather than a disguised dividend, it should involve a significant reduction in the amount of the shareholder's interest in the corporation. The "substantially disproportionate" concept is greatly complicated by the so-called family attribution rules, which consider stock owned by some individuals as being owned indirectly by other family members; one intriguing, although not notably successful strategy has been to argue that the members of a particular family despise each other so intensely that they should be exempted from the application of the attribution rules. This is undoubtedly true in some cases, but rather difficult to prove, and has been greeted with understandable skepticism by the IRS and most courts that have considered the issue.

Tax aspects are also vital in the sale of a business. Here, there are two key decisions: should there be a taxable or tax-free transaction, and (assuming there will be a taxable sale) should it take the form of a sale of the corporation's stock or its assets? As one might expect, these decisions tend to involve a mix of tax and non-tax considerations. As a general rule, a taxable sale of stock tends to be preferable to an equivalent sale of assets, since an asset sale involves two levels of tax — one at the corporate level and one when the profits from the sale are distributed to individual shareholders — and a stock sale is taxed solely at the corporate level.[21] This consideration is particularly important if the corporation has been successful and has a large amount of appreciated assets. But a stock sale may have serious non-tax drawbacks, including the fact that the sale of stock may involve the passage of unwanted liabilities to the new owners, or that the buyer wants to buy some, but not all of the relevant corporate assets. Buyers may also prefer an asset purchase because it will result in a higher basis for the newly acquired items. The end result is that, in most cases, a transaction can be structured as either a stock or asset sale, but the seller will often demand a higher price for the latter in order to compensate for the tax and related disadvantages associated with that format.

Perhaps the quintessential role for the tax planner involves tax-free "reorganizations" under section 368 of the Code. The paradigm here is a simple one. By selling their business for some mixture of stock and other consideration instead of purely for cash — that is, by accepting some kind of continuing role in the acquiring corporation — the acquired corporation and its shareholders can avoid tax, at least temporarily, on profits that would be taxable in an ordinary cash sale. The problem is that one must comply with a veritable parade of rules and regulations in order to secure this tax treatment. First, the courts have imposed requirements with respect to all tax-free sales, the most significant being that at least 50% of the preexisting

---

[20] I.R.C. § 302(b)(2).

[21] This rule applies, whether the assets are sold and the proceeds distributed, or the assets distributed to the shareholders and then sold. *See* I.R.C. § 312(b) (tax treatment on distributions of appreciated property).

owners must continue as owners of the surviving entity (the "continuity of proprietary interest" rule) and that the new owners must continue at least a portion of the same business that was conducted by the old ones (the "continuity of business enterprise" standard). These rules are consistent with the underlying policy of the tax-free reorganization provisions, which is to allow tax-free treatment only when there is significant continuity between the old and new corporate entities.

Second, the statute — like the early bird menu at a Fort Lauderdale restaurant — provides a rather rigid list of possible structures for a tax-free reorganization, each one of which must be perfectly complied with and which permit no substitution of elements between the different alternatives.[22] The rules here are almost entirely arbitrary and mark perhaps the ultimate triumph of form over substance in the entire tax code. As a general rule, "A" reorganizations (statutory mergers or consolidations) are most attractive on tax grounds, since they involve few substantive rules other than the requirement of 50 percent continuous ownership, as described above. However, a statutory merger typically means that the corporate "attributes" (including accumulated earnings and profits) of at least one company carry over to the merged entity and, what is much worse, that the assets of each company are exposed to the other company's preexisting liabilities, a situation which may be extremely undesirable in some cases. "B" reorganizations (stock-for-stock acquisitions) avoid this problem, but require that 100 percent of the purchase price be paid in stock rather than cash or other assets, which may present a problem if one or more of the selling company shareholders want to receive cash for their shares. "C" reorganizations (stock-for-assets) are somewhere between the two other alternatives, providing some flexibility of consideration,[23] but requiring that "substantially all" the assets of the seller be acquired and involving extraordinarily complex calculations, particularly when corporate liabilities are involved. The three principal alternatives are further complicated by the use of "triangular" structures in which a new subsidiary is formed by the acquiring corporation specifically for the purpose of merging with the target entity.[24] This hybrid structure has the advantage of qualifying for tax deferral, but without some of the liability or corporate governance problems that may result from a merger of the original business entity.

A tax-free reorganization involves the delay rather than avoidance of tax, since the surviving corporation takes the acquired stock or assets with their preexisting basis, and will theoretically pay tax at some future point when these are disposed of. In this respect, reorganizations are similar to like-kind exchanges and other deferral mechanisms studied in the previous chapters. But, a tax delayed is sometimes as good as a tax avoided, and the advantages of tax-free treatment — assuming that the statutory and judicial requirements above can be met — are significant enough to engage the skills of many of the best tax practitioners.[25]

---

[22] I.R.C. § 368(a)(1). "A," "B," and "C" reorganizations refer to subparagraphs contained within that provision.

[23] I.R.C. § 368(a)(2)(B).

[24] I.R.C. § 368(a)(2)(D), (E). Taxpayers who receive cash or other "boot" are taxed on the amount of boot received, even in an otherwise tax-free transaction.

[25] The rules for partnerships are if anything more complex than those applicable to corporations, with

Using the Sources

1.   Under section 368(a)(1) of the Code, which qualifies as a tax-free reorganization, and which does not?

   a. A statutory merger effected under New Jersey state law.

   b. A transaction in which Acquisition Corp. acquires all of the stock in Target Corp., compensating the Target Shareholders with a mixture of 80 percent Acquisition Corp. stock and 20 percent cash.

   c. What if the consideration was the same as described in b. above, but Acquiring Corp. acquired Target Corp.'s assets instead of its stock?

Would it matter if Target Corp. had liabilities at the time of the merger? (Hint: *See* I.R.C. § 368(a)(2)(B)).

2.   (Extra credit) What in the world are sections 368(a)(2)(D) and (E) talking about and why would anyone want to bother with them?

3.   (Super extra credit) Which of the two subparagraphs described in item 2. might be preferable to the other in structuring a tax-free reorganization and what additional facts would you want to know before answering?

Law and Planning

Daniel, Erin, and Frances are each one-third owners of SafeSurf Corporation, an Internet-related company which has been in existence for five years. The three owners paid $1 million each for their stock, but the company is now worth at least $15 million (*i.e.*, $5 million each) owing to substantially appreciated assets and a significant amount of retained (*i.e.*, undistributed) earnings. At any given time, the company has about $2 million of cash reserves and $2 million in mortgage and other debts. There is also a $10 million patent infringement lawsuit pending against the company, although the owners believe that is unlikely to succeed.

Daniel, Erin, and Frances are tired of running the business on their own and are thinking about "selling out." Daniel and Frances would be willing to stay on for at least a five year period as part of a reorganized entity, but Erin never wishes to see the others again and is demanding an immediate cash payment in return for her shares.

1. Based on the facts above, and assuming a willing buyer, would it be possible to structure a tax-free reorganization of SafeSurf? If so, which alternative (A, B, C or

---

the difference that the game here tends to involve the timing and character (capital gain or ordinary income) of taxable income and the manipulation of various basis rules, rather than the avoidance of the double tax on corporate income. Particularly challenging are the rules for compensating partners, which provide at least three different alternatives having entirely different tax consequences, and the rules for partnership dissolution, which likewise involve several different alternatives and are at times similar to, but at other times very different from, the equivalent corporate regime. Scholars and practitioners periodically propose that the rules for corporations and partnerships be simpler and more consistent with each other, but the tendency has been for the rules to become more complex, with the rise of the LLC — a hybrid having principally partnership but also some corporate characteristics, especially in its larger versions — providing a further complicating factor.

some type of triangular reorganization) would you recommend and why? (Try your best to parse the actual language of section 368; if this proves overwhelming, you may rely on the pithy description, above.)

2. Assume that all three SafeSurf shareholders demand cash, making a tax-free reorganization impossible. Would you recommend that the parties engage in a taxable stock, or a taxable asset, sale? Would this be an absolute recommendation or would it depend upon the price being offered?

3. What effect, if any, would the existence of the lawsuit have on your answer to either question above?

Politics and Policy

Do the existing rules regarding tax-free reorganizations make any policy sense, and if not, what rule or rules would you suggest to replace them? How about a general rule that said, "A tax-free reorganization is any reorganization in which at least 50 percent of the owners of the target corporation continue on as owners of the acquiring (surviving) corporation for a period of not less than five years," with the Treasury Department authorized to enforce this rule with appropriate regulations? Would this make things any better, or would the problem simply be kicked to the Treasury Department and IRS rather than to the Code? Is there sometimes a value to detailed, even arbitrary rules, or is this just a way to make tax lawyers (before they retire to Fort Lauderdale) richer than everyone else?

V.   CORPORATE TAX SHELTERS

In the 1970s and early 1980s, tax shelters frequently involved aggressive use of depreciation deductions and were often marketed to individual taxpayers. These varieties of tax shelters were mostly shut down by the passive loss rules, which we covered as part of our discussion in Chapter 8.

In contrast, modern tax shelters have generally exploited intricacies in the rules governing business taxation, international taxation, and/or the taxation of financial products. With this chapter's overview of business taxation as a background, we can begin to examine these modern tax shelters.

The following reading discusses one example of a modern tax shelter. The tax shelter in question involves aggressive exploitation of the corporate tax rules. We have briefly covered the basics of the corporate tax provisions upon which this shelter depends, but do not be overly concerned if you find the mechanics of the tax shelter difficult to follow. For many (if not most) of the modern corporate tax shelters, the very success of the shelter depends on the transaction being made sufficiently complicated so that IRS finds it difficult to determine the economic underpinnings of the transaction. If an IRS auditor does not understand that a transaction is designed as a tax shelter, the auditor will not know to challenge the transaction. Hence, tax shelter marketers purposefully make these transaction as convoluted as they can manage.

As you read the following excerpt, try to see if you can understand the gist of the tax shelter transaction. Try to focus on the big picture ("forest") rather than the details ("the trees"). Consider whether you are persuaded by Professor Johnson's view of the transaction, or whether you think he goes too far in criticizing KPMG (the accounting firm that designed the shelter). Ask yourself what role the substance-over-form rules play in combating tax shelters. (The substance-over-form rules — briefly introduced in the Background and Basic Themes Chapter — include a number of tests whereby the IRS can attempt to challenge a taxpayer's characterization of a transaction. Examples of these rules discussed in the following reading include: the "artificial loss," "inevitable pretax loss," "clear reflection of income," and "step transaction" doctrines.)

In evaluating these issues, consider whether taxpayers should be allowed to rely on the language of the Code as passed by Congress? Or should the IRS be permitted to challenge even transactions that appear to comply with the literal language of the Code, if these transactions are at odds with the overall statutory framework (or the Code's "purpose" or "intent")? Should taxpayers be subject to penalties or fines — or even criminal charges — for aggressively exploiting ambiguous statutory language?

Calvin H. Johnson, *Tales From the KPMG Skunk Works: The Basis-Shift or Defective-Redemption Shelter*
108 Tax Notes 431, 431–36, 438–43 (2005)[26]

KPMG, the fourth largest accounting firm, is negotiating with the Justice Department over the terms by which it might avoid criminal indictment for its conduct arising out of its tax shelters. From about 1996 through 2003, KPMG had an extensive operation to invent and sell packaged tax shelters. According to the bipartisan report of the Senate Permanent Subcommittee on Investigations:

> "KPMG devoted substantial resources and maintained an extensive infra-structure to produce a continuing supply of generic tax products to sell to clients, using a process which pressured its tax professionals to generate new ideas, move them quickly through the development process, and approve, at times, illegal or potentially abusive tax shelters."

The KPMG operation was looking for polished "turnkey" tax products that could be sold easily to multiple clients. "The business model," KPMG said internally, "is based upon the simple concept of investing in the development of a portfolio of elegant, high-value tax products and then maximizing the return on this investment though [KPMG's] distribution network." For a participant who purchased a shelter, KPMG offered a package of completed documents and "basically cookie cutter opinions" following a prototype. A "skunk works" operation was once a secret research lab for developing planes to defeat the Nazis and the Communists. The KPMG tax skunk works dreamed up transactions against our *United States*.

KPMG aggressively promoted its products, pressuring its agents to "sell, sell, sell." As one KPMG e-mail put it, "We are dealing with ruthless execution,

---

hand-to-hand combat, blocking and tackling. Whatever the mixed metaphor, let's just do it." The KPMG customers for the shelters were big-gain taxpayers — identified through KPMG's nationwide network as having gains larger than $20 million to shelter. As late as 2003, KPMG listed in its inventory 500 active tax products offered to multiple clients for a fee. Overall, KPMG collected at least $124 million in fees for its skunk works shelters, which would have eliminated $10 billion of gain from the tax base had the shelters been successful.

Within KPMG, there was a lot of professional dissent as to whether KPMG shelters worked, which was picked up in the e-mail traffic the Senate subcommittee reproduced. KPMG decided to go ahead with the marketing of its shelters, however, despite the internal dissent, on the assumption that KPMG would receive enough revenue from their sales to offset the risks of litigation. Philip Weisner, the chief of the KPMG National Tax Office, was responsible for supervising the 100 lawyers and at some point he cut off further discussion of the merits of one shelter. Weisner concluded that "our reputation will be used to market the transaction" and that

> "I do believe the time has come to s**t and get off the pot. The business decisions to me are primarily two: (1) Have we drafted the opinion with the appropriate limiting bells and whistles . . . and (2) Are we being paid enough to offset the risks of potential litigation resulting from the transaction? My own recommendation is that we should be paid a lot of money here for our opinion since the transaction is clearly one that the IRS would view as falling squarely within the tax shelter orbit."

Weisner identified the shelter as a high-risk operation, trading on KPMG's reputation, justified by fees reaching almost $100 million for the shelter at issue and covered by "bells and whistles" limitations on their opinions. Jeffery Stein, No. 2 man at KPMG, responded:

> "I think [the expression is] s**t OR get off the pot. I vote for s**t."

And so KPMG offered its shelters to its customers. To avoid indictment, KPMG itself is willing to admit wrongdoing, calling the operations "unlawful conduct" and an embarrassment that should "never happen again."

KPMG was not alone in marketing packaged shelters. Ernst & Young, Pricewaterhouse Coopers (PwC), and BDO Seidman are being sued for damages by taxpayers who purchased shelters they sold that the IRS has since gone after. PwC is now describing its shelters as an "institutional failure." Arthur Andersen also sold multimillion-dollar tax schemes, and it too suffered "institutional failure."

This report focuses on one shelter, called the FLIP or OPIS shelter by KPMG, but also known as the basis-shift or defective-redemption shelter. KPMG culture considered the shelter to be fair game to apply against the United States, whereas the tax profession as a whole has reached a consensus, demonstrated by its actions in context, that the shelter did not meet minimum professional standards. KPMG was willing to give an opinion that the shelter was more likely than not to prevail in litigation if challenged by the IRS on audit. The tax profession as a whole has concluded that the shelter did not have a realistic possibility of success when the IRS did in fact challenge the shelter.

The KPMG shelters give us a relatively rare window. The Permanent Subcommittee on Investigations collected almost 400 pages of documentation on the FLIP/OPIS shelter, which included many once-very-confidential KPMG internal conversations. There have also been 450 independent, highly qualified tax counsel who have reached a decision on FLIP/OPIS, and it is unusual to have access to such a large sample of independent events. The professional culture seems to have tolerated "aggressive," even vicious, shelters that did not meet lawful "realistic possibility-of-success" standards, when the fees justified the risk of mere monetary damages. The standards of what was fair game in tax were not very high.

There are still no reported cases on the FLIP/OPIS tax issues. The Senate subcommittee that collected the extensive documentation did not analyze the tax issues in the shelter. *Tax Notes* has recently published some fine analyses of other shelter transactions, based on the published court opinions. This report attempts to fill in the literature with a discussion of the tax issues in the FLIP/OPIS shelter.

I. Was FLIP/OPIS Fair Game?

A. Description of the FLIP/OPIS Basis-Shift Shelter

KPMG initially called the shelter the FLIP — short for "Foreign Leveraged Investment Program" — and then changed the name to OPIS — short for "Offshore Portfolio Investment Strategy" — adding complexity with the changing of the name, but without changing the underlying logic of the shelter. The shelter is also reasonably called a "defective-redemption" shelter because it required that a redemption of stock from a Cayman Islands entity fail to qualify as a redemption under U.S. tax law. Union Bank of Switzerland (UBS), which provided financing, called it a "UBS redemption trade." FLIP/ OPIS is also commonly called a "basis-shifting shelter" because it depends on the costs of a shell Cayman Islands entity shifting over to become part of the basis of the domestic taxpayer who purchased the shelter. It is also called a "Notice 2001-45 shelter," after the IRS notice that said it was illegal. KPMG developed the FLIP, but it migrated to PwC when a KPMG professional moved to PwC and began doing copycat deals, and at PwC it was called only FLIP.

FLIP/OPIS was a highly profitable shelter, generating over $45 million fees for KPMG and $16 million fees for PwC, but it was not the biggest of KPMG's shelters. KPMG replaced it in 1999 with another shelter called BLIP or Son-of-BOSS, which generated even more fees. But FLIP/OPIS eliminated reported gain of at least $3.6 billion before the IRS began rolling up the participants, which is a material amount.

In 2001 the IRS gave notice that the tax benefits claimed by FLIP/OPIS were "not properly allowable for Federal income tax purposes" and identified the FLIP/OPIS as a potentially abusive tax shelter that would have to be registered with the IRS and listed on taxpayers' returns. The IRS then announced, in 2003, a very generous settlement offer under which participants in FLIP/OPIS would give up 80 percent of their tax losses and would still face full appropriate penalties. The bar has decided overwhelmingly that the chances of prevailing in litigation were thin enough and that the IRS's offer was generous enough that the shelter is not worth litigating. The IRS has announced that 92 percent of the taxpayers it identified as buying the shelter have taken the IRS settlement offer. FLIP/OPIS transactions are multimillion-dollar transactions, implying that the taxpayers' representatives are top-of-the-bar tax lawyers. The settlements mean that 450 first-class lawyers already have decided independently that FLIP/OPIS will not be upheld if litigated. Substantial tax dollars are still at stake in transactions that have not settled. There have also been malpractice suits by the taxpayers against the professionals participating in the package asking for reimbursement of costs on the argument that FLIP/OPIS was below professional standards.

FLIP is within a family of tax shelters that KPMG called a "loss generator." As UBS candidly described the transaction, "the losses are not real but only tax relevant. The [FLIP/OPIS] uses provisions in the US Tax Code to create a *synthetic* loss." "The structure creates a capital loss from a U.S. tax point of view (but not from an economic point of view) which may be offset against existing capital gains." A "loss generator" must have reported losses that are not lost as a matter of fact or economics. Capital gains tax rates were only 20 percent when FLIP/OPIS was offered, and it is a "fool's shelter" to lose $100 million just to avoid a 20 percent tax ($20 million) on it. The point of a "loss generator" is artificial accounting losses, that is, reporting loss to one's government without losing it.

The FLIP/OPIS shelter depends technically on the cost basis of a Cayman Islands entity shifting over to a related U.S. taxpayer after the Cayman Islands entity was redeemed out. For each purchaser, a shell Cayman Islands Corporation or partnership was set up that was related, within the constructive ownership rules of section 318, to the U.S. taxpayer who purchased the shelter. The Cayman Islands entity bought stock of a foreign bank, either Deutsche Bank or UBS, with funds borrowed on a nonrecourse basis from the same bank, in the amount of the artificial loss to be generated. A few weeks later, the same bank redeemed all the stock, and the Cayman Islands entity repaid the bank with the redemption proceeds. The redemption, however, purported to fail to qualify as a redemption under U.S. tax law.

A shareholder giving up shares in a failed redemption has a dividend rather than a sale or exchange and cannot use its basis in the redeemed shares against the redemption proceeds. FLIP/OPIS rests on the claim that the basis of the Cayman Islands entity that could not be used in the redemption transferred over to bank stock owned by the related U.S. taxpayer who had purchased the shelter. The U.S. taxpayer thus purportedly had an excess, built-in loss on his bank stock by the amount of the original borrowed cost basis of the Cayman Islands entity. The U.S. taxpayer reported the excess loss on the sale of his bank stock. According to KPMG's rather cackling description of its own work, "OPIS is a *clever* application of the section 302 [redemption] rules in a context that was *not* intended."

This report first examines the core basis-shift claim and then looks at a series of equitable substance-over form doctrines. It concludes that the shelter does not have a realistic possibility — defined as a one-in-three chance — of prevailing on the merits in litigation, either because the core technical claim will fail or because the equitable doctrines will defeat it.

Let us assume a hypothetical FLIP/OPIS transaction set up to generate a $100 million loss. An American customer we will call simply Taxpayer or U.S. Taxpayer sold his business for cash in 1998 and would have reported $100 million of capital gain from the cash without the shelter. Taxpayer is approached by a KPMG accountant and buys into the deal, agreeing to pay $7 million in fees. The 7 percent fees are split among the parties that made the sale possible: (1) KPMG, which originated the transaction and gave Taxpayer an opinion that it worked, (2) either Deutsche Bank or UBS, the bank that financed it, (3) an implementer who executed the transactions, including setting up and operating the Cayman Islands entity, and (4) a law firm, usually Brown & Wood, that gave a second opinion that the shelter worked.

KPMG set up a new Cayman Islands entity (let us call Cayman) for each U.S. taxpayer who bought the shelter. Cayman is not subject to U.S. tax. The Cayman Islands is a tax haven without any corporate or income tax, so Cayman also pays no tax at home. U.S. Taxpayer is considered to own 85 percent of Cayman, under constructive ownership rules used in redemptions, because as part of the FLIP package U.S. Taxpayer buys options to buy stock or partnership interests in Cayman. The option to buy 85 percent of Cayman was apparently more expensive than it was worth, but served as a means of delivery of the fees, 7 percent of the tax loss, as well as to establish that Cayman and U.S. Taxpayer were related.

Assume that Cayman borrowed $100 million in cash from UBS in mid-1998 to buy UBS shares. Two months later, UBS redeemed all of the UBS stock from Cayman for the market price, and Cayman used the proceeds of the sale to repay the loan. The $100 million cash never in fact left UBS's hands, from loan through repayment, but there were electronic entries for loan, issuance of stock, redemption back, and repayment of the loan.

For $100 million, Cayman acquired only a trivial fraction of the UBS shares. UBS stock prices fluctuated wildly in 1998, from a high of 657 Swiss francs per share to a low of 270 Swiss francs, but even at the depths of the price, the borrowed $100 million bought only one quarter of 1 percent of UBS's outstanding stock. Let assume a figure within that range, that is, that Cayman acquired 434,000 shares at 338 Swiss francs because, with 217,000,000 UBS shares outstanding in 1998, that would mean that Cayman acquired exactly 0.2 percent of UBS's outstanding shares.

The FLIP/OPIS shelter rests on the claim that Cayman is not entitled to use its $100 million basis on the resale of 434,000 UBS shares back to UBS and that its basis shifts over to the taxpayers under regulations allowing an "appropriate adjustment to basis." Taxpayer as a part of the package purchased a modest amount of UBS stock, say 1,000 shares, and the entire $100 million Cayman cost was purportedly added to Taxpayer's basis for the shares, such that Taxpayer recognized the $100 million loss when he sold his 1,000 UBS shares by the end of 1998.

There were real losses in the FLIP/OPIS. Taxpayer paid fees of $7 million, which were lost. UBS stock collapsed in mid-1998 because UBS was implicated in the Long Term Capital Holding collapse. But Cayman borrowed on a nonrecourse basis so it did not care. UBS bought back its stock for a cheaper price that matched its loss on the loan and lost no cash.

The OPIS shelter also takes full advantage of a tax shelter strategy of using complexity as a defensive camouflage to preclude meaningful review of the transaction. Complexity has a tendency to intimidate and deter any outside review. Still, the core of the deal, ignoring the complexities and fluctuations, is very simple: Taxpayers bought $100 million worth of artificial accounting losses at a price of $7 million in fees. At the 20 percent capital gains tax rate, the losses would have been worth $20 million.

B. The Heart of the Shelter

1. The basis shift. In Notice 2001-45, the IRS announced that it would disallow the losses in basis-shifting shelters like FLIP/OPIS because "(1) the redemption does not result in a dividend (and consequently there is no basis shift) because, viewing the transaction as a whole, the redemption results in a reduction of interest in the redeeming corporation to which section 302(b) applies; (2) the basis shift is not a 'proper adjustment' as contemplated by section 1.302-2(c)." Both IRS claims seem meritorious, as applied to our hypothetical.

The claim that the $100 million cost that Cayman borrowed to buy 0.2 percent of the stock of UBS shifted over to U.S. Taxpayers depends, first, on the premise that Cayman itself is not entitled to use its $100 million cost basis when it was redeemed out of UBS. Section 302(a) and (b)(3) provide together that a "complete redemption" is an exchange in which a shareholder may use basis, but section 302(c) requires that the tax status of the redemption be tested by looking not just to the UBS shares Cayman in fact owned but also to shares Cayman constructively owned. Under the constructive ownership rules, Cayman was deemed to own all the UBS stock in fact owned by Taxpayer. U.S. Taxpayer was deemed to be an 85 percent shareholder of Cayman by reason of its purchase of warrants to buy Cayman stock. Cayman was considered to own the UBS stock actually owned by the plaintiffs.

Just as Cayman was redeemed out of UBS, the American purchasers bought an option, under the package, to buy the same number of UBS shares, 434,000, that Cayman was redeemed out of. Because optioned stock is considered to be constructively owned, without regard to whether exercise of the option was a realistic prospect or not, and because Cayman owned everything Taxpayer owned, Cayman was not completely redeemed out under section 302. Indeed, Cayman had no reduction of its ownership of UBS once constructive ownership was considered.

Section 302(a) and (b)(1) provide that a redemption is a sale or exchange if it is "not essentially equivalent to a dividend." In *United States v. Davis*, the Supreme Court held that a redemption that transfers money to the shareholders without any change in their percentage ownership of the equity of the corporation was not in substance a sale, and would be taxed as a dividend without use of basis. The redemption in *Davis* from a shareholder who started as and remained a 100 percent shareholder was essentially equivalent to a dividend and had no resemblance to a sale disposing of an interest. To be a sale on which basis is used, the Court said, "a redemption must result in a meaningful reduction of the shareholder's proportionate interest in the corporation." In *Davis*, the shareholder may have given up pieces of paper, but he recaptured all fractional value he gave up and remained the 100 percent owner after the redemption.

Under the FLIP/OPIS shelter, Taxpayer's purchased options to buy 434,000 UBS shares (0.2 percent), just as Cayman was redeemed out of its shares. When the plaintiffs' new option purchase is taken into account, and their new shares are considered owned by Cayman, Cayman maintained the same fractional interest in UBS under section 318. KPMG and Brown & Wood therefore concluded that the Cayman redemptions were not qualified under U.S. law as "a sale or exchange" and that Cayman could not use its basis in the redeemed stock against what under U.S. tax law was a dividend. Because Cayman was immune from U.S. tax, its inability to use basis for U.S. tax purposes had no possible effect on Cayman. But an assumption that Cayman could not use its basis, had it been a U.S. taxpayer, is a necessary premise for the next step in the basis-shift argument.

When a redemption is a complete redemption in fact, but a dividend in law because of constructive ownership, the redeemed shareholder does not get to use its cost basis against the redemption and also has no remaining stock to which basis can be attached. That might lead to the inequity of double tax because the basis disappears in cases in which basis is necessary to describe the full situation. Assume, for instance, that a husband makes $1,000 and invests it in stock of a corporation otherwise owned by his wife and the stock is later redeemed for $1,000. The wife continues to own all of the remaining stock of the corporation after the redemption. Because spouses are treated as constructively owning each others' stock, the husband constructively owns all of the stock of the corporation, even after the redemption, and therefore has no reduction of his fractional interest in the corporation, even though he has given up the stock certificates. The $1,000 is accordingly treated as a dividend, taxed in full without recognition of the husband's cost. The husband thus would pay tax on the $1,000 salary he made, and also on the $1,000 redemption proceeds, which are in a meaningful sense just a refund or return of the salary he invested. The husband would own no more stock to which his basis could attach so that the $1,000 cost basis would never be recognized and the husband's basis would simply disappear.

The regulations on redemptions *equitably* prevent the injustice of disappearing basis and double tax in such a case by providing that if an amount received in a redemption is treated as a dividend, "proper adjustment of the basis of the remaining stock will be made." The regulations give an example under which the husband's $1,000 basis in his stock would be added to his wife's basis in her stock and the entire basis would be recognized when the wife sells her stock. In FLIP/OPIS, the argument is that the $100 million basis that Cayman had in UBS stock, similarly shifted over to U.S. Taxpayer, by analogy to the basis shift from husband to wife in the regulation example. When the plaintiffs sold their stock and option interest in UBS they generated an artificial capital loss that was used to eliminate real gain the Taxpayer reported from the otherwise taxable sale of their business.

* * *

C. The Paramount Substance-Over-Form Doctrines

Tax law also has several traditional equitable doctrines that prevent abuse and calculate tax by looking through the form of a transaction to its substance. The doctrines overlap and the expressions of the doctrines vary considerably. Indeed, the doctrines are not so much technical or formal rules as standards or tools to allow the courts to ignore artifice, reach equity, and defeat abuse. Congress has praised the courts for "a commendable tendency to look through the mere form of the transaction into its substance." Denial of the tax losses is "overdetermined," that is, FLIP/OPIS is likely to lose on each of the tax doctrines listed below. Loss on any one issue would be sufficient to deny the claimed loss.

1. Artificial loss. Section 165 allows a deduction only for losses that a taxpayer has really suffered. The regulations under section 165 have long provided that deductions are allowable only when the taxpayer has sustained a "bona fide" loss as determined by its "[s]ubstance and not mere form." The courts must examine "whether the substance of those transactions was consistent with their form," because a transaction that is "devoid of economic substance . . . *simply is not recognized* for federal taxation purposes." The absence of a bona fide loss is fatal to the claim.

The taxpayers did not in economic substance suffer a bona fide loss of the $100 million they claimed under KPMG's FLIP/OPIS shelter. Indeed, Cayman did not lose either: It simply borrowed $100 million, invested it for some weeks in UBS stock, sold the stock back, and returned the borrowed proceeds. It had no bona fide loss to shift.

KPMG's internal documents confess that FLIP has no defense to the argument that the losses were not bona fide. In a February 19, 1998, review of OPIS, Robert Simon of KPMG criticized KPMG's justification for OPIS because:

> "No further attempt has been made to quantify why I.R.C. section 165 should not apply to deny the loss. Instead the argument is again made that because the law is uncertain, we win."

One of the KPMG recipients, who was not identified, responded:

> "As we discussed in our conference call, there simply *is nothing else to say on this topic.* I believe John . . . agreed that, after his extensive review of this area, we could do no better. This, however, is one element of why the strategy is only a "more likely than not." " (Emphasis added.)

Treating a doctrine for which KPMG has no defense and no response as just "one element" of why the strategy is "more likely than not" displays a rather cavalier attitude toward what "more likely than not to succeed if challenged by the IRS in court" means.

2. Inevitable pretax loss. The courts have long taken responsibility to ensure that Potemkin villages erected just for tax do not destroy the tax base. One of the signs by which the courts identify the transactions that have meaning only for tax is that they are profit-losing transactions in absence of tax. The taxpayer must have a "reasonable expectation" of pretax profits to give economic substance to the transaction.

The usual gambit to avoid application of the pretax profit doctrine is to "throw an oil well" or similarly high volatility investment into a transaction. If the thrown-in investment is volatile enough, it *might* appreciate by enough to cover the fees of the transaction.

The appreciation in UBS stock has to be substantial to overcome the 7 percent fees of the transaction. Cayman typically holds UBS stock for only about two months, and 7 percent over two months is like an annualized return of (1+7 percent) or 150 percent of the amount invested, plus a year of ordinary interest. That is not impossible, but it is not the kind of pretax reality that businessmen ordinarily rely on. If the 150 percent appreciation were reliably knowable, the market would have already bid up the price of UBS to take away the extraordinary appreciation before Cayman bought the stock. The chances of appreciation are also offset by chances of loss and UBS stock declined for much of 1998.

UBS was marketable stock with a track record of volatility. That means that under Black-Scholes option pricing, it is possible to appraise the value of an option to purchase UBS stock over a two-month period like Taxpayer's pretax position. The volatility on UBS stock is not a mysterious wildcat oil well, but a quantifiable value, and the taxpayers paid more than was necessary for the option. In any event, if the true purpose of the investment was to speculate on the appreciation of UBS stock, there were countless better transactions with less costs and risks by which Taxpayer could have done that. The Cayman investments were not the stuff of substance that businessmen usually rely on in absence of tax.

The participation of Taxpayer as the purchaser of the deal does nothing to certify that the deal had pretax meaning. A taxpayer purchasing the shelter would go forward even under the expectation that the transaction would lose money in absence of tax, as long as the artificial accounting losses are available, and KPMG assured participants the loss would be available. U.S. taxpayers were purchasing capital losses of $100 million, that were worth $20 million at 1998 capital gains rates. They were, of course, willing to pay $7 million fees and contributions for those tax losses if they were available. The FLIP/OPIS is a tax deal, with a camouflage of some not very important investment in UBS stock.

3. Clear reflection of income. Section 446(b) allows deductions only under a method of accounting that clearly reflects income, in the opinion of the commissioner. Tax losses that fail to reflect income but are mere timing inaccuracies are sometimes tolerated within the conventions of an administrable national tax system, whereas those same inaccuracies are cut off when the errors would otherwise lead to permanent artificial exemptions or losses. The $100 million artificial tax loss claimed by Taxpayer in the FLIP/OPIS shelter was a permanent artificial loss. The loss failed under section 446(b).

4. Step transaction doctrine. Under the step transaction doctrine, the courts determine the meaning of a transaction for tax purposes by looking at the whole transaction from start to finish, collapsing the interim steps into the whole. "The tax consequences of an interrelated series of transactions are not to be determined by viewing each of them in isolation but by considering them together as component parts of an overall plan." Taxpayers "cannot compel a court to characterize the transaction solely upon the basis of a concentration on one facet of it when the totality of circumstances determines its tax status." The dominant judicial rule for testing whether steps may be collapsed is what has been called the "end result test," under which steps will be collapsed if they are "component parts of an overall plan." The doctrine is a subset of the general perspective that taxation depends on the substance of a transaction rather than the form.

KPMG's internal documents show that KPMG accountants believed that the step transaction doctrine destroyed the FLIP. In an e-mail to his sales team, Gregg Ritchie reminded them that they were not to leave FLIP promotional materials with clients because it would "DESTROY any chance the client may have to avoid the step transaction doctrine."

If we collapse the steps between UBS and Cayman, there is no borrowing, no purchase of stock, and no redemption and repayment, only the $100 million staying in the UBS vaults. Nothing rode on the Cayman purchase and sale back of UBS stock, except the generation of a claimed $100 million loss that didn't really happen. If we collapse the steps in the overall transaction into its overall plan, FLIP/OPIS is nothing but the purchase of tax losses. The taxpayer expected to bear a net cost of 7 percent of the tax losses, plus or minus fluctuations. Viewing the transaction according to its net cash flow — $7 million of costs for capital losses of $100 million worth $20 million at capital gains rates — is the best way to see the overall substance.

II. FLIP/OPIS and Professional Standards

KPMG gave an opinion to taxpayers that the tax benefits in FLIP/OPIS were more likely than not to prevail against an IRS challenge. There was a second opinion on the shelters, usually from the law firm then known as Brown & Wood, with the same conclusion. The lawyers who have accepted the IRS settlement offer on behalf of their clients, however, did not think that they were likely to prevail in litigation and the settlements indicate that the FLIP/OPIS does not comply with minimum professional standards.

A. The One-in-Three Chance Test

Since 1989 section 6694 has penalized any return preparer for an understatement of tax due to a position for which there was not a realistic possibility being sustained on its merits if challenged by the IRS. The realistic-possibility-of-prevailing standard requires that a reasonable and well-informed analysis by a person knowledgeable in the tax law would lead such a person to conclude that the position has approximately a *one in three*, or greater, likelihood of being sustained on its merits. Consistently, the Treasury secretary is authorized to disbar from tax practice before the department any accountant who violates Circular 230 standards and Circular 230 requires that a practitioner may not advise a client to take a position on a tax return, or prepare the portion of a tax return on which a position is taken, unless the practitioner determines that the position has a one-in-three realistic possibility of success if challenged. Thus the one-in-three realistic possibility of success test sets the minimum standards that a professional practicing before the IRS must comply with.

In making the one-in-three determination under both section 6694 and Circular 230, the possibility that the position will not be challenged by the IRS is not to be taken into account. Thus, in making the determination as to whether the position will be sustained *on the merits*, the adviser may not consider the "audit lottery" factor that the taxpayer's return may not be audited or the "dumb agent" factor that the issue may not be identified on audit.

The realistic-possibility-of-success standard also seems to be the standard at which accountants confess malpractice and civil liability to taxpayers who buy the shelter. In 2000 the committee of the American Institute of Certified Public Accountants authorized to set standards for the accounting profession on tax services set the realistic-possibility-of-success standard as the "enforceable" standard for CPAs. Before the 2000 promulgation of the AICPA Statement on Standards for Tax Services, the AICPA statements were said to be only educational and advisory in nature, although they were used by courts for malpractice and disciplinary proceedings. In its 2000 revision, the AICPA Statement on Standards for Tax Services conceded that breach of the standard would be grounds for state disciplinary organizations and for malpractice actions. Both Circular 230 and section 6694 are concerned first about breach of a practitioner's duty to the U.S. government. The AICPA Statement of Standards for Tax Services uses the realistic-possibility-of success standard to measure the duty of the accountant to his client, as well.

There are differences between the AICPA expression of realistic possibility of success and the Circular 230 and section 6674 statement, but the differences are not material here. The AICPA announced that it would prefer not to quantify the realistic possibility standard and so it does not repeat the one-in-three chances of success number.90 The difference is not intended to be material, however, because the AICPA testified that "[a]lthough the AICPA . . . prefer[s] not to assign mathematical probabilities to the realistic possibility standard, nevertheless, [the] profession subscribe[s] to the standard."

If an item is disclosed or flagged to the IRS on the tax return as questionable, then an accountant may advise the taxpayer to take the position if there is a "reasonable basis" for the position. It has been suggested that the reasonable basis standard should be quantified as somewhere between a 5 percent and 20 percent chance of success. Cynically, the reasonable basis standard has also been interpreted by practitioners more loosely as equivalent to "anything the taxpayer could say without laughing out loud." Clients do not generally like to have their tax claims flagged for audit as questionable, especially for those claims like the FLIP/OPIS losses that are indeed highly questionable, because that increases the likelihood that the IRS will in fact find and challenge the questionable item. There is no indication that the FLIP/OPIS losses were disclosed on a return anywhere.

B. One-in-Three Applied to Outcomes

Probability is an objective term with exact implications about results. "More likely than not" means that if it were possible to run identical experiments exactly like the FLIP/OPIS a very large number of times, the number of taxpayer victories would approach 50 percent of the taxpayers or money involved, with the results coming closer to 50 percent the greater the number of experiments. Realistic possibility of success implies that 33.33 percent or more of taxpayers would prevail and that no more than 66-2/3 percent of the taxpayers would lose to the IRS, with the results coming closer to one-third prevailing and two-thirds losing the greater the number of experiments in the sample.

For FLIP/OPIS, we have the results of a large sample of experimental outcomes in the form of cases that have already been settled. FLIP/OPIS cases are always large dollar cases, given that the target customers had $20 million or more gain to shelter, so we can presume that the taxpayers were ably represented by experienced, well-respected counsel zealously loyal to their clients' interest. The IRS has identified 488 basis-shifting or Notice 2001-45 shelters and 92 percent of them have taken the IRS offer to settle. If FLIP/OPIS had a "more likely than not chance of succeeding" when contested, 50 percent of the cases should have come down in favor of the taxpayer. If FLIP/OPIS had a "realistic possibility of success," at least a third of the cases should have come down in favor of the taxpayer. Given the settlements so far, the taxpayer can prevail in no more than 8 percent of the cases.

We can also compare KPMG's and Brown & Wood's conclusion with the position of the 450 independent tax attorneys who in fact had to decide whether to challenge the IRS on the merits of the shelter. In 2002 the IRS announced a settlement offer for basis-shifting shelters under which the taxpayer was required to give up 80 percent of the basis-shift loss and 80 percent of the costs of the transaction. Penalties were not waived. An attorney who thought KPMG and Brown & Wood were correct on the merits of FLIP or OPIS would have refused the settlement. Indeed, in a typical hypothetical calculation, taxpayer's representatives would have gone forward if they thought they had more than an 18 percent to 25 percent chance of succeeding. The 18 percent to 25 percent is a ceiling: The chances of success could well have been 2 percent to 15 percent, consistent with the settlements. The consensus of the legal profession, that is, the assessment of the 450 independent tax counsel who had to make a real decision, was that FLIP/OPIS was not more likely than not to succeed and did not have a realistic possibility of success if challenged.

III. Concluding Remarks

KPMG seems to have lost its internal compass as what was fair game to do to our country. By February 1998, FLIP/OPIS had been subjected to scathing internal criticism at KPMG. KPMG counsel internally criticized the KPMG opinion as not handling the argument that the FLIP loss was a sham: "No further attempt has been made to quantify why IRC § 165 should not apply to deny the loss. Instead, the argument is again made that because the law is uncertain, we win." Indeed, KPMG has no defense against the argument that the loss was a sham and yet KPMG went forward with the opinions for FLIP without disclosing its internal criticisms. In a closely related shelter, KPMG's question internally was whether it was receiving enough fees and internally its judgment was that the fees were high enough to assume what would be a huge risk. As long as KPMG was paid "a lot of money for our opinion" and "put enough bells and whistles" on the opinion, it should undertake the recognized high risk. KPMG presents itself in public as a model of "integrity, objectivity and robust independence in everything we do." KPMG's internal operations, however, had evolved into what has been called a "culture of deception." Internally KPMG was selling shelters that were below professional standards because the fees were large enough.

We do not have the luxury of seeing the internal debates and e-mails, or the settlement results, for current tax planning. It is thus speculation to say how far the lessons of FLIP/OPIS and the other KPMG shelters extend to the current culture. Still, the KPMG skunk works shelters tell us what was considered "fair game" against The United States as of two to three years ago, among professionals who appeared respectable, and it is difficult to see why the standards of "fair game" should have shifted very much since then. It seems likely that professionals continue to be willing to issue opinions that various tax benefits are more likely than not to prevail, even for plans without a realistic possibility of success if challenged. Aggressive, even vicious, tax planning has probably not disappeared. Certainly the motive to avoid tax, on the multimillion-dollar level, has not dissipated.

KPMG is a "bad man" under Oliver Wendell Holmes Jr.'s meaning of the term. Holmes has told us, famously, that the law must be written under the assumption that it will need to shape bad men:

> A man who cares nothing for an ethical rule that is believed and practiced by neighbors is likely nonetheless to care a good deal about being made to pay money, and will want to keep out of jail if he can.

We cannot presume that the promoters who sell and give opinions on abusive or potentially abusive tax shelters have ethical feelings toward their Uncle Sam, that is, toward the U.S. or us. A system needs to be constructed under which it is in the objective interest of the promoters and opinion writers not to write erroneous opinions and not to sell transactions that fail to comply with the law as ultimately determined, even if they do not want to do that. Accuracy should be understood here as the amount that would have been required had all issues gone to final judgment after full litigation, but without the full litigation. It must be in the self interest of the promoters and opinion writers not to undercut the accurate reporting of tax ever and to tell their clients that it would be too dangerous to tolerate errors in tax on the down side.

Unfortunately, as a matter of strict economics, the penalties needed to make it in the self interest of the bad man to report tax accurately are rather high. The audit rates are low and IRS auditors do not catch every issue they should beat. The penalty necessary to make it in the interest of a bad man to report tax accurately with only a 1 percent chance of correction must be a no-fault penalty of 100 times the deficiency or 10,000 percent. Jail time for underreporting tax also reduces the monetary penalty we would need to impose to keep the bad man in rein — professionals tend to be easily deterred — but criminal penalties are not all that likely. Minor penalties, say on the order of 10 percent or 20 percent, are not going to do it. With penalties at the 10 percent to 20 percent level, the bad man is going to win this war.

Understanding Corporate Tax Shelters

1.   Do you agree with Professor Johnson that the FLIP/OPIS shelter was likely to lose on each of the substance-over-form doctrines he describes? Should KPMG have known this in advance of any IRS rulings or court decisions? Should the taxpayers who purchased the shelter have suspected that it was likely to lose, despite the advice given by KPMG and by Brown & Wood that it was "more likely than not" to prevail?

2.   Professor Johnson discusses several substance-over-form rules that courts have relied on in deciding against taxpayers. These rules were never explicitly adopted by Congress, but rather have been developed as part of the common law of taxation. Is this appropriate? Assume for the sake of argument that the FLIP/OPIS shelter is valid under a literal (or technical) reading of the Code. Shouldn't taxpayers be allowed to rely on the language of the Code? Even if you agree with Professor Johnson that the FLIP/OPSIS shelter was likely to lose under the substance-over-form rules, should the taxpayers who purchased these shelters be subject to fines or penalties, again assuming that their tax reporting complies with a literal interpretation of the Code?

3.   A famous quote from Judge Learned Hand says: "Anyone may so arrange his affairs that his taxes shall be as low as possible; he is not bound to choose that pattern which will best pay the Treasury. There is not even a patriotic duty to increase one's taxes." Aren't the taxpayers who purchased the FLIP/OPSIS shelter just arranging their affairs so that their taxes are as low as possible? How do we resolve the tension between allowing taxpayers to arrange their affairs so as to reduce their taxes and yet still applying substance-over-form rules?

4.   Arguably, substance-over-form rules are a necessary tool for the IRS and courts to combat tax shelter transactions. If so, should Congress write one or more of the substance-over-form tests into the Code? Or are we better off maintaining the status quo wherein these rules develop through judicial application?

5.   Do you agree with Professor Johnson that KPMG is a "bad man"? Most practicing tax lawyers are in the business of advising their clients on how to arrange their affairs so as to minimize taxes. Does this make these tax lawyers "bad men"? KPMG arguably went much further in providing aggressive tax advice than do most tax lawyers, but this may be a difference in degree, rather than in kind. Is there something morally dubious about being a tax lawyer and giving tax planning advice, even for tax lawyers who would never involve themselves with tax shelters like the FLIP/OPSIS transactions?

VI.   CORPORATE "INTEGRATION" AND THE REFORM OF BUSINESS TAXATION

Having studied the corporate income tax, a frequent response of students and practitioners is, "Who needs it?" Since most of corporate tax law seems to involve efforts to avoid the imposition of a second level of tax — and since this effort is frequently quite successful — why not eliminate the corporate tax altogether and "integrate" the tax treatment of corporations and other businesses with that of the individuals who own them? This argument has grown especially strong with the proliferation of devices (partnerships, sub S corporations, LLCs) that require only one level of tax, and with the widespread acceptance of techniques, like the issuance of debt or the redemption of outstanding stock, for eliminating the second level of tax in Subchapter C corporations. The case for integration is often buttressed by the argument that the corporate tax is, effectively, passed on to individuals in the form of higher prices to consumers and lower returns to shareholders and employees; eliminating the tax would accordingly (or so the argument goes) eliminate this deception and result in a more honest and open tax system.[27]

Proposals for corporate tax integration divide into "full" and "partial" integration schemes. Full integration means essentially a system similar to partnership taxation, in which each shareholder is taxed on his or her percentage of the overall corporate income (whether or not distributed) and the corporation files solely an information return. Because of the difficulty of applying this system to (say) General Motors — and the difficulty of attracting investors who had to pay tax on the undistributed income — relatively few people wish to go that far.

There is broader support for partial integration, which means that some form of corporate tax would exist but with a broad deduction designed to reduce or eliminate taxation of the same income at two distinct levels. This would likely take the form of either a dividends paid deduction at the corporate level (*i.e.*, the corporation would receive a deduction and accordingly avoid tax on amounts distributed to its shareholders), or a dividends received deduction at the level of the shareholders themselves (*i.e.*, the shareholders would receive a deduction and accordingly avoid tax for income already taxed to the corporation).[28] The 2003 tax legislation, which provides a maximum 15 percent tax on dividends received by individuals, is a version of this second proposal.

The good part of integration proposals is that they reduce or eliminate double taxation and thereby limit the distortion inherent in the differing treatment of corporations and other business entities. The problem is that it they tend to reduce taxes on rather wealthy people (and corporations) without any immediate benefit to the rest of the country. Indeed, the reduction of dividend tax rates in 2003 has been sharply criticized on precisely these "vertical equity" grounds. (President Bush

---

[27] The issue of who bears the economic cost of the corporate tax — shareholders, employees, or perhaps even the public in the form of higher prices for corporate products — has confounded economists for many years. *See generally* Joint Committee on Taxation, Methodology and Issues in Measuring Changes in the Distribution of Tax Burdens (JCS-7-93), June 14, 1995.

[28] A dividends received deduction currently exists, but only for dividends paid by one corporation to another, and usually at rates less than 100 percent.

originally proposed the complete elimination of dividend taxes, with the 15 percent rate representing a "compromise" with congressional moderates.) The integration debate is conceptually distinct from, but politically linked to, the debate between an income and consumption tax, with advocates of the latter system frequently suggesting the elimination of corporate taxation as a part of their proposal.

Politics and Policy

Suppose you were a lobbyist for a pro-business organization that supported the partial integration of corporate and individual taxes, that is, the maintenance and perhaps even the further reduction of the 15 percent dividend tax rate enacted in 2003. Which of the following arguments would you emphasize in making your case?

a. Integration will increase fairness by reducing the tax disparity between corporations and partnerships (LLCs) and between corporations that issue debt and those that maintain large stock holdings.

b. Integration will increase economic efficiency, by reducing the volume of corporate taxes and eliminating the distortion associated with excess debt issuance and other existing tax evasion schemes.

c. Foreign countries do it and we need to do it also in order to remain competitive.

Suppose now that you were a "public interest" representative who favored repeal of the 2003 provision, i.e., a return to full "double taxation" of distributed corporate income. How would you respond to the arguments above, and what additional arguments, if any, would you be likely to make against the 2003 bill and similar proposals? Regardless of which side you are on, how do you think the politics of integration will play out in actual fact, and what role if any do you think the above arguments will have in this political process?

Additional Assignment — Chapter 11

The materials above consider business taxation in a bite-sized manner, treating separately the choice of entity issue and the more specific tax problems associated with corporations and partnerships (or LLCs). Sometimes it is useful to consider these together; necessary, in fact, since part of choosing an entity is envisioning the long-range as well as immediate tax consequences of your entity choice. Indeed, tax considerations are typically only one part of a planning decision, which may also reflect managerial, financing, and other business law concerns.

With this in mind, consider the following hypothetical: Alan, Barbara, and Cindy have decided to begin a new business buying and selling used law school textbooks, study aids, and other similar materials at a modest profit to their fellow law students. They plan to begin operations out of a room in Barbara's home but, if they prove successful, to acquire more luxurious quarters and (eventually) to buy and sell textbooks to a regional or national market. Cindy, whose family is rather wealthy, is bringing $100,000 of "seed capital" to the business while the others are making smaller ($5,000-$10,000) cash contributions. Alan, who will be graduating in the spring, plans to work full time on the business for at least three years, while the others will work on a part-time basis as they seek law firm employment. If the company does very well they would consider hiring new employees or seeking additional funds in the future. Barbara is 35 years old and married while the others are somewhere in their mid-20s and remain as yet unattached.

1. Try first to envision the business above as a regular (subchapter C) corporation. What do you see as the tax and business advantages, and disadvantages, of this first option? With respect to tax advantages, consider (i) the impact of a potential double-tax bite on distributed income, (ii) the degree to which the double tax could be reduced by means of debt, salary payments, etc., or else by retaining income in the corporation; and (iii) the tax treatment of losses in the corporate form. With respect to non-tax factors, consider the financial, management, and control structure of a corporation, together with the significance of limited liability, and what role each participant would likely play in the corporate structure.

2. Now try to imagine the same business as a partnership (or if you prefer, LLC). What would be the advantages and disadvantages of this format, and how do they compare to those under the corporate alternative, above? Consider, in particular, (i) the advantages of a single level of taxation that accrues to these entities, (ii) the potential for shifting or special allocations of partnership (LLC) income, and whether the allocations you envision would satisfy the requirement of substantial economic effect; and (iii) the tax treatment of losses, including the effect of the substantial economic effect concept (again) and the passive activity loss rules. Consider also the business aspect of a partnership (LLC), including liability, fundraising, and likely management structure, and whether this form of entity would be better suited to the proposed business than a corporation.

Note: Items 1. and 2. will obviously be easier to answer if you have taken a course in business law, but if not, you can probably answer most of these questions from a mixture of the course materials and your own real-world experience. A good way to begin is by evaluating the goals and interests of the various participants and how they might be accommodated within each different structure. If a large number of students have no business law experience, the problem may be completed on a group basis.

3. Based on the above, which form of entity would you recommend and why? What role did tax and non-tax factors play in your decision? Are there other questions that you would need or like to have answered before making a definite decision?

4. Assume that you chose a corporation in item 3. above. (Note: This is not necessarily the correct answer but is being assumed for pedagogic purposes). It is now ten years later and the business, which has been highly successful and developed a regional and even a national market, has been approached by a larger corporation with respect to a possible takeover. Barbara and Cindy are willing to consider some form of a merger, but Alan, who we will assume has an equal, one-third interest, wants to be "bought out" for cash. The buyer in question typically prefers to acquire assets rather than stock although it may consider the latter if the price is right.

In general terms, what options are available to the corporation, including the various forms of taxable sales and tax-free reorganizations, and how should it choose between them? Again, what role did tax and non-tax factors play in your recommendation and how did you balance them against each other? Does anything in your answer make you want to go back and reevaluate your responses to items 1. through 3. above?

Please prepare a memorandum, *not exceeding five double-spaced pages in length*, discussing the issues above.

Chapter 12

INTERNATIONAL AND COMPARATIVE TAXATION: TOWARD A GLOBAL PERSPECTIVE

In most countries, the study of foreign and comparative law is considered a basic part of a legal education, and a lawyer who knew only his or her own country's rules would be considered something like an American who knew only the rules of his or her own State; that is to say, rather provincial. Because the United States is the ultimate large country — a "hyperpower," as the French like to put it — we tend to think that the world stops at our shores, and regard comparative legal studies as a sort of soft elective for third-year law students. Practitioners know better. Almost any firm of any size has clients with international transactions, and the foreign tax and other legal consequences of these arrangements are no less significant than those on the American side of things. Yet international private law, and especially international tax, remain essentially "boutique" courses in all but a very few law schools.

This chapter aims to redress that imbalance. It is impossible to cover all of international tax in one chapter, and no such effort is made. Instead, the chapter attempts to expose you to a few important concepts and (even more important) to the style of thinking that applies in tax law and policy when more than one lawmaking jurisdiction is involved. This includes the vastly greater number of sources in play for international transactions; the nature of tax planning, when one must be concerned with two distinct sets of rules and their interactions, as well as with the effect of tax treaties and other bilateral or multilateral agreements; the tax policy questions raised by international capital flows, including the concepts of import and export neutrality and the fairness of agreements negotiated between countries of unequal power; and other similar issues. We will also consider a few representative problems in international taxation, emphasizing tax avoidance mechanisms like transfer pricing and the use of tax haven jurisdictions, a perennial source of tension between richer and poorer (or in any event, larger and smaller) countries. The chapter concludes with a look at comparative taxation and at some of the domestic tax issues — notably the imposition of State and local taxes on interstate commerce — that reflect similar themes to international taxation. Many of the concepts in this chapter are common to all multijurisdictional legal practice, so the chapter should be useful even to those who do not see themselves as international tax planners.

I. WHY INTERNATIONAL TAX IS DIFFERENT: THE PROBLEM OF MULTIPLE TAX JURISDICTIONS

One way to approach international taxation is to consider all of the things we have been taking for granted so far in this casebook. Throughout the book, we have emphasized conflicts — between the literal and figurative meaning of statutes; between fairness and efficiency; and between the desire to minimize taxes and a taxpayer's business or personal goals. Yet in almost all cases, we have assumed a single, unitary taxing jurisdiction that has authority to resolve these contradictions. Thus, if the Supreme Court says that section 1001(b) includes nonrecourse mortgages (*Crane*), for all intents and purposes, it does; if Congress decides that the need for a home mortgage interest deduction outweighs the demands of horizontal equity, then such is the case. Where planning and policy problems are concerned, things become more complicated; but the taxpayer (or the public policy-maker) is at least secure in the knowledge that only one principal set of decision-makers has to be taken into account.

All of this changes in an international context. Assume that USCorp wants to open a branch office in the U.K. (United Kingdom) in order to deal more efficiently with European customers. In no particular order, the company must consider both the British and American taxation of its overseas employees; the taxation of profits earned by its overseas operation, including the initial taxation by the home country (in this particular case, the U.K.); the additional taxation, if any, on the transfer of profits from the U.K. back to the U.S.; and whether the answers will be the same if the company operates its office as a subsidiary of its U.S. business, as an independent U.K. entity, or in some alternate manner. To answer each of these questions, the company must consider both the U.S. and U.K. tax laws, including both normal tax provisions (tax rates, tax base, etc.) and any special rules that apply to cross-border transactions, and the provisions of the U.S.-U.K. tax treaty or other, multilateral arrangements that may ignore or amend these rules in particular cases. There is also the matter of tax culture: the U.S. tax lawyer may not even know where to look in order to find U.K. tax law, or what the terms mean when she does look, a problem that is obviously magnified when one switches to non-English speaking tax jurisdictions. In some cases, notably in developing countries, there may not even be a clearly written tax code and the law may be whatever a local official (honest or otherwise) says it is.

The differences above mean that international tax involves intellectual and technical challenges beyond even the most sophisticated domestic provisions: it is no wonder that the best international practitioners are rewarded, well, on an international scale. It also means that international taxation raises a whole new set of tax policy issues.

A first question involves the matter of fairness or horizontal equity. In domestic taxation, horizontal equity means the taxation of similar taxpayers in a similar fashion. International tax tends to speak instead of the equal treatment of money, expressed either as *capital import neutrality* (*i.e.*, the equal treatment of incoming foreign investment with equivalent domestic funds) or its nemesis, *capital export neutrality* (*i.e.*, the equal treatment of outgoing investment flows with the equivalent use of the same money in the country of origin). For example, in a regime of capital import neutrality, British or German funds invested in the United States would be taxed at the same effective rate as American funds invested in our own country. Under a regime of capital export neutrality, the relevant comparison would be somewhat different, with taxation of the British and German funds being compared to the effective tax rates if these same funds had been invested in Britain, Germany, or other European countries. As one might imagine, these two goals come into conflict rather frequently; as one might further imagine, individual countries tend to support, not a consistent set of policies in all cases, but whatever policies support their own selfish interests in a particular instance. These tendencies are exacerbated by the anarchic nature of the international community, in which there is no overarching authority and governments are permitted, even encouraged, to seek their own advantage at the expense of their competitors.

A second set of policy issues — very roughly the equivalent of vertical equity in a domestic tax context — involves the relationship between rich and poor countries. Put simply, an anarchic legal system, dominated by bilateral agreements, will tend over time to reflect the interests of wealthy and powerful nations at the expense of poorer and weaker ones. This situation has long been recognized in areas like environmental and labor law, where multilateral agreements and organizations attempt to combat the tendency for rich nations to exploit the poorer nations or regions of the globe. In tax, with its tradition of national independence and limited, bilateral agreements, such recognition has been slower in coming. However, regional and even some global organizations have begun to redress this balance, and an emerging body of scholarship considers the "vertical" as well as "horizontal" equity of international tax rules and norms.

Finally, although the term "efficiency" is used sparingly in international tax discourse, it continues to have major policy ramifications. This is particularly true in the current era of "globalization," where uninhibited capital flows tend to be seen by Americans as eventually raising the rest of the world to their standard of living, and by many others as a plot to subvert their traditional ways of life and leave them as little more than colonial outposts. This broader perspective also finds expression in tax policy, where the United States and its allies tend to see the purpose of international taxation (like international trade) as providing the least possible interference with international capital flows, *i.e.* as promoting economic efficiency, while other countries may see tax policy as one of the few available levers to maintain fairness and control their domestic economic development. For example, countries like Ireland and Italy have historically used tax incentives to encourage growth in depressed industries or depressed regions like southern Italy, a policy which has sometimes brought them into conflict with the European Union and which may seem inconsistent with a policy of free and undistorted business and capital flows. Similarly, the low tax rates in several Third World countries, while seen as illicit "tax havens" from the rich countries' perspective, may be those countries' only means to encourage investment and may indeed be similar to means employed by the rich countries themselves in an earlier stage of development.

At some point, these international developments begin to impinge on the domestic policies of even the larger countries, as when European countries attempt to "harmonize" (*i.e.*, fix) tax rates in order to prevent low tax countries from taking business and jobs away from their higher-tax competitors. Similar problems arise in the North American Free Trade Association (NAFTA) involving the U.S., Canada, and Mexico. To be sure, there are parallel problems in a domestic context, as when poorer States induce jobs and businesses to relocate with tax holidays and other favors; but these are at least subject to Federal constitutional limitations, whereas in international tax few if any such limits are present.

A description of the international tax system is a tall order for an entire casebook, let alone a single chapter. The following excerpts provide a brief introduction to the existing system and to proposals for its improvement. Do your best to follow the discussion and the principal concepts. As you read the materials, consider which issues are specifically tax problems, and which are merely tax reflections of the broader problem of making and enforcing law in a world that remains divided into sovereign, competing states rather than being subject to a single, universal world order. Consider further the solutions to these problems: can these ever truly be achieved in the existing state system, or is some kind of world government (or at very least a higher level of international cooperation) necessary in order to resolve them more fully?

Description and Analysis of Present-Law Rules Relating to International Taxation (JCX-40-99)
U.S. Congress, Joint Committee on Taxation
June 28, 1999

II. PRESENT LAW

A. U.S. Taxation of U.S. Persons with Foreign Income

1. Overview

The United States taxes U.S. citizens, residents, and corporations (collectively, U.S. persons) on all income, whether derived in the United States or elsewhere. By contrast, the United States taxes nonresident alien individuals and foreign corporations only on income with a sufficient nexus to the United States.

The United States generally cedes the primary right to tax income derived from sources outside the United States to the foreign country where such income is derived. Thus, a credit against the U.S. income tax imposed on foreign-source taxable income is provided for foreign taxes paid on that income. In order to implement the rules for computing the foreign tax credit, the Code and the regulations thereunder set forth an extensive set of rules governing the determination of the source, either U.S. or foreign, of items of income and the allocation and apportionment of items of expense against such categories of income.

The tax rules of foreign countries that apply to foreign income of U.S. persons vary widely. For example, some foreign countries impose income tax at higher effective rates than those of the United States. In such cases, the foreign tax credit allowed by the United States is likely to eliminate any U.S. tax on income from a

U.S. person's operations in the foreign country. On the other hand, operations in countries that have low statutory tax rates or generous deduction allowances or that offer tax incentives (*e.g.*, tax holidays) to foreign investors are apt to be taxed at effective tax rates lower than the U.S. rates. In such cases, after application of the foreign tax credit, a residual U.S. tax generally is imposed on income from a U.S. person's operations in the foreign country.

Under income tax treaties, the tax that otherwise would be imposed under applicable foreign law on certain foreign-source income earned by U.S. persons may be reduced or eliminated. Moreover, U.S. tax on foreign-source income may be reduced or eliminated by treaty provisions that treat certain foreign taxes as creditable for purposes of computing U.S. tax liability.

2. Foreign operations conducted directly

The tax rules applicable to U.S. persons that control business operations in foreign countries depend on whether the business operations are conducted directly (through a foreign branch, for example) or indirectly (through a separate foreign corporation). A U.S. person that conducts foreign operations directly includes the income and losses from such operations on the person's U.S. tax return for the year the income is earned or the loss is incurred.

Detailed rules are provided for the translation into U.S. currency of amounts with respect to such foreign operations. The income from the U.S. person's foreign operations thus is subject to current U.S. tax. However, the foreign tax credit may reduce or eliminate the U.S. tax on such income.

3. Foreign operations conducted through a foreign corporation

a. In general

Income earned by a foreign corporation from its foreign operations generally is subject to U.S. tax only when such income is distributed to any U.S. persons that hold stock in such corporation. Accordingly, a U.S. person that conducts foreign operations through a foreign corporation generally is subject to U.S. tax on the income from those operations when the income is repatriated to the United States through a dividend distribution to the U.S. person. The income is reported on the U.S. person's tax return for the year the distribution is received, and the United States imposes tax on such income at that time. The foreign tax credit may reduce the U.S. tax imposed on such income.

A variety of complex anti-deferral regimes impose current U.S. tax on income earned by a U.S. person through a foreign corporation. Detailed rules for coordination among the anti-deferral regimes are provided to prevent the U.S. person from being subject to U.S. tax on the same item of income under multiple regimes.

The Code sets forth the following anti-deferral regimes: the controlled foreign corporation rules of subpart F (secs. 951-964); the passive foreign investment company rules (secs. 1291–1298); the foreign personal holding company rules (secs.

551–558); the personal holding company rules (secs. 541–547); the accumulated earnings tax rules (secs. 531–537); and the foreign investment company rules (sec. 1246). The operation and application of these regimes are briefly described in the following sections.

b. Controlled foreign corporations

General rules

U.S. 10-percent shareholders of a controlled foreign corporation (a "CFC") are required to include in income for U.S. tax purposes currently certain income of the CFC (referred to as "subpart F income"), without regard to whether the income is distributed to the shareholders (sec. 951(a)(1)(A)). In effect, the Code treats the U.S. 10-percent shareholders of a CFC as having received a current distribution of their pro rata shares of the CFC's subpart F income. In addition, the U.S. 10-percent shareholders of a CFC are required to include in income for U.S. tax purposes their pro rata shares of the CFC's earnings to the extent invested by the CFC in U.S. property (sec. 951(a)(1)(B)). The amounts included in income by the CFC's U.S. 10-percent shareholders under these rules are subject to U.S. tax currently. The U.S. tax on such amounts may be reduced through foreign tax credits.

* * *

4. Transfer pricing rules

In the case of a multinational enterprise that includes at least one U.S. corporation and at least one foreign corporation, the United States taxes all of the income of the U.S. corporation, but only so much of the income of the foreign corporation as is determined to have sufficient nexus to the United States. The determination of the amount that properly is the income of the U.S. member of a multinational enterprise and the amount that properly is the income of a foreign member of the same multinational enterprise thus is critical to determining the amount of income the United States may tax (as well as the amount of income other countries may tax).

Due to the variance in tax rates and tax systems among countries, a multinational enterprise may have a strong incentive to shift income, deductions, or tax credits among commonly controlled entities in order to arrive at a reduced overall tax burden. Such a shifting of items between commonly controlled entities could be accomplished by setting artificial transfer prices for transactions between group members.

As a simple illustration of how transfer pricing could be used to reduce taxes, assume that a U.S. corporation has a wholly-owned foreign subsidiary. The U.S. corporation manufactures a product domestically and sells it to the foreign subsidiary. The foreign subsidiary, in turn, sells the product to unrelated third parties. Due to the U.S. parent's control of its subsidiary, the price which is charged by the parent to the subsidiary theoretically could be set independently of ordinary market forces. If the foreign subsidiary is established in a jurisdiction that subjects its profits from the sale of the product to an effective rate of tax lower than the effective U.S. tax rate, then the U.S. corporation may be inclined to undercharge the foreign subsidiary for the product. By doing so, a portion of the combined profits of the group from the manufacture and sale of the product would be shifted out of a high-tax jurisdiction (the United States) and into a lower-tax jurisdiction (the foreign corporation's home country).[1] The ultimate result of this process would be a reduced worldwide tax liability of the multinational enterprise.

Under section 482, the Secretary of the Treasury is authorized to redetermine the income of an entity subject to U.S. taxation, when it appears that an improper shifting of income between that entity and a commonly controlled entity in another country has occurred. This authority is not limited to reallocations of income between different taxing jurisdictions; it permits reallocations in any common control situation, including reallocations between two U.S. entities.

However, it has significant application to multinational enterprises due to the incentives for taxpayers to shift income to obtain the benefits of significantly different effective tax rates.

Section 482 grants the Secretary of the Treasury broad authority to allocate income, deductions, credits, or allowances between any commonly controlled organizations, trades, or businesses in order to prevent evasion of taxes or clearly to reflect income. The statute generally does not prescribe any specific reallocation rules that must be followed, other than establishing the general standards of preventing tax evasion and clearly reflecting income. Treasury regulations adopt the concept of an arm's length standard as the method for determining whether reallocations are appropriate. Thus, the regulations attempt to identify the respective amounts of taxable income of the related parties that would have resulted if the parties had been uncontrolled parties dealing at arm's length. The regulations contain complex rules governing the determination of an arm's-length charge for various types of transactions. The regulations generally attempt to prescribe methods for identifying the relevant comparable unrelated party transactions and for providing adjustments for differences between such transactions and the related party transactions in question. In some instances, the regulations also provide safe harbors.

Determinations under section 482 that result in the allocation of additional income to the United States might theoretically subject a taxpayer to double taxation, if both the United States and another country imposed tax on the same income and the other country did not agree that the income should be reallocated to the United States. Tax treaties generally provide mechanisms to attempt to resolve such disputes in a manner that may avoid double taxation if both countries agree. Such mechanisms include the designation of a "competent authority" by each country, to act as that country's representative in the negotiation attempting

---

[1] [10] By contrast, U.S. companies owning foreign subsidiaries that are located in countries with effective tax rates that are higher than the U.S. rates may have an incentive to overcharge for sales from the U.S. parent to the foreign subsidiary in order to shift profits, and the resulting tax, into the United States.

to resolve such disputes. However, such competent authority procedures do not guarantee that double tax may not be imposed in a particular case.

One method for addressing the issue of double taxation is through the advance pricing agreement ("APA") procedure. An APA is an advance agreement establishing an approved transfer pricing methodology entered into between the taxpayer, the Internal Revenue Service, and a foreign tax authority. The taxpayer generally is required to use the approved transfer pricing methodology for the duration of the APA. The IRS and the foreign tax authority generally agree to accept the results of such approved methodology. An APA also may be negotiated between just the taxpayer and the IRS; such an APA establishes an approved transfer pricing methodology for U.S. tax purposes. The APA process may prove to be particularly useful in cases involving industries such as financial products and services for which transfer pricing determinations are especially difficult.

5. Foreign tax credit rules

a. In general

Because the United States taxes U.S. persons on their worldwide income, Congress enacted the foreign tax credit in 1918 to prevent U.S. taxpayers from being taxed twice on their foreign source income: once by the foreign country where the income is earned and again by the United States. The foreign tax credit generally allows U.S. taxpayers to reduce the U.S. income tax on their foreign income by the foreign income taxes they pay on that income. The foreign tax credit does not operate to offset U.S. income tax on U.S.-source income.

A credit against U.S. tax on foreign income is allowed for foreign taxes paid or accrued by a U.S. person (sec. 901). In addition, a credit is allowed to a U.S. corporation for foreign taxes paid by certain foreign subsidiary corporations and deemed paid by the U.S. corporation upon a dividend received by, or certain other income inclusions of, the U.S. corporation with respect to earnings of the foreign subsidiary (the "deemed-paid" or "indirect" foreign tax credit) (sec. 902).

The foreign tax credit provisions of the Code are elective on a year-by-year basis. In lieu of electing the foreign tax credit, U.S. persons generally are permitted to deduct foreign taxes (sec. 164(a)(3)). For purposes of the alternative minimum tax, foreign tax credits generally cannot be used to offset more than 90 percent of the U.S. person's pre-foreign tax credit tentative minimum tax (sec. 59(a)).

A foreign tax credit limitation, which is calculated separately for various categories of income, is imposed to prevent the use of foreign tax credits to offset U.S. tax on U.S.-source income. Detailed rules are provided for the allocation of expenses against U.S.-source and foreign-source income. Special rules apply to require the allocation of foreign losses in one category of income for a taxable year to offset foreign income in the other categories for such year and to require the recharacterization of foreign income for a year subsequent to a foreign loss year from one income category to another or from foreign source to U.S. source (sec. 904(f)).

The amount of creditable taxes paid or accrued (or deemed paid) in any taxable year which exceeds the foreign tax credit limitation is permitted to be carried back to the two immediately preceding taxable years and carried forward to the first five succeeding taxable years, and credited in such years to the extent that the taxpayer otherwise has excess foreign tax credit limitation for those years (sec. 904(c)). For purposes of determining excess foreign tax credit limitation amounts, the foreign tax credit separate limitation rules apply.

* * *

c. Foreign tax credit limitation

A premise of the foreign tax credit is that it should not reduce the U.S. tax on a taxpayer's U.S.-source income but should only reduce the U.S. tax on the taxpayer's foreign-source income. Permitting the foreign tax credit to reduce U.S. tax on U.S. income would in effect cede to foreign countries the primary right to tax income earned from U.S. sources.

In order to prevent foreign taxes from reducing U.S. tax on U.S. source income, the foreign tax credit is subject to an overall limitation and a series of separate limitations. Under the overall limitation, the total amount of the credit may not exceed the same proportion of the taxpayer's U.S. tax which the taxpayer's foreign-source taxable income bears to the taxpayer's worldwide taxable income for the taxable year (sec. 904(a)). In addition, the foreign tax credit limitation is calculated separately for various categories of income (sec. 904(d)). Under these separate limitations, the total amount of the credit for foreign taxes on income in each category may not exceed the same proportion of the taxpayer's U.S. tax which the taxpayer's foreign-source taxable income in that category bears to the taxpayer's worldwide taxable income for the taxable year.

* * *

B. U.S. Taxation of Foreign Persons with U.S. Income

1. Overview

The United States imposes tax on nonresident alien individuals and foreign corporations (collectively, foreign persons) only on income that has a sufficient nexus to the United States. In contrast, the United States imposes tax on U.S. persons on all income, whether derived in the United States or in a foreign country.

Foreign persons are subject to U.S. tax on income that is "effectively connected" with the conduct of a trade or business in the United States, without regard to whether such income is derived from U.S. sources or foreign sources.

Such income generally is taxed in the same manner and at the same rates as income of a U.S. person. In addition, foreign persons generally are subject to U.S. tax at a 30-percent rate on certain gross income derived from U.S. sources.

Pursuant to an applicable tax treaty, the 30-percent gross-basis tax imposed on foreign persons may be reduced or eliminated. In addition, an applicable tax treaty may limit the imposition of U.S. tax on business operations of a foreign person to cases where the business is conducted through a permanent establishment in the United States.

2. Source of income rules

The source of income for U.S. tax purposes is determined based on various factors. The relevant factors include the location or nationality of the payor, the location or nationality of the recipient, the location of the recipient's activities that generate the income, and the location of the assets that generate the income. The rules for determining the source of specific types of income are described briefly below.

Interest

Interest income generally is treated as U.S.-source income if it is from obligations of the United States or the District of Columbia or from interest-bearing obligations of U.S. residents or U.S. corporations (sec. 861(a)(1)). Under a special rule, interest paid by certain U.S. persons that conduct active foreign businesses is treated as foreign-source income in whole or in part (sec. 861(c)). Other exceptions from the general rule treating interest paid by U.S. persons as U.S. source income apply to interest on deposits with foreign commercial banking branches of U.S. corporations or partnerships and certain other amounts paid by foreign branches of domestic financial institutions (sec. 861(a)(1)(B)).

Dividends

Dividends from U.S. corporations generally are treated as U.S.-source income (sec. 861(a)(2)(A)). Under a special rule, dividends from certain foreign corporations that conduct U.S. businesses are treated in part as U.S.-source income (sec. 861(a)(2)(B)).

Rents and royalties

Rents or royalties from property located in the United States, and rents or royalties for the use of or privilege of using intangible property in the United States, generally are treated as U.S.-source income (sec. 861(a)(4)).

Income from sales of personal property

Subject to significant exceptions, income from the sale of personal property is sourced on the basis of the residence of the seller (sec. 865(a)). For this purpose, the term "nonresident" is defined to include any foreign corporation (sec. 865(g)). The term "nonresident" also is defined to include any nonresident alien who does not have a "tax home" in the United States.

* * *

Personal services income

Compensation for labor or personal services performed in the United States generally is treated as U.S.-source income, subject to an exception for amounts that meet certain de minimis criteria (sec. 861(a)(3)).

* * *

3. Net-basis taxation

a. Income from a U.S. business

The United States taxes, on a net basis, the income of foreign persons, that is "effectively connected" with the conduct of a trade or business in the United States (secs. 871(b) and 882). Any gross income earned by the foreign person that is not effectively connected with the person's U.S. business is not taken into account in determining the rates of U.S. tax applicable to the person's income from such business (secs. 871(b)(2) and 882(a)(2)).

U.S. trade or business

A foreign person is subject to U.S. tax on a net basis if the person is engaged in a U.S. trade or business. In this regard, partners in a partnership and beneficiaries of an estate or trust are treated as engaged in the conduct of a trade or business within the United States if the partnership, estate, or trust is so engaged (sec. 875).

The question of whether a foreign person is engaged in a U.S. trade or business has generated a significant body of case law. Basic issues involved in the determination include whether the activity constitutes business rather than investing, whether sufficient activities in connection with the business are conducted in the United States, and whether the relationship between the foreign person and persons performing functions in the United States with respect to the business is sufficient to attribute those functions to the foreign person.

* * *

Effectively-connected income

A foreign person that is engaged in the conduct of a trade or business within the United States is subject to U.S. net-basis taxation on the income that is "effectively connected" with such business. Specific statutory rules govern the determination of whether income is so effectively connected (sec. 864(c)).

* * *

Effectively connected taxable income is computed taking into account deductions to the extent that they are associated with income that is effectively connected with the conduct of a U.S. trade or business. For this purpose, the issue of the proper apportionment and allocation of deductions generally is addressed in detailed regulations. The regulations applicable to deductions other than interest expense set forth general guidelines for allocating deductions among classes of income and apportioning deductions between effectively-connected and non-effectively-connected income, providing that, in appropriate cases, deductions may be allocated on the basis of units sold, gross sales or receipts, costs of goods sold, profits contributed, expenses incurred, assets used, salaries paid, space utilized, time spent, or gross income received. More specific guidelines are provided for the allocation of research and experimental expenditures, legal and accounting fees, income taxes, losses on dispositions of property, and net operating losses. Interest deductions are subject to a detailed regulatory regime for the allocation and apportionment to effectively-connected income.

* * *

4. Gross-basis taxation

a. Withholding tax

In the case of U.S.-source interest, dividends, rents, royalties, or other similar types of income (known as fixed or determinable, annual or periodical gains, profits and income), the United States generally imposes a flat 30-percent tax on the gross amount paid to a foreign person if such income or gain is not effectively connected with the conduct of a U.S. trade or business (secs. 871(a) and 881). This tax generally is collected by means of withholding by the person making the payment to the foreign person receiving the income (secs. 1441 and 1442). Accordingly, the 30-percent gross-basis tax generally is referred to as a withholding tax. In most instances, the amount withheld by the U.S. payor is the final tax liability of the foreign recipient and, thus, the foreign recipient files no U.S. tax return with respect to this income.

The United States generally does not tax capital gains of a foreign corporation that are not connected with a U.S. trade or business.

* * *

C. Income Tax Treaties

1. In general

In addition to the U.S. and foreign statutory rules for the taxation of foreign income of U.S. persons and U.S. income of foreign persons, bilateral income tax treaties limit the amount of income tax that may be imposed by one treaty partner on residents of the other treaty partner. Treaties also contain provisions governing the creditability of taxes imposed by the treaty country in which income was earned in computing the amount of tax owed to the other country by its residents with respect to such income. Treaties further provide procedures under which inconsistent positions taken by the treaty countries with respect to a single item of income or deduction may be mutually resolved by the two countries.

The preferred tax treaty policies of the United States have been expressed from time to time in model treaties and agreements. The Organization for Economic Cooperation and Development (the "OECD") also has published model tax treaties. In addition, the United Nations has published a model treaty for use between developed and developing countries. The Treasury Department, which together with the State Department is responsible for negotiating tax treaties, last published a proposed model income tax treaty in September 1996 (the "U.S. model"). The OECD last published a model income tax treaty in 1992 ("the OECD model"). The United Nations last published a model income tax treaty in 1980 ("the U.N. model").

Many U.S. income tax treaties currently in effect diverge in one or more respects from the U.S. model. These divergences may reflect the age of a particular treaty or the particular balance of interests between the United States and the treaty partner. Other countries' preferred tax treaty policies may differ from those of the United States, depending on their internal tax laws and depending upon the balance of investment and trade flows between those countries and their potential treaty partners. For example, certain capital importing countries may be interested in imposing relatively high tax rates on interest, royalties, and personal property rents paid to residents of the other treaty country. Consequently, treaties with such countries may have higher withholding rates on dividends, interest, royalties, and personal property rents. As another example, the other country may demand other concessions in exchange for agreeing to requested U.S. terms. Countries that impose income tax on certain local business operations at a relatively low rate (or a zero rate) in order to attract manufacturing capital may seek to enter into "tax-sparing" treaties with capital exporting countries. In other words, the country may seek to enter into treaties under which the capital exporting country gives up its tax on the income of its residents derived from sources in the first country, regardless of the extent to which the first country has imposed tax with respect to that income. While other capital exporting countries have agreed to such treaties, the United States has rejected proposals by certain foreign countries to enter into such tax-sparing arrangements.

The OECD, the U.N., and the U.S. models reflect a standardization of terms that serves as a useful starting point in treaty negotiations. However, issues may arise between the United States and a particular country that of necessity cannot be addressed with a model provision. Because a treaty functions as a bridge between two actual tax systems, one or both of the parties to the negotiations may seek to diverge from the models to account for specific features of a particular tax system.

2. Model income tax treaty provisions

[The standard features of a "model" U.S. income tax treaty are described here, including concessions with respect to many but not all of the otherwise applicable tax rules. — Ed.]

D. Tax Treatment of U.S. Persons Living Abroad

1. General exclusion

A U.S. citizen or resident generally is taxed on his or her worldwide income, with the allowance of a foreign tax credit for foreign taxes paid on the foreign income. An individual who has his or her tax home in a foreign country and who meets either of two eligibility requirements, however, generally can elect to exclude an amount of foreign earned income from gross income (sec. 911(a)). The maximum exclusion is $70,000 per year, increased in increments of $2,000 per year beginning in 1998. The exclusion is $74,000 for 1999. The exclusion is indexed for inflation beginning in 2008 (for inflation after 2006).

An individual meeting the eligibility requirements generally may also elect to exclude (or deduct, in certain cases) certain housing costs (sec. 911(a)(2)).

* * *

To qualify for the foreign earned income exclusion, an individual must satisfy either a bona fide residence test or a physical presence test. Under the bona fide residence test, a citizen of the United States must establish to the satisfaction of the Treasury Secretary that he or she has been a bona fide resident of a foreign country for an uninterrupted period which includes an entire taxable year (sec. 911(d)(1)). In order to satisfy the physical presence test, the individual must be present overseas for 330 days out of any 12 consecutive month period (sec. 911(d)(2)). In either case, the taxpayer must have a tax home in a foreign country.

The combined earned income exclusion and housing amount exclusion may not exceed the taxpayer's total foreign earned income for the taxable year (sec. 911(d)(7)). Foreign earned income generally means income earned from sources outside the United States as compensation for personal services actually rendered by the taxpayer (sec. 911(d)(2)).

The foreign earned income provision contains a denial of double benefits by reducing such items as the foreign tax credit by the amount attributable to excluded income (sec. 911(d)(6)).

* * *

IV. ANALYSIS OF ISSUES RELATING TO INTERNATIONAL INVESTMENT

A. Capital Export Neutrality, Capital Import Neutrality, and National Neutrality

International investment plays an important role in determining the total amount of worldwide income as well as the distribution of income across nations. In addition, international investment flows can substantially influence the distribution of capital and labor income within nations. Because each government levies taxes by its own method and at its own rates, the resulting system of international taxation can distort investment and contribute to reductions in worldwide economic welfare. A government's tax policies affect the distribution of income directly, by collecting tax from foreigners earning income within its borders and from residents earning income overseas, and indirectly by inducing capital movements across national borders.

The concepts of capital export neutrality and capital import neutrality

Capital movements across national borders in response to tax policy, rather than investment in response to pure economic fundamentals, reduce worldwide economic welfare. The nature of these economic distortions depends on the method of taxing income from international investment. If investment income is taxed only at the source, substantial amounts of capital could be diverted to jurisdictions with the lowest tax rates instead of flowing to investment projects with the highest pre-tax rate of return. If a system of residence taxation is the worldwide norm, enterprises resident in low-tax countries might be able to attract more investment capital or perhaps increase their market share through lower prices to the detriment of enterprises resident in high-tax jurisdictions, even though the latter are more efficient. In either case, capital is diverted from its more productive uses, and worldwide income and efficiency suffer. The most straightforward solution to this problem is equalization of effective tax rates, but this may not be a practical solution given differences in national preferences for the amount and method of taxation.

There is no consensus on what method of taxing international investment income minimizes distortions in the allocation of capital when nations tax income at different effective rates, but the alternatives of capital export neutrality and capital import neutrality are the most cited guiding principles. These two standards are each desirable goals of international tax policy. The problem is that, with unequal tax rates, these two goals are not mutually attainable.

Satisfying both principles at the same time is possible only if effective tax rates on capital income are the same in all countries.

Capital export neutrality. — Capital export neutrality refers to a system where an investor residing in a particular locality can locate investment anywhere in the world and pay the same tax.

Capital import neutrality. — Capital import neutrality refers to a system of international taxation where income from investment located in each country is taxed at the same rate regardless of the residence of the investor.

Chart 1 below, compares capital import neutrality with capital export neutrality. The chart provides a taxonomy of the tax that would apply to income from an investment by location of the investment and by residence of the investor under the principle of capital export neutrality (panel a) and under capital import neutrality (panel b). Tax rates are always equal for investors residing in the same country under capital export neutrality. Tax rates are always equal for investments located in the same country under capital import neutrality.

Chart 1. — The Principles of Capital Export Neutrality and Capital Import Neutrality

a. Capital Export Neutrality

Domestic investor faces domestic tax rate no matter where investment is located. Foreign investor faces foreign tax rate no matter where investment is located. Foreign investment income is subject to foreign tax rate regardless of the residence of the taxpayer.

		Location of Investment	
		Domestic	Foreign
Residence of Investor	Domestic	Tax income at domestic rate	Tax income at domestic rate
	Foreign	Tax income at foreign rate	Tax income at foreign rate

b. Capital Import Neutrality

Domestic investment income subject to the domestic tax rate regardless of the residence of the taxpayer. Foreign investment income subject to foreign tax rate regardless of the residence of the taxpayer.

		Location of Investment	
		Domestic	Foreign
Residence of Investor	Domestic	Tax income at domestic rate	Tax income at foreign rate
	Foreign	Tax income at domestic rate	Tax income at foreign rate

Under capital export neutrality, decisions on the location of investment are not distorted by taxes. Capital export neutrality is a principle describing how investors pay tax, not to whom they pay. Capital export neutrality primarily is a framework for discussing the efficiency and incentives faced by private investors, and not the distribution of the revenues and benefits of international investment. Tax systems may adhere to the principle of capital export neutrality by taxing worldwide income and granting credits for income and profits taxes paid to foreign governments. As an alternative to the system of foreign tax credits, capital export neutrality could be achieved with the source country relinquishing its jurisdiction to tax income derived from investments within its borders and allowing the country of residence the exclusive right to tax this income.

Under capital import neutrality, capital income from all businesses operating in any one locality is subject to uniform taxation. The nationality of investors in a particular locality will not affect the rate of tax. Capital import neutrality may be achieved by the residence country exempting income earned from foreign jurisdictions entirely from tax and allowing the source country's taxation to be the only taxation on the income of international investors. This is commonly referred to as a "territorial" or an "exemption" system of international taxation.

Some commentators refer to the principle of capital import neutrality as promoting "competitiveness." This notion of competitiveness refers to the ability of U.S. multinationals (firms headquartered in the United States that operate abroad) that locate production facilities overseas to compete in foreign markets. Overseas production facilities owned by U.S. interests may compete with firms owned by residents of the host country or with multinational firms based in other countries. The notion of capital import neutrality promoting the competitiveness of such businesses focuses on the after-tax returns to investments in production facilities abroad. As described above, under the principle of capital export neutrality, any business would see the return from its investment in any given foreign country taxed only by that foreign country. Under present law, residual U.S. taxation in the case of a U.S. multinational may apply differently than residual taxation by another capital-exporting country. The result may be that the after-tax return to an investment by a U.S. multinational in a given foreign country may be less than the after-tax return earned by another investor, even if that investor makes an identical investment to that of the U.S. multinational. Some argue that this puts the U.S. multinational at a competitive disadvantage.

The concept of national neutrality

Because countries typically tax income arising within their borders, a nation can increase its income through policies that reduce outbound investment by its residents and encourage inbound investment by foreigners. This is the case even if net outbound investment is driven below the level that would prevail in a free and efficient international capital market. Promoting national economic interest may not coincide with promoting worldwide economic income.

In a world of source taxation, the national interest and the interests of outbound investors do not coincide. Outbound investment is only in the national interest if the return after foreign tax (but before domestic tax) equals or exceeds the before-tax return on domestic investment. To further its national interest, a government can reduce outbound investment by reducing the after-tax rate of return on outbound investment and driving its before-tax return above that on domestic investment. A government can penalize outbound investment by imposing a layer of taxation in addition to foreign taxation at source. This result can be achieved when a capital exporting nation, in response to foreign source taxation, does not cede taxing jurisdiction over foreign source income (for example, through a foreign tax credit) and allows only a deduction for foreign taxes.

The policy of allowing only deductions for foreign taxes is sometimes known as "national neutrality." A deduction penalizes outbound investment and aligns the interests of the taxpayer with the interests of its home country — but only at the expense of reduced worldwide economic welfare. Despite the potential to maximize national welfare, self-interested nations generally do not adopt tax systems designed to achieve national neutrality. There are at least three possible explanations for this. First, there is reason to expect that one nation's unilateral attempt to improve its own welfare through a policy of national neutrality would meet with retaliation by other nations with similar policies. Such tax competition would reduce worldwide income even further. If on the other hand, nations can coordinate their tax policies, a tax system can be designed to increase worldwide income above the inefficient level produced by national neutrality. With international coordination, there is potential for adopting a system in which worldwide income could be maximized (and, if necessary, redistributed) so that all nations could be better off.

Second, the disincentives to outbound investment embodied in the concept of national neutrality only increase national welfare if outbound investment increases at the expense of domestic investment. If the economy responds to increased outbound investment with increased domestic saving instead of reduced domestic investment, policies to discourage outbound investment may have little positive effect on domestic labor and, furthermore, may reduce national welfare in addition to worldwide welfare.

Third, even if the first two rebuttals to national neutrality do not hold, there is some evidence that outbound investment increases exports by more than it increases imports. This increase in net exports may provide benefits to domestic labor and increase overall domestic income. If this is the case, policies discouraging outbound investment could increase the merchandise trade deficit and reduce national output.

Summary

A government can implement capital export neutrality by taxing worldwide income of its residents but also allowing credits for taxes paid to foreign governments. Alternatively, a government can implement national neutrality by replacing credits with deductions for foreign taxes. Finally, a government can implement capital import neutrality by exempting all foreign source income from tax. Since national neutrality is less generous to taxpayers than capital export neutrality, deviations from capital export neutrality that increase tax on foreign income, move the U.S. system closer to a system of national neutrality. Conversely, since capital import neutrality is often more generous to taxpayers than capital export neutrality, deviations from capital export neutrality that decrease tax on foreign income move the U.S. system closer to a system of capital import neutrality.

As a whole, the U.S. system of taxation is a hybrid containing elements consistent with both capital import neutrality and capital export neutrality. With regard to the relative treatment of domestic and outbound investment, many provisions work at cross purposes. Some provisions of current law favor outbound investment, while others discourage it.

* * *

Reuven S. Avi-Yonah, *The Structure of International Taxation: A Proposal for Simplification*
74 TEXAS L. REV. 1301, 1303–05, 1316–17 (1996)[2]

The current international tax regime is a flawed miracle. It is a miracle because taxes are the last topic on which one would expect sovereign nations to reach a consensus. International taxation is, to some extent, a zero-sum game: one country's gain in revenue is another's loss. If income is derived by a resident of one country from sources in another, and if both countries have a legitimate claim to tax that income and the ability to enforce that claim, then either country will lose revenue by agreeing to grant the other the primary right to tax that income.

Nevertheless, and contrary to a prior expectations, a coherent international tax regime exists that enjoys nearly universal support and that underlies the complexities of the international aspects of individual countries' tax systems. This regime was first developed in the 1920s, when the League of Nations first undertook to study ways to avoid international double taxation, and has been embodied both in the model tax treaties developed by the Organization for Economic Co-operation and Development (OECD) and the United Nations and in the multitude of bilateral treaties that are based on those models. The existence of this regime shows that despite each country's claim to sovereignty in tax matters, it is possible to reach an internationally acceptable consensus that will be followed by the majority of the world's taxing jurisdictions. This international tax regime, based on voluntary consensus, can be regarded as one of the major achievements of twentieth-century international law.

Yet the miracle is flawed. The current regime suffers from significant weaknesses, especially in two areas in which the development of the world economy has made the principles that were agreed upon in the 1920s and 1930s obsolete: the growth of internationally mobile capital markets for portfolio investment and the rise of integrated multinational enterprises (MNEs). Thus, as this century nears its end, it is time to re-examine the prevailing international tax regime and ask whether a new consensus can be reached to remedy the regime's major weaknesses and ensure its continued viability in the next century.

This Article seeks to do so in four parts. Part I describes the structure of the international tax regime and how this structure reflects a consensus about the allocation of taxable income among taxing jurisdictions. Specifically, the international consensus allocates active business income to the jurisdiction from which it derives (the source jurisdiction) and passive income to the jurisdiction in which the investor resides (the residence jurisdiction). Part I also discusses two possible alternatives to this consensus — taxing all income in either the residence

---

jurisdiction or the source jurisdiction — but concludes that the current consensus is superior to both. Part II describes how the international aspects of United States tax law fit the international tax regime outlined in Part I and suggests ways in which details of the United States regime that are incongruent with the international consensus may be modified unilaterally. Part III of the Article identifies the two principal weaknesses of the current regime: the difficulty of enforcing residence-based taxation of individuals and the difficulty of allocating the income of MNEs among source jurisdictions. Part III then explains why these problems can only be resolved by multilateral action and describes the recommended solutions: enforcement of residence-based taxation through backup withholding by source jurisdictions and agreement on a unitary method to be used to allocate the profits of MNEs in the absence of comparable transactions. Finally, Part IV describes an alternative international tax regime that is based on the current international consensus, but incorporates the solutions identified in Part III and is considerably simpler than the present structure. Part IV also identifies the implications of the proposal for United States tax law and discusses ways in which the proposal may be applied by jurisdictions that adopt an integrated approach to the taxation of corporations and their shareholders.

* * *

The Active or Passive Distinction and United States International Taxation

This Part of the Article describes how the structure of United States international taxation reflects the active or passive distinction and what changes can be made by the United States unilaterally to make its regime more congruent with the international consensus. The modifications identified in this Part should be distinguished from more profound changes that can only be achieved by multilateral action.

The fundamental distinction underlying the United States international tax regime is between domestic taxpayers (United States citizens, residents, domestic corporations, partnerships, and trusts), who are taxed on their worldwide income, and foreign taxpayers (all others), who are taxed only on their United States source income. Domestic taxpayers are taxed by the United States because of their personal connection to the United States, that is, on the basis of residence; the United States does, however, include nonresident United States citizens in this category. Foreign taxpayers are taxed by the United States on the basis of their territorial connection to the United States, that is, on the basis of source. One problem that is raised by this distinction is that the choice between being taxed on a residence or source basis is initially left to the taxpayer, because corporations are classified as domestic or foreign based on their formal place of incorporation. Therefore, it is possible for a domestic taxpayer to shift income from residence- to source-based taxation by routing it to a corporation incorporated abroad; if the income is foreign source (and not effectively connected with the conduct of a trade or business in the United States), the result is the avoidance of current United States taxation. Much of the complexity of the current United States international tax regime stems from attempts to address this problem through antideferral regimes.

* * *

Robert J. Peroni, *Back to the Future: A Path to Progressive Reform of the U.S. International Income Tax Rules*
51 U. MIAMI L. REV. 975, 980–81 (1997)[3]

A. Introduction

In recent years, many business leaders, politicians, and commentators have taken the position that international tax policy should be driven by concerns about the competitiveness of U.S. multinational corporations in the global economy. These commentators maintain that the U.S. international tax system should be revised to implement capital import neutrality at least with respect to the taxation of active business income earned by U.S. multinationals abroad. Capital import neutrality focuses on taxation in the host country; all firms operating in the same industry in a particular country bear the same level of tax. Under this view, source-based taxation of active business income should be the norm and the residence country should adopt a territorial system of international taxation that would exempt foreign source business income of its multinationals from domestic taxation.

This paper, however, explores and supports a contrary view. It assumes that residence-based taxing jurisdiction of U.S. persons' foreign source income is appropriate and that capital export neutrality should continue to be the main neutrality principle underlying the international tax rules of the United States. Consistent with these assumptions, the United States should not adopt a territorial system for taxing international income. The way to reform the international tax rules is to bring the current system closer to a capital export neutrality ideal by making the following changes: repealing deferral with respect to all foreign income earned by U.S. shareholders through controlled foreign corporations and by any U.S. investors through passive foreign investment companies; reforming and simplifying the foreign tax credit limit; adopting the worldwide fungibility approach for allocating and apportioning interest expense; repealing the inefficient export incentives in the Code such as the FSC provisions and the title-passage source rule for income from inventory sales; and repealing the foreign earned income exclusion in section 911. These changes would simplify the U.S. international tax rules and, more importantly, result in a U.S. international tax system that is more theoretically coherent and that better promotes economic efficiency.

---

[3] Copyright © 1998. All rights reserved. Reprinted by permission.

* * *

Using the Sources

Based on the materials above, and your own reading of the international provisions of the tax code (Subchapter N), answer the following questions:

1.   What is meant by the terms "source" and "resident" taxation, and what is the difference between them? Which of these does the U.S. tax system adopt, and in what cases? Why?

2.   Very briefly, how is the source determined for each of the following items?

   a. Income from services.

   b. Income from sales.

   c. Interest and royalty income.

3.   What are the two ways that income from a foreign corporation can be subject to U.S. tax, and what is the difference between them?

4.   What exactly is meant by the phrase "fixed or determinable, annual or periodical income," and what is its tax treatment?

5.   What is meant by the "basket" system with respect to the foreign tax credit (section 901, *et seq.*), and what incentive, logical or illogical, does it create?

6.   Subpart F (section 951, *et seq.*) addresses the tax treatment of profits earned by controlled foreign corporations (CFCs). Why was this deemed a problem, and how does Subpart F deal with it?

7.   What is the role of tax treaties under U.S. law, and what happens if a treaty conflicts with another previously or subsequently enacted statute?

Law and Planning

Suppose that Java Josephine, an American chain of coffee bars, is thinking of opening a number of outlets in France, to which they hope to attract customers with a mixture of high-test coffee, Internet access, and a generally hip American atmosphere. (Try to ignore the recent trend in Franco-American relations; it is not the first time, and probably won't be the last.) The stores would be managed from a Paris headquarters although ultimately connected, in one form or another, to the American parent company. For purposes of this problem only, assume that the French corporate and individual income tax rate is 40 percent and that there is an additional 20 percent value added tax on all relevant sales; assume further that the tax treaty between the United States and France provides for a maximum 15 percent French tax on dividends paid by a French company to a foreign shareholder. (Note: those are not necessarily the actual provisions of French law but a rough approximation that should give you some idea of the issues faced in this kind of transaction.)

1. In broad outline ("en general," as they say in Paris), what tax questions would you need to ask in order to decide whether to undertake this venture and how to structure it (as a separate French entity, as a unit of the American company, etc.) if you did so? What sources would you need to consult in order to make this evaluation, and in which cases, if any, would you need to consult a French lawyer rather than conducting research on your own? Given the existence of the foreign tax credit (section 901, *et seq.*), does it matter how you structure the venture, or does it all come out the same in the end, anyway? (Note: You do not have enough information, at this point, to provide detailed answers to these problems, but between the Code and the preceding materials you should have more than enough to ask the appropriate questions. That is at least half the battle.)

2. How might the tax laws (U.S. and France) affect your decision with respect to the following?

> a. The decision whether to undertake an investment outside the U.S., at all.

> b. The decision whether to make the investment in France or an alternate European (or non-European) country.

> c. Assuming the investment was to be made in France, the decision whether to establish a separate French entity or operate the business as a unit of the American parent company.

What other factors, besides tax laws, would be likely to affect your decision, and how would you balance these against the tax factors above? (Please feel free to include both nontax legal factors (commercial and business law, labor law, antitrust, etc.) and "real world" business considerations in your analysis.)

3. What do your answers to questions 1. and 2. tell you about the existing tax system and its success in achieving neutrality between different investments?

Politics and Policy

1. Which of the following do you believe should be the most important goals of the international system and (specifically) of U.S. tax law in this area?

> a. Capital export neutrality (*i.e.*, taxes should not affect a decision to invest in the U.S. or in another country).

> b. Capital import neutrality (*i.e.*, foreign investments in the U.S. should be taxed the same as investments from domestic sources).

> c. Promotion of U.S. export industries and protection of our own domestic market.

> d. Promotion of the interests of poorer countries (*i.e.*, redistribution from rich to poor nations).

> e. Promotion of free capital flows between different countries without regard to other issues.

2.   Now shift from a prophet to a hard-eyed observer of existing reality. Of goals a. through e. above, which do you think the present law tax system actually promotes, and why? What specific changes, if any, would you recommend in order to achieve your preferred goals?

3.   What do you think of the idea of a World Tax Organization, modeled after the existing World Trade Organization (WTO) in trade policy, as a means of coordinating and eventually controlling the tax policies of individual countries? What do you think is the likelihood that this will actually happen? Why?

II. A DAY IN THE LIFE OF AN INTERNATIONAL TAX PLANNER: THE PROBLEM OF TRANSFER PRICING

International tax is heavily "proactive" in nature: Even more than in domestic tax, the best practitioners earn their keep not by reacting to existing problems, but by planning ahead in order to reduce or avoid them. Indeed, it is not uncommon for the entire structure of international business enterprises to be determined largely by tax considerations. As you might expect, planning techniques tend to become more rather than less aggressive with the passage of time; this part of the chapter is thus a good opportunity to express your sense of outrage at the injustice of the international tax system as well as to learn a few of its inside tricks.

One of the more intellectually intriguing international planning techniques is the matter of transfer pricing. Let us say that Japancar, Inc. sells cars in the United States that are assembled domestically, but using designs and know-how which by and large originate in Japan. In return for these intangibles the U.S. subsidiary ("Japancar USA") makes royalty payments each year to the Japanese parent, which are deductible to the U.S. subsidiary and (presumably) constitute income to the parent company in Japan. The precise amount of these payments is somewhat arbitrary, since the value of intangibles is difficult to determine and the two companies are part of the same global network, so that there is no arm's-length negotiation between them; but it is obviously proper that some amount should be paid.

Suppose now that, for any number of reasons, taxes in Japan are lower than they are in the United States. What is the firm likely to do? One strategy is to increase the amount of the annual royalty payments described above, which will have the effect of increasing taxes paid in Japan but (owing to the deduction) reducing those paid in the United States. Conversely, if taxes are lower in the United States, the firm could reduce or even eliminate the payments, resulting in an increase in U.S. tax liability but a corresponding decrease, perhaps a dramatic one, in Japanese tax liability. If the company has operations in three or more countries, it could conceivably shift income to whichever of the various countries had the lowest tax rate, using a more sophisticated version of the same strategy.

The concept above is relatively simple, yet a few applications of it are sufficient to enable large multinational corporations to evade literally billions of dollars in taxes. This is especially true when "tax haven" jurisdictions — small or not-so-small countries that use low or nonexistent tax rates in an effort to attract business activity — are entered into the mix. Suppose that, instead of being located in Japan, the company that holds the patents for Japancar's designs and innovations is located in a small Caribbean island that imposes little or no taxes on royalty income. In this not entirely fanciful scenario — and assuming sufficiently generous royalty payments — the tax rate on a large portion of the company's income could be reduced to almost zero.[4]

Obviously, governments are not going to let this happen, and a whole jurisprudence has developed around "transfer pricing" and its tax implications. The problem is exactly what to do about it. In U.S. tax law, the most potent remedy is section 482, rather innocuously labeled "Allocation of income and deductions among taxpayers." Section 482 is sufficiently short and to the point that it bears quotation in full:

> In any case of two or more organizations, trades, or businesses (whether or not incorporated, whether or not organized in the United States, and whether or not affiliated) owned directly or indirectly by the same interests, the Secretary [IRS] may distribute, apportion, or allocate gross income, deductions, credits, or allowances between or among such organizations, trades, or businesses, if he determines that such distribution, apportionment, or allocation is necessary in order to prevent evasion of taxes or clearly to reflect the income of any of such organizations, trades, or businesses. In the case of any transfer (or license) of intangible property . . . the income with respect to such transfer or license shall be commensurate with the income attributable to the intangible.

Taken literally, section 482 would allow the IRS to ignore virtually any arrangements between related companies — domestic or international — and redetermine the companies' income on the basis of a *de novo* evaluation of the relevant economic facts. To prevent this chaos, Treasury Regulations provide a series of highly detailed rules for the application of the reallocation provision.[5] The general rule is that transactions between controlled taxpayers should be compared to those that would have taken place had two uncontrolled (*i.e.*, unrelated) taxpayers engaged in the same transaction under the same circumstances (the so-called "arm's length" standard) (Treas. Reg. section 1.482-1(b)). For example, in the Japancar situation, royalties paid by the U.S. subsidiary to the Japanese parent would be compared to the hypothetical royalties that would be paid in a similar situation involving negotiations between two unrelated taxpayers. If the actual royalties paid were higher than would be determined under an arm's length standard, IRS could reduce the deduction of the U.S. subsidiary resulting in more income being subject to U.S. tax.[6]

At least two problems with this system are readily apparent. One is that it is often extraordinarily difficult to find comparable arm's length situations to which a given royalty or other payment can reasonably be compared. A related problem is

---

[4] The transfer pricing racket involves such vast sums of money that entire careers have been devoted to it. A couple of years ago, one of your authors inquired what a former colleague in Washington had done with the last two decades of his life. "482," came the response. No further questions.

[5] Treas. Reg. § 1.482-1 through -8.

[6] This example assumes that Japanese taxes were lower than those in the United States.

that — given the breadth of section 482 and the difficulty of identifying comparable transactions — it is extremely difficult to predict how section 482 will be interpreted in any given case. To reduce this unpredictability, the regulations allow companies to enter into so-called Advance Pricing Agreements (APAs) which, if they are approved by IRS, essentially insulate the relevant transactions from further section 482 attack. The attraction of an APA — prior knowledge that a company's allocations will be respected by the IRS on audit — is obvious. However, there is always the danger that the IRS will not agree to the company's proposal, and taxpayers may be tempted to adopt a more aggressive position and simply take their chances on a later challenge.

Section 482 is sufficiently complex that no one example can capture it in full. However, the following case serves to capture the flavor of its operation, together with the remarkable creativity (some might say cynicism) of sophisticated international practitioners. As you read, consider whether the transfer pricing issue is really such a difficult one intellectually speaking, or whether taxpayers have manipulated some of the complexity in order (if they get away with it) to achieve monumental tax savings.

E.I. DU PONT DE NEMOURS AND CO. v. UNITED STATES
United States Court of Claims
608 F.2d 445 (1970)

DAVIS, J:

Taxpayer Du Pont de Nemours, the American chemical concern, created early in 1959, a wholly-owned Swiss marketing and sales subsidiary for foreign sales, Du Pont International S.A. (known to the record and the parties as DISA). Most of the Du Pont chemical products marketed abroad were first sold by taxpayer to DISA, which then arranged for resale to the ultimate consumer through independent distributors. The profits on these Du Pont sales were divided for income tax purposes between plaintiff and DISA via the mechanism of the prices plaintiff charged DISA. For 1959 and 1960 the Commissioner of Internal Revenue, acting under section 482 of the Internal Revenue Code which gives him authority to reallocate profits among commonly controlled enterprises, found these divisions of profits economically unrealistic as giving DISA too great a share. Accordingly, he reallocated a substantial part of DISA's income to taxpayer, thus increasing the latter's taxes for 1959 and 1960 by considerable sums. The additional taxes were paid and this refund suit was brought in due course. Du Pont assails the Service's reallocation, urging that the prices plaintiff charged DISA were valid under the Treasury regulations implementing section 482. We hold that taxpayer has failed to demonstrate that, under the regulation it invokes and must invoke, it is entitled to any refund of taxes.

I. *Design, Objectives and Functioning of DISA*

A. Du Pont first considered formation of an international sales subsidiary in 1957. A decreasing volume of domestic sales, increasing profits on exports, and the recent formation of the Common Market in Europe convinced taxpayer's president of the need for such a subsidiary. He envisioned an international sales branch capable of marketing Du Pont's most profitable type of products — Du Pont proprietary products, particularly textile fibers and elastomers specially designed for use as raw materials by other manufacturers. Du Pont had utilized two major marketing techniques to sell such customized products.[7] One mechanism consisted of technical sales services: an elaborate set of laboratory services making technical improvements, developing new applications, and solving customer problems for Du Pont products. The other was "indirect selling," a method of promoting demand for Du Pont products at every point in the distribution chain. These two techniques were to be developed by DISA, Du Pont's international branch in Europe. DISA was not to displace plaintiff's set of independent European distributors, but rather to augment the distributors' efforts by the two marketing methods and to police the independents adequately.

B. Neither in the planning stage nor in actual operation was DISA a sham entity; nor can it be denied that it was intended to, and did, perform substantial commercial functions which taxpayer legitimately saw as needed in its foreign (primarily European) market. Nevertheless, we think it also undeniable that the tax advantages of such a foreign entity were also an important, though not the primary, consideration in DISA's creation and operation. During the planning stages, plaintiff's internal memoranda were replete with references to tax advantages, particularly in planning prices on Du Pont goods to be sold to the new entity. The tax strategy was simple. If Du Pont sold its goods to the new international subsidiary at prices below fair market value, that company, upon resale of the goods, would recognize the greater part of the total profit (*i.e.*, manufacturing and selling profits). Since this foreign subsidiary could be located in a country where its profits would be taxed at a much lower level than the parent Du Pont would be taxed here, the enterprise as a whole would minimize its taxes. *Cf. Baldwin-Lima-Hamilton Corp. v. United States*, 435 F.2d 182, 184 (7th Cir. 1970). The new company's accumulated profits would be used to finance further foreign investments. The details of this planning are set forth in the findings, and they leave us without doubt that a significant objective of plaintiff was to create a foreign subsidiary which would be able to accumulate large profits with which to finance Du Pont capital improvements in Europe.[8]

---

[7] [3] Du Pont also had several other types of products which did not require the specialized sales effort contemplated for DISA. These products included direct "commodity-type" goods (such as household paints) or standard chemical products (*e.g.*, sulfuric acid).

[8] [4] Du Pont is divided into a series of semi-autonomous departments which report to the Executive Committee. An early draft of a memorandum on this subject to the Executive Committee from the International Department (then known as the Foreign Relations Department) stated that the Treasury Department (responsible for Du Pont's tax planning) was considering the possibility of a "transfer of goods to a tax haven subsidiary at prices less than such transfers would be made to other subsidiaries or industrial Departments. . . ." A memorandum from the Treasury Department reviewed the possibility of an IRS attack on such pricing and concluded:

> "It would seem to be desirable to bill the tax haven subsidiary at less than an 'arm's length' price because: (1) the pricing might not be challenged by the revenue agent; (2) if the pricing is challenged, we might sustain such transfer prices; (3) if we cannot sustain the prices used, a transfer price will be negotiated which should not be more than an 'arm's length' price and

C. Consistently with that aim, plaintiff's prices on its intercorporate sales to DISA were deliberately calculated to give the subsidiary the lion's share of the profits. Instead of allowing each individual producing department to value its goods economically and to set a realistic price,[9] Du Pont left pricing on the sales to DISA with the Treasury and Legal Departments. Neither department was competent to set an economic value on goods sold to DISA, and no economic correlation of costs to prices was attempted.[10] Rather, an official of the Treasury Department established a pricing system designed to leave DISA with 75 percent of the total profits. If the goods' cost was greater than DISA's selling price, the department would price the item at its cost *less* DISA's selling expense. This latter provision was designed to insulate DISA from any loss. On the whole, the pricing system was based solely on Treasury and Legal Department estimates of the greatest amount of profits that could be shifted to DISA without evoking IRS intervention.[11]

As it turned out, for the taxable years involved here, 1959 and 1960, the actual division of total profits between plaintiff and DISA was closer to a 50-50 split. In 1959 DISA realized 48.3 percent of the total profits, while in 1960 its share climbed to 57.1 percent. This departure from the original plan was the result of the omission of certain intercorporate transfers — a result not contemplated in the initial pricing scheme.

---

might well be less; thus we would be no worse off than we would have been had we billed at the higher price."

A subsequent Treasury Department report on "Use of a Profit Sanctuary Company by the Du Pont Company" advised pricing goods to the "profit sanctuary" at considerably lower levels than other intercorporate sales, suggesting that such prices could probably be sustained against an IRS challenge. In the spring of 1958, an International Department memorandum stated that the principal advantages of a "profit sanctuary trading company" (dubbed by its initials as a "PST company") depended "largely upon the amount of profits which might be shifted (through selling price) from Du Pont to the 'PST company.' " The report concluded that Du Pont could find "a selling price sufficiently low as to result in the transfer of a substantial part of the profits on export sales to the 'PST company.' " A corporate task force selected Switzerland as the best location for the foreign trading subsidiary, principally because of Swiss tax incentives.

The two industrial departments expected to provide the main source of DISA's sales were not overly enthusiastic about a new layer of company organization. However, both departments agreed to formation of DISA for tax reasons. The Elastomer Department concluded: "The decisive factor in our support of the organization is the potential tax saving." The Textile Fibers Department recognized that tax considerations "will command the establishment of lowest practical transfer prices from the manufacturing subsidiaries to Du Pont Swiss [DISA]. . . ." A memorandum to the Executive Committee in late 1958 (shortly before the Committee approved DISA) spoke of *the modest mark-up* (emphasis in original) of goods sold to the foreign trading subsidiary. A prior draft of the memorandum used the phrase "the 'artificially' low price."

[9] [5] The individual industrial departments which manufactured goods sold to DISA had little reason to care about the pricing of such goods. Under a special accounting system DISA was ignored in computing departmental earnings, bonuses, etc. All profits from DISA were attributed to the department manufacturing the respective goods. This internal treatment of DISA's profits conflicted with Du Pont's standard practice of treating each subsidiary as a distinct profit center.

[10] [6] The responsible official did not solicit the views of the manufacturing departments as to an appropriate pricing system.

[11] [7] Finding 71 summarizes the testimony of the key Treasury Department official, who conceded he would have set prices so as to shift 99 percent of total profits to DISA if he had thought such an allocation would have survived IRS scrutiny.

D. In operation, DISA enjoyed certain market advantages which helped it to accumulate large, tax-free profits. For its technical service function, the subsidiary did not develop its own extensive laboratories (with resulting costs and risks), but could rely on its parent's laboratory network in the United States and England. DISA was not required to hunt intensively (or pay as highly) for qualified personnel, since in both 1959 and 1960 it drew extensively on its parent's reservoir of talent. The international company's credit risks were very low, in part because of a favorable trade credit timetable by Du Pont. DISA also selected its customers to avoid credit losses, having a bad debt provision of less than one-tenth of one percent of sales. Unlike other distributor or advertising service agencies, DISA, because of its special relationship to the Du Pont manufacturing departments, had relatively little risk of termination.[12] And as explained *supra*, Du Pont's pricing formula was intended to insulate DISA from losses on sales.[13]

In operating DISA, Du Pont also maximized its subsidiary's income by funneling a large volume of sales through DISA which did not call for large expenditures by the latter. Many of the products Du Pont sold through DISA required no special services, or already had ample technical services provided. Du Pont routed sales to Australia and South Africa through DISA although the latter provided no additional services to sales in these nonEuropean countries. DISA made sales of commodity-type products and opportunistic spot sales to competitors temporarily short in a raw material, although neither type of sale required DISA's specialized marketing expertise. Du Pont also routed all European sales of elastomers through DISA, even though the parent had a well-established English subsidiary which had all the necessary technical services and marketing ability.

E. We have itemized the special status of DISA — as a subsidiary intended and operated to accumulate profits without much regard to the functions it performed or their real worth — not as direct proof, in itself, supporting the Commissioner's reallocation of profits under Section 482, but instead as suggesting the basic reason why plaintiff's sales to DISA were unique and without any direct comparable in the real world. As we shall see in Part II, *infra*, taxpayer has staked its entire case on proving that the profits made by DISA in 1959 and 1960 were comparable to those made on similar resales by uncontrolled merchandizing agencies. DISA's special status and mode of functioning help to explain why that effort has failed. It is not that there was anything "illegal" or immoral in Du Pont's plan; it is simply that that plan made it very difficult, perhaps impossible, to satisfy the controlling Treasury regulations under Section 482.[14]

---

[12] [8] Du Pont's individual Industrial Departments could terminate sales with DISA, and two smaller departments did terminate. However, there is no evidence that Du Pont as an entity, particularly the important Elastomer and Textile Fiber Departments, would have seriously considered terminating DISA, a child of their own creation. Further, any such termination would have imposed less financial risk to DISA than for an independent distributor.

[13] [9] In actual fact, the pricing system malfunctioned to some extent and DISA incurred some minor losses. As in the case of profit allocation (*see supra*), this discrepancy was the product of a miscalculation in selling costs for a few low-volume goods. The design of Du Pont's pricing policy was to prevent any loss.

[14] [10] The regulations make it clear (§ 1.482-1(c)) that they apply, not only to sham, fraudulent, or shady cases, but "to any case in which either by inadvertence or design the taxable income, in whole or in part, of a controlled taxpayer, is other than it would have been had the taxpayer in the conduct of his

II. *Section 482 and the "Resale Price Method" of Allocating Profits.*

A. Section 482 gives the Secretary of the Treasury (or his delegate) discretion to allocate income between related corporations when necessary to "prevent evasion of taxes or clearly to reflect the income" of any of such corporations. The legislative history parallels the general purpose of the statutory text to prevent evasion by "improper manipulation of financial accounts", "arbitrary shifting of profits," and to accurately reflect "true tax liability." *See* H.R. Rep. No. 350, 67th Cong., 1st Sess. 14 (1921) (section 240(d) of 1921 Act); S. Rep No. 275, 67th Cong., 1st Sess. 20 (1921) (same section); H.R. Rep. No. 2, 70th Cong., 1st Sess. 16 (1928) (predecessor section to § 482); *Young & Rubicam, Inc. v. United States*, 410 F.2d 1233, 1244, 187 Ct. Cl. 635, 654 (1969). *See generally* BITTKER & EUSTICE, FEDERAL INCOME TAXATION OF CORPORATIONS AND SHAREHOLDERS, para. 15.06 (4th ed. 1979) (hereinafter Bittker & Eustice). The overall aim is to enable the IRS to treat controlled taxpayers as if they were uncontrolled. *See Eli Lilly & Co. v. United States*, 372 F.2d 990, 178 Ct. Cl. 666 (1967); *Young & Rubicam, Inc. v. United States, supra; Morton-Norwich Products, Inc. v. United States, ante* at 83.

B. We do not, however, have the initial problem of considering this case on the words of Section 482 alone, or on comparable broad criteria. In 1968 the Secretary of the Treasury issued revised regulations governing action under the statute, and setting forth rules for certain specific situations. Treas. Reg. § 1.482-1, *et seq.* These regulations, which were issued before the trial here, were made retroactive to cover the taxable years before us (1959-1960), and both sides agree that the regulations must control. In some quarters these regulations have been faulted as not giving enough meaningful guidance in specific situations, or as being too narrow in the specific situations they do cover, but there is here no challenge to the validity of the regulations and we have to apply them as they are, with fidelity to both their words and their spirit.

For sales of tangible goods, the directive mandates determination of an arm's length price for the sale by one controlled entity to the other, and then sets out (in order of preference) four methods for calculating such an arm's length price: the comparable uncontrolled price method, the resale price method, the cost plus method, and any other appropriate method. The parties correctly agree upon the inapplicability of the comparable uncontrolled price method (which calls for comparison with an uncontrolled sale of an almost identical product). Plaintiff makes no argument as to the possible application of the cost plus method. Instead it posits its whole case on the resale price method (Treas. Reg. § 1.482-2(e)(3)) — which we now consider.

C. Essentially, the resale price method reconstructs a fair arm's length market price by discounting the controlled reseller's selling price by the gross profit margin (or markup percentage) rates of comparable uncontrolled dealers.[15] Thus,

---

affairs been an uncontrolled taxpayer dealing at arm's length with another uncontrolled taxpayer."

[15] [14] Subpart (vi) of Section 1.482-2(e)(3) declares that the proper markup, described as "the appropriate markup percentage," is "equal to the percentage of gross profit (expressed as a percentage of sales) earned by the buyer (reseller) or another party on the resale of property which is both purchased and resold in an uncontrolled transaction, which resale is most similar to the applicable resale of the property involved in the controlled sale."

if DISA's gross profit margin for resale was 35% and the prevailing margin for comparable uncontrolled resellers was 25%, the Commissioner could reallocate 10% of DISA's gross income. But the vital prerequisite for applying the resale price method is the existence of substantially comparable uncontrolled resellers. Subpart (vi) of Section 1.482-2(e)(3) requires determination of the "most similar" resale or resales, considering the type of property, reseller's functions, use of any intangibles, and similarity of geographic markets.[16] Cases which have considered the regulation uniformly require substantial comparability. *See, e.g., Woodward Governor Co. v. Commissioner*, 55 T.C. 56, 65 (1970) (resale price method applicable only when evidence shows uncontrolled purchases and resales by same or similar reseller); *American Terrazzo Strip Co. v. Commissioner*, 56 T.C. 961, 972–73 (1971) (uncontrolled sales must be comparable in terms of similar goods and circumstances of sale); *Edwards v. Commissioner*, 67 T.C. 224, 236 (1976) (rejecting use of industry gross profit statistic when no evidence that such sales were comparable to taxpayer). Commentators agree on the need for close similarity of uncontrolled sales, and some criticize the regulation when no uncontrolled sales by the *same* party exist. *See* Fuller, *Section 482 Revisited*, 31 TAX L. REV. 475, 505–07, 510–11 (1976); Jenks, *Treasury Regulations under Section 482*, 23 TAX LAWYER 279, 310 (1970) [hereinafter cited as Jenks]; Note, *Multinational Corporations Income Allocation under Section 482 of the Internal Revenue Code*, 89 HARV. L. REV. 1202, 1220 (1976). It is quite plain from the text of the regulation itself that the evident purpose for the use of the particular resale price method, as set forth in the regulation, is to proffer a relatively precise mechanism for determining a realistically comparable, uncontrolled, arm's-length resale price — not to leave the taxpayer, the Service, or the courts to grope at large for some figure drawn out of overly general indices or statistics.

The common starting point for our search in this case for a comparable meeting the requirements of the regulation is our finding 101 which states: "The parties agree, and their agreement is supported by the record, that there is not known to exist, presently or heretofore, an independent organization circumstanced as DISA was during the period in suit and performing the marketing functions that were assigned to it by plaintiff." That being so, the regulation requires us (§ 1.482-2(e)(3)(vi) (a), (b), and (d)) to look for the "most similar" resales and "in determining the similarity of resales" to consider as the "most important characteristics" the type of property sold, the functions performed by the seller with respect to the property, and the geographic market in which the functions are performed by the reseller. There is also special stress on the performance of "comparable functions" by the seller making the "most similar" resales. *See* subpart (vii).

Taxpayer tells us that a group of 21 distributors, whose general functions were similar to DISA's, provides the proper base of comparison. Beyond the most

---

[16] [15] Subpart (vii) directs that, "[w]henever possible markup percentages should be derived from uncontrolled purchases and resale of the buyer (reseller) involved in the controlled sale [here, DISA] . . . In the absence of [such] resales by the same buyer (reseller) . . . evidence of an appropriate markup percentage may be derived from resales by other resellers selling *in the same or a similar market* in which the controlled buyer (reseller) is selling, *providing such resellers perform comparable functions.*" [emphasis added]

general showing that this group, like DISA, distributed manufactured goods, there is nothing in the record showing the degree of similarity called for by the regulation. No data exist to establish similarity of products (with associated marketing costs), comparability of functions, or parallel geographic (and economic) market conditions. Rather, the record suggests significant differences. Defendant has introduced evidence that the six companies plaintiff identifies most closely with DISA all had average selling costs much higher than DISA.[17] Because we agree with the trial judge and defendant's expert that, in general, what a business spends to provide services is a reasonable indication of the magnitude of those services, and because plaintiff has not rebutted that normal presumption in this case, we cannot view these six companies as having made resales similar to DISA's. They may have made gross profits comparable to DISA's but their selling costs, reflecting the greater scale of their services or efforts, were much higher in each instance.[18] Moreover, the record shows that these companies dealt with quite different products (electronic and photographic equipment) and functioned in different markets (primarily the United States).

Other industrial group or individual resales relied on by taxpayer also fall short of comparability to DISA. We are cited to the gross profit margin of certain drug and chemical wholesalers contained in the Internal Revenue Service's Source Book of Statistics of Income for 1960. Because the gross profit for this group of

----

[17] [17] Defendant's comparison is derived from data in various exhibits and is summarized in the following table:

Reseller	Average Annual Markup Percentages	Average Annual Operating Expenses (percentage of net sales)
AIC Photo	38%	27.5%
Superscope	33%	20.5%
Lloyd Electronics	26%	20.5%
DISA	26%	6.7% or 7.1% *
Soundesign	23%	20.0%
Interphoto	20.5%	16.0%
Telecor	19.5%	11.5%

* The trial judge used a 6.7% figure while our own computation shows 7.1% (both figures have been adjusted to exclude certain one-time starting costs in 1959; including such costs our result would be the slightly higher average figure of 7.8%).

Finding 123 summarizes the evidence on DISA's unusually low selling costs: "The evidence shows that DISA so dramatically exceeded the profitability of the independent distributor community [the sample of 21 firms taxpayer relies on] . . . because to earn the dollars represented by that [gross profit] margin it did not have to spend nearly so many dollars to provide service and otherwise operate its business as did the distributors who bought and sold their products and services at prices determined by free market forces."

[18] [18] Taxpayer itself compensated its independent distributors by a system of price discounts ranging from 4% for textile fibers and 5% for elastomers (the two product lines accounting for more than 90% of DISA's sales and earnings) to 35% for photo products and agricultural chemicals, depending on the amount of effort and expense taxpayer thought necessary for the proper merchandising by the independent of the product involved (finding 81).

undisclosed companies in 1960 averaged 21 percent, taxpayer infers that DISA's gross profit of 26 percent was reasonable. Again, the lack of any data establishing comparability between DISA and the category of Source Book companies precludes any such conclusion. The fact that, within the wholesaler category, gross profits varied from 9 to 33 percent indicates that to take a mere arithmetic average, without considering underlying factual details, would risk a total distortion. *See* Simon, *Section 482 Allocations*, 46 Taxes 254 (1968) (criticizing lack of relevance, unavailability of third party data in gauging arm's length prices); *Edwards v. Commissioner*, 67 T.C. 224, 236–37 (1976) (industry average of uncertain reliability in determining arm's length sale price); *cf. Major Coat Co. v. United States*, 543 F.2d 97, 116, 211 Ct. Cl. 1, 34 (1976) (Source Book statistics on profitability of firms in same manufacturing category rejected in renegotiation case; no showing of relative character, efficiencies or risks of other companies). Plaintiff tells us that the IRS itself used these Source Book figures for 1960 and later years (not now before us). But the Service utilized net profit figures, not those for gross profit or gross markup. Whether or not this use of net profit computations contravened the regulations (which call for comparisons of gross profits in using the resale price method) or means that the IRS was following the "fourth method" (*see* Part III *infra*), we cannot say, as plaintiff wants us to, that the Service must have considered these drug and chemical wholesalers as comparable companies making similar resales, but that the IRS simply made a mistake in using net profits. The little we have on the IRS practice does not permit us to conclude anything as to the Service's position on comparability of these companies for the purposes of the resale price method.[19]

The lack of any significantly comparable resale (or group of resales) in this record is underscored by taxpayer's failure to suggest any means for adjusting for differences between DISA and the uncontrolled resellers. Subpart (ix) of section 1.482-2(e)(3) requires "appropriate adjustment" for "any material differences between the uncontrolled purchases and resales used as the basis for the calculation of the appropriate markup percentage and the resales of property involved in the controlled sale." Such material differences must be "differences in functions or circumstances" and must have a "definite and reasonably ascertainable effect on price." The trial judge premised his rejection of plaintiff's case on the failure to suggest appropriate adjustments under this subpart, particularly for

---

[19] [20] Subpart (vii) of the regulation says that "[i]n the absence of data on markup percentages of particular sales or groups of sales, the *prevailing* markup percentage in the *particular industry* involved *may* be appropriate" (emphasis added), but we do not consider that this record (with its wide range of markups and variation in products) shows, with respect to these Source Book companies, the "prevailing" markup in DISA's own "particular industry."

Taxpayer also invites comparison of DISA's gross profits with several other uncontrolled transactions, none of which is apposite. The contract for marketing of film between Du Pont and Bell & Howell involved minimal volume requirements, the expectation of initial marketing losses, and a gross profit contingent on meeting maximum selling cost levels. Such risks are so different from DISA's as to make Bell & Howell's proposed compensation rate "irrelevant for comparative purposes." Finding 105. The rate of return by a Du Pont subsidiary marketing urea herbicides involved special technology loans and missing details which preclude "a meaningful analogy." Finding 109. The sale of a "commodity-type" NA-22 elastomer (not requiring DISA's special selling skills) at a very low volume also precludes the use of such sales as a meaningful comparison. Finding 108. *See also* Findings 106, 107, 110 (discussing in detail other purported comparable profits introduced by taxpayer at trial).

DISA's lack of "entrepreneurial risk." Taxpayer mounts a vigorous assault on this position, arguing that DISA was exposed to all normal risks, including shipping and warehouse risks, sudden European market declines, or termination by manufacturing departments of Du Pont. Even if we assume *arguendo* that DISA did assume full market risks[20] we think taxpayer cannot escape the ultimate point of subpart (ix) — assuming a roughly comparable uncontrolled reseller (or resellers), taxpayer still bears the burden of showing adjustments to arrive at an arm's length price. However, plaintiff proposes no adjustments for differences in marketing locations, selling functions, or production differences between DISA and the "comparable" distributors. Taxpayer's brief selects one of the distributors, Superscope, as the company "most similar in function" to DISA, but fails to suggest the appropriate adjustments for such aspects as Superscope's different product line (tape recorders), different geographic market (the United States), or contractual obligation to make minimum purchases from the manufacturer.

This failure to proffer adjustments reflects the stark fact that, on this record, there is no company or group of companies so near and so comparable to DISA that the few material differences can be properly adjusted for under the regulatory pattern. Subpart (ix) and the example given under it (the same reseller selling two very similar products with only a difference in warranty coverage between the controlled and uncontrolled transactions) reinforce the view that under the resale price method the resales of uncontrolled companies must be substantially similar to those of the controlled reseller before that method can be used. And even if there is greater initial latitude in finding a comparable reseller than seems to us appropriate, subpart (ix) demands "appropriate adjustment . . . to reflect any material differences" which "have a definite and reasonably ascertainable effect on price." Plaintiff, which urges that the resale price method be used, bears the burden of fulfilling all the requirements of the regulation, but has failed to do so.

Plaintiff contends, finally, that requiring it to prove the proper amount of adjustment is an unfair burden. The suggestion is that once Du Pont shows that its prices were arm's length prices (by demonstrating that DISA's gross profit margin was equivalent to that of uncontrolled distributors) any further readjustment should be left to the courts (or perhaps defendant). Our first response is, as we have said above, that taxpayer has not shown that, even apart from subpart (ix), any of its alleged comparables can be accepted as such under the resale price method portion of the regulation. And if we surmount that hurdle, we see no good reason why a taxpayer should be free from suggesting the appropriate adjustments under subpart (ix). As the opening words of the paragraph show, the adjustments called for by the subpart are integral to the determination of an "arm's length price," and the determination of an "arm's length price" is the essence of the resale price method which plaintiff invokes.

---

[20] [21] This is not an easy assumption to accept, since Du Pont's pricing system for DISA was designed to protect the latter from losses, and DISA's operations seemed geared to help it make profits with little risk. *See* Part I, *supra*. Furthermore, the risk of complete termination by the parent which established and operated DISA for a number of particular purposes (including profit accumulation), seems substantially less than that of a wholly independent distributor.

D. The upshot is that plaintiff has failed to bring itself within the resale price method. The record before us does not support use of that formula for this case. Indeed, it may very well be that, because of DISA's unique position, the showing required by the regulation could simply not be made. At any rate, we have to conclude that, on this record, it is not possible to apply the resale price method.

As we have intimated in Part I, D, *supra*, this total failure of proof is no surprise. Taxpayer's prices to DISA were set wholly without regard to the factors which normally enter into an arm's length price (*see* Part I, C, *supra*), and it would have been pure happenstance if those prices had turned out to be equivalent to arm's length prices. This is not a case in which a taxpayer does attempt, the best it can, to establish intercorporate prices on an arm's length basis, and then runs up against an IRS which disagrees with this or that detail in the calculation. Plaintiff never made that effort, and it would have been undiluted luck — which under the regulation it probably could enjoy — if it had managed to discover comparable resales falling within the resale price method as set forth in the regulation (including adjustments to be made under subpart (ix)).

III. *Validity of the Commissioner's Allocation under the Regulation*

In reviewing the Commissioner's allocation of income under Section 482, we focus on the reasonableness of the result, not the details of the examining agent's methodology. *See Eli Lilly & Co. v. United States*, 372 F.2d 990, 997, 178 Ct. Cl. 666, 676 (1967); *Young & Rubicam, Inc. v. United States*, 410 F.2d 1233, 1245, 187 Ct. Cl. 635, 654–55 (1969). Plaintiff contends that the Commissioner's result does not conform to any of the specific methods under the regulations and is therefore unreasonable per se. But the regulations (§ 1.482-2(e)(1)(iii)) specifically allow for another appropriate method — "some appropriate method of pricing other than those described . . . or variations on such methods" — when, as here, none of the three specific methods can properly be used. That alternative "fourth method" now comes into play, and we consider the reasonableness of the Commissioner's result under its very broad delegation. This other "appropriate method of pricing" must, of course, conform to the general directives (stated at the outset of the regulation): "to place a controlled taxpayer on a tax parity with an uncontrolled taxpayer" and "in every case" to apply the standard "of an uncontrolled taxpayer dealing at arm's length with another uncontrolled taxpayer." *See* § 1.482-1(b)(1) and (c).

That some reallocation was reasonable is demonstrated by recalling the facts of DISA's operation. *See* Part I, *supra*. Several of the products sold through DISA received none of its special marketing or technical services. Nonetheless, DISA obtained its usual profit from Du Pont for minimal work on these goods — a result contrary to selling practices in the real world. Examples include: (1) opportunistic sales and sales of commodity-type products; (2) sales to South Africa and Australia routed through DISA; (3) sales of elastomers produced and serviced by Du Pont's British subsidiary. DISA's selling "expertise" was not employed on any of these goods, and the sole reason to sell them through DISA seems to have been to increase the volume of profits for that special subsidiary. Above all of these specific indications that DISA did not earn its profits is the overriding fact (discussed in Parts I and II, *supra*) that Du Pont's prices to DISA were deliberately set high and with little or no regard to economic realities.

The amount of reallocation would not be easy for us to calculate if we were called upon to do it ourselves, but Section 482 gives that power to the Commissioner and we are content that his amount (totaling some $18 million) was within the zone of reasonableness. The language of the statute and the holdings of the courts recognize that the Service has broad discretion in reallocating income. [Citations omitted]. Once past the three specific methods for computing intercompany prices of tangible property, the determiner of realistic intercompany prices is hardly exercising an economic art susceptible of precision. A "broad brush" approach to this inexact field seems necessary and conforms with this court's experience up to now under the Renegotiation Act, requiring *post hoc* and *de novo* determination of excessive profits on war and defense Government business. *See, e.g., A.C. Ball Co. v. United States*, 531 F.2d 993, 996, 209 Ct. Cl. 223, 229 (1976); *Bata Shoe Co. v. United States*, 595 F. 2d 9, 25, 219 Ct. Cl. 240, 269 (1979) (and cases cited). Du Pont has not convinced us, on this record, that the Commissioner abused the broad discretion he possessed (the specific methods being inapplicable), or that he acted unreasonably.

On the contrary, two economic indices presented by defendant support the result of the Commissioner's reallocation. One index compares DISA's ratio of gross income to total operating costs with the ratios for the 32 advertising, management-consultant, and distributor firms functionally similar, in general, to DISA. These are the results

Organization	Average gross income/total cost percentage
6 management-consultant firms	108.3%
5 advertising firms	123.9%
21 distributors	129.3%
DISA (before reallocation)*	281.5(1959); 397.1%(1960)**
DISA (after reallocation)*	108.6(1959); 179.3%(1960)

* DISA's percentages are not averages, but its actual returns for 1959-1960.

** The 281.5% figure for 1959, if readjusted to exclude one-time start-up costs, would be over 336%.

Only twice in over a hundred years of these companies' experience did any of the distributing firms attain income/cost ratios of over 200%, and no distributor ever achieved the 280-400% range experienced by DISA.

The second index does not rely at all on general functional similarities, but rests solely on a very comprehensive study of the rates of return (along with margin and turnover ratios) of over 1,100 companies. The following table illustrates the results:

Index	10-year [avg.] of 1,133 companies	DISA before allocation		DISA after allocation	
		1959	1960	1959	1960
Return on capital	9.47%	450%	147.2%	20%	38%
Margin	7.12%	13.1%	17.3%	-	-
Turnover	1.33	34.0	8.516	-	-

Whether measured by income/cost ratios of functionally similar firms or by capital return rates for industry as a whole, DISA's profits, before reallocation, vastly exceeded the uppermost limits. After reallocation, DISA's return on capital would still be better than over 96% of the 1133 companies surveyed. Using the two indices as a general measure of economic profits, DISA stands supreme before reallocation.[21]

Plaintiff attacks the validity of the two studies, arguing that return on capital is an inaccurate measuring rod, and that the income/cost ratio is inappropriate because profits vary with the skills of the individual companies. Whatever the general limits of any particular gauge of industry profitability, plaintiff cannot escape the basic thrust of defendant's proof. Defendant has shown that DISA made extraordinarily high profits which the Commissioner reallocated to an economically reasonable level. Plaintiff has not shown any specific comparable transactions refuting the general trend, and the record reveals none. *See* Part II, *supra*. Given the Commissioner's general discretion and the necessary inexactitude of such economic allocations, we conclude that the Commissioner's allocation was reasonable and should be accepted.

CONCLUSION OF LAW

Upon the findings of fact, which are made a part of the judgment herein, and the foregoing opinion, the court concludes as a matter of law that plaintiff is not entitled to recover, provided that plaintiff is accorded the opportunity to demonstrate in further proceedings in the Trial Division that it is entitled to relief under the provisions of Rev. Proc. 64-54, 1964-2 Cum. Bull. 1008. The cases are returned to the Trial Division for such further proceedings.

[An Appendix containing excerpts from the relevant Treasury Regulations is omitted here — Ed.]

NICHOLS, Judge, concurring:

I join in the opinion and in the judgment of the court but add a few observations for reasons that will appear.

---

[21] [28] We do not understand the regulation's catch-all (*i.e.* "fourth method") of "some appropriate method of pricing," to outlaw consideration of net profits in appraising the realism of prices charged by one controlled company to another in the circumstances we have here. The net profits index helps in "plac[ing] a controlled taxpayer on a tax parity with an uncontrolled taxpayer" and aids in applying the "standard" "of an uncontrolled taxpayer dealing at arm's length with another uncontrolled taxpayer" (§ 1.482-1(b)(1) and (c), *supra*).

The court says in Part I that plaintiff staked its entire case on proving that the profits made by DISA were comparable to those made on similar resales by uncontrolled merchandising agencies, the "resale price method." That is correct: a study of the briefs and record reveals no effort by plaintiff to sustain its burden by presentation of a fact-based and reason-illuminated case on any alternative theory as a backup if its above theory might fail, as it has, to convince the court. The incorrectness of the methods the Commissioner used when he made the allocations originally is irrelevant by "law of the case," as shown in fn 22, and I believe under accepted practice in tax litigation could not have been made relevant, for the taxpayer must prove he has overpaid, not that the Commissioner erred. Our concern is more with the ultimate results than with his method. *Eli Lilly & Co. v. United States*, 372 F.2d 990, 178 Ct. Cl. 666 (1967). Thus Part III of the opinion is really superfluous and we could have come to our "Conclusion of Law" at the end of Part II. I join in Part III because I believe it is well to show, when happily we can, that the result we reach is not only correct, but also fair and just.

The evidence referred to supports that conclusion, however, in the weakest possible way. In our renegotiation cases under 50 U.S.C. app. §§ 1211-1233 we have elected to make determinations of excessive profits on the basis of proofs as weak, or weaker, where that is all the parties have offered to us. [Citations omitted] Examination of the record in this case will convince anyone that the task of properly reallocating income from subsidiary to parent under § 482, where, as here, one of the Commissioner's express formulae is not applicable, is no whit less difficult or complex than determining how much of the profits a company derived from defense contracts was excessive, while the statutory and regulatory guidelines that are a little help in the renegotiation case are absent here. There are possible for use as many methods as there are experts the parties can afford to hire, and no two methods will lead to the same result. "Whenever a price problem is discussed . . . , divergent figures are likely to be recommended without a semblance of consensus." 38 HARV. BUS. REVIEW 125 (1960) as quoted in *Eli Lilly & Co. v. United States*, 178 Ct. Cl. at 668, 372 F.2d at 992. The theory that one in charge of a controlled group knows exactly the monetary difference between the transactions he engineers, and what they would have been if conducted at arm's-length, will not stand analysis. See my dissent in *Morton-Norwich Products, Inc. v. United States, ante* at 83.

Assuming, still, that no formula prescribed by regulation can be used, if the Commissioner adheres in court to his original method, it would seem we would have to affirm him unless we thought his choice of method arbitrary and capricious. If he abandons his original method and through his counsel supported by expert witnesses, urges the court to adopt another, the taxpayer's task is not much facilitated. *Young & Rubicam, Inc. v. United States*, 410 F.2d 1233, 1245, 187 Ct. Cl. 635, 655 (1969). If the new method justifies the same reallocation or more, and does not look unreasonable, the taxpayer cannot refute it just by showing that other experts, using other methods, would reallocate a lesser amount, or none at all. Where we know from our renegotiation experience that there is no one sure formula to determine excessive profits, and that all methods, or all permitted by law, must be considered and balanced one against another, here, to hold for the taxpayer, it looks as if we would have to hold that *no* acceptable method supports the Commissioner's result. The taxpayer to win, as a practical matter, would have to show that some method favored by him was so much more convincing than others than no such other was reasonable. Rarely will he do it.

The Commissioner it seems to me gets the best of both worlds: as in more ordinary types of tax litigation, his counsel is not committed to having to defend the Commissioner's basic fact finding and reasoning, as in most cases of judicial review of discretionary action; and on the other hand, the determination stands as not arbitrary and capricious, or an abuse of discretion, if any reasonable looking approach sustains it. In *Young & Rubicam, Inc., supra*, at § 482 reallocation was invalidated, but it did not involve issues of pricing judgment.

It is not surprising, therefore, that taxpayer's able counsel here put all his chips on the regulatory resale price method, to the virtual exclusion of any reliance on any "fourth method," really a chaos of any and all methods. After Part II, the sustaining of the determination in Part III involves no real difficulty, their being nothing of substance to oppose it.

Whether the involved regulations leave too many cases for the fourth method is a question the court touches on lightly. The congressional request to write regulations to govern these § 482 reallocations is one sentence long:

It is believed that the Treasury should explore the possibility of developing and promulgating regulations under this authority [§ 482] which would provide additional guidelines and formulas for the allocation of income and deductions in cases involving foreign income. [1962] U.S. Code Cong. & Ad. News 3732, 3739.

Clearly the result of our decision is that this has not been done in respect to the reallocation here involved, and it remains in the almost if not wholly unreviewable discretion of the Treasury, as it was when the suggestion was made. The Treasury wisely believes, or in the past has believed, that it should not have discretion to decide how much money anyone should have to pay to support the government. It was for this reason that it always urged, and always successfully, that the duty of administering the various Renegotiation Acts, now all defunct, should devolve elsewhere than on Treasury. So it is somewhat an anomaly that in the matter of § 482 it is in a position that out renegotiates renegotiation with respect to deciding a taxpayer's liability by exercise of discretion.

Understanding *Du Pont*

1.   Describe, in everyday English, the tax advantages that Du Pont hoped to achieve by setting up DISA and why it ultimately failed.

2.   The court rejects Du Pont's effort to use the resale price method because there were no other companies whose activities were comparable to those of DISA in the relevant accounting period. But if there were no comparable arm's length transactions, how could the IRS know that the prices that Du Pont charged to DISA were too low? Is the IRS really applying the statutory standard, or an arbitrary rule of its own choosing? Is it correct to do so?

3.   There is a Jewish joke that defines *chutzpah* (gall) as killing your own parents and then begging the court's mercy because you are an orphan. How about, "setting deliberately artificial prices in order to reduce taxes and then arguing that

the prices were equivalent to those that would have been set by an independent company that doesn't exist, anyway." Apart from the technical issue, what do you think of the ethics of Du Pont's strategy, *i.e.*, the use of high-priced lawyers to argue one's way out of an essentially disingenuous position entirely of one's own making? Does this "equity" issue turn the court against DuPont, regardless of the statute?

4.   Imagine that you were Du Pont's tax lawyer, and were asked to adjust its internal pricing mechanism in response to this decision. What if anything would you do differently, and why?

The *DuPont* case must have made tax planners either more cautious or more clever: Virtually all subsequent 482 cases were won by the taxpayer or resulted in split decisions. Present law would tax DISA's income to DuPont under the Subpart F (CFC) rules, regardless of the section 482 outcome. Nevertheless, *DuPont* remains an important case for understanding the transfer pricing rules, which are crucially important to the practice of international taxation. Responding to IRS challenges like in *DuPont*, sophisticated taxpayers typically hire accountants or economists to prepare detailed reports backing up the taxpayer's transfer pricing practices. With these reports in hand, taxpayers have made aggressive use of transfer pricing techniques, and the IRS has found it extremely difficult to police taxpayers' use of transfer pricing.[22]

Using the Sources

Review section 482, the section 482 regulations, and the preceding materials and answer the following questions:

1.   What is meant by each of the following terms?

   a. reallocation

   b. comparables

   c. the arm's length standard

   d. the resale price method

   e. advance pricing agreements

2.   Under what circumstances, if any, may a U.S. taxpayer invoke section 482 in her own favor (*i.e.*, report transfer prices different from those actually charged)? In what situation, if any, could you imagine a taxpayer wanting to do this?

3.   By its terms, section 482 applies to both domestic and international transactions. Why then is it in this chapter, and why is it so often thought of as an international provision? Can you think of a possible application of the provision in a wholly domestic context?

---

[22] *See* Reuven S. Avi-Yonah, U.S. International Taxation: Cases and Materials 168 (2002).

Law and Planning

Return to the Java Josephine hypothetical under the Law and Planning section above. Suppose that the company had decided to do business in France using a separately incorporated French company (Java France, be sure to pronounce a soft "J") which entered into various royalty and marketing agreements with the original American company. For purposes of this question only, assume that taxes in France are lower than in the U.S,. so that the business would like, if possible, to shift as much income as possible toward the French corporation.

1.   Based on the materials above, what strategy might you suggest in order to reduce U.S. taxes and shift more income to Java France? Try to be specific about the kinds of contractual agreements (rents, royalties, etc.) you would have the two companies enter into, with respect to what precise assets (tangible or intangible), and whether you would want the transfer of these assets from the U.S. company to Java France to be at a relatively high or low price. Would this strategy be agreeable to the parties themselves, or would the "real-world" costs of the arrangement outweigh any potential tax benefits?

2.   Now assume that tax rates were higher in France and lower in the United States. What alternate strategy might you adopt instead of that chosen in item 1., above? What other information, about French or United States tax law, would you want to have before proceeding?

3.   With respect to each of items 1. or 2. above:

a. How likely would the IRS be to challenge the items in question, using evidence of "comparable" transactions or an alternate method? What if anything would constitute a comparable arm's length transaction?

b. Would you recommend that your clients enter into an advance pricing agreement (APA) in order to deal with this problem? How aggressive would you be (that is, how high or low would you set the relevant transfer price, depending upon the circumstances) in drafting the proposed APA?

c. How would you rate the attractiveness of the transfer pricing mechanism as compared to alternate tax reduction strategies?

Politics and Policy

1.   The transfer pricing scheme is essentially a way of shifting income to the country with the lowest tax rate. A more direct way of fixing this problem would be for all the countries in the world (or at least, the more economically developed ones) to "harmonize" their tax rates at approximately the same level, so that there would be no serious advantage to shifting income between different countries. Such harmonization would also keep business or labor from moving from one country to another in search of the lowest tax rate, and relieve the pressure for reduced tax rates that currently results from fear of such movement. Why doesn't harmonization happen, and would it be a good thing if it did?

2.   Section 482 is an extreme example of a short statute accompanied by very detailed regulations. Many tax reformers believe this is a formula for good tax law,

since the IRS is more expert than Congress in the administration of tax law and will presumably do a better job of creating and enforcing new rules. What does transfer pricing suggest about this theory?

3.   Overall, do you think that section 482 is effective or ineffective at controlling the transfer pricing scheme?

III.   TAX HAVENS, FOREIGN TAX CREDIT, AND THE ECONOMIC SUBSTANCE TEST: THE BRAVE NEW WORLD OF INTERNATIONAL TAX SHELTERS

The transfer pricing conundrum leads to the broader issue of international tax shelters and tax evasion, a subject hinted at in Chapters 8 and 11, but never really treated in depth. In theory, international tax evasion is no different from the domestic version, and should be subject to attack on the same grounds (the substance-over-form doctrines, penalty provisions, and so forth) as its homespun counterpart. In practice, several factors distinguish international tax evasion from its domestic equivalent. The first is the amount of money involved in international transactions, which tends to be high even by tax planning standards. (A one percent difference in tax rate for Toyota or Microsoft may amount to millions of dollars.) A second is the information problem: if companies are incorporated or headquartered overseas it may be difficult even to acquire the information necessary to audit them successfully, especially in countries, *e.g.*, Switzerland, where financial secrecy is not merely tolerated but is a time-honored tradition. Finally, the very complexity of international tax frustrates enforcement efforts: there are perhaps a few hundred people really capable of understanding, say, Chevron's tax return, and a hundred or more of them are probably working for Chevron at any time. Under these circumstances, the "good guys" are at a substantial and possibly growing disadvantage with respect to the tax evaders.

We have already seen one time-honored evasion method in our transfer pricing discussion. The list of alternate techniques is endless. Some are no more complicated than placing all or part of one's business operations in a so-called "tax haven" country — either an exotic location like a Caribbean island or simply an opportunistic larger state — and using the country's low tax rates and informational secrecy in order to shield one's business operations from tax. Others involve more complex, multi-country arrangements. For many years, a favorite technique was the so-called "Dutch sandwich," which employed a variety of Netherlands and Netherlands Antilles corporations in a frequently successful effort to reduce tax on interest and dividend payments. Like some sort of unusual personal habit, for many years a certain embarrassment was attached to such arrangements, but in recent years they have become more widely accepted and even aggressively marketed by investment companies and other tax advisers.

Many of the more recent tax shelters emphasize neither tax havens nor transfer pricing, but simply the manipulation of legitimate, highly complex international and domestic tax rules in order to achieve results not intended by the original draftspersons. For example, a corporation whose income included interest, dividends, and capital gains might attempt, by means of a partnership or similar mechanism, to allocate each type of income to a jurisdiction in which (for whatever reasons) that type of income tended to be taxed at a lower rate. Alternatively, a company with operations in several countries might try to manipulate the foreign tax credit rules so as to achieve perfectly legal, but almost certainly unintended, tax advantages. Viewed from a historical perspective, such transactions are merely the international equivalents of the domestic tax shelter industry, and as such might not seem cause for alarm. Yet the numerous interactions between national tax laws vastly multiply the possibilities for tax evasion, while the corresponding difficulties of enforcement — coupled with the aggressiveness of tax shelter promoters — means that there is a tendency to try evasion schemes that have less and less economic substance. The international tax shelter problem is accordingly both bigger in scope than its domestic equivalent and more difficult to solve.

The following case — something of an "instant classic" in the tax field — concerns a tax reduction effort by a rather well-known and generally respected computer company. The case is interesting because it presents a cross-section of the techniques (transfer pricing, tax havens, foreign tax credit manipulation) alluded to above and (from the Government's perspective) an important effort to apply the business purpose doctrine to an international context. Oh yes, and the good guys won.

COMPAQ COMPUTER CORP. v. COMMISSIONER
United States Tax Court
113 T.C. 214 (1999)

COHEN, J:

The issues addressed in this opinion are whether petitioner's purchase and resale of American Depository Receipts (ADRs) in 1992 lacked economic substance and whether petitioner is liable for an accuracy-related penalty pursuant to section 6662(a). . . .

FINDINGS OF FACT

Some of the facts have been stipulated, and the stipulated facts are incorporated in our findings by this reference. Since 1982, petitioner has been engaged in the business of designing, manufacturing, and selling personal computers. Details concerning petitioner's business operations are set forth in T.C. Memo 1999-220 and are not repeated here.

Petitioner occasionally invested in the stock of other computer companies. In 1992, petitioner held stock in Conner Peripherals, Inc. (Conner Peripherals), a publicly traded, nonaffiliated computer company. Petitioner sold the Conner Peripherals stock in July 1992, recognizing a long-term capital gain of $231,682,881.

Twenty-First Securities Corporation (Twenty-First), an investment firm specializing in arbitrage transactions, learned of petitioner's long-term capital gain from the sale of Conner Peripherals, and on August 13, 1992, Steven F. Jacoby

(Jacoby), a broker and account executive with Twenty-First, mailed a letter to petitioner soliciting petitioner's business. The letter stated that Twenty-First "has uncovered a number of strategies that take advantage of a capital gain", including a Dividend Reinvestment Arbitrage Program (DRIP) and a "proprietary variation on the DRIP", the ADR arbitrage transaction (ADR transaction).

An ADR (American Depository Receipt) is a trading unit issued by a trust, which represents ownership of stock in a foreign corporation that is deposited with the trust. ADRs are the customary form of trading foreign stocks on U.S. stock exchanges, including the New York Stock Exchange (NYSE). The ADR transaction involves the purchase of ADRs "cum dividend", followed by the immediate resale of the same ADRs "ex dividend". "Cum dividend" refers to a purchase or sale of a share of stock or an ADR share with the purchaser entitled to a declared dividend (settlement taking place on or before the record date of the dividend). "Ex dividend" refers to the purchase or sale of stock or an ADR share without the entitlement to a declared dividend (settlement taking place after the record date).

James J. Tempesta (Tempesta) was an assistant treasurer in petitioner's treasury department in 1992. He received his undergraduate degree in philosophy and government from Georgetown University and his master's degree in finance and accounting from the University of Texas. Tempesta's responsibilities in petitioner's treasury department included the day-to-day investment of petitioner's cash reserves, including the evaluation of investment proposals from investment bankers and other institutions. He was also responsible for writing petitioner's investment policies that were in effect during September 1992. Petitioner's treasury department primarily focused on capital preservation, typically investing in overnight deposits, Eurodollars, commercial paper, and tax-exempt obligations.

On September 15, 1992, Tempesta and petitioner's treasurer, John M. Foster (Foster), met with Jacoby and Robert N. Gordon (Gordon), president of Twenty-First, to discuss the strategies proposed in the August 13, 1992, letter from Twenty-First. In a meeting that lasted approximately an hour, Jacoby and Gordon presented the DRIP strategy and the ADR transaction. Following the meeting, Tempesta and Foster discussed the transactions with Darryl White (White), petitioner's chief financial officer. They decided not to engage in the DRIP investment but chose to go forward with the ADR transaction, relying primarily on Tempesta's recommendation. Tempesta notified Twenty-First of this decision on September 16, 1992.

Although cash-flow was generally important to petitioner's investment decisions, Tempesta did not perform a cash-flow analysis before agreeing to take part in the ADR transaction. Rather, Tempesta's investigation of Twenty-First and the ADR transaction, in general, was limited to telephoning a reference provided by Twenty-First and reviewing a spreadsheet provided by Jacoby that analyzed the transaction. Tempesta shredded the spreadsheet a year after the transaction.

Joseph Leo (Leo) of Twenty-First was responsible for arranging the execution of the purchase and resale trades of ADRs for petitioner. Bear Stearns & Co., Inc. (Bear Stearns), was used as the clearing broker for petitioner's trades, and the securities selected for the transaction were ADR shares of Royal Dutch Petroleum Company (Royal Dutch). Royal Dutch ordinary capital shares were trading in 21 organized markets throughout the world in 1992, but primarily on the NYSE in the United States as ADRs. Before agreeing to enter into the transaction, petitioner had no specific knowledge of Royal Dutch, and Tempesta's research of Royal Dutch was limited to reading in the Wall Street Journal that Royal Dutch declared a dividend and to observing the various market prices of Royal Dutch ADRs.

In preparation for the trades, Leo determined the number of Royal Dutch ADRs to be included in each purchase and resale trade. He also selected the market prices to be paid, varying the prices in different trades so the blended price per share equaled the actual market price plus the net dividend. Leo did not, however, discuss the size of the trades or the prices selected for the trades with any employee or representative of petitioner. Leo also chose to purchase the Royal Dutch ADRs from Arthur J. Gallagher and Company (Gallagher). Gallagher had been a client of Twenty-First since 1985 and participated in various investment strategies developed by Twenty-First over the years. During 1991, Gallagher participated in several ADR transaction trades as the purchaser of the ADRs. Tempesta had no knowledge of the identity of the seller of ADRs. He only knew that the seller was a client of Twenty-First.

On September 16, 1992, Leo instructed ABD-N.Y., Inc. (ABD), to purchase 10 million Royal Dutch ADRs on petitioner's behalf from Gallagher on the floor of the NYSE. He also instructed ABD to resell the 10 million Royal Dutch ADRs to Gallagher immediately following the purchase trades. The purchase trades were made in 23 separate cross-trades of approximately 450,000 ADRs each with special "next day" settlement terms pursuant to NYSE rule 64. The aggregate purchase price was $887,577,129, cum dividend.

ABD executed the 23 sale trades, selling the Royal Dutch ADRs back to Gallagher, immediately following the related purchase trade. Accordingly, each purchase trade and its related sale trade were completed before commencing the next purchase trade. The sales transactions, however, had regular settlement terms of 5 days, and the aggregate sales price was $868,412,129, ex dividend. The 23 corresponding purchase and resale trades were completed in about an hour between approximately 2:58 p.m. and 4:00 p.m.

Leo had instructed the ABD floor brokers to execute the trades only if the prices selected were within the range of the current market prices. Thus, when, between the sixth and seventh trades, the market price changed, Leo modified the price for subsequent trades to compensate for the change. In addition, NYSE rule 76 required an open outcry for each cross-trade, and NYSE rule 72 allowed other traders on the floor or the "specialist" responsible for making the cross-trades to break up the transaction by taking all or part of the trade. However, for cross-trades priced at the market price, there was no incentive to break up the transaction.

Pursuant to the "next day" settlement rules, the purchase cross-trades were settled between petitioner and Gallagher on September 17, 1992. On that date, Gallagher's account with Bear Stearns was credited $887,547,543 for the purchase trades, including a reduction for Securities and Exchange Commission fees (SEC fees) of $29,586. Gallagher was subsequently reimbursed for the SEC fees. Also on

September 17, 1992, petitioner transferred $20,651,996 to Bear Stearns, opening a margin account.

On September 18, 1992, at 10:47 a.m., petitioner complied with the applicable margin requirements, transferring $16,866,571 to its margin account with Bear Stearns. The margin requirement for purchase and sale transactions completed on the same day was 50 percent of the purchase price of the largest trade executed on that day. It was not necessary to make payments for each completed trade. Accordingly, this wire transfer was made by petitioner to demonstrate its financial ability to pay under the applicable margin rules. The $16,866,571 was transferred back to petitioner that same day at 1:39 p.m.

Pursuant to the regular settlement rules, the resale cross-trades were settled between petitioner and Gallagher on September 21, 1992. The total selling price credited to petitioner's account with Bear Stearns was $868,412,129 (before commissions and fees). Expenses incurred by petitioner with respect to the purchase and resale trades included: SEC fees of $28,947, interest of $457,846, a margin writeoff of $37, and commissions of $998,929. Petitioner had originally agreed to pay Twenty-First commissions of $1,000,000, but Twenty-First adjusted its commissions by $1,070.55 to offset computational errors in calculating some of the purchase trades.

Due to the different settlement dates, petitioner was the shareholder of record of 10 million Royal Dutch ADRs on the dividend record date and was therefore entitled to a dividend of $22,545,800. On October 2, 1992, Royal Dutch paid the declared dividend to shareholders of record as of September 18, 1992, including petitioner. Contemporaneously with the dividend, a corresponding payment was made to the Netherlands Government representing withholding amounts for dividends paid to U.S. residents within the meaning of the United States-Netherlands Tax Treaty, Convention With Respect to Taxes on Income and Certain Other Taxes, Apr. 29, 1948, U.S.-Neth., art. VII, para. 1, 62 Stat. 1757, 1761. The withholding payment equaled 15 percent of the declared dividend, $3,381,870. Accordingly, a net dividend of $19,163,930 was deposited into petitioner's margin account at Bear Stearns and wired to petitioner on October 2, 1992.

On its 1992 Federal income tax return, petitioner reported the loss on the purchase and resale of Royal Dutch ADRs as a short- term capital loss in the amount of $20,652,816, calculated as follows:

Adjusted basis	$888,535,869
Amount realized	$867,883,053
Capital loss	$ 20,652,816

Petitioner also reported dividend income in the amount of $22,546,800 and claimed a foreign tax credit of $3,382,050 for the income tax withheld and paid to the Netherlands Government with respect to the dividend.

ULTIMATE FINDINGS OF FACT

Every aspect of petitioner's ADR transaction was deliberately predetermined and designed by petitioner and Twenty-First to yield a specific result and to eliminate all economic risks and influences from outside market forces on the purchases and sales in the ADR transaction.

Petitioner had no reasonable possibility of a profit from the ADR transaction without the anticipated Federal income tax consequences.

Petitioner had no business purpose for the purchase and sale of Royal Dutch ADRs apart from obtaining a Federal income tax benefit in the form of a foreign tax credit while offsetting the previously recognized capital gain.

OPINION

Respondent argues that petitioner is not entitled to the foreign tax credit because petitioner's ADR transaction had no objective economic consequences or business purpose other than reduction of taxes. Petitioner argues that it is entitled to the foreign tax credit because it complied with the applicable statutes and regulations, that the transaction had economic substance, and that, in any event, the economic substance doctrine should not be applied to deny a foreign tax credit.

In *Frank Lyon Co. v. United States*, 435 U.S. 561, 583–584 (1978), the Supreme Court stated that "a genuine multiple-party transaction with economic substance . . . compelled or encouraged by business or regulatory realities, . . . imbued with tax-independent considerations, and . . . not shaped solely by tax-avoidance features" should be respected for tax purposes. Innumerable cases demonstrate the difference between (1) closing out a real economic loss in order to minimize taxes or arranging a contemplated business transaction in a tax-advantaged manner and (2) entering into a prearranged loss transaction designed solely for the reduction of taxes on unrelated income. In the former category are *Cottage Sav. Association v. Commissioner*, 499 U.S. 554 (1991); and *Esmark, Inc. & Affiliated Cos. v. Commissioner*, 90 T.C. 171 (1988), *affd. without published opinion* 886 F.2d 1318 (7th Cir. 1989). In the latter category are *ACM Partnership v. Commissioner*, 157 F.3d 231 (3d Cir. 1998), *affg. in part* T.C. Memo 1997-115; *Goldstein v. Commissioner*, 364 F.2d 734 (2d Cir. 1966); and *Friendship Dairies, Inc. v. Commissioner*, 90 T.C. 1054 (1988). Referring to tax shelter transactions in which a taxpayer seeks to use a minimal commitment of funds to secure a disproportionate tax benefit, the Court of Appeals for the Seventh Circuit stated, in *Saviano v. Commissioner*, 765 F.2d 643, 654 (7th Cir. 1985), *affg.* 80 T.C. 955 (1983):

> The freedom to arrange one's affairs to minimize taxes does not include the right to engage in financial fantasies with the expectation that the Internal Revenue Service and the courts will play along. The Commissioner and the courts are empowered, and in fact duty-bound, to look beyond the contrived forms of transactions to their economic substance and to apply the tax laws accordingly.

* * *

Petitioner repeatedly argues, and asks the Court to find, that it could not have had a tax savings or tax benefit purpose in entering into the ADR transaction because:

> In this case, a tax savings or tax benefit purpose cannot be attributed to Compaq because Compaq did not enjoy any tax reduction or other tax benefit from the transaction. Compaq's taxable income INCREASED by approximately $1.9 million as a result of the Royal Dutch ADR arbitrage. Compaq's worldwide tax liability INCREASED by more than $640,000 as a direct result of the Royal ADR arbitrage. The reason for this increase in income taxes is obvious — Compaq realized a net profit with respect to the Royal Dutch ADR arbitrage. That net profit, appropriately, was subject to tax.

Petitioner's calculation of its alleged profit is as follows:

ADR transaction:	
ADR purchase trades	($887,577,129)
ADR sale trades	868,412,129
Net cash from ADR transaction	($19,165,000)
Royal Dutch dividend	22,545,800
Transaction costs	(1,485,685)
PRETAX PROFIT	$1,895,115

Petitioner asserts:

> Stated differently, the reduction in income tax received by the United States was not the result of a reduction in income tax paid by Compaq. Each dollar of income tax paid to the Netherlands was just as real, and was the same detriment to Compaq, as each dollar of income tax paid to the United States. Even Respondent's expert acknowledged this detriment, and that Compaq's worldwide income tax increased as a result of the Royal Dutch ADR arbitrage. A "tax benefit" can be divined from the transaction only if the income tax paid to the Netherlands with respect to Royal Dutch dividend is ignored for purposes of computing income taxes paid, but is included as a credit in computing Compaq's U.S. income tax liability. Such a result is antithetical to the foreign tax credit regime fashioned by Congress.

> In the complete absence of any reduction in income tax, it is readily apparent that Compaq could not have engaged in the transaction solely for the purpose of achieving such an income tax reduction.

Petitioner's rationale is that it paid $3,381,870 to the Netherlands through the withheld tax and paid approximately $640,000 in U.S. income tax on a reported "pretax profit" of approximately $1.9 million. (The $640,000 amount is petitioner's approximation of U.S. income tax on $1.9 million in income.) If we follow petitioner's logic, however, we would conclude that petitioner paid approximately $4 million in worldwide income taxes on that $1.9 million in profit.

Petitioner cites several cases, including *Levy v. Commissioner*, 91 T.C. 838, 859 (1988); *Gefen v. Commissioner*, 87 T.C. 1471, 1492 (1986); *Pearlstein v. Commissioner*, T.C. Memo. 1989-621; and *Rubin v. Commissioner*, T.C. Memo. 1989-484, that conclude that the respective transactions had economic substance because there was a reasonable opportunity for a "pretax profit". These cases, however, merely use "pretax profit" as a shorthand reference to profit independent of tax savings, *i.e.*, economic profit. They do not involve situations, such as we have in this case, where petitioner used tax reporting strategies to give the illusion of profit, while simultaneously claiming a tax credit in an amount (nearly $3.4 million) that far exceeds the U.S. tax (of $640,000) attributed to the alleged profit, and thus is available to offset tax on unrelated transactions. Petitioner's tax reporting strategy was an integrated package, designed to produce an economic gain when — and only when — the foreign tax credit was claimed. By reporting the gross amount of the dividend, when only the net amount was received, petitioner created a fictional $1.9 million profit as a predicate for a $3.4 million tax credit.

While asserting that it made a "real" payment to the Netherlands in the form of the $3,381,870 withheld tax, petitioner contends that that withholding tax should be disregarded in determining the U.S. tax effect of the transaction and the economic substance of the transaction. Respondent, however, persuasively demonstrates that petitioner would incur a prearranged economic loss from the transaction but for the foreign tax credit.

The following cash-flow analysis demonstrates the inevitable economic detriment to petitioner from engaging in the ADR transaction:

Cash-flow from ADR transaction:	
ADR purchase trades	($887,577,129)
ADR sale trades	868,412,129
Net cash from ADR transaction	($19,165,000)
Cash-flow from dividend:	
Gross dividend	22,545,800
Netherlands withholding tax	(3,381,870)
Net cash from dividend	19,163,930
OFFSETTING CASH-FLOW RESIDUAL	(1,070)
Cash-flow from transaction costs:	
Commissions	(1,000,000)
Less: Adjustment	1,071
SEC fees	(28,947)
Margin writeoff	37
Interest	(457,846)
Net cash from transaction costs	(1,485,685)
NET ECONOMIC LOSS	($1,486,755)

The cash-flow deficit arising from the transaction, prior to use of the foreign tax credit, was predetermined by the careful and tightly controlled arrangements made between petitioner and Twenty-First. The scenario was to "capture" a foreign tax credit by timed acquisition and sale of ADRs over a 5-day period in which petitioner bought ADRs cum dividend from Gallagher and resold them ex dividend to Gallagher. Petitioner was acquiring a foreign tax credit, not substantive ownership of Royal Dutch ADRs. *See Friendship Dairies, Inc. v. Commissioner, supra* at 1067.

Petitioner argues that there were risks associated with the ADR transaction, but neither Tempesta nor any other representative of petitioner conducted an analysis or investigation regarding these alleged concerns. Transactions that involve no market risks are not economically substantial transactions; they are mere tax artifices. *See Yosha v. Commissioner*, 861 F.2d 494, 500–501 (7th Cir. 1988), *affg. Glass v. Commissioner*, 87 T.C. 1087 (1986). Tax-motivated trading patterns generally indicate a lack of economic substance. *See Sheldon v. Commissioner*, 94 T.C. 738, 766, 769 (1990). The purchase and resale prices were predetermined by Leo, and the executing floor brokers did not have authority to deviate from the predetermined prices even if a price change occurred. In addition, the ADR transaction was divided into 23 corresponding purchase and resale cross-trades that were executed in succession, almost simultaneously, and within an hour on the floor of the NYSE. Thus, there was virtually no risk of price fluctuation. Special next-day settlement terms and large blocks of ADRs were also used to minimize the risk of third parties breaking up the cross-trades, and, because the cross-trades were at the market price, there was no risk of other traders breaking up the trades. None of the outgoing cash-flow resulted from risks. Accordingly, we have found that this transaction was deliberately predetermined and designed by petitioner and Twenty-First to yield a specific result and to eliminate all market risks.

To satisfy the business purpose requirement of the economic substance inquiry, "the transaction must be rationally related to a useful nontax purpose that is plausible in light of the taxpayer's conduct and . . . economic situation." *AMC Partnership v. Commissioner*, T.C. Memo. 1997-115, *affd. in part, revd. in part, and remanded* 157 F.3d 231 (3d Cir. 1998); *see also Levy v. Commissioner, supra* at 854. This inquiry takes into account whether the taxpayer conducts itself in a realistic and legitimate business fashion, thoroughly considering and analyzing the ramifications of a questionable transaction, before proceeding with the transaction. *See UPS of Am. v. Commissioner*, T.C. Memo. 1999-268.

Petitioner contends that it entered into the ADR transaction as a short-term investment to make a profit apart from tax savings, but the objective facts belie petitioner's assertions. The ADR transaction was marketed to petitioner by Twenty-First for the purpose of partially shielding a capital gain previously realized on the sale of Conner Peripherals stock. Petitioner's evaluation of the proposed transaction was less than businesslike with Tempesta, a well-educated, experienced, and financially sophisticated businessman, committing petitioner to this multimillion-dollar transaction based on one meeting with Twenty-First and on his call to a Twenty-First reference. As a whole, the record indicates and we conclude that petitioner was motivated by the expected tax benefits of the ADR transaction, and no other business purpose existed.

Petitioner also contends that the ADR transaction does not warrant the application of the economic substance doctrine because the foreign tax credit regime completely sets forth Congress' intent as to allowable foreign tax credits.

Petitioner argues that an additional economic substance requirement was not intended by Congress and should not be applied in this case.

Congress creates deductions and credits to encourage certain types of activities, and the taxpayers who engage in those activities are entitled to the attendant benefits. *See, e.g., Leahy v. Commissioner*, 87 T.C. 56, 72 (1986); *Fox v. Commissioner*, 82 T.C. 1001, 1021 (1984). The foreign tax credit serves to prevent double taxation and to facilitate international business transactions. No bona fide business is implicated here, and we are not persuaded that Congress intended to encourage or permit a transaction such as the ADR transaction, which is merely a manipulation of the foreign tax credit to achieve U.S. tax savings.

Finally, petitioner asserts that the enactment of section 901(k) by the Taxpayer Relief Act of 1997, Pub. L. 105-34, sec. 1053(a), 111 Stat. 941, also indicates that Congress did not intend for the economic substance doctrine to apply under the facts of this case. Section 901(k)(1) provides that a taxpayer must hold stock (or an ADR) for at least 16 days of a prescribed 30-day period including the dividend record date, in order to claim a foreign tax credit with respect to foreign taxes withheld at the source on foreign dividends. If the taxpayer does not meet these holding requirements, the taxpayer may claim a deduction for the foreign taxes paid if certain other requirements are met.

Section 901(k) does not change our conclusion in this case. That provision was passed in 1997 and was effective for dividends paid or accrued after September 4, 1997. The report of the Senate Finance Committee indicates that "No inference is intended as to the treatment under present law of tax-motivated transactions intended to transfer foreign tax credit benefits." S. Rept. 105-33, 175, 177 (1997). A transaction does not avoid economic substance scrutiny because the transaction predates a statute targeting the specific abuse. *See, e.g., Krumhorn v. Commissioner*, 103 T.C. 29, 48–50 (1994); *Fox v. Commissioner, supra* 82 T.C. at 1026–1027. Accordingly, section 901(k), enacted 5 years after the transaction at issue, has no effect on the outcome of this case.

ACCURACY-RELATED PENALTY

Respondent determined that petitioner is liable for the section 6662(a) penalty for 1992. Section 6662(a) imposes a penalty in an amount equal to 20 percent of the underpayment of tax attributable to one or more of the items set forth in section 6662(b). Respondent asserts that the underpayment attributable to the ADR transaction was due to negligence. *See* sec. 6662(b)(1). "Negligence" includes a failure to make a reasonable attempt to comply with provisions of the internal revenue laws or failure to do what a reasonable and ordinarily prudent person would do under the same circumstances. See sec. 6662(c); *Marcello v. Commissioner*, 380 F.2d 499, 506 (5th Cir. 1967), *affg. on this issue* 43 T.C. 168 (1964); sec. 1.6662-3(b)(1), Income Tax Regs. Petitioner bears the burden of proving that respondent's determinations are erroneous. *See* Rule 142(a); *Freytag v. Commissioner*, 904 F.2d 1011, 1017 (5th Cir. 1990), *affg.* 89 T.C. 849, 887 (1987), *affd.* 501 U.S. 868 (1991).

The accuracy-related penalty does not apply with respect to any portion of an underpayment if it is shown that there was reasonable cause for such portion of an underpayment and that the taxpayer acted in good faith with respect to such portion. See sec. 6664(c)(1). The determination of whether the taxpayer acted with reasonable cause and in good faith depends upon the pertinent facts and circumstances. *See* sec. 1.6664-4(b)(1), Income Tax Regs. The most important factor is the extent of the taxpayer's effort to assess the proper tax liability for the year. *See id.*

Respondent argues that petitioner is liable for the accuracy-related penalty because petitioner negligently disregarded the economic substance of the ADR transaction; petitioner failed to meet its burden of proving that the underpayment was not due to negligence; and petitioner failed to offer evidence that there was reasonable cause for its return position for the ADR transaction or that it acted in good faith with respect to such item. Petitioner argues that there is no basis for a negligence penalty because the return position was reasonable, application of the economic substance doctrine to the ADR transaction is "inherently imprecise", and application of the economic substance doctrine to disregard a foreign tax credit raises an issue of first impression. We agree with respondent.

In this case, Tempesta, Foster, and White were sophisticated professionals with investment experience and should have been alerted to the questionable economic nature of the ADR transaction. They, however, failed to take even the most rudimentary steps to investigate the bona fide economic aspects of the ADR transaction. *See Freytag v. Commissioner, supra.* As set forth in the findings of fact, petitioner did not investigate the details of the transaction, the entity it was investing in, the parties it was doing business with, or the cash-flow implications of the transaction. Petitioner offered no evidence that it satisfied the "reasonable and ordinarily prudent person" standard or relied on the advice of its tax department or counsel. If any communications occurred in which consideration was given to the correctness of petitioner's tax return position when the return was prepared and filed, petitioner has chosen not to disclose those communications. We conclude that petitioner was negligent, and the section 6662(a) penalty is appropriately applied.

Understanding *Compaq*

1.   The basic economics of *Compaq* are as follows: Compaq bought Royal Dutch stock (ADRs) at a higher price which reflected an anticipated dividend payment, and subsequently sold the stock at a lower price after the dividend had been paid. The Dutch Government withheld a fifteen percent tax on the dividend for which Compaq received a credit against its U.S. taxes. The negative cash flow resulting from the stock purchase and subsequent sale ($19,165,000) almost exactly offset the positive cash flow resulting from receipt of the dividend after the Dutch withholding tax ($19,163,930). However, as a result of these combined transactions, Compaq "manufactured" a foreign tax credit of approximately $3.4 million which it could presumably use to reduce taxes on its other worldwide income.

Admitting that Compaq was a bit clever in its manipulation of the foreign tax credit rules, is there anything wrong with the above result? What statutory provision, if any, did it violate, and, if none, what then is the basis for the court's decision? What is the legislative purpose of the foreign tax credit, and was Compaq's use of the credit consistent with that intended purpose? Does it matter?

2.   What do you think was the significance of the fact that the ADR resale plan was marketed to Compaq as, and understood by Compaq to be, a prepackaged tax reduction plan? Should this be relevant to the court's decision, or should it stick to the technical language of the statute and ignore the taxpayer's motivation? As a general principle, is there anything wrong with aggressive tax avoidance, or does this kind of prearranged plan go too far?

3.   The *Frank Lyon* case held for the taxpayer despite a transaction that seemed expressly designed to reduce the economic risks associated with the acquisition of substantial tax benefits. By contrast *Compaq* held against the taxpayers on parallel, if not entirely similar, facts. The court justifies this difference by stating that "[there is] a difference between (1) . . . arranging a complicated business transaction in a tax-advantaged manner and (2) entering into a prearranged loss transaction designed solely for the reduction of taxes. . . ." How convincing is this distinction? As a general matter, how would you compare the application of the economic substance/business purpose doctrine in the *Frank Lyon*, *KPMG*, and *Compaq* cases, and are they consistent with one another?

4.   Do you think that Compaq (or Twenty-First Securities) will try a scheme like this one again? If they did, what would you advise them to do differently? Would they succeed?

IV.   INTERSTATE COMMERCE, MAIL ORDERS, E-BUSINESS: TOWARD A PARADIGM OF MULTI-JURISDICTIONAL TAXATION

While considering international taxation, it may be interesting to step back and consider a related problem closer to home, *viz.*, the treatment of interstate commerce under the tax laws of the various States that comprise the American federal system. Say, for example, that a company based in New York has its principal manufacturing plant in New Jersey and markets its products through a variety of local distributors, mail orders, and computer sales ultimately reaching consumers in all fifty States. In which State(s) should its income be taxed? And what about sales taxes, which are usually imposed at the point of sale, but which — at least when mail-order or Internet transactions are concerned — may be uncertain in their application? Should the income and sales taxes follow similar rules, or are they dealing with different paradigms?

The problem of multistate taxation differs from that of international transactions because a superior authority — in this case, the federal government — exists to police the states and place limitations on their lawmaking sovereignty. (This is in part what the Civil War was about.) In this connection, the Due Process and Commerce Clause of the United States Constitution have been interpreted to place strict limits on state taxing authority, and specifically to prevent repetitive or "double" taxation which would constitute an impermissible interference with interstate commerce. Since most states have decided to apply their taxing jurisdiction up to the maximum limits permitted by the U.S. Constitution, there is a certain uneasy symmetry between the different state systems, and tax evasion opportunities are perhaps more limited than in an international context. Still, numerous problems do exist which — although involving smaller numbers than their international counterparts — raise many of the same policy and planning issues.

Probably the most famous state tax litigation involves the issue of sales taxes, and specifically the treatment of mail-order and (more recently) computer or Internet sales. The assumption for many years was that interstate mail order sales were effectively exempt from the sales tax, an assumption supported by the Supreme Court's holding in *National Bellas Hess, Inc. v. Illinois Dept of Revenue*, 386 U.S. 753 (1992), which held that mail order companies could not constitutionally be required to collect the sales or use tax on out-of-state purchasers.[23] This result was partly modified by the 1992 decision in *Quill Corp. v. North Dakota*, 504 U.S. 298 (1992), which held that such forced collection was prohibited by the Commerce but not by the Due Process Clause, with the result that Congress could in theory pass legislation that required the states to collect the tax on out-of-state sales. Although this has not yet happened, *Quill* and similar decisions have encouraged some corporations to agree voluntarily to collect the tax and thereby reduce or eliminate their competitive advantage in comparison to ordinary, in-state retailers.

A similar, although potentially much larger, problem exists with respect to Internet sales. At this writing, Congress has barred extension of "new" State taxes to these sales and — given the difficulty of applying the existing sales and use levies — much of the electronic sector remains essentially tax-exempt for the immediate future.

Related to the issue of e-commerce is the taxation of telecommuters, that is, individuals who perform work for an in-State company from a home office or other location physically outside the State. These questions are particularly fascinating because of the intersection of the interstate taxation and home office rules. The New York State Court of Appeals recently held that telecommuters remain subject to New York State income tax provided that (i) any significant portion of the employee's work is performed within the State, and (ii) the employer itself does not require the employee to work outside New York. *Huckaby v. New York State Division of Tax Appeals*, 4 N.Y.3d 427 (Ct. App. 2005).

Beyond telecommuting issues, state income taxes have attracted increased attention in recent years. The usual rule here is to divide the taxation of multistate enterprises between states according to a three-factor formula, based on the volume of sales, property, and employment in the relevant States. Thus, a company with its headquarters and other property in Wisconsin, all of its employees in Minnesota, and all of its sales in Michigan — admittedly an improbable combination — would theoretically pay one-third of its total income taxes to each state. For more complex combinations a weighted average formula would be used. This makes sense as a general principle, but not surprisingly there are numerous controversies, as in the case of passive income which may not fit the three-factor formula or where states apply the three-factor or an alternate formula in different ways. The state and

---

[23] The use tax is the tax imposed on (say) residents of New Jersey who purchase items in New York or another nearby state. (Out-of-state purchasers are typically exempt from sales tax in the state of purchase.) With the exception of cars, boats, and similar large items, as a practical matter few people pay the use tax voluntarily. Thus, failure to collect the tax by the mail order company is for all intents and purposes equivalent to tax evasion.

federal courts have been called in to resolve an increasing number of these controversies, which in the international context would likely be handled by treaty or else by bilateral agreement between the nations involved. Whether the results are better or worse under this system is a matter of some debate.

The experience of multistate taxation becomes more relevant as the world organizes itself along regional and in some cases global lines. Regional groups like the European Union (EU) or perhaps the North American Free Trade Association (NAFTA) may increasingly play roles similar to that of the U.S. Federal Government in "refereeing" tax and trade disputes and in setting general principles for the limits of tax jurisdiction. Yet the U.S. experience suggests that the presence of an arbiter will not make these problems disappear. The problems of multistate taxation — overlapping jurisdictions, inconsistent rules, and the need to consider more than one taxing structure in making business decisions — are simply localized versions of the problems faced by companies doing business in the international marketplace. A clothing store mailing items from Texas to Arkansas may not think itself "international" in nature, but in tax terms it is, and lessons learned at one level have implications for the other.

V.   COMPARATIVE TAXATION AND THE PROBLEM OF TAX CULTURE

Together with international taxation — that is, the taxation of cross-border transactions and capital flows — the tax field is increasingly concerned with comparative taxation, *i.e.*, the comparison of domestic tax regimes with the goal of improving or perhaps even "harmonizing" them in a combined, universal tax system. The process of comparison and convergence tends to be less advanced in the tax field than (say) international trade, labor, or environmental regulation, for reasons which will be explained in a moment.[24] But comparative tax remains an important and growing field, as globalization proceeds apace and countries — yes, even the United States — realize that they can no longer operate completely on their own.

At its most basic level, comparative tax involves the comparison of specific tax provisions in different countries, with an eye toward improving one's own tax law or (for a tax practitioner) of seeking jurisdictions where the treatment of a given item is more favorable than in one's own country. For example, home mortgage interest, which is a deductible expense under the Internal Revenue Code, is not treated as such in many or most foreign countries, which presumably accounts in some part for the relatively high percentage of national income that Americans devote to housing as opposed to other pursuits. This fact is obviously important to U.S. tax reformers, and would likely be of at least some interest to companies engaged in the homebuilding industry, who — at least at the margins — would benefit from an indirect subsidy in the United States that is not available in some other countries. A comparative methodology may also be applied to broader issues of tax base and tax rates. For example many foreign (notably European) countries have substantial

---

[24] *See generally* Robert A. Green, *Antilegalistic Approaches to Resolving Disputes Between Governments: A Comparison of the International Tax and Trade Regimes*, 23 YALE J. INT'L L. 79 (1998).

value added (VAT) and other nonincome taxes in addition to marginal income tax rates as high or higher than their American counterparts. From a taxpayer perspective these differences, no less than specifically "international" tax rules, may be an important factor in locating or structuring a new or continuing business. On a policy level, American tax reformers may look to Europe for guidance in vertical equity or the harmonization of national tax rates, while Europeans (perhaps) can learn from the American experience of tax cuts as an economic stimulus and means of encouraging private enterprise.

Comparative taxation is also fascinating because of the insights it provides into our own legal and tax culture — insights that, without a basis for comparison, might simply be ignored or taken for granted. The Italian tax code, for example, features such alien-seeming items as a credit for fishing enterprises; a credit for female-headed businesses; and a tax incentive for any investment in Sicily, Sardinia, or southern Italy, historically disadvantaged regions. (Anyone who suggested a fishing company headed by a Sicilian woman has a good future as a tax planner.) India exempts all agricultural income from taxation, in a heavily agricultural country. These provisions might seem odd to American eyes, but it helps to focus attention on some of the more unusual credits, deductions, etc. in our own tax code, and may cause one to wonder if perhaps more attention could be devoted to disadvantaged groups or regions at home. Debates about broader tax policy issues[25] are similarly conducted in very different terms: progressivity or vertical equity is enshrined as a constitutional provision in Italy, while in Israel the debate on progressivity is closely tied to the issue of discrimination between Jews and Arabs, as well as between religious and secular Jews, and in India to the issue of colonialism and the caste system with their legacy of unequal wealth and income distribution. The German constitutional court has declared entire taxes unconstitutional for failure to meet norms of equality or fairness in application. None of these things is likely to happen in the United States anytime soon, but awareness of these differences sharpens understanding of our own tax system and opens our eyes to the possibility of reform, both in substantive law and in relevant lawmaking procedure.

In the past decade or so, comparative tax has taken on added significance as a result of several developments. One is the trend toward globalization and the obvious interconnection of the different national tax systems. (It doesn't do much good to reform your own tax laws if the abusers can simply move to a competing jurisdiction.) A second is the trend toward regional integration, most advanced in Europe (the EU) but also beginning to take shape in North America through NAFTA and related international agreements. A third development is the fall of communism and other statist economic systems and the corresponding demand for new tax and commercial laws that reflect the rule of law and at least some respect for private property.

Each of these developments requires the conscious evaluation of conflicting tax rules and the choice between different systems (American, European, etc.) as the "model" for a new, more perfect tax code. For example, the EU and NAFTA eventually must decide whether various domestic tax expenditures (*e.g.*, tax breaks

---

[25] Information about foreign tax systems, in English, can be obtained from the website of the International Bureau of Fiscal Documentation, www.ibfd.nl. (The "nl" is for Netherlands.)

for the U.S. oil or high-tech industries) constitute illegal trade subsidies. Countries like Russia or China must decide which existing tax provisions — the gift exclusion, accelerated depreciation, the substance-over-form rules, etc. — will be incorporated into their own national tax structures. Although at this point largely the work of governments and academics, the process already involves private attorneys at several levels and will likely engage more and more of their time as the new century progresses. A tax lawyer — indeed any good lawyer — will increasingly mean a good international lawyer, as well.

Additional Assignment — Chapter 12

Suppose that you have been hired as a consultant to the Treasury Department with respect to U.S. international tax policy. The Department has asked your advice regarding a number of potentially disturbing trends in international taxation. Specifically, there is concern regarding the following items:

1. The Department is concerned about the number of U.S.-based firms that are evading or reducing taxes by, *inter alia*, the use of transfer pricing and by manipulation of the foreign tax credit rules as observed in *Compaq* above. In this connection, the Department wishes to know what new legislation, if any, could help to prevent this revenue loss. The Department is particularly interested in the prospects for an all-purpose provision, à la the partnership "anti-abuse" rules, which would allow IRS to recharacterize any international transaction that was inconsistent with the purpose of the statute — as determined by them, of course. A rule of this type (section 482) has had at least some success in restricting transfer pricing mechanisms; could a similar approach be extended to a wider range of transactions?

2. A number of Third World and other countries, spurred by the usual anti-American rhetoric, are demanding that the U.S. be more attentive to their needs in tax policy. Specifically, these countries are demanding that the U.S. increase economic assistance as the price for cooperation in fighting international tax haven and tax shelter abuses. "You have progressivity at home, so why not a little bit for us, as well?" they ask with no apparent irony. One specific demand is that the principle of neutrality be compromised in order to allow Third World companies to provide increased tax subsidies to their own, domestic industries.

3. The U.S., Canada, and Mexico are considering expansion of NAFTA to include Brazil, Argentina, and other South American countries. As part of this expansion, the NAFTA countries would begin consultation on the "harmonization" of internal tax policies, with the goal of a uniform tax system by the year 2025. In particular, NAFTA would seek to eliminate domestic tax provisions that function as subsidies to particular regions or industries.

4. Large U.S. corporations are predictably opposed to the first change and somewhat less than wildly enthusiastic about the others. Labor unions and some progressive academics are supportive. Most other people don't care.

How would you advise that the Department respond to the challenges in each of these areas? What political (domestic and international) as well as policy considerations would guide in making your decision, and how would you balance the two? Be as specific as possible, and don't be afraid to cite material from other chapters as appropriate.

TABLE OF CASES

[References are to page numbers. Principal cases are in capital letters.]

[References are to page numbers. Principal cases are in capital letters.]

[References are to page numbers. Principal cases are in capital letters.]

[References are to page numbers. Principal cases are in capital letters.]

[References are to page numbers. Principal cases are in capital letters.]

[References are to page numbers. Principal cases are in capital letters.]

[References are to page numbers. Principal cases are in capital letters.]

[References are to page numbers. Principal cases are in capital letters.]

INDEX

[References are to pages.]

[References are to pages.]

[References are to pages.]

[References are to pages.]

[References are to pages.]